D0535883

# NOTE TO STUDENTS

***STUDY GUIDE***
***to accompany***
***FUNDAMENTALS OF MARKETING***
by Roy Morley

Make studying a breeze! Use this Study Guide as a supplement to the text to ensure that you have a full understanding of marketing theory and its application. This new edition of *Study Guide to accompany Fundamentals of Marketing*, Seventh Canadian Edition, is tailored to meet your study needs. Fully integrated with the text, each Study Guide chapter features eleven sections:

- **Chapter Goals:** target your learning goals
- **Key Terms and Concepts:** understand important terms, cross-referenced to the text
- **Chapter Summary:** review the essential elements of the text chapter
- **Completion Questions:** test your knowledge of the textual material
- **True-False Questions:** self-test your understanding of key issues
- **Multiple-Choice Questions:** self-test your understanding of each chapter
- **Matching Questions:** test your knowledge of the definitions of marketing terms and concepts
- **Problems and Applications:** put your marketing knowledge into practice
- **Exercise:** bridge the gap between knowledge and experience
- **A Real World Case:** short readings illustrate marketing at work
- **Answers to Questions:** grade yourself on your understanding of the chapter material

Get your copy of this complete study aid from your campus bookstore or ask them to order one for you and make your study time worthwhile!

# EX LIBRIS

Name

SEVENTH CANADIAN EDITION

# FUNDAMENTALS OF MARKETING

## SUPPLEMENTARY TITLES AVAILABLE

### Canadian
Study Guide 0-07-552515-1
Issues in Canadian Marketing (Reader) 0-07-551348-X
Basic Canadian Marketing Cases (McDougall & Weinberg) 0-07-551370-6

### American
Marketing Perspectives From Business Week 060965-9
Shoes Marketing Simulation, Student Set, IBM, 5 1/4" 837499-5
Shoes Marketing Simulation, Student Set, IBM, 3 1/2" 837498-7
Planning Your Career in Business Today
Guide to Communication Skills
Critical Thinking Guide

SEVENTH CANADIAN EDITION

# FUNDAMENTALS OF MARKETING


MONTROSE S. SOMMERS
UNIVERSITY OF GUELPH

JAMES G. BARNES
MEMORIAL UNIVERSITY OF NEWFOUNDLAND

WILLIAM J. STANTON
UNIVERSITY OF COLORADO-BOULDER

MICHAEL J. ETZEL
UNIVERSITY OF NOTRE DAME

BRUCE J. WALKER
UNIVERSITY OF MISSOURI-COLUMBIA



McGRAW-HILL RYERSON LIMITED

Toronto Montreal New York Auckland Bogotá
Caracas Lisbon London Madrid Mexico Milan
New Delhi San Juan Singapore Sydney Tokyo

**FUNDAMENTALS OF MARKETING**
*Seventh Canadian Edition*



ISBN 0-07-552514-3

1 2 3 4 5 6 7 8 9 10 ML 4 3 2 1 0 9 8 7 6 5

Care has been taken to trace ownership of copyright material contained in this text. The publisher will gladly take any information that will enable them to rectify any reference or credit in subsequent editions.

SPONSORING EDITOR: Kelly Smyth
DEVELOPMENTAL EDITOR: Lenore Gray
SUPERVISING EDITOR: Margaret Henderson
COPY EDITOR AND PROOFREADER: Wendy Thomas
INDEX: Andrew Little
EDITORIAL ASSISTANT: Susanne Penny
PRODUCTION CO-ORDINATOR: Nicla Dattolico
COVER DESIGN: Brant Cowie/ArtPlus Limited
LAYOUT AND PAGINATION: Heather Brunton/ArtPlus Limited
FILM OUTPUT: TypeLine Express Limited
PRINTING AND BINDING: Metropole Litho
TYPEFACE: Goudy
COVER PHOTO: SuperStock/Roy King

**Canadian Cataloguing in Publication Data**

Main entry under title:

Fundamentals of marketing

7th Canadian ed.
Includes index.
ISBN 0-07-552514-3

1. Marketing. 2. Marketing — Canada. I. Sommers, Montrose S., date — .

HF5415.F85 1995 658.8 C94-932764-6

Printed and bound in Canada

DEDICATED TO

*Jessie, Annie, and Michael*
*Jennifer, Stephanie, and Karen*

## ABOUT THE AUTHORS

**Montrose Sommers** is a Professor of Consumer Studies at the University of Guelph. He received his B. Comm. from the University of British Columbia, his M.B.A. from Northwestern University, and his D.B.A. from the University of Colorado. Dr. Sommers has been a consultant to private- and public-sector organizations involved in petroleum marketing, financial services, telecommunications, various retailing specializations, marketing research, and advertising. His teaching background is extensive; he has worked with Bachelor, Master, and Ph.D. students at the Universities of British Columbia, Texas, Hawaii, Toronto, York, Nairobi in Kenya, Witwatersrand in South Africa, Huazhong and Tianjin in China, and the LSE in Great Britain. Dr. Sommers has also served on the editorial boards of the *Journal of Marketing*, the *Journal of International Management and Organizations*, and the *Journal of the Service Industries*.

**Jim Barnes** is Professor of Marketing at Memorial University of Newfoundland. Dr. Barnes received his B. Comm. and B.A. degrees from Memorial, his M.B.A. from Harvard Business School, and his Ph.D. in Marketing from the University of Toronto. He has been a member of the faculty at Memorial since 1968 and served as Dean from 1978 to 1988. He has held visiting positions at Queen's University and the University of Bath in England. Dr. Barnes has served as a consultant in Marketing and Service Quality to numerous companies in North America and Europe. He is co-founder and Chairman of the Board of Omnifacts Research Limited, the largest full-service marketing and survey research company in Atlantic Canada. He has served on the boards of directors of a number of national organizations, including the Institute of Canadian Bankers. He is currently a director of several Canadian firms, including NewTel Enterprises, the Bristol Group of Companies, and McGraw-Hill Ryerson.

**William J. Stanton** is Professor Emeritus of Marketing at the University of Colorado — Boulder. He received his Ph.D. in Marketing from Northwestern University, where he was elected to Beta Gamma Sigma. He has worked in business and has taught in several management development programs for marketing executives. Professor Stanton has served as a consultant for various business organizations and engaged in research projects for the federal government. He also has lectured at universities in Europe, Asia, Mexico, and New Zealand.

The co-author of the leading text in sales management, Professor Stanton has also published several journal articles and monographs. *Fundamentals of Marketing* has been translated into Spanish, and separate editions have been adapted (with co-authors) for Canada, Italy, Australia, and South Africa. In a survey of marketing educators, Professor Stanton was voted one of the leaders in marketing thought, and he is listed in *Who's Who in America* and *Who's Who in the World.*

**Barnes (*left*), Stanton (*centre*), Sommers (*right*).**

**Michael J. Etzel** received his Ph.D. in Marketing from the University of Colorado in 1970. Since 1980, he has been Professor of Marketing at the University of Notre Dame, where he served as department chairman from 1980 to 1987. He has also been on the faculties at Utah State University and the University of Kentucky. He has held visiting faculty positions at the University of South Carolina and the University of Hawaii. In 1990, he was a Fulbright Fellow at the University of Innsbruck, Austria.

Professor Etzel has taught a wide variety of marketing courses, from fundamentals through the doctoral level. He is also a frequent lecturer in executive training programs.

His research, in the areas of marketing management and buyer behaviour, has appeared in the *Journal of Marketing*, *Journal of Marketing Research*, the *Journal of Consumer Research*, and other publications. He is the co-author of another college level text, *Retailing Today*, and co-editor of *Cases in Retailing Strategy*.

He has been active in the American Marketing Association, most recently serving as vice president of the Education Division. Since 1981 he has directed the Association's School of Marketing Research.

**Bruce J. Walker** is Professor of Marketing and Dean of the College of Business and Public Administration at the University of Missouri — Columbia. He received his undergraduate degree in Economics from Seattle University and his Master's and Ph.D. in Business, both emphasizing marketing, from the University of Colorado.

In his first faculty position, Professor Walker served on the marketing faculty at the University of Kentucky. He then joined the faculty at Arizona State University and served as chair of the Department of Marketing from 1982 to 1989. He moved to the University of Missouri in 1990.

Throughout his teaching career, Professor Walker has taught a variety of courses, including principles of marketing, to undergraduate and graduate students. Besides speaking to business groups in the U.S., he has made presentations and conducted seminars for students and executives in European countries.

Professor Walker's research, focusing primarily on franchising, marketing channels, and survey-research methods, has been published in the *Journal of Marketing*, *Business Horizons*, *Journal of Marketing Research*, and other periodicals. He has also co-authored or co-edited a number of books and conference proceedings, including *Retailing Today*.

Professor Walker has been actively involved with both the American Marketing Association and the Western Marketing Educators Association. He served as vice president of the AMA's Education Division and as president of WMEA.

# CONTENTS IN BRIEF

# CONTENTS

# LIST OF CASES

# PREFACE

## OUR GOAL IS CUSTOMER SATISFACTION, TOO

As we began work on the seventh edition of our textbook, we had a number of objectives that we considered very important. In the first place, we wanted to ensure that the book was as pertinent and valuable to Canadian students as it has been since we published our first edition in 1971. This meant that we had to continue to produce a textbook that was easy and even fun to read and one that was very much related to marketing as it is practised in Canada today. We believe that we have accomplished that objective and that you will find the seventh edition to be simply the best marketing textbook available in Canada.

Secondly, we wanted to ensure that this edition was as practical and current as possible, that it presents Canadian marketing as it really is and not merely from a theoretical perspective. Consequently, you will find that this edition provides you in every chapter with numerous examples of how Canadian companies and organizations are managing marketing. You will find many examples that are extremely current, relating to topics such as the use of technology in data base marketing and the changing face of Canadian retailing. Above all, we wanted to produce a practical book. We believe that students and instructors who use this book will find it interesting because it really does reflect what is going on every day in the offices of Canadian marketing managers.

To achieve these goals, many changes have been made to reflect the dynamic nature of marketing. New concepts have been introduced, established concepts have been expanded and updated, and current developments have been emphasized. We have added new material and chapters to reflect the way in which marketing is developing.

To achieve our goal of presenting Canadian marketing as it is being practised as we prepare for the twenty-first century, we have restructured and revised major sections of the book. This will be most obvious in the addition of two new chapters and in our emphasis on what is really a new way of looking at marketing. This edition will provide comprehensive coverage of the essential topics of marketing that have been covered in depth in our previous editions, as well as a thorough discussion of emerging concepts in marketing. It is designed to be a superior learning tool, a pleasure to read and to learn from.

The changes reflected in this seventh edition have been based to a very great extent on feedback that we have received from students and instructors who have been using our earlier editions in universities and colleges across Canada. We have regularly sought that feedback by talking with instructors across the country and by holding focus group interviews with students. We value this feedback and the contribution it has made to our revision. We are, after all, marketers, and listening to our customers is as important to us as it is to any of the companies you will find discussed in this text.

## WHAT MAKES THIS EDITION SO MUCH BETTER?

### Design

The seventh edition continues the trend established in recent editions of *Fundamentals of Marketing* in providing students and instructors with the most visually appealing textbook available. We have incorporated numerous colour photographs and copies of four-colour advertisements so that students can see real-life examples of marketing in action in Canadian companies and organizations. We believe that you will find it easy to read and even fun.

### Organization

While we have continued to integrate current marketing topics throughout the text, we have responded to feedback from instructors and to a changing emphasis in Canadian marketing and have included separate chapters in this edition dedicated to the important topics of Business-to-Business Marketing and Marketing in Not-for-Profit Organizations. We have continued to integrate into all of our chapters concepts and illustrations on these topics and on other special topics such as services marketing and international marketing. This is done for the most part through our use of Marketing at Work Files, several of which are presented in each chapter.

### New and Expanded Topics

We have made a particular effort to reflect in this edition the new way in which many companies are regarding marketing in their organizations. This involves an emphasis on *keeping* existing customers as well as on *attracting* new ones. Consequently, we emphasize customer satisfaction as the ultimate objective of marketing in any organization and stress the role of service in building relationships with customers, the ultimate goal being to retain them as customers for the long term.

We have added much new material in this edition, reflecting the expanded application of marketing and its increased importance in many organizations. As mentioned above, there are new chapters on Business-to-Business Marketing and Marketing in Not-for-Profit Organizations. The first reflects the fact that many students will find employment after graduation in companies that market to other businesses, and the second acknowledges the fact that marketing is just as important in charitable and cultural organizations, in hospitals and universities, as it is in so-called private-sector businesses. In addition, we have continued to emphasize in this edition the importance of a strategic orientation to marketing. This is reflected in the expansion of our coverage of important strategic concepts such as market segmentation, differentiation, and positioning.

### Canadian Applications

We continue in this edition our emphasis on ensuring that the text is completely Canadian in its orientation and content. We have included in this edition new chapter openers and approximately 100 Marketing at Work Files, liberally sprinkled throughout the chapters. These vignettes deal with what is happening at this moment in Canadian marketing. Each represents an example of an issue or an interesting situation that is facing a Canadian business or not-for-profit organization. These specific examples, coupled with the hundreds of Canadian companies, products, and brands referenced in the text, make this a book that Canadian students will find especially interesting and relevant to their own situations.

### New Cases

The seventh edition contains 20 cases, 13 of which are new for this edition. Most deal with actual businesses with which students will be quite familiar. Many of these cases have been written in a two-part format, providing for interesting discussion of a marketing problem and of the action the company took to address it. We have retained from our sixth edition the two-part cases on W. K. Buckley Limited and The Tea Council of Canada, both of which students have found to be very interesting and useful, particularly for the discussion of marketing strategies. We have also retained the case that describes Peter Taylor's purchase of a new pair of running shoes as we have found it generates excellent class discussion, for it reflects a situation with which most students can readily identify. Our new cases have been carefully chosen and many have been written especially for this edition. They deal with not-for-profit organizations (The Salvation Army), service quality (Acorn Park Hotel), social issues such as Green Marketing and ethics, business-to-business situations (Murray Industrial), new forms of marketing (Catalogue Retailing), and new product introductions (Kodak Photo CD and EJE Trans-Lite). In all, we believe this represents an excellent collection of marketing cases that will challenge the student with examples from a broad cross-section of marketing situations.

## THE BOOK: ITS BASIC APPROACH

Those familiar with the earlier editions of *Fundamentals of Marketing* will notice that, although some major changes have certainly been made, we have retained the essential features that have made this book an outstanding teaching and learning resource. The writing style continues to make the material interesting and easy to read. The basic organization is appropriate in that it reflects new developments as well as the needs of students and instructors. Material flows logically with a section-heading structure that makes for easier reading and outlining.

### Pedagogical Features

We provide many excellent end-of-chapter discussion questions. Most of these are thought-provoking and involve the application of text material rather than simply its recollection. We have added a new feature with this seventh edition. We call it Hands-on Marketing; these are practical assignments that will require the student to go out and talk with practising marketers to get their input on subjects discussed in each chapter. There are two of these "hands-on" assignments at the end of each chapter.

Each of the 20 cases focuses on a topic covered in the text and provides students with an opportunity to apply concepts, practise analysis, and learn decision making.

We have also retained and updated such teaching and learning features as chapter objectives, chapter summaries, appendices dealing with secondary and syndicated data and with marketing arithmetic, and an expanded glossary. The key terms and concepts are summarized in a list at the end of each chapter with a page reference for the first mention.

### "A Total System"

The central theme approach has also been retained from previous editions — that marketing is a total system of business action, rather than a fragmented assortment of functions and institutions. To us, this means that the essential marketing ideas are what matter, not lists of terms and functions or specialized formula approaches. While attention is paid to the role of marketing in the Canadian economic and political system, the book is written largely from the perspective of marketing personnel in an individual organization. This organization may be a manufacturer, a service provider, a not-for-profit organization, or an intermediary in a business or non-business field.

The marketing concept is a philosophy that stresses the need for a marketing orientation compatible with society's long-run interests. This philosophy is evident in the framework of the strategic marketing planning process. A company sets its marketing objectives, taking into consideration the environmental forces that influence its marketing effort. Management next selects target markets. The company then has four strategic elements — its activities — with which to build a marketing program to reach its markets and achieve its objectives. In all stages of the marketing process, management should use marketing research as a tool for problem solving and design making.

### Topic Sequence

This framework for the strategic marketing planning process is reflected generally in the organization of the book's content. The text is divided into seven parts. Part 1 serves as an introduction and includes chapters on the marketing environment and strategic marketing planning. Part 2 is devoted to the analysis and selection of target markets — both consumer and business-to-business markets. It also includes a detailed treatment of the very important strategic concepts of market segmentation and positioning, and the collection and use of marketing information.

Parts 3 through 6 deal with the development of a marketing program, and each of these parts covers one of the above-mentioned components of the strategic marketing mix. In Part 3 various topics related to the product are discussed, including a separate chapter on services marketing. The company's approach to pricing its products and services is the subject of Part 4, and Part 5 covers the distribution system. Part 6 is devoted to the total promotional program, including advertising, personal selling, and sales promotion. Part 7 deals with the implementation and evaluation of the total marketing effort in an individual firm and contains a new chapter on not-for-profit marketing. It also includes a chapter on the increasingly important subject of international marketing. The final chapter presents an appraisal of the role of marketing in our society, including the subjects of consumer criticisms and the social responsibility of an organization.

### Teaching and Learning Supplements

This textbook is the central element in a complete package of teaching and learning resources that have been totally revised and considerably expanded for this edition. The package includes the following supplements:

### For the Student

**Study Guide** by Tom Adams (Sacramento State U) and Roy Morley (Ryerson). This useful study aid provides guidelines for analyzing marketing cases, chapter goals, chapter summaries, key terms and concepts, self-test questions (true/false, multiple choice, matching and completion), problems and applications questions, interesting real-world cases and articles related to chapter concepts, and a new focus on applied, hands-on marketing exercises.

**Shoes: Marketing Simulation** (IBM 5.25", IBM 3.5") by Michael Ursic et al. A straightforward, easy-to-use, one-product simulation about running shoes. Working in teams, students make a series of marketing decisions in a realistic setting regarding market research, price, advertising, consumer promotions, personal selling, dealer promotions, new product development, and more.

**Guide to Communication Skills** A 48-page self-study guide of practical, step-by-step procedures for writing memos, letters, and follow-up notes; writing long and short reports; writing résumés and application letters; interviewing and being interviewed; and preparing and delivering presentations.

**Planning Your Career in Business Today** A 64-page self-study guide on the current job market, assessing occupational preferences, setting career goals, completing the job application process, interviewing, and evaluating job offers.

**Critical Thinking Guide** A 32-page self-study booklet designed to help students interested in assuming responsibility for their own learning. Class-tested for three years, the guide provides practical, results-oriented techniques for applying principles of critical thinking to written and oral assignments within a business curriculum and includes assignments and exercises for enhancing critical thinking.

### For the Instructor

**Instructor's Manual** by Raghu Tadepalli and John Chyzyk. This heavily revised instructor's manual features course organization and development suggestions, thoughts on teaching, chapter overviews, chapter goals, learning objectives, key terms and concepts, suggested overhead transparencies, suggested videos, recommended readings to use with each chapter, lecture outlines for each chapter (including many real-world examples not found in the text), and mini-lectures for each chapter, commentaries on the end-of-chapter questions and on the 20 cases, video-case commentaries, and instructor's materials related to the *Study Guide*, and a guide to the video-cases. The popular five-part Upper Canada Brewery Case has been included to accommodate instructors who may wish to continue using it, along with the three video-cases that do not appear in the textbook (Civilian HUMMER, Southwest Airlines, and Michigan Opera Theater). A "bounce-back" card has been inserted for instructors who wish to receive the Annual Newsletter and Case Update.

**Test Bank** by Pritchett, Pritchett, and Gonthier. Containing over 2,000 questions (20 true/false and 60 to 80 multiple choice per chapter), this test bank features questions that are coded for difficulty level, text page reference, and type of question (definitional, applied, comprehensive, factual, or mathematical).

**Computerized Test Bank** A new test generating system upgrades this ancillary to provide professional-looking tests, expedite creation and editing of test question banks, and accommodates scrambled versions of tests with corresponding printed answer sheets.

**Video-Cases** This package of eclectic, highly polished film footage contains eight video cases, five of which are part-ending cases in the textbook. The three non-part-ending video-cases are reproduced in the *Instructor's Manual*. The running time of each video varies from 10 to 30 minutes. The five part-ending video-cases feature such products, services or subjects as Green Marketing, Kodak Photo CD, Catalogue Retailing, Advertising, and Sneakers. The Buckley's and Salvation Army cases will also have a video component. The Video Guide has been reproduced in the *Instructor's Manual.*

**Venture Video** This 1992 McGraw-Hill Ryerson/CBC "Venture" collaboration provides a professional marketing video that ties segments from the "Venture" series to a variety of marketing concepts and applications from the text. It comes with suggestions for classroom use.

**Overhead Transparencies** Approximately 200 full-colour transparencies including the major illustrations from the text, additional tables and figures not found in the text, and four to eight advertisements (also from outside the text) per chapter to illustrate concepts. A Teaching Note on each left-hand page supplies a script for each acetate including concept, strategy, or technique that is the subject of the acetate, points of emphasis for the acetate, and discussion questions.

**Annual Newsletter and Case Update** *Sommers and Barnes on Marketing* is published annually to provide instructors with current examples and applications, along with additional cases, and updates on cases already in the text. Suggestions are welcome! A "bounce-back" card will be included in the *Instructor's Manual* for instructors who wish to be kept on our data base to receive these items automatically.

## ACKNOWLEDGEMENTS

Through seven editions, many people have made an important contribution to the quality of this book. These include our students, colleagues, clients, marketing managers in Canadian firms, and instructors at many universities and colleges. They have offered their comments and suggestions, which we have incorporated into each new edition.

We wish to acknowledge in particular those research assistants who contributed to the compilation of information and the preparation of cases for the seventh edition. In particular, we wish to thank Jennifer Barnes, Michael Sommers, Kerry Lynn Chaytor, Jennifer Hutchings, Lynn Healey, Darrin Howlett, and Kerri-Lynn Parsons. We are also indebted to the many executives in businesses and other organizations who co-operated in allowing us to write cases on their companies. They are acknowledged specifically in the notes attached to each case. Their contribution is most important in that they have enabled us to ensure that this book continues to demonstrate its commitment to providing students with exposure to real-life examples of marketing problems. We owe particular thanks to Dr. Herbert MacKenzie of Memorial University of Newfoundland who contributed several cases to this edition.

We also thank most sincerely those instructors and students across Canada who have provided helpful suggestions for improvements over almost 25 years since our first edition was published. We would, of course, welcome feedback on this edition as well.

Hundreds of Canadian companies supplied us with photos, videos, advertisements, and other materials that we have incorporated into this book. They are far too numerous to list here, but their input is essential to ensuring that this text is as current, practical, and realistic as possible.

Finally, we would like to acknowledge with much appreciation the support and co-operation we receive from the staff of McGraw-Hill Ryerson. As always we owe particular thanks to Kelly Smyth, our sponsoring editor, who oversaw the process of preparing the book for publication and kept us focused on the task. Special thanks also to our superb copy editor Wendy Thomas, and to the excellent support team at McGraw-Hill Ryerson who worked with us on this project — Margaret Henderson, Lenore Gray, Gary Bennett, Susanne Penny, and Betty Tustin — all of whom provided much-appreciated support and helped us ensure that this edition is the best that we have ever produced.

MONTROSE S. SOMMERS
JAMES G. BARNES

SEVENTH CANADIAN EDITION

# FUNDAMENTALS OF MARKETING

PART

1

# MODERN MARKETING AND ITS ENVIRONMENT

**An overview of marketing, the marketing environment and strategic planning in marketing**

Marketing is often dynamic, challenging, and rewarding. It can also be frustrating and even disappointing. But it is never dull! Welcome to the part of the organization where "the rubber meets the road" — the place where an organization's ideas, planning, and execution are given the acid test of market acceptance or rejection.

To help you understand this activity, Chapter 1 explains what marketing is, how it has developed, and how it is continuing to develop.

In Chapter 2 we discuss the environmental forces that shape an organization's marketing program. Then in Chapter 3 we discuss the management process in marketing and introduce the concept of strategic marketing planning.

## CHAPTER 1 GOALS

"What is marketing?" Chapter 1 answers this question — and the answer may surprise you. After studying this chapter, you should have an understanding of:

- The relationship between exchange and marketing.
- How marketing applies to business and nonbusiness situations.
- The difference between selling and marketing.
- The evolution of marketing.
- The marketing concept.
- The impact of ethics and quality management in marketing.
- Marketing's role in the global economy, in Canada's economy, in an individual organization, and in your life.

CHAPTER 1

# THE FIELD OF MARKETING

## Challenging for U.S. Business

Marketing at the end of the 1990s is nothing if not challenging. The big issues on the road to the twenty-first century concern economic and employment growth, reviving consumer and business spending, increasing innovation and productivity — all in the face of rapid technological change and increasing domestic and global competition. And there is a marketing dimension to each of these issues for all Canadian firms, large or small, that market to consumers, to businesses, or to governments.

Take Challenger Motor Freight of Cambridge, Ontario. The company started operations in 1976, offering transportation services within Canada as well as across the border into the United States. But under American law, a Canadian citizen could not drive a Canadian truck to transport goods between two American locations. Challenger was serious about developing the U.S. market, so it opened an Ohio office. Today, Challenger has a fleet of 450 trucks with 200 of them based in the United States with American drivers. Challenger can provide transportation and logistics services for Canadian and American firms in both countries.

Being Canadian has its marketing advantages for Challenger. It helps when the firm is bidding for cross-border business. Chuck Simpson, waving the flag in the accompanying photo, is director of Challenger Motor Freight's Canadian operations. He says, "We tell them that since we are Canadian, we know the customs regulations. We know the eccentricities of the market. We know how to take care of their customers up there better than an American carrier would."

But sometimes being Canadian in the American market, or any other for that matter, means running up against the "buy local" bias, or in this case, the "buy American" bias. And sometimes this can make marketing difficult. Not impossible, just difficult. Challenger has had to deal with customers who were not happy about using Canadian-supplied services in place of American ones even when price, quality, and service were more than competitive.[1]

Challenger Motor Freight is a successful Canadian marketer of services dealing with all the issues of today and tomorrow: economic growth, consumer and business market needs and perceptions, changing logistics and communications technology, increasing international competition, and the continuous challenge of providing quality service at competitive prices to demanding consumers.

Studying marketing helps you to understand the issues that Challenger faced, how to deal with these issues from a marketing perspective, and how to meet the challenges of today and tomorrow wherever in the world you are.

## NATURE AND SCOPE OF MARKETING

In a business firm, marketing generates the revenues that are managed by the financial people and used by the production people in creating products and services. The challenge of marketing is to generate those revenues by satisfying customers' wants at a profit and in a socially responsible manner.

### Broad Dimensions of Marketing

But marketing is not limited to business. Whenever you try to persuade somebody to do something — donate to the Salvation Army, fasten a seat belt, lower a stereo's noise during study hours, vote for your candidate, accept a date with you (or maybe even marry you) — you are using marketing ideas and engaging in a marketing activity. So-called nonbusiness organizations — they really are in business but don't think of themselves as such — also engage in marketing. Their "product" may be a vacation place they want you to visit, a social cause or an idea they want you to support, a person they are thrusting into the spotlight, or a museum or gallery they want you to attend. Whatever the product is, the organization is using marketing ideas and is engaging in marketing.

Within this broad perspective, there is great variety with respect to (1) marketers, (2) what they are marketing, and (3) their potential markets. For example, marketers might include, in addition to business firms, such diverse social units as the Girl Guides trying to attract new members, the director of the Art Gallery of Ontario selecting exhibits to generate greater attendance and financial support, the Canadian Auto Workers union trying to secure a contract agreement with General Motors, and colleges trying to shift demand from overenrolled to underenrolled courses and majors. Thus, we define **marketers** as people and organizations that wish to make exchanges.

In addition to the range of items normally considered as goods and services, *what is being marketed* may be ideas, such as reducing solid waste through recycling or contributing to the United Way; people, such as rock singer Bryan Adams or country and blues singer k.d. lang; and places, such as Moncton, New Brunswick, as a site for a new data centre, or Venezuela as a place to go for a vacation.

In this general context, *markets* encompass more than the direct consumers of products. For example, in addition to its students, a university's market is made up of government personnel who provide funds, citizens living near the university who may be affected by university activities, and alumni who support university programs. A firm's markets include government regulatory agencies, environmentalists, and stockholders.

Thus, any person or group with whom an individual or organization has an existing or potential exchange relationship can be considered a **market**.

As you may gather, marketing is a very broad-based activity, and consequently, it calls for a broad definition. **The essence of marketing is a transaction — an exchange — intended to satisfy human needs and wants.** That is, marketing occurs any time one social unit (person or organization) strives to exchange something of value with another social unit. Our broad definition then is as follows:

**Marketing consists of all activities designed to generate and facilitate any exchange intended to satisfy human needs or wants.**[2]

**Concept of Exchange** Now let's examine the concept of **exchange** as this term relates to marketing. Exchange is one of three ways in which a person can satisfy a want. Suppose you want some clothes. You can sew them, knit them, or otherwise produce the clothes yourself. You can borrow them or use some form of coercion to get the clothes. Or you can offer something of value (money, service, other products) to another person who will voluntarily exchange the clothes for what you offer. It is only the third approach that we call an exchange in the sense that marketing is taking place.

The following conditions must exist for a marketing exchange to take place:

- Two or more social units — people or organizations — must be involved, and each must have wants to be satisfied. If you are totally self-sufficient in some area, there is no need for an exchange.
- The parties must be involved voluntarily.
- Each party must have something of value to contribute in the exchange, and each must believe that it will benefit from the exchange. In the case of an election, for example, the things of value are the votes of the electorate and the representation of the voters by the candidate.
- The parties must be able to communicate with each other. Assume that you want a new sweater and the Gap has sweaters on sale. If you and the store are not aware of each other — you are not communicating — then there will be no exchange.

**Concept of Relationship in Exchange** When two people or organizations are involved on a voluntary basis, each contributing something of value to an exchange and communicating with each other, a **relationship** exists. A relationship can be transient and exist only for a single act of exchange — a very short-term relationship. On the other hand, a relationship can be of a long-term nature — it can exist over a number of exchanges over a number of years. The longer the exchange relationship, the more likely it is to be of special value to those taking part in it. Buyers and sellers understand each other better; they better understand the value of what they are exchanging; they are able to communicate more easily; both are able to be more efficient and effective. Understanding the exchange relationship between an organization and its customers and clients and how the parties interact is extremely important in allowing a marketer to develop appropriate strategies to satisfy customers.

### Business Dimensions of Marketing

Our broad (or macro) definition tells us something about the pervasive role of marketing in our country. But this is a book about the business of marketing in individual organizations. These organizations may be business firms in the conventional sense of the word *business*. Or they may be what is called a nonbusiness or not-for-profit organization — a hospital, university, Big Brothers, church, police department, or museum, for example. Both groups — business and nonbusiness — face essentially the same basic marketing problems and can make use of the same marketing ideas.

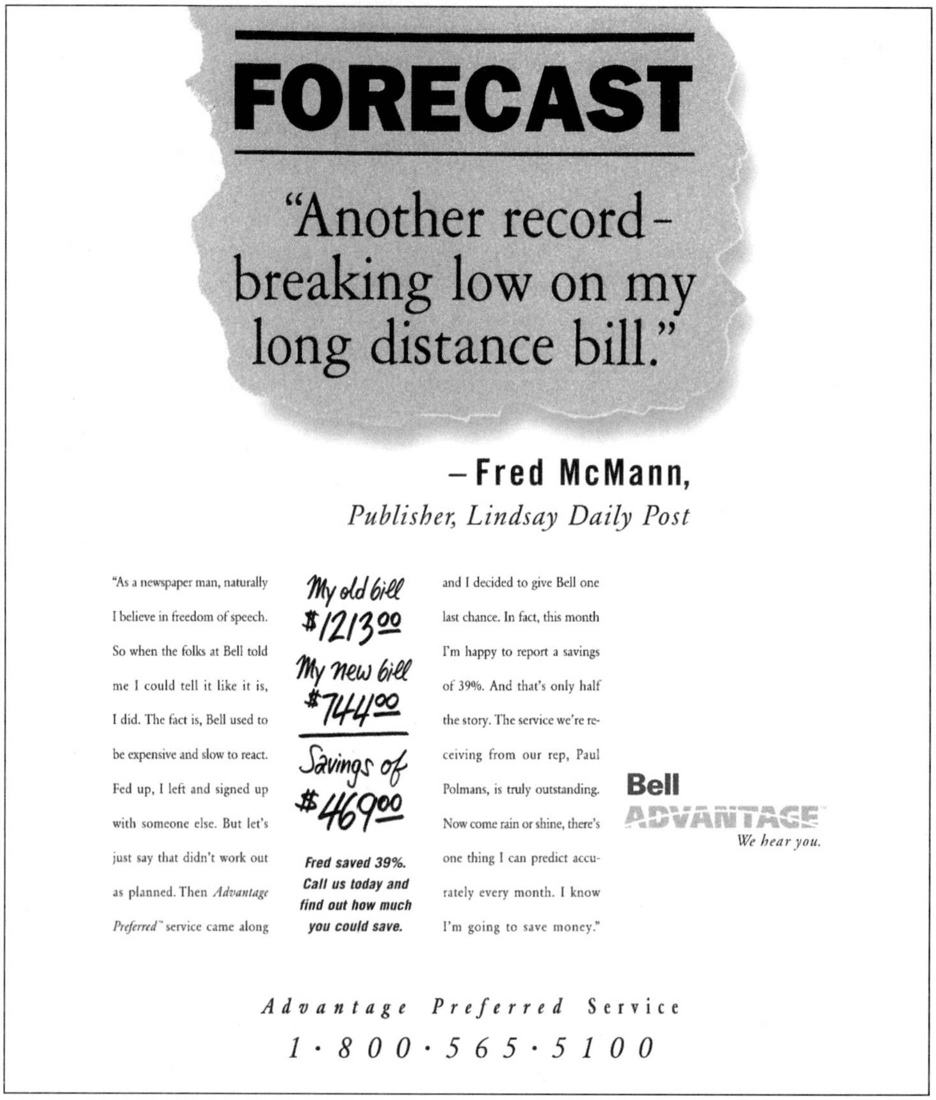


**The service the representative provides makes all the difference in relationship marketing.**

Many executives in those organizations, as well as many household consumers, think they already know a good bit about the business of marketing. After all, churches run newspaper ads and museums sell prints of famous paintings. And people at home watch television commercials that persuade them to buy. These people purchase products on a self-service basis in supermarkets. Some have friends who "can get it for them wholesale." But in each of these examples, we are talking about only one part of the totality of marketing activities. Consequently, we need a micro, business definition of marketing to guide decision makers in business or nonbusiness organizations in the management of their marketing effort.

**Business Definition of Marketing** Our micro definition of marketing — applicable in a business or a nonbusiness organization — is:

**Marketing is a total system of business activities designed to plan, price, promote, and distribute want-satisfying products, services, and ideas to target markets in order to achieve organizational objectives.**[3]

## MARKETING AT WORK

### FILE 1-1 BUILDING SERVICE RELATIONSHIPS

In 1990 the Bank of Montreal came in last in customer satisfaction polls taken by the Canadian Federation of Independent Business. So, between then and the beginning of 1994, while other banks reduced loans to small and independent businesses, the Bank of Montreal increased its by more than 30 percent. It consequently came as no surprise that the next customer satisfaction poll rated the bank first among Canada's five biggest banks.

This radical turnaround is the result of a new commitment to small businesses, learning more about them and their needs, and then building relationships with them. Many small businesses can't get loans because their assets are intellectual as opposed to tangible. The awareness of this problem has led to the bank's launching a program designed to change lending policies to high-tech companies. President Anthony Comper says, "If we can't provide the financing ourselves, we'll direct customers to people who can" — both private lenders and the 200 federal and scores of provincial government sources with available funds. Account managers will also focus on the risks and success factors facing clients as well as plugging them into sources of growth capital and ways of providing interim financing for the period prior to the actual receipt of funds.

Comper says, "The objective is to build relationships, to share our resources and expertise. In return, we expect to learn a great deal . . . that will shape the bank's lending policies for years to come."

Source: Adapted from Margot Gibb-Clark, "B of M Targets High-Tech Firms," *Globe and Mail*, November 25, 1993, p. B4.

| **Marketing is:** | |
|---|---|
| a system: | for business activities |
| designed to: | plan, price, promote, and distribute |
| something of value: | want-satisfying products, services, and ideas |
| for the benefit of: | the target market — present and potential household consumers or business users |
| to achieve: | the organization's objectives. |

This definition has some significant implications:

- It is a managerial, systems definition.
- The entire system of business activities must be customer-oriented. Customers' wants must be recognized and satisfied effectively.
- The marketing program starts with the germ of a product or service idea and does not end until the customer's wants are completely satisfied, which may be some time after the sale is made.
- The definition implies that to be successful, marketing must maximize profitable sales over the *long run*. Thus, customers must be satisfied in order for a company to get the repeat business that ordinarily is so vital to success.

It should be noted that the above definitions, as well as most others commonly used, always include products, services, and ideas in their scope. As a "shorthand," however, products are most frequently referred to and, to a lesser extent, products and services. In fact, the term **product** is now being used in a broader sense than in the past. It stands for various combinations of product, service, and ideas — what could be termed a product/service complex. No longer is it uncommon to hear the term product being used to refer to a "product complex" that consists primarily of services.

From a management perspective, the marketing program comprises four elements known as the organization's marketing mix. The marketing mix consists of (1) an organization's product or service assortment, (2) its pricing structure, (3) the distribution systems used, and (4) the promotional activities. The activities and elements of the marketing mix are continually being reviewed and tested for appropriateness and degree of co-ordination. The marketing mix is expanded on in Chapter 3 in the discussion of marketing planning.

## EVOLUTION OF MARKETING

The foundations of marketing in Canada were laid in pioneer times when French-speaking and then English-speaking settlers traded (exchanged) among themselves and also with the various groups of native peoples. Some settlers even became retailers, wholesalers, and itinerant peddlers. Since then, marketing has evolved through three stages of development. But to understand the *general* evolution of marketing, it is necessary to understand the difference between marketing and selling.

### Difference between Marketing and Selling Orientations

Many people, including some executives, still do not understand the difference between a selling orientation and a marketing orientation. In fact, many think they are synonymous. However, as shown below, there are vast differences between the two activities.

| Selling Orientation | | Marketing Orientation |
|---|---|---|
| **Emphasis is on the product.** | **vs.** | **Emphasis is on customers' wants.** |
| **Company first makes the product and then figures out how to sell it.** | **vs.** | **Company first determines customers' wants and then figures out how to make and deliver a product to satisfy those wants.** |
| **Management is sales-volume-oriented.** | **vs.** | **Management is profit-oriented.** |
| **Planning is short-run-oriented, in terms of today's products and markets.** | **vs.** | **Planning is long-run-oriented, in terms of new products, tomorrow's markets, and future growth.** |
| **Stresses needs of seller.** | **vs.** | **Stresses needs and wants of buyers.** |

When a selling orientation is used, a company makes a product and then persuades customers to buy it. In effect, the firm attempts to alter consumer demand to fit the firm's potential supply of the product. When a marketing orientation is practised, a much different approach is taken. The firm finds out what the customer wants and then develops a product that will satisfy that need and still yield a satisfactory profit. In this case, the company adjusts its supply to the will of consumer demand.

A selling approach may be successful for a while, but as a Korean auto maker discovered, if the customer is not given first priority, problems will occur. Hyundai introduced the Excel first in Canada and then in the United States in 1987. Despite experiencing the fastest growth rate of any new car sold anywhere, by late 1990 the car had all but disappeared. The performance of the product was satisfactory, so what went wrong? To break into the low end of the market, Hyundai priced the Excel very low. As a result, despite selling many units, it didn't generate sufficient profits to invest in critical marketing activities — promotion, customer service, product improvements, and building a strong dealer network — that would have continued to meet the needs of the market. In this instance, a short-run sales-oriented strategy was successful, but the absence of marketing led to disappointing long-run results.[4] Hyundai is now working hard to develop a successful marketing rather than a sales orientation.

**FIGURE 1-1**
**Three stages of marketing evolution.**

The three stages in the development of marketing are shown in Figure 1-1.

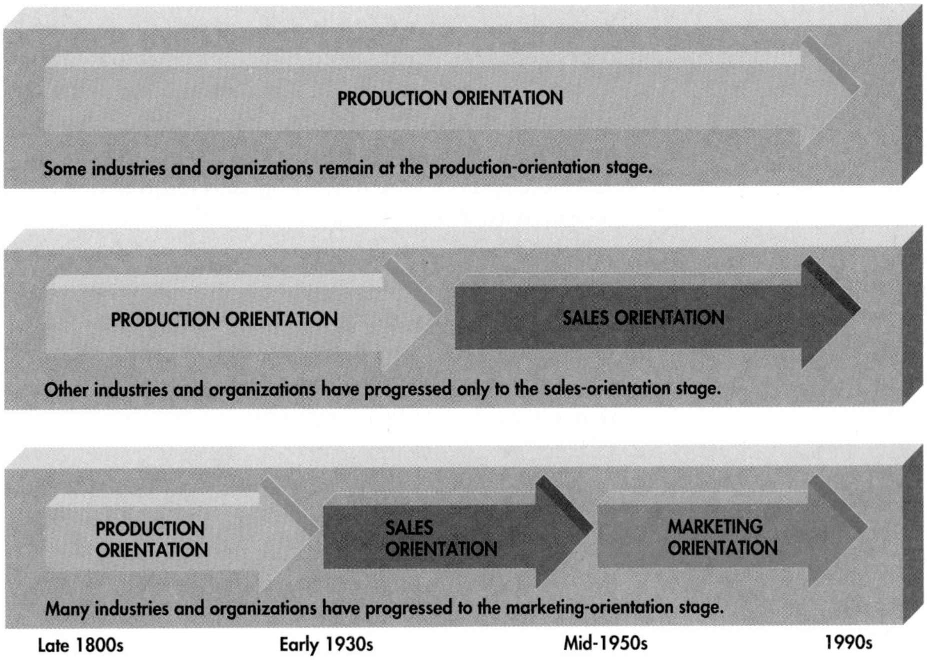


## Production-Orientation Stage

In this first stage, the **production-orientation stage**, a company typically is production-oriented. Executives in production and engineering shape the firm's planning. The function of the sales department is simply to sell the company's output, at a price set by production and financial executives. This is the "build a better mousetrap" stage. The underlying assumption is that marketing effort is not needed to get people to buy a product that is well made and reasonably priced.

During this stage, the term *marketing* is not yet used. Instead, producers have sales departments headed by executives whose job is to manage a sales force. This stage was dominant until the Great Depression in the early 1930s,[5] although some inventors and some small business owners/managers think like this in current times.

## Sales-Orientation Stage

The Depression made it clear that the main problem in the economy no longer was to produce or grow enough but rather was to sell the output. Just making a better product brought no assurance of market success. Firms began to realize that the sale of products required substantial promotional effort. Thus we entered a period — the **sales-orientation stage** — when selling activities and sales executives gained new respect and responsibility from company management.

It was also during this period that selling acquired much of its bad reputation.

## Marketing-Orientation Stage

At the end of World War II there was an enormous pent-up demand for consumer goods created by wartime shortages. As a result, manufacturing plants turned out large quantities of goods that were quickly purchased. However, the postwar surge in consumer spending slowed down as supply caught up with demand, and many firms found they had excess production capacity.

In an attempt to stimulate sales, firms reverted to the aggressive promotional and sales activities of the sales-orientation era. However, this time consumers were less willing to be persuaded. What the sellers discovered was that the war years had also changed the consumer. The service men and women who spent time overseas came home more sophisticated and worldly. In addition, the war effort brought many women out of the home and into the work force for the first time. Because of their experiences, consumers had become more knowledgeable, less naive, and less easily influenced. In addition, they had more choices. The technology developed during the war, when converted to peacetime activity, made it possible to produce a much greater variety of goods.

Thus the evolution of marketing continued. Many companies recognized that to put idle capacity to work they had to produce what consumers wanted. In the **marketing-orientation stage** companies identify what customers want and tailor all the activities of the firm to satisfy those needs as efficiently and effectively as possible.

In this third stage, firms are marketing rather than merely selling. Several tasks that were once associated with other business functions became the responsibility of the top marketing executive, the marketing manager or vice-president of marketing. For instance, inventory control, warehousing, and some aspects of product planning are turned over to the head of marketing as a way of serving customers better. For the firm to be most effective, the top marketing executive must be involved at the beginning of a production cycle, as well as at the end. In addition, marketing must be included in short-term and long-term company planning.

For a firm's marketing to be effective, its top executive must have a favourable attitude towards marketing. Philip Knight, chairman and CEO of Nike, makes this point: "For years we thought of ourselves as a production-oriented company, meaning we put all our emphasis on designing and manufacturing the product. But now we understand that the most important thing we do is market the product."[6]

We are *not* saying that marketing executives should hold the top positions in a company. Nor are we saying that the president of a firm must come up through the marketing department. But it is necessary that the president understand the importance of marketing, that is, be *marketing-oriented.*

Many business firms, as well as some not-for-profit organizations, are presently in this third stage in the evolution of marketing. Others may recognize the importance of a marketing orientation, but have difficulty implementing it for at least two reasons. First, implementation requires accepting the notion that the wants and needs of customers, not the desires of management, direct the organization. As an advertising executive described it, "We must learn to listen [to customers] as a student listens to a mentor."[7] A basic implication of placing customers first is the way an organization describes what it does. Table 1-1 shows how some well-known organizations might define their businesses under a production orientation and how differently the business would be defined using a marketing orientation. Second, managers must understand marketing. On a test of marketing knowledge given recently to over 1,000 chief executives of North American companies, the average score was less than 50 percent![8] Though this particular test may not be a perfect barometer of marketing know-how, the executives' scores raise a question about whether they are or are capable of being marketing-oriented.

Not every organization needs to be marketing-oriented to prosper. A monopolist, such as a provincial power utility, is virtually guaranteed of having customers. Therefore, its management should be much more concerned with low-cost, efficient production than with marketing. There are also instances in which the potential customers consider the product to be so superior that they will seek it out. For example, the world's best heart surgeons or particularly popular artists find a market for their services regardless of their market orientation.

| TABLE 1-1 What business are you in? | | |
|---|---|---|
| Company | Production-oriented answer | Marketing-oriented answer |
| Bell Canada | We operate a telephone company. | We provide multiple forms of reliable, efficient, and inexpensive telecommunications services. |
| Esso | We produce oil and gasoline products. | We provide various types of safe and cost-effective energy. |
| Canadian National | We run a railroad. | We offer a transportation and materials-handling system. |
| Levi Strauss | We make blue jeans. | We offer comfort, fashion, and durability in wearing apparel. |
| Xerox | We make copy machines. | We automate offices. |
| Kodak | We make cameras and film. | We help preserve beautiful memories. |
| Revlon Cosmetics | "In the factory, we make cosmetics." | "In the drugstore, we sell hope" (in the words of its founder). |

## THE MARKETING CONCEPT

As business people began to recognize that marketing is vital to the success of their organizations, a new philosophy of doing business developed. Called the **marketing concept**, it emphasizes customer orientation and co-ordination of marketing activities to achieve the organization's performance objectives. Sometimes the marketing concept is simply stated as "The customer is the boss!" As important as it is to stress customer satisfaction, however, this motto must not be allowed to replace achievement of objectives as the fundamental rationale for the marketing concept.

### Nature and Rationale

The marketing concept is based on three beliefs that are illustrated in Figure 1-2:

**FIGURE 1-2 Components and outcomes of the marketing concept.**

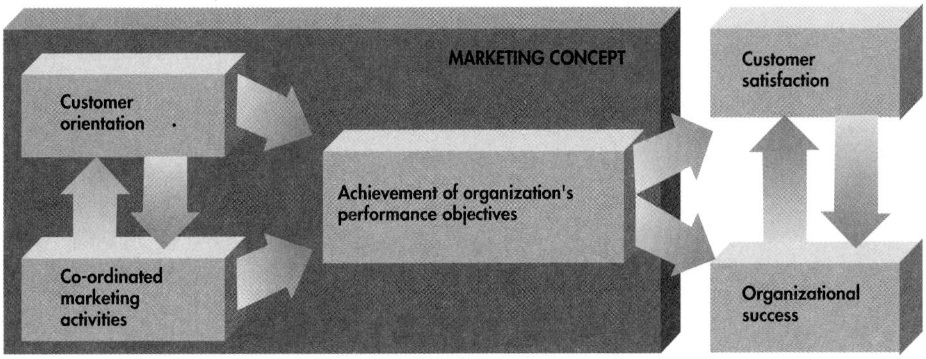


- All planning and operations should be *customer-oriented*. That is, the organization and its employees should be focused on determining and satisfying customers' needs.
- All marketing activities in an organization should be *co-ordinated*. This means that marketing efforts (product planning, pricing, distribution, and promotion) should be designed and combined in a coherent, consistent way, and that one executive should have overall authority and responsibility for the complete set of marketing activities.

- Customer-oriented, co-ordinated marketing is essential to *achieve the organization's performance objectives*. The primary objective for a business is typically a profitable sales volume. In not-for-profit organizations, the objective might be the number of people served or the variety of services offered.

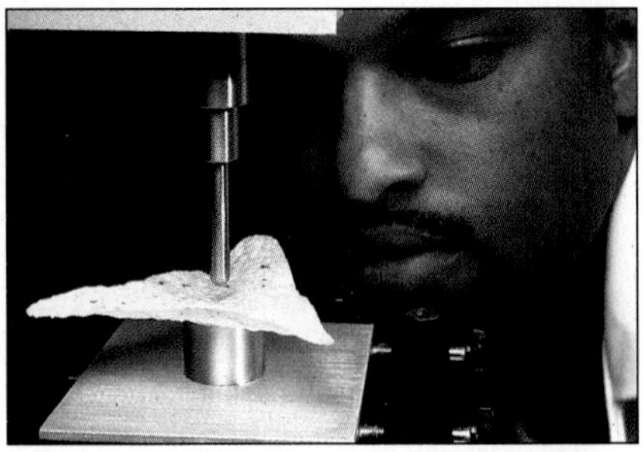

**Frito-Lay chips are tested for the ideal level of crunchiness.**

A customer orientation is demonstrated at Frito-Lay, a company with over 85 varieties of potato chips and over 30 percent of the chip market in Canada and the United States. To stay in touch with what consumers want, it spends over $20 million annually on research and development. That includes over 500,000 consumer interviews each year to investigate such things as preferences in flavours and packaging and the situations in which the product is consumed. But research goes far beyond asking questions. For example, Frito-Lay engineers have developed a simulated human mouth to measure the jaw effort needed to crunch a chip! By comparing taste preference results with test results from the simulated mouth, researchers found that 4 pounds per square inch (2 kg per 2.5 $cm^2$) of oral pressure is the ideal level of crunchiness. Now all chips are tested to meet this standard. As a company executive points out, "We have to be perfect; after all, no one really needs a potato chip."[9]

When we say co-ordinated marketing, we mean combining the marketing elements — product planning, price, distribution, and promotion — so that together they satisfy the market in the most effective and efficient way. In 10 years, Home Depot Inc., which originated in the United States and expanded into Canada, grew into a $2.8-billion home repair chain by bringing together the best feature of the neighbourhood hardware store (advice and information), the attraction of a discount store (low prices), and a selection of products that exceeds both. Home Depot offers over 30,000 separate building supply items and tools, prices that are 30 percent below traditional hardware stores, and knowledgeable, highly motivated sales people.[10]

### The Societal Marketing Concept

Not long after the marketing concept became widely accepted by many firms, it came under fire. For more than 20 years critics have persistently charged that it ignores social responsibility, that although it may lead to an organization achieving its goals, it may at the same time encourage actions that conflict with society's best interests.

From one point of view, these charges are true. A firm may totally satisfy its customers (and in the process achieve a hefty profit), while also adversely affecting society. To illustrate, a Hamilton steel producer might be supplying its customers in Quebec with the right product at a reasonable price, but to do so might be polluting the air and water in Southern Ontario.

However, this need not be the case. A firm's social responsibility can be quite compatible with the marketing concept. Compatibility depends on two things: how broadly a firm perceives its marketing goals, and how long it is willing to wait to achieve those goals. A firm that sufficiently extends the *breadth* and *time* dimensions of its marketing goals to fulfil its social responsibility is practising what has become known as the **societal marketing concept**.

When the marketing concept's *breadth* is extended, a company recognizes that its market includes not only the buyers of its products but also anyone directly affected by its operations. In our example, the Hamilton steel mill has several "customer" groups to satisfy: (1) the Quebec buyers of the steel, (2) the consumers of the air that contains impurities given off by the mill, and (3) the recreational users of the local river and bay where the mill releases its waste matter.

Extending the *time* dimension of its marketing goals means that a firm should take a long-term view of customer satisfaction and performance objectives, rather than concentrating only on tomorrow. For a company to prosper in the long run, it must satisfy its customers' social needs as well as their economic needs.

Thus the marketing concept and a company's social responsibility are compatible if management strives over the long run to (1) satisfy the wants of its product-buying customers, (2) meet the societal needs of others affected by the firm's activities, and (3) achieve the company's performance objectives. The challenges of balancing these three often-conflicting goals frequently place marketers in ethical predicaments. Thus, the issue of ethics in marketing deserves our consideration.

## ETHICS AND MARKETING

The task of marketers is to influence the behaviour of customers. To accomplish this goal, marketers have a variety of tools at their disposal. Broadly speaking, these tools include the design of a product, the price at which it is offered, the message used to describe it, and the place in which it is made available.

Marketers are also responsible to a variety of groups. Certainly their customers depend on them to provide good products at reasonable prices. Also, their employers expect them to generate sales and profits, suppliers and distributors look to them for their continued business, and society expects them to be responsible citizens. The manner in which these marketing tools can be used, and the frequently divergent interests of the groups dependent on the marketer, create a wide variety of ethical challenges.

One response to the need for ethical guidance comes from the American Marketing Association, which has formulated a code of ethics for its members:

> As a member of the American Marketing Association, I recognize the significance of my professional conduct and my responsibility to society and the other members of my profession:
>
> 1. By acknowledging my accountability to the organization for which I work.
> 2. By pledging my efforts to assure that all presentations of goods, services, and concepts be made honestly and clearly.
> 3. By striving to improve marketing knowledge and practice in order to better serve society.
> 4. By supporting free consumer choice in circumstances that are legal and consistent with generally accepted community standards.
> 5. By pledging to use the highest professional standards in my work and in my competitive activity.
> 6. By acknowledging the right of the American Marketing Association, through established procedure, to withdraw my membership if I am found to be in violation of ethical standards of professional conduct.

### What Is Ethical Behaviour?

A discussion of the philosophical underpinnings of ethics is beyond the scope of this book.[11] However, it is safe to say that there is considerable disagreement over what is and what is not ethical conduct. For example, ethics vary from society to society. Take bribery; though repugnant in most societies, it is an accepted and even necessary aspect of business behaviour in many parts of the world. Thus, for our purposes it is sufficient to say that **ethics** are the rules we play by. They are the standards of behaviour generally accepted by a society. Some of these standards are to be found in the various provincial and company human rights codes, more likely in company ethics codes, but most likely of all in individual codes of conduct.

Many organizations have discovered that employees do not necessarily develop a strong sense of ethical standards on their own. Embarrassing scandals and legal proceedings are frequent reminders that ethical behaviour cannot be taken for granted. The results can be costly as well.

### Instilling an Ethical Orientation

Organizations are not ignoring ethical issues. A growing number are holding ethics workshops, and setting up ethics committees. However, as long as there are conflicting goals and the opportunity for people to make judgements, ethical failures will occur. To relieve some of the pressure on employees faced with ethical challenges and perhaps reduce the frequency and severity of ethical problems, organizations have taken several steps.

One dimension of creating an ethical environment is to make sure that the demands on employees to perform are reasonable. Faced with unrealistic quotas and deadlines, people are much more likely to cut corners to accomplish their objectives.

Another important facet of an ethical orientation is communicating clearly what the organization's standards are. Hewlett-Packard, for example, makes sure that all employees are completely familiar with its extensive code of conduct. To constantly remind employees of the importance of ethical behaviour, Texas Instruments includes a weekly column on ethics in its international electronic news service. Included in the column are answers to specific issues raised by employees.

To help employees deal with ethical issues, some companies are creating a position for a full-time ethics officer or ombudsman. This high-level executive gives advice to senior management as well as responds to the complaints and questions of employees at all levels.

Organizations are also taking greater care to reward only ethical performance. It is important that employees see that success is the result of admirable behaviour, not questionable practices.

### The Benefits of Ethical Behaviour

One could argue that ethical behaviour should in itself be rewarding. However, there are tangible benefits as well. Business is built on relationships with suppliers, customers, employees, and other groups. The strength of those relationships is largely a function of the amount of trust the parties have in each other. Unethical behaviour undermines trust and destroys relationships. It is not surprising that a list of companies noted for their attention to ethical standards — Johnson & Johnson, Coca-Cola, Gerber, IBM, Kodak, 3M, Xerox, and Pitney Bowes — had annual growth rates between 1950 and 1990 nearly twice that of a sample of typical firms traded on the New York Stock Exchange. Thus, ethics is a cornerstone of business success through the building of successful relationships.

## QUALITY IN MARKETING

Quality has always been important to consumers. The success of Maytag's "lonely repairman" television commercials is a good indication. The campaign, which communicates the dependability of Maytag appliances, started on Canadian radio in the 1960s and has been running for more than 25 years. Rather than focus on quality, many businesses chose in the past to maximize output through mass production and minimize prices with cost controls. The objective was to have an "acceptable" level of quality, which meant being as good as the competition. This strategy was successful as long as quality remained fairly constant across competitors.

Some argue that North American and even some European managers became complacent about quality, convincing themselves that even minor improvements would raise costs dramatically and thus make a firm uncompetitive. Meanwhile, new state-of-the-art manufacturing techniques were being adopted by firms overseas. Then these foreign firms added quality as a key ingredient of their strategies. The Japanese even created a national award for quality, called the Deming Prize, in 1951. The award is named for W. Edwards Deming, an American quality consultant who for many years was much better received in Japan than elsewhere.

We now see from the success of foreign firms in automobiles, electronics, and computer hardware the benefits of a commitment to quality. Thus, improving quality became a high priority for North American and many European organizations in the 1980s.

### What Is Quality?

One definition of quality is the absence of variation. That doesn't mean that a Chevrolet should perform as well as a Lexus, or that the service at Holiday Inn should be the same as the service at the Ritz Carlton. What it does mean is that a good or service should consistently deliver what it was designed to, without variation from one experience to another. Thus, every Chevrolet or every Holiday Inn should provide consumers with an identical experience. A series of quality experiences is a symptom of a quality relationship.

The most obvious application of variance control is in manufacturing. In fact, most manufacturers have had quality control departments for many years. However, the title "quality control" was misleading since the job was limited to inspecting finished products to prevent defective ones from leaving the plant. But meeting specifications in production did not ensure quality if the product was poorly designed or improperly serviced after it was sold. Thus, we discovered that the real indication of **quality** is how well a product meets the expectations of the customer.

We also learned that quality control cannot be delegated to one department in an organization. It must be the responsibility of every employee. Anywhere that standards for performance can be set and variations measured, there is an opportunity to apply quality management techniques. The modern approach involves all employees in establishing specific programs to determine and maintain the desired level of quality in a firm's entire operation. This ongoing effort involves design, production, marketing, customer service, and all other units within an organization.

**Quality in Marketing** For marketers, the best measure of quality is repeated **customer satisfaction**. In a competitive environment, the ultimate indication of satisfaction is whether the customer returns to buy a product a second, third, or fourth time and forms a long-term relationship. However, a firm can't afford to gamble that its marketing decisions are correct and then wait for repeat purchases to confirm or reject those judgements. Instead, managers realize that satisfaction is determined by how closely *experience* with a product meets or exceeds a customer's *expectations*. Therefore, marketers must do two things:

1. Ensure that all marketing activities, such as the price of a product, the claims made for it in advertising, and the places in which it is sold, contribute to creating reasonable expectations on the part of the customer.
2. Eliminate variations in customers' experiences in purchasing and consuming the product. This means, for example, that not only should every new Chevrolet you buy provide the same level of performance, but also every interaction you have with a Chevrolet dealer should be consistent and without surprises.

**Instilling Quality** As managers have become more concerned about quality, a variety of quality-improvement programs have been developed. Though the programs have some differences, they typically involve:

- Studying competitors and noncompetitors to identify the highest standards of performance in such areas as delivery delays and eliminating defects. This process is called benchmarking.
- Management and labour working closely together in an atmosphere of trust and co-operation to improve performance.
- All employees making a commitment to constantly search for better ways of performing their functions.
- Forming partnerships with suppliers and customers so that their inputs for improvement can be incorporated into the operation.
- Measuring quality and the resulting customer satisfaction.

## MARKETING AT WORK

### FILE 1-2 GETTING THE QUALITY MESSAGE ACROSS

Construction workers have always been tough customers. And these days, they're even tougher. Because they depend more than ever on the quality and durability of their tools, they're usually quite demanding as well as quite sceptical, reluctant to accept at face value marketing claims about quality. Yet what's really tough is that the power tool industry is worth over $300 million in annual sales, and that Makita Canada Inc. has the lion's share of it. Tough, that is, for DeWalt Industrial Tool Co., a unit of Black & Decker Corp., who launched a new line of quality electric portables and accessories. DeWalt plans to get tough on its own by using a fierce sales strategy that will have sales staff making direct contact with trades people on construction sites, where, by placing actual tools in their hands, workers will be able to judge for themselves quality and performance. Thus, sellers will be able to tackle scepticism at its source.

This constitutes only the beginning of DeWalt's grassroots marketing strategy. The company plans on going further, to discover not only where the contractor is, but to find out who he is, what he does, and then to become involved in his life — in ways as various as sponsoring local baseball teams and hosting barbecues. In fact, DeWalt's plans are so long-term that they even take into account the clients of tomorrow — students studying trades at vocational schools. By offering safety courses and sponsoring school contests, DeWalt hopes these future customers will sit up and notice them. Convincing users about quality and then building relationships with them is expected to cause Makita to sit up and take notice.

Source: Adapted from Randall Scotland, "DeWalt Hammers at Makita in See-Saw Canadian Tool Battle," *Financial Post*, March 30, 1993, p. 12.

## IMPORTANCE OF MARKETING

Coca-Cola is sold in virtually every country in the world. Japanese autos continue to be popular in North America, more so in Canada than in the United States. Consumers choose from numerous brands of personal computers and foods. Some students at your school obtained good jobs following graduation last year. Effective marketing is the common denominator in these diverse situations. And, as these examples suggest, marketing plays a major role in the global economy, in the Canadian socioeconomic system, and in any individual organization. It also has significance for you personally — if not in business, then certainly in your role as a consumer.

### In the Global Economy

World War II and its aftermath created the potential for a truly global economy:

- The war produced massive investments in technology that led to peacetime innovations in communications and improvements in transportation. The ability to be in frequent and virtually instantaneous contact with markets around the world and the capability to move goods had the effect of lowering major barriers to international trade.

- The economic development components of international organizations such as the United Nations produced a recognition of potential markets around the world.
- The basic industries in many European and Asian countries that were destroyed in the war were rebuilt and modernized, producing vast industrial potential.

In the early 1980s, the competition facing Canadian firms came primarily from American, Western European, and Japanese companies. Later, firms in the four "Asian tigers" (Hong Kong, Korea, Taiwan, and Singapore) added to the competitive pressures. Canadians became accustomed to more global brands, as well as well-known brands originating in and manufactured in many other countries. In the 1990s, not only will there be continuing competition from these countries, but there will also be new challenges from countries in Eastern Europe, Latin America, Southeast and Southwest Asia. We live in a global economy where products, services, and marketing ideas in one part of the world influence people and businesses in many other parts.

The increases in global competition and international marketing opportunities are enhanced by the developments in global and regional trading agreements. Tariff reductions and other changes in world trading arrangements under the latest GATT (General Agreement on Tariffs and Trade) round will involve over 160 countries in increased marketing activity, both domestic and international. The European Union (EU), which includes most of the major countries of Western Europe, continues to liberalize trade and permit the free movement of goods, services, and capital among its members. For firms within the EU, new marketing opportunities are being created; for those outside it, new competitive challenges as well as opportunities exist. The North American Free Trade Agreement (NAFTA), creates new opportunities for Canadian firms in the Mexican market, in addition to the access already available to the U.S. market. The potential inclusion of Chile, Argentina, and other Latin American countries in the NAFTA promises opportunity as well as competition.

What will determine the future success of international marketers? Leaders in business, government, and academia in Canada, the United States, Japan, Western Europe, and Central Europe were recently asked their opinions. Protecting the environment emerged as the most important issue. That is, consumers will continue to demand quality products, but they will also insist that manufacturing and consuming products not damage the environment. Also, firms that can achieve a high level of standardization around the world while still tailoring their products to meet local preferences will have both cost and market-acceptance advantages.[12] Both are lofty objectives, but not beyond the reach of imaginative firms. Clearly, a global marketplace is emerging. Most nations today — regardless of their degree of economic development or their political philosophy — recognize the importance of marketing beyond their own national borders. Indeed, economic growth in the less developed nations of the world depends greatly on their ability to design effective marketing systems to produce global customers for their raw materials and industrial output.

### In the Canadian Socioeconomic System

Aggressive, effective marketing practices have contributed to the high standard of living in Canada. The efficiency of mass marketing — extensive and rapid communication with customers through a wide variety of media and a distribution system that makes products readily available — combined with mass production has made more products available with increased value. As a result, we enjoy things that once were considered luxuries and in many countries are still available only to people earning high incomes.

## MARKETING AT WORK

### FILE 1-3 GOING INTERNATIONAL WITH HONEY

Canadians are the second biggest consumers of honey in the world, but a healthy appetite for the sweet substance wasn't enough to keep Bee Maid Honey Ltd. alive and buzzing. Until the mid-1980s, the company's owners — the Alberta, Saskatchewan, and Manitoba honey producers' co-operatives — had refused to move south and challenge the turf of fellow westerners, the Iowa-based Sioux Honey Association, a co-operative just like them. However, when the going gets tough . . . it's time to sting. And Bee Maid couldn't refuse the world's richest market when it was sitting right on its doorstep.

So the company began moving into the United States. But one of its biggest initial obstacles was getting American shoppers to recognize the superiority of its product. In Europe, where honey gets dipped into much more often than in North America, Bee Maid can sell its product with no more than a label that says "Pure Canadian Honey," thanks to Canadian honey's worldwide reputation for a lightness in flavour and colour that appeals to mass markets. With taste thus constituting its greatest marketing asset abroad, Bee Maid became the first company to make wide use of in-store sampling when it took on the American market. In doing so, it became a familiar product in 20 states, making it into the number one honey in many markets.

But it's not all sweet victory yet. Low-cost Asian imports coupled with a law permitting U.S. packers to blend up to 25 percent foreign honey with domestic stuff — while still labelling the product as domestic — have created recent problems for Bee Maid. The company is reacting quickly, seizing this occasion as an opportunity to diversify beyond mere honey and offer a range of new products including honey mustards, honey barbecue sauces, flavoured honeys, as well as a dry honey introduced as a substitute for sugar. Ultimately, it hopes to become a food company dealing with food products that may not have anything to do with honey.

Source: Adapted from Pam Bristol, "The Sweet Smell of Survival," *Globe and Mail*, December 7, 1993, p. B26.

Since about 1920 (except during World War II), the available supply of products has far surpassed total demand. Making most products has been relatively easy; the real challenge has been marketing them.

**Employment and Costs** We can get an idea of the significance of marketing in the Canadian economy by looking at how many of us are employed in some way in marketing and how much of what we spend covers the cost of marketing. *Between one-fourth and one-third of the Canadian labour force is engaged in marketing activities*. This figure includes employees in retailing, wholesaling, transportation, warehousing, and communications industries, as well as people who work in marketing departments of manufacturers and those who work in marketing in agricultural, mining, and service industries. Furthermore, over the past century, jobs in marketing have increased at a much more rapid rate than jobs in production, reflecting marketing's expanded role in the economy.

On the average, *about 50 cents of each dollar we spend as consumers goes to cover marketing costs*. The money pays for designing the products to meet our needs, making products readily available when and where we want them, and informing us about products. These activities add want-satisfying ability, or what is called **utility**, to products.

**Creating Utility** A customer purchases a product because it provides satisfaction. That something that makes a product capable of satisfying wants is its utility. And it is through marketing that much of a product's utility is created.

Consider this example. A marketer comes up with an idea for a new product that combines the concept of a single blade from ice skates and the wheels of roller skates, the in-

**What kinds of utilities are provided by home delivery?**

line skate. To produce the product, a company called Rollerblade, Ltd., is begun in Montreal. But Rollerblades made in Montreal in April are of little value to a person in Vancouver who wants to buy a pair for a Christmas present. So the in-line skates must be transported to the west coast (and hundreds of other places) and placed in stores near potential customers. Then, potential buyers must be informed about the product's existence and the benefits it offers through various forms of promotion. Let's see what kinds of utility have been created in this process:

- **Form utility** is associated primarily with production — the physical or chemical changes that make a product more valuable. When lumber is made into furniture, form utility is created. This is production, not marketing. However, marketing research may aid in decision making regarding product design, colour, quantities produced, or some other aspect of a product. For in-line skates, as with most other products, marketing is involved in developing the concept, designing the appearance, and selecting the materials and colours. All these things contribute to the product's form utility.
- **Place utility** exists when a product is readily accessible to potential customers. Rollerblades in Montreal are of little value to customers in Vancouver or most other parts of the country. So, physically moving the product to a store near the customer adds to its value.
- **Time utility** means having a product available when you want it. In the case of Rollerblades, customers like having a selection of skates in stores so they can shop at their convenience. Having a product available when we want it is very convenient, but it means that the retailer must anticipate our desires and maintain an inventory. Thus, there are costs involved in providing time utility.
- **Information utility** is created by informing prospective buyers that a product exists. Unless you know a product exists and where you can get it, the product has no value. Advertising that describes in-line skates or a sales person answering a customer's questions about the durability of Rollerblades creates information utility. **Image utility** is a special type of information utility. It is the emotional or psychological value that a person attaches to a product or brand because of its reputation or social standing. Image utility ordinarily is associated with prestige or high-status products such as designer clothes, expensive foreign automobiles, or certain residential neighbourhoods. However, the image-utility value of a given product may vary considerably depending on different consumers' perceptions. For example, Coca-Cola underestimated the image utility of its traditional product when it tried to replace it with New Coke.
- **Possession utility** is created when a customer buys the product — that is, ownership is transferred to the buyer. Rollerblades in a store's window or on the store's shelf don't provide the customer with any satisfaction. Thus, for a person to consume and enjoy the product, a transaction must take place. This occurs when you exchange your money for a pair of the skates.

### In Organizations

Our primary focus is on the performance of marketing in organizations. We will examine a wide variety of managerially useful concepts that apply to business firms marketing goods and services, as well as not-for-profit organizations.

Marketing considerations should be an integral part of all short-range and long-range planning in any company. Here's why:

- The success of any business comes from satisfying the wants of its customers, which is the social and economic basis for the existence of all organizations.
- Although many activities are essential to a company's growth, marketing is the only one that produces revenue directly. (This is sometimes overlooked by the production managers who use these revenues and the financial executives who manage them.)

## MARKETING AT WORK

### FILE 1-4 WHAT KIND OF UTILITY IS ROCKPORT TRYING TO CREATE?

A new category of shoes that is growing in popularity is called "comfort shoes." They incorporate the technology of athletic shoes in dressier styles for today's active consumers. However, a major problem is the products' appearance. Comfort and style in shoes are not very compatible features. To provide the shoes the market demands, Reebok International, the originator of the category with its Rockport brand, invests heavily in marketing research to gauge what consumers want and also in product development to figure out how to produce it.

Are these utilities likely to be produced by manufacturing or marketing working alone?

When managers are internally focused, products are designed by designers, manufactured by manufacturing people, priced by financial managers, and then given to sales managers to sell. This approach generally won't work in today's environment of intense competition and constant change. Just *building* a good product will not result in sales.

**Service Marketers** Canada has gone from being primarily a manufacturing economy to becoming a more service-oriented economy. As opposed to goods, services are now much more important as the object of a transaction. Examples are communications, entertainment, education, financial services, and repairs.

Because the production of goods dominated our economy until recently, most of the marketing research and writing focused on concepts and strategies related to goods (such as groceries, clothing, machine tools, and automobiles) rather than on services. Now some of the most marketing-oriented firms are in the services sector. Thus, we will investigate what makes services different from goods, and we will see how these differences affect marketing.

**Not-for-Profit Marketers** During the 1980s and early 1990s many not-for-profit organizations realized they needed effective marketing programs to make up for shrinking government subsidies, a decrease in charitable contributions, and other unfavourable eco-

**Blue Cross produces intangible insurance services.**

nomic conditions. Charities with falling donations, service clubs with declining memberships, and symphony orchestras playing to vacant seats all began to understand that marketing was essential to help them turn their situations around.

Today political organizations, museums, and even churches — all organizations that formerly rejected any thought of marketing — are embracing it as a means of growth and, for some, survival. This trend is likely to accelerate during the remainder of the 1990s for two reasons:

- Increasing competition among not-for-profit organizations. For example, the competition among colleges and universities for students interested in specialized programs is intensifying as the number of young people of college age declines, and the search for donors has become more intense as the number of charities has increased.
- Not-for-profit organizations need to improve their images and gain greater acceptance among donors, government agencies, news media, and of course, consumers, all of which collectively determine an organization's success.

**What exchange is this not-for-profit organization interested in stimulating?**

The Canadian Cancer Society is involved in the biggest cover-up in Canadian History.
These people are involved in a nationwide cover-up.
All across Canada, the Society is teaching people to cover-up and protect themselves from skin cancer. One group of volunteers have started the "Mole Patrol", which hands out free sun screen and information about sun exposure and skin cancer. And other Society sponsored events, like "The Sunsational Beach Party", raised awareness of how important proper protection from the sun can be.
These types of education programs are vital - because every year, 47,000 Canadians develop skin cancer. And thanks to the Society's efforts, more Canadians than ever are protecting themselves from this easily preventable disease.
If you would like to find out more, simply contact your local unit of the Canadian Cancer Society. They're doing everything under the sun to help Canadians prevent skin cancer.
CANADIAN CANCER SOCIETY
SOCIÉTÉ CANADIENNE DU CANCER
THE FIGHT AGAINST CANCER HAS MANY FACES

## In Your Life

Okay, so marketing is important globally, in our economy, and in an individual organization. But what's in it for you? Why should you study marketing? There are a number of reasons:

- Marketing pervades so many daily activities. Consider how many marketers view you as part of their market. With people like you in mind, firms such as Nike, Loblaws, Microsoft, and Kellogg's have designed products, set prices, created advertisements, and chosen the best methods of making the product available to you. In response, you watch television with its commercials, buy various articles in different stores, and sometimes complain about prices or quality. Marketing occupies a large part of your daily life. If you doubt this, just imagine for a moment what it would be like if there were no marketing institutions — no retail stores to buy from or no advertising to give you information, for example.
- Studying marketing will make you a better-informed consumer. You'll understand more about what underlies a seller's pricing and how brand names are selected, as well as the role of promotion and distribution.

- Lastly, marketing probably relates — directly or indirectly — to your career aspirations. If you are thinking about a marketing major and employment in a marketing position, you can develop a feel for what marketing managers do. (For an introduction to the many career opportunities in the field, we especially suggest you read Appendix A, "Careers in Marketing.") If you're planning a career in accounting, finance, or other business field, you can learn how marketing affects managerial decision making in these areas. Finally, if you are thinking about a career in a nonbusiness field such as health care, government, music, or education, you will learn how to use marketing in these organizations.

## SUMMARY

Business firms and not-for-profit organizations engage in marketing. Products marketed include goods as well as services, ideas, people, and places. Marketing activities are targeted at markets, consisting of product purchasers and also individuals and groups that influence the success of an organization.

The foundation of marketing is exchange, in which one party provides to another party something of value in return for something else of value. In a broad sense, marketing consists of all activities designed to generate or facilitate an exchange intended to satisfy human needs.

In a business context, marketing is a total system of business activities designed to plan, price, promote, and distribute want-satisfying products to target markets to achieve organizational objectives. The main difference between marketing and selling is that in selling the emphasis is on the product; in marketing the emphasis is on customers' wants.

Marketing's evolution has gone through three stages: It began with a production orientation, passed through a sales orientation, and is now in the marketing orientation. In this third stage a company's efforts are focused on identifying and satisfying customers' needs.

Some organizations remain at the first or second stage, not progressing to the marketing-orientation stage, because they have monopoly power or because their products are in such great demand. Other firms have difficulty implementing a marketing orientation.

A business philosophy called the marketing concept developed to aid companies with supply capabilities that exceed consumer demand. According to the marketing concept, a firm is best able to achieve its performance objectives by adopting a customer orientation and coordinating all its marketing activities. More recently, the societal marketing concept has been proposed as a philosophy by which a company can satisfy its customers and at the same time fulfil its social responsibility.

Marketing is practised today in all modern nations, regardless of their political philosophy. As international competition has heated up, the attention paid to marketing has increased. Between one-fourth and one-third of the work force is involved with marketing, and about one-half of consumer spending covers the cost of marketing. Marketing creates form, information, place, time, and possession utilities.

Depending on circumstances, marketing can be vital to an organization's success. In recent years numerous service firms and not-for-profit organizations have found marketing to be necessary and worthwhile. Marketing also can be useful to individual students, particularly in reference to career opportunities.

## KEY TERMS AND CONCEPTS

The numbers next to the terms refer to the pages on which the terms and concepts are defined. In addition, the glossary at the end of the book defines all key terms and concepts.

**Marketers (4)**
**Market (5)**
**Exchange (5)**
**Relationship (5)**
**Marketing (6)**
**Product (7)**
**Production-orientation stage (9)**
**Sales-orientation stage (9)**
**Marketing-orientation stage (10)**
**Marketing concept (11)**
**Societal marketing concept (12)**
**Ethics (13)**
**Quality (15)**
**Customer satisfaction (15)**
**Utility (18)**
**Form utility (19)**
**Place utility (19)**
**Time utility (19)**
**Information utility (19)**
**Image utility (19)**
**Possession utility (19)**

## QUESTIONS AND PROBLEMS

1. Explain the concept of an exchange, including the conditions that must exist for an exchange to occur, and give an example of an exchange that does not involve money.
2. Name some companies that you believe are still in the production or sales stage in the evolution of marketing. Explain why you chose each of them.
3. Explain the three elements that constitute the marketing concept.
4. "The marketing concept *does not* imply that marketing executives will run the firm. The concept requires only that whoever is in top management be marketing-oriented." Give examples of how a production manager, company treasurer, or personnel manager can be marketing-oriented.
5. For each of the following organizations, describe what is being marketed.
   a. Calgary Stampeders professional football team.
   b. Canadian Airline Pilots Association labour union.
   c. Professor teaching a first-year chemistry course.
   d. Police department in your city.
6. One way of explaining the utilities provided by marketing is to consider how we would live if there were no marketing facilities. Describe some of the ways in which your daily activities would be affected if there were no retail stores or advertising.
7. Name two service firms that, in your opinion, do a good marketing job. Then name some that you think do a poor marketing job. Explain your reasoning in each case.

## HANDS-ON MARKETING

1. Select an organizational unit at your school (e.g., food service, placement office, intramural sports, library), observe the operation, and interview an administrator and some customers to identify: (a) what is being exchanged; and (b) whether the unit is production-, sales-, or marketing-oriented.
2. Find out from a retailer in your community what changes or additions have been made during the last year to better serve customers. Categorize the changes by the six types of utilities discussed in the chapter. Based on your conversation, what utility dimension has the greatest potential for improving the business in the future?

## NOTES AND REFERENCES


1. Adapted from Richard Wright, "Beating America First," *Profit*, September 1993, pp. 38-40.
2. We use the terms *needs* and *wants* interchangeably because marketing is relevant to both. Technically, needs can be viewed in a strict physiological sense (food, clothing, and shelter), with everything else defined as a want. However, from a customer's perspective the distinction is not as clear. For example, many people would consider a phone or a car a necessity.
3. The American Marketing Association, the largest professional organization in the marketing field, recently developed a very similar definition: "Marketing is the process of planning and executing the conception, pricing, promotion, and distribution of ideas, goods, and services to create exchanges that satisfy individual and organizational objectives." See Peter D. Bennett, ed., *Dictionary of Marketing Terms*, American Marketing Association, Chicago, 1988, p. 115.
4. Peter F. Drucker, "Marketing 101 for a Fast-Changing Decade," *The Wall Street Journal*, November 20, 1990, p. A16.
5. Robert J. Keith, "The Marketing Revolution," *Journal of Marketing*, January 1960, p. 37.
6. Geraldine E. Williams, "High Performance Marketing: An Interview with Nike's Phil Knight," *Harvard Business Review*, July-August 1992, p. 92.
7. Lynn B. Upshaw, "It's Time to Let Customers Take the Marketing Wheel," *Marketing News*, March 2, 1992, p. 4.
8. Kevin J. Clancy and Robert S. Shulman, *The Marketing Revolution*, Harper Business, New York, 1991.
9. Robert Johnson, "In the Chips," *The Wall Street Journal*, March 22, 1991, p. B1.
10. Chuck Hawkins, "Will Home Depot Be 'The Wal-Mart of the '90s'?" *Business Week*, March 19, 1990, pp. 124-125.
11. For a thorough discussion of ethics in marketing, see Gene R. Laczniak and Patrick E. Murphy, *Ethical Marketing Decisions: The Higher Road*, Allyn & Bacon, New York, 1993.
12. Michael R. Czinkota and Ilkka Ronkainen, "Global Marketing 2000: A Marketing Survival Guide," *Marketing Management*, Winter 1992, pp. 37-45.

APPENDIX

# A

## CAREERS IN MARKETING

After you graduate, then what? For most people it means looking for a job. But your goal should be more than just finding employment. Your first full-time job after graduation should serve as a springboard to a successful career. No matter how difficult or how easy the economic times are, setting goals and planning a job search will help get you where you want to go.

To get started in the right direction, you should begin your preparation as early as possible in college, and launch your actual job search at least one term, and preferably nine months, before graduation.

To get you thinking about your postgraduation ambitions and upcoming job search, this appendix first discusses choosing a career. Then a variety of career opportunities in marketing are described. Finally, in a section that is relevant to all students regardless of major, guidelines on obtaining a postgraduation job are presented.

### CHOOSING A CAREER

One of the most significant decisions you will ever make is choosing a career. This career decision will influence your future happiness, self-fulfilment, and well-being. Yet, unfortunately, career decisions often seem to be based on insufficient information, analysis, and evaluation of alternatives.

Early in the career-decision process, everyone should spend some time in introspection. Introspection is the process of looking into yourself and honestly assessing what you want and what you have to offer. Let's look briefly at what this involves.

#### What Do You Want?

Perhaps this question would be better worded if we asked, "What is important to you in life?" To answer this broad question, you must answer several more specific ones, such as the following:

- How important are money and other financial rewards?
- Do you want your career to be the main event in your life? Or do you see a career only as the means of financing leisure-time activities?

- How important are the social surroundings, climate, and other aspects of the environment in which you live?
- Would you prefer to work for a large company or a small organization?
- Would you prefer living and working in a small town or in a major urban centre?
- Are you willing to relocate to another part of the country? How often would you be willing to move?
- How important to you is the social prestige of a career?
- Do you prefer work that is evenly paced or occasionally hectic? How do you deal with the pressure of deadlines?
- Do you need tangible signs of results on a job to feel fulfilled?
- Do you prefer to work alone or as part of a team?

Another way to approach the question of what you want from a career is to identify — in writing — your goals in life. List both your intermediate-term goals (3 to 5 years from now) and your long-term goals (10 years or more).

Still another approach is to simply describe yourself in some detail. By writing a description of your personality, likes and dislikes, and hopes and fears, you may be able to identify various careers that would (or would not) fit your self-image.

### What Can You Offer?

Next you need to identify in some detail your strong and weak points. Why would anyone want to hire you? What are your qualifications? What experience—work, education, extracurricular activities—do you have that might be attractive to prospective employers? Since these attributes aren't acquired overnight, you should start developing them early in your college program. However, keep in mind that prospective employers are much more interested in what a person accomplished in various roles than how many different titles he or she had. So be selective, and do a few things well.

## WHAT ARE THE MARKETING JOBS?

In Chapter 1 we noted that about one-quarter to one-third of all jobs are in the field of marketing. These jobs cover a wide variety of activities and a great range of qualifications and aptitudes. For instance, jobs in personal selling call for a set of qualifications that are different from those in marketing research. A person who is likely to be successful in advertising may not be a good prospect in physical distribution. Consequently, the aptitudes and skills of different individuals make them candidates for different types of marketing jobs.

In this section we shall briefly describe the major jobs in marketing, grouping them by title or activity. The types of positions that are most often available to graduating students are summarized in Table A-1.

### Personal Selling

Sales jobs are by far the most numerous of all the jobs in marketing. Personal selling spans a broad array of activities, organizations, and titles. Consider the following people: a driver-sales person for Coca-Cola, a sales clerk in a department store, a sales engineer providing technical assistance in sales of hydraulic valves, a representative for Canadair selling a fleet of airplanes, and a marketing consultant selling his or her services. All these people are engaged in personal selling, but each sales job is different from the others.

Sales jobs of one sort or another are available in virtually every locality. This means that you can pretty well pick the area where you would like to live and still get involved in personal selling.

TABLE A-1 Eight entry-level marketing jobs for university and college graduates

| Job title | Comments |
|---|---|
| Sales representative | Responsible for selling the organization's goods or services to customers. Customers may be ultimate consumers, intermediaries, or other organizations. |
| Sales (or marketing) support person | Assists sales manager and staff in implementing programs, such as trade shows and dealer or sales force incentive programs. Marketing support position involves broader responsibility, including assisting in product development and distribution. |
| Customer service representative | Assists customers after the sale, often by handling complaints and requests for information and/or service. Particularly common in the business-goods sector. |
| Retail management executive trainee | Position is common in department store chains. After training, usually moves through rotating assignment in buying and management of selling department. Ultimately, person focuses on either buying or store management. |
| Assistant store manager | Position is common in chains that have small specialty stores in shopping centres. Assists in overseeing day-to-day activities of the store, especially staffing and display. In effect, is a trainee position. |
| Assistant media buyer | Common starting position in an advertising agency. Assists buyer in purchasing advertising space and time for firms that are the agency's clients. Another entry-level position, working for either an agency or an advertiser, is junior copywriter. |
| Research trainee | Found in various large organizations and in marketing research firms. After or during training, assists with one or more phases of the research process, such as data collection, data analysis, or report preparation. |
| Assistant (or assistant to) product manager | Assists in planning and, especially, implementing marketing program for a specific brand or product line. Most commonly found in large companies that sell consumer goods or services. |

There are opportunities to earn a *very* high income in personal selling. This is especially true when the compensation plan is straight commission or is a combination of salary plus a significant incentive element.

A sales job is the most common entry-level position in marketing. Furthermore, as illustrated in Figure A-1, a sales job is a widely used stepping stone to a management position. Many companies recruit people for sales jobs with the intention of promoting some of these people into management positions. Personal selling and sales management jobs are also a good route to the top in a firm because it is relatively easy to measure a person's performance and productivity in selling.

A sales job is different from other jobs in several significant ways that will be discussed in Chapter 19. Sales people represent their company to customers and to the public in general.

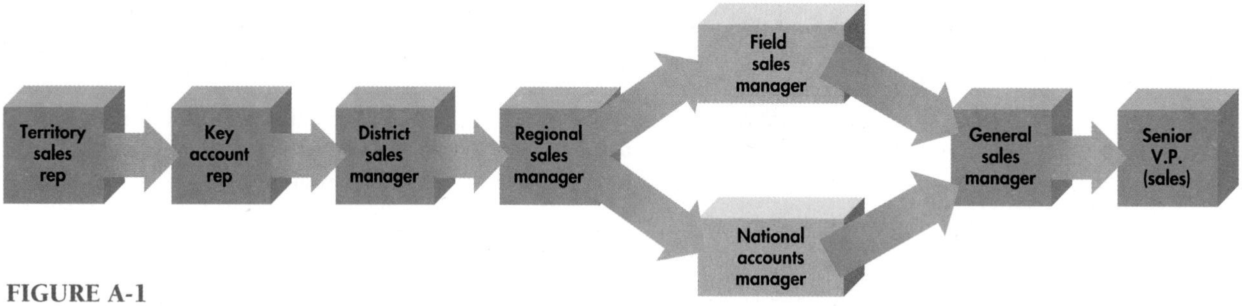


**FIGURE A-1**
**Typical career path starting in personal selling.**

The public ordinarily does not judge a firm by its factory or office personnel. Also, outside sales people (those who go to the customers) operate with very little or no direct personal supervision. They must have considerable creativity, persistence, and self-motivation. Furthermore, sales jobs often involve travelling and require much time away from home and family. Among white-collar jobs, personal selling generally rates low in social status and prestige.

All in all, selling is hard work, but the potential rewards are immense. Certainly no other job contributes as much to the success of an organization. Remember — nothing happens until somebody sells something!

### Store Management

Retailing is second only to personal selling in the number of job opportunities for new graduates. The two primary areas of opportunity in department store, specialty, and discount chains are in merchandising or buying (described in the next section) and store management.

Store managers have a great deal of responsibility and authority. A store manager's authority related to acquiring merchandise (the buying function) varies greatly from one firm to the next. However, once the merchandise arrives in the store, the manager has the responsibility and authority for displaying, selling, and controlling the inventory. Store managers in most companies, either directly or indirectly through department heads, oversee personal selling, promotion, credit, personnel management, and store security.

The entry-level position for store management typically is assistant department manager, department manager, or assistant store manager, depending on the size of the store. The performance of a store or department manager is directly measurable by sales or profits. Therefore, speed of advancement into higher positions is determined primarily by the quality and quantity of results produced by the manager.

### Buying and Purchasing

Most medium-size and larger organizations employ people who specialize in buying, as opposed to selling, goods and services. In one type of position, people select and acquire merchandise for resale. In another type of position, people purchase goods and services not for resale but for use in a manufacturing process or in operating an organization.

Every retail organization needs people to buy the merchandise that is to be resold. Frequently the route to the top in retailing is through the buying (also called merchandising) division of the business. Large retailers have many positions for buyers and assistant buyers. Each merchandise department normally has a buyer. Consequently, you often have a chance to work with particular products that interest you.

There also are centralized buying offices that buy for several different stores or chains. These resident buying offices usually are in Toronto and a few other large cities.

A purchasing agent is the business-market counterpart of the retail store buyer. Virtually all firms in the business market have purchasing departments. People in these departments buy for the production, office, and sales departments in their firms.

Retail buyers and purchasing agents need many of the same skills. They must be able to analyze markets, determine merchandise needs, and negotiate with sellers. It's also necessary to have some knowledge of credit, finance, and physical distribution.

### Advertising

Opportunities in advertising can be found in many different jobs in various organizations. The three primary areas of opportunity are:

- Advertisers, including manufacturers, retailers, and service firms. Many of these organizations prepare and place their own ads. In some of these firms the advertising department is a large one.
- Various media (including newspapers, radio and TV stations, and magazines) that carry ads.
- Advertising agencies that specialize in creating and producing individual ads and entire promotion campaigns.

Jobs in advertising encompass a number of aptitudes and interests — artistic, creative, managerial, research, and sales. The advertising field holds real opportunity for the artistic or creative person. Agencies and advertising departments need copywriters, artists, photographers, layout designers, printing experts, and others to create and produce ads.

Account executive is a key position in advertising agencies. People in this position are the liaisons between the agency and its clients (the advertisers). Account executives coordinate the agency's efforts with the clients' marketing programs.

Another group of advertising jobs involves buying and selling media time and space. Advertisers and agencies also often need people who can conduct buyer-behaviour studies and other marketing research.

### Sales Promotion

The main function of sales promotion is to tie together the activities in personal selling and advertising. Effective sales promotion requires imagination and creativity, coupled with a sound foundation in marketing fundamentals.

One aspect of sales promotion is the design and creation of retailers' in-store displays and window displays. Another aspect deals with trade shows and other company exhibits. Sales promotion activities also include the development and management of premium giveaways, contests, product sampling, and other types of promotion.

### Marketing Research

Marketing research jobs cover a broad range of activities that will be outlined in Chapter 8. People are hired for marketing research jobs by manufacturers, retailers, services marketers, government agencies, and other organizations. There also are a large number of specialized marketing research companies. Generally, however, there are fewer jobs in marketing research than in personal selling or in retailing.

Marketing researchers are problem solvers. They collect and analyze masses of information. Thus they need an aptitude for precise, analytical work. Some quantitative skills are needed, particularly an understanding of statistics.

### Product/Brand Management

In Chapter 9 we discuss briefly the position of product manager in connection with the organizational structure for new product planning and development. Product managers (sometimes called brand managers) are responsible for planning and directing the entire marketing program for a given product or group of products.

Early on, product managers make decisions about packaging, labelling, and other aspects of the product itself. Product managers also are responsible for the marketing research necessary to identify the market. They plan advertising, personal selling, and sales promotional programs for their products. Product managers are concerned with pricing, physical distribution, and legal issues of the product.

In many respects, being a product manager is like running your own business. Product managers must have good analytical skills to keep abreast of what competitors are doing and what is happening in the market. They also need to be tactful and persuasive to gain the co-operation of functional areas such as manufacturing and sales.

### Physical Distribution

Many jobs exist in the field of physical distribution, and the prospects are even brighter as we look ahead to the year 2000. More and more firms are expected to adopt the systems approach in physical distribution to control the huge expenses involved in materials movement and warehousing.

Manufacturers, retailers, and all other goods-handling firms have jobs that involve two stages of physical distribution. First the product must be moved to the firm for processing or resale. Then the finished products must be distributed to the markets. These physical distribution tasks involve jobs in transportation management, warehousing, and inventory control. In addition, many transportation carriers and warehousing firms also provide a variety of jobs that may interest you.

### Public Relations

The public relations department is a valuable connection between an organization and its various publics. The department must deal with, or go through, the news media to reach these publics. Public relations people must be especially good in communications. In fact, these people often have college degrees in communications or journalism, rather than in marketing.

In essence, the job of public relations is to project the desired company image to the public. More specifically, public relations people are responsible for telling the public about the company — its products, community activities, social programs, environmental improvement activities, labour policies, and views regarding controversial issues. Public relations specialists are particularly important — and very visible — when a company responds to adverse publicity. Such publicity may come from a governmental investigation or a charge of unethical practices or unsafe products, as when Johnson & Johnson dealt with the Tylenol tampering and Wal-Mart responded to charges of selling goods made with child labour.

Whether disseminating favourable publicity or responding to adverse publicity, the company's position must be stated in a clear, understandable, and — above all — believable fashion.

### Consumer Affairs and Protection

The broad area of consumer affairs and protection encompasses several activities that provide job and career opportunities. Many of these jobs are an outgrowth of the consumer movement to be discussed in Chapter 24. Many companies have a consumer affairs department to handle consumer complaints. Several federal and provincial agencies keep watch on business firms and provide information and assistance to consumers. Grocery products manufacturers and gas and electric companies regularly hire graduates to aid consumers in product use. Government and private product-testing agencies hire people to test products for safety, durability, and other features.

### Other Career Areas

In this short appendix it is not possible to list all the careers that stem from marketing. We have, however, covered the major areas. You may get additional career ideas from the next section, which deals with organizations that provide these opportunities.

## WHERE ARE THE MARKETING JOBS?

In this section we briefly describe the types of companies and other organizations that provide jobs in marketing. This section also includes comments on jobs in international marketing and a comparison of job opportunities in large versus small organizations.

### Types of Organizations

Literally thousands of organizations provide jobs and career opportunities in marketing. The organizations can be grouped into the following categories.

**Manufacturing** Most manufacturing firms provide career opportunities in all the activities discussed in the previous section. In their promotional mix, some manufacturers stress personal selling while others rely more on advertising. Even small companies offer job opportunities in most of the categories we have mentioned.

Because most manufacturers make products that are used by other businesses, their names are not familiar to the general public. Unfortunately, many college and university graduates overlook some of these potentially excellent employers just because they don't recognize their corporate names. Starting salaries often are higher in manufacturing firms than in retailing and the other organizations described next.

**Retailing** Retailing firms provide more marketing jobs by far than does any other organizational category, but most of these jobs are not intended for college graduates. Careers in retailing are not well understood by students, who may equate retailing with clerking in a department store or filling shelves in a supermarket. Students often perceive that retail pay is low and that retail work-hours include a lot of evenings and weekends.

Actually a career in retailing offers many attractive features for university and college graduates. There are opportunities for very rapid advancement for those who display real ability. Performance results, such as sales and profits, are quickly and highly visible. If you can produce, management will generally note this fact in a hurry.

While the starting pay in many (but not all) stores is lower than in manufacturing, the compensation in higher-level retailing jobs typically is excellent. There are good retailing jobs in virtually every geographic area. Also, large retail chains generally have excellent management-training programs for newly hired college graduates.

Perhaps the main attractions in retailing are less tangible. Retailing can be an exciting field. You are involved constantly with people — customers, suppliers, and other workers. And there are challenges in merchandise buying, especially finding out what will sell well — what customers really want.

It is easier to start a career in retailing than in many other fields. In large stores there are jobs involving personnel management, accounting controls, and store operations (receiving, credit, and customer service departments). However, the lifeblood of retailing is the buying and selling of merchandise or services. Thus the more numerous and better-paying positions are in merchandising and store management. A typical career path is presented in Figure A-2. Note that after several years of experience in both areas, a retail manager often decides to concentrate on merchandising or store management.

**Wholesaling** Career opportunities in wholesaling generally are less well understood and appreciated than those in retailing or manufacturing. Wholesaling firms typically do not recruit on campuses, and they generally have a low profile among students.

Yet opportunities are there. Wholesalers of consumer products and industrial distributors provide many jobs in buying, personal selling, marketing research, and physical dis-

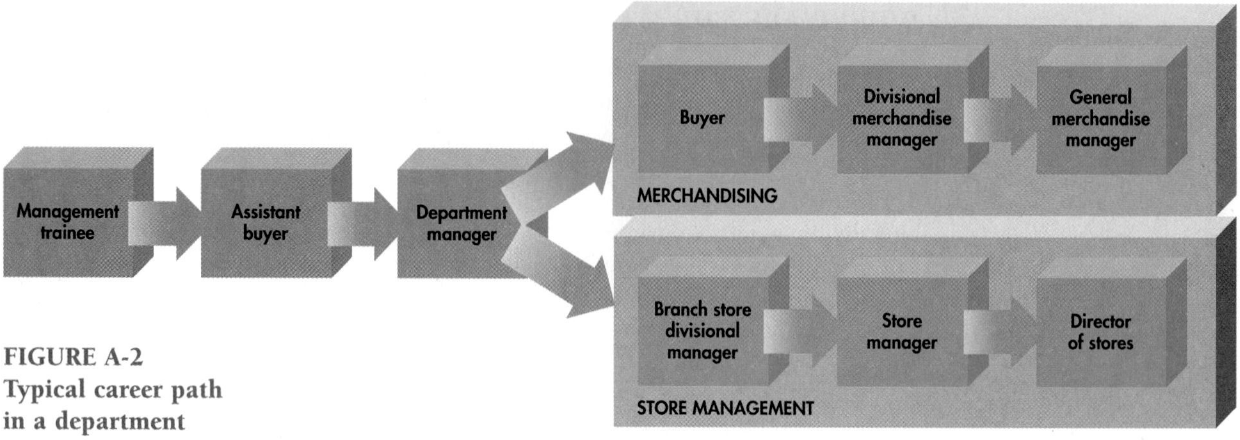


**FIGURE A-2**
**Typical career path in a department store chain.**

tribution. Manufacturers' agents, brokers, and the other agent intermediaries discussed in Chapter 16 also offer jobs and careers. Wholesaling intermediaries are increasing in numbers and in sales volume, and their future is promising.

Services Marketing The broad array of service industries that will be discussed in Chapter 12 provides a bonanza of job and career opportunities in marketing. Many of these fields are expected to experience rapid growth in the future. The travel, hospitality, finance, entertainment, communications, and professional-services fields are prime examples. Recognizing the importance of marketing, many of these industries and organizations within them are now adding marketing-related personnel. Most of these firms really are retailers of services. Consequently, many of the statements we made earlier about retailing careers are relevant here.

Other Business Areas Besides the general types of organizations just described, more specialized business firms hire graduates for marketing-related positions. Entry-level opportunities can be found with communications media (such as TV stations), advertising agencies, franchise systems, participation and spectator sports organizations, public utilities, and transportation firms (such as truck lines).

Not-for-profit Organizations As will be described in Chapter 22, not-for-profit organizations are realizing that marketing is key to their success. Consequently, it is likely that jobs and careers in many not-for-profit organizations will open up in large numbers during the 1990s. Consider the wide variety of not-for-profit organizations — hospitals, museums, educational institutions, religious organizations, foundations, charities, and political parties, among others. Given this diversity, you can expect to find a wide range of marketing-related positions in not-for-profit organizations.

Government Countless federal and provincial government organizations hire people for marketing positions. Here we include the major government departments — agriculture, human services, and the others. We also include all the regulatory agencies. Government organizations employ people in purchasing, marketing research, public relations, physical distribution, consumer affairs and protection, and even advertising and sales promotion. Sometimes students tend to overlook the many marketing career opportunities in government.

### Careers in International Marketing

Students who like to travel and experience different cultures may want to work at least part of the time in foreign countries. They may be interested in careers in international marketing, and they may even major in international business. Typically, however, companies do not hire graduates and immediately assign them to jobs in international marketing. People are normally hired for entry-level positions in the domestic divisions of a company's operations. Then, after some years of experience with the firm, an employee may have an opportunity to move into the firm's international divisions. If you have international aspirations, you would be wise to study a second language and take advantage of opportunities to learn about other cultures.

### Large versus Small Companies

Should you go to work for a large company or a small firm? Or should you go into business for yourself upon graduation? For over a decade now, more and more students have been saying that they want to work for a small company. They feel that there is more freedom of action, more rapid advancement, and less restraint on their life-styles in smaller firms.

Perhaps so. And certainly no one should discourage you from a career in small business. *But* we typically recommend to students (who ask for advice) that they start their careers in a big company. Then, after a few years, they can move into a smaller firm. There are three reasons for this recommendation:

- A large firm is more likely to have a good training program in your chosen field of activity. Many students have little or no practical marketing experience. The fine training programs provided by numerous large manufacturers, retailers, and major service marketers can be critical in launching a career.
- You can learn something about how a big company operates. After all, when you go into a smaller firm, large companies may be your competitors. So the more you know about them, the better able you will be to compete with them.
- After working for a while for a big company, you may change your mind and decide to stay with the larger firm after all. On the other hand, let's say that you want to go to a small company after you have worked a few years at a big firm. At that point it will be relatively easy to move from a large company to a smaller one. If you start in a small firm, however, and later want to move into big business, it is not so easy to move.

We have discussed various career fields and types of organizations that hire people in these fields. Now let's take a brief look at how you should go about getting a job with one of these organizations.

## HOW DO YOU SEARCH FOR A JOB?

This book and your entire course are designed to teach you the fundamentals involved in developing and managing a marketing program. These fundamentals are applicable regardless of whether you are marketing a good, service, idea, person, or place. They are equally applicable to (1) large and small organizations, (2) domestic and international marketing, and (3) business and nonbusiness organizations.

Now let's see whether we can apply these fundamentals to a program designed to market a person — *you*! We shall discuss a marketing approach that you can use to get a job and to start a career. Here we are talking about a *marketing* career. This same approach, however, can be used in seeking jobs and careers in any field.

### Identify and Analyze the Market

The first step in building a marketing program is to identify and analyze the market. In this case the market consists of prospective employers. Right now you don't know exactly who comprises that target market. So you must research several possible markets and then eventually narrow down your choice. In effect, we are talking about "choosing a career." Much of what we discussed in the first section of this appendix is applicable here.

You should initially get as much information as you can regarding various career opportunities in marketing. For information sources you might start with one or two professors whom you know reasonably well. Then turn to the placement office in your school, or wherever postgraduation jobs are listed. Many companies prepare recruiting brochures for students, explaining the company and its career opportunities.

Newspapers and business journals are another good information source. Sometimes, looking carefully through a series of company annual reports can give you ideas of firms you might like to work for. You should exchange information with other students who also are in the job market.

In summary, learn all you can about various firms and industries. Then, from this information search, zero in on the group of companies that are your leading choices. You will now be ready to develop the marketing mix that will be effective in marketing yourself to your target markets.

### Product

In this case the "product" you are planning and developing is yourself and your services. You want to make yourself as attractive as possible to your market — that is, prospective employers.

Start your product planning by listing in some detail your strong and weak points. These will lead into another list — your qualifications and achievements. This introspection is something we discussed in the first section of this appendix in connection with choosing a career.

When you are considering your qualifications, it may help to group them into broad categories such as these:

- Education — schools attended, degree earned, grade-point average, major, favourite subjects.
- Work experience — part-time and full-time, responsibilities.
- Honours and awards.
- Extracurricular activities and organizations — memberships, offices, committees, accomplishments.
- Hobbies.

Later we will discuss the presentation of your qualifications in a personal data sheet.

An important aspect of product planning is product differentiation. How can you differentiate yourself from all the other grads? What have you done that is different, unusual, or exceptional? This doesn't have to be earth-shaking — just something that shows a trait such as initiative, imagination, or perseverance.

Another part of product planning is packaging. When you go for an interview, be sure that the external package looks attractive. People do judge you by your appearance, just as you judge products by the way they look. This means paying attention to what you wear and how you are groomed. A good impression starts with prospective employers' first meetings with you.

### Price

"What salary do you expect?" "How much do you think we should pay you?" These are two of the questions a prospective employer might ask in a job interview. If you have not done some thinking in advance regarding the price you want for your services, these questions may throw you.

As part of your marketing program, find out what the market price is for people entering your field. Talk with placement officers, career counsellors, professors, and other students who are in the job market. From these sources you should get a pretty good idea of starting salaries in entry-level positions. Use this information to decide *before* the interview on a range of salaries for yourself. Remember that income can be stated in several different ways. For example, there may be a base salary, the possibility of a bonus, and fringe benefits such as the use of a company-supplied car.

### Distribution Channel

There are only a few major channels you are likely to use in marketing yourself to prospective employers. The simplest channel is your placement office, assuming that there is one on your campus. Most colleges and universities, through their placement offices, host and assist companies that send job recruiters to do on-campus interviewing.

Another channel is help-wanted ads in business journals, trade journals, and newspapers. Perhaps the most difficult, but often the most rewarding, channel is going directly to firms in which you are especially interested — knock on doors or write letters seeking a job interview. Many employers look favourably on people who display this kind of initiative in their job search.

### Promotion

Other than planning and developing an excellent product, the most important ingredient in your marketing mix is a good promotion (or communications) program. Your promotion will consist primarily of written communications (a form of advertising) and interviewing (a form of personal selling).

To stand out from the crowd and be noticed, job applicants have tried everything from singing telegrams to skywriting. One enterprising student paid $400 to rent the sides of an 18-wheeler. Soon after his name, phone number, and plea for a job began cruising the highways, he received several hundred calls.

Most applicants use more conventional approaches. Frequently your first contact with a prospective employer is a cover letter in which you state briefly why you are writing to that company and what you have to offer. You enclose a personal résumé, and you request an appointment for an interview.

**Cover Letter** In the opening paragraph of your cover letter, you should indicate why you want to work for the firm. Mention a couple of key points regarding the firm — points you learned from your research. In the second paragraph, you can present a few highlights of your own experience or personality that make you an attractive prospect. In the third paragraph, state that you are enclosing your résumé, and request an appointment for an interview, even suggesting some dates and a time when you will telephone to arrange the meeting.

**Résumé** A résumé (also called a personal data sheet) is really a brief history of yourself. Personal computers and word processing packages make it possible to design a distinctive and very professional-appearing résumé. You can start with biographical information such as your name, address, and phone number. Then divide your résumé into sections, including education, work experience, and activities that were described in the product section.

At the end of your résumé, provide information about your references. One approach is simply to state, "References furnished upon request." The rationale for this approach is that interested employers will ask for names and addresses of references if or when they want to contact them. An alternative approach is to list your references by name (along with their titles, addresses, and phone numbers) at the bottom of your résumé or on a separate sheet. The thinking behind this approach is that you should make it as easy as possible for a prospective employer to check your references.

It is difficult to overstate the value of a persuasive cover letter and a distinctive résumé. They are critically important elements in your job search. They certainly are two of the most important ads you will ever write.

**Interview** Rarely is anyone hired without one or more interviews. In some cases, as when recruiters visit your campus, the interview is your initial contact with the firm. In other situations the interviews come as a result of your letter of introduction and résumé.

The interview is an experience in personal selling — in this case, you are selling yourself. People are often uncomfortable and uptight in interviews, especially their first few, so don't be surprised or disappointed if you are. One way to reduce your anxiety and increase the likelihood of impressing the interviewer is to prepare yourself to answer tough questions that may be asked:

- Why should we hire you?
- What are your distinctive strengths?
- Do you have any weaknesses, and how do you plan to overcome them?
- What kind of job do you expect to have in five years?

Your performance in an interview often determines whether you get the job. So be on your toes — be honest in your answers, and try to look more relaxed and confident than you may feel!

After interviews with a company have been completed, it is worthwhile to write a letter to each of the interviewers. Thank them for the opportunity to learn about their company, and, if appropriate, restate your interest in the job.

**Evaluating Job Offers** You are likely to receive multiple job offers *if*:

- The economy is fairly healthy, *and*
- You have at least an acceptable academic record,
- You conduct an aggressive job search,
- You develop a persuasive cover letter and professional résumé, and
- You perform well in job interviews.

You should evaluate the suitability of a single job offer or compare multiple job offers against a set of criteria that are important to you. The criteria you select and the importance you place on them require some careful thought. Below are examples of criteria you might consider.

- Will you be happy in your work? It is no accident that we frequently hear about "Monday blues" (the weekend of freedom is finished and I have to go back to work) and "TGIF" (thank God it's Friday). Many people in society are not happy with their jobs. Normally, half or more of your waking hours will be spent at work, commuting to and from work, or doing job-related work at home. So you should look for a job and career that you will enjoy.
- Does the career fit your self-image? Are the job and career in line with your goals, dreams, and aspirations? Will they satisfy you? Will you be proud to tell people about your job? Will your spouse (and someday your teenage children) be proud of you in that career?

- What demands or pressures are associated with the career? Some people thrive on pressure. They constantly seek new challenges in their work. Other people look for a more tranquil work experience. They do not want a job with constant demands and deadlines to meet.
- Do the financial factors meet your needs? How does the starting salary compare with those of other jobs? Consider what the job is likely to pay after you have been there three to five years. Some engineering jobs, for example, have high starting salaries, but soon hit a salary ceiling. In contrast, some marketing jobs have lower starting salaries but no upper limits.
- Are there opportunities for promotion? You should evaluate the promotion patterns in a job or in a firm. Try to find out how long it normally takes to reach a given executive level. Study the backgrounds of presidents of a number of large companies in the industry. Did they come up through engineering, the legal department, sales or marketing, accounting, or some other area?
- Are the travel considerations suitable? Some jobs involve a considerable amount of travel whether you are an entry-level worker or an executive. Other jobs are strictly in-house, with no travel at all. You need to assess which situation would meet your needs.
- Is there job or career "transportability"? Are there similar jobs in many other geographic areas? If you and your spouse both are career-oriented, what will happen to you if your spouse is transferred to another city? One nice thing about such careers as teaching, retailing, nursing, and personal selling is that generally these jobs exist in considerable numbers in many different locations.
- What is the supply-and-demand situation in this field? Determine generally how many job openings currently exist in a given field, as compared with the supply of qualified applicants. At the same time, study the future prospects regarding this supply-and-demand condition. Determine whether a present shortage or overcrowding of workers in a field is a temporary situation or is likely to exist for several years.

## WHERE IS THERE MORE INFORMATION?

We encourage you to keep in mind the questions and guidelines presented in this appendix as you take this course and progress through your academic program. To provide you with additional advice and guidance, some excellent reference sources are listed below. It's not too early to start thinking about — and planning — your search for a postgraduation job!


- Richard Nelson Bolles, *What Color Is Your Parachute? A Practical Manual for Jobhunters and Career Changers*, Ten Speed Press, Berkeley, CA, 1992.
- Lila B. Starr, *Careers in Marketing*, VGM Career Horizons, Lincolnwood, IL, 1991.

# CHAPTER 2 GOALS

After studying this chapter, you should have an understanding of:

- The concept of environmental monitoring (environmental scanning).
- How external environmental forces such as demography, economic and competitive conditions, social and cultural forces, and the political and legal system can influence a company's marketing program.
- How external forces such as suppliers and intermediaries that are specific to a firm can influence its marketing program.
- How the nonmarketing resources and departments within a firm can influence how it practises marketing.

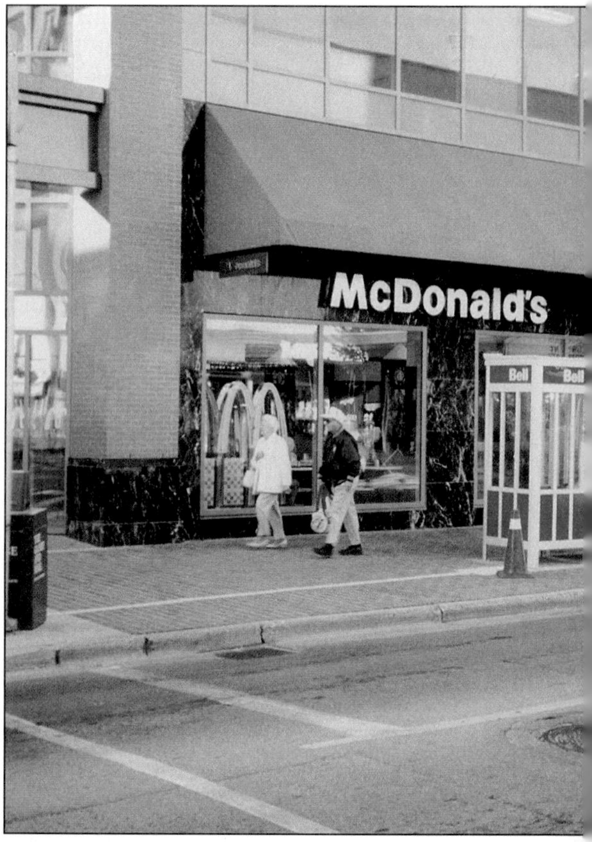

CHAPTER 2

# THE CHANGING MARKETING ENVIRONMENT

## How McDonald's Stays Current in the Changing Food Market

Over the past 30 years or so, McDonald's Restaurants has enjoyed success in North America and in an increasing number of countries around the world because of its commitment to giving its customers value based on a simple menu — hamburgers, French fries, milkshakes, and soft drinks. The prices were low, the quality was consistent, the service was very fast, and all McDonald's restaurants were virtually identical and spotlessly clean.

But McDonald's has changed. It no longer has its standard hamburgers-and-fries menu; it offers a wide variety of products, including eggs and sausage for breakfast, pizza, and salads — even lobsterburgers in eastern Canada. The company has opened outlets in unusual locations, including zoos, airports, schools, universities, and in Wal-Mart stores in the United States and Canada. McDonald's meals for children are even served on United Airlines flights out of Chicago. Abandoning its policy of opening stores only with a minimum of 80 seats, the company has opened stores in small towns such as Fergus, Ontario, and Marystown, Newfoundland, with as few as 40 seats. McDonald's even operated a mobile restaurant in the resort area of Grand Bend, Ontario, a program that the company plans to expand to different special events such as concerts.

Why the changes? Simply put, McDonald's is responding to changes that are taking place in the company's external environment. In recent years, its growth rate has slowed down and its position at the top of the fast-food industry has been slipping.

The most obvious change that McDonald's and virtually every other company and organization is facing relates to the composition of the Canadian population. For many years, McDonald's main target customer group was young couples with children. In fact, a theme of one of the company's early advertising campaigns was "You deserve a break today." Today, people are marrying later in life and are having fewer children. As a result, McDonald's traditional customer base has eroded.

There are also cultural changes with which the company has had to contend. As consumers have become more health-conscious, their consumption of beef and other red meats has declined. McDonald's original menu of burgers, fries, and shakes is not exactly the diet most recommended by dietitians today. The pressures of time, the number of people working outside the home, and the decreasing number of traditional families have combined to increase the total market for fast-food restaurants.

Consumers want convenience. In the past, they jumped in the car and drove to McDonald's or other restaurants — many of the early fast-food restaurants, such as A&W, were drive-ins. Today, they can pop something into the microwave oven or telephone Pizza Pizza or one of hundreds of other pizza restaurants to have a pizza delivered. Another challenge to the way in which the fast-food industry had been doing business came as consumers became more concerned about their physical environment. The "clamshell" polystyrene hamburger packaging McDonald's had been using for years was criticized by people who demanded the use of recycled and biodegradable packaging, prompting McDonald's and others to return to cardboard packages.

At the same time all these changes were taking place, competitors were getting stronger. Restaurants such as The Keg, Red Lobster, and Mother Tucker's cut into the higher end of the family restaurant market by offering extensive menus, all-you-can-eat salad bars, and a casual family atmosphere. At the other end of the market, long-established fast-food chains such as Burger King, Wendy's, and A&W represented more competition with lower prices, fast service, and expanded menu offerings.[1]

Adjusting to these environmental changes is the big problem facing McDonald's and other companies today. What other environmental factors should McDonald's consider? What courses of action are open to George Cohon, CEO of McDonald's Restaurants of Canada, as he plans a competitive strategy for his company for the future?

McDonald's Restaurants and other companies and organizations are responding to changes in their external environment — especially the demographic, economic, competitive, and cultural environment. The strategic changes being considered by McDonald's and others are the result of environmental monitoring, a practice that more and more companies are adopting in order to stay on top of the changing world in which they operate.

Environmental forces influence the way in which a company does its marketing. Some of these forces are external to the company, while others come from within. There isn't much that management can do about controlling the external forces, but it generally can control the internal ones. McDonald's, like any organization, must manage its marketing program within its combined external and internal environments.

## ENVIRONMENTAL MONITORING

**Environmental monitoring** — also called *environmental scanning* — is the process of: (1) gathering information regarding a company's external environment, (2) analyzing it, and (3) forecasting the impact of whatever trends the analysis suggests.

Today, much of the environmental discussion is about our *physical* environment — air quality, water pollution, disposal of solid waste, and conserving natural resources. However, we will use the term *environment* in a much broader sense in this chapter.

An organization operates within an *external* environment that it generally *cannot* control. At the same time, there are marketing and nonmarketing resources *within* the organization that generally *can* be controlled by its executives.

There are two levels of external forces:

- *Macro* influences (so called because they affect all firms) include demographics, economic conditions, culture, and laws.
- *Micro* influences (so called because they affect a particular firm) consist of suppliers, marketing intermediaries, and customers. Micro influences, while external, are closely related to a specific company and are part of its total marketing system.

Successful marketing depends largely on a company's ability to manage its marketing programs within its environment. To do this, a firm's marketing executives must determine what makes up the firm's environment and then monitor it in a systematic, ongoing fashion. These marketing executives must be alert to spot environmental trends that could be opportunities or problems for their organization. And they must be able to respond to these trends with the resources they can control.

## EXTERNAL MACROENVIRONMENT

The following six interrelated macroenvironmental forces have a considerable effect on any organization's marketing system. Yet they are largely not controllable by management. See Figure 2-1.

- Demography.
- Economic conditions.
- Competition.
- Social and cultural forces.
- Political and legal forces.
- Technology.

Note that we just said that these forces are *largely*, but not *totally*, uncontrollable by management in a firm. That is, a company must be able to manage its external environment to some extent. For example, through company and industry lobbying in Ottawa or provincial capitals, a company may have some influence on the political-legal forces in its environment. Or new-product research and development that is on the technological frontier can influence a firm's competitive position. In fact, it may be *our* company's technology that is the external environmental force of technology that is affecting *other* organizations.

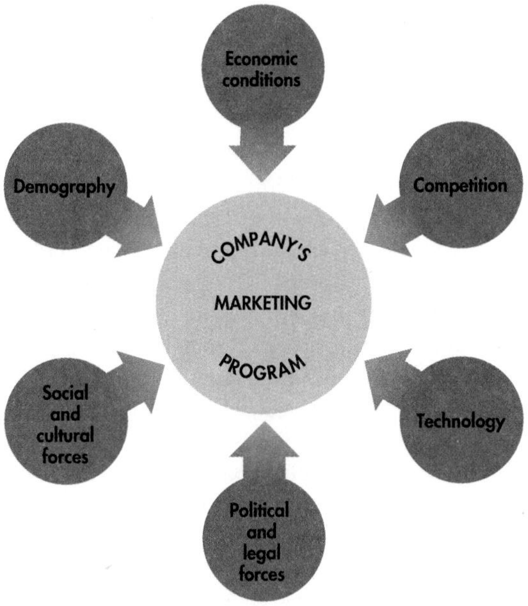


**FIGURE 2-1**
**External macroenvironment of a company's marketing program.**

**Six largely uncontrollable external forces influence an organization's marketing activities.**

If there is one similarity in these six environmental factors, it is that they are all subject to considerable change — and at different rates. Also, an important point from a marketing perspective is that not all markets or all consumers are affected by these changes in the same way. For example, some consumers cope with difficult economic times better than others do; some people are more adept at using the latest technological innovations; some accept new ideas and new ways of doing things much more readily than others do. The result is an extremely complex marketplace that is influenced by external factors that the marketer cannot influence but must understand and appreciate. In the following section, we will examine each of the six major environmental forces.

## Demography

We may define **demography** as the statistical study of human population and its distribution. It is especially important to marketing executives, because people constitute markets. Demography will be discussed in greater detail in the section on markets. At this point we shall mention just a couple of examples of how demographic factors influence marketing systems.

In the mid-1980s, for the first time in history, the number of people 65 and older surpassed the number of teenagers — and this gap will widen considerably as we progress towards the end of the century. Retired and near-retired Canadians now represent 26 percent of the population but control 75 percent of personal wealth and account for 60 percent of discretionary buying power. In 1996, the over-50 population will total 7.6 million; by 2006, it will have reached 9.5 million.[2] The marketing implications of such a trend are obvious. More and more companies are turning their attention towards meeting the needs of older Canadians. Some have added products like Jhirmack's shampoo for greying hair. Airlines, movie theatres, and many retail stores offer discounts to customers aged 65 and older. Banks have established special seniors' banking areas in their branches to serve older customers, only to find that not all retired and older customers want the special treatment. One study found that such initiatives aimed at the older market often do not meet with success because many healthy and active older people would prefer not to admit that they are getting older; many reject such terms as "senior citizen" and "golden years." When asked how old they feel, most people reply with a number that is 75 percent of their actual age.[3]

Another important demographic change relates to the growing market segment made up of single people. Today, well over 20 percent of Canadian households are made up of people who live alone. An increasing percentage of these single-person households contain older people, mostly women, who have been widowed. Many of these single, older consumers are healthy and lead active lives and represent an attractive target market segment for travel and tour companies.

The marketing implications of this demographic force are almost limitless. The frozen-food industry caters to this market with high-quality frozen entrées in a wide variety of menu offerings, many of which involve single servings. Automobile manufacturers and banks recognize the increased buying power of single women and have developed marketing programs and services specifically for this segment. Homebuilders are designing homes, condominium units, and housing developments with older singles in mind, while tour companies regularly offer bus tour vacations and cruises for this increasingly affluent group.

The aging of the baby-boom generation will, 10 years from now, bring changes in middle-aged values, tastes, and concerns as most of that age group will be into their fifties. With their children grown, they will indulge themselves with well-earned vacations and luxury cars instead of the family minivan. Their expanding waistlines will bring a boom in larger-sized jeans and more conservative casual clothes. As they forsake their city and suburban residences for cottage country, the price of recreational property will rise. Their continued interest in healthy living will see them into their fifties and sixties, with renewed emphasis on sensible eating and less active sports such as curling, golf, and bowling.[4]

But it is not just the baby boomers who represent a lucrative and challenging target segment for the rest of the century and beyond. Their children, now in their late teens and early twenties — a group often referred to as Generation X — themselves constitute an attractive age segment. Because there were so many babies born between 1947 and 1966, they produced lots of children, even though they had fewer children per family. This generation, who faces the challenge of entering the work force in circumstances less attractive than those their parents faced, tends to react differently to conventional approaches to marketing.[5]

## MARKETING AT WORK

### FILE 2-1 WHAT IS A CUSTOMER, ANYWAY?

It is generally accepted these days that the objective of marketing is to produce satisfied customers. Marketers in customer-focused companies concentrate their efforts on attracting and keeping customers. But rarely do we stop and ask ourselves who these customers are or how we define a "customer."

David Foley, writing in *Strategy* magazine, suggests there are four customer types common in most organizations. This way of looking at the customer marketplace focuses on the concept that not everyone is a customer or even has the prospect of becoming a customer. Another lesson that is often difficult for some companies to learn is that there are some customers and prospective customers the company may not want to attract or keep, because they are not profitable or because they simply do not fit with the company's objectives.

Foley's four customer types are:

**Advocates:** These are satisfied customers who become goodwill ambassadors for the company, its products, and its services. They are so satisfied that they promote the company to others and are more valuable than these purchases may indicate. They are not necessarily heavy buyers but are more likely to have an emotional commitment to the company.

**Customers:** These are people, excluding the advocates, who do business with a company. Unless customers are upgraded to advocate status, there is a very real risk of losing them, particularly if they perceive the company and its products as offering no distinct competitive advantage — and thus no reason for them to deal with it. Many companies have introduced loyalty marketing programs such as Zellers' Club Z and Air Canada's Aeroplan to attempt to retain customers in a market where competitors may be perceived to be offering much the same products and services.

**Prospects:** These are people who are aware of the company and may have bought its products and services in the past. All former customers and inactive customers are prospects who have to be given a reason to come back.

**Rejectors:** These are most likely dissatisfied former customers who probably complained and were not satisfied. They have had a bad experience and not only will not be back, but will tell all their friends.

Source: David Foley, "How Does One Define a Customer?" *Strategy*, February 22, 1993, p. 29.

### Economic Conditions

People alone do not make a market. They must have money to spend and be willing to spend it. Consequently, the **economic environment** is a significant force that affects the marketing system of just about any organization. A marketing system is affected especially by such economic considerations as the current stage of the business cycle, inflation, and interest rates.

**Stage of the Business Cycle** Marketing executives should understand what stage of the business cycle the economy currently is in, because this cycle has such an impact on a company's marketing system. The traditional business cycle goes through four stages — prosperity, recession, depression, and recovery. However, various economic strategies have been adopted by the federal government; these strategies have averted the depression stage in Canada and other developed countries for 60 years. Consequently, today we think of a three-stage **business cycle** — prosperity, recession, recovery — then returning full cycle to prosperity.

Essentially, a company usually operates its marketing system quite differently during each stage. Prosperity is characterized typically as a period of economic growth. During this stage, organizations tend to expand their marketing programs as they add new products and enter new markets. A recession, on the other hand, involves higher rates of unemployment and reduced consumer spending and typically is a period of retrenchment for consumers and businesses. People can become discouraged, scared, and angry. Naturally these feelings affect their buying behaviour, which, in turn, has major implications for the marketing programs in countless firms.

Recovery finds the economy moving from recession to prosperity: the marketers' challenge is determining how quickly prosperity will return and to what level. As the unemployment rate declines and disposable income increases, companies expand their marketing efforts to improve sales and profits.

**Inflation** **Inflation** is a rise in price levels. When prices rise at a faster rate than personal income, there is a decline in consumer buying power. During the late 1970s and early 1980s, Canada experienced what for us was a high inflation rate of 10 to 15 percent. Although inflation rates declined in recent years to less than 5 percent, with economic growth there is a fear that higher rates may return. Consequently, this spectre continues to influence government policies, consumer psychology, and business marketing programs.

Inflation presents some real challenges in the management of a marketing program — especially in the area of pricing and cost control. Consumers are adversely affected as their buying power declines. At the same time, they may overspend today for fear that prices will be higher tomorrow.

**Interest Rates** **Interest rates** are another external economic factor influencing marketing programs. When interest rates are high, for example, consumers tend to hold back on long-term purchases such as housing. Consumer purchases also are affected by whether they think interest rates will increase or decline. Marketers sometimes offer below-market interest rates (a form of price cut) as a promotional device to increase business. Auto manufacturers have used this tactic extensively in recent years, for example.

**Employment Rates** One of the most important indicators of the strength of an economy is the percentage of people who are employed and the percentage looking for work. During a strong economic period, unemployment rates are generally lower. At other times, or in certain parts of Canada, unemployment is higher. This affects greatly the amount of disposable income that consumers have to spend on products and services and is of considerable interest to marketers.

A marketer must pay considerable attention to the condition of the economy in which his or her company is operating. Purchasers of certain products and services may react quickly to changes or expected changes in economic conditions. The marketer must be ready to respond with changes in the marketing program.

### Competition

A company's competitive environment obviously is a major influence shaping its marketing system. Any executives worth their salt should be constantly gathering intelligence and otherwise monitoring all aspects of competitors' marketing activities — that is, their products, pricing, distribution systems, and promotional programs. Under expanded trade with other countries, Canadian firms will have to pay greater attention to *foreign competition* and, with the movement towards global free trade, increasingly find opportunities for Canadian products and services in foreign markets. The 1990s have, for example, been characterized by the entry into Canada of large American retailers such as Home Depot and Wal-Mart, prompting Canadian retailers to mount a defence strategy.[6] Two aspects of competition we shall consider briefly here are the types of competition and the competitive market structure in which the companies may be operating.

A firm generally faces competition from three sources:

**Watch out, Mr. Christie! Gourmet cookie maker Paige Sillcox of Aurora, Ontario, represents a small-business, niche competitor for the major bakers.**

- Direct *brand competition* and *store competition* from marketers of similar and directly competing products and services. Air Canada competes with Canadian Airlines International on many domestic routes and with KLM, British Airways, United Airlines, Cathay Pacific, and other foreign carriers on international routes. Bauer competes with Micron, Lange, and CCM in the skate business. Cooper competes with overseas companies such as Karhu and Koho for the Canadian hockey stick business. Domestic retailers face competition from international retailers such as Wal-Mart, IKEA, and Marks and Spencer. Even charitable organizations such as the Canadian Cancer Society, the Canadian Heart Foundation, and the Salvation Army compete for our donations and for the time of canvassers and volunteers.
- *Substitute products* that satisfy the same basic need. For example, vinyl records have all but disappeared in the face of competition first from tape cassettes and then from compact discs. Local courier companies and Canada Post have seen a portion of their business taken away by business use of facsimile (fax) machines. Many conventional delivery services are threatened by the use of electronic delivery systems. The use of mail services and long-distance telephone calling is being challenged by electronic mail, and even business air travel may be under threat from teleconferencing and video conferencing offered by telephone companies. Many department stores and clothing retailers are realizing that their competition is coming not only from other stores down the street or in the same town, but from catalogue companies such as Sears and Tilley Endurables, some of which, including L. L. Bean and Lands' End, are in other countries.
- In the third type of competition — more general in nature — *every company or organization* is competing for the consumer's limited buying power. In this regard, the competition faced by a marketer of tennis rackets may come from other companies that are marketing slacks or shoes, or from a car repair bill, or a weekend ski holiday.

On the international scene, two major competitive environmental developments in the 1990s have created important challenges for Canadian marketers. One is the creation of blocs of nations around the world who have combined into free-trade zones, thereby allowing a less restricted flow of products and services across international borders. The unification of the European Community has created one such bloc, while the North American Free Trade Agreement has linked Canada, the United States, and Mexico in an economic union. The second development involves the radical change from a government-controlled system to a relatively free market economy in many countries, particularly in Eastern Europe and the countries of the former Soviet Union. Prices have been decontrolled and government subsidies removed on many products in Poland, Russia, and Estonia, for example. In addition, some major companies and industries, formerly 100 percent government-owned, have been sold to private interests. We will discuss some of these developments in greater detail in our chapter on international marketing.

### Social and Cultural Forces

The task facing marketing executives is becoming more complex because our cultural patterns — life-styles, social values, beliefs — are changing much more quickly than they used to. Here are a few changes in **social and cultural forces** that have significant marketing implications.

**Changing Values — Emphasis on Quality of Life** Our emphasis today is increasingly on the *quality* of life rather than the *quality* of goods. The theme is "Not more — but better." We seek value, durability, comfort, and safety in the products and services we buy. Looking ahead, we will worry more about inflation, health, and the environment, and less about keeping up with the neighbours in autos, dress, and homes. Our growing concern for the environment and our discontent with pollution and resource waste are leading to significant changes in our life-styles. And when our life-styles change, of course marketing is affected.

This change in values among Canadians is evident in a number of areas, as consumers reject the accumulation of assets that characterized the 1980s in favour of a return to products that reflect the values of old. An important influence on the changing values of which Canadian marketers should be aware is the effect the large number of recent immigrants has had on shaping values in certain parts of the country. Each immigrant group brings with it a unique set of values shaped by the culture of its home country. One group of authors has identified the following as characteristic of many of the immigrant groups who have recently made Canada their home:

- A high degree of control by family elders over purchasing power and buying decisions
- A suspicion of government and government-sponsored programs
- An aversion to the use of credit cards and to the accumulation of debt
- A focus on household and family goals, including securing a job, home ownership, and education for the children.

Such values lead to recurrent patterns of behaviour among these consumers, which marketers must consider when plotting marketing strategy to appeal to them.[7]

**Role of Men and Women** One of the most dramatic shifts in our culture has been the changing role of women. What is especially significant is the erosion of stereotypes regarding male-female roles in families, jobs, recreation, and product use.

The evolving roles of women have many implications for marketers. Well over one-half of the women in Canada are working outside the home today. This has changed some traditional buying patterns in households. Many men now shop for groceries, while women buy gas and arrange for auto maintenance. Women working outside the home buy different clothing than women working at home. With both spouses working, the demand for microwave ovens and household services, for example, has increased because time-saving and convenience are major factors in buying. Many women with young children work outside the home, increasing the demand for day-care centres and nursery schools. The sharing of family responsibility is a characteristic of most modern Canadian families, to the point where many employers have begun to extend programs to men that had been available only for women, including paternity leave, pregnancy-education programs, and parenting seminars.

**Attitudes Towards Physical Fitness and Eating** In recent years, an increased interest in health and physical fitness seems generally to have cut across most demographic and economic segments of our society. Participation in physical fitness activities from aerobics to yoga (we could not think of any activity beginning with a Z) is on the increase. Stores supplying activity products and service organizations catering to this trend have multiplied. Public facilities (bicycle paths, hiking trails, jogging paths, and playgrounds) have been improved.

Paralleling the physical fitness phenomenon, we are experiencing significant changes in the eating patterns of Canadians. We are becoming more sensitive to the relationship between our diet and major killing diseases such as heart attacks and cancer. Consequently, there is a growing interest in weight-control eating, foods low in salt, additives, and choles-

terol, and foods high in vitamins, minerals, and fibre content. Health foods now occupy large sections in many supermarkets. Over the past 20 years, per capita consumption of chicken in Canada has increased by more than 35 percent, while consumption of fish increased by almost 50 percent. Similar increases were noted in the consumption of fresh fruit and vegetables, while dramatic declines have been experienced in consumption of beef and canned vegetables. These trends in our food preferences and consumption have contributed to the dramatic changes that have been made in the menu at McDonald's and other restaurants.[8]

**Canadians are eating more pasta than ever before, prompting Italpasta of Brampton, Ontario, to expand its line of pasta products.**

## MARKETING AT WORK

### FILE 2-2 LAYING OUT THE WELCOME PACK

Canada is constantly priding itself on its multiculturalism. But up until recently, marketers had been mystified as to how to reach the 250,000 immigrants who arrive each year and who constitute a market both frustratingly fragmented and yet alluringly lucrative. Knut Brundtland, a marketing expert who immigrated to Canada from Norway 25 years ago, thought back to the jug of Becker's 2% milk that he first purchased back then and still purchases today and came up with the Canada Welcome Pack.

The Pack is composed of 20 basic food and household products — ranging from Cloverleaf tuna and Shreddies cereal to Ivory soap and Crisco oil — worth approximately $40. These are offered free to new Canadians in order to win their loyalty to a particular brand. Although the concept of distributing free samples to promote sales is not original, the fact that the target audience is composed of new citizens instead of new brides, new homeowners or new mothers, is a fresh departure. "Sampling works particularly well among new consumers," claims Brundtland. "Immigrants are the only ready-made new consumers we've got. And no business relationship starts without trial. The company that gets to trial early has a competitive advantage."

Now in its fourth year of operation, Brundtland's program has distributed 75,000 Welcome Packs through supermarkets in Ontario, Quebec, and British Columbia. Considerable success has been achieved, with 75 percent of products being repurchased, compared with the usual 30 percent buyback rate that occurs in most sampling programs. Yet such success comes at a high price. For each product it manufactures for the Welcome Pack, a company spends around $1 — a figure more than four times the cost demanded by regular sampling programs with home drop-offs. It's a program difficult to sustain during times when marketing budgets are drying up. Because of the expense, original participants such as Kraft General Foods Canada have withdrawn from the program, in spite of the fact that Kraft's peanut butter achieved an 80 percent repurchase rate.

Source: Marina Strauss, "Marketers Reach Out to Immigrants," *Globe and Mail*, September 30, 1993.

**Emphasis on Service Quality** As consumers have become more confident of their rights and the power they wield in the marketplace, they have become increasingly demanding concerning the manner in which they are treated by business. Although companies have long appreciated that they must produce quality products in order to compete effectively for the consumer's loyalty, most are now beginning to realize that quality is equally important in the delivery of service. Increasingly, consumers are making decisions to shop at certain stores or to stay at certain hotels not only on the basis of tangible products or the decor of the room or the quality of food in the restaurant (although these are important) but on the much more intangible factor of the level of service. Customers now regularly tell businesses they want to be treated as if they are important and their business is welcomed and appreciated. The best companies have responded with sophisticated programs to measure the satisfaction of customers and with quality programs designed to deliver a higher level of service quality.

**Concern for the Environment** Possibly one of the most important forces that will influence Canadian business and marketing in the coming years is Canadians' concern for the physical environment. As we have seen the damage that has been done to the quality of water, air, and the land during this century, there has been a collective outpouring of support for programs and products that allow us to take action to protect the environment.

Consequently, governments have moved to control the emissions of automobiles and factories; food manufacturers package products in less wasteful and more biodegradable packages; and municipalities across the country have established recycling programs in which many householders and most businesses participate. Supermarket chains stock many products labelled "environmentally friendly," meaning that their packages and ingredients are not harmful to the environment. The result is a major movement driven by the changing values of consumers, who are concerned about air and water pollution, acid rain, holes in the ozone layer, destruction of forests, overfishing, and the disposal of chemicals and solid waste. The environmental movement is a global concern, as consumers in most countries of the world have adopted similar concerns.

Contribute to the green movement.
green³
Samsung makes the contribution easy.
Our new Green³ line of monitors save *energy* with advanced, low power consumption technology. They save *resources*, through the use of recycled and recyclable materials. They also save *money*, by reducing operating costs – up to $75 per year, in the average office*. Green³ monitors offer an assortment of available features, including low radiation technology, Samsung's own colour control system and on-screen programming.
Contribute to the green movement at your Samsung dealer today.
Samsung. Thinking ahead.
SAMSUNG
Samsung Electronics Canada Inc. Tel: (905) 542-3535. Fax: (905) 542-3835
*contact Samsung for test results.

**Even computer monitors are designed to be environmentally friendly by using less electricity and through the use of recycled materials.**

The implications for business should be obvious:

- As many as 50 percent of consumers are expected to make purchases in the future on the basis of environmental factors.
- McDonald's and other fast-food retailers have replaced their polystyrene containers with cardboard and paper containers.
- Companies such as The Body Shop have successfully positioned themselves on the basis of their concern for the environment and other social issues.[9]
- A number of cosmetics manufacturers have begun to offer products that are packaged in recyclable containers and that were developed without testing on animals.
- Many consumers are altering their purchase behaviour significantly as they look for products that do not contain harsh or unnecessary chemicals.[10]

**Desire for Convenience** As an outgrowth of the increase in discretionary purchasing power and the importance of time, there has been a continual increase in the consumer's desire for convenience. We want products ready and easy to use, and convenient credit plans to pay for them. We want these products packaged in a variety of sizes, quantities, and forms. We want stores located close by and open at virtually all hours.

Every major phase of a company's marketing program is affected by this craving for convenience. Product planning is influenced by the need for customer convenience in packaging, quantity, and selection. Pricing policies must be established in conformity with the demand for credit and with the costs of providing the various kinds of convenience. Distribution policies must provide for convenient locations and hours of business. As a result, Canada's banks have placed thousands of automated banking machines in various locations in cities and towns across Canada, so that their customers now have access to banking services in off-premise locations and at any time of the day or night. Most also offer bank-by-phone services. Another example of business responding to the consumer's desire for convenience is the increasing use of catalogues to order products. Even people who live in major cities and who have access to a wide variety of retail stores find it less time-consuming and more convenient to shop from catalogues. These catalogue retailers make shopping from home as easy as possible through the use of toll-free 1-800 telephone numbers, acceptance of major credit cards, and relatively risk-free shopping through generous exchange and refund policies.

**Impulse Buying** Recently there has been a marked increase in impulse buying — purchases made without much advance planning. A shopper may go to the grocery store with a mental note to buy meat and bread. In the store, he may also select some fresh peaches because they look appealing or are priced attractively. Another shopper, seeing cleansing tissues on the shelf, may be reminded that she is running low and so may buy two boxes. These are impulse purchases.

A key point to understand is that some impulse buying is done on a very rational basis. Self-service, open-display selling has brought about a marketing situation wherein planning may be postponed until the buyer reaches the retail outlet. Because of the trend towards impulse buying, emphasis must be placed on promotional programs designed to get people into a store. Displays must be appealing because the manufacturer's package must serve as a silent sales person.

Even the new breed of nonstore retailers, those who sell their products through vending machines, catalogues, and home demonstration parties, must be mindful of the phenomenon of impulse shopping. Again they make their offerings as attractive as possible and facilitate the process by offering free delivery, free catalogues, credit, and toll-free telephone numbers.

## POLITICAL AND LEGAL FORCES

To an increasing extent, every company's conduct is influenced by the political-legal processes in society. Legislation at all levels exercises more influence on the *marketing* activities of an organization than on any other phase of its operations. The political-legal influences on marketing can be grouped into six categories. In each, the influence stems both from legislation and from policies established by the maze of government agencies. The categories are:

1. *General monetary and fiscal policies*. Marketing systems obviously are affected by the level of government spending, the money supply, and tax legislation.
2. *Our legislative framework and codes and policies set by government agencies*. Human rights codes and programs to reduce unemployment fall in this category. Also included is legislation controlling the environment. For example, marketers in the direct mail business are coming under increasing attack for what some consumers feel is the waste involved in flyers and mailing pieces that arrive unsolicited in their mailboxes, much of which ends up in the garbage unread. Legislators are being pressured by environmental groups to pass legislation regulating the sending of such mail. The City of Montreal passed a law in 1991 that forbids private companies distributing flyers to any residence displaying special "no junk mail" stickers.[11] The Government of Ontario, in 1994, proposed legislation that would prohibit drugstores and pharmacies from selling tobacco products.[12]
3. *Social legislation*. Governments often pass legislation that is intended to protect members of society. A ban on smoking in airplanes, mandatory seat belt use, and the prohibition of cigarette advertising are examples of this type of legislation.
4. *Government relationships with individual industries*. Here we find subsidies in agriculture, shipbuilding, passenger rail transportation, culture, and other industries. Tariffs and import quotas also affect specific industries. Throughout the 1990s, governments in Canada and in many other countries have moved to reduce the extent to which they are involved in the operation of businesses. Many have sold government-owned corporations to the private sector. There has been a major move towards *deregulation*, as industries such as banking, airlines, trucking, telecommunications, and broadcasting have been freed to a greater extent from regulations imposed by government. Through subsidies and tariff protection, Canadian governments have been involved in such traditional industries as the production of agricultural products. Some of these industries have been threatened with the removal of that protection as industries are deregulated throughout the world and as tariff barriers are removed.[13] Such barriers will continue to fall as the movement towards freedom in international trade expands and as such government involvement in industry is seen to be an impediment to free trade.[14]
5. *Legislation specifically related to marketing*. Marketing executives do not have to be lawyers. But they should know something about these laws, especially the major ones — why they were passed, what are their main provisions, and what are the current ground rules set by the courts and government agencies for administering these laws.

   The federal department Industry Canada, through its Consumer Products, Marketing Practices, and Competition Policy divisions, administers much of the legislation that is included in categories 3 and 4 above. Table 2-1 contains a number of examples of the legislation that is administered by that department that is relevant for marketers. In addition, there are many other pieces of legislation relating to such topics as food products and advertising that are administered by other departments of the federal government. We shall discuss these laws and regulations at the appropriate places throughout this book.
6. *The provision of information and the purchase of products*. This sixth area of government influence in marketing is quite different from the other five. Instead of telling mar-

TABLE 2-1 Marketing-related legislation administered by Industry Canada

| | |
|---|---|
| • Bankruptcy Act and Bankruptcy Rules | • Industrial Design Act |
| • Boards of Trade Act | • Insurance Companies Act |
| • Canada Business Corporations Act | • Integrated Circuit Topography Act |
| • Canada Co-operative Association Act | • Lobbyists Registration Act |
| • Canada Corporations Act | • Patent Act |
| • Competition Act | • Pension Fund Societies Act |
| • Consumer Packaging and Labelling Act | • Precious Metals Marking Act |
| • Copyright Act | • Public Servants Inventions Act |
| • Department of Consumer and Corporate Affairs Act | • Tax Rebate Discounting Act |
| • Electricity and Gas Inspection Act | • Textile Labelling Act |
| • Farmers' Creditors Arrangement Act | • Timber Marking Act |
| • Gas Inspection Act | • Trade Marks Act |
| • Government Corporations Operation Act | • Weights and Measures Act |

keting executives what they must do or cannot do — instead of the legislation and regulations — the government is clearly helping them. The federal government, through Statistics Canada, is the largest source of secondary marketing information in the country. And the government is the largest single buyer of products and services in the country.

## TECHNOLOGY

**Technology** has a tremendous impact on our lives — our life-styles, our consumption patterns, and our economic well-being. Just think of the effect of major technological developments such as the airplane, plastics, television, computers, antibiotics, lasers, and compact discs. Except perhaps for the airplane, all these technologies reached the large-scale marketing stage only in your lifetime or your parents' lifetime. Think how your life in the future might be affected by cures for the common cold, development of energy sources to replace fossil fuels, low-cost methods for making ocean water drinkable, or even commercial travel to the moon.

Consider for a moment some of the dramatic technological breakthroughs that are expanding our horizons in the 1990s. The role of robots undoubtedly will expand considerably. At the heart of a robot's operating mechanism is a miniature electronic computer system, which leads us into another technological breakthrough area — miniature electronic products. It's hard to grasp the fantastic possibilities in this field. Then there is the awesome potential of the superconductor — a means of transmitting electrical energy with virtually no resistance. Further developments in fibre optics, high-definition television, digital transmission, and CD-ROM technology will open vistas of communication that were not possible even five years ago. For example, the "information highway" will see virtually every home and office in Canada linked over interactive telephone lines, thereby allowing families to shop and do their banking from their living rooms and to order video movies from a catalogue for instant viewing. The advancement of CD-ROM technology will change the way we buy books, videos, and records. In the future, we will buy recordings that combine text, graphics, sound, video, and music on a single disc or in central computers, available for the use of the individual consumer when he or she wants them. Such digital storage will permit text to be retrieved from computers and books to be printed instantly, thereby eliminating problems such as storage and the aging of inventory.[15]

## MARKETING AT WORK

### FILE 2-3 THE WEST *IS* DIFFERENT

It should be obvious to all of us that there are many ways in which Canadians are different from coast to coast. The easiest way to express those differences is in terms of the cultural and demographic differences across provinces and regions of the country. But Canadians also differ considerably in how they shop and how they spend their incomes. Such differences have very important implications for marketers and how they target their products and services to particular regions of the country. Some interesting differences between the highest and lowest provinces are outlined below. What factors contribute to these differences across provinces and what do they mean for marketers? What do differences such as these tell us about life-style differences across provinces?

**Restaurant expenditures:** While consumers in British Columbia spend an average of $774 each in restaurants and taverns each year, Newfoundlanders spend only $340 (the Canadian average is $661).

**Cable television:** While 84 percent of homes in British Columbia have cable television, only 55 percent in Saskatchewan do (the Canadian average is 71 percent).

**Home computers:** Twenty-five percent of homes in British Columbia have computers, but only 11 percent in Prince Edward Island do (Canadian average is 20 percent).

**Video recorders:** Seventy-eight percent of homes in Alberta have VCRs, as compared with 69 percent in Quebec (Canadian average is 74 percent).

**Clothes dryers:** In Saskatchewan, 84 percent of homes have clothes dryers, while only 70 percent do in Ontario (Canadian average is 74 percent).

**Microwave ovens:** Eighty-one percent of Saskatchewan homes have microwave ovens, as compared with 69 percent in Newfoundland (Canadian average is 76 percent).

Source: *Market Research Handbook 1993-1994*, Ottawa: Statistics Canada, catalogue number 63-224, annual, 1994.

Major technological breakthroughs have a threefold impact on marketing. They are:

- To start entirely new industries, such as computers, robots, lasers, facsimile machines, and microwave ovens have done, and as CD-ROM and other digital technologies will do in the future;
- To alter radically or virtually destroy existing industries. Television had a significant impact on movies and radio when it was introduced in the 1950s. Compact discs have virtually eliminated vinyl records and threaten cassette tapes. Facsimile (fax) machines have certainly cut into the conventional mail business of Canada Post, which now offers its own courier and electronic mail services. Sensors imbedded in toll highways will be able to record cars as they pass over them and will bill their owners for the tolls they have used, thereby eliminating toll booths and speeding up traffic.[16] Movie companies in the United States are experimenting with sending movies to theatres directly from the studio through digital transmission over the telephone lines, thereby eliminating traditional distribution channels and companies.[17]
- To stimulate other markets and industries not related to the new technology. New home appliances and entertainment products have certainly altered the pattern of time use within the home and outside. Cable television, the VCR, CD players, video games, and microwave ovens have revolutionized how consumers use their time. Their development has also led to new industries providing entertainment products and food products that are used with these new devices and that were not available a few years ago.

There is virtually no aspect of our lives that is not being affected in a significant way by new technology. In the home, more than three-quarters of Canadian families have a VCR and a microwave oven; 13 percent have a second VCR.[18] Banks are offering their customers the use of a debit card, which allows shoppers to pay for items by direct debit to their bank accounts, thereby eliminating the use of cheques and the incurring of interest charges, although some financial institutions may charge a fee to customers each time they use the service. Supermarkets are using computerized systems that give shoppers instant coupons, thereby eliminating the wasted paper involved in millions of printed coupons that are not redeemed. Multimedia services being tested in Great Britain will allow customers to view catalogues and menus on their television sets and order from their living rooms.[19]

Despite the advances that have been made, technology is often a mixed blessing. A new technology may improve our lives in one area, while creating environmental and social problems in other areas. The automobile makes life great in some ways, but it also creates traffic jams and air pollution. Television provides built-in baby-sitters, but it also can have an adverse effect on family discussions and on children's reading habits. It is a bit ironic that technology is strongly criticized for creating problems (air pollution, for example), but at the same time is expected to solve these problems.

## EXTERNAL MICROENVIRONMENT

Three environmental forces that are external, but are a part of a company's marketing system, are that firm's market, its suppliers, and its marketing intermediaries. While they are generally uncontrollable, these external forces can be influenced more than the macro forces. A marketing organization, for example, may be able to exert pressure on its suppliers or intermediaries. And, through its advertising, a firm should have some influence on its market (see Figure 2-2).

**FIGURE 2-2**
**External microenvironment of a company's marketing program.**

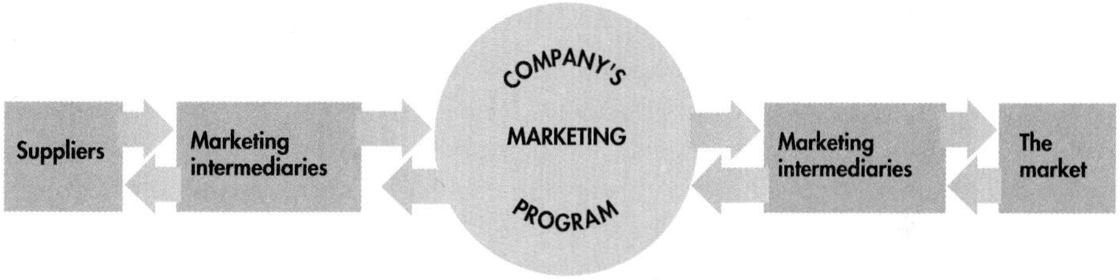


### The Market

The market really is what marketing is all about — how to reach it and serve it profitably and in a socially responsible manner. The market should be the focus of all marketing decisions in an organization. But just what is a market? A *market* may be defined as a place where buyers and sellers meet, goods or services are offered for sale, and transfers of ownership occur. A *market* may also be defined as the demand made by a certain group of potential buyers for a good or service. For instance, there is a farm *market* for petroleum products.

These definitions are not sufficiently precise to be useful to us here. For business purposes we define a **market** as people or organizations with *wants (needs) to satisfy, money to spend, and the willingness to spend it*. Thus, in the market demand for any given product or service, there are three factors to consider:

- People or organizations with wants (needs).
- Their purchasing power.
- Their buying behaviour.

When we say "needs," we mean what the dictionary says it means: the lack of anything that is required, desired, or useful. We do not limit needs to the physiological requirements of food, clothing, and shelter essential for survival. In our discussions about marketing, the words *needs* and *wants* are used synonymously and interchangeably.

### Suppliers

You can't sell a product if you can't first make it or buy it. That's why the people or firms who supply the goods or services that we need to produce what we sell are critical to our marketing success. And that's why we consider a firm's **suppliers** as part of its marketing system.

Marketing executives often are not concerned enough with the supply side of the marketing system. But they do become very concerned when shortages occur. Shortages make clear the need for co-operative relationships with suppliers.

### Marketing Intermediaries

**Marketing intermediaries** are independent business organizations that directly aid in the flow of goods and services between a marketing organization and its markets. There are two types of intermediaries: (1) the firms we call *middlemen* or *intermediaries*[20] — wholesalers and retailers, and (2) various *facilitating organizations* that provide such services as transportation, warehousing, and financing that are needed to complete exchanges between buyers and sellers.

These intermediaries operate between a company and its markets and between a company and its suppliers. Thus they are part of what we call *channels of distribution*.

In some cases it may be more efficient for a company to "do-it-yourself," not using marketing intermediaries. A producer can deal *directly* with its suppliers or sell *directly* to its customers and do its own shipping, financing, and so on. But marketing intermediaries are specialists in their respective fields. They often do a better job at a lower cost than the marketing organization can do by itself.

## ORGANIZATION'S INTERNAL ENVIRONMENT

An organization's marketing system is also shaped by internal forces that are controllable by management. (See Figure 2-3.) These internal influences include a firm's production, financial, and personnel activities. If Procter & Gamble is considering adding a new brand of soap, for example, it must determine whether existing production facilities and expertise can be used. If the new product requires a new plant or machinery, financial capability enters the picture.

Other nonmarketing forces are the company's location, its research and development (R&D) strength, and the overall image the firm projects to the public. Plant location often determines the geographic limits of a company's market, particularly if transportation costs are high or its products are perishable. The R&D factor may determine whether a company will lead or follow in its industry.

Another thing we must consider in a firm's internal environment is the need to co-ordinate its marketing and nonmarketing activities. Sometimes this can be difficult because of conflicts in goals and executive personalities. Production people, for example, like to see long production runs of standardized items. However, marketing executives may want a variety of models, sizes, and colours to satisfy different market segments. Financial executives typically want tighter credit and expense limits than the marketing people feel are necessary to be competitive.

To wrap up our discussion of the marketing environment, Figure 2-4 shows how all environmental forces combine to shape an organization's marketing program. Within the framework of these constraints, management should develop a marketing program to provide want-satisfaction to its markets. The strategic planning of marketing programs is the topic of the next chapter. Permeating the planning and operation of a marketing program is a company's marketing information system — a key marketing subsystem intended to aid management in solving its problems and making decisions. Chapter 7 is devoted to the subjects of marketing research and a company's flow of information.

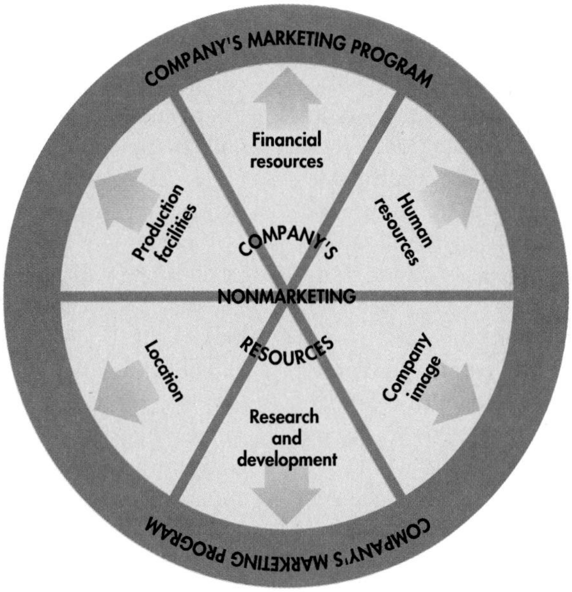


**FIGURE 2-3**
**Internal environment affecting a company's marketing activities.**

**A company's internal, nonmarketing resources influence and support its marketing program.**

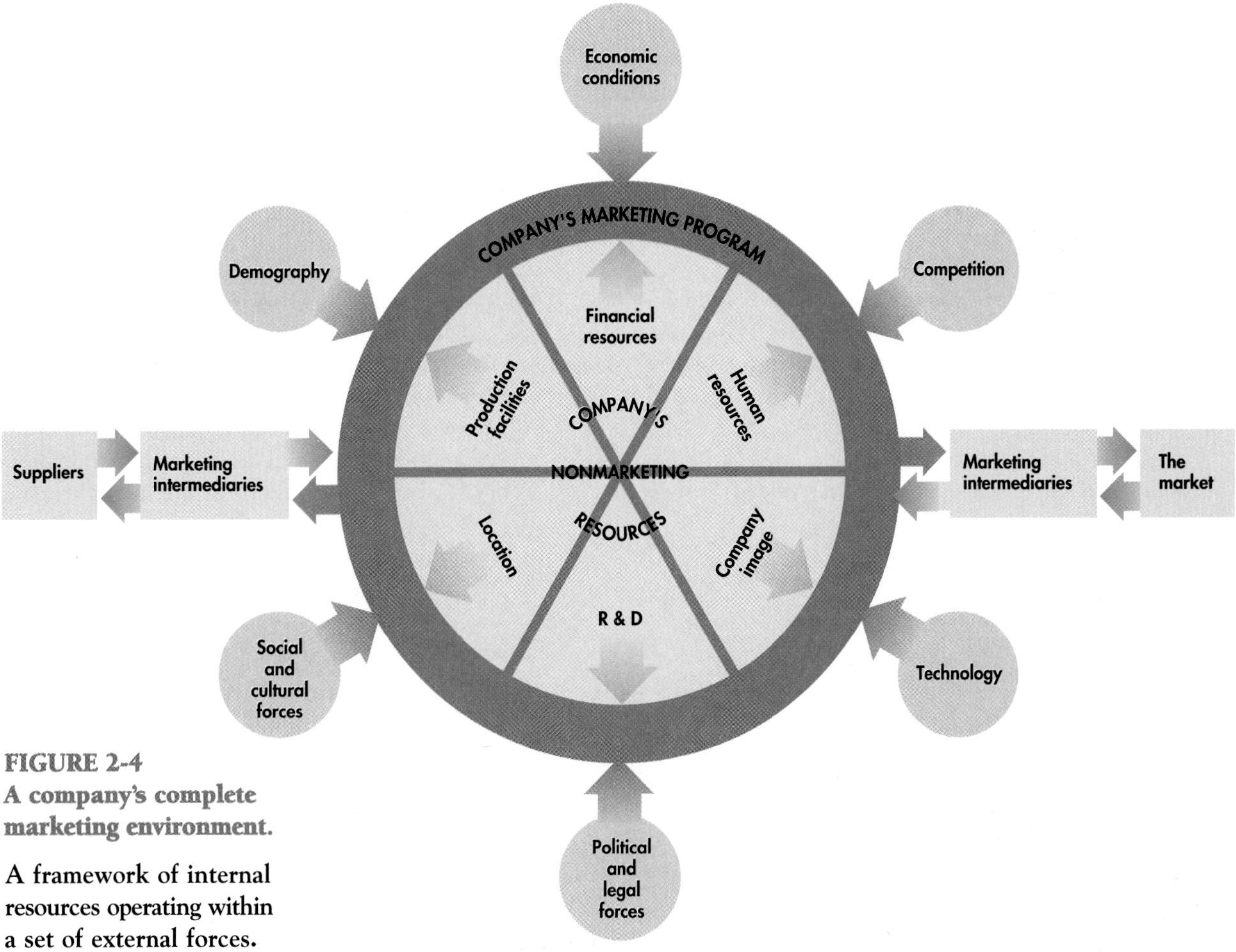


**FIGURE 2-4**
**A company's complete marketing environment.**

A framework of internal resources operating within a set of external forces.

## SUMMARY

Various environmental forces influence an organization's marketing activities. Some are external to the firm and are largely uncontrollable by the organization. Other forces are within the firm and are generally controllable by management. A company manages its marketing system within this external and internal environment. To start with, management should set up a system for environmental monitoring — the process of gathering and evaluating environmental information.

Six broad variables constitute the external environment that generally cannot be controlled by an organization. Demographic conditions are one of these macro influences. Another is economic conditions such as the business cycle, inflation, and interest rates. Management must be aware of the various types of competition and the competitive structure within which a given firm operates. Social and cultural forces, including cultural changes, are another factor with which to contend. Political and legal forces, along with technology, round out the group of external macroenvironmental influences.

Another set of environmental factors — suppliers, marketing intermediaries, and the market itself — is also external to the firm. But these elements are part of the firm's marketing system and can be controlled to some extent by the firm. At the same time, a set of nonmarketing resources within the firm — production facilities, personnel, finances, location, research and development, and company image — influences its marketing system. These variables generally are controllable by management.

## KEY TERMS AND CONCEPTS

**Environmental monitoring (40)**
**Demography (42)**
**Economic environment (43)**
**Business cycle (43)**
**Inflation (44)**
**Interest rates (44)**
**Social and cultural forces (45)**
**Political and legal forces (50)**
**Technology (51)**
**Market (53)**
**Suppliers (54)**
**Marketing intermediaries (54)**

## QUESTIONS AND PROBLEMS

1. It is predicted that university and college enrolments will decline during the next several years. What marketing measures should your school take to adjust to this forecast?
2. For each of the following companies, give some examples of how its marketing program is likely to differ during periods of prosperity as contrasted with periods of recession.
   a. McCain's orange juice.
   b. CCM skates.
   c. Adidas athletic shoes.
   d. Sony Walkman.
3. If interest rates are high, how is the situation likely to affect the market for the following products?
   a. Roots sweatshirts.
   b. Building materials.
   c. Videocassette recorders.
   d. Day-care programs.
4. Explain the three types of competition faced by a company. What marketing strategies or programs would you recommend to meet each type?
5. Give some examples of how the changing attitudes of Canadians towards the environment and their changing food consumption patterns have been reflected in the marketing programs of various companies.
6. What are some of the marketing implications of the increasing public interest in health and physical fitness?
7. What should be the role of marketing in treating the following major social problems?
   a. Air pollution.
   b. The depletion of irreplaceable resources.
   c. Seasonal unemployment.
8. Give some examples of the effects of marketing legislation in your own buying, recreation, and other everyday activities. Do you believe these laws are effective? If not, what changes would you recommend?
9. Using examples other than those in this chapter, explain how a firm's marketing system can be influenced by the environmental factor of technology.
10. Explain how each of the following resources within a company might influence that company's marketing program.

a. Plant location.
b. Company image.
c. Financial resources.
d. Personnel capability.

11. Specify some internal environmental forces affecting the marketing program of:
    a. Shoppers Drug Mart.
    b. Your school.
    c. A local restaurant.
    d. Air Canada.
12. Explain how or under what conditions a company might exert some control over its suppliers and intermediaries in its marketing program.

## HANDS-ON MARKETING

1. Identify two controversial social-cultural issues in the community where your school is located, and explain their impact on firms that market in the community.
2. After interviewing some consumers and/or business people in your community, identify two products or companies (national or local) that you think are doing very well regarding the physical environment. Identify two that you think are doing a poor job.

## NOTES AND REFERENCES


1. Adapted from "Big Mac's Counter Attack," *The Economist*, November 13, 1993, pp. 71-72; and Barnaby J. Feder, "McDonald's Makes a Comeback," *Globe and Mail*, January 22, 1994, p. B8.
2. Jo Marney, "Do You Know Where the OPALs Are?" *Marketing*, November 9, 1992, p. 8.
3. "The Rich Autumn of a Consumer's Life," *The Economist*, September 5, 1992, pp. 67-68.
4. David K. Foot, "Let Us Now Appraise Famous Trends," *Canadian Business*, November 1992, pp. 63-72.
5. Cyndee Miller, "Xers Know They're a Target Market, and They Hate That," *Marketing News*, vol. 27, no. 25, December 6, 1993, p. 2.
6. Richard Wright, "Battleplan for the Retail Counter Attack," *Profit*, vol. 13, no. 1, March 1994, pp. 22-27.
7. Milton Parissis and Michael Helfinger, "Ethnic Shoppers Share Certain Values," *Marketing*, January 11, 1993, p. 16.
8. David Menzies, "Serving It Up Healthy and Nutritious," *Food in Canada*, vol. 52, no. 4, May 1992, pp. 12-14.
9. Margot Franssen, "Beyond Profits," *Business Quarterly*, Autumn 1993, pp. 15-20.
10. Kathleen Deveny, "Fifth Column: There's a New Wave of Pure Consumers Out There," *Globe and Mail*, August 3, 1993, p. A16.
11. Marina Strauss, "Junk-mail Marketing Riles Homeowners," *Globe and Mail*, January 25, 1991, p. B6.
12. James Pollock, "Smoke Bill Sparks Fiery Debate," *Marketing*, January 3/10, 1994, p. 3.
13. Andrew Reed, "A System That Milks Consumers," *Globe and Mail*, January 10, 1994, p. A9.
14. Gary A. Knight, "NAFTA Holds Promise for Stronger, Prosperous North America," *Marketing News*, October 25, 1993, pp. 14-15.
15. Jacquie McNish, "Instant Books, Music Riding Digital Wave," *Globe and Mail*, January 22, 1994, p. B1.
16. "Big Brother Is Clocking You," *The Economist*, August 7, 1993, pp. 71-72.
17. "Test Will Send Movies to Theatres by Phone Line," *Ottawa Citizen*, March 26, 1994, p. F6.
18. Bruce Little, "Gadgets and Gismos Go Gonzo," *Globe and Mail*, December 13, 1993, p. A7.
19. Paul Penrose, "Sit Down and Go Shopping," *The Times* (London), March 11, 1994, p. 35.
20. The terms *middlemen* and *intermediaries* may be used interchangeably. We have chosen to use intermediaries throughout this book.

## CHAPTER 3 GOALS

In this chapter we'll examine how a company plans its total marketing program. After studying this chapter, you should have an understanding of:

- The nature and scope of planning and how it fits within the management process.
- Similarities and differences among mission, objectives, strategies, and tactics.
- The essential difference between strategic company planning and strategic marketing planning.
- The steps involved in strategic marketing planning.
- The purpose and contents of an annual marketing plan.
- Similarities and differences as well as weaknesses and strengths across several models used in strategic planning.

CHAPTER 3

# STRATEGIC MARKETING PLANNING

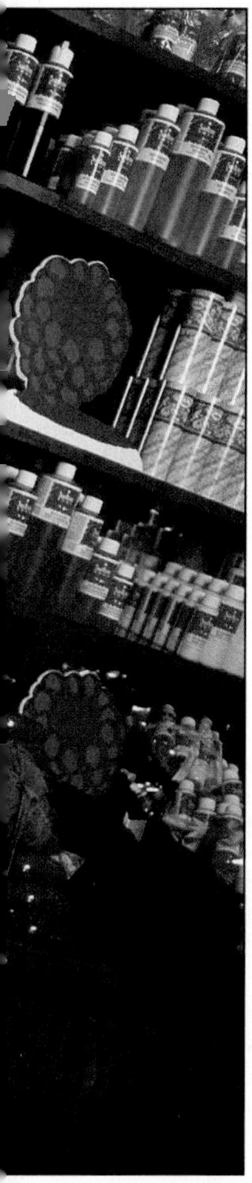

## Exporting Success Demands More than Common Scents

The story of Northern Telecom's mission to be a global competitor and its strategy and plans for continued expansion, its latest marketing successes being in China and Mexico, are well documented. You've also heard about the strategy of McDonald's of Canada expanding into international markets, specifically Moscow, and all the planning and implementation difficulties that had to be dealt with. But the success of new small companies and the missions, strategies, and tactics they develop are much less well known. An example of one such company is Soapberry Shops of Toronto.

Natasha Rajewski, Soapberry's founder, had a mission in her commitment to the environment and matters environmental. She had seen a similar growing public interest in the environment, in environmental issues, and environmentally friendly products. Since she also had a strong interest and expertise in the cosmetics business, she put cosmetics and the environment together and formed Soapberry Shops. Before long, Soapberry cosmetic products were being successfully marketed through 51 retail stores, including five franchised U.S. locations.

And then Natasha and her father visited St. Petersburg, where the family had originally come from. She "fell in love with the Russian people" and was moved to spread her environmental message there and to give something back to them. She saw a tremendous potential in Russia and wanted to be part of its future development.

With this mission, she decided, after meeting with Russian bureaucrats and business people, to enter the market by building a store in Moscow to provide her line of environmentally friendly cosmetics, all to be imported initially to the Moscow market. Her original target was going to be expatriates and diplomats living in the Russian capital. She has discovered that with Russia's privatization efforts has come "a new upper class," and most of the 700 customers per day served in her Moscow outlet are Russians, not foreigners. Building on her success, Natasha now plans to open a second outlet in Moscow and a third in St. Petersburg. Natasha says, "This is no place to go for quick profit. You have to want to be there and to do business there. You've got to think long-term."[1]

As the Soapberry example suggests, success for any organization requires skilful and effective marketing management. The *marketing* part of the term *marketing management* was defined in Chapter 1, but what about the *management* part? **Management** is the process of planning, implementing, and evaluating the efforts of a group of people working towards a common goal. In this chapter we provide an overview of the management process and examine planning in some detail. We also discuss an essential element of marketing planning, the forecasting of marketing demand. Later, when you have learned more about the strategies and techniques of marketing, we will cover implementation and evaluation, the other two steps in the management process.

## PLANNING AS PART OF MANAGEMENT

The management process, as applied to marketing, consists basically of (1) planning a marketing program, (2) implementing it, and (3) evaluating its performance. This process is illustrated in Figure 3-1.

The *planning* stage includes setting goals and designing strategies and tactics to reach these goals. The *implementation* stage entails forming and staffing the marketing organization and directing the actual operation of the organization according to the plan. The *evaluation* stage consists of analyzing past performance in relation to organizational goals.[2] This third stage indicates the interrelated, continuing nature of the management process. That is, the results of this stage of the management process are used in *planning* goals and strategies for future periods. And the cycle continues.

**FIGURE 3-1**
**The management process in marketing.**

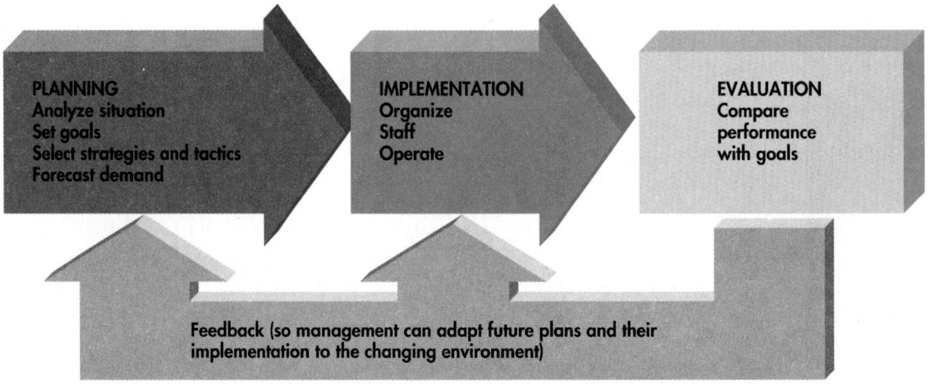


### The Nature of Planning

"If you don't know where you're going, any road will get you there." The point of this axiom is that all organizations need both general and specific plans to be successful. Management first should decide what it intends to accomplish as a total organization and develop a strategic plan to achieve these results. Based on this overall plan, each division of the organization should determine what its own plans will be. Of course, the role of marketing in these plans needs to be considered.

If planning is so important, exactly what is it? Quite simply, **planning** is deciding now what we are going to do later, including how and when we are going to do it. Without a plan, we cannot get things done effectively and efficiently, because we don't know what needs to be done or how to do it.

In **strategic planning**, managers match an organization's resources with its market opportunities over the long run. Market and economic conditions during the past two decades prompted many companies to consider more formally and more frequently how best to match their opportunities and their resources. The intent was to seize the opportunities and to avoid the threats associated with changing markets. Formal strategic planning was recognized as an effective management tool to do this.

## Key Planning Concepts

We'll begin by becoming familiar with the basic terms we use in discussing marketing management, especially the planning phase.

### Mission

An organization's **mission** states what customers it serves, what needs it satisfies, and what types of products it offers. A mission statement indicates in general terms the boundaries for an organization's activities.

A mission statement should be neither too broad and vague nor too narrow and specific. To say that a firm's mission is "to benefit Canadian consumers" is too vague; to state that its purpose is "to make tennis balls" is too narrow. Neither statement outlines meaningful benefits for customers or provides much guidance to management. Unless the firm's purpose is clear to executives, strategic planning will likely result in disagreement and confusion.

Traditionally, companies stated their missions in production-oriented terms, such as "We make furnaces" (or telephones or tennis racquets). Today, firms following the marketing concept express their mission in customer-oriented terms. Executives should think about the wants they are satisfying and the benefits they are providing. Thus, instead of "We make furnaces," Lennox Company's statement of mission should be "We provide home climate control." Recall that Table 1-1 illustrated different ways of stating a company's mission.

**Rather than making film and cameras, Kodak really helps preserve beautiful memories.**

### Objectives and Goals

We treat *objectives* and *goals* as synonyms. An **objective** is simply a desired outcome. Effective planning must begin with a set of objectives that are to be achieved by carrying out plans.

To be worthwhile and workable, objectives should be:

- Clear and specific.
- Stated in writing.
- Ambitious, but realistic.
- Consistent with one another.
- Quantitatively measurable wherever possible.
- Tied to a particular time period.

Consider these examples:

| Weak (too general) | | Workable |
|---|---|---|
| **Increase our market share.** | → | **Increase our market share to 25% next year from its present 20% level.** |
| **Improve our company's public image.** | → | **Receive favourable recognition awards next year from at least three consumer or environmental groups.** |

Strategies and Tactics The term *strategy* originally applied to the art of military leadership. In business, a **strategy** is a broad plan of action by which an organization intends to reach its objectives. In marketing, the relationship between objectives and strategies may be illustrated as follows:

| Objective | | Possible strategies |
|---|---|---|
| **Increase sales next year by 10% over this year's figure.** | → | **1. Intensify marketing efforts in domestic markets.** **2. Expand into foreign markets.** |

Two organizations might have the same objective but use different strategies to reach it. For example, two firms both might aim to increase their market shares by 20 percent over the next three years. To do that, one firm might intensify its efforts in household markets, while the other might concentrate on expanding into institutional markets (e.g., food-service organizations). Conversely, two organizations might have different objectives but select the same strategy to reach them.

A **tactic** is a means by which a strategy is implemented. A tactic is a more specific, detailed course of action than is a strategy. Also, tactics generally cover shorter time periods than strategies. Here's an illustration:

| Strategy | | Tactics |
|---|---|---|
| **Direct our promotion to males, ages 25-40.** | → | **1. Advertise in magazines read by this group of people.** **2. Advertise on television programs watched by this group.** |

To be effective, a tactic must coincide with and support the strategy with which it is related.

### Scope of Planning

Planning may cover long or short periods. Strategic planning is usually long-range, covering 3, 5, 10, or (infrequently) 25 years. It requires the participation of top management and often involves a planning staff.

Long-range planning deals with company-wide issues such as expanding or contracting production, markets, and product lines. For example, all firms in the North American auto industry must look ahead to the next century to identify key markets, plan new products, and update production technologies.

## MARKETING AT WORK

### FILE 3-1 COFFEE WITH A SKYSCRAPER STRATEGY

Several years ago, Becky McKinnon, president of the Toronto-based chain of specialty coffee shop/cafés, Timothy's Coffee of the World Inc., evaluated the performance of her 47 stores. What emerged was that her most profitable outlets were those located in office towers. The bigger the tower, the longer the line-up of harried executives in need of a quick caffeine fix. If Timothy's was going to achieve its objective of expansion into high-profit markets only, it was going to have to do so in big-city skyscrapers. The problem is that Canada is rather limited in big-city skyscrapers — Toronto had only 25 towers that had 70,000 square metres of rented space, the amount McKinnon calculated would sustain a Timothy's shop. In New York, however, there were over 150 such beasts. The strategy was clear — it was time to look at expansion into Manhattan.

There are many stories of Canadian businesses, particularly retailers, who went south with a great idea only to return less than successful soon after — a result of insufficient research and underestimation of the competition. This had happened often enough that nervous Canadian banks were loath to lend McKinnon the money required for Timothy's expansion. So McKinnon took the move slowly and spent a lot of time on tactical detail — such as personally training her New York staff. She found, surprisingly, that renting real estate in Manhattan cost less than a third of what it had cost in Toronto. Even more surprising, however, was the fact that in the middle of the sophisticated Big Apple, the closest thing New Yorkers could get to coffee was a Styrofoam cup of watery black stuff sold in delis and from sidewalk carts. They quickly became gourmet coffee converts. In the first year, Timothy's two midtown coffee bars surpassed McKinnon's sales expectations by 25 percent and quickly became Timothy's greatest sources of revenue, with average sales of $900 dollars (U.S.) a square foot, compared with a Canadian store average of $600 dollars (U.S.) a square foot.

Since then, American investors have woken up to smell the coffee and have helped to finance nine more Timothy's stores in New York, as well as one in Boston. With things brewing the way they are, McKinnon predicts New Yorkers will be able to quench their caffeine craving at more than 50 outlets by 1995.

Source: Adapted from Jacquie McNish, "Timothy's Cup Runs over in Crowded Manhattan," *Globe and Mail*, November 15, 1993, pp. B1-B2.

### KEY QUESTIONS FOR AN ORGANIZATION TO ANSWER

The concepts of mission, objectives, strategies, and tactics each raise an important question that must be answered by an organization seeking success in business or, more specifically, in marketing:

| Concept | | Question |
|---|---|---|
| **Mission** | → | **What business are we in?** |
| **Objectives** | → | **What do we want to accomplish?** |
| **Strategies** | → | **In general terms, how are we going to get the job done?** |
| **Tactics** | → | **In specific terms, how are we going to get the job done?** |

Short-range planning typically covers one year or less and is the responsibility of middle and lower-level managers. It focuses on such issues as determining which target markets will receive special attention and what will be the marketing mix. Looking again at the auto industry, Chrysler annually decides which target markets it will concentrate on and whether its marketing mixes for each of these markets should be changed. Naturally, short-range plans must be compatible with the organization's long-range plans.

Planning the marketing strategies in a firm should be conducted on three different levels:

- **Strategic company planning.** At this level management defines an organization's missions, sets long-range goals, and formulates broad strategies to achieve these goals. These company-wide goals and strategies then become the framework for planning in the firm's different functional areas, such as production, finance, human resources, research and development, *and* marketing.
- **Strategic marketing planning.** The top marketing executives set goals and strategies for an organization's marketing effort. Strategic *marketing* planning obviously should be co-ordinated with *company-wide* planning.
- **Annual marketing planning.** Short-term plans should be prepared for a firm's major functions. Covering a specific period, usually one year, the annual marketing plan is based on the firm's strategic marketing planning.

## STRATEGIC COMPANY PLANNING

**Strategic company planning** consists of four essential steps:

1. Defining the organizational mission.
2. Analyzing the situation.
3. Setting organizational objectives.
4. Selecting strategies to achieve these objectives.

The process is shown in the top part of Figure 3-2.

The first step, defining the organizational mission, influences all subsequent planning. For some firms, this step requires only reviewing the existing mission statement and confirming that it is still suitable. Still, this straightforward step is too often ignored.

**FIGURE 3-2 Three levels of organizational planning.**

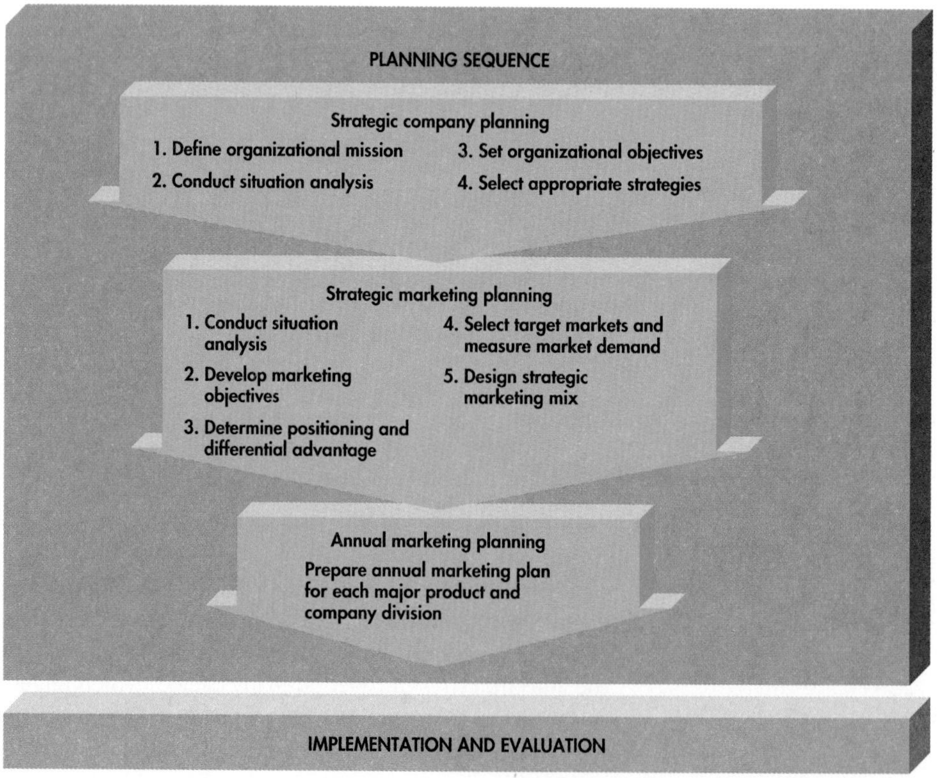

PLANNING SEQUENCE
Strategic company planning
1. Define organizational mission
2. Conduct situation analysis
3. Set organizational objectives
4. Select appropriate strategies
Strategic marketing planning
1. Conduct situation analysis
2. Develop marketing objectives
3. Determine positioning and differential advantage
4. Select target markets and measure market demand
5. Design strategic marketing mix
Annual marketing planning
Prepare annual marketing plan for each major product and company division
IMPLEMENTATION AND EVALUATION

Conducting a situation analysis, the second step, is vital because strategic planning is influenced by many factors beyond and within an organization. By **situation analysis**, we simply mean gathering and studying information pertaining to one or more specified aspects of an organization. We'll talk more about conducting a situation analysis in an upcoming section.

The third step in strategic company planning requires management to decide on a set of objectives to guide the organization in fulfilling its mission. Objectives also provide standards for evaluating an organization's performance.

By this point in its strategic planning, the organization has determined where it wants to go. The fourth step, selecting appropriate strategies, indicates how the firm is going to get there. **Organizational strategies** represent broad plans of action by which an organization intends to achieve its goals and fulfil its mission. Strategies are selected either for the entire company if it is small and has only a single product or for each division if the company is large and has multiple products or units.

Do companies actually engage in this kind of planning and then prepare a written plan? According to a recent survey, almost 70 percent of firms have strategic plans in place; among them, nearly 90 percent believe their strategic plans have been effective.[3] Interestingly, a larger proportion of younger firms (one to ten years old) than older firms have formal strategic plans.

## STRATEGIC MARKETING PLANNING

After completing the strategic planning for its organization as a whole, management needs to lay plans for each major functional area, such as marketing or production. Of course, planning for each function should be guided by the organization-wide mission and objectives.

**Strategic marketing planning** is a five-step process:

1. Conduct a situation analysis.
2. Develop marketing objectives.
3. Determine positioning and differential advantage.
4. Select target markets and measure market demand.
5. Design a strategic marketing mix.

These five steps are shown in the middle of Figure 3-2, indicating how they relate to the four steps of strategic company planning. Each step is discussed below.

### Situation Analysis

The first step in strategic marketing planning, situation analysis, involves analyzing where the company's marketing program has been, how it has been doing, and what it is likely to face in the years ahead. Doing this enables management to determine if it's necessary to revise the old plans or devise new ones to achieve the company's objectives.

Situation analysis normally covers external environmental forces[4] and internal nonmarketing resources (such as R&D capabilities, finances, and skills and experience levels of personnel) that surround the marketing program. A situation analysis also considers the groups of consumers served by the company, the strategies used to satisfy them, and key measures of marketing performance.

As the basis for planning decisions, situation analysis is critical. But it can be costly, time-consuming, and frustrating. For example, it's usually difficult to extract timely, accurate information from the "mountains" of data compiled during a situation analysis. Moreover, some valuable information, such as sales or market-share figures for competitors, is often unavailable.

As part of a situation analysis, many organizations perform a **SWOT assessment**. In this activity, a firm identifies and evaluates its most significant strengths, weaknesses, opportunities, and threats. To fulfil its mission, an organization needs to capitalize on its key strengths, overcome or alleviate its major weaknesses, avoid significant threats, and take advantage of the most promising opportunities in order to fulfil its mission.

We're referring to strengths and weaknesses in an organization's own capabilities. For example, Eaton's strength is its large size, that gives it — among other things — clout in dealing with suppliers. However, a weakness may be its comparatively high operating expenses.

Opportunities and threats often originate outside the organization. For example, an opportunity identified by Wal-Mart in expanding into Canada is the large number of metropolitan areas in which it can open stores. But a threat is the group of competitors (such as K mart and Zellers) that await Wal-Mart in metropolitan locations.

### Marketing Objectives

The next step in strategic marketing planning is to *determine marketing objectives*. Marketing goals should be closely related to company-wide goals and strategies. In fact, a *company strategy* often translates into a *marketing goal*. For example, to reach an organizational objective of a 20 percent return on investment next year, one organizational strategy might be to reduce marketing costs by 15 percent. This company strategy would become a marketing goal. In turn, converting all sales people from salaried compensation to a commission basis might be one of the marketing strategies adopted to achieve this marketing goal.

We already know that strategic planning involves matching an organization's resources with its market opportunities. With this in mind, each objective should be assigned a priority based on its urgency and potential impact on the marketing area and, in turn, the organization. Then resources should be allocated in line with these priorities.[5]

### Positioning and Differential Advantage

The third step in strategic marketing planning actually involves two complementary decisions: how to position a product in the marketplace, and how to distinguish it from competitors. **Positioning** refers to a product's image in relation to directly competitive products as well as other products marketed by the same company.[6] For example, given rising health consciousness among many consumers, manufacturers of mayonnaise, corn oil, and other food products recognized the need to introduce products that would be perceived as more wholesome.[7] CPC International is trying to position its Hellmann's Dijonnaise, which combines no-fat mustard with mayonnaise ingredients (but no egg yolks), as a healthful *and* tasty product.

After the product is positioned, a viable differential advantage has to be identified. **Differential advantage** refers to any feature of an organization or brand perceived by customers to be desirable and different from those of the competition.[8] At the same time, a company has to avoid a **differential disadvantage** for its product. Consider Apple computers.[9] For many years, the Macintosh's "user friendliness" represented a strong advantage for the product. As the 1990s began, however, the Macintosh's relatively high prices created a disadvantage in relation to comparable IBM and Compaq computers.

### Target Markets and Market Demand

Selecting target markets is the fourth step in marketing planning. A **market** consists of people or organizations with needs to satisfy, money to spend, and the willingness to spend it. For example, many people need transportation and are willing to pay for it. However, this large group is made up of a number of segments (that is, parts of markets) with various transportation needs. One segment may want low-cost, efficient transportation, for instance, while another may prefer luxury and privacy. Ordinarily it is impracti-

**Eggs have to combat the perceived differential disadvantage that they are high in cholesterol.**

cal for a firm to satisfy all segments with different needs. Instead, a company targets its efforts on one or more of these segments. Thus a **target market** refers to a group of people or organizations at which a firm directs a marketing program.

In a new company, management should analyze markets in detail to identify potential target markets. In an existing firm, management should routinely examine any changes in the characteristics of its target markets and alternative markets. At this point, management should decide to what extent and in what manner to divide up total markets and then pursue only those segments (that is, parts of markets) that show the best potential for successful marketing.

## MARKETING AT WORK

### FILE 3-2 RED LOBSTER PLANS WITHOUT CANADIAN ANALYSIS

Too bad the prosperous U.S. Red Lobster Restaurants chain didn't do their situation analysis, work out good target markets, and position themselves well. If they had, perhaps in 1993 they wouldn't have been forced to close 13 out of 70 of their seafood restaurants — a fifth of the Canadian total.

Based on their U.S. performance, Red Lobster had no reason to doubt itself. With more than $1.5 billion (U.S.) in sales in 1992, it is the largest sit-down, full-service restaurant chain in the United States, conquering more than 25 percent of the full-service restaurant market while boasting the title of world's largest buyer of shrimp. With 600 restaurants already in operation and another 50 in the works, the chain saw no reason it wouldn't match its success with an expansion north of the border. The plan was to duplicate its operations in Canada.

Where Red Lobster floundered, however, was in failing to analyze the Canadian market thoroughly and adapt the product to the market. Unlike Americans, who seem to like the dependability and uniformity of chain restaurants, Canadians tend to be more adventurous when dining out cheaply. They either take advantage of their much-touted multiculturalism and opt for souvlaki, pasta, or pad thai, or they drop into the corner greasy spoon for a hearty chunk of home-made meat pie.

It also turns out that in general Canadians tend to be choosier than their southern neighbours. And their taste buds are simply not so easily tempted by the seafood favourites that sold at such high volumes in the United States, allowing Red Lobster to charge rock-bottom prices and still make a healthy profit. In a scrambling attempt to please our northern palates, the chain tried introducing lower margin but more expensive specialties such as escargots, but this ploy only succeeded in diminishing the high sales volumes they required.

Furthermore, perplexed by a country with such a small and dispersed population, Red Lobster decided it had better venture out from its usual strongholds in suburbia and open restaurants in downtown centres, where it hoped to drum up more customers. Unfortunately, business was poor. They might perhaps have considered that Canada's city slickers, health-conscious and on-the-run, have neither the time nor the tummies for much vaunted frills such as unlimited cheese bread, Orange Icicles (amaretto, orange juice, and ice cream) and Fudge Overloads (brownie-fudge-pecan pie à la mode). Not knowing the Canadian market, coupled with a large staff and heavy investment in sophisticated computer equipment, represented an obvious obstacle to success. Mat Reime, president of Hospitality Consulting Associates, commented, "The suburbs were the only place they could work. As soon as they moved into the cities, they killed themselves. You can't just throw out food and hope you hit somebody. You really have to target your audience, and you have to target your menu, and your environment, to that audience."

Source: Adapted from Danielle Bochove, "Change in Tastes at Canadian Border an Expensive Lesson," *Globe and Mail*, July 8, 1993, pp. B1-2.

A firm may select a single segment as its target, as was done by the publisher of the highly specialized trade magazine, *Progressive Grocer*. In contrast, CB Publications aims its periodical, *Canadian Business*, at several market segments.

Target markets must be selected on the basis of opportunities. And to analyze its opportunities, a firm must forecast demand (that is, sales) in its target markets. The results of demand forecasting will indicate whether the firm's targets are worth pursuing, or whether alternatives should be identified. We'll take a look at demand forecasting later in Chapter 5.

### Marketing Mix

Next, management must design a **marketing mix** — the combination of a product, how it is distributed and promoted, and its price. These four elements together must satisfy the needs of the organization's target market(s) and, at the same time, achieve its marketing objectives. Let's consider the four elements and some of the concepts and strategies you'll learn about in later chapters:

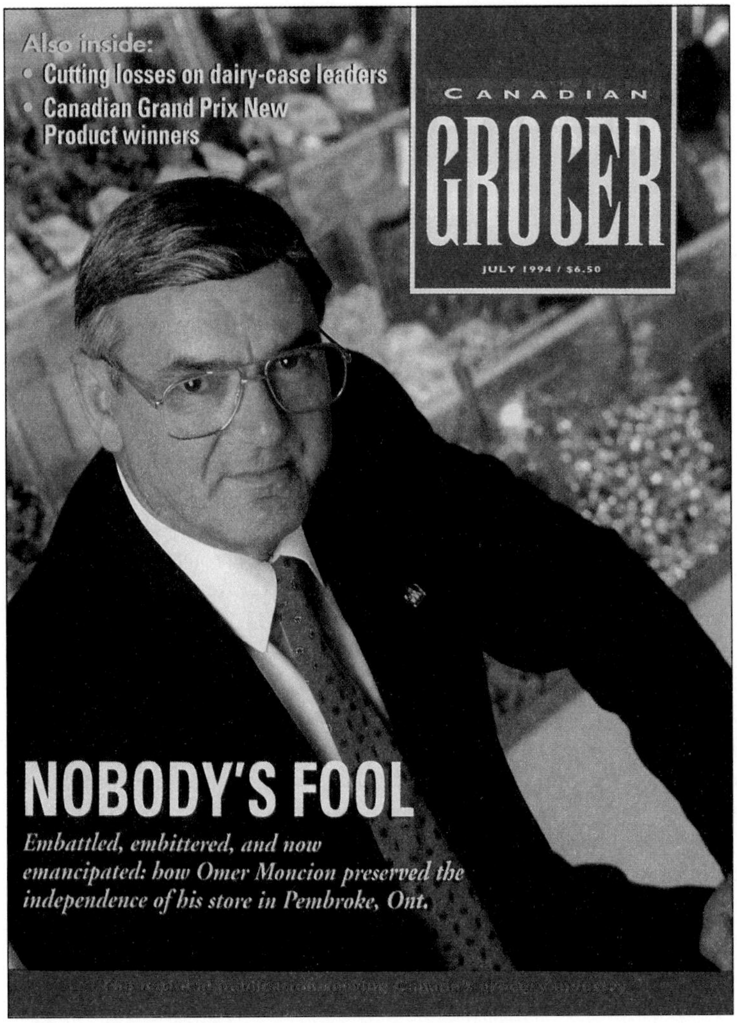

Also inside:
• Cutting losses on dairy-case leaders
• Canadian Grand Prix New Product winners
CANADIAN
GROCER
JULY 1994 / $6.50
NOBODY'S FOOL
Embattled, embittered, and now emancipated: how Omer Moncion preserved the independence of his store in Pembroke, Ont.


**This trade magazine is targeted at the retail food segment of the business market.**

- **Product.** Strategies are needed for managing existing products over time, adding new ones, and dropping failed products. Strategic decisions must also be made regarding branding, packaging, and other product features such as warranties.
- **Price.** Necessary strategies pertain to the locations of customers, price flexibility, related items within a product line, and terms of sale. Also, pricing strategies for entering a market, especially with a new product, must be designed.
- **Distribution.** Here, strategies involve the management of the channel(s) by which ownership of products is transferred from producer to customer and, in many cases, the system(s) by which goods are moved from where they are produced to where they are purchased by the final customer. Strategies applicable to intermediaries, such as wholesalers and retailers, must be designed.
- **Promotion.** Strategies are needed to combine individual methods such as advertising, personal selling, and sales promotion into a co-ordinated campaign. In addition, promotional strategies must be adjusted as a product moves from the early stages to the later stages of its life. Strategic decisions must also be made regarding each individual method of promotion.

The four marketing-mix elements are interrelated; decisions in one area often affect actions in another. To illustrate, design of a marketing mix is certainly affected by whether a firm chooses to compete on the basis of price *or* on one or more other elements. When a firm relies on price as its primary competitive tool, the other elements must be designed to support aggressive pricing. For example, the promotional campaign likely will be built around a theme of "low, low prices." In nonprice competition, however, product, distribution, and/or promotion strategies come to the forefront. For instance, the product must have features worthy of a higher price, and promotion must create a high-quality image for the product.

Each marketing-mix element contains countless variables. For instance, an organization may market one product or many, and they may be related or unrelated to each other. The product(s) may be distributed through wholesalers, to retailers without the benefit of wholesalers, or even directly to final customers. Ultimately, from the multitude of variables, management must select a combination of elements that will satisfy target markets and achieve organizational and marketing goals.

## ANNUAL MARKETING PLANNING

Besides strategic planning for several years into the future, more specific, shorter-term planning is also vital. Thus, strategic marketing planning in an organization leads to the preparation of an annual marketing plan, as shown in the bottom part of Figure 3-2. An **annual marketing plan** is the master blueprint for a year's marketing activity for a specified organizational division or major product. Note that it is a written document.

A separate plan normally should be prepared for each major product and company division. Sometimes, depending on a company's circumstances, separate plans are developed for key brands and important target markets.[10] As the name implies, an annual marketing plan usually covers one year. However, there are exceptions. For instance, because of the seasonal nature of some products or markets, it is advisable to prepare plans for shorter time periods. For fashionable clothing, plans are made for each season, lasting just several months.

## Purposes and Responsibilities

An annual marketing plan serves several purposes:

- It summarizes the marketing strategies and tactics that will be used to achieve specified objectives in the upcoming year. Thus it becomes the "how-to-do-it" document that guides executives and other employees involved in marketing.
- The plan also points to what needs to be done with respect to the other steps in the management process — namely, implementation and evaluation of the marketing program.
- Moreover, the plan outlines who is responsible for which activities, when they are to be carried out, and how much time and money can be spent.

The executive responsible for the division or product covered by the plan typically prepares it. Of course, all or part of the task may be delegated to subordinates.

Preparation of an annual marketing plan may begin nine months or more before the start of the period covered by the plan. Early work includes necessary research and arranging other information sources. The bulk of the work occurs one to three months prior to the plan's starting date. The last steps are to have the plan reviewed and approved by upper management. Some revision may be necessary before final approval is granted. The final version of the plan, or relevant parts of it, should be shared with all employees who will be involved in implementing the agreed-upon strategies and tactics. Since an annual plan contains confidential information, it should not be distributed too widely.

## Recommended Contents

The exact contents of an annual marketing plan should be determined by an organization's circumstances. For example, a firm in an intensely competitive industry would assess its competitors in a separate section. A firm in another industry would present this assessment as part of the situation analysis. Likewise, some organizations include alternative (or contingency) plans; others don't. An example of a contingency plan is the set of steps the firm will take if a competitor introduces a new product, as is rumoured.

Annual marketing planning follows a sequence similar to strategic marketing planning. However, annual planning has a shorter time frame and is more specific — both with respect to the issues addressed and to the plans laid. Still, as shown in Table 3-1, the major sections in an annual marketing plan are similar to the steps in strategic marketing planning.

In an annual marketing plan, more attention can be devoted to tactical details than is feasible in other levels of planning. As an example, strategic marketing planning might stress personal selling within the marketing mix. If so, the annual plan might recommend increased college recruiting as a source of additional sales people.

Also note that an annual marketing plan actually relates to all three steps of the management process, not just planning. That is, sections 5 through 7 deal with implementation and section 8 is concerned with evaluation.

## MARKETING AT WORK

### FILE 3-3 AN ETHICAL ISSUE

Assume you are the manager responsible for a line of hand-held calculators used by executives and engineers. In the past year, your brand has fallen from second to third in sales. You attribute the decline to an unfair comparative advertising campaign run by the new second-place firm. The firm used ads that pointed to alleged shortcomings in your calculators. Unexpectedly, you are presented with an opportunity to regain the upper hand when one of your sales people brings you a copy of that competitor's marketing plan for next year. The sales person found it on a chair following a seminar attended by representatives from a number of calculator makers. After studying this plan, you could adjust your plans to counter the other firm's strategies.

Even though you didn't buy or steal the plan, is it ethical to read and use it?

TABLE 3-1 Contents of an annual marketing plan

1. *Executive Summary.* In this one- or two-page section, the thrust of the plan is described and explained. It is intended for executives who desire an overview of the plan but need not be knowledgeable about the details.
2. *Situation Analysis.* Essentially, the marketing program for the strategic business unit (SBU) or product covered by the plan is examined within the context of pertinent past, present, and future conditions. Much of this section might be derived from the results of strategic marketing planning. Additional information of particular relevance to a one-year planning period may be included in this section.
3. *Objectives.* The objectives in an annual plan are more specific than those produced by strategic marketing planning. However, annual objectives must help achieve organizational goals and strategic marketing goals.
4. *Strategies.* As in strategic marketing planning, the strategies in an annual plan should indicate which target markets are going to be satisfied through a combination of product, price, distribution, and promotion.
5. *Tactics.* Specific activities, sometimes called action plans, are devised for carrying out each major strategy included in the preceding section. For ease of understanding, strategies and tactics may be covered together. Tactics specifically answer the question of *what, who,* and *how* for the company's marketing efforts.
6. *Financial Schedules.* This section normally includes two kinds of financial information: projected sales, expenses, and profits in what's called a pro-forma financial statement; and the amounts of resources dedicated to different activities in one or more budgets.
7. *Timetable.* This section, often including a diagram, answers the question of *when* various marketing activities will be carried out during the upcoming year.
8. *Evaluation Procedures.* This section addresses the questions of *what, who, how,* and *when* connected with measuring performance against goals, both during and at the end of the year. The results of evaluations during the year may lead to adjustments in the plan's strategies and/or tactics or even the objectives to be achieved.

## SELECTED PLANNING MODELS

Over the past 20 to 25 years, a number of frameworks or tools — we'll call them *models* — have been designed to assist with strategic planning. Most of these models can be used with both strategic company planning *and* strategic marketing planning. In this section, therefore, we briefly discuss several planning models that have received ample attention in recent years. First, however, you need to be familiar with a form of organization, the strategic business unit, that pertains to these planning models.

### Strategic Business Units

Most large and medium-sized companies — and even some smaller firms — consist of multiple units and produce numerous products. In such diversified firms, company-wide planning cannot serve as an effective guide for executives who oversee the organization's various divisions. Bombardier Inc., a company probably best known to most Canadians as the manufacturer of Ski-Doo snowmobiles, provides a good example. The mission, objectives, and strategies of the divisions within the *motorized consumer products group* (which includes the Sea-Doo/Ski-Doo Division) are — and must be — quite different from those that guide marketing and other activities in its *aerospace group* (where the SBUs include Canadair and De Havilland — manufacturers of airplanes) and its *transportation equipment group*, where the SBUs are involved in the manufacture of subway and railway cars, shuttle-train cars for the tunnel under the English Channel, and PeopleMover Transportation systems.

Consequently, for more effective planning and operations, a multibusiness or multiproduct organization should be divided according to its major markets or products. Each such entity is called a **strategic business unit (SBU)**. Each SBU may be a major division in an organization, a group of related products, or even a single major product or brand.

To be identified as an SBU, an entity should:

- Be a separately identifiable business.
- Have a distinct mission.
- Have its own competitors.
- Have its own executive group with profit responsibility.

The trick in setting up SBUs in an organization is to arrive at the *optimum* number. Too many can bog down top management in details associated with planning, operating, and reporting. Too few SBUs can result in each one covering too broad an area for managerial planning. Of course, most companies have fewer SBUs than Bombardier.

Let's now consider several different planning models.

### The Boston Consulting Group Matrix

Developed by a management consulting firm, the **Boston Consulting Group (BCG) matrix** dates back at least 25 years.[11] Using this model, an organization classifies each of its SBUs (and, sometimes, major products) according to two factors: its market share relative to competitors, and the growth rate of the industry in which the SBU operates. When the factors are divided simply into high and low categories, a $2 \times 2$ grid is created, as displayed in Figure 3-3.

#### DIVIDING UP THE "PIE"

Possible SBUs for two giant companies and a not-for-profit organization are as follows:

- **Canadian General Electric:** Electrical motors, major appliances, jet engines, lighting equipment, commercial credit, and broadcasting.
- **PepsiCo Canada:** Soft drinks, snack foods, and restaurants (and further subdivision of each of these areas is possible).
- **Your university or college:** Different schools (such as business and engineering) *or* different delivery systems (such as on-campus curricula and televised courses).

**FIGURE 3-3 The Boston Consulting Group matrix.**

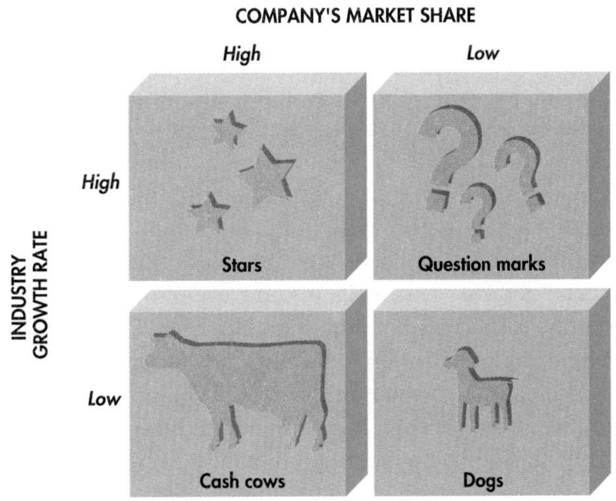


In turn, the four quadrants in the grid represent distinct categories of SBUs or major products. The categories differ with respect not only to market share and industry growth rate but also to cash needs and appropriate strategies.

- **Stars.** High market shares and high industry growth rates typify SBUs in this category. However, an SBU that falls into this category poses a challenge for companies because it requires lots of cash to remain competitive in growing markets. Aggressive marketing strategies are imperative for stars to maintain or even build market share.
- **Cash cows.** These SBUs have high market shares and do business in mature industries (those with low growth rates). When an industry's growth diminishes, stars move into this category. Because most of their customers have been with them for some time and are still loyal, a cash cow's marketing costs are not high. Consequently, it generates more cash than can be reinvested profitably in its own operations. As a result, cash cows can be "milked" to support the firm's other SBUs that need more resources. Marketing strategies for cash cows seek to defend market share, largely by reinforcing customer loyalty.
- **Question marks** (sometimes called *problem children*). SBUs characterized by low market shares but high industry growth rates fit in this category. A question mark has not achieved a strong foothold in an expanding, but highly competitive market. The question surrounding this type of SBU is whether it can gain adequate market share and be profitable. If management answers "no," then the SBU should be divested or liquidated. If management instead answers "yes," the firm must come up with the cash to build market share — more cash than the typical question mark generates from its own profits. Appropriate marketing strategies for question marks focus on creating an impact in the market by displaying a strong differential advantage and, thereby, building customer support.
- **Dogs.** These SBUs have low market shares and operate in industries with low growth rates. A company normally would be unwise to invest substantial funds in SBUs in this category. Marketing strategies for dogs are intended to maximize any potential profits by minimizing expenditures *or* to promote a differential advantage to build market share. The company can instead say "Enough's enough!" and divest or liquidate an SBU that's a dog.

Ordinarily, one firm cannot affect the growth rate for an entire industry. (An exception might be the dominant firm in a fairly new, rapidly growing industry. An example would be Rollerblade, in what's called the in-line roller skating market.) If growth rate cannot be influenced, companies must turn their attention to the other factor in the BCG matrix, market share. Hence, marketing strategies based on the BCG matrix tend to concentrate on building or maintaining market share, depending on which of the four SBU categories is involved. Various strategies require differing amounts of cash, which means that management must continually allocate the firm's limited resources (notably cash) to separate marketing endeavours.

In the financial arena, an investor needs a balanced portfolio with respect to risks and potential returns. Likewise, a company should seek a balanced portfolio of SBUs. Certainly, cash cows are indispensable. Stars and question marks are integral to a balanced portfolio, because products in growing markets determine a firm's long-term performance. While dogs are undesirable, it is rare that a company doesn't have at least one. Thus, the portfolios of most organizations with numerous SBUs or major products include a mix of stars, cash cows, question marks, and dogs.

## MARKETING AT WORK

### FILE 3-4 PLANNING IN CHANGING SOCIETIES

The planning models discussed in this section were developed in competitive economies. As a result, it's safe to say that they are most useful for companies operating in a mature, free-market economy (as found in North America, Japan, and the European Union). However, do these planning models have any value for companies in other types of economies?

One Hungarian economist, Magdolna Csath, believes they do. Since the economic reforms of 1968, strategic planning has become more and more common in Hungarian industries. According to Csath, if strategic planning is to have value, firms must be able to make their own decisions rather than having them mandated by the government.

The Hungarian economy is still vastly different from the North American economy. For instance, there is still much more government ownership of industry in Hungary than in most Western countries. Besides operating in its home market, a Hungarian company may operate in other, very different types of markets, including developing countries and the nations of Western Europe.

Given the nature of the business environment in Hungary, Csath found it necessary to alter the Boston Consulting Group matrix for use by Hungarian companies. The two factors in Csath's modified model are *environmental opportunities*, rather than industry growth rate, and *company's competitive strength*, rather than company's market share. Like the BCG matrix, the resulting four areas in the matrix have distinct strategic implications. Csath advocates using the model not only to assess a company's present product portfolio, but also to plan a desired portfolio.

Does the revised model have practical value? To date, it has been applied in more than 20 enterprises in Hungary. According to Csath, the most successful applications have occurred when the head of a company initiated use of the model *and* told lower-level managers why it was being used.

Source: Magdolna Csath, "Corporate Planning in Hungarian Companies," *Long Range Planning*, August 1989, pp. 89-97.

### Porter's Generic-Strategies Model

Michael Porter, a Harvard business professor, advises firms to assess two factors, scope of target market and differential advantage, and then choose an appropriate strategy.[12] **Porter's generic-strategies model** recommends three alternatives for consideration:

- **Overall cost leadership.** A company or an SBU, typically large, seeks to satisfy a broad market by producing a standard product at a low cost and then underpricing competitors.

The competition among Federal Express, United Parcel Service, and Canada Post in overnight package delivery largely revolves around cost leadership at the present time.

- **Differentiation.** An organization creates a distinctive, perhaps even a unique, product through its unsurpassed quality, innovative design, or some other feature and, as a result, can charge a higher-than-average price. This strategy may be used to pursue either a broad or narrow target market.
- **Focus.** A firm or an SBU concentrates on part of a market and tries to satisfy it with either a very low-priced or highly distinctive product. The target market ordinarily is set apart by some factor such as geography or specialized needs. For example, a small company in the auto-parts business might target owners of cars that are no longer produced (such as Volkswagen beetles and Avantis).

The strategies making up Porter's model are displayed in Figure 3-4. Porter stresses that profitability depends on having a clear, distinctive strategy. Firms or SBUs that wind up "in the middle," without cost leadership, focus, or differentiation, are unlikely to achieve satisfactory financial performance.

**FIGURE 3-4**
**Porter's generic-strategies model.**

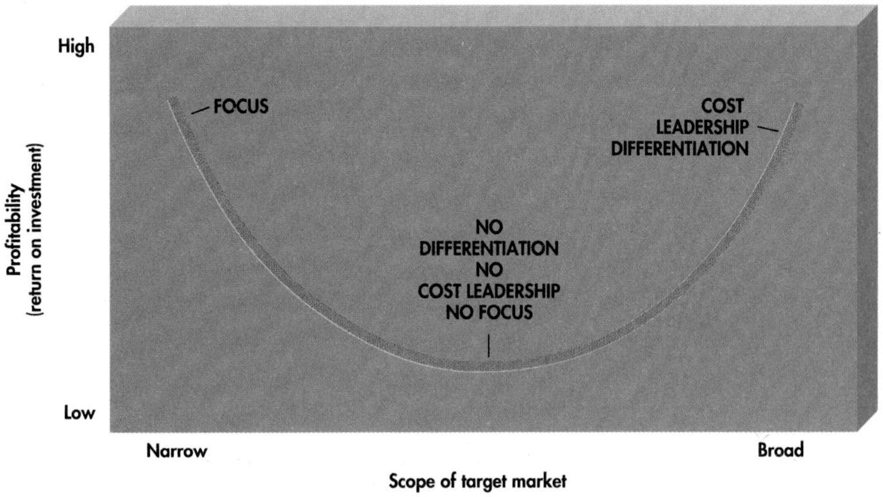


Each of the three strategies is based on having a strong differential advantage so this factor is not plotted.

Unlike the BCG model, Porter's model indicates that financial success does not necessarily require high market share. Instead, using either a focus or a differentiation strategy, a firm can achieve success by doing a great job of satisfying part of a total market. While its share of the total market is small, the company achieves a dominant position in part of the market.

## Product-Market Growth Matrix

Most organizations' statements of mission and objectives focus on growth — that is, a desire to increase revenues and profits. In seeking growth, a company has to consider *both* its markets and its products. Then it has to decide whether to continue doing what it is now doing — only do it better — *or* establish new ventures. The **product-market growth matrix**, first proposed by Igor Ansoff, depicts these options.

Essentially, as shown in Figure 3-5, there are four product-market growth strategies:[13]

- **Market penetration.** A company tries to sell more of its present products to its present markets. Supporting tactics might include greater spending on advertising or personal

**FIGURE 3-5 Product-market growth matrix.**

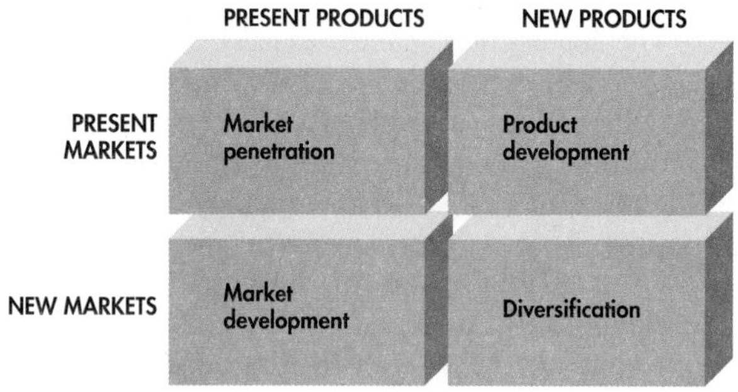


selling. For example, the Wrigley gum company relies on this strategy, most recently encouraging smokers to chew gum where smoking is prohibited.[14] Or a company tries to become a single source of supply by offering preferential treatment to customers who will concentrate all their purchases with it.

- **Market development.** A firm continues to sell its present products, but to a new market. For example, ski resort operators' efforts to attract families and foreigners represent market development.
- **Product development.** This strategy calls for a company to develop new products to sell to its existing markets. One example is Sony's introduction of the Watchman TV following its success with the Walkman personal stereo. To remain competitive, Kodak has to develop and introduce improved colour film as often as every two years. Even more boldly, in the early 1990s, Kodak launched a major product-development effort in electronic imaging (also called filmless cameras).[15]
- **Diversification.** A company develops new products to sell to new markets. This strategy is risky because it doesn't rely on either the company's successful products or its position in established markets. Sometimes it works, but sometimes it doesn't.

As market conditions change over time, a company may shift product-market growth strategies. For example, when its present market is fully saturated, a company may have no choice other than to pursue new markets.

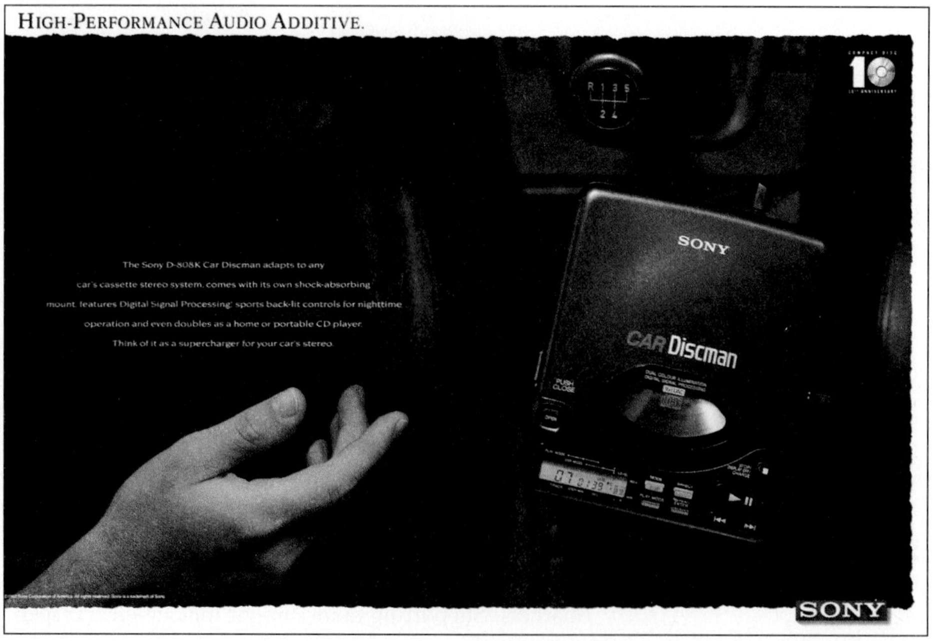

HIGH-PERFORMANCE AUDIO ADDITIVE.
The Sony D-808K Car Discman adapts to any car's cassette stereo system, comes with its own shock-absorbing mount, features Digital Signal Processing, sports back-lit controls for nighttime operation and even doubles as a home or portable CD player.
Think of it as a supercharger for your car's stereo.
SONY
CAR Discman
SONY

**New products like the Watchman TV and the Car Discman make Sony's product-development strategy a success.**

### Assessment of the Planning Models

Each of these three planning models has been praised and criticized.[16] While each is somewhat distinctive, all share some common weaknesses and strengths.

The primary weakness is probably oversimplification. Each model bases its assessment of market opportunities and subsequent decisions on only two or three key factors.

Another weakness is the possibility of placing an SBU on a grid or choosing a strategy without relevant, reliable information. For example, whether market share is critical to a product's profitability is still debated. A third possible weakness is that the results from one of the models might be used to contradict or substitute for the critical business judgements made by line managers (such as a marketing vice-president).

However, these models also possess noteworthy strengths. Most notable is straightforward classification. That is, each model permits an organization to examine its entire portfolio of SBUs or major products in relation to criteria that influence business performance. A second strength is that the models can pinpoint attractive business opportunities and suggest ventures to avoid. Another strength of the models is that they encourage careful, consistent assessment of opportunities, allocation of resources, and formulation of strategies. Without planning models, these activities might be haphazard — for example, using one set of criteria this month and, with no good reason, another set next month.

Overall, we believe these planning models can help management in allocating resources and also in developing sound business and marketing strategies. Of course, any planning model should supplement, rather than substitute for, managers' judgements and decisions.

## SUMMARY

The management process consists of planning, implementation, and evaluation. Planning is deciding now what we are going to do later, including when and how we are going to do it. Planning provides direction to an organization. Strategic planning is intended to match an organization's resources with its market opportunities over the long run.

In any organization, there should be three levels of planning: strategic company planning, strategic marketing planning, and annual marketing planning. In strategic company planning, management defines the organization's mission, assesses its operating environment, sets long-range goals, and formulates broad strategies to achieve the goals. This level of planning guides planning in different functional areas, including marketing.

Strategic marketing planning entails five steps: conduct a situation analysis; develop objectives; determine positioning and differential advantage; select target markets and measure market demand; and design a marketing mix. Based on strategic marketing plans, an annual marketing plan lays out a year's marketing activities for each major product and division of an organization. An annual plan includes tactics as well as strategies. It is typically prepared by the executive responsible for the division or product.

Management can rely on one or more of the following models for assistance with strategic planning: Boston Consulting Group matrix, Porter's generic-strategies model, and Ansoff's product-market growth matrix. A planning model helps management see how best to allocate its resources and to select effective marketing strategies.

## KEY TERMS AND CONCEPTS

**Management (60)**
**Planning (61)**
**Strategic planning (61)**
**Mission (61)**
**Objective (61)**
**Strategy (62)**
**Tactic (62)**
**Strategic company planning (64)**
**Situation analysis (65)**
**Organizational strategies (65)**
**Strategic marketing planning (65)**
**SWOT assessment (66)**
**Positioning (66)**
**Differential advantage (66)**
**Differential disadvantage (66)**
**Market (66)**
**Target market (67)**
**Marketing mix (68)**

**Annual marketing plan (70)**
**Strategic business unit (SBU) (73)**
**Boston Consulting Group (BCG) matrix (73)**
**Stars (74)**
**Cash cows (74)**
**Question marks (74)**
**Dogs (74)**
**Porter's generic-strategies model (75)**
**Overall cost leadership (75)**
**Differentiation (75)**
**Focus (75)**
**Product-market growth matrix (76)**
**Market penetration (76)**
**Market development (76)**
**Product development (76)**
**Diversification (76)**

## QUESTIONS AND PROBLEMS

1. Should a small firm (either a manufacturer or a retailer) engage in formal strategic planning? Why or why not?
2. Using a customer-oriented approach (benefits provided or wants satisfied), answer the question "What business are we in?" for each of the following companies:
   a. Holiday Inn.
   b. Adidas athletic shoes.
   c. Apple computers.
3. In the situation-analysis step of strategic marketing planning, what specific external environmental factors should be analyzed by a manufacturer of equipment used for backpacking in the wilderness?
4. If you were the vice-president of marketing for a large airline, which of the three planning models would you find most useful? Why?
5. "The economic unification of the European Community means absolute chaos for firms trying to market to consumers in these countries. For a number of years, the situation will be so dynamic that executives should not waste their time on formal strategic planning related to European markets." Do you agree with this statement? Support your position.
6. Use an example to explain the concept of a strategic business unit.
7. What market factors might you logically use in estimating the market potential for each of the following products?
   a. Central home air conditioners.
   b. Electric milking machines.
   c. Luxury airline travel.
   d. Sterling silver flatware.
   e. Personal computer repair services.

## HANDS-ON MARKETING

1. Go to your school's library and obtain a copy of an annual report for a major corporation. Based on your examination of the year-end review, which of the following product-market growth strategies is being used by this company: market penetration, market development, product development, and/or diversification?
2. Talk with a marketing executive at a local firm. Which of the various methods of forecasting demand does this company employ, and why?

## NOTES AND REFERENCES

1. Adapted from Marlene Cartash, "Waking up the Neighbours," *Profit*, vol. 12, no. 3, September 1993, pp. 24-28.
2. Many writers and executives use the terms *control* and *evaluation* synonymously. We distinguish between them. To speak of control as only one part of the management process is too restrictive. Rather than being an isolated managerial function, control permeates virtually all other organizational activities. For example, management *controls* its operations through the goals and strategies it selects. Also, the type of organizational structure used in the marketing department determines the degree of *control* over marketing operations.
3. *Pulse of the Middle Market — 1990*, BDO Seidman, New York, 1990, pp. 12-13.
4. Techniques for identifying and monitoring nontraditional competitors are discussed in William E. Rothschild, "Who Are Your Future Competitors?" *The*

*Journal of Business Strategy*, May/June 1988, pp. 10-14; a technique for assessing a firm's strengths and weaknesses in relation to other firms in an industry is presented in Emilio Cvitkovic, "Profiling Your Competitors," *Planning Review*, May-June 1989, pp. 28-30.

5. Malcolm H. B. McDonald, "Ten Barriers to Marketing Planning," *The Journal of Business and Industrial Marketing*, Winter 1992, p. 15.
6. Edward DiMingo, "The Fine Art of Positioning," *The Journal of Business Strategy*, March/April 1988, pp. 34-38.
7. Suein L. Hwang, "Its Big Brands Long Taunted as Fatty, CPC Tries a More 'Wholesome' Approach," *The Wall Street Journal*, April 20, 1992, pp. B1, B4.
8. An excellent article stressing that strategy should focus on customer needs, not just on beating competition, is Kenichi Ohmae, "Getting Back to Strategy," *Harvard Business Review*, November- December 1988, pp. 149-156.
9. Barbara Buell, "Apple: New Team, New Strategy," *Business Week*, October 15, 1990, pp. 86-89.
10. An excellent source of information on how various companies prepare their marketing plans is Howard Sutton, *The Marketing Plan*, The Conference Board, New York, 1990.
11. *The Experience Curve Reviewed, IV. The Growth Share Matrix of the Product Portfolio*, Boston Consulting Group, Boston, 1973.
12. Michael E. Porter, *Competitive Advantage: Creating and Sustaining Superior Performance*, The Free Press, New York, 1985, pp. 11-26.
13. First proposed by H. Igor Ansoff, "Strategies for Diversification," *Harvard Business Review*, September–October 1957, pp. 113-124.
14. Brett Pulley, "Wrigley Is Thriving, Despite the Recession, in a Resilient Business," *The Wall Street Journal*, May 29, 1991, pp. A1, A8.
15. James S. Hirsch, "Kodak Hopes Electronic Imaging Clicks as Company Faces Fuzzy Photo Future," *The Wall Street Journal*, July 16, 1990, p. B4.
16. Improvements worth considering are suggested in the following articles: R. A. Proctor and J. S. Hassard, "Towards a New Model for Product Portfolio Analysis," *Management Decision*, vol. 28, no. 3, 1990, pp. 14-17, and Rick Brown, "Making the Product Portfolio a Basis for Action," *Long Range Planning*, February 1991, pp. 102-110.

## CASES FOR PART 1

# CASE 1-1

# THE SALVATION ARMY RED SHIELD APPEAL (A)

When Lt. Col. Melvyn Bond, territorial public relations secretary of The Salvation Army, met with Julian Elwes, senior vice-president of BBDO Canada[1], to discuss the 1994 Salvation Army Red Shield advertising program, there were a number of things on his mind. Col. Bond knew that the 1993 Red Shield Appeal had raised more than $30 million to support the work of the Salvation Army in Canada, but he also knew that the demands being placed on the Army were greater than ever and that even more funds were needed.

Col. Bond was aware that the expectations for support and assistance from the Salvation Army were almost greater than the Army was able to provide, because of the many social and economic problems facing a Canadian population dealing with a recession and the resulting effects on families and individuals. But Col. Bond also had other objectives for The Salvation Army's advertising. He wanted to make sure that the advertising communicated a message to Canadians about The Salvation Army and its work, that it not simply be an appeal for funds. He felt it was not enough to have a successful fund-raising campaign; the advertising should also tell Canadians something about "who we are and why we do what we do."

The Salvation Army is an internationally respected religious and charitable organization that is represented in more than 100 countries. The Army originated in England, where, in 1865, a Methodist minister, William Booth, and his wife, Catherine, began to preach to residents of East London who they believed were not being reached by the established churches. The Booths directed their ministry to the working class, the sick, and the poor. The evangelists realized that, to help these people, they would need to combine practical support and material assistance with their Christian teachings. Social programs for the betterment of all members of society have been an integral part of The Salvation Army's work since its establishment.

The Salvation Army was originally referred to as the Christian Revival Association and later was named the Christian Mission. It was not until 1878 that the name, The Salvation Army, was adopted. With this name also came the adoption of a quasi-military command structure that was derived from a combination of the military traditions of nineteenth-century Europe and biblical reference to spiritual warfare. The "Army" uses military ranks and terminology and all officers, or ordained clergy, are required to wear its uniform.

### THE SALVATION ARMY IN CANADA

The work of The Salvation Army spread rapidly after its establishment in London; adherents were working in Wales by 1874 and in Scotland by 1879. During 1880, the Army began its work in Ireland, the United States, and Australia, and operations were begun in France in 1881. Canadian operations of The Salvation Army were established in 1882 in London, Ontario.

For organizational purposes, Canada and Bermuda are combined into a single "territory" or geographical area of administration. Worldwide, there are more than 50 such territories covering more than 100 countries. The Salvation Army's International Headquarters are in London, England, while the administrative headquarters for the Canada and Bermuda territory is in Toronto, where plans for the Army's religious, health, social services, and fund-raising programs are prepared. Regional administration of approximately 400 local "corps" or church congregations and of community service programs is handled by the 15 divisional headquarters located in major cities across Canada and in Bermuda.

The Salvation Army's mission today is a reflection of the original objectives of its founders William and Catherine Booth — to preach the Gospel and to improve social conditions so as to enhance the physical and spiritual well-being

[1] BBDO Canada has been the advertising agency of The Salvation Army in Canada and Bermuda for more than 40 years. The agency began as McKim Advertising, changed its name to McKim Baker Lovick/ BBDO in 1992, and became BBDO Canada in 1994.

 The authors wish to thank Lt. Col. Mel Bond of The Salvation Army and Julian Elwes of BBDO Canada for their support and assistance in the preparation of this case.

of all people. For this reason, members express their faith not only through religious activity, but also through participation in a wide variety of community service activities. However, in translating religious conviction into acts of practical, philanthropic assistance, The Salvation Army requires both the active and financial support of many individuals from all faiths and all walks of life. Thousands of individuals willingly contribute their time and skills as volunteers and advisors for The Salvation Army.

## COMMUNITY ACTIVITIES AND SOCIAL PROGRAMS

The Salvation Army is world-renowned for its multifaceted community services programs, which involve many different types of social service. A list of many of the activities, programs, and organizations supported by The Salvation Army in Canada is presented at the end of this case.

Understanding the public's concern that its programs and services are operated using sound financial principles and integrity, The Salvation Army consistently ensures that it ranks among the most efficient and cost-effective charities. In addition to continuous internal audits, the accounts of all programs that receive government assistance are subject to audit by external professional accountants, and all financial records are available for public inspection on request. Less than 10 percent of funds received from its members and the Canadian public is directed to fund raising and administration expenses.

## THE PUBLIC RELATIONS DEPARTMENT

It is the responsibility of The Salvation Army's public relations department to ensure that fund raising and media relations are professionally organized and conducted. The Salvation Army in Canada operates a national public relations department and communications services unit centralized in Toronto, headed by the territorial public relations secretary. This national office is supported by 20 regional offices throughout the territory of Canada and Bermuda. Each office is managed by a Salvation Army officer, assisted by skilled professionals who may or may not be Salvationists or hold Salvation Army rank. Each regional office is operated by a public relations director, with the support of a public relations officer.

The responsibilities of the regional public relations offices include not only ensuring and collecting financial support, but also enlisting practical support of the thousands of volunteers who organize and canvass for the annual Red Shield Blitz held across Canada at the community level each May. Each local public relations office is supplied with brochures and materials on Salvation Army programs and activities for members of the media and anyone else interested in learning about the Army. The offices also provide speakers, films, and videos on many aspects of The Salvation Army to church groups, service clubs, and other community organizations.

The territorial public relations department, through its advertising agency, purchases and solicits complementary or public service media coverage, such as newspaper or magazine space or radio and television time. All such marketing activities, including the development of campaign themes and slogans and the printing of promotional material, are carried out at the national level. A major factor that contributes to The Salvation Army's economic efficiency is this national direction policy. The result is less expenditure on marketing and administration and more on social services. In addition to initiating large, and usually cheaper, contracts with national companies, this technique establishes strong relationships with companies that are then motivated to complete some services for the Army free of charge. This system of centralized, top-down direction also avoids expensive repetition of efforts.

## THE FUND-RAISING PROGRAM

The public relations department is responsible for fund raising aimed at corporations and the general public. Most of the contributions received each year by the Salvation Army are the result of the National Red Shield Appeal, which consists of a door-to-door collection blitz in May, as well as postal donation requests sent to selected households in both May and December, and the traditional Christmas Appeal with the Army's famous "red kettles," which are seen on street corners and in shopping centres across the country. Additional income is received from "offerings" during Sunday religious services and the ongoing Planned Giving program, which encourages arrangements such as bequests from wills or gift annuities. In addition, since 1985, The Salvation Army has held an annual World Services Appeal, which raises money to assist the needy in Third World countries and in areas subject to natural disasters.

## THE HISTORY OF THE RED SHIELD APPEAL

In 1993, The Salvation Army marked the 75th anniversary of the Red Shield Appeal and the use of the Red Shield as the official symbol for the Army's social services. The use of the Red Shield originated in Canada and has since spread worldwide. In the early 1900s, a silver metal shield carrying The Salvation Army's name was worn by uniformed Salvationists or converts who did not have the resources to purchase a full uniform. This lapel badge or pin was worn on street-corner or door-to-door collecting missions. Use of the shield evolved when British Salvationists serving or helping during World War I began to use shields to identify their Naval and Military League rest huts.

Although Canadian Salvation Army workers were not required to serve in Europe during World War I, at the end of the war, the Canadian government asked the Army to set up military hostels for returning soldiers and a visiting program for wives, widows, and orphaned children. The fourth military hostel, opened in Winnipeg in 1918, was the first to receive "Red Shield" designation. The significant increase in the need for Salvation Army services required more than local funding, and plans for a national "Red Shield" Appeal were prepared in late 1918. Calgary became the first place in the world to use the reputation of the Red Shield to create a link between The Salvation Army's social services and public funding. Calgary Army workers, in 1918, began campaigning for funds using the Red Shield with white lettering to stimulate donations from the public. The world's first official Red Shield Appeal, which was not formally undertaken until January 1919, raised $4.5 million.

The Red Shield Appeal, in the form it is known today, began in the late 1940s and, since its inception, Salvation Army officers and others from across the globe have adopted the principles and methods of the Canada and Bermuda territory's Red Shield Appeal. Today, the Red Shield is one of the most widely recognized and universally respected symbols in the world, communicating a practical expression of hope to the countless people who turn to The Salvation Army for help. A summary of the fund-raising objective for the Red Shield appeal and the amounts actually raised for selected years since 1965 are presented in Exhibit 1.

**EXHIBIT 1 Red Shield Campaign Objectives and Amounts Collected (Selected Years 1965-1993)**

| Year | Objective | Amount Collected |
|---|---|---|
| 1965 | 3,257,568 | 3,458,738 |
| 1970 | 3,712,968 | 4,189,726 |
| 1971 | 3,819,961 | 4,380,271 |
| 1972 | 4,002,641 | 4,720,227 |
| 1976 | 5,204,937 | 6,772,710 |
| 1977 | 5,875,903 | 7,509,148 |
| 1978 | 7,408,462 | 8,237,814 |
| 1979 | 7,916,526 | 9,001,730 |
| 1980 | 8,741,000 | 9,997,957 |
| 1981 | 10,101,136 | 11,430,564 |
| 1982 | 12,000,000 | 13,590,380 |
| 1983 | 14,000,000 | 15,908,129 |
| 1984 | 15,450,000 | 17,160,795 |
| 1985 | 18,100,000 | 20,937,652 |
| 1986 | 20,000,000 | 23,082,280 |
| 1987 | 22,150,000 | 25,873,394 |
| 1988 | 26,427,906 | 28,858,655 |
| 1989 | 29,000,000 | 31,345,944 |
| 1990 | 31,045,523 | 32,905,890 |
| 1991 | 32,693,534 | 34,321,975 |
| 1992 | 34,096,724 | 34,861,490 |
| 1993 | 36,255,949 | 34,692,243 |

## RED SHIELD ADVERTISING

The annual Red Shield Appeal of The Salvation Army has been supported for many years by a national advertising campaign, which has been co-ordinated for more than 40 years by the Army's advertising agency, BBDO Canada. While most of the advertising appears in mass media across Canada in a six-week period leading up to the May door-to-door blitz, some advertising exposure is obtained throughout the year, largely in the form of public service announcements and billboard placements.

In keeping with The Salvation Army's objective of ensuring that the largest possible percentage of funds donated reaches people in need, the budget for the annual advertising campaign is necessarily small. Placing advertisements in local newspapers, radio stations, magazines, billboards, television, and on public transit systems across the country is co-ordinated by BBDO Canada. Each year, the agency solicits input from the Army's regional public relations directors, concerning which media they feel should be used in their regions. BBDO Canada is also successful in getting air time and advertising space donated by the various media. In 1993, the Salvation Army spent approximately $300,000 on paid advertising, but received additional advertising worth three times that amount as public service announcements and donated space.

Again, in order to keep the costs of advertising to a manageable level, BBDO Canada has been preparing new advertising materials for the Red Shield Campaign in four- to five-year cycles. Each campaign contains a simple message captured in a slogan that represents the focal point of all advertising materials. The slogans used in recent years have included:

"Who says you can't buy happiness? Please give." (1973-76)

"If you don't need our help, we need yours." (1977-79)

"All you need is love. Please give." (1980-83)

"For the love of God, give." (1984-88)

"God knows, you can make a difference." (1989-93)

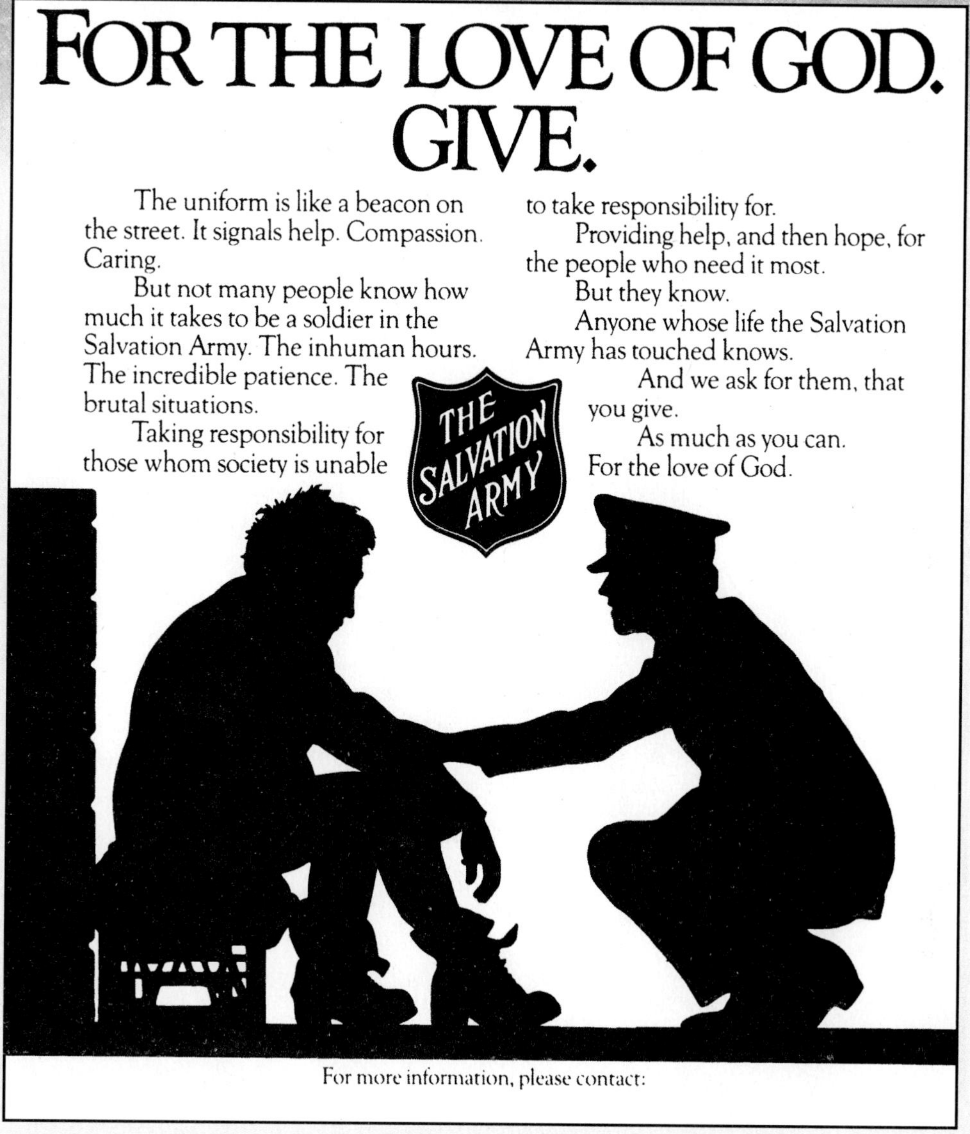
FOR THE LOVE OF GOD. GIVE.
The uniform is like a beacon on the street. It signals help. Compassion. Caring.
But not many people know how much it takes to be a soldier in the Salvation Army. The inhuman hours. The incredible patience. The brutal situations.
Taking responsibility for those whom society is unable to take responsibility for.
Providing help, and then hope, for the people who need it most.
But they know.
Anyone whose life the Salvation Army has touched knows.
And we ask for them, that you give.
As much as you can.
For the love of God.
THE SALVATION ARMY
For more information, please contact:

Examples of recent advertising for the Red Shield Appeal are presented here and on page 84.

## THE 1993 DECISION

While there was little information available to The Salvation Army and its advertising agency concerning how successful past advertising campaigns for the Red Shield Appeal had been, apart from the fact that actual amounts raised had exceeded annual objectives in every year up to 1993, Lt. Col. Bond and Julian Elwes were familiar with a research study that had been conducted in 1987 by Decima Research. It indicated that The Salvation Army was extremely well regarded by Canadians, but not necessarily as a religious organization. There appeared to be some confusion about whether the Army is a charity or a religious denomination. There was also evidence from the Decima study that the Army's message may not be getting through to younger Canadians.

Partly as a result of the conclusions drawn from the Decima study, a decision was made to reposition The Salvation Army slightly in the Red Shield advertising campaign that was introduced in 1989 and that continued to run through 1993. In that campaign, it was decided to reinforce the image of The Salvation Army as a religious denomination, but to do so softly, through the slogan "God knows, you can make a difference."

In planning the 1994 Red Shield advertising program, Col. Bond and Elwes considered the increasing demands

being placed on The Salvation Army's programs across Canada and the fact that the competition for charitable donations had become fierce in an economy where many people could not afford to donate as much as they had in the past. They were facing the question of whether the appeal embodied in the slogan for the 1994 campaign should be much more blunt than that used for the past four years and whether the advertising should make the religious side of the Salvation Army more obvious.

Friday night is Red Shield Appeal Night
Your generosity can shed light into someone's life.
The lonely heart crying out for comfort. The lost soul searching for a haven.
The child crying for compassion. These are the people for whom the Salvation Army
provides help, and then hope, the people who need it most.
We ask for them that you give. As much as you can.
THE NATIONAL RED SHIELD APPEAL
THE SALVATION ARMY
God knows
you can make a difference

## QUESTIONS

1. What are the factors that influence a person's decision to donate to a charitable organization? What do you feel is the image of The Salvation Army among prospective donors in Canada? Is it perceived to be a religious organization or a charity?
2. How are the attitudes of Canadians towards charitable donations affected by the changing environment in which they live? What are the implications for The Salvation Army?
3. How do your answers to questions 1 and 2 influence the decision The Salvation Army and its advertising agency have to make concerning the direction of the advertising campaign to support the 1994 Red Shield Appeal?

## ACTIVITIES OF THE SALVATION ARMY IN CANADA

- Emergency services, which offer material and emotional support in emergency situations and at times of natural disaster.
- Suicide prevention services to counsel individuals in distress.
- Senior citizens' residences.
- "Fresh Air" camps for less privileged children from low-income families, for the physically and mentally challenged, and for single mothers and their children.
- Public hospitals, including maternity hospitals and palliative care centres.
- Addiction and rehabilitation services for victims of alcohol and drug abuse; hostels, rehabilitation centres, and industrial units where recovering victims are provided with a place where they can receive guidance as well as material assistance.
- Emergency shelters for the homeless and for arriving immigrants.
- Family thrift stores where people can purchase refurbished clothing, furniture, and household items at affordable prices.
- Many different programs of social services for women: maternity homes for prenatal and postnatal single mothers and their infants, facilities for developmentally handicapped women, battered women, post-psychiatric women, and women with alcohol and substance addiction problems, emergency shelters, and day-care centres.
- Correctional and justice-related social services such as parole supervision, legal aid assistance, victim witness assistance, bail verification and supervision, shoplifter programs, and employment assistance.
- Visiting the sick, shut-in, elderly, hospitalized, and imprisoned; dedicated volunteers visit individuals in institutions such as convalescent or children's homes, and also visit private homes.
- Material aid to overseas countries in need; The Salvation Army provides food products, accommodations, and training to many developing countries.
- Sheltered workshops where physically and mentally challenged adults are given work assignments and the ability to earn an income.
- Family services, which provide counselling and support groups, pastoral care, and material assistance for a variety of individuals such as teen mothers, single parents, seniors, and those in search of employment or homes. In addition, food and toy hampers are distributed during the Christmas season.
- Youth camps where children can receive training in music or drama and learn about the Bible; Guide and Scout camps are also available at Salvation Army camp grounds.
- Social and educational groups for men, women, seniors, and children, which offer character-building programs and activities that assist in the social and spiritual development of members and promote the sanctity of the family.

# CASE 1-2

# GREEN MARKETING

## DESIGNING A MARKETING STRATEGY

Although there is no generally accepted definition of green marketing, the term is used to describe any marketing activity that is intended to create a positive impact or to lessen the negative impact of a product on the environment and as a result capitalize on consumers' concerns about environmental issues. It encompasses everything from using recycled material in making a product to environmentally specific claims in advertising or on package labels. A question faced by many managers is whether green marketing can or should become part of their firm's marketing strategy.

Green marketing grew out of firms' attempts to respond to the criticisms of individuals and groups concerned about pollution and waste. At first, these criticisms were viewed as public relations issues that could be ignored or refuted with some facts and figures about customer preferences and the high costs of products friendly to the environment. However, criticism continued and the critics became more vocal. Here are some examples of products under fire:

- **Aseptic boxes.** Every day, Canadians pack hundreds of thousands of aseptic boxes in their lunches for school or work. These boxes have many positive attributes; they use less energy and fewer raw materials to produce, fill, and ship than any other ready-to-drink package; they are shelf-stable, which means they are able to maintain a drink's freshness for a long time without refrigeration; and finally, a typical aseptic box is 96 percent beverage and 4 percent package, thus creating one-twelfth the waste of a glass container. On the downside, these boxes have been described as an environmental nightmare. The boxes are made of multiple layers of plastic, paper and aluminum, all of which are individually recyclable, but very few facilities exist for recycling the aseptic boxes. A handful of communities in Canada have pilot programs for gathering these boxes through municipal curbside collection programs. The boxes ultimately end up in Mississauga, Ontario, where Superwood, a plastic lumber company, uses them to make items such as park benches and picnic tables. Tetra Pak Inc. claimed in a newspaper advertisement that their aseptic boxes were 100 percent recyclable. However, the facilities do not exist in most Canadian cities to recycle the boxes. Even if recycling centres were built throughout the country, 900 million Tetra Paks are sold annually in Canada, most of which are packed in lunches and end up being discarded at offices, schools, and other places that are unlikely to be part of recycling programs. Thus millions of aseptic boxes would still end up in garbage dumps.
- **Disposable diapers.** Two major manufacturers of disposable diapers, Kimberly-Clark and Procter & Gamble (P & G), have found ways to reduce the bulk of diapers and their packaging by as much as 50 percent, and both are experimenting with recycling projects. Despite these efforts, the criticisms continue. P & G advise purchasers that demonstration projects in the United States have shown that disposable diapers are compostable in municipal closed-vessel composting units, and that opportunities to do this in Canada are under review. No facilities exist right now for composting disposable diapers in Canada. P & G includes a note on the plastic wrapping that Pampers come in: "This package is recyclable where plastic bag recycling facilities are available." As fewer than a dozen Canadian cities have such facilities, most of the packages will end up in the garbage dump.
- **Garbage bags.** Loblaw Companies Limited began green marketing in 1989 when it introduced a line of what it calls "environmentally friendly" products under the GREEN brand name. The line consists of 100 products, including disposable diapers made from non-chlorine bleached pulp, Alar-free apple juice, and high-efficiency light bulbs. Though GREEN items account for only one-half of 1 percent of Loblaw's products and the chain continues to offer products that may be viewed as environmentally unfriendly, the results have been positive in sales and publicity. Loblaw remains the leader in environmental

---

Adapted in part, from: Bob Mackin Jr., "Gas Goes 'Green'," *Marketing*, March 16, 1992, pp. 1, 3; Eugene J. Casey Jr., "A Plan for Environmental Packaging," *Business Strategy*, July/August 1992, vol. 13, no. 4, pp. 18-20; Julia Moulden, "Even Greener Marketing," *Marketing*, February 8, 1993, pp. 1, 3; Arthur Johnson, "Eco-hype," *Financial Post Magazine*, May 1991, pp. 17-22; Colin Isaacs, "What Does 'Green' Really Mean?," *Marketing*, July 8, 1991, pp. 1, 3; James Rusk, "Green Loses Sheen as Shoppers Try to Stay out of Red," *Globe and Mail*, February 12, 1993, pp. A1, A2.

hype. Its garbage bags, for example, are labelled "94% biodegradable and photodegradable." Only the drawstring, which represents 6 percent of the garbage bag by weight, is not biodegradable. The bags are certainly capable of biodegrading (breaking down naturally) and photodegrading (breaking down when exposed to sunlight) under optimal conditions — full exposure to sunlight. The result is the bags break down into small pieces of plastic and plastic dust. In reality, most of the bags will wind up buried beneath soil and other garbage in a landfill site, and the amount of breakdown will be much less. Even worse, the starches and other substances added to the plastic to make the bags break down, even partially, render them nonrecyclable. The National Research Council of Canada says such garbage bags have no environmental advantage whatsoever.

Firms have responded to environmental concerns with four strategic versions of green marketing:

- **Making environmental claims about existing products on labels or in ads.** Label banners such as "all natural ingredients," "recyclable," and "biodegradable" have become quite common. Some may help consumers make informed decisions, but can they also be misleading? Makers of many products sold in aerosol containers indicate on their labels that the products contain no chlorofluorocarbons (CFCs). However, the use of CFCs as a propellant in aerosols has been banned in Canada since 1980 because CFCs damage the ozone layer and critics feel the information misleads consumers into thinking that the manufacturers making the claims are more environmentally friendly than their competitors. Similarly, The Body Shop products, until recently, carried the label "Not Tested on Animals." However, this statement is false as every product in the world has at some time been tested on animals. The Body Shop has since begun phasing out the "Not Tested on Animals" label, and now uses a much more vague statement: "Against Animal Testing."
- **Introducing entirely new products designed to appeal to environmentally conscious consumers or respond to legal mandates.** Markham, Ontario-based Black's Photo noted that consumers respond most favourably to products that are truly innovative and/or ahead of the regulations. Consequently, Black's developed the country's first closed-loop photofinishing system, investing three years of R & D and more than $1 million. Two years later, Black's still leads the industry in chemical waste management. Black's System Crystal was created partly in recognition that a zero discharge law is inevitable; the company reasoned that one major redesign was preferable to periodic adjustments over a number of years. Another example is Toro Company. Toro, a leading lawn mower company, invented "bagged" lawn mowers several decades ago. Bagging, then, was deemed to be the most efficient way to get a manicured look for the lawn. Toro has since become aware that upwards of 10 percent of the solid waste accumulating in landfills comes from lawn clippings stored in plastic bags. In response, Toro has designed a recycling, mulching lawn mower that cuts the grass into such tiny clippings that there is no need to rake and bag the grass.

  For some companies green marketing is not just a fad, it is the company's entire positioning strategy. Mohawk Oil, of Burnaby, British Columbia, is such a company. Mohawk has built its entire marketing strategy around the environment, to the extent that it has dubbed itself "Mother Nature's Gas Station." Mohawk began selling ethanol-blended gasoline in Manitoba in 1980 and is the only oil company approved by Environment Canada (Mohawk's ads include the EcoLogo Symbol). Mohawk has also been recognized for its re-refined motor oil.
- **Adapting products and/or packages to make them more environmentally sound.** This green marketing strategy requires more substantive effort. A firm might replace an offensive ingredient with a more acceptable one, change production or distribution methods to reduce pollutants and waste, or design a product for easier recycling. For instance, under the Kodak recycling program, consumers will see their single-use, Fun-Saver cameras being returned by photo finishers to Kodak for recycling. As an incentive, the photo finishers are paid by Kodak to return the cameras, which are designed so that 86 percent of their parts can be recycled and reused. In 1991, 1 million Fun-Saver cameras were returned. In addition, Kodak has introduced a self-contained plastic package for its Ektar film. The new film canister has a compatible plastic label that makes the total package recyclable.
- **Linking brands with environmental causes to create goodwill.** Since its inception in England in 1976, The Body Shop has aligned itself closely with the animal rights movement. As The Body Shop does not advertise per se, it promotes environmental causes with point-of-purchase displays, such as having labels bearing the statement "Against Animal Testing" displayed on its products. Toronto-based Lever Brothers Ltd. is also a supporter of environmental charities and is a founding partner of Global Relief, a reforestation campaign administered by Friends of the Earth.

Green marketing is a strategy that will work only if enough consumers find it appealing. Environmental concerns are high on the list of priorities for Canadians; however, that does not necessarily mean they are willing to pay higher prices for green products. A 1992 survey conducted by the Grocery Products Manufacturers of Canada found that only 15 percent of respondents were willing to pay a premium for products friendly to the environment. Even among the 31 percent of shoppers who claimed to be the most concerned about the environment, only 28 percent said they would pay extra. The slow-growth economy has left consumers more worried about their pocket books than the environment. Consequently, consumers are now much more price sensitive and are looking for "value" as opposed to "green" products.

Green marketing is far from dead and interest in environmentally friendly products remains strong, despite the recession. Forty-five percent of respondents in a Gallup/Marketing survey said that a product's environmental friendliness is an important factor in their purchasing decisions. Consumers have grown very sophisticated about companies' environmental claims for their products and many dismiss such claims as gimmicks. As a result, successful green marketers these days must do a lot more than relabel, repackage, and reposition their products. Packaging will now have to include information about *why* a product is better for the environment.

## QUESTIONS

1. Is green marketing consistent with the marketing concept?
2. What dimensions of a firm's internal and external environment might be affected by a green marketing strategy?
3. How would the five steps in strategic marketing planning apply to green marketing?

PART 2

# TARGET MARKETS

**An analysis of the people and organizations who buy, why they buy, and how they buy**

In Part 1, we stressed the importance of customer orientation in an organization's marketing efforts. We also defined strategic planning as the process of matching an organization's resources with its marketing opportunities. These notions suggest that, early in the strategic marketing process, an organization should determine who its potential customers are. Only then can management develop a marketing mix intended to satisfy the wants of these customers. Therefore, in Part 2 we discuss the selection of an organization's intended customers — that is, its target market.

In Chapter 4, we examine the concept of market segmentation as it relates to the selection of target markets, and we discuss several approaches to the segmentation of markets. In Chapter 5, we explore the strategic concept of positioning as a means to ensure that a company's offerings are found appealing by its target segments. We also discuss the important topic of forecasting. Chapter 6 is devoted to consumer buying behaviour and the buying process involved in the purchase of products and services. In Chapter 7, we examine in detail the important target market known as the business-to-business market, thereby reminding ourselves that there is a massive market that many end consumers rarely see — the one that involves businesses marketing to businesses and other organizations. Finally in this part, Chapter 8 covers the important topics of marketing research and marketing information systems, the means whereby marketers learn about their markets and the target consumers and customers who comprise them.

## CHAPTER 4 GOALS

After studying this chapter, you should have an understanding of:

- The fundamental principles behind target market identification and selection.
- The concept of market segmentation — its meaning, benefits, limitations, and situations where it finds greatest use.
- The difference between ultimate consumer markets and business markets.
- The principal bases for segmenting consumer markets.
- Segmentation of the market through examination of the distribution and composition of the population of Canada.
- Segmentation of the market through examination of consumer groups on the basis of income distribution and spending patterns.

How to get your toddler to open up.
HEINZ
TODDLER
Introducing Toddler Foods from Heinz.

# CHAPTER 4

# FOUNDATIONS FOR MARKET SEGMENTATION

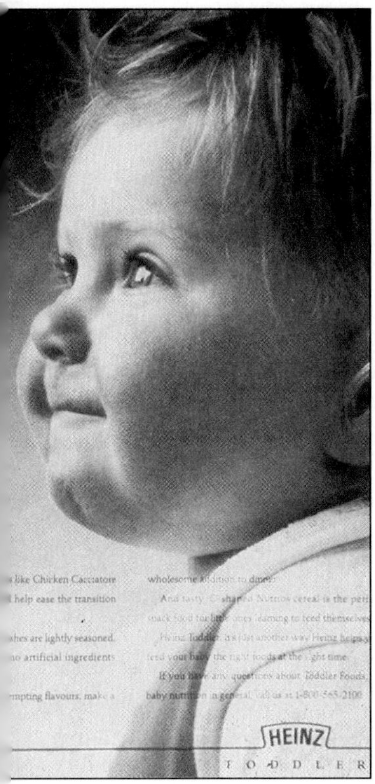


## Who Is the Target Segment for Toddler Foods from Heinz?

When you think of Heinz, do you think of its market-leading ketchup, or maybe of baby foods or junior foods, or even beans? The H. J. Heinz Company has been manufacturing and distributing food products in Canada for generations and the brand name is very familiar to most Canadians.

Recently, Heinz introduced a line called Toddler Foods, which is directed towards 12- to 24-month-old children who have outgrown baby foods and junior foods, but who may not yet be ready for "grown-up" meals. The new line of Toddler Foods contains a full range of menu items, including cereals, main courses, and desserts.

This new product introduction represents a good example of a company targeting a specific market segment and positioning its product to appeal to that segment. On the surface, it may appear that this is a new food product targeted at a specific age segment, namely children aged 12 to 24 months. But there may be more to this new product launch than meets the eye.

In order to gain a more complete understanding of the background to the introduction of Heinz Toddler Foods, we need to think a little more about the concept of target segments as discussed in this chapter. We also need to have some feel for the behaviour of consumers as they buy food products of this type. It may help us if we consider such questions as: Who buys food products for infants and small children? Who makes the purchase decision? What factors are taken into consideration?

Once we deal with such questions, it should become obvious that the target market is, in fact, the *parents* of these young children, and that Heinz is trying to appeal to certain motives and needs of these parents. This example serves to introduce a number of very important topics in marketing: the selection of a target market segment; the fact that the target segment should be characterized on the basis of a number of factors, only some of which may be demographic; and the need to position a new product so that it appeals to the target segment.

The introduction of Heinz Toddler Foods provides us with an example that is relevant for the next three chapters. We will discuss in this chapter the factors that a company takes into account in selecting a target segment for its product. In Chapter 5, we will deal with the positioning of that product so it has greatest appeal for the target segment. In Chapter 6, we will gain a better understanding of consumer psychology and behaviour that guide the marketer in making strategic decisions about segmentation and positioning.

## SELECTING A TARGET MARKET

In Chapter 1 we defined a *market* as people or organizations with (1) wants (needs) to satisfy, (2) money to spend, and (3) the willingness to spend it. A **target market** is a group of customers (people or firms) at whom the seller specifically aims its marketing efforts. The careful selection and accurate definition (identification) of target markets are essential for the development of an effective marketing program. One of the fundamental principles underlying the practice of market segmentation is that most companies and brands can no longer aspire to be "all things to all people." With the fragmentation of the Canadian marketplace and the increased level of competition from local, domestic, and international competitors, most marketers practise a strategy of carving out of the mass market a manageable target group of consumers upon which they will concentrate.

### Guidelines in Market Selection

Four general guidelines govern the selection of target markets. The first one is that target markets should be compatible with the organization's goals and image. A firm that is marketing high-priced personal computers should not sell through discount chain stores in an effort to reach a mass market.

A second guideline — consistent with our definition of strategic planning — is to match the market opportunity with the company's resources. In many ways, Heinz did this when it introduced its line of Toddler Foods. The company had enjoyed many years of market success as a manufacturer of quality food products and had created a particularly strong presence in the market for children's foods. Therefore, it was a logical extension of its expertise and image into the "toddler" market. However, there was also an obvious appreciation for the fact that a viable segment existed for the introduction of a product directed at the parents of children in the fairly narrow age bracket, 12 to 24 months. Consequently, Heinz matched its considerable expertise and positive image with the recently identified emerging market segment.

Over the long run, a business must generate a profit if it is to survive. This rather obvious, third guideline translates into what is perhaps an obvious market selection guideline. That is, an organization should consciously seek markets that will generate sufficient sales volume at a low enough cost to result in a profit. Surprisingly, companies often have overlooked the profit factor in their quest for high-volume markets. The goal was sales volume alone, not *profitable* sales volume.

Finally, a company ordinarily should seek a market wherein the number of competitors and their size are minimal. An organization should not enter a market that is already saturated with competition unless it has some overriding competitive advantage that will enable it to take customers from existing firms.

### Market Opportunity Analysis

Theoretically a market opportunity exists any time and any place there is a person or an organization with an unfilled need or want. Realistically, of course, a company's market opportunity is much more restricted. Thus selecting a target market requires an appraisal of market opportunities available to the organization. A market opportunity analysis begins with a study of the environmental forces (as discussed in Chapter 2) that affect a firm's marketing program. Then the organization must analyze the three components of a market — people or organizations, their buying power, and their willingness to spend. Analysis of the "people" component involves a study of the geographic distribution and demographic composition of the population. The second component is analyzed through the distribution of consumer income and consumer expenditure patterns. Finally, to determine consumers' "willingness to spend," management must study their buying behaviour. Population and buying power are discussed more fully later in this chapter. Buying behaviour is covered in Chapter 6.

### Target-Market Strategy: Aggregation or Segmentation

In defining the market or markets it will sell to, an organization has its choice of two approaches. In one, the total market is viewed as a single unit — as one mass, aggregate market. This approach leads to the strategy of *market aggregation*. In the other approach, the total market is seen as many smaller, homogeneous segments. This approach leads to the strategy of *market segmentation*, in which one or more segments is selected as top target market(s). Deciding which of the two strategies to adopt is a key in selecting target markets. We shall discuss market aggregation and segmentation in more detail in Chapter 5.

### Measuring Selected Markets

When selecting target markets, a company should make quantitative estimates of the potential sales volume of the market for its product or service. This process requires estimating, first, the total industry potential for the company's product in the target market or among the target segment and, second, its share of this total market. It is essential that management also prepare a sales forecast, usually for a one-year period. A sales forecast is the foundation of all budgeting and short-term operational planning in all departments — marketing, production, and finance. Sales forecasting will be discussed in more detail in Chapter 5 after we build a better knowledge of market segmentation.

## NATURE OF MARKET SEGMENTATION

The total market for most types of products is too varied — too heterogeneous — to be considered a single, uniform entity. To speak of the market for vitamin pills or electric razors or education is to ignore the fact that the total market for each product or service consists of submarkets that differ significantly from one another. This lack of uniformity may be traced to differences in buying habits, in ways in which the product or service is used, in motives for buying, or in other factors. Market segmentation takes these differences into account.

Not all consumers want to wear the same type of clothing, use the same shampoo, or participate in the same recreational activities. Nor do all business firms want to buy the same kind of computers or delivery trucks. At the same time, a marketer usually cannot afford to tailor-make a different product or service for every single customer.

Consequently market segmentation is the strategy that most marketers adopt as a compromise between the extremes of one product or service for all and a different one for each customer. A major element in a company's success is its ability to select the most effective location on this segmentation spectrum between the two extremes.

### What Is Market Segmentation?

Market segmentation is the process of dividing the total heterogeneous market for a product or service into several segments, each of which tends to be homogeneous in all significant aspects. Management selects one or more of these market segments as the organization's target market. A separate marketing mix is developed for each segment or group of segments in this target market.

### Benefits of Market Segmentation

Market segmentation is a customer-oriented philosophy and thus is consistent with the marketing concept. We first identify the needs of customers within a submarket (segment) and then satisfy those needs.

By tailoring marketing programs to individual market segments, management can do a better marketing job and make more efficient use of marketing resources. A small firm with limited resources might compete very effectively in one or two market segments, whereas the same firm would be buried if it aimed for the total market. By employing the strategy of market segmentation, a company can design products that really match market demands. Advertising media can be used more effectively because promotional messages — and the media chosen to present them — can be aimed specifically towards each segment of the market.

Some of the most successful marketers are small or medium-sized firms that have decided to concentrate on a small number of market segments and to gain a strong market position and disproportionate market share in these segments. This relates to the principle of niche marketing, which will be discussed in greater detail in Chapter 5.

Even very large companies with the resources to engage in mass marketing supported by expensive national advertising campaigns are now abandoning mass marketing strategies. Instead these companies have accepted market segmentation as a more effective strategy to reach the fractured fragments that once constituted a mass, homogeneous market. Procter & Gamble's marketing program nicely illustrates these changing conditions. Once the epitome of a mass marketer with innovative but utilitarian products, P&G advertised heavily on network television. But today it's a different ball game. Fewer people are at home during the day to watch television. Those who spend time in front of the television may be watching programs, viewing videos, or a film or program that was taped a day or two earlier, or playing video games. Even if they are watching TV, viewers may be tuned to any one of 30 or more channels. With such a variety of programming to choose from, many viewers spend much of their time "flicking" from channel to channel, using their remote-control devices.

Faced with this "fragmentation" of the television audience, Procter & Gamble has developed a variety of marketing campaigns, each designed to appeal to a different target market segment. The company now offers five varieties of its market-leading Tide detergent, each targeted to consumers with different needs and reasons for buying laundry detergent. Within its line of hand and bath soaps, P&G offers Ivory, Zest, Coast, Safeguard, Camay, and Oil of Olay. Many of these brands come in different sizes for sink and tub, colours to match bathroom decor, and liquid soap in pump dispensers. Procter & Gamble, by offering such a wide range of options to the consumer, is competing in a soap market that is segmented by skin type (oily versus dry), fragrance, aesthetics, the desire for convenience, and the primary benefit sought (clean hands or a pleasant, deodorized fragrance). It is clear that all consumers buy soap for cleansing, but they also expect other benefits from the soap they use. Hence, many segments exist.

Advances in technology have made market segmentation easier for companies in many industries as they have created efficiencies by permitting the targeting of specific segments. For example, many companies regularly collect data on their customers and their purchasing patterns. By maintaining data bases on such purchasing behaviour, it is possible for these companies to target products and brands to customers who have certain characteristics and needs. Such targeting of products and services to specific segments or even to specific customers through the use of data bases makes marketing much more cost-effective than was ever possible in the past.

### Limitations of Market Segmentation

Although market segmentation can provide a lot of marketing benefits to an organization, this strategy also has some drawbacks with respect to costs and market coverage. In the first place, market segmentation can be an expensive proposition in both the production and marketing of products. In production, it obviously is less expensive to produce mass quantities of one model and one colour than it is to produce a variety of models, colours, and sizes.

Segmentation increases marketing expenses in several ways. Total inventory costs go up because adequate inventories of each style, colour, and the like must be maintained. Advertising costs go up because different ads may be required for each market segment. Or some segments may be too small for the seller to make effective use of television or another advertising medium. Administrative expenses go up when management must plan and implement several different programs.

### Conditions for Effective Segmentation

Ideally, management's goal should be to segment markets in such a way that each segment responds in a homogeneous fashion to a given marketing program. Three conditions will help management move towards this goal.

- The basis for segmenting — that is, the characteristics used to categorize customers — must be *measurable*, and the data must be *accessible*. The "desire for ecologically compatible products" may be a characteristic that is useful in segmenting the market for a given product. But data on this characteristic may not be readily accessible or easily quantified.
- The market segment itself should be *accessible* through existing marketing institutions — distribution channels, advertising media, company sales force — with a minimum of cost and waste. To aid marketers in this regard some national magazines, such as *Maclean's* and *Chatelaine*, publish separate geographical editions. This allows an advertiser to run an ad aimed at, say, a Western segment of the market, without having to pay for exposure in other, nontarget areas.
- Each segment should be *large enough* to be profitable. In concept, management could treat each single customer as a separate segment. (Actually this situation may be normal in business markets, as when Canadair markets passenger airplanes to commercial airlines or when the Royal Bank of Canada makes a loan to a company planning to export to Europe.) But in segmenting a consumer market, a firm must not develop too broad an array of styles, colours, sizes, and prices. Usually the diseconomies of scale in production and inventory will put reasonable limits on this type of oversegmentation.

From a customer-oriented perspective, the ideal method for segmenting a market is on the basis of customers' desired benefits. Certainly, using benefits to segment a market is consistent with the idea that a company should be marketing benefits and not simply the physical characteristics of a product. After all, a carpenter wants a smooth surface (benefit), not sandpaper (the product). However, in many cases benefits desired by customers do not meet the first condition described above. That is, they are not easily measured, because customers are unwilling or unable to reveal them. For example, what benefits do people derive from clothing that has the label on the outside? Conversely, why do others refuse to wear such clothing?

Even when benefits are identified, possibly in focus-group studies, it is difficult to determine how widely they exist in the market. As a result, a variety of indirect indicators of benefits are often used to describe segments. These indicators, such as age, are not the reason customers buy, but they are easily measured characteristics that people seeking the same benefit frequently have in common. For example, middle-aged people are more likely to read *Canadian Business* than are teenagers, not because they are middle aged but because the content of the magazine is more directly relevant to their lives. Marketers of *Canadian Business* find it easier to measure age than relevance, so age becomes a segmentation variable for them. Several of these commonly used, indirect bases for segmentation are discussed next.

## BASES FOR MARKET SEGMENTATION — ULTIMATE CONSUMERS AND BUSINESS USERS

A company can segment its market in many different ways. And the bases for segmentation vary from one product to another. At the top of the list, however, is the division of the entire potential market into two broad categories: ultimate consumers and business users.

The sole criterion for placement in one of these categories is the customer's *reason for buying*. **Ultimate consumers** buy goods or services for their own personal or household use. They are satisfying strictly nonbusiness wants, and they constitute what is called the "consumer market."

**Business users** are business, industrial, or institutional organizations that buy goods or services to use in their own businesses or to make other products. A manufacturer that buys chemicals with which to make fertilizer is a business user of these chemicals. Farmers who buy the fertilizer to use in commercial farming are business users of the fertilizer. (If homeowners buy fertilizer to use on their yards, they are ultimate consumers because they buy it for personal, nonbusiness use.) Supermarkets, museums, and paper manufacturers that buy the service of a chartered accountant are business users of this service. Business users constitute the "business market" — discussed in greater detail in Chapter 7.

The segmentation of all markets into two groups — consumer and business — is extremely significant from a marketing point of view because the two markets buy differently. Consequently the composition of a seller's marketing mix — products, distribution, pricing, and promotion — will depend on whether it is directed towards the consumer market or the business market.

## BASES FOR CONSUMER MARKET SEGMENTATION

Dividing the total market into consumer and business segments is a worthwhile start towards useful segmentation, but it still leaves too broad and heterogeneous a grouping for most products. We need to identify some of the bases commonly used to segment these two markets further.

As shown in Table 4-1, the consumer market may be segmented on the basis of the following characteristics:

- Geographic.
- Demographic.
- Psychographic.
- Behaviour towards product (product-related bases).

TABLE 4-1 Segmentation bases for consumer markets

| Segmentation basis | Examples of typical market segments |
|---|---|
| GEOGRAPHIC | |
| Region | Atlantic provinces; Quebec; Ontario; Prairie provinces; B.C.: census regions. |
| City or CMA size | Under 25,000; 25,000 to 100,000; 100,000 to 250,000; 250,000 to 500,000; 500,000 to 1,000,000; over 1,000,000. |
| Urban-rural | Urban; rural; suburban; farm. |
| Climate and topography | Mountainous; seacoast; rainy; cold and snowy; etc. |
| DEMOGRAPHIC | |
| Age | Under 6, 6-12, 13-19, 20-34, 35-49, 50-64, 65 and over. |
| Gender | Male, female. |
| Family life cycle | Young single, young married no children, etc. |
| Education | Grade school only, high school graduate, college graduate. |
| Occupation | Professional, manager, clerical, skilled worker, sales, student, homemaker, unemployed. |
| Religion | Protestant, Catholic, Jewish, other. |
| Ethnic background | White; black; Asian.<br>British; French; Chinese; German; Ukrainian; Italian; Indian; etc. |
| Income | Under \$10,000, \$10,000-\$25,000, \$25,000-\$35,000, \$35,000-\$50,000, over \$50,000. |
| PSYCHOGRAPHIC | |
| Social class | Upper class, upper middle, lower middle, upper lower, etc. |
| Personality | Ambitious, self-confident, aggressive, introverted, extroverted, sociable, etc. |
| Life-style | Conservative, liberal, health and fitness oriented, adventuresome. |
| BEHAVIOUR TOWARDS PRODUCT (OR PRODUCT-RELATED BASES) | |
| Benefits desired | Examples vary widely depending upon product:<br>appliance: cost, quality, life, repairs.<br>toothpaste: no cavities, plaque control, bright teeth, good taste, low price. |
| Usage rate | Nonuser, light user, heavy user. |

Marketing managers should be particularly aware of trends taking place in the demographic, psychographic, and behavioural characteristics of the markets in which they are operating. For example, if the population of Victoria, British Columbia, is increasing because of a large number of people moving there to retire, this has obvious implications for businesses that operate in and around Victoria. Similarly, a company should be interested in knowing if the customers it has been serving are gradually reducing their usage of the product and are using more of an indirectly competing product. This is precisely what has been happening in the beer market in Canada in recent years, as per capita consumption of the product has been declining gradually, as consumers have switched to consuming more wine and non-alcoholic drinks. The key word that marketers should keep in mind when examining such trends or changes in consumption and other segmentation variables is implications. The marketer should always look into the implications of such change and should be seeking information to guide an appropriate response to the market.

In using these bases outlined in Table 4-1 to segment markets, we should bear in mind two points. First, buying behaviour is rarely traceable to only one segmentation factor. Useful segmentation is developed by including variables from several bases. To illustrate, the market for a product rarely consists of all people living in British Columbia or all people over 65. Instead, the segment is more likely to be described with a few of these variables. Thus a market segment for a financial service might be families living in British Columbia, having young children, and earning above a certain income. As another example, one clothing manufacturer's target market might be affluent young women (income, age, gender).

The other point to observe is the interrelationships among these factors, especially among the demographic factors. For instance, age and life-cycle stage typically are related. Income depends to some degree on age, life-cycle stage, education, and occupation.

We shall discuss the two most commonly used bases for segmentation — geographic and demographic — in this chapter, leaving to Chapter 5 a detailed discussion of the more complex bases of market segmentation.

## Geographic Segmentation

Subdivisions in the geographical distribution and demographic composition of the population are widely used bases for segmenting consumer markets. The reason for this is simply that consumers' wants and product usage often are related to one or more of these subcategories. Geographic and demographic groupings also meet the conditions for effective segmentation — that is, they are measurable, accessible, and large enough. Let's consider how the geographic distribution of population may serve as a segmentation basis.

### Total Population

A logical place to start is with an analysis of total population, and here the existence of a "population explosion" that has fizzled becomes evident. The population of Canada did not reach 10 million until about 1930. However, it took only another 35 years to double, and by 1966 the total population of the country stood at just over 20 million. But then the rapid growth in population that had been experienced during the baby boom years from 1945 to the early 1960s began to slow down and by 1992 the Canadian population had reached only 27.4 million. With the current low birth rate expected to continue, projections are that the total population will not go much beyond 32 million by 2011. Unless the federal government relaxes restrictions on immigration, Canada could face a situation of *declining* population early in the twenty-first century. The result of a decline in the birth rate from almost four children per family to 1.7 and reduced immigration levels is a static, aging population.

The total market is so large and so diverse that it must be analyzed in segments. Significant shifts are occurring in regional and urban-rural population distribution patterns. Market differences traceable to differences in age, gender, household arrangements, life-styles, and ethnic backgrounds pose real challenges for marketing executives.

### Regional Distribution

Figure 4-1 shows the distribution of Canadian population in 1992 and its projected growth to 2011 by province. The biggest markets and the largest urban areas are located in central Canada, where the provinces of Ontario and Quebec together account for 62 percent of Canadian population. However, the greatest rate of population growth since the early 1980s has occurred in Ontario and Western Canada, in particular in British Columbia where the population increased by 17.4 percent from 1983 to 1992.

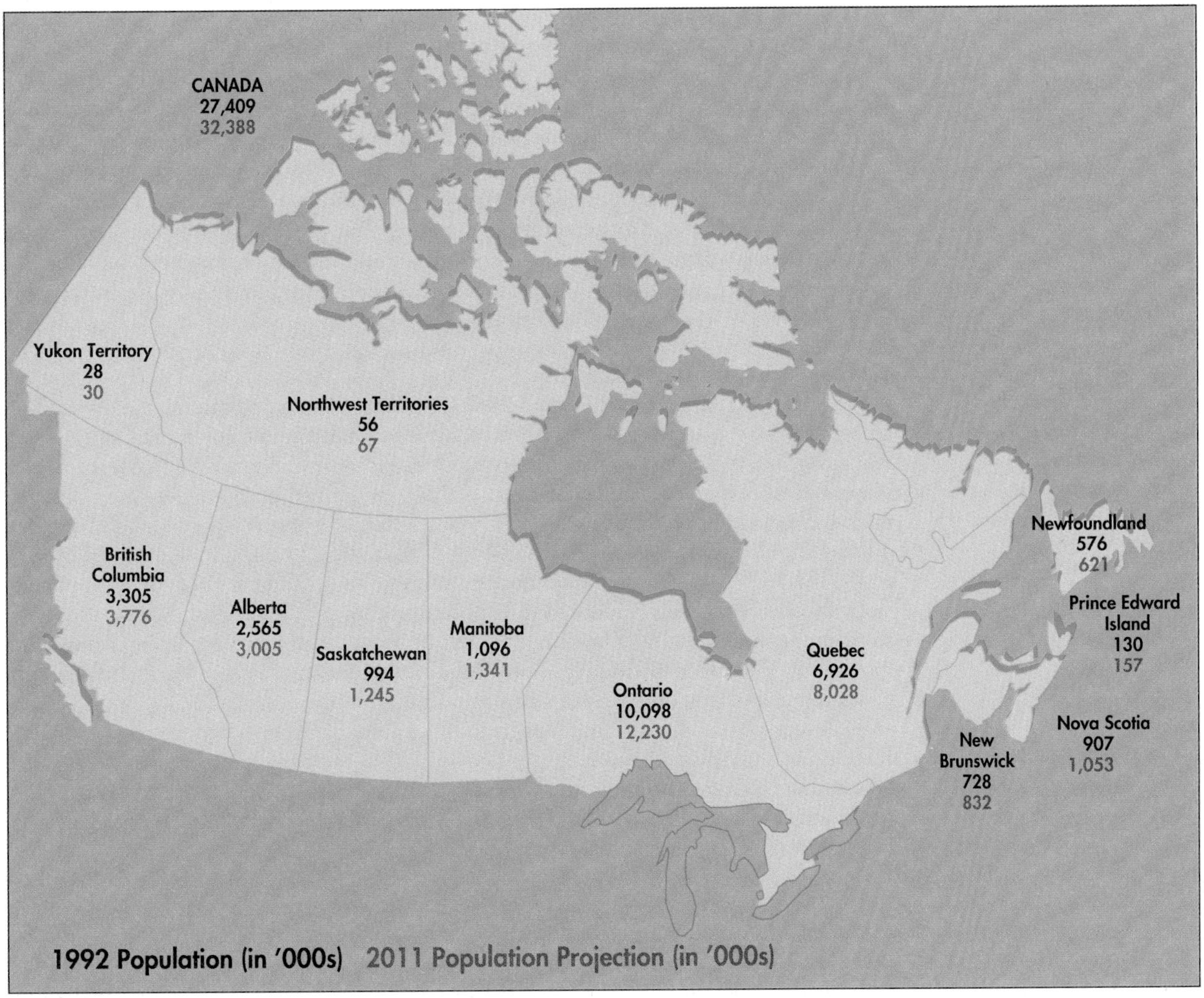


**FIGURE 4-1 Provincial distribution of Canadian population, 1992, and projected growth to 2011.**

Source: Statistics Canada, *Market Research Handbook*, 1993-94, catalogue no. 63-224, pp. 160, 607. Note: The projections of provincial population figures to 2011 are based on a series of assumptions. In this case, it is assumed that the birth rate continues at approximately the level that pertained at the end of the 1980s, namely, approximately 1.67 births per woman, and that the level of immigration is approximately 200,000 per year. Life expectancy is expected to increase to 77.2 years for men and 84.0 years for women by 2011.

The regional distribution of population is important to marketers, because people within a particular geographic region broadly tend to share the same values, attitudes, and style preferences. However, significant differences do exist among the various regions, because of differences in climate, social customs, and other factors. Ontario is a more urbanized province and represents the greatest concentration of people in Canada, especially in the corridor between Oshawa and Niagara Falls. This market is attractive to many marketers because of its sheer size and the diversity of consumers living there. On the other hand, the Atlantic region and the Prairie provinces are characterized by a much more relaxed and rural life-style, which suggests demand for different types of products and services. People in the West appear to be more relaxed and less formal than Eastern Canadians, and they spend more time outdoors. As this Western Canadian market grows, there will be a growth in demand for products associated with an outdoors life-style.

### Urban, Rural, and Suburban Distribution

For many years in Canada there has been both a relative and an absolute decline in the farm population, and this decline in the rural market is expected to continue. The declining farm population has led some people to underestimate the importance of rural markets. However, both as an industrial market for farm machinery and other resource industry equipment and supplies, and as a consumer market with increased buying power and more urban sophistication, the rural market is still a major one. Sociological patterns (such as average family size and local customs) among rural people differ significantly from those of city dwellers. These patterns have considerable influence on buying behaviour. Per capita consumption of cosmetics and other beauty aids, for example, is much lower in farm and rural markets than in city markets.

### Census Metropolitan Areas

As the farm population has shrunk, the urban and suburban population has expanded. In recognition of the growing urbanization of the Canadian market, some years ago the federal government established the concept of a Census Metropolitan Area (CMA) as a geographic market-data-measurement unit. A CMA is defined by Statistics Canada as the main labour market of a continuous built-up area having a population of 100,000 or more. Table 4-2 indicates the growth in the population of the 25 CMAs in Canada from 1979 to 1991. By 1991 these 25 areas accounted for more than 60 percent of the total population of Canada, and this percentage is expected to continue to increase. This is especially so as immigration to Canada increases, and as most immigrants settle in urban areas. Obviously, these Census Metropolitan Areas represent attractive, geographically concentrated market targets with considerable sales potential.

In several places in Canada, the metropolitan areas have expanded to the point where there is no rural space between them. This joining of metropolitan areas has been called "interurbia." Where two or more city markets once existed, today there is a single market. For example, there is virtually no space between Quebec City and Niagara Falls that is not part of a major urban area.

### Suburban Growth

As the metropolitan areas have been growing, something else has been going on *within* them. The central cities are growing very slowly, and in some cases the older established parts of the cities are actually losing population. The real growth is occurring in the fringe areas of the central cities or in the suburbs outside these cities. For the past 40 years, one of the most significant social and economic trends in Canada has been the shift of population to the suburbs. As middle-income families have moved to the suburbs, the economic, racial, and ethnic composition of many central cities (especially core areas) has changed considerably, thus changing the nature of the markets in these areas.

TABLE 4-2 Census metropolitan areas population, 1979, 1986, and 1991 (in thousands)

| | 1979 | 1986 | 1991 |
|---|---|---|---|
| Calgary, Alberta | 530.9 | 671.3 | 754.0 |
| Chicoutimi-Jonquière, Quebec | 132.3 | 158.5 | 160.9 |
| Edmonton, Alberta | 608.2 | 785.5 | 839.9 |
| Halifax, Nova Scotia | 274.1 | 296.0 | 320.5 |
| Hamilton, Ontario | 537.5 | 557.0 | 599.7 |
| Kitchener, Ontario | 281.8 | 311.2 | 356.4 |
| London, Ontario | 279.4 | 342.3 | 381.5 |
| Montreal, Quebec | 2,799.8 | 2,921.4 | 3,127.2 |
| Oshawa, Ontario | 149.4 | 203.5 | 250.1 |
| Ottawa-Hull, Ontario-Quebec | 712.6 | 819.3 | 920.8 |
| Quebec, Quebec | 562.4 | 603.3 | 645.5 |
| Regina, Saskatchewan | 159.6 | 186.5 | 191.6 |
| St. Catharines-Niagara Falls, Ontario | 305.5 | 343.3 | 364.5 |
| St. John's, Newfoundland | 148.8 | 161.9 | 171.8 |
| Saint John, New Brunswick | 114.0 | 121.3 | 124.9 |
| Saskatoon, Saskatchewan | 143.7 | 200.7 | 210.0 |
| Sherbrooke, Quebec | — | 130.0 | 139.1 |
| Sudbury, Ontario | 151.5 | 148.9 | 157.6 |
| Thunder Bay, Ontario | 121.8 | 122.2 | 124.4 |
| Toronto, Ontario | 2,910.0 | 3,427.2 | 3,893.0 |
| Trois-Rivières, Quebec | — | 128.9 | 136.3 |
| Vancouver, British Columbia | 1,207.6 | 1,380.7 | 1,602.5 |
| Victoria, British Columbia | 223.5 | 255.5 | 287.8 |
| Windsor, Ontario | 250.4 | 254.0 | 262.0 |
| Winnipeg, Manitoba | 583.0 | 625.3 | 652.3 |

Source: *Census Metropolitan Areas and Census Aggregates: Population and Dwelling Counts*. Ottawa: Statistics Canada, catalogue No. 93-303, 1993.

## MARKETING AT WORK

### FILE 4-1 RICH KIDS

When you were younger, you may have thought you deserved an increase in your weekly allowance. It would appear that many parents have given in to such demands in recent years, as the allowances and money earned by Canadians under the age of 18 now exceed $864 million annually. When you add money received as gifts and entrusted to them for family shopping, Canadian kids control well over $1 billion annually.

Recent research by Dialogue Canada also shows that kids exert considerable influence over many of the purchases made by Canadian households. As a result, many marketers are beginning to target children with their advertising in an effort to establish early in life brand preferences that will carry over into adulthood. *Sports Illustrated* now has an edition for kids and Delta Airlines signed up 600,000 children in the two years following the launch of its Fantastic Flyer program aimed at young jet-setters.

While the 5-to-17 age group will decline as a percentage of the Canadian population over the next few years, their numbers will remain fairly stable at about 5 million. They represent a lucrative target segment as they come to have more money and do more discretionary shopping. They are very aware consumers and are knowledgeable and sophisticated about advertising and brand names.

Source: Ray Whalen, "Kids as Consumers," *Imprints*, Summer 1993, p. 8. (*Imprints* is a publication of the Professional Marketing Research Society.)

The growth of the suburban population has some striking marketing implications. Since a great percentage of suburban people live in single-family residences, there is a vastly expanded market for lawn mowers, lawn furniture, home furnishings, and home repair supplies and equipment. Suburbanites are more likely to want two cars than are city dwellers. They are inclined to spend more leisure time at home, so there is a bigger market for home entertainment and recreation items.

As we near the end of the century, marketing people are watching two possible counter-trends. One is the movement from the suburbs back to the central cities by older people whose children are grown. Rather than contend with commuting, home maintenance, and other suburban challenges, older people are moving to new apartments located nearer to downtown facilities. And it is not just older people who are returning to the downtown areas. In many Canadian cities, young professional families are locating close to their downtown places of work, preferring to renovate an older home, rather than contend with commuting and other perceived shortcomings of suburban living.

The other reversal is that there has been an increase in the rural population near larger cities. Although the rural population of Canada has increased very little in recent years, most of that growth occurred in close proximity to the large Census Metropolitan Areas. This growth has been brought about, not only because some people wish to live in a more rural setting, but also because of rising real estate prices in or near many Canadian cities. Some of the growth that has been experienced in the population of Census Metropolitan Areas as shown in Table 4-2 has occurred because some of the areas around these CMAs have been incorporated into the cities.

In recent years, geographic segmentation has become much more refined through the use of **geodemographic clustering**, a process that uses census and other statistical data to cluster postal code areas into similar groups or segments. By examining such data, a marketer can identify groups of postal code areas that have similar patterns of education, income, household size, age, housing, occupation, and other factors. Thus, companies can then make their direct marketing efforts much more efficient by targeting their advertising to those homes located in postal code areas that best reflect the characteristics of the target markets they wish to reach. Such an approach is also useful for making efficient decisions on new store locations, to determine the best products and brands to offer in specific stores, and to direct mail order catalogues with appropriate merchandise featured.[1]

### Demographic Segmentation

The most common basis for segmenting consumer markets is some demographic category such as age, gender, family life-cycle stage, income distribution, education, occupation, or ethnic origin.

### Age Groups

Analyzing the consumer market by age groups is a useful exercise in the marketing of many products and services. Age is one of the most fundamental bases for demographically segmenting markets, as we can see from the large number of products and services directed at seniors, children, teens, young adults, and so on. But marketers must be aware of the changing nature of the age mix of the Canadian population. Looking ahead again to the year 2011, we see an aging population and one that is not growing very quickly. In 1992, for example, there were 3.71 million people in Canada aged between 10 and 19. By 1996, this age group will have become slightly larger at 3.77 million; but by 2011, there will be only 3.53 million Canadians in this age bracket, assuming the birth rate remains at the present level. On the other hand, in 1986, there were only 2.7 million Canadians aged 65 and older. By 1992, this age bracket contained 3.2 million; by 1996, this group will increase in number to 4.0 million and to 4.8 million by 2011.[2]

**The teen segment is probably the heaviest purchasers of CDs.**

The youth market (roughly aged 5 to 13) carries a three-way market impact. First, these children can influence parental purchases. Second, millions of dollars are spent on this group by their parents. Third, these children themselves make purchases of goods and services for their own personal use and satisfaction, and the volume of these purchases increases as the children get older. Promotional programs are often geared to this market segment. Manufacturers of breakfast cereals, snack foods, and toys often advertise on television programs that are directed at children — except on the CBC television network, which prohibits advertising on children's programs.[3]

Playing on the success of the Toronto Blue Jays, World Series Champions in 1992 and 1993, the Jr. Jays club boasted a membership in early 1994 of 150,000, which was expected to double by the end of 1994. New members, primarily in the 7-to-12 age group, are recruited on Jr. Jays days at SkyDome, where free copies of the *Jr. Jays Magazine* are distributed, along with information about the club. The magazine is distributed free to more than 1.2 million kids annually, and the club has spawned a YTV cable television program *Jr. Jays Newsmagazine*. This represents a good example of marketing to children by an organization whose target market is principally adults, but which is clearly interested in expanding its market in the future.[4]

The *teenage* market is also recognized as an important one, and yet many companies find it difficult to reach. The mistake might be in attempting to lump all teenagers together. Certainly, the 13-to-16 age group is very different from the 17-to-20 age bracket. Yet marketers must understand the teenage market because of the size of the segment and because its members have a great deal of money to spend. This group has considerable discretionary buying power, because of their part-time jobs and allowances that often come from two income-earning parents. Although the total number of teens has decreased, this group still represents a major market segment for marketers of clothing, cosmetics, fast food, tapes and compact discs, driving lessons, and other products and services.[5]

In the 1990s the early *middle-age* population segment (35 to 50) is an especially large and lucrative market. These people are the products of the post-World War II baby boom and were the rebels of the 1960s and 1970s. They also were a very big and profitable teenage and young adult market for many companies during those years. Now, as they move towards middle age in the late 1990s, they are reaching their high earning years. Typically, their values and life-styles are far different from those found among the people of the same age category in previous generations. Already, companies are adjusting to these changing demographics. While toothpaste manufacturers like Procter & Gamble and Colgate-Palmolive capitalized on concern about cavity prevention in children's teeth in the 1950s and 1960s, 30 or more years later they are producing toothpaste to fight tartar — an adult dental problem. This generation, with more dual-income families and fewer children, have more money to spend on themselves. As a result, they are a prime market for products that promise convenience and for home and garden services.

The aging baby-boom generation makes an attractive market segment for a number of other reasons. Many are in the process of seeing their children graduate from college and university and have likely paid off the mortgage on the family home. Suddenly, they have a lot more disposable money to spend on themselves and on indulging their new grandchildren. Coupled with the fact that this age group has reached this stage in their family life cycle is the fact that, as a result of the recession that gripped Canada in the early 1990s, many have opted to take early retirement from their jobs. As a result, many have a lot of leisure time on their hands. Consequently, this age group makes an attractive target for vacation travel, smaller homes and condominiums, and long-term investments intended to finance a long retirement.

At the older end of the age spectrum are two market segments that should not be overlooked. One is the group of people in their fifties and early sixties. This *mature* market is large and financially well off. Its members are at the peak of their earning power and typically no longer have financial responsibility for their children. Thus, this segment is a good target for marketers of high-priced, high-quality products and services.

The other older age group is made up of people over 65 — a segment that is growing both absolutely and as a percentage of the total population. Manufacturers and intermediaries alike are beginning to recognize that people in this age group are logical prospects for small, low-cost housing units, cruises and foreign tours, health products, and cosmetics developed especially for older people. Many firms are also developing promotional programs to appeal to this group because their purchasing power is surprisingly high. Also, the shopping behaviour of the over-65 market typically is different from that found in other age segments. On a per capita basis, seniors are increasing their spending faster than average in areas such as health care, entertainment, recreation, gifts, and contributions. In this latter category, seniors give more dollars than the average Canadian, making them an attractive market segment for charities and religious groups.

We should not fall into the trap of assuming that all older seniors are inactive or financially disadvantaged. Interesting research on those Canadians aged 75 and older shows that this is not only a rapidly growing market segment, but that most are in good health, and an increasing percentage are living alone and enjoying an active life. More than 50 percent of men aged 75 and older are still driving their cars. In 1991, 14 percent of men and 11 percent of women in this age bracket said they had travelled away from home for more than four weeks in the preceding year.[6]

## Gender

Gender is an obvious basis for consumer market analysis. Many products are made for use by members of one gender, not both. In many product categories — autos, for example — women and men typically look for different product benefits. Market analysis by gender is also useful because many products have traditionally been purchased by either men only or women only.

"Woman In Repose"
LEVI'S
JEANS FOR WOMEN
Levi's® 501®, 512™ and 550™ Jeans. Now Cut, Styled and Sized for Women.
Bus stop shelter (68" x 47")

**When a market is segmented by gender, ads take on a very different look.**

**Targeting a growing market approaching retirement.**

However, some of these traditional buying patterns are breaking down, and marketers certainly should be alert to changes involving their products. Not too many years ago, for example, women did most of the grocery shopping, and men bought hardware and products and services needed for automobiles. Today, men are frequent food shoppers, and women buy auto accessories and arrange for repairs and maintenance. Many products and services that were once considered the near-exclusive domain of either men or women are now purchased regularly by both sexes.

The number of women, both married and single, who are employed outside the home is increasing dramatically. By 1992, almost 60 percent of women in Canada were employed outside the home. Women now account for almost 47 percent of the Canadian work force in the age bracket between 15 and 44. It is expected that the labour force participation rates for men and women will be approximately the same in the age bracket from 25 to 44, as we near the end of the 1990s. These facts are significant for marketers. Not only are the life-style and buying behaviour of women in the labour force quite different from those of women who do not work outside their homes, but many of those women are members of households where their spouses also are employed, thereby producing Canadian households with considerable buying power.[7]

### Family Life Cycle

Frequently the main factor accounting for differences in consumption patterns between two people of the same age and sex is that they are in different life-cycle stages. The concept of the family life cycle implies that there are several distinct stages in the life of an ordinary family. The traditional six-stage family cycle is shown in Figure 4-2, along with three alternative stages that reflect significant changes from traditional patterns. Life-cycle position is a major determinant of buyer behaviour and thus can be a useful basis for segmenting consumer markets.[8]

A young couple with two children (the full-nest stage) has quite different needs from those of a couple in their mid-fifties whose children no longer live at home (the empty-nest stage). A single-parent family (divorced, widowed, or never married) with dependent children faces social and economic problems quite different from those of a two-parent family. Young married couples with no children typically devote large shares of their income to clothing, autos, and recreation. When children start arriving, expenditure patterns shift as many young families buy and furnish a home. Families with teenagers find larger portions of the budget going for food, clothing, and educational needs.[9]

One of the most rapidly growing segments among the Canadian population is the *singles*. In 1961, only 9.3 percent of Canadian households consisted of just one person — a **single**. By 1991, just 30 years later, almost 23 percent of Canadian homes had only a single occupant, although the percentage of people living alone differs considerably from province to province. In Manitoba, for example, 25.6 percent of the households have only a single occupant, while the corresponding percentage in Newfoundland is only 12.6 percent. The total number of one-person households is increasing at a much faster rate than that of family units. Among the reasons for this increase in the number of one-person households are:

- The growing number of working women.
- People marrying at a later age.
- The reduced tendency for single people to live with their parents.
- A rising divorce rate.

The impact that single people of both sexes have on the market is demonstrated by such things as apartments for singles, social clubs for singles, and special tours, cruises, and eating places seeking the patronage of singles. Even in the mundane field of grocery products the growing singles market (including the divorced and widowed) is causing changes by retailers and food manufacturers.

Singles in the 25-to-39 age bracket are especially attractive to marketers because they are such a large group. Compared with the population as a whole, this singles group is:

- More affluent.
- More mobile.
- More experimental and less conventional.
- More fashion- and appearance-conscious.
- More active in leisure pursuits.
- More sensitive to social status.

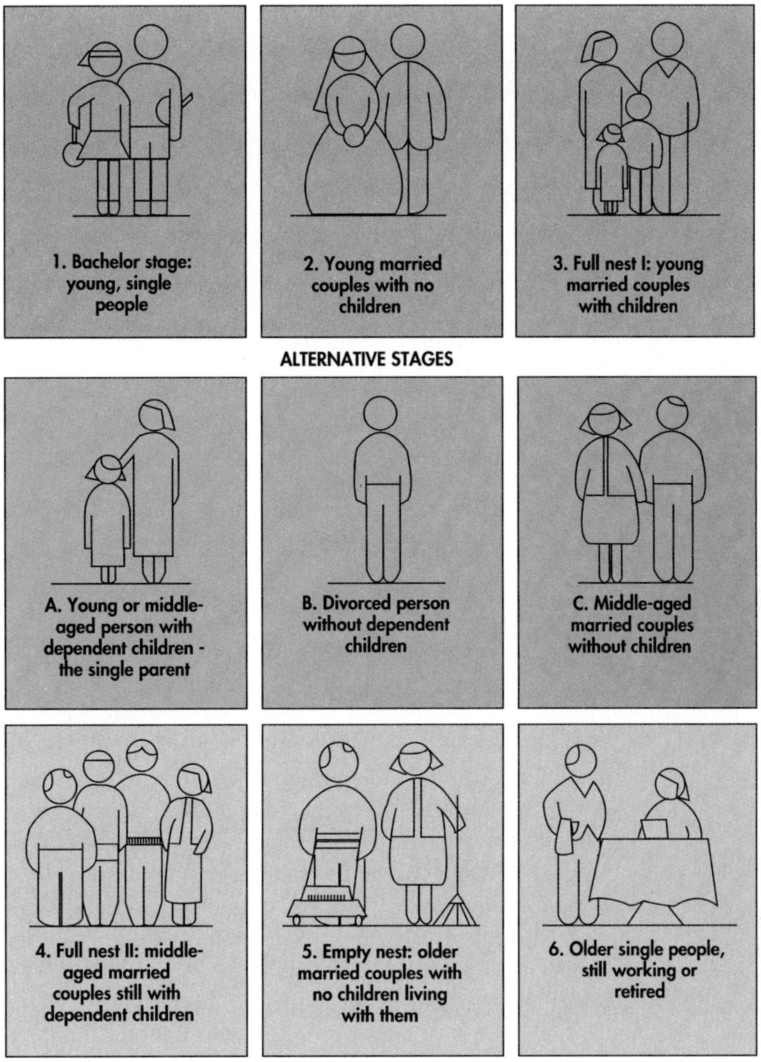


**FIGURE 4-2**
**The family life cycle.**

## Other Demographic Bases for Segmentation

The market for some consumer products is influenced by such factors as education, occupation, religion, or ethnic origin. With an increasing number of people attaining higher levels of **education**, for example, we can expect to see (1) changes in product preferences and (2) buyers with more discriminating taste and higher incomes. **Occupation** may be a more meaningful criterion than income in segmenting some markets. Truck drivers or auto mechanics may earn as much as young retailing executives or college professors. But the buying patterns of the first two are different from those of the second two because of attitudes, interests, and other life-style factors.

For some products, it is useful to analyze the population on the basis of **religion** or **ethnic origin**. The most important distinction in Canada is between the two founding races. French-English differences are fundamental to doing business in Canada and will be dealt with in much greater detail in Chapter 6. Marketers have known for some time that certain products such as instant coffee and tomato juice sell much better in Quebec.

In larger Canadian cities, the cultural diversity of the population creates an increasing marketing opportunity for companies that specialize in products and services directed

## MARKETING AT WORK

### FILE 4-2 THE CHANGING CANADIAN FAMILY

In 1971, 64 percent of family units in Canada followed what was the traditional family model — a married couple with children at home. By the time the 1991 census rolled around, only 48 percent of families in the country were in that category. Almost 30 percent of families were married couples without kids, 13 percent were single-parent homes, 6 percent were common-law couples without children, and 4 percent were common-law couples with kids.

Alanna Mitchell, writing in the *Globe and Mail*, observed: "The family is being reinvented. Common-law relationships are flourishing. Many couples are choosing not to have children. Single-parent families are moving into the mainstream as divorce becomes more common and having children outside marriage becomes more acceptable."

In addition, there are many other changes going on in Canadian families. For example, only 64.9 percent of families had children at home in 1991, as compared with 73.2 percent in 1971. Those families who did have children were much smaller with an average of 1.2 children in 1991, down from 1.8 in 1971.

Consider how the changing composition of the Canadian family affects how certain products and services are marketed today, compared with 20 years ago.

Source: Alanna Mitchell, "Family Portraits," *Globe and Mail*, February 11, 1994, p. A15; and *A Portrait of Families in Canada*, Ottawa: Statistics Canada, catalogue number 89-523, 1993.

towards a particular ethnic community. In Toronto, for example, almost half the population was born outside Canada. Persons of Italian heritage represent almost 5 percent of the population in Ontario and more than 8 percent in Toronto. Almost 8 percent of the population of Alberta have German roots, as do almost 13 percent of people in Saskatchewan. Almost 7 percent of the population of Manitoba are Ukrainian.

In certain areas of the country, such as the large German population around Kitchener-Waterloo, Ontario, and in many of the larger cities, ethnic groups represent a viable target market segment for certain specialty products and services. The large number of recent immigrants from Hong Kong and other Asian countries has transformed some neighbourhoods in some cities, as did immigrants from Portugal, Italy, and the Caribbean before them.

The Chinese community in Toronto was labelled the fastest-growing ethnic group in Canada in the 1991 census, having increased in number from 126,000 in 1986, to 232,000 in 1991, and estimated at being closer to 350,000 in the Toronto area in 1994. The importance of this market segment to the Toronto business community is reflected in the fact that the market is served by three Chinese-language daily newspapers, two of which have been published since the late 1970s. The newest entrant, *Ming Pao Daily News*, began publishing in Toronto and Vancouver in 1993, targeting primarily recent immigrants from Hong Kong. Major advertisers such as the Royal Bank of Canada and Canadian Airlines International have used these newspapers to reach this lucrative market segment.[10]

## CONSUMER INCOME AND ITS DISTRIBUTION

People alone do not make a market; they must have money to spend. Consequently, income, its distribution, and how it is spent are essential factors in any quantitative market analysis.

### Nature and Scope of Income

What is income? There are so many different concepts of income that it is good to review some definitions. The following outline is actually a "word equation" that shows how the several concepts are related.

**National income:** Total income from all sources, including employee compensation, corporate profits, and other income

*Less:* Corporate profits, and pension and social program contributions

*Plus:* Dividends, government transfer payments to persons, and net interest paid by government

*Equals:*

**Personal income:** All forms of income received by persons and unincorporated businesses; including wages, salaries, and supplementary labour income; military pay and allowances; net income of nonfarm business including rent; net income of farm operators from farm production; interest, dividends, and miscellaneous investment income; and transfer payment income from government, corporations, and non-residents

*Less:* All personal federal, provincial, and municipal taxes

*Equals:*

**Personal disposable income:** Personal income less personal direct taxes and other current transfers to government from persons; represents the amount available for personal consumption expenditure and savings

*Less:* (1) Essential expenditures for food, clothing, household utilities, and local transportation and (2) fixed expenditures for rent, house mortgage payments, insurance, and instalment debt payments

*Equals:*

**Discretionary purchasing power:** The amount of disposable personal income that is available after fixed commitments (debt repayments, rent) and essential household needs are taken care of. As compared with disposable personal income, discretionary purchasing power is a better (more sensitive) indicator of consumers' ability to spend for *nonessentials*.

In addition, we hear the terms "money income," "real income," and "psychic income." **Money income** is the amount a person receives in actual cash or cheques for wages, salaries, rent, interest, and dividends. **Real income** is what the money income will buy in goods and services; it is purchasing power. If a person's money income rises 5 percent in one year but the cost of purchases increases 2 percent on average, then real income increases by only 3 percent. **Psychic income** is an intangible, but highly important, income factor related to comfortable climate, a satisfying neighbourhood, enjoyment of one's job, and so on. Some people prefer to take less real income so they can live in a part of the country that features a fine climate — greater psychic income.

As measured by income, the Canadian economy has grown dramatically in recent years. With the exception of recessions in the early 1980s and early 1990s, the economy has enjoyed almost uninterrupted growth since the end of World War II. Personal disposable income, which stood at $154 billion in 1978 and at $233 billion in 1981, had jumped to $607 billion by 1991; this represents an increase of almost 400 percent in 13 years, despite two periods of recession. In the 10 years from 1981 to 1991, per capita personal disposable income increased from $9,587 to $22,495. Discretionary purchasing power has, therefore, increased considerably during the past 15 years or so. Particularly when one considers that inflation has been at very low levels in Canada in recent years, the improvement in consumer buying power is impressive.[11]

### Income Distribution

To get full value from an analysis of income, we should study the variations and trends in the distribution of income among regions and among population segments. Regional income data are especially helpful in pinpointing the particular market to which a firm wishes to appeal. Income data on cities and even on areas within cities may indicate the best locations for shopping centres and suburban branches of downtown stores.

## MARKETING AT WORK

### FILE 4-3 CHINESE CANADIANS: GROWTH SEGMENT

With declining birth rates in this country, much of the future growth in the Canadian population will come from immigration. In recent years, a wave of new immigrants to Canada has come primarily from Asian countries, with the result that Chinese is the third most frequently spoken language in Canadian homes. This rapid growth in the Chinese-speaking population, primarily in larger cities such as Toronto and Vancouver, where 75 percent of recent Chinese immigrants have settled, has created a concentration of consumers in these urban markets with particular needs.

Studies of Chinese Canadians have shown that approximately one in ten residents of Toronto and Vancouver is Chinese. The majority of these came to Canada in an influx of immigrants from Hong Kong, Taiwan, and China, beginning in 1987. They tend to be under 40 years of age and better off than the average Canadian. A large percentage of Chinese immigrants in recent years have come from Hong Kong under Canadian laws that attract business immigrants. Many have sold homes and property in Hong Kong and have transferred their wealth to Canada. As a result, they are much more likely than are other Canadian families to own their own homes and to own home computers and other luxury durables. They represent an attractive target segment for many businesses.

Source: David Chilton, "Study Profiles Chinese Canadians," *Strategy*, September 20, 1993, p. 17; and Julie Manyee Lui, "What Marketers Should Know About Chinese Immigrants," *Imprints*, September 1993, p. 8.

**Jimmy Hung, general manager of the *Ming Pao Daily News*, started a third Chinese daily newpaper in Toronto and Vancouver in 1993 to reach the growing Asian-Canadian market.**

There has been a genuine income revolution going on in Canada over the past 30 years or so. During the second half of the twentieth century, the pattern of income distribution has been dramatically altered. (See Table 4-3.) There has been a tremendous growth in the middle-income and upper income segments and a corresponding decrease in the percentage of low-income groups.

The purchasing power of the average Canadian family is expected to continue to increase over the next 10 years. We will see the effects of higher personal incomes and higher participation rates in the labour force. It is very likely that more than half of all Canadian families will have a total annual income in excess of $50,000 by the year 2000. This anticipated increase in the number of affluent households is the result of several factors. These include (1) the large growth in the number of people in the prime earning years 25 to 45, (2) the increase in dual-income families, and (3) the wider distribution of inherited wealth. We will still have low-income families. However, there will be fewer below the poverty line, even though that level (by government definition) is moving up, in recognition of both inflation and a society that is generally better able to provide its members with a reasonable income.

**TABLE 4-3 Percentage distribution of families by income groups in Canada Annual income 1979, 1984, 1992**

| Income group | 1979 | 1984 | 1992 |
|---|---|---|---|
| less than $10,000 | 15.2 | 6.7 | 2.4 |
| $10,000 to $14,999 | 11.5 | 9.3 | 3.8 |
| $15,000 to $19,999 | 14.7 | 9.5 | 5.9 |
| $20,000 to $24,999 | 16.0 | 9.0 | 7.5 |
| $25,000 to $29,999 | 13.4 | 10.1 | 6.7 |
| $30,000 to $34,999 | 10.0 | 10.1 | 6.6 |
| $35,000 to $39,999 | 6.8 | 9.6 | 7.1 |
| $40,000 to $44,999 | 4.2 | 8.1 | 6.3 |
| $45,000 to $49,999 | 2.6 | 6.5 | 6.6 |
| $50,000 to $59,999 | 2.9 | 9.1 | 12.5 |
| $60,000 and over | 2.5 | 12.1 | 34.5 |

Source: *Income Distribution by Size in Canada*, Ottawa: Statistics Canada, catalogue No. 13-707 annual, 1992, p. 53.

## Marketing Significance of Income Data

The declining percentage of families in the poverty bracket, coupled with the sharp increases in the upper-income groups, presages an explosive growth in discretionary purchasing power. And, as discretionary income increases, so too does the demand for items that once were considered luxuries.

The middle-income market is a big market and a growing market, and it has forced many changes in marketing strategy. Many stores that once appealed to low-income groups have traded up to the huge middle-income market. These stores are upgrading the quality of the products they carry and are offering additional services.

In spite of the considerable increase in disposable income in the past 30 years, many households are still in the low-income bracket or find their higher incomes inadequate to fulfil all their wants. Furthermore, many customers are willing to forgo services in order to get lower prices. One consequence of this market feature has been the development of self-service retail outlets, discount houses, and the more recent superstores such as those operated by furniture and appliance retailers like The Brick Warehouse in

Ontario and Western Canada and by specialists in electronic sound equipment such as Majestic Electronic Stores.

Earlier in this chapter we noted the dramatic increase in the number of working women. This demographic factor also has had a tremendous impact on family income levels. The increase in two-income families has significant marketing and sociological implications. Dual incomes generally enable a family to offset the effects of inflation. But more than that, two incomes often enable a family to buy within a short time the things their parents worked years to acquire.

## CONSUMER EXPENDITURE PATTERNS

*How* consumers' income is spent is a major market determinant for most products and services. Consequently, marketers need to study consumer *spending patterns*, as well as the *distribution* of consumer income. Marketers also should be aware of the significant *shifts* in family spending patterns that have occurred over the past two or three decades. Energy costs, inflation, and heavy consumer debt loads have had a major impact on our spending patterns. As examples, let's consider just a few of the changes in spending patterns that have occurred between the 1960s and the 1990s. Over that time span, families have *increased* the percentage of their total expenditures going for housing, health, and utilities. Spending (as a percentage of total) has *decreased* for food, beverage, clothing, and home expenses (except utilities).

But expenditure patterns are not the same for all families. These patterns vary considerably, depending on family income, life-cycle stage, and other factors.

### Relation to Stage of Family Life Cycle

Consumer expenditure patterns are influenced by the consumer's stage in the life cycle. There are striking contrasts in spending patterns between, say, people in the full-nest stage with very young children and people in the empty-nest stage. Table 4-4 summarizes the behavioural influences and the spending patterns for families in each stage of the cycle. (This table expands the number of stages shown earlier in Figure 4-2.) Young married couples with no children typically devote large shares of their income to clothing, autos, and recreation. When children start arriving, expenditure patterns shift as many young families buy and furnish a home. Families with teenagers find larger portions of the budget going for food, clothing, and educational needs. Families in the empty-nest stage, especially when the head is still in the labour force, are attractive to marketers. Typically, these families have more discretionary buying power.

### Relation to Income Distribution

The pattern of consumer expenditures is influenced significantly by the income level of the household. For example, as we can see in Table 4-5, families with incomes in the range of $15,000 to $19,999 spend an average of 18.5 percent of their expenditures on food. This percentage drops to 13.9 percent for those with annual incomes between $35,000 and $39,999, and to 12.4 percent for those with incomes above $60,000 per annum. These and other findings from the analysis of Statistics Canada data suggest the type of information that marketers might obtain from analyzing spending patterns by income groups. Some additional generalizations from such data are summarized below.

- There is a high degree of uniformity in the expenditure patterns of *middle-class* spending units. As we shall note in Chapter 6, however, social-class structure is often a more meaningful criterion for determining expenditure patterns.

- For each product category, there is a considerable *absolute increase* in dollars spent as income rises (or, more correctly, as we compare one income group with a higher income group). In other words, people in a given income bracket spend significantly more *dollars* in each product category than those in lower brackets. However, the lower-income households devote a larger *percentage* to their total expenditures to some product categories, such as food. Marketers are probably more concerned with the total *dollars* available from each income group than with the *percentage* share of total expenditures.
- In each successively higher income group, the amount spent for food declines as a *percentage* of total expenditures.
- The percentage of expenditures devoted to housing, household operation, and utilities totals approximately 21 percent. This varies from more than 32 percent for consumers with incomes between \$15,000 and \$20,000 to 18 percent for those whose family incomes are more than \$60,000 annually.
- Dramatic differences are observed across income groups in their actual dollar expenditures on recreation. Whereas a family in the lower-income bracket may spend as little as \$483 annually, the higher-income family will spend as much as \$5,000.
- The percentage spent on clothing remains fairly constant across income groups, ranging from 4.8 percent to 5.9 percent. Dollar expenditures, however, range from \$688 to more than \$5,500 annually.
- A major difference between low-income and higher-income Canadian families lies in the percentage of their total income that goes to government in the form of taxes. Whereas a family whose total income is in the top 20 percent in Canada may pay 25 percent or more of total personal income in taxes, lower-income families may pay no tax at all.
- Major differences in expenditure patterns are also found when the Canadian population is examined across geographic regions. This is related in part to income differences, but also is caused to a degree by the differences in the cost of certain items in different areas of the country. For example, the average family in Montreal spends 13.6 percent of total expenditures on food, while a family in Halifax spends only 11.7 percent. On the other hand, a family in Victoria will spend 17.4 percent of its total expenditures on housing, as compared with only 15.3 percent in St. John's, Newfoundland.

THOSE WHO WANT THE FINEST CAR IN THE WORLD
CHOOSE MERCEDES-BENZ.
THOSE WHO WANT THE FINEST MERCEDES-BENZ IN THE WORLD
CHOOSE THE S-CLASS.
Nothing in your life has prepared you for this. Call 1-800-387-4632 to arrange a private appointment at your local showroom.
The S-Class. Starting at $94,650.
© Mercedes-Benz Canada Inc.,1994. Member of the Daimler-Benz Group.


**No doubt which income segment Mercedes-Benz is targeting.**

TABLE 4-4 Behavioural influences and buying patterns, by family life-cycle stage

| Bachelor stage; young single people not living at home | Newly married couples; young, no children | Full nest I; youngest child under 6 | Full nest II; youngest child 6 or over | Full nest III; older married couples with dependent children |
|---|---|---|---|---|
| Few financial burdens.<br>Fashion opinion leader.<br>Recreation-oriented.<br>Buy: Basic kitchen equipment, basic furniture, cars, equipment for the mating game, vacations. | Better off financially than they will be in near future.<br>Highest purchase rate and highest average purchase of durables.<br>Buy: Cars, refrigerators, stoves, sensible and durable furniture, vacations. | Home purchasing at peak.<br>Liquid assets low.<br>In some cases, both spouses work outside the home.<br>Dissatisfied with financial position and amount of money saved.<br>Interested in new products.<br>Like advertised products.<br>Buy: Washers, dryers, TV sets, baby food, chest rubs and cough medicine, vitamins, dolls, wagons, sleds, skates. | Financial position better.<br>In many cases, both spouses work outside the home.<br>Less influenced by advertising.<br>Buy larger-sized packages, multiple-unit deals.<br>Buy: Many foods, cleaning materials, bicycles, music lessons, pianos. | Financial position still better.<br>In many cases, both spouses work outside the home.<br>Some children get jobs.<br>Hard to influence with advertising.<br>High average purchase of durables.<br>Buy: New, more tasteful furniture, auto travel, nonnecessary appliances, boats, dental services, magazines. |

| Empty nest I; older married couples, no children living with them, head in labour force | Empty nest II; older married couples, no children living at home, head retired | Solitary survivor, in labour force | Solitary survivor, retired |
|---|---|---|---|
| Home ownership at peak.<br>Most satisfied with financial position and money saved.<br>Interested in travel, recreation, self-education.<br>Make gifts and contributions.<br>Not interested in new products.<br>Buy: Vacations, luxuries, home improvements. | Drastic cut in income.<br>Keep home.<br>Buy: Medical appliances, medical care, products that aid health, sleep, and digestion. | Income still good but likely to sell home. | Same medical and product needs as other retired group; drastic cut in income.<br>Special need for attention, affection, and security. |

Source: William D. Wells and George Gubar, "Life Cycle Concept in Marketing Research," *Journal of Marketing Research*, November 1966, p. 362.

TABLE 4-5 Detailed family expenditure by selected family income categories all families and unattached individuals 1990

| Expenditure Category | Family Income | | |
|---|---|---|---|
| | $15,000-<br>$19,999 | $35,000-<br>$39,999 | $60,000<br>and over |
| Food | 18.5 | 13.9 | 12.4 |
| Shelter | 27.3 | 19.0 | 16.7 |
| Household operation | 5.4 | 4.1 | 3.7 |
| Household furnishings and equipment | 3.3 | 2.8 | 2.7 |
| Clothing | 5.9 | 4.8 | 5.5 |
| Transportation | 10.0 | 13.2 | 11.9 |
| Health care | 3.2 | 1.9 | 1.6 |
| Personal care | 2.8 | 2.0 | 1.8 |
| Recreation | 4.9 | 5.1 | 5.1 |
| Reading materials and other printed matter | 0.8 | 0.5 | 0.5 |
| Education | 1.0 | 0.7 | 0.8 |
| Tobacco products and alcoholic beverages | 3.3 | 3.1 | 2.7 |
| Miscellaneous | 2.1 | 3.2 | 2.9 |
| Personal taxes | 6.5 | 16.9 | 22.5 |
| Security | 1.5 | 4.3 | 5.0 |
| Gifts and contributions | 3.4 | 4.5 | 4.5 |

Source: *Market Research Handbook*, Ottawa: Statistics Canada, 1993-94, catalogue No. 63-224, p. 226-7.

Generalizations such as these provide a broad background against which marketing executives can analyze the market for their particular product or service. People with needs to satisfy and money to spend, however, must be *willing* to spend before we can say a market exists. Consequently, in Chapter 6 we shall look into consumer motivation and buying behaviour — the "willingness-to-buy" factor in our definition of a market.

## SUMMARY

A sound marketing program starts with the identification and analysis of target markets for whatever it is that an organization is selling. A market consists of people or organizations with needs or wants, money to spend, and the willingness to spend it. There are some general guidelines to follow when selecting target markets.

Some form of market segmentation is the strategy that most marketers adopt as a compromise between the extremes of an aggregate, undifferentiated market and a different product tailor-made for each customer. Market segmentation is the process of dividing the total heterogeneous market into several homogeneous segments. A separate marketing mix is developed for each segment that the seller selects as a target market. Market segmentation is a customer-oriented philosophy that is consistent with the marketing concept.

Market segmentation enables a company to make more efficient use of its marketing resources. Also, this strategy allows a small company to compete effectively in one or two segments. The main drawback of market segmentation is that it requires higher production and marketing costs than does a one-product, mass-market strategy. The requirements for effective segmentation are that (1) the bases for segmentation be measurable with accessible data; (2) the segments themselves be accessible to existing marketing institutions; and (3) the segments be large enough to be potentially profitable.

The total market may be divided into two broad segments — ultimate consumers and business users. The four major bases that may be used for further segmenting the consumer market are: (1) geographic — the distribution of population; (2) demographic — the composition of population such as age, gender, and income distribution; (3) psychographic — personality traits and lifestyles; and (4) product-related — product benefits desired and product usage rates.

In the consumer market, the makeup of the population — its distribution and composition — has a major effect on target-market selection. For some products it is useful to analyze population on a regional basis. Another useful division is by urban, suburban, and rural segments. In this context, the bulk of the population is concentrated in metropolitan areas. Moreover, these areas are expanding and joining together in several parts of the country.

The major age groups of the population make up another significant basis for market analysis — young adults, teenagers, the over-65 group, and so on. The stage of the family life cycle influences the market for many products. Other demographic bases for market analysis include education, occupation, religion, and ethnic origin.

Consumer income — especially disposable income and discretionary income — is a meaningful measure of buying power and market potential. The distribution of income affects the markets for many products. Income distribution has shifted considerably during the past 25 years. Today, a much greater percentage of families are in the over $60,000 bracket and a much smaller percentage earn under $10,000. A family's income level and life cycle are, in part, determinants of its spending patterns.

## KEY TERMS AND CONCEPTS

**Market (92)**
**Target market (92)**
**Target market strategy (93)**
**Market segmentation (94)**
**Conditions for effective segmentation (95)**
**Ultimate consumers (96)**
**Business users (96)**
**Bases for segmenting consumer market (96)**
**Regional distribution of population (99)**
**Urban-suburban-rural distribution (100)**
**Census Metropolitan Areas (CMA) (100)**
**Geodemographic clustering (102)**
**Demographic segmentation (102)**
**Market segmentation by gender (104)**
**Family life cycle (106)**
**Single (106)**
**Education (107)**
**Occupation (107)**
**Religion (107)**
**Ethnic origin (107)**
**Consumer income (108)**
**Personal disposable income (109)**
**Discretionary purchasing power (109)**
**Money income (109)**
**Real income (109)**
**Psychic income (109)**
**Income distribution (109)**
**Expenditure patterns (112)**

## QUESTIONS AND PROBLEMS

1. Outline some reasons why a company might adopt a strategy of market segmentation.
2. What benefits can a company expect to gain from segmenting its market?
3. Cite some regional differences in product preferences caused by factors other than climate.
4. Give several examples of products whose market demand would be particularly affected by each of the following population factors:
   a. Regional distribution.
   b. Marital status.
   c. Gender.
   d. Age.
   e. Urban-rural-suburban distribution.
5. List three of the major population trends noted in this chapter (for instance, a growing segment of the population is over 65 years of age). Then carefully explain how *each* of the following types of retail stores might be affected by *each* of the trends.
   a. Supermarket.
   b. Sporting goods store.
   c. Drugstore.
   d. Restaurant.
6. In which stage of the life cycle are families likely to be the best prospects for each of the following products or services?
   a. Braces on teeth.
   b. Suntan lotion.
   c. Second car in the family.
   d. Vitamin pills.
   e. Refrigerators.
   f. Life insurance.
   g. Aerobics classes.
   h. Fourteen-day Caribbean cruise.

7. In what ways has the rise in disposable personal income since 1960 influenced the marketing programs of a typical department store? A supermarket?
8. Give examples of products whose demand is substantially influenced by changes in discretionary purchasing power.
9. Using the demographic and income segmentation bases discussed in this chapter, describe the segment likely to be the best market for:
   a. Skis.
   b. Good French wines.
   c. Power hand tools.
   d. Birthday cards.
   e. Gas barbecues.
10. Describe what you believe to be the demographic characteristics of heavy users of:
    a. Dog food.
    b. Ready-to-eat cereal.
    c. CD players.
    d. Electronic mail.
11. Suppose you are marketing automobiles. How is your marketing mix likely to differ when marketing to each of the following market segments?
    a. High school students.
    b. Husbands.
    c. Blue-collar workers.
    d. Homemakers.
    e. Young single adults.
12. Why should a marketer of children's clothing be interested in expenditure patterns on this product category across income levels and across provinces and cities? Consult Statistics Canada data to identify whether major differences exist in expenditures on children's clothing by these categories of consumers.

## HANDS-ON MARKETING

1. Interview three friends or acquaintances who all own running shoes, but who are from different demographic groups (for example, education, age, or gender). Using demographic characteristics only, describe in as much detail as possible the market segment each of your friends represents. Is yours a very complete segment picture? Why?
2. Consider three retailers or three restaurants in your home town or the town or city in which your university or college is located, and describe in as much detail as possible the target market segment each of the stores or restaurants is presently serving.

## NOTES AND REFERENCES

1. For an interesting and detailed discussion of the use of geodemographic clustering in marketing, see the December 1993 issue of *research PLUS*, a magazine published by the Market Research Society, London, England.
2. For additional information on the market represented by seniors in Canada, see *A Portrait of Seniors in Canada*, Ottawa, Statistics Canada, catalogue No. 89-519, 1990.
3. For additional information on the market represented by children in Canada, see *A Portrait of Children in Canada*, Ottawa, Statistics Canada, catalogue No. 89-520, 1990.
4. Henry Mietkiewicz, "Jr. Jays Go Big League," *Toronto Star*, May 22, 1994, pp. F1, F12.
5. For additional information on the buying power of the teen market in Canada, see *Youth in Canada*, Ottawa, Statistics Canada, catalogue No. 89-511, 1989.
6. Gordon E. Priest, "Seniors 75+: Living Arrangements," and Sandrine Prasil, "Seniors 75+: Lifestyles," *Canadian Social Trends*, no. 30, Autumn 1993, pp. 23-29.
7. For an additional perspective on the changing segmentation of the women's market, see *Women in Canada: A Statistical Report*, Ottawa: Statistics Canada, catalogue No. 89-503, 1989.
8. For a view of the family life cycle that reflects the growing number of single adults, with or without dependent children, see Patrick E. Murphy and William A. Staples, "A Modernized Family Life Cycle," *Journal of Consumer Research*, June 1979, pp. 12-22; and *New Trends in the Family: Demographic Facts and Features*, Ottawa: Statistics Canada, catalogue No. 91-535E occasional, 1991.
9. For an excellent statistical overview of the modern Canadian family, see *A Portrait of Families in Canada*, Ottawa: Statistics Canada, catalogue No. 89-523, 1993.
10. Andrew Trimble, "Metro's Other Paper War," *Toronto Star*, Sunday, May 22, 1994, pp. D1, D5.
11. *Market Research Handbook, 1993-1994*, Ottawa: Statistics Canada, catalogue No. 63-224, 1993, p. 207.

## CHAPTER 5 GOALS

In this chapter, we continue our discussion of market segmentation and introduce the important strategic concept of positioning. Positioning involves occupying a position in the minds of consumers by creating an image that distinguishes a brand or store or company from the competition.

We conclude the chapter with a detailed discussion of forecasting, the last stage in the marketer's quest for target markets. To do an effective job of targeting, the marketer must not only know the characteristics of the segments, but also must be aware of their buying potential. After studying the chapter, you should have an understanding of:

- How to approach the segmentation of markets from a life-style or product-related perspective.
- How to deal with a number of different segments.
- The importance of positioning a brand or company so as to appeal to target market segments.
- Niche marketing and other positioning strategies to appeal to different consumers or segments.
- The importance of being able to forecast market demand and the market potential of each target segment.

CHAPTER

5

# SEGMENTATION, POSITIONING, AND FORECASTING

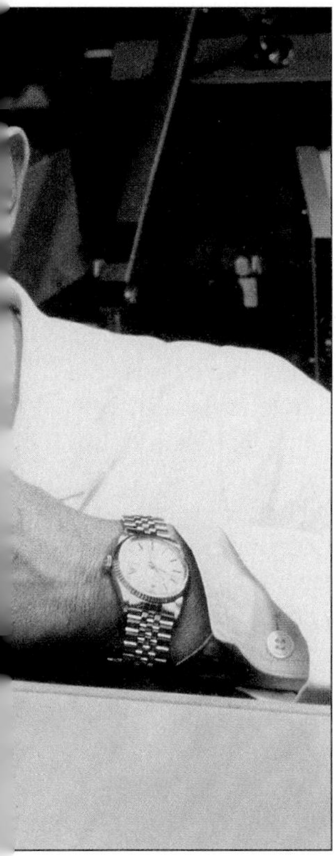

## Much More than a Wristwatch

This chapter brings together two of the most important concepts in marketing — segmentation and positioning. Most successful marketing organizations, whether in the private, public, or not-for-profit sectors, have effectively combined segmentation with positioning to ensure that they appeal to a particular target segment of their market and that they occupy a position in the minds of target customers that sets them apart from their competitors.

Rolex has created an image for its famous watches that has certainly ensured it appeals only to a most discriminating owner. This image is created in part by the price of the Rolex watch, but more particularly through an emphasis on craftsmanship and precision. The famous Swiss-made movement of the Rolex and its Oyster case guarantee that the watch functions flawlessly and is waterproof to a depth of at least 100 m.

But it is Rolex's association with people and events that has guaranteed its appeal to a discriminating segment and a position in the chronometer market that sets it above imitators. In 1914, Kew Observatory in London awarded Rolex a class A certificate indicating that the wristwatch was of the same standard as a marine chronometer. In 1927, a young British girl swam the English Channel wearing a Rolex Oyster; it was working perfectly at the end of the swim.

Rolex was with Sir Edmund Hillary when he made the first successful ascent of Mount Everest and has been regular equipment for many high-altitude climbers ever since. A Rolex watch kept perfect time to a depth of 10,916 m while strapped to the outside of the bathyscaphe "Trieste" when it explored the Marianas Trench in the Pacific Ocean. Julian Nott chose Rolex when he made his record-breaking hot air balloon ascent to 16,800 m.

The market segment targeted by Rolex is reflected in its advertising, which features famous people such as the soprano Dame Kiri Te Kanawa, the golfer Arnold Palmer, polar explorers, deep-sea divers, symphony conductors, prima ballerinas, and astronauts. The Rolex market position is captured in the following paragraph from a promotional brochure. "The owners of Rolex watches can be seen equally at home battling the Atlantic Ocean single handed or lounging on Bahamian beaches. Such is the versatility of this tough, elegant and famous watch. It is the clear choice of those who, for reasons of profession or prestige, demand the ultimate in dependability, durability and distinction."

This example reflects the principal topics of Chapter 5. We see how Rolex has segmented the market for wristwatches, not only on demographics, but on the life-styles and psychological makeup of prospective buyers. The result is an effective positioning of Rolex in the minds of consumers. The positioning ensures that the brand appeals to certain types of consumers and is distinct from other brands of watches available at the high end of the price range.

## Psychological Segmentation

Demographic data are used to segment markets because these data are related to behaviour and because they are relatively easy to gather. However, demographics are not in themselves the causes of behaviour. Consumers don't buy windsurfing equipment because they are young. They buy it because they enjoy an active, outdoor life-style, and it so happens that such people are also typically younger. Thus, demographics often correlate with behaviour, but they do not explain it.

Marketers have gone beyond demographic attributes in an effort to better understand why consumers behave as they do. They now engage in **psychological segmentation**, which involves examining attributes such as personality and life-styles. When demographics and psychological attributes are combined, richer descriptions of segments are produced. Consider, for example, the segmentation of business travellers described in the box on page 122.

### Personality Characteristics

An individual's **personality characteristics** are usually described in terms of traits that influence behaviour. Theoretically, they would seem to be a good basis for segmenting markets. Our experience tells us that compulsive people buy differently from cautious consumers, and quiet introverts do not buy the same things nor in the same way as gregarious, outgoing people. However, personality characteristics pose problems that limit their usefulness in practical market segmentation. First, the presence and strength of these characteristics in the population are virtually impossible to measure. For example, how many people in Canada could be classified as aggressive? Another problem is associated with the accessibility condition of segmentation. There is no advertising medium that provides unique access to a particular personality type. That is, television reaches introverts as well as extroverts, aggressive people as well as timid people. So one of the major goals of segmentation, to avoid wasted marketing effort, is not likely to be accomplished using personality.

Nevertheless, many firms tailor their advertising messages to appeal to certain personality traits. Even though the importance of the personality dimension in a particular decision may be unmeasurable, the seller believes that it does play an influential role. Thus we see products and services advertised to consumers who are "on the way up," or are "men of distinction," or "want to break away from the crowd."

**Life-styles** The term **life-style** is a broad concept that sometimes overlaps personality characteristics. Being cautious, sceptical, ambitious, a workaholic, a copycat — are these personality or life-style traits? Life-styles relate to your activities, interests, and opinions. They reflect how you spend your time, what books you read, television programs you watch, where you take vacations, and what your beliefs are on various social, economic, and political issues.

There is no commonly accepted terminology of life-style categories for segmenting markets. Nevertheless, people's life-styles undoubtedly affect their choice of products and their brand preferences. Marketers are well aware of this and often attempt to segment their markets on a life-style basis.

As consumer tastes and life-styles have changed in recent years, most companies have had to make adjustments in their products and services to ensure that they remained attractive to their target customers. Food manufacturers and retailers have responded to a decline in brand loyalty and a growing tendency on the part of consumers to shop around and save money to introduce increased numbers of private-label products. More major food chains are challenging Loblaws' dominance of the private-label food market by introducing their own upscale private brands.[1] Harley-Davidson maintains success in the market by positioning its brand of motorcycles to appeal to "closet Brandos": older, professional riders (the average Harley purchaser is 40 years old and earns $50,000 U.S. a year) who want to capture the Harley mystique and to emulate Marlon Brando in *The Wild One*.[2] A new advertising campaign for the Canadian Imperial Bank of Commerce is designed to appeal to "real people" who have hopes and dreams for a new home, a car, or vacation. The ads also reinforce a move that the CIBC has been stressing in recent years, that of making the bank more accessible to its busy customers by enabling them to contact the bank through a 1-800 number — another response to the changing life-styles of consumers.[3]

Although it is a valuable marketing tool, life-style segmentation has some of the same serious limitations ascribed to segmentation based on personality characteristics. It is very difficult to measure accurately the size of life-style segments in order to determine their viability. Another problem that may affect the marketer's ability to deal with specific life-style segments relates to their accessibility. Although certain of the mass media (particularly magazines and television) offer options that appeal to particular life-style groups, such options for advertising may be out of the cost range of many smaller companies, thereby making it difficult for them to reach their life-style targets in a cost-effective manner.

**Psychographics** The term **psychographics** was coined to describe a wide variety of psychological and behavioural descriptions of a market. The development of psychographics evolved from attempts by marketers to find measures more directly related to purchase and consumption than demographics.

*Values* are one such descriptor. According to psychologists, values are a reflection of our needs adjusted for the realities of the world in which we live. Research at the Survey Research Center at the University of Michigan has identified nine basic values that relate to purchase behaviour.[4] The nine, which they call the **List of Values (LOV)**, are:

- Self-respect
- Self-fulfilment
- Security
- Sense of belonging
- Excitement
- Sense of accomplishment
- Fun and enjoyment in life
- Being well-respected
- Having warm relationships

## MARKETING AT WORK

### FILE 5-1 ADDING VALUE TO FREQUENT-FLYER SEGMENTATION

The use of psychological, behavioural, and life-style characteristics provides for a much more valuable and detailed description of the various segments that exist within a particular market. For example, the 1993 Canadian Business Travel Survey described the travel patterns, attitudes, behaviour, and motivations of a sample of 2,009 frequent business travellers (six or more round trips for business purposes in the past year).

The study profiled five distinct segments within the frequent business traveller market:

**High Flyers:** (20 percent of frequent travellers) These are last-minute, self-motivated people who will pay for quality to some extent. They tend to need things now, and don't have time to wait. They travel more, tending to fly in first class, and they stay at the best hotels.

**Comfortable Establishment:** (26 percent) This is the core group of business travellers, accounting for 31 percent of business trips and 34 percent of car rentals. They tend to stick with the same service suppliers.

**Reluctant/No Frills:** (22 percent) The people in this group tend to be frugal, book in advance, stay in less expensive hotels, and don't spend as much money on trips. They would prefer to do business in their own cities.

**Experimental:** (14 percent) Many of the members of this group own their own companies or are CEOs of smaller firms. They tend to be among the first to try new things, such as new telecommunications devices. They spend more money when travelling, although they would like to spend less on air fares and more on hotels.

**Status Seekers:** (18 percent) These are would-be High Flyers, and they want to be seen as successful. They want to travel more. They are aware of the image conveyed by a particular airline and hotel and take that into consideration when making travel plans.

If you were preparing a marketing program for a new regional airline, how would you use this information?

Source: Jo Marney, "Frequent Flyers," *Marketing*, December 20/27, 1993, p. 15.

While most people would view all these values as desirable, their relative importance differs among people, and their importance changes over a person's life. For example, people who value fun and enjoyment especially like skiing, dancing, bicycling, and backpacking, and people who value warm relationships give gifts for no particular reason. Thus, the relative strength of values could be the basis for segmenting a market.

Probably the best-known psychographic segmentation tool is **VALS**, developed in 1978 by the research firm SRI International. The VALS system was developed from a large study that divided adults into nine segments based on similarities in their *values* (beliefs, desires, and prejudices) and their *life-styles* — hence, the VALS acronym. In what has become a classic and successful application of VALS, Merrill Lynch switched its advertising from depicting a herd of bulls charging across the prairie to a single bull, described as a "breed apart." The reason? The herd is more consistent with the VALS segment known as "belongers." Belongers are traditionalists who are content to follow others and are unlikely to be heavy investors. But Merrill Lynch wants to appeal to "achievers," the VALS segment characterized by independent thinkers who see themselves as being above the crowd. The result? After changing the ads from a herd to a single bull, Merrill Lynch's advertising had a much greater impact on consumers, and its market share went up.[5]

In 1990 SRI introduced **VALS2** to reflect changes in how we live and make decisions. The two primary dimensions used to segment the population in VALS2 are an individual's resources and self-orientation. Resources are broadly defined to include not only income but other factors such as health, education, and self-confidence. Self-orientation reflects a person's self-image and the behaviour used to communicate that image to others. Three self-orientation patterns are included in VALS2: principle-oriented (your choices are directed by your beliefs), status-oriented (your choices are directed by your desire for the approval of others), and action-oriented (your choices are directed by your desire for physical or social activity, variety, or risk taking). Resources range from abundant to minimal. Based on a representative sample of the population, and using resources and self-orientation, eight consumer segments of approximately equal size have been identified. For example, one segment, called "actualizers," is characterized as optimistic, involved, outgoing, and growth-oriented. Actualizers have wide intellectual interests, engage in varied leisure activities, are well informed, and are politically active. In contrast, another segment, called "experiencers," are unconventional, active, impetuous, and energetic. They like new and offbeat things, are concerned about image, admire wealth and fame, and are uninterested in political issues.[6]

Several organizations have used VALS2 to develop or refine their marketing strategies. For example, Transport Canada, the agency that operates major Canadian airports, used VALS2 to study the flying public passing through Vancouver, British Columbia. Though actualizers make up about 12 percent of the general population, the study found that 37 percent of the travellers belonged to this group. Since actualizers are a good market for quality arts and crafts, the results suggested that stores such as Sharper Image or Nature Company could do well at the airport.[7]

### Behavioural Segmentation

Some marketers regularly attempt to segment their markets on the basis of product-related behaviour — they utilize **behavioural segmentation**. In this section we briefly consider two of these: the benefits desired from a product, and the rate at which the consumer uses the product.

**Benefits Desired** Russell Haley is credited with drawing attention to the notion of benefit segmentation when he described a hypothetical division of the toothpaste market based on the benefits desired. The segment names, benefits sought by each segment, and the likely preferred brands were:

- Sensories: flavour and appearance — Colgate or Stripe.
- Sociables: brightness of teeth — MacLeans or Ultra Brite.
- Worriers: decay prevention — Crest.
- Independents: low price — any brand on sale.[8]

If Haley were to prepare a similar division today, he might include "plaque control" as a fifth benefit segment.

Two things determine the effectiveness of benefit segmentation. First, the specific benefits consumers are seeking must be identified. This typically involves several research steps, beginning with the identification of all possible benefits related to a particular product or behaviour through brainstorming, observing consumers, and listening to focus groups. Then, more focus groups are conducted to screen out unlikely or unrealistic benefits and to amplify and clarify the remaining possibilities. Finally, large-scale surveys are conducted to determine how important the benefits are and how many consumers seek each one.

To illustrate, a recent study subdivided supermarket shoppers according to their shopping strategies. The segments, their sizes, and the benefits each sought are:

- Practical loyalists (29 percent of shoppers): Brand loyal but always alert to ways of saving money on preferred brands.

**Appealing to a customer's need for safety.**

- Bottom-liners (26 percent of shoppers): Select the lowest-priced alternative, with little or no regard for brand.
- Opportunistic switchers (24 percent of shoppers): Use coupons and sales to select from among a defined set of acceptable brands.
- Deal hunters (13 percent of shoppers): View shopping as a "game" and consider getting a bargain as more important than how well the product or brand meets their needs.
- Nonstrategists (8 percent of shoppers): Do not consider the time and effort necessary to find bargains as worth the effort.[9]

The second task, once the separate benefits are known, is to describe the demographic and psychographic characteristics of the people seeking each benefit. Remember, "accessibility" is a requirement of successful segmentation. For example, among the shopper segments described above, "opportunistic switchers" tend to have some college education. So, to reach this group with advertising for a new product, a firm would select media that appeal to college-educated consumers.

More recently, a new twist has been added to the concept of benefit segmentation. Some researchers have extended the concept beyond the original idea of user-based benefit segmentation to include segmentation based on the occasions that customers would associate with use of the product or service. This is an approach to segmentation that emerged in the 1970s, but has not received a great deal of attention among marketers. It may, however, have increasing relevance in the face of declining brand loyalty, where consumers may be more willing to switch brands and to use different brands on different occasions.[10]

**Usage Rate** Another product-related basis for market segmentation is the rate at which people use or consume a product. Thus we can have categories for nonusers, light users, medium users, and heavy users. Normally a company is most interested in the heavy users of its product. The 50 percent of the people who are the "heavy half" of the users of a product typically account for 80 to 90 percent of the total purchases of a given product or service.

That is not to say that this percentage applies precisely in all product or service categories. Rather, it is the principle that is important. Typically, a company can identify a number of different segments among its target customers. Among these segments, there are usually one or two that contain disproportionally heavier consumers of the product or service. For example, one segment may contain only 15 percent of customers, but these customers may account for 24 percent of all purchases of the company's product. Another segment may have a comparatively small number of consumers, accounting possibly for only 8 percent of potential customers, but their consumption patterns may be such that they account for 20 percent of all sales of the product or service. These segments, because they contain such heavy consumers, represent important target segments. In such circumstances, most companies would prefer to be the market leader among the heaver users, rather than targeting their marketing efforts at customers who use relatively little of the product.

The remarkable feature of usage patterns is that they seem to be fairly constant across industries and over time. In most of the situations a marketer might encounter, there are bound to be heavy-user and light-user segments. Thus this segmentation base becomes an effective predictor of future buying behaviour. Comparable studies in the 1960s and 1980s showed similar patterns in the percentage of total purchases accounted for by the heavy-user half in several product categories. Some sample products and percentages of the total market accounted for by the heavy half in 1962 and 1982 were as follows: shampoo, 81 and 79 percent; cake mixes, 85 and 83 percent; beer, 88 and 87 percent; soaps and detergents, 80 and 75 percent.[11]

Sometimes the target market is the nonuser or light user, and the objective is to woo these customers into a higher use category. Or light users may constitute an attractive niche for a seller simply because they are being ignored by other firms that are targeting heavy users. Once the characteristics of these light users have been identified, management can go to them directly with an introductory low-price offer. Or a seller might increase usage rates by promoting (1) new uses for a product (baking soda as a deodorant); (2) new times for uses (off-season vacations); or (3) multiple packaging (a 12-pack of soft drinks).

## MARKETING AT WORK

### FILE 5-2 WHO'S DRINKING NON-ALCOHOLIC BEER?

One of the most useful purposes of marketing research data is to allow the marketing manager to prepare a profile of the target consumer in certain segments or categories. As the data presented below illustrate, the consumers of non-alcoholic beer in Canada represent only 4 percent of Canadians over the age of 12, but they do constitute a very interesting and attractive target segment when profiled on their demographic and life-style characteristics. They are over-represented in certain categories — for example, they are 71 percent more likely than other Canadians aged 12 and older to have a post-graduate education and 65 percent more likely to have annual household income greater than $75,000.

The profile of the non-alcoholic beer drinker may be summarized as follows. He is more likely to be aged 25 to 34; a well-educated, higher-income, professional; from Quebec or British Columbia; and more active in sports such as cross-country skiing, squash, and jogging.

Source: "A Marketing Profile of Drinkers of Non-alcoholic Beer," *Marketing*, March 14, 1994, p. 11.

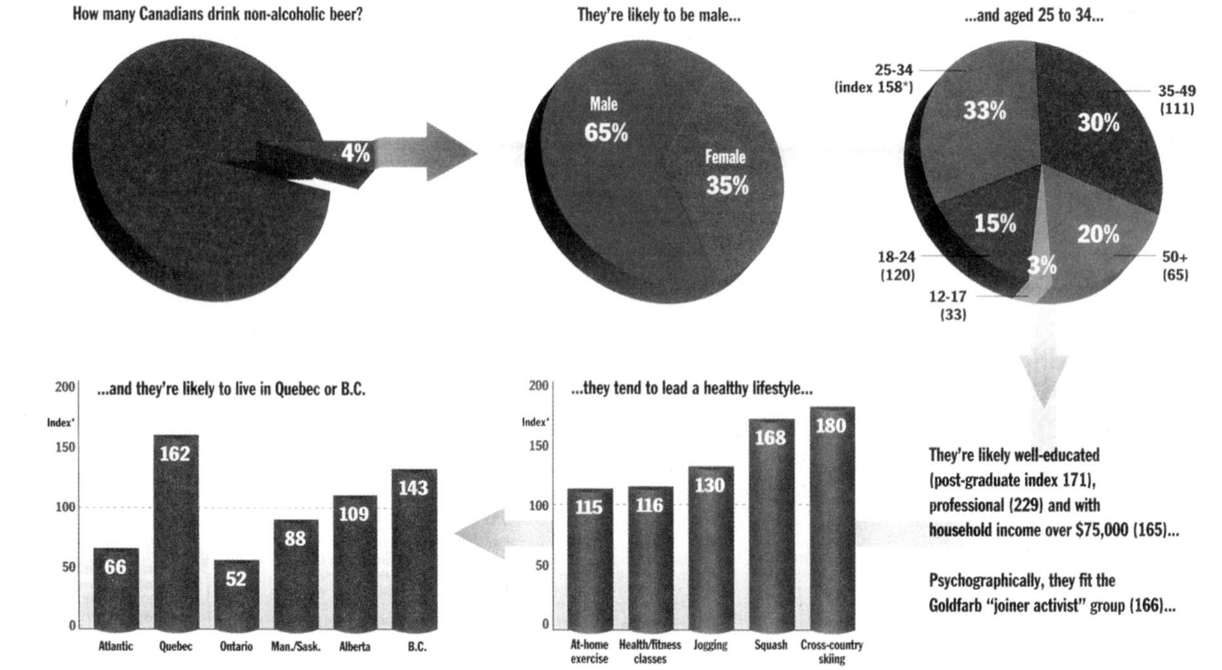


*This compares people 12+ who drink non-alcoholic beer with all people 12+. For instance, those who drink non-alcoholic beer are 58% more likely to be 25 to 34 than is the average person 12 or older.
Source: PMB '93. Prepared by Jim McElgunn (Marketing Magazine) and Steve Ferley (Print Measurement Bureau).

Reproduced with permission of Print Measurement Bureau/*Marketing Magazine*.

## TARGET-MARKET STRATEGIES

Let's assume that a company has segmented the total market for its product. Now management is in a position to select one or more segments as its target markets. The company can follow one of three strategies — market aggregation, single-segment concentration, or multiple-segment targeting — as illustrated in Figure 5-1. To evaluate the strategies, management must determine the market potential of each of the segments it has identified. But before a strategy is chosen, the potential of the identified segments must be determined. This calls for establishing some guidelines for target-market selection.

## Guidelines in Selecting a Target Market

Four guidelines govern how to determine which segments should be the target markets. The first is that target markets should be compatible with the organization's goals and image. For years many manufacturers resisted distributing their products through K mart because of the chain's discount image. However, as K mart achieved a high level of acceptability with consumers, image concerns seemed to disappear.

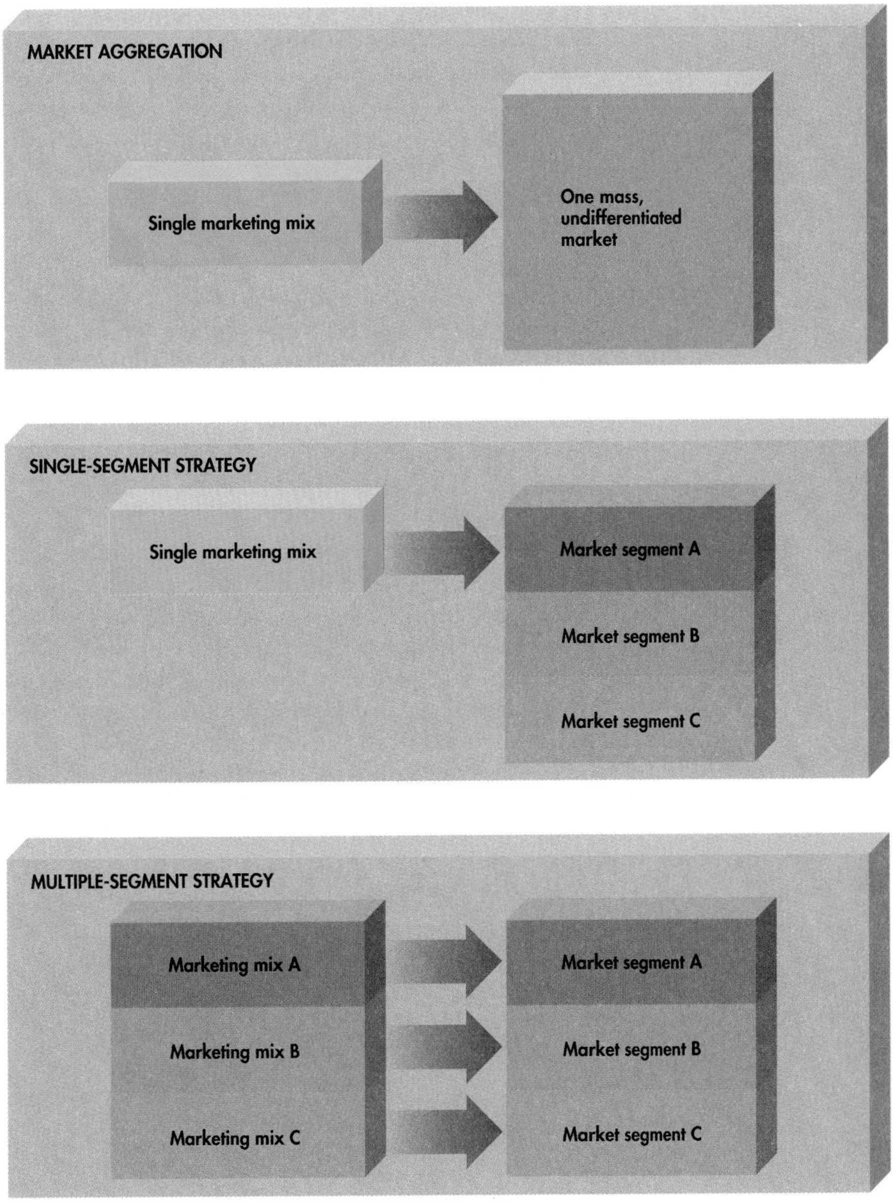


**FIGURE 5-1**
**The three target-market strategies.**

A second guideline — consistent with our definition of strategic planning — is to match the market opportunity represented in the target markets with the company's resources. In examining new product opportunities, 3M considered many options but chose the do-it-yourself home improvement market due to the marketing economies that could be achieved. The firm's name was already well known to consumers, and the products could be sold through many of the retail outlets already selling 3M products. Thus, entering this market was much less expensive than entering a market in which 3M was inexperienced.

Over the long run, a business must generate a profit to survive. This rather obvious statement translates into our third market-selection guideline. That is, an organization should seek markets that will generate sufficient sales volume at a low enough cost to result in a profit. Surprisingly, companies often have overlooked profit in their quest for high-volume markets. Their mistake is going after sales volume, not *profitable* sales volume.

Fourth, a company ordinarily should seek a market where there are the fewest and smallest competitors. A seller should not enter a market that is already saturated with competition unless it has some overriding differential advantage that will enable it to take customers from existing firms. When Häagen-Dazs, a brand of premium ice cream, entered Europe and Asia in the late 1980s, it had little competition at the high end of the market. Because per capita ice cream consumption on these continents is well below that of North America, many viewed the prospects of a high-price brand in a low-usage market as not very attractive. However, Häagen-Dazs, with sales of over $500 million in 1991, proved the doubters wrong. It wasn't that consumers disliked ice cream; rather, many simply had not been exposed to a high-quality version. By getting to the market first, Häagen-Dazs now has a significant advantage over later entrants.[12]

These are only guidelines. A seller still has to decide how many segments to pursue as its target market, as we will see next.

### Market Aggregation

By adopting a strategy of *market aggregation* — also known as a *mass-market* or an *undifferentiated-market* strategy — an organization treats its total market as a single unit. This unit is one mass, aggregate market whose parts are considered to be alike in all major respects. Management then develops a single marketing mix to reach as many customers as possible in this aggregate market. That is, the company develops a single product for this mass audience; it develops one pricing structure and one distribution system for its product; and it uses a single promotional program that is aimed at the entire market.

When is an organization likely to adopt the strategy of market aggregation? Generally when a large group of customers in the total market tends to have the same perception of the product's want-satisfying benefits. This strategy often is adopted by firms that are marketing a nondifferentiated, staple product such as gasoline, salt, or sugar. In the eyes of many people, sugar is sugar, regardless of the brand. All brands of table salt are pretty much alike, and one unleaded gasoline is about the same as another.

Basically, market aggregation is a production-oriented strategy. It enables a company to maximize its economies of scale in production, physical distribution, and promotion. Producing and marketing one product for one market means longer production runs at lower unit costs. Inventory costs are minimized when there is no (or a very limited) variety of colours and sizes of products. Warehousing and transportation efforts are most efficient when one product is going to one market.

Market aggregation will work only as long as the seller's single marketing mix continues to satisfy enough customers to meet the company's sales and profit expectations. The strategy of market aggregation typically is accompanied by the strategy of product differentiation in a company's marketing program. **Product differentiation** is the strategy by which one firm attempts to distinguish its product from competitive brands offered to the same aggregate market. By differentiating its product, an organization hopes to create the impression that its product is better than the competitors' brands. The seller also hopes to engage in nonprice competition and thus avoid or minimize the threat of price competition.

A seller implements this strategy either (1) by changing some feature of the product — packaging, colour, or label design, for example; (2) by using a promotional appeal that features a differentiating benefit; or (3) by using advertising and other promotional strategies to create a differentiating image for the brand, product, or service. Oral-B has differentiated its toothbrushes by introducing a band of blue bristles on each toothbrush that indicates the extent of wear and, therefore, when the toothbrush should be replaced. Diet Pepsi has sought to differentiate itself from other brands of soft drinks by indicating a "best before" date on the bottom of its cans.

Differentiation is an important strategy in any situation where there is little difference across the offerings of various companies, or where the consumer is unable to understand or appreciate differences that do exist. Increasingly, companies are turning to service to differentiate their products and even their companies. With so many products now being perceived by consumers to be quite similar, it is those companies that can offer the best service to their customers that are getting the business. In many industries, the highly competitive marketplace brought about by the recession of the early 1990s has forced companies to compete on the basis of service, thereby attempting to set themselves apart from their competitors.[13] In the retail gasoline industry, where most consumers would perceive the product to be similar, if not identical, across competing companies, Imperial Oil has featured its employees and great customer service in its advertising to set the Esso brand apart from its many competitors.

## Single-Segment Strategy

A strategy of **single-segment concentration** involves selecting as the target market one homogeneous segment from within the total market. One marketing mix is then developed to reach this single segment. A small company may want to concentrate on a single market segment, rather than to take on many competitors in a broad market. For example, an Alberta guest ranch got started by appealing only to guest horseback riders who also enjoyed square dancing. A large cruise-ship company, offering a round-the-world luxury cruise, targets its marketing effort at one market segment — older, affluent people who also have time to travel.

When manufacturers of foreign automobiles first entered the North American market, they typically targeted a single market segment. The Volkswagen Beetle was intended for the low-priced, small-car market. Honda originally sold only lower-powered motorcycles, and Mercedes-Benz targeted the high-income market. Today, of course, most of the original foreign car marketers have moved into a multisegment strategy. Only a few, such as Jaguar and Ferrari, continue with a concentration strategy.

This strategy enables a company to penetrate one small market in depth and to acquire a reputation as a specialist or an expert in this limited market. A company can enter such a market with limited resources. And as long as the single segment remains a small market, large competitors are likely to leave the single-segment specialist alone. However, if the small market should show signs of becoming a large market, then bigger companies may well jump in. This is exactly what happened in the market for herbal and specialty teas. Prior to the 1980s, rose-hip, camomile, Earl Grey, and similar specialty teas were sold primarily in health-food stores and specialty shops and were available from only a small number of manufacturers and importers. With changing consumer tastes and preferences during the past ten years or so, specialty teas have become more popular. The growth of the herbal and specialty segment was such that new tea companies entered this expanding corner of the market, including some major competitors such as Tetley and Lipton.

The big risk and limitation to a single-segment strategy is that the seller has all its eggs in one basket. If that single segment declines in market potential, the seller can suffer considerably. Also, a seller with a strong name and reputation in one segment may find it difficult to expand into another segment.

The strategy of not concentrating the entire marketing effort on a single segment is also reflected in other industries. Both Volkswagen and Honda have traded their lines up to compete with the higher-priced models of BMW and Mercedes: VW with its Audi line, and Honda with its Acura. Nestlé has successfully marketed its instant coffees Nescafé and Taster's Choice for many years and later entered the ground coffee segment with its Taster's Choice ground.

**Multiple-Segment Strategy** Under a **multiple-segment strategy**, two or more different groups of potential customers are identified as target markets. A separate marketing mix is developed to reach each segment. A marketer of personal computers, for example, may identify three distinct market segments — university and college students, small businesses, and a home market — and then design a different marketing mix to reach each segment. In segmenting the automobile market, General Motors originally developed separate marketing programs for each of its five brands of passenger cars — the company had different marketing programs for its Chevrolet and GMC trucks. The five divisions — Chevrolet, Buick, Pontiac, Oldsmobile, and Cadillac — essentially tried to reach the total market for automobiles on a segmented basis. This segmentation has been further enhanced with the addition of the Geo and Saturn brands, each of which is targeted at a different segment than the five established brands or makes offered by General Motors. The distinction across the various GM brands has diminished over the years, however, as models offered by Chevrolet, Buick, and the others overlap in price, appearance, and features. As a result, the target markets for the brands are no longer clearly defined, and GM brands find themselves competing with one another.

In a multiple-segment strategy, a seller frequently will develop a different version of the basic product for each segment. However, market segmentation can also be accomplished with no change in the product, but rather with separate distribution channels or promotional appeals, each tailored to a given market segment. Wrigley's, for example, targets smokers by promoting chewing gum as an alternative in situations where smoking is unwelcome. And Evian bottled water has broadened its market beyond athletes and fitness-oriented consumers to other groups including pregnant women and environmentalists.

## POSITIONING

The concept of market *positioning* is closely related to segmentation; a marketer must determine how the company's brands or stores or image are perceived by the public in general and more particularly by the segment of the market that has been selected as the principal target. As part of a company's marketing strategy, decisions must be made concerning how the company and its brands are to be portrayed to convey the correct image to the target segment. Positioning, therefore, relates to the use of various marketing techniques and marketing-mix variables to create the image or perception that will best fit with what the company wishes to be known for.[14]

A company may develop a positioning strategy for a particular brand or group of brands, for a retail store or chain, or for the company itself. The process involves answering questions such as the following: Who are the target-market segments for this brand or store or company? On what basis do we wish to appeal to this segment? What do we

## MARKETING AT WORK

### FILE 5-3 GETTING GREENER ALL THE TIME

Canada produces more garbage per person than any other country in the world. A recent study for the Canadian Council of Ministers of the Environment showed that each Canadian produces an average of 1.7 kg of garbage each day, compared with less than 1.5 kg for the Germans, Dutch, and Swiss, and less than 1 kg per day for the British, Japanese, and Swedes. Despite this rather negative perspective on the Canadian environmental scene, there is some evidence that attitudes are changing and that North Americans are becoming more aware of environmental issues and are more prepared to act to protect the environment from further damage.

Consumers come in different shades when it comes to concern for the environment and willingness to act to protect it. So-called "deep-green" consumers are characterized as upscale, educated women with children, while lighter-green consumers are less easily motivated, but can be reached with cost-effective and easily used environmental-product solutions such as phosphate-free, ultra-concentrated laundry detergent, fabric softener refills, and reductions in packaging.

The willingness of consumers to adopt more environmentally friendly practices stems from recent changes in attitudes and values, which include:

- Consumers moving from passive to active on the environmental-action scale;
- Greater acceptance of products made from recycled materials;
- Greater likelihood to view disposable as bad and durable as good;
- Rejection of paper products that are white because of the use of chlorine bleach;
- Greater acceptance of packaging alternatives that fit the solid-waste disposal system available to the consumer.

Source: Jo Marney, "Trash Can Be Cash," *Marketing*, April 11, 1994, p. 27.

want people to think of when they hear our name? How do we wish to be seen to be different from our competitors or from other brands or companies in the market? In dealing with questions such as these, the company is really asking: what *position* do we wish to occupy in this market?

The company's positioning strategy may be applied at the brand level, at the level of the retail store, or for entire companies. For example, while the Bank of Montreal has been staking out a position in the Canadian banking industry as the price leader and the bank that is first to lower interest rates, the Canadian Imperial Bank of Commerce has been moving into a position as the bank of the future with increased levels of automation, reliance on automatic banking machines and telephone banking, and increased use of customer data bases to identify the most lucrative customer segments.[15] At the same time, the Royal Bank of Canada, having solidified its position as Canada's largest financial institution following its merger with Royal Trust, reinforces that dominant position with advertising, stating that the bank became Canada's largest "one customer at a time."

The enRoute credit card, purchased by Diners Club from Air Canada, does not go head-to-head with VISA and MasterCard, but is rather positioned as the country's leading corporate travel card. Loblaws has positioned itself for many years as the leading food retailer in the introduction of quality private-label brands. Four Seasons Hotels has carved out a position at the top end of the quality hotel market where they can charge premium rates and offer exceptional service.[16] In the ongoing battle for market share in the deregulated financial services industry, the Bank of Montreal has positioned itself as the price leader by continually being the first to announce reductions in interest rates payable on loans and mortgages. The small Red Rock Brewery of Calgary has developed its own unique position by promoting premium-priced, additive-free brands with unorthodox names like Buzzard Breath and Warthog, and by exporting their products to the western United States and other foreign markets.[17] At the corporate level, Dofasco is a company that has positioned itself as a caring employer through corporate advertising that features the corporate slogan "Our product is steel, our strength is people."

Positioning, therefore, is a strategy for locating a brand or store in the consumer's mind, with respect to its rating on certain dimensions or attributes that the consumer considers important. It involves staking out a place in the collective perception of consumers in which the brand or store or company can establish an image that will be appropriate for certain segments of the market. This image is created through effective use of marketing-mix variables, including advertising, product design, pricing, packaging, store decor, and sales promotions.

The creation of the appropriate image may be approached in a combination of ways. In the first place, a firm may wish to occupy a position in a market *in relation to that occupied by competitors*. It may choose a position that is distinct from that occupied by a competitor or may choose to challenge a competitor directly, thereby trying to occupy roughly the same position.

On the other hand, the positioning strategy may be developed so as to position the brand or store through the creation of an image tailored to the characteristics, preferences, attitudes, and feelings of a *particular segment of the market*. This approach is dependent on the company having selected certain target segments. The image of the product, brand, or store is then tailored to appeal to those segments.

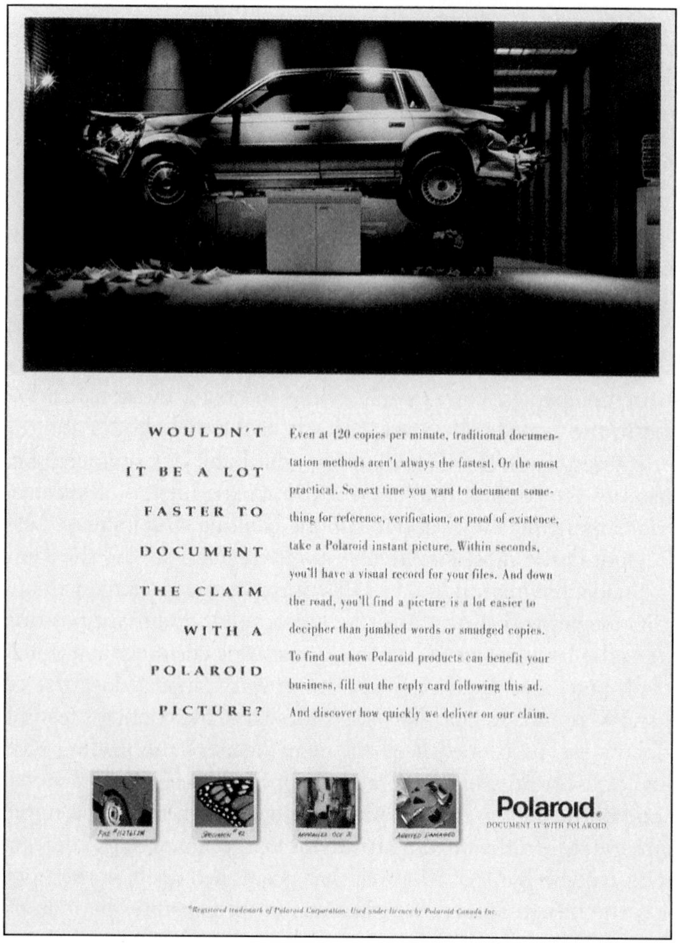


**Polaroid positioned as a business tool to document evidence.**

Finally, a brand or store may be positioned on the basis of its *inherent characteristics*. In other words, the marketing staff of the company would have to decide what the brand or retailer is to be known for and set about creating the appropriate image. Such an approach deals implicitly with positioning against competition and meeting the needs of particular segments, but is often undertaken in response to the identification of a market gap, where no company has established a dominant position.

**Positioning Maps** One of the easiest ways to get a feel for the concept of positioning is to examine products, brands, or stores as they are arrayed on a *positioning map*. Such maps are developed through marketing research, which explores the image that consumers have of the various brands or stores in the market and rates each competing brand or store on a series of attributes. In such research, consumers are typically asked to identify the elements of the purchase situation and the product or store attributes that are important in influencing the purchase decision. Once these attributes and elements have been identified, research is undertaken to determine which are most important in influencing the consumer to select one brand over another. Finally, consumers are asked to rate the competing brands or stores in the market on each of the important dimensions or attributes. Such research data allow the researcher to present the brands or stores of interest in a map similar to that shown in Figure 5-2.

**FIGURE 5-2**
**Perceptual Map Based on Data in Table 5.1.**

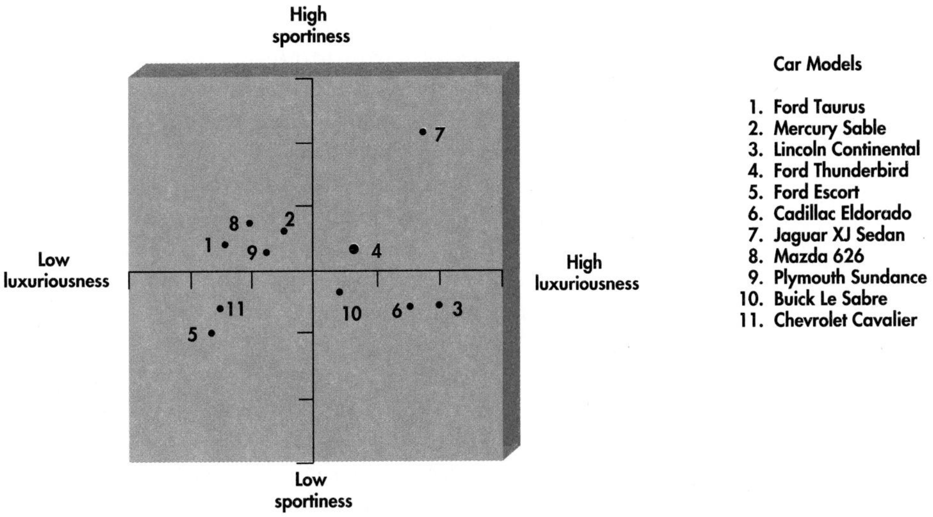


TABLE 5-1 Rank order of similarities between pairs of car models

| Stimuli | 1 | 2 | 3 | 4 | 5 | 6 | 7 | 8 | 9 | 10 | 11 |
|---|---|---|---|---|---|---|---|---|---|---|---|
| 1 | — | 8 | 50 | 31 | 12 | 48 | 36 | 2 | 5 | 39 | 10 |
| 2 | | — | 38 | 9 | 33 | 37 | 22 | 6 | 4 | 14 | 32 |
| 3 | | | — | 11 | 55 | 1 | 23 | 46 | 41 | 17 | 52 |
| 4 | | | | — | 44 | 13 | 16 | 19 | 25 | 18 | 42 |
| 5 | | | | | — | 54 | 53 | 30 | 28 | 45 | 7 |
| 6 | | | | | | — | 26 | 47 | 40 | 24 | 51 |
| 7 | | | | | | | — | 29 | 35 | 34 | 49 |
| 8 | | | | | | | | — | 3 | 27 | 15 |
| 9 | | | | | | | | | — | 20 | 21 |
| 10 | | | | | | | | | | — | 43 |
| 11 | | | | | | | | | | | — |

**The rank number "1" represents the most similar pair.**

Source: Paul E. Green and Frank J. Carmone, *Multidimensional Scaling and Related Techniques in Marketing Analysis*. Copyright © 1970 by Allyn and Bacon. Reprinted with permission.

Positioning maps allow the marketer to see where his or her brand is perceived to lie in the market in comparison with competing brands, how it is rated on various attributes, and where it lies in relation to the various segments that have been identified. Typically, a number of brands that are perceived to have similar characteristics are clustered together in close proximity to those large segments of the market that have considerable buying power. Other brands occupy positions in the market where they are seen to appeal to different segments and to display different characteristics.

One benefit of examining perceptual market maps is that the marketer can identify how his or her brand or store is perceived by consumers in comparison with competitors. Such examination often leads to a decision to reposition a brand, a topic we will cover later in this chapter. Also, examination of market maps may lead to the identification of market gaps — positions in the market that are not now filled by existing brands or stores and where untapped market demand may be said to exist. One of the most interesting markets for which to prepare a market map is the restaurant business in any medium-sized to large city. There are usually enough restaurants and residents are sufficiently familiar with many of them that they can rate them on various dimensions, such as price, atmosphere, menu selection, value for money, speed of service, target market group, and so on. Once such data are collected, a positioning map may be prepared that will identify those restaurants perceived by consumers to be located close to one another and that, therefore, are competing directly with one another. At the same time, it is likely the case that certain parts of the map will be "empty," suggesting there are no restaurants presently occupying those positions and, therefore, reflecting a gap in the local restaurant market.

**Niche Marketing** Some marketers may choose to stake out "niche" positions for their brands; they create an image that is quite distinct and intended to appeal to a fairly narrow segment of the market. Within the Canadian beer market, for example, brands such as Black Label and O'Keefe's Extra Old Stock and the newer "handmade" brands are considered to be "niche" brands, while mainstream brands such as Molson Canadian and Labatt's Blue are positioned to appeal to much larger segments. Niche brands generally are not positioned to take on the major competitors head-on, but rather to be a leader in a very narrow area of the market. Smaller companies often successfully "carve out a niche" for themselves. To continue with our beer examples, successful microbrewers such as Upper Canada Brewing, Sleeman's, Red Rock, and Granville Island Brewery are really niche marketers; they are satisfied with occupying a relatively small position in a very large market by catering to the tastes and preferences of consumers who want something different.

Niche marketing, therefore, is generally a successful strategy for smaller companies that do not have the financial and other resources generally available to large companies. In the travel business, for example, many travel agencies are seeking ways to set themselves apart from their competitors by specializing in narrow parts of the market. As travel has become more complex and travellers more demanding, some travel agencies have found it impossible to serve all segments equally well. Consequently, some become niche players, specializing in cruises, business travel, the ethnic market, or theme travel — tours organized around a theme such as a murder mystery or a spring-training boat cruise for baseball fans.

Large organizations often target small market niches. For example, within the Canadian banking industry, most of the foreign banks (known as Schedule II banks) that have entered the Canadian market in recent years have chosen not to compete at the "retail" level by opening branches; rather, some, such as Citibank Canada, have chosen to target specific niches. In the case of Citibank, the decision was to target recent Chinese immigrants to Canada through a strategy known as remote banking, which would involve dealing with customers through telephone, mail, and automated banking machines.[18] Niche markets are also not restricted to local situations. A small Canadian electroplating firm, Dalcan Services of Burlington, Ontario, which specializes in brush-plating, received a contract to undertake the gold replating of the Dome of the Rock in Jerusalem, the third holiest Muslim site in the world.[19]

To be successful in positioning itself as a niche player in the market, a company or the managers of a niche brand must have identified a segment of the market that is not now being served adequately by the brands and companies that are in the market; that segment must have sufficient potential buying power to warrant the development of a marketing program; it must be sufficiently small that larger companies are unlikely to retaliate if the niche brand is successful; and the niche marketer must have detailed knowledge of the characteristics of the members of the segment and their needs and preferences.

One author has suggested that a company should follow four steps in implementing a successful niche marketing strategy.[20]

1. *Identify an appropriate niche* through marketing research that will identify segments of the market not now being well served by existing brands.
2. *Exploit the niche* by determining the likelihood of competitive retaliation and the length of time the company will enjoy a competitive advantage.
3. *Expand the niche* by meeting changing needs of the market segment, expanding the customer base, and making more effective use of marketing variables.
4. *Defend the niche* by continuing to meet the needs of segment members through improving the product and offering better service or lower prices.

**Positioning Strategies** Once a company has determined its market segmentation objectives and has identified the segments towards which its brands are to be targeted, it may adopt a number of positioning strategies to accomplish its objectives.

1. Take on the competition head-on: By deciding to challenge the market leader or to target large segments of the market with a broad appeal, a marketer is saying, "Our brand is as good as or better than the leader." Such a strategy is exemplified in the so-called "cola wars" in which Pepsi-Cola and Coca-Cola have been fighting for market leadership by attempting to create the widest appeal to attract as many consumers as possible.
2. Occupy a gap in the market: A number of companies have moved to fill a gap in a market by positioning a brand to appeal to a certain segment of consumers or to take advantage of the disappearance of a competitor. For example, Michelin differentiates its tires from those of competitors by emphasizing safety.
3. Set a brand apart from the competition: Often a company will decide to employ a strategy that says, "Our brand is not like all the others; this is why you should buy ours." This involves positioning a brand or store so as to avoid head-to-head competition with market leaders or with brands that have an established image or reputation and a secure market share.
4. Occupy position of leadership: Some companies that are clearly market leaders are not particularly interested in positioning themselves against the competition, but rather are likely to stake out a position as clear market leader, known to be ahead of the pack and leader in such areas as product quality, service to customers, profitability, innovations, or technology. Companies such as Loblaws, Northern Telecom, and the Royal Bank of Canada tend to be regarded by many consumers as market leaders whose market franchise is so large and well established that competitors often try to emulate them and to position themselves against them.
5. Position to appeal to life-style segments: Often a company will position its brands or retail stores to appeal to certain segments of the market that are defined not only by demographic characteristics but also by their life-styles. IKEA, the Swedish home furnishings retailer, has been rethinking its market position in recent years. In addition to the fact that the company has struggled, along with other furniture retailers, with the prolonged Canadian recession, IKEA was saddled with an image as a place to buy cheap modular furniture for the first apartment or the rec room. In an attempt to alter that image and to move the chain to a new position in the Canadian market, IKEA launched a new approach to advertising that depicted the company as a more up-market supplier of a complete range of household items, more appropriate for families as they move from the household formation stage and into the "cocooning" stage of their life cycles.[21]

**Repositioning** Repositioning is a variation of a positioning strategy that involves changing the market position of a brand or store in response to changes taking place in the broader market environment. The need to reposition a brand or retail store may result from one of three market conditions. First, management may identify a gap in the market that may be filled by altering the image of the store or brand — that is, changing the position it occupies in the minds of consumers. For example, a retailer in a local market may realize that the average age of its customer base is increasing and may decide to reposition the store to have greater appeal to a younger market segment.

Second, repositioning may be required by an increase in competitive activity. For example, the economic downturn in the late 1980s and early 1990s created considerable turmoil in the Canadian retail apparel field. Major clothing retailers found themselves in extremely competitive situations that demanded they seek out new positions in the market. Marks & Spencer Canada sought to shed the consumer perception that it operates dowdy stores by undertaking extensive renovations, better merchandise displays, and its first advertising campaign. K mart Canada also sought to reposition itself through a new look brought about by store renovations, more brand-name merchandise, and additional displays. Fairweather moved away from catering to its traditional teenage market and sought to occupy a position as supplier to a more affluent, older market segment.[22] With the influx of large U.S. retailers into the Canadian market in the past five years, many of these same retailers are again having to rethink their position in the market, in light of new competition.

Third, it may be necessary to reposition a brand or store in response to a change in the demographic characteristics or attitudes or values of the target consumer market. In moving its major evening newscast, "Prime Time News," back into its traditional time slot of 10 P.M., from the 9 P.M. slot it had occupied for 18 months, the CBC was acting in a manner consistent with its plan to reposition the network to address the needs and wishes of its target audience.[23]

**Repositioning Canada's largest utility.**

Let the sceptics fade away.
Hold out the hand to those who yearn
and work to build.
Welcome those who have the fire.
THE NEW ONTARIO HYDRO
It Has Begun.
There's a new Ontario Hydro, born out of a tradition of commitment to Ontario: its industry, its people. We believe it's our responsibility to ensure that a promising, energy-efficient future will be there for all of us and for those who come after.
Reducing the cost of how we operate will help stabilize the cost of electricity. So, as difficult as it may be, we're cutting the cost of our operations, maintenance and administration by at least 25%. And the good news is we're already ahead of schedule. Our customers agree that moves like these will help Ontario businesses compete more efficiently. And that helps keep jobs right where they belong.
"Ontario Hydro is helping us manage our costs. That helps us be more competitive"
John Queenan, Plant Manager, St. Marys Cement Company
If you would like to learn more about how the new Ontario Hydro is helping business, call us at:
1-800-263-9000

## MARKETING AT WORK

### FILE 5-4 SEARS REPOSITIONS TO STAY AHEAD

Facing an increasingly competitive retail industry, in 1994 Sears Canada undertook a major repositioning in order to strengthen its position in a market where it faced aggressive established competitors in the form of Zellers, The Bay, Eaton's, and K mart, and a new threat from Wal-Mart, which was in the position of taking over the 122 Woolco stores in Canada. In revamping the Sears operation, management undertook to present the retailer's stores as more upscale, offering value rather than price alone, and putting its name behind specific brands where it had the potential to dominate a product category. In so doing, Sears undertook to segment its market on psychographic, rather than demographic grounds, thereby creating an image for the chain that would appeal to two major life-style segments of Canadian consumers.

Sears adopted the segmentation approach that had been developed by Goldfarb Consultants of Toronto, who had identified six psychographic groups among Canadian consumers. The retail chain decided to target two of these segments, the "day-to-day watchers," fairly conservative people who tend to conform to popular trends, and the "joiner-activists," less conservative and prepared to embrace new ideas. Working with its advertising agency, Prism Communications, Sears has selected advertising media that are more likely to reach these target market segments.

Beyond the use of psychographics to better target Sears' marketing efforts, the company has undertaken a number of other marketing initiatives, designed to strengthen its position in the new retailing environment. These include:

- Increasing direct marketing efforts by sending specific advertising messages to its data base of more than 7 million Canadian households.
- Undertaking store renovations in those 21 locations where it shares a mall with new Wal-Mart (former Woolco) stores.
- Increasing focus on customer service through employee training.
- Adding more brand names in categories where Sears' brands such as Kenmore and Craftsman have traditionally been prominent in Sears stores.
- Meeting competition, including Wal-Mart, on price.
- Developing distinctive catalogues to reach urban and rural markets.
- Developing direct response television advertising campaigns, so that consumers watching a Sears ad on television can telephone the company's call centre in Belleville on a toll-free number to place an order.

These steps in Sears' strategy illustrate that repositioning is a multidimensional approach to giving a company or its products a new image or "position" in the market and in the minds of consumers. In addition to targeting its efforts at specific groups of consumers, the company is relying on a number of different but related strategic changes to achieve its objective.

Source: James Pollock, "Sears' New Tack," *Marketing*, March 14, 1994, pp. 9-10.

## FORECASTING MARKET DEMAND

As the final step in selecting its target markets, a company should forecast the market demand for its product or service. Forecasting market demand means to estimate the sales-volume size of a company's total market and the sales volume expected in each market segment. This step involves estimating the total industry potential for the company's product in the target market. (This industry figure is called the *market potential* for the product.) Then the seller should estimate its share of this total market. (This company figure is called the *sales potential*.)

The key requirement in demand forecasting is the preparation of a sales forecast, usually for a one-year period. A sales forecast is the foundation of all budgeting and operational planning in all departments of a company — marketing, production, and finance.

## Definition of Some Basic Terms

Before we discuss forecasting methods, we need to define several terms, because they often are used loosely in business.

Market Factor and Market Index  A market factor is an item or element that (1) exists in a market, (2) may be measured quantitatively, and (3) is related to the demand for a product or service. To illustrate, the "number of cars three years old and older" is a market factor underlying the demand for replacement tires. That is, this element affects the number of replacement tires that can be sold. A **market index** is simply a market factor expressed as a percentage, or in some other quantitative form, relative to some base figure. To illustrate, one market factor is "households owning appliance X"; in 1995, the market index for this factor was 132 (relative to 1980 equals 100). An index may also be composed of multiple market factors, such as the number of cars three years old and older, population, and disposable personal income.

Market Potential and Sales Potential  The **market potential** for a product is the total expected sales of that product by all sellers during a stated period of time in a stated market. **Sales potential** (synonymous with **market share**) is the share of a market potential that an individual company expects to achieve.

Thus we may speak of the "market potential" for automatic washing machines, but the "sales potential" (or market share) for one company's brand of machine. In the case of either market potential or sales potential, the market may encompass the entire country, or even the world. Or it may be a smaller market segmented by income, by geographic area, or on some other basis. For example, we may speak of the *market potential* for washing machines in the Atlantic provinces, or the *sales potential* for Whirlpool washers in homes with incomes of $50,000 to $75,000. The market potential and sales potential are the same when a firm has a monopoly in its market, as in the case of some public utilities.

Sales Forecast  A **sales forecast** may be defined as an estimate of sales (in dollars or product units) during some specific future period of time and under a predetermined marketing plan in the firm. A sales forecast can ordinarily be made more intelligently if the company first determines its market and/or sales potential. However, many firms start their forecasting directly with the sales forecast. See Figure 5-3.

**The Sales Forecast and the Marketing Plan.** The marketing goals and broad strategies — the core of a marketing plan — must be established before a sales forecast is made. That is, the sales forecast depends on these predetermined goals and strategies. Certainly, different sales forecasts will result, depending on whether the marketing goal is (1) to liquidate an excess inventory of product A or (2) to expand the firm's market share by aggressive advertising.

However, once the sales forecast is prepared, it does become the key controlling factor in all operational planning throughout the company. The forecast is the basis of sound budgeting. Financial planning for working-capital requirements, plant utilization, and other needs is based on anticipated sales. The scheduling of all production resources and facilities, such as setting labour needs and purchasing supplies and materials, depends on the sales forecast.

**Sales-forecasting Periods.** The most widely used period for sales forecasting is one year, although many firms will review annual forecasts on a monthly or quarterly basis. Annual sales forecasts tie in with annual financial planning and reporting and are often based on estimates of the coming year's general economic conditions.

Forecasts for less than a year may be desirable when activity in the firm's industry is so volatile that it is not feasible to look ahead for a full year. As a case in point, many firms

**FIGURE 5-3**
**A simple approach to demand forecasting.**

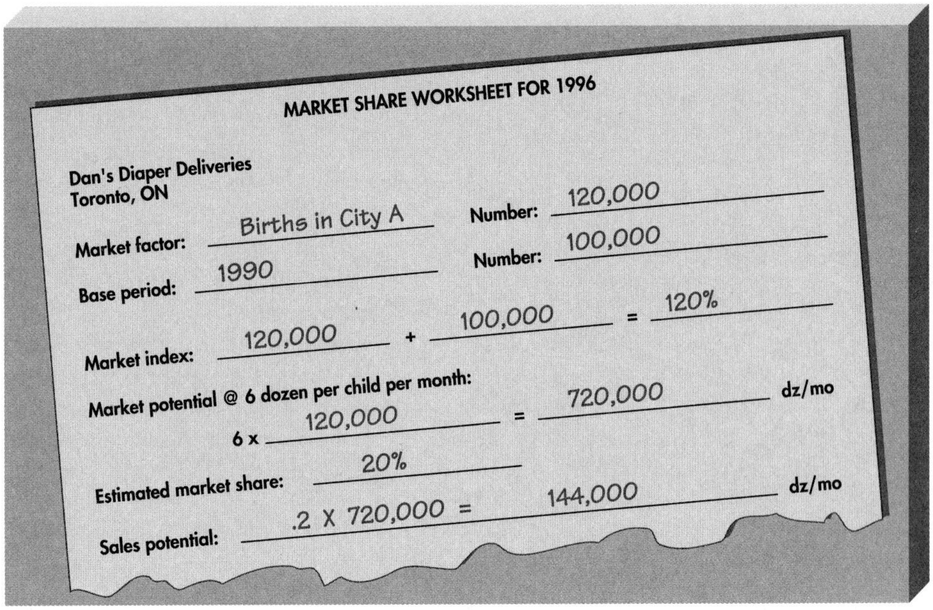


engaged in fashion merchandising — producers and retailers alike — prepare a forecast that covers only one fashion season.

## Methods of Forecasting Demand

A company can forecast its sales by using either of two basic procedures — the "top-down" or the "buildup" approach.[24]

Using the **top-down** (or **breakdown**) approach, management generally would:

1. *start with a forecast of general economic conditions*, as the basis to
2. *determine the industry's total market potential for a product or service*; then
3. *measure the share of this market the firm is getting*; the measurements in items 2 and 3 form the basis to
4. *forecast the sale of the product or service*.

In the **buildup** technique, management would generate estimates of future demand in segments of the market or from organizational units (sales people or branches) in the company. Then management would simply add the individual estimates to get one total forecast.

Predictions of future market demand — whether they are sales forecasts or estimates of market potential — may be based on techniques ranging from uninformed guesses to sophisticated statistical methods. Marketing executives do not need to know how to do the statistical computations. However, they should understand enough about a given technique to appreciate its merits and limitations. They should also know when each method is best used, and they should be able to ask intelligent questions regarding the assumptions underlying the method.

Here are some of the commonly used methods of predicting demand.

**Market-Factor Analysis** This method is based on the assumption that the future demand for a product is related to the behaviour of certain market factors. If we can determine what these factors are and can measure their relationship to sales activity, we can forecast future sales simply by studying the behaviour of the factors.

The key to the successful use of this method lies in the selection of the appropriate market factors. It is also important to minimize the number of market factors used. The greater the number of factors, the greater the chance of erroneous estimates and the more difficult it is to tell how much each factor influences the demand. The two procedures used to translate market-factor behaviour into an estimate of future sales are the direct-derivation method and the correlation-analysis technique.

**Direct Derivation.** Let's illustrate the use of this method to estimate *market potential*. Suppose that a manufacturer of automobile tires wants to know the market potential for replacement tires in Canada in 1996. The primary market factor is the number of automobiles on the road. The first step is to estimate how many cars are likely prospects for new tires. Assume (1) that the seller's studies show that the average car is driven about 16,000 km a year and (2) that the average driver gets about 45,000 km from a set of four tires. This means that all cars that become three years old during 1996 can be considered a part of the potential market for replacement tires during that year. The seller can obtain a reasonably accurate count of the number of cars sold in 1993. (These are the cars that will become three years old in 1996.) The information sources are provincial vehicle licensing offices or private organizations. In addition, the seller can determine how many cars will become 6, 9, or 12 years old in 1996. (These ages are multiples of three. That is, in 1996, a six-year-old car presumably would be ready for its second set of replacement tires.) The number of cars in these age brackets times four (tires per car) should give a fair approximation of the market potential for replacement tires in 1996. We are, of course, dealing in averages. Not all drivers will get 45,000 km from a set of tires, and not all cars will be driven exactly 16,000 km per year.

The direct-derivation method has much to recommend it. It is relatively simple and inexpensive to use, and it requires little statistical analysis. It is reasonably easy to understand, so that executives who are not statistics-oriented can follow the method and interpret the results.

**Correlation Analysis.** This technique is a mathematical refinement of the direct-derivation method. When correlation analysis is used, the degree of association between potential sales of the product and the market factor is taken into account. In effect, a correlation analysis measures, on a scale of 0 to 1, the variations between two series of data. Consequently, this method can be used only when a lengthy sales history of the industry or firm is available, as well as a history of the market factor.

Correlation analysis gives a more exact estimate of market demand, provided that the method is applied correctly. In direct derivation, the correlation measure is implicitly assumed to be 1.00. But rarely does this perfect association exist between a market factor and the sales of a product. Correlation analysis therefore takes the past history into account in predicting the future. It also allows a researcher to incorporate more than one factor into the formula.

There are at least two major limitations to this method. First, as suggested above, a lengthy sales history must be available. To do a really good job, researchers need about 20 periods of sales records. Also, they must assume that approximately the same relationship has existed between the sales and the market factors during this entire period. And, furthermore, they must assume that this relationship will continue in the next sales period. These can be highly unrealistic assumptions. The other major drawback is that not all marketing people understand correlation analysis and can actually do the necessary computations. Thus support of statistical staff may be necessary.

**Survey of Buyer Intentions** Another commonly used method of forecasting is to survey a sample of potential customers. These people are asked how much of the stated product or service they would buy or use at a given price during a specified future time period. Some firms maintain consumer panels on a continuing basis to act as a sounding board for new-product ideas, prices, and other features.

A major problem is that of selecting the sample of potential buyers. For many consumer products, a very large, and thus very costly, sample would be needed. Aside from the extremely high cost and large amount of time this method often entails, there is another very serious limitation. It is one thing for consumers to *intend to buy* a product, but quite another for them to *actually buy* it. Surveys of buying intentions inevitably show an inflated measure of market potential.

Surveys of buying intentions are probably most effective when (1) there are relatively few buyers; (2) these buyers are willing to express their buying intentions; and (3) their past record shows that their follow-up actions are consistent with their stated intentions.

**Test Marketing** In using this technique, a firm markets its products in a limited geographic area. Then, from this sample, management projects the company's sales potential (market share) over a larger area. Test marketing is frequently used in deciding whether sufficient sales potential exists for a new product. The technique also serves as a basis for evaluating various product features and alternative marketing strategies. The outstanding benefit of test marketing is that it can tell management how many people *actually buy* the product, instead of only how many *say they intend* to buy. If a company can afford the time and money for this method, and can run a valid test, this is the best way of measuring the potential for its product.

These are big "ifs," however. Test marketing is expensive in time and money. Great care is needed to control the test-marketing experiment. A competitor, learning you are test marketing, is usually adept at "jamming" your experiment. That is, by unusual promotional or other marketing effort, a competitor can create an artificial situation that distorts your test results. To avoid such test-market "wars," some companies are using simulations of test markets. In effect, these marketers are conducting a test market in a laboratory, rather than in the field.[25]

**Past Sales and Trend Analysis** A favourite method of forecasting is to base the estimate *entirely* on past sales. This technique is used frequently by retailers whose main goal is to "beat last year's figures." The method consists simply of applying a flat percentage increase to the volume achieved last year or to the average volume of the past few years.

This technique is simple, inexpensive, and easy to apply. For a firm operating in a stable market, where its market share has remained constant for a period of years, past sales alone might be used to predict future volume. On balance, however, the method is highly unreliable.

Trend analysis is a variation of forecasting based on past sales, but it is a bit more complicated. It involves either (1) a long-run projection of the sales trend, usually computed by statistical techniques, or (2) a short-run projection (forecasting for only a few months ahead) based upon a seasonal index of sales. The statistical sophistication of long-run trend analysis does not really remove the inherent weakness of basing future estimates only on past sales activity. Short-run trend analysis may be acceptable if the firm's sales follow a reliable seasonal pattern. For example, assume that sales reach 10,000 units in the first quarter (January-March) and, historically, the second quarter is always about 50 percent better. Then we can reasonably forecast sales of 15,000 units in the April-June period.

**Sales-Force Composite** This is a buildup method that may be used to forecast sales or to estimate market potential. As used in sales forecasting, it consists of collecting from all sales people and intermediaries an estimate of sales in their territories during the forecasting period. The total (the composite) of these separate estimates is the company's sales forecast. This method can be used advantageously if the firm has competent high-calibre sales people. The method is also useful for firms selling to a market composed of relatively few, but large, customers. Thus, this method would be more applicable to sales of large electrical generators than small general-use motors.

The sales-force composite method takes advantage of the sales people's specialized knowledge of their own market. Also, it should make them more willing to accept their assigned sales quotas. On the other hand, the sales force usually does not have the time or the experience to do the research needed in forecasting future sales.

**Executive Judgement** This method covers a wide range of possibilities. Basically, it consists of obtaining opinions regarding future sales volume from one or more executives. If these are really informed opinions, based on valid measures such as market-factor analysis, then the executive judgement is useful and desirable. Certainly all the previously discussed forecasting methods should be tempered with sound executive judgement. On the other hand, forecasting by executive opinion alone is risky. In some instances, such opinions are simply intuition or guesswork.

## SUMMARY

One of the most important lessons to be learned concerning the use of market segmentation as a marketing strategy is to get beyond the rather simplistic geographic and demographic bases for segmenting a market. Many marketers today are successful in segmenting markets on psychographic and product-usage bases, which involve targeting products and services at groups of consumers based on their personality and life-style characteristics and on why they select a product, how much of it they use, or how often they buy it.

There are three alternative segmentation strategies that a marketer can choose from when selecting a target market. The three are market aggregation, single-segment concentration, or multiple segmentation. Market aggregation involves using one marketing mix to reach a mass, undifferentiated market. In single-segment concentration, a company still uses only one marketing mix, but it is directed at only one segment of the total market. The third alternative involves selecting two or more segments and then developing a separate marketing mix to reach each one.

The concept of market positioning involves developing a position for a product, brand, retail store, or company in the minds of the members of the target segment or even in the minds of the general public. In essence, it involves management asking what they want the brand or store to be known for, as compared with the customer's image of the competition; what do they want consumers to think of when they hear the brand or store name? The task of creating the right position or image for a brand or store is accomplished through strategic use of the marketing mix variables.

One of the most effective ways to determine the current position that a brand or store occupies in the consumer's mind is to develop a positioning map based on research into consumer perceptions of the various competitors in the market. Such maps may be used to identify gaps in the market, to determine whether there exists a niche towards which a brand may be directed, and to identify a need to reposition a brand for some other reason.

A company may take a number of approaches to position a brand, a retail store, or the company itself in the minds of target consumers: (1) it may decide to take on competitors head-on; (2) it may reposition a brand to occupy a gap in the market; (3) it may decide to distance a brand from its main competitors; (4) it may stake out a position as the market leader; or (5) it may position it to appeal to certain life-style segments. Often a decision is made to reposition a brand or store because of changes that have taken place within the market environment. Decisions to reposition may result from the identification of a market gap, an increase in competitive activity, or a decision to respond to changing consumer demographics, attitudes, and values.

Before deciding on a target market, the company should forecast the demand in the total market and in each segment under consideration. Demand forecasting involves measuring the industry's market potential, then determining the company's sales potential (market share), and finally preparing a sales forecast. The sales forecast is the foundation of all budgeting and operational planning in all major departments of a company. There are several major methods available for forecasting market demand.

## KEY TERMS AND CONCEPTS

**Psychological segmentation (120)**
- **Personality characteristics (120)**
- **Life-styles (121)**
- **Psychographics (121)**
- **List of Values (LOV) (121)**
- **VALS (122)**
- **VALS2 (122)**

**Behavioural segmentation (123)**
- **Benefits desired (123)**
- **Usage rate (125)**

**Target-market strategies (126)**
- **Market aggregation (128)**
- **Product differentiation (128)**

**Single-segment concentration strategy (129)**

**Multiple-segment strategy (130)**

**Positioning (130)**

**Positioning maps (132)**

**Niche marketing (134)**

**Positioning strategies (135)**

**Repositioning (136)**

**Forecasting market demand (137)**
- **Market factor and market index (138)**
- **Market potential and sales potential (138)**
- **Sales forecast (138)**

**Methods of forecasting demand (139)**
- **Top-down (breakdown) (139)**
- **Buildup (139)**
- **Market factor analysis (139)**
- **Survey of buyer intentions (140)**
- **Test marketing (141)**
- **Past sales and trend analysis (141)**
- **Sales-force composite (142)**
- **Executive judgement (142)**

## QUESTIONS AND PROBLEMS

1. Consult back issues of your local newspaper and a number of consumer magazines and identify examples of companies that are positioning their brands to appeal to target life-style segments of the consumer market. Identify examples of other brands that are targeted at consumers on the basis of product usage.
2. Explain the similarities and differences between a single-segment and a multiple-segment target-market strategy.
3. How might the following organizations implement the strategy of market segmentation?
   a. Manufacturer of personal computers.
   b. Canadian Red Cross.
   c. CBC.
   d. Producer of laser-disc style of stereo records.
4. Assume that a company has developed a new type of portable headphone-type cassette player in the general product category of a Sony Walkman. Which of the three target-market strategies should this company adopt?
5. What positioning strategy has each of the following marketers chosen?
   a. Harry Rosen menswear.
   b. Your provincial liquor board or commission.
   c. IKEA furniture stores.
   d. Colgate toothpaste.
   e. Toronto-Dominion Bank.
   f. Mr. Big chocolate bar.
6. Identify a number of brands, retailers, or restaurants with which you are familiar and that have chosen to occupy a niche in the market. How would you describe the niche each occupies? Why do you feel each has chosen this niche?
7. Why would a company decide that one of its brands needs to be repositioned? What market conditions are likely to lead to a decision to reposition a brand or store? Can you think of any brands or stores with which you are familiar that have recently been repositioned? What were their original positions? How would you describe the new positions each occupies in the market? How was the repositioning accomplished in each case?
8. Carefully distinguish between market potential and a sales forecast, using examples of consumer or industrial products.

9. What are some logical market factors that you might use in estimating the market potential for each of the following products?
   a. Central home air conditioners.
   b. Electric milking machines.
   c. Golf clubs.
   d. Sterling flatware.
   e. Safety goggles.
10. How would you determine the market potential for a textbook written for the introductory course in marketing?
11. Explain the direct-derivation method of sales forecasting, using a product example other than automobile tires. How does this forecasting method differ from the correlation-analysis method?
12. What are some of the problems a researcher faces when using the test-market method for determining market potential or sales potential?

## HANDS-ON MARKETING

1. Identify a number of brands of breakfast cereal (both hot and cold) available in supermarkets in your town or city, and indicate how each of the brands is differentiated and how each is positioned to appeal to a specific segment of the market.
2. Prepare a positioning map of the restaurants in the area around your college or university. On what dimensions should the restaurants be positioned? What gaps in the market have you identified?

## NOTES AND REFERENCES


1. Marina Strauss, "Oshawa Group Plans to Fire up Private-Label War," *Globe and Mail*, June 3, 1994, p. B1.
2. Oliver Bertin, "Harley Finds Success Cultivating Closet Brandos," *Globe and Mail*, June 23, 1994, p. B8.
3. Marina Strauss, "CIBC Campaign Keeps It Simple," *Globe and Mail*, March 31, 1994, p. B5.
4. Lynn R. Kahle, Sharon E. Beatty, and Pamela Homer, "Alternative Measurement Approaches to Consumer Values: The List of Values (LOV) and Values and Lifestyles (VAL)," *Journal of Consumer Research*, December 1986, pp. 405-409.
5. James Atlas, "Beyond Demographics," *Atlantic Monthly*, October 1984, pp. 49-58.
6. For a more complete discussion of VALS and VALS2, see William L. Wilkie, *Consumer Behavior*, 2nd ed., John Wiley & Sons, New York, 1990.
7. Rebecca Piirto, "VALS the Second Time," *American Demographics*, July 1991, p. 6.
8. See Russell J. Haley, "Benefit Segmentation: A Decision Oriented Research Tool," *Journal of Marketing*, July 1968, pp. 30-35. For an update on this classic article and the concept of benefit segmentation, see Haley, "Benefit Segmentation — 20 Years Later," *The Journal of Consumer Marketing*, vol. 1, no. 2, 1983, pp. 5-13.
9. Laurie Petersen, "The Strategic Shopper," *Adweek's Marketing Week*, March 30, 1992, pp. 18-20.
10. Joel S. Dubow, "Occasion-Based vs. User-Based Benefit Segmentation: A Case Study," *Journal of Advertising Research*, March/April 1992, pp. 11-18.
11. Victor J. Cook, Jr., and William A. Mindak, "A Search for Constants: The 'Heavy User' Revisited," *The Journal of Consumer Marketing*, vol. 1, no. 4, 1984, pp. 79-81.
12. Mark Maremont, "They're All Screaming for Häagen-Dazs," *Business Week*, October 14, 1991, p. 121.
13. Ann Kerr, "Service Is the Inn Thing as Prices Hit Floor," *Globe and Mail*, September 14, 1993, p. C2.
14. For additional insight into the concept of positioning, the reader is referred to Edward DiMingo, "The Fine Art of Positioning," *The Journal of Business Strategy*, March/April 1988, pp. 34-38; and G. Lynn Shostack, "Service Positioning Through Structural Change," *Journal of Marketing*, vol. 51, January 1987, pp. 34-43.
15. Tamsen Tillson, "CIBC Unveils Bank of the Future," *Globe and Mail*, June 2, 1994, pp. B1, B2.
16. John Saunders and Carolyn Leitch, "Sharp Seeks Graceful Checkout," *Globe and Mail*, May 21, 1994, p. B1.
17. Cathryn Motherwell, "Alberta Brewer Not Just California Dreaming," *Globe and Mail*, August 5, 1993, p. B16.
18. John Partridge, "Citibank Targets Niche Market," *Globe and Mail*, January 12, 1993, p. B12.
19. Danielle Bochove, "Tiny Firm Strikes Gold in Jerusalem," *Globe and Mail*, September 20, 1993, pp. B1, B8.

20. Allan J. Magrath, "Niche Marketing: Finding a Safe, Warm Cave," *Sales and Marketing Management in Canada*, May 1987, p. 40. The reader is also referred to Robert E. Linneman and John L. Stanton, Jr., "Mining for Niches," *Business Horizons*, vol. 35, no. 3, May/June 1992, pp. 43-51.
21. Stan Sutter, "Ikea's Mission: Convincing Consumers It's Grown Up, Too," *Financial Times of Canada*, May 15, 1993, p. 6.
22. Mark Evans, "The Tricky Art of Changing Formats," *The Financial Post*, January 11/13, 1992, p. 3.
23. Christopher Harris, "CBC Opts for Re-positioning," *Globe and Mail*, May 11, 1994, p. A10.
24. For a detailed review of various methods of estimating and forecasting market demand, see James G. Barnes, *Research for Marketing Decision Making*, Toronto: McGraw-Hill Ryerson Limited, 1991, Chapter 5, pp. 83-99.
25. For more detail on the use of test markets and simulated test markets, see James G. Barnes, *Research for Marketing Decision Making*, Toronto: McGraw-Hill Ryerson Limited, 1991, pp. 516-522.

## CHAPTER 6 GOALS

In Chapters 4 and 5, our discussions of market segmentation, positioning, and forecasting focused on the target market. In this chapter, we consider the consumer's *willingness to buy* as determined by information sources, social environment, psychological forces, and situational factors. After studying this chapter, you should have an understanding of:

- The process consumers go through in making purchase decisions.
- The importance of commercial and social information sources in buying decisions.
- The influence of culture, subcultures, and social class characteristics on buying behaviour.
- The direct impact of reference groups on buying behaviour.
- Family and household buying behaviour.
- The roles of motivation, perception, learning, personality, and attitudes in shaping consumer behaviour.
- The importance of situational factors in buying.

CIBC
"I see our time together as very precious... too precious to spend running around doing errands."
Apply for CIBC LinkUp® and enjoy the convenience of banking by phone

CHAPTER 6

# SOCIAL AND PSYCHOLOGICAL INFLUENCES ON BUYER BEHAVIOUR

## "Everyone has a dream"

When Paul Bailey took over as vice-president of marketing services at the Canadian Imperial Bank of Commerce (CIBC), he was concerned that the bank really did not understand what it takes to build close relationships with its customers. One of the first questions that he asked when he arrived at CIBC was whether the bank had ever researched the aspirations of its customers. Bailey had moved to CIBC from London Life, where he had been responsible for the insurance company's "Freedom 55" program and had learned a lot about having a customer focus.

The CIBC had been running an advertising campaign that featured bank employees and a conventional product-oriented appeal. Bailey launched a research program to better understand how consumers feel about life. "When I came in, CIBC had researched what people thought about banks but not their hopes, dreams, and aspirations. So we set up focus groups around the country where people simply talked about themselves — where they were going in their lives, the pressures they felt, their aspirations for themselves and their families," he explained. The focus groups revealed that most Canadians dream about home ownership, travel, saving for retirement and education, and buying things like new cars and boats. Not exactly earth-shattering news, but results that gave Paul Bailey a clear direction for a new advertising campaign.

He handed the assignment to Padulo Advertising of Toronto, the agency that had been handling CIBC's direct-mail account. Padulo came up with the Personal Vision campaign, positioning CIBC as a bank that will help people achieve their dreams. The new campaign takes the emphasis off the bank's products and focuses on helping customers achieve their dreams. Richard Padulo, the agency's CEO observed, "Everyone has hopes, and we wanted to speak to that. No one wants a mortgage for the rest of their lives, but everyone dreams of being a homeowner. People want a car, but not a car loan."

By focusing on customers' dreams and how they might be achieved, the CIBC is emphasizing an understanding of consumer psychology and needs that is often not revealed in advertising. The Personal Vision ad for CIBC LinkUp, the bank's bank-by-phone service, addresses the consumer's need for time to spend with family. CIBC travel and medical insurance promotes peace of mind and freedom from worry. This theme is carried through all of the bank's advertising — television, radio, business newspaper ads, direct mail, and in-branch materials — focusing on the customers' Personal Vision and on how CIBC can help them realize their dreams.[1]

As this CIBC example illustrates, marketing to consumers has become more complicated. The reason is simple. The domestic and international marketplaces have become more competitive and complex, and our understanding of consumer buying behaviour is constantly improving. But there is much more to learn. And because marketing success largely depends on the ability to anticipate what buyers will do, in this chapter we examine the challenging topic of consumer buying behaviour. First we develop an overview with a description of the buying-decision process. Next we consider the sources of information used by consumers — without information there are no decisions. We then describe the various social and group forces in society that influence decision making and the psychological characteristics of the individual that affect the decision process in buying. In the final section, our focus shifts to the role in buying played by situational factors.

Figure 6-1 brings all the dimensions of buying behaviour together in a model that provides the structure for our discussion. The model features a six-stage **buying-decision process** influenced by four primary forces.

## DECISION MAKING AS PROBLEM SOLVING

To deal with the marketing environment and make purchases, consumers engage in a decision process. The process, which divides nicely into six stages, can be thought of as a problem-solving approach. When faced with a buying problem ("I'm bored. How do I satisfy my need for entertainment?"), the consumer goes through a series of logical stages to arrive at a decision.

As shown in the centre of Figure 6-1, the stages are:

1. *Need recognition:* The consumer is moved to action by a need.
2. *Choice of an involvement level:* The consumer decides how much time and effort to invest in the remaining stages.
3. *Identification of alternatives:* The consumer collects information about products and brands.
4. *Evaluation of alternatives:* The consumer weighs the pros and cons of the alternatives identified.
5. *Purchase and related decisions:* The consumer decides to buy or not to buy.
6. *Postpurchase behaviour:* The consumer seeks reassurance that the choice made was the correct one.

**FIGURE 6-1**
**The consumer buying-decision process and the factors that influence it.**

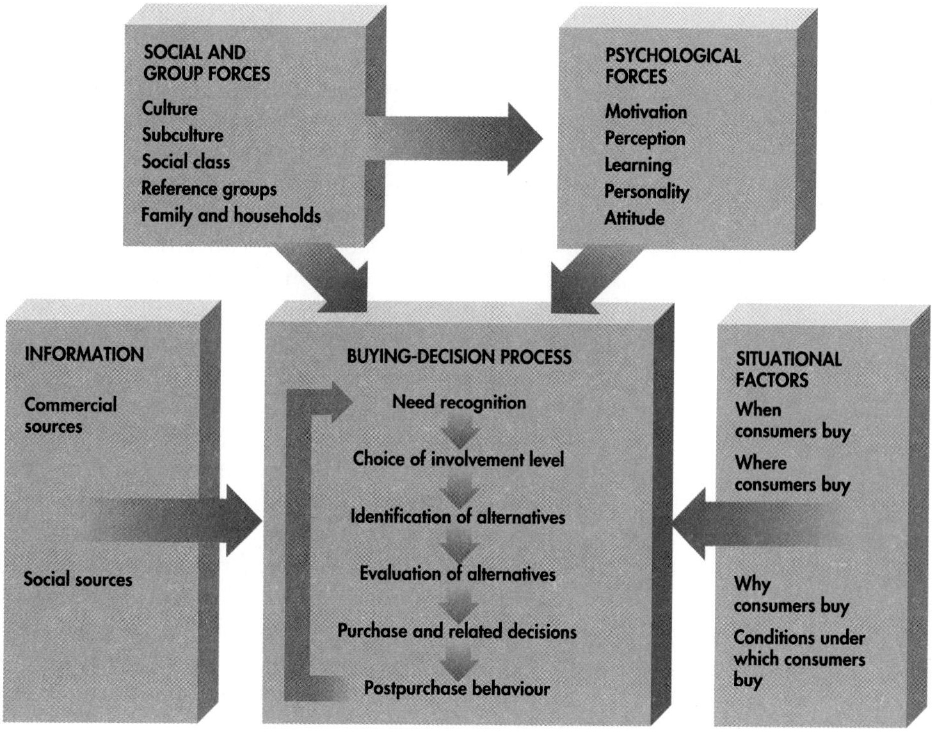


Though this model is a useful starting point for examining purchase decisions, the process is not always as straightforward as it may appear. Consider these variations:

- The consumer can withdraw at any stage prior to the actual purchase. If, for example, the need diminishes or no satisfactory alternatives are available, the process will come to an abrupt end.
- It is not uncommon for some stages to be skipped. All six stages are likely to be used only in certain buying situations — for instance, when buying high-priced, infrequently purchased items. However, for frequently purchased, familiar products, purchasing is routine. The aroused need is satisfied by repurchasing a familiar brand, and the third and fourth stages are bypassed.
- The stages are not necessarily of the same length. When a mechanic tells you that your car's engine needs an overhaul, it may take only a moment to recognize the need for a new car. However, the identification and evaluation of alternative models may go on for weeks.
- Some stages may be performed consciously in certain purchase situations and subconsciously in others. For example, we don't consciously calculate for every purchase the amount of time and effort we will put forth. Yet the fact that we spend more time on some purchases and less on others indicates that level of involvement is part of the process.

In the following discussion we assume that this six-stage process generally characterizes buying decisions. However, keep in mind that the stages may have to be adjusted to fit the circumstances of a particular purchase situation.

### 1. Recognition of an Unsatisfied Need

The process begins when an unsatisfied need creates tension or discomfort. This condition may arise internally (for example, a person feels hungry). Or the need may be dormant until it is aroused by an external stimulus, such as an ad or the sight of a product. Another possible source of tension is dissatisfaction with a product currently being used.

Once the need has been recognized, consumers often become aware of conflicting or competing uses for their scarce resources of time and money. Let's say a student wants to purchase a personal computer for school, but for the same amount of money she could buy a nice stereo on sale. Or she is concerned that if she buys the computer her friends will think she is becoming "too studious." She must resolve these conflicts before proceeding. Otherwise the buying process stops.

### 2. Choice of an Involvement Level

Very early in the process the consumer consciously or subconsciously decides how much effort to exert in satisfying a need. Sometimes when a need arises, a consumer is dissatisfied with the quantity or quality of information about the purchase situation and decides to actively collect and evaluate more. These are **high-involvement** purchases that entail all six stages of the buying-decision process. If, on the other hand, a consumer is comfortable with the information and alternatives readily available, the purchase situation is viewed as **low involvement**. In such a case, the buyer will likely skip directly from need recognition to purchase, ignoring the stages in between.

Some of the major differences in consumer behaviour in high- and low-involvement situations are:

| Behaviour | High involvement | Low involvement |
|---|---|---|
| **Time invested** | **Large amount** | **Small amount** |
| **Information search** | **Active** | **Little or none** |
| **Response to information** | **Critically evaluate** | **Ignore or accept without evaluation** |
| **Brand evaluations** | **Clear and distinct** | **Vague and general** |
| **Likelihood of brand loyalty developing** | **Strong** | **Weak** |

Though it is somewhat risky to generalize since all consumers are different, involvement tends to be greater under any of the following conditions:

- The consumer lacks information about the purchase.
- The product is viewed as important.
- The risk of making a bad decision is perceived as high.
- The product has considerable social importance.
- The product is seen as having a potential for providing significant benefits.

Since they rarely meet any of these conditions, most buying decisions for relatively low-priced products that have close substitutes would be low-involvement. Typical examples are the majority of items sold in supermarkets, variety stores, and hardware stores. However, for a wealthy person the purchase of a car could be a low-involvement experience, while for a person with a high need for social acceptance, purchasing toothpaste might be highly involving. Thus it is important to remember that involvement must be viewed from the perspective of the consumer, not the product.

**Impulse buying**, or purchasing with little or no advance planning, is an important form of low-involvement decision making. A shopper who goes to the grocery store with

**High-involvement purchases include all six buying-decision stages.**

the intention of buying meat and bread and on noticing a display of peaches at an attractive price decides to buy some engages in impulse buying.

Self-service, open-display retailing has conditioned shoppers to postpone planning and engage in more impulse buying. Because of the growth of this type of low-involvement purchasing, greater emphasis must be placed on promotional programs to get shoppers into a store. Also, displays and packages must be made appealing since they serve as silent sales people.

### 3. Identification of Alternatives

Once a need has been recognized and the level of involvement is selected, the consumer must next identify the alternatives capable of satisfying the need. First, alternative products and then alternative brands are identified. Product and brand identification may range from a simple memory scan of previous experiences to an extensive external search. Consider this example. Suppose a couple decides not to cook but to have an already-prepared item for their evening meal. Identifying alternatives might entail checking the freezer to see if any frozen dinners are on hand, examining the newspaper for specials or discount coupons, and recalling a radio advertisement that described a new restaurant.

The search for alternatives is influenced by:

- How much information the consumer already has from past experiences and other sources.
- The consumer's confidence in that information.
- The expected value of additional information or, put another way, what the additional information is worth in terms of the time and money costs to get it.

### 4. Evaluation of Alternatives

Once all the reasonable alternatives have been identified, the consumer must evaluate them before making a decision. The evaluation involves establishing some criteria against which each alternative is compared. In the preceding meal example, the decision maker may have a single criterion ("How quickly can we complete the meal?") or several criteria (speed, taste, nutrition, and price). When multiple criteria are involved, they typically do not carry equal weight. For example, preparation time might be more important than nutrition.

The criteria that consumers use in the evaluation result from their past experience and feelings towards various brands, as well as the opinions of family members and friends. Differences in the criteria or in the relative importance that different consumers place on them are what determine market segments.

Because experience is often limited or dated and information from sources such as advertising or friends can be biased, evaluations can be factually incorrect. That is, a consumer may believe that the price of brand A is higher than that of brand B, when in fact the opposite is true. Marketers monitor consumers to determine what choice criteria they use, to identify any changes that may be taking place in their criteria, and to correct any damaging misperceptions.

### 5. Purchase and Related Decisions

After searching and evaluating, the consumer must decide whether to buy. Thus the first outcome is the decision to purchase or not to purchase the alternative evaluated as most desirable. If the decision is to buy, a series of related decisions must be made regarding features, where and when to make the actual transaction, how to take delivery or possession, the method of payment, and other issues. So the decision to make a purchase is really the beginning of an entirely new series of decisions that may be as time-consuming and difficult as the initial one. Alert marketers recognize that the outcome of these additional decisions affects satisfaction, so they find ways to help consumers make them as efficiently as possible. For example, car dealers have speeded up loan approval, streamlined the process of tracking down a car that meets the buyer's exact specifications, and made delivery of the car a "miniceremony" to make the customer feel important.

Selecting a source from which to make a purchase is one of the buying decisions. Sources can be as varied as mail-order houses or manufacturers' outlets. The most common source is a retail store, and the reasons a consumer chooses to shop at a certain store are called **patronage buying motives**. People want to feel comfortable when they shop. They want the assurance of being around people like themselves and in an environment that reflects their values. There are consumers, for example, who would feel uncomfortable shopping in an upscale store such as Holt Renfrew.

Patronage motives can range from something as simple as convenience when you want a soft drink, to something more complex, such as the atmosphere of a restaurant. For example, there has been a resurgence in the popularity of diners, simple restaurants with informal surroundings that offer home-style cooking at moderate prices. Many attract a loyal following with a design that is reminiscent of the roadside diners that were commonplace along highways in the 1950s.[2]

Some common patronage motives are:

- Location convenience
- Service speed
- Merchandise accessibility
- Crowding
- Prices
- Merchandise assortment
- Services offered
- Store appearance
- Sales personnel
- Mix of other shoppers

Like the criteria consumers use to choose products and brands, their patronage motives will vary depending on the purchase situation. Successful retailers evaluate their target customers carefully and design their stores accordingly. For example, some shoppers might be surprised to learn that such different women's wear stores as Braemar, Fairweather, Fashion Rack, La Senza, Suzy Shier, and LA Express all are operated by Dylex Ltd. A manufacturer, in turn, selects retailers with the patronage characteristics that complement its product and appeal to the desired target market.

The marketing concept emphasizes customer satisfaction, yet only in the last few years has a serious effort been made to understand what satisfaction means. The level of **satisfaction** is determined when a consumer compares the *performance expected* from a product with the *performance experienced* in consuming the product.[3] If performance equals or exceeds expectations, the consumer is satisfied. However, if performance falls short of expectation, dissatisfaction results. Consumers' expectations come from past product use, information from social sources, and sales presentations and advertising.

Establishing and maintaining a balance between expectations and experience is tricky. It requires more than making a good product. Consider two examples of how expectations and experience can be distorted:

- Because advertising claims and sales presentations influence expectations, marketers must be careful not to promise more than can be delivered. If expectations are created but not fulfilled, consumers will certainly be disappointed and future sales will be lost.
- Marketers must also do what they can to see that consumers use products properly. If a consumer runs a snowblower on an incorrect mixture of gas and oil or overloads a washing machine, problems will result and expectations will not be met. As a result, marketers work hard through product design, printed instructions, demonstrations, and even training to ensure that products are used correctly.

### Postpurchase Behaviour

What a consumer learns from going through the buying process has an influence on how he or she will behave the next time the same need arises. Having gathered information, evaluated alternatives, and arrived at a decision, the consumer has acquired additional knowledge about the product and various brands. Furthermore, new opinions and beliefs have been formed and old ones have been revised. It's this change in the consumer that is indicated by an arrow in Figure 6-1 from the **postpurchase behaviour** stage of the buying-decision process model back to the need-recognition stage.

Something else often occurs following a purchase. Have you ever gone through a careful decision process for a major purchase (say, a set of tires for your car or an expensive item of clothing), selected what you thought was the best alternative, but then had doubts about your choice after the purchase? What you were experiencing is postpurchase **cognitive dissonance** — a state of anxiety brought on by the difficulty of choosing from among several alternatives. Unfortunately for marketers, dissonance is quite common; and if the anxiety is not relieved, the consumer may be unhappy with the chosen product even if it performs adequately!

Postpurchase cognitive dissonance occurs when each of the alternatives seriously considered by the consumer has both attractive and unattractive features. For example, in purchasing tires, the set selected may be the most expensive (unattractive), but they provide better traction on wet roads (attractive). The brand not chosen was recommended by a friend (attractive), but came with a very limited warranty (unattractive). After the purchase is made, the unattractive features of the product purchased grow in importance in the consumer's mind, as do the attractive features offered by the rejected alternatives. As a result, we begin to doubt the wisdom of the choice and experience anxiety over the decision.

Dissonance typically increases: (1) the higher the dollar value of the purchase; (2) the greater the similarity between the item selected and item(s) rejected; and (3) the greater the importance of the purchase decision. Thus buying a house or car creates more dissonance than buying a candy bar.

Consumers try to reduce their postpurchase anxieties. They avoid information (such as ads for the rejected products) that is likely to increase the dissonance. And they seek out information that supports their decision, even to the extreme of reading ads for a product after it has been purchased. Also, prior to the purchase, putting more effort into evaluating alternatives can increase a consumer's confidence and reduce dissonance.

Some useful generalizations can be developed from the theory of cognitive dissonance. For example, anything sellers can do in their advertising or personal selling to reassure buyers — say, by stressing the number of satisfied owners — will reduce dissonance. Also, the quality of a seller's follow-up and postsale service programs can be significant factors in reducing dissonance.

With this background on the buying-decision process, we can examine what influences buying behaviour. We'll begin with the sources and types of information used by consumers.

## INFORMATION AND PURCHASE DECISIONS

Consumers must find out what products and brands are available, what features and benefits they offer, who sells them at what prices, and where they can be purchased. Without this market information there wouldn't be a decision process because there wouldn't be any decisions to make.

## MARKETING AT WORK

### FILE 6-1 GETTING INFORMATION, NEGOTIATING, AND DECISION MAKING MADE EASY

Many people hate having to go out and buy a car. Might it have something to do with all the confusion, haggling, and pressure they know they're doomed to confront on the showroom floor? Might it have something to do with not knowing what you think you ought to know to make a good decision? To boot, if you're a woman, you probably find — as did 66 percent of women in a *Chatelaine* magazine survey — that you don't get taken very seriously by sales staff.

All in all, recent consumer studies show that frustration with the retail end of the automobile industry is high. And though a few automobile dealers have attempted to change by adopting no-dicker pricing — a strategy in which dealers attach a non-negotiable price tag to every car in their inventory — the majority of dealers still prefer a system that relies on haggling and information overload.

What's a poor uninformed car shopper to do? Simple. Let Car$mart give you the real low-down. For a $100 fee, Jim Davidson, a former car salesman who founded the Toronto-based car-buying consulting service, recommends car makes and models that suit his customers' needs before leading clients through a step-by-step method of how to negotiate a purchase. If you want, he'll even go a few steps further — accompany you on a test drive or even shop the market for a good price and set up a dealer appointment for you.

"Originally I thought my service would mainly appeal to women, senior citizens, or first-time car buyers," says Davidson. "But a lot of my customers have been professionals who just don't have the time and detest the whole process. It's almost impossible to get accurate, unbiased information in this industry and when you're only in the market once every six years, it's really hard to become an overnight expert."

Source: Adapted from Laura Fowlie, "Easing the Car-Buying Hassle," *Financial Post*, March 13, 1993, p. 18.

What are some of the sources and types of information that exist in the buying environment? As shown in Figure 6-1 two information sources, the commercial environment and the social environment, influence the buying-decision process. The **commercial information** environment consists of all marketing organizations and individuals that attempt to communicate with consumers. It includes manufacturers, retailers, advertisers, and sales people whenever any of them are engaged in efforts to inform or persuade. The other source is the **social information** environment made up of family, friends, and acquaintances who directly or indirectly provide information about products. If you think for a moment about how often your conversation with friends or family deals with purchases you are considering or those you have made, you will begin to appreciate the marketing significance of these social sources.

Advertising is the most common type of commercial information. Other commercial sources are direct sales efforts by store clerks, telemarketing, and direct mail to consumers' homes, as well as consumers' physical involvement with products (examining packages, trial product use, and sampling).

The normal kind of social information is word-of-mouth communication, in which two or more people simply have a conversation about a product. Other social sources include the observations of others using products and exposure to products in the homes of others.

When all the different types of information are taken into consideration, it becomes apparent that there is enormous competition for the consumer's attention. It was recently estimated that the typical adult is exposed to about 300 ad messages a day, or almost 10,000 per month.[4] Coincidentally, the consumer's mind has to be a marvellously efficient machine to sort and process this barrage of information. To understand how the consumer functions, we will begin by examining the social and group forces that influence the individual's psychological makeup and also play a role in specific buying decisions.

**The EnerGuide label is a form of commercial information available to purchasers of appliances.**

What To Look For
In A New Appliance.
It's black and white and rectangular.
You can find it on every new refrigerator, freezer, clothes washer, dryer, range and dishwasher sold in Canada.
It's the new EnerGuide label and it shows the typical amount of energy an appliance will use *in one year*. By looking at the label, you can compare the energy consumption of one appliance to others with similar features.
The lower the number, the more energy efficient the appliance. It's that simple.
ENERGUIDE
684 kWh
If you consider that a modern refrigerator can often last up to 20 years, choosing an energy efficient model today can add up to a lot of savings over the lifetime of the appliance.
So become an energy wise consumer. The next time you're shopping for an appliance, look for the EnerGuide label.
Choose the appliance that's the least power hungry. You'll save money and help the environment at the same time.
And isn't that what everybody is looking for?
It pays to read the new EnerGuide Label
Energy, Mines and Resources Canada
Énergie, Mines et Ressources Canada
Canada


## SOCIAL AND GROUP FORCES

The way we think, believe, and act is determined to a great extent by social forces and groups. In addition, our individual buying decisions — including the needs we experience, the alternatives we consider, and the way in which we evaluate them — are affected by the social forces that surround us. To reflect this dual impact, the arrows in Figure 6-1 extend from the social and group forces in two directions — to the psychological makeup of the individual and to the buying-decision process. Our description begins with culture, the force with the most *indirect* impact, and moves to the force with the most *direct* impact, the household.

### Definition of Culture and Cultural Influence

A **culture** is the complex of symbols and artifacts created by a given society and handed down from generation to generation as determinants and regulators of human behaviour. The symbols may be intangible (attitudes, beliefs, values, languages, religions) or tangible (tools, housing, products, works of art). A culture implies a totally learned and "handed-down" way of life. It does *not* include instinctive acts. However, standards for performing instinctive biological acts (eating, eliminating body wastes, and sexual relationships) can be culturally established. Thus everybody gets hungry, but what people eat and how they act to satisfy the hunger drive will vary among cultures.

Actually, much of our behaviour is culturally determined. Our sociocultural institutions (family, schools, churches, and languages) provide behavioural guidelines. Years ago, Kluckhohn observed: "Culture . . . regulates our lives at every turn. From the moment we are born until we die there is constant conscious and unconscious pressure upon us to follow certain types of behaviour that other men have created for us."[5] People living in a culture share a whole set of similarities — and these can be different from those in or from another culture.

### Cultural Change

Cultural influences do change over time, as old patterns gradually give way to the new. During the past 10 to 25 years, cultural changes — that is, life-style changes — of far-reaching magnitude have been occurring. Marketing executives must be alert to these changing life-styles so that they can adjust their planning to be in step with, or even a little ahead of, the times. In Chapter 2 we mentioned some of these cultural changes when we discussed social and cultural forces as an environmental factor influencing a company's marketing system. Now at this point we shall simply summarize a few of the sociocultural changes that significantly affect consumer buying behaviour.

- *Time has become as valuable as money*. Canadians feel overcommitted, with more obligations and demands on their time than they can fulfil. Across all demographic groups, they are willing to sacrifice some income for more time. They also would like more leisure time, despite the fact that on average Canadians actually have more free time now than they did in the recent past.
- *Two-income families are the norm*. Families with two incomes are no longer the exception. Some view it as a necessity to achieve a reasonable standard of living. For others, particularly households that include two professionals, it has made the ownership of many luxuries possible. When both adults in a household work outside the home, it affects not only the ability to buy, but also the choice of products and the time in which to buy and consume them.
- *Gender roles are losing their identity*. The distinction between the roles of men and women or husbands and wives is becoming less clear. It is reflected in educational opportunities, careers, clothing, and language.
- *Young and healthy is in, old and sick is out*. Canadians want to be fit and stay active. To be thought of as younger than your chronological age (once you're over 21!) is seen by most as a compliment. To remain healthy and free from disease, Canadians have made exercise a regular part of their lives and changed their eating and drinking behaviour. The growing opposition to smoking and alcohol consumption reflects this trend.

### Subcultures

Given the multicultural nature of Canadian society, marketers should understand the concept of subcultures and analyze them as potentially profitable market segments. Any

You Decide
BRAN
Catelli Healthy Harvest Moisson Santé
Catelli Healthy Harvest Moisson Santé SPAGHETTI
Healthy
True, this bag of bran contains many of the dietary requirements you need to maintain a healthy lifestyle. But it lacks any taste or excitement as food. There is a better way.
Healthy Harvest™
Healthy Harvest™ Pastas and Sauces are low in fat and high in fibre. What makes them different is that they are good for you and they taste great. Healthy Harvest™ is a delicious way to eat healthy.
Healthy Harvest™ Pasta and Sauce Make A Great Tasting Nutritional Dish.
Catelli
Healthy Harvest
Healthy Made Delicious.

**Advertisers such as Catelli take advantage of consumers' interest in healthy living by developing appropriate new products.**

time there is a culture as heterogeneous as ours, there are bound to be significant subcultures based upon factors such as race, nationality, religion, geographic location, age, and urban-rural distribution. Some of these were recognized in Chapter 4, when we analyzed the demographic market factors. Ethnicity, for example, is a cultural factor that has significant marketing implications. Concentrations of Middle or Eastern Europeans in the Prairies provide a market for some products that would go unnoticed in Italian or Chinese sections of Toronto.

The cultural diversity of the Canadian market has taken on increased importance for some companies in recent years. Twenty years ago, most companies ignored the ethnic market, but the Canadian census shows that almost 40 percent of Canada's population had origins other than British, French, or native. Slightly more than 4 million Canadians claimed a mother tongue other than English or French.

The most obvious efforts to reach ethnic market segments are, of course, found in major urban markets such as Toronto and Vancouver. In Toronto, for example, a multicultural television channel, MTV, carries European soccer and other programming directed to ethnic markets. These and similar media represent attractive advertising outlets for companies who wish to reach this growing market segment.

The sharpest subcultural differences are portrayed in behavioural differences between English- and French-Canadian communities on a country-wide basis, although to the urban dweller in Toronto or Montreal the acceptance (or ritual avoidance) of the obvious differences between a diversity of ethnic minorities is now a matter of course. As indicated in Chapter 4, marketing to French Canada involves considerably more than cursory acknowledgement of ethnic differences.

### The Changing Nature of the French-Canadian Market

French Canada, as a subculture, has undergone a revolution during the past 30 years. This has had a profound effect on the nature of the French-Canadian market.

French Canadians have taken major steps to preserve their cultural identity in the English-dominated North American society and to prevent the assimilation of French Canada into this society. They developed programs to preserve the French language, improved health and education programs, and renewed interest in French-Canadian crafts and culture. The roles of religion, the family, and women have changed dramatically during this revolutionary period. No longer do the traditional professions of the

## MARKETING AT WORK

### FILE 6-2 INTERNATIONAL MARKETS — BECOMING MORE CULTURALLY SIMILAR?

Many changes will ensue now that trade barriers between the members of the European Union (formerly called the European Economic Community) are being removed to create a single European market. Among the most significant benefits are 5 to 6 million new jobs in Europe, an increase in the European gross national product of 6 percent, and more goods and services for consumers to choose from. But there are also problems for marketers related to the different cultures. Even without trade restrictions, differences in languages, tastes, customs, climates, and distribution systems hamper the development of a single market.

Some firms are now experiencing problems because their previous marketing efforts were geared to distinct national markets. For example:

- Lever Europe has a fabric softener sold in 10 European countries under seven names, in different containers, and sometimes with different formulations. The names, packages, and product designs were originally intended to complement local language and tastes. However, the cost of manufacturing and marketing so many brands puts Lever at a differential disadvantage as the European markets become more integrated. The solution seems easy: Standardize. The problem with the solution: Consumers have become accustomed to the existing brands, and changes in the names, packages, or formulations could be devastating. To go from selling Cif, its liquid cleaner, in an orange bottle to a white bottle, for example, was a major undertaking for Lever. First, an ad campaign showed the new bottle. Then, to ease the transition, the new bottle was initially sold in an orange wrapper that the consumer had to peel off.
- In an effort to standardize its products, Mars, Inc., has eliminated highly successful European brand names. In Britain, the Marathon chocolate bar was renamed Snickers. Europe's most successful chocolate biscuit, the Raider, became Twix. And Bonitos in France are now called M&Ms. Although costly, these efforts were less complicated than what the firm is faced with in trying to standardize Milky Way and Mars bars. Both brands exist worldwide, but they are different products in different places!

The problems for a new entrant to the European market may be less severe. Whirlpool, virtually unknown in Europe before 1989, evaluated more than 20 proposed advertising campaigns before selecting one that was designed to appeal to consumers across all of Western Europe. Emphasizing high technology and the desire for more free time, Whirlpool has achieved a high level of awareness and positive associations for its home appliances in several countries.

Source: E. S. Browning, "In Pursuit of the Elusive Euroconsumer," *The Wall Street Journal*, April 23, 1992, p. B1.

priesthood, law, and medicine dominate the cultural hierarchy. A new middle class has developed in French Canada that is less traditional in its outlook and is more attuned to youth and business. The Quebec business scene is vibrant and entrepreneurial. New, exciting opportunities are developing for Quebec-owned businesses and hundreds of new businesses have been established in the province in recent years. Quebec now accounts for more than one-third of all business graduates from Canadian universities.

### Differences in Consumption Behaviour

Cultural differences lead to differences in consumption behaviour between English and French Canadians. Certain products sell in much larger quantities in Quebec than in other provinces, while other products that sell well in English Canada are rarely purchased by French Canadians. Some examples of differences in product preferences and buying behaviour follow.[6]

**"Coming Home to Dempster's" is communicated to Greek-speaking customers.**

- There is a better acceptance in Quebec of premium-priced products such as premium-grade gasoline and expensive liquors.
- French Canadians spend more per capita on clothing, personal care items, tobacco, and alcoholic beverages.
- The French Canadian consumes more soft drinks, maple sugar, molasses, and candy per capita than does the English Canadian.
- French Canadians have much higher consumption rates for instant and decaffeinated coffee.
- French Canadians watch more television and listen to radio more than do English Canadians.
- Premiums and coupons are more popular in Quebec.
- French Canadians buy more headache and cold remedies than do English Canadians.
- In many Quebec homes a full meal is served both at noon and in the evening.
- French-Canadian consumers may experience higher levels of dissatisfaction with repairs and general consumer services and with professional and personal services than is the case for English-speaking Canadians.[7]

### Factors Influencing French-English Consumption Differences

Although it is relatively easy to determine where actual differences in consumption behaviour exist between French and English Canadians, it is somewhat more difficult to identify reasons for the existence of such differences. And yet, it is important for marketers to have some understanding of the factors that contribute to these differences if they are to market effectively to both market segments.

In the past, authors have pointed out that French Canadians have a lower per capita income than do English Canadians, that they have lower average education levels, and that they are a much more rural population. These differences along income and other demographic lines might suggest that the differences in product purchase rates and shopping behaviour between French Canadians and English Canadians may be attributable simply to demographic differences and that the consumption behaviour of French Canadians is really no different from that of English Canadians with similar demographic characteristics. At least two studies have refuted this argument.

An early one indicated that consumption behaviour was significantly different between Quebec and Ontario households when households of *similar size and income levels were compared*.[8] A second study found significant differences in household expenditure levels between English-Canadian and French-Canadian households for eight consumption expenditure categories after certain noncultural differences (such as the rural-urban breakdown of the groups and stage of the family life cycle) between the two groups were controlled.[9] Such findings suggest that the consumption behaviour differences between French and English Canadians are not attributable solely to demographic differences but, rather, are more likely explained by cultural differences.

### The Impact of Cultural Differences on Marketing

The fact that French Canada represents a distinctively different culture from that found in English Canada requires that marketers who wish to be successful in the French-Canadian market develop unique marketing programs for this segment. There must be an appreciation of the fact that certain products will not be successful in French Canada simply because they are not appropriate to the French-Canadian culture and life-style. In other cases, products that are successful in English Canada must be marketed differently in French Canada because the French Canadian has a different perception of these products and the way in which they are used. It may be necessary for companies to develop new products or appropriate variations of existing products specifically for the French-Canadian market. Similarly, the retail buying behaviour of French Canadians may necessitate the use of different channels of distribution in Quebec.

In the area of advertising, many national companies have encountered problems in reaching the French-Canadian market. In the past, much of the national advertising in Canada was prepared by English-Canadian advertising agencies (usually based in Toronto) that developed advertisements for use in both English and French Canada. These agencies generally employed translators whose responsibility it was to translate the advertisements, which had been developed by English Canadians for the English culture, so that they might be used in the Quebec market. In many cases, literal translations were demanded and the end results were inappropriate for the French market.

The challenges of advertising in French Canada go far beyond those of translating English to French. Even where the translation is a good one and English expressions and slang are converted into expressions that are meaningful to French Canadians, the problem still remains that the basic approach to the advertisement is based in English-Canadian or even American culture. Many advertisements contain illustrations, themes, and representations of life-styles that are quite appropriate in English Canada but quite inappropriate in Quebec. What is needed is that advertising to be directed to the French-Canadian market be planned from "scratch" with that market in mind. The advertising content must be consistent with the culture of the market, and this requires that it be developed and written by French Canadians. Many national advertisers now place their English-language advertising with an English-Canadian agency, but use a Montreal-based French-language agency to develop advertising for the Quebec market.[10]

## REFERENCE GROUP INFLUENCES

Consumers' perceptions and buying behaviour are also influenced by the reference groups to which they belong. These groups include the large social classes and smaller reference groups. The smallest, yet usually the strongest, social-group influence is a person's family.

## MARKETING AT WORK

### FILE 6-3 THE QUEBEC MARKET: THE DIFFERENCES CONTINUE

In contrast with Canada's other provinces, Quebecers make the fewest long-distance phone calls, give the least to charity, buy more lottery tickets, eat more pasta, use more laxatives, and drink more gin. They also possess that ever intangible but undeniable "*joie de vivre*" — a combination of passion, impulsiveness, open sexuality, and provocative humour that sets them apart from English Canada and allows for BMW ads to be run in which breasts are bared, while in the rest of Canada one sees only bras.

These days, with advertising becoming "globalized" in an efficient attempt to appeal to greater worldwide similarities, Quebec provides an exception, an example of a new "tribalism" that defines the powerful regional marketing campaigns geared expressly towards the province. So don't go selling Quebecers Pepsi using Michael Jackson commercials. With 90 percent of the province's most popular TV shows being local productions and an entire tabloid and magazine industry that caters to a stable of home-grown stars such as Roch Voisine and Céline Dion, American icons — while hits in the rest of the country — fall flat here. It wasn't Jackson, but Montreal comedian Claude Meunier, whose irreverent send-ups of provincial stereotypes sent Quebecers buying Pepsi in droves, making it one of the few provinces in Canada in which Pepsi is the number one soft drink. Sorry, Coca-Cola and the U.S.A., but if you want to do business in Quebec, you have to do it on Quebec's terms. Which up until recently has meant devising an English advertising campaign in Toronto or New York — one that is logical and explains the features and benefits of a product — and then a separate French campaign in Montreal — appealing to Quebecers' passions, off-beat humour, and more "modern" views on the environment, equality of women, and human rights. Lately, however, the tides have begun to turn. With advertisers preferring the increased efficiency of working with only one agency, more and more Montreal ad firms are being handed entire national accounts, in both French and English. Big firms such as General Motors of Canada Ltd., BMW Canada, and Labatt Dry have already jumped on the Montreal bandwagon, much to the chagrin of their Toronto counterparts, who claim the English ads are written in a sort of "franglais."

Yet it would be a mistake to write off the Quebec phenomenon as a simple language showdown between Francophone Quebec and Anglophone Canada, for that would be ignoring the English-speaking Quebecers who, culturally, if not linguistically, share the habits and characteristics, not of English Canadians, but of French Quebecers. It would also be ignoring the fact that Montreal constitutes the third largest Anglophone market in Canada.

Source: Adapted from Pauline Couture, "Vive la Difference," *Report on Business Magazine*, November 1993, pp. 104-112; Anne Darche, "Differences Getting Too Much Attention," *Marketing*, March 25, 1991, p. 35; Brian Dunn, "Why Quebec Ads Are Different," *Montreal Gazette*, September 26, 1992, pp. F10-F11.

### Influence of Social Class

People's buying behaviour is often influenced by the class to which they belong, or to which they aspire, simply because they have values, beliefs, and life-styles that are characteristic of a social class. This occurs whether they are conscious of class notions or not. The idea of a social-class structure and the terms *upper*, *middle*, and *lower* class may be repugnant to many Canadians. However, it does represent a useful way to look at a market. We can consider social class as another useful basis for segmenting consumer markets.[11]

A social-class structure currently useful to marketing managers is one developed by Richard Coleman and Lee Rainwater, two respected researchers in social-class theory. The placement of people in this structure is determined primarily by such variables as *education*, *occupation*, and *type of neighbourhood of residence*.[12]

Note that "amount of income" is *not* one of the placement criteria. There may be a general relationship between amount of income and social class — people in the upper classes usually have higher incomes than people in the lower classes. But *within* each social class there typically is a wide range of incomes. Also, the same amount of income may be earned by families in different social classes.

For purposes of marketing planning and analysis, marketing executives and researchers often divide the total consumer market into five social classes. These classes and their characteristics, as adapted from Warner and the Coleman structure previously noted, are summarized below. The percentages are only approximations and may vary from one city or region to another.

**Social Classes and Their Characteristics** The **upper class**, about 2 percent of the population, includes two groups: (1) the socially prominent "old families" of inherited wealth and (2) the "new rich" of the corporate executives, owners of large businesses, and wealthy professionals. They live in large homes in the best neighbourhoods and display a sense of social responsibility. They buy expensive products and services, but they do not conspicuously display their purchases. They patronize exclusive shops.

The **upper-middle class**, about 12 percent of the population, is composed of moderately successful business and professional people and owners of medium-sized companies. They are well educated, have a strong drive for success, and want their children to do well. Their purchases are more conspicuous than those in the upper class. This class buys status symbols that show their success, yet are socially acceptable. They live well, belong to private clubs, and support the arts and various social causes.

The **lower-middle class**, about 32 percent of the population, consists of the white-collar workers — office workers, most sales people, teachers, technicians, and small-business owners. The **upper-lower class**, about 38 percent of the population, is the blue-collar "working class" of factory workers, semi-skilled workers, and service people. Because these two groups together represent the mass market and thus are so important to most marketers, the attitudes, beliefs, and life-styles they exhibit are the focus for much marketing research.

The **lower-lower class**, about 16 percent of the population, is composed of unskilled workers, the chronically unemployed, unassimilated immigrants, and people frequently on welfare. They typically are poorly educated, with low incomes, and live in substandard houses and neighbourhoods. They tend to live for the present and often do not purchase wisely. The public tends to differentiate (within this class) between the "working poor" and the "welfare poor."

**Marketing Significance of Social Classes** Now let's summarize the basic conclusions from social-class research that are highly significant for marketing:

- A social-class system can be observed whether people are aware of it or not. There are substantial differences between classes regarding their buying behaviour.
- Differences in beliefs, attitudes, and orientations exist among the classes. Thus the classes respond differently to a seller's marketing program.
- For many products, class membership is a better predictor of buyer behaviour than is income.

This last point — the relative importance of income versus social class — has generated considerable controversy. There is an old saying that "a rich man is just a poor man with money — and that, given the same amount of money, a poor man would behave exactly like a rich man." Studies of social-class structure have proved that this statement simply is not true. Two people, each earning the same income but belonging to different social classes, will have quite different buying patterns. They will shop at different stores, expect different treatment from sales people, and buy different products and even different brands. Also, when a family's income increases because more family members get a job, this increase almost never results in a change in the family's social class.

### Influence of Small Reference Groups

Small-group influence on buyer behaviour introduces to marketing the concept of reference-group theory, which we borrow from sociology. A **reference group** may be defined as a group of people who influence a person's attitudes, values, and behaviour. Each group develops its own standards of behaviour that then serve as guides, or "frames of reference," for the individual members. The members share these values and are expected to conform to the group's normative behavioural patterns. It is likely that a person's reference groups are to be found in their own social class category.

Consumer behaviour is influenced by the small groups to which consumers belong or aspire to belong. These groups may include family, social organizations, labour unions, church groups, athletic teams, or a circle of close friends or neighbours. Studies have shown that personal advice in face-to-face groups is much more effective as a behavioural determinant than advertising in newspapers, television, or other mass media. That is, in selecting products or changing brands, we are more likely to be influenced by word-of-mouth advertising from satisfied customers in our reference group. This is true especially when the speaker is considered to be knowledgeable regarding the particular product.

A person may agree with all the ideas of the group or only some of them. Also, a person does not have to belong to a group to be influenced by it. Young people frequently pattern their dress and other behaviour after that of an older group that the younger ones aspire to join.

Another useful finding pertains to the flow of information between and within groups. For years marketers operated in conformity with the "snob appeal" theory. This is the idea that if you can get social leaders and high-income groups to use your products, the mass market will also buy them. The assumption has been that influence follows a *vertical* path, starting at levels of high status and moving downward through successive levels of groups. Contrary to this popular assumption, studies by Katz and Lazarsfeld and by others have emphasized the *horizontal* nature of opinion leadership. Influence emerges on each *level* of the socioeconomic scale, moving from the opinion leaders to their peers.[13]

The proven role of small groups as behaviour determinants, plus the concept of horizontal information flow, suggests that a marketer is faced with two key problems. The first is to identify the relevant reference group likely to be used by consumers in a given buying situation. The second is to identify and communicate with two key people in the group — the innovator (early buyer) and the influential person (opinion leader). Every group has a leader — a taste-maker, or **opinion leader** — who influences the decision making of others in the group. The key is for marketers to convince that person of the value of their products or services. The opinion *leader* in one group may be an opinion *follower* in another. Married women with children may be influential in matters concerning food, whereas unmarried women are more likely to influence fashions in clothing and makeup.

### Family and Household Influence

A **family** is a group of two or more people related by blood, marriage, or adoption living together in a household. During their lives many people will belong to at least two families — the one into which they are born and the one they form at marriage. The birth family primarily determines core values and attitudes. The marriage family, in contrast, has a more direct influence on specific purchases. For example, family size is important in the purchase of a car.

A **household** is a broader concept than a family. It consists of a single person, a family, or any group of unrelated persons who occupy a housing unit. Thus an unmarried homeowner, college students sharing an off-campus apartment, and cohabiting couples are examples of households.

This distinction between family and household stems from relatively recent changes in the "typical" household. At one time, marketers could safely assume that a household consisted of a married couple and their children. As discussed in previous chapters, this is no longer the case. When research indicated that singles found mealtime particularly lonely, preferred to spend little time on food preparation and eating, and often combined a meal with another activity such as reading or working to reduce the loneliness, marketers responded. Campbell's LeMenu, Stouffer's Lean Cuisine upscale frozen dinners, and Swanson's Great Start Breakfast Sandwiches are products that combine quality and convenience and are targeted at this market.

Sensitivity to household structure is important in designing marketing strategy. If affects such dimensions as product size (How large should refrigerators be?) and the design of advertising (Is it appropriate to depict a traditional family in a TV ad?).

In addition to the direct, immediate impact households have on the purchase behaviour of members, it is also interesting to consider the buying behaviour of the household as a unit. Who does the buying for a household? Marketers should treat this question as four separate ones, because each may call for different strategies:

**Sunlight is sensitive to the effect of a new addition on family life.**

- Who influences the buying decision?
- Who makes the buying decision?
- Who makes the actual purchase?
- Who uses the product?

Social life. Sex life. Sleeping habits. Laundry powder.
Having a baby changes everything. Almost.

Sunlight actually rinses cleaner than Ivory Snow (no soapy residue is left behind), making it perfect for your entire family's wash. So even if the rest of your life has been turned upside down, when it comes to laundry, all you'll have to change are diapers.

Soft on babies. Tough on stains.

Different people may assume these various roles, or one individual may play several roles in a particular purchase. In families, for many years the female household head did most of the day-to-day buying. However, this behaviour has changed as more women have entered the work force, and men have assumed greater household responsibility. Night and Sunday business hours in stores in suburban shopping centres in some provinces also encourage men to play a bigger role in family purchasing.

In recent years, teenagers and young children have become decision makers in family buying, as well as actual shoppers. Canadian teenagers could represent a $10 billion market by the year 2000, up from $6 billion today. This certainly is enough to warrant the attention of many manufacturers. Even very young children influence buying decisions today because they watch TV advertising and ask for products when they shop with their parents. Purchasing decisions are often made jointly by husband and wife. Young couples are much more likely to make buying decisions on a joint basis than older couples are. Apparently the longer a couple lives together, the more they feel they can trust each other's judgement.

Knowing which family member is likely to make the purchase decision will influence a firm's entire marketing mix. If children are the key decision makers, as is often the case with breakfast cereals, then a manufacturer will produce something that tastes good to children, design the package with youngsters in mind, and advertise on Saturday morning cartoon shows. This would be done regardless of who actually makes the purchase and who else (besides the children) in the household might eat cereal.

## PSYCHOLOGICAL FACTORS

In discussing the psychological component of consumer behaviour, we will continue to use the model in Figure 6-1. One or more motives within a person activates goal-oriented behaviour. One such behaviour is perception — that is, the collection and processing of information. Other important psychological activities are learning and attitude formation. We then consider the roles that personality and self-concept play in buying decisions. These psychological variables help to shape a person's life-style and values. The term psychographics is being used by many researchers as a synonym for those variables and life-style values.

### Motivation — The Starting Point

To understand why consumers behave as they do, we must first ask why a person acts at all. The answer is, "Because he or she experiences a need." All behaviour starts with a recognized need. A **motive** is a need sufficiently stimulated that an individual is moved to seek satisfaction. Security and prestige are examples of needs that may become motives.

A need must be aroused or stimulated before it becomes a motive. We have many dormant needs that do not activate behaviour because they are not sufficiently intense. Thus hunger that is strong enough that we search for food and fear great enough that we seek security are examples of aroused needs that become motives for behaviour.

Explanations for behaviour can range from simple to unexplainable. To illustrate, buying motives may be grouped on three different levels depending on consumers' awareness of them and their willingness to divulge them. At one level, buyers recognize, and are quite willing to talk about, their motives for buying certain products. At a second level, they are aware of their reasons for buying but will not admit them to others. A man may buy a luxury car because he feels it adds to his social position in the neighbourhood. Or a woman may buy a leather coat to keep up with her peer group. But when questioned about their motives, they offer other reasons that they think will be more socially acceptable. The most difficult motives to uncover are those at the third level, where even the buyers themselves cannot explain the real factors motivating their buying actions.

To further complicate our understanding, a purchase is often the result of multiple motives. Moreover, various motives may conflict with one another. In buying a new dress, a young woman may want to (1) please herself, (2) please her boyfriend, (3) be considered a fashion leader by other young women in her social circle, and (4) strive for economy. To accomplish all these objectives in one purchase is truly a difficult assignment. Also a person's buying behaviour changes because of changes in income, life-style, and other factors. Finally, identical behaviour by several people may result from quite different motives, and different behaviour by the same person at various times may result from the same motive.

**Classification of Motives** Psychologists generally agree that motives can be grouped in two broad categories: (1) needs aroused from *physiological states* of tension (such as the need for sleep) and (2) needs aroused from *psychological states* of tension (such as the needs for affection and self-respect).

The psychologist Abraham Maslow formulated a theory of motivation based on needs. He identified a hierarchy of five levels of needs, arrayed in the order in which people seek to gratify them.[15] This hierarchy is shown in Figure 6-2. Maslow recognized that a normal person is most likely to be working towards need satisfaction on several levels at the same time and that rarely are all needs on a given level fully satisfied. However, the hierarchy indicates that the majority of needs on a particular level must be reasonably well satisfied before a person is motivated at the next higher level.

In their attempts to market products or communicate with particular segments, marketers often must go beyond a general classification like Maslow's to understand the specific motives underlying behaviour. For example, to observe that a consumer on a shopping trip may be satisfying physiological and social needs because he or she purchases food and talks to friends in the store may be correct, but it is not very useful. Addressing this issue, Edward Tauber described 13 specific motives reported by shoppers, including recreation, self-gratification, sensory stimulation, peer group attraction, and status.[16] Using these motives, marketers are better prepared to design appealing products and stores. Much more needs to be done, however, to identify marketing-specific motives and to measure their strengths.

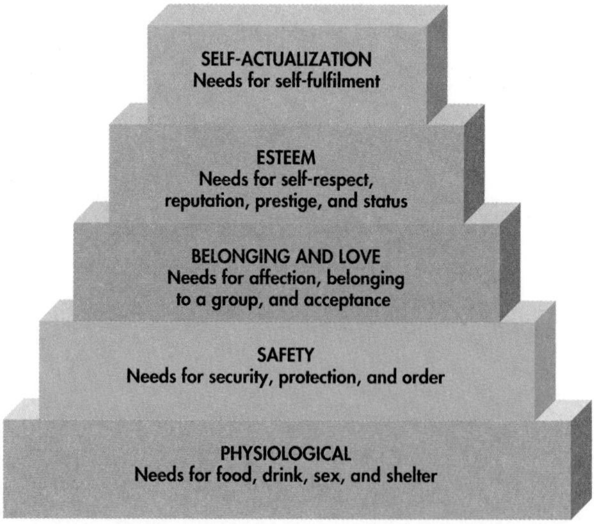


**FIGURE 6-2 Maslow's hierarchy of needs.**

## Perception

A motive is an aroused need. It, in turn, activates behaviour intended to satisfy the aroused need. One form that behaviour takes is collecting and processing information from the environment, a process known as **perception**. We constantly receive, organize, and assign meaning to stimuli detected by our five senses. In this way, we interpret or give meaning to the world around us. Perception plays a major role in the alternative identification stage of the buying-decision process.

What we perceive — the meaning we give something sensed — depends on the object and our experiences. In an instant, the mind is capable of receiving information, comparing it to a huge store of images in memory, and providing an interpretation.

Though important, visual stimuli are just one factor in perception. Consumers make use of all five senses. Scents, for example, are powerful behaviour triggers. Who can resist the aroma of popcorn in a theatre or of fresh cookies in a supermarket bakery? As with all perception, memory plays a large part with aromas. A recent study of common odours that evoke pleasant childhood memories found that older consumers identified natural smells of horses, flowers, and hay. However, younger subjects associated pleasant recollections with the scent of Play-Doh and even jet fuel! Marketers are using this type of information to odourize products and shopping environments to create positive perceptions.

Every day we come in contact with an enormous number of marketing stimuli. However, a process of selectivity limits our perceptions. As an illustration, consider that:

- We pay attention by exception. That is, of all the marketing stimuli our senses are exposed to, only those with the power to capture and hold our attention have the potential of being perceived. This phenomenon is called **selective attention**.
- We may alter information that is inconsistent with our beliefs and attitudes. Thus someone may say, "Despite the evidence, I don't believe smoking will be hazardous to my health." This is **selective distortion**.
- We retain only part of what we have selectively perceived. We may read an ad but later forget it. This is known as **selective retention**.

There are many communication implications in this selectivity process. For example, to grasp and hold attention, an ad must be involving enough to stimulate the consumer to seek more information. If the ad is too familiar, it will be ignored. On the other hand, if it is too complex, the ad will be judged not worth the time and effort to figure out. Thus, the goal is a mildly ambiguous first impression that heightens the consumer's interest. A recent print ad for the Isuzu Trooper picturing the truck on a frozen lake surrounded by shopping carts is a good example. The incongruity of the situation sparks the reader's curiosity. The copy then explains how the quality of the Isuzu's paint helps the car resist "the attraction of shopping carts to automobiles."

As part of perception, new information is compared with a person's existing store of knowledge, or frame of reference. If an inconsistency is discovered, the new information will be distorted to conform to the established beliefs. Thus if a consumer believes foreign-made cars are better built than domestic ones, a claim of superior quality by Ford will be viewed as an exaggeration or an attempt at deception rather than as fact.

To reduce distortion, advertisers strive for meaningful, strong messages that will be believed. A major factor influencing the believability of a message is the credibility of the source. Advertisers use recognized experts to endorse their products — Michael Jordan for Nike shoes and Wayne Gretzky for Zurich Canada insurance to add credibility to their messages.

Even messages received undistorted are still subject to selective retention. Consequently ads are repeated many times. The hope is that numerous exposures will etch the message into the recipient's memory.

**Sellers have discovered that besides providing information, sale signs produce a conditioned response in many consumers.**

## Learning

**Learning** may be defined as changes in behaviour resulting from previous experiences. Thus it excludes behaviour that is attributable to instinct such as breathing or temporary states such as hunger or fatigue. The ability to interpret and predict the consumer's learning process enhances our understanding of buying behaviour, since learning plays a role at every stage of the buying-decision process. No simple learning theory has emerged as universally workable and acceptable. However, the one with the most direct application to marketing strategy is the stimulus-response theory.[17]

**Stimulus-response theory** holds that learning occurs as a person (1) responds to some stimulus and (2) is rewarded with need satisfaction for a correct response or penalized for an incorrect one. When the same correct response is repeated in reaction to the same stimulus, a behaviour pattern or learning is established.

Research has shown that attitudes and other factors also influence a consumer's response to a given stimulus. Thus a learned response does not necessarily occur every time a stimulus appears.

Five factors are fundamental to learning:

- **Drives:** Internal or external forces that require the person to respond in some way.
- **Cues:** Signals from the environment that determine the pattern of response.
- **Responses:** Behavioural reactions to the drive and cues.
- **Reinforcement:** Results when the response is rewarding. Reinforcement can be either positive or negative. **Positive reinforcement** involves experiencing a desirable outcome as a result of engaging in the behaviour. **Negative reinforcement** occurs when a behaviour allows a person to avoid an undesirable outcome.
- **Punishment:** A penalty inflicted for incorrect behaviour.

If the response is rewarded by either positive or negative reinforcement, a connection among the drive, cues, and response will be established. Learning, then, emerges from reinforcement, and repeated reinforcement leads to a habit or brand loyalty. For example, a person motivated to shop (drive) who has found bargains (positive reinforcement) when going into stores (response) that have "sale" signs in their windows (cues) will respond (learn) by going into other stores with "sale" signs. Similarly, a consumer who finds it satisfying to avoid having problems (negative reinforcement) due to poor quality by paying premium prices will learn this response pattern.

Marketers have taught consumers to respond to certain cues:

- End-of-aisle displays in supermarkets suggest that the item is on sale.
- Sale signs in store windows suggest that bargains can be found inside.
- Large type in newspaper grocery ads suggests that the item is a particularly good bargain.

Once a habitual behaviour pattern has been established, it replaces conscious, willful behaviour. In terms of our model, this means that the consumer would go directly from the recognized need to purchase, skipping the steps in between. The stronger the habit (the more it has been reinforced), the more difficult it is for a competitive product to break in. On the other hand, if the learned response is not rewarding, the consumer's mind is open to another set of cues leading to another response. The consumer will try a substitute product or switch to another brand.

## Personality

The study of human personality has given rise to many, sometimes widely divergent, schools of psychological thought. As a result, attempts to inventory and classify personality traits have produced a variety of different structures. In this discussion, **personality** is defined broadly as an individual's pattern of traits that influence behavioural responses. We speak of people as being self-confident, aggressive, shy, domineering, dynamic, secure, introverted, flexible, or friendly and as being influenced (but not controlled) by these personality traits in their responses to situations.

It is generally agreed that personality traits do influence consumers' perceptions and buying behaviour. However, there is considerable disagreement as to the nature of this relationship; that is, *how* personality influences behaviour. Although we know that people's personalities often are reflected in the clothes they wear, the cars they drive (or whether they use a bike or motorcycle instead of a car), and the restaurants they eat in, we have not been successful in predicting behaviour from particular personality traits. The reason is simple: many things besides personality enter into the consumer buying-decision process.

**The Self-Concept** Your **self-concept**, or self-image, is the way you see yourself. At the same time it is the picture you think others have of you. Psychologists distinguish between (1) the **actual** self-concept (the way you really see yourself) and (2) the **ideal** self-concept (the way you want to be seen or would like to see yourself). To some extent, the self-concept theory is a reflection of other psychological and sociological dimensions already discussed. A person's self-concept is influenced, for instance, by innate and learned physiological and psychological needs. It is conditioned also by economic factors, demographic factors, and social-group influences.

Studies of purchases show that people generally prefer brands and products that are compatible with their self-concept. There are mixed reports concerning the degree of influence of the actual and ideal self-concepts on brand and product preferences. Some psychologists contend that consumption preferences correspond to a person's *actual* self-concept. Others hold that the *ideal* self-concept is dominant in consumers' choices.

Perhaps there is no consensus here because in real life we often switch back and forth between our actual and our ideal self-concepts. A middle-aged man may buy some comfortable, but not fashionable, clothing to wear at home on a weekend, where he is reflecting his actual self-concept. Then later he buys some expensive, high-fashion exercise clothing, envisioning himself (ideal self-concept) as a young, active, upwardly mobile guy. This same fellow may drive a beat-up pickup truck for his weekend errands (actual self-concept). But he'll drive his new foreign sports car to work where he wants to project a different (ideal) self-concept.[18]

### Attitudes

A classic definition of **attitude** is: a learned predisposition to respond to an object or class of objects in a consistently favourable or unfavourable way.[19] In our model of the buying-decision process, attitudes play a major role in the evaluation of alternatives. Numerous studies have reported a relationship between consumers' attitudes and their buying behaviour regarding both types of products selected and brands chosen. Surely, then, it is in a marketers' best interest to understand how attitudes are formed, the functions they perform, and how they can be changed.

All attitudes have the following characteristics in common:

- Attitudes are *learned*. The information individuals acquire through their direct experiences with a product or an idea, indirect experiences (such as reading about a product in *Canadian Living*), and interactions with their social groups all contribute to the formation of attitudes. For example, the opinions expressed by a good friend about garage sales plus the consumer's favourable or unfavourable experience as a result of going to garage sales will contribute to an attitude towards garage sales in general.
- Attitudes have an *object*. By definition, we can hold attitudes only towards something. The object can be general (professional sports) or specific (Toronto Blue Jays); it can

be abstract (campus life) or concrete (the computer centre). In attempting to determine consumers' attitudes it is very important to carefully define the object of the attitude since a person might have a favourable attitude towards the general concept (health food) but a negative attitude towards a specific dimension (broccoli).
- Attitudes have *direction* and *intensity*. Our attitudes are either favourable or unfavourable towards the object. They cannot be neutral. In addition, they have a strength. For example, you may mildly like this text or you may like it very much (we hope!). This factor is important for marketers since both strongly held favourable and strongly held unfavourable attitudes are difficult to change.
- Finally, attitudes are arranged in structures that tend to be *stable* and generalizable. Once formed, attitudes usually endure, and the longer they are held, the more resistant to change they become. People also have a tendency to generalize attitudes. For instance, if a person is treated nicely by a sales clerk in a particular store, there is a tendency to form a favourable attitude towards the entire store.

A consumer's attitudes do not always predict purchase behaviour. A person may hold very favourable attitudes towards a product but not buy it because of some inhibiting factor. Typical inhibitors are not having enough money or discovering your preferred product or brand is not available when the purchase must be made. Under such circumstances, purchase behaviour may even contradict attitudes.

As the preceding discussion suggests, it is extremely difficult to change strongly held attitudes. Consequently when the marketer is faced with negative or unfavourable attitudes, there are two options. The first is to try to change the attitude to be compatible with the product. The second is to determine what the consumers' attitudes are and then change the product to match those attitudes. Ordinarily it is much easier to change the product than it is to change consumers' attitudes.

Nevertheless, in some situations, attitudes have been changed. Consider how negative attitudes have changed in favour of small cars, yellow tennis balls, off-season vacations, and coed dorms in universities.

### Values and Life-styles

One of the most valuable ways of looking at a market and its potential involves consideration of consumer life-styles and values. Marketers now develop marketing programs based not only on how old their customers are or where they live, but also on how they spend their leisure time, what type of movies they like to watch, and what things they consider important in their lives. This is an integral part of the concept of market segmentation, which we discussed in Chapters 4 and 5. Essentially, the Canadian market is made up of many different types of people. Once we can identify how these various groups think and live, we can do a better job of developing products, services, advertising, and other marketing techniques to appeal to them.

The field of psychographic research was developed in the 1960s and initially examined consumer activities, interests, and opinions. A more recent development has been the use of a program known as VALS (Values, Attitudes, and Life-style), which was developed in the United States at the Stanford Research Institute and is discussed in Chapter 5. VALS research involves the study of thousands of consumers and measures their opinions, interests, attitudes, values, beliefs, and activities in a variety of different areas. Using sophisticated computer-based data analysis techniques, the developers of VALS have identified nine different segments or clusters of consumers in the U.S. population. In Canada, a similar study has revealed 14 different "life-style segments," eight female and six male (see box on next page). The company that developed this way of looking at the market in Canada has given each segment a name and can describe personal attributes of its members.

## CANADIANS AS LIFE-STYLE SEGMENTS

Trying to get a fix on the real you? According to the first Canada Lifestyle study, English Canadians over the age of 18 can be neatly divided into the following 14 "lifestyle segments":

**Diana**, "The Working Mother" (20%): Not a "mother who works" but a "worker with kids." Aggressively social, active, mobile and practical.

**Sue**, "The Social Single" (17%): A remnant of the "Me Generation." Well educated and a voracious cultural consumer but incapable of making commitments and fearful of marriage, family, and romance.

**Liz**, "The Upscale Pacesetter" (15%): An affluent, sophisticated homemaker who runs her home as if it were a business. Cultured, well educated, well informed, and confident.

**Sara**, "The Traditionalist" (12%): A middle-aged, middle-class housewife who lives according to the values she was brought up on. Thoughtful and articulate, she is constantly looking for ways to improve herself.

**Brenda**, "Blue Jeans Mother" (10%): A young, lower-income homemaker trying to cope with the transition from being a carefree single to the responsibilities of family life. Depends on a "strong leader" — either husband or father — and exercises thrift in her spending.

**Fran**, "The Happy Homemaker" (9%): Her interests are the family, home, and church, and she pours most of her energy into the home. Traditional, security conscious, and sceptical of women's lib.

**Gran** (9%): Old-fashioned and traditional, she lives morally in the nineteenth century. More family oriented than any other segment.

**Edna**, "The Malcontent" (8%): Emotionally and intellectually negative, she is a homebody who hides within the fortress of her family. She sees only deterioration in the world around her.

**Steve**, "The Hardhat" (21%): Usually employed in a skilled trade, he is well paid but depressed by the routine of the working day. Conservative and materialistic, he admires strong leaders and can be prone to violence.

**Ross**, "The Urban Businessman" (20%): Well educated and status conscious, he is probably in a professional or executive position. Although he observes some traditions, he is progressive and modern in his thinking. He enjoys competition but lives in constant fear of failure.

**Dave**, "The Playboy" (17%): Extremely social, a swinger and a sportsman. Sensitive about his self-image, he avoids personal commitment but is determined to succeed professionally.

**Henry**, "The Old Guard" (16%): A gentleman, a churchman, and a traditionalist. Ultraconservative, he is disillusioned by the decline of morals in the contemporary world but is content with his own achievements.

**Bert**, "The Egotist" (13%): Chauvinistic and macho, he is obsessed with his masculinity. Most likely to work at a job that requires more strength than skill, he harbours fantasies about becoming a person of great strength who defies danger and wins the day.

**Roy**, "The Homespun Handyman" (13%): Canada's cowboy, fisherman, farmer, or artisan. Dedicated to his trade and his family, he has no illusions about social status and is happy with the old-fashioned way he has chosen to live.

Reprinted with permission from Ian Pearson, "Social Studies," *Canadian Business*, December 1985, p. 73.

## SITUATIONAL INFLUENCES

These life-style or psychographic definitions of market segments are much more interesting and useful to the marketer than are segments based only on demographic characteristics such as age, income levels, and marital status. For example, groups for which convenience is of considerable importance represent target segments for home cleaning services and automatic teller machines. Often the situations in which we find ourselves play a large part in determining how we behave. Students, for example, act differently in a classroom than they do when they are in a stadium watching a football game. The same holds true of buying behaviour. You might get your hair cut because of an upcoming job interview. On vacation you might buy a souvenir that seems very strange when you get home. For a close friend's wedding gift, you might buy a fancier brand of small appliance than you would buy for yourself. These are all examples of **situational influences**, temporary forces associated with the immediate purchase environment that affect behaviour. Situational influence tends to be less significant when the consumer is very loyal to a brand and when the consumer is highly involved in the purchase. However, it often plays a major role in buying decisions. The five categories of situational influences are explained next.

### When Consumers Buy — The Time Dimension

Marketers should be able to answer at least two time-related questions about consumer buying: Is it influenced by the season, week, day, or hour? What impact do past and present events have on the purchase decision?

The time dimension of buying has implications for promotion scheduling. Promotional messages must reach consumers when they are in a decision-making frame of mind. Marketers also adjust prices in an attempt to even out demand. For instance, supermarkets may offer double coupons on Wednesdays, usually a slow business day. If seasonal buying patterns exist, marketers can sometimes extend the buying season. There is obviously little opportunity to extend the buying season for Easter bunnies or Christmas ornaments. But the season for vacations has been shifted to such an extent that winter and other "off-season" or "shoulder-season" vacations are now quite popular.

The second question concerns the impact of past or future events. For example, the length of time since you last went out to dinner at a nice restaurant may influence a decision on where to go tonight. Or the significance of an upcoming event, such as a vacation trip to a resort area, could result in a greater than normal amount of clothing purchases. Marketers need to know enough about the targeted consumers to anticipate the effects of these past and future events.

The growth and popularity of fast-food restaurants, quick-service oil-change outlets, and catalogue retailers are marketers' responses to consumers experiencing time pressures. Dual-income households, job activity (including business trips and travel time to and from work), and mandatory leisure-time activities (such as car pooling children to social and sports events) leave little time for relaxed shopping. The results are measurable. In 1988 the average consumer spent 90 minutes on a mall shopping trip. The figure today is 68 minutes.[20] To help consumers conserve time, marketers are making large and small changes. For example, some photoprocessing operations return the developed prints by mail to eliminate the customers' second trip to pick up the pictures.

### Where Consumers Buy — The Physical and Social Surroundings

Physical surroundings are the features of a situation that are apparent to the senses, such as lighting, smells, weather, and sounds. Think of the importance of atmosphere in a restaurant or the sense of excitement and action created by the sights and sounds in a gambling casino. Music can be an important element in a store's strategy.

The social surroundings are the number, mix, and actions of other people at the purchase site. You probably would not go into a strange restaurant that has an empty parking lot. And in a crowded store with other customers waiting, you will probably ask the clerk fewer questions and spend less time comparing products.

### How Consumers Buy — The Terms and Conditions of the Purchase

How consumers buy refers to the terms and conditions of sale as well as the transaction-related activities that buyers are willing to perform. Many more retailers sell on credit today than just a few years ago. Not only do consumers use credit for instalment purchases (to buy things today with future income), but many now use credit for convenience. The ability to use VISA or MasterCard to make a wide variety of purchases while not carrying cash is an attractive option to many consumers. Another recent development is the increase in purchases made by mail and phone. The growth of catalogue distribution and telephone shopping services has enabled consumers to buy everything from jewellery to food without setting foot in a store. Finally, the trend towards one-stop shopping has encouraged retailers to add even unrelated items to their basic mix of products. Consider, for example, the wide variety of goods found in what we call a drugstore.

Marketers have also experimented with transferring functions or activities to consumers. What were once called "service stations" are now called "gas stations" because you pump your own gas and wash your own windshield. Consumers have shown a willingness to assemble products, bag their own groceries, and buy in case quantities — all in exchange for lower prices.

### Why Consumers Buy — The Objective of the Purchase

The intent or reason for a purchase affects the choices made. We are likely to behave very differently if we are buying a product for a gift as opposed to buying the same product for our personal use. When purchasing a wristwatch, a consumer may be most interested in one that will provide accurate time at a reasonable price. However, the appearance of a watch bought as a graduation present can be very important.

A marketer must understand the consumer's objective in buying the product in order to design an effective marketing mix. For example, the failure by most watchmakers to appeal to the functional, nongift watch market is what allowed Timex to be so successful with its reasonably priced product.

### Conditions under Which Consumers Buy — States and Moods

Sometimes consumers are in a temporary state that influences their buying decisions. When you are ill or rushed, you may be unwilling to wait in line or you do not take the time or care that a particular purchase deserves. Moods can also influence purchases. Feelings such as anger or excitement can result in purchases that otherwise would not have been made. In the exciting atmosphere of a rock concert, for example, you might pay more for a commemorative T-shirt than you would under normal circumstances. Sales people must be trained to recognize consumers' moods and adjust their presentations accordingly.

Marketers must also monitor long-term situational influences. The optimistic consumers of the 1980s were free-spending and apparently care-free. Household debt grew 50 percent faster than disposable income during the decade as the baby-boom generation acquired cars, homes, and household possessions. However, the recession that rocked the economy at the end of the decade produced many changes. It created more conservative buyers, who save more, avoid debt, and purchase more carefully. One outcome of these changes was the disappearance of a large number of car dealerships in the early 1990s. Though it is obviously difficult to predict if these changes in consumer psychology are temporary or permanent, they have important implications for virtually all marketers.

When a particular situational influence becomes widely accepted and strongly embedded (such as shopping on particular days of the week), overcoming it can be difficult. The marketer may have to carry out an extensive campaign with no guarantee of success.

## MARKETING AT WORK

### FILE 6-4 ENVIRONMENT, MOOD, AND THE SWEET SMELL OF SUCCESS

With such intense competition these days, everybody's always looking for the competitive marketing edge that will boost personal productivity and sales. Companies have been quick to stick plants in offices to boost worker morale or to use more colourful packaging when displaying their products in retail stores. All this care is lavished on that which is visual, when the real competitive advantage might lie, literally, under marketer's very noses — in the great impact odours can have on people and their moods.

Smelling success, a Japanese firm began selling a "fragrance processor" to workplaces, a device that pumps cinnamon into the air to relieve tiredness, jasmine to soothe stress, and citrus or woody aromas with the aim of keeping workers more alert. Tests discovered that in perfumed offices, typists managed to hit 14 percent more keys an hour, while committing 21 percent fewer errors, than in odourless offices.

Meanwhile on the retail front, marketers have hit upon odours as a way of plunging consumers simultaneously into their memories and their wallets. The smell of baked goods, for example, softens the most hardened and wary consumer by conjuring up his or her childhood, while the smell of new leather can awaken a thirst for action and adventure. Scents don't always make sense, however. For instance, while people born before 1930 become nostalgic when confronted with natural smells such as pine and hay, younger folk tend to associate happy childhoods with "artificial smells" such as Play-Doh and VapoRub. And while the big American lingerie chain, Victoria's Secret, became famous in part for the floral scent of its stores, when racier lingerie stores tried to emulate their success, they only ended up scaring off their predominantly male clientele.

Source: Adapted from Kenneth Kidd, "Making Scents of Marketing," *Report on Business Magazine*, June 1992, p. 14.

## SUMMARY

The buying behaviour of ultimate consumers can be examined using a five-part model: the buying-decision process, information, social and group forces, psychological forces, and situational factors.

The buying-decision process is composed of six stages consumers go through in making purchases. The stages are need recognition, choice of an involvement level, identification of alternatives, evaluation of alternatives, purchase and related decisions, and postpurchase behaviour.

Information fuels the buying-decision process. Without it, there would be no decisions. There are two categories of information sources: commercial and social. Commercial sources include advertising, personal selling, selling by phone, and personal involvement with a product. Word of mouth, observation, and experience with a product owned by someone else are social sources.

Social and group forces are composed of culture, subculture, social class, reference groups, family, and households. Culture has the broadest and most general influence on buying behaviour, while a person's household has the most immediate impact. Social and group forces have a direct impact on individual purchase decisions as well as a person's psychological makeup.

Psychological forces that affect buying decisions are motivation, perception, learning, personality, and attitudes. All behaviour is motivated by some aroused need. Perception is the way we interpret the world around us and is subject to three types of selectivity: attention, distortion, and retention. Learning is a change in behaviour as a result of experience. Stimulus-response learning involves drives, cues, responses, reinforcement, and punishment. Continued reinforcement leads to habitual buying and brand loyalty.

Personality is the sum of an individual's traits that influence behavioural responses. The Freudian psychoanalytic theory of personality has had a significant impact on marketing. It has caused marketers to realize that the true motives for behaviour are often hidden. The self-concept is related to personality. Because purchasing and consumption are very expressive actions, they allow us to communicate to the world our actual and ideal self-concepts.

Attitudes are learned predispositions to respond to an object or class of objects in a consistent fashion. Besides being learned, all attitudes are directed towards an object, have direction and intensity, and tend to be stable and generalizable. Strongly held attitudes are difficult to change.

Situational influences deal with when, where, how, and why consumers buy, and the consumer's personal condition at the time of purchase. Situational influences are often so powerful that they can override all of the other forces in the buying-decision process.

## KEY TERMS AND CONCEPTS

**Buying-decision process (148)**
**Need recognition (148)**
**High involvement (150)**
**Low involvement (150)**
**Impulse buying (150)**
**Patronage buying motives (152)**
**Satisfaction (152)**
**Postpurchase behaviour (153)**
**Cognitive dissonance (153)**
**Commercial information (154)**
**Social information (154)**
**Culture (156)**
**Subculture (156)**
**Social class (161)**
  **Upper class (162)**
  **Upper-middle class (162)**
  **Lower-middle class (162)**
  **Upper-lower class (162)**
  **Lower-lower class (162)**
**Reference groups (163)**
**Opinion leader (163)**
**Family and household (163)**
**Motive (165)**
**Maslow's hierarchy of needs (166)**
**Perception (167)**
**Selective attention (167)**
**Selective distortion (167)**
**Selective retention (167)**
**Learning (168)**
**Stimulus-response theory (168)**
**Drives (168)**
**Cues (168)**
**Responses (168)**
**Positive reinforcement (168)**
**Negative reinforcement (168)**
**Punishment (168)**
**Personality (168)**
**Self-concept (169)**
**Actual self (169)**
**Ideal self (169)**
**Attitude (169)**
**Life-styles and values (170)**
**Situational influence (171)**

## QUESTIONS AND PROBLEMS

1. When might the purchase of a colour television be a low-involvement decision?
2. When a consumer's experience with a product *equals* her expectations for the product, the person is satisfied. Is there any disadvantage to a marketer whose product causes consumers' experience to *greatly exceed* expectations?
3. From a consumer behaviour perspective, why is it incorrect to view the European Union or the countries of Asia as single markets?
4. Explain why reference-group influence would affect the choice of the product, the brand, or neither for the following items:
   a. Bath soap.
   b. Auto tune-up.
   c. Office furniture.
   d. Waterbed.
5. What roles would you expect a husband, a wife, and their young child to play in the purchase of the following items?
   a. Nintendo.
   b. Choice of a fast-food outlet for dinner.
   c. Personal computer.
   d. Lawn-care service.
6. Explain how self-concept might come into play in the purchase of the following products:
   a. Eyeglasses.
   b. New suit.
   c. Eye shadow.
   d. College education.
7. What situational influences might affect a family's choice of a motel in a strange town while on a vacation?

## HANDS-ON MARKETING

1. Interview the manager of a store that sells big-ticket items (furniture, appliances, electronic equipment) about what methods, if any, the store uses to reinforce purchase decisions and to reduce the cognitive dissonance of its customers. What additional methods can you suggest?
2. Have a friend describe a high-involvement purchase that he or she recently made. Show how each of the six stages described in the chapter are reflected in the description. Identify the primary social influences that played a part in the decision.

## NOTES AND REFERENCES


1. Adapted from Angela Kryhul, "Dream Financing," *Marketing*, May 30, 1994, pp. 9-10.
2. Andrea Gerlin, "Diners Get Back on Track with Recipes for a New Age," *The Wall Street Journal*, September 8, 1992, p. B2.
3. The relationship between expectations and experience is described in Richard I. Oliver, "A Cognitive Model of the Antecedents and Consequences of Satisfaction Decisions," *Journal of Marketing Research*, November 1980, pp. 460-469.
4. R. Craig Endicott, "Advertising Fact Book," *Advertising Age*, January 6, 1992, p. S-11.
5. Clyde Kluckhohn, "The Concept of Culture," in Richard Kluckhohn (ed.), *Culture and Behaviour*, The Free Press, New York, 1962, p. 26.
6. See Nariman K. Dhalla, *These Canadians: A Sourcebook of Marketing and Socioeconomic Facts*, McGraw-Hill, Toronto, 1966, pp. 287-300; Frederick Elkin and Mary B. Hill, "Bicultural and Bilingual Adaptation in French Canada: The Example of Retail Advertising," *Canadian Review of Sociology and Anthropology*, August 1965, pp. 132-148; M. Brisebois, "Marketing in Quebec," in W. H. Mahatoo (ed.), *Marketing Research in Canada*, Thomas Nelson and Sons, Toronto, 1968, pp. 88-90; Bruce Mallen, "The Present State of Knowledge and Research in Marketing to the French-Canadian Marketing," in Donald N. Thompson and David S. R. Leighton (eds.), *Canadian Marketing: Problems and Prospects*, Wiley Publishers of Canada Limited, Toronto, 1973, pp. 100-101; and Jean-Charles Chebat and Georges Hénault, "The Cultural Behavior of Canadian Consumers," in Vishnu H. Kirpalani and Ronald H. Rotenberg (eds.), *Cases and Readings in Marketing*, Holt, Rinehart and Winston of Canada Limited, Toronto, 1974, pp. 178-180.
7. S. B. Ash, Carole P. Duhaime, and John A. Quelch, "Consumer Satisfaction: A Comparison of English- and French-Speaking Canadians," in Vernon J. Jones (ed.), *Marketing*, vol. 1, part 3, *Proceedings* of the Administrative Sciences Association of Canada, Marketing Division, Montreal, 1980, pp. 11-20.
8. Kristian S. Palda, "A Comparison of Consumer Expenditures in Quebec and Ontario," *Canadian Journal of Economics and Political Science*, February 1967, p. 26.
9. Dwight R. Thomas, "Culture and Consumption Behavior in English and French Canada," in Bent Stidsen (ed.), *Marketing in the 1970s and Beyond*, Canadian Association of Administrative Sciences, Marketing Division, Edmonton, 1975, pp. 255-261.
10. For a discussion of the evolution of advertising agencies in Quebec, see Madeleine Saint-Jacques and Bruce Mallen, "The French-Canadian Market," in Peter T. Zarry and Robert D. Wilson (eds.), *Advertising in Canada: Its Theory and Practice*, McGraw-Hill Ryerson Limited, Toronto, 1981, pp. 349-368; and Robert MacGregor, "The Impact of the Neo-Nationalist Movement on the Changing Structure and Composition of the Quebec Advertising Industry," in the *Proceedings* of the Administrative Sciences Association of Canada, Marketing Division, 1980, p. 237.
11. D. W. Greeno and W. F. Bennett, "Social Class and Income as Complementary Segmentation Bases: A Canadian Perspective," in *Proceedings* of the Marketing Division, Administrative Sciences Association of Canada, 1983, pp. 113-122.
12. W. Lloyd Warner and Paul Lunt, *The Social Life of a Modern Community*, Yale University Press, New Haven, Conn., 1941; and W. Lloyd Warner, Marchia Meeker, and Kenneth Eells, *Social Class in America*, Science Research Associates, Inc., Chicago, 1949.
13. See Elihu Katz and Paul Lazarsfeld, *Personal Influence*, Free Press, New York, 1955, especially p. 325.
14. Kenneth Kidd, "Teen Pockets Run Deep," *Globe and Mail*, March 3, 1991, pp. B1-B2.
15. A. H. Maslow, *Motivation and Personality*, Harper & Row, New York, 1954, pp. 80-106.

16. Edward M. Tauber, "Why Do People Shop?" *Journal of Marketing*, October 1972, pp. 46-49.
17. Other schools of thought on learning, principally the cognitive approach and gestalt learning, are discussed in books on consumer behaviour. See David Loudon and Albert J. Della Bitta, *Consumer Behavior*, 3rd ed., McGraw-Hill, New York, 1988.
18. For an analytical review of self-concept studies, the research problems connected with these studies, and a comprehensive bibliography, see M. Joseph Sirgy, "Self-Concept in Consumer Behaviour: A Critical Review," *Journal of Consumer Research*, December 1982, pp. 287-300.
19. Gordon W. Allport, "Attitudes," in C. A. Murchinson (ed.), *A Handbook of Social Psychology*, Clark University Press, Worcester, Mass., 1935, pp. 798-844.
20. Eugene Fram, "The Time Compressed Shopper," *Marketing Insights*, Summer 1991, pp. 34-39.

# CHAPTER 7 GOALS

In many ways business markets are similar to the consumer markets we have been examining, but there are also important differences. After studying this chapter, in addition to being able to describe how business markets differ from consumer markets, you should have an understanding of:

- The nature and scope of the business market.
- The components of the business market.
- The characteristics of business market demand.
- The determinants of business market demand.
- The buying motives, buying processes, and buying patterns in business markets.

The Industrial Group of Funds
YELLOW PAGES
Air Canada
MR SUB
"WE DID TWO MAIN THINGS TO BECOME CANADA'S FASTEST GROWING CAR RENTAL COMPANY. WE ADDED GRETZKY TO OUR TEAM AND FOUND THE VERY BEST PLACE FOR HIM TO PLAY. TSN." RON KERR, Director of National Marketing, Thrifty Car Rental

CHAPTER 7

# THE BUSINESS MARKET

## In Business-to-Business Marketing, Confidence Counts and So Do Recommendations

Business-to-business marketing, even more than consumer marketing, has a lot to do with getting the right kind of personal services and business resources put together so that your goals can be achieved. As TSN says in this ad, "real TV" provides real solutions and real results by putting together the right mix of business services and resources.

The real TV is The Sports Network (TSN), Canada's national, English-language, 24-hour sports specialty television service, delivered primarily to consumers via cable. TSN's major league schedule covers every major sport in the world, complemented by extensive coverage of Canadian and amateur sport. The network has been in business for over ten years. During this period, it has increased its coverage of different sports to broaden the appeal of the network and has improved the quality of what was programmed both by judicious selection of sporting events and by using advanced technology to cover them. At the same time, it has faced increased competition from other channels as well as other media. This is the specialized and continuous sports entertainment service that we as viewers are aware of and enjoy at the push of a button.

But as an organization that earns its livelihood from business-to-business marketing, TSN presents itself to marketers of products and services and other organizations as a vehicle for launching and promoting their ideas, services, and brands and for reinforcing the images of existing brands or meeting other marketing and communications objectives. It has to demonstrate to potential buyers of commercial time that it can reach a large number of viewers with certain characteristics that are appropriate for the products and services offered by those advertisers. And it has to work well with advertisers and provide the kind of service that results in a mutually beneficial relationship of the type illustrated in the business advertisement sponsored by TSN on pages 178-179.

When Ron Kerr, director of national marketing for Thrifty Car Rental, is prepared to endorse TSN with the kind of statements found in the ad, other businesses have to pay attention. After all, it's not often that a television network gets this kind of credit from a marketing manager. The selection of Wayne Gretzky as a spokesperson for Thrifty illustrates another dimension of business-to-business marketing — namely, selecting a spokesperson who is right for the audience and can work well with the advertising network, station, or publication.

Whatever marketing strategies TSN and other business marketers adopt, one thing is clear. The target markets for each of their services and products are business firms that will use them in making other products and in providing other services. The business market is big, rich, and widely diversified. It employs tens of thousands of employees in thousands of different jobs.

## NATURE AND SCOPE OF THE BUSINESS MARKET

The **business market** consists of all **business users**, organizations that buy goods and services for one of the following purposes:

- **To make other goods and services.** Campbell's buys fresh vegetables to make soup, and Bombardier buys various metal products to make Ski-Doos.
- **To resell to other business users or to consumers.** Loblaws buys canned tuna fish to sell to consumers, and Western Pipe Supply Company buys lawn sprinkler equipment and supplies from manufacturers and resells them to sprinkler contractors.
- **To conduct the organization's operations.** The University of Calgary buys office supplies and electronic office equipment for use in the registrar's office, and Vancouver General Hospital buys supplies to use in its surgical operating rooms.

In the business market we deal with both consumer products and business products. **Business marketing**, then, is the marketing of goods and services to business users, as contrasted to ultimate consumers.

Because the business market is largely unknown to the average consumer, we are apt to underrate its significance. Actually, it is huge when measured by total sales volume and the number of firms involved. About 50 percent of all manufactured products are sold to the business market. In addition, about 80 percent of all farm products and virtually all mineral, forest, and sea products are business goods. These are sold to firms for further processing.

The magnitude and complexity of the business market are also evident from the many transactions required to produce and market a product. Consider, for example, the business marketing transactions and total sales volume involved in getting leather workshoes to their actual users. First, cattle are sold through one or two intermediaries before reaching a meatpacker. Then the hides are sold to a tanner, who in turn sells the leather to a shoe manufacturer. The shoe manufacturer may sell finished shoes to a wholesaler, who markets them to retail stores, or to factories that supply shoes to their workers. Each sale is a business marketing transaction.

In addition, the shoe manufacturer buys metal eyelets, laces, thread, glue, steel safety toe plates, heels and soles, and shoe polish. Consider something as simple as the shoelaces. Other industrial firms must first buy the raw cotton and then spin, weave, dye, and cut it so that it becomes shoestring material. All the manufacturers involved have factories and offices with furniture, machinery, furnaces, lights, and maintenance equipment and supplies required to run them — and these also are business goods that have to be produced and marketed. In short, thousands of business products and business marketing activities come into play before almost any product — consumer good or business good — reaches its final destination.

The magnitude and complexity of the business market loom even larger when we consider all the business services involved throughout our workshoe example. Each firm engaged in any stage of the production process probably uses outside accounting and law firms. Several of the producers may use advertising agencies. And all the companies will use services of various financial institutions.

Every retail store and wholesaling establishment is a business user. Every bus company, airline, and railroad is part of this market. So is every hotel, restaurant, bank, insurance company, hospital, theatre, and school. In all, there are close to half a million business users in Canada. While this is far short of the approximately 28 million consumers, the total sales volume in the business market far surpasses total sales to consumers. This difference is due to the very many business marketing transactions that take place before a product is sold to a single ultimate user.

## MARKETING AT WORK

### FILE 7-1 PRODUCT TESTING SERVICE OPTIONS INCREASE FOR BUSINESS

In Canada, all manufactured products are obliged to pass safety certification tests before being placed on the market. Prior to the Canada–U.S. Free Trade Agreement of 1988, only designated Canadian firms were allowed to certify Canadian products, resulting in a market controlled by only two organizations — namely the Toronto-based Canadian Standards Association (CSA) and Underwriters Laboratories of Canada (ULC). However, with trade barriers down and an estimated $100-million market up for grabs, it was only a matter of time before a new player decided to join — the Illinois-based Underwriters Laboratories Inc., whose trademark UL is already a familiar logo on more than 6 billion American products each year.

The fact that most certification firms are not-for-profit organizations doesn't mean they can't be big business as well. UL boasts over 4,000 employees and $300 million (U.S.) in sales. And their arrival on the Canadian market after two years spent trying to drum up the necessary federal and provincial approval threatens to create some serious competition. While the CSA welcomes the challenge, its Canadian rival is worried about safety and an end to independent Canadian standards. Peter Higginson, president of ULC, feels that increased competition could lead disreputable manufacturers to shop around for a certifier who will charge less as well as give certification more easily. "In a competitive market," he warns, "corners will be cut. Safety certification is a public service like fire protection. You don't do yourself any service by having competing fire departments."

Source: Adapted from Barrie McKenna, "U.S. Giant Bids to Make Its Mark in Canada's Safety," *Globe and Mail*, January 15, 1994, p. B5.

## COMPONENTS OF THE BUSINESS MARKET

Traditionally, business markets were referred to as industrial markets. This caused many people to think the term referred only to approximately 40,000 Canadian manufacturing firms. But as you can see from what we just explained, the business market is a lot more than that. Certainly manufacturers constitute a major portion of the business market, but there are also six other components — agriculture, resellers, government agencies, service companies, and not-for-profit organizations. Although they are often underrated or overlooked because of the heavy attention devoted to manufacturing, each is a significant part of the business market. Keep in mind that some of our most important business markets are outside Canada — in the United States and many other countries.

### The Agriculture Market

The worldwide income from the sale of Canadian agricultural products gives farmers, as a group, the purchasing power that makes them a highly attractive market. Moreover, world population forecasts and food shortages in many countries undoubtedly will keep pressure on farmers to increase their output. Companies hoping to sell to the farm market must analyze it carefully and be aware of significant trends. For example, both the proportion of farmers in the total population and the number of farms have been decreasing and probably will continue to decline. Counterbalancing this has been an increase in large corporate or "business" types of farms. Even the remaining "family farms" are expanding in order to survive. Farming is becoming more automated and mechanized. This means, of course, that capital investment in farming is increasing. **Agribusiness** — farming, food processing, and other large-scale farming-related businesses — is big business in every sense of the word.

**Agriculture is one of the major business markets.**

Agriculture has become a modern industry. Like other business executives, farmers are looking for better ways to increase their productivity, cut their expenses, and manage their cash flows. Technology is an important part of the process. For example, one large business farmer has developed a sensor and remote steering system that guides a tractor between the rows in a field to avoid destroying any crops. And, as farmers become fewer and larger, marketing to them effectively requires carefully designed strategies. For example, some large fertilizer producers have sales people who visit individual farms. There, working with the farmer, the sales rep analyzes the soil and crops to determine exactly what fertilizer mix is best for the particular farm. Based on the analysis, the manufacturer prepares the appropriate blend of ingredients as a special order.

### The Reseller Market

Intermediaries in the Canadian marketing system — approximately 500,000 wholesalers, retailers, and other organizations — constitute the **reseller market**. The basic activity of resellers — unlike any other business market segment — is buying products from supplier organizations and reselling these items in essentially the same form to the resellers' customers. In economic terms, resellers create time, place, and possession utilities, rather than form utility.

Resellers also buy many goods and services for use in operating their businesses — items such as office supplies and equipment, warehouses, materials-handling equipment, legal services, electrical services, and janitorial supplies. In these buying activities, resellers are essentially no different from manufacturers, financial institutions, or any other segment of the business market.

It is their role as buyers for resale that differentiates resellers and attracts special marketing attention from their suppliers. To resell an item, you must please your customer. Usually it is more difficult to determine what will please an outside customer than to find out what will satisfy someone within your own organization. For example, an airline that decides to redesign the uniforms of its flight crews can carefully study the conditions under which the uniforms will be worn and work closely with the people who will be wearing the uniforms to get their views. As a result, the airline should be able to select a design that will be both functional and acceptable. Contrast that with a retailer trying to anticipate what clothing fashions will be popular next spring. In both cases clothing is being purchased, but the opportunity for interaction with the users and the greater interest by those likely to be affected by the purchase make buying for internal use less difficult and less risky than buying for resale.

Buying for resale, especially in a large reseller's organization, can be a complex procedure. For a supermarket chain such as Sobey's or Safeway, buying is frequently done by a buying committee made up of experts on market demand, trends, supply, and prices. Department stores may retain resident buyers — independent buying agencies — located in Toronto, London, Hong Kong, or other major market centres to be in constant touch with the latest fashion developments.

### The Government Market

The large government market includes federal, provincial, municipal governments, and various Crown agencies and corporations that spend millions each year buying for institutions such as schools, offices, hospitals, and military bases. At the federal level, Supply and Services Canada purchases billions of dollars of goods and services annually for other government units. Provincial and local governments taken together are more important markets than the federal government.

Government procurement processes are different from those in the private sector of the business market. A unique feature of government buying is the competitive bidding system. Much government procurement is done on a bid basis. That is, the government agency advertises for bids using a format that states specifications for the intended purchase. Then it must accept the lowest bid that meets these specifications.

In other buying situations, the government may negotiate a purchase contract with an individual supplier. This marketing practice might be used, for instance, when the Department of National Defence wants someone to develop and build a new aircraft tracking system and there are no comparable products on which to base bidding specifications.

A glance at an issue of the *Weekly Bulletin of Business Opportunities*, a government publication that lists business opportunities with the government, will give you some idea of the size of this market. The potential is sufficiently attractive that some firms concentrate almost exclusively on government markets.

Despite the opportunities, many companies make no effort to sell to the government, because they are intimidated by the red tape. There is no question that dealing with the government to any significant extent usually requires specialized marketing techniques and information. Some firms, such as Spar Aerospace and Bombardier, have established special departments to deal with government markets. Also, there are information and guidelines available from Supply and Services Canada on the proper procedures for doing business with the government.

### The Services Market

Currently, firms that produce services greatly outnumber firms that produce goods. That is, there are more service firms than the total of all manufacturers, mining companies, construction firms, and enterprises engaged in farming, forestry, and fishing. The **services market** includes all transportation carriers and public utilities, and the many financial, insurance, legal, and real estate firms. This market also includes organizations that produce and sell such diverse services as rental housing, recreation and entertainment, repairs, health care, personal care, and business services.

Service firms constitute a huge market that buys goods and other services. Four Seasons Hotels, for example, buy blankets and sheets from textile manufacturers. Hospitals in Canada and abroad buy supplies from Baxter Healthcare. The Toronto Blue Jays, Montreal Expos, and other Major League teams buy their baseball bats from Louisville Slugger in the United States and Cooper Sporting Goods in Canada. And all these service firms buy legal, accounting, and consulting advice from other service marketers. The importance to Canadian marketers of the services market is dealt with in greater detail in Chapter 12.

### The "Nonbusiness" Business Market

In recent years we have been giving some long-overdue marketing attention to the multi-million-dollar market made up of so-called nonbusiness or not-for-profit organizations. The **nonbusiness market** includes such diverse institutions as churches, colleges and universities, museums, hospitals and other health institutions, political parties, labour unions, and charitable organizations. Actually, each of these so-called nonbusiness organizations is a business organization. However, our society (and the institutions themselves) in the past did not perceive a museum or a hospital as being a business. And many people today still feel uncomfortable thinking of their church, school, or political party as a business organization. Nevertheless, these organizations do virtually all the things that businesses do — offer a product or service, collect money, make investments, hire employees — and therefore require professional management.

Not-for-profit organizations also conduct marketing campaigns — albeit under a different name — in an effort to attract millions of dollars in contributions. In turn, they spend millions of dollars buying goods and services to run their operations.

## CHARACTERISTICS OF BUSINESS MARKET DEMAND

Four demand characteristics differentiate the business market from the consumer market: Demand is derived, demand tends to be inelastic, demand is widely fluctuating, and the market is well informed.

### Demand Is Derived

The demand for a business product is derived from the demand for the consumer products in which that business product is used. Thus the demand for steel depends partially on consumer demand for automobiles and refrigerators, but it also depends on the demand for butter, hockey pads and equipment, and CD players. This is because the tools, machines, and other equipment needed to make these items are made of steel. Consequently, as the demand for hockey equipment increases, Cooper Sporting Goods may buy more steel sewing machines or filing cabinets.

There are two significant marketing implications in the fact that business market demand is a derived demand. First, to estimate the demand for a product, a business marketer must be very familiar with how it is used. This is fairly easy for a company like Pratt & Whitney, a maker of jet engines. But what about the manufacturer of rubber O-rings (doughnut-shaped rings of all sizes that are used to seal connections)? Considerable research may be necessary to identify uses and users.

Second, the producer of a business product may engage in marketing efforts to encourage the sale of its buyers' products. For example, Du Pont advertises to consumers, urging them when buying carpeting to ask specifically for products made with Du Pont's stain-resistant Stainmaster fibre. Similarly, the NutraSweet Company ran a consumer advertising campaign designed to build consumer loyalty for products sweetened with NutraSweet. The idea, of course, is that increases in consumer demand will, in turn, trigger increases in derived demand for these business products.

### Demand Is Inelastic

Another characteristic of the business market is demand elasticity of business products. Elasticity of demand refers to how responsive demand is to a change in the price of a product. (To review some economics, demand elasticity is explained early in Chapter 13.)

The demand for many business products is relatively inelastic, which means that the demand for a product responds very little to changes in its price. If the price of buttons for men's jackets should suddenly rise or fall considerably, how much effect would it have on the price of jackets? Because the buttons are such a small part of the jacket, the price increase would not likely change the price of jackets. As a result, demand for jackets would remain the same, so there would be no appreciable change in the demand for buttons either.

The demand for business products is inelastic because ordinarily the cost of a single part or material is a small portion of the total cost of the finished product. The cost of the chemicals in paint is a small part of the price a consumer pays for paint. The cost of the enamel on a refrigerator is a small part of its retail price. Even the cost of expensive capital equipment, such as a robot used in assembling automobiles, when spread over the thousands of units it helps produce, becomes a very small part of the final price of each one. As a result, when the price of the business product changes, there is very little change in the price of the related consumer products. Since there is no appreciable shift in the demand for the consumer goods, then — by virtue of the derived-demand feature — there is no change in the demand for the business product.

**The derived-demand feature of business markets stimulates some business producers to advertise to final consumers.**

You could go to great lengths to keep ugly spills off your carpets.
Or you could simply get DuPont Certified Stainmaster carpet.
Then, you can handle most common household spills with soap and water.
Even if they've sat for hours.
And that'll leave you leaping for joy.
Instead of other things.
What would you do without Stainmaster carpet?
DUPONT
CARPET FIBERS

From a marketing point of view, there are three factors that can moderate inelasticity of business demand.

- Price changes must occur throughout an entire industry, not in a single firm. An industry-wide cut in the price of steel belts used in tires will have little effect on the price of tires and therefore little effect on the demand for automobile tires. Consequently, it will cause little shift in the total demand for steel belts. The pricing policy of an individual firm, however, can substantially alter the demand for its products. If one supplier cuts the price of its steel belts significantly, the drop in price may draw a great deal of business away from competitors. Thus, in the short run, the demand curve faced by a single firm may be quite elastic. However, any advantage will likely be temporary, because competitors will almost certainly retaliate in some way to recapture their lost business.
- The second marketing factor that can affect the inelasticity of demand is time. Much of our discussion here applies to short-term situations. Over the long run, the demand for a given industrial product is more elastic. If the price of cloth for women's suits rises, there probably will be no immediate change in the price of the finished garment. However, the increase in the cost of materials could very well be reflected in a rise in suit prices for next year. This rise could then influence the demand for suits, and thus for cloth, a year or more hence.
- The third factor is the relative importance of a specific business product in the cost of the finished good. We may generalize to this extent:

  **The greater the cost of a business product as a percentage of the total price of the finished good, the greater the elasticity of demand for this business product.**

### Demand Is Widely Fluctuating

Although the demand for business goods does not change much in response to price changes, it does respond to other factors. In fact, market demand for most classes of business goods fluctuates considerably more than the demand for consumer products. The demand for installations — major plant equipment, factories, and so on — is especially subject to change. Substantial fluctuations also exist in the market for accessory equipment — office furniture and machinery, delivery trucks, and similar products. These tend to accentuate the swings in the demand for business raw materials and fabricating parts. We can see this very clearly when declines in demand in the construction and auto industries affect suppliers of lumber, steel, and other materials and parts.

A major reason for these fluctuations is that individual businesses are very concerned about having a shortage of inventory when consumer demand increases or being caught with excess inventory should consumer demand decline. Thus they tend to overreact to signals from the economy, building inventories when they see signs of growth in the economy and working inventories down when the signs suggest a slowdown. When the actions of all the individual firms are combined, the effect on their suppliers is widely fluctuating demand. This is known as the *acceleration principle*. One exception to this generalization is found in agricultural products intended for processing. Because people have to eat, there is a reasonably consistent demand for animals intended for meat products, for fruits and vegetables that will be canned or frozen, and for grains and dairy products used in cereals and baked goods.

Fluctuations in the demand for business products can influence all aspects of a marketing program. In product planning, fluctuations in demand may stimulate a firm to diversify into other products to ease production and marketing problems. For example, IBM has moved from concentrating on large, mainframe computers to personal computers, software, microcomputer chips, and consulting. Distribution strategies may be affected. When demand declines, a manufacturer may discover that selling to some resellers is unprofitable, so they are dropped as customers. In its pricing, management may attempt to stem a decline in sales by cutting prices, hoping to attract customers away from competing firms.

### Buyers Are Well Informed

Typically, business buyers are better informed about what they are buying than are ultimate consumers. They know more about the relative merits of alternative sources of supply and competitive products for three reasons. First, there are relatively few alternatives for a business buyer to consider. Consumers typically have many more brands and sellers from which to choose than do business buyers. Consider, for example, how many options you would have in purchasing a 19-inch TV set. However, in most business situations a buyer has only a few firms that offer the particular combination of product features and service desired. Second, the responsibility of a buyer in an organization is ordinarily limited to a few products. Unlike a consumer who buys many different things, a purchasing agent's job is to be very knowledgeable about a narrowly defined set of products. Third, for most consumer purchases, an error is only a minor inconvenience. However, in business buying the cost of a mistake may be thousands of dollars or even the decision maker's job!

This need for information has a significant marketing implication. Sellers of business products place greater emphasis on personal selling than do firms that market consumer products. Business sales people must be carefully selected, properly trained, and adequately compensated. They must give effective sales presentations and furnish satisfactory service both before and after each sale is made. Sales executives are devoting increased effort to the assignment of specialized sales people to key accounts to ensure that they are compatible with business buyers.

## DETERMINANTS OF BUSINESS MARKET DEMAND

To analyze a consumer market, a marketer would study the distribution of population and various demographics such as income, and then try to determine the consumers' buying motives and habits. Essentially the same type of analysis can be used by a firm selling to the business market. The factors affecting the market for business products are the number of potential business users and their purchasing power, buying motives, and buying habits. In the following discussion we'll identify several basic differences between consumer markets and business markets.

### Number and Types of Business Users

The business market contains relatively few buying units compared to the consumer market. There are approximately a half million business users, with about 40,000 of these being manufacturing establishments. In contrast, there are about 28 million consumers divided among more than 9 million households. The business market will seem even more limited to most companies, because they sell to only a segment of the total market. A firm selling to meat-processing plants, for example, would have about 45 potential customer plants. If you were interested in providing services to battery manufacturers, you would find about 25 companies as basic prospects. Consequently, marketing executives must try to pinpoint their market carefully by type of industry and geographic location. A firm marketing hard-rock mining equipment is not interested in the total business market, nor even in all firms engaged in mining and quarrying.

## MARKETING AT WORK

### FILE 7-2 STATSCAN MARKETS TO BUSINESS — UNFAIR COMPETITION?

How many people do you think are interested in reading "Production, Shipments and Stocks on Hand of Sawmills East of the Rockies"? Not many? Well, that's what Ivan Fellegi thought too, when he took over the reins of Statistics Canada in 1985. For years, the agency had been dutifully publishing everything possibly publishable about Canada and Canadians. The only problem was that there was virtually no demand for much of this superspecialized information, and with budget cuts looming, it became evident that StatsCan could no longer afford to publish such statistics.

What StatsCan could do — and what Fellegi did do — was to transform the plodding numbers cruncher into an aggressive supplier of information, analysis, and services to Canadian businesses. This strategy has been earning the agency close to $35 million a year — $12 million of which comes from selling statistics it already produces for the public good. The rest comes from conducting special surveys.

Although Statistics Canada is not the only government agency for whom selling information for profit has become a driving force, it is in the vanguard and as such is an inspiration to other federal departments looking to hawk their wares as well. Says Denis Desjardins, director-general of the agency's marketing and information services branch, "We, as public servants, have a culture that has always been to give stuff away. . . . (Now) we've become more marketing-oriented."

The agency has done this by identifying its two distinct types of clients: the general public, who obtain statistical information from the media and public libraries, and specialists, such as private economists and academics who require highly specialized information. It is to the latter that StatsCan has been directing marketing efforts that go beyond the mere publication of figures by providing analysis, explanation, and even custom-tailored information packages that the agency offers to private-sector clients — for a fee. "Should the Canadian taxpayer subsidize (this) sort of use?" asks Fellegi. "If you want your own copy on your desk or electronically, maybe you should pay for it. Somebody pays for it, either the taxpayer or the client."

Not only have such initiatives proved financially profitable, but they have done much to bolster StatsCan's public image as cutting-edge "information consultants." Fellegi says, "We really came to this realization that we were not doing a good job for either class of clients by trying to put out one grey ream of information — undigested numbers." But the good job is not being done for altruistic reasons. "What is very important is that we want quite consciously to engender profit. . . . Those revenues have become quite significant."

However, although other government agencies are inspired, some, such as academics, economists, and business people, feel that StatsCan should charge enough money to offset its costs, but that it is being unethical in seeking to make a profit. Michael McCracken, president of the Ottawa economic information firm Informetrica Ltd., which depends on StatsCan's data for its forecasts, protests that not only are prices prohibitively high, but they can be raised at any time. As examples, he points to a tape of import and export data that recently tripled in price to $3,000 and to the *Canadian Economic Observer*, essential for economists, which is sold for $220; the comparable American publication sells for $28 (U.S.). And while a CD-ROM full of information cost about $35 (U.S.) from American agencies, in Canada, a purchaser is obliged to fork out hundreds or thousands of dollars. The upshot of such prices, according to McCracken, is that "we end up being a data-poor country. . . (with only) the information that is most marketable." Fellegi counters, "To charge less would be to subsidize private enterprise. If the government wants to subsidize. . . it should be [done] out in the open, not through the acquisition of cheap statistics."

Source: Adapted from Alanna Mitchell, "Numbers for Sale: Call StatsCan," *Globe and Mail*, August 18, 1993, pp. A1, A5.

One very useful source of information is the **Standard Industrial Classification (SIC)** system, which enables a company to identify relatively small segments of its business market. All types of businesses in Canada are divided into 12 groups, as follows:

1. Agriculture.
2. Forestry.
3. Fishing and trapping.
4. Mines, quarries, and oil wells.
5. Manufacturing industries (20 major groups).
6. Construction industry.
7. Transportation, communication, and other utilities.
8. Trade.
9. Finance, insurance, and real estate.
10. Community, business, and personal service industries (8 major groups).
11. Public administration and defence.
12. Industry unspecified or undefined.

A separate number is assigned to each major industry within each of the above groups; then, three- and four-digit classification numbers are used to subdivide each major category into finer segments. To illustrate, in division 5 (manufacturing), major group 4 (leather) contains:

| SIC code | Industrial group |
|---|---|
| 172 | Leather tanneries |
| 174 | Shoe factories |
| 175 | Leather-glove factories |
| 179 | Luggage, handbag, and small-leather goods manufacturers |

**Size of Business Users** Although the market may be limited in the total number of buyers, it is large in purchasing power. As one might expect, business users range in size from very small companies with fewer than five employees to firms with staff numbering more than 1,000. A relatively small percentage of firms account for the greatest share of the value added by a given industry. For example, Statistics Canada data on the manufacturing sector in Canada indicate that slightly more than 1 percent of manufacturing firms — those with 500 or more employees — account for approximately 40 percent of the total value added by manufacturing and for more than 30 percent of the total employment in manufacturing. The firms with fewer than 50 employees, while accounting for more than 80 percent of all manufacturing establishments, produce less than 15 percent of the value added by manufacturing. Table 7-1 shows the selected statistics on manufacturing establishments, employment, and value added by firms for the ten provinces and two territories. **Value added** is the dollar value of firm's output minus the value of the inputs it purchased from other firms. If a manufacturer buys lumber for $40 and converts it into a table that it sells for $100, the value added by the manufacturer is $60.

The marketing significance in these facts is that buying power in the business market is highly concentrated in relatively few firms. This market concentration has considerable influence on a seller's policies regarding its channels of distribution. Intermediaries are not as essential as in the consumer market.

**Regional Concentration of Business Users** There is substantial regional concentration in many of the major industries and among business users as a whole. A firm selling products usable in oil fields will find the bulk of its market in Alberta, the Northwest Territories, offshore Newfoundland, and the United States and abroad. Rubber products manufacturers are located mostly in Ontario, shoes are produced chiefly in Quebec, and most of the nation's garment manufacturers are located in southern Ontario and Quebec. There is a similar regional concentration in the farm market.

WE PROCESS THE FUEL THAT DRIVES CANADIAN BUSINESS
To Such Strict Tolerances Its Performance Is 100% Accurate
The fuel that drives employees is their salary. That is why Comcheq, Canada's largest full-service payroll company, processes payrolls with speed, accuracy, and economy. Because on the road to success our clients demand that their fuel be on time and perfectly formulated. Always.
PAYROLLS ARE FOR COMCHEQ
Comcheq


**Comcheq serves a vertical business market.**

Although a large part of a firm's market may be concentrated in limited geographic areas, a good portion may lie outside these areas. Consequently, a distribution policy must be developed that will enable a firm to deal directly with the concentrated market and also to employ intermediaries (or a company sales force at great expense) to reach the outlying markets.

**Vertical and Horizontal Business Markets** For effective marketing planning, a company should know whether the market for its products is vertical or horizontal. If a firm's product is usable by virtually all firms in only one or two industries, it has a **vertical business market**. For example, some precision instruments are intended only for the marine market, but every boatbuilder or shipbuilder is a potential customer. If the product is usable by many industries, then it is said to have a broad or **horizontal business market**. Business supplies, such as Esso lubricating oils and greases, Canadian General

Electric small motors, and MacMillan Bloedel paper products, may be sold to a wide variety of industries.

A company's marketing program ordinarily is influenced by whether its markets are vertical or horizontal. In a vertical market, a product can be tailor-made to meet the specific needs of one industry. However, the industry must buy enough to support this specialization. In addition, advertising and personal selling can be directed more effectively in vertical markets. In a horizontal market, a product is developed as an all-purpose item, to reach a larger market. However, because of the larger potential market, the product is likely to face more competition.

TABLE 7-1 Selected principal statistics of the manufacturing industries of Canada, by province 1990 annual survey of manufacturers

| Province | Manufacturing activity | | | | | | | |
|---|---|---|---|---|---|---|---|---|
| | | Production and related workers | | | Cost of fuel and electricity | Cost of materials and supplies used | Value of shipments of goods of own manufacture | Value added |
| | No. of establishments | Number | Person-hours paid '000,000 | Wages | | | | |
| | | | | $'000,000 | | | | |
| Newfoundland | 341 | 13,134 | 26.9 | 309.9 | 88.5 | 714.2 | 1,551.8 | 742.1 |
| Prince Edward Island | 141 | 2,663 | 5.6 | 50.8 | 9.7 | 229.1 | 396.4 | 155.7 |
| Nova Scotia | 760 | 27,772 | 57.5 | 724.8 | 183.1 | 3,202.4 | 5,150.5 | 1,856.2 |
| New Brunswick | 714 | 25,104 | 52.2 | 686.5 | 259.2 | 3,724.8 | 5,865.5 | 1,912.5 |
| Quebec | 13,362 | 381,882 | 782.5 | 10,246.7 | 2,431.6 | 38,488.1 | 73,973.6 | 33,477.5 |
| Ontario | 15,563 | 706,346 | 1,480.1 | 21,058.6 | 3,253.9 | 89,803.8 | 155,995.2 | 62,629.0 |
| Manitoba | 1,167 | 39,973 | 82.5 | 998.4 | 181.1 | 3,435.9 | 6,739.5 | 3,154.6 |
| Saskatchewan | 809 | 14,481 | 30.3 | 407.9 | 123.9 | 2,227.2 | 3,786.0 | 1,475.1 |
| Alberta | 2,827 | 64,292 | 133.7 | 1,900.9 | 541.0 | 12,651.6 | 20,048.8 | 7,029.6 |
| British Columbia | 4,126 | 117,346 | 241.3 | 4,013.5 | 862.5 | 14,145.4 | 25,335.9 | 10,507.2 |
| Yukon | 30 | 189 | 0.4 | 4.6 | 0.4 | 7.7 | 19.3 | 11.1 |
| Northwest Territories | 24 | 142 | 0.3 | 4.0 | 1.0 | 34.1 | 56.1 | 21.8 |
| Canada – 1990 | 39,864 | 1,393,324 | 2,893.3 | 40,406.5 | 7,936.1 | 168,664.3 | 298,918.5 | 122,972.5 |

Source: Statistics Canada, *The Daily*, January 21, 1993, Cat. No. 11-001E.

## Buying Power of Business Users

Another determinant of business market demand is the purchasing power of business users. This can be measured either by the expenditures of business users or by their sales volume. Many times, however, such information is not available or is very difficult to estimate. In such cases, it is more feasible to use an **activity indicator** — that is, some market factor that is related to income generation and expenditures. Sometimes an activity indicator is a combined indicator of purchasing power and the number of business users. Following are examples of activity indicators that might be used to estimate the purchasing power of business users.

**Measures of Manufacturing Activity** Firms selling to manufacturers might use as market indicators such factors as the number of employees, the number of plants, or the dollar value added by manufacturing. One firm selling work gloves used the number of employees in manufacturing establishments to determine the relative value of various geographic markets. Another company that sold a product that controls stream pollution used two indicators — (1) the number of firms processing wood products (paper mills, plywood mills, and so forth) and (2) the manufacturing value added by these firms.

**Measures of Mining Activity** The number of mines operating, the volume of their output, and the dollar value of the product as it leaves the mine all may indicate the purchasing power of mines. This information can be used by any firm marketing industrial products to mine operators.

**Measures of Agricultural Activity** A company marketing fertilizer or agricultural equipment can estimate the buying power of its farm market by studying such indicators as cash farm income, acreage planted, or crop yields. The chemical producer that sells to a fertilizer manufacturer might study the same indices, because the demand for chemicals in this case is derived from the demand for fertilizer.

**Measures of Construction Activity** If a firm is marketing building materials, such as lumber, brick, gypsum products, or builders' hardware, its market is dependent on construction activity. This may be indicated by the number and value of building permits issued or by the number of construction starts by type of housing (single-family residence, apartment, or commercial).

## BUSINESS BUYING BEHAVIOUR

Business buying behaviour, like consumer buying behaviour, is initiated when an aroused need (a motive) is recognized. This leads to goal-oriented activity designed to satisfy the need. Once again, marketers must try to determine what motivates the buyer, and then understand the buying process and buying patterns of business organizations in their markets.

### The Importance of Business Buying

Business buying or purchasing, formerly a relatively minor function in most firms, is now an activity that top management is very much interested in. Once viewed as an isolated activity that focused primarily on searching out low prices, purchasing has become an important part of overall strategy for at least three reasons:[1]

- Companies are making less and buying more. For example, 93 percent of the cost of an Apple computer is purchased content, and for all manufacturers, purchased content is over 50 percent of their final products. For many years General Motors has owned the plants that made many of the parts for its cars. But in 1992 it announced the closing of seven parts plants that were no longer competitive. As a result, General Motors will become much more reliant on independent parts suppliers in both Canada and the United States. With outside suppliers so significant, buying becomes a prime strategic issue.
- Firms are under intense quality and time pressures. To reduce costs and improve efficiency, firms no longer buy and hold inventories of parts and supplies. Instead, they demand that raw materials and components that meet specifications be delivered "just in time" to go into the production process. Compaq's Prolinea line of personal computers is a good example.[2] The firm had an established reputation for high quality and

high prices. However, intense competition from lower-priced clones forced a change. Compaq established a goal of developing the Prolinea in six months to sell for less than one-third of the price of its similar Deskpro model without a cut in quality. To accomplish its goal, Compaq searched around the world for suppliers that combined the best prices with consistent quality and on-time delivery.

- To get what they need, firms are concentrating their purchases with fewer suppliers and developing long-term "partnering" relationships. This level of involvement extends beyond a purchase to include such things as working together to develop new products and providing financial support.[3]

## Buying Motives of Business Users

One view of **buying motives** is that business purchases are methodical and structured. Business buying motives, for the most part, are presumed to be practical and unemotional. Business buyers are assumed to be motivated to achieve the optimal combination of price, quality, and service in the products they buy. An alternative view is that business buyers are human, and their business decisions are certainly influenced by their attitudes, perceptions, and values. In fact, many sales people would maintain that business buyers seem to be motivated more towards personal goals than organizational goals, and the two are often in conflict.

The truth is actually somewhere in between. Business buyers have two goals — to further their company's position (in profits, in acceptance by society) and to protect or improve their position in their firms (self-interest). Sometimes these goals are mutually consistent. For example, the firm's highest priority may be to save money, and the buyer knows that she will be rewarded for negotiating a low price. Obviously the more consistent the goals are, the better for both the organization and the individual, and the easier it is to make buying decisions.

However, there are often significant areas where the buyer's goals do not coincide with those of the firm, as when the firm insists on dealing with the lowest-price supplier, but the buyer has developed a good relationship with another supplier and doesn't want to change. In these cases a seller must appeal to the buyer both on a rational, "what's good for the firm" basis and on a self-interest "what's in it for me" basis. Promotional appeals directed to the buyer's self-interest are particularly useful when two or more competing sellers are offering essentially the same products, prices, and postsale services.[4]

## Types of Buying Situations

In Chapter 6 we observed that consumer purchases can range from routine to complex buying decisions. Similarly, the buying situations in business organizations vary widely in their complexity, number of people involved, and time required. Researchers in organizational buying behaviour have identified three classes of business buying situations. The three **buy classes** are new-task buying, straight rebuy, and modified rebuy. The stages in the business buying-decision process and the three buy classes are illustrated in Table 7-2.

- **New-task buying.** This is the most difficult and complex buying situation because it is a first-time purchase of a major product. Typically more people are involved in new-task buying than in the other two situations because the risk is great. Information needs are high and the evaluation of alternatives is difficult because the decision makers have little experience with the product. Sellers have the challenge of finding out the buyer's needs and communicating the product's ability to provide satisfaction. A hospital's first-time purchase of laser surgical equipment or a company buying robots for a factory (or buying the factory itself) are new-task buying conditions.

TABLE 7-2 The buy-grid framework

Stages in the business buying process (buy phases) in relation to buying situations (buy classes)

| Buy phases (stages in buying-decision process) | Buy classes | | |
|---|---|---|---|
| | New class | Modified rebuy | Straight rebuy |
| **1. Recognize the problem.** | Yes | Maybe | No |
| **2. Determine product needs.** | Yes | Maybe | No |
| **3. Describe product specifications.** | Yes | Yes | Yes |
| **4. Search for suppliers.** | Yes | Maybe | No |
| **5. Acquire supplier proposals.** | Yes | Maybe | No |
| **6. Select suppliers.** | Yes | Maybe | No |
| **7. Select an order routine.** | Yes | Maybe | No |
| **8. Evaluate product performance.** | Yes | Yes | Yes |

Source: Adapted from Patrick J. Robinson, Charles W. Faris, and Yoram Wind, *Industrial Buying and Creative Marketing*, Allyn and Bacon, Inc., Boston, 1967, p. 14.

- **Straight rebuy.** This is a routine, low-involvement purchase with minimal information needs and no great consideration of alternatives. The buyer's extensive experience with the seller has been satisfactory, so there is no incentive to search. An example is the repeat purchase of steering wheels by Freightliner, a truck manufacturer. These buying decisions are made in the purchasing department, usually from a predetermined list of acceptable suppliers. Suppliers who are not on this list may have difficulty getting in to make a sales presentation to the buyer.
- **Modified rebuy.** This buying situation is somewhere between the other two in time and people involved, information needed, and alternatives considered. In selecting diesel engines for the trucks it manufactures, Freightliner considers Cummins and Caterpillar products among others. However, because these engine makers frequently introduce new design and performance features, Freightliner evaluates each on a regular basis.

### Buying-Decision Process in Business

The buying-decision process in business markets is a sequence of five stages similar to the ones followed by consumers, as discussed in the preceding chapter. Not every purchase involves all five steps. Straight-rebuy purchases usually are low-involvement situations for the buyer, so purchasers typically skip some stages. But a new-task purchase of an expensive product or service is likely to be a high-involvement, total-stage buying decision.

To illustrate the process, let's assume that Weston Bakeries is considering a fat substitute in baked goods:

- **Need recognition.** Weston's marketing executives are sensitive to the concerns of many consumers about fat in their diets. The opportunity to produce high-quality, good-tasting baked goods without fat is very attractive, but finding the right substitute is the challenge.
- **Identification of alternatives.** The marketing staff draws up a list of product-performance specifications for the fat-free baked goods — attractive appearance, good taste, and reasonable cost. Then the purchasing department identifies the alternative brands and supply sources of fat substitutes that generally meet these specifications.

- **Evaluation of alternatives.** The production, research, and purchasing people jointly evaluate both the alternative products and sources of supply. They discover that some brands cannot withstand high temperatures, there are differences in how well they simulate the taste and texture of fat, and some have not received final approval from federal health authorities. The complete evaluation considers such factors as product performance and price as well as the suppliers' abilities to meet delivery schedules and provide consistent quality.
- **Purchase decision.** Based on the evaluation, the buyer decides on a specific brand and supplier. Next, the purchasing department negotiates the contract. Since large sums are involved, the contract will likely include many details. For example, the contract might go beyond price and delivery schedules to include the producer of the fat substitute providing marketing support for Weston's finished baked goods.
- **Postpurchase behaviour.** Weston continues to evaluate the performances of the fat substitute and the selected supplier to ensure that both meet expectations. Future dealings with a supplier will depend on this performance evaluation and on how well the supplier handles any problems that may later arise involving its product.

### Multiple Buying Influences — The Buying Centre

One of the biggest challenges in business-to-business marketing is to determine which individuals in the organization play the various buying roles. That is, who influences the buying decision, who determines product specifications, and who makes the buying decision? In the business market these activities typically involve several people. In other words, there are **multiple buying influences**, particularly in medium-sized and large firms. Even in small companies where the owner-managers make all major decisions, knowledgeable employees are usually consulted before certain purchases are made.

Understanding the concept of a buying centre is helpful in identifying the multiple buying influences and understanding the buying process in business organizations. A **buying centre** may be defined as all the individuals or groups who are involved in the process of making a decision to purchase. Thus a buying centre includes the people who play any of the following roles:

- **Users.** The people who actually use the business product — perhaps a secretary, an executive, a production-line employee, or a truck driver.
- **Influencers.** The people who set the specifications and aspects of buying decisions because of their technical expertise, their organizational position, or even their political power in the firm.
- **Deciders.** The people who make the actual buying decision regarding the business product and the supplier. A purchasing agent may be the decider in a straight-rebuy situation. But someone in top management may make the decision regarding whether to buy an expensive computer.
- **Gatekeepers.** The people who control the flow of purchasing information within the organization as well as between the firm and potential vendors. These people may be purchasing agents, secretaries, receptionists, or technical personnel.
- **Buyers.** The people who interact with the suppliers, arrange the terms of sale, and process the actual purchase orders. Typically this is the purchasing department's role. But again, if the purchase is an expensive, complex new buy, the buyer's role may be filled by someone in top management.

Several people in an organization may play the same role: There may be several users of the product. Or the same person may occupy more than one role: A secretary may be a user, an influencer, and a gatekeeper in the purchase of word-processing equipment.

## MARKETING AT WORK

### FILE 7-3 ETHICAL ISSUES IN BUSINESS NEGOTIATIONS

In business marketing, the participants engage in bargaining or negotiations to determine the actual terms of sale. In these negotiations, purchasers use a variety of tactics to gain an advantage. In a recent study of rebuying decisions of component parts, it was found that the four most common tactics employed by purchasing agents are:

- Creating the impression that there are other vendors aggressively competing for the business.
- Imposing time pressure on the seller to reach an agreement.
- Implying that the selling firm is in danger of losing the contract.
- Suggesting that a competitor is offering a significantly better deal.

Other tactics used by purchasing agents are:

- Suggesting that the selling firm's performance has slipped.
- Testing the seller's limits by making excessive demands.
- Creating the impression that the buyer's boss won't allow him or her to accept the seller's terms.

Would the use of all or any of these tactics be unethical if the situation suggested did not actually exist?

Source: Barbara C. Perdue and John O. Summers, "Purchasing Agents' Use of Negotiation Strategies," *Journal of Marketing Research*, May 1991, pp. 175-189.

The size and composition of a buying centre will vary among business organizations. In one study, the average size of buying centres ranged from 2.7 to 5.1 persons.[5] Within a given organization, the size and makeup of the buying centre will vary depending on the product's cost, the complexity of the decision, and the stage of the buying process. The buying centre for a straight rebuy of office supplies will be quite different from the centre handling the purchase of a building or a fleet of trucks.

The variety of people involved in any business buying situation, plus the differences among companies, present real challenges to sales people. As they try to determine "who's on first" — that is, determine who does what in a buying situation — sales reps often call on the wrong executives. Even knowing who the decision makers are at a certain time is not enough, because these people may be very difficult to reach and people move into and out of the buying centre as the purchase proceeds through the decision process. This, in part, explains why a sales person typically has only a few major accounts.

Certainly the challenges presented in the business buying-decision process should suggest the importance of co-ordinating the selling activities of the business marketer with the buying needs of the purchasing organization.

### Buying Patterns of Business Users

Buying behaviour in the business market differs significantly from consumer behaviour in several ways. These differences stem from the products, markets, and buyer-seller relationships in business markets.

**Direct Purchase** In the consumer market, consumers rarely buy directly from the producer except in the case of services. In the business market, however, direct purchase by the business user from the producer is quite common even for goods. This is true especially when the order is large and the buyer needs much technical assistance. Computer

**This major law firm wishes to establish relationships with corporate clients.**

chip makers deal directly with personal computer manufacturers because the chip technology is changing so rapidly. From a seller's point of view, direct sale in the business market is reasonable, especially when there are relatively few potential buyers, they are big, or they are geographically concentrated.

**Nature of the Relationship** Many business marketers take a broad view of exchanges. Rather than focus only on the immediate customer, they approach marketing as a value chain. That is, they consider the roles of suppliers, producers, distributors, and end users to see how each adds value to the final product. This perspective leads to a recognition of the importance of all the parties involved in successfully bringing a product to market and an emphasis on building and maintaining relationships. For example, Apple Computer, which once relied exclusively on dealers, recognized that many of its larger customers needed specialized service. To satisfy this segment of the market and maintain strong ties to these key customers, the computer firm now has its own sales force calling directly on large accounts. However, many of the orders taken by the sales force are contracted out to dealers to ensure that they are protected.[6]

**Frequency of Purchase** In the business market, firms buy certain products very infrequently. Large installations are purchased only once in many years. Small parts and materials to be used in the manufacture of a product may be ordered on long-term contracts, so that a selling opportunity exists as seldom as once a year. Even standard operating supplies, such as office supplies or cleaning products, may be bought only once a month.

Because of this buying pattern, a great burden is placed on the personal-selling programs of business sellers. The sales force must call on potential customers often enough to keep them familiar with the company's products and to know when a customer is considering a purchase.

**Size of Order** The average business order is considerably larger than its counterpart in the consumer market. This fact, coupled with the infrequency of purchase, highlights the importance of each sale in the business market. Losing the sale of a pair of shoes to a consumer is not nearly as devastating as Canadair losing the sale of 10 airplanes.

**Length of Negotiation Period** The period of negotiation in a business sale is usually much longer than in a consumer transaction. General Electric, for example, negotiated over a five-year period before completing the purchase of a $9.5-million Cray supercomputer to aid in managing operations and research activities in Canada and the United States. Some reasons for extended negotiations are:

- Several executives participate in the buying decision.
- The sale involves a large amount of money.
- The business product is made to order and considerable discussion is required to establish the specifications.

**Reciprocity Arrangements** A highly controversial business buying practice is reciprocity: the policy of "I'll buy from you if you'll buy from me." Traditionally, reciprocity was common among firms marketing homogeneous basic business products (oil, steel, rubber, paper products, and chemicals).

There has been a decline, but not an elimination, of reciprocity. This decline has occurred for two reasons, one legal and the other economic. The Competition Act applies to reciprocity when the practice is similar to price discrimination. A firm can buy from a customer, but it must be able to prove that it is not given any special privileges regarding price, quality, or service that are not made available to competing buyers.

From an economic point of view, reciprocity may not make sense because the price, quality, or service offered by the seller may not be competitive. In addition, when a firm fails to pursue objectives that maximize profits, morale of both the sales force and the purchasing department may suffer.

Reciprocity is an area in which firms run into problems in doing business overseas. In many parts of the world, it is taken for granted that if I buy your product, you will buy mine.

**Demand for Service** The user's desire for excellent service is a strong business buying motive that may determine buying patterns. Frequently a firm's only differentiating feature is its service, because the product itself is so standardized that it can be purchased from any number of companies. Consider the choice of suppliers to provide elevators for a major office building or hotel. The installation of the elevators is no more important than keeping them operating safely and efficiently. Consequently, in its marketing efforts a firm such as Otis emphasizes its maintenance service as much as its products.

Sellers must be ready to furnish services both before and after the sale. For example, suppliers such as Kraft General Foods conduct a careful analysis of a supermarket's customers and sales performance and then suggest a product assortment and layout for the store's dairy department. In the case of office copiers, manufacturers train the buyers' office staffs in the use of the equipment, and after the machines have been installed, offer other services, such as repairs by specially trained technicians.

## MARKETING AT WORK

### FILE 7-4 NEGOTIATING INTERNATIONALLY IN BUSINESS MARKETS

In doing business around the world, executives have found that economic and political environments are major factors in determining success or failure. But what have they learned about the styles of their international business counterparts? Consider these tips on what marketers going abroad can expect:

- In Germany, executives are thorough, systematic, well prepared, and quite rigid. They tend to be assertive, even intimidating, and not very willing to compromise. They are punctual and prize efficiency and directness.
- In France, managers may insist that negotiations be conducted in French. Because they consider speaking to be an art, the French dislike being interrupted. Lengthy lunches with lots of wine are more likely to affect the negotiating skills of Americans than French executives, who are more used to such meals.
- In England, the style is friendly and easygoing. Executives are more likely to be underprepared than overprepared. They are flexible and open to initiatives. However, their kindly posture can be misleading, and they can become very stubborn if they sense a lack of respect.
- In Mexico, personal relationships are very important, so face-to-face contact is a must. Unlike in Canada, the rule is to socialize first and work later. Mexicans are very ego-involved in business decisions, so concessions that make the decision maker look good are important. They are quite flexible when it comes to trade-offs, but it is often best to negotiate them in private, one-on-one conversations rather than in front of others.
- In China, small courtesies and follow-up gifts are important in establishing friendship. Being meticulous in preparation and consistent in presentations is crucial, because the Chinese are very thorough. Decision making cannot be rushed, so business deals take a lot of time.
- In Japan, the Japanese executive often considers the long-term relationship with a business contact as important as the immediate negotiations, so negotiators should keep the future as well as the present in mind. Because decisions often involve more people and more levels of management than in Canada, meetings tend to be large. The Japanese avoid saying no directly. As a result, any answer other than a definite yes may, in fact, be a no. If circumstances change after an agreement is reached, the Japanese assume the right to renegotiate.
- In Russia, the tone of negotiations will be very bureaucratic, and the red tape will be extensive. Decision makers must be prepared for many delays. It is likely that managers will be unfamiliar with many free-market concepts and will require detailed explanations of costs and pricing strategies. The price of a mistake is very large, so a manager's job or even career may be at stake in the negotiations.

Source: Sergy Frank, "Global Negotiating: Vive Les Differences!" *Sales & Marketing Management*, May 1992, pp. 65-69.

**Dependability of Supply** Another business buying pattern is the user's insistence on an adequate quantity of uniform-quality products. Variations in the *quality* of materials going into finished products can cause considerable trouble for manufacturers. They may be faced with costly disruptions in their production processes if the imperfections exceed quality control limits. Adequate *quantities* are as important as good quality. A work stoppage caused by an insufficient supply of materials is just as costly as one caused by inferior quality of materials. In one study of problems faced by purchasing agents for smaller manufacturers, the problem most often reported was the failure of sellers to deliver on schedule.

The emphasis on total quality management (TQM) has increased the significance of dependability. Now that it has been established that firms can operate with virtually zero defects, buyers expect a very high standard of performance.

**Leasing Instead of Buying** A growing tendency among firms in the business market is leasing business goods instead of buying them. In the past this practice was limited to large equipment, such as mainframe computers, packaging equipment, and heavy construction equipment. Presently, industrial firms are expanding leasing arrangements to include delivery trucks, automobiles used by sales people, machine tools, and other items that are generally less expensive than major installations.

Leasing has several merits for the lessor — the firm providing the equipment:

- Total net income — the income after charging off repairs and maintenance expenses — is often higher than it would be if the equipment were sold.
- The lessor's market may be expanded to include users who could not afford to buy the product, especially for large equipment.
- Leasing offers an effective method of getting users to try a new product. They may be more willing to rent a product than to buy it. If they are not satisfied, their expenditure is limited to a few monthly payments.

From the lessee's — or customer's — point of view, the benefits of leasing are:

- Leasing allows users to retain their investment capital for other purposes.
- Firms can enter a new business with less capital outlay than would be necessary if they had to buy equipment.
- Leased products are usually repaired and maintained by lessors, eliminating one headache associated with ownership.
- Leasing is particularly attractive to firms that need equipment seasonally or sporadically, as in food canning or construction.

## BASES FOR BUSINESS MARKET SEGMENTATION

Several of the bases used to segment the consumer market can also be used to segment the broad business market. For example, we can segment business markets on a geographical basis. Several industries are geographically concentrated, so any firm selling to these industries could nicely use this segmentation basis. Sellers also can segment on product-related bases such as usage rate or benefits desired.[7]

Let's look at three of the bases that are used solely for segmenting business markets — type of customer, size of customer, and type of buying situation.[8]

**Type of Customer** Any firm that sells to customers in a variety of business markets may want to segment this market on the basis of customer types. We discussed the Standard Industrial Classification (SIC) code as a very useful tool for identifying business and institutional target markets. A firm selling display cases or store fixtures to the retail market, for example, might start out with potential customers included in the two-digit code number 61 for shoe, apparel, fabric and yarn industries — retail. Then the three-digit code 612 identifies potential customers in the retail clothing business. Finally, the four-digit code number 6121 pinpoints men's clothing specialty stores.

A firm selling janitorial supplies or small electric motors would have a broad potential market among many different industries. Management in this firm could segment its market by type of customer and then perhaps decide to sell to firms in only a limited number of these segments.

**Size of Customer** In this situation, size can be measured by such factors as sales volume, number of production facilities, or number of sales offices. Many business-to-business marketers divide their potential market into large and small accounts, using separate distribution channels to reach each segment. The large-volume accounts, for example,

**Targeting the segment that does business in the United States.**

may be sold to directly by the company's sales force. But to reach the smaller accounts, the seller will use a manufacturers' agent or some other form of intermediary.

**Type of Buying Situation** Earlier in this chapter, we discussed the three types of buying classes — new buy, modified rebuy, and straight rebuy. We also recognized in that discussion that a new buy is significantly different from a straight rebuy in several important respects. Consequently, a business seller might well segment its market into these three buy-class categories. Or the seller could at least set up two segments by combining new buy and modified rebuy into one segment. Then different marketing programs would be developed to reach each of these two or three segments.[9]

## SUMMARY

The business market consists of organizations that buy goods and services to produce other goods and services, to resell to other business users or consumers, or to conduct the organization's operations. It is an extremely large and complex market spanning a wide variety of business users that buy a broad array of business goods and services. Besides manufacturing, the business market includes the agriculture, reseller, government, services, not-for-profit, and international markets.

Business market demand generally is derived, inelastic, and widely fluctuating. Business buyers usually are well informed about what they are buying. Business market demand is analyzed by evaluating the number and kinds of business users and their buying power.

Business buying, or purchasing, has taken on greater strategic importance because organizations are buying more and making less, under intense time and quality pressures, and developing long-term partnering relationships with suppliers.

Business buying motives are focused on achieving a firm's objectives, but the business buyer's self-interest must also be considered.

The buying-decision process in business markets may involve as many as five stages: need recognition, identification of alternatives, evaluation of alternatives, purchase decision, and postpurchase behaviour. The actual number of stages in a given purchase decision depends largely on the buying situation, whether new-task buy, straight rebuy, or modified rebuy.

The concept of a buying centre reflects the multiple buying influences in business purchasing decisions. In a typical buying centre are people playing the roles of users, influencers, deciders, gatekeepers, and buyers.

Buying patterns (habits) of business users often are quite different from patterns in the consumer market. In the business market, direct purchases (without intermediaries) are more common, purchases are made less frequently, and orders are larger. The negotiation period usually is longer, and reciprocity arrangements are more common. The demand for service is greater, and the dependability of supply is more critical. Finally, leasing (rather than product ownership) is quite common in business marketing.

Three segmentation bases that are used solely for segmenting the business market are customer type, customer size, and type of buying situation.

## KEY TERMS AND CONCEPTS

**Business market (180)**
**Business users (180)**
**Business marketing (180)**
**Agribusiness (182)**
**Reseller market (183)**
**Services market (184)**
**Nonbusiness market (184)**
**Standard Industrial Classification (SIC) system (188)**
**Value added (189)**
**Vertical business market (190)**
**Horizontal business market (190)**
**Activity indicators of buying power (191)**
**Buying motives (193)**
**Buy classes: (193)**
- **New-task buy (193)**
- **Straight rebuy (194)**
- **Modified rebuy (194)**

**Multiple buying influences (buying centre): (195)**
- **Users (195)**
- **Influencers (195)**
- **Deciders (195)**
- **Gatekeepers (195)**
- **Buyers (195)**

## QUESTIONS AND PROBLEMS

1. What are some marketing implications of the fact that the demand for business goods:
   a. Fluctuates widely?
   b. Is inelastic?
   c. Is derived?
2. What are the marketing implications for a seller of the fact that business customers are geographically concentrated and limited in number?
3. What differences would you expect to find between the marketing strategies of a company that sells to horizontal business markets and those of a company that sells to vertical business markets?
4. A manufacturer has been selling word processors to a large oil company in Norway. In which of the three buy classes would you place this buyer-seller relationship? Is there any aspect of the relationship that is likely to fall into the straight-rebuy category?

5. Explain how the five stages in the buying-decision process might be applied in the following buying situations:
   a. New-task buying of a conveyor belt for a soft-drink bottling plant.
   b. Straight rebuying of maintenance services for that conveyor belt.
6. How would you go about determining who influences the buying decisions of business users?
7. NCR, IBM, Xerox, and other manufacturers of office equipment make a substantial proportion of their sales directly to business users. At the same time, wholesalers of office equipment are thriving. Are these two market situations inconsistent? Explain.

## HANDS-ON MARKETING

1. Find an ad for a business product or service that is directed towards the business market and another ad for the same product that is directed towards consumers (such as an ad for leasing fleets of Chevrolets and an ad for Chevrolet aimed at consumers). Discuss the buying motives appealed to in the ads.
2. Interview a purchasing agent about buying a product that would qualify as a modified rebuy. Draw a diagram that shows the purchasing agent's perceptions of: (a) the stages of the decision process; (b) who was in the buying centre at each stage of the decision process; and (c) what role(s) each person played at each stage of the process. Comment on how this diagram might be useful to a sales person representing the product in question.

## NOTES AND REFERENCES


1. Louis J. DeRose, "How Industrial Markets Buy Value Selling: A Strategy for Dealing with Change," *The Journal of Business and Industrial Marketing*, Winter 1992, pp. 65-69.
2. Joanne Lipmann, "Compaq Pushing New Line, New Images," *The Wall Street Journal*, June 2, 1992, p. B5; Michael Allen, "Developing New Lines of Low-Priced PCs Shakes Up Compaq," *The Wall Street Journal*, June 15, 1992, pp. A1, A4.
3. Some background on relationship building is described in F. Robert Dwyer, Paul H. Schurr, and Sejo Oh, "Developing Buyer-Seller Relationships," *Journal of Marketing*, April 1987, pp. 11-27. A simple approach to building relationships is described in Barry J. Farber and Joyce Wycoff, "Relationships: Six Steps to Success," *Sales & Marketing Management*, April 1992, pp. 50-58.
4. An interesting description of value imaging, the psychological influences on business buying behaviour, can be found in Paul Sherlock, "The Irrationality of 'Rational' Business Buying Decisions," *Marketing Management*, Spring 1992, pp. 8-15.
5. Robert D. McWilliams, Earl Naumann, and Stan Scott, "Determining Buying Center Size," *Industrial Marketing Management*, February 1992, pp. 43-49.
6. Ken Yamada, "Apple to Unveil Mail Order Catalog and Sell Directly to Big Companies," *The Wall Street Journal*, September 17, 1992, p. B7.
7. For examples of benefit segmentation as used in the business market, see Mark L. Bennion, Jr., "Segmentation and Positioning in a Basic Industry," *Industrial Marketing Management*, February 1987, pp. 9-18; Susan A. Lynn, "Segmenting a Business Market for a Professional Service," *Industrial Marketing Management*, February 1986, pp. 13-21; Rowland T. Moriarty and David J. Reibstein, "Benefit Segmentation in Industrial Markets," *Journal of Business Research*, December 1986, pp. 483-86; and Cornelis A. de Kluyver and David B. Whitlark, "Benefit Segmentation for Industrial Products," *Industrial Marketing Management*, November 1986, pp. 273-86.
8. For some additional approaches to business marketing segmentation, see Benson P. Shapiro and Thomas V. Bonoma, "How to Segment Industrial Markets," *Harvard Business Review*, May/June 1984, pp. 104-110. See also James G. Barnes and Ronald McTavish, "Segmenting Industrial Markets by Buyer Sophistication," *European Journal of Marketing*, vol. 17, no. 6, 1983, pp. 16-33.
9. For an excellent review of the literature on industrial market segmentation — some 30 articles spanning 20 years — see Richard E. Plank, "A Critical Review of Industrial Market Segmentation," *Industrial Marketing Management*, May 1985, pp. 79-91. Also, a detailed coverage of the topic is contained in Thomas V. Bonoma and Benson P. Shapiro, *Segmenting the Industrial Market*, Lexington, MA: Lexington Books, 1983.

## CHAPTER 8 GOALS

The experience of Volvo in launching the new 850 reflects one thing all organizations have in common — the need for information. To be effective, marketing managers need current, accurate information about the markets they are trying to reach, the macroenvironment affecting their particular industry, and the internal and external factors that affect their specific market. We're about to see where this information can be obtained and how to use it. After studying this chapter, you should have an understanding of:

- What marketing research is and the role it plays in improving marketing decision making.
- The systems that have been developed to increase the usefulness of data.
- The appropriate way to conduct a marketing research project.
- Who actually does marketing research.
- The current status of marketing research.

CHAPTER

8

# MARKETING RESEARCH AND INFORMATION

## Marketing Research Supports Launch of the Volvo 850

Behind most successful new product introductions lies a great deal of research. The introduction of a new automobile is no exception. In the case of a new car, however, there must be effective use of research and development that results in a design that is technically advanced and that offers features buyers will find attractive. Coupled with this engineering-based research must be marketing research that addresses the issue of what the customer wants and how it can best be offered in the new car. The combination of both forms of research were obvious in the launch of Volvo's new 850 model.

Work on the development of Volvo's first front-drive car began in the late 1970s when Volvo started to address the question of what type of cars Volvo should manufacture for the next century. The company launched the Galaxy project, which would try to predict the values and standards the world would set for the automobile, particularly in light of environmental and energy issues. From the Galaxy project sprang a number of concept cars that led ultimately to the introduction of the Volvo 400 series of cars in Europe and to the launch of the Volvo 850 in 1991.

For more than 10 years, Volvo engineers worked on the design of various Galaxy prototype cars, each of which was developed with certain objectives in mind. It was to be efficient, but with the ability to absorb enough energy in a crash to protect its occupants, thereby protecting Volvo's reputation for safety. An early decision was made that the new car was to be front-drive, and after much testing it was decided that it would be powered by a unique transversely-mounted inline five-cylinder engine, which would offer enough power to drive a five-passenger mid-sized automobile. Finally, after testing many prototype designs and exhaustive performance testing of the final design, the first Volvo 850 rolled off the production line on April 16, 1991.

The marketing of the new Volvo in Great Britain provides a valuable insight into how marketing research is used to support the launch of an automobile resulting from more than 10 years of engineering research and design. In the first place, the Volvo 850 was to be positioned in a manner consistent with Volvo's reputation for safety. The design features of the new 850 were such that it is reputed to be the world's safest car. However, as well as safety, this image was to reflect the superior driving performance, handling, and responsiveness. The positioning of the new 850 had to minimize cannibalization from other Volvo models, including the 940.

Research into the positioning strategy for the new 850 began in late 1991 and included a series of nine extended focus group interviews with existing Volvo owners (three groups) and non-owners (six groups). All were from white-collar and professional backgrounds, reflecting the Volvo target segment, and typically bought their cars new. These focus group interviews centred on the respondents' views of the car market and on Volvo's current image and standing. They also provided an opportunity to review competitive advertising materials and to see the initial advertising theme for the 850 and the car itself. During the focus-group sessions, participants viewed the new 850 as sleek, sumptuous, and "softer" than conventional Volvos, and above all "not boring." The 850 was expected to compete with makes such as Saab, BMW, and Audi. Even without driving the car, participants viewed the 850 as responsive and a driver's car.

The second stage of the consumer research was carried out in early 1992 and offered 153 target consumers the opportunity to test drive the 850 against two competing cars, the Rover 827 and the BMW 525. This stage of the research also allowed for testing a revised advertising concept that centred on the use of horses in a television commercial to convey an impression of grace, power, and the characteristics of a thoroughbred. This stage of the research led to two important recommendations: that Volvo should emphasize the nature of the driving experience to ensure that the 850 is seen to be different from other Volvos and to reinforce the message of responsiveness; and that the advertising should embody a greater sense of gracefulness and style, so as to overcome any impression that the 850 is a "speed machine."

Finally, the "horses" advertising theme was developed into a finished television commercial and examined through the third stage of the research, a series of 155 semi-structured interviews among upscale males aged 35 to 55. Each respondent was shown a reel of five television commercials with the test advertising for the Volvo 850 in the middle. Recall and communications measures were taken for the Volvo commercial, before it was shown again in isolation to allow for more detailed discussion of its communication effectiveness. The 850 commercial tested very well, with high levels of recall and respondents commenting favourably on the image being conveyed of power and excitement. The advertising was seen to break away from the traditional image of Volvo.[1]

This example demonstrates how various forms of marketing research are used to follow on from the design and engineering work to ensure the successful introduction of a new product. While the specific forms of research used may differ by product category and from company to company, the basic principles are the same, that a marketer can learn much about how a product should be positioned and promoted by collecting relevant information from target customers before such marketing decisions are made.

## NEED FOR MARKETING RESEARCH

Management in any organization needs information — and lots of it — about potential markets and environmental forces in order to develop successful strategic marketing plans and to respond to changes in the marketplace. A mass of data is available both from external sources and from within a firm. The challenge is how to transform the raw data into information and how to use it effectively. To see how to do this, we will begin by briefly discussing why organizations need to do research. Then we will focus our attention on how organizations manage their research efforts.

Today many forces dictate that every firm have access to timely information. Consider some of these factors and their relationship to information management:

- **Competitive pressure.** To be competitive, companies must develop and market new products more quickly than ever before.
- **Expanding markets.** Marketing activity is becoming increasingly complex and broader in scope as more firms operate in both domestic and foreign markets.
- **Cost of a mistake.** Introducing and marketing a new product is enormously expensive. A product failure can cause severe — even fatal — damage to a firm.
- **Growing customer expectations.** The lack of timely, adequate information about a problem with some aspect of an organization's marketing program can result in lost business.

### What Is Marketing Research?

Marketing research includes all the activities that enable an organization to obtain the information it needs to make decisions about its environment, its marketing mix, and its present or potential customers and consumers. More specifically, **marketing research** is the development, interpretation, and communication of decision-oriented information to be used in the strategic marketing process. Businesses and other organizations spend millions of dollars each year obtaining information to improve the quality of decision making. Obviously, research is an important part of marketing!

To understand what modern marketing research is and what it does, we must keep in mind that:

- It plays a role in all three phases of the management process in marketing: planning, implementation, and evaluation.
- It is more than just collecting data.
- It recognizes the researcher's responsibility to develop information that will be useful to managers.[2]

## SCOPE OF MARKETING RESEARCH ACTIVITIES

The scope of marketing research activities that are typically practised by larger companies in particular is reflected in Table 8-1. These results from a recent Canadian study indicate the percentage of companies that currently engage in each of these types of research.[3] Some of the results are particularly interesting and reflect the activities and interests of businesses in the 1990s. For example, approximately 90 percent of companies indicated that they monitor market share and market trends, and close to 80 percent analyze profits and costs and perform market and sales forecasts. The relatively small percentage engaged in plant location studies and channel performance research probably reflects the fact that many companies are not engaged in the manufacture and distribution of physical products. It is encouraging to see that a very large percentage of the companies who responded to the study indicated that they are carrying out research in the areas of service quality and customer satisfaction. Possibly surprising is the fact that only 20.9 percent of respondents indicated that they are conducting export or international research.

Much of the marketing research conducted by Canadian business tends to be done on behalf of larger companies. Among companies with annual sales in excess of $5 million, 50 percent have an organized marketing research department and an additional 28 percent have at least one person with responsibility for marketing research. Typically in these companies, marketing research departments are quite small, averaging 3.8 employees, including researchers and support staff. The small size reflects the fact that most companies have the actual marketing research studies conducted on their behalf by outside marketing research specialists. The staff of the marketing research departments in most cases carry out studies of the economy and industry trends and will supervise the purchase of specialized research services from outside suppliers.

In addition to the research studies conducted by a company's own marketing research department or on its behalf by an external research supplier, there are two other sources that provide the marketing information needed by managers.

- The marketing information system, which provides a continuous, scheduled flow of standardized reports to managers.
- The decision support system, which permits managers to interact directly with data through personal computers to answer specific questions.

## MARKETING AT WORK

### FILE 8-1 CULTURE OUTDRAWS SPORTS

A recent survey conducted by Statistics Canada has confirmed that in 1992 more Canadians over the age of 15 attended a concert, play, or dance performance than went to a professional sporting event — 42 percent had attended at least one cultural event, while only 31 percent took in at least one sporting event. The results also indicated different preferences for events across the country. Nova Scotians were most likely to have attended performances of popular music, while residents of Saskatchewan were the biggest supporters of country and western music. Quebecers were most likely to have gone to a concert featuring pop, rock, jazz, and blues music.

During the year, only 32 percent of those surveyed had visited a museum at least once; the lowest was New Brunswick at 23 percent, and highest was British Columbia at 45 percent. British Columbians were the most avid readers of both magazines and books. Only 38 percent of residents in New Brunswick and Newfoundland had gone to a movie in 1992, while the percentage renting movie videos was lowest in Quebec at 62 percent.

Such results from Statistics Canada's annual survey of social activities in which Canadians engage provide an interesting insight into how various groups across the country lead their lives. The differences in life-style can be very revealing and relevant to marketers. Why might a marketing manager of an art gallery or a symphony orchestra be interested in such research results?

Source: "Culture Outdraws Sports, Survey Says," *Globe and Mail*, April 21, 1994, p. E1.

TABLE 8-1 Selected marketing research activities of larger Canadian companies

| Subject areas examined | % doing |
|---|---|
| *Business/economic and corporate research:* | |
| Industry/market characteristics and trends | 91.5 |
| Market share analyses | 89.7 |
| Corporate image research | 72.3 |
| *Quality/satisfaction research:* | |
| Customer satisfaction research | 81.6 |
| Customer profiling and segmentation research | 74.1 |
| Service quality research | 70.9 |
| Product quality research | 68.4 |
| *Pricing Research:* | |
| Profit analysis | 80.9 |
| Demand analysis research: | |
| Market potential | 77.0 |
| Sales potential | 74.5 |
| Sales forecasts | 77.0 |
| Cost analysis | 76.2 |
| *Product Research:* | |
| Concept development/testing | 66.3 |
| Competitive product studies | 52.5 |
| Testing existing products | 50.0 |
| Test marketing | 45.4 |
| *Distribution Research:* | |
| Plant/warehouse location studies | 38.7 |
| Channel performance studies | 31.6 |
| *Advertising and Promotion Research:* | |
| Copy testing | 52.5 |
| Sales force compensation studies | 51.4 |
| Media research | 48.9 |
| Public image studies | 47.9 |
| Advertising post-testing | 42.9 |
| *Buyer Behaviour Research:* | |
| Market segmentation research | 56.4 |
| Brand awareness research | 48.2 |
| Brand image/attitudes | 47.5 |
| Purchase intentions research | 46.5 |

Source: The data presented in this table are unpublished background data from the project reported in Eva E. Kiess-Moser and James G. Barnes, "Emerging Trends in Marketing Research: The Link with Customer Satisfaction," Ottawa: The Conference Board of Canada, Report 82-92, 1992.

## MARKETING INFORMATION SYSTEMS

As computers became common business tools over the past 20 or 30 years, firms were able to collect, store, and manipulate larger amounts of data to aid marketing decision makers. Out of this capability developed the **marketing information system (MkIS)** — an ongoing, organized procedure to generate, analyze, disseminate, store, and retrieve information for use in making marketing decisions. Figure 8-1 illustrates the characteristics and operation of an MkIS.

The ideal MkIS:

- Generates regular reports and recurring studies as needed.
- Integrates old and new data to provide information updates and identify trends.
- Analyzes data using mathematical models that represent the real world.

**FIGURE 8-1**
**The structure of a marketing information system.**

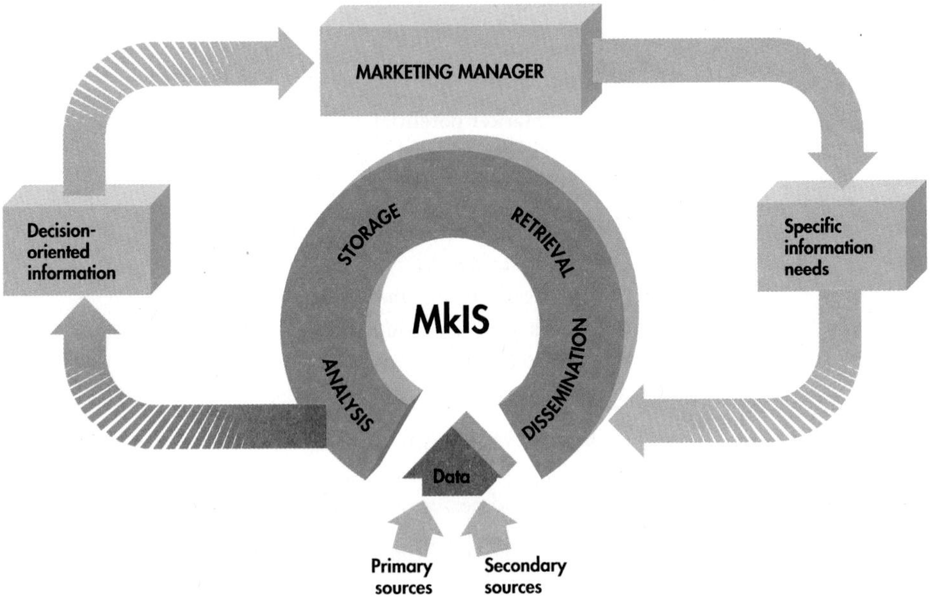


### Designing an MkIS

To build an MkIS, marketing managers must identify what information will help them make better decisions. Working with researchers and systems analysts, managers then determine whether the data needed are available within the organization (for example, in the daily reports made by sales people or cost data from the accounting department) or must be procured, how the data should be organized, the form in which they should be reported, and the schedule according to which they will be delivered. For example, the manager at Procter & Gamble who is responsible for Tide wants to know the retail sales of all detergent brands by geographic area on a monthly basis. The same manager may want quarterly reports on the prices that competitors are charging and how much advertising they are doing. Less frequently, possibly once a year, this manager needs to know about developments in the marketplace such as demographic changes that might affect Tide in the long term. In addition to these (and probably other) regular reports, the manager may periodically request special reports that can be compiled from existing data. For example, the Tide manager may want to see what share of the total market each detergent brand had by quarter over the last five years and a projection of how each is likely to perform over the next three years.

A well-designed MkIS can provide a continuous flow of this type of information for management decision making. The storage and retrieval capability of an MkIS allows a wide variety of data to be collected and used. With this capability, managers can continually monitor the performance of products, markets, sales people, and other marketing units.

An MkIS is of obvious value in a large company, where information for management is likely to get lost or distorted as it becomes widely dispersed. However, experience shows that even relatively simple information systems can upgrade management's decision making in small and medium-sized firms.

How well an MkIS functions depends on three factors:

- The nature and quality of the data available.
- The ways in which the data are processed to provide usable information.
- The ability of the operators of the MkIS and the managers who use the output to work together.

### The Global MkIS

As firms expand their operations beyond national borders, their need for information also grows. Centrally managed international organizations must be informed about what is happening around the world. However, a recent study identified two problems associated with developing a global MkIS.[4]

- Data that managers in a particular country use for making operating decisions may be considerably different from the data needed by higher management at headquarters in another country in order to evaluate their performance.
- Computer hardware and software preferred in various parts of the world may not be compatible.

Thus, designing and operating a global MkIS can be more complex than developing one at the domestic level. It requires co-ordinating across all subsidiaries of a firm, recognizing differences in management styles and cultures, and an internal marketing effort to convince each unit of the value of timely, accurate information.

### MkIS Limitations

When an MkIS doesn't do what management expects it to do, there are several possible explanations:

- It is not always obvious what information is needed on a regular basis to make better decisions. Some managers are comfortable using their experience and intuition and may find that information produced by an MkIS is "interesting" but not necessarily useful. Thus, an MkIS can produce exactly what has been requested, but the results may not improve decisions because the managers have not identified what will help them.
- Gathering, organizing, and storing data and disseminating reports customized to the needs of many managers can be extremely expensive. Beyond the cost of operating an MkIS, there is the need to keep it updated as more sophisticated data become available and managers recognize new and different information needs.
- Possibly most important, an MkIS is not well suited to the solution of unanticipated problems. The biggest challenges managers face are situations in which a decision must be made quickly, without all the details clearly defined, nor the implications of the options known. Under these conditions, standard reports produced according to predetermined schedules are unlikely to be of much value.

The features of an MkIS — a focus on preplanned, structured reports and centralized control over the information by computer specialists — resulted from the skills required to operate computers. Organizations were forced to depend on highly trained programmers working on large computers to produce the information requested by managers. However, advances in computer hardware and software have reduced both problems and led to the development of decision support systems.[5]

## DECISION SUPPORT SYSTEMS

A **decision support system (DSS)** is a sophisticated management tool that allows a manager to interact with data and methods of analysis to gather, analyze, and interpret information. Like an MkIS, the heart of a DSS is data — different types of data from a wide variety of sources. Typically, there are data describing customers, competitors, economic and social trends, and the organization's performance. Also like an MkIS, the DSS has methods for analyzing data. These methods range from simple procedures such as computing ratios or graphs to sophisticated statistical techniques and mathematical models. Where the methods differ is in the extent to which they permit managers to interact directly with the data. Through the use of personal computers and greatly simplified computer software, managers can retrieve data, examine relationships, and even produce reports to meet their specific needs. This interactive capability allows managers to react to what they see in a set of data by asking questions and getting immediate answers. Figure 8-2 depicts the relationships in a DSS.

Consider this example. Midway through the year, a manager wants to compare actual sales of a product to what was forecast. Sitting down at her computer, she calls up the monthly forecasts and the actual sales figures. Discovering that sales fell slightly below the forecast in the most recent month, she commands the system to provide similar data for the company's other products. Finding that the other products are on target, she concludes that there may be a problem with the product in question. Next, she asks the system to break down the total sales figure by geographic areas and discovers that the poor sales results occurred in only two of seven regions. Suspecting competitive activity, she then compares advertising levels and prices of her product and those of competitors in

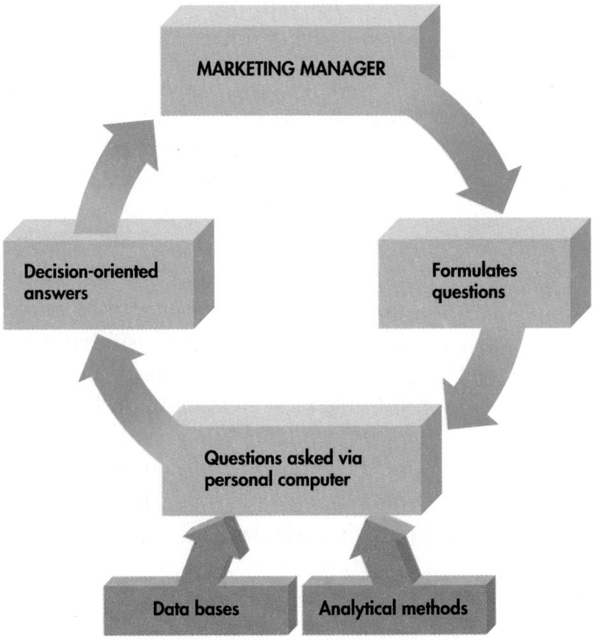


**FIGURE 8-2**
**The structure of a decision support system.**

the markets where sales forecasts were achieved and where they weren't. Finding nothing out of the ordinary, she decides to examine distribution levels for the sales regions. Requesting data on the size and types of retail outlets over time, she finds that in the two regions where sales have slipped there has been a slow but steady decline in the type of small, independent retailers that account for a significant portion of the product's sales. Thus, her strategy is to investigate the use of alternative outlets for selling the product in these problem regions. Notice that, with an adequate DSS, this entire task was done in a short time by simply asking for information, analyzing it, and moving on to another question suggested by the analysis.

The DSS adds speed and flexibility to the MkIS by making the manager an active part of the research process. The increased use of desktop computers, "user-friendly" software, and the ability to link computer systems at different locations (networking) have greatly enhanced the potential of DSS. However, these systems are costly to implement and maintain. As a result, the DSS may be limited to large organizations for the time being.[6]

## DATA BASES

An MkIS or a DSS uses data from a variety of sources both within the organization and from outside suppliers. These data are organized, stored, and updated in a computer in what is called a **data base**. Often a data base will contain separate data modules on such topics as customers, competitors, industry trends, and environmental changes.

## MARKETING AT WORK

### FILE 8-2 WHERE'S THE HIGHWAY PATROL?

A recent study of more than 1,000 people over the age of 18 conducted for Andersen Consulting has shown that Canadians are generally quite knowledgeable about the "information superhighway" that will combine telephone, computer, and cable television technology to deliver a vast array of new services to our homes and offices. But, while more than 54 percent of Canadians interviewed were familiar with the coming technological revolution, nearly 85 percent of them are worried that it will bring with it a threat to individual privacy. Nevertheless, 55 percent of them said they would be prepared to pay as much as $15 a month to be hooked up.

While Canadians generally seem to feel that the information highway is a positive development, they rate business and educational uses much higher than entertainment. While 59 percent were interested in educational services, such as home study, only 21 percent were interested in shopping from home, and only 16 percent would be interested in accessing video games.

Concerns about confidentiality of information suggest that Canadians are aware of the use of data-base information by companies that are expected to travel the information highway. Thomas Healey of Andersen Consulting's electronic highway division indicated that companies are going to have to address the issue to the satisfaction of consumers or they will refuse to do business electronically. He says that the response to abuse will be quick; consumers will simply stop doing business with companies that misuse confidential information.

Is this a research issue? How can companies provide assurances of privacy and confidentiality of information even before consumers embark on their journey on the information highway? Is such assurance necessary, or should consumers wait and see how such information will be handled?

Source: Geoffrey Rowan, "Snoopophobia Haunts Information Highway," *Globe and Mail*, May 3, 1994, p. B1.

Internally, data come from the sales force, marketing, manufacturing, and accounting departments. One of the most lucrative sources of customer data, for example, already exists within customer accounts and billing files in many companies. Some organizations, such as banks and telephone companies, maintain such detailed accounts that they know precisely what a customer has purchased. Some users of data bases have begun using their data for *predictive modelling*, which seeks to determine which customers would be interested in a particular type of product or service. For example, by scanning its data base of credit card customers for individuals who have used their gold card to purchase a computer in the past year, a bank could develop an excellent list of customers who would likely be interested in on-line banking and investment services.[7]

One of the most successful users of customer data bases in Canada is Zellers, which operates almost 300 stores across Canada and now accounts for one-quarter of all discount department store sales in the country. Zellers introduced its Club Z customer loyalty program in 1986. Club Z now has almost 8 million members, reaching an incredible 65 percent of all Canadian households. Club members earn 100 points for every dollar spent at Zellers and can redeem their points for gifts from the Club Z catalogue. But the greatest value of Club Z to Zellers is the information that it provides on every item purchased by Club Z members. Douglas Ajram, director of Club Z, observed, "We use our data base to paint a picture of our customers, what they like about us, and what kind of merchandise they are interested in."[8] Many companies such as Zellers are using internally generated data to establish data bases on their customers. The way in which a company analyzes and combines the data from such data bases will determine their usefulness in planning and implementing marketing strategy.

The development and selling of mailing lists and data bases is normal business practice, and a new industry has evolved to rent computerized lists of potential customers who have certain characteristics and spending habits. A number of Canadian *mailing list brokers* rents more than 2,000 lists to marketers wishing to target certain types of potential customers. These brokers do not sell the names and data on their lists but will rent them for one-time use to clients who wish to target direct mail materials. Most brokers will want to approve samples of the material to be mailed before supplying the names.[9] There is growing pressure on mailing list brokers and on users of data bases generally to ensure that the information they have at their disposal is used in an ethical and responsible manner. Because of the availability of such computer-based data, there are many situations where the privacy of consumers may be violated and information misused.[10]

Research has allowed marketers to move from undifferentiated, mass marketing to focusing on well-defined market segments. It is now suggested that through the management of data bases, marketers will be able to reach the ultimate level of segmentation — the individual. For example, L.L. Bean, a mail-order catalogue marketer, uses a customer's past purchases from the catalogue to calculate a probability of future purchases for each of its merchandise lines. The firm then sends the customer only the specialized catalogues for which the likelihood of a purchase exceeds a minimum level.[11]

### Scanners and Single-Source Data

An important data source for data bases is scanners, the electronic devices at retail checkouts that read the bar code on each item purchased. Scanners were originally intended to speed up checkout and reduce errors in supermarkets. By matching an item's unique code with price information stored in a computer, the scanner eliminated the need for clerks to memorize prices and reduced mistakes from hitting the wrong cash register key. However, retailers quickly discovered that scanners could also produce information on purchases that could be used to improve decisions about how much of a product to keep in inventory and the appropriate amount of shelf space to allocate to each product.

Knowing what customers buy is even more important if a firm knows what advertising they have been exposed to. In many countries, research companies such as A.C. Nielsen have developed consumer household panels to create data bases of information on advertising exposure and retail purchases. A representative sample of households agree to have their television viewing monitored by an electronic device known as a people meter and to have their purchases recorded when they buy groceries at scanner-equipped retail stores. Demographic information is obtained from each household when its members agree to be part of the scanner panel. The result is that household demographics can be correlated to television advertising exposure *and* product purchases. The result is called **single-source data** because exposure to television advertising and product purchases can be traced to individual households, providing a *single source* for both types of data.[12]

TABLE 8-2 Typical marketing research projects

| Project | Objective |
|---|---|
| **Concept test** | **To determine if a new product idea is attractive to potential customers** |
| **Copy test** | **To determine if the intended message in an advertisement is being communicated effectively** |
| **Price responsiveness** | **To gauge the effect a price change would have on demand for a brand** |
| **Market-share analysis** | **To determine a firm's proportion of the total sales of a product or service** |
| **Segmentation studies** | **To identify distinct groups within the total market for a particular product or service** |
| **Customer satisfaction studies** | **To monitor how customers feel about an organization and its products or services** |

## MARKETING RESEARCH PROJECTS

Before MkIS and DSS, much of what was called marketing research consisted of nonrecurring projects to answer specific managerial questions. Projects, some that are nonrecurring and others that are repeated periodically, are still a major part of marketing research. The results of a project may be used to make a particular decision. They could also become part of a data base to be used in an MkIS or DSS. Examples of marketing research projects are described briefly in Table 8-2. According to a recent study, the most common projects are studies of industry and market trends and market share analyses (see Table 8-1 earlier in this chapter).

Most marketing research projects follow the procedure outlined in Figure 8-3. Let's examine what goes into conducting a marketing research project.

### Define the Objective

Researchers need a clear idea of what they are trying to learn — the objective of the project. Usually the objective is to solve a problem, but this is not always so. Often the objective is to *define* the problem. Sometimes it's simply to determine if there is a problem. To illustrate, a manufacturer of commercial air-conditioning equipment had been enjoying a steady increase in sales volume over a period of years. Management decided to conduct a

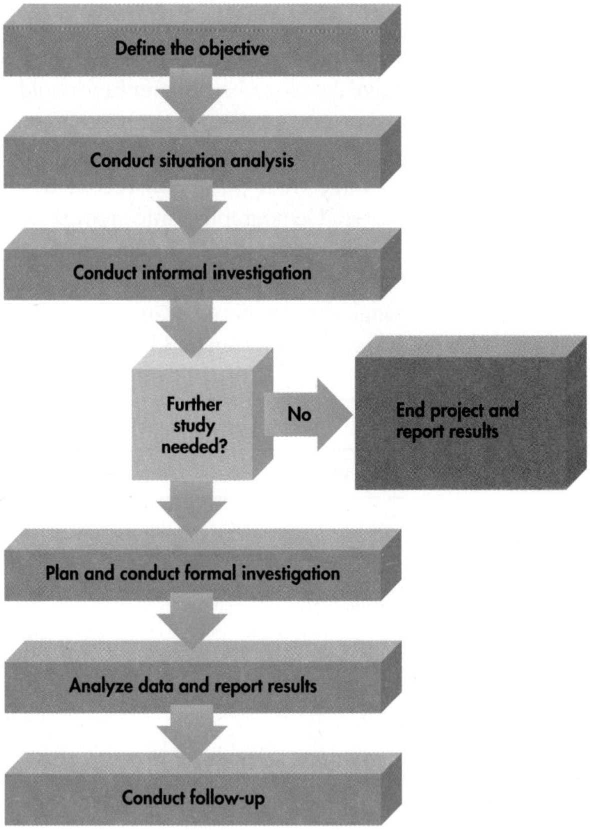


**FIGURE 8-3 Marketing research procedure.**

sales analysis. This research project uncovered the fact that, although the company's volume had been increasing, its share of the market had declined because the industry was growing even faster. In this instance, marketing research uncovered a problem that management did not know existed. After specifying the objective, the researcher is ready for the next step — the situation analysis.

## Conduct a Situation Analysis

Next, the researchers try to get a "feel" for the situation surrounding the problem. They analyze the company, its market, its competition, and the industry in general. The **situation analysis** is a background investigation that helps in refining the research problem. It involves obtaining information about the company and its business environment by means of library research and extensive interviewing of company officials.

In the situation analysis, researchers also try to refine the problem definition and develop hypotheses for testing. A research **hypothesis** is a tentative supposition that if proven would suggest a possible solution to a problem. Some examples of testable hypotheses are:

- There is adequate demand to support an additional national cola brand.
- Customers prefer to buy home computers from specialized computer stores rather than from department stores.
- The rate at which technology is advancing will likely make video discs obsolete in two years.
- The supply of nursing homes is growing faster than the demand for their services.

The project then turns to generating data that can be used to test the correctness of the hypotheses.

### Conduct an Informal Investigation

Having gotten a feel for the problem, the researchers are now ready to collect some preliminary data from the marketplace. This **informal investigation** consists of gathering readily available information from people inside and outside the company — intermediaries, competitors, advertising agencies, and consumers.

The informal investigation is a critical step in a research project because it will determine whether further study is necessary. Decisions can frequently be made with information gathered in the informal investigation. For example, a company that is considering opening sales offices for its computer software support service in Western Canada might first talk with representatives of trade associations representing the personal computer industry and with officials of companies that supply computers and software. Before contacting any prospective clients for their new service, the company would be interested in getting a "feel" for the market and for the extent to which demand for software support is being satisfied. The conclusion at this stage may be that the market is large enough to warrant further investigation. The company's representatives might then meet with office managers or computer centre managers of prospective clients in cities such as Edmonton, Calgary, and Vancouver to discuss informally their needs for software support, where they are currently buying the service, and what they would look for in a new entrant into the market.

Much valuable information is obtained through an informal market investigation. The company not only will learn a great deal about the market it proposes to enter, but it will also determine whether further study is needed. A decision on the main problem can often be made with information gathered at the informal investigation stage.

### Plan and Conduct a Formal Investigation

If the project warrants continued investigation, the researcher must determine what additional information is needed and how to gather it.

**Select Sources of Information** Primary data, secondary data, or both can be used in an investigation. **Primary data** are original data gathered specifically for the project at hand. **Secondary data** have already been gathered for some other purpose. For example, when researchers stand in a supermarket and observe whether people use shopping lists, they are collecting primary data. When they get information from Statistics Canada, they are using a secondary source.

One of the biggest mistakes made in marketing research is to collect primary data before exhausting the information available in secondary sources. Ordinarily, secondary information can be gathered much faster and at far less expense than primary data.

**Syndicated data** represent a third source of information that is a hybrid between primary and secondary data. Syndicated data are collected by a research supplier and may be purchased from that supplier by a number of clients, some of whom may be in direct competition with one another. The most common form of syndicated data involves the collection of data on a regular basis from an established sample or panel of consumers or retail stores. Clients subscribe to the reports, which are produced by the research company and essentially share the cost of collecting the data from the large sample. Although syndicated research does not provide privileged information to a single company, it does allow companies to obtain information on a shared-cost basis.

**Sources of Secondary and Syndicated Data** Several excellent sources of secondary information and syndicated data are available to marketers and marketing researchers in Canada. The following represents a summary of such sources; a much more detailed review of the main sources of secondary and syndicated data in this country may be found in Appendix B.

1. *Internal company records*. Information that the company already has in its files may be considered secondary data in the sense that it already exists. Companies regularly maintain orderly records of the reports of sales personnel, customer complaints, and sales by territory, product, and type of customer. When a problem must be addressed, the first place a company should go for information is its own files.
2. *Parent company records*. Many Canadian companies are subsidiaries of larger multinational companies. The parents and affiliates of these companies can often provide useful data on worldwide market conditions and on their experiences in foreign markets.
3. *Federal government*. The Government of Canada can furnish more marketing data than any other single source. Because of its legal powers to collect data, it has access to information that cannot be collected by private companies. Statistics Canada, as the statistical arm of government, collects much of the available information on behalf of government. Annual catalogues list the many publications of Statistics Canada and other departments and agencies of government.
4. *Provincial governments*. The provincial and territorial governments regularly produce reports and statistical summaries of broad economic interest. Many operate their own statistical offices, which produce reports of provincial statistics.

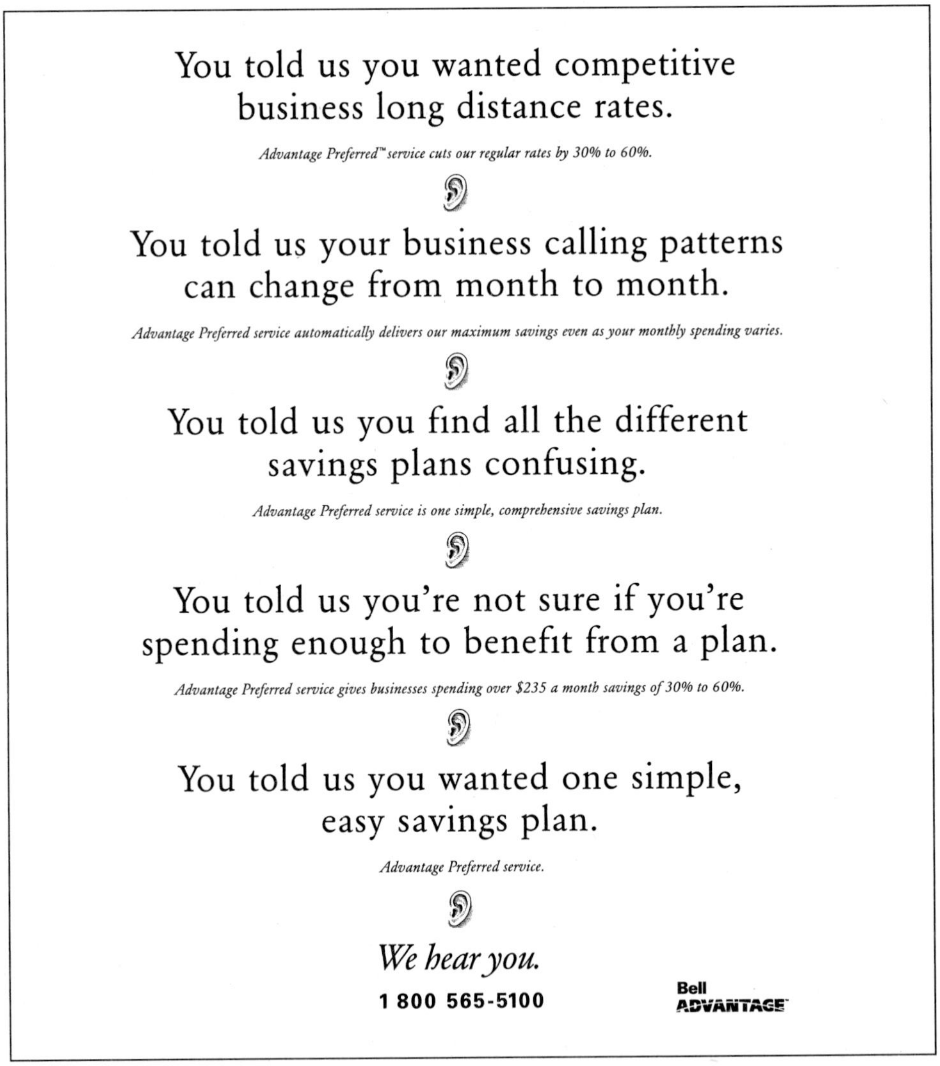


**This ad suggests that Bell Canada really listens to its customers through research.**

5. *Trade, professional, and business organizations*. Associations are excellent sources of information for their members. They often publish reports on surveys of members, and supply data of interest to outside groups. Some groups, such as the Conference Board of Canada and the Canadian Chamber of Commerce, which represent members with a wide variety of interests, will produce reports on an appropriately wide variety of topics. Others, such as the Canadian Bankers' Association, produce studies and reports specific to their industry.
6. *Advertising media*. Many magazines, newspapers, radio and television networks and stations, and outdoor advertising companies publish information that marketing researchers find useful. Such information usually relates to circulation data, station reach and coverage maps, and statistics on trading areas.
7. *University research organizations*. Some universities operate research units and publish research results that are of interest to business.
8. *Foundations*. Not-for-profit research foundations and related groups carry out many research projects of interest to business. Such groups include the Conference Board of Canada, the C.D. Howe Institute, and the Institute for Research in Public Policy.

**Sources of Primary Data.** After exhausting all the available secondary sources considered pertinent, researchers may still lack sufficient data. If so, they must turn to primary sources and gather or purchase the information. In a company's research project, for instance, a researcher may interview the firm's sales people, intermediaries, or customers to obtain the market information needed.

Determine How to Gather Primary Data There are four widely used methods of gathering primary data: survey, qualitative research, observation, and experimentation. Normally not all three are used on the same project. Because each method has strengths and weaknesses, the choice of which to use depends on the nature of the problem, but it will also be influenced by how much time and money are available for the project.

**Survey Method.** A **survey** consists of gathering data by interviewing people. The advantage of a survey is that information is firsthand. In fact, it may be the only way to determine the opinions or buying intentions of a group.

Inherent in the survey method are certain limitations. There are opportunities for error in the construction of the survey questionnaire and in the interviewing process. Moreover, surveys can be very expensive, and they are time-consuming. Other weaknesses are that potential respondents sometimes refuse to participate and the ones who do respond often cannot or will not give true answers.

Survey data collection may be done by the researcher in person, by telephone, or by mail. **Personal interviews** are more flexible than the other two types because interviewers can probe more deeply if an answer is incomplete. Ordinarily it is possible to obtain more information by personal interview than by telephone or mail. Also the interviewer, by observation, can obtain data regarding the respondents' socioeconomic status — their home, neighbourhood, and apparent standard of living.

Rising costs and other problems associated with door-to-door interviewing have prompted many marketing researchers to survey people in central locations, typically regional shopping centres. This technique is called the **shopping mall intercept** method of interviewing. By interviewing people as they pass through a shopping mall, the interviewer is better able to encounter large numbers of people, as the urban mall has essentially become the "main street" of North America. Although data collection is made somewhat easier by this method, the researcher is less confident that he or she is obtaining a representative sample of the population of interest. In such a situation, the ability to access large numbers of people at relatively low cost outweighs concerns about the representativeness of the sample.[13]

In a **telephone survey**, the respondent is approached by telephone, and the interview is completed at that time. Telephone surveys can usually be conducted more rapidly and at less cost than either personal or mail surveys. Since a few interviewers can make any number of calls from a few central points, this method is quite easy to administer. Computer-assisted techniques have broadened the scope of telephone interviewing. These techniques involve automated random-number dialling and a facility for the interviewer to record the respondent's answers directly into the computer as they are received. This technology speeds up the entry and processing of data and the production of reports.

A telephone survey can be timely. For instance, people may be asked whether they are watching television at the moment and, if so, the name of the program and the advertiser. One limitation of the telephone survey is that interviews cannot be too long, although telephone interviews that take 20 to 30 minutes to complete are not uncommon. In fact, one of the myths of telephone interviewing is that the questionnaire must be very short, because participants will not be willing to stay on the line for more than a minute or so. This is simply not so, as many Canadians appear quite co-operative in participating in surveys that take five to ten minutes to complete. What is making it more difficult to conduct telephone survey research is that progressively fewer people are at home, and those that are at home are becoming more difficult to reach. Although there appears to be no dramatic increase in the frequency of unlisted numbers, more and more people are installing telephone answering machines or subscribing to services such as voice mail and call display available from telephone companies. Many people who have such devices or services are using them to screen incoming calls, forcing callers to leave messages, or are electing not to answer the call if they do not recognize the number or name displayed. The result is that telephone interviewers are unable to reach an increasing percentage of the population, thereby making telephone interviewing more costly and resulting in more biased samples.

Telephone surveys have been used successfully with executives at work. When preceded by a letter introducing the study and a short call to make an appointment for the actual interview, these surveys can elicit a very high co-operation rate.

**Interviewing by mail** involves mailing a questionnaire to potential respondents and having them return the completed form by mail. Since no interviewers are used, this type of survey is not hampered by interviewer bias or problems connected with the management of interviewers. Mailed questionnaires are more economical than personal interviews and are particularly useful in national surveys. If the respondents remain anonymous, they are more likely to give true answers because they are not biased by the presence of an interviewer.

A major problem with mail questionnaires is the compilation of a good mailing list, especially for a *broad-scale* survey. If the sample can be drawn from a *limited* list, such as property taxpayers in certain counties, regions, or municipalities or subscribers to a certain magazine, the list presents no problem. Another significant limitation concerns the reliability of the questionnaire returns. The researchers have no control over who actually completes the questionnaire or how it is done. For example, a survey may be addressed to an adult male member of the household but because he is unavailable or not interested, his teenage daughter "helps out" by completing it. In addition, because there is no personal contact with the respondents, it is impossible to judge how much care and thought went into providing the answers.

Still another limitation is that there is usually a low response rate to a mail survey. It is not uncommon to receive completed replies from only 10 to 30 percent of those contacted. This is particularly important because if the respondents have characteristics that differentiate them from nonrespondents on certain dimensions of the survey, the results will be invalid. Techniques for improving mail response rates have been the subject of hundreds of experiments.[14]

**Qualitative Research.** While a survey is generally intended to collect numeric data, so that a researcher can say that a certain percentage of respondents preferred a certain brand or regularly watch a certain television program, qualitative research is intended to probe more deeply into the opinions and attitudes of people interviewed. To do so, the researcher must use different techniques. Consequently, qualitative research usually employs much smaller samples and interviews people in greater depth and for as long as 90 minutes or two hours. The two most widely used qualitative research techniques are the individual depth interview and the focus group interview.[15]

The **individual depth interview** is used in situations where the marketing researcher wishes to probe into the consumer's thoughts concerning his or her purchase and use of a certain product or service. It is conducted in an individual rather than a group format often because the topics to be discussed are sensitive ones or because the people are difficult to reach and would be unlikely to attend a focus group session. For example, the individual depth interview is often used to interview business executives and professionals. Such interviews often take one hour or more to complete and range over a number of different topics. The interviewer generally conducts the interview from a prepared interview guide or questionnaire.

In the case of the **focus group interview**, approximately eight to ten people are "recruited" to participate. They are usually selected to meet certain criteria relating to demographic characteristics, the use of a particular brand, frequent visits to certain vacation destinations, or similar criteria of interest to the researcher and client. The focus group interviewer or moderator orchestrates the discussion using a fairly unstructured interview guide, rather than the more structured questionnaire of the typical one-on-one interview. Many interesting and enlightening findings are revealed through focus group interviews, which have become one of the most widely used techniques in marketing research.[16]

**Focus groups represent an excellent way to learn what consumers really think.**

Because these are qualitative marketing research techniques, their results are completely nonquantifiable. They do produce valuable insights into how consumers feel about certain concepts and why they make decisions as they do. The principal use of the focus group interview, for example, is to allow the marketer to really understand why customers are buying one brand over another, what they like and dislike about each, how they feel about the various brands in the marketplace, and what would have to happen for them to switch brands. Occasionally, marketing researchers will use the focus group technique to learn more about how consumers think about certain product categories or approach certain purchase decisions. They are then in a better position to design larger research surveys that may involve several hundred interviews with consumers.

## MARKETING AT WORK

### FILE 8-3 LISTENING AS A FORM OF RESEARCH

Most managers would agree that listening is important in a variety of contexts, but at Labatt Breweries, listening has been elevated to the status of competitive strategic tool. Hugo Powell, Labatt's president, defines listening as understanding what people mean, not merely what they say. Consequently, Powell, in collaboration with a team of researchers from Research Management Group, embarked on a special project to "listen to — and challenge — every traditional belief that constituted the conventional understanding of the Canadian beer drinker." They began a process of "future listening," which begins with the premise "what if we don't understand?"

The listening process involved talking with the same people who had been included in earlier Labatt research, but they were asked different types of questions in different ways by different types of interviewers. The result was that Labatt learned some things they had not heard before by asking beer drinkers to do such things as design their ideal brewing company — how should it be run, what kind of marketing activities it would engage in, and so on. Through the process, Labatt may have developed a radically different approach to marketing research. They have at least formulated the following listening principles:

- Recognize that listening is a prime leadership responsibility;
- Rethink who and what is listened to;
- Rediscover the art of asking questions;
- Realize that one reason people avoid listening is because it creates reasons to change;
- Listening takes time.

Is this really a new approach to research? Should other companies follow Labatt's lead?

Source: Hugo Powell and Richard Kelly, "Listening at Labatt," *Marketing*, April 25, 1994, p. 15.

**Observational Method.** In the **observational method**, the data are collected by observing some action of the respondent. No interviews are involved, although an interview may be used as a follow-up to get additional information. For example, if customers are observed buying beer in cans instead of bottles, they may be asked why they prefer that one form of packaging to the other.

Information may be gathered by personal or mechanical observation. In one form of **personal observation**, the researcher poses as a customer in a store. This technique is useful in getting information about the calibre of the sales people or in determining what brands they promote. **Mechanical observation** is illustrated by an electric cord stretched across a highway to count the number of cars that pass during a certain time period.

The observation method has several merits. It can be highly accurate. Often it removes all doubt about what the consumer does in a given situation. The consumers are usually unaware they are being observed, so presumably they act in their usual fashion.

The observation technique reduces interview bias. However, the technique is limited in its application. Observation tells *what* happened, but it cannot tell *why*. It cannot delve into motives, attitudes, or opinions.

To overcome the biases inherent in the survey method, some firms are using sophisticated observational techniques that involve a combination of cable TV, electronic scanners in supermarkets, and computers. For example, some marketing research companies in Canada and the United States have established "scanner panels." Selected households are invited to participate in a program that involves recording electronically every TV commercial watched in participants' homes; every purchase the participants make in supermarkets that are equipped with checkout scanners is electronically recorded. With this observational method, researchers can measure which products members of the households are buying and determine which TV commercials they have seen. It provides an improved link between advertising and purchase that allows for more accurate measurement of which advertising works and which does not.

The A.C. Nielsen Company and the BBM Bureau of Measurement have installed "people meters" in more than 2,000 Canadian homes. These devices record electronically the channels to which TV sets are tuned and who is watching the programs. Computers are already programmed with data on each member of the households that participate in the panel. Data are recorded continuously and fed to a central computer each night, providing the TV networks and advertisers with detailed, timely, and accurate information concerning program audiences and the exposure of TV commercials.

**Experimental Method.** An **experiment** is a method of gathering primary data in which the researcher is able to observe the result of changing one variable in a situation while holding all others constant. Experiments are conducted in laboratory settings and in the field. In marketing research, the word laboratory is used to describe an environment over which the researcher has complete control during the experiment.

Consider this example. A small group of consumers is assembled and presented with a brief product description and proposed package for a new breakfast cereal. After examining the package, the people are asked whether they would buy the product and their responses are recorded. Next a similar group of consumers is brought together and presented with the identical package and product information, except that a nutritional claim is printed on the package. This group is also asked if it would buy the product. Because the researcher had complete control over the test environment and the only thing changed was the nutritional claim on the package, any difference in buying intentions can be attributed to the claim.

Laboratory experiments can be used to test virtually any component of marketing strategy. However, it is important to recognize that the setting is unnatural and consumers' responses may be biased by the situation.

An experiment in the *field* is called test marketing. It is similar to a laboratory experiment but is conducted under more realistic conditions. The researcher therefore has less control. In **test marketing**, the researcher duplicates real market conditions in a small geographic area to measure consumers' responses to a strategy before committing to a major marketing effort. Test marketing may be undertaken to forecast sales or to evaluate different marketing mixes.

The advantage of field experiments over laboratory experiments is their realism. However, there are several disadvantages. Test marketing is expensive ($500,000 is not uncommon), time-consuming (9 to 12 months is normal), and impossible to keep secret from competitors (who may intentionally disrupt the test by temporarily changing their marketing mixes). Another problem is the researcher's inability to control the situation. For example, a company that is test marketing a new product may encounter a certain amount of publicity while the product is in the test market, simply because of the innovativeness of the product. Although such publicity would normally be considered a good thing, when faced with it in a test market situation, the marketer is not sure to what extent it has distorted the sales results. In other words, what volume of sales resulted from the product and the regular marketing efforts of the company (what was actually being tested?), and what resulted from the publicity that was generated?

Because of its inherent limitations, the use of traditional test marketing declined as faster, less expensive alternatives were developed. One of these alternatives is the **simulated test market**, in which a sample of consumers is shown ads for the product being tested as well as for other products. The subjects are then allowed to "shop" in a test store that resembles a small grocery store. Follow-up interviews may be conducted immediately and also after the products have been used to better understand the consumers' behaviour. The entire set of data goes into a statistical model and sales for the product are forecast.

The potential benefits of simulated test marketing include:

- Lower costs than a traditional test market.
- Results in as little as eight weeks.
- A test can be kept secret.

The drawbacks are:

- Questionable accuracy for unique, new products.
- Application limited to traditional packaged goods.
- Inability to predict the response of competitors or retailers.
- Inability to test changes in marketing variables like packaging or distribution because of the simulation's short duration.[17]

Simulated test marketing has not replaced traditional test markets because of these limitations. In fact, the two methods are often used together, with the simulation results used to make marketing mix modifications before beginning the traditional test market.[18]

**Prepare Forms for Gathering Data** Whether interviewing or observing subjects, researchers use a questionnaire or form on which there are instructions and spaces to record observations and responses. It is not easy to design a data-gathering form that elicits precisely the information needed. Here are several fundamental considerations:

- **Question wording.** If a question is misunderstood, the data it produces are worthless. Questions should be written with the potential respondent in mind. Vocabulary, reading level, and familiarity with jargon all must be considered. A common wording error is to inadvertently include two questions in one. For example, the question "How would you evaluate the speed and efficiency of our service?" followed by a scale from good to bad is likely to cause problems. Some respondents may see the service as fast, which is good, but with too many mistakes, which is bad.
- **Response format.** Questions are either designed for check-mark responses (such as yes–no, multiple choices, agree–disagree scales) or open-ended replies. Open-ended questions are often easier to write and frequently produce richer answers, but they require more effort from the respondent and therefore lower the level of co-operation. In addition, in a mail survey it is often difficult to read and interpret open-ended responses. Open-ended questions are used most often in personal or telephone interviews, where the interviewer can probe for explanations and additional details. When they are used, they are usually placed near the end of a questionnaire to avoid discouraging respondents early in the interview.

- **Questionnaire layout.** The normal procedure is to begin with easier questions and move to the more difficult or complicated questions. To understand behaviour, researchers must sometimes ask questions about possibly sensitive topics (for example, personal hygiene) or private matters (age, income). These questions are normally placed at the very end of a questionnaire.
- **Pretesting.** All questionnaires should be pretested on a group of respondents similar to the intended sample. Pretesting is designed to identify problems and make corrections and refinements prior to the actual study.

Complete books are available on questionnaire design. Extreme care and skill are needed to produce a questionnaire that maximizes the likelihood of getting a response while minimizing bias, misunderstanding, and respondent irritation.

**Plan the Sample** It is unnecessary to survey or observe every person who could shed light on a research problem. It is sufficient to collect data from a sample if its reactions are *representative* of the entire group. We all employ sampling in our everyday activities. Often we base our opinion of a person on only one or two conversations. And we taste food before taking a larger quantity. The key in these personal issues and in marketing research is whether the sample provides accurate information.

**If this questionnaire is handed to all customers at the counter of the store, will the completed responses be a random sample?**

The fundamental idea underlying sampling is that a small number of items — a sample — if properly selected from a larger number of items — a population — will have the same characteristics and in about the same proportion as the larger number. Obtaining reliable data with this method requires the right technique in selecting the sample.

COOKIE MUNCHER'S
PARADISE
A UNIQUE BAKERY

A COOKIE FOR YOUR THOUGHTS!

*Your comments are important to us. Please fill out this card and give it to our manager. We'd like to show our appreciation for your time by giving you a freshly baked Chipper!*

*Please rate your experience today at Paradise Bakery. A 5 rating is excellent, a 3 rating is good and a 1 rating is poor.*

1. Friendliness of staff 5 4 3 2 1
2. Helpfulness 5 4 3 2 1
3. Promptness of service 5 4 3 2 1
4. Value 5 4 3 2 1
5. Freshness of product 5 4 3 2 1
6. Overall quality of menu 5 4 3 2 1
7. Cleanliness 5 4 3 2 1
8. Would you come back to Paradise? Yes_____ No_____
9. What is your favorite menu item?
10. How did you hear about Paradise?
11. How could we improve on your experience at Paradise?

*Thanks for being a "COOKIE MUNCHER." If you would like a personal response, please put your name, address and phone number on the back of this card.*

Improper sampling is a source of error in many studies. One firm, for example, selected a sample of calls from all the calls made to its 1-800 number and used the information to make generalizations about its customers. Would you be comfortable saying these callers are representative of all the firm's customers or even all the dissatisfied ones?[19] Though numerous sampling techniques are used, only random samples are appropriate for making generalizations from a sample to a population. A **random sample** is selected in such a way that every member of the population has an equal chance of being included.

All other (nonrandom) samples are known as **convenience samples**. Convenience samples are quite common in marketing research, for two reasons. First, random samples are very difficult to get. Even though the researcher may *select* the subjects in a random fashion, there is no guarantee that they all will *participate*. Some will be unavailable and others will refuse to co-operate. As a result, researchers often resort to carefully designed convenience samples that reflect the characteristics of the population as closely as possible. Second, not all research is done with the objective of generalizing to a population. For example, to confirm the judgement of the advertising department, a researcher may be satisfied with the finding that a small group of respondents all take a similar message away from an ad.

A common question regarding sampling is: How large should a sample be? With random methods, a sample must be large enough to be truly representative of the population. Thus the size will depend on the diversity of characteristics within the population. All basic statistics books contain general formulas for calculating sample size. In the case of nonrandom samples, since the objective is not to make generalizations, researchers can select any size sample with which they and the managers using the data feel comfortable.

**Collect Data** Collecting primary data by interviewing, observation, or both, is often the weakest link in the research process. Ordinarily, in all other steps, it's possible to ensure accuracy. However, the fruits of these labours may be lost if the data gatherers are inadequately trained or supervised.

Motivating data gatherers is difficult, because they frequently are part-time workers doing what is often a monotonous task. As a result, many problems may crop up at this point. For instance, poorly trained data gatherers may fail to establish rapport with respondents or may change the wording of questions. In extreme cases, there have even been instances where interviewers have attempted to fake the responses!

### Analyze the Data and Present a Report

The value of research is determined by its results. And since data cannot speak for themselves, analysis and interpretation are key components of any project. Computers have made it possible for researchers to tabulate and process masses of data quickly and inexpensively. This tool can be abused, however. Managers have little use for reams of computer printouts. Researchers must be able to identify pivotal relationships, spot trends, and find patterns — that's what transforms data into useful information.

The end product of the investigation is the researcher's conclusions and recommendations. Most projects require a written report, often accompanied by an oral presentation to management. Here communication skill becomes a factor. Not only must researchers be able to write and speak effectively, they must adopt the perspective of the manager in presenting research results.

### Conduct Follow-up

Researchers should follow up their studies to determine whether their results and recommendations are being used. Management may choose not to use a study's findings for several reasons. The problem that generated the research may have been misdefined, become less urgent, or even disappeared. Or the research may have been completed too late to be useful. Without a follow-up, the researcher has no way of knowing if the project was on target and met management's needs or if it fell short, and an important source of information for improving research in the future would be ignored.

By this point you have probably realized that doing good research is not easy. As a result, it shouldn't surprise you that many research projects are done poorly. You should also be aware that some research is intentionally misleading.

## WHO DOES MARKETING RESEARCH?

Marketing research can be done by a firm's own personnel or by outside researchers. Sometimes a job is divided, with company personnel doing parts of a project and using a research specialist for such tasks as collecting data or developing analytical models.

### Within the Company

Separate marketing research departments exist primarily in larger companies and are usually quite small. The marketing research department may consist of only a single manager

## MARKETING AT WORK

### FILE 8-4 WE KNOW WHAT YOU BOUGHT

In the summer of 1994, Nielsen Marketing Research announced a new Canadian marketing research service that offers faster and more complete tracking of consumer purchases of groceries and other household items. This in-home, scanner-based approach to data collection will replace the now-outdated diary method whereby householders were asked to record their purchases by hand in diaries that were mailed to them. It also represents an improvement over the system Nielsen had been using in Toronto, Montreal, and Calgary. This system involved consumers presenting scannable cards at supermarket checkouts when they shopped.

Under the new system, Nielsen will equip more than 6,000 households across Canada with telephone-sized scanner devices that shoppers will use to scan the UPC codes on items they have purchased and brought home. The data stored in these scanning devices will be transmitted each week by modem to Nielsen's central computer for inclusion in the company's continuous tracking study of Canadians' grocery purchases.

The in-home scanning of grocery purchases will provide Nielsen's clients — most of the large manufacturers of grocery products — with data within three weeks of purchase and will cover all of Canada. It will also deliver data on all products that have UPC codes, not only those purchased at scanner-equipped participating retailers, as was the case with systems previously in use.

Despite the advances made by this new system, are there still concerns about the accuracy of such data? What information are Nielsen's clients particularly interested in and how will it be used?

Source: Jim McElgunn, "Nielsen's Fast Track," *Marketing*, January 3/10, 1994, p. 3.

or may be as large as four or five professionals in large consumer products companies. In most such situations, the marketing research department rarely conducts research utilizing its own staff, but rather contracts the work out to suppliers outside the company. The primary role of the marketing research department, therefore, is to organize, monitor, and co-ordinate marketing research, which may be done by a number of different suppliers throughout the country. The manager of the marketing research department reports either to the chief marketing executive or directly to top management. The researchers who staff this department must be well versed in company procedures and know what information is already available within the company. They must also be familiar with the relative strengths and weaknesses of potential marketing research suppliers.

### Outside the Company

A sign of maturity in marketing research is the fact that it has already developed many institutions from which a company may seek help in marketing research problems. There exist in Canada today well over 100 companies that operate in the field of marketing research. When a marketing manager requires information on Canadian marketing research suppliers, a number of sources exist that may be consulted in order to obtain a list of potential suppliers. One listing of such suppliers is the *Directory of Canadian Marketing Research Organizations*, produced by the Professional Marketing Research Society. This directory provides detailed information on those companies that operate in Canada in marketing research and related fields.

There are more than 30 full-service marketing research companies in Canada. These companies include such firms as the Creative Research Group, Canadian Facts, Market Facts of Canada, and Thompson Lightstone. They provide a full range of marketing research services, from the design of a research study to the submission of a final report. In addition to the full-service marketing research companies, there are in Canada dozens of smaller firms that operate in various specialized areas of marketing research. These companies are usually small and may specialize by geographic region, by industry, or by service performed. Some concentrate in either consumer or industrial research or carry out studies that involve the application of specialized techniques. Other companies provide specialized marketing research services, such as the analysis of survey data. Some marketing research is also conducted in Canada by advertising agencies and by management consulting firms.

## STATUS OF MARKETING RESEARCH

Significant advances have been made in both quantitative and qualitative research methodology, and researchers are making effective use of the behavioural sciences, mathematics, and statistics. Still, far too many companies are spending dollars on manufacturing research, but only pennies on determining market opportunities for their products.

Several factors account for this less-than-universal acceptance of marketing research. Unlike the results of a chemical experiment, the results of marketing research cannot always be measured quantitatively. The research director or brand manager cannot conduct a research project and then point to x percent increase in sales as a result of that project. Also, if management is not convinced of the value of marketing research, it will not spend the amount of money necessary to do a good job. Good research costs money. Executives may not realize that it is a false economy to spend less money: half the amount of money spent will usually result in a job that's less than half as good.

Marketing research cannot predict future market behaviour accurately in many cases, yet often that is what is expected of it. In fact, when dealing with consumer behaviour, the research is hard-pressed to get the truth regarding *present* attitudes or motives, much less those of next year.

Possibly a more fundamental reason for the relatively modest status of marketing research in some companies has been the failure of researchers to communicate adequately with management. Admittedly, there are poor researchers and poor research. Moreover, sometimes the mentality of the quick-acting, pragmatic executive may be at odds with the cautious, complex, hedging-all-bets mentality of some marketing researchers. However, researchers, like many manufacturers, are often product-oriented when they should be market-oriented. They concentrate on research methods and techniques, rather than on showing management how these methods can aid in making better marketing decisions. Executives are willing to invest heavily in technical research because they are convinced there is a payoff in this activity. Management is often not similarly convinced of a return on investment in marketing research.

Another basic problem is the apparent reluctance of management (1) to treat marketing research as a continuing process and (2) to relate marketing research and decision making in a more systematic fashion. Too often, marketing research is viewed in a fragmented, one-project-at-a-time manner. It is used only when management realizes it has a marketing problem. One way to avoid such a view is to incorporate marketing research as one part of a marketing information system — a system that provides a continuous flow of data concerning the changing marketing environment.[20]

Looking to the future, however, we think the prospects for marketing research are encouraging. As more top marketing executives embrace the concept of strategic marketing planning, we should see a growing respect for marketing research and marketing information systems. The strategic planning process requires the generation and careful analysis of information. Marketing researchers have the particular training, capabilities, and systems techniques that are needed for effective information management.

## SUMMARY

Competitive pressure, expanding markets, the cost of making a mistake, and growing customer expectations all contribute to the need for marketing research. For a company to operate successfully today, management must develop a method for gathering and storing relevant data and converting it into usable information. Three tools used in research are the marketing information system, decision support systems, and the research project.

A marketing information system (MkIS) is an ongoing set of procedures designed to generate, analyze, disseminate, store, and retrieve information for use in making marketing decisions. An MkIS provides a manager with a regularly scheduled flow of information and reports. A decision support system (DSS) differs from an MkIS in that the manager, using a personal computer, can interact directly with data.

A marketing research project is undertaken to help resolve a specific marketing problem. The problem must first be clearly defined. Then a researcher conducts a situation analysis and an informal investigation. If a formal investigation is needed, the researcher decides which secondary and primary sources of information to use. To gather primary data, a survey, observation, or an experiment may be used. The project is completed when data are analyzed and the results reported. Follow-up provides information for improving future research.

Researchers have recently developed a stronger interest in finding out what competitors are currently doing and forecasting what they are likely to do in the future. Research is conducted internally by marketing research staff members and purchased externally from firms that specialize in doing research.

Marketing research has not yet achieved its potential because the value of research often cannot be directly measured, research does not always accurately predict the future, and researchers are too production-oriented. Further, researchers do not always communicate effectively with management, and research is frequently used in an ad hoc manner.

## KEY TERMS AND CONCEPTS

**Marketing research (207)**
**Marketing information system (MkIS) (210)**
**Decision support system (DSS) (212)**
**Data base (213)**
**Single-source data (215)**
**Situation analysis (216)**
**Hypothesis (216)**
**Informal investigation (217)**
**Primary data (217)**
**Secondary data (217)**
**Syndicated data (217)**
**Survey (219)**
**Personal interviews (219)**
**Shopping mall intercept (219)**
**Telephone survey (220)**
**Interviewing by mail (220)**
**Individual depth interview (222)**
**Focus group interview (221)**
**Observational method (222)**
**Personal observation (222)**
**Mechanical observation (222)**
**Experiment (223)**
**Test marketing (223)**
**Simulated test market (224)**
**Random sample (225)**
**Convenience sample (225)**

## QUESTIONS AND PROBLEMS

1. Explain how a marketing information system differs from a decision support system.
2. How involved do you think marketing researchers should be in setting strategy for their organizations?
3. A group of wealthy business executives regularly spends some time each winter at a popular ski resort — Whistler, British Columbia; Banff, Alberta; or Grey Rocks, Quebec. They were intrigued with the possibility of forming a corporation to develop and operate a large ski resort in the B.C. Rockies near the Alberta border. This would be a totally new venture and would be on federal park land. It would be a complete resort with facilities appealing to middle- and upper-income markets. What types of information might they want to have before deciding whether to go ahead with the venture? What sources of information would be used?
4. Evaluate surveys, observation, and experimentation as methods of gathering primary data in the following projects:
   a. A sporting goods retailer wants to determine college students' brand preferences for skis, tennis racquets, and golf clubs.

b. A supermarket chain wants to determine shoppers' preferences for the physical layout of fixtures and traffic patterns, particularly around checkout stands.
c. A manufacturer of conveyor belts wants to know who makes buying decisions for his product among present and prospective users.

5. Using the steps in the research process from the text, describe how you would go about investigating the feasibility of a copy shop adjacent to your campus.
6. What kind of sample would you use in each of the research projects designed to answer the following questions?
   a. What brand of shoes is most popular among the students on your campus?
   b. Should the department stores in or near your hometown be open all day on Sundays?
   c. What percentage of the business firms in the large city nearest your campus have automatic sprinkler systems?
7. Would it be appropriate to interview 200 students as they left your college hockey arena about their feelings towards funding for athletics and then generalize the results to the student body? Why or why not?
8. If you were the research manager, what suggestions would you have for your management if they proposed that you conduct a consumer study to determine the feasibility of introducing a new laundry detergent in several Asian countries?

## HANDS-ON MARKETING

1. Assume you work for a manufacturer of a liquid glass cleaner that competes with Windex and Glass Wax. Your manager wants to determine the amount of the product that can be sold throughout the country. To help her in this project, prepare a report that shows the following information for your home province and, if possible, your home city or region. Carefully identify the sources you use for this information.
   a. Number of households or families.
   b. Income or buying power per family or per household.
   c. Total retail sales in the most recent year for which you can find reliable data.
   d. Total annual sales of food stores, hardware stores, and drugstores.
   e. Total number of food stores.
2. Interview the manager of the bookstore that serves your school about the marketing information system it uses (keep in mind that it may be a very informal system).
   a. What are the data sources?
   b. How are the data collected?
   c. What reports are received and on what schedule?
   d. What problems arise with the MkIS?
   e. How could the MkIS be improved?

## NOTES AND REFERENCES

1. Adapted from Martin Peters, "The Evolution of Volvo's Automotive Revolution," *Road & Track Guide to the All-New Volvo 850 GLT*, 1992, pp. 36-47; and Sarah Newton and David Iddiols, "From Hearses to Horses: Launching the Volvo 850," *Journal of the Market Research Society*, vol. 35, no. 2, 1993, pp. 145-159.
2. In "New Marketing Research Definition Approved," *Marketing News*, January 2, 1987, p. 1, the American Marketing Association defines marketing research as follows: Marketing research links the consumer, customer, and public to the marketer through information — information used to identify and define marketing opportunities and problems; generate, refine, and evaluate marketing actions; monitor marketing performance; and improve understanding of marketing as a process. Marketing research specifies the information required to address these issues; designs the methods for collecting information; manages and implements the data collection process; analyzes the results; and communicates the findings and their implications.
3. Eva E. Kiess-Moser and James G. Barnes, "Emerging Trends in Marketing Research: The Link with Customer Satisfaction," Ottawa: The Conference Board of Canada, Report 82-92, 1992.
4. Lexis F. Higgins, Scott C. McIntyre, and Cynthia G. Raine, "Design of Global Marketing Information Systems," *The Journal of Business and Industrial Marketing*, Summer/Fall 1991, pp. 49-58.
5. For an overview of the development of marketing information systems, the reader may wish to see Kimball P. Marshall and Stephen W. LaMotte, "Marketing Information Systems: A Marriage of Systems Analysis and Marketing Management," *Journal of Applied Business Research*, vol. 8, no. 3, Summer 1992, pp. 61-73.

6. For more information on the development of marketing decision support systems, see James G. Barnes, *Research for Marketing Decision Making*, Toronto: McGraw-Hill Ryerson Limited, 1991, pp. 15-16; Louis A. Wallis, *Decision-Support Systems for Marketing*, Conference Board Research Report No. 923, New York: The Conference Board, Inc., 1989; and Rajendra S. Sisodia, "Marketing Information Systems and Decision Support Systems for Services," *The Journal of Services Marketing*, vol. 6, no. 1, Winter 1992, pp. 51-64.
7. Gordon Arnaut, "Getting to Know You; Getting to Know All About You," *Globe and Mail*, February 15, 1994, p. B27.
8. Maurice Simms, "Retailers Pin Their Hope on Marketing Skill," *Globe and Mail*, February 15, 1994, p. B28.
9. Jim Steinhart, "Their Aim Is True — For Rent: 2,000 Mailing Lists," *Globe and Mail*, February 15, 1994, p. B28.
10. For more information on the issue of privacy in the use of data bases, see Joe Clark, "Privacy Issues Are Never Far from the Surface," *Globe and Mail*, February 15, 1994, p. B28; and Linda Morris and Steven Pharr, "Invasion of Privacy: A Dilemma for Marketing Research and Database Technology," *Journal of Systems Management*, vol. 43, no. 10, October 1992, pp. 10-43.
11. Robert C. Blattberg and John Deighton, "Interactive Marketing: Exploiting the Age of Addressability," *Sloan Management Review*, Fall 1991, pp. 5-14.
12. For a more detailed discussion of scanner panels and single-source data, see James G. Barnes, *Research for Marketing Decision Making*, Toronto: McGraw-Hill Ryerson Limited, 1991, pp. 137-140.
13. For discussion of the issue of the representativeness of the sample in mall-intercept surveys, as compared with other approaches to data collection, see Alan J. Bush and A. Parasuraman, "Mall Intercept versus Telephone-Interviewing Environment," *Journal of Advertising Research*, vol. 25, no. 2, April/May 1985, pp. 36-43; and Thomas D. Dupont, "Do Frequent Mall Shoppers Distort Mall-Intercept Survey Results?" *Journal of Advertising Research*, vol. 27, August/September 1987, pp. 45-51.
14. See, for example, Srinivasan Ratneshwar and David W. Stewart, "Nonresponse in Mail Surveys: An Integrative Review," *Applied Marketing Research*, Summer 1989, pp. 37-46; Bruce J. Walker, Wayne Kirchmann, and Jeffery S. Conant, "A Method to Improve Response to Industrial Mad Surveys," *Industrial Marketing Management*, November 1987, pp. 305-14 and A.J. Faria and John R. Dickinson, "Mail Survey Response, Speed, and Cost," *Industrial Marketing Management*, February 1992, pp. 51-60.
15. For additional detail on the use of the individual depth interview and the focus group interview, see James G. Barnes, *Research for Marketing Decision Making*, Toronto: McGraw-Hill Ryerson Limited, 1991, Chapter 12.
16. For two interesting articles on the use of focus group interviews by Canadian firms, see Suanne Kelman, "Consumers on the Couch," *Report on Business Magazine*, February 1991, pp. 50-53; and Jared Mitchell, "The Truth Is Not for the Squeamish," *Report on Business Magazine*, March 1987, pp. 75-76.
17. Howard Schlossberg, "Simulated Vs. Traditional Test Marketing," *Marketing News*, October 23, 1989, pp. 1-2, 11.
18. A useful comparison of various test marketing techniques is found in Patricia Greenwald and Marshall Ottenfeld, "New Product Testing: A Review of Techniques," *Applied Marketing Research*, Summer 1989, pp. 17-24 and in Leslie Brennan, "Meeting the Test," *Sales & Marketing Management*, March 1990, pp. 57-65.
19. Kathy Gardner Chadwick, "Some Caveats Regarding the Interpretation of Data from 800 Number Callers," *Journal of Services Marketing*, Summer 1991, pp. 55-61.
20. For an insight into how some Canadian marketers are making use of new approaches to marketing research, see James Pollock, "The Need to Know," *Marketing*, May 23, 1994, pp. 12-13.

APPENDIX

# B

# SOURCES OF SECONDARY AND SYNDICATED DATA

"**Secondary data**" refers to information that has been collected by other organizations, such as governments, foundations, trade and industry associations, and similar bodies, for their own use and for publication and use by the general public. There are two generic sources of secondary data: **original sources** and **acquired sources**. An acquired source is one that obtained the data from the original source. For example, demographic data appearing in *Canadian Markets*, published by the *Financial Post*, represents publication by an acquired source, as the data were initially obtained from Statistics Canada, the original source.

When using secondary data, it is sometimes preferable to gather it from original sources rather than from acquired sources. Acquired sources may omit important statements, footnotes, and other information that could influence the perceived accuracy of the data reported. In addition, original sources tend to provide more details and citations than do acquired sources, both of which may be important to researchers. This does not mean that acquired sources are unimportant to researchers; the publishers of an acquired source, for example the *Financial Post*, in the case of its annual publication, *Canadian Markets*, provide a valuable service in compiling secondary data into a single volume, thereby saving the user considerable time and effort.

Often, the organizations that collected the data (whether collected from original or acquired sources) will have done so for purposes that may differ significantly from those of the company investigating the sources. Caution must be used in interpreting and relying upon such data, as they may be biased or unsuitable for the intended use. Despite these drawbacks, secondary data are typically readily available, relatively inexpensive, and in many cases allow a marketer to gain valuable insights into a problem area.

In addition to secondary data, there often exist suitable "**syndicated sources**" for data that can be applied to the solution of a marketing problem. The most common form of syndicated research involves the collection of data on a regular basis from a predetermined sample or panel of consumers or retail stores. Syndicated data are made available by a research supplier and may be purchased by several clients, some of whom may be in competition with one another. Clients subscribe to the reports from such a service and, by so doing, essentially share the cost of collecting data from a very large sample. These services allow the clients to monitor changes taking place in their markets in such critical indicators as market share, consumer attitudes, and the acceptance of new brands.

## SECONDARY SOURCES OF RESEARCH INFORMATION

Numerous secondary sources of data useful for marketing managers exist within Canada and internationally. A description of the most important of these sources follows.

### Internal Data

Internal data are considered a secondary source as the data have already been collected. Most businesses, whether independent retailers or large international organizations, collect some kind of internal data as part of their daily operation. The exact type of data collected will vary by the nature of the business; in small companies, it may be limited to basic accounting reports, whereas in large international organizations, the data collected may cover the entire range of operations. Some large businesses even have information departments whose sole purpose is to gather and disseminate information about the company, its competitors, its markets, etc. Becoming familiar with the various types of information that are available internally, including where to find them, is an important requirement of any marketing manager. Examples of internal data that are typically available in many companies are cost and sales figures, advertising and promotion data, mail order records, credit and charge account data, subscription and donor lists, manufacturing reports, inventory records, production schedules, research and development reports, and annual reports.

Although primarily collected for accounting purposes, cost and sales information can be used by marketing managers to determine levels and trends, broken down by types of customer, sales territories, and even specific products. By using such data in conjunction with advertising and promotional information, measures of marketing effectiveness can be obtained. Retailers can use credit and charge account data and mail order records to identify just who their customers are and the brands or products they purchase most often. This information can then be used, for example, to target promotional material at specific subgroups of customers or to determine what other types of products customers may be interested in. Not-for-profit organizations and publishing companies can review their subscription and donor lists to identify potential locations and population segments from which to obtain new customers or donors.

Researchers can often find a great deal of useful information on companies in their annual reports, although these are usually available only for publicly owned companies listed on stock exchanges. Annual reports typically contain sections on operations, financial aspects of the company, information on products and services provided by the company, together with shareholder information and lists of directors, principal officers, and subsidiaries. By analyzing annual reports over a five- to ten-year period, a researcher can prepare a profile of a company and its performance over time. This information could be useful for forecasting industry trends.

For industrial marketers, valuable information can be obtained by combining manufacturing reports, production schedules, inventory control data, and research and development material. When utilized in conjunction with cost and sales data, such information can offer important insights into new product and process possibilities, pricing flexibility, etc.

In addition, internal data can often be collected from parent or affiliated companies. Many Canadian companies are subsidiaries of larger multinational companies. The parent companies can sometimes provide useful data on market conditions in other countries as well as their experiences in foreign markets and with relevant products. Canadian companies may also be affiliated with one or more other businesses (either in Canada or abroad) as a result of joint ventures, minority ownership of shares, or simply through friendly agreements to share resources. The companies may then be able to share internal data that will assist all parties involved.

The foregoing are just a few of the types of internal data that are usually accessible and that marketing researchers should not overlook. It is especially important to consider internal data during the initial stages of a research project if information is required in order to design a questionnaire or carry out a survey about a company's customers. By using internal data sources, time and money can be saved and reliable, relevant baseline data obtained.

### Federal Government Publications

The Canadian government is the largest source of valuable secondary information in Canada. It gathers, analyzes, and publishes a vast quantity of information, mainly through Statistics Canada, the national statistical agency. Statistics Canada maintains regional offices across the country in St. John's, Halifax, Montreal, Ottawa, Toronto, Winnipeg, Regina, Edmonton, and Vancouver. Each reference centre is equipped with a library, microcomputer diskettes, microfiche, census maps, and the facilities to access and retrieve information from two computerized systems, CANSIM and Telichart. For communities where there is no Statistics Canada office, a toll-free telephone number can be used to gain access to the many services the agency provides. These services include providing statistical information to users in person, by mail or by telephone; assisting users with statistical needs and data problems; providing information and training on how to find and use the data held by Statistics Canada; and arranging for the design and management of surveys and statistical research projects on behalf of the Canadian government, institutions, and private agencies.

In addition to the regional offices, there are more than 50 libraries across Canada that carry all Statistics Canada publications. These full depository libraries automatically receive all federal publications not designated as confidential and provide public access to these documents and materials.

The agency publishes a broad spectrum of material of interest to marketing managers:

The *Statistics Canada Current Publications Index* (Catalogue #11-204) is an annual index referencing all numbered publications released by Statistics Canada during the year. (Statistics Canada publications are given a *catalogue number* to facilitate finding and using them.) The Current Publications Index is divided into two sections; the first section gives a listing of publications by catalogue number and subject and the second lists publications by title and subject.

Statistics Canada also publishes a *Guide to Statistics Canada's Programs and Products* (Catalogue #12-575), which describes in detail the many survey activities of the agency and provides valuable information on how its many research projects are conducted. This guide represents a valuable background reference for companies and others who are interested in knowing exactly how research data have been collected.

The *Census of Population* is the most important source of information collected by Statistics Canada. The census is conducted on the whole of the Canadian population once every five years; the latest census was conducted in 1991. Statistics Canada publishes an impressive array of reports based on the census. For example, a series of *census profiles* based on the census allows a marketing manager to collect detailed data on the population of every geographic area of Canada, from urban neighbourhoods of approximately 200 households to the 295 federal electoral districts. An entrepreneur who is considering opening a pet store and grooming service can put together a profile of the population of a specific area of a city by obtaining data on more than 200 characteristics of the population of that area.

*Market Research Handbook* (Catalogue #63-224) is an annual handbook containing a wide variety of Canadian marketing information derived from a number of Statistics Canada sources, including the census, other federal government agencies, and international organizations. The handbook covers a number of topics of interest to marketers including:

- Economic indicators.
- Government finances and employment.
- Socioeconomic characteristics of the population.
- Personal income and expenditure.
- Housing and household facilities and equipment.
- International trade.
- Merchandising and service industries data.
- Small area data, including Census Metropolitan Areas (CMAs) and Census Agglomerations (CAs).

Statistics Canada has also published a valuable series of reports based on the results of the 1991 Census. The *Nation Series* contains reports such as the following:

*Age, Sex and Marital Status* (Catalogue #93-310)
*Dwellings and Households* (Catalogue #93-311)
*Families: Number, Type and Structure* (Catalogue #93-312)
*Mother Tongue* (Catalogue #93-313)

Statistics Canada has produced three useful reports that provide a valuable overview of Canadian consumers and how they live — extremely important information for marketers:

*Family Expenditures in Canada* (Catalogue #62-5550)
*Family Food Expenditure in Canada* (Catalogue #62-5540)
*Homeowner Repair and Renovation Expenditure in Canada* (Catalogue #62-2010)

Each publication includes data presented in easy-to-read tables and charts, together with a description of the main characteristics and trends observed. Many contain comparative data from previous censuses.

Other publications of interest to marketing researchers include:

*The Daily* (Catalogue #11-001) — contains news summaries and announcements of reports, reference papers, and other releases, together with a list of titles of the publications released.

*Infomat* (Catalogue #11-002) — a weekly digest that highlights major Statistics Canada reports and other material, containing charts and other summary statistics.

*Canada Year Book* (Catalogue #11-402) — a biennial reference work providing textual and tabular information on Canada, including demography, social and economic conditions, transportation, and communications.

*Canada: A Portrait* (Catalogue #11-403) — a biennial publication that provides a synopsis of life in Canada, covering such topics as government, technology, arts, and culture.

Finally, Statistics Canada publishes the *Listing of Supplementary Documents*, which covers works that are usually tentative or speculative in nature, such as discussion and working papers published by government departments.

The publications listed above are just a small sample of those available through Statistics Canada. For a complete listing, the reader should consult the Current Publications index.

In addition to publications, another method of gaining access to Statistics Canada data is through the agency's computerized data bank and information retrieval service called the *Canadian Socio-Economic Information Management System* (CANSIM). CANSIM provides public access, in a number of formats, to current and historical statistics, together with specialized data manipulation and analysis packages, graphics facilities, and a bibliographic search service.

The CANSIM system comprises three data bases:

1. *Time Series data base:* consists primarily of economic and business statistics, allowing the user to examine how certain indicators or variables have changed over time. Some of the information covered includes:

    - Prices and price indexes.
    - Primary industries.
    - Merchandising and services.
    - Finance.
    - Transportation.
    - Health and welfare.
    - Labour.
    - External trade.

2. *Cross-Classified data base:* contains multidimensional tables of social and economic data gathered from the Agriculture, Health, Justice, Education, Science, and Culture divisions of Statistics Canada. This data permits the examination of interaction among several factors, such as income levels across regions or by sex or age groups.
3. *Census Summary Data Service:* contains summary data from each census since 1961, permitting the user to examine the characteristics of various cities and towns across Canada.

Researchers can gain on-line access to the CANSIM data bases through Statistics Canada regional offices, privately owned computer service bureaus across the country, or through national data transmission networks that are accessed by private terminals or microcomputers equipped with modems. Users of the CANSIM data bases can access a main data base (Main Base) of more than 400,000 entries, or a Mini Base of 25,000 of the more popular time series, both of which are updated daily. Data can be retrieved on paper, tape, or diskette. Time series data can also be produced in graphic form, on paper or slides, through the Telichart interactive colour graphic display service, which produces colour prints on paper, overhead transparencies, 35 mm slides, or diskettes.

The vast coverage and level of detail of the data collected by Statistics Canada makes it one of the most valuable secondary data sources in Canada. The information that a researcher can gather from Statistics Canada publications, especially when combined with other complementary sources of data, can usually provide some insights into most marketing problems dealing with the Canadian public or business sector. For example, direct mail marketers often find it quite effective to combine small area data from Statistics Canada with information from Canada Post on where their customers or prospective customers live. For relatively low cost, these direct marketers can determine the characteristics of various postal areas, including the larger Forward Sortation Areas (those areas identified by the first three digits of the postal code) or smaller "postal walks" (each postal walk contains 200 to 300 households). By obtaining from Statistics Canada the demographic characteristics of those postal areas in which they are interested, these marketers can direct advertising campaigns and telemarketing programs only to those areas determined to hold the greatest potential for sales.

In addition to Statistics Canada publications, the Government of Canada also publishes thousands of other documents through its many departments and agencies. One valuable source to assist researchers in sorting through these many publications is the Publishing Centre of the Canada Communications Group, which operates under Supply and Services Canada in Ottawa. The Canada Communications Group is responsible for a number of activities relating to government publications, including:

- Providing warehousing and distribution services for federal government publications.
- Processing orders for government publications by mail, telex, fax, and telephone.
- Co-ordinating all publishing activities with the author departments.
- Helping design and implement marketing plans and strategies that promote its publications.
- Offering Canadian publishers the opportunity to share in the promotion of the federal government's best works (Co-publishing Program).
- Assisting individuals and organizations to obtain access to Crown copyright material and granting permission to reproduce these texts.

### Provincial Government Publications

While Statistics Canada is the major publisher of statistical data on Canadian society, each of the provinces also operates a statistical office that produces regular reports on trends and economic indicators. Statistics Canada reports generally deal with national and regional data and allow the user of the information to make comparisons across regions and provinces. On the other hand, in many cases, the provincial governments produce data that will allow a more detailed examination of specific aspects of the economy or of business in a particular province.

In addition, provincial governments also publish a tremendous amount of information through the various governmental departments. Subjects typically covered in provincial government publications include:

- Agriculture.
- Education.
- Environment.
- Energy.
- Health.
- Lands.
- Mines.
- Social services.
- Tourism.

Additional information is available through the Queen's Printer, which publishes most provincial works, and through the general guide *Canadiana*, which includes a regular listing of provincial and municipal government publications.

### Newspapers and Magazines

Newspapers and magazines can provide a wealth of general business and marketing information. The two newspapers that provide the widest "business" coverage in Canada are the *Financial Post* and the *Globe and Mail*, both published daily. Both of these newspapers provide information on business, including advertising and marketing information, issues, and trends. The *Globe and Mail* Report on Business is published daily as a section of the newspaper and contains a comprehensive review of business matters, including a weekly section devoted to marketing topics. Both these newspapers also periodically publish Special Report supplements on areas such as transportation, communications, technology, banking and business finance, small business, and computers. A third newspaper, the *Financial Times of Canada*, is published weekly and also provides a good source of information on more general financial aspects of business in Canada.

*The Report on Business Magazine* is a monthly publication distributed with the *Globe and Mail*. It contains full-length articles on Canadian business topics. *The Financial Post Magazine*, a monthly business magazine available to subscribers of the parent newspaper, is also of value on a wide range of business topics. Two other general business magazines of interest are *Canadian Business* and *Profit*.

### Trade, Professional, and Business Publications

There are numerous trade, professional, and business magazines and journals that cover a wide range of topics dealing with business in Canada. These include:

- *Au Courant*, published by the Information Section of the Economic Council of Canada on a quarterly basis, presents reports that reflect the viewpoint of the Economic Council and covers research studies, discussion papers, and other background papers prepared for the council by staff members and others.
- *Canadian Social Trends*, published quarterly by Statistics Canada (Catalogue #11-008), provides an interesting interpretation of statistical trends in Canadian society.
- *The Business Quarterly*, published by the School of Business Administration, the University of Western Ontario, contains articles of interest to a business audience, written by practising managers and by university business school professors.
- *The Canadian Banker* is the journal of the Canadian Bankers' Association. Published six times annually, this journal contains articles of particular interest to bankers.
- *The Canadian Journal of Economics*, published quarterly by the University of Toronto Press, discusses Canadian economic developments.
- The quarterly, *Canadian Public Administration*, covers a variety of topics dealing with administration, politics, and public policy.

Publications by such organizations as chambers of commerce and boards of trade can also be useful. These organizations usually have access to and publish economic, demographic, governmental, and other information on a municipal level. Examples of such publications include the *Metropolitan Business Journal*, published by the Board of Trade of Metropolitan Toronto, and *News and Views*, published by the St. John's Board of Trade in Newfoundland.

### Regional Publications

There are a number of regional publications that report on activities within the regions covered; for example, the Atlantic Provinces Economic Council publishes a variety of useful material on the Atlantic provinces; *Business Life in Western Canada* reports on the Western business climate; and *Alberta Report* reports on business and commerce in the province of Alberta.

### Foundations

A number of research foundations and "think tanks" regularly publish reports on topics of interest to marketers that are of assistance in understanding markets and how they are changing. These include the Institute for Research in Public Policy, the Conference Board of Canada, the C.D. Howe Institute, the Hudson Institute of Canada, the Atlantic Provinces Economic Council, and the Fraser Institute. Publications by these groups include *Policy Options*, the bimonthly publication of the Institute for Research on Public Policy, which provides a forum for diverse views on public policy and related areas, and *Canadian Business Review*, published quarterly by the Conference Board of Canada, which contains articles of general business interest.

The Conference Board of Canada also produces a number of other publications. The *Handbook of Canadian Consumer Markets* contains data on consumer markets gathered from numerous government, trade, and Conference Board sources. The main topics of the handbook include population, labour and employment, income and expenditures, production and retail trade, and price indices. *Canadian Outlook: Economic Forecast* and *Provincial Outlook: Economic Forecast* are quarterly publications that provide forecasts of a number of economic indicators including prices, costs, employment, and housing. The Canadian version provides the information for the country as a whole, whereas the provincial version has separate sections for each province. The Conference Board also offers a marketing data base that contains time-series and cross-sectional data. This data base is part of the AERIC System, the board's on-line analysis and forecasting system. The AERIC System allows immediate access to, and manipulation of, data base information. Available software permits the user to perform immediate and straightforward data manipulation, for example, percentage change, plotting, correlations, and regression.

In recognition of 1994 as the International Year of the Family, the Vanier Institute of the Family produced a very interesting report entitled *Canadian Families*, which contains extremely comprehensive information and data on the structure and characteristics of Canadian families and how they live.

### Advertising Media

For researchers looking for information directly pertaining to advertising in Canada, there are a number of publications that may be of assistance:

*Canadian Advertising Rates and Data*, published monthly by Maclean Hunter Limited, is the most comprehensive source of data on the advertising industry in Canada, containing advertising rates, circulation data, mechanical requirements, addresses, personnel, and ownership information on virtually all advertising media in Canada.

*The National List of Advertisers*, an annual publication of Maclean Hunter Limited, contains detailed information on more than 3,000 national advertisers, their brand names, advertising agencies and their accounts, advertising budgets, media used, and companies that provide direct marketing and advertising services.

Maclean Hunter also publishes the annual *Report on Advertising Revenues in Canada*, which contains total expenditures on advertising in Canada, broken down by the various media. Billings for major advertising agencies are also presented.

Finally, the company also publishes the *Media Editorial Profile* once a year. This publication provides abbreviated information on the subject matter and editorial focus of more than 700 Canadian consumer, farm, and business magazines.

*The Canadian Marketing Goldbook*, published annually by Roger E. Murray, contains more than 20,000 listings covering all aspects of the Canadian marketing industry, including sections on media, services and supplies, event facilities, design, advertising, direct response, and photography.

### Marketing Publications

One of the leading sources of information and publications on marketing in general is the American Marketing Association (AMA). The association publishes a number of marketing periodicals, some of which are more technical in nature than others.

The *Journal of Marketing* is published quarterly by the AMA. This journal contains a regular feature entitled "Marketing Abstracts," in which articles from a variety of periodicals are listed under major subject headings and subheadings. Researchers will appreciate the abstracts that accompany each article as they can substantially reduce the amount of time spent searching for the listed publications.

The American Marketing Association also publishes the *Journal of Marketing Research*, which deals with quantitative aspects of marketing research; the *Journal of Health Care Marketing*, which covers the health care field and related topics; *Marketing News*, a biweekly newspaper that deals with marketing topics; and a quarterly journal entitled *Marketing Research*.

Most AMA publications can be found in university libraries, or through the association's Canadian chapters, which are located in Quebec City, Montreal, Ottawa, Toronto, and Vancouver.

Other marketing-related publications include the Canadian weekly, *Marketing*, published by Maclean Hunter, which deals with the marketing and advertising industries. *Strategy* (formerly called *Playback Strategy*) is a biweekly newspaper devoted to marketing topics, published by Brunico Publishing of Toronto. American publications that also contain articles relating to the marketing and advertising industries and that occasionally present Canadian material, include *Sales and Marketing Management*, *Advertising Age*, and *Applied Marketing Research*, the latter published by the Marketing Research Association.

### Indexing Services and Data Bases

The publications and secondary sources of information listed above obviously constitute only a fraction of those available. With this huge number of sources, how is a marketer to quickly and easily find the sources of most value to the problem being studied? Fortunately, the work is greatly simplified by the use of published indexes and commercial data bases.

Published indexes contain listings of references to articles and studies that have been published on particular topics. Such indexes are available in most public and corporate libraries.

*The Canadian Business Index* (formerly the *Canadian Business Periodicals Index*) is a reference guide to Canadian periodicals and reports in business, industry, economics, and related areas. It is published monthly along with an annual cumulative index published at the end of each year. The index covers more than 45,000 articles a year from more than 160 Canadian business publications, including the *Globe and Mail*, the *Financial Post* and the *Financial Times of Canada*, as well as from many very specialized periodicals.

In addition, researchers can save themselves hours of work in libraries by accessing commercial data bases to search for information pertinent to a marketing problem. There are more than 500 on-line services in existence offering more than 4,000 data bases on a variety of topics. All that is needed to gain access to these data bases is a personal computer equipped with a telephone hook-up. In addition, most major university and public libraries offer data base search services.

Computerized data bases are searched for information on a subject by entering one or more keywords or terms that describe the topic of interest. The computer then searches for data that are related to the keywords and provides a listing of citations for the user. The listings can vary in format, but most contain at minimum a basic bibliographical citation consisting of author, title, publication name, date, and page numbers.

While there are literally thousands of different data bases covering almost every topic imaginable, there are four main categories:

1. **Bibliographic.** These data bases offer on-line bibliographies or indexes, as well as abstracts of books, journals, reports, and other such information. One such data base of specific interest to marketers and researchers is the Canadian Business and Current Affairs (CBCA) data base, an on-line version of three indexes (*Canadian Business Index*, *Canadian News Index*, and *Canadian Magazine Index*). It contains bibliographic reference to articles on business and management subjects that may be printed in any of the major Canadian business newspapers and periodicals. The CBCA is published by Micromedia Limited and is available on that company's DIALOG service.

Another bibliographic data base is the PTS Marketing and Advertising Reference Service (PTS MARS), offered by Predicasts Inc. This data base contains abstracts on information relating to the advertising and marketing of consumer goods and services.

2. **Full text.** These data bases contain the entire text of articles, reports, and other secondary source data. The PTS New Product Announcements (PTA NPA) data base, also published by Predicasts Inc., is an example of a full-text data base of interest to marketers and researchers. The PTA NPA contains the full text of company press releases dealing with the introduction of new products.
3. **Directory.** Directory data bases provide on-line lists of names, services, companies, publications, and other sources. The National Standards Association provides a directory data base entitled FINDEX Reports and Studies, available through the DIALOG on-line service. FINDEX provides a listing of more than 10,000 published, commercially available business and market research reports, studies, and surveys from more than 300 international publishers, including a number in Canada. FINDEX is published annually with a mid-year supplement.
4. **Statistical.** Statistical data bases provide numerical data, including financial statistics, in preformatted or raw form. The CANSIM system of Statistics Canada described earlier is an example of a statistical data base.

A number of companies have been established in recent years to serve the growing market for on-line data base information. Three of the largest in Canada are Micromedia Limited, Info Globe, and Infomart Online.

Micromedia Limited is a business information supplier established in the early 1970s to supply data bases, on-line services, and publications. Micromedia is the Canadian entity in the SVP International network and is also the official agent for DIALOG Information Services Inc., the Ontario Securities Commission, University Microfilms International, and Statistics Canada, among others. The data bases available through Micromedia include Canadian Business and Current Affairs, the Canadian Corporations Database, the Directory of Associations in Canada, and Microlog, a Canadian research index that provides access to more than 7,000 Canadian government and institutional reports.

Many national publishers now offer "on-line" versions of their publications accessible by any researcher who has access to a microcomputer and modem. Such publications may be "searched" electronically for articles of interest to marketers and marketing researchers. These include Info Globe, the electronic publishing division of the *Globe and Mail.* In addition to providing an on-line version of the daily newspaper, Info Globe publishes the *Canadian Periodicals Index* and acts as marketing agent for a number of other on-line services, including the Dow Jones News/Retrieval and Profile data bases.

Infomart Online, a division of Southam, Inc., provides access to numerous business and news information sources in Canada and the United States, by offering on-line versions of many daily newspapers and news wire services.

The Financial Post Information Service offers FP OnLine Electronic Editions, which feature the full text of such publications as the *Financial Post*, *Maclean's*, the *Directory of Directors*, the *Survey of Industrials*, and the *Survey of Mines and Energy Resources*.

### Bibliographies

Bibliographies, especially those that offer annotated descriptions of entries, are another source of data that can save researchers a considerable amount of time. Bibliographies offer information on a number of topics; one bibliography of particular interest to marketing researchers is the *Bibliography of Marketing Research Methods* compiled by John R. Dickinson of the University of Windsor. Other bibliographies provide information about recent Canadian publications, such as *Books in Canada*, issued 10 times a year, and

*Canadian Studies*, an annual publication of the Canadian Book Publishers' Council. *Canadian Books in Print* is published annually by the University of Toronto Press and lists by subject all books published in Canada.

### Directories

Directories are an often overlooked source of information, especially when a marketing manager is interested in identifying individuals or companies who could be of assistance or offer market potential. The Yellow Pages of telephone directories can be a valuable source of information, and city directories are also useful. For example, R. L. Polk and Company Limited publishes annual city directories for most of the larger urban centres in Canada. These directories include four main sections: a buyer's guide; an alphabetical list of names of residents and business and professional concerns; a directory of householders, including street and avenue guide; and a numerical telephone guide.

Numerous trade directories are published and may be classified into three categories: (1) general trade directories, such as the *Canadian Trade Index*; (2) specific industry directories, such as the *Pulp and Paper Directory*; and (3) regional trade directories, such as *Scott's Directories: Atlantic Manufacturers*. Financial directories, such as the *Financial Post Survey of Industrials*, *Survey of Mines & Energy Resources*, and *Survey of Investment Funds*, provide information on an annual basis about companies involved in these industries.

Other general directories such as *Who's Who in Canada*, the *Financial Post Directory of Directors*, and *Canadian Who's Who* provide information on prominent Canadians. Canadian almanacs can be useful sources of data as well. The only exclusively Canadian almanac is the *Canadian World Almanac*, published annually by Global Press.

*Canadian Markets*, published annually by the *Financial Post*, is a handbook of marketing data and facts gleaned mainly from Statistics Canada sources. It also includes Buying Power Indices, which are indicators of the relative strength of consumer markets across Canada, and a Focus on Industrial Development section, which includes the names and addresses of industrial contacts for more than 250 cities and towns across Canada. As well, there are comparative rankings of major metropolitan markets and comprehensive listings of media by market area.

*Sales and Marketing Management* publishes two issues each year that are devoted to its "Survey of Buying Power." These issues contain a considerable volume of data on the U.S. market, but the publisher offers similar Canadian data to readers who may write and order a Canadian report. The Canadian "Survey of Buying Power" contains information on retail sales, population, effective buying income, and buying power indexes for provincial and metropolitan markets.

The Industrial Marketing and Research Association of Canada (IMRAC) publishes the *Canadian Guide to Industrial Marketing Information*, a comprehensive directory of sources of information about business-to-business marketing in Canada.

The *Financial Post* and *Canadian Business* publish a ranking of Canada's top 500 companies in May and June each year. *Report on Business Magazine* publishes a ranking of the top 1,000 companies in Canada in July, and together these provide a wealth of information on corporate performance in Canada.

As well as these secondary sources, there are numerous private research organizations that undertake a large variety of research and data collection projects. The section on syndicated data that follows deals with a number of such organizations and describes the manner in which they collect syndicated data.

### International Sources

The sources described so far have concentrated mainly on Canada; however, many of the same types of sources are also available in other countries. Some information can be provided by foreign governments; census data similar to those collected in Canada are also available in the United States and most other nations with statistical agencies. A number of international organizations also offer sources of data. The United Nations publishes the *Statistical Yearbook*, which contains data on international trade, broken down by imports and exports for individual countries. The World Bank publishes the *World Atlas*, which provides general data on population, growth, trends, and economic conditions. It also publishes the *World Tables*, which are a series of tables giving economic, demographic, and social data for a large number of countries.

Private publishers may also provide data on foreign countries. For example, Predicasts Inc. offers *World Studies*, providing information on markets, product prices, trends, capital, producers, trend forecasts, and geopolitical data on a number of countries. Euromonitor publishes *International Marketing Data and Statistics*, which provides marketing related statistics for more than 100 countries around the world. It also publishes *European Marketing Data and Statistics*, covering European countries in more detail than the international edition. As well, Gower Publishing offers a *World Index of Economic Forecasts*, which provides information on a large number of organizations that make economic forecasts of countries around the world.

Trade associations in other countries, such as foreign chambers of commerce, can often provide information similar to that of their Canadian counterparts. In general, most Canadian sources of data can also be found for foreign countries, although the exact nature and detail of these sources will obviously vary.

### Other Secondary Sources

University research departments, royal commissions, private institutions, review boards, and the like also provide considerable information that can be of use to marketing departments and researchers. The intention has not been to provide in this section an exhaustive list of secondary data sources, but rather an illustrative one. As can be seen, there are many such sources in Canada.

## SYNDICATED SOURCE DATA

"Syndicated data" refers to data that are gathered from samples on a subject of interest and made available to clients who share the cost of the project. Typically, a private supplier of syndicated data, such as a marketing research firm, will develop and conduct a syndicated study and sell the results to organizations interested in the results. Long-term agreements for such studies will often be arranged as they benefit both the supplier and subscriber; such agreements allow the supplier to cover the typically high fixed and overhead costs of the study and ensure the subscriber receives continuous information that is important for monitoring and valuative purposes. Often, the supplier will allow the subscribing organizations to include private questions in the study for an additional fee. The results of these private questions are then analyzed and reported only to the client who paid for them. Subscribers may also be given the exclusive rights to certain portions of the study, again for an extra fee.

Data collection methods used in conducting syndicated research vary with the syndicated suppliers, depending on the sample size, type of data required by the clients, and the geographic regions to be included. Some studies use telephone surveys or mailed questionnaires sent to a recruited panel of consumers or to a random sample. Other studies are more technically complex and involve the use of technical measurement equipment to monitor television viewing, magazine readership, purchase behaviour, etc. The specific methods used will also depend on what the study is measuring. Syndicated studies are typically used for tracking, performance monitoring, and for market penetration, brand share, and brand awareness.

The principal advantage of syndicated data to subscribers is that they often allow companies to receive valuable information at a lower cost and more quickly than if the study was conducted for just one subscriber. The drawbacks to such data are that the results are usually shared by a number of companies, thus preventing any one company from gaining an informational advantage, and that the data may not specifically meet the needs of the subscriber. The study may use secondary data that in turn could be out of date or inaccurate, or the study may not cover the exact markets or products and services of interest to the user.

There are a number of syndicated services that serve the Canadian market. For purposes of description, these can be classified into syndicated services that provide either general data, specialized data, retail data, or media and audience measurement data.

### General Data Services

*Canadian Facts* is a full-service research company based in Toronto that operates the *C.F. Monitor*, a continuous, shared-cost survey that supplies information on large representative samples. Each month, a personal survey of 2,000 individuals aged 15 years and over is conducted throughout all of Canada except for the Northwest Territories and Yukon. The survey provides representative coverage of the country as a whole as well as for five, more focused regions: British Columbia, the Prairies, Ontario, Quebec, and the Atlantic provinces.

*Contemporary Research Centre* operates the *CRC Omnibus*, a bimonthly, shared-cost survey of representative samples of 2,000 respondents 15 years of age and older across Canada. All the interviews are conducted in-home with a family member being selected at random. *Criterion Research Corporation* also conducts a quarterly omnibus survey that covers social and public affairs issues in Manitoba.

*Gallup Canada Inc.* carries out periodic syndicated studies that are either market-based or population-based, the former focusing on the market for specific products and the latter designed to examine sub-populations, such as farmers. For instance, the *Gallup National Omnibus* is a personal in-home omnibus survey conducted weekly with a different sample of 1,000 Canadian adults. Subscribers to the Omnibus provide questions to be included in the survey and receive the resulting tabulated data on a confidential and exclusive basis. For clients who need information only on a provincial or regional basis, Gallup also periodically conducts the *Regional Omnibus Program* in British Columbia, Alberta, Saskatchewan, Ontario, Quebec, and the Atlantic region.

*Market Facts of Canada Limited* conducts the quarterly *CMP National Omnibus* among proportionate samples of all Canadian households, either nationally or regionally. Sample sizes range from 1,000 to 10,000. The company also offers a syndicated telephone survey called *Telenation*, which surveys 1,000 different adults twice each month.

*Omnifacts Research Limited*, with offices in St. John's, Dartmouth, Moncton, and Fredericton, offers the *Omnifacts Atlantic Report*, a syndicated, semi-annual survey of social, economic, and political issues conducted with more than 1,500 households throughout the four Atlantic provinces. For an additional fee, clients can submit specialized questions of interest and receive an exclusive analysis and report of the findings.

*Omnitel* is a monthly omnibus offered by *Thompson Lightstone & Company Limited*. From a network of central telephone facilities in a number of urban centres, this omnibus surveys random national samples of 2,000 Canadians 18 years of age and older on issues of interest to subscribers.

### Specialized Data Services

There are also a number of syndicated services that offer data on more specialized subjects:

For the agriculture sector, *Criterion Research Corporation* offers *Agwatch*, an omnibus survey of farm operators in the Prairies, Ontario, and Quebec. A typical Agwatch study would sample 1,000 farm operators: 300 in Ontario, 200 each in Alberta, Saskatchewan, and Manitoba, and 100 in Quebec.

*ISL International Surveys Ltd.* provides specialized, syndicated services for the medical and health care markets, computing and home electronics, together with a *National Omnibus Survey* that is conducted five times a year with a probability sample of 2,000 adults. *Schema Research Ltd.* provides a service called Contact, which allows access to a national sample of physicians five times a year, as well as several other health care market monitors.

In addition to its general omnibus, *Market Facts of Canada* also conducts a number of specialized studies:

- The *Household Equipment Audit* provides market information on more than 70 home appliance and electronic products for 8,000 households at the end of each year;
- *Infostudy* measures eating-out behaviour based on a sample of 1,000 households per quarter;
- The quarterly *Household Flow of Funds and Customer Service Survey* measures ownership and dollar value of all major savings and investments, based on a sample of 1,200 households;
- The *Canadian Eating Habits Study* consists of a population-based sample of 4,000 Canadians who report consumption data throughout one year;
- The *Health Care Monitor* provides information on more than 60 ailments and illnesses, with 30,000 Canadians reporting annually on chronic illness and 8,000 reporting at six-month intervals on common ailments;
- Market Facts of Canada also operates a *farm panel*, a *baby panel*, and a *microwave oven owner panel*.

*Compusearch Market and Social Research Limited* offers clients a different form of syndicated research reports. Compusearch compiles data from Statistics Canada and other secondary sources and repackages the information in a form that is useful to the client. The company presents detailed demographic and other relevant data by neighbourhoods, trading areas, sales territories, or any other geographic areas of interest to purchasers of the data. Data can be provided by neighbourhoods as small as 200 households and can be used by clients to identify the characteristics of target markets, to determine where new branches or stores should be located, and to target the most promising consumer groups.

### Retail Data Services

*A.C. Nielsen Company of Canada Limited* offers a number of retail indices such as the Food Index, the Drug Index, the Confectionery/Tobacco Index and the Mass Merchandiser Index, collectively known as Nielsen's *Retail Index Services*. In developing these indices, a disproportionate sample of retail chains, voluntary group associations, and unaffiliated independent retailers are audited by A.C. *Nielsen*. Every two months, auditors enter the stores and take in-store inventory counts and review store purchase invoices. They may also collect observable information such as prices, sales, display space, and point of purchase promotions. By collecting this information, the company can determine such measures as what products and brands are being bought, general trends for specific products and product groups, and market share data.

For example, the grocery industry is served by the Food Index. This index is based on a sample of 475 grocery stores across Canada, measuring more than 200 product categories. The reports are tailored to clients' needs and contain quantitative results of market size and direction, brand/size sales volume and share, plus a host of "reasons why" data.

Also serving the grocery industry is Nielsen's *Warehouse Shipment Service*, which provides a measurement of grocery shipments from chain/wholesale warehouses to individual retail stores. More than 500 categories are covered in regions from Newfoundland to British Columbia, with reports based on four-week intervals covering all items shipped through the warehouse. The major advantage of data collected from warehouses is that it permits companies to monitor the effectiveness of promotions by comparing movement of products before, during, and after promotions are offered.

### Media and Audience Measurement Data Services

Media and audience-measurement data represent another important segment of syndicated data. A number of services exist to provide users with data on print media readership and radio and television audiences.

#### PRINT MEDIA MEASUREMENT

Most publishers of print media are interested in determining who is reading their publications, as are companies trying to plan and evaluate their print advertising programs. The Print Measurement Bureau (PMB) is a not-for-profit, tripartite industry association that offers standardized readership information on the publications of its member companies. Samples of Canadian residents 12 years of age and older are interviewed regularly and the results of the last two years' worth of data are compiled into an annual report made available exclusively to PMB members. The role of the Print Measurement Bureau has also been expanded to include the collection of data on the exposure of consumers to other media, their life-styles, and product usage.

To provide information on print advertising, there is a syndicated readership service called the *Starch Readership Studies*, produced by *Starch Research Services Inc*. This service examines receivers and readers of print media and the extent to which they read specific editorials, articles, and advertisements. On a continuing basis, the Starch Readership Studies cover more than 10,000 advertisements in more than 50 Canadian publications, although almost any issue of any publication can be Starch measured, including magazines, newspapers, and the business press.

Starch also offers a readership study for advertising on posters, superboards, backlights, mall posters, car cards, bus boards, and bus shelter posters. In-home interviews with 400 to 500 people are used to compile information on the awareness and penetration of advertisements in these locations. Syndicated readership studies for specialized print media are also offered by the company. For example, to measure penetration and readership of medical journals among Canadian physicians, Starch offers a continuous research program called the Canadian Medical Media Study.

#### RADIO AUDIENCES

One of the best known organizations involved in determining audience estimates for radio stations and programs in Canada is the BBM Bureau of Measurement, an independent, not-for-profit organization with approximately 1,000 members and associates from the broadcasting industry. BBM conducts surveys of radio audiences up to four times a year, depending on the size and competitive nature of the areas surveyed. The first step BBM takes in conducting a survey is to select a random sample of telephone listings from more than 346 sampling "cells" across Canada that are consistent with Statistics Canada market definitions. Once demographic data from the telephoned households are collected and verified to be representative of the Canadian population in size, location, and demographics, BBM recruits entire households to take part in the survey. In exchange for a small cash token of appreciation, each member of a recruited household agrees to record the listening done over a seven-day period. From this sample, radio audiences for more than 150 markets are developed and published in syndicated reports that are made available to members as part of their membership entitlement.

#### TELEVISION AUDIENCES

The BBM Bureau of Measurement also undertakes television surveys up to 10 times a year, using the same sampling approach and seven-day period as with radio surveys.

Household members record in their diaries when they watch television, for how long, and on which sets. The results are published in "market" and "reach" report books, consisting of ratings and audiences.

The A.C. Nielsen Company of Canada also surveys Canadian television households and until 1989 also used a television diary. However, these diaries have now been phased out by Nielsen, in favour of a new technological approach to the recording of television viewing. A small device known as a people meter is connected to the television set in the home of each participant, and this device is connected to a microprocessor installed inside the television. The computer measures when the set is on and in what format, that is, local television channels, cable, VCR, pay TV, and so on. All individuals in the household are assigned numbers that they use to enter data into the people meter to indicate when they and any others are watching television.

The people meter was a technological breakthrough that opened the door for a new concept in research, that of "single-source data." Single-source data gathering involves the measurement of television viewing and product/service purchases. This concept allows a more accurate and detailed analysis of the links between television viewership and products purchased in stores; it encompasses a number of areas including product/service tracking, television audience measurement, casual data collection, data processing on a large scale, and the production of action-oriented reports for clients.

Under the single-source system, A.C. Nielsen monitors a national panel of households in major cities. Households agree to have their television viewing monitored using a people meter and to have their purchases recorded whenever they buy products at retail stores equipped with scanners. Each member of the panel is assigned a number that is used to record purchases at the retail stores and to register television viewing patterns through the people meter. Information from the retail scanners is transmitted via telephone lines to a central computer for analysis. Advertisements watched on television by the same consumer panel are charted by viewers entering appropriate information into the people meter through a hand-held device similar to a television remote-control unit. Again this information is transmitted daily to a central computer. Single-source data represent a tool for planning, purchasing, and evaluating television advertising, based on actual customer purchase behaviour.

Another company involved in the single-source data area, but which uses slightly different techniques, is PEAC Media Research Inc. of Toronto. This company has developed a customized, microcomputer-based diagnostic and valuative system called the Program Evaluation Analysis Computer (PEAC) system. It is used for testing advertising and television programs in a group setting. Use of the PEAC system involves a two-stage group meeting. In the first stage, a target group is exposed to advertisements or television programs, and the PEAC system collects the group's reaction to the advertising individually, spontaneously, and anonymously. In the second stage, these results are put in a graphical form and synchronized with the test material to see reactions to specific sections of the advertisement or program. Using these results, the group moderator can solicit further group discussions about the viewing session, probing for reasons to explain the observations.

PEAC Media Research also offers a technological system used for electronic test marketing and electronic single source systems. For example, the Viewfacts division of the company offers a single-source measurement service for the Toronto market. This service records program audiences and actual purchase or service usage obtained by equipping all households in a consumer panel with a hand-held scanning device. Viewing information is recorded using a proprietary "on-screen prompt" people meter.

## CASES FOR PART 2

# CASE 2-1

# PETER TAYLOR BUYS RUNNING SHOES

April was drawing to a close and the signs of spring were evident throughout the nation's capital. Peter Taylor was in the process of writing the final set of examinations for his Master's Degree in Business Administration at the University of Ottawa. As a marketing major and sports enthusiast, his primary job-search objective was to find a position in sports marketing, preferably in Toronto. Peter knew that Canada's largest city contained an established base of sports and fitness organizations that could be targeted as employment prospects. In addition, Toronto contained the head offices of many large corporations that are involved in sports sponsorship. He had already made tentative plans to be in Toronto by June 1.

Peter had been involved in sports and athletics for as long as he could remember. His father, also an athlete and a soccer coach, encouraged Peter's initial involvement in hockey and baseball from the time Peter was five or six years old. Up to high school, Peter's active involvement in the local minor hockey program was maintained throughout the fall and winter, and he was active in baseball during the spring and summer seasons. The high school hockey schedule demanded early morning and evening practices, which eventually led him to decrease his hockey participation to a recreational level.

As a natural athlete, Peter enjoyed the competition offered by court sports. He became an avid competitor throughout the school year — soccer in the fall, volleyball until Christmas, basketball in the new year until Easter, and then track and field in the spring.

Peter has always felt that a physically active life-style enhanced his academic performance and general well-being. His parents were very outdoors-oriented and concerned about health and diet. These factors contributed to Peter's performance and drive in all his athletic endeavours. After he completed high school in Peterborough and began his undergraduate program at Trent University, a heavy course schedule prevented him from participating in team sports as actively as he had previously. For recreation and to keep the old gang together, Peter and a group of his high school friends arranged for free gym time in their old school. Every couple of weeks they would round up players for an afternoon or evening of basketball or volleyball.

Peter was also an active intramural competitor. Twenty or so of Peter's friends in his Business Administration class were athletically inclined. They competed in a variety of intramural sports as the nucleus of the Business Administration teams throughout their four years at Trent. The team performed reasonably well, although the Arts and Physical Education teams were very competitive.

When Peter went on after graduation to the University of Ottawa for his MBA, few of his friends were surprised. They had expected for some time that Peter would try to combine his interest in marketing with his love for sports. During the often-gruelling two-year MBA program, Peter found less and less time for organized team sports. He rarely played hockey and did not compete in intramural sports. He did find time each week to swim in the university pool and he cycled to the university regularly from his apartment in the Glebe area of the city. He also took squash more seriously, playing at least twice a week, although he had played only a little at Trent. This was a sport he felt he could continue to play after graduation.

Now that Peter was nearing the end of his MBA program, he realized that an active involvement in team sports would become difficult. He intended to continue playing squash, as he required only one partner to play. However, he wished to pursue an alternative form of exercise to balance and enhance his overall fitness. He considered weight training, but preferred more active sports. Having done quite well in middle-distance track and field competitions during high school, Peter decided to take running more seriously. During his two years in Ottawa, he had done a lit-

---

 This case was written by James G. Barnes and Bernita Kiefte of Memorial University of Newfoundland and is intended to stimulate discussion of a marketing problem and not to illustrate either effective or ineffective handling of that problem. The authors wish to acknowledge the input of Kenneth Thornicroft of Memorial University, who reviewed an earlier draft, and Ed Ayres, editor of *Running Times*, for his comments and for permission to reproduce the exhibit in this case.

tle jogging from time to time along the Rideau Canal, which runs near the university, but the cold Ottawa winters discouraged him from maintaining a year-round schedule. He realized, however, that running was one physical activity he could do according to his own schedule. He felt he might even consider competing in some of the middle and longer distance runs that he knew were held on a regular basis in and around Toronto.

Although Peter considered himself quite knowledgeable about most sports, he also felt there was probably more to running than just putting on a pair of sneakers and going out for a jog. He decided he should take advantage of the fact that the head office of Athletics Canada was located in Ottawa to obtain some technical information on the sport. Intuition told him that he should expand his common-sense list of "do's" and "don'ts." By placing a telephone call to the office of Athletics Canada, he was able to obtain the address of the Ontario Track and Field Association, which he was advised could provide him with a list of track and roadrunning clubs he might wish to join in the Toronto area.

As he walked through the Rideau Centre on a Saturday afternoon, following the exam in his Marketing Strategy course, he stopped into W. H. Smith, a bookstore that carried a wide range of magazines. He was particularly interested in buying a running magazine that might tell him something more about the right equipment for the sport. He found two such magazines in the sports and fitness section of the magazine rack, *Runner's World* and *Running Times*. He was not familiar with either magazine, but as he thumbed through them he was surprised by the number of advertisements for running shoes, and by the "high-tech" descriptions of many of the shoes. He selected *Running Times*, primarily because of the section labelled "Annual Running Shoe Guide," which seemed to be just what he needed.

Of particular concern to Peter was the financial investment he would need to make if he was to take running seriously. Although he owned an ample supply of basic sportswear such as shorts, sweatshirts, and T-shirts, he knew that top-of-the-line running shoes and a rainsuit were two necessities that together might cost him $300 or more. Peter did not yet have a salary, but he was never one to scrimp on sports equipment. He rationalized that the time he invested in such activities deserved a comparable monetary investment. His father had always taught him the value of good equipment as insurance against accidents and injuries.

Peter decided that he would wait until he moved to Toronto to join a running club and to learn more about the technique of the sport. Right now, he determined that he needed to get back to exercising regularly again, following the past few months of the MBA program, which had left him little time to work out. The more he thought about running, and stimulated by the articles in *Running Times*, the more anxious he was to begin running regularly as soon as his exams were over. He realized that he needed to know what running shoes to purchase and how best to prevent running injuries.

He was also beginning to realize that he knew very little about the engineering and technology of running shoes. Although he had bought other athletic footwear during the past few years, he had not appreciated the diversity of styles and models available. Advertisements in *Running Times* stressed materials such as Hexalite and Dynalite, cushioning based on air, fluids, gel, and foam, and glitzy colours and styles. Peter was unaware of the benefits each system offered. He read terms such as "rearfoot control," "heel counter," and "shock distribution," but felt ignorant about what shoe he should buy.

The wide variety of running shoes displayed in retail stores and featured in running magazines and the range of prices, colours, and styles made the decision even more complex. Rapidly changing technology, eye-catching innovations, and clever marketing tended to sway Peter from brand to brand without his knowing if the shoe matched his own needs and requirements. Running-shoe purchases, as Peter had learned through consumer behaviour textbooks, seemed to be determined by how the buyer wishes to be perceived, whether to be trendy or athletic. Running-shoe buyers often appeared to Peter to be very fickle, depending on what appealed to them or caught their eye at the point of purchase. He knew that serious runners often buy two or three different pairs, rotating them from day to day. He concluded that, as advanced engineering has transformed running shoes into technical and fashionable articles, their purchase had become a conspicuous activity and their wearing a "fashion statement."

Peter wanted to make sure he bought the right brand of running shoe. As he mulled over his decision, he identified criteria he felt he should consider in the selection process. Despite the wide price range of the shoes advertised in the magazine, high price was not a deterrent to Peter's purchase decision. Although he expected to pay more than $100 for a pair of quality running shoes, he preferred to keep the expense close to that level if at all possible. Comfort, availability, and protection against injury were critical to Peter. Colour was not at all important, although some shoes seemed a little too flashy. He was tending towards a lighter-weight shoe, which seemed to be preferred for longer distances, to protect against tiring. Peter felt that if each of these criteria was satisfied, he could run at his optimal capability.

To ensure that he was on the right track, he arranged a meeting with Sheila Cambridge at Athletics Canada. Sheila was a consultant with the association and held the provincial record for the 10 km distance. Peter had met Sheila at a campus party several weeks ago and knew that she was held in high regard in the local athletic community. She would also be well versed in the technical aspects of running-shoe construction, as she had graduated from the University of Ottawa a year earlier having specialized in kinesiology. Peter felt confident that she would be able to provide the expert advice he needed to pick the *right* pair of running shoes. "Besides," thought Peter as he walked along the canal towards Sheila's office, "it will be nice to see Sheila again."

Peter enjoyed the meeting with Sheila, as they discussed mutual friends and Sheila's training for the summer road-racing season. Peter learned that she had been training for the past four months in preparation for her first attempt at the marathon distance, to take place in mid-May in Ottawa's National Capital Marathon. Peter began to feel a little ill at ease, as he realized that Sheila was obviously far more knowledgeable about running than he was. He wondered whether he would ever reach the same level of training that she had achieved and felt a little uncomfortable at the thought of asking very basic questions about what shoes he should buy. He wondered whether he shouldn't just end the conversation.

It was too late when Sheila said, "Enough about my running. You wanted to talk about running shoes, didn't you? How much running are you planning to do?" Peter explained that he had participated in track and field in high school, but at distances from 400 to 1,500 m. He now wanted to try running some longer distances, primarily to get back in shape. He also thought he might like to run some road races and even try a little cross-country. With that, Sheila pulled from a pile of magazines and books on her desk a back issue of *Running Times*. She turned to a page that contained a diagram of the various components of a running shoe (Exhibit 1). She explained to Peter those components to which he should pay particular attention. "In selecting a running shoe," she explained, "the factor that I consider most important is fit. If the shoe doesn't fit well, you are likely to encounter problems down the road."

Sheila further suggested that one of the main criteria Peter must satisfy in his purchase of running shoes was protection against injury and overload. Research into the causes of injury has pointed to the type of running surface as one of the possible causes. She explained that common running injuries and ailments include leg fractures, muscle pulls and tears, heel spurs, shin splints, and knee injuries.

Although Peter felt he would prefer cross-country training through wooded and grassy areas, he observed that access to scenic trails would likely be limited once he moved to Toronto. "In that case," explained Sheila, "your running shoe must provide stability and protection against the high impact of pounding on the pavement. Not only do the interior components of the shoe have to protect your feet but the exterior components such as the outsole will be important in cushioning against impact."

Other factors Sheila mentioned as contributing to injury were the type of movement, the training distance per week, and the intensity of training. She went on to explain that protection against overloading is also important. "Load is the external force acting upon a body. It results both from dynamic factors such as the type of movement, the velocity of limbs, posture, muscular activity, and the number of repetitions, and also from boundary conditions such as the shoe surface, obstacles, anthropometric factors, and individual situation," she explained.

Peter found himself listening less intently as the information that Sheila was offering began to sound much more technical than he had expected. He really just wanted her to recommend a pair of running shoes and was not interested in all the technical jargon. When Sheila suggested that he attend a running clinic to check out what some of the local runners were wearing, Peter asked her what she would buy if she was in his position.

Sheila said that she really couldn't recommend a brand or model that would be best for him, as there were many acceptable shoes available. She did say that she ran in Nike shoes and that Nike is, in her opinion, the leading running shoe in the market. She suggested that he probably wouldn't be disappointed if he bought a Nike shoe, possibly an Air Stab or an Air Span. Peter wondered if her opinion might be biased by her personal choice. He thanked her, but felt a little disappointed to have left without knowing why Nike would be a good choice.

Heading home the next day, following his final exam in marketing research, Peter decided to visit Sports Experts, a sporting goods store in the Rideau Centre, to look at the selection of running shoes and to price the various brands and styles that he had seen in a recent advertising flyer from the store. He had often found the sales clerks in sporting goods stores to be knowledgeable and hoped he might get some advice concerning running shoes. Although he was familiar with a number of sporting goods stores in the Ottawa area, Peter decided to visit only three of them, all located within the downtown area. Over the next day or two, he would check the variety and prices at Sports Experts, Elgin Sports, and Sports-4.

Sports Experts had a reputation for a wide selection and good service. Generally, Peter did not appreciate being hounded by sales clerks in stores. He had never found the

# Glossary of Terms

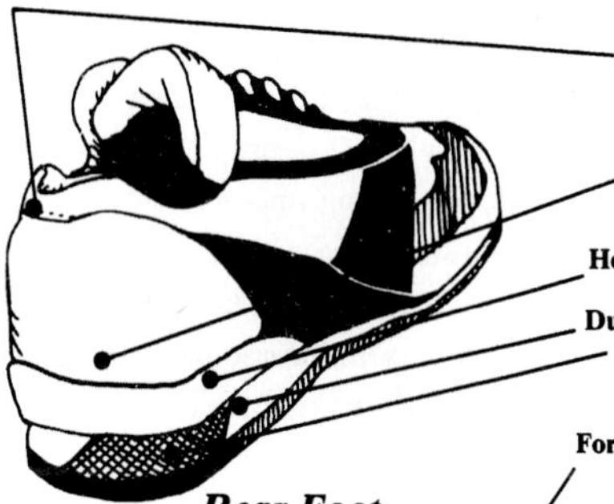

*Rear Foot*

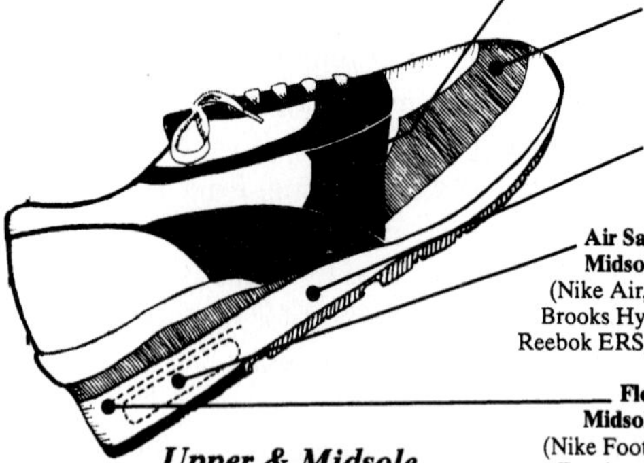

*Upper & Midsole*

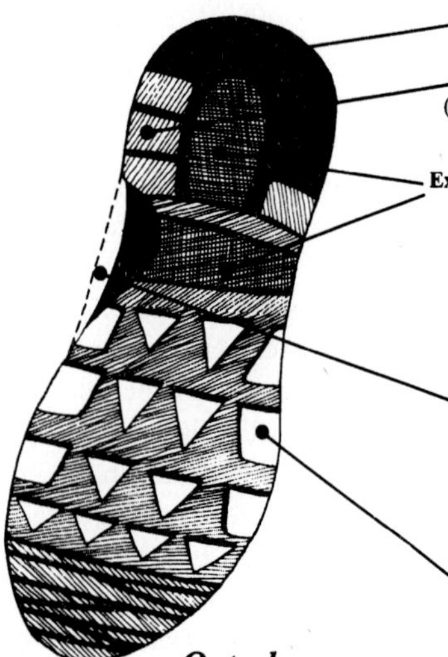

*Outsole*

| Term | Explanation |
|---|---|
| **Rearfoot Stability** | Prevents excessive lateral wobble or sag, and is important to severe pronators (see opposite page). |
| **Achilles Notch** | Soft, padded material above heel counter cushions Achilles tendon and is sometimes notched to prevent irritation of the tendon. |
| **Heel Counter** | Rigid cup holds heel firmly in place to prevent lateral motion. |
| **Heel Counter Collar** | Reinforces heel counter. |
| **Dual-density midsole** | Higher density on medial (inner) side of shoe resists compression and makes it harder for the foot to pronate (roll or sag sideways toward the inward side). |
| **Forefoot stability strap** | Helps to keep the upper material (usually a light nylon fabric or mesh) from sagging or bursting out; also helps to prevent excessive lateral motion of the forefoot. |
| **Toe Box** | Should be roomy enough to let toes wiggle freely, with at least a thumb's width of space between toe and front wall of box. Foot should be snug around the heel, roomy around the toes. |
| **Midsole** | Cushions the foot. Simplest midsoles are pieces of EVA foam. A more durable material is lightweight polyurethane (PU). |
| **Air Sac and Fluid Sac Midsole Components** (Nike Air, Etonic StableAir, Brooks Hydroflow, Asics Gel, Reebok ERS, Hi-Tec AirBall, etc.) | Cushions impact of heel on the road, lengthens life of the shoe by preventing squashing of midsole (units are usually contained in strong PU casings) and may help stabilize ride by distributing impact. |
| **Flexible Plate Midsole Components** (Nike Footbridge, Avia ARC, Etonic graphite plate, etc.) | Cushions impact by distributing impact over a wider area, and ARC combines this cushioning with a trampoline effect for greater energy return or "bounce." |
| **Heel Plug** | Carbon/rubber resists abrasion, prevents wearing through prematurely at outside corner of the heel. |
| **Horseshoe Outsole** (Nike Center-of-Pressure, Avia Cantilever) | Distributes weight to perimeter to maximize stability, while allowing center of rearfoot outsole to be scooped out (see Exposed Midsole, below). |
| **Exposed (Recessed) Midsole** | Often in the center of the rearfoot bottom, and sometimes across the midfoot bottom, sections of dense outsole are scooped out in areas where foot contact with the ground isn't needed. This cuts down on the weight of the shoe, helps to keep the heel centered (by allowing it to sink down more in the center than on either side), and allows the foot to trampoline for better energy return. |
| **Filled-in Medial Arch** | Resists pronation by preventing sag at instep. Similarly, **straight-lasted** shoe has straight shape suitable for stabilizing motion for hard heel-hitters and severe pronators. **Curved-lasted** models facilitate natural motion for forefoot-strikers and faster-paced runners. |
| **Outsole Studs or Lugs** | Provide traction, especially important in the forefoot area, for both heel-strikers and forefoot-strikers. Tread patterns vary widely, but generally the smoother patterns are more effective for roads, the toothier patterns better in snow or mud or off-road. |

sales clerks in this particular store to be pushy, but rather genuinely helpful and friendly. Many seemed to be students who were working in the store part-time. After he had been given a few minutes to scan the huge wall display of running, court, squash, tennis, aerobic, basketball, cross-training, volleyball, sprinting, cycling, and windsurfing shoes, a sales clerk approached him and offered her assistance.

Peter had been looking closely at several Nike and Brooks styles, as he had worn both brands in the court and cross-training styles in the past and had been very satisfied with them. He asked the sales clerk which of the brands was considered best and what benefits each had to offer.

The Sports Expert sales clerk, Donna Williams, proceeded to explain that neither was necessarily the best brand. She suggested that Peter's decision should be based on comfort and ensuring that the width was neither too narrow nor so wide that the foot shifted from side to side. She felt that price was generally a good measure of the quality of the shoe, but not necessarily of the brand. She recommended that Peter try one style of each of the major brands, so that he could determine the fit of each of the shoes, and whether the cushioning felt right.

Donna went on to suggest that sturdiness could be tested by bending the shoe from right to left, and by ensuring that the heel components of the shoe felt firm. The lightness of the various shoes could be compared easily. Once the most comfortable brand of shoe was identified, price could be used along with a visual test of features to determine which shoe fulfilled his need. Donna suggested that generally the higher the price, the more stability and features were associated with the running shoe. She felt that gimmicks, such as endorsements by personalities, Velcro closures, and fluorescent colours, would probably inflate the price, but did not necessarily enhance the shoe's quality. So the quality-conscious consumer, as compared to the socially conscious one, would need to search beyond superficial features. Donna Williams indicated that it was often very difficult to tell, having been influenced by advertising and other marketing strategies, which features were truly beneficial for a runner such as Peter and which had merely been promoted to make a shoe stand out from the competition. She felt that the consumer did not necessarily need to be a technical expert or sports engineer to perceive the difference, but should be educated as to what was most necessary given his or her running style, training schedule, desired features, and price range.

Peter proceeded to try one Nike, one Brooks, one Reebok, and one Asics running shoe, all within the same price range. Donna Williams suggested that he walk and jog down the mall corridor outside the store for a more realistic indication of comfort and stability. This comparison would give him a better basis for comparing the features offered by each brand. Peter declined the offer to jog in the mall. Instead, he tried on each pair of shoes and walked around the store. He decided that he felt most comfortable with the Nike shoes, as the air cushioning and light weight seemed to offer more spring, and he felt this would diminish some of the impact he would experience running on hard surfaces.

Peter remembered Sheila Cambridge's recommendation. Although Peter was sold on the Nike brand, the particular style he had tried, the Air Max, felt a little wide on his narrow foot. Donna Williams explained that the only shoe manufacturer who offered shoes in a full range of widths was New Balance and asked whether he would like to try a pair. Peter explained that he really liked the feel of the Nike shoe, but he wanted to find one that felt a little less wide. Donna suggested another Nike shoe, the Air Stab, which Peter proceeded to try. Feeling satisfied with the shoe, he jogged on the spot as a test of this new style. He felt that he had finally found what he had been looking for.

Peter asked Donna to hold the shoes for him until closing that night. This would provide ample time for him to ensure that the other stores were not offering the Nike Air Stab at a lower price than $129.99. Peter thanked Donna Williams for her help and left Sports Experts to see what the other stores had to offer. As he walked towards the mall exit on Laurier Street, he passed another sporting goods store and was attracted by a large wall display of athletic shoes. Athlete's World was offering Nike Air Stab at the same price he had found at Sports Experts, so Peter left the store quickly, feeling that Sports Experts deserved the sale, considering that Donna Williams had invested considerable time helping him. Peter decided to head for Bank Street, where he could see the offerings at Elgin Sports and Sports-4. Elgin Sports was an established Ottawa sporting goods store, with its original outlet on Elgin Street. A couple of years ago, the company had opened a second store on Bank Street, which offered a wide variety of sports clothing and shoes. Sports-4 was a newer store, having opened just two or three years ago. Peter felt that the Sports-4 outlet was much more of a running specialty store, as a display near the door contained notices of forthcoming road races and triathlons.

The Elgin Sports store on Bank Street also had the Air Stabs priced at $129.99, which left Peter wondering if he was needlessly running around the city when he could have purchased the pair of shoes he had seen at Sports Experts. On entering Sports-4, Peter was pleasantly surprised, as the Nike Air Stab was on a special promotion for $99.99. Peter was thrilled with this $30 savings and asked if he could try on a size 9, feeling he really couldn't buy a pair of shoes without trying them on. The sales clerk disappeared into the storage room for a few minutes only to walk out empty-handed. He looked at Peter apologetically and informed him that unfortunately a 9 1/2 was the smallest size they had in stock.

Peter decided to try them on anyway. Perhaps the extra half-size wouldn't make much difference to the fit. After all, he would be saving $30 in the process. However, the extra space in the toe was quite noticeable, even with the thick socks the clerk had handed him to try with the shoes. Peter wondered how this difference might affect his running performance. His past experience with athletic footwear suggested that the shoe would stretch a little with wear, especially if exposed to wet conditions. Disappointed, Peter felt he would have to forfeit the $30 savings and be satisfied with the fact that he was still fairly close to this initial price range.

Geoff Wallace, the clerk at Sports-4, suggested that he measure Peter's foot to make sure that he did indeed require a size 9. Having confirmed that this was Peter's correct size, he advised strongly against buying a half-size larger, indicating it was his opinion that fit is of critical importance when selecting a pair of running shoes. He then asked Peter to walk up and down in front of the shoe display so that he might examine how his feet struck the floor as he walked.

Geoff observed that Peter tended to strike the floor first with the outer edge of his foot, a tendency referred to as supination, and suggested that Peter might like to try a pair of Brooks GFS-105 shoes, explaining that this was a shoe that offered excellent fit and the Hydroflow cushioning system. He also explained that the GFS-105 featured a curved last, which was recommended for people who tended to supinate. Peter was impressed at the time Geoff was taking to help him select the right shoe and with the fact that the Brooks GFS-105 shoe was on sale at a special price of $109. Peter declined Geoff's suggestion politely, explaining that he had decided on the Nike Air Stab.

Peter was wondering, as he left Sports-4, if he might be able to strike a deal at Sports Experts, considering he should probably think about buying a rainsuit anyway. After dinner, he walked back to the Rideau Centre, wandered into Sports Experts, and was met by Donna Williams, who had been so helpful earlier in the day. Peter requested the running shoes that he had asked her to hold for him, but expressed his dismay over the better deal offered by Sports-4. Peter asked if he might speak with the manager about the possibility of matching the Sports-4 price.

While Donna disappeared to get the manager, Peter spotted a Nike rainsuit that appealed to him and had been marked down in price. As he took the rainsuit off the display rack, he was greeted by the manager who had been directed to Peter by Donna Williams. Peter explained his dilemma and asked if Sports-4's sale price on the Nike Air Stab might be matched, provided that he purchase the rainsuit he had selected. The manager was eager for business and goodwill, especially since he considered Sports-4 to be Sports Experts' main competitor for running and triathlon equipment in the city. He nodded and offered to ring in the sale for him, all the while making conversation about running in Ottawa. Peter appreciated the concession that Sports Experts had made and thanked the manager and Donna Williams, telling them he would be sure to shop at Sports Experts stores in Toronto on a regular basis.

While running slowly along the Rideau Canal later that evening, Peter met Sheila Cambridge, who had just finished a 10 km run. The clean white of Peter's new shoes caught her eye and she commented that he had made an excellent choice. Peter continued on his run towards his apartment on the other side of the canal, feeling satisfied with his purchase. He could sense that he was going to enjoy running, and he was already thinking about entering his first road race later that summer.

## QUESTIONS

1. Identify the various factors that influenced Peter Taylor's behaviour in selecting a pair of running shoes. Why did he select the Nike brand?
2. What objectives do you feel Peter was trying to accomplish in the selection of running shoes? What motivated his final selection?
3. Why did he buy his shoes at Sports Experts? What could Geoff Wallace have done to persuade Peter to buy the Brooks shoe (or any other) at Sports-4?

# CASE 2-2

# RUBBERMAID, INC.

Who can get excited about utilitarian household products such as dust pans, dish drainers, and lunch boxes? Apparently, an awful lot of North American consumers can, judging by the continuing success of Rubbermaid, Inc. The company generates sales of more than $2 billion annually, and its profits are also enviable. Over a 10-year period, Rubbermaid provided investors with an average annual rate of return of 25.7 percent, far above the average return of 16.2 percent for all firms among the Standard and Poor's 500.

As it has satisfied numerous consumers and shareholders, it also has impressed the business community. In a survey conducted by *Fortune*, Rubbermaid shows up every year among America's most admired corporations. Of the 311 companies in the study, Rubbermaid ranked number two overall in 1993 in the eyes of the 8,000 senior executives, directors, and security analysts participating in the survey. Further, Rubbermaid ranked among the top three firms with respect to five of the eight key attributes of a corporate reputation: quality of management, use of corporate assets, quality of products, community and environmental responsibility, and innovativeness (for which Rubbermaid was ranked number one).

The origins of Rubbermaid's present success date back to the late 1950s, when the firm started to work with plastic as a substitute for rubber or wood in various products. Its first breakthrough was a plastic "lazy Susan," a revolving tray for dining-room tables. Eventually, Rubbermaid became well known for helpful plastic or rubber products for the kitchen and the bathroom.

More recently, the firm has introduced products for the rest of the house — other rooms, the garage, and the yard. Now Rubbermaid is extending some of its products for use at industrial sites. More often than not, the company's products store or hold things — dust, lunches, garbage, tools, makeup, and so on. Contrary to popular perception, not all its products are wildly successful. For example, its line of office products faltered, and its line of lawn furniture has been caught in a price war.

Rubbermaid applies its name to virtually all its products. Often the Rubbermaid brand is used in conjunction with a name for the product line, such as Roughneck garbage cans, Drain Tainer oil pans, and Littlerless Lunch Kits. Due to this strategy, Rubbermaid enjoys 97 percent brand awareness among consumers.

Rubbermaid distributes its products widely — through more than 100,000 retail stores. To achieve such intensive distribution, the company places its products not only in department stores but also in discount houses. Potentially, using different types of outlets can confuse consumers or aggravate retailers, or both. Explaining the company's strategy, a vice-president said that Rubbermaid "let consumers decide which was better for them. They decided they got better selection, better pricing, and better in-stock situations at discount chains."

Now Rubbermaid is trying to go a step further and establish Everything Rubbermaid sections in selected retail stores. Under this concept, all Rubbermaid's housewares products are displayed together. This section provides added convenience to shoppers and also enhances Rubbermaid's brand image. The concept has been tested in K mart stores. Early results showed a 40 percent increase in sales of Rubbermaid products in stores with the new section.

Rubbermaid's stated goal is to derive 30 percent of its annual sales from products that did not exist five years ago. To achieve this goal, the company introduces new products at a rate of one per day. According to one "rule of thumb," it takes 20 to 25 ideas to come up with a successful new product and 10 new products to yield a " home run." How does Rubbermaid come up with the storehouse of ideas that are needed to generate a steady flow of new products? Several approaches have proven fruitful:

Sources: Jennifer Reese, "America's Most Admired Corporations," *Fortune*, February 8, 1993, pp. 44-47, 53; Elaine Underwood, "Rubbermaid Rolls into a Hot New Niche — Beauty Organizers," *Brandweek*, January 11, 1993, p. 3; Rahul Jacob, "Thriving in a Lame Economy," *Fortune*, October 5, 1992, pp. 45-46; "Rubbermaid: Breaking All the Molds," *Sales & Marketing Management*, August 1992, p. 42; Jon Berry, "The Art of Rubbermaid," *Adweek's Marketing Week*, March 16, 1992, pp. 22-25; Brian Dumaine, "Closing the Innovation Gap," *Fortune*, December 2, 1991, pp. 56-59; and Zachary Schiller, "At Rubbermaid, Little Things Mean a Lot," *Business Week*, November 11, 1991, p. 126.

- **Being market-driven.** According to a company vice-president, "It's a misnomer that Rubbermaid is *marketing*-driven. We're *market*-driven, and all functions are devoted to improving the product." Thus, recognizing that the North American population is aging, Rubbermaid introduced a variety of storage products. The rationale is that as people age, they accumulate — and need to store — all kinds of possessions. Rubbermaid also asks consumers, "What's wrong?" That means inquiring about small problems encountered on a daily basis and about problems with existing products. The answers provide the basis for developing products with small but meaningful advantages. Hence, Rubbermaid introduced products such as a shower caddy that holds the bottle of shampoo upside down (so every drop of shampoo can be used easily), and a lunch box that has three plastic containers for a sandwich, a drink, and another item (so there's no litter).
- **Using cross-functional teams.** New-product teams in each product line include employees not just from marketing and sales but also from the areas of finance, manufacturing, purchasing, and research and development. This team approach seeks to enhance both the creativity and efficiency of new-product development.
- **Entering new product categories.** Rubbermaid constantly searches for new opportunities that complement its current strengths and marketing activities. Typically the company enters a new product category every 12 to 18 months. For example, in 1993, Rubbermaid moved into beauty organizers, a product category that generates more than $200 million in annual sales — mostly to teenaged girls. With this new line of plastic containers for makeup and hair accessories, Rubbermaid hopes to get a substantial share of this category's sales.
- **Holding an internal product fair.** Over two days, new-product managers and research-and-development staff members from all Rubbermaid's divisions exchanged and discussed ideas. The outcome was 2,000 ideas for new products.

In the future, Rubbermaid intends to maintain a steady flow of new products. By doing so, it will avoid what the company chairman described as "years of drought."

Rubbermaid also plans to build its offshore international presence. In 1991, 15 percent of the company's sales came from foreign markets; the goal is 25 percent by the year 2000. Part of that growth will be achieved by acquiring foreign companies, and some will come from joint ventures with other foreign firms.

## QUESTIONS

1. Is the Rubbermaid brand name a good one, and does it possess brand equity?
2. Which of the following features are important to Rubbermaid products — packaging, labelling, design, quality, warranty, and postsale service?
3. What other product categories should Rubbermaid consider entering?

# PART 3

# PRODUCTS AND SERVICES

**The planning, development, and management of the want-satisfying goods and services that are a company's products**

Part 2 focuses on the selection and identification of target markets in accordance with the firm's marketing goals. The next step in the strategic marketing planning process is to develop a marketing mix that will achieve these goals in the selected target markets. The marketing mix is a strategic combination of four variables — the organization's product, pricing structure, distribution system, and promotional program. Each of these is closely interrelated with the other three variables in the mix.

Part 3, consisting of four chapters, is devoted to the product component of the marketing mix. In Chapter 9 we define the term *product*, consider the importance of product planning and innovation, and discuss the new-product development process. Chapter 10 deals mainly with product-mix strategies, the management of the product life cycle, and a consideration of style and fashion. Chapter 11 is concerned with branding, packaging, labelling, and other product features. Chapter 12 introduces the subject of services and their delivery to consumers.

# CHAPTER 9 GOALS

After studying this chapter, you should have an understanding of:

- The meaning of the word *product* in its fullest sense.
- What a "new" product is.
- The classification of consumer and business products.
- The relevance of these product classifications to marketing strategy.
- The importance of product innovation.
- The steps in the product-development process.
- Criteria for adding a product to a company's line.
- Adoption and diffusion processes for new products.
- Organizational structures for product planning and development.

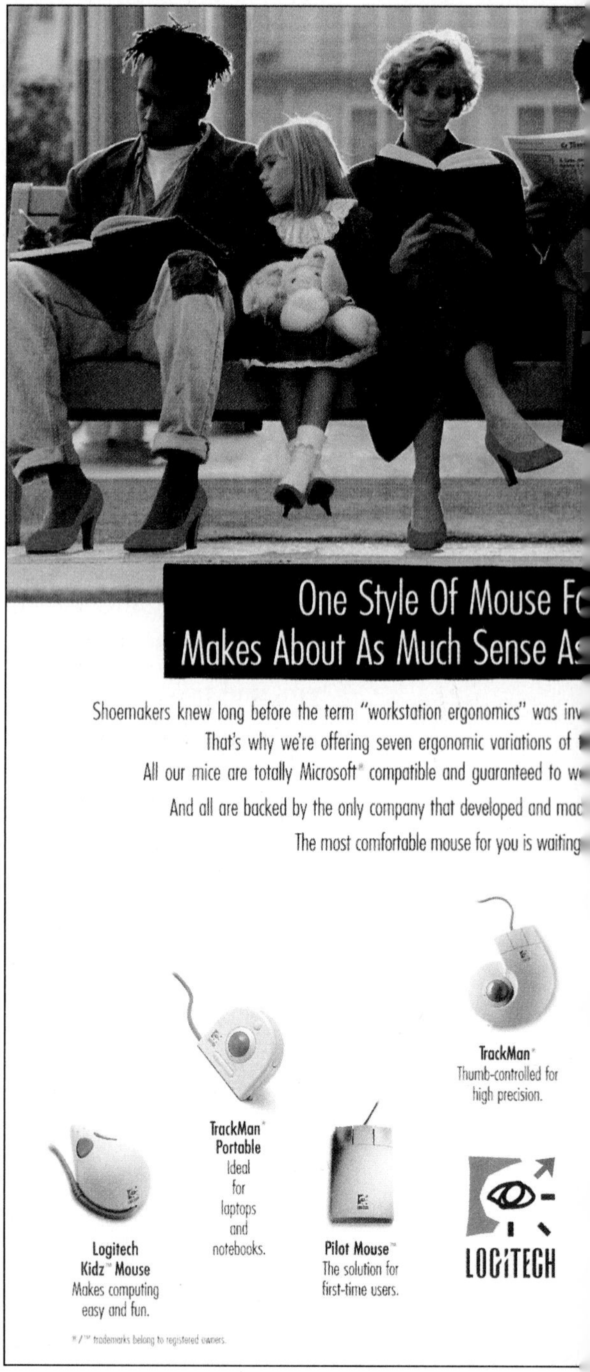

# CHAPTER 9

# PRODUCT PLANNING AND DEVELOPMENT

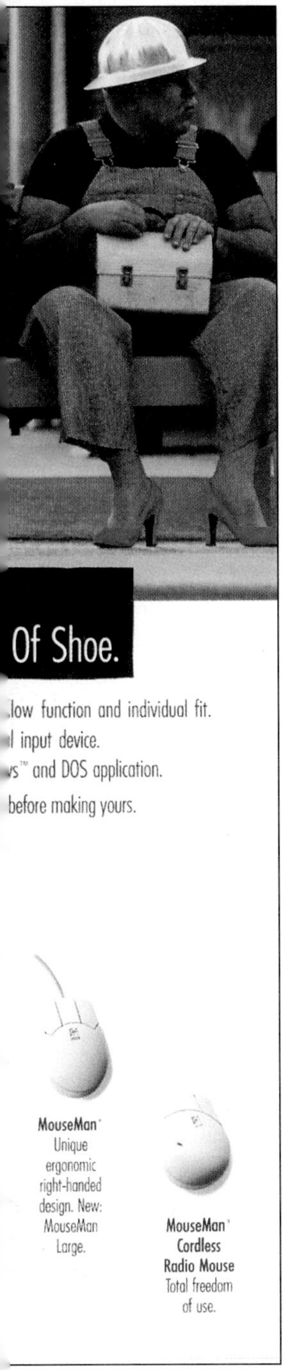

Of Shoe.
low function and individual fit.
input device.
and DOS application.
before making yours.
MouseMan Unique ergonomic right-handed design. New: MouseMan Large.
MouseMan Cordless Radio Mouse Total freedom of use.


## Computer Product and Service Innovation Races to Keep Pace with Innovation-Hungry Consumers

Computer and computer-related technology seems to change more rapidly than almost every other kind. Every week, if not every day, or so it seems, there is the announcement of a new piece of Corel or Alias software, a new Canon ink-jet printer, a new Compaq laptop, a new and faster Intel chip, even a new mouse. The new product and service development process for computing equipment is truly working overtime.

And which market is first to take up these myriad innovations? It's not the big companies of Canada, it's practitioners who buy computers and equipment for their home-based businesses (26 percent of PC sales), or to bring work home (16 percent), or to give their children a high-tech tutor (27 percent). These are the buyers — the consumer innovators and early adopters — who are willing to be the first to pay for extra computing power, the convenience of more specialized software, or the comfort and precision of a refined mouse. Together with the rest of the industry, Logitech™, a company that produces computer mice, continues to develop new input devices to satisfy the needs of newly discovered and eager customers. As the ad copy attests, there is a Logitech™ mouse for every need — be it ease of use, fun, portability, lack of experience, ergonomics, high precision — even if you're left-handed there's a mouse designed for you.

The process of creating new products and services for the ever-growing and ever-changing computer market is fraught with risk. Innovating firms that are too technologically driven run the risk of having superior technical products but no apparent market demand for the technology. The success of many firms in this industry comes from their recognition that technical superiority by itself does not guarantee markets. It is necessary that your product be "user friendly" and easy to use right from the start. Compaq Canada's Presario single-unit desktop computer took off in sales to the home-user market in 1993 and 1994 simply because it was so user friendly in set-up and start-up; just plug it in and after 10 to 20 minutes of guided instruction, the user can be productive. Today, the consumer's need for ease of use, ease of understanding, and ease of getting quality service plays an increasing role in the design and marketing of various computers and computer-related products. As consumers start to regard computer equipment more like appliances, markets will continue to grow beyond the small number of users who are technically sophisticated. And, of course, this means more and more mice in various styles for Logitech™ to work on. But there is always the problem for an innovative firm like Logitech™ — what product is under development that can make the mouse, as we know it today, obsolete?[1]

## THE MEANING OF PRODUCT

In a *narrow* sense, a product is a set of attributes assembled in an identifiable form. Each product is identified by a commonly understood descriptive (or generic) name, such as steel, insurance, tennis racquets, or entertainment. Product attributes such as brand name and postsale service that appeal to consumer motivation or buying patterns play no part in this narrow interpretation. According to this interpretation, an Apple and a Compaq would be the same good — a personal computer. And Canada's Wonderland and Ontario Place would be an identical service — an amusement park.

In marketing we need a broader definition of product to indicate that consumers are not really buying a set of attributes, but rather benefits that satisfy their needs. Thus consumers don't want sandpaper; they really want a smooth surface. To develop a sufficiently broad definition, let's start with *product* as an umbrella term covering goods, services, places, persons, and ideas. Throughout this book, when we speak of products, we are using this broad connotation.

Thus a product that provides benefits can be something other than a tangible *good*. The Holiday Inn's product is a *service* that provides the benefit of a comfortable night's rest at a reasonable price. The Vancouver Visitors Bureau's product is a *place* that provides romance, sun and sea, relaxation, cross-cultural experiences, and other benefits. In a political campaign, the New Democratic or Reform party's product is a *person* (candidate) whom the party wants you to buy (vote for). The Canadian Cancer Society is selling an *idea* and the benefits of not smoking. In Chapter 12 we discuss in more detail the marketing of intangible products such as services and ideas.

To further expand our definition, we treat each *brand* as a separate product. In this sense, Kodacolor film and Fujicolor film are different products. Lantic Sugar and St. Lawrence are also separate products, even though the only physical difference may be the brand name on the package. But the brand name suggests a product difference to the consumer, and this brings the concept of consumer want satisfaction into the definition.

Any change in a feature (design, colour, size, packaging), however minor, creates another product. Each such change provides the seller with an opportunity to use a new set of appeals to reach what essentially may be a new market. Pain relievers (Tylenol, Anacin) in capsule form are a different product from the same brand in tablet form, even though the chemical contents of the tablet and the capsule are identical. Seemingly minor product changes can be the key to success (or failure) in international markets. For example, to satisfy Japanese consumers, two modified versions of Oreo cookies were developed. One has less sugar in the cookie batter, the other omits the cream filling.[2] (Can you believe it — Oreos that can't be twisted apart?)

We can broaden this interpretation still further. A Sony TV bought in a discount store on a cash-and-carry basis is a different product than the identical model purchased in a department store. In the department store, the customer may pay a higher price for the TV but buys it on credit, has it delivered free of charge, and receives other store services. Our concept of a product now includes the services that accompany it when purchased. Occasionally, a seller's support and assurances may be extraordinary. For example, to stimulate sales during the recent recession, Volkswagen marketers in the United States expanded its product to the point of assuring customers that it would pay their car loan and car insurance for up to 12 months should they be laid off from their jobs.[3]

We're now ready for a definition that is useful to marketers: A **product** is a set of tangible and intangible attributes, including packaging, colour, price, quality, and brand, plus the seller's services and reputation. A product may be a good, service, place, person, or idea. (See Figure 9-1.) In essence, then, consumers are buying much more than a set of physical attributes when they buy a product. They are buying want satisfaction in the form of the benefits they expect to receive from the product.

## CLASSIFICATIONS OF PRODUCTS

To design effective marketing programs, organizations need to know what kinds of products they are offering to consumers. Thus it's helpful to separate *products* into homogeneous categories. First we will divide all products into two categories — consumer products and business products — that parallel our description of the market. Then we will subdivide each category still further.

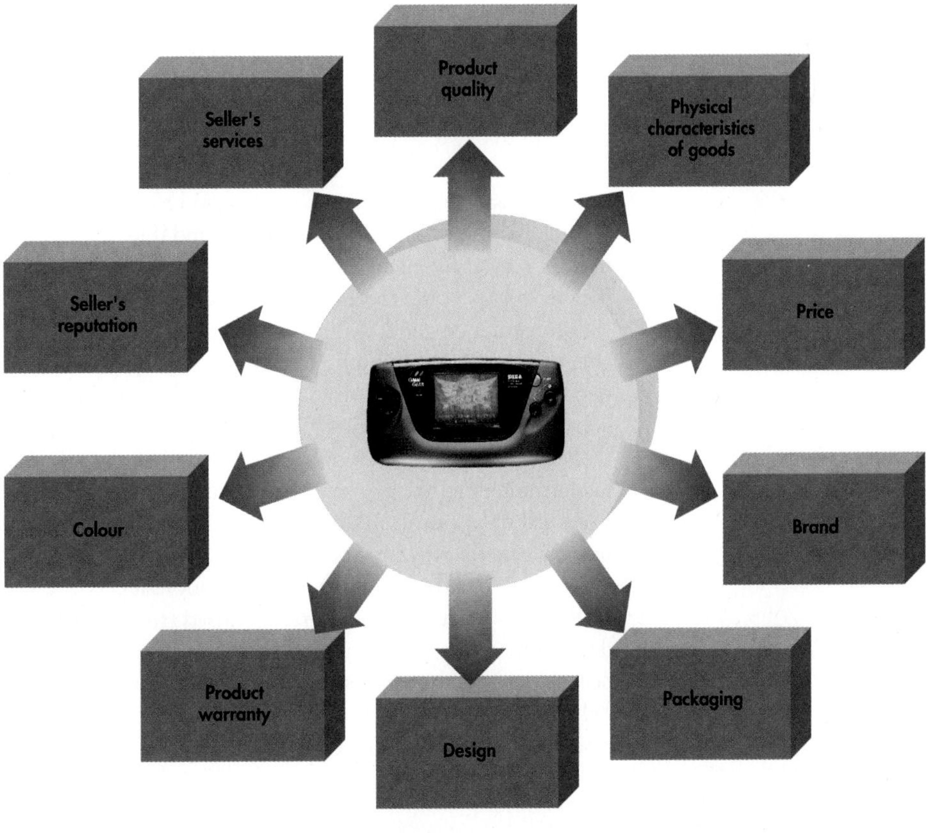


**FIGURE 9-1**
**A product is much more than a set of physical attributes.**

### Consumer and Business Products

**Consumer products** are intended for use by household consumers for nonbusiness purposes. **Business products** are intended for resale, for use in producing other products, or for providing services in an organization. Thus the two types of products are distinguished based on *who will use them* and *how they will be used.*

The position of a product in its distribution channel has no bearing on its classification. Kellogg's cornflakes are categorized as consumer products, even if they are in the manufacturers' warehouses, in a freight line's trucks, or on retailers' shelves, *if ultimately they will be used in their present form by household consumers.* However, Kellogg's cornflakes sold to restaurants and other institutions are categorized as business products no matter where they are in the distribution system.

Often it is not possible to place a product in only one class or the other. Seats on a Canadian Airlines International flight from Toronto to Vancouver may be considered a consumer product if purchased by students or a family going on vacation. But a seat on the same flight bought by a sales rep for business use is categorized as a business product. Canadian Airlines International, or any other company in a similar situation, recognizes that its product falls into both categories and therefore develops separate marketing programs for each market.

These distinctions may seem like "splitting hairs," but they are necessary for the strategic planning of marketing programs. Each major category of products ultimately goes to a distinctive type of market and thus requires different marketing methods.[4]

### Classification of Consumer Goods

For marketing purposes, distinguishing consumer goods from business goods is helpful but only a first step. The range of consumer goods is still too broad. Consequently, as shown in Table 9-1, they are further classified as convenience goods, shopping goods, specialty goods, and unsought goods. This classification is not based on intrinsic differences in the products themselves. Rather, it is based on how consumers go about buying a particular product. Depending on the buying behaviour of different consumers, a single product — such as wine or dress slacks — can fall into more than one of the four categories.

**Convenience Goods** A tangible product that the consumer knows enough about before going out to buy it and then actually buys it with a minimum of effort is termed a **convenience good**. Normally the advantages resulting from shopping around to compare price and quality are not considered worth the extra time and effort required to shop and compare. A consumer is willing to accept any of several brands and thus will buy the one that is most accessible. For most buyers, convenience goods include many food items, inexpensive candy, drug sundries such as shampoo and toothpaste, and staple hardware items such as light bulbs and batteries.

Convenience goods typically have a low unit price, are not bulky, and are not greatly affected by fad and fashion. They usually are purchased frequently, although this is not a necessary characteristic. Items such as Christmas tree lights or Mother's Day cards are convenience goods for most people, even though they may be bought only once a year.

Because a convenience good must be readily accessible when consumer demand arises, a manufacturer must be prepared to distribute it widely and rapidly. However, because most retail stores sell only a small volume of the total output of a convenience good (such as a particular brand of candy bar), it is not economical for the manufacturer to sell directly to all retail outlets. Instead the producer relies on wholesalers to sell the product to selected retailers.

Retailers usually carry several brands of the same type of convenience item, so they seldom promote any single brand. They are not interested in advertising convenience goods because many other stores carry the same brands (such as Canadian General Electric and Sylvania light bulbs). Thus any advertising by one retailer would help its competitors. As a result, virtually the entire advertising burden is shifted to the manufacturer.

TABLE 9-1 Categories of consumer goods: characteristics and marketing considerations

| | Type of product* | | |
|---|---|---|---|
| | Convenience | Shopping | Specialty |
| EXAMPLES: | Canned fruit | Furniture | Expensive suits |
| CHARACTERISTICS | | | |
| Time and effort devoted by consumer to shopping | Very little | Considerable | Cannot generalize; consumer may go to nearby store and buy with minimum effort or may have to go to distant store and spend much time and effort |
| Time spent planning the purchase | Very little | Considerable | Considerable |
| How soon want is satisfied after it arises | Immediately | Relatively long time | Relatively long time |
| Are price and quality compared? | No | Yes | No |
| Price | Usually low | High | High |
| Purchase frequency | Usually frequent | Infrequent | Infrequent |
| MARKETING CONSIDERATIONS | | | |
| Length of channel | Long | Short | Short to very short |
| Retailer | Relatively unimportant | Important | Very important |
| Number of outlets | As many as possible | Few | Few; often only one in a market |
| Stock turnover | High | Lower | Lower |
| Gross margin | Low | High | High |
| Responsibility for advertising | Producer's | Retailer's | Joint responsibility |
| Point-of-purchase display | Very important | Less important | Less important |
| Brand or store name important | Brand name | Store name | Both |
| Packaging | Very important | Less important | Less important |

*Unsought products are not included. See text explanation.

Shopping Goods A tangible product for which consumers want to compare quality, price, and perhaps style in several stores before making a purchase is considered a **shopping good**. Examples of shopping goods — at least for most consumers — are fashionable apparel, furniture, major appliances, and automobiles. The process of searching and comparing continues as long as the customer believes that the potential benefits from a better purchase more than offset the additional time and effort spent shopping. A *better* purchase might be saving several hundred dollars on the purchase of a new car or finally finding a software package that prepares financial statements in the manner desired by the buyer.

With shopping goods, buying habits affect the distribution and promotion strategies of both intermediaries (as retail stores) and manufacturers. Shopping-goods manufacturers require fewer retail outlets because consumers are willing to look around for what they want. To facilitate comparison shopping, manufacturers that believe their products are superior in price and/or quality try to place their products in stores located near other stores carrying competing items. Similarly, department stores and other retailers that carry primarily shopping goods like to be near each other.

Manufacturers usually work closely with retailers in marketing shopping goods. Since manufacturers use fewer retail outlets, they are more dependent on those they do select. Retail stores typically buy shopping goods in large quantities. And it's common for manufacturers to distribute directly to retailers. To buyers of a shopping good, the reputations of the stores carrying the product often are more important than the images of the manufacturers. For example, a consumer may be more loyal to a local Future Shop store than to various brands of audio and video equipment, such as JVC and Sanyo.

**Specialty Goods** A tangible product for which consumers have a strong brand preference and are willing to expend substantial time and effort in locating the desired brand is called a **specialty good**. The consumer is willing to forgo more accessible substitutes to search for and purchase the desired brand. Examples of products usually categorized as specialty goods include expensive men's suits, stereo sound equipment, health foods, photographic equipment, and, for many people, new automobiles and certain home appliances. Various brands, such as Armani, Nikon, and BMW, have achieved specialty-good status in the minds of some consumers.

**Some highly satisfying and well-respected brands achieve specialty-good status.**

Since consumers *insist* on a particular brand and are willing to expend considerable effort to find it, manufacturers can use fewer retail outlets. Ordinarily the manufacturer deals directly with these retailers. The retailers are extremely important, particularly if the manufacturer uses only one in each area. And where the opportunity to handle the product is highly valued, the retailer may be quite willing to abide by the producer's policies regarding the amount of inventory that must be maintained, how the product should be advertised, or other marketing factors.

Because relatively few outlets are used *and* the product's brand name is important to buyers, both manufacturer and retailer advertise the product extensively. Often the manufacturer pays a portion of the retailer's advertising costs, and the name of the store carrying the specialty good frequently appears in the manufacturer's ads.

**Unsought Goods** There's one more, quite different category of goods. In fact, it's so unlike the other three categories that we have not included it in Table 9-1. Nevertheless, because some firms sell unsought goods, this category deserves brief discussion.

An **unsought good** is a new product that the consumer is not yet aware of *or* a product that the consumer is aware of but does not want right now. For many people, unknown new products include computers that speak and video telephones. However, telephone companies are betting that new promotional programs will remove the latter product from the unsought category.

Currently unwanted products might include gravestones for those who have not lost a loved one and snow tires in the summer. An electric car might be an unsought good for most people, either because they are unaware of it or do not want one after learning about it. As the name suggests, a firm faces a very difficult, perhaps impossible, advertising and personal-selling job when trying to market unsought goods. The best approach may be to make consumers aware of the products so they will buy the advertised brand when the need arises.

TABLE 9-2 Categories of business goods: characteristics and marketing considerations

| | Type of product | | | | |
|---|---|---|---|---|---|
| | Raw materials | Fabricating parts and materials | Installations | Accessory equipment | Operating supplies |
| EXAMPLES: | Iron ore | Engine blocks | Blast furnaces | Storage racks | Paper clips |
| CHARACTERISTICS | | | | | |
| Unit price | Very low | Low | Very high | Medium | Low |
| Length of life | Very short | Depends on final product | Very long | Long | Short |
| Quantities purchased | Large | Large | Very small | Small | Small |
| Frequency of purchase | Frequent delivery; long-term purchase contract | Infrequent purchase, but frequent delivery | Very infrequent | Medium frequency | Frequent |
| Standardization of competitive products | Very much; grading is important | Very much | Very little; custom-made | Little | Much |
| Quantity of supply | Limited; supply can be increased slowly or not at all | Usually no problem | No problem | Usually no problem | Usually no problem |
| MARKETING CONSIDERATIONS | | | | | |
| Nature of channel | Short; no intermediaries | Short; intermediaries only for small buyers | Short; no intermediaries | Intermediaries used | Intermediaries used |
| Negotiation period | Hard to generalize | Medium | Long | Medium | Short |
| Price competition | Important | Important | Varies in importance | Not main factor | Important |
| Presale/postsale service | Not important | Important | Very important | Important | Very little |
| Promotional activity | Very little | Moderate | Sales people very important | Important | Not too important |
| Brand preference | None | Generally low | High | High | Low |
| Advance buying contract | Important; long-term contracts | Important; long-term contracts | Not usual | Not usual | Not usual |

### Classification of Business Goods

As with consumer goods, the general category of *business goods* is too broad to use in developing a marketing program. Consequently, as shown in Table 9-2, we separate business goods into five categories: raw materials, manufactured parts and materials, installations, accessory equipment, and operating supplies. This classification is based on the product's broad *uses*. For example, a business good may be used in producing other products, in operating an organization, and in other ways we will discuss.

Raw Materials Business goods that become part of another tangible product prior to being processed in any way (except as necessary to assist in handling the product) are considered **raw materials**. Raw materials include:

- Goods found in their natural state, such as minerals, land, and products of the forests and the seas, and
- Agricultural products, such as cotton, fruits, livestock, and animal products including eggs and raw milk.

Due to their distinctive attributes, these two groups of raw materials should be marketed differently. For instance, the supply of raw materials in their natural state is limited, cannot be substantially increased, and often involves only a few large producers. Further, such products generally are of a commodity nature, must be carefully graded, and, consequently, are highly standardized. Consider coal as an example; it is extracted in great quantities and then is graded by hardness and sulphur content.

The characteristics of raw materials in their natural state affect how they are marketed:

- Prices are normally set by supply and demand, approximating the conditions of perfect competition. As a result, producers have little or no control over prices.
- Because of their great bulk, low unit value, and the long distances between producer and business user, transportation is an important consideration for natural raw materials. Consider grain and fish as examples.
- Due to these same factors, natural raw materials frequently are marketed directly from producer to business user with a minimum of physical handling.
- There is very little branding or other product differentiation of this type of product. It is tough to distinguish one producer's coal from another producer's.
- It's also rare for marketers of natural raw materials to advertise or try to stimulate demand in other ways.

For raw materials in their natural state, competition is built around price and the assurance that a producer can deliver the product as specified.

Agricultural products are supplied by many small producers located some distance from their markets. The supply is largely controllable by producers — frequently through marketing boards — but it cannot be increased or decreased rapidly. The product is perishable and is not produced at a uniform rate throughout the year. Most Okanagan and Niagara soft fruits, for example, ripen in late summer and thus are readily available at that time

ONE OF THE FEW THINGS
TALON DOESN'T MAKE A ZIPPER FOR.
Talon has hatched so many zippers that you'll find our name in more than two billion products.
In fact, the consistent excellence and proven performance of our zippers have made the Talon name a symbol of quality. A reliable sign that tells you the rest of the product will be well-made, too.
So be a smart shopper. Always look for and select the products that carry the Talon name.
Of course, we don't make a zipper for an egg. But that's only because the manufacturer hasn't asked us for one.
The Talon® zipper says a lot about what it's in.

**Some products are purchased by both consumer and business markets.**

of year and become less available in subsequent months. Standardization and grading are commonplace for agricultural products. Also, transportation costs are likely to be high relative to the product's unit value.

Close attention must be given to transportation and warehousing. Transportation costs are high relative to unit value, and standardization and grading are very important. Because producers are small and numerous, many producer co-operatives, intermediaries, and long channels of distribution are needed. Promotional activity is usually carried out by marketing boards.

**Manufactured Parts and Materials** Business products that become part of other finished products fit into the category of manufactured parts and materials. Some of these undergo further processing and may be referred to as **fabricating materials**; examples include yarn that is woven into cloth and flour used in making bread. What distinguishes them from raw materials is that they have already been processed. Some manufactured parts, such as engine blocks in automobiles, may undergo further processing, but most parts are already fully manufactured and are bought by manufacturers for assembly into their final products. Some examples are the small motors that are bought by manufacturers of furnaces and lawnmowers, the zippers used by clothing manufacturers, and computer chips that are bought from companies such as Intel by IBM, Compaq, and others.

Manufactured materials and parts are usually purchased in large quantities. Normally, buying decisions are based on the price and the service provided by the seller. To ensure an adequate, timely supply, a buyer may place an order a year or more in advance. Because customers are concerned about price, service, and reliability of supply, most manufactured products are marketed directly from producer to user. Intermediaries are used most often when the buyers are small and/or when buyers have small fill-in orders (after the large initial order) requiring rapid delivery.

Branding manufactured materials and parts is generally unimportant. However, some firms have successfully pulled their business goods out of obscurity by branding them. Talon zippers and the NutraSweet brand of sweetener are examples.

**Installations** Manufactured products that are an organization's major, expensive, and long-lived equipment are termed **installations**. Examples are large generators in a dam, a factory building, diesel engines for a railroad, and blast furnaces for a steel mill. The characteristic of installations that differentiates them from other categories of business goods is that they *directly affect the scale of operations in an organization producing goods or services*. Adding 12 new Steelcase desks will not affect the scale of operations at Air Canada, but adding 12 Airbus jet aircraft certainly will. Therefore, jet aircraft are categorized as installations, but desks normally are not.

The marketing of installations presents a real challenge, because each unit sold represents a large dollar amount. Often each unit is made to the buyer's detailed specifications. Also, much presale and postsale servicing is essential. For example, a large printing press requires installation, maintenance, and — inevitably — repair service. Sales are usually made directly from producer to business user; no intermediaries are involved. Because installations are technical in nature, a high-calibre, well-trained sales force is needed to market installations. Because installations require careful, detailed explanation, promotion emphasizes personal selling. Some advertising might be used, though.

**Accessory Equipment** Tangible products that have substantial value and are used in an organization's operations are called **accessory equipment**. This category of business goods neither becomes an actual part of a finished product nor has a significant impact on the organization's scale of operations. The life of accessory equipment is shorter than

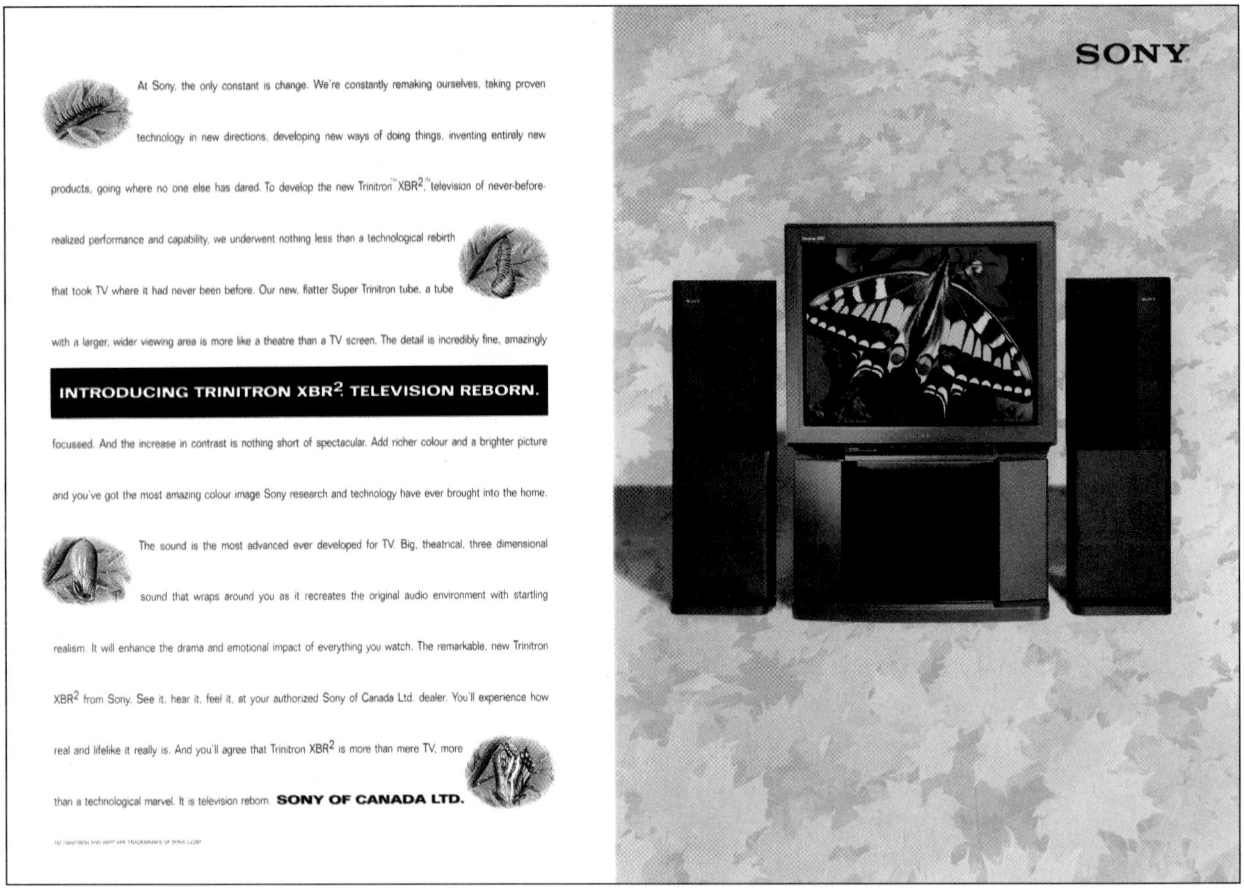


**Successful companies continually update and refresh their product mixes.**

that of installations but longer than that of operating supplies. Some examples are point-of-sale terminals in a retail store, small power tools, forklift trucks, and office desks.

It is difficult to generalize about how accessory equipment should be marketed. For example, direct sale is appropriate for some products in this category. This is true particularly when an order is for several units or when each unit is worth a lot of money. A manufacturer of forklift trucks may sell directly to customers because the price of a single unit is large enough to make this form of distribution profitable. Normally, however, manufacturers of accessory equipment use intermediaries — for example, office-equipment distributors. The reasons: typically, the market is geographically dispersed, there are many different types of potential users, and individual orders may be relatively small.

Operating Supplies Business goods that are characterized by low dollar value per unit and a short life and that aid in an organization's operations without becoming part of the finished product are called **operating supplies**. Examples are lubricating oils, pencils and stationery, and heating fuel. Purchasers want to buy operating supplies with fairly little effort. Thus operating supplies are the convenience goods of the business sector.

As with the other categories of goods, the characteristics of operating supplies influence how they should be marketed. Because they are low in unit value and are bought by many different organizations, operating supplies — like consumer convenience goods — are distributed widely. Thus the producing firm uses wholesaling intermediaries extensively. Also, because competing products are quite standardized and there is little brand insistence, price competition is normally stiff.

MARKETING AT WORK

FILE 9-1 **WHAT KIND OF GOOD IS THIS . . . BUSINESS OR CONSUMER? IS IT AN INSTALLATION OR ACCESSORY?**

"We wanted to see robots becoming commonplace in industry — and even at the consumer level," says Vivek Burhanpurkar, the founder and president of Cyberworks, a small firm in Orillia, Ontario. Cyberworks makes robots that can see and learn and be human-like, not like those uninspiring competitors' boxes that perform simple repetitive tasks.

Burhanpurkar founded his company in 1985, after dropping out of university. His firm makes robots that are intelligent, are non-programmed, and operate autonomously. He has sales of about $1 million a year currently and employs 10 engineers and designers. While he now manufactures robots for a variety of niche markets, what he wants to do is be the supplier of the core technology — the "eyes" of the robot — to the makers of hundreds of robotic products. Then his product can be all things to all buyers, business and consumer, installation and accessory.

When Burhanpurkar started his firm and started developing the core technology, what he really had was an unsought good — a product for which there was no apparent business or consumer demand. This is pretty normal for a lot of entrepreneurs. He needed a commercial product, not just a technology. By loading some brushes and suction onto the basic "seeing" technology, he had a robotic vacuum cleaner that could navigate around a room and not bump into the furniture, even if it was moved every day. Again, using the basic "seeing" technology, he developed a security guard robot. His sales grew with each niche application. Cyberworks robots were marketed in Japan and the United States, and distributorships were set up in Japan, Singapore, and South Korea — all high-demand robotic markets.

To achieve his goal of being the marketer of the core technology, Burhanpurkar has a number of customers and universities working on applications. He says, "Let the world build robots, but let's have them use our technology. You can't be the manufacturer of 500 different robotic products."

Adapted from Carolyn Leitch, "When Boxes Have Brains," *Globe and Mail*, April 12, 1994, p. B26.

## IMPORTANCE OF PRODUCT INNOVATION

A business exists to satisfy consumers while making a profit. Fundamentally, a company fulfils this dual purpose through its products. New-product planning and development are vital to an organization's success. A company cannot successfully sell a bad product over the long run.

### Requirement for Growth

A guideline for management is "innovate or die." For many companies a substantial portion of this year's sales volume and net profit will come from products that did not exist 5 to 10 years ago. Consider, for example, Hewlett-Packard Co., a maker of computers, microprocessor chips, and measurement and testing instruments with markets all over the world. In 1991, 60 percent of the orders received by the firm were for products it did not offer in 1989. In fact, Hewlett-Packard replaced its entire line of 21 computers in 1991. In the early 1990s, both Rubbermaid and Johnson & Johnson generated more than 25 percent of their sales from products that had been introduced during the past five years.[5]

Because products, like people, go through a life cycle, new products are essential for sustaining a company's revenues and profits. Sales of a product grow and then, almost inevitably, decline; eventually, most products are replaced. The concept of the product life cycle is discussed in more detail in Chapter 10, but we mention it here because it has two significant implications for product innovation:

- Every company's present products eventually become obsolete as their sales volume and market share are reduced by changing consumer desires and/or superior competing products.
- As a product ages, its profits generally decline. Introducing a new product at the right time can help maintain a company's profits.

Companies that develop innovative products can reap financial benefits. According to a recent study, 39 percent of highly successful firms had introduced an innovative product during the previous five years, compared to only 23 percent of less successful firms.[6] Consider specific examples such as microwave popcorn, fibre optic cable, and Post-It notes. Each provided benefits that were not previously available. Most recently, Procter & Gamble developed Pert Plus, a combined shampoo-conditioner. Because the unique new product worked well and saved time for consumers, it quickly became a leading shampoo in the Canadian and U.S. markets.[7]

### Increased Consumer Selectivity

In recent years, consumers have become more selective in their choices of products. Many consumers' disposable income and many organizations' resources were dissipated by the recent recession. With reduced buying power, these individuals, households, and organizations have to be very careful in their purchases. Even households and individuals who escaped the negative effects of the recession are being selective in making additional purchases because they are already reasonably well fed, clothed, housed, transported, and equipped. The same can be said of companies that were not hurt by the recession.

Another reason for more selective buying is that consumers have to sort through an abundance (or, some would say, an excess) of similar products. Many new products are mere imitations of existing products and, as such, offer few if any added benefits. How many of the 124 new condiments that were introduced in a recent month are really new?[8] This deluge of new products may lead to "product indigestion." The remedy is to develop *truly* new products — to *innovate*, not just *imitate*.

### High Failure Rates

For many years, the "rule of thumb" has been that about 80 percent of new products fail. In the early 1990s, the rate of failure was even higher. According to one survey, 86 percent of new products introduced in 1991 were expected to fall short of their business objectives.[9]

Why do new products fail? Most fail because they are no different than existing products. Other factors contributing to failures include poor positioning and lack of marketing support. Another reason a new product fails is that it is perceived as offering poor value in relation to its price.

Despite high failure rates, there is still a torrent of product introductions. For instance, in each of the first two years of the 1990s, more than 15,000 new products (including different varieties, formats, and sizes) were introduced in grocery and drugstores. Some large internationally based companies, such as Unilever, Procter & Gamble, and Avon, annually introduce hundreds of new products of their own.[10]

Considering how vital new products are to a company's growth, the large number of new-product introductions, and the high failure rates, product innovation deserves special attention. Firms that are inattentive to their new products may face financial ruin due to the high cost of product failures. Companies that effectively manage product innovation can expect to reap a variety of benefits — differential advantage, higher sales and profits, and a solid foundation for the future.

## DEVELOPMENT OF NEW PRODUCTS

It's often said that nothing happens until somebody sells something. This is not entirely true. First there must be something to sell — a product, service, person, place, or idea. And that "something" must be developed.

### What Is a "New" Product?

Just what is a "new" product? Are the auto manufacturers' annual models new products? GM's recently introduced Saturn automobile? Or, in other product categories, is Cheerios with an apple-cinnamon flavour a new product? How about Ultra, a superconcentrated liquid detergent that Procter & Gamble tested in 1992? Or must a product be revolutionary, never before seen, before we can class it as *new*?

How new a product is affects how it should be marketed. There are numerous connotations of "new product," but we will focus our attention on three distinct categories of **new products**:

- Products that are *really innovative* — truly unique. A recent example is a gadget developed by Hewlett-Packard that permits viewers to participate in "interactive" TV programs. Another example is a fat substitute developed by Unilever for use in ice cream, mayonnaise, and other traditionally high-fat food products. Still-to-be-developed products in this category would be a cancer cure and easily, inexpensively repaired automobiles. Any new product in this category satisfies a real need that is not being satisfied at the time it is introduced.
- Replacements that are *significantly different* from existing products in form, function, and — most important — benefits provided. Johnson & Johnson's Acuvue disposable contact lenses and Sharp Corp.'s very thin (only 3 inches/7.5 cm deep) TV, which hangs on a wall like a picture, are replacing some traditional models. Compact-disc players are gaining favour over conventional record and tape players. In some years, new fashions in clothing are different enough to fit into this category. Referring back to the earlier examples, probably GM's Saturn line and P&G's Ultra detergent fall in this category.
- Imitative products that are new to a particular company but not new to the market. Usually, annual models of autos and new versions of cereals are appropriately placed in this category. In another situation, a firm may simply want to capture part of an existing market with a "me too" product. To maximize company-wide sales, makers of cold and cough remedies routinely introduce imitative products, some of which compete with a nearly identical product *from the same company*. That's the case with Dristan Sinus and CoAdvil, both put out and marketed in Canada by American Home Products. In a different field, following the early success of hotels featuring two-room suites rather than single rooms, Quality Inns added similar products.

Ultimately, of course, whether a product is new or not depends on how the intended market perceives it. If buyers consider it to be significantly different from competitive products in some relevant characteristic (such as appearance or performance), then it is indeed a new product. As in other situations, *perception is reality*!

### New-Product Strategy

To achieve strong sales and healthy profits, every producer of business goods or consumer goods should have an explicit strategy with respect to developing and evaluating new products. This strategy should guide every step in the process of developing a new product.

A **new-product strategy** is a statement identifying the role a new product is expected to play in achieving corporate and marketing goals. For example, a new product might be designed to protect market share or maintain the company's reputation as an innovator.

Or a new product's role might be to meet a specific return-on-investment goal or establish a position in a new market.

A new product's intended role also will influence the *type* of product to be developed. To illustrate:

| Company goal | | Product strategy | | Recent examples |
|---|---|---|---|---|
| **To defend market share.** | → | **Introduce an addition to an existing product line or revise an existing product.** | → | **Dairy desserts to complement other Healthy Choice "healthful" frozen foods.** |
| **To strengthen a reputation as an innovator.** | → | **Introduce a *really* new product — not just an extension of an existing one.** | → | **Palmtop computers introduced by Hewlett-Packard.** |

Only in recent years have many companies consciously identified new-product strategies. The process of developing new products has become more efficient *and* more effective for firms with strategies because they have a better idea of what they are trying to accomplish.

## Stages in the Development Process

Guided by a company's new-product strategy, a new product is best developed through a series of six stages, as shown in Figure 9-2. Compared to unstructured development, the formal development of new products provides benefits such as higher success rates, increased customer satisfaction, and greater achievement of time, quality, and cost objectives for new products.[11]

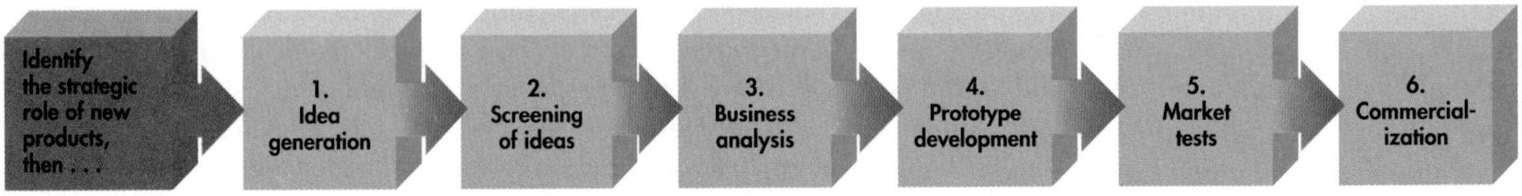


**FIGURE 9-2 Major stages in the new-product development process.**

At each stage, management must decide whether to proceed to the next stage, abandon the product, or seek additional information.[12] Here's a brief description of what should happen at each stage of the **new-product development process**:

1. **Generating new-product ideas.** New-product development starts with an idea. A system must be designed for stimulating new ideas within an organization and then acknowledging and reviewing them promptly. Customers should also be encouraged to propose innovations. In a recent study, 80 percent of companies pointed to customers as their best source for new-product ideas.[13]
2. **Screening ideas.** At this stage, new-product ideas are evaluated to determine which ones warrant further study.[14] Typically, a management team screens the pool of ideas.
3. **Business analysis.** A surviving idea is expanded into a concrete business proposal. That means management (a) identifies product features, (b) estimates market demand, competition, and the product's profitability, (c) establishes a program to develop the product, and (d) assigns responsibility for further study of the product's feasibility.
4. **Prototype development.** If the results of the business analysis are favourable, then a prototype (or trial model) of the product is developed. In the case of goods, a small quantity of the trial model is manufactured to designated specifications. Laboratory

## MARKETING AT WORK

### FILE 9-2 SOURCES OF NEW PRODUCT IDEAS FOR GROWING SMALL AND MEDIUM-SIZED FIRMS

Growing small and medium-sized firms are not like large firms when it comes to sources for new product ideas. While the customer is still the single most important source of product ideas, management comes a strong second — a situation you would be unlikely to easily find in a large firm. Statistics Canada surveyed almost 1,500 growing small and medium-sized enterprises (GSMEs) with average sales of $6.6 million. When companies were asked to rank their sources of product innovation on a scale of zero to five, customers headed the list with a score of 3.51, demonstrating once again the importance of focusing on the buyer.

In close second place were the company's own managers with a score of 3.14 out of five. Managers are the internal innovators and entrepreneurs in companies of this size. The third most important source of new product ideas were suppliers with a score of 2.84.

Outsiders — customers, suppliers, and competitors — ranked higher than insiders as sources of new product ideas. The importance of customers and management as sources of innovations indicates that firms of this size (GSMEs) are demand-driven and top-down firms. Larger firms are less likely to be top down in the same way — but they are trying to organize to achieve the flexibility of smaller size.

Adapted from Bruce Little, "Listen to the Customer," *Globe and Mail*, May 2, 1994, p. B 6.

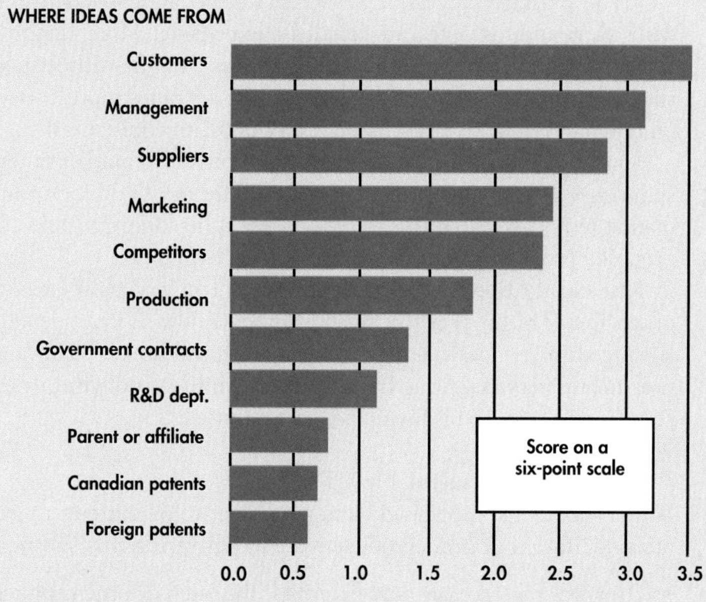


*Source: Statistics Canada*

tests and other technical evaluations are carried out to determine whether it is practical to produce the product. A firm may be able to construct a prototype of a new type of cellular telephone but be unable to manufacture the new product in large quantities or at a cost that is low enough to stimulate sales and still yield a profit. In the case of services, the facilities and procedures necessary to produce and deliver the new product are designed and tested. That certainly is a necessary step in the development of a new rollercoaster ride at an amusement park!

5. **Market tests.** Unlike the internal tests conducted during prototype development, these tests involve actual consumers. A new tangible product may be given to a sample of people for use in their households (in the case of a consumer good) or their organizations (a business good). Following this trial, consumers are asked to evaluate the product. Consumer-use tests are less practical for services due to their intangible nature.

This stage in new-product development often entails **test marketing**, in which the product is placed on sale in a limited geographic area. Results, including sales and repeat purchases, are monitored by the company that developed the product and perhaps by competitors as well. In this stage, the product's design and production plans may have to be adjusted as a result of test findings. Following market tests, management must make a final "go-no go" decision about introducing the product.

6. **Commercialization.** In this stage, full-scale production and marketing programs are planned and, finally, implemented. Up to this point in development, management has virtually complete control over the product. Once the product is "born" and enters its life cycle, however, the external competitive environment becomes a major determinant of its destiny.

Note that the first two stages — idea generation and screening — are tied closely to the overall new-product strategy. This strategy can provide a focus for generating new-product ideas *and* a basis for evaluating them.

In the six-stage process, the first three stages are particularly critical because they deal with ideas and, as such, are the least expensive. More important, many products fail because the idea or the timing is wrong — and the first three stages are intended to identify such situations. Each subsequent stage becomes more costly in terms of the dollars and human resources necessary to carry out the required tasks.

Some companies, trying to bring new products to market faster than their competitors, skip stages in the development process. The most common omission is the fifth stage, market tests.[15] Without this stage, however, the company lacks consumer reactions to the proposed product.

Historically, the marketing of goods has received more attention than the marketing of services. Thus it is not surprising that the new-product development process is not as advanced in services fields as it is in goods industries.[16] However, on the positive side, that means services firms have more flexibility to devise a new-product development process that suits their distinctive circumstances.

### Producer's Criteria for New Products

When should a company add a new product to its current assortment of products? Here are guidelines that some producers use in answering this question:

- There must be *adequate market demand.* Too often management begins with the wrong question, such as "Can we use our present sales force?" or "Will the new item fit into our production system?" The necessary first question is "Do enough people really want this product?"
- The product must *satisfy key financial criteria.* At least three questions should be asked: "Is adequate financing available?" "Will the new item reduce seasonal and cyclical fluctuations in the company's sales?" And, most critical, "Can we make sufficient profits with the product?"
- The product must be *compatible with environmental standards.* Key questions include: "Do the production processes avoid polluting the air or water?" "Will the finished product, including its packaging, be friendly to the environment?" And, "After being used, does the product have recycling potential?"

**Where do you suppose this new product idea came from?**

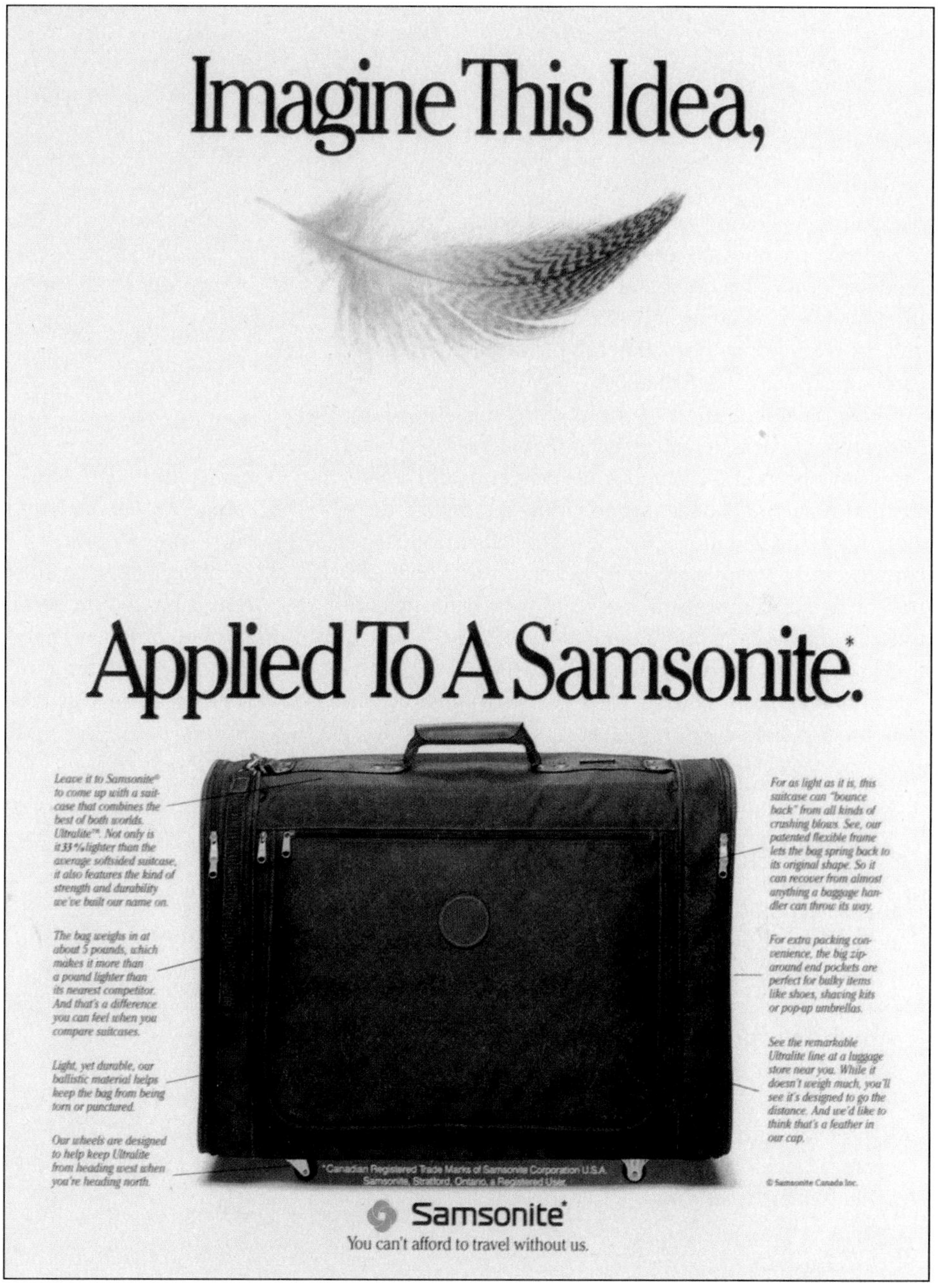


- The product must *fit into the company's present marketing structure.* Sherwin Williams Paint Company would probably find it quite difficult to add margarine to its line of paints. Specific questions related to whether a new product will fit the company's marketing expertise and experience include: "Can the existing sales force be used?" "Can the present channels of distribution be used?"

Besides these four issues, a proposed product must satisfy other criteria. For instance, it must be in keeping with the company's objectives and image. The product also must be compatible with the firm's production capabilities. And it must satisfy any pertinent legal requirements.

## MARKETING AT WORK

### FILE 9-3 FINDING INNOVATIONS ABROAD

Seeking a marketing edge and added sales, a growing legion of companies are scanning foreign markets for new-product ideas. The origins of various products recently introduced — including Whiskas cat food from Mars Inc. and the Symphony chocolate bar from Hershey Foods — can be traced to foreign markets.

Why haven't businesses been shopping abroad for new-product ideas for many years? Two reasons: First, firms have been preoccupied with competing effectively in their home markets, going so far as to monitor virtually every strategic move and new-product introduction carried out by key competitors. Second, there has been too little communication between the domestic and overseas divisions of most companies.

Nevertheless, several factors have prompted many companies to look beyond their domestic markets for new-product ideas:

- Bored with mere imitations, consumers are willing to accept novel products. In fact, many desire them.
- Adapting a foreign product for sale in the firm's home country can be much cheaper, especially with respect to research and development costs, than starting the development process from scratch. That was one reason why Mars decided to use the Whiskas brand in the North American market.
- An existing foreign product may be the best way of satisfying an ethnic market segment in the home country. For example, Colgate-Palmolive thinks the lighter texture and pleasing smell of its Fabuloso cleaner, developed in a foreign country, will appeal to some North Americans.
- Unlike brands and inventions, product concepts are not legally protected, so they can be easily "borrowed" by an interested firm.

Bringing a foreign product that is successful in its home country to North America does not guarantee success. How can the chances for success be maximized? Here are several guidelines:

- Concentrate on products that have achieved widespread success in foreign markets. Dry beers in Japan are a case in point.
- Don't just rely on the product's newness, but ensure that it has a differential advantage.
- Stick to products that coincide with North American trends. A greater interest in healthful foods helped Kellogg achieve success with Mueslix, a cereal combining grains, nuts, and fruits that was invented in Switzerland.

How are companies searching for new-product ideas in foreign markets? Some hire consultants to do the legwork. Others, including Unilever Group, dedicate small teams of employees to this task. Still others rely on the most direct approach — they ask their foreign subsidiaries which of their products have achieved fame and fortune in other countries.

Sources: Michael J. McCarthy, "More Companies Shop Abroad for New-Product Ideas," *The Wall Street Journal*, March 14, 1990, pp. B1, B6; Bob Hagerty, "Unilever Scours the Globe for Better Ideas," *The Wall Street Journal*, April 25, 1990, p. A11.

### Intermediary's Criteria for New Products

Intermediaries, such as retailers and wholesalers, considering whether to buy a new product for resale should apply all the preceding criteria except those related to production. In addition, an intermediary should apply the following guidelines:

- The intermediary must have *a good working relationship with the producer*. By distributing a new product, an intermediary should stand to benefit from the producer's reputation, the possibility of getting the right to be the only company to sell the product in a given territory, and the promotional and financial help given by the producer.

- The producer and intermediary must have *compatible distribution policies and practices.* Pertinent questions include: "What kind of selling effort is required for the new product?" "How does the proposed product fit with the intermediary's policies regarding repair service, alterations (for clothing), credit, and delivery?"
- As in the case of producers, the product must *satisfy key financial criteria.* At least two questions should be asked: "If adding a new product necessitates eliminating another product due to a shortage of shelf or storage space, will the result be a net gain in sales?" And "Can we make sufficient profits with the product?"

## NEW-PRODUCT ADOPTION AND DIFFUSION

The likelihood of achieving success with a new product, especially a really innovative product, is increased if management understands the adoption and diffusion processes for that product. Once again, we are stressing that organizations need to understand how consumers behave. The **adoption process** is the set of successive decisions *an individual* makes before accepting an innovation. **Diffusion** of a new product is the process by which an innovation spreads throughout a *social system* over time.[17]

By understanding these processes, an organization can gain insight into how a product is or is not accepted by consumers and which groups of consumers are likely to buy a product soon after it is introduced, later on, or never. This knowledge of consumer behaviour can be valuable in designing an effective marketing program.

### Stages in Adoption Process

A prospective user goes through six **stages in the adoption process** — deciding whether to purchase something new:

| Stage | Activity in that stage |
|---|---|
| **Awareness** ↓ | **Individual is exposed to the innovation; becomes a prospect.** |
| **Interest** ↓ | **Prospect is interested enough to seek information.** |
| **Evaluation** ↓ | **Prospect judges the advantages and disadvantages of a product.** |
| **Trial** ↓ | **Prospect adopts the innovation on a limited basis. A consumer buys a sample, if the product can be sampled.** |
| **Adoption** ↓ | **Prospect decides whether to use the innovation on a full-scale basis.** |
| **Confirmation** | **After adopting the innovation, prospect becomes a user who immediately seeks assurances that decision to purchase the product was correct.** |

### Adopter Categories

Some people will adopt an innovation soon after it is introduced. Others will delay before accepting a new product, and still others may never adopt it. Research has identified five **innovation adopter categories**, based on the point in time when individuals adopt a given innovation. Nonadopters are excluded from this categorization. Characteristics of early and late adopters are summarized in Table 9-3.

Innovators Representing about 3 percent of the market, **innovators** are venturesome consumers who are the first to adopt an innovation. In relation to later adopters, innovators are likely to be younger, have higher social status, and be in better financial shape. Innovators also tend to have broad social relationships involving various groups of people in more than one community. They are likely to rely more on nonpersonal sources of information, such as advertising, rather than on sales people or other personal sources.

TABLE 9-3 Characteristics of early and late adopters of innovations

| | Early adopters | Late adopters |
|---|---|---|
| KEY CHARACTERISTICS | | |
| **Venturesome** | **Innovators (3% of total adopters)** | |
| **Respected** | **Early adopters (13%)** | |
| **Deliberate** | **Early majority (34%)** | |
| **Sceptical** | | **Late majority (34% of total adopters)** |
| **Tradition-bound** | | **Laggards (16%)** |
| OTHER CHARACTERISTICS | | |
| **Age** | **Younger** | **Older** |
| **Education** | **Well educated** | **Less educated** |
| **Income** | **Higher** | **Lower** |
| **Social relationships: within or outside community** | **Innovators: outside**<br>**Others: within** | **Totally local** |
| **Social status** | **Higher** | **Lower** |
| **Information sources** | **Wide variety; many media** | **Limited media exposure; limited reliance on outside media; reliance on local peer groups** |

Early Adopters Making up about 13 percent of the market, **early adopters** purchase a new product after innovators but sooner than other consumers. Unlike innovators, who have broad involvements *outside* a local community, early adopters tend to be involved socially *within* a local community. Early adopters are greatly respected in their social system; in fact, other people are interested in and influenced by their opinions. Thus the early-adopter category includes more opinion leaders than any other adopter group. Sales people are probably used more as information sources by early adopters than by any other category.

In the process of diffusion, a **change agent** is a person who seeks to accelerate the spread of a given innovation. In business, the person responsible for introducing an innovative new product must be a change agent. Consider the new generation of light bulbs that use less energy and last 10 to 20 years but cost $15 to $20 apiece. The marketers of these light bulbs must be effective change agents, convincing consumers that it is worthwhile to spend 15 times the normal cost of a light bulb.[18] A change agent focuses the initial persuasive efforts on early adopters because other people respect their opinions and eventually will emulate their behaviour. If a firm can get early adopters to accept its innovative product, then the broader market eventually will accept the product as well.

**Early Majority** The **early majority**, representing about 34 percent of the market, includes more deliberate consumers who accept an innovation just before the "average" adopter in a social system. This group is a bit above average in social and economic measures. Consumers in the early-majority group rely quite a bit on ads, sales people, and contact with early adopters.

**Late Majority** The **late majority**, another 34 percent of the market, is a sceptical group of consumers who usually adopt an innovation to save money or in response to social pressure from their peers. They rely on their peers — late or early majority — as sources of information. Advertising and personal selling are less effective with this group than is word-of-mouth communication.

**Laggards** **Laggards** are consumers who are bound by tradition and, hence, are last to adopt an innovation. They make up about 16 percent of the market. Laggards are suspicious of innovations and innovators; they wonder why anyone would pay a lot more for a new kind of light bulb, for example. By the time laggards adopt something new, it may already have been discarded by the innovators in favour of a newer concept. Laggards are older and usually are at the low end of the social and economic scales.

We are discussing only *adopters* of an innovation. For most innovations, there are many people who are *not* included in our percentages. They are **nonadopters**; they never adopt the innovation.

### Innovation Characteristics Affecting Adoption Rate

There are five **innovation characteristics that affect the adoption rate:**[19]

- **Relative advantage:** the degree to which an innovation is superior to currently available products. Relative advantage may be reflected in lower cost, greater safety, easier use, or some other relevant benefit. Safest Stripper, a paint and varnish remover introduced by 3M, scores high on this characteristic. The product contains no harmful chemicals, has no odour, and allows the user to refinish furniture indoors rather than having to work outdoors.
- **Compatibility:** the degree to which an innovation coincides with the cultural values and experiences of prospective adopters. Since many consumers want to save time *and* satisfy their desires now rather than later, microwave popcorn certainly satisfies this characteristic.
- **Complexity:** the degree of difficulty in understanding or using an innovation. The more complex an innovation is, the more slowly it will be adopted — if it is adopted at all. Combined shampoo-conditioners certainly are simple to use, so adoption of them was not impeded by complexity. However, many forms of insurance and some consumer-electronics products have problems with this characteristic.
- **Trialability:** the degree to which an innovation may be sampled on some limited basis. Setting aside the other characteristics, the greater the trialability, the faster will be the adoption rate. For instance, a central home air-conditioning system is likely to have a slower adoption rate than a new seed or fertilizer, which may be tried on a small plot of ground. In general, due to this characteristic, costly products will be adopted more slowly than will inexpensive products. Likewise, many services (such as insurance) are difficult to use on a trial basis, so they tend to be adopted rather slowly.
- **Observability:** the degree to which an innovation actually can be seen to be effective. In general, the greater the observability, the faster the adoption rate. For example, a new weed killer that works on existing weeds probably will be accepted sooner than a product that prevents weeds from sprouting. The reason? The latter product, even if highly effective, produces no dead weeds to show to prospective buyers!

A company would like an innovative product to satisfy all five characteristics discussed above. But few do. One-time cameras come close, however.[20] These cameras, which are usable for only one roll of film, come prepacked with film (reducing *complexity*), cost only $15-$25 (contributing to *trialability*), and offer good value (representing *relative advantage*). They are widely distributed, which enhances *compatibility* with consumers' desire for convenient purchase — especially when we forget to bring our regular camera on a trip. The leading makers of one-time cameras, Kodak and Fuji, addressed *observability* by giving many of the cameras away in promotions so that consumers could use the product and see the results without bearing any risk or cost.

## ORGANIZING FOR PRODUCT INNOVATION

For new-product programs to be successful, they must be supported by a strong, long-term commitment from top management. This commitment must be maintained even when some new products fail. To implement this commitment to innovation effectively, new-product programs must be soundly organized.

### Types of Organization

There is no "one best" organizational structure for product planning and development. Many companies use more than one structure to manage these activities. Some widely used organizational structures for planning and developing new products are:

- **Product-planning committee.** Members include executives from major departments — marketing, production, finance, engineering, and research — and, especially in small firms, the president and/or another top-level executive.
- **New-product department.** These units are small, consisting of five or fewer people. The department head reports to the president (which, in a large firm, may be the president of a division).
- **Venture team.** A small group, with representatives from engineering, production, finance, and marketing research, operates like a separate small business. Typically the team reports directly to top management.[21]
- **Product manager.** This individual is responsible for planning new products as well as managing established products. Although still effective in some firms, we'll discuss in the next section why this structure is being displaced in many firms by one of the other structures discussed above.

Which organizational structure is chosen is not the key point here — each has strengths and weaknesses. What's critical is to make sure that some person or group has the specific responsibility for new-product development — and is backed by top management. Product innovation is too important an activity to handle in an unorganized, nonchalant fashion, figuring that somehow the job will get done.[22] To maximize the chances for successful new-product development, it is vital that employees responsible for product planning have the right skills, particularly the ability to work well with other people, and operate in a supportive environment.[23]

As the new product is completed, responsibility for marketing it usually is shifted either to an existing department or a new department established just for this new product. In some cases the team that developed the product may continue as the management nucleus of the new unit.

Integrating new products into departments that are already marketing established products does carry at least two risks, however. First, executives who are involved with ongoing products may have a short-term outlook as they deal with day-to-day problems of existing products. Consequently, they may not recognize the long-term importance of new products and, as a result, neglect them. Second, managers of successful existing products often are reluctant to assume the risks inherent in marketing new products.

## MARKETING AT WORK

### FILE 9-4 THE ONE-MAN PRODUCT INNOVATION ORGANIZATION

Back in the 1960s, Mark Lowman wanted to be a drummer in a rock'n'roll band. He didn't make it then, but now he's going on a major world tour with legendary rock bank Pink Floyd. Only not as a drummer, but as the supplier of an estimated $1 million of laser special effects with which the group will astound its audiences.

In the late eighties, Lowman founded a Markham, Ontario, company called Rocklite International, which provides special laser effects to a variety of clients. He was convinced that lasers, which had many scientific applications, could also be applied to a vast untapped special effects market. He invested heavily in research and development and came up with some uniquely innovative laser technology that had never been seen before.

Rocklite got its feet wet by creating the Laserium light shows at Toronto's McLaughlin Planetarium and then moving on to develop computer-controlled projection systems that allowed lasers to project pictures on the walls of buildings, giant screens, or even clouds. The company built up a library of corporate events for the likes of McDonald's, IBM, Apple, Reebok, John Labatt, General Motors, Xerox, and the Royal Bank of Canada.

The next step was expanding into theme parks such as Canada's Wonderland and special events such as the opening of the SkyDome stadium, the CN Tower's New Year's party, and the 1994 Superbowl in Atlanta. At the same time, Rocklite also began designing, manufacturing, and selling laser systems to night clubs, first in North America, then in Europe. And along the way, Lowman couldn't resist returning to the rock'n'roll arena — where he created effects for stars ranging from the Jeff Healey Band and Deep Purple to Def Leppard, Michael Jackson, and now Pink Floyd. Declares Lowman, "We've landed the biggest tour in two decades because we're good. We've been spending a lot of time and effort on development and the Pink Floyd contract is a result of (this) R&D."

Source: Adapted from Harvey Enchin, "Pink Floyd Picks Canadian Firm," *Globe and Mail*, January 20, 1994, p. B5.

### Product Manager

In many companies, a **product manager** — sometimes called a *brand manager* — is responsible for planning related to *new* products as well as to *established* ones. A large company may have many product managers who report to higher marketing executives.

In many large firms — Procter & Gamble, and Kraft General Foods, to name a few — the product manager's job is quite broad. Responsibilities include *planning the complete marketing program* for a brand or group of products. Setting marketing goals, preparing budgets, and developing plans for advertising and personal-selling activities are some of the product manager's tasks. Developing new products along with improving established products may also be part of the job description. At the other extreme, some companies limit product managers' activities to the areas of selling and sales promotion.

Probably the biggest problem with this structure is that a company often saddles product managers with great responsibility but provides them with little authority. For instance, product managers are expected to develop the plan by which the sales force will market the product to wholesalers and retailers, but they have no real authority over the sales force. They are responsible for drafting advertising plans, but typically do not select the advertising agencies that will fully develop and execute them. Product managers have a profit responsibility for their brands, yet are often denied any control over product costs, prices, or advertising budgets. Their effectiveness depends largely on their ability to influence other executives to co-operate with their plans.

The product-manager structure was widely adopted and thrived from the 1950s through the 1970s, a period of economic growth and market expansion. In the 1980s, however, many industries experienced slow growth in maturing markets, coupled with a trend towards strategic planning that stressed centralized managerial control. Because of these environmental forces, the product-manager structure has been abolished in some firms and is being modified in many other companies. For instance, in preparing for the 1990s on a worldwide basis, Procter & Gamble established **category managers** who oversee the activities of a related group of product managers. P&G also decided to rely more on business teams that are formed to serve the needs of a particular marketing project.[24]

## SUMMARY

The first commandment in marketing is "Know thy customer," and the second is "Know thy product." The relative number and success of a company's new products are a prime determinant of its sales, growth rate, and profits. A firm can best serve its customers by producing and marketing want-satisfying goods or services. The scarcity of some natural resources and a growing concern for our environment make social responsibility a crucial aspect of product innovation.

To manage its products effectively, a firm's marketers must understand the full meaning of *product*, which stresses that consumers are buying want satisfaction. Products can be classified into two basic categories — consumer products and business products. Each category is then subdivided, because a different marketing program is required for each distinct group of products.

There are many views as to what constitutes a *new* product. For marketing purposes, three categories of new products need to be recognized — innovative, significantly different, and imitative.

A clear statement of the firm's new-product strategy serves as a solid foundation for the six-stage development process for new products. The early stages in this process are especially important. If a firm can make an early *and correct* decision to stop the development of a proposed product, a lot of money and labour can be saved.

In deciding whether to add a new product, a producer or intermediary should consider whether there is adequate market demand for it. The product also should fit in with the firm's marketing, production, and financial resources. Management needs to understand the adoption and diffusion processes for a new product.

A prospective user goes through six stages in deciding whether to adopt a new product. Adopters of an innovation can be divided into five categories, depending on how quickly they accept an innovation such as a new product. These categories are innovators, early adopters, early majority, late majority, and laggards. In addition, there usually is a group of nonadopters.

Five characteristics of an innovation seem to influence the adoption rate. They are relative advantage, compatibility, complexity, trialability, and observability.

Successful product planning and development require long-term commitment and strong support from top management. Furthermore, new-product programs must be soundly organized. Most firms use one of four organizational structures for new-product development: product-planning committee, new-product department, venture team, or product manager.

## KEY TERMS AND CONCEPTS

**Product (260)**
**Consumer products (262)**
**Business products (262)**
**Convenience good (262)**
**Shopping good (263)**
**Specialty good (264)**
**Unsought good (265)**
**Raw materials (266)**
**Manufactured parts and materials (267)**
**Fabricating materials (267)**
**Installations (267)**
**Accessory equipment (267)**
**Operating supplies (268)**
**New products (271)**
**New-product strategy (271)**
**New-product development process (272)**
**Business analysis (272)**
**Market tests (274)**
**Test marketing (274)**
**Adoption process (277)**
**Diffusion (277)**
**Stages in the adoption process (277)**
**Innovation adopter categories (277)**
- **Innovators (278)**
- **Early adopters (278)**
- **Early majority (279)**
- **Late majority (279)**
- **Laggards (279)**

**Change agent (278)**
**Nonadopters (279)**
**Innovation characteristics that affect the adoption rate (279)**
**Product-planning committee (280)**
**New-product department (280)**
**Venture team (280)**
**Product manager (281)**
**Category manager (282)**

## QUESTIONS AND PROBLEMS

1. In what respects are the products different in each of the following cases?
   a. A Whirlpool dishwasher sold at an appliance store and a similar dishwasher sold by Sears under its Kenmore brand name. Assume that Whirlpool makes both dishwashers.
   b. Sunbeam Mixmaster sold by a leading department store and the same model sold by a discount house.
   c. An airline ticket purchased through a travel agent and an identical ticket purchased directly from the airline.
2. a. Explain the various interpretations of the term *new product*.
   b. Give some examples, other than those cited in this chapter, of products in each of the three new-product categories.
3. "Because brand preferences are well established with regard to many items of women's clothing, these items — traditionally considered shopping goods — will move into the specialty-goods category. At the same time, however, other items of women's clothing can be found in supermarkets and variety stores, thus indicating that some items are convenience goods."
   a. Explain the reasoning in these statements.
   b. Do you agree that women's clothing is shifting away from the shopping-goods classification? Explain.
4. Compare the elements of a producer's marketing mix for a convenience good with those of the mix for a specialty good.
5. In which of the five categories of business goods should each of the following be included? And which products may belong in more than one category?
   a. Trucks.
   b. Medical X-ray equipment.
   c. Typing paper.
   d. Copper wire.
   e. Printing presses.
   f. Nuts and bolts.
   g. Paper clips.
   h. Land.
6. In developing new products, how can a firm make sure that it is being socially responsible with regard to scarce resources and our environment?
7. Assume that the following organizations are considering additions to their product lines. In each case, does the proposed product meet the criteria for adding a new product? Explain your decisions.
   a. McDonald's — salad bar.
   b. Safeway — automobile tires.
   c. Esso — personal computers.
   d. Banks — life insurance.
   e. General Motors Canada — outboard motors for boats.
8. Describe the kinds of people who are most likely to be found in (a) the innovator category of adopters and (b) the late-majority category.
9. What are some of the problems typically connected with the product-manager organizational structure?

## HANDS-ON MARKETING

1. Arrange a meeting with the manager of a large retail outlet in your community. Discuss two topics with the manager:
   a. What recently introduced product has been a failure or appears destined to fail?
   b. Did this product, in retrospect, satisfy the criteria for adding a new product? (Remember to consider not just the intermediary's criteria but also applicable producer's criteria.)
2. Design (either in words or drawings) a new product that fits into one of the first two categories of new products — that is, a really innovative product or a significant replacement, not just an imitative product. Then evaluate how your proposed product rates with respect to the five characteristics of an innovation that influence the adoption rate.

## NOTES AND REFERENCES


1. Adapted, in part, from Andrew Tausz, "Novelty Begins at Home," *Globe and Mail*, January 14, 1994, p. B19.
2. Yumiko Ono, "Some Kids Won't Eat the Middle of an Oreo," *The Wall Street Journal*, November 20, 1991, p. B1.
3. Jacqueline Mitchell, "Buyers of VWs Receive Cushion against Layoffs," *The Wall Street Journal*, January 29, 1992, p. B1.
4. For a different classification scheme that provides strategic guidelines for management by relating products and prices, along with an excellent bibliography on product classification, see Patrick E. Murphy and Ben M. Enis, "Classifying Products Strategically," *Journal of Marketing*, July 1986, pp. 24-42. Also see Ernest F. Cooke, "The Relationship between a Product Classification System and Marketing Strategy," *Journal of Midwest Marketing*, Spring 1987, pp. 230-240.
5. The examples in this paragraph are drawn from Robert D. Hof, "Suddenly, Hewlett-Packard Is Doing Everything Right," *Business Week*, March 23, 1992, pp. 88-89; Zachary Schiller, "At Rubbermaid, Little Things Mean a Lot," *Business Week*, November 11, 1991, p. 126; and Joseph Weber, "A Big Company That Works," *Business Week*, May 4, 1992, pp. 124-127.
6. "Study: Launching New Products Is Worth the Risk," *Marketing News*, January 20, 1992, p. 2.
7. Alecia Swasy, "How Innovation at P&G Restored Luster to Washed-Up Pert and Made It No. 1," *The Wall Street Journal*, December 6, 1990, p. B1.
8. "124 New Condiments Burst onto the Market," *St. Louis Post-Dispatch*, August 26, 1991, p. 24BP. One area in which "product indigestion" exists is cold medicines, as described in Kathleen Deveny, "Copycat Cold Medicines Proliferate, Creating Confusion among Consumers," *The Wall Street Journal*, February 1, 1991, p. B1.
9. These failure rates and also the reasons for failure presented in the next paragraph were drawn from "The 1991 Innovation Survey," conducted by Group EFO Limited of Weston, CT.
10. These statistics and examples were compiled by Marketing Intelligence Service Ltd. of Naples, NY, as reported in Laura Bird, "New-Product Troubles Have Firms Cutting Back," *The Wall Street Journal*, January 13, 1992, p. B1.
11. The benefits cited are from a study reported in Robert G. Cooper and Elko J. Kleinschmidt, "New Product Processes at Leading Industrial Firms," *Industrial Marketing Management*, May 1991, pp. 137-147. For an approach to improve the management of multiple new-product development projects, see Steven C. Wheelwright and Kim B. Clark, "Creating Project Plans to Focus Product Development," *Harvard Business Review*, March-April 1992, pp. 70-82.
12. For a report on the criteria used in making "go-no go" decisions in the product-development process, see Ilkka A. Ronkainen, "Criteria Changes across Product Development Stages," *Industrial Marketing Management*, August 1985, pp. 171-178.
13. "Study: Launching New Products Is Worth the Risk," loc. cit.
14. For more on the first two stages, termed *opportunity identification*, see Linda Rochford, "Generating and Screening New Product Ideas," *Industrial Marketing Management*, November 1991, pp. 287-296.
15. "Study: Launching New Products Is Worth the Risk," loc. cit.
16. Howard Schlossberg, "Services Development Lags Behind New Products," *Marketing News*, November 6, 1989, p. 2.

17. For foundations of diffusion theory and a review of landmark studies on diffusion of innovation, see Everett M. Rogers, *Diffusion of Innovations*, 3d ed., The Free Press, New York, 1983.
18. Joan E. Rigdon and Meredith K. Wadman, "New Long-Life Bulbs May Lose Brilliance in a Crowded Market," *The Wall Street Journal*, June 2, 1992, p. B6.
19. Rogers, op. cit.
20. Joan E. Rigdon, "For Cardboard Cameras, Sales Picture Enlarges and Seems Brighter Than Ever," *The Wall Street Journal*, February 11, 1992, p. B1.
21. See Frank G. Bingham and Charles J. Quigley, Jr., "Venture Team Application to New Product Development," *Journal of Business and Industrial Marketing*, Winter-Spring 1989, pp. 49-59.
22. For support of this point, see Cooper and Kleinschmidt, op. cit., and C. Merle Crawford, "The Dual-Drive Concept of Product Innovation," *Business Horizons*, May-June 1991, pp. 32-38. The latter article also emphasizes that, regardless of which organizational structure is used, it is vital for product innovation to be driven by *both* technology and markets.
23. For further discussion of the differences between more and less successful product-development leaders, see Gloria Barczak and David Wilemon, "Successful New Product Team Leaders," *Industrial Marketing Management*, February 1992, pp. 61-68.
24. For more on P&G's preparation for product planning and development in the 1990s, see Alecia Swasy, "In a Fast-Paced World, Procter & Gamble Sets Its Store in Old Values," *The Wall Street Journal*, September 21, 1989, pp. A1, A18; Jolie Solomon and Carol Hymowitz, "P&G Makes Changes in the Way It Develops and Sells Its Products," *The Wall Street Journal*, August 11, 1987, pp. 1, 12.

## CHAPTER 10 GOALS

At any given time, a firm may be marketing some new products and some old ones, while others are being planned and developed. In this chapter we'll cover a number of strategic decisions pertaining to an organization's assortment of products. After studying this chapter, you should have an understanding of:

- The difference between product mix and product line.
- The major product-mix strategies:
  - Positioning
  - Expansion
  - Alteration
  - Contraction
- Trading up and trading down.
- Managing a product throughout a life cycle.
- Planned obsolescence.
- Style and fashion.
- The fashion-adoption process.

CHAPTER

10

# PRODUCT-MIX STRATEGIES

## Thirsty?

In most industries, companies would not even consider keeping exactly the same products in their product lines year after year. The effective management of product lines demands that companies react quickly to changing customer needs and tastes and to the introduction of new products by competitors. The result is that marketers are constantly changing their lines in response to market pressures — introducing new products, modifying existing products, altering packages, repositioning. By examining how companies modify their product lines over time, we can gain considerable insight into their marketing strategies and how they approach the market.

The beverage industry is no exception. This highly competitive industry is in a constant state of change as consumer tastes in hot and cold beverages lead to new preferences and as companies try to gain an upper hand on their competitors. While not direct competitors, coffee manufacturers are competing with soft drink companies, as well as with tea producers and with brewers. As a result, recent years have brought a number of new products into the market, as illustrated in the examples below.

- Canadians are obviously taking their coffee drinking very seriously, as indicated by the success of retail chains like Second Cup, Tim Horton's, and Starbuck's. Coffee manufacturers are taking advantage of the growing interest in brewing good coffee at home by introducing new lines of exotic and flavoured coffees.

Nabob's line includes African and Columbian blends, as well as Dark Roast, South Pacific, and Espresso.

- Not to be outdone, tea manufacturers are riding a wave of rapid growth in the iced-tea sector, where sales of ready-to-serve iced tea increased an impressive 24 percent in the 12-month period ending February 1994. Tetley responded to the growth in demand with new bottle designs, new label designs, and new flavours, including natural raspberry and natural lemon.[1]
- In a flat beer market, brewers such as Molson and Labatt are looking to product-line changes to gain even the slightest competitive edge. Consequently, recent years have seen a spate of new brand introductions, including Carlsberg Traditional Dark from Labatt, a draft beer positioned as a fuller-flavoured alternative for urban beer drinkers who have been attracted to the more natural products of the microbrewers. In a different niche of the market, Molson and Labatt both have leading brands in the no-alcohol and low-alcohol category, where sales in supermarkets grew an impressive 70 percent in 1993.[2]
- In the soft drink business, the world leader, Coca-Cola, is forced to introduce literally dozens of new products and brands each year merely to keep up with private label manufacturers in North America and Europe and with competing drinks producers in other countries. In Japan, more than half of Coke's sales now come from non-fizzy products, and the company's product line contains ginseng-based and milk-based drinks and a honey-and-lemon flavoured juice. In Canada, Coke's arch-rival Pepsi-Cola introduced Pepsi Max, and both companies launched packaging innovations that included a cube-shaped 24-bottle pack.[3]

Labatt announces another addition to its product line.

A common thread runs through these examples from the various beverage industries. That is, over time a company must make numerous decisions about the array of products it offers consumers. Whether the correct decisions are made — and made at the right time — greatly affects a company's success, not just for a single year, but for many years to come.

## PRODUCT MIX AND PRODUCT LINE

Very few firms rely on a single product or service; instead most sell many products. The set of all products offered for sale by a company is called a **product mix**. The structure of a product mix has both breadth and depth. Its **breadth** is measured by the number of product lines carried, its **depth** by the variety of sizes, colours, and models offered within each product line. A product-mix structure is illustrated in Figure 10-1.

A broad group of products, intended for essentially similar uses and having similar physical characteristics, constitutes a **product line**. Firms may delineate a product line in different ways. For Labatt Breweries, its various brands of Labatt beer (such as the long-established Blue and the newer Ice Beer) represent a product line. However, for your campus pub or a restaurant chain, all brands of beer, both domestic and imported, represent one of the product lines carried.

## PRODUCT-MIX STRATEGIES

Many large corporations, such as Kraft General Foods, Sony, and Procter & Gamble, offer a vast array of products to consumers. In service industries today, telecommunications companies such as Bell Canada and retail giants such as Sobey's and the Hudson's Bay Company offer customers many services and many different ways to access them. Did these diverse assortments of products and services develop by accident? No — it reflects a planned strategy by the company. To be successful in marketing, producers and intermediaries need carefully planned strategies for managing their product mixes, as we'll see next.

**FIGURE 10-1**
**Product mix — breadth and depth.**

**Part of the product mix in a lawn and garden store.**

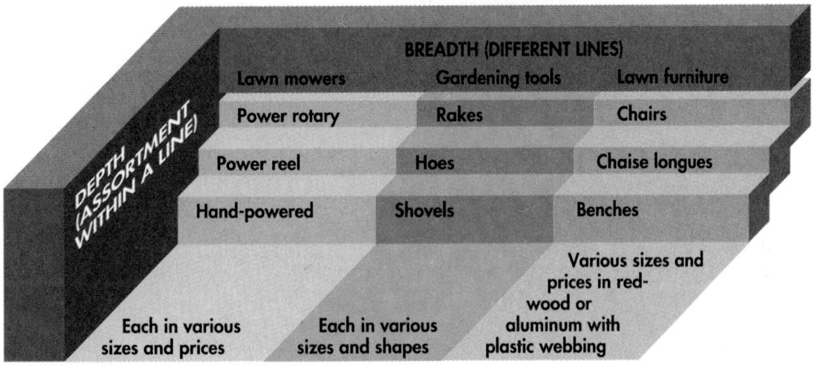


### Product Positioning

Management's ability to position a product appropriately in the market is a major determinant of company profit. A product's **position** is the image the product projects in the minds of consumers compared to competitive products and to other products marketed by the same company.

Marketing executives can choose from a variety of positioning strategies, in order to create the most useful meaning in the minds of consumers.[4]

**Positioning in Relation to a Competitor** For some products (Coca-Cola and Pepsi-Cola, for example), the best position is directly against the competition. For other products, head-to-head positioning is exactly what *not* to do, especially when a competitor has a strong market position. Canon's desktop copier avoids competing against the Xerox floor models, but Midas Muffler went head-to-head with Speedy Muffler King, terming its mechanics the "top guns." This strategy is especially suitable for a firm that already has a solid differential advantage or is trying to solidify such an advantage. To fend off rival makers of microprocessors, Intel Corp. launched a campaign to convince buyers that its product is superior to competitors'. The company even paid computer makers to include the slogan, "Intel Inside," in their ads.[5]

Companies in the Canadian record-store industry are using different strategies to position themselves in relation to competitors. For example, HMV Canada positions itself as a "pure music retailer"; Sam the Record Man offers a mix of products, including videos, while A&A had been a retailer positioning itself as a store that provides complete home entertainment systems, including videos, computer gadgets, and other high-tech accessories — a strategy that apparently did not work, as A&A is no longer in business.[6]

**Intel is trying to convince both manufacturers and buyers that its microprocessor is superior to competitors'.**

**To run an entire library of software, look for this symbol.**

**Ask for PCs with the Intel Inside® symbol.**

When you see the Intel Inside sticker on the outside of a PC, you know there's an Intel 32-bit microprocessor

inside. What you may not know is that Microsoft, Borland, Lotus, Novell, plus thousands of other software developers write and test their applications on that same vital ingredient: a genuine Intel CPU.

At Intel we subject all our microprocessors

to extensive testing. For example, each Intel486™ CPU actually goes through over 10 million tests. This assures you that it functions identically to the one your software was tested on.

So look for the Intel Inside symbol on

your next PC. It's your library card to the world's most popular software applications.

For more information, call 1-800-228-4549.

**intel.**

©1992 Intel Corporation. Intel486 is a trademark, and Intel Inside and the Intel Inside logo are registered trademarks of Intel Corporation.

**Positioning in Relation to a Product Class or Attribute**    Sometimes a company's positioning strategy entails associating its product with (or dissociating it from) a product class or attribute. Some firms promote their wares as being in a desirable class, such as "Made in Canada" or having an attractive attribute, such as "low energy consumption" or "environmentally friendly."

Occasionally, a company or a province or region can position its products based on the fact that they are manufactured in the province or country of the target market, appealing to the consumer's sense of patriotism. A recent survey of consumers' opinions of manufactured goods made in different countries revealed that Canadians rate their own manufactured goods more favourably than products produced in Japan, Germany, and other countries.[7] These results are good news for Canadian firms that wish to position their products on a "made in Canada" basis.

The strategy of differentiating or positioning products on the basis of an attractive attribute is widely used in the food industry. For example, McCain, Aylmer, Del Monte, Campbell's, Kellogg's, and competing companies have introduced lines of vegetables, soups, cereals, and other foods with one common denominator — they contain no (or very little) salt. These items are positioned against products that are packed with the conventional amounts of salt. Similarly, makers of healthful frozen foods really are positioning their products in relation to not just salt but also calories, cholesterol, and fat content. Sometimes what's *in* (rather than left out of) the product is emphasized. That's the case with Volvo, which constructed a steel frame around the passenger compartment of its brand of automobile.

Positioning is a strategy that can work for services as well as for tangible products. The Mighty Ducks of Anaheim have been positioned as the "fun" team of the National Hockey League. The Disney-owned club chose teal and purple as the team colours, and Ducks merchandise is sold in retail stores throughout North America, including Disney stores. The team's logo and colour scheme were selected with merchandising in mind and to appeal not only to hockey's traditional audience, men, but to women and children as well.[8]

## MARKETING AT WORK

### FILE 10-1 REPOSITIONING TEA: COLD IS HOT

In the 1990s tea is trendy. But not the plain old stuff that comes in bags. For decades sales of tea in bags have been declining. Yet, thanks to some timely innovations — the first to come about within the last century — a host of high-quality, high-tech teas are seeping their way onto the Canadian beverage market. Runaway successes have been specialty flavoured teas — ranging from tried and true Earl Grey to more alternative mango and caramel, decaffeinated teas, and especially ready-to-drink iced teas — sales of which rose 19 percent between 1992 and 1993.

With consumers obsessively searching for the perfect healthy cold drink, tea makers have jumped on the fitness bandwagon with iced tea, teaming up with soft-drink giants to take advantage of their sophisticated distribution networks. As such, Thomas J. Lipton Inc. has joined forces with Pepsi-Cola Canada Beverages Ltd., while Nestlé Canada Inc. has hooked up with Coca-Cola Ltd. These unions are fruitful for Coke and Pepsi as well, since soda pop sales have tapered off in favour of more healthy alternatives such as mineral water and fruit juice.

Trying to align its marketing of iced tea with the healthy concerns of the 1990s consumer, the Tea Council of Canada has taken to touting tea as "all natural," with no calories, additives, or preservatives. And iced tea manufacturers have created advertising campaigns that focus on young, active people for whom playing sports is inseparable from drinking tea. While Nestlé's Nestea is marketed as having a "clean and fresh" taste, commercials for Lipton's iced tea feature a basketball player downing an iced tea with the tag line: "This ain't no sippin' tea." And it doesn't hurt either that Canada's new Food Guide to Healthy Living recommends that a moderate daily intake of caffeine is in fact beneficial to most people.

Source: Marina Strauss, "Tea Industry Looking for Ways to Boost Sales," *Globe and Mail*, February 10, 1994, p. B4.

**Positioning in Relation to a Target Market** Regardless of which positioning strategy is used, the needs of the target market always must be considered. This positioning strategy doesn't suggest that the other ones ignore target markets. Rather, with this strategy, the target market — rather than another factor such as competition — is the focal point in positioning the product.

Johnson & Johnson repositioned its mild baby shampoo for use by mothers, fathers, and people who must wash their hair frequently. Air Canada and Canadian Airlines International aim their frequent flyer programs at regular business travellers in an attempt to build "brand" loyalty. Nestlé Canada launched its new Quik chocolate bar, an extension of the company's long-established chocolate milk powder, to appeal to children aged two to nine, with an emphasis on those in the six-to-eight age bracket. Nestlé made it quite clear that this was to be a new product aimed almost exclusively at children.[9]

**Positioning by Price and Quality** Some retail stores are known for their high-quality merchandise and high prices (Harry Rosen, Birks). Positioned at the other end of the price and quality scale are discount stores such as K mart and Zellers.

In the automotive field, positioning by price and quality is common. In recent years, "luxury" cars that accentuate quality and carry comparatively high prices have proliferated; Infiniti and Lexus are the latest noteworthy entries. However, the makers of luxury cars are having trouble differentiating themselves from each other with respect to important attributes such as performance, comfort, and safety. As a result, consumers are confused.[10]

**Sometimes a company will feel it is necessary to *reposition* a product or brand to give it a new image.**

It'll do you good, but not the way your mother thought.
Mom thought Welch's® Prune Nectar was a laxative. She was wrong, but she was right, too. Because Welch's Prune Nectar is a good source of dietary fibre, which helps keep your system regular, and it contains other good things such as potassium, iron, and vitamin C. Made from sun-ripened California prune plums, Welch's Prune Nectar has a smooth, dry, non-acidic, plummy taste. Serve it well chilled. It'll do you and your family good.
Welch's

## Product-Mix Expansion

**Product-mix expansion** is accomplished by increasing the depth within a particular line and/or the number of lines a firm offers to consumers. Let's look at these options.

When a company adds a similar item to an existing product line with the same brand name, this is termed a **line extension**. For examples, pull the coupons out of your local newspaper or take a look at coupons that appear in your mailbox. You will probably see lots of examples of new products that are really line extensions. Procter & Gamble added to the existing versions of Tide, its leading laundry detergent, by launching a new Ultra Tide, which keeps cotton fabrics looking newer longer. Christies added Mini-Ritz to its line of Ritz crackers along with five-grain and low-salt Ritz, Kraft added a "light" version of its Cracker Barrel cheese. DowBrands of Canada expanded its line of Ziploc refrigerator bags by adding a new line of vegetable bags with holes to keep vegetables fresher by allowing them to "breathe."

The line-extension strategy is also used by organizations in services fields. For example, universities now offer programs to appeal to prospective older students, and the Roman Catholic church broadened its line of religious services by adding Saturday and Sunday evening masses. Many hospitals have added nutrition counselling clinics and even exercise classes to their product lines, acknowledging that an important part of their role is to keep people well.

There are many reasons for line extensions. The main one is that the firm wants to appeal to more market segments by offering a wider range of choices for a particular product. Another reason is that companies want to take advantage of the considerable value that resides in their established brands. There is often a much lower risk involved in introducing a new product as an extension to an existing line under a recognized brand than there would be to launch a completely separate line with a new brand name. To increase the success rate of new product introductions, a line extension strategy is a very obvious part of the marketing program of many companies in the 1990s.

Another way to expand the product mix, referred to as **mix extension,** is to add a new product line to the company's present assortment. To illustrate, when Johnson & Johnson introduced a line of Acuvue disposable contact lenses, that was mix extension because it added another product to the company's product mix. In contrast, line extension adds more items within the same product line. When J&J adds new versions of Tylenol pain reliever, that's line extension.

Under a mix-extension strategy, the new line may be related or unrelated to current products. Furthermore, it may carry one of the company's existing brand names or may be given an entirely new name. Here are examples of these four alternatives:

- **Related product, same brand:** To allow their customers to enjoy their favourite cup of coffee at home, Tim Horton's added canned ground coffee and then introduced a line of Tim Horton's coffee makers that customers could buy to take home; Kimberley-Clark added Kleenex toilet tissue to the long-established facial tissues; Nestlé added the Quik chocolate bar.
- **Unrelated product, same brand:** Forschner Group, Inc., maker of the Original Swiss Army Knives, extended its mix by adding Swiss Army watches and sunglasses; and Swatch, a Swiss watch company, added a clothing line and then announced an even more, unlikely mix extension — small cars![11] 3M, the maker of Scotch Tape and other adhesive and abrasive products, expanded into audio and video tapes and then to computer discs, Scotch-Brite soap pads that never rust, and the famous Post-it notes.
- **Unrelated product, different brand:** This reflects a diversification strategy, such as when a company adds a new division in a different field; for example, Pepsi-Cola owns and operates Pizza Hut restaurants, and McDonald's in the United States explored the possibility of introducing a new indoor playground for kids and their parents, branded "Leaps and Bounds."[12]
- **Related product, different brand:** Procter & Gamble introduced Luvs as a companion to its Pamper disposable diapers.

Most often, the new line is related to the existing product mix because the company wants to capitalize on its expertise and experience. Given the success of Reese's peanut butter cups, Hershey's thinks the brand says "peanut butter" to consumers, so it introduced a line of Reese's peanut butters. However, CPC International holds the same view about its Skippy brand, so it developed Skippy peanut butter cookies. In both cases, the new lines carry one of the company's popular brands to benefit from consumers' familiarity with and good feelings towards that brand. We'll consider this approach in more detail when we discuss *brand equity* in the next chapter.

### Trading Up and Trading Down

The product strategies of trading up and trading down involve a change in product positioning *and* an expansion of product line. **Trading up** means adding a higher-price product to a line to attract a broader market. Also, the seller intends that the new product's prestige will help the sale of its existing lower-price products.

Consider some examples of trading up. Facing stiff competition in the middle-price market, Holiday Inns introduced the higher-price Crowne Plaza Hotels, with nicer surroundings and more amenities. To its line of inexpensive sport watches, Swatch added an $80 Chrono stopwatch and other upgraded watches. And even pet-food manufacturers have traded up to "superpremium" lines, as illustrated by Kal Kan's Pedigree and Quaker Oats' King Kuts.

## MARKETING AT WORK

### FILE 10-2 TIMEX MARCHES ON

An industry leader in the 1960s, Timex found itself losing money and market share in the 1970s as a result of its failure to cash in on the growth in digital technology. When C. Michael Jacobi became vice-president of marketing in 1981, he beefed up Timex market research on the transition of the watch from functional object to fashion accessory. Appointed company president in 1992, Jacobi has reinforced Timex's position as industry leader by increasing the depth of the company's product line over the past decade: in 1985, Timex locked in to the sports watch craze by introducing its "Ironman"; a plastic line called "Watercolours" was produced to go head-to-head with Swiss watchmaker Swatch; following Watercolours, the company developed Carriage, a more classic-look timepiece. To expand its line, in 1992 Timex acquired rivals Guess and Monet jewellers, and then did a deal with Nautica Apparel to market a line of Nautica dressy men's watches. The 1990s have seen products such as wall clocks and clock radios licensed with the Timex name, a line of Disney character watches, and one of its latest innovations, "Indiglo," a watch with an illuminated dial. The Timex line has grown from 300 styles in 1970 to more than 1,500 today, ranging in price from $20 to more than $300. The strategy has resulted in sales increases at Timex of 15 percent annually in 1992 and 1993, and a market share increase since the mid-1980s to more than 30 percent today.

Source: Chris Roush, "At Timex, They're Positively Glowing," *Business Week*, July 12, 1993, p. 141.

A company is said to be **trading down** when it adds a lower-priced item to its line of prestige products. The company expects that people who cannot afford the original product will want to buy the new one because it carries some of the status of the higher-priced good. In line with this strategy, major manufacturers of 35 mm single lens reflex (SLR) cameras, such as Pentax, Canon, and Minolta, have introduced smaller, simplified cameras for photography buffs who want to be seen to be using the major brands but who do not want to be bothered with the intricacies of 35 mm photography. Mont Blanc, the West German manufacturer of the "world's most famous fountain pen," introduced a lower-priced ballpoint pen, thereby allowing its purchasers to own a Mont Blanc without having to pay more than $300 for the top-of-the-line fountain pen.

**Swatch has broadened its market by adding higher-price watches with extra features.**

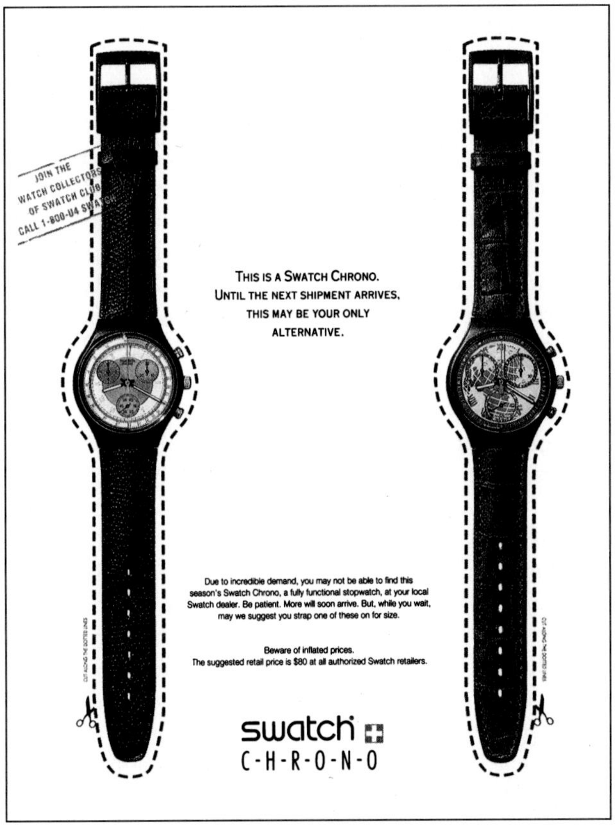


Sometimes the effect of trading down can be achieved through advertising, without introducing new, lower-priced products. A manufacturer of fine crystal or chinaware might accomplish this by advertising some of the lower-priced items in its existing product lines.

Trading up and trading down are perilous strategies because the new products may confuse buyers, resulting in negligible net gain. It is equally undesirable if sales of the new item or line are generated at the expense of the established products. When *trading down*, the new offering may permanently hurt the firm's reputation and that of its established high-quality product. To reduce this possibility, new lower-price products may be given brand names unlike the established brands.

In *trading up*, on the other hand, the problem depends on whether the new product or line carries the established brand or is given a new name. If the same brand name is used, the firm must change its image enough so that new customers will accept the higher-priced product. At the same time, the seller does not want to lose its present customers. The new offering may present a cloudy image, not attracting new customers but driving away existing customers. If a different brand name is used, the company must create awareness for it and then stimulate consumers to buy the new product.

### Alteration of Existing Products

As an alternative to developing a completely new product, management should take a fresh look at the organization's existing products. Often, improving an established product — **product alteration** — can be more profitable and less risky than developing a completely new one. The substitution of NutraSweet for saccharin in diet soft drinks increased sales of those drinks. However, product alteration is not without risks. When

Coca-Cola Co. modified the formula for its leading product and changed its name to New Coke, sales suffered so much that the old formula was brought back three months later under the Coca-Cola Classic name.

For some products, *redesigning* is the key to their relaunching or repositioning. Many companies frequently redesign or reformulate their products to give them a fresh appeal. In recent years, disposable diapers have been redesigned to be less bulky and are now available in separate styles for girls and boys. Sometimes the redesign might simply involve the addition of a new flavour, in which case the product becomes more of a line extension, as when General Mills launched Apple Cinnamon Cheerios.

Alternatively, especially for consumer products, the product itself is not changed but its *packaging* is altered. This strategy is employed to gain a competitive advantage, as when Kraft began to package its cheese slices as Singles. Kraft, Black Diamond, and other manufacturers of cheese products are now offering their sliced and shredded cheeses in packages that reseal using zipper-like closures. Thus, packages can be altered to enhance appearance or to improve the product's usability.

### Product-Mix Contraction

Another product strategy, **product-mix contraction**, is carried out either by eliminating an entire line or by simplifying the assortment within a line. Thinner and/or shorter product lines or mixes can weed out low-profit and unprofitable products. The intended result of product-mix contraction is higher profits from fewer products. General Mills decided to concentrate on its food business and, consequently, sold its interest in Izod (the "alligator" apparel maker) and its lines of children's toys and games. In services fields, some travel agencies have shifted from selling all modes of travel to concentrate on specialized tours and trips to exotic places.

During the early 1990s, most companies expanded — rather than contracted — their product mixes. Numerous line extensions document this trend. As firms find that they have an unmanageable number of products or that various items or lines are unprofitable, or both, product-mix pruning is likely. The result in many organizations will be fewer product lines, with the remaining lines thinner and shorter.

## THE PRODUCT LIFE CYCLE

As we saw in Chapter 9, a product's life cycle can have a direct bearing on a company's survival. The life cycle of a product consists of four stages: introduction, growth, maturity, and decline. The concept of product life *applies to a generic category of product* (microwave ovens, for example) and not to specific brands (such as Sony or Braun). A **product life cycle** consists of the aggregate demand over an extended period of time for all brands making up a generic product category.

A life cycle can be graphed by plotting aggregate sales volume for a generic product category over time, usually years. It is also worthwhile to accompany the sales-volume curve with the corresponding profit curve for the product category, as shown in Figure 10-2. After all, we are interested ultimately in profitability, not just sales.

The *shapes* of these two curves vary from one product category to another. Still, for most categories, the basic shapes and the relationship between the sales and the profit curves are as illustrated in Figure 10-2. In this typical life cycle, the profit curve for most new products is negative (signifying a loss) through much of the introductory stage. In the latter part of the growth stage, the profit curve starts to decline while sales volume is still rising. Profits decline because the companies in an industry usually must increase their advertising and selling efforts or cut their prices (or both) to sustain sales growth in the face of intensifying competition during the maturity stage.

Introducing a new product at the proper time will help maintain a company's desired level of profit. Striving to maintain its dominant position in the wet-shaving market, the Gillette Company has faced that challenge often. A while back, a large French firm cut into Gillette's market share by introducing the highly successful Bic disposable razors. After considerable research and development, Gillette counterattacked in 1989 with the new Sensor razor, featuring independently suspended blades. The strategy has worked, as many consumers have left the convenience of low-price disposable razors in favour of the better shaves provided by the higher-price Sensor razor.[13] If a new product is particularly appealing to consumers and it lacks competition, a firm can charge a fairly high price and achieve strong profits. To date, that's been the case with Sensor, so Gillette is reaping healthy profits from the wet-shaving market.

**FIGURE 10-2**
**Typical life cycle of a product category.**

**During the introduction stage of a life cycle, a product category — and virtually all brands within it — is unprofitable. Profits are healthy during the growth stage but then start to decline while a product's sales volume is still increasing.**

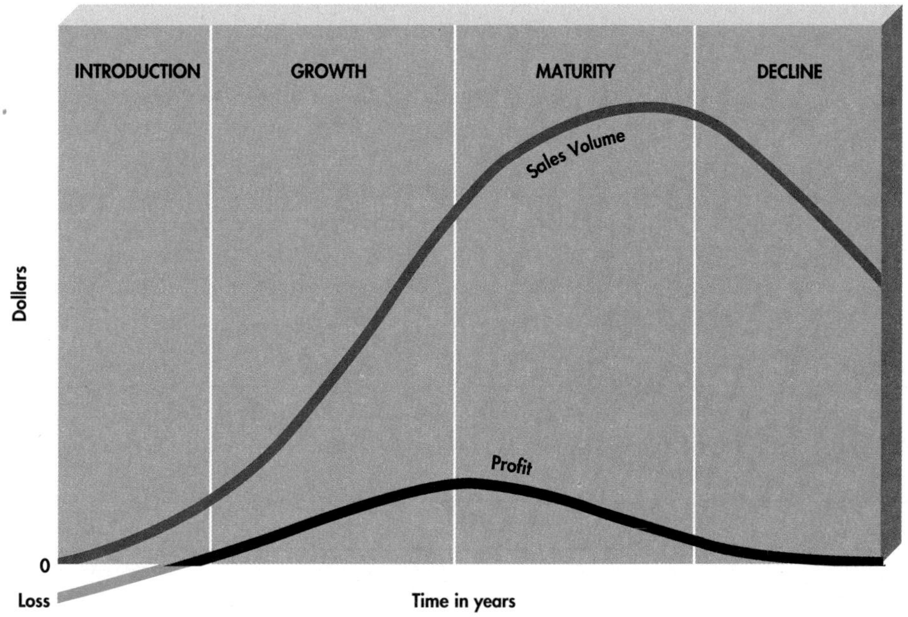


## MARKETING AT WORK

### FILE 10-3 3M COMES TO THE RESCUE

Minnesota Mining and Manufacturing Co. — more commonly known as 3M — the Scotch Tape manufacturers — is thinking of branching out and producing another line of sticky substances: bandages. However, they have no intention of competing directly with market giant Johnson & Johnson, whose Band-Aids have been healing generations of North American scrapes and scratches.

Instead, 3M is creating a line of flexible, foam Active Strips that stretch and conform to fingers, knees, and elbows. In doing so, they are targeting customers "with an active life-style, whether children or adults," says Dave Berkley, general manager of 3M's consumer and professional care division. After all, he clarifies carefully, "3M is not about to enter product categories with broad lines of 'me too' products."

Source: "3M Designs Bandage for People with Active Lifestyles," *Globe and Mail*, February 11, 1994, p. B4.

The product life-cycle concept has been criticized as lacking empirical support and being too general to be useful in specific cases.[14] Although the product life cycle is not perfect and it must be adapted to fit different circumstances, we believe this model is both straightforward and powerful. A company's marketing success can be affected considerably by its ability to determine and adapt to the life cycles for each of its product categories.

### Characteristics of Each Stage

Management must be able to recognize what part of the life cycle its product is in at any given time. The competitive environment and marketing strategies that should be used ordinarily depend on the particular life-cycle stage. Table 10-1 contains a synopsis of all four stages. Each stage is highlighted below.

#### Introduction

During the **introduction stage**, a product is launched into the market in a full-scale marketing program. It has gone through product development, including idea screening, prototype, and market tests. The entire product may be new, such as a substitute for fat in prepared foods. Or it may be well known but have a significant new feature that, in effect, creates a new product category; the fax machine and electronic mail are examples.

This introductory (sometimes called *pioneering*) stage is the most risky and expensive one, because substantial dollars must be spent in seeking consumer acceptance of the product. But many products are not accepted by a sufficient number of consumers and fail at this stage. For really new products, there is very little direct competition. Thus the promotional program is designed to stimulate demand for the entire product category rather than only the seller's brand.

TABLE 10-1 Characteristics and implications of different product life-cycle stages

***Each stage of a product's life-cycle has different characteristics; as a result, marketing must be modified over the course of the cycle***

| | Stage | | | |
|---|---|---|---|---|
| | Introduction | Growth | Maturity | Decline |
| CHARACTERISTICS | | | | |
| **Customers** | **Innovators** | **Mass market** | **Mass market** | **Loyal customers** |
| **Competition** | **Little if any** | **Increasing** | **Intense** | **Decreasing** |
| **Sales** | **Low levels, then rising** | **Rapid growth** | **Slow/no annual growth** | **Declining** |
| **Profits** | **None** | **Strong, then at a peak** | **Declining annually** | **Low/none** |
| MARKETING IMPLICATIONS | | | | |
| **Overall strategy** | **Market development** | **Market penetration** | **Defensive positioning** | **Efficiency or exit** |
| **Costs** | **High per unit** | **Declining** | **Stable or increasing** | **Low** |
| **Product strategy** | **Undifferentiated** | **Improved items** | **Differentiated** | **Pruned line** |
| **Pricing strategy** | **Most likely high** | **Lower over time** | **Lowest** | **Increasing** |
| **Distribution strategy** | **Scattered** | **Intensive** | **Intensive** | **Selective** |
| **Promotion strategy** | **Category awareness** | **Brand preference** | **Brand loyalty** | **Reinforcement** |

Source: Adapted from material provided by Professor David Appel, University of Notre Dame, Notre Dame, IN.

Growth In the **growth stage**, or *market-acceptance stage*, sales and profits rise, often at a rapid rate. Competitors enter the market, often in large numbers if the profit outlook is particularly attractive. Mostly as a result of competition, profits start to decline near the end of the growth stage. Appropriate marketing strategies for this stage, as well as the other three, are summarized in Table 10-1.

Maturity During the first part of the **maturity stage**, sales continue to increase, but at a decreasing rate. When sales level off, profits of both producers and intermediaries decline. The primary reason: intense price competition. Seeking to differentiate themselves, some firms extend their product lines with new models. During the latter part of this stage, marginal producers, those with high costs or without a differential advantage, are forced to drop out of the market. They do so because they lack sufficient customers and/or profits.

Decline For most products, a **decline stage**, as gauged by sales volume for the total category, is inevitable for one of the following reasons:

- The need for the product disappears, as when frozen orange juice generally eliminated the market for juice squeezers.
- A better or less expensive product is developed to fill the same need. Electronic microprocessors made possible many replacement products such as hand-held calculators (which made slide rules obsolete) and video games (which may have pushed the category of board games such as Monopoly and Clue into their decline stage).
- People simply grow tired of a product (a clothing style, for instance), so it disappears from the market.

Seeing little opportunity for revitalized sales or profits, most competitors abandon the market during this stage. However, a few firms may be able to develop a small market niche and remain moderately successful in the decline stage. Some manufacturers of wood-burning stoves have been able to do this. Whether a product at this stage has to be abandoned or can be continued on a profitable basis often depends on the skills and creativity of the marketing manager responsible for the product.

## Length of Product Life Cycle

The total length of the life cycle — from start of the introduction stage to the end of the decline stage — varies across product categories. It ranges from a few weeks or a short season (for a clothing fashion) to many decades (for autos or telephones). And it varies due to differences in the length of individual stages from one product category to the next. Furthermore, although Figure 10-2 suggests that all four life-cycle stages cover nearly equal periods of time, the stages in any given product's life cycle usually last for different periods.

Three variations on the typical life cycle are shown in Figure 10-3:

- In one, the product gains widespread consumer acceptance only after an extended introductory period (see part a). A case can be made that the videophone is following this path, since early models of this product were introduced, but attracted few customers, some years ago. The category of fat substitutes, which are used in making foods ranging from ice cream to salad dressings, appears to be languishing in the introduction stage of its life cycle.
- In another variation, the entire life cycle begins and ends in a relatively short period of time (part b). This variation depicts the life cycle for a **fad**, a product or style that becomes immensely popular nearly overnight and then falls out of favour with consumers almost as quickly. Hula hoops and pet rocks are examples of past fads; troll dolls and beaded seat covers for cars may be 1990s fads.

**FIGURE 10-3**
**Product life-cycle variations.**

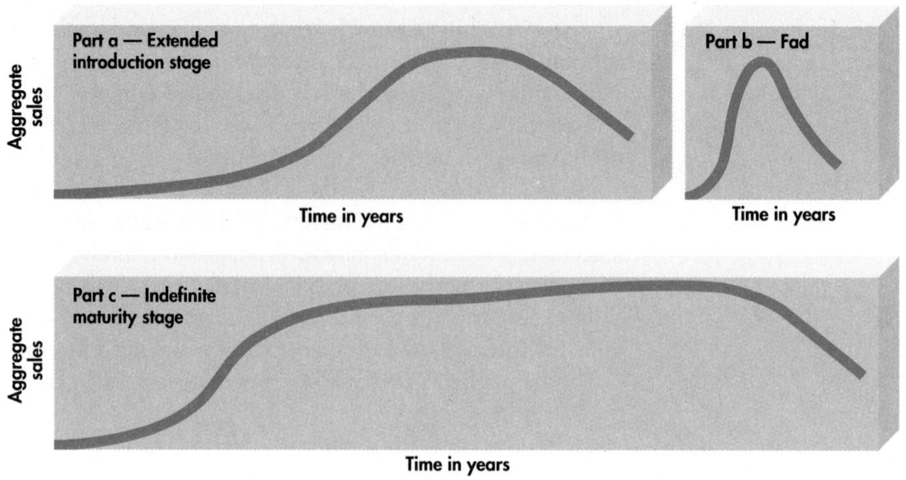


- In a third variation, the product's mature stage lasts almost indefinitely (part c). This life cycle is illustrated by canned, carbonated soft drinks and also by the automobile with a gasoline-powered, internal-combustion engine. Other forms, such as electric- and solar-powered cars, have been proposed, but the automobile as we know it remains dominant.

Setting aside fads, which represent a special case, product life cycles are getting shorter generally. If competitors can quickly introduce a "me too" version of a popular product, it may move swiftly into the maturity stage. Or rapid changes in technology can make a product obsolete virtually overnight. Could this happen in the audio field as digital audio tapes (DATs) are seen by some as a replacement for compact discs (CDs)?

Moreover, a number of product categories do not make it through all four stages of the life cycle. Some fail in the introductory stage. That appeared to be the case in the 1980s with a product that plays videodiscs rather than videotapes. Now the product is appearing again, so perhaps it was just in a very extended introduction stage!

## Life Cycle Is Related to a Market

When we say that a product is in a specific stage of its life cycle, implicitly we are referring to a specific market. A product may be well accepted (growth or maturity stage) in some markets but still be striving for acceptance in other markets. At the time Ortho Pharmaceuticals introduced Retin-A as a treatment for acne, existing products already served this purpose. Thus the acne-treatment category probably was in the maturity stage. However, then it was discovered that Retin-A might be effective in reducing facial wrinkles. In effect, it created a new product category. Hence, as the 1990s began, Retin-A fit into both the acne-treatment category that was in the maturity stage among teenagers and into the wrinkle-remover category that was in the introductory or perhaps early-growth stage among the middle-aged.

In terms of geographic markets, a product may be in its maturity stage in one country and its introductory stage or perhaps even unknown in another country. For example, brewed coffee in cans and bottles is widely accepted in Japan — a $5 billion market, in fact.[15] Yet it is largely unknown in North America. Nevertheless, Maxwell House and other companies are introducing new ready-to-drink coffee products (most sweet, flavoured, and intended to be served chilled). Steel-belted radial tires were in their maturity stage in Western Europe well before they were introduced widely in this country. In contrast, so-called fast foods are a mature product category in North America but are much less common in most other parts of the world.

## MARKETING AT WORK

### FILE 10-4 THE RAPID RISE OF THE COMPACT DISC

It seems difficult to believe that compact discs have been with us for little more than 10 years. In that rather short time in the evolution of a product, the now-ubiquitous CD has virtually replaced vinyl records and has sent the audio cassette into the decline stage of its life cycle. It is interesting to examine the life cycles of the various forms in which recordings have appeared in recent years as technology has evolved. It wasn't too many years ago that long-playing records (LPs) replaced the 78s and 45s that usually contained only one song per side. Then, we saw the rapid rise and fall of eight-track tapes, before the popular audio cassette came on the scene in the 1970s. But it was the CD that really sounded the death knell for the LP. In only seven or eight years after CDs became widely available, production of LPs was stopped by almost all record companies, this despite the fact that less than 50 percent of North American households had CD players.

It is useful to think of the relative advantages that CDs offer over LPs and cassettes, in an attempt to explain its rapid rise. What might the future hold? Will digital audio tape begin to replace CDs within the next few years?

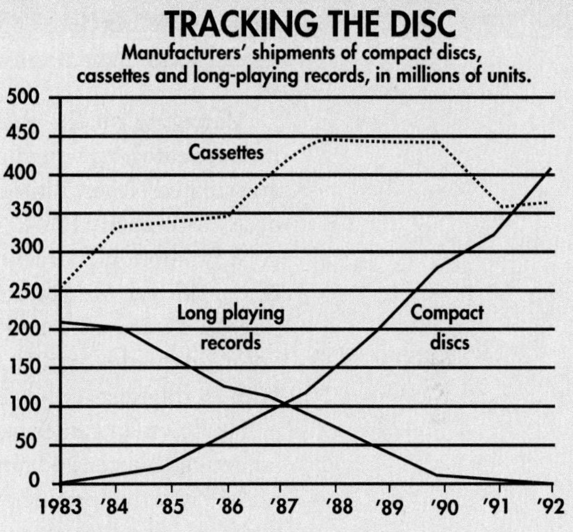


Source: Recording Industry Association of America.

Source: Allan Kozinn, "Why Vinyl Really Slipped Its Disc," *Globe and Mail*, September 16, 1993, p. A11.

### Life-Cycle Management

To a surprising extent, the shape of the sales and profit curves for a product category can be controlled. The collective actions of firms offering competing products in the same category shape the curves. But even single companies can have an impact. A giant firm may be able to shorten the introductory stage by broadening the distribution or increasing the promotional effort supporting the new product.

Most firms, however, cannot substantially affect the sales and profit curves for a product category. Thus their task is to determine how best to achieve success with their own brands within the life cycle for an entire product category. For an individual firm, successful life-cycle management depends on (1) predicting the shape of the proposed product's cycle even before it is introduced and (2) successfully adapting marketing strategies at each stage of the life cycle.

**Entry Strategies** A firm entering a new market must decide whether to plunge in during the introductory stage. Or it can wait and make its entry during the early part of the growth stage, after innovating companies have proven there is a viable market.

The strategy of entering during the introductory stage is prompted by the desire to build a dominant market position right away and thus lessen the interest of potential competitors and the effectiveness of actual competitors. This strategy worked for Sony with the Walkman; Perrier with bottled sparkling water; and Nike with running shoes. Evidently, there is benefit to getting a head start in marketing a new type of product. The hurdles may be insurmountable when you enter with a "me too" product and try to play catch-up.

However, delaying entry until the market is proven can sometimes pay off. Pioneering requires a large investment, and the risks are great — as demonstrated by the high failure rate among new products. Large companies with the marketing resources to overwhelm smaller innovating firms are most likely to be successful with a delayed-entry strategy. In one such case, Coca-Cola introduced Tab and Diet Coke, and Pepsi-Cola introduced Diet Pepsi, and the two giants surpassed Diet Rite Cola, an early pioneer.

It's not clear-cut which is the better entry strategy. Each has its advantages and disadvantages, its successes and failures. As with nearly all marketing decisions, sound managerial judgement is critical.[16]

**Managing on the Rise** When sales are growing strongly and profits are robust in a product category, you might think a marketing manager has little to do except tally up an anticipated bonus. Unfortunately, that's not the case. During the growth stage of the life cycle, a company has to devise the right strategies for its brand(s) in that product category. Promotion that will cause consumers to desire the company's brand of product must be considered. Distribution must be expanded. And product improvements must be considered. Decisions made during the growth stage influence (a) how many competitors enter the market and (b) how well the company's brand within a product category does both in the near and distant future.

Home video games were introduced in the 1970s, but the more captivating (perhaps addictive) Nintendo brand, in effect, created a new product category in the 1980s. In the mid-1990s, this product was in the growth stage of its life cycle. To sustain the growth and avoid the flattening out of the sales curve, Nintendo introduced an improved game console; created additional video games for adults; launched Game Boy, a hand-held model; and targeted Europe as a prime new market.[17]

**Managing during Maturity** Various strategies may be effective in maintaining or boosting sales of a product during the maturity stage of its life cycle. Of course, what works magnificently for one product may perform dismally for another.[18] Common strategies during maturity include modifying the product, designing new promotion, and devising new uses for the product.[19] Such steps may lead to added purchases by present customers and/or may attract new customers. As sales in the North American cruise industry flattened out, some cruise lines modified their services by adding fitness programs and offering special theme cruises (sometimes in conjunction with a professional sports team). Even Aspirin — the epitome of a mundane, mature product — found a new market among people who have survived one heart attack. The reason? Aspirin was found to reduce considerably the chances of a second attack.

The Du Pont Co. appears to be particularly adept at sustaining mature products, most recently Teflon and Lycra.[20] Teflon launched an entire category of special-use protective-coating products. Now, more than 50 years later, Du Pont's marketing managers keep the product vibrant by devising new uses for it. For instance, Teflon was packaged in a spray can to be used, among other purposes, on walls to protect against fingerprints and on ski clothes to keep them dry in snow. Du Pont followed a similar path with its Lycra brand of spandex, a fibre the company invented in 1959. Even though the company's patent expired a while back, demand for Lycra is growing. Du Pont's primary strategy to generate continuing interest in Lycra has been to develop improved versions of it. Having done this, the product now is used in a variety of fashionable clothing.

**Surviving the Decline Stage** Perhaps it is in the decline stage that a company finds its greatest challenges in life-cycle management. For instance, the advent of video camcorders and filmless cameras may hint at the decline of photographic film as a product category. Kodak Canada is trying to prevent the decline of this product while keeping pace with competitors in examining bold new products. With one such product, which Kodak calls Photo CD, consumers take pictures as they normally have; the big difference comes at the time of film processing, when the prints can be stored on a compact disc. Then they can be shown on a TV, if you have a new videodisc player![21]

When sales are declining, management has the following alternatives:

- Ensure that marketing and production programs are as efficient as possible.
- Prune unprofitable sizes and models. Frequently this tactic will *decrease* sales but *increase* profits.
- "Run out" the product; that is, cut all costs to the bare minimum to maximize profitability over the limited remaining life of the product.
- Best (and toughest) of all, improve the product in a functional sense, or revitalize it in some manner. Publishers of printed dictionaries may have done this. Other reference materials, including dictionaries on personal computers, seemed to have pushed the traditional dictionary into — or at least towards — decline. However, some publishers are working hard to maintain the appeal of the dictionary. Houghton Mifflin, for instance, added 16,000 new words to its latest edition and backed it with $2 million in promotion.[22]

If one of these alternatives doesn't work, management will have to consider **product abandonment**. The expense of carrying profitless products goes beyond what shows up on financial statements. For example, there is a very real cost to the managerial time and effort that is diverted to terminally ill products. Management often is reluctant to discard a product, however, partly because it becomes attached to the product over the years.

In the final analysis, the most compelling — but often painful — alternative may be product abandonment. Knowing when and how to abandon products successfully may be as important as knowing when and how to introduce new ones. Certainly management should develop systematic procedures for phasing out weak products.[23]

## PLANNED OBSOLESCENCE AND FASHION

Consumers seem to be constantly searching for "what's new" but not "too new." They want newness — new products, new styles, new colours. However, they want to be moved gently out of their habitual patterns, not shocked out of them. Consequently, many manufacturers use a product strategy of planned obsolescence. The intent of this strategy is to make an existing product out of date and thus to increase the market for replacement products. Consumers often satisfy their thirst for newness through fashion. And producers of fashions rely heavily on planned obsolescence, as we'll now see.

### Nature of Planned Obsolescence

The term **planned obsolescence** may be interpreted two ways:

- **Technological or functional obsolescence.** Significant technical improvements result in a more effective product. For instance, audio cassette tapes made phonograph records obsolete; now digital audio tapes threaten to make cassettes and compact discs obsolete. This type of obsolescence is generally considered to be socially and economically desirable, because the replacement product offers more benefits and/or a lower cost.
- **Style obsolescence.** Superficial characteristics of a product are altered so that the new model is easily differentiated from the previous model. Style obsolescence, sometimes called "psychological" or "fashion" obsolescence, is intended to make people feel out of date if they continue to use old models. Products subject to this type of obsolescence include clothing, furniture, and automobiles.

When people criticize planned obsolescence, they usually mean style obsolescence. In our discussion, when we refer to planned obsolescence, we will mean *only* style obsolescence, unless otherwise stated.

### Nature of Style and Fashion

Although the words *style* and *fashion* are often used interchangeably, there is a clear distinction. A **style** is a distinctive manner of construction or presentation in any art, product, or endeavour (singing, playing, behaving). Thus we have styles in automobiles (sedans, station wagons), in bathing suits (one-piece, bikini), in furniture (Early American, French Provincial), and in dancing (waltz, "break").

A **fashion** is any style that is popularly accepted and purchased by successive groups of people over a reasonably long period of time. Not every style becomes a fashion. To be considered a fashion, or to be called "fashionable," a style must be accepted by many people. All of the styles listed in the preceding paragraph, except perhaps for break dancing, qualify as fashions. All societies, ranging from contemporary primitive groups to medieval European societies, have fashions.

Fashion is rooted in sociological and psychological factors. Basically, most of us are conformists. At the same time, we yearn to look and act a *little* different from others. We probably are not in revolt against custom; we simply wish to be a bit distinctive but not be accused of bad taste or disregard for norms. Fashion furnishes the opportunity for self-expression.

### Fashion-Adoption Process

The fashion-adoption process reflects the concepts of (1) large-group and small-group influences on consumer buying behaviour and (2) the diffusion of innovation, as discussed in Chapters 6 and 9. People usually try to imitate others at the same or the next higher socioeconomic level. One way people do that is purchasing a product that is fashionable in the group they want to be like.

Thus the **fashion-adoption process** is a series of buying waves that arise as a particular style is popularly accepted in one group, then another group and another, until it finally falls out of fashion. This movement, representing the introduction, rise, popular culmination, and decline of the market's acceptance of a style, is referred to as the **fashion cycle**. A case can be made that synthetic fibres, such as polyester, in clothing and the convertible model of automobile are two products that have run the full fashion cycle.

There are three theories of fashion adoption (see Figure 10-4):

- **Trickle-down**, where a given fashion cycle flows *downward* through several socio-economic levels.
- **Trickle-across**, where the cycle moves *horizontally* and *simultaneously within* several socioeconomic levels.
- **Trickle-up**, where a style first becomes popular at lower socioeconomic levels and then flows *upward* to become popular among higher levels.

Traditionally, the *trickle-down* theory has been used to explain the fashion-adoption process. As an example, designers of women's apparel first introduce a style to opinion leaders in the upper socioeconomic groups. If they accept the style, it quickly appears in leading fashion stores. Soon the middle-income and then the lower-income markets want to emulate the leaders, and the style is mass-marketed. As its popularity wanes, the style appears in bargain-price stores and finally is no longer considered fashionable.

**FIGURE 10-4**
**Fashion-adoption processes.**

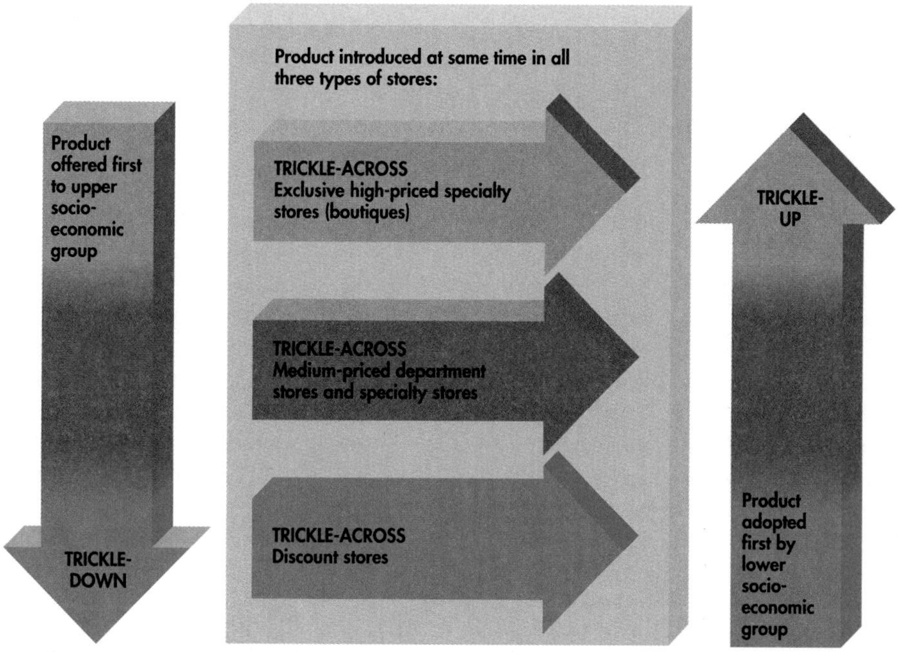


## MARKETING AT WORK

### FILE 10-5 GIVING NEW MEANING TO OLD PRODUCTS — CASHING IN ON PRODUCTS THAT MAKE A STATEMENT

In fashion these days, the hippest thing for North American consumers seems to be going back to the simple products of yore — functional, sturdy, trustworthy back-to-basics items that give off an air of toughness in these tough times and evoke a myth of rebellion in a period where people feel increasingly fed-up and helpless. Such seems to be the case with respect to Levi's 501 jeans, Doc Martens boots and Harley-Davidson motorcycles; they have rapidly replaced glitzy status symbols of the 1980s such as Armani suits, $150 Nike cross trainers, and BMWs with car phones.

Levi's jeans of course are a classic. Originally worn by Yukon gold miners, they remained exclusively the stuff of hard-working, rough, and rugged proletarians before being adopted as the uniforms of rebellious youth in the 1950s and '60s. In the 1970s and '80s, Levi's got fancy and spiffed their jeans up, offering a wide array of colours and cuts, such as green, acid-washed, and Levi's for women. In the 1990s, however, it's hip to dress down and customers — both men and women — are clamouring for the original 501 pure old-fashioned blue jeans with the old-fashioned buttons (none of this high-tech zipper stuff). These days, anti-glamour is glamour and Levi's itself is focusing on this cultural shift in its latest ad campaign, which plays up the authenticity of original 501s by symbolically linking the jeans with the tough but truth-seeking generation of today. Shot in a raw MTV style, the commercials — aired during hip shows such as "The Simpsons" and "Late Night with David Letterman" — feature characters such as a young man on rollerblades who says, "Be yourself always. Don't let anyone stop you" or another on a Los Angeles street who confesses, "I think it's good to get away from everything you've known in order to learn something new. But I still haven't found what I'm looking for." Haphazardly inserted in the commercials is the slogan "Can't Fake It," implying that you can't fake life and neither can you fake jeans.

Another product whose humble utilitarian beginnings have suddenly become the fashionable rage are Doc Martens shoes and boots. Invented during World War II by Dr. Klaus Maertens, the clunky, orthopedic shoes were originally bought by elderly customers with foot ailments. After the war, Doc Martens came to be manufactured in

England, where the British working class adopted them, before being appropriated in the 1960s and '70s by skinheads, then punks and neo-fascists who especially liked the military style of the boots. They appropriated the cherry red boot as their political trademark and created a series of codes based on lace colour. White, for example, indicated white supremacists. By the end of the 1980s, Docs had travelled the globe with British music groups, been adopted by Seattle's scruffy grunge movement, and transformed themselves from an underground racist icon to a hip status symbol in an era when it's fashionable to be alternative.

Anthropologist Grant McCracken of Toronto's Royal Ontario Museum says, "When you get the trickle-up phenomenon, as something moves into the centre of society, it gives up some of its street credibility, but carries some of its symbolism with it." According to McCracken, well-heeled, fashion-conscious folk now wear Docs as a protest against mainstream society, bourgeois values, and adult convention. Just as in the 1980s people wore high-tech fitness shoes without actually getting fit, in the '90s they are wearing Docs to feel powerful, tough, and intimidating without actually being alternative. And women, in particular, are embracing Docs, rebelling against the notion of traditional feminine footwear and challenging traditional gender codes by mixing the boots with long flowery dresses.

Another product associated with myths of down-to-earth ruggedness and no-nonsense simplicity is the Harley-Davidson motorcycle. Once the symbol of the Wild One Brando rebel, the Easy Rider outcast, or the tough Hell's Angel, Harleys, like 501s and Docs, are becoming the new status symbol of fortysomething doctors, lawyers, agents, and film executives looking to drown out the noisy angst of their midlife crisis with the roar of their motorcycle. Rejecting the values conferred by past flashy status symbols, "rubbies" — rich urban bikers — are taking to the streets (in 501s and Docs) and rebelling, having missed out the first time because they were so busy getting into Harvard. Harley-Davidson says that close to 70 percent of its customers have college degrees and are an average age of 40. Accordingly, the company has moved to sell its product as not just a bike, but a life-style. A spokesman says, "Nothing feels or sounds like a Harley . . . . You're buying into the Harley-Davidson family — the riding with friends, the rallies, the leather clothing." In catering to this vision, the manufacturer recently opened New York's Harley-Davidson Café, in which rubbies and their female counterparts — "frubbies" — can get together for a Harley Hogg sandwich and listen to tunes interspersed with the sound of revving bikes while fake exhaust pours from display motorcycles.

Sources: Amy Willard Cross, "Why Docs' Rise Is No Mean Feat," *Globe and Mail*, December 15, 1993, p. A15; Michael Janofsky, "Levi Puts Some Life into Jeans Pitch," *New York Times*. Reprinted by the *Globe and Mail*, July 29, 1993, p. B4; Kate Muir, "Their Hearts Belong to Harley-Davidson," *Times* (London). Reprinted by the *Globe and Mail*, October 23, 1993, p. A2.

Today the *trickle-across* theory best explains the adoption process for most fashions. It's true that there is some flow downward, and obviously there is an upward flow. But, by means of modern production, communication, and transportation, we can disseminate style information and products so rapidly that all social levels can be reached at about the same time. For example, within a few weeks of the beginning of the fall season, the same style of dress (but at different quality levels) appears (1) in small, exclusive dress shops appealing to the upper social class, (2) in large department stores appealing to the middle social class, and (3) in discount houses and low-price women's ready-to-wear chain stores, where the appeal is to the portion of the lower social class that has some disposable income.

Most apparel manufacturers produce a wide *variety* of essentially one style. They also produce different *qualities* of the same basic style so as to appeal to different income groups. When an entire cycle may last only one season, sellers cannot afford to wait for style acceptance to trickle down. They must introduce it to many social levels simultaneously.

Within each class, the dresses are purchased early in the season by the opinion leaders — the innovators. If the style is accepted, its sales curve rises as it becomes popular with the early adopters and then with the late adopters. Eventually, sales decline as the style loses popularity. This cycle is a horizontal movement, occurring virtually simultaneously within each of several socioeconomic levels.

The *trickle-up* process also explains some product-adoption processes. Consider how styles of music such as jazz and rap became popular. Also look at blue jeans, denim jackets, T-shirts, athletic footwear, and even pasta in the 1990s. They all have one thing in common: They were popular first with lower socioeconomic groups, and later their popularity "trickled up" to higher-income markets.

### Marketing Considerations in Fashion

When a firm's products are subject to the fashion cycle, management must know what stage the cycle is in at all times. Managers must decide at what point to get into the cycle and when to get out.

Accurate forecasting is critical to success in fashion merchandising. This is extremely difficult, however, because the forecaster must deal with complex sociological and psychological factors. Frequently a retailer or manufacturer operates largely on intuition and inspiration, tempered by considerable experience.

Ordinarily a retailer cannot participate successfully in all stages of the fashion cycle at the same time. Thus a specialty apparel store — whose stocks are displayed in limited numbers without price tags — should get in at the start of a fashion trend. And a department store appealing to the middle-income market should plan to enter the cycle in time to mass-market the style as it is climbing to its peak of popularity. Fundamentally, retail executives must keep in mind the product's target market in deciding at which stage(s) of the life cycle its stores should offer fashionable apparel.

## SUMMARY

Many strategic decisions must be made to manage a company's assortment of products effectively. To start, a firm must select strategies regarding its product mix. One decision is how to position the product relative to competing products and other products sold by the firm.

Another strategic decision is whether or how to expand the product mix by adding items to a line and/or introducing new lines. Alternatively, management may elect to trade up or trade down relative to existing products. Altering the design, packaging, or other features of existing products is still another option among the strategies of selecting the best mix. The product mix also can be changed by eliminating an entire line or by simplifying the assortment within a line.

Executives need to understand the concept of a product life cycle, which reflects the total sales volume for a generic product category. Each of the cycle's four stages — introduction, growth, maturity, and decline — has distinctive characteristics that have implications for marketing. Managing a product as it moves through its life cycle presents challenges and opportunities. Eventually, a product category may lack adequate acceptance from consumers; at that point, all or most companies will abandon their versions of this product.

Planned obsolescence is a controversial product strategy, built around the concepts of style, fashion, and the fashion cycle. Fashion — essentially a sociological and psychological phenomenon — follows a reasonably predictable pattern. With advances in communications and production, the fashion-adoption process has moved away from the traditional trickle-down pattern. Today the process is better described as trickle-across. There also are examples of fashions trickling up. Managing a product, such as expensive apparel, through a fashion cycle may be even more challenging than adjusting another type of product's strategies during its life cycle.

## KEY TERMS AND CONCEPTS

**Product mix (288)**
**Breadth (288)**
**Depth (288)**
**Product line (288)**
**Positioning (289)**
**Product-mix expansion (292)**
**Line extension (292)**
**Mix extension (293)**
**Trading up (294)**
**Trading down (294)**
**Product alteration (295)**
**Product-mix contraction (296)**
**Product life cycle (296)**
**Introduction stage (298)**
**Growth stage (299)**
**Maturity stage (299)**
**Decline stage (299)**
**Fad (299)**
**Product abandonment (303)**
**Planned obsolescence (303)**
**Technological (functional) obsolescence (303)**
**Style (fashion or psychological) obsolescence (303)**
**Style (304)**
**Fashion (304)**
**Fashion-adoption process (304)**
**Fashion cycle (304)**
**Trickle-down theory (304)**
**Trickle-across theory (304)**
**Trickle-up theory (304)**

## QUESTIONS AND PROBLEMS

1. "It is inconsistent for management to follow concurrently the product-line strategies of *expanding* its product mix and *contracting* its product mix." Discuss.
2. "Trading up and trading down are product strategies closely related to the business cycle. Firms trade up during periods of prosperity and trade down during recessions." Do you agree? Why?
3. Name one category of good and one category of service you believe are in the introductory stage of their life cycles. For each product, identify the market that considers your examples to be truly new.
4. What are two products that are in the decline stage of the life cycle? In each case, point out whether you think the decline is permanent. What recommendations do you have for rejuvenating the demand for either of these products?
5. How might a company's advertising strategies differ, depending on whether its brand of a product is in the introduction stage or the maturity stage of its life cycle?
6. What products, other than apparel and automobiles, stress fashion and style in marketing? Do styles exist among business products?
7. Is the trickle-across theory applicable to the fashion-adoption process in product lines other than women's apparel? Explain, using examples.
8. Planned obsolescence is criticized as a social and economic waste because we are urged to buy things we do not like and do not need. What is your opinion? If you object to planned obsolescence, what are your recommendations for correcting the situation?

## HANDS-ON MARKETING

1. Select a product category in which you are interested. Go to the library and identify the national or provincial trade association for this product category. Then write to the association, requesting sales figures for this product over its history and other information that will allow you to plot the life cycle for this product. What stage of the life cycle is this product in? Explain.
2. Arrange a meeting with a supermarket manager or a department manager in a supermarket. Discuss how the manager handles the challenge of line extensions. In which product category are line extensions most common? When new items are added to the line, how does the manager find space for the new entries — by giving more space to this category, dropping other items carrying this same brand, pruning other brands in this category, or some other means?

## NOTES AND REFERENCES


1. James Pollock, "Tetley Heats up Iced Tea to Retain Its Lead," *Marketing*, March 21, 1994, p. 4.
2. Mark Smyka, "Labatt to Launch Carlsberg Dark," *Strategy*, February 21, 1994, p. 7; and Terry Brodie, "No-buzz Beers Give Breweries a Blast," *Financial Times*, December 11, 1993, p. 14.
3. "Fizzing," *The Economist*, September 4, 1993, pp. 63-65; and Marina Strauss, "Coke Switches Marketing Strategy," *Globe and Mail*, January 18, 1994, p. B16.
4. Adapted from David A. Aaker and J. Gary Shansby, "Positioning Your Product," *Business Horizons*, May/June 1982, pp. 56-58.
5. Russell Mitchell, "Intel Isn't Taking This Lying Down," *Business Week*, September 30, 1991, pp. 32-33.
6. Gayle MacDonald, "Record Retailers Use Different Strategies," *The Financial Post*, March 20, 1992, p. 12.
7. Marina Strauss, "Canada Rated 6th in Quality of Its Manufactured Goods," *Globe and Mail*, February 10, 1994, p. B6.
8. Kathy Tyrer, "Selling Hockey in the Land of La La and Disney," *Marketing*, November 8, 1993, p. 5.
9. Patrick Allossery, "Nestlé Quik Bar Aims at Children," *Strategy*, December 13, 1993, pp. 1, 19.
10. Melinda G. Guiles, "Quiet Ride Ends for Luxury-Car Makers as a Crowded Market Befuddles Buyers," *The Wall Street Journal*, March 22, 1990, p. B1.
11. Ariane Sains, "Swiss Army Swells Ranks," *Adweek's Marketing Week*, June 4, 1990, p. 24; Kathleen Deveny, "If Swatch Name Sells Watches, Why Not Cars?" *The Wall Street Journal*, September 20, 1990, p. B1.
12. "McDonald's Grows by 'Leaps & Bounds,'" *Daily Camera* (Boulder, Colo.), September 3, 1991, p. 22.
13. Lawrence Ingrassia, "Gillette Holds Its Edge by Endlessly Searching for a Better Shave," *The Wall Street Journal*, December 10, 1992, pp. A1, A6.
14. The criticisms are summarized in Geoffrey L. Gordon, Roger J. Calantone, and C. Anthony di Benedetto, "Mature Markets and Revitalization Strategies: An American Fable," *Business Horizons*, May-June 1991, pp. 39-50. Alternative life cycles are proposed in Edward D. Popper and Bruce D. Buskirk, "Technology Life Cycles in Industrial Markets," *Industrial Marketing Management*, February 1992, pp. 23-31; and C. Merle Crawford, "Business Took the Wrong Life Cycle from Biology," *The Journal of Product and Brand Management*, Winter 1992, pp. 51-57.
15. Dorian Friedman, "Get Your Iced, Cold Java," *U.S. News & World Report*, April 29, 1991, p. 59.
16. For more on this subject, see Steven P. Schnaars, "When Entering Growth Markets, Are Pioneers Better than Poachers?" *Business Horizons*, March-April 1986, pp. 27-36.
17. Susan Moffat, "Can Nintendo Keep Winning?" *Fortune*, November 5, 1990, pp. 131-132, 136.
18. For a study examining business products, see Jorge Vasconcellos, "Key Success Factors in Marketing Mature Products," *Industrial Marketing Management*, November 1991, pp. 263-278.
19. For discussion of four strategies — recapture, redesign, refocus, and recast — that are particularly applicable to *business* products, see Paul C. N. Michell, Peter Quinn, and Edward Percival, "Marketing Strategies for Mature Industrial Products," *Industrial Marketing Management*, August 1991, pp. 201-206; for discussion of five strategies used by the Quaker Oats Company for *consumer products*, see James R. Tindall, "Marketing Established Brands," *The Journal of Consumer Marketing*, Fall 1991, pp. 5-10.
20. Laurie Hays, "Teflon Is 50 Years Old, But Du Pont Is Still Finding New Uses for Inventions," *The Wall Street Journal*, April 7, 1988, p. 30; Monica Roman, "How Du Pont Keeps 'Em Coming Back for More," *Business Week*, August 20, 1990, p. 68.
21. Joan E. Rigdon, "Kodak Tries to Prepare for Filmless Era without Inviting Demise of Core Business," *The Wall Street Journal*, April 18, 1991, p. B1.
22. Meg Cox, "Ad Blitz Turns Dictionary into Best Seller," *The Wall Street Journal*, October 23, 1992, p. A9A.
23. For suggestions on how to recognize the technological limits of an existing product — in effect, knowing when to get off the curve for an existing product and to jump on the curve for the next product — see Richard Foster, "When to Make Your Move to the Latest Innovation," *Across the Board*, October 1986, pp. 44-50.

## CHAPTER 11 GOALS

As the Country Style case illustrates, the success of a product or service will depend to a very great extent on the image that is communicated by the brand name. Otherwise, how do you account for some people buying Bayer Aspirin, while others prefer to buy a private-label brand of ASA tablet, when both products are virtually identical? Consumer choice is influenced not only by the brand name, but also in the case of tangible products by the package, warranty, design, and other product features. It is important to recognize that Country Style was making the equivalent of package and design changes when it redesigned its stores and signs. Because these features of products and services are important elements in a marketing program, we devote this chapter to them. After studying this chapter, you should have an understanding of:

- The nature and importance of brands.
- Characteristics of a good brand name.
- Branding strategies of producers and intermediaries.
- Why and how a growing number of firms are building and using brand equity.
- The nature and importance of packaging and labelling.
- Major packaging strategies.
- The marketing implications of other product features — design, quality, warranty, and postsale service — that can satisfy consumers' wants.

CHAPTER 11

# BRANDS, PACKAGING, AND OTHER PRODUCT FEATURES

## A New Look for Country Style

The first Country Style Donuts store opened in downtown Toronto in March 1963. The concept was a simple one: offer the customer a cup of freshly brewed coffee, along with a large selection of doughnuts baked fresh daily, keep the store spotlessly clean at all times, and provide fast and friendly service 24 hours a day, seven days a week. Sounds great, and it was exactly what customers wanted in the early 1960s.

However, over the past 30 years, customers have changed and their expectations of what a coffee and doughnut shop should offer have changed as well. Not only have the demographic characteristics of Canadian households changed, as we reviewed in Chapter 4, but the way in which people lead their lives is also different. People are more mobile, they have less time on their hands, and competition in the coffee shop business has become fierce. In response to such changes, Country Style no longer locates its stores on the "drive home" side of the road in larger cities so that "dad" can drop in to pick up a dozen doughnuts for the family on his way home from work. The company now locates on the "way to work" side of the road, as well as in shopping centres, office complexes, and industrial parks. The product line has also changed to meet customer demands, and reduces emphasis on its 56 varieties of doughnuts, and now features specialty coffees, thick home-style soup, fresh salads, deli-style sandwiches, hearty chili, and Yogen Früz frozen yogurt.

Changes in the consumer and in the competitive marketplace led management in the early 1990s to develop a strategic plan that would distinguish Country Style from all competing coffee and doughnut shops. To begin, consumer research was conducted in three of the company's distinctively different major markets in order to determine strengths and weaknesses as perceived by the customer, to explore the image of Country Style, and to examine consumers' likes and dislikes. The results pointed the company towards a program that would undertake a complete redesign of the visual aspects of Country Style and how it is perceived by the public.

Working with a design company, Shikatani LaCroix Design Inc., Country Style designed facilities that would meet the needs of the company and its customers for many years. A complete redesign was undertaken of the exterior of stores, inside and outside signs, interior layouts, service areas, display areas, product presentation, merchandising, and product line components. A new colour scheme, a more comfortable store ambience, and new graphics on all point-of-purchase materials and packaging were part of the new look for Country Style. All components of the program were incorporated into new stores and renovated premises beginning in late 1993.

According to Peter Mertens, executive vice-president, customer response to the new look has been excellent and results are better than anticipated. Changing the image of Country Style by virtually repackaging the entire company is an integral part of a strategy that involves an aggressive expansion across Canada in the near future.[1]

When we think of brand names, most of us probably tend to think of products that we use often and that we have been using or at least have been familiar with for many years. Certainly, many well-established brands have been part of our consumer lives for 50 years or more. They include Tetley tea, Campbell's soup, Kodak film, Christie's biscuits, and Wrigley chewing gum. But brand names are just as important in the marketing of services. A retail store name is really a brand, as are such names as Air Canada, Delta Hotels, and Canada's Wonderland, although these are not applied to tangible products. As we will see in this chapter, some retailer names have become so trusted and accepted by Canadians that they constitute widely regarded brand names in their own right.

The approach that Country Style is taking to differentiate itself from the competition is the equivalent of a brand repositioning, as we discussed in Chapter 10. Management at Country Style, a brand that has been prominent in coffee and doughnut retailing for more than 30 years, has decided that the brand needs some rejuvenation. If it is to remain competitive, this brand must be seen by prospective customers to be able to offer as much as or more than competitors such as Tim Horton's, Second Cup, A.L. Van Houtte, Starbucks, and Timothy's. The market is heating up as Canadians continue to increase their consumption of coffee. A stale brand, like stale doughnuts, won't succeed in this business.

## BRANDS

The word *brand* is a comprehensive term, and it includes other, narrower terms. A **brand** is a name, term, symbol, or special design, or some combination of these elements, that is intended to identify the goods or services of one seller or a group of sellers. A brand differentiates one seller's products or services from those of competitors. A brand **name** consists of words, letters, and/or numbers that can be *vocalized.* A brand **mark** is the part of the brand that appears in the form of a symbol, design, or distinctive colouring or lettering. It is recognized by sight but may not be expressed when a person pronounces the brand name. Ski-Doo, McCain, Gillette, and Robin Hood are brand names. Brand marks are illustrated by the picture of Robin Hood on the flour package, the distinctive CN logo of Canadian National, and the Root Bear character who promotes A&W. These marks, logos, or designs are usually registered and may be used only by the company that owns the mark.

**A company with a well-known trademark must defend itself.**

XEROX
You can't Xerox a Xerox on a Xerox.
But we don't mind at all if you copy a copy on a Xerox copier.
In fact, we prefer it. Because the Xerox trademark should only identify products made by us. Like Xerox copiers and Xerox printing systems.
As a trademark, the term Xerox should always be used as an adjective, followed by a noun. And it is never used as a verb. Of course, helping us protect our trademark also helps you.
Because you'll continue to get what you're actually asking for.
And not an inferior copy.
XEROX The Document Company
© 1991 XEROX CORPORATION. XEROX® The Document Company and Document Machines are trademarks of XEROX CORPORATION.

A **trademark** is defined as a brand that is given legal protection because, under the law, it has been appropriated by one seller. Thus *trademark* is essentially a legal term. All trademarks are brands and thus include the words, letters, or numbers that can be pronounced. They may also include a pictorial design (brand mark). Some people erroneously believe that the trademark is only the pictorial part of the brand.

One major method of classifying brands is on the basis of who owns them — producers or retailers. Major brands such as Sony, Zenith, Arrow, Sunlight, GWG, and Kellogg are producers' brands, while Motomaster, President's Choice, Birkdale, Viking, Kenmore, Body Shop, and Life are all brands that are owned by retailers.

The term *national* has been used for many years to describe producer-brand ownership, while brands owned by retailers are generally referred to as *private* brands or private labels. However, more acceptable terminology for many marketers would be the terms *producer* and *retailer* brands. To say that a brand of a small manufacturer of poultry feed in British Columbia, who markets in only two or three Western provinces, is a *national brand*, while those of Canadian Tire, Shoppers Drug Mart, Eaton's, Loblaws, and Sears are private brands, seems to be misusing these terms to some extent. Nevertheless, the brands of retailers continue to be referred to as *private labels*.

The issue of trademark protection arises quite often in marketing. In 1994, a Canadian retailer, Business Depot Limited, was granted a preliminary injunction by the Federal Court of Canada to prevent the largest office-supply warehouse chain in the United States, Office Depot Inc., from opening stores in Ontario. The court decided there was a serious legal question involved in the use of similar trademarks by competing companies in the same location and that Business Depot had established extensive goodwill with its trademark in Ontario and could lose market share if customers were to go to an Office Depot store thinking it was a Business Depot outlet.[2] It is important to note that trademark protection under Canadian law extends not only to exact copies but to similar representations of brands as well.

The similarity of private-label and national-brand products also has the potential to cause concerns over trademark infringement. In 1994, a giant British retail food chain, Sainsbury's, joined with Canadian private-label soft drinks producer, Cott Corporation, to introduce a new Sainsbury's cola into the company's stores throughout the United Kingdom. The problem was that the new Sainsbury's cola can was strikingly similar to Coca-Cola's Classic Coke. Both were red and white cans. Where Coke had the words "Coca-Cola" running vertically down the can, Sainsbury's had substituted "Cola," written in a similar script. The Sainsbury's can also bore the word "Classic." Probably in the interest of preserving good retailer-supplier relations, the case never got to court as Sainsbury's eventually agreed to withdraw the offending design.[3]

## WHAT'S IN A NAME?

A history of brand marketing will tell us that once a brand establishes a position of brand leadership in a product category, this position is often maintained over a very long period of time. Many of the leading brands that we buy today were purchased regularly by our parents and even our grandparents. Brands that continue to dominate their consumer product categories include Kodak, General Electric, Kellogg, Levi, Kraft, Nabisco, Tide, and Campbell.

The development and protection of brand names has become a very important element of marketing management and one that demands increased attention all the time. Companies such as Colgate-Palmolive have made conscious decisions to manage their brand names in such a way as to dominate a product category. For example, this company has made a commitment to position Colgate as an all-purpose supplier of oral-health products. The importance of the Colgate name is summed up in a comment from Patrick Knight, former vice-president of marketing for Colgate-Palmolive: "We now consider the most valuable assets we have to be our trademarks."[4]

Such an attitude towards successful brands has led major companies to ensure that their brand names are assigned a value and are shown as assets on their balance sheets. Many of the leading brands have been the major targets in corporate takeovers as the purchasing companies have realized that the equity represented in successful brands is considerably more valuable than factories and distribution systems.[5]

Equally important is the value of established brands in allowing their owners to apply the brands to new products. As the cost of acquiring established brands increases, as does the cost and risk of introducing new products, many companies have been turning in recent years to the launching of *brand extensions* as a way of trading on the success of established brands and reducing the risk of new product failure. Procter & Gamble now offers several varieties of its market-leading Tide laundry detergent. Mars chocolate bars are now sold in a white chocolate version, as well as a frozen ice-cream product.

Some companies have succeeded in keeping their brands successful and before the purchasing public for many years. Christie Brown and Company, the makers of such cookies and crackers as Oreo, Ritz, Arrowroot, Chips Ahoy, and Triscuit, have been making cookies in Canada since 1861. Triscuit Crackers date from 1895, Honey Maid Graham Wafers from 1900, and Ritz from 1935. Today, the success of the Christie's brands is obvious, and many have spawned brand extensions. More than 29 million Ritz crackers, in several varieties, are baked *daily*. More than 500 million Oreo cookies are consumed annually in Canada, and the brand is now available in double crème, chocolate-covered, and mint varieties, as well as several produced for special occasions.[6]

By stretching the original successful brand name to cover a number of brand extension products, the marketer is trading on the success of the original brand, but is running some risk at the same time. Clearly, there may be some new products to which the original brand should not be applied. This raises the question of how far the successful brand can be "extended" before the marketer is stretching the credibility of the link between the brand and the product. Colgate can with confidence launch a line of toothbrushes, dental floss, and mouthwash, but would consumers buy Colgate sunglasses or suntan lotion?[7] When Pepsi Max was launched, there was some question concerning whether it was an appropriate extension to the Pepsi-Cola brand. Because the new product was a super-sweetened diet cola, some Pepsi executives were concerned that it would cannibalize sales of Diet Pepsi.[8]

Brands make it easy for consumers to identify goods or services. Brands also help assure purchasers they are getting comparable quality when they reorder. For sellers, brands can be advertised and recognized when displayed on shelves in a store. Branding also helps sellers control their market because buyers will not confuse one branded product with another. Branding reduces price comparisons because it is hard to compare prices on two items with different brands. Finally, for sellers branding can add a measure of prestige to otherwise ordinary commodities (Sunkist oranges, Sifto salt, Lantic sugar, Highliner fish, Chiquita bananas).

### Reasons for Not Branding

The two major responsibilities inherent in brand ownership are (1) to promote the brand and (2) to maintain a consistent quality of output. Many firms do not brand their products because they are unable or unwilling to assume those responsibilities.

Some items are not branded because of the difficulty of differentiating the products of one firm from those of another. Clothespins, nails, and industrial raw materials (coal, cotton, wheat) are examples of goods for which product differentiation (including branding) is generally unknown. The physical nature of some items, such as fresh fruits and vegetables, may discourage branding. However, now that these products are often packaged in typically purchased quantities, brands are being applied to the packages.

Producers frequently do not brand that part of their output that is below their usual quality. Products graded as seconds or imperfects are sold at a cut price and are often distributed through channels different from those used for usual-quality goods.

**Mr. Christie sure makes successful brands.**

## MARKETING AT WORK

### FILE 11-1 MOST MAJOR BRANDS TRAVEL VERY WELL

Politically, aspirations of a unified Europe might have been placed on the back burner, but in terms of pan-European marketing, dreams have become the reality. With a select group of six multinationals (the first five of which are American) owning half the companies on the Nielsen-Checkout Top 100 list of Europe's top 100 brands, Europeans are witnessing a homogenization of everything from the brands they buy to their eating and washing habits to their very cultures. Not only is Coca-Cola one of the top three brands in the United Kingdom, it is also in the top three in Germany, France, Italy, and Spain.

All of this Europeanization is the result of recent multibillion-dollar takeovers that have created new food empires. The cigarette company Philip Morris, for example, has swallowed up Kraft Foods and Jacob Suchard, while Nestlé has gobbled up Rowntree and Perrier. Michael Perry, chairman of Unilever, which leads the pack with sales of $5.7 billion among the top 100 brands alone, claims: "Well-defined and genuine consumer constituencies are developing — groups of people in different countries and cultures who share common tastes and interests." Unilever's aim is "to define the need, create the brand and move it around the world at the marketing equivalent of the speed of light," a goal achieved by classic brand building, joint ventures, and the mopping up of small companies.

Such steps have been accompanied by the concentration of production and marketing centres in order to maximize economies of scale. Yet many, including Perry himself, are aware of the danger of becoming producer-driven, lowest-common-denominator marketers. After all, just how far can a brand be stretched across national and regional boundaries before it snaps?

Source: Alan Mitchell, "One Europe, One Taste?" *The Times* (London), November 10, 1993, p. 30.

### Selecting a Good Brand Name

Some brand names are so good that they contribute to the sales success of the product or service; others appear to be so poor or inappropriate that they would appear to contribute little if anything to sales success and may even seem to be a factor in market failures. Some products seem to have been successful despite having names that may appear to add little to their appeal. Some brand names attain considerable value over time and remain consumer favourites for many years.

**The Challenge** Today, selecting a good name for a product or service is more challenging than ever. The reason is that we are running out of possibilities — and many of the good names have already been used. There are about 10,000 new products launched annually in North America, yet the standard desk-size dictionary contains only about 50,000 words. When one considers that a new brand can't be labelled Panasonic, Oreo, Esso, or Timex, because these brands have been used successfully for many years, and that there are many other words one would not want to have associated with one's product or service, it is no surprise that companies often resort to words that aren't really words, or that they bring out the new product as an extension of an already-successful brand.

The need for names and brands that are likely to contribute to a product's success has led to the establishment of companies that specialize in coming up with attractive and appealing brand names. These firms will use data base searches and will rely on unusual sources to identify likely names. Some even employ qualified linguists on staff. They often come up with names that aren't part of any language: Pentium (Intel's new microprocessor chip), Zoloft (a new pharmaceutical product), Lexus, Acura, and Compaq. The

TABLE 11-1 The leading beer brands in Canada

***Some of the market leaders have been in the market for many years, while some market share is being captured by new market entrants such as the ice beers. The top 12 brands accounted for 62% of the market in 1993, up from 55% in 1992.***

| Rank | | | 1993* | | 1992* | |
|---|---|---|---|---|---|---|
| 1993 | 1992 | Brand | Million hectolitres | Share % | Million hectolitres | Share % |
| 1 | 1 | Blue/Blue Light (L) | 2,595 | 15.0 | 2,992 | 16.0 |
| 2 | 2 | Canadian/Cdn. Light (M) | 1,211 | 7.0 | 2,244 | 12.0 |
| 3 | 3 | Export (M) | 1,038 | 6.0 | 1,309 | 7.0 |
| 3 | 4 | Budweiser (L) | 1,038 | 6.0 | 935 | 5.0 |
| 4 | – | Labatt Ice (L) | 865 | 5.0 | – | – |
| 5 | 4 | Coors/Coors Light (M) | 692 | 4.0 | 935 | 5.0 |
| 5 | 4 | Molson Special Dry (M) | 692 | 4.0 | 935 | 5.0 |
| 6 | 4 | Labatt Genuine Draft (L) | 605 | 3.5 | 935 | 5.0 |
| 7 | – | Canadian Ice (M) | 519 | 3.0 | – | – |
| 7 | 5 | Labatt 50 (L) | 519 | 3.0 | 748 | 4.0 |
| 7 | – | Wildcat/Wildcat Strong (L) | 519 | 3.0 | – | – |
| 8 | 5 | O'Keefe Ale (M) | 432 | 2.5 | 748 | 4.0 |
| | | Other | 8,574 | 38.0 | 8,415 | 45.0 |
| | | Total Market (Estimated) | 17,300 | 100.0 | 18,700 | 100.0 |

* 12 months ended November; (L) = Labatt; (M) = Molson; 1 hectolitre = 100 litres

Data Source: *Equity Research Associates*. Table adapted from Marina Strauss, "Brewers Concentrate on the Flagship Labels," *Globe and Mail*, June 9, 1994, p. B6. Reprinted with permission from *The Globe and Mail.*

creation of a new brand name will often involve research to determine that consumers will react positively to the brand being proposed. It also is not an inexpensive process, as some firms will charge $25,000 or more for a new brand name.[9]

**Desirable Characteristics** Five characteristics determine the desirability of a brand name for a product or service.[10] It is difficult to think of a brand that has all five. Still, a brand should possess as many of these characteristics as possible:

- Suggest something about the product's characteristics — its benefits, use, or action. Some names that suggest desirable benefits include Beautyrest, Cold-spot, Motomaster, and La-Z-Boy. Product use and action are suggested by Minute Rice, Dustbuster, Spic and Span, Gleem, and Easy-Off.
- Be easy to pronounce, spell, and remember. Simple, short, one-syllable names such as Tide, Ban, Aim, and Raid are helpful.
- Be distinctive. Brands with names like National, Star, Ideal, or Standard fail on this point.
- Be adaptable to new products that may be added to the product line. An innocuous name such as Kellogg, Lipton, or Jelinek may serve the purpose better than a highly distinctive name suggestive of product benefits. Frigidaire is an excellent name for a refrigerator and other cold-image products. But when the producer expanded its line of home appliances and added Frigidaire kitchen ranges, the name lost some of its sales appeal.
- Be capable of being registered and legally protected under the Trade Marks Act and other statutory or common laws.

### Protecting a Brand Name

Over a period of years, some brands have become so well accepted that the brand name is substituted for the **generic** name of the particular product. Examples of brand names that legally have become generic are linoleum, celluloid, cellophane, kerosene, shredded wheat, and nylon. Originally, these were trademarks limited to use by the owner.

A brand name can become generic in several ways. Sometimes the patent on a product expires. There is no simple generic name available and so the public continues to use the brand name as a generic name. This happened with shredded wheat, nylon, and cellophane. Sometimes a firm just does too good an advertising and selling job with an outstanding brand name. While not yet legally generic, names such as Xerox, Band-Aid, Scotch Tape, Ski-Doo, and Kleenex are on the borderline. They are outstanding brand names for the original product and have been promoted so well that many people use them generically.

It is the responsibility of the trademark owner to assert the company's rights in order to prevent the loss of the distinctive character of the trademark. A number of strategies are employed to prevent the brand name from falling into generic usage. The most common strategy is to ensure that the words "trade mark" or the letters "TM"® appear adjacent to the brand name wherever it appears.

A second strategy is to use two names — the brand name together with either the company's name or the generic name of the product. An example of this is the name "Thermos Vacuum Bottle," which is designed to suggest to the public that "Thermos" is but one brand of vacuum bottle and that the name "Thermos" should not be applied to all products in that product category.

A third strategy for protecting a trademark involves the incorporation into the trademark of a distinctive signature or logo. Many companies have adopted distinctive ways of presenting the brand name of their products so that the consumer is able to identify their products whenever they encounter the particular brand written as a certain script or type face.

Finally, the owner of a registered trademark must be willing to prosecute any other companies attempting to market products under a brand name that is identical to or similar to the registered brand name. By prosecuting such infringements of the trademark protection, the company is demonstrating to the courts that it is actively protecting its right to use of the brand and is guarding against the brand falling into generic usage. If the owner company fails to prosecute infringements, even if it decides to prosecute at a later date after other companies have adopted the brand, the distinctive character of the trademark will be lost and the courts are likely to rule that the original owner no longer has exclusive right to use of the brand name, as it is in the public domain. Some companies seek to show competitors or others who wish to make use of registered trademarks that they are willing to take legal action to protect their trademarks. An example of advertising that is designed to achieve this purpose is presented on page 313.

## BRANDING STRATEGIES

Both producers and intermediaries face strategic decisions regarding the branding of their goods or services.

### Producers' Strategies

Producers must decide whether to brand their products and whether to sell any or all of their output under intermediaries' brands.

**Marketing Entire Output under Producers' Own Brands** Companies that market their entire output under their own brands usually are very large, well-financed, and well-managed. Polaroid, Maytag, and IBM are examples. They have broad product lines, well-established distribution systems, and large shares of the market. Only a small percentage of manufacturers follow this policy, and their number seems to be decreasing.

Some reasons for adopting this policy have already been covered in the section on the importance of branding to the seller. In addition, intermediaries often prefer to handle producers' brands, especially when the brands have high consumer acceptance.

**Branding of Fabricating Parts and Materials** Some producers of fabricating materials and parts (products used in the further manufacturing of other goods) will brand their products.[11] This strategy is used in the marketing of Fiberglas insulation, Pella windows, Acrilan fabrics, and many automotive parts — spark plugs, batteries, oil filters, and so on.

Underlying this strategy is the seller's desire to develop a market preference for its branded part of material. For instance, G.D. Searle wants to build a market situation in which customers will insist on food products sweetened with NutraSweet. In addition, the parts manufacturer wants to persuade the producer of the finished item that using the branded materials will help sell the end product. In our example, the Searle Company hopes to convince food manufacturers that their sales will be increased if their products contain NutraSweet.

Certain product characteristics lend themselves to the effective use of this strategy. First, it helps if the product is also a consumer good that is bought for replacement purposes. This factor encourages the branding of Champion spark plugs, Atlas batteries, and Fram oil filters, for example. Second, the seller's situation is improved if the item is a major part of the finished product — a microprocessor within a personal computer, for instance. Intel Corp. developed the slogan "Intel Inside" to strengthen its product's position.[12]

**Marketing under Intermediaries' Brands** A widespread strategy is for producers to brand part of all their output with the brands of their intermediaries' customers. For the manufacturer, this intermediaries' brand business generates additional sales volume and profit dollars. Orders typically are large, payment is prompt, and a producer's working-capital position is improved. Also, manufacturers may utilize their production resources more effectively, including their plant capacities. Furthermore, refusing to sell under a retailer's or wholesaler's brand will not eliminate competition from this source. Many intermediaries want to market under their own brands, so if one manufacturer refuses their business, they will simply go to another.

Probably the most serious limitation to marketing under intermediaries' brands is that a producer may be at the mercy of the intermediaries. This problem grows as the proportion of that producer's output going to intermediaries' brands increases.

### Intermediaries' Strategies

The question of whether or not to brand must also be answered by intermediaries. There are two usual strategies, as follows:

**Carry Only Producers' Brands** Most retailers and wholesalers follow this policy because they are not able to take on the dual burdens of promoting a brand and maintaining its quality.

**Carry Intermediaries' Brands Alone or with Producers' Brands** Many large retailers and some large wholesalers have their own brands. Intermediaries may find it advantageous to market their own brands for several reasons. First, this strategy increases their control over their market. If customers prefer a given retailer's brand, they can get it only from that retailer's store. Furthermore, intermediaries can usually sell their brands at prices below those of producers' brands and still earn higher gross margins. This is possible because intermediaries can buy at lower costs. The costs may be lower because (1) manufacturers' advertising and selling costs are not included in their prices, or (2) producers are anxious to get the extra business to keep their plants running in slack seasons.

Intermediaries have more freedom in pricing products sold under their own labels. Products carrying a retailer's brand become differentiated products, and this hinders price comparisons that might be unfavourable to that retailer. Also, prices on manufacturers' brands can be cut drastically by competing retail stores. This last point is what has been happening in recent years in the marketing of clothing with designer labels such as Calvin Klein, Simon Chang, Ralph Lauren, and Alfred Sung. Some of the large retailers in their upper-priced clothing departments have increased their stocks of apparel carrying the store's own brand. These stores (Eaton's, The Bay, Harry Rosen, for example), have cut back on products with designer brands such as Calvin Klein and others. The reason for this brand-switching is that some designer-labelled products are now available at much lower prices in stores such as K mart, Zellers, and other "off-price retailers."

The strategy of marketing as many products as possible under the retailer's own label has met with considerable success for such Canadian retailers as Loblaw and Canadian Tire. In fact, Loblaw is among the leading companies in the world at the private-label game, creating a situation where more than 30 percent of all Loblaw sales is accounted for by private-label products such as President's Choice Decadent Chocolate Chip cookies, Memories of Szechwan Peanut Sauce and Dressing, and PC Cola. In fact, Loblaw has been so successful at developing the market for private-label products that the company has licensed the President's Choice brand to chains around the world. Loblaw is an excellent example of how private-label products can replace national brands in the consumer's mind when the retailer develops products and value in which the consumer can be confident. Brand loyalty is certainly not dead, but more and more consumers are transferring their loyalty to brands that are manufactured (often by the major makers of national brands) for the retail chains. The success of Loblaw's private-label products is reflected in the fact that at one point in 1992, PC Memories of Kobe, a "two-minute Miracle Tamari Dressing," outsold all pourable salad dressings in Loblaw stores; in some stores, Memories of Szechwan Peanut Sauce and Dressing outsells all varieties of ketchup![13]

## MARKETING AT WORK

### FILE 11-2 THE COLA WARS HAVE SOME NEW WARRIORS

It used to be that there was Coca-Cola and there was Pepsi-Cola. These two soft drink superpowers regularly took to the arena of glitzy, high-priced advertising campaigns to wage continuous wars against each other for domination of Canada's fizzy beverage market.

But while this terrible twosome was locked in battle, along came Gerry Pencer and the Cott Corporation, who, while the big boys' backs were turned, instigated a revolution in beverage retailing by transforming a small, private-label product into a profitable and formidable foe. Beginning in 1989 as a regional bottler who supplied mainly Quebec retailers, Cott's fortunes took off when it became the private-label supplier of President's Choice Cola for Loblaw Co. Ltd. of Ontario. With the purchase of Cott's generic cola, Loblaw was considerably increasing its profit margins by selling the cola as a premium product under its own private label. Meanwhile, the concept of buying high-quality, high-value beverages, trendily packaged, and at a third of the price of its two national competitors ($4.99 for a 24 case of President's Choice compared with $6.99 for a case of Coke or Pepsi), made it an instant hit with consumers, who were soon buying six cases of President's Choice soft drinks for every four cases of Coke and Pepsi combined. Before long, Cott expanded and was putting fizz in the glasses of more than half of Ontario's soft-drink guzzlers, in the meantime allowing Ontario retailers to earn more from soft drinks than retailers in any other market.

It was a hit strategy. Cott could compete on price with Coke and Pepsi but make big savings on advertising and distribution costs. It could also compete with the new warehouse stores such as Price Club and Costco by offering distinct products that had an image of value for the dollar. Moreover, by going further and offering retailers not just a generic product but an entire consulting package developed to offer services ranging from advice on marketing and promotion to packaging and store layout, Cott made itself a force to be reckoned with. It also witnessed its sales rocketing from $31 million in 1989 to close to $600 million in 1993. Having successfully branched into the United States, Cott is now the largest private-label bottler in North America and is already moving into markets in Europe, Australia, and South Africa.

In addition, in 1993 Coca-Cola's sales volume dropped 23 percent from the year before (giving it 24.5 percent of the Canadian market, and Pepsi-Cola's increased a mere 6 percent (allowing it to hold onto 32.4 percent of the market), while private labels grew a whopping 54 percent to grab a 27.3 percent share of the market. Cott's phenomenal success seems to have done the trick in forcing Coke and Pepsi to finally wake up and smell the cola. And the two are each preparing some brutal offensives in order to beat Cott at its own game.

Toronto-based Coca-Cola Canada, for instance, is cutting costs by closing plants and laying off workers in an attempt to shift from decentralized warehousing to a more efficient distribution system based on information technology that will move the product from the producer to the retailer, and hence to the consumer, at a much quicker rate. The company's overall approach is to offer more value to the consumer by toning down its glitzy ads in favour of more solid information that will tout new initiatives such as easy-to-handle contour Coke bottles and the Easy Pak, easy-to-carry cube-shaped boxes that hold 24 cans. Practical benefits will be emphasized and promotional price "specials" will be offered — such as the $1-off coupons Canadians will receive for the purchase of an Easy Pak. Other new tactics include printing "best-before-dates" on Coke packaging in response to complaints about stale products and to the marked shift away from Coke's traditional youth market; the company will target older, female consumers — 35 years and up — who now constitute the principal buyers of soft drinks.

Like Coke, Pepsi-Cola Canada is also overhauling, streamlining, and downsizing its operations as well as turning its attentions to new packaging and lower prices. It has introduced one-litre, wide-mouth bottles of Pepsi called Big Slams, aimed at teenagers who can drink it all in one serving, as well as 355-mL cans of Pepsi Max, which boasts one-third the calories of regular Pepsi, in order to entice the third of cola drinkers who switch back and forth between regular and diet sodas. It will be delivering free samples of Pepsi Max to homes across Canada accompanied by coupons offering customers 50 cents off on future purchases.

Both cola giants are also placing increased emphasis on distributing their "New-Age alternative beverages" — Coke's Minute Maid juices and Nestlé iced tea and Pepsi's Clearly Canadian mineral water, Ocean Spray juices, and Lipton iced tea — which have sold consistently well and offer healthier profit margins than soft drinks. Pepsi has even gone so far as to install, free of charge for retailers, thousands of new coolers, including compact coolers at checkout counters in order to stimulate "impulse buying" of these drinks. Both Coke and Pepsi, however, swear that price slashing will not be the main focus of their competitive strategies. They maintain they'll try to remain competitive within the market, but add that they intend to do so by concentrating on other elements in the marketing mix. In the meantime, the soft drink war wages on.

Sources: Bud Jorgensen, "Cott Cashes in, Makes Enemies," *Globe and Mail*, January 8, 1994, pp. B1, B6; John Heinzl, "Cott Shares Sink on Pop War Fears," *Globe and Mail*, January 19, 1994, p. B9; Marina Strauss, "Coca Cola Closing 16 Plants," *Globe and Mail*, November 25, 1993, p. B1, B10; Marina Strauss, "Cola Price War Looms as Pepsi Cuts Predicted," *Globe and Mail*, November 30, 1993, p. B1, B8; Marina Strauss, "Pepsi-Cola Launches 'All-Out Assault'," *Globe and Mail*, December 2, 1993, p. B4; Marina Strauss, "Coke Switches Marketing Strategy," *Globe and Mail*, January 18, 1993, p. B16.

### Strategies Common to Producers and Intermediaries

Producers and intermediaries alike must adopt some strategy with respect to branding their product mix and branding for market saturation.

**Branding a Line of Products** At least four different strategies are widely used by firms that sell more than one product.

- The same "family" or "blanket" brand may be placed on all products. This policy is followed by Heinz, Catelli, Campbell's, McCain's, and others in the food field, as well as by Proctor-Silex and Black & Decker.
- A separate name may be used for each product. This strategy is employed by Procter & Gamble and Lever Brothers.
- A separate family brand may be applied to each grade of product or to each group of similar products. Sears groups its major home appliances under the Kenmore name, its paints and home furnishings under Harmony House, and its insurance under Allstate.
- The company trade name may be combined with an individual name for the product. Thus there is Johnson's Pledge, Kellogg's Rice Krispies, Molson Golden, and Ford Mustang.

When used wisely, a **family-brand strategy** has considerable merit. This strategy makes it much simpler and less expensive to introduce new related products to a line. Also, the general prestige of a brand can be spread more easily if it appears on several products rather than on only one. A family brand is best suited for a marketing situation where the products are related in quality, in use, or in some other manner. When Black & Decker, a manufacturer of power tools, purchased General Electric's line of small appliances, the Black & Decker brand was put on those appliances, *but* not immediately. Because of the perceived differences between kitchen products and workroom products, Black & Decker realized it was a risky proposition to switch brands. Consequently, the company mounted a year-long brand-transition campaign before making the change. Also, during those years, Black & Decker introduced several other houseware products, and this helped in the General Electric-Black & Decker brand transition.

The success of major brands and families of brands certainly makes it easier for companies, whether manufacturers or intermediaries, to introduce new products under the established family brand or as brand extensions to well-established brands. This is obvious when one considers the number of varieties of Oreo cookies and Ritz crackers now produced by Christie Brown and the wide array of products marketed under the Motomaster label by Canadian Tire. But the use of family brands and established brands to launch new products places a burden on the brand owner to maintain consistently high quality across all products marketed under that brand. One bad item can reflect unfavourably on other products that carry the brand and may even lead to the creation of a negative image for the overall brand.

**Branding for Market Saturation** Frequently, to increase its degree of market saturation, a firm will employ a **multiple-brand strategy**. Suppose, for example, that a company has built one type of sales appeal around a given brand. To reach other segments of the market, the company can use other appeals with other brands. For example, Procter & Gamble markets a line of detergents that includes Tide, Bold, Cheer, Oxydol, and Ivory Snow. There may be some consumers who feel that Tide, even with its many varieties (phosphate-free, with bleach, unscented, liquid, and "regular"), is not suitable for washing lingerie and other delicate clothing. For these people, Procter & Gamble offers Ivory Snow, a detergent whose image is gentler than that of Tide and one that trades on its association with the purity and gentleness of Ivory soap. With this brand line-up, Procter & Gamble is assured of having a brand or a brand variation to appeal to every segment of the detergent market.

### Building and Using Brand Equity

Companies as diverse as Sears, Canadian Tire, The Gap, Hilton, Christie, and Imperial Oil recognize that the brands they own may be more valuable than their physical assets such as buildings and equipment.[14] What we are talking about here is *brand equity*, one of the hottest topics in marketing during the 1990s. **Brand equity** is the value a brand adds to a product.[15] In the minds of many consumers, just having a brand name such as Sony, Kenmore, or Reebok on a product adds value to it. Beyond a product's value in its potential to do what it's supposed to do, a brand adds value to that product through its name awareness and its connotations of favourable attributes (such as quality or economy).

We tend to think of brand equity as a positive aspect of a product or service. Occasionally, a brand will lack equity or will even have a negative equity. That is, the brand adds nothing to or even detracts from the value of the basic product or service. In the 1970s, there were so many problems with the Firenza car that the brand came to epitomize negative brand equity in the auto industry.

If you're not convinced that a brand name by itself can have much value, consider the results of two studies. In one, the proportion of subjects choosing cornflakes cereal jumped from 47 percent when the brand was not known to 59 percent when the brand was identified as Kellogg's. In another study, when physically identical TV sets were sold under both the General Electric and Hitachi brands, Hitachi outsold GE by two to one — even though the Hitachi sets were priced $75 higher than the GE models![16] It's evident that Kellogg's, Hitachi, and many other brands have substantial equity.

Building a brand's equity consists of developing a favourable, memorable, and consistent image — no easy task.[17] Product quality and advertising play vital roles in this endeavour. Substantial brand equity provides many benefits to the firm that owns the brand:

- The brand itself can become a differential advantage, influencing consumers to buy a particular product. Examples include BMW, Häagen Dazs, and Kenmore (Sears' brand of home appliances), to name several.
- Because it is expensive and time consuming to build brand equity, it creates a barrier for companies that want to enter the market with a similar product.
- Brand equity can help a product survive changes in the operating environment, such as a business crisis or a shift in consumer tastes. Tylenol seemed to fare better than Perrier when both products faced crises involving their purity.

Brand equity is most often used to expand a product line, especially to extend a brand into new varieties or even new products. In fact, it may be argued that brand extensions are not possible unless the brand has established considerable equity.[18] We have cited a number of examples in this chapter of brands that have been extended in this way — an expanded line of Oreo cookies from Christie, Tetley's extension into flavoured iced teas, and the ever-growing line of coffee, food, and related products at Tim Horton's. The rationale for using an existing, strong brand name on a new item or line is that the brand's equity will convey a favourable impression of the product and increase the likelihood that consumers will at least try it.

If a brand has abundant equity, that does not necessarily mean it should be applied to other products. Procter & Gamble decided its hugely successful Crest name should be used on different kinds of toothpaste but not on other product categories such as mouthwash. When it was developing a spaghetti sauce, Campbell determined its popular brand name would not convey an Italian image, so it selected Prego as the name for its new sauce. Also, strong equity does not guarantee success for new items or lines using the well-regarded brands. There are many examples of new products carrying well-known brands that have failed nevertheless, simply because they were not acceptable to consumers.

The issue of relative brand equity is most obvious in the 1990s in the battle that is raging between established national brands on the one hand and generally newer private-label or retailers' own brands on the other. In fact, this has developed into one of the most important issues in marketing today. This battle of the brands is most obvious in grocery and personal care products — the items that most households buy regularly from their neighbourhood supermarkets and drugstores. As consumer confidence in the quality of such private-label products has grown, so too has their share of the packaged-goods business. These retailer-owned brands now account for 36 percent of the grocery business in Britain and more than 20 percent in both Canada and the United States. Such well-known and successful private brands as President's Choice (Loblaw), Life (Shoppers Drug Mart), and Master Choice (A&P) have carved out a significant niche in the market for many products.

The rising success of private-label brands has been described by some commentators as a reflection of a decline in brand loyalty and the tendency for consumers to stick with their favourite brands. But, in fact, the consumer has simply replaced loyalty to national brands with loyalty to the brands of specific retailers. The equity in retailer brands has increased in recent years, while that of some of the large manufacturers of national brands has undoubtedly slipped. This phenomenon of growing acceptance of private-label products is international in scope and has been attributed to three related causes:

- The first is perceived product parity. Research conducted by the advertising agency BBDO indicates that nearly two-thirds of consumers around the world believe there are no relevant or discernible differences between brands across a broad range of products. Technological advances have raised the standards of manufacturing and the quality of products to the point where they are generally correct.
- The proliferation of new products that characterizes many product categories led to a fiercely competitive retail environment in which retailers sold shelf space to the highest bidder; many suppliers were forced to pay fees to retailers just to get their brands stocked. One result was that power in the distribution chain passed to the retailer who could control shelf space and pricing.
- As private-label products proliferated, consumers began to gain greater confidence in their quality and value. They were no longer the drab "no-name" products that had first appeared as generic brands in the 1970s. In fact, many of the private-label products are manufactured by the same companies that make the national brands, in the same factories, to the same high standards. Many private-label products now occupy premium status.[19]

## Trademark Licensing

An effective branding strategy that has grown by leaps and bounds in recent years is brand (or trademark) licensing. Under this strategy, the owner of a trademark grants permission (a licence) to other firms to use the owner's brand name, logotype (distinctive lettering and colouring), and/or character on the licensee's products. To illustrate, Coca-Cola has allowed (licensed) Murjani International to use the Coca-Cola name and distinctive lettering on a line of clothing (blue jeans, sweaters, shirts, jackets). The owner of the trademark characters in the "Peanuts" cartoon strip (Snoopy, Charlie Brown, Lucy, etc.) has licensed the use of these characters on many different products and services. Sears has introduced McKids, a line of children's clothing featuring McDonald's characters. The licensee typically pays a royalty of about 5 percent on the wholesale price of the product that carries the licensed trademark. However, this figure can vary depending on the perceived strength of the licensor's brand.

Strategy decisions must be made by both parties — the licensor and the licensee. Alfred Sung (a licensor) must ask, "Should we allow other firms to use our designer label?" A manufacturer of eyeglasses (a licensee) must ask, "Do we want to put out a line of high-fashion eyeglasses under the Alfred Sung name?"

Owners of well-known brands are interested in licensing their trademarks for various reasons. First, it can be very profitable since there is no expense involved on the part of the licensor. Second, there is a promotional benefit, because the licensor's name gets cir-

## MARKETING AT WORK

### FILE 11-3 SUCCESS MEANS MAKING YOUR MARK

Everybody knows the age-old motto: "A picture is worth a thousand words." Yet these days perhaps nobody is more aware of it than Canada's big companies, to whom corporate symbols have become an essential tool in visually stamping their identity on the public's consciousness. When the average Canadian's eyes alight on a blue squiggle and a stripe, they immediately conjure up "money, stability," and other elements associated with the Bank of Montreal. Such symbols are often used as trademarks, but a trademark can also be words, designs, or a combination of both. "Uh-huh!" is a registered trademark of Pepsi-Cola Co., while the phrase "Membership has its privileges" is owned by American Express.

The adoption of a corporate trademark is a complex affair. It should fit not only an individual organization's product or service, but the nature and aspirations of the people associated with it. To be successful, a trademark must flood the marketplace so that it becomes ingrained in the public's consciousness, yet simultaneously, it must reflect consumers' values. For example, consumers originally rejected the pillars that accompanied the Mutual Group's slogan, "Life is a mutual affair." The pillars were meant to evoke bank-like stability, but the public felt they lacked the warmth and humanity of the slogan. A subsequent logo — two faces joined in a stylized "M" — proved much more successful.

According to Toronto designer Chris Yaneff, "The key to a trademark is to be unique and different . . . . It has to be able to go on a sign five feet high . . . and to fit on the back of your fingernail." According to Yaneff, 85 percent of "marks" don't stick with the public because they are too complicated. Ultimately, in order to endure, a trademark must be clean and simple. After all, look at the Christian church. In its adoption of the cross, it has created one of the most successful corporate identities in the world, one that has stood the test of quite a few centuries.

Source: Sally Ritchie, "Powerful Symbols," *Globe and Mail*, August 31, 1993, p. B30.

culation far beyond the original trademarked article. Third, licensing can help protect the trademark. If Coca-Cola licenses its brand for use in a variety of product categories, it can block any other company from using that brand legally in those product categories.

For the company receiving the licence — the licensee — the strategy is a quick way to gain market recognition and to penetrate a new market. Today there is a high financial cost involved in establishing a new brand name. Even then there is no guarantee of success. It is a lot easier for an unknown firm to gain consumer acceptance of its product if that item carries a well-known brand.

### Strategic Branding of Services

Throughout this chapter, we have discussed the competitive edge that a well-selected brand can give to a product. These advantages are equally applicable to tangible goods and intangible services. Furthermore, the marketers of services have to make many of the same strategic branding decisions as do the marketers of tangible products. Perhaps the first of these decisions is to select a good brand name for the service.[20] In services marketing, more so than in the marketing of tangible goods, the company name typically serves as the brand name.

The characteristics of an effective service brand are much the same as for tangible goods. Thus, a service brand should be:

- *Relevant to the service or its benefits*. Ticketron, the sales agency that sells tickets to sporting events, concerts, and other major attractions, conveys the nature of the service and the electronic speed with which it is delivered. VISA suggests an international activity and is relevant for a global financial service. Instant Teller is a good name for the automatic

banking machines of the CIBC. Budget implies the best price for people who rent cars from that company. Four Seasons suggests a hotel chain that has something to offer year-round.
- *Distinctive*. This characteristic is difficult to communicate. The point is that companies should avoid branding their service with names that others could use. Thus, names like National, Canadian, and Royal should probably be avoided because, standing alone, they tell us nothing about the service or its benefits. When names such as these are used, the company will usually add words that tell us what service is being offered, such as Canadian *Airlines International*, Royal *Trust*, and National *Life Insurance*.

  Some service marketers differentiate themselves from the competition by using a symbol (usually referred to as a *logo*) or a distinctive colour. We are all familiar with the golden arches of McDonald's, the lion of the Royal Bank of Canada, and Air Canada's maple leaf. For colour, we see the green of the Toronto-Dominion Bank, the red of Scotiabank, the claret of CIBC, and the blue of the Bank of Montreal. The use of a person's name such as Harvey's, Eaton's, and Tilden, or a coined word, such as Avis, Re/Max, and AMEX, also offers distinctiveness, but it tells us little about the service being offered. This is the case until the name has been firmly established and it comes to mean something to the consumer. Certainly, many such names have become very well established in the marketplace.
- *Easy to pronounce and remember*. Simple, short names, such as Delta and A&W usually meet this criterion. Others, such as Aetna and Overwaitea, pose pronunciation problems for some people. Sometimes, unusual spelling aids in having the consumer remember the name — the reverse R in Toys " Я " Us, for example.
- *Adaptable to additional services or regions*. Companies that change their mix of services and their geographical locations over time should be flexible enough to adapt to these extensions of their operations. One Canadian bank, the Canadian Imperial Bank of Commerce, has shortened its name to CIBC in anticipation of expanding its range of financial services beyond banking. Many successful companies (Bank of Montreal, London Life, Great-West Life) have been able to establish national reputations despite the fact that their names suggest a regional association, although it may be easier for companies with names like Canada Life and Canada Trust to do so. When companies have names with geographic connotations, such as Canadian Pacific, they are often abbreviated when expansion takes place, as in CP Hotels. Airlines with names like Air BC and Air Atlantic are obviously regional carriers, while one named Air Nova may find it easier to expand beyond its original market area.

Another decision is whether to use family branding. Insurance companies and financial services firms often use the same brand name for the variety of services offered. On the other hand, the Canadian chartered banks generally operate their brokerage arms as separate entities. The Dylex Group operates its many different retail chains under a variety of names — including Fairweather, Tip Top, Harry Rosen, and Braemar.

Whether to get into trademark licensing is a strategic branding decision for many services firms. Companies, entertainers, and many professional sports teams, such as the Montreal Canadiens, Edmonton Oilers, and Toronto Blue Jays, license their names for use on many different products.

## PACKAGING

**Packaging** may be defined as all the activities of designing and producing the container or wrapper for a product. There are three reasons for packaging:

- Packaging serves several *safety and utilitarian purposes*. It protects a product on its route from the producer to the final customer, and in some cases even while it is being used by the customer. Effective packaging can help prevent ill-intentioned persons from tampering with products. Some protection is provided by "child-proof" closures on containers of medicines and other products that are potentially harmful to children. Also, compared with bulk items, packaged goods generally are more convenient, cleaner, and less susceptible to losses from evaporation, spilling, and spoilage.

- Packaging may be *part of a company's marketing program*. Packaging helps identify a product and thus may prevent substitution of competitive products. At the point of purchase, the package can serve as a silent sales person. Furthermore, the advertising copy on the package will last as long as the product is used in its packaged form. A package may be the only significant way in which a firm can differentiate its product. In the case of convenience goods or business operating supplies, for example, most buyers feel that one well-known brand is about as good as another.

  Some feature of the package may add sales appeal — a no-drip spout, a reusable jar, or a self-applicator (a bottle of shoe polish or glue with an applicator top, for example). By packaging their toothpaste in a pump dispenser — a product long used in Europe — Colgate and Close-Up brands increased their sales considerably. Crest and Aim later adopted the same type of packaging.
- A firm can package its product in a way that *increases profit and sales volume*. A package that is easy to handle or minimizes damage losses will cut marketing costs, thus boosting profit. On the sales side, packaged goods typically are more attractive and therefore better than items sold in bulk. Many companies have increased the sales volume of an article simply by redesigning its package. The Pears shampoo container is a good example of a package that holds appeal for both consumers and retailers. Its square shape and interlocking sides provide more efficient use of shelf space and, consequently, greater sales and profit per square foot.

### Importance of Packaging in Marketing

Historically, packaging was a production-oriented activity in most companies, performed mainly to obtain the benefits of protection and convenience. Today, however, the marketing significance of packaging is fully recognized, and packaging is truly a major competitive force in the struggle for markets. The widespread use of self-service selling and automatic vending means that the package must do the selling job at the point of purchase. Shelf space is often at a premium, and it is no simple task for manufacturers even to get their products displayed in a retail outlet. Most retailers are inclined to cater to producers that have used effective packaging.

In addition, the increased use of branding and the public's rising standards in health and sanitation have contributed to a greater awareness of packaging. Safety in packaging has become a prominent marketing and social issue in recent years. Extensive consumer use of microwave ovens has had a significant impact on packaging. Many food products are now packaged so they can go straight from the shelf or freezer into a microwave oven.

New developments in packaging, occurring rapidly and in a seemingly endless flow, require management's constant attention. We see new packaging materials replacing traditional ones, new shapes, new closures, and other new features (measured portions, metered flow). These all increase convenience for consumers and selling points for marketers. One relatively new development in packaging that will be particularly interesting to watch in the coming years is the use of aseptic containers — the well-known "drinking boxes" made of laminations of paper, aluminum foil, and polyethylene. The air-tight features of this container allow beverages and other products to be kept fresh for as long as five months without refrigeration, and it costs only about half as much as cans and 30 percent as much as bottles. It has been used widely in Canada to package juice and other drink products and is widely regarded as extremely convenient. We are likely to see its uses expand in the future, provided that issues related to its environmental impact are resolved.

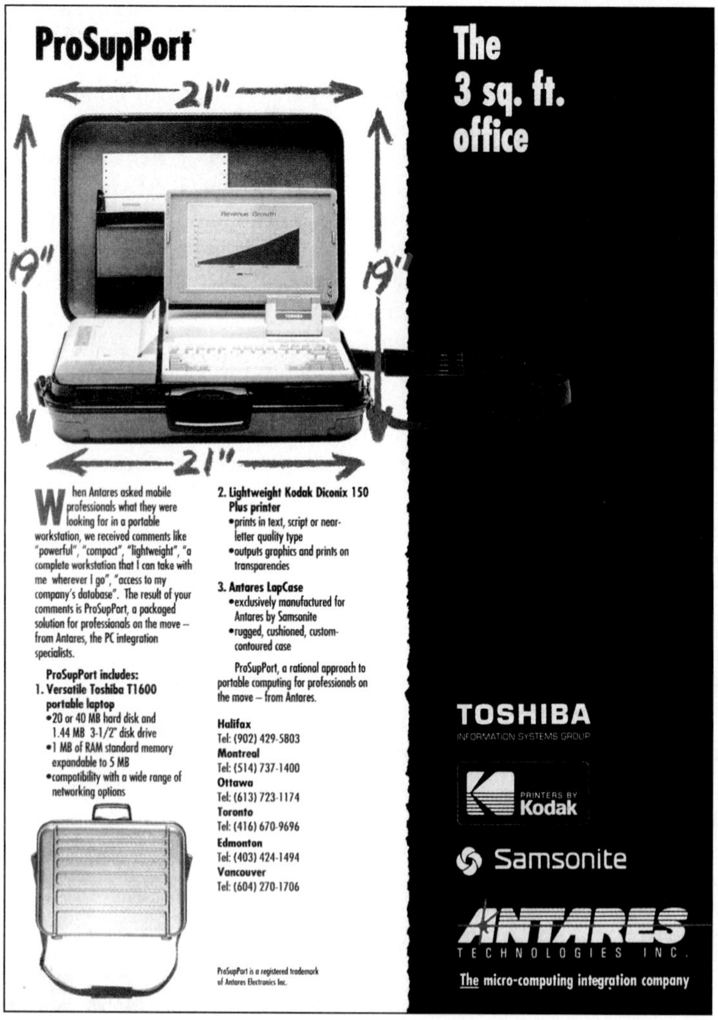


**Four companies combined to create this functional package.**

Packaging is an important marketing tool for companies that operate in international markets. Most countries have regulations governing the packaging of products and the wording that must appear on labels. A company that wishes to export its product to another country must, therefore, be aware of the packaging laws of that country. For example, companies in other countries that export to Canada and the Canadian importers that represent them have to be aware of Canadian packaging regulations pertaining to metric package sizes, bilingual labelling, and the standard sizes of packages used in some industries. In addition to regulations, exporters must understand that packages that work in one country may not be accepted in another, because of design, illustration, or colour.

## Packaging Strategies

**Changing the Package** In general, management has two reasons for considering a package change — to combat a decrease in sales and to expand a market by attracting new groups of customers. More specifically, a firm may want to correct a poor feature in the existing container, or a company may want to take advantage of new materials. Some companies change their containers to aid in promotional programs. A new package may be used as a major appeal in advertising copy, or because the old container may not show up well in advertisements.

**Packaging the Product Line** A company must decide whether to develop a family resemblance in the packaging of its several products. **Family packaging** involves the use of identical packages for all products or the use of packaging with some common feature. Campbell's, for example, uses virtually identical packaging on its condensed soup products. Management's philosophy concerning family packaging generally parallels its feelings about family branding. When new products are added to a line, promotional values associated with old products extend to the new ones. On the other hand, family packaging should be used only when the products are related in use and are of similar quality.

**Reuse Packaging** Another strategy to be considered is **reuse packaging**. Should the company design and promote a package that can serve other purposes after the original contents have been consumed? Glasses containing cheese can later be used to serve fruit juice. Baby-food jars make great containers for small parts such as nuts, bolts, and screws. Reuse packaging also should stimulate repeat purchases as the consumer attempts to acquire a matching set of containers.

**Multiple Packaging** For many years there has been a trend towards **multiple packaging**, or the practice of placing several units in one container. Dehydrated soups, motor oil, beer, golf balls, building hardware, candy bars, towels, and countless other products are packaged in multiple units. Test after test has proved that multiple packaging increases total sales of a product.

### Criticisms of Packaging

Packaging is in the forefront today because of its relationship to environmental pollution issues. Perhaps the biggest challenges facing packagers is how to dispose of used containers, which are a major contributor to the solid-waste disposal problem. Consumers' desire for convenience (in the form of throw-away containers) conflicts with their desire for a clean environment.

In many ways, the debate over the environmental impact of packaging often appears impossible to resolve, as the issue of the disposability of packaging is weighed against that of the use of energy and other effects associated with manufacturing it. For example, we are seeing a growing number of consumer and industrial products packaged in environmentally friendly packages. LMG Reliance, a Winnipeg company, manufactures the Enviro-Chem agricultural chemical container, part of a closed-loop recycling system that involves the collection of used containers from landfill sites for recycling. Dow Canada produces its Fantastik cleaner in a stand-up pouch refill, as do many other makers of cleaners and detergents. Kraft General Foods Canada introduced its barbecue sauces in a plastic bottle that contains 25 percent recycled plastic content.[21] Such examples suggest the lengths to which manufacturers and packaging suppliers have gone to respond to consumer concerns for the environment.

The issue is, however, not a simple one. Environmentalists argue that companies should abandon disposable products, but the alternatives are often fraught with problems as considerable energy may be required for their production and in recycling them for reuse. The controversy over the impact of packaging on the environment can be expected to rage for some time to come, as scientists and governments try to resolve the question of what types of packaging are most harmful. Clearly some companies and industries are more affected than others, but there are implications for practically all businesses.

Soft drink and beer companies are pressured to move towards a completely refillable packaging strategy, involving the exclusive use of glass bottles. The makers of the convenient aseptic containers are under pressure from environmentalists because the juice boxes are not recyclable and end up in municipal garbage dumps. Companies that have for years been supplying the restaurant industry and providing Canadians with convenient disposable products have been greatly affected by the environmental movement and have had to adopt strategies aimed at developing products that are less harmful to the environment. Major corporations are doing their part to address this global issue by moving to the use of less packaging, refillable containers, and recyclable materials. The support of consumers for such actions is obvious and will guarantee that recycling will represent one of the major growth areas in this country well into the future.

Other criticisms of packaging are:

- Packaging depletes our natural resources. This criticism is offset to some extent as packagers increasingly make use of recycled materials. Another offsetting point is that effective packaging reduces spoilage (another form of resource waste).
- Packaging is excessively expensive. Cosmetic packaging is often cited as an example here. But even in seemingly simple packaging — beer, for example — as much as half the production cost goes for the container. On the other hand, effective packaging reduces transportation costs and losses from product spoilage.
- Health hazards occur from some forms of plastic packaging and some aerosol cans. Government regulations have banned the use of several of these suspect packaging materials.
- Packaging is deceptive. Government regulation plus improvements in business practices regarding packaging have reduced the intensity of this criticism, although it is heard on occasion.

Truly, marketing executives face some real challenges in satisfying these complaints while at the same time retaining the marketing-effectiveness, consumer-convenience, and product-protection features of packaging.

## LABELLING

Labelling is another product feature that requires managerial attention. The **label** is part of a product that carries verbal information about the product or the seller. A label may be part of a package, or it may be a tag attached directly to the product. Obviously there is a close relationship among labelling, packaging, and branding.

### Types of Labels

Typically, labels are classified as brand, grade, or descriptive. A **brand label** is simply the brand alone applied to the product or to the package. Thus, some oranges are brand-labelled (stamped) Sunkist or Jaffa, and some clothes carry the brand label Sanforized. A **grade label** identifies the quality with a letter, number, or word. Canadian beef is grade-labelled A, B, or C and each grade is subdivided by number from 1 to 4 indicating an increasing fat content. **Descriptive labels** give objective information about the use, construction, care, performance, or other features of the product. On a descriptive label for a can of corn, there will be statements concerning the type of corn (golden sweet), the style (creamed or in niblet kernels), and the can size, number of servings, other ingredients, and nutritional content. There is also growing interest in **eco-labelling**, such as the Canadian government's Environmental Choice program, which encourages environmentally safe products through awarding seals of approval. Many companies are now redesigning their products to qualify for environmental labels offered through such programs, which are now in operation in almost 40 countries worldwide.[22]

Relative Merits Brand labelling creates very little stir among critics. While it is an acceptable form of labelling, its severe limitation is that it does not supply sufficient information to a buyer. The real fight centres on grade versus descriptive labelling and on whether grade labelling should be made mandatory.

The proponents of grade labelling argue that it is simple, definite, and easy to use. They also point out that if grade labels were used, prices would be more closely related to quality, although grade labelling would not stifle competition. In fact, they believe that grade labelling might increase competition, because consumers would be able to judge products on the basis of both price and known quality.

Those who object to grade labelling point out that a very low score on one grading characteristic can be offset by very high scores on other factors. Companies selling products that score high *within* a given grade would be hurt by grade labelling. These companies could not justify a higher price than that charged for a product that scored very low in the same grade. And some people feel that grades are an inaccurate guide for consumer buying. It is not possible to grade the differences in flavour and taste, or in style and fashion, yet these are the factors that often influence consumer purchases.

### Statutory Labelling Requirements

The importance of packaging and labelling in its potential for influencing the consumer's purchasing decision is reflected in the large number of federal and provincial laws that exist to regulate this marketing activity. At the federal level, the Competition Act regulates the area of misleading advertising and a number of companies have been convicted of misleading advertising for the false or deceptive statements that have appeared on their packages. In this case, the information that appears on a package or label has been considered to constitute an advertisement.

## MARKETING AT WORK

### FILE 11-4 HOW DOES THAT BAR CODE WORK?

*You have probably wondered from time to time why virtually every package in a retail store now sports a bar code (more correctly termed a "Universal Product Code") which is swiped across the scanner at the checkout.*

The picture of a bee with a bar code stuck to its side, which appeared recently on the cover of a trade magazine, raises the question: How do you know where the bar code ends and the bee begins?

You don't, of course, but the laser scanners that read the little black-and-white stripes used by everyone from beekeepers to barkeepers do know, and the 50-year-old technology is enjoying a remarkable resurgence.

Bar codes long ago moved out of the grocery and retail stores into every realm of life where organization and record-keeping are necessary. Auto parts, overnight parcels and aircraft-carrier parts all carry the little label.

Some political pundits have even credited the humble bar code with deep-sixing former U.S. president George Bush's re-election attempt. When Mr. Bush was wowed by a supermarket scanner reading bar codes — a technological trick that anyone who has been grocery shopping in the past 10 years has seen — he revealed just how out of touch he was with the middle class, and the rest is history.

A scanner reads a bar code by shining a light on it, usually a laser, and measuring the light reflected back.

With the hand-held scanners in many retail outlets, for example, the clerk picks up the price tag, positions the bar code so the lines are vertical and pulls the trigger, and we see what looks like a line of light hitting the bar code.

That beam is actually 36 pulses of laser light a second. Inside the scanner, a mirror is mounted on a motor that is oscillating — moving the mirror at high speed. As the laser hits that mirror it reflects the tiny bursts of light out the end of the scanner, spraying them across the bar code.

Each one of those pulses bounces back into the scanner. Pulses that have bounced off a dark area are weaker because the dark colour has absorbed some of the light. Pulses that have bounced off a light area are stronger because more light has been reflected.

The scanner converts what it has read — the number of dark or light bars and their width — into a digital code of zeroes and ones that a computer or cash register can read.

So, for example, a wide light bar, wide dark bar, narrow light bar and narrow dark bar might represent the letter A, or the number 6.

Grocery-store scanners, like the one that undid Mr. Bush, work a little differently. They have up to 20 different beams coming up through the glass on the counter at different angles. Whichever one of those beams spots the bar code first (bearing in mind that it takes only a fraction of a second for the scanner to read the code and check it) is the one that reads it. With counter-top scanners, because of the multiple beams, it doesn't matter how the bar code is positioned as long as a beam can find it.

At the beginning and end of bar codes are so-called "quiet zones," which tell the scanner where the bar codes begin and end. And each code has a check digit, which is a way for the scanner to determine whether it is reading the information correctly. Using a specific mathematical equation, the scanner will compare all the information it has read with the check digit. If the answer to the equation is not the check digit, the scanner knows it has misread something and will not give a reading at the cash register.

Most bar codes serve only as a sort of address. They tell a computer where to look for a detailed description of what the item is that has been scanned.

There are about 40 different commercial bar codes, although only a handful are regularly used, the most common being the universal product code or UPC. They use numbers or letters, or numbers and letters, or odd numbers only, or even numbers only, or some other variation. The challenge with bar codes has always been how to make them smaller, hence the reference to bar-coded bees. (The trick to bar-coding bees, by the way, is to get just the right amount of adhesive. Too little and if falls off, too much and the bee can't fly.)

But even with the advent of tiny, bee-sized bar codes, their shortcoming has always been that they can represent only a small amount of information. Bar coders have finally figured a way around that — two-dimensional bar coding.

Historically, whether on the side of a honeybee or a jet fighter, the bar code is the same at the top as in the middle as at the bottom. The scanner has only to make one pass through the bars and it has all the information they can hold.

But by changing the width of the bars at several intervals from top to bottom, the tiny codes can be made to contain a great deal more information.

With two-dimensional bar codes it's possible to have a tractor trailer full of products and a single bar code on a shipping document that tells you everything inside the truck.

Or you could carry your entire medical history in bar-code form on a medical card, and have an updated history printed on a bar code after each visit to the doctor.

Or you could keep a record of every bee in your hive, its name, honey production and personal preferences.

Source: Geoffrey Rowan, "Deciphering the Bar Code," *Globe and Mail*, August 3, 1993, p. A7.

The **Hazardous Products Act** gives the federal government the power to regulate the sale, distribution, advertising, and labelling of certain consumer products that are considered dangerous. A number of products have been banned from sale under this Act and all hazardous products, such as cleaning substances, chemicals, and aerosol products, must carry on their labels a series of symbols that indicate the danger associated with the product and the precautions that should be taken with its use. The symbols illustrate that the product is poisonous, inflammable, explosive, or corrosive in nature.

Similarly the federal Food and Drugs Act regulates the sale of food, drugs, cosmetics, and medical devices. Under this Act, regulations deal with the manufacture, sale, advertising, packaging, and labelling of such products. Certain misleading and deceptive packaging and labelling practices are specifically prohibited.

Without question, the strictest regulations applied to packaging in Canada pertain to the cigarette industry. Amendments to the Tobacco Products Control Act in 1993 required manufacturers to make a number of very detailed changes to their cigarette packages, including:

- The area in which health warnings are displayed must increase to 25 percent of the main display panel of the cigarette package.
- The warning must be placed at the top of the package.
- The warning must be either in black type on a white background, or in white lettering on black.
- A total of eight different warning messages are available for tobacco companies to choose from to appear on their packages, among them "Smoking can kill you" and "Cigarettes cause strokes and heart disease."[23]

The Textile Labelling Act requires that manufacturers label their products, including wearing apparel, yard goods, and household textiles, according to the fibre content of the product. In the past, more than 700 fabric names have appeared on products, but most of these were brand names of individual companies. For example, the fibre known generically as polyester has been labelled as Terylene, Trevira, Dacron, Kodel, Fortrel, Tergal, Tetoron, and Crimplene, all of which are manufacturers' brand names for polyester. In order to reduce confusion among the buying public, products now have to be labelled according to the generic fibre content, with the percentage of each fibre in excess of 5 percent listed.

There also exist in Canada two government-sponsored consumer product labelling schemes that are informative in nature. These programs are the Canada Standard Size program and the Textile Care Labelling program. The Textile Care Labelling program involves the labelling of all textile products with symbols that indicate instructions for washing and dry cleaning the product.

The **Consumer Packaging and Labelling Act** regulates all aspects of the packaging and labelling of consumer products in this country. The regulations that have been passed under this Act require that most products sold in Canada bear bilingual labels. The net quantity of the product must appear on the label in both metric and imperial units. If the quantity of a food product is expressed in terms of a certain number of servings, the size of the servings must also be stated. Where artificial flavourings are used in the manufacture of a food product, the label must contain the information that the flavour is imitation or simulated. The Act makes provision for the standardization of container sizes. The first set of regulations to be passed under the Act set down the standard package sizes for toothpaste, shampoo, and skin cream products, and it is in contravention of the regulations to manufacture these products in other than the package sizes approved.

The Consumer Packaging and Labelling Act requires that manufacturers of consumer products, especially in the food industry, incorporate the bilingual and metric requirements into the design of their labels.

The provinces have also moved into the field of regulating packaging and labelling. A number of provinces have passed legislation regarding misleading advertising and any information that appears on a package or label is considered an advertisement. In Quebec, that province's Official Language Act requires that all labels be written in French or in French and another language. If both English and French appear on the label, at least equal prominence must be given to the French.

Largely in response to complaints from people who suffer from allergies, the federal government moved in 1990 to require the listing of all ingredients on the labels of cosmetics products. Regulations under the Food and Drugs Act cover approximately 4,000 ingredients commonly found in shampoos, soaps, deodorants, and makeup. We can expect to see further changes in the labels required on food and grocery items in the future as consumers demand more information about the products they are consuming and using. The most likely changes relate to the listing of nutritional information on food products, brought about by the increasing interest of consumers in their health and nutrition.

## OTHER IMAGE-BUILDING FEATURES

A well-rounded program for product planning and development will include a company policy on several additional product attributes: product design, colour, quality, warranty, and after-sale service.

### Product Design and Colour

One way to satisfy customers and gain a competitive advantage is through skilful **product design**. In fact, a distinctive design may be the only feature that significantly differentiates a product. Many firms feel that there is considerable glamour and general promotional appeal in product design and the designer's name. In the field of business products, *engineering* design has long been recognized as extremely important. Today there is a realization of the marketing value of *appearance* design as well. Office machines and office furniture are examples of business products that reflect recent conscious attention to product design, often with good sales results. The marketing significance of design has been recognized for years in the field of consumer products, from big items like automobiles and refrigerators to small products like fountain pens and apparel.

Good design can improve the marketability of a product by making it easier to operate, upgrading its quality, improving its appearance, and/or reducing manufacturing costs. Recognizing the strategic importance of design, many companies have elevated the design function in the corporate hierarchy. In a number of firms, the director of design (sometimes called the director of human factors) participates in strategic planning and reports directly to top management.

**Colour** often is the determining factor in a customer's acceptance or rejection of a product, whether that product is a dress, a table, or an automobile. Colour by itself, however, is no selling advantage because many competing firms offer colour. The marketing advantage comes in knowing the right colour and in knowing when to change colours. If a garment manufacturer or a retail store's fashion co-ordinator guesses wrong on what will be the fashionable colour in this season's clothing, disaster may ensue.

### Product Quality

The quality of a product is extremely significant, but it is probably the most difficult of all the image-building features to define. Users frequently disagree on what constitutes quality in a product, whether it be a cut of meat or a work of art or music. Personal tastes are deeply involved. One guideline in managing **product quality** is that the quality level should be compatible with the intended use of a product; the level need not be any higher. In fact, *good* and *poor* sometimes are misleading terms for quality. *Correct* and *incorrect* or *right* and *wrong* may be more appropriate. If a person is making a peach cobbler, grade B or C peaches are the correct quality. They are not necessarily the best quality, but they are right for the intended use. It is not necessary to pay grade-A prices for large, well-formed peaches when these features are destroyed in making the cobbler. Another key to the successful management of quality is to maintain *consistency* of product output at the desired quality level.

In recent years, North American manufacturers have been increasingly concerned about the quality of their products.[24] And well they should be! For many years, consumers have complained about the poor quality of some products — both materials and workmanship. Foreign products — Japanese cars, for example — made serious inroads into the market because these products are perceived as being of better quality than their North American counterparts.

Quality of output also is a primary consideration in the production and marketing of services. The quality of its service can determine whether a firm will be successful. Yet it is virtually impossible for a firm to standardize performance quality among its units of service output. We frequently experience differences in performance quality from the same organization in appliance repairs, haircuts, medical exams, football games, or marketing courses. Consequently, it is essential that management do all it can to ensure consistency of quality at or above the level expected by the firm's present and potential customers.

To aid in determining and maintaining the desired level of quality in its goods and services, a company should establish a quality-improvement program. This should be an ongoing group effort of the design, production, marketing, and customer-service departments. Such a program is in sharp contrast to a simple inspection of finished goods or parts on a production line — what some firms call quality control. A total-quality-management program should also include provisions for communicating to the market its commitment to quality. A firm may then justifiably claim in its advertising that its product quality has improved. The problem is getting consumers to believe this fact.

Product quality should be a primary consideration not only for manufacturers of goods but also for producers of services, as will be discussed in Chapter 12. It is virtually impossible for a services firm to achieve the same level of quality in all units of output. Quality varies because people, not just machines, are normally involved in producing services.

In recent years, many organizations have implemented **total quality management** (TQM) programs. TQM entails not just specific procedures, policies, and practices, but a philosophy that commits the organization to continuous quality improvement in all of its activities. All kinds of organizations — manufacturers, services firms, government agencies, and educational institutions — are adopting TQM.[25]

### Warranties

The purpose of a **warranty** is to assure buyers they will be compensated in case the product does not perform up to reasonable expectations. In years past, courts seemed to recognize only **express warranties** — those stated in written or spoken words. Usually these were quite limited in their coverage and seemed mainly to protect the seller from buyers' claims. As a result, the following caution was appropriate: "Caveat emptor," which means "Let the buyer beware."

But times change! Consumer complaints led to a campaign to protect the consumer in many areas, including product warranties. Courts and government agencies have broadened the scope of warranty coverage by recognizing **implied warranty**. This means that a warranty was *intended*, although not actually stated, by the seller. Furthermore, producers are being held responsible, even when the sales contract is between the retailer and the consumer. Now the caution is: "Caveat venditor," or "Let the seller beware."

In recent years manufacturers have responded to legislation and consumer complaints by broadening and simplifying their warranties. Many sellers are using their warranties as promotional devices to stimulate purchase by reducing consumers' risks. The effective handling of consumers' complaints related to warranties can be a significant factor in strengthening a company's marketing program.

The Hazardous Products Act indicates how the law has changed regarding **product liability** and injurious products. This law prohibits the sale of certain dangerous products and requires that other products that may be potentially dangerous carry an indication on their labels of the dangers inherent in their use. As further indication of the growing interest on the part of consumer groups and governments in the protection that existing forms of warranties offer the consumer, the Ontario Law Reform Commission in 1972 issued its Report on Consumer Warranties and Guarantees in the Sale of Goods. This report recommended broad and sweeping changes in the law respecting warranties and guarantees, which would provide the consumer with greater protection. In recent years, some provinces have passed Consumer Products Warranty Acts. The Saskatchewan Act provides for statutory warranties that are deemed to be given by the retailer to the original purchaser and to subsequent owners. It also prescribes the form that written warranties must take.

### Postsale Service

Many companies have to provide **postsale service**, notably repairs, to fulfil the terms of their warranties. Other firms offer postsale services such as maintenance and repairs not only to satisfy their customers but also to augment their revenues. Companies such as Otis and Montgomery, which sell elevators, rely on their service contracts for a substantial portion of their sales and profits. With more complex products and increasingly demanding and vocal consumers, postsale service has become essential. A constant consumer gripe is that manufacturers and retailers do not provide adequate repair service for the products they sell.

A manufacturer can shift the main burden for postsale service to intermediaries, compensate them for their efforts, and possibly even train their service people. This approach is evident in the automobile and personal-computer industries. Or a manufacturer can establish regional factory service centres, staff them with well-trained company employees, and strive to make product servicing a separate profit-generating activity. This is common in the appliance industry; for example, Black & Decker uses this approach.

Consumers become frustrated if they cannot voice their complaints and get their postsale-service problems solved. They want someone to listen and respond to their complaints. Many responsive companies have established toll-free 1-800 telephone numbers that connect the customer directly with a customer service representative. Many actually invite customers to complain, acting on the principle that if the customer doesn't complain the company won't know there is a problem and can't take steps to correct it. Many companies post their 1-800 customer service numbers on the doors of their stores and feature them in their advertising. While it may not always be pleasant to listen to customer complaints, the alternative of customers taking their business elsewhere is much worse in the long run.[26]

Like packaging and the other need-satisfying product features discussed in this chapter, postsale service can be either a differential advantage or a disadvantage for an organization. Thus it certainly should be on the list of matters managers need to heed constantly.

## SUMMARY

Effective product management involves developing and then monitoring the various features of a product — its brand, package, labelling, design, quality, warranty, and postsale service. A consumer's purchase decision may take into account not just the basic good or service but also the brand and perhaps one or more of the other want-satisfying product features.

A brand is a means of identifying and differentiating the products of an organization. Branding aids sellers in managing their promotional and pricing activities. The dual responsibilities of brand ownership are to promote the brand and to maintain a consistent level of quality. Selecting a good brand name — and there are relatively few really good ones — is difficult. Once a brand becomes well known, the owner may have to protect it from becoming a generic term.

Manufacturers must decide whether to brand their products and/or sell under an intermediary's brand. Intermediaries must decide whether to carry producers' brands alone or to establish their own brands as well. In addition, intermediaries must decide whether to carry generic products. Both producers and intermediaries must set policies regarding branding of groups of products and branding for market saturation.

A growing number of companies are recognizing that the brands they own are — or can be — among their most valuable assets. They are building brand equity — the added value that a brand brings to a product. It's difficult to build brand equity but, if it can be done, it can be the basis for expanding a product mix. Products with abundant brand equity also lend themselves to trademark licensing, a marketing arrangement that is growing in popularity.

Packaging is becoming increasingly important as sellers recognize the problems, as well as the marketing opportunities, associated with it. Companies must choose among strategies such as family packaging, multiple packaging, and changing the package. Labelling, a related activity, provides information about the product and the seller. Many consumer criticisms of marketing target packaging and labelling. As a result, there are several laws regulating these activities.

Companies are now recognizing the marketing value of both product design and quality. Good design can improve the marketability of a product; it may be the only feature that differentiates a product. Projecting the appropriate quality image and then delivering the level of quality desired by customers are essential to marketing success. In many cases, firms need to enhance product quality to eliminate a differential disadvantage; in others, firms seek to build quality as a way of gaining a differential advantage.

Warranties and postsale service require considerable management attention these days because of consumer complaints and governmental regulations. Product liability is an issue of great consequence to companies because of the financial risk associated with consumers' claims of injuries caused by the firms' products.

Many companies provide postsale service, mainly repairs, to fulfil the terms of their warranties and/or to augment their revenues. To promote customer satisfaction, a number of firms are improving their methods of inviting and responding to consumer complaints.

## KEY TERMS AND CONCEPTS

**Brand (312)**
**Brand name (312)**
**Brand mark (312)**
**Trademark (313)**
**Generic products (318)**
**Family brand strategy (322)**
**Multiple-brand strategy (322)**
**Brand equity (323)**
**Trademark (brand) licensing (324)**
**Packaging (326)**
**Family packaging (328)**
**Reuse packaging (328)**
**Multiple packaging (328)**
**Label (330)**
**Brand label (330)**
**Grade label (330)**
**Descriptive label (330)**
**Eco-labelling (330)**
**Statutory labelling requirements (330)**
**Hazardous Products Act (332)**
**Consumer Packaging and Labelling Act (333)**
**Product design (333)**
**Product colour (334)**
**Product quality (334)**
**Total quality management (334)**
**Warranty (335)**
**Express warranty (335)**
**Implied warranty (335)**
**Product liability (335)**
**Postsale service (335)**

## QUESTIONS AND PROBLEMS

1. List five brand names you think are good ones and five you consider poor. Explain the reasoning behind your choices.
2. Evaluate each of the following brand names in light of the characteristics of a good brand, indicating the strong and weak points of each name.
   a. Xerox (office copiers).
   b. Kodak (cameras).
   c. Bauer (skates).
   d. Dack's (shoes).
   e. A-1 (steak sauce).
   f. Far West (clothing).
3. Suggest some brands that are on the verge of becoming generic. What course of action should a company take to protect the separate identity of its brands?
4. What are brand extensions? Why would a company launch a new product as a brand extension rather than as a completely new brand? What are the risks associated with such a strategy?
5. In which of the following cases should the company adopt the strategy of family branding?
   a. A manufacturer of men's underwear introduces essentially the same products for women.
   b. A manufacturer of women's cosmetics adds a line of men's cosmetics to its product assortment.
   c. A manufacturer of hair-care products introduces a line of portable electric hair dryers.
6. Suppose you are employed by the manufacturer of a well-known brand of skis. Your company is planning to add skates and water skis to its product line. It has no previous experience with either of these two new products. You are given the assignment of selecting a brand name for the skates and water skis. Your main problem is in deciding whether to adopt a family-brand policy. That is, should you use the snow-ski brand for either or both of the new products? Or should you develop separate names for each of the new items? You note that Campbell's (soups) and McCain (french fries) use family brands. You also note that Sears and Procter & Gamble generally do the opposite. They use different names for each *group of products* (Sears) or each *separate product* (P&G). What course of action would you recommend? Why?
7. A manufacturer of a well-known brand of ski boots acquired a division of a company that marketed a well-known brand of skis. What brand strategy should the new organization adopt? Should all products (skis and boots) now carry the boot brand? Should they carry the ski brand? Is there some other alternative that you feel would be better?
8. Why do some firms sell an identical product under more than one of their own brands?
9. Assume that a large department-store chain proposed to Black & Decker that the latter company supply the chain with a line of power tools carrying the store's own label. What factors should Black & Decker management consider in making such a decision? Would the situation be any different if a supermarket chain had approached Kraft General Foods with a request to supply a private-label jelly dessert similar to Jell-O?
10. A Canadian manufacturer of camping equipment (stoves, lanterns, tents, sleeping bags) plans to introduce its line into several Eastern European countries. Should management select the same brand name for all countries or market under the

name that is used in Canada? Should they consider using a different name in each country? What factors should influence this decision?

11. What changes would you recommend in the typical packaging of these products?
    a. Soft drinks.
    b. Hairspray.
    c. Potato chips.
    d. Toothpaste.
12. If grade labelling is adopted, what factors should be used as bases for grading the following products?
    a. Lipstick.
    b. Woollen sweaters.
    c. Diet-food products.
13. Give examples of products for which the careful use of the colour of the product has increased sales. Can you cite examples to show that poor use of colour may hurt a company's marketing program?
14. Explain the relationship between a product warranty on small electric appliances and the manufacturer's distribution system for these products.
15. How would the warranty policies set by a manufacturer of skis differ from those adopted by an automobile manufacturer?

## HANDS-ON MARKETING

1. Visit a large local supermarket and:
   a. Obtain the store manager's opinions regarding which products are excellently packaged and which are poorly packaged. Ask the manager for reasons.
   b. Walk around the store and compile your own list of excellent and poor packages. What factors did you use to judge quality of packaging?
2. Ask five students who are not taking this course to evaluate the following names for a proposed expensive perfume: Entice, Nitespark, At Risk, and Foreglow. For evaluation purposes, share with the students the characteristics of a good brand name. Also ask them to suggest a better name for the new perfume.

## NOTES AND REFERENCES


1. Based on correspondence with Maureen Lane, regional marketing representative, Country Style Donuts, and adapted from articles supplied by Country Style. The authors wish to thank Peter Mertens and Maureen Lane for their co-operation.
2. Eric Swetsky, "The Naming of Names," *Marketing*, February 21, 1994, p. 30.
3. Madelaine Drohan, "British Await Coke's Reply to Grocer's Look-Alike Cola," *Globe and Mail*, April 29, 1994, p. B5; and "Unreal," *The Economist*, May 14, 1994, p. 20.
4. Derek Suchard, "How the Pros Build Brands," *Canadian Business*, January 1991, p. 70.
5. Larry Black, "What's in a Name?" *Report on Business Magazine*, November 1989, pp. 98-110.
6. Ken Riddell, "Cookies Ahoy!" *Marketing*, November 15, 1993, p. 26.
7. For an interesting review of the value of brand names and the risks associated with brand extensions, the reader is referred to "Brand-Stretching Can Be Fun — and Dangerous," *The Economist*, May 5, 1990, pp. 77-80.
8. James Pollock, "Pepsi Tries Supersweet Diet Pop," *Marketing*, October 11, 1993, p. 6.
9. Jamie Beckett, "Inventing a Product Name Is Part Science, Part Art," *Globe and Mail*, October 27, 1992, p. B4.
10. See also Kim Robertson, "Strategically Desirable Brand Name Characteristics," *The Journal of Product and Brand Management*, Summer 1992, pp. 62-72.
11. For an excellent discussion of the nature and benefits of this strategy, see Donald G. Norris, "Ingredient Branding: A Strategy Option with Multiple Beneficiaries," *The Journal of Consumer Marketing*, Summer 1992, pp. 19-31.
12. Russell Mitchell, "Intel Isn't Taking This Lying Down," *Business Week*, September 30, 1991, pp. 32-33.
13. For a very interesting look at the success of Loblaw in the private-label business and at the developer of the program, Dave Nichol, the reader is referred to Mark Stevenson, "Global Gourmet," *Canadian Business*, July 1993, pp. 22-33; see also Anne Kingston, *The Edible Man: Dave Nichol, President's Choice and the Making of Popular Taste*. Toronto: Macfarlane, Walter & Ross, 1994.

14. Howard Schlossberg, "Brand Value Can Be Worth More than Physical Assets," *Marketing News*, March 5, 1990, p. 6.
15. This definition is drawn from the comprehensive examination of brand equity in Peter H. Farquar, "Managing Brand Equity," *Journal of Advertising Research*, August/September 1990, pp. RC-7-RC-12. For even more on brand equity, see the first book devoted entirely to this important topic: David A. Aaker, *Managing Brand Equity: Capitalizing on the Value of a Brand Name*, The Free Press, New York, 1991.
16. The Kellogg's example was described by Farquar, op. cit., p. RC-7; the Hitachi-GE example was originally reported by Norman C. Berry, "Revitalizing Brands," *The Journal of Product and Brand Management*, Spring 1992, pp. 19-24.
17. Farquar, op. cit., pp. RC-8-RC-10.
18. For a discussion of the potential advantages and disadvantages of using brand equity in this way, see David Aaker, "Brand Extensions: The Good, the Bad, and the Ugly," *Sloan Management Review*, Summer 1990, pp. 47-56.
19. A very good overview of the issues involved in this "battle of the brands" can be obtained from three excellent articles: "Shoot out at the Check-Out," *The Economist*, June 5, 1993, pp. 69-72, reprinted as "Brands on the Run from the Store Shelf," *Globe and Mail*, June 5, 1993, p. A7; "Death of the Brand Manager," *The Economist*, April 9, 1994, pp. 67-68; and "Behind the Battle of the Brands," *Globe and Mail*, June 6, 1994, p. A10.
20. For a good discussion of this topic, see Leonard L. Berry, Edwin F. Lefkowith, and Terry Clark, "In Services, What's in a Name?" *Harvard Business Review*, September/October 1988, pp. 38-30. Some of the examples in this section are drawn from this source.
21. Larry Dworkin, "The Best in Technology and Design," *Strategy*, 1993, p. 14.
22. "Labeling cooperation urged," *Marketing News*, May 9, 1994, p. 17.
23. Ann Gibbon, "Smoking's Labelling Perils," *Globe and Mail*, May 5, 1994, p. B1.
24. For a list of reasons why product quality is so important and for a discussion of the marketing function's role in quality management, see Neil A. Morgan and Nigel F. Piercy, "Market-Led Quality," *Industrial Marketing Management*, May 1992, pp. 111-118.
25. For a thorough discussion of the status and prospects for TQM, see the following special issue: "The Quality Imperative," *Business Week*, October 25, 1991; for some concerns about effectiveness of TQM, see Gilbert Fuchsberg, "Quality Programs Show Shoddy Results," *The Wall Street Journal*, May 14, 1992, p. B1.
26. For useful recommendations, see Mary C. Gilly and Richard W. Hansen, "Consumer Complaint Handling as a Strategic Marketing Tool," *The Journal of Product and Brand Management*, Summer 1992, pp. 5-16. Also see Roland T. Rust, Bala Subramanian, and Mark Wells, "Making Complaints a Management Tool," *Marketing Management*, vol. 1, no. 3, 1992, pp. 41-45.

## CHAPTER 12 GOALS

This chapter will focus on the major differences between marketing services and marketing tangible products, as well as on the tremendous growth in emphasis recently on quality of service in the marketplace. After studying this chapter, you should have an understanding of:

- What services are and are not.
- The importance of services in our economy.
- The characteristics of services, and the marketing implications in these characteristics.
- The attitudes of service organizations towards marketing.
- Planning a marketing mix for services marketing.
- The future of services marketing.

# CHAPTER 12

# MARKETING AND DELIVERY OF SERVICES

## Developing a Warm Relationship

The Canadian banking business is not what it used to be. In fact, it is probably not accurate to describe it as banking any more. With all the mergers and purchases by the major banks of trust companies, brokerage houses, and insurance firms, we have witnessed in recent years the emergence of an integrated financial services industry in this country.

In addition to the structural changes that have taken place in banking there has been another, equally important change; the banks have discovered marketing and the customer. In recent years, there has been a transformation in banking that has seen the banks move from a product and interest-rate emphasis to a genuine interest in serving the customer as conveniently and as warmly as possible. In fact, most have embraced completely the philosophy of "relationship marketing."

A number of reasons account for this change of emphasis on the part of Canadian banks, and indeed of banks throughout the world. In the first place, banking has become far less regulated and far more competitive in recent years. The major Canadian chartered banks have faced increasing competition from foreign-owned banks that have been allowed to operate in Canada since the 1980s. Competition has also grown from other financial organizations and from retailers and manufacturing companies such as Sears and General Electric who are now operating in fields such as leasing and credit that were once the preserve of the banking business.

Secondly, technological developments have made it possible for banks to operate differently and to compete more effectively. This has had a considerable effect on the banks' product lines. Because most of the "products" that are sold by banks are variations on deposits and loans, it is possible to vary the features of a product quickly or even to tailor a product to the needs of a particular customer. This also means that the competition can offer an identical product almost immediately. Therefore, gaining any form of strategic advantage through conventional bank products is unlikely. Technology has also made it possible for banks to deliver their services much more conveniently through automated banking machines, telephone banking, and on-line bank services.

Finally, the banks, like many other businesses, have come to the realization that the most profitable customers are those who stay with them for a long time, who give them most of their business, and who are so satisfied that they will tell their friends. There has been a marked change in emphasis in bank marketing towards the development and preservation of positive relationships with customers and on keeping them satisfied. This has meant the development of specific products and programs for growing segments of the market, such as seniors, and on attempts to satisfy the customer at every turn. The Toronto Dominion Bank is so serious about its commitment to service that it offers a guarantee. Taking a leaf out of the book of pizza-delivery companies, the TD offers customers $5 if they have to wait in line for more than five minutes in their branches.[1]

These examples are indicative of the changes that have been taking place in Canadian financial institutions. They also reflect how many service organizations have become much more marketing-oriented in recent years as they realize that their principal basis for competing is the quality of the services they offer.

## NATURE AND IMPORTANCE OF SERVICES

In concept, tangible products marketing and services marketing are essentially the same. In each case the marketer must select and analyze target markets. Then a marketing program must be built around the parts of the marketing mix — the product or service, the price structure, the distribution system, and the promotional program. In practice, there often are substantial similarities as well. However, the basic characteristics that differentiate services from tangible products typically lead to a quite different marketing program. The strategies and tactics used in conventional product marketing frequently are inappropriate for services marketing.

### Definition and Scope of Services

We are talking about the marketing of services, but what do we mean by "services"? The term is difficult to define, because invariably services are marketed in conjunction with tangible products. Services require supporting products (you need an airplane to provide air transportation services), and products require supporting services (to sell even a shirt or can of beans calls at least for a cashier's service). Furthermore, a company may sell a combination of goods and services. Thus, along with repair service for your car, you might buy spark plugs or an oil filter. It may be helpful to think of every product as a mix of goods and services located on a continuum ranging from pure goods to pure services, as shown in Figure 12-1.

To move closer to a useful definition, we identify two classes of services. In the first group are services that are the *main purpose or object of a transaction*. As an example, suppose you want to rent a car from Avis. Avis needs a car (tangible good) to provide the rental service. But you are buying the rental use of the car, not the car itself. The second group consists of *supplementary* services that support or facilitate the sale of a tangi-

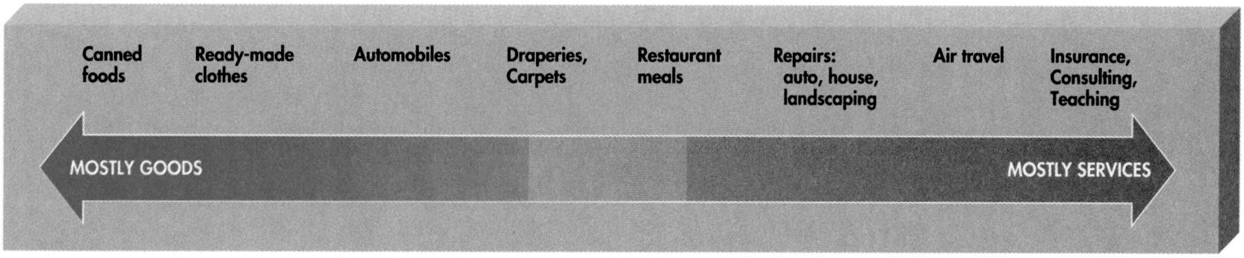


**FIGURE 12-1**
**A goods-services continuum.**

ble good or another service. Thus, when you buy a compact disc player, you may want technical information service from a sales person and the opportunity to pay with a credit card service.

Consequently, our definition of services in this chapter is as follows: **Services** are identifiable, intangible activities that are the main object of a transaction designed to provide want-satisfaction to customers. By this definition we exclude supplementary services that support the sale of tangible goods or other services. Although we are interested primarily in the marketing of services that are the principal objective of a transaction, as in financial services, air travel, hotel accommodations, and car rentals, we must not overlook the very important services associated with the marketing of literally every product, whether tangible or intangible. Increasingly, marketers are realizing that one of the most effective ways to compete and to differentiate one's company from the competition is to offer excellent service. Thus, even to a company selling industrial supplies, there is a challenge to deliver the product on time and in good condition and to ensure that the customer is billed correctly and called on regularly.

We are concerned here primarily with the services marketed by business or professional firms with profit-making motives — commercial services. This is in contrast to services of not-for-profit organizations, such as churches, universities, colleges, and the government. A useful classification of commercial services by industry is as follows:

- Housing (includes rental of hotels, motels, apartments, houses, and farms).
- Household operations (includes utilities, house repairs, repairs of equipment in the house, landscaping, and household cleaning).
- Recreation and entertainment (includes rental and repair of equipment used to participate in recreation and entertainment activities; also admission to all entertainment, recreation, and amusement events).
- Personal care (includes laundry, dry cleaning, beauty care).
- Medical and other health care (includes all medical services, dental, nursing, hospitalization, optometry, and other health care).
- Private education.
- Business and other professional services (includes legal, accounting, management consulting, and computer services).
- Insurance, banking, and other financial services (includes personal and business insurance, credit and loan services, investment counselling, and tax services).
- Transportation (includes freight and passenger services on common carriers, automobile repairs and rentals).
- Communications (includes telephone, facsimile, computer, and specialized business communication services).

Note that no attempt was made to separate the above groups into consumer and business services, as we did with tangible products. In fact, most are purchased by both market groups.

## Importance of Services

North America has genuinely become a service economy. More than 70 percent of all jobs in Canada are now accounted for by the service sector, and almost 70 percent of the country's gross domestic product is accounted for by services. Also, service jobs typically hold up better during a recession than do jobs in industries that produce tangible products. Canadians have become more dependent on the service sector for their jobs. Much of that employment, particularly in retail organizations, is now on a part-time basis.

While the share of total output accounted for by manufacturing has dropped to less than 20 percent in Canada, there is some evidence that even this value is overstated, as many of the activities that add value or contribute to final output in manufacturing companies are really services. *The Economist* has observed that the distinction between services and manufacturing is becoming less useful. Nevertheless, governments in particular continue to classify companies as manufacturing or services firms, despite the fact, for example, that the largest single supplier to General Motors is not a parts manufacturer, but Blue Cross-Blue Shield, a health-care provider. More than 20 percent of the value of final output of such "manufacturers" as Sony and General Motors is in the form of services.[2]

Close to one-half of all consumer expenditures are for the purchase of services. During the 1950s and 1960s, much of the employment growth in services involved jobs in government and other public sector organizations, such as education and health. Since the 1970s, most of the growth has been in the provision of business and personal services. We have seen dramatic growth through the 1980s, for example, in the business services sector, including accounting, engineering, legal and management consulting, and in the provision of personal services, including accommodation and food, amusement, and recreation. The number of people employed in each of these industries rose more than 20 percent through the 1980s.

Moreover, most of this explosive growth in services employment is not in low-paying jobs, contrary to the beliefs of many economists, business and labour leaders, and politicians. For several years the fastest-growing occupational category has been "professional, technical, and related work." These jobs pay well above the average, and most are in service industries.

The growth in the market for **personal services** is at least partially explained by the relative prosperity that Canadians have enjoyed during the past 40 years. As consumers became better able to satisfy their demand for tangible items, they turned to services either to provide things that they could not afford before or to do things for them that they no longer wished to do for themselves.

The growth of **business services** may be attributed to the fact that business has become increasingly complex, specialized, and competitive. As a consequence, management has been forced to call in experts to provide services in research, taxation, advertising, labour relations, and a host of other areas.

The rate of growth has not been uniform for all categories of consumer services. As disposable personal incomes have increased and life-styles have changed, the demand for some services has grown relatively faster than for others. Projections through to the end of the 1990s suggest that high growth rates in jobs and spending will occur especially in temporary employment, auto repairs, banking and finance fields, leisure-time industries, and home shopping.

## Characteristics of Services

The special nature of services stems from a number of distinctive characteristics. These features create special marketing challenges and opportunities. As a result, service firms often require strategic marketing programs that are substantially different from those found in the marketing of tangible goods.

**Intangibility** Because services are intangible, it is impossible for customers to sample — taste, feel, see, hear, or smell — a service before they buy it. Consequently, a company's promotional program must portray the *benefits* to be derived from the service, rather than emphasizing the service itself. Four promotional strategies that may be used to suggest service benefits are as follows.[3]

- *Visualization*. For example, Carnival Cruise Lines depicts the benefits of its cruises with ads that show people dancing, dining, playing deck games, and visiting exotic places.
- *Association*. Connect the service with a tangible good, person, object, or place. The Australian airline, Qantas, uses a cuddly koala bear in its advertising to project a warm, friendly image of Australia. Prudential Insurance suggests stability and security with its Rock of Gibraltar. Imperial Oil features its employees in its advertising to add a personal touch to retailing Esso gasoline.
- *Physical representation*. American Express uses colour — green, gold, or platinum — for its credit-card services to symbolize wealth and prestige. Fast-food chains, telephone companies, and many other firms dress their service representatives in clean, distinctive uniforms to stress visibility, cleanliness, and dependability.
- *Documentation*. Air Canada and other airlines cite facts and figures in their ads to support claims of dependability, performance, care for passengers, and safety.

**Inseparability** Services typically cannot be separated from the creator-seller of the service. Moreover, many services are created, dispensed, and consumed simultaneously. For example, dentists create and dispense almost all their services at the same time, *and* they require the presence of the consumer for the services to be performed. Because of this inseparability feature, many people are involved concurrently in the production operations and the marketing effort in services firms. And the customers receive and consume the services at the production site — in the firm's "factory," so to speak. Consequently, customers' opinions regarding a service frequently are formed through contacts with the production-marketing personnel and impressions of the physical surroundings in the "factory." Too often, contact personnel think of themselves as producers-creators of the service rather than as marketers.

From a marketing standpoint, inseparability frequently means that direct sale is the only possible channel of distribution, and a seller's services cannot be sold in very many markets. This characteristic limits the scale of operation in a firm. One person can repair only so many autos in a day or treat only so many medical patients.

As an exception to the inseparability feature, services may be sold by a person who is representing the creator-seller. A travel agent, insurance broker, or rental agent, for instance, may represent and help promote services that will be sold by the institutions producing them. Another way in which services are delivered by intermediaries is through franchising. Companies such as Swiss Chalet and Tilden Rent-a-Car are in the service business, but their head offices deal with customers through franchise holders in various cities.

The inseparability of a service from the people providing it has important implications for companies that are operating in service-oriented businesses. This includes not only those companies in true "service" industries, such as financial services, entertainment, hotels, and restaurants, but also those who must pay particular attention to the services that support the marketing of their tangible products. For example, although Eastern Bakeries is technically a manufacturer of bakery products such as breads and cakes, it is also in the business of making sure that its products are delivered on time and in the quantity and condition the customer ordered.

For the most part, it is employees of a company who have the greatest influence on the level of service provided to its customers. Eastern Bakeries may bake the most wholesome bread in eastern Canada, but if employees cannot get it to the retail stores in time for consumers to buy it, then any product advantage Eastern may have had will be lost.

In fact, in many industries, particularly those where the products or services are technologically advanced or difficult for the consumer to understand, or where the customer cannot see important differences among the offerings of the various competitors, the ability to compete comes down to whether a company can deliver superior service. Most progressive companies have come to realize that their employees are extremely important in providing a level of service that will keep their customers happy.

This applies to employees who come into direct contact with the customer — sales staff, repair technicians, and flight attendants — as well as to support personnel who can damage a company's relationship with its customers even though they may never meet them directly. A clerk in the accounting department who fails to credit a customer's account correctly, or a baggage handler who sends a passenger's suitcase to Halifax when the passenger was travelling to Calgary, is just as responsible for service and customer relations as those staff members who meet and talk with customers.

## MARKETING AT WORK

### FILE 12-1 PIZZA DELIVERY IS A SERVICE BUSINESS

In business today, everybody keeps talking about becoming global, global, and more global. Not so in Quebec, where Mike's Restaurants have concentrated on remaining regional in order to remain far ahead of all competing national and international Italian food home-delivery chains, such as Pizza Hut and Domino's. Owned by Montreal-based M-Corp, Mike's boasts annual network-wide sales of $130 million and has gobbled up more than 25 percent of the home-delivery market, crowning it the market's uncontested leader. M-Corp's vice-president, Neil Zeidel, attributes Mike's success to three fundamental factors: a commitment to product quality, efficient customer service through the fulfilment of a "30-minutes or free" guarantee, and careful selection of target consumers accompanied with appropriate marketing strategies.

Aside from quality food, its claim to "30 minutes or free" delivery has fashioned Mike's into a food service customers can count on. Investment in a sophisticated, single-number computer call-in centre, with more than 100 receptionists and a team of well-trained dispatchers, has enabled Mike's to back up all its promises. On top of this fundamental delivery service, however, are the company's astute marketing efforts — such as its recent introduction of SuperMikes, a 30-piece pie, which drove sales to an all-time record high.

With a campaign aimed at families headed by parents between the ages of 19 and 49 and with children under 18, the company created the Super-Delivery Man character, symbolizing the strength of the concept and the speed of its service. The slogan "30 pieces in 30 minutes" was the focal point of commercials that aired on Thursday, Friday, and Saturday nights on Quebec network television programs selected for their high ratings and family orientation, as well as their coinciding with peak periods for home delivery. The strategy — effective throughout the province — provoked an increase of delivery sales of almost 75 percent from the previous year.

Source: Neil Zeidel, "On a Regional Roll," *Marketing*, February 28, 1994, pp. 13-14.

**Heterogeneity** It is impossible for a service industry, or even an individual seller of services, to standardize output. Each "unit" of the service is somewhat different from other "units" of the same service. For example, an airline does not give the same quality of service on each trip. All repair jobs a mechanic does on automobiles are not of equal quality. An added complication is the fact that it is often difficult to judge the quality of a service. (Of course, we can say the same for some goods.) It is particularly difficult to forecast quality in advance of buying a service. A person pays to see a ball game without knowing whether it will be an exciting one (well worth the price of admission) or a dull performance.

The heterogeneity of services is of concern to service providers, but the ability to deliver customer satisfaction is further complicated by the fact that customer expectations are not at all consistent. Although a student on a short lunch break may spend only 15 minutes grabbing a quick meal at a restaurant near campus, the same student may take more than an hour to enjoy a pizza with a friend after a Saturday-night movie. In the first case, the customer wants to be served as quickly as possible; in the second, he or she is prepared to wait a little longer for service. Because service expectations differ across customers and even over time for the same customers, it is very difficult for service businesses to standardize their level of service.

In recent years, some service companies have turned to technology in an attempt to standardize the type and quality of service provided, but at the expense of losing personal contact and the ability to respond to customers' questions or concerns. Nevertheless, some services, such as those provided by automated banking machines, telephone banking, and self-service gas stations, can become standardized and are accepted by a large number of customers. Similarly, many companies and other organizations have installed telephone-answering and voice-mail systems that allow callers to leave messages for staff members who are out of the office or unable to answer their calls when the telephone rings. Canada's telephone companies have automated directory assistance services and have introduced a voice-response system for handling third-party collect calls. To automate service even further, the telephone industry has encouraged customers to sign up for Calling Cards, which eliminate the need to contact an operator to place long-distance calls billed to a third number.

While such technology-based services achieve standardization of service, in part by delegating much of the service provision or delivery to the customers themselves, there are at least some risks inherent in their use. On the other hand, some customers may resent having to do all the work, especially when they are paying for the service. Also, some customers simply prefer to deal with real people and get confused or irritated when they encounter technology. Finally, in some industries management is faced with the dilemma of not being able to keep in touch with customers or to establish relationships with them, when the customers are dealing primarily with machines or computers.

Service companies should pay special attention to the product-planning stage of their marketing programs. From the beginning, management must do all it can to ensure consistency of quality and to maintain high levels of quality control. This important issue of service quality will be discussed in a later section of this chapter.

**Perishability and Fluctuating Demand** Services are highly perishable, and they cannot be stored. Unused telephone time, empty seats in a stadium, and idle mechanics in a garage all represent business that is lost forever. Furthermore, the market for services fluctuates considerably by season, by day of the week, and by hour of the day. Most ski lifts lie idle all summer, whereas golf courses go unused in the winter. The use of city buses fluctuates greatly during the day.

There are notable exceptions to this generalization regarding the perishability and storage of services. In health and life insurance, for example, the service is purchased by a person or a company. Then it is held by the insurance company (the seller) until needed by the buyer or the beneficiary. This holding constitutes a type of storage.

The combination of perishability and fluctuating demand offers product-planning, pricing, and promotion challenges to services executives. Some organizations have developed new uses for idle plant capacity during off-seasons. Thus, during the summer, sev-

**If the flight for Hong Kong leaves with empty seats, they can never be sold.**

eral ski resorts operate their ski lifts for hikers and sightseers who want access to higher elevations. Advertising and creative pricing are also used to stimulate demand during slack periods. Hotels offer lower prices and family packages on weekends. Telephone companies offer lower rates at nights and weekends.

## SERVICE ORGANIZATIONS' ATTITUDES TOWARDS MARKETING

The growth in services has generally *not* been a result of marketing developments in service industries, but rather to the maturation of our economy and our rising standard of living. Traditionally, executives in services companies have not been marketing-oriented. They have lagged behind sellers of tangible products in accepting the marketing concept and have generally been slow in adopting marketing techniques. Marketing management in service firms has not been especially creative. Innovations in services marketing have usually come from companies in the consumer-products industries.

We can identify some reasons for this lack of marketing orientation. No doubt the intangibility of services creates more difficult marketing challenges for sellers of services than for sellers of goods. In many service industries — particularly professional services — the sellers think of themselves as producers or creators, and not as marketers, of the service. Proud of their abilities to represent a client in court, diagnose an illness, or give a good haircut, they often do not consider themselves business people.

The all-encompassing reason, however, is that top management in many cases does not understand (1) what marketing is or (2) its importance to a company's success. Service executives often seem to equate marketing with selling, and they fail to consider other parts of a marketing system. Many service firms also lack an executive whose sole responsibility is marketing — the counterpart of the vice-president of marketing in a goods-producing company.

In defence of firms in certain service industries, however, we note that external influences have contributed to the neglect of marketing. Up until the 1980s, several significant service industries were heavily regulated by governments or professional associations. Banking and all major forms of transportation services, for example, were severely restricted in marketing practices such as pricing, distribution, market expansion, and product expansion. In the fields of law, accounting, and health care, various laws and professional association regulations have prevented the providers from engaging in advertising, price competition, and other marketing activities. During the past 10 to 15 years, though, consumer protests and relaxing of regulations have removed many of these restrictions — thus creating genuine competition and a growing awareness of marketing in these industries.

There are, of course, exceptions to these negative generalizations. The success of such organizations as Four Seasons, American Express, Avis, and Federal Express is due in large part to their marketing orientation. In many services industries, the organizational concept of franchising (discussed in Chapter 17) has been applied successfully. Examples of franchising in services fields include equipment rentals, beauty salons, tax services, printing, lawn care services, and of course, restaurants. Under the umbrella philosophy of a marketing orientation, franchising organizations have used attributes such as good locations, training, and capital investment to meet services marketing challenges of intangibility, labour intensity, and quality control.[4]

The hotel industry provides an interesting example of a service industry that was not particularly marketing-oriented in the past, but that has more recently become extremely competitive and service oriented. As more and more people began to travel on business and vacations during the past 20 years, the hospitality industry in general has responded with promotions and marketing programs to attract various segments of the travelling market.

Some hotel chains, such as Four Seasons and Hyatt, have positioned themselves to appeal to the high end of the business travel market, offering superior service and amenities. Others, including CP Hotels, Sheraton, Hilton, Radisson, Delta, and Westin, are firmly in the business travel and convention business, while others, such as Ramada Inn and Journey's End, are marketing aggressively at a more budget-minded market segment, including the economy-minded business traveller. This latter segment is also being targeted by a relatively new entrant into the hotel business, the all-suite hotels now being opened across Canada by companies such as Cambridge Suites and Journey's End Suites. Still other hotel chains, including some of the CP Hotels, are in the resort business, catering largely to conventions and vacationers.

The hotel industry also is beginning to understand how to make effective use of two other powerful marketing tools — creative pricing and skilful promotion. Several chains now offer lower rates for weekend nights, and charge nothing for children accompanying their parents. Realizing that their long-term success lies in being able to attract business travellers to make return visits, many chains are now paying particular attention to regular customers. Some have established "frequent-guest" or **"membership" programs**, modelled after the airlines' frequent-flyer programs, which reward regular guests with points for each visit. Members of the Westin Premier or Hilton Honors programs, for example, can redeem their points for free nights at Westin and Hilton hotels around the world. This "membership" in an exclusive club, coupled with superior service for program members, is intended to create a feeling among regular customers that their business is welcomed and appreciated.

One hotel chain that has virtually all segments of the hospitality market covered is Choice Hotels Canada, which resulted from a 1993 joint-venture deal between Journey's End and Choice Hotels International of the United States. The agreement created the largest hotel chain in Canada, operating the 120 Journey's End properties and 54 Choice International locations in Canada. The new chain immediately began to rebrand the hotels in the product line by linking the Journey's End name with the seven levels of Choice Hotels from the Friendship Inns (one-star locations), to the two-and-a-half-star Comfort Inns and Suites, to the four-star Clarion network. The company has also entered joint promotion arrangements with Via Rail, Thrifty Car Rental, and Pepsi-Cola.[5]

## STRATEGIC PLANNING FOR SERVICES MARKETING

Because of the characteristics of services (notably intangibility), the development of a total marketing program in a service industry is often uniquely challenging. However, as in the marketing of goods, management first should define its marketing goals and select its target markets. Then management must design and implement marketing-mix strategies to reach its markets and fulfil its marketing goals.

### Selecting Target Markets

The task of analyzing a firm's target markets is essentially the same, whether the firm is selling a tangible product or a service. Marketers of services should understand the components of population and income — the demographic factors — as they affect the market for the services. In addition, marketers must try to determine for each market segment why customers buy the given service. That is, what are their buying *motives*? Sellers must determine buying patterns for their services — when, where, and how do customers buy, who does the buying, and who makes the buying decisions? The psychological determinants of buying behaviour — attitudes, perceptions, and personality — become even more important when marketing services rather than goods, because typically we cannot touch, smell, or taste a service offering. In like manner, the sociological factors of social-class structure and small-group influences are market determinants for services. The fundamentals of the adoption and diffusion of innovation are also relevant in the marketing of services.[6]

Some of the trends noted in Chapters 4 to 6 are particularly worth watching because they carry considerable influence in the marketing of services. As an example, increases in disposable income and discretionary buying power mean a growing market for health care services, insurance, and transportation services. Shorter working hours result in increased leisure time. More leisure time plus greater income means larger markets for recreation and entertainment services.

Market segmentation strategies also can be adopted by services marketers. We find apartment rental complexes for students, for single people, and for the over-65 crowd. Some car repair shops, such as Autotrend of Calgary, target owners of foreign cars. Limited-service motel chains cater to the economy-minded market segment, while all-suite hotels seek to attract families and business travellers.

## Planning of Services

New services are just as important to a service company as new products are to a goods-marketing firm. Similarly, the improvement of existing services and elimination of unwanted, unprofitable services are also key goals.

Product planning and development has its counterpart in the marketing program of a service organization. Management must select appropriate strategies based on answers to these questions:

- What services will be offered?
- What will be the breadth and depth of the service mix?
- How will the services be positioned?
- What attributes, such as branding, packaging, and service quality, will the service have?

**Services Offering** New services are just as important to a service company as new products are to a goods-producing company. Many firms have become successful by identifying a previously unsatisfied consumer need, and then developing a service to address that need. A good example is the number of regional airlines that now serve smaller cities and towns in Canada, operating small aircraft and charging low prices to fly passengers to larger centres. The introduction of new services should involve a process very similar to that which may be used by manufacturers in introducing new tangible products. Attention must be paid to addressing customer needs and to knowing what will appeal to the customer. Failure to do so will lead to the same lack of success that manufacturers encounter when they do not follow these principles in launching new tangible products.[7]

**Service-Mix Strategies** Several of the product-mix strategies discussed in Chapter 10 can be employed effectively by services marketers. Consider the strategy of *expanding or enhancing the line of services offered*. This is often referred to as a process of adding value for the customer. In fact, one of the most effective ways of adding value to existing products and services is by adding new support services. Some retail chains such as Sears have expanded into financial and travel services. Rental car companies offer no-smoking cars and rent cellular telephones. United Parcel Service enhanced its existing parcel delivery service by including electronic, on-line tracking of all ground and air packages. By using a cellular data service, UPS can provide the status of customers' packages and confirm delivery in seconds. Nearly 1 million cellular calls are made from UPS delivery vans in Canada and the United States every day, making UPS the largest cellular telephone user in the world.[8]

Some companies have taken a hard look at certain of the services they offer their customers in light of the recent recession. Some airlines, for example, have begun to offer no-frills service where the passenger pays only for the flight — no meal, no drinks, no magazines. Unprofitable services have been cut from the lines of some firms, suggesting that business may be doing a better job of assessing the profitability of intangible offerings. In the public sector this has been even more obvious, as universities, colleges, hospitals, and some government departments have reduced the services they have been offering or have begun to charge customers for services that were previously offered "free."

## MARKETING AT WORK

### FILE 12-2 GETTING CLOSE TO THE LISTENER

"To build brand loyalty in the 1990s, you have to create a bond with your audience by giving them what they're looking for, when they're looking for it," says Rob Mise, operations manager at Toronto radio station CFRB-AM. And Mise hit on the perfect way of creating such a bond — by copying retailers and creating a loyalty program for its listeners, a program not unlike Zeller's "Club Z."

Now people tuning in to CFRB can call in and join the Listener's Club by simply responding to a three-to-five-minute questionnaire. This places them on a marketing data base that allows the radio station to more precisely determine the nature and desires of its listeners. Furthermore, it also attracts advertisers, who — with these lists — can target particular goods and services to potentially hot sales prospects. As a result, CFRB boosts its market share, generates new revenues, and solidifies relationships with both listeners and advertisers.

Although creating a data base of loyal listeners takes time — two years in CFRB's case — the effort required is relatively simple and of minimal cost. And once it gets going, a loyalty club can branch out in many directions. CFRB launched a daily newsletter that it faxes to advertisers and produces a Listener Club magazine featuring behind-the-scenes articles, program guides, and contest opportunities that proved interesting to members. Furthermore, at CFRB-sponsored events such as store openings and home shows, members are invited to bring their magnetic cards and "swipe" them through a magnetic card reader that offers them instant prizes from CFRB draws and instant discounts from advertisers. Bringing a card reader on location not only increases traffic, but draws more listeners when club members tune in to the on-air draws. At the same time, within minutes, CFRB and its advertisers have a list of who attended a given event.

Source: Ron Mise, "How a Database Can Boost Loyalty," *Marketing*, March 7, 1994, p. 19.

Many firms have moved to *alter their services offering* in response to competition or to customer demands. To better serve customers who may be having difficulty coping with tough economic times, the Bank of Montreal began to offer a free financial planning service available to customers and noncustomers through a 1-800 number, mail, or fax.[9] Some car-wash operators in the United States have equipped their waiting rooms with rabbit-petting pens, aquariums, sundecks, cable television, games tables for kids — and free popcorn! The Clean Duds franchise chain now operates more than 70 Duds'n'Suds laundromat locations in Canada, Northern Ireland, and England that serve beer and snacks to customers while they wait for their laundry to wash and dry. It is estimated that 90 percent of laundromats in North America now offer some form of ancillary services, ranging from sit-down restaurants, video games, tanning salons, to exercise rooms — and even dating services![10]

*Managing the life cycle of a service* is another strategy that is being practised more and more by services marketers. Recognizing that the credit card industry is in its maturity stage, Canadian banks have explored new ways of getting their cards into the hands of new customers and of expanding use of the cards. The result in many cases is that consumers now carry several credit cards where they had only one previously. The new variations on the VISA card include a deal between the Toronto Dominion Bank and General Motors which sees 5 percent of all charges on the TD VISA held as a rebate that can be saved (up to a maximum of $500 per year for five years) and applied towards the purchase of a GM vehicle. CIBC offers a similar deal with Ford Motor Company of Canada, allowing for savings of up to $700 per year. This "co-branding" of credit cards has really extended the concept of the credit card as a means of savings towards a major purchase. The Bank of Montreal is one bank that has developed "affinity cards" on behalf of major universities, including McGill, Queen's, and Dalhousie; a percentage of cardholders' (usually alumni) purchases on Bank of Montreal's affinity MasterCard are donated to the participating university. Probably the most successful "new" credit card launch in recent years was the CIBC Aerogold VISA card, which allows holders to accumulate Air Canada Aeroplan points by using the card. The objective of all such programs is to extend the life of the credit card by developing new uses and increased usage.[11]

Service Features In some respects, product planning is easier for services than for goods. Packaging and labelling really are nonexistent in services marketing. However, other features — branding and quality management, for example — present greater challenges for services industries.

**Branding of services** is a problem because maintaining consistent quality (a responsibility of brand ownership) is difficult. Also, a brand cannot be physically attached to a label or to the service itself. A services marketer's goal should be to create an effective brand image. The strategy to reach this goal is to develop a total theme that includes more than just a good brand name. To implement this strategy, the following tactics may be used:[12]

- *Include a tangible good as part of the brand image* — like the umbrella of Travelers Insurance, Prudential's Rock of Gibraltar, or the koala bear of Qantas.
- *Tie in a slogan with the brand* — for instance, "You're in good hands with Allstate" or "Membership has its privileges" (American Express).
- *Use a distinctive colour scheme* — such as Avis's red or the green of the Toronto Dominion Bank.

**UPS not only delivers; they know where the package is at all times.**

Life is unpredictable. Your courier shouldn't be.
If you'd like to be absolutely sure of at least one thing tomorrow, call UPS today.
We've invested more than 12 months and 20 million dollars to give you more control over every item you send.
Four new levels of service let you pick your speed — and your price. Canada's first cellular tracking network monitors every move.
And our money-back delivery guarantees ensure on-time arrival. Even on Saturday.*
If there's room in your life for that kind of reliability, put us to the test. Just dial our new toll-free hotline, 1-800-PICK-UPS, for a prompt pickup today. And the confidence of knowing exactly what's going to happen tomorrow. United Parcel Service Canada Ltd.
UPS
Every address in every province and territory. UPS guarantees on-time delivery to places many couriers don't deliver at any time.
UPS EXPRESS
UPS EXPEDITED
UPS STANDARD
UPS ECONOMY
10:30 AM — NOON — 2:00 PM — 5:00 PM — GUARANTEED
Tell us when you want it there; we guarantee it. Not just to the day, but the hour. All at rates that can save you real money. With four new levels of time-definite service, only one courier in Canada offers you that kind of control.
Need a quick pickup? Pick up the nearest phone and call 1-800-PICK-UPS, our new toll-free hotline.
Thanks to the only cellular network in Canada, you can monitor your urgent documents and packages 24 hours a day, 7 days a week, and even confirm delivery within seconds.
Only UPS captures the recipient's actual signature with this powerful hand-held computer.
North America's ninth-largest airline speeds your documents and packages to over 190 countries worldwide.
United Parcel Service
4,800 employees and 1,400 vehicles across Canada could make your life more predictable.
*See service guide for guarantee and time-in-transit details. ©1993 United Parcel Service Canada Ltd.

**Management of Service Quality** In our brief discussion of product quality in Chapter 11, we noted the elusiveness of this important product feature. Quality is difficult to define, measure, control, and communicate. Yet in services marketing, the quality of the service is critical to a firm's success. Two airlines each fly a Boeing 747 for the same fare; two auto repair shops each use Ford or Chrysler parts and charge the same price; and two banks each offer the same investment accounts at identical interest rates. Assuming similar times and locations, quality of service is the only factor that differentiates the offerings in each of these paired situations.

However difficult it may be to define the concept of service quality, management must understand one thing: *Quality is defined by the consumer and not by the producer-seller of a service*. Your hairstylist may be delighted with the job she did on your hair. But if you think your hair looks terrible, then the service quality was poor. What counts is what consumers think about a service. Service quality that does not meet customer expectations can result in lost sales from present customers and a failure to attract new customers. Consequently, it is imperative that management strives to maintain *consistent* service quality at or above the level of consumer expectations. Yet it is sometimes virtually impossible to standardize service quality — that is, to maintain consistency in service output. Performance quality typically varies even within the same organization. This is true in such diverse fields as opera, legal services, landscaping, baseball, health care, and marketing courses.[13]

As part of managing service quality, an organization should design and operate an ongoing quality-improvement program that will monitor the level and consistency of service quality. A related, but also difficult, task is to evaluate service quality by measuring customer satisfaction — that is, customers' perceptions of the quality of an organization's services.[14]

Most successful marketers of services and those responsible for the services associated with tangible products have begun to introduce programs that will allow them to measure the quality of the service they provide, as perceived by their customers. Many businesses have existed for years under the assumption that management knew what the customer wanted and how he or she wished to be treated. The most successful have now abandoned that way of thinking and have subscribed to the maxim that "good service is whatever the customer says it is." Thus, a program to measure the perceived quality of a business's service must start by defining the aspects of the contact with the company the customer considers to be most important.[15]

Research with a number of Canadian and foreign companies in various industries has confirmed that consumers consider three components of service to be important: (1) the nature of the *service itself* or of services required to ensure that a product performs to expectations; (2) the *process* by which the product or service is delivered; and (3) interaction with the *people* who deliver the service (see Figure 12-2).

For example, customers of Bell Canada and other telephone companies are interested in ensuring that their telephone systems work properly, that calls go through, and that reception is clear (the "product" aspects of the service). In fact, as technology has improved in the telecommunications industry, customers do not expect their telephone systems ever to fail. The next component of service relates to the processes the telephone company has in place to provide and support the service — the accuracy of telephone bills, the speed with which new lines are installed, and how often sales people call to explain new services. Finally, the quality of service as perceived by customers is related to the way in which employees of the company treat their customers — whether operators are courteous and polite, whether sales people know the technology, and how complaints are resolved.

**FIGURE 12-2**
**The domain of customer service.**

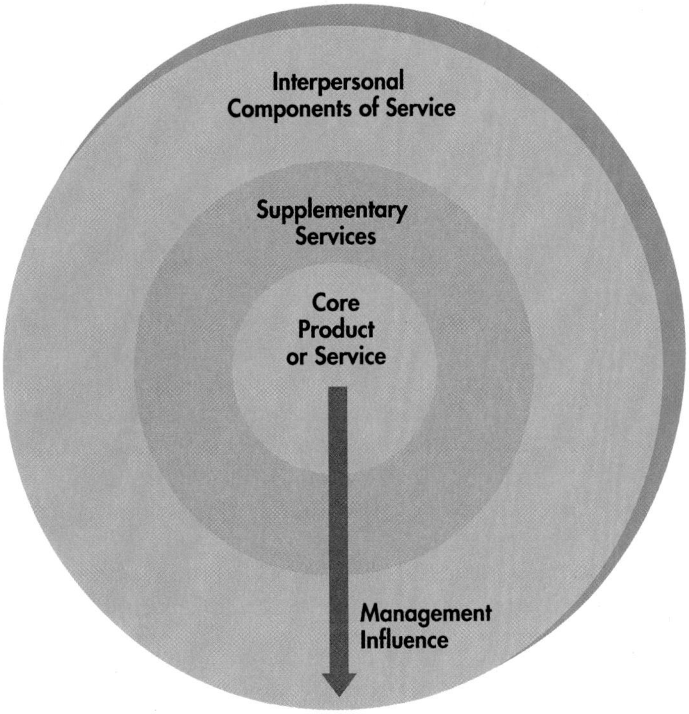


One author has suggested that as the nature of service moves farther away from the actual product or service, and more towards the "people" aspects of service, the less control management has over the delivery, and therefore the quality, of the service offered.[16] For example, an airline company can control the actual flight from Toronto to Vancouver (the basic service, getting passengers from one city to another). Barring unforeseen circumstances management can control, to a greater or lesser extent, the services that support that basic product: the frequency of flights, departure and arrival times, the number of ticket agents at the counter, baggage-handling systems, and type of meals served.

Management loses much more control over the details of the service provided at the interface between customer and employee — how the ticket agent greets the customer at the check-in counter, whether the baggage handler puts the suitcase on the right plane, whether the flight attendants are pleasant and helpful. In fact, it is in this latter component of service that many companies feel their greatest potential lies to differentiate themselves from the competition. Among international airlines, Air Canada, Singapore Airlines, and Cathay Pacific try to feature superior service and "cabin comfort" in their advertising.

It is this realization that employees have the potential to make or break a relationship with a customer that has led many companies to introduce programs of **internal marketing**. These are programs intended to ensure that employees "buy in" to the concept of customer service and appreciate that every satisfied customer means a returning customer. Again, the more progressive companies, and those that are most committed to exceptional levels of customer service, have developed elaborate training and motivation programs that emphasize excellence in treating the customer and reward those employees who treat customers well.

## Pricing of Services

In the marketing of services, nowhere is there a greater need for managerial creativity and skill than in the area of pricing. Earlier we noted that services are extremely perishable, they usually cannot be stored, and demand for them often fluctuates considerably. All these features carry significant pricing implications. To further complicate the situation, customers may perform some services themselves (auto and household repairs, for example).

These considerations suggest that the elasticity of demand for a service should influence the price set by the seller. Interestingly enough, sellers often do recognize inelastic demand. They then charge higher prices. But they fail to act in opposite fashion when faced with an elastic demand — even though a lower price would increase unit sales, total revenue, utilization of facilities, and probably net profit.

Certainly, perfect competition does not apply to any great extent, if at all, in the pricing of services. Because of the heterogeneity and difficulty of standardizing quality, most services are highly differentiated. Also, it is virtually impossible to have complete market information. As an example, consider how difficult it is to get reliable, detailed information on accountants' or lawyers' fees. In any given market, such as a neighbourhood, often there are geographic limits within which a buyer will seek a service. Consequently, there are not a large number of sellers. The heavy capital investment required to produce certain services (transportation, broadcasting, communications) often greatly limits the freedom of entry.

Nevertheless, in recent years price competition in many service areas has increased considerably, going through three identifiable phases:

- In the first phase, price is barely mentioned in the organization's advertising. For example, the Royal Bank of Canada, in advertising its V.I.P. Service, will emphasize the various aspects of the service and how to contact an Account Manager, but will not mention price.
- In the second phase, the seller uses a market segmentation strategy to target a given market at a specific price. To illustrate, the Royal Bank of Canada may advertise its Royal Certified Service and may also mention that this enhanced package of banking services may be had for a certain low monthly charge.
- The third phase involves out-and-out price competition as firms stress comparative prices in their advertising. As banking has become more and more competitive, we have seen advertising for the Royal Bank and others stressing their mortgage rates and the interest rates being paid on deposit accounts.

Many of the pricing strategies discussed in Chapter 13 are applicable to services marketing. Quantity discounts, for instance, are used by car-rental agencies. Daily rates are lower if you agree to rent the car for a week or a month at a time. Cash discounts are offered when insurance premiums are paid annually instead of quarterly. Accountants and management consultants can use a variable-price policy. Geographic pricing policies may apply, although the variable here is time, not freight charges. Mechanics will charge more if they must travel out of town, and engineers will usually command higher fees for work in foreign countries.

## Channels of Distribution for Services

Traditionally, most services have been sold directly from producer to consumer or business user. No intermediaries are used when the service cannot be separated from the seller or when the service is created and marketed simultaneously. For example, public utilities, medical care, and repair services are typically sold without intermediaries. Not using intermediaries does limit the geographic markets that services sellers can reach. But it also enables sellers to personalize their services and get quick, detailed customer feedback.

The only other frequently used channel includes one agent intermediary. Some type of agent or broker is often used in the marketing of securities, travel arrangements, enter-

**Professional service firms are advertising more and more.**

tainment, and housing rentals. Sometimes dealers are trained in the production of the service and then are **franchised** to sell it. This is the case with Sanitone dry cleaning, Midas Muffler shops, Computerland, and similar franchises.

In recent years, some firms have realized that the characteristic of inseparability is not an insurmountable limitation to a seller's distribution system. With a little imagination, a services marketer can broaden distribution considerably. Let's look at some examples, starting with location.

The service seller or seller's agent should be conveniently located for customers, because many services cannot be delivered. Many motels and restaurants have gone out of business when a new highway bypassed their locations, thereby drawing away customer traffic. On the other hand, banks have increased business by installing 24-hour automated banking machines and by launching telephone banking and allowing customers to access their accounts by computer from their offices. Dental centres, chiropractors, and optometrists have opened offices in shopping-centre malls. Retail-store locations have been especially successful for dental centres, and the idea is spreading to all sections of the country. They offer convenience of location, extended hours, and parking.

The use of intermediaries is another way to expand distribution. Some banks have arranged for companies to deposit employees' pay cheques directly into their bank accounts. The employer thus becomes an intermediary in distributing the bank's service. Insurance firms have broadened distribution by setting up vending machines in airports. Canada Post now operates post offices in drugstores across Canada.

The characteristic of intangibility essentially eliminates physical distribution problems for most service producers. For example, other than office and other supplies, accountants have no physical inventory to store or handle. However, not all service producers are free from physical distribution headaches. A chain of equipment-rental stores, for example, would certainly have to contend with inventory problems.

### Promoting a Service

Several forms of promotion are used extensively in services marketing, but personal selling plays the dominant role. Whether or not they realize it, any employee of a service firm who comes in contact with a customer is, in effect, part of that firm's sales force. In addition to a regular sales force, customer contact personnel might include airline counter attendants, law-office receptionists, Federal Express delivery people, bank tellers, and ticket-takers and ushers at ballparks or theatres. We use the term **service encounter** to describe a customer's interaction with any service employee or with any tangible element such as a service's physical surroundings (bank, ballpark, legal office). Customers often form opinions of a company and its service on the basis of service encounters. Consequently, it is essential that management recognizes the strategic importance of service encounters and prepares contact personnel and physical surroundings accordingly. A key step in preparing to sell a service is to provide sales training and service information for contact personnel, impressing on them the importance of their role.[17]

For years, of course, *advertising* has been used extensively in many service fields — hotels, transportation, recreation, and insurance, for example. What is new is the use of advertising by professional-services firms, including legal, accounting, and health services such as physiotherapists and chiropractors. Previously, professional associations in such fields prohibited advertising on the grounds that it was unethical. While some associations still control the type of advertising that may be done, the promotion of professional services is much more open and accepted than ever before.

In *sales promotion*, while point-of-purchase displays of services offered are often impossible, displays of the *results* of using a service can be effective. Many service firms, especially in the recreation and entertainment fields, benefit considerably from free *publicity*. Sports coverage by newspapers, radio, and television provides publicity, as do newspaper reviews of movies, plays, and concerts. Travel sections in newspapers have helped sell transportation, accommodation, and other services related to the travel industry.

As an *indirect type of promotion*, engineers, accountants, lawyers, and insurance agents may participate actively in community affairs as a means of getting their names before the public. Some professional firms are even offering guarantees.[18] Service firms (banks, public utilities, lawyers) may advertise to attract new industry to the community. They know that anything that helps the community grow will automatically mean an expanded market for their services.

## THE FUTURE OF SERVICES MARKETING

The boom in the service economy in recent years has been accompanied by a significant increase in competition in many service industries. This competition has been stimulated by several factors. One is the reduction in government regulation in some industries — airlines, trucking, and banking, for example. Relaxed regulations by professional organizations now permit advertising in the medical, legal, and other professions. New techniques have opened new service fields — in solar energy and information processing, for instance. Technological advances have also brought automation and other "industrial" features to formerly all-hand-labour service industries. Service chains and franchise systems are replacing the small-scale independent in many fields, including take-out food, auto repairs, beauty shops, and real estate brokerage.

### MARKETING AT WORK

### FILE 12-3 SHOPPING BY MAIL REQUIRES EXCELLENT SERVICE

The Canadian Direct Marketing Association, in a 1991 study, estimated that Canada's mail-order industry was generating annual sales of about $2.2 billion and had grown at a rate of 7 percent annually from 1977 to 1985, and at about 3 percent annually thereafter. The industry continues to be a bright spot in retailing. A spokesman for Sears Canada, the largest Canadian catalogue operation, says that sales are "going stronger than ever."

Sales by catalogue are expected to continue to grow through the 1990s before their place in the market begins to be eroded by the effect of television home shopping networks, whose impact has yet to be felt in Canada. To take advantage of the continuing boom in catalogue sales, some established catalogue retailers such as Regal Greetings and Gifts, whose traditional business has been in cards and gifts, have branched into new areas of operation. Regal, for example, has signed a deal with Walt Disney Co. to distribute children's clothing by mail in Canada.

Much of the mail order business in clothing in Canada flows out of the country to massive catalogue operations such as L. L. Bean and Lands' End, south of the border. These U.S. retailers have been so successful in Canada that they are making every effort to make catalogue shopping as easy as possible for their Canadian customers. These companies have set up separate departments to process Canadian orders. Rather than have the customer do all the work or paying duty and clearing customs, the U.S. catalogue giants add the appropriate rate of duty and the GST to the customer's bill, clear the order through Canada Customs, and have it delivered right to the customer's door.

Source: "Mail-order Firms Putting Shoppers First," *Globe and Mail*, August 8, 1994, p. B11.

### Need for Increased Productivity

The growth in service businesses has also brought about deterioration in the quality of many services. In general, service industries are often plagued by poor management, inefficiency, and low productivity. This inefficiency — and the need to increase productivity — is probably the biggest problem facing service industries. Low productivity also has significant implications for the health of the total economy. Service industries are very labour-intensive compared with manufacturing. Thus wage increases in the service sector of the economy have a major impact on price levels and inflation. Furthermore, the forecast for the remainder of the 1990s is for continued growth in the service sector, but a decrease in the labour pool for these industries. This projected labour shortage is likely to result in fundamental changes as service industries seek ways to improve productivity rates.

Service firms are employing various strategies to improve productivity. One is to invest in education and training programs, not just to teach basic skills but also to improve employees' efficiency. Another strategy is to bring in new technology and adopt methods used in manufacturing. Machines have enhanced or even replaced labour in a wide range of service industries. The most widely adopted technology has been some form of computer-based information system. Computers have increased the efficiency of operations in countless service firms. But the flip side is that computers (or computer users) many times have fallen short of their potential. Sometimes the users are not properly trained, or existing systems are not adapted to make the most effective use of new technologies. A third productivity improvement strategy is to restructure jobs so that each employee can accomplish a lot more in the same amount of time. Thus, auto repair shops have employees who specialize in brakes, transmissions, or mufflers. The introduction of assembly-line techniques at Burger King, Harvey's, and McDonald's has increased output per employee.

However, the basic premise of the manufacturing model is that machines and technology are the primary keys to increased productivity and successful operations. The people who deliver the services are less important — so goes the premise. But this premise simply no longer works in the competitive services environment of the 1990s. Instead, we need a model that puts customer-contact employees first and then designs the business operations around these people. Four key elements in this new model are:[19]

- Companies value investments in people at least as much as investments in machines.
- Firms use technology to *support* the work of customer-contact people, rather than using it to monitor or replace these workers.
- Companies make recruiting and training as important for sales people and other customer-contact employees as for executives.
- Management ties compensation to performance for employees at every level from bottom to top.

McDonald's, Taco Bell, and ServiceMaster are examples of firms working to implement this new services model. They would agree with Ron Zemke, the president of Performance Research Associates, who said, "No amount of marketing money and moxie can wash away the effect of poor frontline service." Michael Quinlan, McDonald's CEO, summed up the changing times when he said, "In the seventies, we focused on *serving* the customer; in the eighties, we emphasized *satisfying* the customer, and now, in the nineties, our goal is to *exceed customer expectations*."[20]

## Performance Measurement in Services Organizations

Profit-seeking service firms can evaluate their performance by using quantitative measures such as market share or return on investment, and then compare these figures with industry averages and trends. Unfortunately, many firms, particularly smaller businesses, do not have access to such comparative data and are unable to *benchmark* themselves against other companies. For many, it would be inappropriate to compare themselves to much larger firms or those that operate in quite different markets. In any event, market share and return on investment are much too broad to serve as good measures of how the service company is performing.

To measure their performance, therefore, companies that operate in service industries must address the question of how consumers perceive the quality of the service provided and how well they are doing in meeting customers' expectations of service. One of the principal issues relates to how such measurement of perceived service quality is to be carried out; another deals with what should be measured. There are many ways to measure service quality, some of which have been mentioned in this chapter. But it is not a simple process and is made all the more difficult by the fact that we are dealing with intangibles and that every customer's definition of acceptable quality is different. This issue of developing a sound basis for measuring the quality of service is one that will command the attention of services marketers in the future.

Another issue relating to measurement deals with the question of measuring payback on investment in service and with determining where such investment should be directed. For example, should a bank or airline or hotel chain spend much to provide superb service to a customer who may bring them little business and whose account may cost the company a great deal to service? Should a retail store invest in superior service if most of the customers it serves are passing traffic and very few can be counted on for repeat business? These are questions that must be addressed by services marketers in deciding where to invest in the improvement of service. Dealing with this issue will also require improved cost accounting systems in many companies so that they can track the effectiveness of spending money on service improvements.[21]

The analysis and management of customer complaints is an evaluation tool that can be used by both not-for-profit and profit-seeking organizations. The complaint-management process involves keeping track of: (1) customer complaints; (2) how they are resolved by company employees; and (3) whether the complaint handling was satisfactory enough so that the complaining customer ends up as a returning customer. One hotel chain effectively uses this complaint-management process to:

- Determine where to concentrate its customer-satisfaction attention.
- Compare the profitability of various complaint-handling activities.
- Demonstrate to customer-contact employees the importance of complaint management.[22]

### Prospects for Growth

Services will continue to take an increasing share of the consumer dollar, just as they have done over the past 40 years. This forecast seems reasonable even for periods of economic decline. History shows that the demand for services is less sensitive to economic fluctuations than the demand for goods. The demand for *business* services should also continue to expand as business becomes more complex and as management further recognizes its need for business-service specialists. In *professional* services especially, the use of marketing programs is expected to increase considerably during the coming decade. This expansion will occur as physicians, lawyers, and other professionals come to understand the economic benefits they can derive from an effective marketing program.

Unfortunately, many service firms today still do not provide a satisfactory level of service quality. Most consumers undoubtedly would agree with this assessment by Leonard Berry, for many years a researcher in services marketing. Any prediction of profitable growth in services firms is based on senior management's raising their aspirations, learning from past mistakes, and providing effective leadership. More specifically, future profitability depends on a company's ability to correct the following basic mistakes related to service quality:[23]

- **Spending money on the wrong priorities.** A major hotel planned to install colour TV sets in some guest bathrooms when 66 percent of customer calls to the housekeeping department were requests for irons and ironing boards. The hotel later reversed these priorities.
- **Reducing quality by flaws in service design.** Computer-generated billing statements that are impossible for customers to understand; clothing store dressing rooms that lack a minimum of two hooks — one for street clothes and one for try-on clothes.
- **Seeking easy solutions to quality problems.** Short-term, superficial, pep-talk solutions when the real need is an investment in managerial time, energy, and ego to change employee and management habits and attitudes regarding service quality.

- **Shortchanging fairness to customers.** Hotels and airlines that do not honour confirmed reservations; insurance companies that inadequately disclose important information.
- **Underinvesting in leadership development.** At all managerial levels, companies need leadership of employees faced with large numbers of demanding, sometimes rude, customers and other conditions that breed stress, fatigue, and discouragement.

Even manufacturers are taking an increasing interest in services as a basis for growth. Most tangible goods can be quickly and easily imitated. Consequently, manufacturers see their accompanying services as a key factor in giving a company a competitive advantage. The idea is to bundle services with goods to respond to a full range of customers' wants.[24]

## SUMMARY

Most product offerings are a mix of tangible goods and intangible services, located on a spectrum ranging from pure goods to pure services. Services are separately identifiable, intangible activities that are the main object of a transaction designed to provide want-satisfaction for customers. Conceptually, goods marketing and services marketing are essentially the same. In reality, however, the characteristics that differentiate services from goods usually call for quite different marketing programs.

The scope of services marketing is enormous. About half of what we spend goes for services, and about two-thirds of nongovernmental jobs are in service industries. Not only are services of considerable significance in our economy today, but it is predicted that the services sector will continue to grow faster than the goods sector of the economy. Services generally are intangible, inseparable from the seller, heterogeneous, and highly perishable, and they have a widely fluctuating demand. Each of these distinctive characteristics has several marketing implications.

The growth in services has not yet been matched by widespread understanding or acceptance of the marketing concept. Service organizations have been slow to adopt marketing programs and techniques that, in goods marketing, have brought satisfaction to consumers and profits to producers.

The development of a program for the marketing of services parallels that for goods, but takes into account the special characteristics of services. Management first identifies its target market and then designs a marketing mix to provide want-satisfaction for that market. In the product-planning stage, the element of service quality is critical to a company's success. Similar pricing strategies are used by services and goods producers. In distribution, intermediaries are used very sparingly, and location of the service marketer in relation to the market is important. Personal selling is the dominant promotional method used in services marketing.

As we move towards 2000, the service environment will continue to change. Probably the biggest challenge for service industries today is to develop ways to improve productivity. Productivity becomes more important as services account for a growing share of consumer expenditures and as consumers pay increasing attention to service.

## KEY TERMS AND CONCEPTS

**Services (343)**
**Personal services (344)**
**Business services (344)**
**Intangibility (345)**
**Inseparability (345)**
**Heterogeneity (346)**
**Perishability (347)**
**Fluctuating demand (347)**
**"Membership" programs (350)**
**Branding of services (353)**
**Service quality (354)**
**Internal marketing (355)**
**Services franchising (357)**
**Service encounter (358)**

## QUESTIONS AND PROBLEMS

1. How do you explain the substantial increase in expenditures for services relative to expenditures for tangible products in the last 40 years?
2. What are some marketing implications in the fact that services possess the characteristic of intangibility?
3. Why are intermediaries rarely used in the marketing programs of service firms?
4. Services are highly perishable and are often subject to fluctuations in demand. In marketing its services, how can a company offset these factors?
5. Cite some examples of service marketers that seem to be customer-oriented, and describe what these firms have done in this vein.
6. "Traditionally, marketers of services have *not* been marketing-oriented." Do you agree? If so, how do you account for this deficiency?
7. Present a brief analysis of the market for each of the following service firms. Make use of the components of a market discussed in Chapters 4 to 7.
   a. Canadian Airlines International.
   b. Hotel near large airport.
   c. Indoor tennis club.
   d. Credit union.
8. What are some of the ways in which each of the following service firms might expand its services mix?
   a. Chartered Accountant.
   b. Hairstyling salon.
   c. Bank.
9. Explain the importance of demand elasticity in the pricing of services.
10. "Personal selling should be the main ingredient in the promotional mix for a marketer of services." Do you agree? Discuss.
11. Present in brief form a marketing program for each of the following services. Your presentation should start with a description of the target market you have selected for the service. Then explain how you would plan, price, promote, and distribute the service.
    a. A disc jockey for private parties in the community.
    b. Your electric company.
    c. Household cleaning.

## HANDS-ON MARKETING

1. Identify a company in your town that manufactures tangible products (a woodworking shop, a metal fabricating plant, or similar operation) and examine the services this company also must supply in supporting the sale of its tangible products.
2. Review a service encounter in which you have recently participated where you were not pleased with the outcome. Consider what went wrong, using the model shown in Figure 12-2. Was the problem with the "core" product or service, or in one of the outer rings? What could the service provider do to improve your experience next time?

## NOTES AND REFERENCES


1. Sandy Fife, "Have a Nice Day," *Report on Business Magazine*, October 1991, pp. 49-56; and Marina Strauss, "Time Is Money, TD Bank Pledges," *Globe and Mail*, September 25, 1993, p. A1.
2. "The Final Frontier," *The Economist*, February 20, 1993, p. 63.
3. Leonard L. Berry and Terry Clark, "Four Ways to Make Services More Tangible," *Business*, October/December 1986, p. 53. Also see Betsy D. Gelb, "How Marketers of Intangibles Can Raise the Odds for Consumer Satisfaction," *Journal of Services Marketing*, Summer 1987, pp. 11-17.
4. James C. Cross and Bruce J. Walker, "Service Marketing and Franchising: A Practical Business Marriage," *Business Horizons*, November/December 1987, pp. 50-58.
5. Carolyn Green, "Room to Expand," *Marketing*, January 24, 1994, p. 9.
6. For an example of buying behaviour of firms when purchasing architectural and engineering services, see Ellen Day and Hiram C. Barksdale, Jr., "How Firms Select Professional Services," *Industrial Marketing Management*, May 1992, pp. 85-91.

7. For a model of new-service development, see Eberhard E. Scheuing and Eugene M. Johnson, "A Proposed Model for New Service Development," *The Journal of Services Marketing*, Spring 1989, pp. 25-34. Also see G. Lynn Shostack, "Service Positioning through Structural Change," *Journal of Marketing*, January 1987, pp. 34-43. For an insight into the process for introducing new services to the business-to-business market, see Ulrike de Brentani, "Success and Failure in New Industrial Services," *Journal of Product Innovation Management*, vol. 6, 1989, pp. 238-258.
8. Daniel DiMaggio, "Hitting the Right Track," *Marketing*, July 18, 1994, p. 18.
9. "B of M Cultivates Positive Image," *Globe and Mail*, May 17, 1994, p. B3.
10. Melissa Lee, "How to Enjoy Being Taken to the Cleaners," *Globe and Mail*, July 16, 1993, p. A7.
11. Tony Van Alphen, "GM, TD Hail New Card as Savings 'Vehicle'," *Toronto Star*, March 10, 1993, pp. D1, D6; and Kirk Makin, "The Lures of the Credit Card," *Globe and Mail*, June 18, 1993, p. B1.
12. Leonard L. Berry, Edwin F. Lefkowith, and Terry Clark, "In Services, What's in a Name?" *Harvard Business Review*, September-October 1988, pp. 28-30. Also see Sak Onkvisit and John J. Shaw, "Service Marketing: Image, Branding, and Competition," *Business Horizons*, January/February 1989, pp. 13-18.
13. For a good summary of service quality, see Leonard L. Berry, A. Parasuraman, and Valarie A. Zeithaml, "The Service-Quality Puzzle," *Business Horizons*, September/October 1988, pp. 35-43. Also, the topic of services and service quality is addressed from a number of different perspectives in a special issue of the *Journal of Retailing*, Spring 1993 (vol. 69, no. 1); finally, a rich collection of articles on the subject may be found in Roland T. Rust and Richard L. Oliver (eds.), *Service Quality: New Directions in Theory and Practice*, Thousand Oaks, CA: Sage Publications, 1994.
14. For more on the measurement of customers' perceptions of service quality, see A. Parasuraman, Valarie A. Zeithaml, and Leonard L. Berry, "SERVQUAL: A Multiple-item Scale for Measuring Consumer Perceptions of Service Quality," *Journal of Retailing*, Spring 1988, pp. 12-40; Stephen W. Brown and Teresa A. Swartz, "A Gap Analysis of Professional Service Quality," *Journal of Marketing*, April 1989, pp. 92-98; J. Joseph Cronin, Jr., and Steven A. Taylor, "Measuring Service Quality: A Reexamination and Extension," *Journal of Marketing*, vol. 56, July 1992, pp. 55-68; and A. Parasuraman, Leonard L. Berry, and Valarie A. Zeithaml, "Refinement and Reassessment of the SERVQUAL Scale," *Journal of Retailing*, vol. 67, no. 4, Winter 1991, pp. 420-450.
15. James G. Barnes and William J. Glynn, "The Customer Wants Service: Why Technology Is No Longer Enough," *Journal of Marketing Management*, vol. 9, 1993, pp. 43-53.
16. James G. Barnes, "The Role of Internal Marketing: If the Staff Won't Buy It, Why Should the Customer?" *Irish Marketing Review*, vol. 4, no. 2, 1989, pp. 11-21.
17. For further discussion of personal selling and service encounters, see William R. George, Patrick Kelly, and Claudia E. Marshall, "The Selling of Services: A Comprehensive Model," *Journal of Personal Selling & Sales Management*, August 1986, pp. 29-37; Mary Jo Bitner, Bernard H. Booms, and Mary Stanfield Tetreault, "The Service Encounter: Diagnosing Favorable and Unfavorable Incidents," *Journal of Marketing*, January 1990, pp. 71-84; and Mary Jo Bitner, "Evaluating Service Encounters: The Effects of Physical Surroundings and Employee Responses," *Journal of Marketing*, April 1990, pp. 69-82.
18. Christopher W. L. Hart, Leonard A. Schlesinger, and Dan Maher, "Guarantees Come to Professional Service Firms," *Sloan Management Review*, vol. 33, no. 3, Spring 1992, pp. 19-29.
19. Leonard A. Schlesinger and James L. Heskett, "The Service-Driven Service Company," *Harvard Business Review*, September-October 1991, pp. 71-81.
20. Both quotations from "How Does Service Drive the Service Company?" (letters to the editor regarding article in preceding footnote), *Harvard Business Review*, November-December 1991, pp. 146-147.
21. James G. Barnes and Judith A. Cumby, "The Cost of Quality in Service-oriented Companies: Making Better Customer Service Decisions Through Improved Cost Information," *Proceedings of the 23rd Annual Conference of the Atlantic Schools of Business*, Saint John, New Brunswick, November 4-6, 1993, pp. 241-250.
22. Roland T. Rust, Bala Subramanian, and Mark Wells, "Making Complaints a Management Tool," *Marketing Management*, vol. 1, no. 3, pp. 41-45.
23. Leonard L. Berry, "Improving America's Service," *Marketing Management*, vol. 1, no. 3, pp. 28-38. For each of the five fundamental mistakes, the author discusses several examples, the reasons for the mistakes, and suggestions for correcting the situation.
24. For a further discussion of developing manufacturers' services, with several company examples, see Richard B. Chase and David A. Garvin, "The Service Factory," *Harvard Business Review*, July/August 1989, pp. 61-69.

## CASES FOR PART 3

# CASE 3–1

# ACORN PARK HOTEL

*The Acorn Park Hotel was opened in 1946 and is located in South Kensington, a quiet area of London, not far from Harrods and other fashionable shops, and very close to a number of museums and art galleries. With only 80 rooms, the Acorn Park was typical of the properties in the Redpath Group of Inns, who prided themselves as hotels that created a special atmosphere for their guests. It was Monday, July 18 and Geoffrey Thornton, guest relations manager, had just entered his office. The morning mail had arrived and the first envelope Thornton opened contained the following letter.*

**Martha K. Stone, QC**
**Barrister and Solicitor**
**3265 Main Street**
**Fredericton, NB, Canada**
**E3B 4K6**

July 13, 1994

Mr. Geoffrey Thornton
Guest Relations Manager
Acorn Park Hotel
100 Bromley Road, London

Dear Mr. Thornton:

My husband and I have just returned home, having spent the past ten days in London on a combined business and pleasure trip. We decided to end our trip with a short weekend stay at the Acorn Park before returning to Canada, as your hotel had been recommended by some good friends of ours who stayed there last summer. Our friends had nothing but good things to say about the Acorn Park Hotel. But, despite the hotel's excellent reputation, the service we received during our stay was quite the opposite. I have decided to write to you to describe the treatment my husband and I received from what can only be described as your tactless and unhelpful staff.

When we arrived last Friday, we were quite tired and were looking forward to relaxing in our room for a few hours before dinner. Upon checking in we were assigned room 216 which was, if I may say, not what one would expect in a four-star hotel. The room had not been cleaned, as items of clothing had been left by the previous guest. The window looked out on scaffolding and the room was unbearably hot. The person at the front desk, when I finally was able to get through, informed me that there was nothing she could do to find us an alternate room.

The next morning, we experienced totally unacceptable treatment when we ate breakfast in the dining room. The lady on the desk as we entered the dining room pointed out to us that, as we were not part of one of the tours staying at the hotel, our breakfast was not included in our room rate and we would have to pay for it! This was no surprise as we had fully expected to pay.

---

We were quite surprised as we were leaving the dining room to be stopped again by this lady who insisted that we either pay in cash or by credit card. Despite our protests that we were guests in the hotel and that she should simply put the charge on our room bill, she insisted that she had instructions to accept only cash or credit card payment from us, referring to the fact that our name was on a list that had been provided to her by the front office.

While I began the process of paying by credit card, my husband went looking for the front desk manager, who was most helpful and responded immediately. He accompanied my husband to the dining room where he ascertained that an error had been made and that the name opposite room 216 on the list which had been provided to the dining room staff was not ours. He apologized and the charge was allowed to go to our room bill. The dining room staff involved were totally unaccommodating and tactless in the manner in which they handled the matter. Needless to say, we did not eat breakfast at the hotel the following morning.

My second complaint refers to your telephone system. Shortly after arriving on Friday evening, I wanted to make an outside telephone call and dialled 9 to get an outside line. I did not get a second dial tone, but rather the line rang and rang for 15 or 20 rings with no answer. I tried two or three times before I could get an answer from the switchboard, only to be told that I should dial 9. Only when I explained that I had been dialling 9 was there an effort made to find out what had happened. Evidently, my line had been switched over in some way so that dialling 9 resulted in the telephone ringing at the front desk. Once this was rectified, I was able to make outside calls.

Checking out on Sunday morning was the final frustration. It was 9 o'clock; others were checking out, bus tours were leaving, guests were trying to have travellers' cheques cashed before their buses left, and the telephones were ringing constantly. The young lady who was working alone on the front desk was trying to deal with this confusion. Guests were becoming upset, the departure of the tours was being delayed, and your employee became so frustrated with the ringing telephones that she simply lifted them and placed them back down again, without answering them!

I do not blame the employee; she was doing her best under the circumstances. I find it totally unacceptable that a hotel would have one employee serving the front desk during what is one of the busiest periods of the day, and have her try to answer the telephones at the same time.

Despite the recommendation from our friends and the Acorn Park's excellent location, I would have to say that it is very unlikely that we will be back unless we have some assurance that the problems with customer service have been overcome. I would welcome your comments.

Sincerely

Martha K. Stone, QC

## QUESTIONS

1. Why did Martha Stone write her letter?
2. What factors contributed to her dissatisfaction?
3. How important were the following factors in affecting the service the Stones had received?
   - Product
   - Process
   - Performance
   - People
4. What were the Stones' expectations when they arrived at the Acorn Park Hotel?
5. What does Martha Stone expect to happen now that she has written?
6. What could or should the front desk manager have done when he was called to the dining room on Saturday morning?
7. What should Geoffrey Thornton do now? What factors will influence how he responds?

# CASE 3–2

# KODAK PHOTO CD

In 1990 Kodak announced a new technology for storing, working with, and viewing photographic images. It is a plastic compact disc that contains pictures in the form of digital information. Now Kodak faces the challenge of marketing this system to consumers and business users. It hopes gradually to phase in the new technology without cannibalizing its enormous stake in conventional film and colour-paper processing.

During the 1980s the development of self-focusing 35-mm cameras and improvements in film formulas made amateur photography easier and the quality of the photographs better. Meanwhile, the process of storing and retrieving photographs remained virtually unchanged — hence, an alternative, the Kodak Photo CD system, a method of digitizing photography.

Kodak developed the Photo CD system in conjunction with Philips NV, a Dutch electronics firm. In its simplest form, Photo CD allows the user to store photographs on a CD and display them on a TV screen. A single CD holds up to 100 pictures, which can be viewed, rearranged, and combined with sound. In addition, images on a CD can be copied endlessly, electronically transmitted anywhere in the world, and, with the help of a computer, trimmed, tinted, sharpened, shaded, and combined.

To use the Photo CD system, a consumer takes pictures using a standard 35-mm camera and film. The film is processed conventionally into negatives or slides. Each picture is then scanned and transferred into digital form, and the compressed digital image is written to a compact disc, called a CD master disc. Another major technological stride taken by Kodak was to shrink the images so they do not take up too much hard disc space. By compressing algorithms, images are able to be stored in fewer than six megabytes.

The pictures are displayed by inserting the disc into a remote-controlled Photo CD player, built by Philips. The units can be plugged into a TV and will also play back regular audio CDs when plugged into a stereo. The viewer can select specific pictures, program them to appear in a particular order, rotate the images, or zoom in for a close-up. Even better, each shot can be cropped to eliminate unwanted features and expand the portion users like best. In addition to the Photo CD player, the discs are compatible with two different types of computer CD players, the CD-1 and the CD-ROM XA.

Besides viewing convenience, the CDs offer other advantages over prints and negatives. They are non-erasable, so pictures cannot be inadvertently lost. They provide images whose resolution is 16 times greater than the standard required for television, so the reproduction quality is excellent. A Photo CD also functions as a negative from which a photofinisher can make an unlimited number of prints with no loss in picture quality. Finally, pictures can be added to a disc until it reaches capacity.

Kodak began by marketing its Photo CD imaging workstations to a few large photofinishing shops across Canada. The necessary equipment to produce Photo CDs cost a photofinisher under $150,000 for the whole package. The workshop consisted of five components: a high-resolution film scanner, a Sun SPARCstation computer, imaging processing software, a disc writer and a thermal printer. Having a roll of 24-exposure film developed and put on a CD master disc cost consumers about $30. The cost of a Photo CD player, necessary to view the pictures, varied depending on the features the player offered. There were models to choose from. The entry-level PCD 250 retailed for $550. The PCD 850, which had a "zoom-in" capacity, sold for $650, and the PCD 5850 came with a carousel much like that on a slide projector and was priced at $850. The Photo CD player was available across Canada through photographic retail outlets and other music and home-entertainment stores.

In 1993 Kodak introduced a more advanced Photo CD system for the consumer market called the Portfolio disc. This product allowed the user to merge Photo CD images with text, graphics, and sound. For example, a person could arrange the photos from a vacation trip with the voices of those in the pictures describing the scenes, a recording made on the trip, background music, maps, and dates. Portfolio discs could be created in two ways, both requiring a consumer's direct involvement. One approach was to visit a photofinisher with a minilab equipped with authoring software that would enable the consumer to combine photos with sound, text, or graphics. The other option was for

Adapted, in part, from James Pollock, "Coming to TV: Silent Pictures," *Marketing*, August 3, 1992, p. 3; "CD Player Can Show Photos on TV," *The Gazette*, September 19, 1990, p. D4; Frances Misutka, "Photo CD Systems Changing the Focus of Photography," *The Financial Post*, vol. 5 (172), December 1, 1992, p. 26; Andrew Tausz, "Picture CDs Portray Colourful Future," *Globe and Mail*, July 22, 1992, p. B4.

computer buffs. By adding a CD input attachment to a personal computer and using software available from Kodak, consumers could create their own productions at home. A Portfolio disc held up to 800 images.

Kodak also anticipates commercial applications of Portfolio discs. Publishers are expected to use the Portfolio format to develop and distribute prerecorded educational and entertainment discs. For example, a company could produce baseball card discs for all the major league teams. A disc might include pictures as well as statistics and audio interviews with the players.

Kodak has also targeted various segments of the business market by identifying a variety of Photo CD commercial uses. Some of them are:

- **Professional photographers.** Photo CD discs provide them with an enhanced way of storing and retrieving the thousands of photos they take.
- **Corporate records storage.** Insurance companies and credit card companies make digital images of insurance claims and convert their paper receipts for storage. Police departments (with "mug shots" and fingerprints), driver's licence bureaus, and numerous other organizations that need ready access to thousands of records are potential customers.
- **Real estate agents.** Potential buyers can examine the exterior and interior of homes in a particular price range or location and hear a description of each without leaving the agent's office.
- **Health professions.** A physician or dentist can get a second opinion or a diagnosis by electronically sending a patient's visual and audio record to another health care professional.
- **Photo editors.** The people who track down the photographs for publications like this book and the companies that assemble and offer thousands of photos from which they make their selections can systematize the search process.
- **Entertainment and education.** For a generation raised on television, Photo CD offers an attractive medium. For example, a book about a young woman's solo trip across Australia, entitled *From Alice to Ocean*, is accompanied by a Photo CD. While reading the book, a person can also view pictures on TV that include narration by the author and indigenous sounds of the region.
- **Catalogues.** A catalogue of vacation destinations, various products, works of art, or anything else — combined with text, graphics, and sound — can be supplied to consumers.
- **Graphic designers.** Because of the computer power needed to store them, photographs typically create problems for graphic designers. In addition, once the information gets transferred on to a computer it tends to degenerate after a while. The Kodak CD system provides a solution. One CD will store anywhere from a dozen to a few thousand images, which makes one CD worth hundreds of computer discs. As well, with a CD the quality of the image does not deteriorate over time or with use.

To meet the needs of particular business applications, Kodak has adapted the basic disc. For example, catalogue CDs need more images but can get by with lower-quality pictures. By using a lower video resolution, Kodak was able to develop the Photo CD Catalogue disc, which can store 6,000 images and provide on-screen menus that allow a shopper to move through the catalogue quickly and easily. For professional photographers, Kodak designed the Pro Photo CD Master, which allows them to store the larger film formats they prefer. This model also offers them several security features to prevent the unauthorized use or reproduction of their pictures.

In addition to the Photo CDs, a number of camera makers, including Kodak, have their first versions of the computer-based camera on the market. Digital cameras, of course, rely on memory chips and not film. With digital cameras, the photo processing lab and scanner become obsolete as images can be incorporated directly into an electronic layout. However, computer-based cameras still cannot match the resolution of film-based cameras.

For both consumers and business users, Kodak has also developed Photo CD technology to make it possible to incorporate high-quality pictures in desktop publishing. Photos in a digital format on a disc can be read by computers with the appropriate hardware. Then anyone, from a consumer composing a family newsletter to an art director designing page layouts for a magazine, can use this technology.

Though Photo CD has many possible applications, Kodak initially focused its efforts on the consumer market because consumers worldwide take 60 billion photographs a year. However, consumers may not be as quick as businesses to see the advantages of Photo CD. Another problem is that using the system requires having both a disc and a disc player. This creates a predicament for consumers. They will not want to spend $30 to have their pictures put on a disc they cannot play, and they will not want to buy a player without a collection of discs to view.

## QUESTIONS

1. How new a product is Photo CD? Given your answer, what special marketing challenges does Kodak face?
2. Examine the benefits Photo CD offers consumers. Which of the three target-market strategies would you recommend?
3. How should the marketing effort directed to business users differ from the marketing aimed at consumers?

PART 4

# PRICE

**The development of a pricing structure and its use as part of the marketing mix**

We are in the process of developing a marketing mix to reach our target markets and achieve our marketing goals. Having completed product planning, we turn now to pricing, where we face two tasks. First, we must determine the base price for a product that is consistent with our pricing objectives; this endeavour is covered in Chapter 13. Second, we must decide on strategies (such as discounts and value pricing) to employ in modifying and applying the base price; these strategies are discussed in Chapter 14.

## CHAPTER 13 GOALS

In this chapter we cover the role of price in the marketing mix — what price is, how it can be used, and how it is set relative to such factors as product costs, market demand, and competitors' prices. After studying this chapter, you should have an understanding of:

- The meaning of price.
- The significance of price in our economy, to an individual firm, and in a consumer's mind.
- The concept of value and how it relates to price.
- Major pricing objectives.
- Key factors influencing price.
- The types of costs incurred in producing and marketing a product.
- Approaches to determining prices, including cost-plus pricing, marginal analysis, and setting prices in relation only to other prices in the market.
- Break-even analysis.

CHAPTER 13

# PRICE DETERMINATION

## Superior Cost Control Leads to Attractive Prices

IKEA, with eight large stores across Canada and many more around the world, is well known for its attractively designed products at very affordable prices. It also has appealing award-winning advertising, like the three newspaper campaign ads shown here. The ads by themselves tell you a bit about a firm that decided years ago to provide beautiful and well-designed home furnishings at popular and affordable prices and then developed a whole marketing system to achieve that.

IKEA started in a small office in Småland, Sweden, that sold pencils and seeds to local farmers. But soon, the office began to sell furniture as well. The owners wanted to let ordinary people enjoy what only the very rich could enjoy, a beautifully furnished home. This became IKEA's mission: to contribute to a better everyday life for the majority of people. They do this by offering a wide range of home furnishing items of good design and function, at prices so low that the majority of people can afford to buy them. This meant providing style, design, durability, variety, accessibility, and dependability in a different way. IKEA wanted its company, its products, and its prices to express the region's virtues of diligence and thrift.

IKEA concluded that traditional manufacturing and retailing was too expensive to allow it to achieve its mission of passing on attractive prices and value to its customers. It examined every detail of the growing business to find ways of saving money. By designing their own furniture, the owners could control the process from start to finish.

Ways were found to cut costs without affecting quality — like not lacquering the underside of a table as many times as the top or using pieces trimmed from table legs, which would ordinarily become waste, to create candleholders.

It also meant searching all over the world to find the least expensive manufacturers who could meet IKEA's strict quality standards. Placing large orders meant IKEA could get volume discounts plus the manufacturer's care and attention. Doing things differently to maintain quality at a good price meant using different materials than would normally be the case as well as manufacturing and assembling in a different way.

But the most unique way IKEA had of keeping costs down in order to deliver superior value was by making it easy for consumers to shop on their own without sales help and take their purchases home with them. Because IKEA furniture is designed for quick and easy assembly, and because it is flat-packed, there are huge savings in manufacturing, transportation, and storage. And as their catalogue says: "If your car won't hold all your IKEA furniture . . . simply add a roof rack. We sell them at cost . . . Return the rack and we'll return your money."[1]

The issue of how much a company should charge for its products and services will depend on many factors. In the IKEA example, we have illustrated the important role of costs in influencing the price that can be charged. There are, of course, many other factors that must be considered, including the target segment for the product or service and the prices being charged by competitors. These factors must be considered when a company introduces a new product or service or considers changing the price of an existing one.

In this chapter we will discuss major methods used to determine a price. Before being concerned with actual price determination, however, executives — and you — should understand the meaning and importance of price.

## MEANING OF PRICE

Some pricing difficulties occur because of confusion about the meaning of *price*, even though the concept is easy to define in familiar terms. Simply, **price** is the amount of money and/or other items with utility needed to acquire a product. Recall that **utility** is an attribute that has the potential to satisfy wants.

Thus price may involve more than money. To illustrate, the price of a rare Bobby Hull hockey card may be (1) $500, (2) the rookie cards for 10 players, or (3) some combination of dollars and baseball cards. Exchanging goods and/or services for other products is termed **barter**. Because our economy is not geared to a slow, ponderous barter system, we typically state price in monetary terms and use money as our medium of exchange.

### PRICE IS WHAT YOU PAY FOR WHAT YOU GET

Here are prices under various names:

- Tuition → Education
- Interest → Use of money
- Rent → Use of living quarters or a piece of equipment for a period of time
- Fare → Taxi ride or airline flight
- Fee → Services of a physician or lawyer
- Retainer → Lawyer's or consultant's services over a period of time
- Toll → Long-distance phone call or travel on some highways
- Salary → Services of an executive or other white-collar employee
- Wage → Services of a blue-collar employee
- Commission → Sales person's services
- Dues → Membership in a union or a club

And in socially undesirable situations, there are prices called blackmail, ransom, or bribery.

Source: Suggested in part by John T. Mentzer and David J. Schwartz, *Marketing Today*, 4th ed., Harcourt Brace Jovanovich, San Diego, 1985, p. 599.

Practical problems arise when we try to state simply the price of a product. Suppose you paid $325 for a desk, but your instructor paid only $175 for one of similar size. At first glance, it looks as if the instructor taught the student a lesson! Your desk — which has a beautiful finish — was delivered to your apartment, and you had a year to pay for it. Your instructor, a do-it-yourself buff, bought a partially assembled desk with no finish on it. It had to be assembled and then stained and varnished. The seller provided neither delivery nor credit. Now who paid the higher price? The answer is not as easy as it first appeared.

This example indicates that the definition depends on determining exactly what is being sold. A seller usually is pricing a combination of (1) the specific good or service that is the object of the transaction, (2) several supplementary services (such as a warranty), and (3) in a very real sense, the want-satisfying benefits provided by the product. Sometimes it is difficult even to define the price of the predominant good or service itself. On one model of automobile, a stated price may include radio, power steering, and power brakes. For another model of the same brand of auto, these three items may be priced separately. So, to know the real price of a product, you need to look at the identifiable components that make up that product.

## IMPORTANCE OF PRICE

Price is significant in our economy, to an individual firm, and in the consumer's mind. Let's consider each situation.

### In the Economy

A product's price influences wages, rent, interest, and profits. That is, a product's price influences the amounts paid for the factors of production: labour, land, capital, and entrepreneurship. Price thus is a basic regulator of the economic system because it influences the allocation of the factors of production. High wages attract labour, high interest rates attract capital, and so on. As an allocator of resources, price determines what will be produced (supply) and who will get the goods and services produced (demand).

Criticism of our system of reasonably free enterprise and, in turn, public demand for added restraints on the system are often triggered by negative reactions to prices or pricing policies. For example, concerns about rapidly rising prices (that is, inflation) may lead to a call for price controls. To reduce the risk of government intervention, businesses need to establish prices in a manner and at a level that consumers and government officials consider socially responsible. Of course, this prescription applies not just to pricing but to all marketing activities.

### In the Individual Firm

A product's price is a major determinant of the market demand for it. Price affects a firm's competitive position and its market share. As a result, price has a considerable bearing on a company's revenues and net profits. Through prices, money comes into an organization.

Nevertheless, several factors can limit how much effect pricing has on a company's marketing program. Differentiated product features, a favourite brand, high quality, convenience, or some combination of these and other factors may be more important to consumers than price. As we saw in Chapter 11, one object of branding is to *decrease* the effect of price on the demand for a product.

At the retail level, surveys consistently show that about one-fifth of shoppers are, generally, interested primarily in low prices.[2] This means that four-fifths are more concerned with other factors, such as those we just mentioned. In fact, about one-fourth of consumers are not at all concerned about price in making most of their purchases. To put the role of pricing in a company's marketing program in its proper perspective, it is only one of four marketing-mix elements that must be skilfully combined — and then adapted over time — to achieve business success.

### In the Consumer's Mind

Some consumers' perceptions of product quality vary directly with price. Typically, the higher the price, the better the quality is perceived to be. Haven't you been concerned about product quality — such as when you are looking at ads for compact disc players — if the price is unexpectedly low? Or, at the other extreme, have you selected a restaurant for a special dinner because you heard it was fairly high priced so you thought it would be very nice?

Shoppers make price-quality judgements particularly when they lack other information about product quality. Consumers' quality perceptions can also be influenced by such factors as store reputation and advertising.[3]

In the 1990s a growing number of consumers are concerned about price. Why? One reason is that price is a component of value. And more and more prospective buyers, both in consumer and business markets, are demanding better value in the goods and services they purchase.

**Value** is the ratio of perceived benefits to price and any other incurred costs. Time associated with shopping for the product, time and gasoline used travelling to the place of purchase, and time and perhaps aggravation assembling the product are examples of these *other incurred costs*. When we say a product has value, we don't necessarily mean it is inexpensive. Rather, value indicates that a particular product has the kinds and amounts of potential benefits — such as product quality, image, and purchase convenience — consumers expect from that product at a particular price level.

Many businesses are responding to consumers' calls for more value by devising new products. The intent is to improve value — essentially, the ratio of benefits to price. This can be accomplished by maintaining essential elements, adding a new element or two, dropping other elements to cut costs, and lowering prices.[4]

Other businesses are striving for better value with existing products. Fast-food firms, including McDonald's and Taco Bell, have reduced prices on basic items. "Combination meals," consisting of several items that collectively cost less than if purchased separately, are also gaining popularity.[5]

Attention to value was certainly heightened by the recent recession. However, don't expect concern about real value to dissipate. In the opinion of Jack Welch, chairman of General Electric, the 1990s is the "value decade."[6] According to market researchers, the increased emphasis on value reflects a more fundamental shift in consumer attitudes. At least in Canada and the United States, individuals, households, and organizations alike are now more cautious in their spending. Consumers' greater interest in the ratio of benefits to price has created a new approach to pricing, not surprisingly called "value pricing," which we will discuss in Chapter 14.

## PRICING OBJECTIVES

Every marketing activity — including pricing — should be directed towards a goal. Thus management should decide on its pricing objective before determining the price itself.[7] Yet, as logical as this may sound, few firms consciously establish, or explicitly state, a pricing objective.

To be useful, the pricing objective management selects must be compatible with the overall goals set by the company and the goals for its marketing program. Let's assume that a *company's goal* is to increase return on investment from its present level of 15 percent to 20 percent within three years. It follows that the *pricing goal* during this period must be to achieve some stated percentage return on investment. It would not be logical, in this case, to adopt the pricing goal of maintaining the company's market share or of stabilizing prices.

## MARKETING AT WORK

### FILE 13-1 PRICE MEANS COST AND VALUE

There is no question that the pricing decision is a very important one for the company trying to decide what to charge for its product or service. But how important is it to the consumer who is expected to buy that product or service? Marketers occasionally fall into the trap of believing that price is all-important in influencing the consumer's decision of whether to buy. Such is not always the case. Just a few years ago, a study was conducted of the retail price of food products in 50 cities and towns in Newfoundland to determine what factors contributed to differences in the prices paid by consumers in different towns. The main conclusion of the study was that the level of food prices is attributable mainly to factors such as the presence of large chain stores, the amount of competition, and the distance from main wholesale distribution centres. What was more surprising was that consumers in small, more isolated towns did not express as much concern about the level of food prices as had been expected. Consumers were more concerned about the variety of food products available and the quality of fresh fruit and vegetables. Many said that they would be prepared to pay even more for better quality and greater variety. Although consumers may complain about *price*, what they really want is better *value*.

We shall discuss the following **pricing objectives**:

- Profit-oriented:
  - To achieve a target return
  - To maximize profit
- Sales-oriented:
  - To increase sales volume
  - To maintain or increase market share
- Status quo-oriented:
  - To stabilize prices
  - To meet competition

Recognize that all these objectives can be sought — and hopefully attained — not just through pricing but also through other marketing activities such as product design and distribution channels. And all these objectives are ultimately aimed at satisfactory performance over the long run. For a business, that requires ample profits.

### Profit-Oriented Goals

Profit goals may be set for the short or long run. A company may select one of two profit-oriented goals for its pricing policy.

Achieve a Target Return  A firm may price its product to **achieve a target return** — a specified percentage return on its *sales* or on its *investment*. Many retailers and wholesalers use a target return *on sales* as a pricing objective for short periods such as a year or a fashion season. They add an amount to the cost of the product, called a **markup**, to cover anticipated operating expenses *and* provide a desired profit for the period. Safeway or Loblaws, for example, may price to earn a net profit of 1.5 percent on a store's sales. A chain of men's clothing stores may have a target profit of 6 percent of sales, and price its products accordingly. (Markup and other operating ratios are discussed fully in Appendix C following this chapter.)

Achieving a target return *on investment* is measured in relation to a firm's net worth (its assets minus its liabilities). This pricing goal is often selected by the leading firm in an industry. Target-return pricing is used by industry leaders such as Du Pont, Alcan, and

Saab appeals to value-sensitive luxury-conscious consumers to increase share and profit.

Esso because they can set their pricing goals more independently of competition than can smaller firms in the industry. The leaders may price so that they earn a net profit that is 15 or 20 percent of the firm's net worth.

**Maximize Profits** The pricing objective of making as much money as possible is probably followed more than any other goal. The trouble with this goal is that to some people, **profit maximization** has an ugly connotation, suggesting profiteering, high prices, and monopoly.

In both economic theory and business practice, however, there is nothing wrong with profit maximization. Theoretically, if profits become high in an industry because supply is short in relation to demand, new capital will be attracted to increase production capacity. This will increase supply and eventually reduce profits to normal levels. In the marketplace it is difficult to find many situations where profiteering has existed over an extended period of time. Substitute products are available, purchases are postponable, and competition can increase to keep prices at a reasonable level.

Where prices are unduly high and entry into the field is severely limited, public outrage soon balances the scales. Such was the case with AZT, a drug that purports to prolong the lives of AIDS patients. At first, Burroughs Wellcome set AZT's price equivalent to about $8,000 for a one-year supply per patient. Following outcries from AIDS patients and their supporters, the company cut the price of AZT by 20 percent. If market conditions and public opinion do not bring about reasonable prices, government may intervene.[8] Extra-billing doctors and auto insurers in some provinces are accused of being greedy, and provincial governments have responded with regulated fees and rates.

A profit-maximization goal is likely to be far more beneficial to a company if it is pursued over the *long term*. To do this, however, firms may have to accept modest profits or even losses over the short term. For example, a company entering a new geographic market or introducing a new product frequently does best by initially setting low prices to build a large clientele. Repeat purchases from this large group of customers may allow the firm to maximize its profits over the long term.

The goal should be to maximize profits on *total output* rather than on each single product. In fact, a company may maximize total profit by setting low, relatively unprofitable prices on some products in order to stimulate sales of others. In its advertising on televised athletic events, the Gillette Company frequently promotes razors at very low prices. The firm hopes that once customers acquire Gillette razors, they will become loyal customers for Gillette blades, which generate healthy profits for the company.

### Sales-Oriented Goals

In some companies, management's pricing is focused on sales volume. The pricing goal may be to increase sales volume or to maintain or increase the firm's market share.

**Increase Sales Volume** This pricing goal of **increasing sales volume** is typically adopted to achieve rapid growth or to discourage potential competitors from entering a market. The goal is usually stated as a percentage increase in sales volume over some period, say, one year or three years. Management may seek higher sales volume by discounting or by some other aggressive pricing strategy, perhaps even incurring a loss in the short run. Thus, clothing stores run end-of-season sales, and auto dealers offer rebates and below-market financing rates on new cars to stimulate sales. Many vacation spots, such as golf courses and resorts, reduce prices during off-seasons to increase sales volume.

**Maintain or Increase Market Share** In some companies, both large and small, the pricing objective is to **maintain or increase market share**. Why is market share protected or pursued so vigorously? Most industries today are not growing much, if at all, *and* have excess production capacity. Many firms need added sales to more fully utilize their production capacity and, in turn, gain economies of scale and better profits. Since the size of the "pie" isn't growing in most cases, businesses that need added volume have to grab a bigger "slice of the pie" — that is, greater market share. The North American auto and airline industries illustrate these situations.

Other firms are intent on maintaining their market shares. In recent years, for instance, the Japanese yen rose considerably in relation to the Canadian and U.S. dollars.

Consequently, Japanese products — autos, for example — became more expensive in dollars and Japanese companies faced the prospect of losing market share. To maintain their shares, Toyota, Nissan, and Honda accepted smaller profit margins and reduced their costs so that they could lower their selling prices.

Occasionally a price war is started when one firm cuts its price in an effort to increase its market share. A gas station may lower the price of its gasoline below market level, or an airline may cut fares on certain routes. Other gas stations and airlines in those markets usually are forced to cut their prices just to maintain their market shares.

### Status Quo Goals

Two closely related goals — **stabilizing prices** and **meeting competition** — are the least aggressive of all pricing goals. They are intended simply to maintain the firm's current situation — that is, the status quo. With either of these goals, a firm seeks to avoid price competition.

Price stabilization often is the goal in industries where the product is highly standardized (such as steel or bulk chemicals) *and* one large firm historically has acted as a leader in setting prices. Smaller firms in these industries tend to "follow the leader" when setting their prices. What is the reason for such pricing behaviour? A price cut by any one firm is likely to be matched by all other firms in order to remain competitive; therefore, no individual firm gains, but all may suffer smaller profits. Conversely, a price boost is unlikely to be matched, but the price-changing firm faces a differential disadvantage because other elements of a standardized product such as gasoline are perceived to be fairly similar.

Even in industries where there are no price leaders, countless firms deliberately price their products to meet the prevailing market price. This pricing policy gives management an easy means of avoiding difficult pricing decisions.

Firms that adopt status-quo pricing goals to avoid price competition are not necessarily passive in their marketing. Quite the contrary! Typically these companies compete aggressively using other marketing-mix elements — product, distribution, and especially promotion. This approach is called *nonprice competition*.

**Gas stations' pricing goal usually is to meet competition.**

## FACTORS INFLUENCING PRICE DETERMINATION

Knowing the objective of its pricing, a company then can move to the heart of price management: determining the base price of a product. **Base price**, or *list price*, refers to the price of one unit of the product at its point of production or resale. This price does not reflect discounts, freight charges, or any other modification (discussed in the next chapter) such as leader pricing and value pricing.

The same procedure is followed in pricing both new and established products. Pricing an established product usually is less difficult than pricing a new product, however, because the exact price or a narrow range of prices may be dictated by the market.[9] Other factors, besides objectives, that influence price determination are discussed next.

### MARKETING AT WORK

#### FILE 13-2 THE ROLE OF TAXES IN PRICING

There used to be the manufacturer's sales tax, which was hidden, so few if any consumers knew that it existed. It was replaced by the Goods and Services Tax (GST), which was not hidden. Every consumer in the country knew it was there, hated it, hated the government that brought it in, and used it — together with a not bad exchange rate — as an excuse to shop in the United States. The GST was said to be a "good" tax, in theory, because it was visible and people knew they were paying it. Regardless of its merits or lack thereof, the presence of the GST, as well as provincial sales taxes (PSTs), in all provinces except Alberta, make pricing more difficult today than in the past. To complicate matters further, in a few weeks, months, or years, the GST will be changed, re-named, and/or modified — and there will be a lot of discussion and many heated arguments about how it should be designed and implemented — hidden or visible — and on what it will be levied. Also, the federal government will attempt to blend it with the various provincial taxes so that only one value-added or consumption tax regime exists instead of the 11 we now have. From a marketer's perspective, a uniform blended tax that is simple to administer and collect and that stays hidden seems to be ideal — if one has to have a value-added or sales tax at all, which most marketers might deny. It is clear from our GST experiences that the effects of federal and provincial taxes on consumer perceptions of value for money must be determined and calculated when developing pricing strategies. The confusion on these types of taxes and their effects on Canadian consumers' behaviour is a tax/price phenomenon unique in the world.

A second phenomenon associated with new taxes and their effects on prices and consumer responses has to do with "anti-social" products — cigarettes, tobacco, and alcoholic beverages being prime examples. Canada has some of the highest "sin" taxes in the world. Although the federal government was regarded by approximately 6 million smokers as a villain because of the level of tobacco taxes, the provinces were taking their tax-revenue share as well. But a major increase in smuggling cheaper American cigarettes resulted in such a steep drop in provincial and federal revenues, that the tobacco tax was decreased in an attempt to wipe out the smuggling, a move that appears to be working for the time being. Of course, a lot of nonsmoking Canadians are unhappy with being forced to subsidize smokers in this fashion. But various U.S. tax and quota initiatives are being put in place which will increase the price of cigarettes in the United States and thus allow both the federal and provincial governments in Canada to raise taxes again.

So the role of taxes has greater commercial, moral, and ethical implications than ever before and price and response to price (tax included or not) is one place to start to look at these matters. It seems clear that it's not easy to predict consumer response to taxes, hidden or otherwise.

### Estimated Demand

In pricing, a company must estimate the total demand for the product. This is easier to do for an established product than for a new one. The steps in estimating demand are (1) determine whether there is a price the market expects and (2) estimate what the sales volume might be at different prices.

The **expected price** of a product is the price at which customers consciously or unconsciously value it — what they think the product is worth. Expected price usually is expressed as a **range** of prices rather than as a specific amount. Thus the expected price might be "between $250 and $300" or "not over $20."

A producer must also consider an intermediary's reaction to price. Intermediaries are more likely to promote a product if they approve its price. Retail or wholesale buyers can frequently make an accurate estimate of the selling price that the market will accept for a particular item.

It's possible to set a price too low. If the price is much lower than what the market expects, sales may be lost. For example, it probably would be a mistake for L'Oreal, a well-known cosmetics maker, to put a $1.49 price tag on its lipstick or to price its imported perfume at $3.49 for 3 mL. Either customers will be suspicious about product quality or their self-concept will not let them buy such low-priced products.

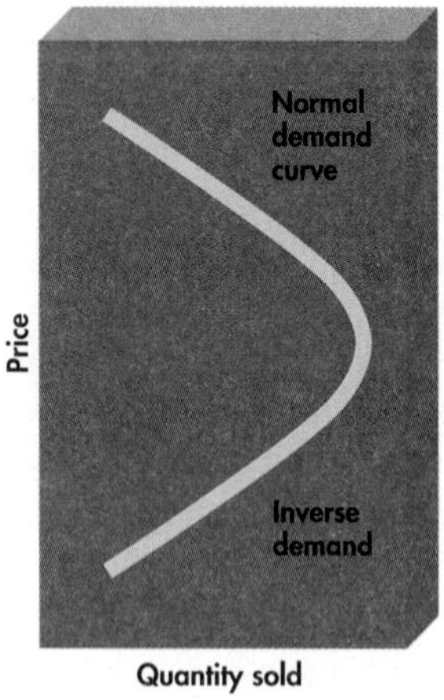


**FIGURE 13-1**
**Inverse demand.**

After raising a product's price, some organizations have experienced a considerable increase in sales. This situation is called **inverse demand** — the higher the price, the greater the unit sales. Inverse demand usually exists only within a given price range and only at low price levels. At some point (see Figure 13-1), inverse demand ends and the usual-shaped demand curve is evident. That is, demand declines as prices rise.

How do sellers determine expected prices? They may submit products to experienced retailers or wholesalers for appraisal. A business-goods manufacturer might get price estimates by showing models or blueprints to engineers working for prospective customers. Another alternative is to ask a sample of consumers what they would expect to pay for the product or which item in a list of alternatives is most similar to the test product. Using such methods, a seller can determine a reasonable range of prices.

It is extremely helpful to estimate what the sales volume will be at several different prices. By doing this, the seller is, in effect, determining the demand curve for the product. Moreover, the seller is gauging **price elasticity of demand**, which refers to the responsiveness of quantity demanded to price changes. (Price elasticity of demand is covered in more detail in Appendix C following this chapter.) Estimates of sales at different prices also are useful in determining break-even points (we'll get to this topic shortly).

Sellers can choose from several methods to estimate sales at various prices. Recall some of the demand-forecasting methods discussed in Chapter 5 — survey of buyer intentions, test marketing, and sales-force composite, for example. These methods can be used in this situation as well.[10]

### Competitive Reactions

Competition greatly influences base price. A new product is distinctive only until the inevitable arrival of competition. The threat of *potential* competition is greatest when the field is easy to enter *and* profit prospects are encouraging. Competition can come from these sources:

- **Directly similar products:** Nike versus Adidas or Reebok running shoes.
- **Available substitutes:** Air freight versus truck shipping or rail freight.
- **Unrelated products seeking the same consumer dollar:** Videocassette recorder (VCR) versus a bicycle or a weekend excursion.

In the case of directly similar products, a competitor may adjust its prices. In turn, other firms have to decide what price adjustments, if any, are necessary to retain their customers.

### Other Marketing-Mix Elements

A product's base price is influenced considerably by the other ingredients in the marketing mix.

**Product** We have already observed that a product's price is affected by whether it is a new item or an established one. Over the course of a life cycle, price changes are necessary to keep the product competitive. The end use of the product must also be considered. For instance, there is little price competition among manufacturers of packaging materials or producers of industrial gases, so their price structure is stable. These business products are only an incidental part of the final article, so customers will buy the least expensive product consistent with the required quality. The price of a product is also influenced by whether (1) the product may be leased as well as purchased outright, (2) the product may be returned to the seller, and (3) a trade-in is involved.

**Distribution Channels** The channels and types of intermediaries selected will influence a producer's pricing. A firm selling both through wholesalers and directly to retailers often sets a different factory price for these two classes of customers. The price to wholesalers is lower because they perform services that the producer would have to perform — such as providing storage, granting credit to retailers, and selling to small retailers.

**Promotion** The extent to which the product is promoted by the producer or intermediaries and the methods used are added considerations in pricing. If major promotional responsibility is placed on retailers, they ordinarily will be charged a lower price for a product than if the producer advertises it heavily. Even when a producer promotes heavily, it may want its retailers to use local advertising to tie in with national advertising. Such a decision must be reflected in the producer's price to these retailers.

### VARIOUS KINDS OF COSTS

- A **fixed cost**, such as rent, executive salaries, or property tax, remains constant regardless of how many items are produced. Such a cost continues even if production stops completely. It is called a fixed cost because it is difficult to change in the short run (but not in the long run).
- **Total fixed cost** is the sum of all fixed costs.
- **Average fixed cost** is the total fixed cost divided by the number of units produced.
- A **variable cost**, such as labour or materials, is directly related to production. Variable costs can be controlled in the short run simply by changing the level of production. When production stops, for example, all variable production costs become zero.
- **Total variable cost** is the sum of all variable costs. The more units produced, the higher is this cost.
- **Average variable cost** is the total variable cost divided by the number of units produced. Average variable cost is usually high for the first few units produced. It decreases as production increases, due to such things as quantity discounts on materials and more efficient use of labour. Beyond some optimum output, it increases due to such factors as crowding of production facilities and overtime pay.
- **Total cost** is the sum of total fixed cost and total variable cost for a specific quantity produced.
- **Average total cost** is total cost divided by number of units produced.
- **Marginal cost** is the cost of producing and selling one more unit. Usually the marginal cost of the last unit is the same as that unit's variable cost.

## Cost of a Product

Pricing of a product also should consider its cost. A product's total unit cost is made up of several types of costs, each reacting differently to changes in the quantity produced.

The cost concepts in the box on the previous page are fundamental to our discussion of pricing. These concepts and their interrelationships are illustrated in Table 13-1 and Figure 13-2. The interrelationship among the various *average costs per unit* from the table is displayed graphically in the figure. It may be explained briefly as follows:

- The **average fixed cost curve** declines as output increases, because the total of the fixed costs is spread over an increasing number of units.
- The **average variable cost curve** usually is U-shaped. It starts high because average variable costs for the first few units of output are high. Variable costs per unit then decline as the company realizes efficiencies in production. Eventually the average variable cost curve reaches its lowest point, reflecting optimum output with respect to variable costs (not total costs). In Figure 13-2 this point is at three units of output. Beyond that point the average variable cost rises, reflecting the increase in unit variable costs caused by overcrowded facilities and other inefficiencies. If the variable costs per unit were constant, then the average variable cost curve would be a horizontal line at the level of the constant unit variable cost.
- The **average total cost curve** is the sum of the first two curves — average fixed cost and average variable cost. It starts high, reflecting the fact that total *fixed* costs are spread over so few units of output. As output increases, the average total cost curve declines because unit fixed cost and unit variable cost are decreasing. Eventually the point of lowest total cost per unit is reached (four units of output in the figure). Beyond that optimum point, diminishing returns set in and average total cost rises.
- The **marginal cost curve** has a more pronounced U-shape than the other curves in Figure 13-2. The marginal cost curve slopes downward until the second unit of output, at which point the marginal costs start to increase.

TABLE 13-1 An example of costs for an individual firm

***Total fixed costs do not change in the short run, despite increases in quantity produced. Variable costs are the costs of inputs — materials and labour, for example. Total variable costs increase as production quantity rises. Total cost is the sum of all fixed and variable costs. The other measures in the table are simply methods of looking at costs per unit; they always involve dividing a cost by the number of units produced.***

| (1) Quantity produced | (2) Total fixed costs | (3) Total variable costs | (4) Total costs (2) + (3) | (5) Marginal cost per unit | (6) Average fixed cost (2) ÷ (1) | (7) Average variable cost (3) ÷ (1) | (8) Average total cost (4) ÷ (1) |
|---|---|---|---|---|---|---|---|
| 0 | $256 | $ 0 | $256 | | **Infinity** | **Infinity** | **Infinity** |
| 1 | 256 | 84 | 340 | $ 84 | $256.00 | $84 | $340.00 |
| 2 | 256 | 112 | 368 | 28 | 128.00 | 56 | 184.00 |
| 3 | 256 | 144 | 400 | 32 | 85.33 | 48 | 133.33 |
| 4 | 256 | 224 | 480 | 80 | 64.00 | 56 | 120.00 |
| 5 | 256 | 400 | 656 | 176 | 51.20 | 80 | 131.20 |

**FIGURE 13-2**
**Unit cost curves for an individual firm.**

**This figure is based on data in Table 13-1. Here we see how unit costs change as quantity increases. Using cost-plus pricing, two units of output would be priced at $184 each, whereas four units would sell for $120 each.**

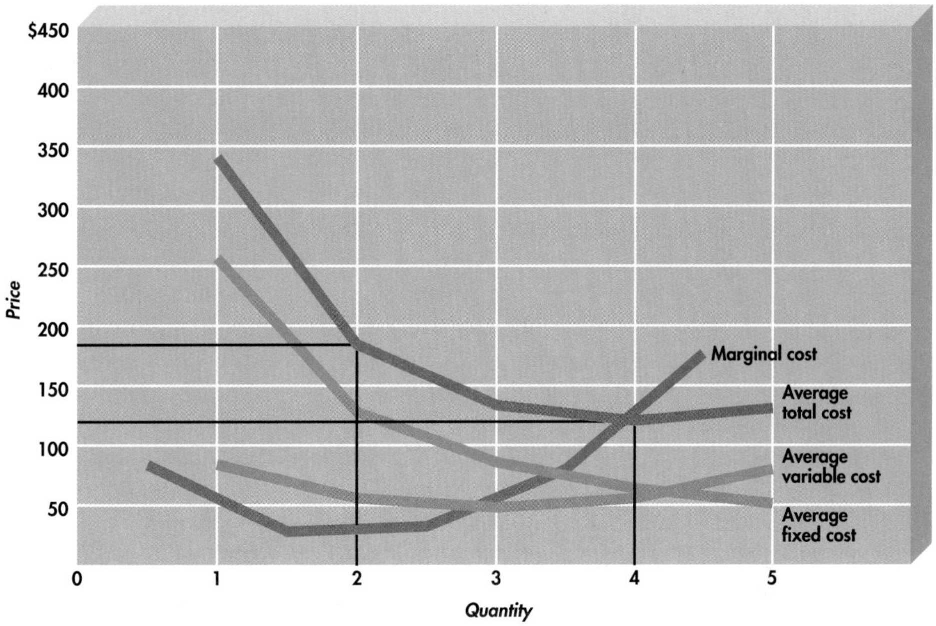


Note the relationship between the marginal cost curve and the average total cost curve. The average total cost curve slopes downward *as long as the marginal cost is less than the average total cost.* Even though marginal cost increases after the second unit, the average total cost curve continues to slope downward until the fourth unit. This occurs because marginal cost — even when going up — is still less than average total cost.

The two curves — marginal cost and average total cost — intersect at the lowest point of the average total cost curve. Beyond that point (the fourth unit in the example), the cost of producing and selling the next unit is higher than the average cost of all units. The data in Table 13-1 show that producing the fifth unit reduces the average fixed cost by $12.80 (from $64 to $51.20), but causes the average variable cost to increase by $24. From then on, therefore, the average total cost rises. This occurs because the average variable cost is increasing faster than the average fixed cost is decreasing.

## COST-PLUS PRICING

We now are at the point in price determination to talk about setting a *specific* selling price. Most companies establish their prices using one of the following methods:

- Prices are based on total cost plus a desired profit. (Break-even analysis is a variation of this method.)
- Prices are based on marginal analysis — a consideration of both market demand and supply.
- Prices are based only on competitive market conditions.

Let's first discuss **cost-plus pricing**, which means setting the price of one unit of a product equal to the total cost of the unit plus the desired profit on the unit. Suppose that King's Kastles, a contractor, figures the labour and materials required to build and sell 10 condominiums will cost $750,000, and other expenses (office rent, depreciation on equipment, management salaries, and so on) will be $150,000. The contractor wants to earn a profit of 10 percent on the total cost of $900,000. Cost plus desired profit is $990,000, so each of the 10 condos is priced at $99,000.

## MARKETING AT WORK

### FILE 13-3 WHAT GUIDES PRICE DETERMINATION BY FOREIGN FIRMS?

Do firms actually set pricing objectives and consider various factors as they determine appropriate prices for their products? According to one survey conducted in Great Britain, the answer is a qualified "Yes."

Among industrial distributors in Great Britain, price competition is the name of the game. For such firms, most of which are fairly small, competing on the basis of price can be risky and costly, perhaps hurting profits. In fact, though, the situation is probably similar to what occurs in Canada and the United States.

This survey focused on British industrial distributors that purchase paper- and engineering-related products from manufacturers and other suppliers and then resell them to other firms. The large majority have less than 50 employees and annual sales in pounds that convert to under $20 million. When they need to set prices, do these firms establish pricing objectives? The following results suggest that most distributors not only establish objectives but employ multiple objectives:

| Objectives | Firms designating as "a very important objective" |
|---|---|
| Target profit or return on investment | 77% |
| Prices fair to firm and customers | 61% |
| Target sales revenue | 49% |
| Target price competitiveness | 44% |
| Target market share | 18% |
| Target market image | 18% |

Overall, these objectives parallel those we presented earlier in this chapter. Interestingly, the researchers did not ask the distributors whether they use two objectives — profit maximization and price stabilization — that are sometimes criticized as being socially undesirable.

As the distributors proceed with pricing, what factors guide their thinking? More than 70 percent of the firms indicate they considered all nine of the influences listed by the researchers. However, the results reveal that some factors carry more influence than others:

| Influences on pricing decisions | Firms designating as "a very important influence" |
|---|---|
| Quality of products offered | 69% |
| Pricing objectives | 55% |
| Competitors' prices | 48% |
| Demand in different market segments | 30% |
| Suppliers' requirements | 27% |
| Effect on demand for other products | 12% |

These results are surprising in two ways. First, 45 percent of the firms apparently are not greatly influenced by the pricing objectives they set. The obvious question then becomes: Why set pricing objectives? Second, more than 50 percent of the distributors are not particularly concerned about competitors' prices. Perhaps these firms are more concerned about their own situations (such as product quality) and their customers' *and* are trying to avoid a profit-eroding price war with competitors.

Source: David Shipley and Elizabeth Bourdon, "Distributor Pricing in Very Competitive Markets," *Industrial Marketing Management*, August 1990, pp. 215-224.

While it is an easily applied method, cost-plus pricing has limitations. One is that it does not recognize various types of costs or the fact that these costs are affected differently by changes in level of output. In our housing example, suppose that King's Kastles built and sold only eight condos at the cost-plus price of $99,000 each. As shown in Table 13-2, total sales would then be $792,000. Labour and materials chargeable to the eight condos would total $600,000 ($75,000 per house). Since the contractor would still incur the full $150,000

**Should the builder use the cost-plus method when pricing these condominiums?**

in overhead expenses, the total cost would be $750,000. This would leave a profit of only $42,000, or $5,250 per condominium instead of the anticipated $9,000. On a percentage basis, profit would be only 5.6 percent of total cost rather than the desired 10 percent.

A second limitation of this pricing approach is that market demand is ignored. That is, cost-plus pricing assumes that all the output will be produced and sold. If fewer units are produced, each would have to sell for a higher price to cover all costs and show a profit. But if business is slack and output must be cut, it is not wise to raise the unit price. Another limitation of this method is that is doesn't recognize that total unit cost changes as output expands or contracts. However, a more sophisticated approach to cost-plus pricing can take such changes into consideration.

### Prices Based on Marginal Costs Only

Another approach to cost-plus pricing is to set **prices based on marginal costs only**, not total costs. Refer again to the cost schedules shown in Table 13-1 and Figure 13-2, and assume that a firm is operating at an output level of three units. Under marginal cost pricing, this firm could accept an order for one more unit at $80 or above, instead of the total unit cost of $120. The revenue from a unit sold at $80 would cover its variable costs. However, if the firm can sell for a price above $80 — say, $85 or $90 — the excess contributes to the payment of fixed costs.

TABLE 13-2 King's Kastles: an example of cost-plus pricing
***Actual results often differ from planned outcomes because various types of costs react differently to changes in output.***

| | Number of condominiums built and sold by King's Kastles | |
|---|---|---|
| King's Kastles costs, selling price, and profit | Planned = 10 | Actual = 8 |
| **Labour and materials costs ($75,000 per condo)** | $750,000 | $600,000 |
| **Overhead (fixed) costs** | 150,000 | 150,000 |
| **Total costs** | $900,000 | $750,000 |
| **Total sales at $99,000 per condo** | 990,000 | 792,000 |
| **Profit: Total** | $ 90,000 | $ 42,000 |
| **Profit: Per condo** | $ 9,000 | $ 5,250 |
| **Profit: As percent of cost** | 10% | 5.6% |

Not all orders can be priced to cover only variable costs. Marginal cost pricing may be feasible, however, if management wants to keep its labour force employed during a slack season. It may also be used when one product is expected to attract business for another. Thus a department store may price meals in its café at a level that covers only the marginal costs. The reasoning is that this café will bring shoppers to the store, where they will buy other, more profitable products.

### Pricing by Intermediaries

At first glance, cost-plus pricing appears to be widely used by retailing and wholesaling intermediaries. A retailer, for example, pays a given amount to buy products and have them delivered to the store. Then the retailer adds an amount, called a markup, to the acquisition cost. This markup is estimated to be sufficient to cover the store's expenses and provide a reasonable profit. Thus a building materials outlet may buy a power drill for $30 including freight, and price the item at $50. The $50 price reflects a markup of 40 percent based on the selling price, or 66⅔ percent based on the merchandise cost. Of course, in setting prices, intermediaries also should take into account the expectations of their customers.

Various types of retailers require different percentage markups because of the nature of the products handled and the services offered. A self-service supermarket has lower costs and thus can have a lower average markup than a full-service delicatessen. Figure 13-3 shows examples of markup pricing by intermediaries. (Markups are discussed in more detail in Appendix C.)

Is cost-plus pricing really used by intermediaries? For the following reasons, it's safe to say that cost-plus pricing is *not* used widely by intermediaries:

- Most retail prices are really only offers. If customers accept the offer, the price is fine. If they reject it, the price usually will be changed quickly, or the product may even be withdrawn from the market. Prices thus are always on trial.
- Many retailers don't use the same markup on all the products they carry. A supermarket will have a markup of 6 to 8 percent on sugar and soap products, 15 to 18 percent on canned fruit and vegetables, and 25 to 30 percent on fresh meats and produce. These different markups for distinctive products reflect competitive considerations and other aspects of market demand.

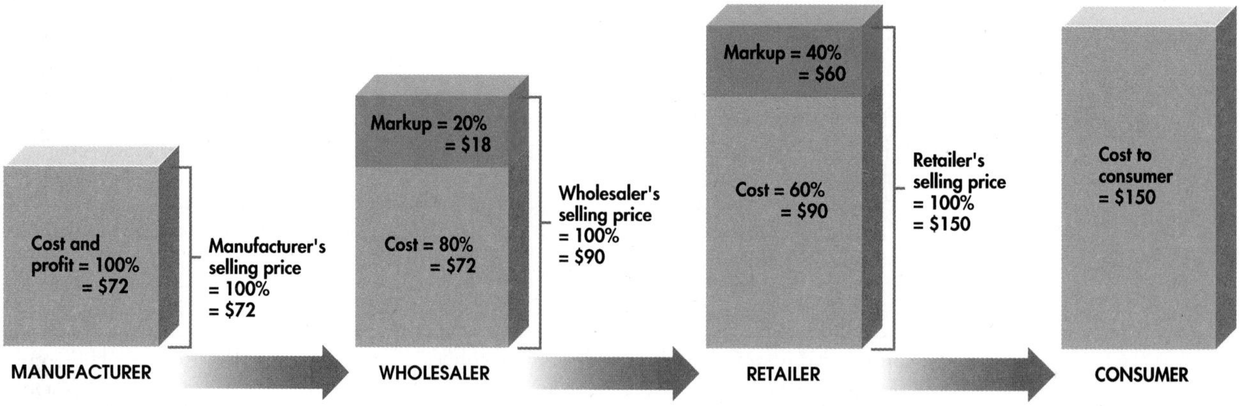


**FIGURE 13-3 Examples of markup pricing by retailers and wholesalers.**

- The intermediary usually doesn't actually set a base price but only adds a percentage to the price already set by the producer. The producer's price is set to allow each intermediary to add a reasonable markup and still sell at a competitive retail price. The key price is set by the producer, with an eye on the final market.

Thus what seems to be cost-plus pricing by intermediaries is usually market-influenced pricing.

### Evaluation of Cost-Plus Pricing

Since a firm should be market-oriented and cater to consumers' wants, why are we considering cost-plus pricing? Simply, cost-plus pricing must be understood because it is referred to often in business. Further, it is used by numerous industrial firms.[11]

An appropriate perspective is that costs should be a determinant of prices, *but not the only one*. Costs are a floor under a firm's prices. If goods are priced under this floor for a long time, the firm will be forced out of business. But when it is used by itself, cost-plus pricing is a weak and unrealistic method because it ignores competition and market demand.

## BREAK-EVEN ANALYSIS

One way to consider both market demand and costs in price determination is to use **break-even analysis** to calculate break-even points. A **break-even point** is that quantity of output at which total revenue equals total costs, *assuming a certain selling price*. There is a different break-even point for each different selling price. Sales exceeding the break-even point result in a profit on each additional unit. The higher sales are above the break-even point, the higher will be the total and unit profits. Sales below the break-even point result in a loss to the seller.

### Determining the Break-Even Point

The method of determining a break-even point is illustrated in Table 13-3 and Figure 13-4. In our example, the Futon Factory's fixed costs are $25,000 and variable costs are constant at $30 per unit. Recall that in our earlier example (Table 13-1 and Figure 13-2), we assumed that unit variable costs are *not* constant but fluctuate. To simplify our break-even analysis, we now assume that variable costs *are* constant.

The total cost of producing one unit is $25,300 — the Futon Factory obviously needs more volume to absorb its fixed costs! For 400 units the total cost is $37,000 ($30 multiplied by 400, plus $25,000). In Figure 13-4 the selling price is $80 a unit and variable costs of $30 per unit are incurred in producing each unit. Consequently, any revenue over $30 contributes to covering fixed costs (sometimes termed *overhead*). When the price is $80, that would be $50 per unit. At a price of $80, the break-even point is 500 units, because a $50 per-unit contribution will just cover overhead of $25,000.

Stated another way, variable costs for 500 units are $15,000 and fixed costs are $25,000, for a total cost of $40,000. This amount equals the revenue from 500 units sold

TABLE 13-3 Futon Factory: computation of break-even point

***At each of several prices, we wish to find out how many units must be sold to cover all costs. At a unit price of $100, the sale of each unit contributes $70 to cover overhead expenses. The Futon Factory must sell about 357 units to cover its $25,000 in fixed costs. See Figure 13-4 for a depiction of the data in this table.***

| (1) Unit price | (2) Unit variable costs | (3) Contribution to overhead (1) – (2) | (4) Overhead (total fixed costs) | (5) Break-even point (rounded) (4) ÷ (3) |
|---|---|---|---|---|
| $ 60 | $30 | $ 30 | $25,000 | **833 units** |
| 80 | 30 | 50 | $25,000 | **500 units** |
| 100 | 30 | 70 | $25,000 | **357 units** |
| 150 | 30 | 120 | $25,000 | **208 units** |

at $80 each. So, at an $80 selling price, the break-even volume is 500 units. Figure 13-4 shows a break-even point for an $80 price, but it is highly desirable to calculate break-even points for several different selling prices.

The break-even point may be found with this formula:

$$\text{Break-even point in units} = \frac{\text{total fixed costs}}{\text{unit contribution to overhead}}$$

Because unit contribution to overhead equals selling price less the average variable cost, the working formula becomes:

$$\text{Break-even point in units} = \frac{\text{total fixed costs}}{\text{selling price} - \text{average variable cost}}$$

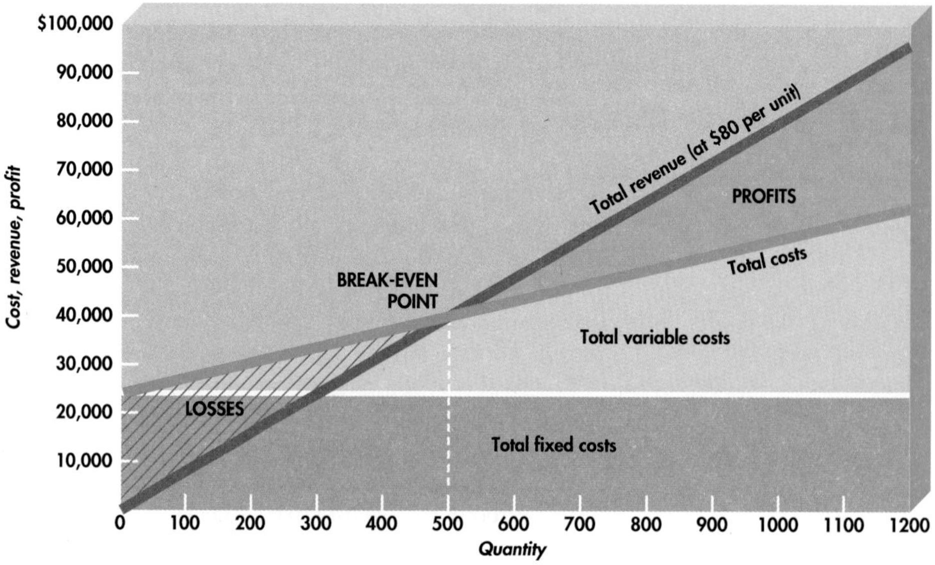


**FIGURE 13-4**
**Break-even chart for the Futon Factory with an $80 selling price.**

**Here the break-even point is reached when the company sells 500 units. Fixed costs, regardless of quantity produced and sold, are $25,000. The variable cost per unit is $30. If this company sells 500 units, total costs are $40,000 (variable cost of 500 × $30, or $15,000, plus fixed costs of $25,000). At a selling price of $80, the sale of 500 units will yield $40,000 revenue, and costs and revenue will equal each other. At the same price, the sale of each unit above 500 will yield a profit.**

Two basic assumptions underlie these calculations:

- Total fixed costs are constant. In reality they may change, although usually not in the short run.
- Variable costs remain constant per unit of output. Actually, average variable costs usually fluctuate.

## Evaluation of Break-Even Analysis

Key assumptions underlying break-even analysis usually are not valid in the actual business world. Consequently, break-even analysis cannot be used conclusively in companies where demand and/or average unit costs fluctuate. But it still can provide general guidance.

Another drawback of break-even analysis is that it cannot tell us whether we *can* actually sell the break-even amount. Table 13-3, for example, shows what revenue will be at the different prices *if* the given number of units can be sold at these prices. The number the market will buy at a given price could well be below the break-even point. If that happens, the firm will not break even — it will show a loss.

Despite these limitations, management should not dismiss break-even analysis as a pricing tool. Even in its simplest form, break-even analysis is helpful because in the short run many firms experience reasonably stable cost and demand structures.[12]

## PRICES BASED ON MARGINAL ANALYSIS

Another pricing method, marginal analysis, also takes account of both demand and costs to determine the best price for profit maximization. Firms with other pricing goals might use **prices based on marginal analysis** to compare prices determined by different means.

### Determining the Price

To use marginal analysis, the price setter must understand the concepts of average and marginal revenue as well as average and marginal cost. **Marginal revenue** is the income derived from the sale of the last unit. **Average revenue** is the unit price at a given level of unit sales; it is calculated by dividing total revenue by the number of units sold.

Referring to the hypothetical demand schedule in Table 13-4, we see that Limos for Lease can sell one unit (that is, lease one limousine for a two-hour period on a weekend night) at $80. To attract a second customer and thereby lease two limos on the same night, it must reduce its price to $72 for each unit. Thus the company receives an additional $64 (marginal revenue) by selling a second unit. After the fourth unit, total revenue declines each time the unit price is lowered in order to sell an additional unit. Hence, there is a negative marginal revenue.

TABLE 13-4 Limos for Lease: demand schedule for an individual firm

***At each market price a certain quantity of the product — in this example, a two-hour rental of a limousine on a weekend night — will be demanded. Marginal revenue is simply the amount of additional money gained by selling one more unit. Limos for Lease gains no additional marginal revenue after it has rented its fourth limo at a price of $53.***

| Units sold (limos leased) | Unit price (average revenue) | Total revenue | Marginal revenue |
|---|---|---|---|
| 1 | $80 | $ 80 | |
| 2 | 72 | 144 | $64 |
| 3 | 63 | 189 | 45 |
| 4 | 53 | 212 | 23 |
| 5 | 42 | 210 | −2 |
| 6 | 34 | 204 | −6 |

Marginal analysis is illustrated in Figure 13-5. We assume that a company — a services firm like Limos for Lease or a manufacturer — will continue to produce and sell its product as long as revenue from the last unit sold exceeds the cost of producing this last unit. That is, output continues to increase as long as marginal revenue exceeds marginal cost. At the point where they meet, production theoretically should cease. Ordinarily a company will not want to sell a unit at a price less than its out-of-pocket (variable) costs of producing a good or a service. The optimum volume of output is the quantity level at which *marginal cost equals marginal revenue*, or quantity Q in Figure 13-5a.

Thus the unit price is determined by locating the point on the average revenue curve that represents an output of quantity Q — the level at which marginal cost equals marginal revenue. Remember that average revenue represents the unit price. Referring to Figure 13-5b, in which the average revenue curve has been added, the unit price at which to sell quantity Q is represented by point C — that is, price B.

The average total cost curve has been added in Figure 13-5c. It shows that, for output quantity Q, the average unit cost is represented by point D — that is, unit cost A. Thus, with a price of B and an average unit cost of A, the company enjoys a unit profit given by B minus A in the figure. Total profit is quantity Q times the unit profit.

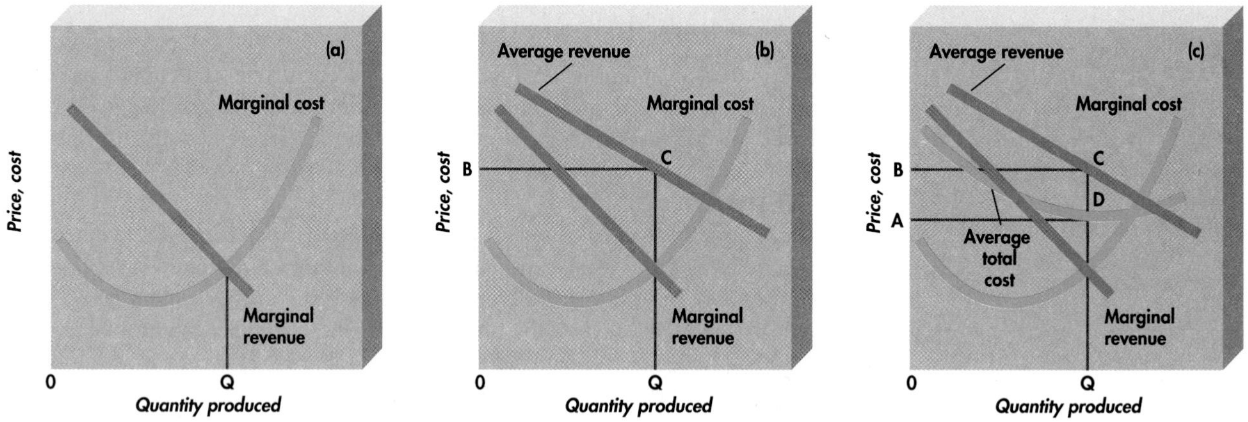


**FIGURE 13-5**
**Price setting and profit maximization through marginal analysis.**

### Evaluation of Marginal Analysis Pricing

Marginal analysis has been used sparsely as a basis for price setting. According to business people, it can be used to study past price movements. However, many managers think that marginal analysis cannot serve as a practical basis for setting prices unless accurate, reliable data can be obtained for plotting the curves.

On the brighter side, management's knowledge of costs and demand is improving. Computerized data bases are bringing more complete and detailed information to management's attention all the time. And experienced management in many firms can do an accurate job of estimating marginal and average costs and revenues.

## PRICES SET IN RELATION TO MARKET ALONE

Cost-plus pricing is one extreme among pricing methods. At the other extreme are methods where a firm's prices are set in relation *only* to the market price. The seller's price may be set right at the market price to meet the competition, or it may be set above or below the market price.

### Pricing to Meet Competition

**Pricing to meet competition** is simple to carry out. A firm ascertains what the market price is and, after allowing for customary markups for intermediaries, arrives at its own selling price. To illustrate, a manufacturer of women's shoes knows that retailers want to sell the shoes for $70 a pair. The firm sells directly to retailers, who want an average markup of 40 percent of their selling price. Consequently, after allowing $28 for the retailer's markup, the producer's price is $42. This manufacturer then has to decide whether $42 is enough to cover costs and provide a reasonable profit. Sometimes a producer faces a real squeeze if its costs are rising but the market price is holding firm.

One situation in which management might price a product right at the market level is when competition is keen and the firm's product is not differentiated significantly from competing products. To some extent, this pricing method reflects the market conditions of **perfect competition**. That is, product differentiation is absent, buyers and sellers are well informed, and the seller has no discernible control over the selling price. Most producers of agricultural products and small firms marketing well-known, standardized products use this pricing method.

The sharp drop in revenue occurring when the price is raised above the prevailing market level indicates that the individual seller faces a **kinked demand** (see Figure 13-6). The prevailing price is at A. Adjusting this price is not beneficial to the seller:

- Above the prevailing price, demand for the product drops sharply, as indicated by the fairly flat average revenue curve above point P. Above price A, demand is highly elastic and, as a result, total revenue declines.

- Below price A, demand for the product increases very little, as shown by the steeply sloping average revenue curve and the negative marginal revenue curve below point P. Demand is highly inelastic and, as a result, total revenue still declines.

In the case of kinked demand, total revenue decreases each time the price is adjusted from the prevailing price, A in Figure 13-6. The prevailing price is strong. Consequently, when a single firm reduces its price, its unit sales will not increase very much — certainly not enough to offset the loss in average revenue.

So far in our discussion of pricing to meet competition, we have observed market situations that involve *many* sellers. Oddly enough, this same pricing method is often used when the market is dominated by a *few* firms, each marketing similar products. This type of market structure, called an **oligopoly**, exists in such industries as copper, aluminum, soft drinks, breakfast cereals, auto tires, and even among barber shops and grocery stores in a small community. When the demand curve is kinked, as in Figure 13-6, oligopolists should simply set prices at a competitive level and leave them there. Typically they do.

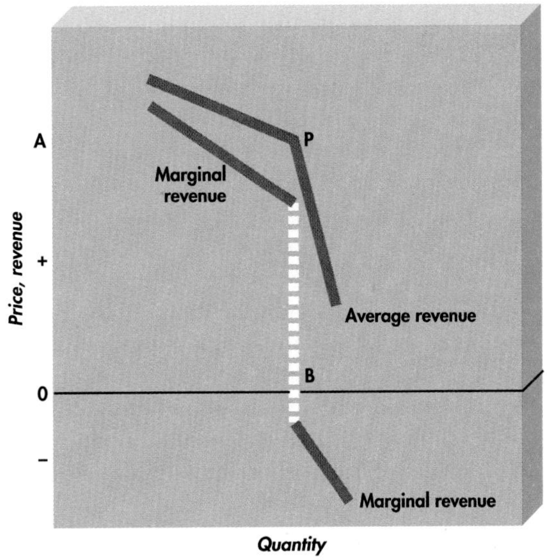


FIGURE 13-6
Kinked demand curve.

**This type of curve faces firms selling well-known, standardized products as well as individual firms in an oligopolistic market structure. The kink occurs at the point representing the prevailing price A. At prices above A, demand declines rapidly. A price set below A results in very little increase in volume, so revenue is lost; that is, marginal revenue is negative.**

## Pricing below Competition

A variation of market-based pricing is to set a price *below* the level of your main competitors. **Pricing below competition** is done by discount retailers, such as Zellers and Wal-Mart, which stress low markup, high volume, and few customer services (including sales people). They price some heavily advertised, well-known brands 10 to 30 percent below the suggested list price, which is normally charged by full-service retailers. Even full-service retailers may price below the competitive level by eliminating specific services. Some gas stations offer a discount to customers who pay with cash instead of a credit card.

The risk in pricing below competition is that consumers begin to view the product as an undifferentiated commodity, such as coal and bulk salt, with all the focus on price differences. If that happens, and some would say it already has in fields such as personal computers, then consumers choose the brand with the lowest price. In turn, competing firms are likely to wind up in a price war that diminishes or eliminates profits. One observer asked a question that applies to any industry in which firms rely on price as a way to gain an edge over competitors: "How can restaurant chains ever expect to charge top dollar again after relentlessly pushing value [low] prices?"[13]

## MARKETING AT WORK

### FILE 13-4 CAN YOU DEAL WITH A KINKED DEMAND CURVE?

Intense price competition has characterized the airline industry in Canada since it was deregulated. Attempting to increase the number of passengers, Canadian Airlines International cuts its price on a heavily travelled route, Vancouver to Toronto, for example. However, Air Canada usually matches that lower fare immediately. As a result, there is no significant shift in the market share held by each airline on that route. But another result is that the market price settles — at least temporarily — at the lower level. Unless the number of passengers increases substantially, the profits of both airlines flying this route are likely to suffer.

What marketing strategies might an airline use to avoid having to match a competitor's price cut?

### Pricing above Competition

Producers or retailers sometimes set their prices *above* the prevailing market level. Usually, **pricing above competition** works only when the product is distinctive or when the seller has acquired prestige in its field. Most communities have an elite clothing boutique and a prestigious jewellery store where price tags are noticeably above the level set by other stores with seemingly similar products. However, a gas station that has a strong advantage based on a superior location (perhaps the only such station for many kilometres on the Trans-Canada Highway) may also be able to use above-market pricing.

Above-market pricing often is employed by manufacturers of prestige brands of high-cost products such as autos (Ferrari, Mercedes), crystal (Waterford), leather products (Gucci, Fendi), and watches (Breguet, Rolex). Patek Philippe, a Swiss firm, makes only about 15,000 watches per year, but they are priced in the range of $5,000 to $400,000 — that's per watch! One new Patek Philippe watch, with 1,728 parts and 33 uses, was sold for around $3.5 million several years ago.[14] Above-market pricing is sometimes found even among relatively low-cost products — candies, for example. Godiva, a brand of imported Belgian chocolates, follows this practice in Canada and the United States.

In the "thrifty 1990s," compared to the "free-spending 1980s," some businesses are finding it difficult to maintain above-market prices. They have either lowered some prices or introduced less expensive — but still expensive — brands or product lines. In the North American financial services industry, American Express traditionally charged merchants higher fees than other credit card companies. Recently it adjusted its price structure so that some merchants would qualify for lower fees. American Express also enhanced its services to its merchant customers as a way of justifying its above-market prices.[15]

The basic pricing methods covered in this chapter (cost-plus and marginal analysis, for instance) are equally applicable in the marketing of goods *and* services by businesses. Pricing of services was discussed in more detail in Chapter 12. Pricing in not-for-profit organizations, however, involves different considerations — also discussed in Chapter 22.

## SUMMARY

In our economy, price influences the allocation of resources. In individual companies, price is one significant factor in achieving marketing success. And in many purchase situations, price can be of great importance to consumers. However, it is difficult to define price. A rather general definition is: Price is the amount of money and/or other items with utility needed to acquire a product.

Before setting a product's base price, management should identify its pricing goal. Major pricing objectives are to (1) earn a target return on investment or on net sales, (2) maximize profits, (3) increase sales, (4) hold or gain a target market share, (5) stabilize prices, and (6) meet competition's prices.

Besides the firm's pricing objective, other key factors that influence price setting are: (1) demand for the product, (2) competitive reactions, (3) strategies planned for other marketing-mix elements, and (4) cost of the product. The concept of elasticity refers to the effect that unit-price changes have on the number of units sold and on total revenue.

Three major methods used to determine the base price are cost-plus pricing, marginal analysis, and setting the price in relation only to the market. For cost-plus pricing to be effective, a seller must consider several types of costs and their reactions to changes in the quantity produced. A producer usually sets a price to cover total cost. In some cases, however, the best policy may be to set a price that covers marginal cost only. The main weakness in cost-plus pricing is that it completely ignores market demand. To partially offset this weakness, a company may use break-even analysis as a tool in price setting.

In actual business situations, price setting is influenced by market conditions. Hence, marginal analysis, which takes into account both demand and costs to determine a suitable price for the product, is a useful price-determination method. Price and output level are set at the point where marginal cost equals marginal revenue. The effectiveness of marginal analysis in setting prices depends on obtaining reliable cost data.

For many products, price setting is relatively easy because management simply sets the price at the level of competition. Pricing at prevailing market levels makes sense for firms selling well-known, standardized products and sometimes for individual firms in an oligopoly. Two variations of market-level pricing are to price below or above the levels of primary competitors.

## KEY TERMS AND CONCEPTS

**Price (372)**
**Utility (372)**
**Barter (372)**
**Value (374)**
**Pricing objectives (375)**
**Achieve target return (375)**
- **Profit maximization (376)**
- **Increase sales volume (377)**
- **Maintain or increase market share (377)**
- **Stabilize prices (378)**
- **Meet competition (378)**

**Markup (375)**
**Base price (list price) (379)**
**Expected price (380)**
**Range of prices (380)**
**Inverse demand (380)**
**Price elasticity of demand (380)**
**Fixed cost (381)**
**Total fixed cost (381)**
**Average fixed cost (381)**
**Variable cost (381)**
**Total variable cost (381)**
**Average variable cost (381)**
**Total cost (381)**
**Average total cost (381)**
**Marginal cost (381)**
**Average fixed cost curve (382)**
**Average variable cost curve (382)**
**Average total cost curve (382)**
**Marginal cost curve (382)**
**Cost-plus pricing (383)**
**Prices based on marginal costs only (385)**
**Break-even analysis (387)**
**Break-even point (387)**
**Prices based on marginal analysis (389)**
**Marginal revenue (389)**
**Average revenue (389)**
**Pricing to meet competition (390)**
**Perfect competition (390)**
**Kinked demand (390)**
**Oligopoly (391)**
**Pricing below competition (391)**
**Pricing above competition (392)**

## QUESTIONS AND PROBLEMS

1. Explain how a firm's pricing objective may influence the promotional program for a product. Which of the six pricing goals involves the largest, most aggressive promotional campaign?
2. What marketing conditions might logically lead a company to set "meeting competition" as a pricing objective?
3. What is your expected price for each of the following articles? How did you arrive at your estimate in each instance?
   a. A new type of cola beverage that holds its carbonation long after it has been opened; packaged in 355-mL and 2-L bottles.
   b. A nuclear-powered 23-inch table-model television set, guaranteed to run for 10 years without replacement of the original power-generating component; requires no battery or electric wires.
   c. An automatic garage-door opener for residential housing.
4. Name at least three products for which you think an inverse demand exists. For each product, within which price range does this inverse demand exist?
5. In Figure 13-2, what is the significance of the point where the marginal cost curve intersects the average total cost curve? Explain why the average total cost curve is declining to the left of the intersection point and rising beyond it. Explain how the marginal cost curve can be rising while the average total cost curve is still declining.
6. What are the merits and limitations of the cost-plus method of setting a base price?
7. In a break-even chart, is the total *fixed* cost line always horizontal? Is the total *variable* cost line always straight? Explain.
8. Referring to Table 13-3 and Figure 13-4, what would be the Futon Factory's break-even points at prices of $50 and $90, if variable costs are $40 per unit and fixed costs remain at $25,000?
9. A small manufacturer sold ballpoint pens to retailers at $8.40 per dozen. The manufacturing cost was 50 cents for each pen. Expenses, including all selling and administrative costs except advertising, were $19,200. How many dozen must the manufacturer sell to cover these expenses and pay for an advertising campaign costing $6,000?
10. In Figure 13-5, why would the firm normally stop producing at quantity Q? Why is the price set at B rather than at D or A?

## HANDS-ON MARKETING

1. Select 10 items that college students purchase frequently at a supermarket. Be specific in describing the items (e.g., a six-pack of Diet Coke). Conduct separate interviews with five of your fellow students, asking them to indicate the price of each item at the supermarket closest to campus. Compare the students' answers with the actual prices charged by that supermarket. How many of the 50 answers were within 5 percent of the actual price? Within 10 percent? Do these results, admittedly from a small sample, suggest that consumers are knowledgeable and concerned about grocery prices?
2. Identify one store in your community that generally prices *below* the levels of most other firms and one that prices *above* prevailing market levels. Arrange an interview with the manager of each store. Ask both managers to explain the rationale and procedures associated with their pricing approaches. Also ask the manager of the store with below-market prices how profits are achieved with such low prices. Ask the manager of the store with above-market prices how customers are attracted and satisfied with such high prices.

## NOTES AND REFERENCES


1. Adapted from, "IKEA, 1994," published by IKEA Systems B.U., 1993.
2. Survey conducted for *Progressive Grocer* magazine, as reported in Albert D. Bates, "Pricing for Profit," *Retailing Issues Newsletter*, September 1990, pp. 1-2. This newsletter is published by Arthur Andersen & Co. in conjunction with the Center for Retailing Studies at Texas A&M University.
3. For an in-depth discussion of this topic, along with excellent bibliographies, see David J. Curry and Peter C. Riesz, "Prices and Price/Quality Relationships: A Longitudinal Analysis," *Journal of Marketing*, January 1988, pp. 36-51; Valarie A. Zeithaml, "Consumer Perceptions of Price, Quality, and Value: A Means-End Model and Synthesis of Evidence," *Journal of Marketing*, July 1988, pp. 2-22. For evidence that price can also affect consumer perceptions of a new product's function, see Alfred S. Boote, "Price Inelasticity: Not All That Meets the Eye," *The Journal of Product and Brand Management*, Spring 1992, pp. 41-46.
4. Pauline Yoshihashi, "Limited-Service Chains Offer Enough to Thrive," *The Wall Street Journal*, July 27, 1992, p. B1; Amy E. Gross, "'Value' Brands Head for Shelves," *Adweek's Marketing Week*, October 29, 1990, p. 6.
5. Richard Gibson and Laurie M. Grossman, "Fast-Food Chains Hope Diners Swallow New 'Value' Menu of Higher-Priced Items," *The Wall Street Journal*, March 13, 1992, p. B1.
6. As quoted in Stratford Sherman, "How to Prospect in the Value Decade," *Fortune*, November 30, 1992, p. 91. For more on this topic, see Joseph B. White, "'Value Pricing' Is Hot as Shrewd Consumers Seek Low-Cost Quality," *The Wall Street Journal*, March 12, 1991, p. A1.
7. For a list of 21 pricing objectives and a discussion of objectives as part of a strategic pricing program for industrial firms, see Michael H. Morris and Roger J. Calantone, "Four Components of Effective Pricing," *Industrial Marketing Management*, November 1990, pp. 321-329.
8. Marilyn Chase, "Burroughs Wellcome Cuts Price of AZT under Pressure from AIDS Activists," *The Wall Street Journal*, September 19, 1989, p. A3.
9. For a discussion of new-product pricing, taking into account the product's perceived benefits and entry time, see Eunsang Yoon, "Pricing Imitative New Products," *Industrial Marketing Management*, May 1991, pp. 115-125.
10. For a report on how this is done in the business market, see Michael H. Morris and Mary L. Joyce, "How Marketers Evaluate Price Sensitivity," *Industrial Marketing Management*, May 1988, pp. 169-176.
11. Morris and Calantone, op. cit., p. 323.
12. For an approach to break-even analysis that includes semifixed costs and is of more practical value in situations typically faced by marketing executives, see Thomas L. Powers, "Breakeven Analysis with Semifixed Costs," *Industrial Marketing Management*, February 1987, pp. 35-41.
13. Dan Koeppel, "Fast Food's New Reality," *Adweek's Marketing Week*, March 30, 1992, pp. 22-23.
14. Margaret Studer, "Switzerland's Luxury-Watch Industry Continues to Defy Economic Downturn," *The Wall Street Journal*, August 10, 1992, p. A5B.
15. Peter Pae, "Amex to Cut Some Card Fees for Merchants," *The Wall Street Journal*, February 24, 1992, p. A3.

APPENDIX C

# MARKETING MATH

Marketing involves people — customers, intermediaries, and producers. Much of the business activity of these people is quantified in some manner. Consequently, knowledge of certain concepts in economics, accounting, and finance is essential for decision making in many areas of marketing. With that in mind, this appendix presents an overview — or, for many of you, a review — of (1) price elasticity of demand, (2) the operating statement, (3) markups, and (4) analytical ratios.

## PRICE ELASTICITY OF DEMAND

**Price elasticity of demand** refers to the responsiveness of quantity demanded to price changes. Specifically, it gauges the effect that a change in the price of a product has on amount sold and on total revenue. (Total revenue — that is, total sales in dollars — equals the unit price times the number of units sold.)

We say demand is **elastic** when (1) reducing the unit price causes an increase in total revenue *or* (2) raising the unit price causes a decrease in total revenue. In the first case, the lower price results in a boost in quantity sold that more than offsets the price cut — hence, the increase in total revenue. In the second case, the higher price results in a large drop in quantity sold that more than counters the potential gain from the price rise — hence, the decrease in total revenue.

These elastic demand situations are illustrated in Figure C-1. We start with a situation where, at $5 a sandwich, the Campus Sandwich Company sells 100 units and the total revenue (TR) equals $500. When the firm lowers price to $4, the quantity sold increases to 150 and total revenue also goes up — to $600. When the price is boosted to $6, however, the quantity sold drops off so much (to 70 sandwiches) that total revenue also declines (to $420). Thus demand is *elastic* when the price change (either up or down) and total revenue change move in the *opposite* direction.

Demand is **inelastic** when (1) a price cut causes total revenue to decline *or* (2) a price rise results in an increase in total revenue. In each of these situations, the changes in unit price more than offset the relatively small changes in quantities sold. That is, when the price is cut, the increase in quantity sold is not enough to offset the price cut, so total revenue goes down. And when the unit price is raised, it more than counters the decline in quantity sold, so total revenue goes up. Simply, demand is *inelastic* when the price change and the resulting change in total revenue go in the *same* direction.

Inelastic demand situations are illustrated in Figure C-2. Again we start with a unit price of $5, Paperbacks and More sells 100 units, and total revenue is $500. When the store lowers the unit price to $4, the quantity of books sold increases to 115. But this is not enough to offset the price cut, so total revenue declines to $460. When the unit price is raised to $6, the quantity sold falls off to 90. But the price increase more than offsets the drop in quantity sold, so total revenue goes up to $540.

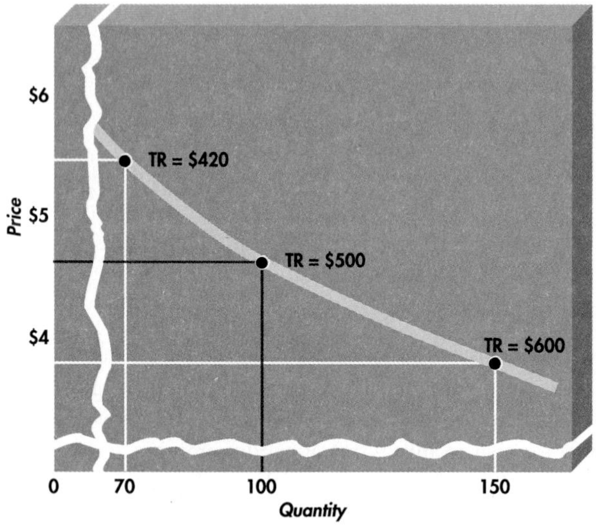


**FIGURE C-1 Elastic demand.**

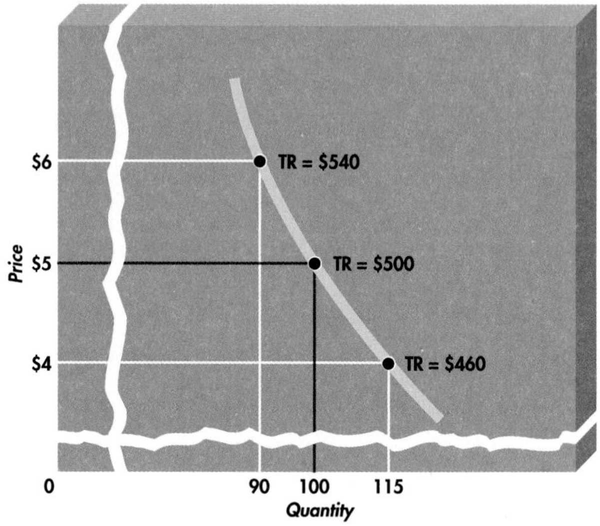


**FIGURE C-2 Inelastic demand.**

In general, the demand for necessities (salt, sugar, gasoline, telephone service, gas and electric service) tends to be inelastic. If the price of gasoline goes up or down, say 5 or 10 cents a litre, the total number of litres sold does not change very much. Simply, consumers need gasoline for their car. Conversely, the demand for products purchased with discretionary income (luxury items, large appliances, furniture, autos) typically is much more elastic. That is why the demand for new electronics products often soars as prices decline in the early stages of the life cycle.

Moreover, the demand for individual *brands* is more elastic than is the demand for the broader *product* category. If consumers encounter an unsatisfactory price on an individual brand, they ordinarily can purchase an alternative brand. However, if they are displeased with the prices in an entire product category, they may not be able to find an alternative type of product to meet their needs. Thus the demand for Air Canada or Tilden rental cars is far more elastic (price-sensitive) than is the demand for air travel or rental cars in general.

Price elasticity of demand is not just a theoretical concept in economics. It has practical value. By gauging whether demand for a product is elastic or inelastic, marketing executives are better able to establish suitable prices for their products.

## THE OPERATING STATEMENT

A company prepares two main financial statements — a balance sheet and an operating statement. A **balance sheet** shows the assets, liabilities, and net worth of a company at a given time — for example, at the close of business on December 31, 1995.

The focus of our attention here, however, is the operating statement. Often called a *profit-and-loss statement* or an *income statement*, an **operating statement** is a summary of the firm's income and expenses over a period of time, for example the 1995 calendar year. The operating statement shows whether the business earned a net profit or suffered a net loss during the period covered.

An operating statement can cover any period of time. To fulfil income tax requirements, virtually all firms prepare a statement covering operations during a calendar year or another 12-month period called a fiscal year. It is also common for businesses to prepare monthly, quarterly, and/or semiannual operating statements.

Table C-1 is an operating statement for a hypothetical firm, the Alpha-Zeta Company Ltd., which could be either a wholesaler or a retailer. The major difference between the operating statement of an intermediary and that of a manufacturer is the cost-of-goods-sold section. A manufacturer shows the cost of goods *manufactured*, whereas the intermediary's statement shows net *purchases*.

The essence of business is very simple. A company buys or makes a product and then (hopefully) sells it for a higher price. From the sales revenue, the seller intends to cover the cost of the merchandise and the expenses of the business and have something left over, which is called **net profit**. These relationships form the basic structure of an operating statement:

- Sales minus cost of goods sold equals gross margin; and
- Gross margin minus expenses equals net profit.

An example based on the Alpha-Zeta Company in Table C-1 follows:

| | | |
|---|---|---|
| | Sales | $80,000 |
| *less* | Cost of goods sold | 48,000 |
| *equals* | Gross margin | 32,000 |
| *less* | Expenses | 27,200 |
| *equals* | Net profit | $ 4,800 |

Now let's look at the primary components in an operating statement.

## Sales

The first line in an operating statement records **gross sales** — the total amount sold by an organization, stated in dollars. From this figure the Alpha-Zeta Company (hereafter, A-Z) deducts sales returns and sales allowances. A-Z also deducts discounts granted to employees when they purchase merchandise or services.

In virtually every firm at some time during an operating period, customers want to return or exchange merchandise. In a **sales return**, the customer is refunded the full purchase price in cash or credit. In a **sales allowance**, the customer keeps the merchandise but is given a reduction from the selling price because of some dissatisfaction. The income from the sale of returned merchandise is included in a company's gross sales, so returns and allowances must be deducted to calculate net sales.

## Net Sales

The most important figure in the sales section of the statement is **net sales**, which represents the net amount of sales revenue, out of which the company will pay for the products and all its expenses. The net sales figure is also the one on which many operating ratios are based. It is designated as 100 percent (of itself), and the other items are then expressed as a percentage of net sales.

TABLE C-1 Example of an operating statement for a wholesaler or a retailer

The Alpha-Zeta Company Ltd.
Operating Statement for Year Ending December 31, 1995

| | | | |
|---|---|---|---|
| Gross sales | | $87,000 | |
| *Less*: Sales returns and allowances | $ 5,500 | | |
| *Less*: Cash discounts allowed | 1,500 | 7,000 | |
| Net sales | | | $80,000 |
| Cost of goods sold: | | | |
| Beginning inventory, January 1 (at cost) | | $18,000 | |
| Gross purchases | $49,300 | | |
| *Less*: Cash discounts taken on purchases | 900 | | |
| Net purchases | $48,400 | | |
| *Plus*: Freight in | 1,600 | | |
| Net purchases (at delivered cost) | | 50,000 | |
| Cost of goods available for sale | | $68,000 | |
| *Less*: Ending inventory, December 31 (at cost) | | 20,000 | |
| Cost of goods sold | | | 48,000 |
| Gross margin | | | $32,000 |
| Expenses: | | | |
| Sales-force salaries and commissions | | $11,000 | |
| Advertising | | 2,400 | |
| Office supplies | | 250 | |
| Taxes (except income tax) | | 125 | |
| Telephone and fax | | 250 | |
| Delivery expenses | | 175 | |
| Rent | | 800 | |
| Heat, light, and power | | 300 | |
| Depreciation | | 100 | |
| Insurance | | 150 | |
| Interest | | 150 | |
| Bad debts | | 300 | |
| Administrative salaries | | 7,500 | |
| Office salaries | | 3,500 | |
| Miscellaneous expenses | | 200 | |
| Total expenses | | | 27,200 |
| Net profit before taxes | | | $ 4,800 |

## Cost of Goods Sold

As we work towards determining A-Z's net profit, we deduct from net sales the cost of the merchandise. To calculate the **cost of goods sold** in a retail or wholesale operation, we start with the value of any merchandise on hand at the beginning of the period. To this we add the net cost of what is purchased during the period. From this total we deduct the value of whatever remains unsold at the end of the period.

In Table C-1 the firm started with an inventory worth $18,000, and it purchased goods that cost $50,000. Thus A-Z had a total of $68,000 worth of goods available for sale. If all were sold, the cost of goods sold would have been $68,000. At the end of the year, however, there was still $20,000 worth of merchandise on hand. Thus, during the year, A-Z sold goods that cost $48,000.

We just spoke of merchandise *valued at* a certain figure or *worth* a stated amount. Actually, the problem of inventory valuation is complicated and sometimes controversial. The rule of thumb is to value inventories at cost or market, whichever is lower. The application of this rule in the real world may be difficult. Assume that a store buys six beach balls at $5 each and the following week buys six more at $6 each. The company places all 12, jumbled, in a basket display for sale. Then one is sold, but there is no marking to indicate whether its cost was $5 or $6. Thus the inventory value of the remaining 11 balls may be $60 or $61. If we multiply this situation by thousands of purchases and sales, we begin to see the depth of the problem.

A figure deserving some comment is the **net cost of delivered purchases**. A company starts with its gross purchases at billed cost. Then it must deduct any purchases that were returned or any purchase allowances received. The company should also deduct any discounts taken for payment of the bill within a specified period of time. Deducting purchase returns, allowances, and discounts gives the net cost of purchases. Freight charges paid by the buyer (called **freight in**) are added to net purchases to determine the net cost of *delivered* purchases.

In a manufacturing concern, the cost-of-goods-sold section has a slightly different form. Instead of determining the cost of goods *purchased*, the firm determines the cost of goods *manufactured*, as in Table C-2. Cost of goods manufactured ($50,000) is added to the beginning inventory ($18,000) to ascertain the total goods available for sale ($68,000). Then, after the ending inventory of finished goods has been deducted ($20,000), the result is the cost of goods sold ($48,000).

To find the cost of goods *manufactured*, a company starts with the value of goods partially completed (beginning inventory of goods in process — $24,000). To this beginning inventory figure is added the cost of raw materials, direct labour, and factory overhead expenses incurred during the period ($48,000). The resulting figure is the total goods in process during the period ($72,000). By deducting the value of goods still in process at the end of the period ($22,000), management finds the cost of goods manufactured during that span of time ($50,000).

## Gross Margin

**Gross margin** is determined by subtracting cost of goods sold from net sales. Gross margin, sometimes called *gross profit*, is a key figure in the entire marketing program. When we say that a certain store has a *margin* of 30 percent, we are referring to the gross margin.

## Expenses

**Operating expenses** are deducted from gross margin to determine net profit. The operating expense section includes marketing, administrative, and miscellaneous expenses. It does not, of course, include the cost of goods purchased or manufactured, since these costs have already been deducted.

## Net Profit

**Net profit** is the difference between gross margin and total expenses. Obviously, a negative net profit is a loss.

TABLE C-2 Cost-of-goods-sold section of an operating statement for a manufacturer

| | | | |
|---|---|---|---|
| **Beginning inventory of finished goods (at cost)** | | | **$18,000** |
| **Cost of goods manufactured:** | | | |
| **Beginning inventory, goods in process** | | **$24,000** | |
| ***Plus:* Raw materials** | **$20,000** | | |
| **Direct labour** | **15,000** | | |
| **Overhead** | **13,000** | **48,000** | |
| **Total goods in process** | | **$72,000** | |
| ***Less:* Ending inventory, goods in process** | | **22,000** | |
| **Cost of goods manufactured** | | | **50,000** |
| **Cost of goods available for sale** | | | **$68,000** |
| ***Less:* Ending inventory, finished goods (at cost)** | | | **20,000** |
| **Cost of goods sold** | | | **$48,000** |

## MARKUPS

Many retailers and wholesalers use markup percentages to determine the selling price of an article. Normally the selling price must exceed the cost of the merchandise by an amount sufficient to cover operating expenses and still leave the desired profit. The difference between the selling price of an item and its cost is the **markup**, sometimes referred to as the *mark-on*.

Typically, markups are expressed in percentages rather than dollars. A markup may be expressed as a percentage of either the cost or the selling price. Therefore, we must first determine which will be the *base* for the markup. That is, when we speak of a 40 percent markup, do we mean 40 percent of the *cost* or 40 percent of the *selling price?*

To determine the markup percentage when it is based on *cost*, we use the following formula:

$$\text{Markup \%} = \frac{\text{dollar markup}}{\text{cost}}$$

When the markup is based on *selling price*, the formula to use is:

$$\text{Markup \%} = \frac{\text{dollar markup}}{\text{selling price}}$$

All interested parties must know which base is being used in a given situation. Otherwise there can be considerable misunderstanding. To illustrate, suppose that Allan Aaron runs a clothing store and claims he needs a 66⅔ percent markup to make a small net profit. Blanche Brister, who runs a competitive store, says she needs only a 40 percent markup and that Aaron must be either inefficient or a big profiteer.

Actually, both merchants are using identical markups, but they are using different bases. Each seller buys hats at $6 apiece and sets the selling price at $10. This is a markup of $4 per hat. Aaron is expressing his markup as a percentage of cost — hence the 66⅔ percent figure ($4 ÷ $6 = 0.67, or 66⅔ percent). Brister is basing her markup on the selling price ($4 ÷ $10 = 0.4, or 40 percent).

It would be a mistake for Aaron to try to get by on Brister's 40 percent markup, as long as Aaron uses cost as his base. If Aaron used the 40 percent markup, but *based it on cost*, the markup would be only $2.40. And the selling price would be only $8.40. This $2.40

markup, averaged over the entire hat department, would not enable Aaron to cover his usual expenses and make a profit.

*It is conventional to state markup percentages as a percentage of selling price.*

### Markup Based on Selling Price

The following diagram shows the relationships among selling price, cost, and markup. It can be used to calculate these figures regardless of whether the markup is stated in percentages or dollars, and whether the percentages are based on selling price or cost:

| | | Dollars | Percentage |
|---|---|---|---|
| | **Selling price** | | |
| *less* | **Cost** | ______ | ______ |
| *equals* | **Markup** | | |

As an example, suppose a merchant buys an article for $90 and knows the markup based on selling price must be 40 percent. What is the selling price? By filling in the known information in the diagram, we obtain:

| | | Dollars | Percentage |
|---|---|---|---|
| | **Selling price** | | 100 |
| *less* | **Cost** | 90 | ___ |
| *equals* | **Markup** | | 40 |

The percentage representing cost must then be 60 percent. Thus the $90 cost is 60 percent of the selling price. The selling price is then $150. That is, $90 equals 60 percent of the selling price. Then $90 is divided by 0.6 (or 60 percent) to get the selling price of $150.

A common situation facing merchants is to have competition set a ceiling on selling prices. Or possibly the sellers must buy an item to fit into one of their price lines. Then they want to know the maximum amount they can pay for an item and still get their normal markup. Assume that the selling price of an article is set at $60 — set by competition or by a $59.95 price line. The retailer's normal markup is 35 percent. What is the most the retailer should pay for this article? Again let's fill in what we know in the diagram:

| | | Dollars | Percentage |
|---|---|---|---|
| | **Selling price** | 60 | 100 |
| *less* | **Cost** | ___ | ___ |
| *equals* | **Markup** | | 35 |

The dollar markup is $21 (35 percent of $60). So by simple subtraction we find that the maximum cost the merchant will want to pay is $39.

### Series of Markups

Markups are figured on the selling price at *each level of business* in a channel of distribution. A manufacturer applies a markup to determine its selling price. The manufacturer's selling price then becomes the wholesaler's cost. The wholesaler must determine its own selling price by applying its usual markup percentage based on its — the wholesaler's — selling price. The same procedure is carried out by the retailer, using the wholesaler's selling price as its — the retailer's — cost.

The following calculations illustrate this point:

| | | |
|---|---|---|
| Producer's cost | \$ 7 | Producer's markup = \$3, or 30% |
| Producer's selling price | \$10 | |
| Wholesaler's cost | \$10 | Wholesaler's markup = \$2, or $16\frac{2}{3}$% |
| Wholesaler's selling price | \$12 | |
| Retailer's cost | \$12 | Retailer's markup = \$8, or 40% |
| Retailer's selling price | \$20 | |

### Markup Based on Cost

If a firm customarily deals in markups based on cost — and sometimes this is done among wholesalers — the same diagrammatic approach may be employed. The only change is that cost will equal 100 percent. The selling price will be 100 percent plus the markup based on cost. As an example, a firm bought an article for \$70 and wants a 20 percent markup based on cost. The markup in dollars is \$14 (20 percent of \$70). The selling price is \$84 (\$70 plus \$14):

| | | Dollars | Percentage |
|---|---|---|---|
| | **Selling price** | 84 | 120 |
| *less* | **Cost** | 70 | 100 |
| *equals* | **Markup** | 14 | 20 |

The relationship between markups on cost and markups on selling price is important. For instance, if a product costs \$6 and sells for \$10, there is a \$4 markup. This is a 40 percent markup based on selling price, but a $66\frac{2}{3}$ percent markup based on cost. The following may be helpful in understanding these relationships and in converting from one base to another:

| **If selling price = 100%** | | | | | **If cost = 100%** |
|---|---|---|---|---|---|
| **\$10 = 100%** | 60% → | **Cost = \$6.00** | ← 100% | | **\$10 = $166\frac{2}{3}$%** |
| | 40% → | **Markup = \$4.00** | ← $66\frac{2}{3}$% | | |

The relationships between the two bases are expressed in the following formulas:

$$\%\text{ markup on selling price} = \frac{\%\text{ markup on cost}}{100\% + \%\text{ markup on cost}}$$

$$\%\text{ markup on cost} = \frac{\%\text{ markup on selling price}}{100\% - \%\text{ markup on selling price}}$$

To illustrate the use of these formulas, let's say that a retailer has a markup of 25 percent on *cost*. This retailer wants to know what the corresponding figure is, based on selling price. In the first formula we get:

$$\frac{25\%}{100\% + 25\%} = \frac{25\%}{125\%} = 0.2,\text{ or } 20\%$$

A markup of 33 percent based on *selling price* converts to 50 percent based on cost, according to the second formula:

$$\frac{33\frac{1}{3}\%}{100\% - 33\frac{1}{3}\%} = \frac{33\frac{1}{3}\%}{66\frac{2}{3}\%} = 0.5,\text{ or } 50\%$$

The markup is closely related to gross margin. Recall that gross margin is equal to net sales minus cost of goods sold. Looking below gross margin on an operating statement, we find that gross margin equals operating expenses plus net profit.

Normally the initial markup in a company, department, or product line must be set a little higher than the overall gross margin desired for the selling unit. The reason? Some reductions will be incurred before all the articles are sold. Due to one factor or another, certain items will not sell at the original price. They will have to be marked down — reduced in price from the original level. Some pilferage and other shortages also may occur.

## ANALYTICAL RATIOS

From a study of the operating statement, management can develop several ratios to evaluate the results of its marketing program. In most cases net sales is used as the base (100 percent). In fact, unless specifically mentioned to the contrary, all ratios reflecting gross margin, net profit, or any operating expense are stated as a percentage of net sales.

### Gross Margin Percentage

The ratio of gross margin to net sales is termed simply **gross margin percentage**. In Table C-1 the gross margin percentage for A-Z is $32,000 ÷ $80,000, or 40 percent.

### Net Profit Percentage

The ratio called **net profit percentage** is determined by dividing net profit by net sales. For A-Z this ratio is $4,800 ÷ $80,000, or 6 percent. This percentage may be calculated either before or after income taxes are deducted, but the result should be labelled to show which it is.

### Operating Expense Ratio

When total operating expenses are divided by net sales, the result is the **operating expense ratio**. Using the figures in Table C-1, this ratio for A-Z is $27,000 ÷ $80,000, or 34 percent. In similar fashion we may determine the expense ratio for any given cost. Thus we note in the figure that rent expense was 1 percent, advertising 3 percent, and sales-force salaries and commissions 13.75 percent.

### Stockturn Rate

Management often measures the efficiency of its marketing operations by means of the **stockturn rate**. This figure represents the number of times the average inventory is *turned over*, or sold, during the period under study. The rate is calculated on either a cost or a selling-price basis. Both the numerator and the denominator of the fraction must be expressed in the same terms, either cost or selling price.

On a *cost* basis, the formula for stockturn rate is:

$$\text{Stockturn rate} = \frac{\text{cost of goods sold}}{\text{average inventory at cost}}$$

The average inventory is determined by adding beginning and ending inventories and dividing the result by 2. In Table C-1 the average inventory is ($18,000 + $20,000) ÷ 2 = $19,000. The stockturn rate then is $48,000 ÷ $19,000 = 2.53. Because inventories usually are abnormally low at the first of the year in anticipation of taking physical inventory, this average may not be representative. Consequently, some companies find their average inventory by adding the book inventories at the beginning of each month and then dividing this sum by 12.

Now let's assume inventory is recorded on a *selling-price* basis, as is done in most large retail organizations. Then the stockturn rate equals net sales divided by average inventory at selling price. Sometimes the stockturn rate is computed by dividing the number of *units* sold by the average inventory expressed in *units*.

Wholesale and retail trade associations in many types of businesses publish figures showing the average stockturn rate for their members. A firm with a low rate of stockturn is likely to be spending too much on storage and inventory. The company runs a higher risk of obsolescence or spoilage. If the stockturn rate gets too high, the company's average inventory may be too low. Often a firm in this situation is using hand-to-mouth buying (that is, buying small quantities and selling all or most of them before replenishing inventory). In addition to incurring high handling and billing costs, the company is likely to be out of stock on some items.

### Markdown Percentage

Sometimes retailers are unable to sell products at the originally stated prices. When this occurs, they often reduce these prices to move the products. A **markdown** is a reduction from the original selling price.

Management frequently finds it helpful to determine the markdown percentage. Then the size and number of markdowns and the reasons for them can be analyzed. Retailers, particularly, analyze markdowns.

Markdowns are expressed as a percentage of net sales and *not* as a percentage of the original selling price. To illustrate, a retailer purchases a hat for $6 and marks it up 40 percent to sell for $10. The hat does not sell at that price, so it is marked down to $8. Now the seller may advertise a price cut of 20 percent. Yet, according to our rule, this $2 markdown is 25 percent *of the $8 selling price*.

**Markdown percentage** is calculated by dividing total dollar markdowns by total net sales during a given period. Two important points should be noted. First, the markdown percentage is determined in this fashion whether the markdown items were sold or are still in the store. Second, the percentage is calculated with respect to total net sales, and not only in connection with sales of marked-down articles. As an example, assume that a retailer buys 10 sports hats at $6 each and prices them to sell at $10. Five hats are sold at $10. The other five are marked down to $8, and three are sold at the lower price. Total sales are $74 and total markdowns are $10. The retailer has a markdown ratio of $10 $74, or 13.5 percent.

Markdowns do not appear on the profit-and-loss statement because they occur *before* an article is sold. The first item on an operating statement is gross sales. That figure reflects the actual selling price, which may be the selling price after a markdown has been taken.

### Return on Investment

A commonly used measure of managerial performance and of the operating success of a company is its rate of return on investment. We use both the balance sheet and the operating statement as sources of information. The formula for calculating **return on investment** (ROI) is as follows:

$$\text{ROI} = \frac{\text{net profit}}{\text{sales}} \times \frac{\text{sales}}{\text{investment}}$$

Two questions may come to mind. What do we mean by "investment"? Why do we need two fractions? It would seem that the sales component in each fraction would cancel out, leaving net profit divided by investment as the meaningful ratio.

To answer the first query, consider a firm whose operating statement shows annual sales of $1,000,000 and a net profit of $50,000. At the end of the year, the balance sheet reports:

| | | | | |
|---|---|---|---|---|
| Assets | $600,000 | Liabilities | | $200,000 |
| | | Capital stock | $300,000 | |
| | | Retained earnings | 100,000 | 400,000 |
| | $600,000 | | | $600,000 |

The ROI figure is obviously affected by which figure we use. But is the investment $400,000 or $600,000? The answer depends on whether we are talking to the stockholders or to the company executives. Stockholders are more interested in the return on what they have invested — in this case, $400,000. The ROI calculation then is:

$$\text{ROI} = \frac{\text{net profit } \$50{,}000}{\text{sales } \$1{,}000{,}000} \times \frac{\text{sales } \$1{,}000{,}000}{\text{investment } \$400{,}000} = 12\tfrac{1}{2}\%$$

Management, on the other hand, is more concerned with total investment, as represented by total assets ($600,000). This is the amount that the executives must manage, regardless of whether the assets were acquired by stockholders' investment, retained earnings, or loans from outside sources. Within this context the ROI computation becomes:

$$\text{ROI} = \frac{\text{net profit } \$50{,}000}{\text{sales } \$1{,}000{,}000} \times \frac{\text{sales } \$1{,}000{,}000}{\text{investment } \$600{,}000} = 8\tfrac{1}{3}\%$$

Regarding the second question, we use two fractions because we are dealing with two separate elements — the rate of profit on sales and the rate of capital turnover. Management really should determine each rate separately and then multiply the two. The rate of profit on sales is influenced by marketing considerations — notably, sales volume, price, product mix, and advertising effort. Capital turnover is a financial consideration that is not involved directly with costs or profits — only with sales volume and assets managed.

To illustrate, say our company's profits doubled with the same sales volume and investment because of an excellent marketing program this year. In effect, we doubled our profit rate with the same capital turnover:

$$\text{ROI} = \underbrace{\frac{\text{net profit } \$100{,}000}{\text{sales } \$1{,}000{,}000}}_{10\%} \times \underbrace{\frac{\text{sales } \$1{,}000{,}000}{\text{investment } \$600{,}000}}_{1\frac{2}{3}} = 16\tfrac{2}{3}\%$$

$$10\% \times 1\tfrac{2}{3} = 16\tfrac{2}{3}\%$$

As expected, this 16 percent is twice the ROI calculated above.

Now assume that we earned our original profit of $50,000 but did it with an investment of only $500,000. We cut the size of our average inventory, and we closed some branch offices. By increasing our capital turnover from 1.67 to 2, we raised the ROI from 8 percent to 10 percent, even though sales volume and profits were unchanged:

$$\text{ROI} = \underbrace{\frac{\$50{,}000}{\$1{,}000{,}000}}_{5\%} \times \underbrace{\frac{\$1{,}000{,}000}{\$500{,}000}}_{2} = 10\%$$

$$5\% \times 2 = 10\%$$

Now let's say that we increased our sales volume — we doubled it — but did not increase our profit or investment. The cost-profit squeeze has brought us "profitless prosperity." The following results occur:

$$\text{ROI} = \underbrace{\frac{\$50{,}000}{\$2{,}000{,}000}}_{2\frac{1}{2}\%} \times \underbrace{\frac{\$2{,}000{,}000}{\$600{,}000}}_{3\frac{1}{3}} = \begin{matrix}10\% \\ 8\frac{1}{3}\%\end{matrix}$$

The profit rate was cut in half, but this was offset by a doubling of the capital turnover rate. The result was that the ROI was unchanged.

## QUESTIONS AND PROBLEMS

1. Construct an operating statement from the following data and compute the gross margin percentage:

| | |
|---|---|
| Purchases at billed cost | $15,000 |
| Net sales | 30,000 |
| Sales returns and allowances | 200 |
| Cash discounts given | 300 |
| Cash discounts earned | 100 |
| Rent | 1,500 |
| Salaries | 6,000 |
| Opening inventory at cost | 10,000 |
| Advertising | 600 |
| Other expenses | 2,000 |
| Closing inventory at cost | 7,500 |

2. Prepare a retail operating statement from the following information and compute the markdown percentage:

| | |
|---|---|
| Rent | $ 9,000 |
| Closing inventory at cost | 28,000 |
| Sales returns | 6,500 |
| Cash discounts allowed | 2,000 |
| Salaries | 34,000 |
| Markdowns | 4,000 |
| Other operating expenses | 15,000 |
| Opening inventory at cost | 35,000 |
| Gross sales | 232,500 |
| Advertising | 5,500 |
| Freight in | 3,500 |
| Gross margin as percentage of sales | 35 |

3. What percentage markups *on cost* correspond to the following percentages of markup on selling price?
   a. 20 percent.
   b. $37\frac{1}{2}$ percent.
   c. 50 percent.
   d. $66\frac{2}{3}$ percent.
4. What percentage markups *on selling price* correspond to the following percentages of markup on cost?
   a. 20 percent.
   b. $33\frac{1}{3}$ percent.
   c. 50 percent.
   d. 300 percent.
5. A hardware store bought a gross (12 dozen) of hammers, paying $602.40 for the total order. The retailer estimated operating expenses for this product to be 35 percent of sales and wanted a net profit of 5 percent of sales. The retailer expected no markdowns. What retail selling price should be set for each hammer?
6. Competition in a line of sporting goods limits the selling price on a certain item to $25. If the store owner feels a markup of 35 percent is needed to cover expenses and return a reasonable profit, what is the most the owner can pay for this item?
7. A retailer with annual net sales of $2 million maintains a markup of $66\frac{2}{3}$ percent based on cost. Expenses average 35 percent. What are the retailer's gross margin and net profit in dollars?
8. A company has a stockturn rate of five times a year, a sales volume of $600,000, and a gross margin of 25 percent. What is the average inventory at cost?
9. A store has an average inventory of $30,000 at retail and a stockturn rate of five times a year. If the company maintains a markup of 50 percent based on cost, what are the annual sales volume and cost of goods sold?
10. From the following data, compute the gross margin percentage and the operating expense ratio:
    Stockturn rate = 9
    Average inventory at selling price = $45,000
    Net profit = $20,000
    Cost of goods sold = $350,000
11. A ski shop sold 50 pairs of skis at $90 a pair, after taking a 10 percent markdown. All the skis were originally purchased at the same price and had been marked up 60 percent on cost. What was the gross margin on the 50 pairs of skis?

12. A women's clothing store bought 200 suits at $90 each. The suits were marked up 40 percent. Eighty were sold at that price. The remaining suits were each marked down 20 percent from the original selling price, and all were sold. Compute the sales volume and markdown percentage.
13. An appliance retailer sold 60 portable cassette players at $40 each after taking markdowns equal to 20 percent of the actual selling price. Originally all the cassette players had been purchased at the same price and were marked up 50 percent on cost. What was the gross margin percentage earned in this situation?
14. An appliance manufacturer produced a line of small appliances advertised to sell at $30. The manufacturer planned for wholesalers to receive a 20 percent markup, and retailers a 33$^1/_3$ percent markup. Total manufacturing costs were $12 per unit. What did retailers pay for the product? What were the manufacturer's selling price and percentage markup?
15. A housewares manufacturer produces an article at a full cost of $4.80. It is sold through a manufacturers' agent directly to large retailers. The agent receives a 20 percent commission on sales, the retailers earn a margin of 30 percent, and the manufacturer plans a net profit of 10 percent on the selling price. What is the retail price of this article?
16. A building materials manufacturer sold a quantity of a product to a wholesaler for $350, and the wholesaler in turn sold it to a lumberyard. The wholesaler's normal markup was 15 percent, and the retailer usually priced the item to include a 30 percent markup. What is the selling price to consumers?
17. From the following data, calculate the return on investment, based on a definition of *investment* that is useful for evaluating managerial performance:

| | |
|---|---|
| Net sales | $800,000 |
| Gross margin | 280,000 |
| Total assets | 200,000 |
| Cost of goods sold | 520,000 |
| Liabilities | 40,000 |
| Average inventory | 75,000 |
| Retained earnings | 60,000 |
| Operating expenses | 240,000 |
| Markup | 35% |

## CHAPTER 14 GOALS

In this chapter we discuss ways in which a firm adjusts a product's base price to coincide with its overall marketing program. After studying this chapter, you should have an understanding of:

- Pricing strategies for entering a market, notably market skimming and market penetration.
- Price discounts and allowances.
- Geographic pricing strategies.
- Special strategies, including one-price and flexible-price approaches, unit pricing, price lining, resale price maintenance, leader pricing, and odd pricing.
- Legal issues associated with pricing.
- Price competition versus nonprice competition, including the concepts of value pricing and a price war.

CHAPTER 14

# PRICING STRATEGIES AND POLICIES

## Pricing to Keep the National a Prima Ballet

Pricing strategy is about positioning yourself competitively and working out the details of discounts, allowances, geographic pricing strategies, special strategies to counter competition, and a host of other details. Does the National Ballet of Canada really worry about such straightforward commercial matters? You bet it does. While the cover of its 1994-95 season brochure communicates the essence of classical ballet, the copy of the bottom line, "Subscribe now and save up to 43%," introduces the story of the National's pricing strategies.

The National Ballet of Canada sees itself as the leading Canadian ballet company and positions itself at the forefront of international dance. It is a not-for-profit organization with a mission to bring the absolute best in classical and contemporary ballet to Canadians. This mission is tempered by the fact that the early nineties have been a financially difficult period for all the performing arts — financial support from government, donors, and patrons has been under pressure. This means that the National works with a reasoned and cautious approach to budgets. Its pricing strategy is to lower ticket prices in keeping with its aim to make ballet more accessible to everyone. "Ballet for all" is the operating credo for the nineties and this is reflected in the pricing strategies used to support this goal.

The schedule inside the brochure tells us that quantity discounts are at work with savings up to 43 percent for seven performances, 33 percent for five and 23 percent for four. It also shows discounts for matinées and for combinations of performances; 50 percent discounts for students and senior subscriptions; and special discounts for family subscriptions.

The National also makes the case for donations. Rather than leaving the amount up to the donor, it suggests, "Donations make a difference. Please help us bring you world class ballet with a donation of $25. Become a special member of the National Ballet (donations of $60)."[1]

Fundamentally, in managing the price element in a company's marketing mix, management first must decide on its pricing goal and then set the base price for a good or service. The final task, as shown in Figure 14-1, is to design pricing strategies that are compatible with the rest of the marketing mix. Many strategic questions related to price must be answered by all firms. These questions include: What kind of discount schedule should be adopted? Will the firm occasionally absorb freight costs? Will the firm compete primarily on the basis of price, or on other factors? Are our approaches to pricing ethical and legal?

We will use the term *strategy* frequently in this chapter, so let's review its meaning. A **strategy** is a broad plan of action by which an organization intends to reach its goal. To illustrate, a company may adopt a strategy of expanding product lines that enjoy substantial brand equity. Another strategy would be to offer quantity discounts to achieve the goal of a 10 percent increase in sales next year.

## MARKET-ENTRY STRATEGIES

In preparing to enter the market with a new product, management must decide whether to adopt a skimming or a penetration pricing strategy.

### Market-Skimming Pricing

Setting a relatively high initial price for a new product is referred to as **market-skimming pricing**. Ordinarily the price is high in relation to the target market's range of expected prices. That is, the price is set at the highest possible level that the most interested consumers will pay for the new product.

Market-skimming pricing has several purposes. Since it should provide healthy profit margins, it is intended primarily to recover research and development costs as quickly as possible. Further, lofty prices can be used to connote high quality. Moreover, market-

**FIGURE 14-1**
**The price-determination process.**

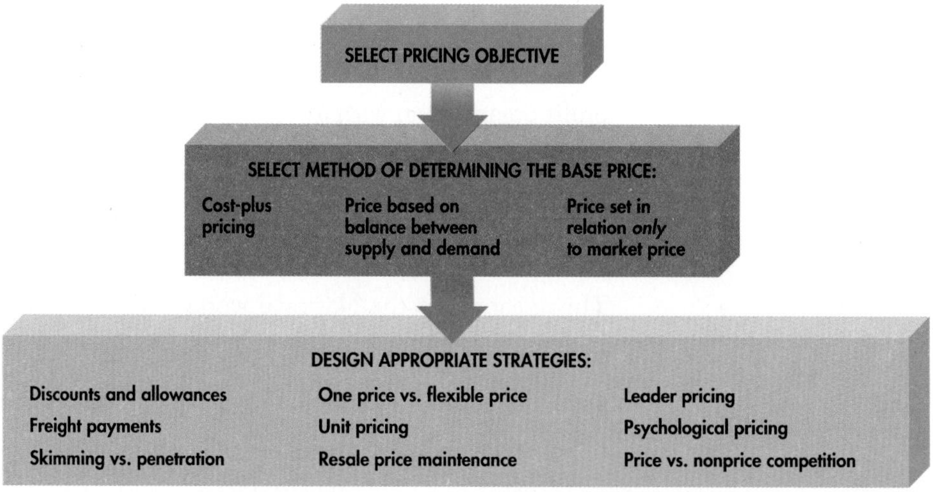

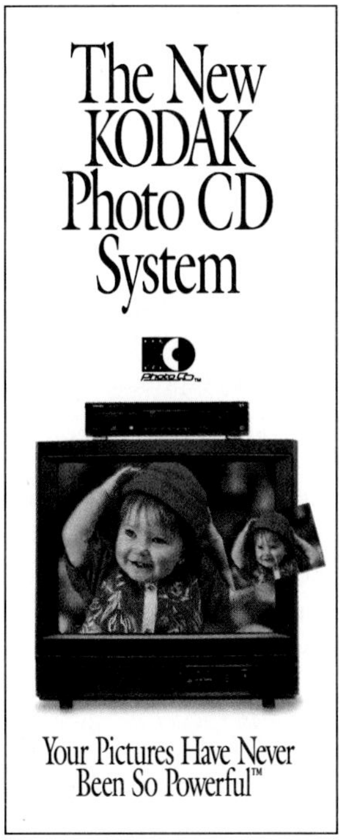


**In introducing this product, should Kodak use market-skimming or market-penetration pricing?**

skimming pricing is likely to curtail demand to levels that do not outstrip the firm's production capacities. Finally, it provides the firm with flexibility, because it is much easier to lower an initial price that meets with consumer resistance than it is to raise an initial price that has proven to be too low to cover costs.

Market-skimming pricing is suitable under the following conditions:

- The new product has distinctive features strongly desired by consumers.
- Demand is fairly inelastic, most likely the case in the early stages of a product's life cycle. Under this condition, lower prices are unlikely to produce greater total revenues.
- The new product is protected from competition through one or more entry barriers such as a patent.

Market skimming is often used in pricing new technological products such as cellular telephones and high-definition TVs. Over time, the initial price may be lowered gradually. Still, the high initial prices associated with market skimming are subject to criticism from consumers and others.

### Market-Penetration Pricing

In **market-penetration pricing**, a relatively low initial price is established for a new product. The price is low in relation to the target market's range of expected prices. The primary aim of this strategy is to penetrate the mass market immediately and, in so doing, generate substantial sales volume and a large market share. At the same time, it is intended to discourage other firms from introducing competing products.

Market-penetration pricing makes the most sense under the following conditions:

- A large mass market exists for the product.
- Demand is highly elastic, typically in the later stages of the life cycle for a product category.
- Substantial reductions in unit costs can be achieved through large-scale operations. In other words, economies of scale are possible.
- Fierce competition already exists in the market for this product or can be expected to materialize soon after the product is introduced.

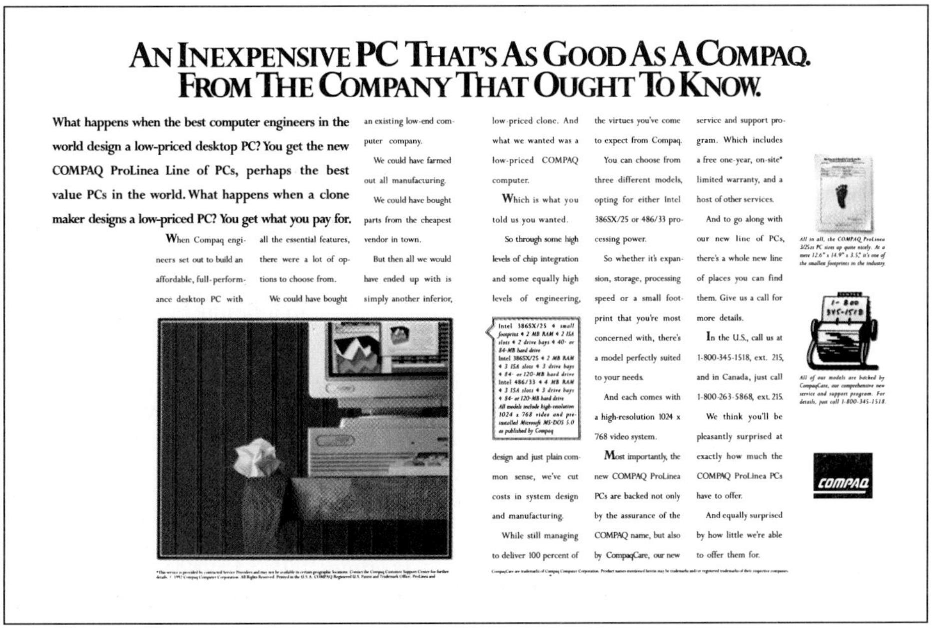


**Facing stiff competition and elastic demand, Compaq used market-penetration pricing in introducing a new line of PCs.**

Computer firms introducing clones that imitate IBM or Apple models rely on market-penetration pricing. In retaliation, leading computer makers apply the same pricing strategy for their new products. Apple has developed new Macintosh PCs, and Compaq has launched an entire new line of Prolinea PCs, with both firms using penetration pricing.[2]

## DISCOUNTS AND ALLOWANCES

Discounts and allowances result in a deduction from the base (or list) price. The deduction may be in the form of a reduced price or some other concession, such as free merchandise or advertising allowances. Discounts and allowances are commonplace in business dealings.

### Quantity Discounts

**Quantity discounts** are deductions from a seller's list price intended to encourage customers to buy in larger amounts or to buy most of what they need from the seller offering the deduction. Discounts are based on the size of the purchase, either in dollars or in units.

A **noncumulative discount** is based on the size of an *individual order* of one or more products. A retailer may sell golf balls at $2 each or at three for $5. A manufacturer or wholesaler may set up a quantity discount schedule such as the following, used by a manufacturer of industrial adhesives:

| Boxes purchased in single order | Percent discount from list price |
|---|---|
| 1-5 | None |
| 6-12 | 2.0 |
| 13-25 | 3. 5 |
| Over 25 | 5.0 |

Noncumulative quantity discounts are intended to encourage large orders. Many expenses, such as billing, order filling, and salaries of sales people, are about the same whether the seller receives an order totalling $10 or one totalling $500. Consequently, selling expense as a percentage of sales decreases as orders grow in size. With a noncumulative discount, a seller shares such savings with a purchaser of large quantities.

A **cumulative discount** is based on the total volume purchased *over a specified period.* This type of discount is advantageous to a seller because it ties customers more closely to that firm. The more total business a buyer gives a seller, the greater is the discount. Airline frequent-flyer and hotel frequent-guest programs are a form of cumulative discount. IBM offers an assortment of volume-over-time discounts. And Unitel competes with Bell Canada and other telephone companies by offering deep discounts to high-volume users of long-distance telephone service.[3] Cumulative discounts also are common in selling perishable products. These discounts encourage customers to buy fresh supplies frequently, so that the buyer's merchandise will not become stale.

Quantity discounts can help a producer achieve real economies in production as well as in selling. On the one hand, large orders (motivated by a noncumulative discount) can result in lower production and transportation costs. On the other hand, frequent orders from a single customer (motivated by a cumulative discount) can enable the producer to make much more effective use of production capacity, even though individual orders are small and do not generate savings in marketing costs.

### Trade Discounts

**Trade discounts**, sometimes called *functional discounts*, are reductions from the list price offered to buyers in payment for marketing functions the buyers will perform — functions such as storing, promoting, and selling the product. A manufacturer may quote a retail price of $400 with trade discounts of 40 percent and 10 percent. The retailer pays the wholesaler $240 ($400 less 40 percent), and the wholesaler pays the manufacturer $216 ($240 less 10 percent). The wholesaler is given the 40 and 10 percent discounts. The wholesaler is expected to keep the 10 percent to cover costs of the wholesaling functions and pass on the 40 percent discount to retailers. Sometimes, however, wholesalers keep more than the 10 percent — and it's not illegal for them to do so.

Note that the 40 and 10 percent discounts do not constitute a total discount of 50 percent off list price. They are not additive; rather, they are discounts on discounts. Each discount is computed on the amount remaining after the preceding discount has been deducted.

### Cash Discounts

A **cash discount** is a deduction granted to buyers for paying their bills within a specified time. The discount is computed on the net amount due after first deducting trade and quantity discounts from the base price. Every cash discount includes three elements, as indicated in Figure 14-2:

- The percentage discount
- The period during which the discount may be taken
- The time when the bill becomes overdue

Let's say a buyer owes $360 after other discounts have been granted and is offered terms of 2/10, n/30 on an invoice dated November 8. This means the buyer may deduct a discount of 2 percent ($7.20) if the bill is paid within 10 days of the invoice date — by November 18. Otherwise the entire (net) bill of $360 must be paid in 30 days — by December 8.

**FIGURE 14-2**
**Parts of a cash discount.**

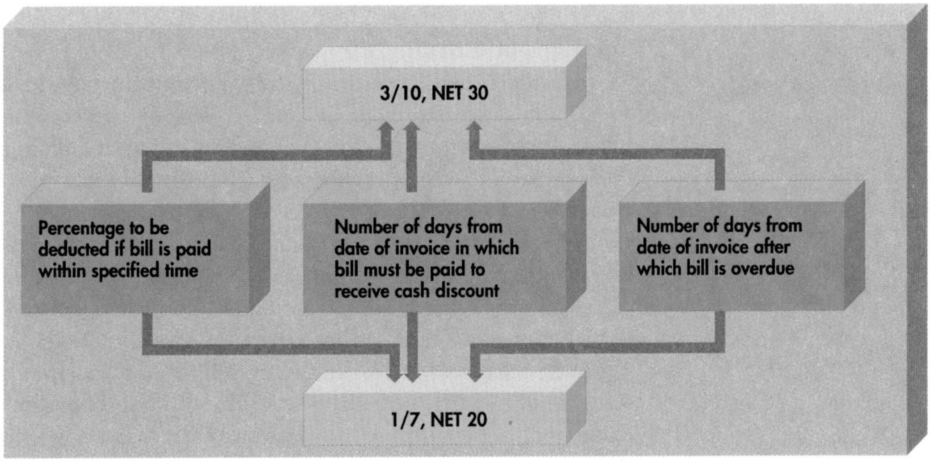


There are almost as many different cash discounts as there are industries. For example, in women's fashions, large discounts and short payment periods have been common; thus a cash discount of 5/5, n/15 would not be surprising. Such differences persist not so much for business reasons but because of tradition in various industries.

Most buyers are eager to pay bills in time to earn cash discounts. The discount in a 2/10, n/30 situation may not seem like very much. But this 2 percent is earned just for paying 20 days in advance of the date the entire bill is due. If buyers fail to take the cash discount in a 2/10, n/30 situation, they are, in effect, borrowing money at a 36 percent annual rate of interest. Here's how we arrived at that interest rate: In a 360-day business year, there are 18 periods of 20 days. Paying 2 percent for one of these 20-day periods is equivalent to paying 36 percent for an entire year.

### Other Discounts and Allowances

A manufacturer of goods such as air conditioners or toys purchased on a seasonal basis may consider granting a **seasonal discount**. This discount of, say, 5, 10, or 20 percent is given to a customer who places an order during the slack season. Off-season orders enable manufacturers to better use their production facilities and/or avoid inventory-carrying costs. Many services firms also offer seasonal discounts. For example, Club Med and many other vacation resorts lower their prices during the off-season.

**Forward dating** is a variation on both seasonal and cash discounts. A manufacturer of fishing tackle might seek and fill orders from wholesalers and retailers during the winter months. But the bills would be dated April 1, with terms of 2/10, n/30 offered as of that date. Orders filled in December and January help to maintain production during the slack season for more efficient operation. The forward-dated bills allow the wholesale or retail buyers to pay their bills after the season has started and they can generate some sales revenue from the products delivered earlier.

A **promotional allowance** is a price reduction granted by a seller as payment for promotional services performed by buyers. To illustrate, a producer of builders' hardware gives a certain quantity of free goods to dealers who prominently display its line. Or a clothing manufacturer pays one-half the cost of a retailer's ad featuring its product.

## THE COMPETITION ACT AND PRICE DISCRIMINATION

The discounts and allowances discussed in this section may result in different prices for different customers. Whenever price differentials exist, there is **price discrimination**. The terms are synonymous. In certain situations, price discrimination is prohibited by the **Competition Act**. This is one of the most important federal laws affecting a company's marketing program.

### Background of the Act

Competition legislation in Canada was first introduced in 1888. Small businesses that suffered from the monopolistic and collusive practices in restraint of trade by large manufacturers pressured Parliament into setting up a Combines Investigation Commission. Investigators attempting to verify the allegations of the small businesses unearthed a widespread range of restrictive practices and measures.

The results of the investigation led Parliament in 1889 to pass the Act for the Prevention and Suppression of Combinations Formed in Restraint of Trade. The intent of the Act was to declare illegal monopolies and combinations in restraint of trade. Although the Act was incorporated into the Criminal Code as section 520 in 1892, it proved ineffectual, because to break the law an individual would have to commit an illegal act within the meaning of the "common law." In 1900 the Act was amended to remove this loophole and undue restriction of competition became, in itself, a criminal offence.

Additional legislation was passed in 1910 after a rash of mergers involving 58 business firms, to complement the Criminal Code and assist in the application of the Act. In 1919 the Combines and Fair Prices Act was passed, which prohibited undue stockpiling of the "necessities of life" and also prohibited the realization of exaggerated profits through "unreasonable" prices.

In 1923, Canadian combines legislation was finally consolidated and important sections remain in force to this day. Following the presentation of a report by the Economic Council of Canada in 1969,[4] the Government of Canada introduced into Parliament, in 1971 and 1975, a number of important amendments to the Combines Investigation Act to form the basis for a new competition policy for Canada. However, it was not until 1986, when the new Competition Act (the successor to the Combines Investigation Act) became law, that major Economic Council recommendations were implemented.

Below are some of the Competition Act implications for common pricing strategies and policies.[5]

### Predatory Pricing as an Offence

The provisions respecting predatory pricing are contained in paragraph 34(1)(*c*) of the Competition Act, which states:

> 34.(1) Every one engaged in a business who
> (c) engages in a policy of selling products at prices unreasonably low, having the effect or tendency of substantially lessening competition or eliminating a competitor, or designed to have such effect; is guilty of an indictable offence and is liable to imprisonment for two years.

In order for a conviction to result under paragraph 34(1)(*c*), it must be shown that prices are unreasonably low and that such prices have the effect of reducing competition. The amendments to the Combines Investigation Act that were passed in 1975 extended the predatory pricing provisions to the sale of both articles and services. The word "products" is now defined in the Competition Act to include articles *and* services.

### Price Discrimination as an Offence

At present, price discrimination is regulated under paragraph 34(1)(*a*) of the Competition Act, which states:

> 34.(1) Every one engaged in a business who
> (a) is a party or privy to, or assists in, any sale that discriminates to his knowledge, directly or indirectly, against competitors of a purchaser of articles from him in that any discount, rebate, allowance, price concession or other advantage that, at the time the articles are sold to such purchaser, is available to such competitors in respect of a sale of articles of like quality and quantity; is guilty of an indictable offence and is liable to imprisonment for two years.

This section goes on to state in paragraph 34(2):

> (2) It is not an offence under paragraph (1)(a) to be a party or privy to, or assist in any sale mentioned therein unless the discount, rebate, allowance, price concession or other advantage was granted as part of a practice of discriminating as described in that paragraph.

The following conditions must, therefore, be met in order for a conviction to be registered for price discrimination: (1) a discount, rebate, allowance, price concession, or other advantage must be granted to one customer and not to another; (2) the two customers concerned must be *competitors*; (3) the price discrimination must occur in respect of *articles* of similar quality and quantity; (4) the act of discrimination must be part of a *practice* of discrimination.

Not all price discrimination is, *per se*, an offence. It is lawful to discriminate in price on the basis of quantities of goods purchased. The cost justification defence that is used in the United States — that of a seller differentiating the price to a favoured competitor because of a difference in the costs of supplying that customer — is not viewed as an acceptable basis for discrimination in Canada. On the other hand, a seller does not have to demonstrate a cost difference in order to support a quantity discount structure. Rather, the basis for such price discrimination is accepted only on a quantity of goods-purchased basis. Establishing volume discount pricing structures that are available to competing buyers who purchase in comparable quantities is a major basis for discriminating under the provision.

It is also of note that the buyer is seen as being as liable as the seller in cases of discrimination. The legislation applies to those who are party to a sale and this includes both buyer and seller. This wording was intended to restrain large-scale buyers from demanding discriminatory prices. In addition, the buyer (as well as the seller) must know that the price involved is discriminatory.

### Granting Promotional Allowances as an Offence

The Competition Act in section 35 requires that promotional allowances be granted proportionately to all competing customers. This section states:

> 35.(1) In this section "allowance" means any discount, rebate, price concession or other advantage that is or purports to be offered or granted for advertising or display purposes and is collateral to a sale or sales of products but is not applied directly to the selling price.
>
> (2) Everyone engaged in a business who is a party or privy to the granting of an allowance to any purchaser that is not offered on proportionate terms to other purchasers in competition with the first-mentioned purchaser, (which other purchasers are in this section called "competing purchasers"), is guilty of an indictable offence and is liable to imprisonment for two years.
>
> (3) For the purposes of this section, an allowance is offered on proportionate terms only if
> (a) the allowance offered to a purchaser is in approximately the same proportion to the value of sales to him as the allowance offered to each competing purchaser is to the total value of sales to such competing purchaser.
> (b) in any case where advertising or other expenditures or services are exacted in return therefor, the cost thereof required to be incurred by a purchaser is in approximately the same proportion to the value of sales to him as the cost of such advertising or other expenditures or services required to be incurred by each competing purchaser is the total value of sales to such competing purchaser, and
> (c) in any case where services are exacted in return therefor, the requirements thereof have regard to the kinds of services that competing purchasers at the same time or different levels of distribution are ordinarily able to perform or cause to be performed.

The provisions of section 35 apply to the sale of both articles and services. Discrimination in the granting of promotional allowances is a per se offence, not requiring proof of the existence of either a practice of discrimination or a lessening of competition. A company that wishes to discriminate among its customers may do so through the legal practice of granting quantity discounts.

## GEOGRAPHIC PRICING STRATEGIES

In pricing, a seller must consider the costs of shipping goods to the buyer. These costs grow in importance as freight becomes a larger part of total variable costs. Pricing policies may be established whereby the buyer pays all the freight expense, the seller bears the entire cost, or the seller and buyer share this expense. The strategy chosen can influence the geographic limits of a firm's market, locations of its production facilities, sources of its raw materials, and its competitive strength in various geographic markets.

### F.O.B. Point-of-Production Pricing

In one widely used geographic pricing strategy, the seller quotes the selling price at the factory or at some other point of production or origin. In this situation the buyer pays the entire cost of transportation. This is usually referred to as **f.o.b. mill** or **f.o.b. factory** pricing. Of the four strategies discussed in this section, this is the only one in which the seller does not pay *any* of the freight costs. The seller pays only the cost of loading the shipment aboard the carrier — hence the term **f.o.b.**, or **free on board**.

Under f.o.b. factory pricing strategy, the seller nets the same amount on each sale of similar quantities. The delivered price to the buyer varies according to the freight charge. However, this pricing strategy has serious economic and marketing implications. In effect, f.o.b. mill pricing tends to establish a geographic monopoly for a given seller, because freight rates prevent distant competitors from entering the market. The seller, in turn, is increasingly priced out of more distant markets.

### Uniform Delivered Pricing

Under the **uniform delivered pricing** strategy, the same delivered price is quoted to all buyers regardless of their locations. This strategy is sometimes referred to as "postage stamp pricing" because of its similarity to the pricing of first-class mail service. The net revenue to the seller varies, depending on the shipping cost involved in each sale.

A uniform delivered price is typically used where transportation costs are a small part of the seller's total costs. This strategy is also used by many retailers who feel that "free" delivery is an additional service that strengthens their market position.

Under a uniform delivered price system, buyers located near the seller's factory pay for some of the costs of shipping to more distant locations. Critics of f.o.b. factory pricing are usually in favour of a uniform delivered price. They feel that the freight expense should not be charged to individual customers any more than any other single marketing or production expense.

### Zone-Delivered Pricing

Under a **zone-delivered pricing** strategy, a seller would divide the Canadian market into a limited number of broad geographic zones. Then a uniform delivered price is set within each zone. Zone-delivered pricing is similar to the system used in pricing parcel post services and long-distance telephone service. A firm that quotes a price and then says "Slightly higher west of the Lakehead" is using a two-zone pricing system. The freight charge built into the delivered price is an average of the charges at all points within a zone area.

When adopting this pricing strategy, the seller must walk a neat tightrope to avoid charges of illegal price discrimination. This means that the zone lines must be drawn so that all buyers who compete for a particular market are in the same zone. Such a condition is most easily met where markets are widely distributed.

### Freight-Absorption Pricing

A **freight-absorption pricing** strategy may be adopted to offset some of the competitive disadvantages of f.o.b. factory pricing. With an f.o.b. factory price, a firm is at a price disadvantage when it tries to sell to buyers located in markets nearer to competitors' plants. To penetrate more deeply into such markets, a seller may be willing to absorb some of the freight costs. Thus, seller A will quote to the customer a delivered price equal to (1) A's factory price plus (2) the freight costs that would be charged by the competitive seller located nearest to that customer.

A seller can continue to expand the geographic limits of its market as long as its net revenue after freight absorption is larger than its marginal cost for the units sold. Freight absorption is particularly useful to a firm with excess capacity whose fixed costs per unit of product are high and whose variable costs are low. In these cases, management must constantly seek ways to cover fixed costs, and freight absorption is one answer.

The legality of freight absorption is reasonably clear. The strategy is legal if it is used independently and not in collusion with other firms. Also, it must be used only to meet competition. In fact, if practised properly, freight absorption can have the effect of strengthening competition because it can break down geographic monopolies.

## MARKETING AT WORK

### FILE 14-1 THE MODULAR APPROACH TO PRICING

Interleaf is a producer of high-end publishing software and is a company that uses price bundling as an important part of its marketing strategy. Interleaf sells its core Technical Publishing Software for $2,500. Then there are options that can be added, such as the Advanced Graphics module ($4,500) and the Book Catalogue module ($2,500). The full version of Technical Publishing Software, including other modules, sells for $15,000. Because its product is sold in optional parts, Interleaf is able to adopt a high-price strategy in its less price-sensitive markets (where they have few rivals), while remaining competitive in lower-end markets, where competition is fierce and consumers are more price sensitive. With this strategy, Interleaf is able to standardize on one basic system while catering to the individual needs of specific customers — already they have designed add-on modules that appeal to the graphic arts, technical document, and newspaper market segments. Because potential and future modules can all be added to the core product, Interleaf is constantly able to expand its markets vertically.

Source: Adapted from Denes Bartakovich, "Building Competitive Advantage Through Creative Pricing Strategies," *Business Quarterly*, Summer 1990, pp. 47-48.

## SPECIAL PRICING STRATEGIES

To set initial prices and evaluate existing prices, a firm needs to consider a number of distinctive strategies. It's likely that at least one, but probably not all, will apply to a particular pricing situation.

### One-Price and Flexible-Price Strategies

Rather early in its pricing deliberations, management should decide whether to adopt a one-price strategy or a flexible-price strategy. Under a **one-price strategy**, a seller charges the *same* price to all similar customers who buy similar quantities of a product. Under a **flexible-price** (also called a **variable-price**) strategy, similar customers may each pay a *different* price when buying similar quantities of a product.[6]

In Canada and the United States, a one-price strategy has been adopted more than variable pricing. Most retailers, for example, typically follow a one-price policy — except in cases where trade-ins are involved, and then flexible pricing abounds. A one-price policy builds customer confidence in a seller, whether at the manufacturing, wholesaling, or retailing level. Weak bargainers need not feel that they are at a competitive disadvantage.

When a flexible pricing policy is followed, often the price is set as a result of buyer-seller bargaining.[7] In automobile retailing — with or without a trade-in — price negotiating (bargaining) is quite common, even though window-sticker prices may suggest a one-price policy. Variable pricing may be used to meet a competitor's price. Airlines have used an aggressive flexible-price strategy to enter new markets and to increase their market share on existing routes. Their new business comes from two sources — passengers now flying on other airlines and passengers who would not fly at higher prices. In the second group, especially, the demand for air travel is highly elastic. The trick is to keep the market segment of price-sensitive passengers separate from the business-traveller segment, whose demand is inelastic. Airlines keep these segments apart by placing restrictions on the lower-priced tickets — requiring advance purchases, over-the-weekend stays in destination cities, etc.

Even in automobile retailing, where flexible pricing has been the norm, the one-price strategy is gaining favour. In launching the Saturn model, General Motors stressed a one-price policy so as to minimize haggling over prices between the consumer and the dealer's sales person. The number of dealers that have curtailed bargaining over price is growing, but it is still only a small fraction of all dealerships and is concentrated mainly in the Toronto and Montreal markets. The majority of dealers doing so report improved sales. However, most of the dealers using a one-price strategy still bargain on trade-ins.[8]

A **single-price strategy** is an extreme variation of the one-price strategy. Not only are all customers charged the same price, but all items sold by the firm carry a single price! The origins of this approach may be traced to budget motels of 30 years ago. For instance, Motel 6 in the United States (where they "leave the light on" for you) originally priced all rooms at $6 a night for single occupancy.

Now single-price stores are a rapidly growing, but still very small, segment of retailing.[9] Retailers offer frugal shoppers a variety of merchandise ranging from grocery items to cosmetics at a price of $1. Others appeal to customers with assorted clothing at a single price. These stores typically purchase close-out and discontinued products as well as production overruns from a variety of sources at a small fraction of their original costs. Some analysts question whether single-price stores can be successful not just during a recession but during prosperous times as well.

## Price Lining

**Price lining** involves selecting a limited number of prices at which a business will sell related products. It is used extensively by retailers of apparel. The Athletic Store, for instance, sells several styles of shoes at $39.88 a pair, another group at $59.95, and a third assortment at $79.99.

For the consumer, the main benefit of price lining is that it simplifies buying decisions. For the retailer, price lining helps in planning purchases. The buyer for The Athletic Store can go to market looking for shoes that can be retailed at one of its three prices.

Rising costs can put a real squeeze on price lines. That's because a company hesitates to change its price line every time its costs go up. But if costs rise and prices are not increased accordingly, profit margins shrink and the retailer may be forced to seek products with lower costs.

## Odd Pricing

Earlier, we briefly discussed pricing strategies that might be called *psychological* pricing: pricing above competitive levels, raising an unsuitably low price to increase sales, and

**Recently, there's been a resurgence of single-price stores.**

price lining. All these strategies are intended to convey desirable images about products. Odd pricing, another psychological strategy, is commonly used in retailing. **Odd pricing** sets prices at uneven (or odd) amounts, such as 49 cents or $19.95, rather than at even amounts. Autos are priced at $13,995 rather than $14,000, and houses sell for $119,500 instead of $120,000. Odd pricing is often avoided in prestige stores or on higher-priced items. Expensive men's suits, for example, are priced at $750, not $749.95.

The rationale for odd pricing is that it suggests lower prices and, as a result, yields greater sales than even pricing. According to this reasoning, a price of 98 cents will bring in greater revenue than a $1 price for the same product. Recent research indicates that odd pricing can be an effective strategy for a firm that emphasizes low prices.[10]

## MARKETING AT WORK

### FILE 14-2 UNIT PRICING FOR CUSTOMER SATISFACTION

It's generally agreed that consumers have certain rights, including the right to be informed. Recognizing these rights — and desiring to fully satisfy their customers and create store loyalty — numerous supermarket chains have adopted unit pricing. In **unit pricing**, for each separate product and package size, there is a shelf label that states (1) the price of the package and (2) this price expressed in dollars and cents per 100 grams or millilitres.

Unit pricing really is a business response to consumer complaints about the proliferation of package sizes. Numerous package sizes made it virtually impossible to compare prices of similar products. For example, is a can labelled 10 oz liq/284 mL for $1.29 a better deal than two 1-pound, 1-ounce liq/482 mL cans for $2.89?

Studies covering the early years of unit pricing showed that customers ignored unit-pricing data. More recent studies indicate that an increasing number of consumers are aware of and use unit-pricing information. However, urban residents (more likely to include lower-income consumers) still use this information much less than suburban residents (typically higher-income consumers).

How about you? Do you use unit pricing when shopping in supermarkets?

Source: David A. Aaker and Gary T. Ford, "Unit Pricing Ten Years Later: A Replication," *Journal of Marketing*, Winter 1983, pp. 118-122.

## RESALE PRICE MAINTENANCE

Some manufacturers want control over the prices at which retailers resell the manufacturers' products. This is most often done in Canada by following a policy of providing manufacturers' suggested list prices, where the price is just a guide for retailers. It is a list price on which discounts may be computed. For others, the suggested price is "informally" enforced. Normally enforcement of a suggested price, termed resale price maintenance, has been illegal in Canada since 1951. In this country, attempts on the part of the manufacturers to control or to influence upward the prices at which their products are sold by retailers have been considered akin to price fixing.

Section 38 of the Competition Act prohibits a manufacturer or supplier from requiring or inducing a retailer to sell a product at a particular price or not below a particular price. On occasion, a supplier may attempt to control retail prices through the use of a "suggested retail price." Under section 38, the use of "suggested retail prices" is permitted *only* if the supplier makes it clear to the retailer that the product *may* be sold at a price below the suggested price and that the retailer will not in any way be discriminated against if the product is sold at a lower price. Also, where a manufacturer advertises a product, and in the advertisement mentions a certain price, the manufacturer must make it clear in the advertisement that the product may be sold at a lower price.

Prior to 1975 it was legal in Canada for a manufacturer to refuse to supply a product to a retailer if that retailer was selling that product as a loss leader or was using the product in "bait advertising" to attract people to his or her store. The 1975 amendments to the Combines Investigation Act eliminated this provision, and it is now illegal for a manufacturer to refuse to supply a product to a retailer because of the pricing policies of the retailer. In other words, a retailer is free to sell a product at whatever price he or she deems appropriate, and the manufacturer of that product is not permitted to exert any pressure on the retailer to sell at a particular price.

## LEADER PRICING AND UNFAIR-PRACTICES ACTS

Many firms, primarily retailers, temporarily cut prices on a few items to attract customers. This price and promotional strategy is called **leader pricing** and the items whose prices may be reduced below the retailer's cost are called **loss leaders**. These leader items should be well-known heavily advertised articles that are purchased frequently. The idea is that customers will come to the store to buy the advertised leader items and then stay to buy other regularly priced merchandise. The net result, the firm hopes, will be increased total sales volume and net profit.

Three provinces, British Columbia, Alberta, and Manitoba, have had legislation dealing with loss leader selling. The approach has been to prohibit a reseller from selling an item below invoice cost, including freight, plus a stated markup, which is usually 5 percent at retail.

The general intent of these laws is commendable. They eliminate much of the predatory type of price-cutting; however, they permit firms to use loss leaders as a price and promotional strategy. That is, a retailer can offer an article below full cost but still sell above cost plus 5 percent markup. Under such acts, low-cost, efficient businesses are not penalized, nor are high-cost operators protected. Differentials in retailers' purchase prices can be reflected in their selling prices, and savings resulting from the absence of services can be passed on to the customers.

On the other hand, the laws have some glaring weaknesses. In the first place, the provinces do not establish provisions or agencies for enforcement. It is the responsibility and burden of the injured party to seek satisfaction from the offender in a civil suit. Another limitation is that it is difficult or even impossible to determine the cost of doing business for each individual product. The third weakness is that the laws seem to disregard the fundamental idea that the purpose of a business is to make a profit on the total operation, and not necessarily on each sale of each product.

## PRICE VERSUS NONPRICE COMPETITION

In developing a marketing program, management has to decide whether to compete primarily on the basis of price or the nonprice elements of the marketing mix. This choice obviously affects other parts of the firm's marketing program.

### Price Competition

A firm engages in **price competition** by regularly offering products priced as low as possible and accompanied by a minimum of services. Discount houses and off-price retailers compete in this way. A firm can also use price to compete by (1) changing its prices and (2) reacting to price changes made by a competitor.

## MARKETING AT WORK

### FILE 14-3 AN INTERNATIONAL PERSPECTIVE ON PRICE SETTING

Price setting becomes more complex when the firm's goods and services are aimed at foreign markets. To prevent a migraine — actually, to achieve profits — what factors does a firm need to consider in setting base prices and then developing various pricing strategies for its products in foreign markets? Let's take a look at three factors that are more or less distinctive to pricing in international settings:

- **Fluctuating exchange rates.** Different currencies around the world exchange at various rates. Exchange rates fluctuate daily. The strength of a nation's currency affects foreign demand for products from that country. In the first half of the 1980s, the value of the U.S. dollar rose sharply, which meant that foreign currencies were worth less in relation to the dollar. As a result, because the Canadian dollar tends to fluctuate with the American dollar on foreign-currency markets, Canadian-made products were more costly in most foreign markets, which would have hurt exports by Canadian companies. Since then, the value of the dollar has declined, which is good for exporting (but bad in other economic matters). Fluctuating exchange rates require marketers to monitor their prices in foreign markets and, in turn, to adjust them frequently.
- **Price controls.** Following severe inflation or a change in the ruling government, price controls are sometimes instituted in a country. That happened recently in Brazil, Argentina, and Mexico. Price controls either freeze prices at existing levels or place ceilings on prices that can be charged for products such as essentials. How does a Canadian firm deal with price controls in a foreign market? One possibility is to anticipate them (by detecting severe inflation, for example) and adjust prices upward prior to when controls are expected. Another approach is to introduce a modified product that is not covered by the price controls.
- **Antidumping laws.** Increasingly common, such laws are intended to prevent foreign companies from pricing their products so low as to harm domestic producers of similar products. For example, country A's antidumping law would stipulate that a firm from country B cannot set the price of its product sold in country A below either the presumed cost to produce it or its price in country B. Although they are the subject of sharp debate as part of the General Agreement on Tariffs and Trade (GATT) negotiations, antidumping laws appear to be spreading around the globe. Frankly, there's not much a Canadian firm can do when it encounters antidumping laws except abide by them.

Other factors, such as costs and competitors' present and potential prices, must be taken into account when a firm sets prices for foreign markets. Moreover, as discussed in Chapter 13, a firm should consider its pricing objectives prior to establishing prices for products sold in different markets around the world. Low prices may be used to establish a foothold in a country a company believes has long-term potential. In contrast, relatively high prices may be appropriate in a country perceived only as a short-term opportunity.

Whether the market is Argentina, Zambia, or the U.S., some fundamentals of pricing (such as considering objectives and competition) always apply. However, pricing for foreign markets presents challenges *and opportunities*, due to such factors as fluctuating exchange rates, price controls, and antidumping laws.

Source: James K. Weekly, "Pricing in Foreign Markets: Pitfalls and Opportunities," *Industrial Marketing Management*, May 1992, pp. 173-179.

As you will see in this section, there is tremendous price competition in our economy today. This form of competition is spreading to other parts of the world as well. For example, price reductions became commonplace throughout Europe in the early 1990s. This switch in competitive strategy was due to the elimination of various trade barriers and also to the continent's continuing economic woes. All kinds of products — consumer electronics, computers, air travel, and autos — were available at discounted prices. One economist explained the situation as follows: "What you're now seeing is a scramble for limited volume through price competition."[11]

**Value Pricing** In Chapter 13 we discussed how more and more consumers are seeking better value in their purchases. In response, many companies in diverse industries are using what's called **value pricing**. This form of price competition aims to improve a product's value — that is, the ratio of its benefits to its price and related costs. Using value pricing, a firm: (1) offers products with lower prices but the same, or perhaps added, benefits; and (2) at the same time seeks ways to slash expenses so that profits do not suffer.

During the 1990s, value pricing has become a pivotal marketing trend in fields as diverse as air travel, groceries, personal computers, and fast food. Consider two examples:

- In 1990, Taco Bell trimmed prices on some of its mainstays such as tacos and burritos and introduced some cheaper snack-size items (since dropped). Equally important, the fast-food chain attacked its cost structure, particularly labour costs. Its employees now "assemble" tacos and other items from meats and vegetables cooked, sliced, and otherwise prepared by outside suppliers and delivered to the outlets.[12]
- In mid-1992, Compaq Computer Corp. introduced about two dozen new desktop and laptop personal computers (PCs). Compared to their predecessors, these PCs not only were priced about 50 percent less but also had enhanced capabilities. To achieve a profit on the new PCs, Compaq pruned its manufacturing costs and business expenses by, among other things, changing suppliers for many components and assembling the products in Singapore.[13]

Value pricing certainly emphasizes the price element of the marketing mix. But that's not enough. The chairman of Compaq, the computer maker, stated it in this way: "If all you have to offer is price, I don't think it's a successful long-term strategy in the value decade."[14] Consequently, value pricing depends on creatively combining all elements of the marketing mix in order to maximize benefits in relation to price and other costs. With a value-pricing strategy, products often have to be redesigned to expand benefits and/or shave costs. Relationships among channel members and customers have to be strengthened to generate repeat sales. Steps towards this end include frequent-buyer programs, toll-free customer-service lines, and hassle-free warranties. And advertising has to be revamped to provide more facts and fewer emotional appeals.

**Proactive and Reactive Changes** After an initial price is set, a number of situations may prompt a firm to change its price. As costs increase, for instance, management may decide to raise its price rather than to maintain price and either cut quality or promote the product aggressively. Temporary price cuts may be used to sell excess inventory or to introduce a new product.

Also, if a company's market share is declining because of strong competition, its executives may react initially by reducing price. Monsanto Co. did this with its weedkiller.[15] Faced with not only a drought but also new competitors, the price was cut to attract more customers. Monsanto hoped a lower price would prompt more farmers to use chemicals, rather than tilling, to kill weeds. For many products, however, a better long-term alternative to a price reduction is improving the overall marketing program.

Any firm can safely assume that its competitors will change their prices — sooner or later. Consequently, every firm should have guidelines on how it will react. If a competitor *boosts* price, a short delay in reacting probably will not be perilous. However, if a competing firm *reduces* price, a prompt response normally is required to avoid losing customers.

Occasional price reductions occur even in an oligopoly, because all sellers of the product cannot be controlled. In the absence of collusion, every so often some firm will cut its price. Then all others usually follow to maintain their respective market shares. For instance, in the field of long-distance telephone services, it has been suggested that the

**Air Canada appeals to an international business market with price cuts.**

prices of the leading firms would be coming closer together.[16] However, vigorous short-term discount plans indicate that the major competitors are engaging in vigorous price competition at the initial stage of market and brand development.

Price Wars From a seller's standpoint, the big disadvantage in price cutting is that competitors will retaliate — and not let up. A **price war** may begin when one firm decreases its price in an effort to increase its sales volume and/or market share. The battle is on if other firms retaliate, reducing price on their competing products. Additional price decreases by the original price cutter and/or its competitors are likely to follow until one of the firms decides it can endure no further damage to its profits. Most businesses would like to avoid price wars.

Always part of business, price wars seem to be epidemic in the 1990s, breaking out in numerous fields ranging from groceries to computer software. In 1991 computer makers began to cut their prices more rapidly than their costs declined from technological gains. The price war continued into 1993, with Apple and Dell dropping their prices by more than 35 percent. As a result of the ongoing price war, there are now two tiers in the personal computer field: technological innovations carrying high prices and fairly standard "commodities" with low, and declining, prices.[17]

In the short term, consumers benefit from price wars through sharply lower prices. But over the longer term, the net effects on consumers are not clear-cut. What is evident is that price wars can be harmful to many firms, especially the weaker ones, in an industry. As one consultant advised retailers, "Long-term price competition can take a devastating toll on profits."[18] Lower profits typically decrease the number of competitors and, over a longer period, possibly the vigour of competition. After extended price wars, some companies in industries as different as groceries and personal computers have gone out of business. Ultimately, a smaller number of competing firms might translate to fewer product choices and/or higher prices for consumers.[19]

**FIGURE 14-3**
**Shift in demand curve for skis.**

**Nonprice competition can shift the demand curve for a product. A company selling skis in the European market used a promotional program to sell more skis at the same price, thereby shifting DD to D′D′. Volume increased from 35,000 to 55,000 units at $250 (point X to point Y). Besides advertising, what other devices might this firm use to shift its demand curve?**

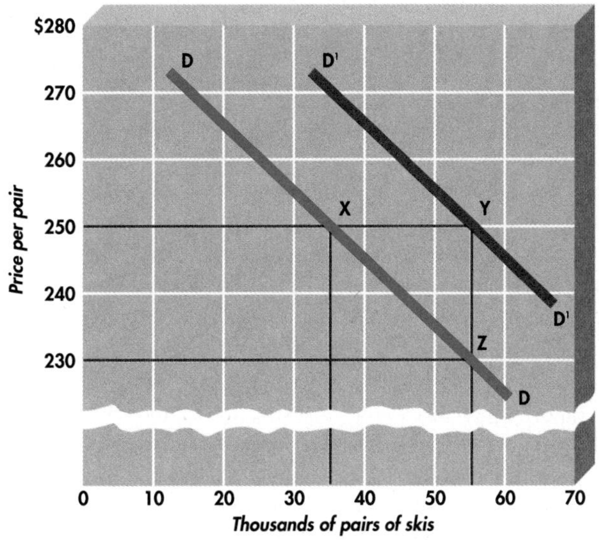


## Nonprice Competition

In **nonprice competition**, sellers maintain stable prices and attempt to improve their market positions by emphasizing other aspects of their marketing programs. Of course, competitors' prices still must be taken into consideration, and price changes will occur over time. Nevertheless, in nonprice competition, the emphasis is on something other than price.

Using terms familiar in economic theory, we can differentiate price and nonprice competition. In *price* competition, sellers attempt to move up or down their individual demand curves by changing prices. In *nonprice* competition, sellers attempt to shift their demand curves to the right by means of product differentiation, promotional activities, or some other technique. In Figure 14-3, the demand curve faced by the producer of a given model of skis is DD. At a price of $250, the producer can sell 35,000 pairs a year in the European market. On the basis of price competition alone, sales can be increased to 55,000 if the producer is willing to reduce the price to $230. The demand curve is still DD.

However, the producer is interested in boosting sales without any decrease in selling price. Consequently, the firm embarks on a fresh promotional program — a form of nonprice competition. Suppose that enough new customers are persuaded to buy at the original $250 price that unit sales increase to 55,000 pairs a year. In effect, the firm's entire demand curve has been shifted to position D′D′.

Many firms stress nonprice competition — and others would like to rely on it rather than price competition. Wanting to be masters of their own destinies, companies believe they have more control in nonprice competition. With price competition, many consumers will buy a brand only as long as it has the lowest price. There is little customer loyalty when price is the only feature differentiating products from each other.

With nonprice competition, however, a seller keeps some advantage when a competitor decides to undersell. The best approach in nonprice competition is to build strong — if possible, unassailable — brand equity for the firm's products. Two methods of accomplishing this are to develop distinctive, hopefully unique, products and to create a novel, appealing promotional program. In addition, some firms emphasize the variety and quality of the supplementary services they offer to customers.[20]

## SUMMARY

After deciding on pricing goals and setting the base (or list) price, marketers must establish pricing strategies that are compatible with the rest of the marketing mix. When a firm is launching a new product, it must choose a market-skimming or a market-penetration pricing strategy. Market skimming uses a relatively high initial price, market penetration a low one.

Strategies also must be devised for discounts and allowances — deductions from the list price. Management has the option of offering quantity discounts, trade discounts, cash discounts, and/or other types of deductions.

Freight costs must be considered in pricing. A producer can require the buyer to pay all freight costs (FOB factory pricing), or a producer can absorb all freight costs (uniform delivered pricing). Or the two parties can share the freight costs (freight absorption). Decisions on discounts and allowances must conform to the Competition Act, a federal law regulating price discrimination.

Management also should decide whether to charge the same price to all similar buyers of identical quantities of a product (a one-price strategy) or to set different prices (a flexible-price strategy). Many organizations, especially retailers, use at least some of the following special strategies: Unit pricing — providing not only the total price but also the price per some standard measure; price lining — selecting a limited number of prices at which to sell related products; odd pricing — setting prices at uneven (or odd) amounts; and leader pricing — temporarily cutting prices on a few items to attract customers.

Many manufacturers are concerned about resale price maintenance, which means controlling the prices at which intermediaries resell products. Some approaches to resale price maintenance are stronger than others; moreover, some methods may be illegal.

Another basic decision facing management is whether to engage primarily in price or nonprice competition. Although price competition is widespread in the 1990s, most firms prefer nonprice competition. Price competition establishes price as the primary, perhaps the sole, basis for attracting and retaining customers. A growing number of businesses are adopting value pricing to improve the ratio of benefits to price and, in turn, win customers from competitors. Market opportunities and/or competitive forces may motivate companies to initiate price changes or, in other situations, to react to other firms' price changes. A series of successive price cuts by competing firms creates a price war, which can harm the profits of all participating companies.

In nonprice competition, sellers maintain stable prices and seek a differential advantage through other aspects of their marketing mixes. Common methods of nonprice competition include offering distinctive and appealing products, promotion, and/or customer services.

## KEY TERMS AND CONCEPTS

**Strategy (412)**
**Market-skimming pricing (412)**
**Market-penetration pricing (413)**
**Quantity discount (414)**
**Noncumulative discount (414)**
**Cumulative discount (414)**
**Trade (functional) discount (414)**
**Cash discount (415)**
**Seasonal discount (416)**
**Forward dating (416)**
**Promotional allowance (416)**
**Price discrimination (416)**
**Competition Act (416)**
**F.O.B. factory (mill) pricing (418)**
**Uniform delivered pricing (419)**
**Zone-delivered pricing (419)**
**Freight-absorption pricing (419)**
**One-price strategy (420)**
**Flexible-price (variable-price) strategy (420)**
**Single-price strategy (421)**
**Price lining (421)**
**Unit pricing (422)**
**Odd pricing (422)**
**Leader pricing (424)**
**Loss leaders (424)**
**Price competition (424)**
**Value pricing (426)**
**Price war (427)**
**Nonprice competition (427)**

## QUESTIONS AND PROBLEMS

1. For each of the following products, should the seller adopt a market-skimming or a market-penetration pricing strategy? Support your decision in each instance.
   a. High-fashion dresses styled and manufactured by Yves St. Laurent.
   b. An exterior housepaint that wears twice as long as any competitive brand.
   c. A cigarette that is *totally* free of tar and nicotine.
   d. A tablet that converts a litre of water into a litre of automotive fuel.
2. As economic unification is attained and trade barriers are being removed throughout the European Union (EU), numerous companies are deliberating how best to achieve sales and profits in all or part of this huge market. Name two non-European brands that well might adopt a market-skimming pricing strategy in the EU, and another two that should use a market-penetration strategy.
3. Carefully distinguish between cumulative and noncumulative quantity discounts. Which type of quantity discount has the greater economic and social justification? Why?
4. A manufacturer of appliances quotes a list price of $800 per unit for a certain model of refrigerator and grants trade discounts of 35, 20, and 5 percent. What is the manufacturer's selling price? Who might get these various discounts?
5. The Craig Charles Company (CCC) sells to all its customers at the same published price. One of its sales managers discerns that Jamaican Enterprises is offering to sell to one of CCC's customers, Mountain Sports, at a lower price. CCC then cuts its price to Mountain Sports but maintains the original price for all other customers. Is CCC's price cut a violation of the Competition Act?
6. "An FOB point-of-production price system is the only geographic price system that is fair to buyers." Discuss.
7. An Eastern firm wants to compete in Western markets, where it is at a significant disadvantage with respect to freight costs. What pricing alternatives can it adopt to overcome the freight differential?
8. Under what conditions is a company likely to use a variable-price strategy? Can you name firms that employ this strategy other than when a trade-in is involved?
9. On the basis of the topics covered in this chapter, establish a set of price strategies for the manufacturer of a new glass cleaner that is sold through an intermediary to supermarkets. The manufacturer sells the cleaner at $15 for a case of a dozen 482 mL bottles.

## HANDS-ON MARKETING

1. Talk to the owner or a top executive of a firm in your community regarding whether this company emphasizes price or nonprice competition and the reasons for following this course. Also ask whether its approach is similar to or dissimilar from the normal approach used by competitors to market the primary product sold by this firm.

## NOTES AND REFERENCES


1. Adapted in part from *The National Ballet of Canada Souvenir Magazine, 1993-94*. Published by Canadian Controlled Media Communications.
2. Stephanie A. Forest, "Compaq Declares War on the Clones," *Business Week*, June 15, 1992, p. 43; Kate Bertrand, "Apple Bites Back," *Business Marketing*, August 1991, pp. 12, 14, 16, 17.
3. George S. Day and Adrian B. Ryans, "Using Price Discounts for a Competitive Advantage," *Industrial Marketing Management*, February 1988, pp. 1-14.
4. Economic Council of Canada, *Interim Report on Competition Policy*, Queen's Printer, Ottawa, July 1969.
5. The materials presented in this section are based on *Competition Law Amendments*, Ministry of Supply and Services 1986; and *A Guide to Competition Law Amendments*, Ministry of Supply and Services 1985. Both are sponsored by Industry Canada.
6. For a report on the managerial, legal, and ethical aspects of flexible pricing in business markets, see Michael H. Morris, "Separate Prices as a Marketing Tool," *Industrial Marketing Management*, May 1987, pp. 79-86.
7. For an in-depth discussion of flexible pricing including a theoretical model and managerial implications, see Kenneth R. Evans and Richard F. Beltramini, "A Theoretical Model of Consumer Negotiated Pricing: An Orientation Perspective," *Journal of Marketing*, April 1987, pp. 58-73.
8. "Car Buyers Like Single Price," *St. Louis Post-Dispatch*. September 1, 1992, p. 6B.
9. Christina Duff, "Single-Price Stores' Formula for Success: Cheap Merchandise and a Lot of Clutter," *The Wall Street Journal*, June 30, 1992, p. B1; Kate Fitzgerald, "$1 Store Fills the Bill," *Advertising Age*, December 16, 1991, p. 26.
10. Robert M. Schindler and Lori S. Warren, "Effects of Odd Pricing on Price Recall," *Journal of Business*, June 1989, pp. 165-177; Robert Blattberg and Kenneth Wisniewski, "How Retail Price Promotions Work: Empirical Results," Marketing Working Paper No. 42, University of Chicago, 1987.
11. Bill Javetski, "Price War I Is Raging in Europe," *Business Week*, July 6, 1992, pp. 44-45.
12. Bill Saporito, "Why the Price Wars Never End," *Fortune*, March 23, 1992, pp. 68-71.
13. Forest, loc. cit.; Michael Allen, "Developing New Line of Low-Priced PCs Shakes Up Compaq," *The Wall Street Journal*, June 15, 1992, pp. A1, A4.
14. Stratford Sherman, "How to Prosper in the Value Decade," *Fortune*, November 30, 1992, p. 98. For more on this topic, see Christopher Power, "Value Marketing," *Business Week*, November 11, 1991, pp. 132-135.
15. Robert Steyer, "Weedkiller's Price Cut to Fight Drought, Competition," *St. Louis Post-Dispatch*, March 18, 1991, p. 7BP.
16. Peter Coy, "Sounding More and More Like a Three-Man Band," *Business Week*, April 23, 1990, p. 30.
17. Andrew Kupfer, "Who's Winning the PC Price Wars," *Fortune*, September 21, 1992, pp. 80-82; Kathy Rebello, "They're Slashing as Fast as They Can," *Business Week*, February 7, 1992, p. 40; Bertrand, loc. cit.
18. Albert D. Bates, "Pricing for Profit," *Retailing Issues Newsletter*, September 1990, p. 1.
19. John R. Wilke, "PC Giants' Price War Hurts Tiny Makers," *The Wall Street Journal*, November 2, 1992, p. B1; Katia Hetter, "Grocery Rivals Plunge Houston into a Price War," *The Wall Street Journal*, August 20, 1992, p. B1.
20. For three recommended forms of nonprice competition for retailers, see Bates, op. cit., p. 4.

## CASES FOR PART 4

# CASE 4-1

# EJE TRANS-LITE INC.

In early 1994, Paul Edison, marketing director of EJE Trans-Lite Inc., was trying to decide what to do concerning the price of the Digi-Lite, the company's principal product. Paul had helped design the original Digi-Lite soon after he joined EJE in 1989. His technical background was in radio operations and electronic communications. He had completed a course in this at Red River College in Winnipeg before spending eight years in the offshore oil industry immediately prior to joining EJE.

When the Digi-Lite was introduced in 1990, it was the world's smallest rescue light; it measured 4.2 x 5.0 cm and weighed only 33 g. It could be tied to or sewn on any survival system (life jacket, survival suit, or life raft) by means of a plastic tie or specially designed patch. The light was visible for 1.2 nautical miles, and the lithium battery, when activated, would last 12 hours, 50 percent longer than competitive products. The Digi-Lite was the only product that operated automatically when in contact with water, a great advantage in marine applications where the user could be unconscious or seriously injured.

Sales growth was rapid, and by 1993, it was sold through approximately 45 independent distributors in 40 countries. EJE had a sales agent in the United States who sold to the distributors there. Ninety-seven percent of sales were outside Canada, with 60 percent going to the United States. Two of the largest distributors that EJE had were Unitor and Jotron, both Scandinavian-based companies that sold a broad range of products to the marine industry. Unitor advertised daily delivery to 837 ports throughout the world, and it had offices and warehouses in many of these ports. Jotron sold mainly to independent distributors throughout the world; EJE manufactured Digi-Lites for them with the Jotron brand name.

Besides using distributors, EJE sold direct to cruise lines and manufacturers of water survival clothing. Both were considered original equipment manufacturers (OEM) accounts, and the volume justified lower pricing. In fact, price was the major purchasing decision criterion among OEM accounts, followed by availability of inventory. For distributors, the decision criteria varied depending on the size of the distributor. The larger distributors placed more emphasis on price as they often sold to smaller distributors and sometimes to large user accounts. Smaller distributors generally sold in small quantities to final customers such as fishermen or recreational users, and price was less important as the final customer was not so price-sensitive. Availability was often the most important purchase criterion, along with the convenience of being able to purchase many items from a single source of supply. In some instances, for example, EJE and Jotron sold to the same distributors. EJE had the price advantage when large orders were involved, but Jotron had the advantage when smaller quantities were involved as it could offer the convenience of a broad range of items that could be bought at one time.

Paul estimated that his 1993 North American market share was 35 percent and market share in the rest of the world was 46 percent. There were two main competitors, ACR Electronics in the United States and McMurdo in the United Kingdom. Both had larger units that required manual operation and were slightly higher priced. ACR Electronics sold about the same number of units as EJE in North America, but its total annual sales were at least 10 times greater due to an expanded product line. It also sold strobe lights, buoy lights, search and rescue transponders, electronic positioning devices, and other electronic equipment.

The original unit, model A-12M, was for marine applications. In 1993, Paul introduced model A-12A, a similar model for aviation applications, and had sold one trial order of 500 units. Government approval for general sale was expected at any time, and Paul expected to sell 6,000 units in 1994. A final model was the A-12EWS, identical to model A-12M, but with a copper wire attached to it to ensure contact with the water in the event it was on an inflatable life jacket and was too high above the water to be activated automatically. The Canadian Coast Guard purchased 3,600 units in 1993 and was expected to buy another 4,800 in 1994. Paul also expected to sell 7,200 units of model A-12EWS to the United Kingdom in 1994. Paul estimated the world market would grow by 20.4 percent in 1994, but his own sales should increase by 23 percent because of expected increases in sales of models A-12A and A-12EWS.

All Digi-Lites, while designed by EJE, were assembled by another firm in St. John's, Newfoundland, and were sold to EJE in lots of 10,000 units. Exhibit 1 shows the sales and profit data for 1993.

In January 1994, Paul was contacted by one of his major distributors and informed that unless he dropped his price by 12½ percent, the distributor would have to buy elsewhere. Both competitors had dropped their prices, and although the distributor preferred to buy EJE Digi-Lites, the price differential was too great.

After a careful assessment, Paul determined that he stood to lose 27 percent of his 1994 projected sales. He thought that he would maintain proposed sales of model A-12A as these would be domestic sales, and there was no competitive product. He also thought he would maintain proposed sales of model A-12EWS in Canada, but would probably lose the U.K. order. Model A-12M would account for the balance of lost sales.

Paul was trying to decide what to do. This was the first major pricing decision he had to make. He really didn't want to lower his price as he worked on a 70 percent markup over cost and had used this markup for every product and every customer since the company started in business. EJE had just designed a unit with a slightly smaller, lighter lens that would be cheaper to produce, but, unfortunately, approval to design changes would take about a year, and production would delay introduction another six months.

Another alternative Paul had was to introduce units identical in size and appearance to the present units, only with flashing bulbs. These could be available in one month, would extend battery life to 40 hours, and would be the only flashing units on the market. It would cost about $15,000 for engineering and production set-up; otherwise, the additional cost per unit would be $0.60 to EJE. If they were introduced in 1994, and Paul kept his full markup on all models, he expected that his sales would still be 22 percent below his 1994 projections. He also anticipated sales for model A-12A would change totally to flashing units due to the extended battery life; sales of model A-12EWS would remain totally with regular bulbs as many users were uncomfortable with flashing bulbs because they believed they might be less visible due to wave action that could hide them at times. For model A-12M, Paul thought that 30 percent of his sales would be for flashing units.

**EXHIBIT 2**

DIGI-LITE
PERSONAL
RESCUE
LIGHT
DIGI-LITE
Aviation A-12A
Marine A-12M
This product is the world's smallest personal rescue light for marine/aviation use. It activates upon contact in water and will last in excess of 12 hours. No exterior wires to tangle and no plugs to pull. This light is cost effective and built with safety in mind. Its bright light is powered by a lithium cell and can be easily tested. Digi-Lite is available in a marine and aviation model, with minor differences to the power supply and lamp. The complete unit measures 4.2 x 5cm and weighs 33g. For the Aviation version ask for Digi-Lite model A-12A. For the Marine version ask for Digi-Lite model A-12M.
EJE
TRANS-LITE INC.
HEAD OFFICE
P.O. Box 427
70 Brookfield Road
St. John's, Newfoundland
Canada, A1C 5K4
Telephone: (709) 747-3772
Fax: (709) 368-1337
DIGI-LITE A-12M (above) and A-12A powered by Duracell Lithium XL # DL123A
DURACELL LITHIUM XL

## QUESTIONS

1. What impact will the competitor's price reduction have on EJE?
2. What would be the financial impact on EJE if Paul decided to introduce the new models with flashing bulbs?
3. What should Paul Edison do?

**EXHIBIT 1 EJE sales and profit data, 1993**

| Model | Units Sold | Cost | Selling Price | Contribution/Unit | Contribution/Total |
|---|---|---|---|---|---|
| A-12M | 90,871 | 7.74 | 13.16 | 5.42 | 492,520.82 |
| A-12A | 500 | 7.74 | 13.16 | 5.42 | 2,710.00 |
| A-12EWS | 3,600 | 8.94 | 15.20 | 6.26 | 22,536.00 |

# CASE 4-2

# HORIZON VIDEO COMPANY: PRICING A RENTAL SERVICE

Henry and Frances Seybold were discussing how they might increase the weekday customer traffic in their store — Horizon Video Company. They had done a limited amount of advertising during the past year and concluded that the slight improvement in store traffic did not justify the advertising costs. Now they were devoting their attention to the current pricing schedule for their products.

Horizon Video was a retail store that rented movies and videocassette recorders (VCRs). The store also sold a line of VCR-related products. It was located in a small shopping centre in a Western college town with a population of about 80,000. Henry and Frances Seybold had purchased the store from its original owners a little over a year ago.

Horizon carried a rental stock of 1,350 movies and 10 VCRs. Products for sale included used movies, blank videocassette tapes, videocassette holders, VCR connectors, and VCR head cleaners. The inventory of rental films included various categories, such as romance, horror, science fiction, war, comedy, classics, and even some "adult" movies. Horizon purchased two to six new films each month, some in multiple copies, depending on what was available and the store's financial condition. The cost of a new film ranged from $50 to $70.

Horizon's owners identified their market broadly as any person or family who owned a TV set. One segment of this market included people who owned a VCR and rented movies; another segment rented both the VCR and the movies. Henry noted that over half of Horizon's customers were between the ages of 23 and 50, about equally divided between men and women. The majority seemed to be middle-income adults or lower-income college students. The students were more price-conscious and less store-loyal than the older customers.

Frances said that Horizon faced considerable competition in the city. The Yellow Pages telephone directory listed 21 retail stores under the heading of "videotapes and discs — renting and leasing." Frances also noted that their main competition came from four nearby stores, including a supermarket in the same shopping centre as Horizon. Each of the three video-store competitors had about two and a half times as much store space as Horizon and all were more attractively furnished. However, Frances felt that their store was "a nice clean place with a pleasant, friendly atmosphere." Two of the four competitors offered an annual membership deal that included lower rental charges to members. The pricing schedule in the four competing stores is shown in Exhibit 1.

**EXHIBIT 1 Pricing schedules of Horizon's main competitors**

| Store | Annual membership charge | Movie rental per day, any day | | | VCR rental per day | |
|---|---|---|---|---|---|---|
| | | | Member | Nonmember | Member | Nonmember |
| Sunset Video | $10 | One movie<br>Additional movies | $3<br>$2 | $5<br>$4 | $6.95 (Mon.-Fri.)<br>$9.95 (Sat.-Sun.) | Same |
| Laser Sound Video | $40 | One movie<br>Additional movies | $3<br>$2 | $5<br>$4 | $7.98 (Mon.-Fri.)<br>$9.98 (Sat.-Sun.) | $9.98 per day |
| Hollywood-at-Home | None | One movie<br>Additional movies | $2.99<br>$1.99 | —<br>— | $9.95 (Sun.-Thurs.)<br>$12.95 (Fri.-Sat.) | —<br>— |
| Supermarket | None | One movie<br>Additional movies | $2.99<br>$ .99 | —<br>— | $9.95 (Sun.-Thurs.) | — |

Adapted from a case prepared by Scott Hansen, under supervision of Professor William J. Stanton.

In Henry's opinion, the most serious difficulty facing Horizon was the lack of store traffic during the week. Many days were extremely slow, and the problem seemed to be getting worse. Weekends, especially Friday nights, were better, but still not what they had hoped for.

The Seybolds had done a limited amount of advertising in the classified section of student newspapers on the college campus in the city. However, the slight improvement in customer traffic was not enough to justify the advertising costs.

As Henry and Frances continued the discussion of the customer-traffic situation, their attention shifted to their pricing structure for rental video movies and VCRs. At the time, their rental schedule was as follows:

**For movies:**

Monday, Tuesday, Thursday: 2 for $5 or $3 each.
Wednesday: 2 for $3; additional movies $3 each.
Friday, Saturday, Sunday: $3 each with no quantity discount.

**For VCRs:**

$10.95 per day, any day, including 2 "free" movies.

Horizon did not charge a membership fee, but did use a "punch-card" system. By purchasing a punch card, a customer, in effect, paid for movie rentals in advance and in so doing, received a substantial discount. Punch-card prices were as follows:

7-movie punch card: $15.
12-movie punch card: $25.
17-movie punch card: $30.

The cards had no expiration date and could be used by anyone whose name was listed on the back of the card. The Seybolds believed that the punch cards had helped to increase store loyalty and repeat business. About 150 punch cards had been sold.

The Seybolds also distributed "2 for 1" cards to local appliance stores that sold VCRs. These cards were given to customers who bought a new VCR and entitled them to 20 "2 for 1" movie rentals. With a "2 for 1" card, the rental price was $3 for two movies any day of the week. Currently about 100 customers were using these cards.

As they reviewed their own pricing structure and compared it with competitors' prices, Henry raised the question of whether their pricing structure was too complicated and thus confusing to customers. He noted that some other video stores in town charged the same rental price every day of the week. He also considered cutting Horizon's price to $2 per movie every day of the week. But Frances said this might upset the punch-card holders.

## QUESTION

What changes, if any should Horizon make in its pricing schedule?

# CASE 4-3

# PRICING

## A GREAT DEAL ON HEATING OIL

The Maxwell Oil Company had been marketing home heating oil to homeowners in the Westville area for more than 50 years. This company operated an annual payment/purchase plan that offered customers a package that, for $99 per year, gave them regular maintenance, service and insurance on their furnaces, and the fuel at 34 cents per litre.

During the past year or so, the company had noticed they were receiving a number of telephone calls from customers who were calling to cancel their annual plan because a local competitor was offering them home heating oil at 30 cents per litre. Maxwell management agreed to match the deal for any customer who called in the future, thereby giving anyone who called a reduction of 4 cents per litre from the current contract price.

The net result was that many customers started to call, once it became generally known in certain Westville neighbourhoods that Maxwell was prepared to match the competitor's price. Then the company began to receive a number of calls from very angry customers who were upset at the fact that some of their neighbours, who apparently had signed up for the same contract, had been receiving their fuel at 4 cents per litre less — merely because they had called up and asked for it. Those who were still paying the higher price were not happy and threatened to leave. Some had been Maxwell customers for 30 years or more and felt "hurt" at being treated this way.

### QUESTIONS

1. What obligation, if any, did the Maxwell company have to offer the same price reduction to all customers who were currently under contract with the annual plan?
2. What options did the company have when it first encountered the fact that the competition was offering fuel at 4 cents per litre less? Should it have let some of its customers go or tried to keep as many as possible?
3. Is there an ethical issue involved when prices are lowered for some customers and not for others?

## SALE DAY AT THE BAY

Bob Jones was walking through the men's wear department of The Bay department store in downtown Westville, taking a short cut to the restaurant where he was meeting Gail for lunch. As he neared the door, Bob noticed a rack of men's cotton slacks above which was displayed a large sign announcing "SPECIAL! 50% OFF." Although Bob had not intended to buy slacks that day, he was attracted by the sign and stopped to look at the goods.

As Bob examined the slacks on the rack, he noticed that the brand was Ruff Hewn and that the original price was $80. He thought, "I could use a pair of slacks and this is a really good price." He had a couple of Ruff Hewn cotton shirts hanging in his closet, and he thought the sweater Gail had given him for his birthday was Ruff Hewn as well. He picked out a dark green pair, size 32 waist, and tried them on. They fitted perfectly, so he decided to buy them.

"Is that on your Bay account, sir?" asked the sales clerk. Bob replied that he would be paying cash and took a $50 bill from his wallet. The clerk then asked, "Do you have your Bay Day card?" Bob indicated that he wasn't familiar with a Bay Day card. The clerk explained that he should have picked up a Bay Day card as he entered the store and that, since this was Bay Day, he was entitled to scratch a certain part of the card to reveal the discount that he would receive on his purchase. As Bob didn't have a card, she reached under the counter and gave him one. Bob scratched the latex portion of the card and saw the words "30% OFF."

"Too bad I can't use this," Bob commented. "The pants are already 50 percent off." "Oh no," replied the sales clerk. "You get an additional 30 percent off the sale price. Let's see, that's another $12, so the price of the slacks will be $28." Bob was delighted. He really hadn't expected to get the pants for that low a price. He had thought he was getting a good deal at $40. He paid the $28, plus tax, thanked the sales clerk, and rushed off to apologize to Gail for being late.

## QUESTIONS

1. What was the price of the pants that Bob bought?
2. What factors influenced his decision to buy?
3. What would Bob have done if he had seen a rack of pants at The Bay with a sign reading "COTTON SLACKS $28" or a sign that said "COTTON SLACKS $80"?

## SANDSTROM STEREOTACTIC SYSTEM

Pia Sandstrom of Welland, Ontario, was studying medical technology at the University of Umea, Sweden, when her mother, Monica, came to see her and to visit her homeland. Monica, trained as a chemical engineer, was looking for a new career, having retired from her research job at a Hamilton chemical company. She decided to check out the possibility of importing Swedish medical devices to Canada. She and Pia came upon a revolutionary device that helps locate brain tumours. They decided to begin importing the product into North America, only to find that the product could not meet U.S. health standards.

They decided to begin manufacturing the device themselves and, three years later, having dipped into savings, sold off investments, and mortgaged the family home, the Sandstroms expected to sell 40 of their Stereotactic Systems a year at $25,000 each. They rely on a chain of suppliers in the Hamilton area to make the components of the system and to assemble the final product.

Most North American hospitals have been using a device that is screwed into the patient's forehead with sheet-metal screws. These machines are heavy, painful, and expensive — at $60,000 to $100,000 each. The Sandstrom system attaches painlessly to the patient's ears and nose and can be worn all day without discomfort. And it sells for only $25,000.

Stereotactic systems work much like a sailor's sextant. A technician, working from x-rays or ultrasound, reads off the co-ordinates of the tumour and gives the information to the neurosurgeon. By pinpointing the location of the tumour, 85 percent of the cost of the surgery is saved. A professor of neurosurgery at the University of Saskatchewan observed, "The patient can go home the next day, instead of being hospitalized for three weeks. That makes the patient cheaper to look after."

The Sandstroms are a two-person company. They spend their time networking at medical trade shows where they meet doctors and academics and develop leads, which they then follow up. They have come to realize that it takes a considerable amount of time and effort to generate sales. It also took them some time to accept that a machine that costs only $1,700 to manufacture can be sold for 15 times that amount when it reaches the market.

## QUESTIONS

1. What is the relationship between cost and price in the marketing of the Sandstrom Stereotactic System?
2. How would you explain to a professor of neurosurgery why the price of the device is $25,000?
3. How important is price to a senior hospital administrator who must justify the purchase of this device in an economic climate where hospital budgets are being severely cut by governments?

PART 5

# DISTRIBUTION

**Channels of distribution from producer to user, wholesaling and retailing institutions.**

We are in the process of developing a marketing program to reach the firm's target markets and achieve the goals established in strategic marketing planning. So far, we have considered the product and pricing structure in that marketing mix. Now we turn our attention to the distribution system — the means for getting products and services to the market.

The distribution ingredient in the marketing mix encompasses two broad topics: (1) strategies for selecting and operating channels of distribution — Chapter 15, and (2) the wholesaling and retailing institutions used in distribution — Chapters 16 and 17.

# CHAPTER 15 GOALS

We will discuss distribution channels in this chapter from the point of view of the producer or the developer of the product or service. As you will see, however, the problems and opportunities that intermediaries face in managing their channels are similar to those faced by distributors. After studying this chapter, you should have an understanding of:

- The nature and importance of intermediaries.
- What a distribution channel is.
- The sequence of decisions involved in designing a channel.
- The major channels for consumer goods, business goods, and services.
- Vertical marketing systems.
- Intensity of distribution.
- How to choose individual intermediaries.
- The nature of conflicts and control within distribution channels.
- Legal considerations in channels management.

CHAPTER 15

# CHANNELS OF DISTRIBUTION: CONFLICT, CO-OPERATION, AND MANAGEMENT

## When the Dealin's Done ...

The establishment of a chain of fast-food restaurants involves just as much a distribution decision as does the question of whether to distribute a line of children's clothing by catalogue, through specialty stores, or through large department stores. The issue involves how to get the new restaurant service to the target consumer segment in a way that is most acceptable and so that it offers convenience, access, and service.

Kenny Rogers Roasters, with only a few outlets operating in Canada at the moment, represents a relative newcomer to the vast $5.3 billion-a-year Canadian fast-food industry, which is dominated by giants like McDonald's and KFC. But the competitiveness of the marketplace does not deter Bruce Raba and Boyd Simpson, who bought the Canadian rights to the Kenny Rogers Roasters name in late 1992 and opened their first restaurant in Mississauga, Ontario, in January 1993. They are convinced theirs is a new concept that will allow Roasters to occupy a position in the market that will allow them to take sales from the dominant chicken restaurants, KFC and Swiss Chalet.

Kenny Rogers Roasters restaurants began operations in the United States in 1991 and are jointly owned by the famous country and western singer and the former governor of Kentucky, John Brown, the man who bought Kentucky Fried Chicken from Colonel Sanders in 1964. The concept that Raba and Simpson brought to Canada is a different one, involving a positioning somewhere between KFC and Swiss Chalet. They realized that chicken is big; Canadian per capita consumption increased by 15 percent between 1986 and 1993. But consumption of fried chicken is on a decline, as is consumption of red meat, reflecting the interest of Canadians in more wholesome, leaner foods.

You also won't find any fried chicken at Roasters. The chicken is marinated in citrus and natural herbs and spices and is roasted over a hardwood fire in full view of customers. In fact, the oven is the centrepiece of the restaurant and customers select their own chicken buffet-style, along with 12 side dishes, eight hot and four cold. As Boyd Simpson explains, "At all times the customer is in control; you can see what is going on your plate."

Once their first restaurant was open, Raba and Simpson set their sights on expansion. By early 1994, they had six restaurants, stretching from Halifax to Toronto, with plans for 22 others on the drawing board. The goal is to have 100 open by 1998. The first six operations were all company-owned, but the partners intend to have about half its restaurants franchised in the future. One major decision is where these new Roasters restaurants are to be opened — not just in what cities but on what street corners and in what malls. Two of the early stores were opened directly across the street from Swiss Chalet, part of a company strategy to lure customers away from the competition.[1]

When we think of distribution channels, we tend to consider first the steps that a tangible product follows in moving from the manufacturing plant to the home of the end consumer. This chapter will discuss such channels. But we should not lose sight of the fact that services must be distributed to customers as well. In the restaurant business, the product is more than the food that is served; it is also the concept or image of the restaurant itself. Companies in a service business such as this must establish strategies for distribution channels and delivery of the product in much the same way as would a manufacturer of clothing, food products, or auto parts.

The distribution decisions that Bruce Raba and Boyd Simpson had to make deal with the layout of their restaurants, how the food is to be served, location of restaurants, and whether they are to be operated as company-owned or franchised outlets.

## INTERMEDIARIES AND DISTRIBUTION CHANNELS

Ownership of a product has to be transferred somehow from the individual or organization that makes it to the consumer who needs and buys it. Goods also must be physically transported from where they are produced to where they are needed. Services ordinarily cannot be shipped but rather are produced and consumed in the same place (as we discussed in Chapter 12).

Distribution's role within a marketing mix is getting the product or service efficiently and conveniently to its target market. The most important activity in getting a product to market is arranging for its sale (and the transfer of title) from producer to final customer. Other common activities (or functions) are promoting the product, storing it, and assuming some of the financial risk during the distribution process.

A producer can carry out these functions in exchange for an order (and, hopefully, payment) from a customer. Or producer and consumer can share these activities. Typically, however, firms called intermediaries perform some of these activities on behalf of the producer or the consumer.

An **intermediary** is a business firm that renders services related directly to the sale and/or purchase of a product as it flows from producer to consumer. An intermediary either owns the product at some point or actively aids in the transfer of ownership. Often, but not always, an intermediary takes physical possession of the product.

Intermediaries are commonly classified on the basis of whether they take title to the products being distributed. **Merchant intermediaries** actually take title to the products they help to market. The two groups of merchant intermediaries are wholesalers and retailers. **Agents** never actually own the products, but they do arrange the transfer of title. Real estate brokers, manufacturers' agents, and travel agents are examples of agents.

### How Important Are Intermediaries?

Some critics say prices are high because there are too many intermediaries performing unnecessary or redundant functions. During the recent recession, some manufacturers also reached this conclusion and sought to cut costs by eliminating wholesaling intermediaries. While intermediaries can be eliminated from channels, lower costs may not always be achieved. The outcome is not predictable, because of a basic axiom of marketing: *You can eliminate intermediaries, but you cannot eliminate essential distribution activities that they perform*. These activities — such as creating assortments and storing products — can be shifted from one party to another in an effort to improve efficiency. However, someone has to perform the various activities — if not an intermediary, then the producer or the final customers.[2]

Intermediaries may be able to carry out distribution activities better or more cheaply than either producers or consumers. Moreover, it is usually not practical for a producer to deal directly with ultimate consumers. Think for a moment how inconvenient your life would be if there were no retail intermediaries — no supermarkets, gas stations, or ticket sales outlets, for instance.

As illustrated in Figure 15-1, intermediaries serve as purchasing agents for their customers and as sales specialists for their suppliers. They provide financial services for both suppliers and customers. Intermediaries' storage services, capability to divide large shipments into smaller ones for resale, and market knowledge benefit suppliers and customers alike.

### What Is a Distribution Channel?

A **distribution channel** consists of the set of people and firms involved in the transfer of title to a product as the product moves from producer to ultimate consumer or business user.

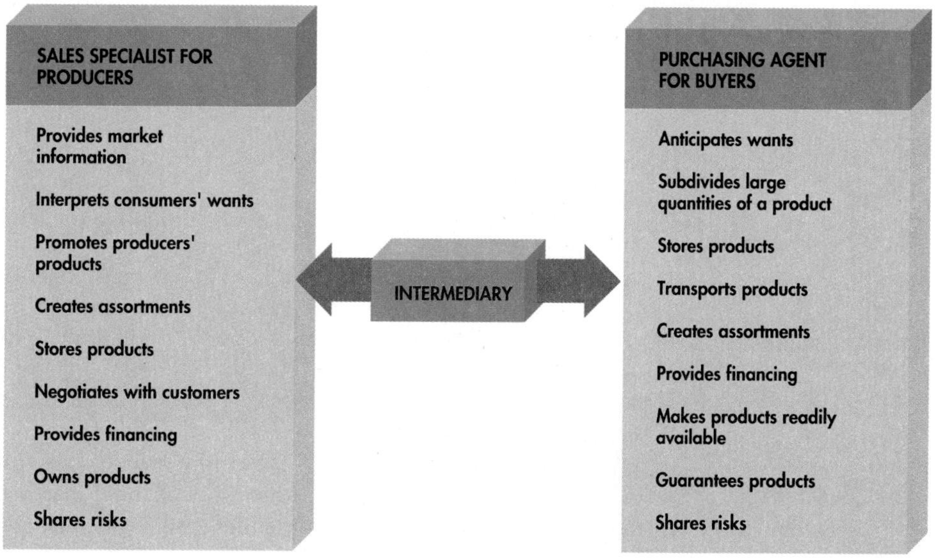


**FIGURE 15-1**
**Typical activities of an intermediary.**

A channel of distribution always includes both the producer and the final customer for the product in its present form as well as any intermediaries such as retailers and wholesalers.

The channel for a product extends only to the last person or organization that buys it without making any significant change in its form. When its form is altered and another product emerges, a new channel is started. When lumber is milled and then made into furniture, two separate channels are involved. The channel for the *lumber* might be lumber mill → broker → furniture manufacturer. The channel for the *finished furniture* might be furniture manufacturer → retail furniture store → consumer.

Besides producer, intermediaries, and final customer, other institutions aid the distribution process. Among these intermediaries are banks, insurance companies, storage firms, and transportation companies. However, because they do not take title to the products and are not actively involved in purchase or sales activities, these intermediaries are not formally included in the distribution channel.

This chapter focuses on the flow (or transfer) of ownership for a product, while part of Chapter 16 examines the physical flow of goods. These flows are distinct; consequently, different institutions may carry them out. For example, a contractor might order roofing shingles from a local building-materials distributor. To minimize freight and handling costs, the product might be shipped directly — that is, shingles manufacturer → contractor. But the channel for title (and ownership) would be manufacturer → distributor → contractor.

**Sofas, like many goods, are typically distributed through a channel that includes manufacturer, retailer, and final consumer.**

## DESIGNING DISTRIBUTION CHANNELS

Companies that appear to be similar often have very dissimilar channels of distribution. For example, Tupperware sells its housewares primarily through a party-plan arrangement, where customers buy products at Tupperware "parties" held in the homes of friends and neighbours. Rubbermaid, on the other hand, sells its similar line of housewares through conventional department and variety stores. Avon cosmetics are sold through a sales force and catalogues, while most other major brands of cosmetics are sold in drugstores and at the cosmetics counters of department stores.

Why do seemingly similar firms wind up with such different channels? One reason is that there are numerous types of channels and intermediaries from which to choose. Also a variety of factors related to the market, product, intermediaries, and company itself influence which channel is actually used by a firm.

A company wants a distribution channel that not only meets customers' needs but also provides an edge on competition. Some firms gain a differential advantage with their distribution channels. Major corporations such as Caterpillar in construction equipment and John Deere in farm equipment use dealers to provide many important services, ranging from advice about financing programs to rapid filling of orders for repair parts. Some car dealerships in the Toronto area have sought to gain a competitive edge by installing information kiosks on their premises that provide customers with comparative information on various makes and models of cars without having them go all over town to competing dealerships.[3]

To design channels that satisfy customers and outdo competition, an organized approach is required.[4] As shown in Figure 15-2, we suggest a sequence of four decisions:

**FIGURE 15-2**
**Sequence of decisions to design a distribution channel.**

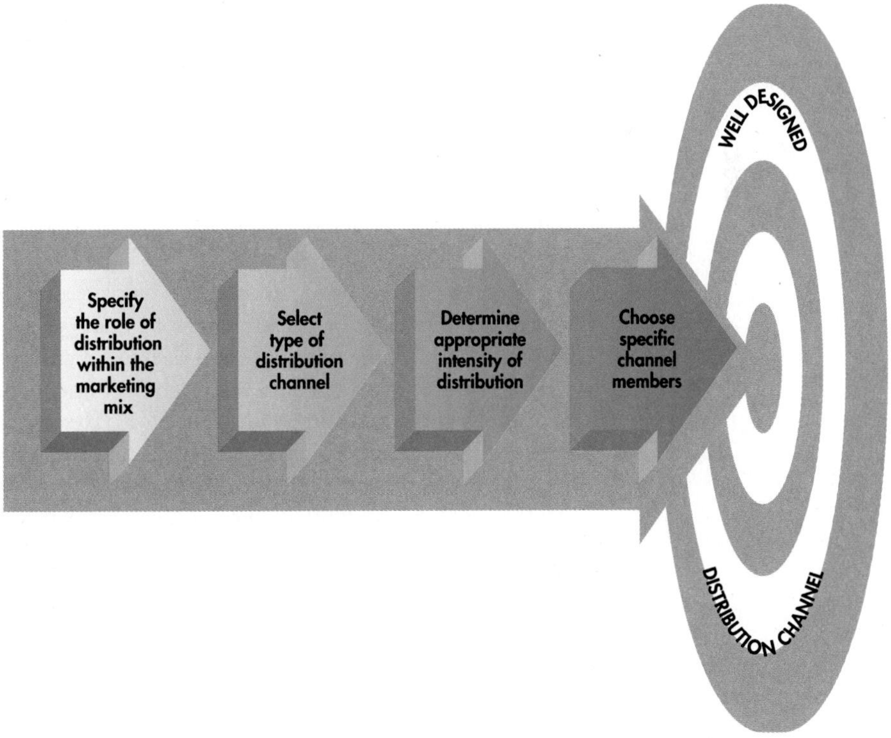


1. **Specifying the role of distribution.** A channel strategy should be designed within the context of the entire marketing mix. First the firm's marketing objectives are reviewed. Next the roles assigned to product, price, and promotion are specified. Each element may have

a distinct role, or two elements may share an assignment. For example, a manufacturer of pressure gauges may use both intermediaries and direct-mail advertising to convince prospective customers that it is committed to servicing the product following the sale.

A company must decide whether distribution will be used defensively or offensively. Under a defensive approach, a firm will strive for distribution that is as good as, but not necessarily better than, other firms' distribution. With an offensive strategy, a firm uses distribution to gain an advantage over competitors. General Motors decided to seek an advantage for its Saturn line of value-priced cars by establishing separate Saturn dealerships rather than relying on existing GM dealerships; Honda did likewise with its Acura line of luxury cars. However, some Acura dealers have faltered because they depend on a single brand of automobile that is aimed at a fairly small segment of the total car-buying market.

2. **Selecting the type of channel.** Once distribution's role in the overall marketing program has been agreed on, the most suitable type of channel for the company's product must be determined. At this point in the sequence, a firm needs to decide whether intermediaries will be used in its channel and, if so, which types of intermediaries.[5]

   To illustrate the wide array of institutions available, as well as the difficulty of channel selection, consider a manufacturer of compact disc (CD) players. If the firm decides to use intermediaries, it must choose among many different types. At the retail level, the range of institutions includes specialty audio-video outlets, department stores, discount houses, and mail-order firms. Which single type or combination of types would permit the manufacturer to achieve its distribution objectives? Another choice must be made if the firm decides to also use wholesaling intermediaries. In a subsequent section, this decision as well as the major types of channels for goods and services will be discussed in detail.
3. **Determining intensity of distribution.** The next decision relates to intensity of distribution, or the number of intermediaries used at the wholesale and retail levels in a particular territory. The target market's buying behaviour and the product's nature have a direct bearing on this decision, as we will see later.
4. **Choosing specific channel members.** The last decision is selecting specific firms to distribute the product. For each type of institution, there are usually numerous specific companies from which to choose.

   Recalling our compact disc player example, assume that the manufacturer prefers two types of intermediaries: department stores and specialty outlets. If the CD players will be sold in Toronto, the producer must decide which department stores — Eaton's or The Bay — will be asked to distribute its product line. Also one or more audio-video chains — from a group including Multitech, Stereo Express, and Electronic Station — must be selected. Similar decisions must be made for each territory in the firm's market.

   When selecting specific firms to be part of a channel, a producer should assess factors related to the market, the product, its own company, and intermediaries. Two additional factors are whether the intermediary sells to the market that the manufacturer wants to reach and whether the intermediary's product mix, pricing structure, promotion, and customer service are all compatible with the manufacturer's needs.

## SELECTING THE TYPE OF CHANNEL

Firms may rely on existing channels, or they may use new channels to better serve current customers and reach prospective customers. In selecting their channels, a firm should seek to gain a differential advantage. For instance, after relying for years strictly on its own sales force, IBM has added 18 new channels to reach its ever-broadening market.[6] Breaking with the tradition of selling computer software through direct selling or

## MARKETING AT WORK

### FILE 15-1 LOGISTICS: THE NEW ROUTE TO PROFITS

The combination of cost pressures and modern technology has led many manufacturers and intermediaries to take a hard look at transportation and logistics. It is rather obvious that business profits depend on only two things: revenues and costs. In a competitive environment, with its pressures to keep prices down and where the economy has not experienced much growth, business is turning its attention to cost cutting. While marketers continue to try to bring in more revenue, others, usually out of sight from the customer, are busily looking for new ways to bring costs down without impairing customer service or quality. The approaches they are using include:

**The supply pipeline:** Retailers today are focusing on speed and costs. Wal-Mart spends only 1.8 percent of sales on logistics, while the average retailer spends 3.5 percent. They make complete use of point-of-sale data, and they have special partnering arrangements with suppliers, so that products move quickly through distribution centres, minimizing inventory and warehousing costs.

**Outsourcing:** Many firms are contracting out the operation of their warehouses and transportation systems, realizing that specialists can provide the services more cheaply and efficiently.

**Wholesaling:** Many manufacturers are distributing their products directly to high-volume customers, while some of those customers are banding together to form buying groups, which then deal directly with suppliers. The result is pressure on the conventional wholesaling business.

**Warehousing:** As more companies adopt a system of just-in-time delivery, the need for conventional warehousing will diminish. Products simply won't lie in warehouses for weeks or months as they did in the past.

**Attention to details:** Companies are realizing more and more that they can save money on paying attention to details like buying trucks with common axles and other parts so that parts inventories can be kept low. Installing lighting on trucks improves safety, reduces accidents, thereby not only cutting repair costs, but keeping the trucks on the road where they make money. Taking precautions to reduce theft also saves money.

Source: Adam Corelli, "How Businesses Can Cut Costs and Keep Rolling," *Globe and Mail*, March 1, 1994, p. B22.

computer resellers, Microsoft recently began to distribute its best-selling DOS disc operating system through bookstore chains.[7] Shiseido, the Japanese cosmetics company, is growing at a rate of 10 percent annually, in part because of some clever distribution strategies. Shiseido is not only operating a thriving mail- and telephone-ordering catalogue system, but has also launched a co-branded VISA card that sends cardholders a full-sized Shiseido magazine with their VISA statements.[8]

Most distribution channels include intermediaries, but some do not. A channel consisting only of producer and final customer, with no intermediaries providing assistance, is called **direct distribution**. ServiceMaster uses a direct approach to sell its building cleaning services to both residential and commercial customers.

In contrast, a channel of producer, final customer, and at least one level of intermediaries represents **indirect distribution**. Canadian Airlines International depends heavily on an indirect approach, involving travel agents, to market its air travel services to consumers. One level of intermediaries — retailers but no wholesaling intermediaries, for example — or multiple levels may participate in an indirect channel. (For consumer goods, sometimes a channel in which wholesalers are bypassed but retailers are used is termed *direct*, rather than indirect, distribution.) With indirect distribution a producer must determine the type(s) of intermediaries that will best serve its needs. The range of options at the wholesale and retail levels will be described in the next two chapters.

Now we'll look at the major channels traditionally used by producers and at two special channels. Then we can consider the factors that most influence a company choice of channels.

### Major Channels of Distribution

Diverse distribution channels exist today. The most common channels for consumer goods, business goods, and services are described next and are summarized in Figure 15-3.

Distribution of Consumer Goods Five channels are widely used in marketing tangible products to ultimate consumers:

- **Producer → consumer.** The shortest, simplest distribution channel for consumer goods involves no intermediaries. The producer may sell from door to door or by mail. For instance, Regal Stationery uses students and other part-time sales people to market its cards and gift items on a direct marketing basis.
- **Producer → retailer → consumer.** Many large retailers buy directly from manufacturers and agricultural producers. To the chagrin of various wholesaling intermediaries, Wal-Mart has increased its direct dealings with producers.
- **Producer → wholesaler → retailer → consumer.** If there is a traditional channel for consumer goods, this is it. Small retailers and manufacturers by the thousands find this channel the only economically feasible choice.
- **Producer → agent → retailer → consumer.** Instead of using wholesalers, many producers prefer to use agents to reach the retail market, especially *large-scale* retailers. For example, a manufacturer of a glass cleaner selected a food broker to reach the grocery store market, including large chains.
- **Producer → agent → wholesaler → retailer → consumer.** To reach *small* retailers, producers often use agents, who in turn call on wholesalers that sell to large retail chains and/or small retail stores.

Distribution of Business Products A variety of channels are available to reach organizations that incorporate the products into their manufacturing process or use them in their operations.[9] In the distribution of business products, the terms *industrial distributor* and *merchant wholesaler* are synonymous. The four common channels for business goods are:

- **Producer → user.** This direct channel accounts for a greater *dollar* volume of business products than any other distribution structure. Manufacturers of large installations, such as airplanes, generators, and heating plants, usually sell directly to users.
- **Producer → industrial distributor → user.** Producers of operating supplies and small accessory equipment frequently use industrial distributors to reach their markets. Manufacturers of building materials and air-conditioning equipment are two examples of firms that make heavy use of industrial distributors.
- **Producer → agent → user.** Firms without their own sales departments find this a desirable channel. Also, a company that wants to introduce a new product or enter a new market may prefer to use agents rather than its own sales force.
- **Producer → agent → industrial distributor → user.** This channel is similar to the preceding one. It is used when, for some reason, it is not feasible to sell through agents directly to the business user. The unit sale may be too small for direct selling. Or decentralized inventory may be needed to supply users rapidly, in which case the storage services of an industrial distributor are required.

Distribution of Services The intangible nature of services creates special distribution requirements. There are only two common channels for services:[10]

**FIGURE 15-3 Major marketing channels for different categories of products.**

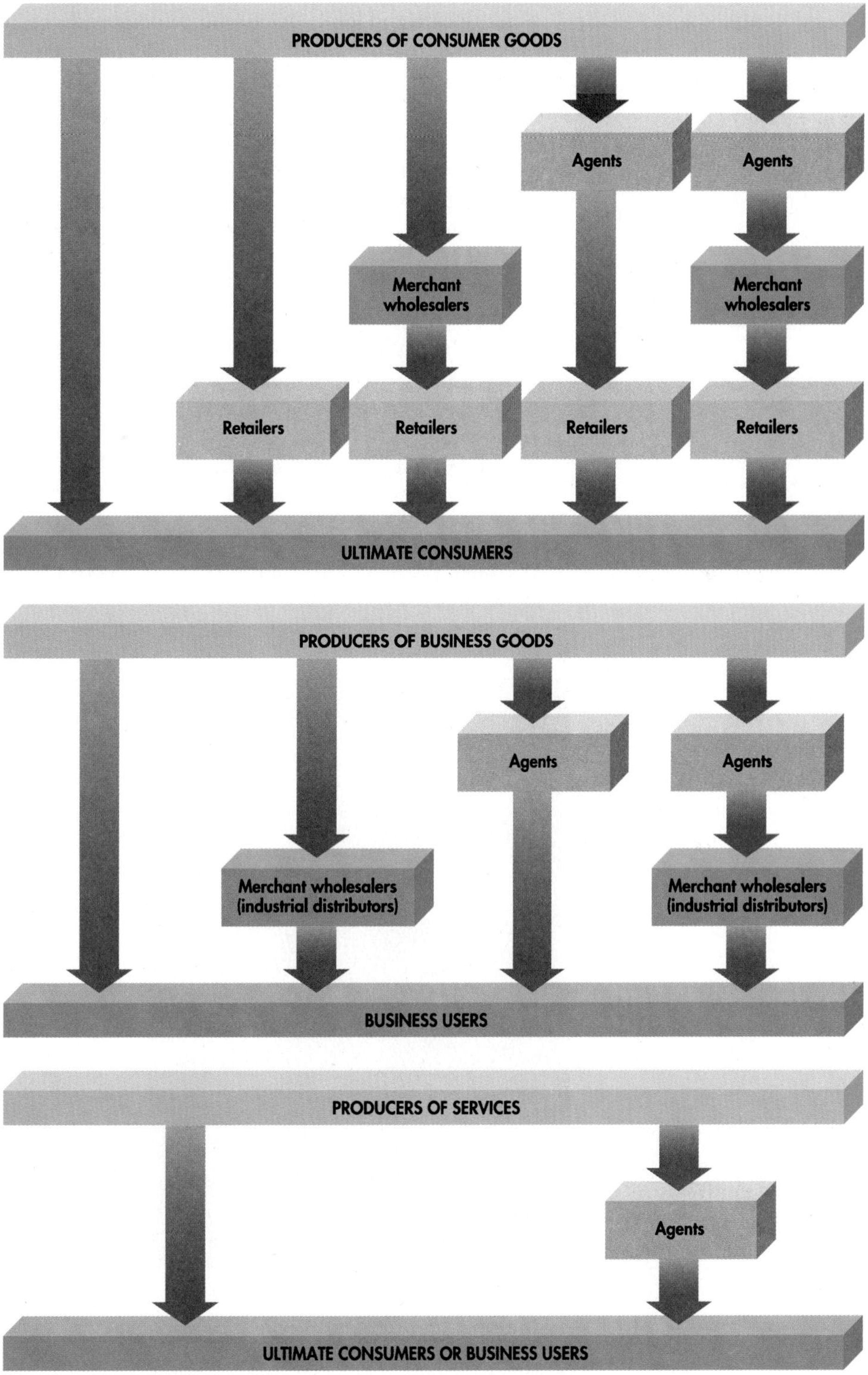


- **Producer → consumer.** Because a service is intangible, the production process and/or sales activity often require personal contact between producer and consumer. Thus a direct channel is used. Direct distribution is typical for many professional services, such as health care and legal advice, and personal services, such as haircutting and weight-loss counselling. However, other services, including travel, insurance, and entertainment, may also rely on direct distribution.

- **Producer → agent → consumer.** While direct distribution often is necessary for a service to be performed, producer-consumer contact may not be required for distribution activities. Agents frequently assist a services producer with transfer of ownership (the sales task) or related tasks. Many services, notably travel, lodging, advertising media, entertainment, and insurance, are sold through agents.

### Multiple Distribution Channels

Many, perhaps most, producers are not content with only a single distribution channel. Instead, for reasons such as achieving broad market coverage or avoiding total dependence on a single arrangement, they employ **multiple distribution channels**. (Similarly, many companies establish multiple *supply* channels to ensure that they have products when needed.)

Use of multiple channels, sometimes called *dual distribution*, occurs in several distinct situations.[11] A manufacturer is likely to use multiple channels to reach *different types of markets* when selling:

- The same product (for example, sporting goods or computer printers) to both consumer and business markets[12]
- Unrelated products (margarine and paint; rubber products and plastics)

**Responding to socio-cultural trends, Avon now uses multiple channels to reach its primarily female market.**

Multiple channels are also used to reach *different segments within a single market* when:

- Size of the buyers varies greatly. An airline may sell directly to travel departments in large corporations but use travel agents to reach small businesses and end consumers.
- Geographic concentration differs across parts of the market. A manufacturer of industrial machinery may use its own sales force to sell directly to customers that are located close together, but may employ agents in sparsely populated markets.

## MARKETING AT WORK

### FILE 15-2 HIRE A COURIER TO MANAGE INVENTORY

In the 1980s, overnight air courier delivery services were making a fortune. Then competition and discounting drove prices down. In 1984, Federal Express Corp. of Memphis was raking in (U.S.) $21.03 per package delivered, whereas today they make less than $15. In frantically casting around for a new way to make a buck, air couriers have happened upon a new retailing trend called "quick response," a logistical concept whereby a manufacturer manages its inventory, transportation, and distribution so that the right stock is always available at the right time. With the courier acting as a liaison between buyers and suppliers, manufacturers gain efficiency and expertise, without having to make enormous investments by creating their own in-house transportation and distribution networks.

Although third-party logistics have become de rigueur for businesses in Europe, Asia, and the United States, cautious Canadian companies have been slower to jump on the "quick response" bandwagon. Recently however, a breakthrough occurred as Sears Canada Inc. became the first department store chain in Canada to employ air express for logistics. Using the services of Belgian industry leader DHL Worldwide Express, Sears will be paying the courier company millions to quickly fly in plane loads of textiles from Asia. Yet, in order to woo an initially hesitant Sears, DHL also agreed to throw in services ranging from the co-ordination of production schedules with offshore manufacturers and the packaging of fabrics, to packing and transportation of goods to distribution centres, and even retail stores, in Canada.

Do all these services sound too good not to take advantage of? K mart, Eaton's, and Canadian Tire think so. Already, they're in the midst of carving out similar logistical support programs with DHL Worldwide, who, thanks to this new niche, is once again soaring.

Source: Andrew Tausz, "Quick Response a New Trend in Retailing," *Globe and Mail*, April 12, 1994, p. C1.

A significant trend involves selling the *same brand to a single market* through channels that compete with each other. Dack's shoes, Sherwin-Williams paints, and Goodyear tires are distributed through the manufacturers' own retail stores as well as through wholesalers, independent retailers, and large retail chains. Producers may open their own stores, thereby creating dual distribution, when they are not satisfied with the market coverage provided by existing retail outlets. Or they may establish their own stores primarily as testing grounds for new products and marketing techniques.

Although multiple distribution channels provide benefits to the producer, they can aggravate intermediaries. Disputes between producers and intermediaries may occur. For example, owners of franchised Häagen-Dazs stores rebelled when faced with multiple channels. The franchisees (who are intermediaries) claimed their marketing efforts were undermined (and sales and profits reduced) when the producer decided to sell its premium ice cream in supermarkets as well as in franchised stores. It is sometimes, but not always, possible to arrange multiple channels in such a way that a firm's intermediaries do not get upset. One approach, which is difficult to achieve, is to develop separate pricing and promotion strategies for each different channel.[13]

### Vertical Marketing Systems

Historically, distribution channels stressed the independence of individual channel members. That is, a producer used various intermediaries to achieve its distribution objectives; however, the producer typically was not concerned with intermediaries' needs. Conversely, wholesalers and retailers were more interested in maintaining their freedom than in co-ordinating their activities with a producer. These priorities of conventional distribution channels provided an opportunity for a new type of channel.

During the past three decades, the vertical marketing system has become perhaps *the* dominant form of distribution channel. A **vertical marketing system** (VMS) is a tightly co-ordinated distribution channel designed specifically to improve operating efficiency and marketing effectiveness. A VMS illustrates the concept of function shifting discussed earlier. In a VMS no marketing function is sacred to a particular level or firm in the channel. Instead, each function is performed at the most advantageous position in the channel.

The high degree of co-ordination or control characterizing a VMS is achieved through one of three means: common ownership of successive levels of a channel, contracts between channel members, or the market power of one or more members. As shown in Table 15-1, there are three distinct forms of vertical marketing systems.

In a **corporate vertical marketing system**, a firm at one level of a channel owns the firms at the next level or owns the entire channel. Sherwin-Williams and Goodyear, for example, own retail outlets. Also, a growing number of apparel makers such as Roots and Ralph Lauren have opened retail stores to feature their brands of clothing.

Intermediaries may also engage in this type of vertical integration. For example, some grocery chains own food-processing facilities, such as dairies, which supply their stores. And some large retailers, including Sears, own all or part of manufacturing facilities that supply their stores with many products.

In a **contractual vertical marketing system**, independent producers, wholesalers, and retailers operate under contracts specifying how they will try to improve the effectiveness and efficiency of their distribution. Three kinds of contractual systems have developed: wholesaler-sponsored voluntary chains (for example, IGA grocery stores), retailer-owned co-operatives (Canadian Tire), and franchise systems (Pizza Delight pizza and Midas automotive maintenance and repairs). All will be discussed in Chapter 16.

TABLE 15-1 Types of vertical marketing systems

| Type of system | Control maintained by | Examples |
|---|---|---|
| **Corporate** | **Ownership** | **Singer (sewing machines), Goodyear (tires), Radio Shack (electronics), Bata (shoes)** |
| **Contractual:** | | |
| **Wholesaler-sponsored voluntary chain** | **Contract** | **IDA and Guardian Drugs, IGA stores** |
| **Retailer-owned co-operative** | **Stock ownership by retailers** | **Canadian Tire stores** |
| **Franchise systems:** | **Contract** | |
| **Manufacturer-sponsored retailers** | | **Ford, Chrysler, and other auto dealers** |
| **Manufacturer-sponsored wholesalers** | | **Coca-Cola and other soft-drink bottlers** |
| **Marketers of services** | | **Wendy's, Speedy Muffler, Harvey's, Holiday Inn, Tilden car rentals** |
| **Administered** | **Economic power** | **Samsonite luggage, General Electric, Labatt** |

An **administered vertical marketing system** co-ordinates distribution activities through the market and/or economic power of one channel member or the shared power of two channel members. This is illustrated by Corning in ovenware, Rolex in watches, and Kraft General Foods in food products. Sometimes a producer's brand equity and market position are strong enough to gain the voluntary co-operation of retailers in matters such as inventory levels, advertising, and store display. However, retailers — especially giant ones such as Loblaw and The Bay — are more likely to dominate channel relationships now than in prior years.

In a variation on an administered VMS, a **systems integrator** pulls together all the goods and services that are needed to present a business solution to a customer. This type of firm, which is seen more and more often in business markets, represents multiple products, suppliers, and subcontractors. For instance, Harnischfeger Engineers offers automated materials-handling equipment to factories. As a systems integrator, it assembles a package of goods and services from many sources to provide a customer with a plant-wide solution. Typically, an intermediary becomes a systems integrator; however, some huge manufacturers such as IBM and Digital Equipment Corp. also are moving into this role.[14]

In the distant past, competition in distribution usually involved two different conventional channels. For instance, one Producer → Retailer → Consumer channel tended to compete with another Producer → Retailer → Consumer channel. More recently, competition pitted a conventional channel against some form of VMS. Thus a traditional Producer → Retailer → Consumer channel battled a contractual VMS for business. Increasingly, the most common competitive battles are between different forms of vertical marketing systems. For example, a corporate system (such as the stores owned by Goodyear) competes with a contractual system (such as General Tire's franchised dealers). Considering the potential benefits of vertical marketing systems with respect to both marketing effectiveness and operating efficiencies, they should continue to grow in number and importance.

**In this administered VMS, Ralph Lauren and a retailer work towards shared goals.**

### Factors Affecting Choice of Channels

If a firm is customer-oriented (and it had better be, if it hopes to prosper), its channels are determined by consumer buying patterns. The nature of the market should be the key factor in management's choice of channels. Other considerations are the product, the intermediaries, and the company itself.

**Market Considerations** A logical starting point is to consider the target market — its needs, structure, and buying behaviour:

- **Type of market.** Because ultimate consumers behave differently than business users, they are reached through different distribution channels. Retailers, by definition, serve ultimate consumers, so they are not in channels for business goods.
- **Number of potential customers.** A manufacturer with few potential customers (firms or industries) may use its own sales force to sell directly to ultimate consumers or business users. Canadair uses this approach in selling its jet aircraft. For a large number of customers, the manufacturer would likely use intermediaries. Reebok relies on numerous intermediaries, notably retailers, to reach the large number of consumers in the market for athletic footwear. A firm using intermediaries does not need as large a sales force as a company selling directly to final consumers.
- **Geographic concentration of the market.** When most of a firm's prospective customers are concentrated in a few geographic areas, direct sale is practical. This is the situation in the textile and garment manufacturing industries. When customers are geographically dispersed, direct sale is likely to be impractical due to high travel costs. Sellers may establish sales branches in densely populated markets and use intermediaries in less concentrated markets.
- **Order size.** When either order size or total volume of business is large, direct distribution is economical. Thus a food-products manufacturer would sell directly to large grocery chains. The same manufacturer, however, would use wholesalers to reach small grocery stores, whose orders are usually too small to justify direct sale.[15]

**Product Considerations** While there are numerous product-related factors to consider, we will highlight three:

- **Unit value.** The price attached to each unit of a product affects the amount of funds available for distribution. For example, a company can afford to use its own employee to sell a large aircraft engine part that costs more than $10,000. But it would not make sense for a company sales person to call on a household or a business firm to sell a $2 ballpoint pen. Consequently, products with low unit value usually are distributed through indirect channels (that is, through one or more levels of intermediaries). There are exceptions, however. For instance, if order size is large because the customer buys many products at the same time from the company, then a direct channel may be economically feasible.
- **Perishability.** Some goods, including many agricultural products, physically deteriorate fairly quickly. Other goods, such as clothing, perish in a fashion sense. As was discussed in Chapter 12, services are perishable due to their intangible nature. Perishable products require direct or very short channels.
- **Technical nature of a product.** A *business* product that is highly technical is often distributed directly to business users. The producer's sales force must provide considerable presale and postsale service; wholesalers normally cannot do this. *Consumer* products of a technical nature provide a real distribution challenge for manufacturers. Ordinarily, manufacturers cannot sell the goods directly to the consumer. As much as possible, producers try to sell directly to retailers, but even then product servicing often poses problems.

**Intermediaries Considerations** Here we begin to see that a company may not be able to arrange exactly the channels it desires:

- **Services provided by intermediaries.** Each producer should select intermediaries that will provide those marketing services that the producer either is unable to provide or cannot economically perform.
- **Availability of desired intermediaries.** The intermediaries preferred by a producer may not be available. They may be carrying competitive products and may not want to add another line.
- **Attitude of intermediaries towards producers' policies.** Sometimes manufacturers' choices of channels are limited because their marketing policies are not acceptable to certain types of intermediaries. Some retailers or wholesalers, for example, are interested in carrying a line only if they receive assurance that no competing firms will carry the line in the same territory.

**Company Considerations** Before choosing a distribution channel for a product, a company should consider its own situation:

- **Desire for channel control.** Some producers establish direct channels because they want to control their product's distribution, even though a direct channel may be more costly than an indirect channel. By controlling the channel, producers can achieve more aggressive promotion and can better control both the freshness of merchandise stocks and their products' retail prices. In mid-1992, IBM started experimenting with mail-order sales of its personal computers. In bypassing intermediaries, IBM hoped to improve service to final customers and improve customer-satisfaction ratings for its PCs.[16]
- **Services provided by seller.** Some producers make decisions about their channels based on the distribution functions desired (and occasionally demanded) by intermediaries. For instance, numerous retail chains will not stock a product unless it is presold through heavy advertising by the producer.
- **Ability of management.** The marketing experience and managerial capabilities of a producer influence decisions about which channel to use. Many companies lacking marketing know-how turn the distribution job over to intermediaries.
- **Financial resources.** A business with adequate finances can establish its own sales force, grant credit to its customers, and/or warehouse its own products. A financially weak firm uses intermediaries to provide these services.

In a few cases, virtually all factors point to a particular length and type of channel. In most cases, however, the factors send mixed signals. Several factors may point to the desirability of direct channels, others to the use of wholesalers and/or retailers. Or the company may find the channel it wants is unavailable. If a company with an unproven product having low profit potential cannot place its product with intermediaries, it may have no other option but to try to distribute the product directly to its target market.

## DETERMINING INTENSITY OF DISTRIBUTION

At this point in designing a channel, a firm knows: what role has been assigned to distribution within the marketing mix; whether direct or indirect distribution is better; and which types of intermediaries will be used (assuming indirect distribution is appropriate). Next the company must decide on the **intensity of distribution** — that is, how many intermediaries will be used at the wholesale and retail levels in a particular territory.

There are many possible degrees of intensity. As shown in Figure 15-4, we will consider the three major categories — ranging from intensive to selective to exclusive. Distribution intensity ordinarily is thought to be a single decision. However, if the channel has more than one level of intermediaries (wholesaler and retailer, for example), the appropriate intensity must be selected for each level.

Different degrees of intensity may be appropriate at successive levels of distribution. A manufacturer can often achieve intensive retail coverage with selective, rather than intensive, wholesale distribution. Or selective intensity at the retail level may be gained through exclusive intensity at the wholesale level. Of course, the wholesaling firm(s) will determine which retail outlets actually receive the product. Despite this lack of control, a producer should plan the levels of intensity needed at both the wholesale and retail levels. Making only one decision about distribution intensity is simplistic and can create serious problems.

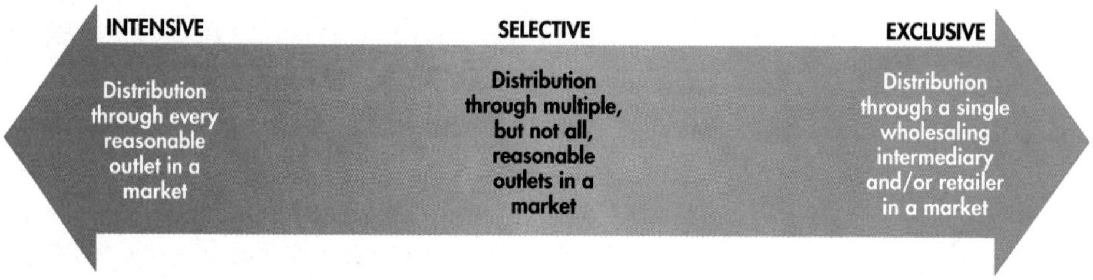
INTENSIVE
SELECTIVE
EXCLUSIVE
Distribution through every reasonable outlet in a market
Distribution through multiple, but not all, reasonable outlets in a market
Distribution through a single wholesaling intermediary and/or retailer in a market

**FIGURE 15-4 The intensity-of-distribution continuum.**

## Intensive Distribution

Under **intensive distribution**, a producer sells its product through every available outlet in a market where a consumer might reasonably look for it. Ultimate consumers demand immediate satisfaction from convenience goods and will not defer purchases to find a particular brand. Thus intensive distribution is often used by manufacturers of this category of product. Retailers often control whether a strategy of intensive distribution actually can be implemented. For example, a new manufacturer of toothpaste or a small producer of potato chips may want distribution in all supermarkets, but these retailers may limit their assortments to four fast-selling brands.

Retailers typically will not pay to advertise a product that is sold by competitors. Therefore, intensive distribution places most of the advertising and promotion burden on the producer.

## Selective Distribution

In **selective distribution**, a producer sells its product through multiple, but not all possible, wholesalers and retailers in a market where a consumer might reasonably look for it. Selective distribution is appropriate for consumer shopping goods, such as various types of clothing and appliances, and for business accessory equipment, such as office equipment and handheld tools.

A company may shift to a selective distribution strategy after some experience with intensive distribution. The decision to change usually hinges on the high cost of intensive distribution or the unsatisfactory performance of intermediaries. Certain intermediaries perennially order in small, unprofitable amounts; others may be poor credit risks. Eliminating such marginal intermediaries may reduce the number of outlets *but* increase a company's sales volume. Many companies have found this to be the case simply because they were able to do a more thorough selling job with a smaller number of accounts.

A firm may move towards more selective distribution to enhance the image of its products, strengthen customer service, and/or improve quality control. For instance, the

Italian firm of Guccio Gucci concluded that its brand was on too many leather goods and fashion accessories and they were carried by too many retailers. Hence, as part of a new marketing strategy, Gucci slashed both its product line and the number of outlets carrying its goods.[17]

### Exclusive Distribution

Under **exclusive distribution**, the supplier agrees to sell its product only to a single wholesaling intermediary and/or retailer in a given market. At the wholesale level, such an arrangement is normally termed an exclusive *distributorship*; at the retail level, an exclusive *dealership*. A manufacturer may prohibit an intermediary that holds an exclusive distributorship or dealership from handling a directly competing product line.

Producers often adopt an exclusive distribution strategy when it is essential that the retailer carry a large inventory. Thus exclusive dealerships are frequently used in marketing consumer specialty products such as expensive suits. This strategy is also desirable when the dealer or distributor must furnish installation and repair service. For this reason, manufacturers of farm machinery and large construction equipment grant exclusive distributorships.

Exclusive distribution helps a manufacturer control the last level of intermediary before the final customer. An intermediary with exclusive rights is usually willing to promote the product aggressively. Why? Interested customers will have to purchase the product from this intermediary because no other outlets in the area carry the same brand. However, a producer suffers if its exclusive intermediaries in various markets do not serve customers well. Essentially a manufacturer has "all its eggs in one basket."

An exclusive dealer or distributor has the opportunity to reap all the benefits of the producer's marketing activities in a particular area. However, under exclusive distribution, an intermediary may become too dependent on the manufacturer. If the manufacturer fails, the intermediary also fails (at least for that product). Another risk is that once sales volume has been built up in a market, the producer may add other dealers or, worse yet, drop all dealers and establish its own sales force.

## CONFLICT AND CONTROL IN CHANNELS

Distribution occasionally is characterized by goals shared by suppliers and customers and by co-operative actions. But conflicts as well as struggles for control are more typical. To manage distribution channels effectively requires an understanding of both conflict and control, including techniques to (1) decrease conflict, or at least its negative effects, and (2) increase a firm's control within a channel.

**Channel conflict** exists when one channel member perceives another channel member to be acting in a way that prevents the first member from achieving its distribution objectives. Firms in one channel often compete vigorously with firms in other channels; this represents horizontal conflict. Even within the same channel, firms argue about operating practices and try to gain control over other members' actions; this illustrates vertical conflict.

### Horizontal Conflict

**Horizontal conflict** occurs among firms on the same level of distribution. The personal-computer field provides an excellent example. Virtually all PCs used to be sold through conventional computer stores. Now PCs can be purchased at a multitude of other outlets — office-supply outlets, department stores, warehouse clubs, consumer-electronics retailers, and gigantic new computer superstores.

## MARKETING AT WORK

### FILE 15-3 DORITOS, JUST-IN-TIME

According to Duffy Smith, vice-president of operations with Hostess Frito-Lay, in order to keep the many consumers of Doritos and the company's other products as happy as possible, they must ensure a continuous supply of fresh products on store shelves. That means that Smith must be able to rely on his suppliers of packaging and other materials to get *their* products to him on time. If there's no packaging material available, Hostess can't package chips, and the result is obvious.

To ensure that they meet the expectations of Hostess Frito-Lay, the company's main supplier of packaging materials, Mobil Chemical Canada, of Belleville, Ontario, established a capacity planning system that matches the plant's manufacturing capability with customers' order patterns. Mobil Chemical has developed a computer model that allows for the efficient scheduling of production to utilize plant capacity and to ensure that customer orders are produced on time.

Such a system works only if the supplier and customer are prepared to share data in an "information alliance." The Mobil system would not work if Hostess Frito-Lay was not prepared to make sales and order data available to the packaging manufacturer. Such partnerships are becoming more common in supplier-customer relationships, and the results are impressive. Mobil Chemical has improved the percentage of orders shipped on time to more than 90 percent.

Source: Gordon Arnaut, "Snack Food Goes Just-in-time," *Globe and Mail*, March 1, 1994, p. B24.

**Duffy Smith of Hostess Frito-Lay.**

Basically, horizontal conflict may occur between:

- *Intermediaries of the same type:* Maryvale Home Hardware versus Fred's Friendly Hardware, for example.
- *Different types of intermediaries on the same level:* Maryvale Home Hardware versus St. Clair Paint and Wallpaper versus K mart.

The main source of horizontal conflict is **scrambled merchandising**, in which intermediaries diversify by adding product lines not traditionally carried by their type of business. Supermarkets, for instance, expanded beyond groceries by adding health and beauty aids, small appliances, records, snack bars, and various services. Retailers that originally sold these product lines became irritated both at supermarkets for diversifying and at producers for using multiple distribution channels.

Scrambled merchandising and the resulting horizontal competition may stem from consumers, intermediaries, or producers. Many *consumers* prefer convenient, one-stop shopping, so stores broaden their assortments to satisfy this desire. *Intermediaries* constantly strive for higher gross margins and more customer traffic, so they increase the number of lines they carry. *Producers* seek to expand their market coverage and reduce unit production costs, so they add new outlets. Such diversification intensifies horizontal conflict.

### Vertical Conflict

Perhaps the most severe conflicts in distribution involve firms at different levels of the same channel. **Vertical conflict** typically occurs between producer and wholesaler or producer and retailer.

#### Producer Versus Wholesaler

Tensions occasionally arise between producers and wholesalers. A producer and wholesaler may disagree about aspects of their business relationship. For instance, John Deere has argued with distributors about whether they should sell farm equipment made by other companies or should restrict their efforts to the Deere brand.

Why do conflicts arise? Basically manufacturers and wholesalers have differing points of view. On the one hand, manufacturers think that wholesalers neither promote products aggressively nor provide sufficient storage services. And wholesalers' services cost too much. On the other hand, wholesalers believe producers either expect too much or do not understand the wholesaler's primary obligation to customers.

Channel conflict typically stems from a manufacturer's attempts to bypass wholesalers and deal directly with retailers or consumers. Direct sale occurs because (1) producers are dissatisfied with wholesalers' services or (2) market conditions call for direct sale. Ordinarily battles about direct sale are fought in *consumer* goods channels. Such conflicts rarely arise in channels for business goods because there is a tradition of direct sale to ultimate customers in business markets.

To bypass wholesalers, a producer has two alternatives:

- **Sell directly to consumers.** Producers may employ house-to-house or mail-order selling. They also may establish their own distribution centres in different areas or even their own retail stores in major markets.
- **Sell directly to retailers.** Under certain market and product conditions, selling directly to retailers is feasible and advisable. An ideal retail market for this option consists of retailers that buy large quantities of a limited line of products.

Direct distribution — a short channel — is advantageous when the product (1) is subject to physical or fashion perishability, (2) carries a high unit price, (3) is custom-made, or (4) requires installation and technical service. Direct distribution, however, places a financial and managerial burden on the producer. Not only must the manufacturer operate its own sales force and handle physical distribution of its products, but a direct-selling manufacturer also faces competition from its former wholesalers, which no doubt now sell competitive products.

Wholesalers too can improve their competitive position and thereby reduce channel conflict. Their options include:

- **Improve internal management.** Many wholesalers have modernized their operations and upgraded the calibre of their management. Functional, single-store warehouses have been built outside congested downtown areas, and mechanized materials-handling equipment has been installed. Computers have improved order processing, inventory control, and billing.

- **Provide management assistance to retailers.** Wholesalers have realized that improving retailers' operations benefits all parties. Wholesalers help meet certain retailers' needs, such as store layout, merchandise selection, promotion, and inventory control.
- **Form voluntary chains.** In a voluntary chain (discussed in Chapter 16), a wholesaler enters into a contract with a group of retailers, agreeing to furnish them with management services and volume buying power. In turn, retailers promise to buy all, or almost all, of their merchandise from the wholesaler.
- **Develop private brands.** Some large wholesalers have successfully established their own brands. A voluntary chain of retailers provides a built-in market for the wholesaler's brand.

Producer Versus Retailer Another struggle for channel control takes place between manufacturers and retailers. Conflict can arise over terms or conditions of the relationship between the two parties. Or producers may compete with retailers by selling from house to house or through producer-owned stores. A number of apparel makers — including Ralph Lauren, Levi's, and Liz Claiborne — have opened retail outlets. In doing so, they have aggravated department stores and specialty retailers that also carry their brands.

Producer and retailer may also disagree about terms of sale or conditions of the relationship between the two parties. For example, some retailers demand a so-called **slotting allowance** to place a manufacturer's product on store shelves. This trend is most evident in the grocery-products field. In some cases, companies with new products are required to pay a fee of $100 to over $1,000 per store for each version of the product. Or payment may be in the form of free products. Of course, not all manufacturers are paying all of these fees. And some small producers cannot afford them. Manufacturers criticize slotting allowances, claiming they stifle the introduction of new products, particularly those developed by small companies. Retailers vigorously defend slotting allowances. Supermarkets contend they must find a way to recoup the costs of reviewing the flood of new products, stocking some of them, and removing failures.

Producers and retailers both have methods to gain more control. Manufacturers can:

- **Build strong consumer brand loyalty.** Creative and aggressive promotion is a key in creating such loyalty.
- **Establish one or more forms of vertical marketing system.**
- **Refuse to sell to unco-operative retailers.** This tactic has to be defensible from a legal standpoint.

Effective marketing weapons are also available to retailers. They can:

- **Develop store loyalty among consumers.** Skilful advertising and strong store brands are means of creating loyal customers.
- **Improve computerized information systems.** Information is power. Knowing what sells and how fast it sells is useful in negotiating with suppliers.
- **Form a retailer co-operative.** In this form of vertical marketing system, a group of retailers (usually fairly small ones) bands together to establish and operate a wholesale warehouse. Their primary intent is to gain lower merchandise costs through volume buying power.[18]

### Who Controls Channels?

Every firm would like to regulate the behaviour of the other companies in its distribution channel. When a channel member is able to do this, it has **channel control**. In many situations, including distribution channels, power is a prerequisite for control. **Channel**

**power** is the ability to influence or determine the behaviour of another channel member. There are various sources of power in the context of channels. They include expertise (for example, possessing vital technical knowledge about the product), rewards (providing financial benefits to co-operative channel members), and sanctions (removing unco-operative members from the channel).

Traditionally, manufacturers have been viewed as controlling channels — that is, making the decisions regarding types and number of outlets, participation of individual intermediaries, and business practices to be followed by a channel. But this is a one-sided, outdated point of view.

Intermediaries often have considerable freedom to establish their own channels. Certainly the names Safeway, Loblaw and Eaton's mean more to consumers than the names of most brands sold in these stores. Large retailers are challenging producers for channel control, just as many manufacturers seized control from wholesalers years ago. Even small retailers can be influential in local markets, because their prestige may be greater than their suppliers' prestige.

Manufacturers contend they should assume the leader's role in a channel because they create the new products and need greater sales volume to benefit from economics of scale. Conversely, retailers also stake a claim for leadership, because they are closest to final customers and, as a result, are best able to know customers' wants and to design and oversee channels to satisfy them. Various factors have contributed to retailers' growing ability to control channels. For instance, many retailers have implemented electronic scanning devices, which has given them access to more accurate, timely information about sales trends of individual products than producers have.[19]

### A Channel Viewed As a Partnership

Sometimes, members see a channel as a fragmented collection of independent, competing firms. Suppliers and intermediaries should not think of channels as something they "command and control," but rather as partnerships aimed at satisfying end users' needs.[20] Thus co-ordination is needed throughout a distribution channel.

One possible reason for channel problems is that most producers do not have a person in the organization who is responsible for co-ordinating the firm's channel activities. While most producers have an *advertising* manager and a *sales* manager, few have a *channels* manager. Perhaps it is time for producers to create this position.

## LEGAL CONSIDERATIONS IN CHANNEL MANAGEMENT

In various ways, organizations may try to exercise control over the distribution of their product as it moves through the channel. Generally speaking, any attempts to control distribution may be subject to legal constraints. In this section, we shall discuss briefly four control methods that are frequently considered by suppliers (usually manufacturers):

- **Dealer selection.** The manufacturer wants to select its customers and refuses to sell to some intermediaries.
- **Exclusive dealing.** The manufacturer prohibits its dealers from carrying products of the manufacturer's competitors.
- **Tying contracts.** The manufacturer sells a product to an intermediary only under the condition that this intermediary also buys another (possibly unwanted) product from the manufacturer. Or, at least, the intermediary agrees not to buy the other product from any other supplier.
- **Exclusive (closed) territories.** The manufacturer requires each intermediary to sell *only* to customers who are located within the intermediary's assigned territory.

None of these arrangements is automatically illegal. The Competition Act deals with such practices under Part VII in which certain dealings between manufacturers and intermediaries are deemed illegal if they restrict competition.

### Dealer Selection

Under Section 47 of the Competition Act, it is illegal for a manufacturer or supplier to refuse to supply an intermediary with the supplier's products. Under certain circumstances, however, a supplier may refuse to deal with retailers or other intermediaries if they are unwilling or unable to meet the usual trade terms of the supplier. In other words, for example, if the intermediary engaged in a practice of selling the supplier's product as a loss leader, or failed to provide adequate postpurchase service, or in some other way failed to support the product, the supplier could refuse to deal with that company. Generally, it would be illegal to refuse to supply an intermediary if the company carried a competitor's product or resisted a tying contract.

### Exclusive Dealing

Exclusive dealing contracts have been declared unlawful if the manufacturer's sales volume is a substantial part of the total volume in a market or if the volume done by the exclusive dealers is a significant percentage of the total business in an area. That is, the law is violated when the competitors of a manufacturer are essentially shut out from a substantial part of the market because of this manufacturer's exclusive dealing contract.

By inference, it is clear that exclusive dealing is not illegal in all situations. In fact, where the seller is just getting started in a market or where its share of the total market is so small as to be negligible, its negotiation of exclusive dealing agreements may not only improve its competitive position but also strengthen competition in general.

Ordinarily there is no question of legality when a manufacturer agrees to sell to only one retailer or wholesaler in a given territory, provided there are no limitations on competitive products. Also, a manufacturer can sell to dealers who do not carry competitors' products, as long as this is a voluntary decision on the part of the franchise holder.

### Tying Contracts

A supplier is likely to push for a tying agreement when:

- There are shortages of a desired product, and the supplier also wants to push products that are less in demand.
- The supplier grants a franchise (as in fast-food services) and wants the franchisee to purchase all necessary supplies and equipment from this supplier.
- The supplier has exclusive dealers or distributors (in appliances, for example) and wants them to carry a full line of the supplier's products.

With regard to tying contracts, apparently a dealer can be required to carry a manufacturer's full line as long as this does not impede competition in the market. The arrangement may be questionable, however, if a supplier forces a dealer or a distributor to take slow-moving, less attractive items in order to acquire the really desirable products.

### Exclusive Territories

Traditionally, the strategy of exclusive (or closed) sales territories has been used by manufacturers in assigning market areas to retailing or wholesaling intermediaries. However, closed sales territories can create area monopolies, lessen competition, and restrict trade among intermediaries who carry the same brand. Exceptions are generally provided when a company is small or is a new entrant to the market, in order to facilitate market entry.

## MARKETING AT WORK

### FILE 15-4 SHOPPING IS JUST A KEYSTROKE AWAY

As more and more people shop by telephone, television, and computer, retail shopping has become immediate, convenient, and efficient. For many Canadians, going shopping is becoming less convenient and less necessary. Many products can now be purchased from home and delivered within days. In some product categories, conventional store-based retailing is being threatened, as shopping from home and office increased by more than 30 percent in North America from 1988 to 1992.

A number of factors are driving this revolution. In the first place, consumers are becoming much more confident in their ability to make decisions, and the quality of products has improved to the point that the risk in shopping from home has been minimized. Secondly, many consumers have neither the time nor the desire to deal with the congestion and hassle of shopping. Finally, technology has made it easy as 1-800 numbers and direct computer links become standard tools of the direct marketing trade.

Retailers such as Macy's in the United States are planning their own cable television channels to serve their shoppers. Blockbuster Video is entering the instant CD market, in which they will download a selection of music to custom-ordered CDs while the customer waits, thereby eliminating inventories that currently fill record stores. Dell Computers have created a whole new system of direct-to-the-customer retailing of personal computers, with the resulting elimination of retail inventories.

Such changes herald a dramatic shift in how products are created, moved, and delivered to the customer. The net effect is better service for the customer, elimination of many conventional retail services, and a squeezing of the distribution function.

Source: Don Libey, "A New Generation of Buyers: New Marketing Techniques and a Changing Society Are Driving Forces Behind a New Revolution in Retailing," *Direct Marketing News*, vol. 15, no. 11, August 1993, pp. 10, 11.

These limitations on closed sales territories are likely to foster vertical marketing systems, where the manufacturer retains ownership of the product until it reaches the final buyer. That is, the manufacturer could either (1) own the retail or wholesale outlet or (2) consign products on an agency basis to the intermediaries but retain ownership. In either of these situations, exclusive territories are quite legal.

## THE CHANGING FACE OF DISTRIBUTION

Largely as a result of advancing technology and the changing balance of power within distribution channels, we are witnessing a change in the nature of distribution and in the means by which products and services reach the end consumer. It should be obvious from the examples in this chapter that many of the traditional channels by which products and services moved from their producers to consumers are under threat and may be expected to undergo considerable change in the years to come.

In many cases, entirely new channels of distribution have been established. For example, in some Canadian cities, formal networks have been established to barter goods and services. In Toronto, BarterPlus Systems Inc. has 1,400 members who barter and trade their various products and services through a network that involves millions of dollars worth of transactions, without a dollar ever changing hands[21] — not a conventional distribution channel.

As we have seen earlier in this chapter, shopping from home is expected to be a major growth area in retailing in the future as systems become more sophisticated and as catalogue companies and other direct retailers become even better at serving their customers.

We will see increased use of direct response television, which will involve customers ordering directly from the supplier's computer through touch-tone telephone, or by placing more conventional "voice" orders via 1-800 numbers.[22] As many consumers tire of the retail shopping-mall experience and have less time to indulge in it, more will turn to electronic shopping.

Finally, with the advances in technology today, it is not always clear what constitutes a distribution channel, as compared with an advertising or promotional tool. For example, many Canadian companies are installing information kiosks in retail stores, shopping malls, and other public locations. One kiosk is installed in the small New Brunswick town of Paquetville, where the nearest pharmacy is 30 km away. The kiosk, operated by MediTrust Pharmacy of Toronto, uses Northern Telecom multimedia software to allow the customer at the kiosk to speak with a pharmacist who may be hundreds of kilometres away. The prescription is scanned at the kiosk, and the order is filled and delivered within 48 hours. Other kiosks allow customers to obtain information on in-store specials, to compare prices at competing car dealers, and to buy life and travel insurance.[23] Apple Computer launched a CD-ROM containing text, sound, and images from leading mail-order catalogues, including Lands' End, Williams-Sonoma, and Tiffany.[24] The service, known as En Passant, is initially to be updated quarterly. Eventually it will be made available on computer networks that can be immediately updated with fresh information.

Do these examples represent new channels of distribution or merely variations on existing practices? Certainly, they will revolutionize the way in which many manufacturers, suppliers, and intermediaries conduct their business.

## SUMMARY

The role of distribution is getting a product to its target market. A distribution channel carries out this assignment with intermediaries performing some tasks. An intermediary is a business firm that renders services directly related to the purchase and/or sale of a product as it flows from producer to consumer. Intermediaries can be eliminated from a channel, but someone still has to carry out their essential functions.

A distribution channel is the set of people and firms involved in the flow of title to a product as it moves from producer to ultimate consumer or business user. A channel includes producer, final customer, and any intermediaries that participate in the process.

Designing a channel of distribution for a product occurs through a sequence of four decisions: (1) delineating the role of distribution within the marketing mix; (2) selecting the proper type of distribution channel; (3) determining the appropriate intensity of distribution; and (4) choosing specific channel members. A variety of channels are used to distribute consumer goods, business goods, and services. Firms often employ multiple channels to achieve broad market coverage, although this strategy can alienate some intermediaries. Because of deficiencies in conventional channels, vertical marketing systems have become a major force in distribution. There are three forms of vertical marketing systems: corporate, contractual, and administered.

Numerous factors need to be considered prior to selecting a distribution channel for a product. The primary consideration is the nature of the target market; other considerations relate to the product, the intermediaries, and the company itself.

Distribution intensity refers to the number of intermediaries used at the wholesale and retail levels in a particular territory. It ranges from intensive to selective to exclusive.

Firms distributing goods and services sometimes clash. There are two types of conflict: horizontal (between firms at the same level of distribution) and vertical (between firms at different levels of the same channel). Scrambled merchandising is a prime cause of horizontal conflict. Vertical conflict typically pits producer against wholesaler or retailer. Manufacturers' attempts to bypass intermediaries are a prime cause of vertical conflict.

Channel members frequently strive for some control over one another. Depending on the circumstances, either producers or intermediaries can achieve the dominant position in a channel. All parties may be served best by viewing channels as a system requiring co-ordination or distribution activities. Moreover, attempts to control distribution may be subject to legal constraints.

## KEY TERMS AND CONCEPTS

**Intermediary (440)**
**Merchant intermediary (441)**
**Agent (441)**
**Distribution channel (441)**
**Intensity of distribution (444)**
**Direct distribution (445)**
**Indirect distribution (445)**
**Multiple distribution channels (448)**
**Dual distribution (448)**
**Vertical marketing system (450)**
**Corporate vertical marketing system (450)**
**Contractual vertical marketing system (450)**
**Administered vertical marketing system (451)**
**Systems integrator (451)**
**Intensity of distribution (453)**
**Intensive distribution (454)**
**Selective distribution (454)**
**Exclusive distribution (455)**
**Channel conflict (455)**
**Horizontal conflict (455)**
**Scrambled merchandising (456)**
**Vertical conflict (457)**
**Slotting allowance (458)**
**Channel control (458)**
**Channel power (458)**
**Dealer selection (459)**
**Exclusive dealing (459)**
**Tying contracts (459)**
**Exclusive territory (459)**

## QUESTIONS AND PROBLEMS

1. "You can eliminate intermediaries, but you cannot eliminate their functions." Discuss this statement.
2. Which of the following institutions are intermediaries? Explain.
   a. Avon sales person.
   b. Electrical wholesaler.
   c. Real estate broker.
   d. Railroad.
   e. Auctioneer.
   f. Advertising agency.
   g. Grocery store.
   h. Stockbroker.
   i. Bank.
   j. Radio station.
3. Which of the channels illustrated in Figure 15-3 is most apt to be used for each of the following products? Defend your choice in each case.
   a. Fire insurance.
   b. Single-family residences.
   c. Farm hay balers.
   d. Washing machines.
   e. Hair spray.
   f. An ocean cruise.
4. "The great majority of business sales are made directly from producer to business user." Explain the reason for this first in relation to the nature of the market, and then in relation to the product.
5. Explain, using examples, the differences among the three major types of vertical systems — corporate, administered, contractual. Which is the best kind?
6. A small manufacturer of fishing lures is faced with the problem of selecting its channel of distribution. What reasonable alternatives does it have? Consider particularly the nature of its product and the nature of its market.
7. Is a policy of intensive distribution consistent with consumer buying habits for convenience goods? For shopping goods? Is intensive distribution normally used in the marketing of any type of business goods?
8. From a producer's viewpoint, what are the competitive advantages of exclusive distribution?
9. What are the drawbacks to exclusive distribution from a retailer's point of view? To what extent are these alleviated if the retailer controls the channel for the particular brand?
10. A manufacturer of a well-known brand of men's clothing has been selling directly to one dealer in a small Canadian city for many years. For some time the market has been large enough to support two retailers very profitably. Yet the present dealer objects strongly when the manufacturer suggests adding another outlet. What alternatives does the manufacturer have in this situation? What course of action would you recommend?
11. "Manufacturers should always strive to select the lowest-cost channel of distribution." Do you agree? Should they always try to use the intermediaries with the lowest operating costs? Why or why not?
12. What are reasons for producers' dissatisfaction with the wholesalers' performance? Do you agree with the producers' complaints?
13. Why are full-service wholesalers relatively unimportant in the marketing of women's high-fashion wearing apparel, furniture, and large electrical equipment?

## HANDS-ON MARKETING

1. Arrange an interview with either the owner or a top-level manager of a small manufacturing firm. Inquire about (a) what distribution channel(s) the company uses for its primary product, (b) what factors were the greatest influences in arriving at the channel(s), and (c) whether the company would prefer some other channel(s).
2. Visit with either a supermarket manager or a buyer for a supermarket chain to learn more about slotting allowances and any other charges they levy on manufacturers. Inquire whether such charges have led to channel conflict and how the supermarket chain is handling this type of situation. Also ask whether any grocery-products manufacturers refuse to pay slotting allowances and whether the chain ever waives the fees.

## NOTES AND REFERENCES


1. Adapted from Laura Pratt, "The Gamblers," *Foodservice and Hospitality*, October 1993, pp. 15, 17; and John Greenwood, "Playing Chicken," *The Financial Post Magazine*, April 1994, pp. 26-29.
2. The concept of shifting activities, the possibility of manufacturers shifting some functions away from their firms, and the opportunity for small wholesalers to perform added functions to maintain their economic viability are all discussed in Ronald D. Michman, "Managing Structural Changes in Marketing Channels," *The Journal of Business and Industrial Marketing*, Summer/Fall 1990, pp. 5-14.
3. "Auto Shopping via ATM," *Marketing*, November 15, 1993, p. 15.
4. An alternative approach, which emphasizes market analysis, is presented in Allan J. Magrath and Kenneth G. Hardy, "Six Steps to Distribution Network Design," *Business Horizons*, January-February 1991, pp. 48-52.
5. For more on selecting channels for international markets, especially the decision of whether to use intermediaries, see Saul Klein, "Selection of International Marketing Channels," *Journal of Global Marketing*, vol. 4, 1991, pp. 21-37.
6. Rowland T. Moriarty and Ursula Moran, "Managing Hybrid Marketing Systems," *Harvard Business Review*, November-December 1990, p. 146.
7. Patrick Allossery, "DOS Enters Book Stores," *Strategy*, November 15, 1993, pp. 1, 35.
8. Stan Rapp, "Shiseido, Amil Use TRC to Rack up Growth in Hard Times," *Direct Marketing News*, vol. 15, no. 5, January 1993, pp. 15, 18.
9. An excellent discussion of distribution channels for business goods and services is found in Michael D. Hutt and Thomas W. Speh, *Business Marketing Management*, 4th ed., The Dryden Press, Ft. Worth, TX, 1992, pp. 359-392.
10. For an admirable discussion of this topic, see Donald H. Light, "A Guide for New Distribution Channel Strategies for Service Firms," *The Journal of Business Strategy*, Summer 1986, pp. 56-64.
11. Moriarty and Moran, op. cit., pp. 146-155, use the term *hybrid marketing system* and stress the importance of analyzing basic marketing tasks to determine how many and what types of channels are needed.
12. For extensive discussion of this strategy, see John A. Quelch, "Why Not Exploit Dual Marketing?" *Business Horizons*, January-February 1987, pp. 52-60.
13. For further discussion of the advantages and disadvantages of multiple channels as well as ways to minimize conflict resulting from multiple channels, see Martin Everett, "When There's More Than One Route to the Customer," *Sales & Marketing Management*, August 1990, pp. 48-50.
14. Martin Everett, "Systems Integrators: Marketing's New Maestros," *Sales & Marketing Management*, November 1990, pp. 50.
15. For more on the idea that market considerations should determine a producer's channel structure, see Louis W. Stern and Frederick D. Sturdivant, "Customer-Driven Distribution Systems," *Harvard Business Review*, July-August 1987, pp. 34-41.
16. Paul B. Carroll, "IBM Will Test Selling Its PCs by Mail Order," *The Wall Street Journal*, April 29, 1992, p. B5.
17. John Rossant, "Can Maurizio Gucci Bring the Glamour Back?" *Business Week*, February 5, 1990, pp. 83-84.
18. For further discussion of strategies that either create or offset conflict between manufacturers and retailers, see Allan J. Magrath and Kenneth G. Hardy, "Avoiding the Pitfalls in Managing Distribution Channels," *Business Horizons*, September-October 1987, pp. 29-33.
19. The emerging dominance of gigantic retailers and their dictates to manufacturers are described in Zachary

Schiller and Wendy Zellner, "Clout!" *Business Week*, December 21, 1992, pp. 66-69. Customer market power in relation to channel control is covered in Gul Butaney and Lawrence H. Wortzel, "Distributor Power versus Manufacturer Power: The Customer Role," *Journal of Marketing*, January 1988, pp. 52-63.

20. Allan J. Magrath, "The Hidden Clout of Middlemen," *The Journal of Business Strategy*, March/April 1990, pp. 38-41. For further ideas on how to build a good producer-intermediary relationship, see James A. Narus and James C. Anderson, "Distributor Contributions to Partnership with Manufacturers," *Business Horizons*, September-October 1987, pp. 34-42.
21. John Heinzl, "Sultans of Swap," *Globe and Mail*, March 1, 1994, p. B26.
22. Dan Plashkes, "The Revolution in Television Shopping," *Marketing*, November 15, 1993, p. 53.
23. Steve McLuskie, "Firms Embrace Interactive Kiosks," *Globe and Mail*, May 26, 1994, p. C4.
24. "Apple to Produce CD for Home Shopping," *Globe and Mail*, November 24, 1993, p. B8.

## CHAPTER 16 GOALS

This chapter will provide you with insight into how wholesale markets, wholesaling institutions, and physical-distribution activities relate to marketing. After studying this chapter, you should have an understanding of:

- The nature and economic justification of wholesaling and the role of wholesaling intermediaries.
- Differences across three categories of wholesaling intermediaries.
- Major types of merchant wholesalers, agent wholesalers, and manufacturers' sales facilities, and the services they render.
- What physical distribution is.
- The systems approach to physical distribution.
- How physical distribution is used to strengthen a marketing program and reduce marketing costs.
- The five subsystems within a physical distribution system: inventory location and warehousing; materials handling; inventory control; order processing; and transportation.
- Trends in wholesaling and physical distribution.

CHAPTER 16

# WHOLESALING: MARKETS AND INSTITUTIONS

## Delivering Service Results in Real Growth

Nir Shafrir started out by driving around town delivering computer parts himself. He was sure that it would all pay off. This was in 1985. In 1994, his company, Computer Brokers of Canada, had shipped more than $175 million of computers and accessories to dealers across Canada, and in the same period its recent Minneapolis acquisition sold $100 million in the U.S. market. Today, CBC is among the top five North American computer distributors. As far as Nir Shafrir is concerned, "what made it for us was quick response time and service." Undoubtedly, being able to spot industry trends and moving quickly on them were also important.

Computer distributors are big business these days. They offer product lines from the United States and foreign manufacturers for resale to more than 10,000 Canadian mass merchants, department stores, electronic superstores, large original equipment manufacturers, and even small independents. A single distributor can carry a stock that consists of hundreds of product lines from suppliers around the world. In total, Canadian distributors have revenues of roughly $2.4 billion and experience annual growth rates of something like 50 percent. Computer Brokers of Canada carries the products of more than 65 suppliers and distributes them to more than 6,000 retailers across Canada.

In 1985, Shafir had just graduated from college and had spotted the trend to hard-drive replacement and upgrades. Working out of the second bedroom of his Toronto apartment, he sold $6 million worth of hard drives, tape drives, and monitors in 1986. In the next year, he had sales of $34 million and distribution and sales offices in Montreal and Vancouver. By 1988, CBC had expanded its product lines to include computers, and sales were at $71 million. In 1989, because of its rapid growth, CBC was selected as the Canadian distributor for the sought-after line of hard drives manufactured by California-based Quantum Corporation. CBC is now Quantum's leading North American distributor with more than 30 percent of Quantum's hard drives moving through CBC warehouses and into Compaq, IBM, and Apple computers. By January of 1993, CBC had opened a warehouse in Memphis, Tennessee, adjacent to the Federal Express transportation hub putting it within 24-hours' delivery of all U.S. markets.

Since Quantum selected CBC as a distributor, other manufacturers of computer parts (Seagate drives) and computers (AST, Compaq) have joined it in making use of CBC's distribution services and systems. What makes them seek out CBC is its service orientation and its no-nonsense approach with dealers. Shafrir says, "They (the dealers) aren't looking for someone in a fancy suit to take them out to lunch. They're looking for convenience because this is a real-time business.

Driving around town delivering parts is still important at CBC. While other distributors may stall for weeks before replacing a part for a dealer, CBC is there to make replacements on the spot. "This bought us a lot of loyalty," says Shafrir. With dealer loyalty and some skill at sorting out what will sell and what won't, CBC is looking to take on the biggest in the industry.[1]

Although consumers shop regularly at the stores of retailing intermediaries, they rarely see the establishments of wholesaling intermediaries such as Computer Brokers of Canada. Also, beyond noticing transportation carriers such as trucks and trains, consumers have little exposure to how products actually are moved from the point of production to the point of final sale and consumption. As a result, wholesaling and physical distribution are often misunderstood — and occasionally criticized — by consumers. Nevertheless, wholesaling intermediaries can be essential members of a distribution channel, and physical distribution is an integral aspect of marketing most goods. Therefore, it's critical that you understand the nature and managerial issues of both wholesaling and physical distribution.

## NATURE AND IMPORTANCE OF WHOLESALING

Wholesaling and retailing enable what is produced to be purchased for consumption. We already know that retailing involves sales to ultimate consumers for their personal use. Now we'll see that wholesaling has a different role in the marketing system.

### Wholesaling and Wholesaling Intermediaries

**Wholesaling** (or *wholesale trade*) is the sale, and all activities directly related to the sale, of goods and services to businesses and other organizations for (1) resale, (2) use in producing other goods or services, or (3) operating an organization. When a business firm sells shirts and blouses to a clothing store that intends to resell them to final consumers, this is wholesaling. When a mill sells flour to a large bakery for making bread and pastries, this is also a wholesale transaction. And when a firm sells uniforms to a business or another organization for its employees to wear in carrying out their duties, this is wholesaling as well.

Sales made by one producer to another are wholesale transactions, and the selling producer is engaged in wholesaling. Likewise, a discount house is involved in wholesaling when it sells calculators and office supplies to a business firm. Thus wholesaling includes sales by any firm to any customer *except* an ultimate consumer who is buying for personal, nonbusiness use. From this perspective, all sales are either wholesale or retail transactions — distinguished only by the purchaser's intended use of the good or service.

In this chapter we will focus on firms engaged *primarily* in wholesaling. This type of company is called a **wholesaling intermediary**. We will not be concerned with retailers involved in occasional wholesale transactions. And we will not focus on manufacturers and farmers because they are engaged primarily in production rather than wholesaling. Keep in mind, then, that *wholesaling* is a business *activity* that can be carried out by various types of firms, whereas a *wholesaling intermediary* is a business *institution* that concentrates on wholesaling.

## Economic Justification for Wholesaling

Most manufacturing firms are small and specialized. They don't have the capital to maintain a sales force to contact the many retailers or final users that are (or could be) their customers. Even for manufacturers with sufficient capital, some of their products or lines generate such a small volume of sales that it would not be cost-effective to establish a sales force to sell them.

At the other end of the distribution channel, most retailers and final users buy in small quantities and have only a limited knowledge of the market and sources of supply. Thus there is often a gap between the seller (producer) and the buyer (retailer or final user). A wholesaling intermediary can fill this gap by providing services of value to manufacturers and/or retailers. For example, a wholesaling intermediary can pool the orders of many retailers and/or final users, thereby creating a market for the small producer. At the same time, a wholesaling intermediary selects various items from among many alternatives to form its product mix, thereby acting as a buying service for small retailers and final users. Essentially, as we will see at various points in this chapter, the activities of a wholesaling intermediary create time, place, and/or possession utility.

From a broad point of view, wholesaling brings to the total distribution system the economies of skill, scale, and transactions:

- Wholesaling *skills* are efficiently concentrated in a relatively few hands. This saves the duplication of effort that would occur if many producers had to perform wholesaling functions themselves. For example, one wholesaler's warehouse in Memphis, Tennessee, saves many manufacturers from having to build their own warehouses to provide speedy service to customers in this area.
- Economies of *scale* result from the specialization of wholesaling intermediaries performing functions that might otherwise require several small departments run by producing firms. Wholesalers typically can perform wholesaling functions more efficiently than can most manufacturers.
- *Transaction* economies come into play when wholesaling or retailing intermediaries are introduced between producers and their customers. Let's assume that four manufacturers want to sell to six retailers. As shown in Figure 16-1, *without* an intermediary, there are 24 transactions; *with* one wholesaling intermediary, the number of transactions is cut to 10. Four transactions occur when all the producers sell to the intermediary, and another six occur when the intermediary sells to all the retailers.

## Size of the Wholesale Market

In 1990, there were more than 71,000 wholesaling establishments in Canada, with a total annual sales volume of about $314 billion. As is the case in retailing, the sales generated by wholesaling establishments have increased dramatically in recent years. Part of this increase is accounted for by increases in prices that have occurred during the past ten years or so, but even if sales were expressed in constant dollars, we would still see a substantial increase.

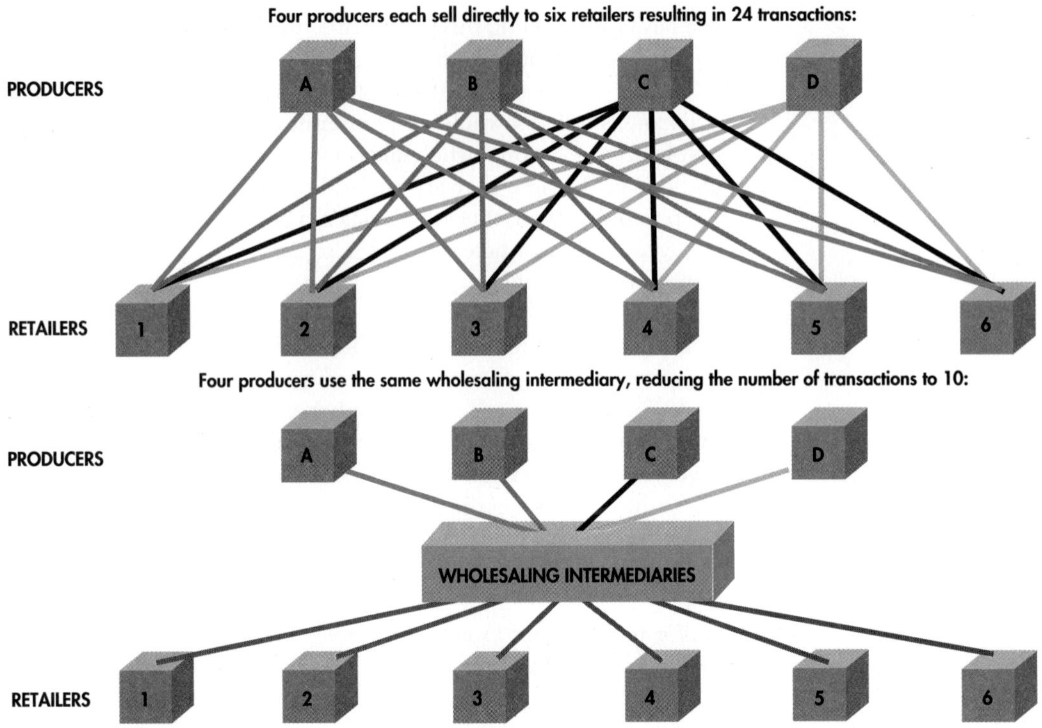


**FIGURE 16-1**
**The economy of transactions in wholesaling.**

## PROFILE OF WHOLESALING INTERMEDIARIES

A producer or retailer considering indirect distribution and the use of wholesaling intermediaries must know what alternatives are available, whom these intermediaries serve, and how they operate. Having this information increases the likelihood of establishing effective distribution arrangements.

### Four Major Categories

Classifying wholesaling intermediaries is difficult because they vary greatly in (1) products they carry, (2) markets to which they sell, and (3) methods of operation. To minimize the confusion, we will use the classification scheme shown in Figure 16-2. There, all wholesaling intermediaries are grouped into only four broad categories — wholesale merchants, manufacturers' sales branches and offices, agents and brokers, and primary product dealers. These four groups are the classifications used by Statistics Canada, which is the major source of quantitative data covering wholesaling institutions and markets. Later in this chapter we shall discuss merchant wholesalers, agents and brokers, and primary products dealers in more detail.

**Merchant Wholesalers** These are firms we usually refer to as wholesalers, jobbers, or industrial distributors. They typically are independently owned, and they take title to the merchandise they handle. They form the largest single segment of wholesaling firms when measured either by sales or by number of establishments. Statistics Canada reports that wholesale merchants, along with manufacturers' sales branches and primary-product dealers discussed below, account for almost 85 percent of total wholesale trade.[2]

**Manufacturers' Sales Branches and Offices** These establishments are owned and operated by manufacturers, but they are physically separated from the manufacturing plants. The distinction between a sales branch and a sales office is that a branch carries merchandise stock and an office does not.

## MARKETING AT WORK

### FILE 16-1 WHOLESALING GOES RETAILING

A recent development in Canadian distribution is the wholesale or warehouse club. These large bulk merchandisers are located in large urban areas such as Vancouver, Toronto, Edmonton, and Montreal and sell in volume to retail customers and to small independent businesses, many of whom buy at attractive discounts to resell in their own stores. Costco Wholesale opened the first warehouse club in Burnaby, B.C., in 1985. It now has stores in Edmonton and Calgary. Steinberg opened its first Price wholesale club in Montreal, and Titan Warehouse Club is based in Toronto. By 1993, Price and Costco had merged to become a more formidable wholesale/retail competitor.

The wholesale club stocks food and other merchandise and operates on thin margins and no-frills service. Consumers must be members and they buy in bulk at attractive discounts. About 25 percent of warehouse club sales are from food, 20 percent from appliances, and the rest from a wide range of products including sporting goods, automotive products, and toys. The clubs attract small convenience store operators, professionals, restaurant operators, and other small businesses who have no efficient route to buy supplies wholesale. Provided they can show a commercial licence, they buy at special wholesale prices and pay no sales tax. These business customers typically account for between 50 percent and 70 percent of sales. Warehouse clubs also appeal to consumer groups, such as credit unions and government employees.

TABLE 16-1 Wholesale trade in Canada, 1992

| | Number of Establishments | Number of Locations | Sales Volume ($ millions) |
|---|---|---|---|
| **Wholesaler merchants** | 63,121 | 73,801 | 248,681.9 |
| **Agents and brokers** | 1,758 | 1,982 | 38,561.1 |
| **TOTAL** | 64,879 | 75,783 | 287,243.0 |

Source: *Wholesale Trade Statistics*, cat. no. 63-226, 1992. Reproduced with permission of the Minister of Supply and Services Canada.

Agents and Brokers These firms are principally engaged in buying for resale primary products such as grain, livestock, furs, fish, tobacco, fruit, and vegetables from the primary producers of these products. On occasion, they will act as agents of the producer. Co-operatives that market the primary products of their members are also included in this category.

Some other subcategories used in classifying the wholesaling business are reflected in Figure 16-2. For example, wholesaling intermediaries may be grouped by:

- **Ownership of products** — wholesale merchants versus agents.
- **Ownership of establishments** — manufacturers' sales branches versus independent merchants and agents.
- **Range of services offered** — full-service wholesalers versus limited-service firms.
- **Depth and breadth of the line carried** — general-line wholesalers (drugs, hardware) versus specialty firms (frozen foods, dairy products).

### Customers of Wholesaling Intermediaries

One might expect that total retail sales would be considerably higher than total wholesale trade, because the retail price of a given product is higher than the wholesale price. Also, many products sold at retail never pass through a wholesaler's establishment and so are excluded from total wholesale sales.

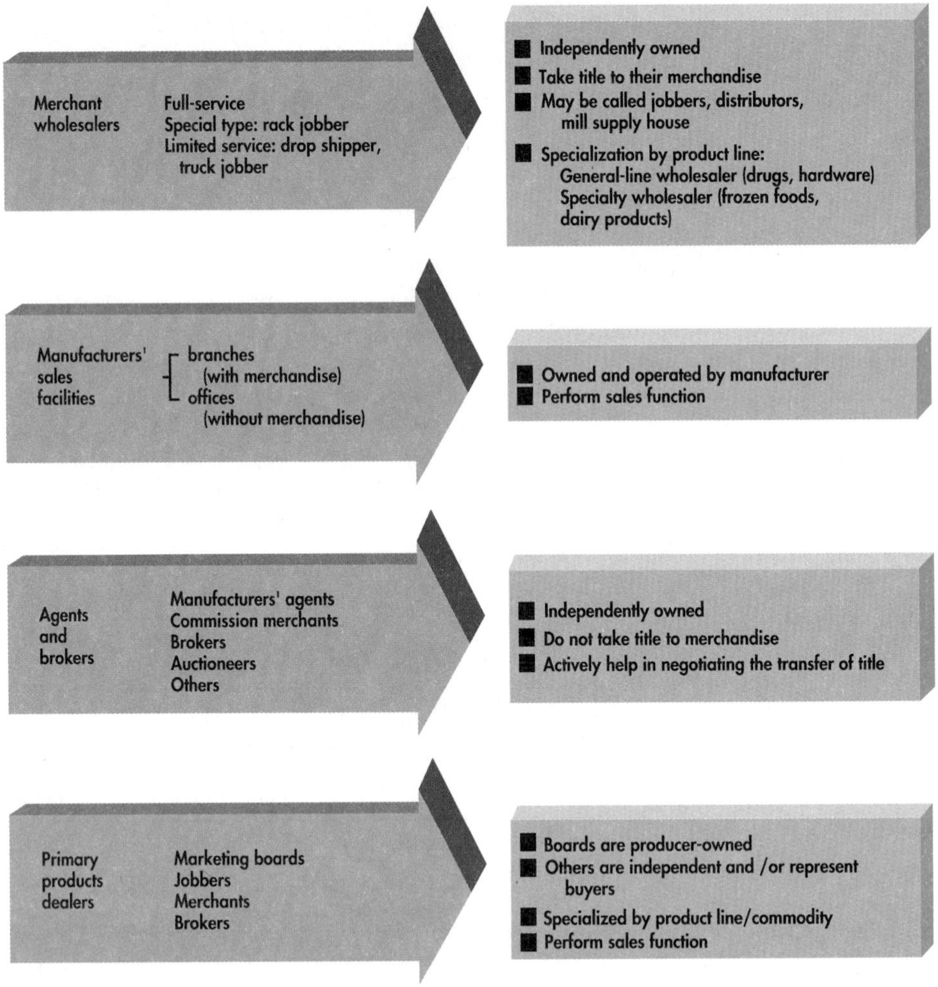


**FIGURE 16-2**
**Types of wholesaling institutions.**

Total sales figures belie this particular line of reasoning (see Table 16-2). In each year, the volume of wholesale trade is considerably higher than total retail sales.

The explanation for this situation may be found in an analysis of the customers of wholesaling intermediaries (see Figure 16-3).

Most wholesale merchants' sales are made to customers other than retailers. That is, large quantities of business and industrial products are now sold through wholesale merchants. Moreover, sales by the other types of wholesaling intermediaries show this same pattern. Thus, overall, sales to retailers account for much less than total sales by wholesale merchants.

Another trend that has become obvious in recent years is the increase in the percentage of consumer goods sold directly to retailers by manufacturers. Yet, in spite of this increased bypassing of the wholesaler, wholesaling is on the increase, an indication of the usefulness of wholesaling to the business world.

## Operating Expenses and Profits of Wholesaling Intermediaries

The average total operating expenses for wholesaling intermediaries combined has been estimated at about 17 percent of *wholesale* sales. It has also been estimated that operating expenses of retailers average about 25 percent of *retail* sales (omitting bars and restaurants, which do some processing of products). Therefore, on a broad average, the expenses of wholesaling intermediaries take less than 8 percent of the consumer's dollar.

TABLE 16-2 Total wholesale and retail trade, selected years

| Year | Wholesale Trade | Retail Trade |
|---|---|---|
| 1980 | 128,932.6 | 84,026.6 |
| 1982 | 170,061.0 | 97,638.5 |
| 1984 | 213,747.5 | 116,079.9 |
| 1986 | 171,848.5 | 146,734.7 |
| 1987 | 191,637.1 | 156,713.9 |
| 1990 | 310,431.2 | 192,558.2 |
| 1992 | 287,243.0 | 184,895.4 |

Source: Statistics Canada, *Market Research Handbook*, cat. no. 63-224; Canadian Statistical Review, cat. no. 11-003E; *Corporate Financial Statistics*, cat. no. 61-207; and *Wholesale Trade Statistics*, cat. no. 63-226 (various years). Reproduced with permission of Supply and Services Canada.

**FIGURE 16-3 Wholesale trade customers.**

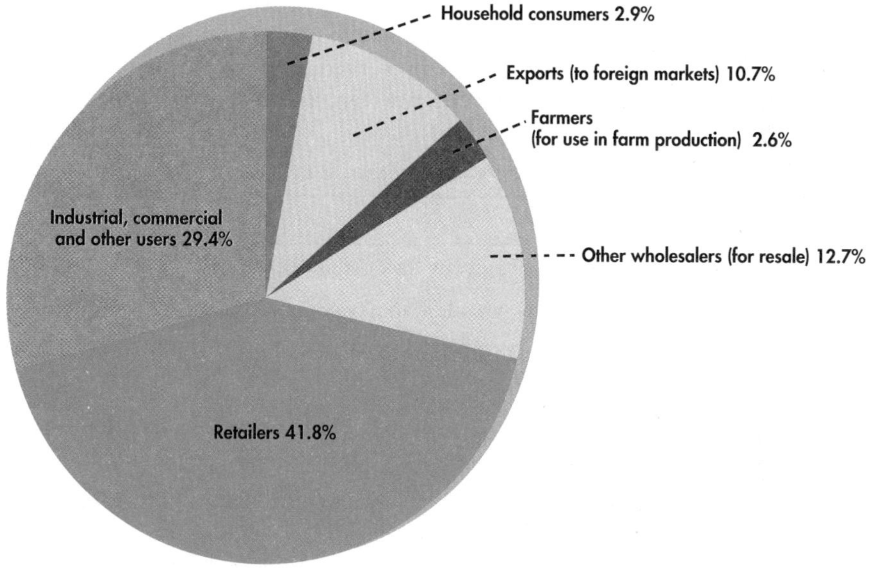


Net operating profit after taxes, expressed as a percentage of total income, is extremely modest for wholesaling intermediaries and is considerably lower than that for retailing intermediaries. The most current data collected by Statistics Canada from wholesalers showed an average after-tax profit of only 1.7 percent. This compares with an average of 3.3 percent profit after taxes among retailers. The highest after-tax profits were reported by wholesalers of motor vehicles and parts. Several categories of wholesalers reported after-tax profits of less than 1.5 percent of total income. These included petroleum wholesalers and those engaged in the wholesaling of paper, food, and livestock products.

## MERCHANT WHOLESALERS

Wholesale merchants are the wholesaling intermediaries that take title to the products they handle, and they account for the largest segment of wholesale trade.

### Full-Service Wholesalers

An independent merchant intermediary that performs a full range of wholesaling functions (from creating assortments to warehousing) is a **full-service wholesaler**. This type of intermediary may handle consumer and/or business products that may be manufactured or nonmanufactured (such as grown or extracted), and imported, exported, or made and sold domestically.

Full-service wholesalers comprise the majority of merchant wholesaling intermediaries. They have held their own in competitive struggles with other forms of indirect distribution, including manufacturers' sales facilities and agent wholesaling intermediaries. Actually, there has been an increase in full-service wholesalers' share of wholesale trade. But this trend may be a bit misleading. While full-service wholesalers have made gains in some industries, they have lost ground in others.

Individual manufacturers in some industries have begun to distribute their products directly, eliminating some or all of the wholesalers in their channels. Amana Refrigeration, a maker of home appliances, decided to end its relationships with merchant wholesalers and deal directly with appliance retailers. Obviously, this action displeased — and perhaps devastated — many wholesalers that had carried the Amana line.[3]

Full-service wholesalers survive and prosper by providing services needed by both their customers and producers. These services are summarized in Table 16-3. Large wholesalers use their clout to obtain good prices from producers. They also apply the latest technology to develop computerized inventory systems for their customers. By helping customers keep their inventories lean, a full-service intermediary can garner added loyalty.

TABLE 16-3 Full-service wholesalers' typical services to customers and to producers

| Service | Description |
|---|---|
| **Buying** | **Act as purchasing agent for customers.** |
| **Creating assortments** | **Buy from many suppliers to develop an inventory matching needs of customers.** |
| **Subdividing** | **Buy in large quantities (such as a truckload) and then resell in smaller quantities (such as a dozen).** |
| **Selling** | **Provide a sales force for producers to reach small retailers and other businesses, at a lower cost than producers would incur by having their own sales forces.** |
| **Transportation** | **Make quick, frequent deliveries to customers, reducing customers' risks and investment in inventory.** |
| **Warehousing** | **Store products in facilities that are nearer customers' locations than are manufacturing plants.** |
| **Financing** | **Grant credit to customers, reducing their capital requirements. Aid producers by ordering and paying for products before purchase by customers.** |
| **Risk taking** | **Reduce a producer's risk by taking title to products.** |
| **Market information** | **Supply information to customers about new products and producers' special offers and to producer-suppliers about customers' needs and competitors' activities.** |
| **Management assistance** | **Assist customers, especially small retailers, in areas such as inventory control, allocation of shelf space, and financial management.** |

### Other Merchant Wholesalers

We should also consider two types of merchant wholesalers with distinctive operations:

- **Truck jobbers**, also called *truck distributors*, carry a selected line of perishable products and deliver them by truck to retail stores. Truck jobbers are common in the food-products field. Each jobber carries a nationally advertised brand of fast-moving, perishable or semiperishable goods, such as candies, dairy products, potato chips, and tobacco products. Truck jobbers furnish fresh products so frequently that retailers can buy perishable goods in small amounts to minimize the risk of loss. But truck jobbers are saddled with high operating costs, caused primarily by the small order size and inefficient use of their trucks (for example, only during parts of the day).

- **Drop shippers**, also known as *desk jobbers*, sell merchandise for delivery directly *from the producer to the customer*. Drop shippers do not physically handle the product. They are common in only several product categories, including coal, lumber, and building materials, that are typically sold in very large quantities and that have high freight costs in relation to their unit value.

## AGENT WHOLESALERS

As distinguished from merchant wholesalers, agent wholesalers (1) do *not* take title to products and (2) typically perform fewer services. Agent wholesalers receive a commission intended to cover their expenses and to provide a profit. Commission rates vary greatly, ranging from about 3 to 10 percent, depending mainly on the nature of the product and the services performed.

Agent wholesalers have lost one-third of their wholesale trade since the late 1960s. In the case of agricultural products, agents are being replaced by merchant wholesalers or by direct sales to food-processing companies and grocery stores. Likewise, for manufactured goods, agents are being replaced by merchant wholesalers or direct distribution. As shown in Table 16-4, product characteristics and market conditions determine whether a distribution channel should include agent or merchant wholesalers.

On the basis of sales volume, the most significant types of agent wholesalers are manufacturers' agents, brokers, and commission merchants. These three types as well as several special types of agent wholesalers are described next.

TABLE 16-4 Factors suggesting which type of wholesaling intermediaries should be used in a channel

| Factors | Favouring agent wholesalers | Favouring merchant wholesalers |
|---|---|---|
| **Nature of product** | **Nonstandard, perhaps made to order** | **Standard** |
| **Technicality of product** | **Simple** | **Complex** |
| **Product's gross margin** | **Small** | **Relatively large** |
| **Number of customers** | **Few** | **Many** |
| **Concentration of customers** | **Concentrated geographically and in a few industries** | **Dispersed geographically and in many industries** |
| **Frequency of ordering** | **Relatively infrequently** | **Frequently** |
| **Time between order and receipt of shipment** | **Customer satisfied with relatively long lead time** | **Customer requires or desires shorter lead time** |

Source: Adapted from Donald M. Jackson and Michael F. d'Amico, "Products and Markets Served by Distributors and Agents," *Industrial Marketing Management*, February 1989, pp. 27-33.

### Manufacturers' Agents

An independent agent wholesaler that sells part or all of a manufacturer's product mix in an assigned geographic territory is a **manufacturers' agent**, or *manufacturers' representative*. Agents are not employees of the manufacturers; they are independent business firms.

Still, they have little or no control over prices and terms of sale, which are established by the manufacturers they represent.

Because a manufacturers' agent sells in a limited territory, each producer uses multiple agents for full coverage of its markets. Manufacturers' reps have continuing, year-round relationships with the companies (often called principals) they represent. Each agent usually serves several noncompeting manufacturers of related products. For example, a manufacturers' agent may specialize in toys and carry an assortment of noncompeting lines in board games, dolls, learning materials, and outdoor play equipment.

When a manufacturer finds it is not feasible to have its own sales force, a manufacturers' agent is often practical. An agent can be cost-effective because its major expenses (travel and lodging) are spread over a number of product lines. Also, producers pay agents a commission, which is a percentage of sales volume, so agents are paid only for what they actually sell.

Manufacturers' agents are used extensively in distributing many types of consumer and business goods, ranging from sporting goods to heating and air-conditioning vents and ductwork. Their main service to manufacturers is selling. Because a manufacturers' agent does not carry nearly as many lines as a full-service wholesaler, an agent can be expected to provide knowledgeable, aggressive selling.

Manufacturers' agents are most helpful to:

- A small firm that has a limited number of products and no sales force.
- A business that wants to add a new and possibly unrelated line to its existing product mix, but its present sales force either is not experienced in the new line or cannot reach the new market. In this situation, a company's own sales force and its agents may cover the same geographic market, but for different product lines.
- A firm that wants to enter a new market that is not yet sufficiently developed to warrant the use of its own sales force.

There are limitations to what manufacturers' agents do. Agents do not carry an inventory of merchandise, usually do not install machinery and equipment, and typically are not equipped to furnish customers with extensive technical advice or repair service.

Depending on how difficult the product is to sell and whether it is stocked by the agent, operating expenses of manufacturers' agents can vary greatly. However, they average about 7 percent of sales. Some reps operate on a commission as low as 2 percent of net sales; others earn as much as 20 percent; the average is about 5.5 percent.

### Brokers

Brokers ordinarily neither physically handle products being distributed nor work on a continuing basis with sellers or buyers. Instead, a **broker** is an independent agent wholesaler that brings buyers and sellers together and provides market information to either party. It furnishes information about many topics, including prices, products, and general market conditions. In recent years, manufacturers' agents and brokers have become more similar with respect to attributes and services.

Most brokers work for sellers, although some represent buyers. Brokers have no authority to set prices. They simply negotiate a sale and leave it up to the seller to accept or reject the buyer's offer.

Brokers are used in selling real estate and securities, but they are most prevalent in the food field. For example, a seafood broker handles the output from a salmon cannery, which operates only about three months each year. The canner employs a broker to find buyers among retail stores, wholesalers, and other outlets. When the entire output has been sold, the canner-broker relationship is discontinued — although it may be renewed the next year.

## MARKETING AT WORK

### FILE 16-2 AN INTERNATIONAL PERSPECTIVE ON "UNAUTHORIZED DISTRIBUTION"

Products distributed by wholesaling intermediaries do not always wind up where their manufacturers intend. Occasionally products are sold through distribution channels that are not authorized by the manufacturer. This practice, called *grey marketing*, usually involves products made in one country and destined for sale in another country.

Cameras, computer disc drives, perfumes, cars, liquor, and personal computers are among the diverse products that are sold through grey markets. Ordinarily, grey marketing arises when a product with a well-known brand name carries different prices under different circumstances. For example, a product's wholesale price may vary depending on the country to which it is sold or the quantity purchased.

Grey marketing takes many forms. Usually, a wholesaling intermediary, such as an import or export agent, purchases a product made in one country and agrees to distribute it in a second country, but instead diverts the product to a third country (sometimes Canada). Because the product typically is sold at a discount in a reputable outlet, not on the "black market" or from the trunks of cars, it isn't apparent that normal distribution has not been used.

So what's wrong with grey marketing? After spending time and money to promote the product, authorized distributors lose sales to other distributors selling the same product through the grey market. Manufacturers then have to placate their authorized distributors. Grey marketing disrupts a producer's distribution and pricing strategies. And when consumers buy products through the grey market, they may wind up without warranties or service contracts valid in Canada.

Still, some parties (but definitely not authorized distributors) see benefits in grey marketing. Unauthorized distributors are able to sell products they normally cannot acquire. To sell excess output, some manufacturers quietly participate in, or at least do not discourage, grey marketing. Consumers pay lower prices for popular products and may also find them at more outlets.

Most manufacturers would like to eliminate grey marketing. However, some have concluded that it's too difficult and costly to fight. Other producers try to minimize grey marketing by revising price schedules and distribution policies and taking unauthorized distributors to court. Grey marketing represents one more challenge for both producers and wholesaling intermediaries.

Sources: Robert E. Weigand, "Parallel Import Channels — Options for Preserving Territorial Integrity," *Columbia Journal of World Business*, Spring 1991, pp. 53-60; Peter Engardio et al., "There's Nothing Black-and-White about the Gray Market," *Business Week*, November 7, 1988, pp. 172-173ff ; and Larry S. Lowe and Kevin McCrohan, "Gray Markets in the United States," *Journal of Consumer Marketing*, Winter 1988, pp. 45-51.

Brokers provide limited services and, as a result, incur fairly low expenses, about 3 percent of sales. Likewise, they receive relatively small commissions — normally less than 5 percent.

### Other Agent Wholesalers

Four additional types of agent wholesalers account for smaller shares of wholesale trade than manufacturers' reps and brokers. Nevertheless, they provide valuable services for certain products and in specific markets. These intermediaries are:

- **Commission merchants**, common in the marketing of many agricultural products, set prices and terms of sale, sell the product, and perhaps physically handle it. (Despite the word *merchant*, a commission merchant is an *agent* wholesaler that normally does not take title to the products being handled and sold.)
- **Auction companies** help assembled buyers and sellers complete their transactions. They provide (1) auctioneers who do the selling and (2) physical facilities for displaying the sellers' products. Although they make up only about 1 percent of total wholesale trade, auction companies are extremely important in the wholesaling of used cars and certain agricultural products (such as tobacco, livestock, and fruit).

- **Selling agents** essentially substitute for a marketing department by marketing a manufacturer's entire output. Although selling agents transact only about 1 percent of wholesale trade, they play a key role in the distribution of textile products and coal and, to a lesser extent, apparel, food, lumber, and metal products.
- **Import-export agents** bring together sellers and buyers in different countries. Export agents work in the country in which the product is made; import agents are based in the country where the product will be sold.

## MARKETING AT WORK

### FILE 16-3 THE PERILS AND PLEASURES OF IMPORTING

Brian Taylor loves fast motorcycles so much that in the mid-1970s he dropped out of the engineering program at the University of Alberta to set up his own motorcycle shop in Cochrane, Alberta. When things went well, he moved to Calgary and became a dealer for Ducati, a popular line of Italian sports motorcycles. Working with Ducati taught Taylor something about dealing with foreign suppliers as he learned to adjust to Italy's haphazard working hours, uncertain dealer support, and frustrating bureaucracy. Yet it also whetted his appetite for more. It was the nineties now, and Taylor decided he'd like to stop being just a dealer and move into distribution. He decided to begin by adding to his Ducatis a line of Moto Guzzis, another top line of high-priced motorcycles made by Italy's GBM SpA.

The timing seemed perfect. Moto Guzzi's North American importer had retired several years before, leaving a gap on the market and die-hard motorcycle lovers in withdrawal. Through talking with dealers and potential customers, Taylor realized there was enough interest in Canada to make his scheme worthwhile. Now all he needed was to place his order, pay a tariff, and steer the motorcycles past the Canadian Department of Transport. Or so he thought.

Right off, he encountered difficulties trying to get four demo bikes into the country. Customs officials refused to let them past the border and relented only when he promised not to sell the bikes in Canada. Taylor was stuck with $60,000 worth of idle machines and heavy financing costs. In order to sell the bikes, he had to convert them to Ottawa's standards — a job that took $20,000 and 10 months' worth of effort, following 20-page regulation books, writing letters to Ottawa, and arranging for federal inspectors to visit his dealership on several occasions. Not only did Taylor have to install new $300 speedometers, but he required new windshields, reflectors, and special wiring for the headlights. Other conversions — such as bilingual vehicle identification numbers, safety warnings, and instructions, as well as a thorough series of brake tests — could be carried out only by the manufacturer in Italy. GBM grudgingly complied, but warned that it would make a special line of Canadian bikes only if Taylor could sell 100 a year. If he could sell only two or three, it wouldn't be worth it.

Taylor finally got permission for his company, Moto Italia of Canada Inc., to import and license Moto Guzzi products. Now Taylor had to assure himself that GBM was serious about entering the Canadian market and then convince the Italian company that he was the best person to handle its product. At first GBM was wary: "This industry is plagued with people who are enthusiastic, but don't have the business skills to stay alive. They drive us crazy." But after examining Taylor's business plans and financing, his drive and responsibility, the company decided to sign a contract with him.

Finally, after a year, expenditures totalling $500,000, six trips across Canada, and a voyage to Italy and back, Brian Taylor is now selling the fire-engine red Moto Guzzi machines. But to the countless other entrepreneurs, who, as devoted fans of exotic products, take the leap into importing them without a thought to the complex web of accompanying rules and regulations, Taylor offers this warning: "Anybody who is here for a quick buck has to be crazy. It's been a real headache."

Source: Adapted from Oliver Bertin, "Born to Be Riled," *Globe and Mail*, January 10, 1994, p. B6.

## NATURE AND IMPORTANCE OF PHYSICAL DISTRIBUTION

After a company establishes its channels of distribution, it must arrange for the physical distribution of its products through these channels. **Physical distribution**, which we use synonymously with *logistics*, consists of all the activities concerned with moving the right amount of the right products to the right place at the right time. In its full scope, physical distribution for manufacturers includes the flow of *raw materials* from their sources of supply to the production line *and* the movement of *finished goods* from the end of the production line to the final users' locations. Intermediaries manage the flows of goods *onto* their shelves as well as *from* their shelves to customers' homes, stores, or other places of business.

The activities making up physical distribution are:

- Inventory location and warehousing.
- Materials handling.
- Inventory control.
- Order processing.
- Transportation.

A decision regarding any one of these activities affects all the others. Location of a warehouse influences the selection of transportation methods and carriers; the choice of a carrier influences the optimum size of shipments.

### Increasing Attention to Physical Distribution

Through the years, management has made substantial progress in reducing production costs. Reductions have also been achieved in other costs of marketing. Physical distribution may be the last marketing area with substantial opportunities for cost cutting. And the potential savings are great. For certain products, such as furniture and building materials, the largest operating expenses are related to physical distribution. For other products, as much as one-half the wholesale cost is incurred in transportation and warehousing. For some businesses engaged in distribution, profits are small, so any savings are appreciated. A supermarket, for instance, may earn a net profit of 1 percent on sales. Thus every $1 a supermarket saves in physical distribution costs has the same effect on profit as a $100 increase in sales!

Effective physical distribution also can be the basis by which a firm gains and sustains a strong differential advantage. On-time delivery, which requires effective physical distribution, can provide a competitive edge. With that in mind, Caterpillar is able to deliver replacement parts within 72 hours for 99.7 percent of all orders.[4]

A business faces a problem (or maybe it's an opportunity) when it has a warehouse full of goods in Edmonton but unsatisfied customers in Calgary or too many ski parkas in Regina and too few in Winnipeg. These examples point up the importance of location in marketing, especially with respect to merchandise. That is, the appropriate assortment of products must be in the right place at the right time to maximize the opportunity for profitable sales. That's what physical distribution can help achieve.

Opportunities to cut costs, gain a competitive edge, and/or better satisfy customers expanded greatly around 1980 when marketing activities (notably pricing) in the transportation industries were freed from many federal and provincial regulations.[5] Previously, pricing by railroads, airlines, and trucking companies had been subject to restrictive regulations.

Since deregulation, transportation firms have been able to decide which rates (prices) and levels of service would best satisfy their target markets. For example, Challenger Motor Freight promises on-time deliveries and works hard to keep its promise. Toward this end, Challenger has equipped its trucks with satellite tracking devices that allow the company to monitor their progress and to communicate with its drivers. From another perspective, companies that ship goods shop around for rates and service levels that best meet their needs.

## Systems Approach to Physical Distribution

We have occasionally alluded to marketing as a *total system* of business action rather than a fragmented series of operations. Nowhere is this clearer than in physical distribution. But it has not always been this way. Traditionally, physical distribution activities were fragmented.

**In a deregulated environment, trucking companies are guaranteeing on-time delivery, competitive pricing, and delivery information.**

ROADWAY PACKAGE SYSTEM LTD
Flexible Pricing.
Fax Proofs of Delivery.
Accurate Shipment Information.
Your Customers Deserve This.
When your customers want special consideration, RPS is the answer. Thanks to the RPS bar code on every parcel, you get accurate and detailed shipment information, right up to delivery and afterward. Fast. Proofs of delivery by fax. Free. Delivery information the day after delivery. Flexible pricing. Plus RPS weighs and rates your parcels for you, and minimizes parcel paperwork. RPS has a high weight limit (100 lbs.), too. Your customers deserve this. For more information, call 1-800-762-3725.
RPS
We take care of business ... to business.


In many firms, physical distribution is still unco-ordinated. Managerial responsibility for it is delegated to various units that often have conflicting, perhaps opposite, goals. The production department, for instance, is interested primarily in long production runs to minimize unit manufacturing costs, even though the result may be high inventory costs. In contrast, the finance department wants a minimum of funds to be tied up in inventories. At the same time, the sales department wants to have a wide assortment of products available at locations near customers. Of course, there's always the temptation to select carriers with low rates, even though this may mean longer time in transit.

Unco-ordinated conditions like these make it impossible to achieve a flow of products that satisfies the firm's goals. However, the **systems approach to physical distribution** can bring together these individual activities in a unified way.

### The Total Cost Concept

As part of the systems approach to physical distribution, executives should apply the **total cost concept**. That is, a company should determine the set of activities that produces the best relationship between costs and profit for the *entire* physical distribution system. This approach is superior to focusing strictly on the separate costs of individual distribution activities.

Too often, a company attempts to minimize the cost of only one aspect of physical distribution — transportation, for example. Management might be upset by the high cost of air freight. But the higher costs of air freight may be more than offset by savings from (1) lower inventory costs, (2) less insurance and interest expense, (3) lower crating costs, and (4) fewer lost sales due to out-of-stock conditions. The point is *not* that air freight is the best method of transportation. Rather, the key point is that physical distribution should be viewed as a *total* process, with all the related costs being analyzed.

### Strategic Use of Physical Distribution

The strategic use of physical distribution may enable a company to strengthen its competitive position by providing more customer satisfaction and/or by reducing operating costs. The management of physical distribution can also affect a firm's marketing mix — particularly product planning, pricing, and distribution channels.[6] Each opportunity is described below.

**Improve Customer Service** A well-run logistics system can improve the service a firm provides its customers — whether they are intermediaries or ultimate users. Furthermore, the level of customer service directly affects demand. This is true especially in marketing undifferentiated products (such as chemicals and most building materials), where effective service may be a company's only differential advantage.

To ensure reliable customer service, management should set standards of performance for each subsystem of physical distribution. These standards should be quantitatively measurable. Some examples:

- Electronics manufacturer: Make delivery within seven days after receiving an order.
- Sporting goods wholesaler: Fill 98 percent of orders accurately.
- Industrial distributor: Maintain inventory levels that enable fulfilment of at least 85 percent of orders received from inventory on hand.

**Reduce Distribution Costs** Many avenues to cost reductions may be opened by effective physical distribution management. For example, eliminating unneeded warehouses will lower costs. Inventories — and their attendant carrying costs and capital investment — may be reduced by consolidating stocks at fewer locations.

**Create Time and Place Utilities** Storage, which is part of warehousing, creates *time utility*. Storage is essential to correct imbalances in the timing of production and consumption. An imbalance can occur when there is *year-round consumption* but only *seasonal production*, as in the case of agricultural products. For instance, time utility is created and value is added when bananas are picked green and allowed to ripen in storage. And skilful use of warehousing allows a producer to store a seasonal surplus so that it can be marketed long after the harvest has ended. In other instances warehousing helps adjust *year-round production* to *seasonal consumption*. A manufacturer may produce lawn mowers on a year-round basis; during the fall and winter, the mowers are stored for sale in the spring and summer.

Transportation adds value to products by creating *place utility*. A fine suit hanging on a manufacturer's rack in Montreal has less value than an identical suit displayed in a retailer's store in Vancouver. Transporting the suit creates place utility and adds value to it.

**Stabilize Prices** Careful management of warehousing and transportation can help stabilize prices for an individual firm or for an entire industry. If a market is temporarily glutted with a product, sellers can store it until supply and demand conditions are better balanced. Such use of warehousing facilities is common in the marketing of agricultural products and other seasonally produced goods. Moreover, the judicious movement of products from one market to another may enable a seller to (1) avoid a market with depressed prices or (2) take advantage of a market that has a shorter supply and higher prices. If demand for heating oil is stronger in Kamloops than in Kelowna, a producer should be able to achieve greater revenues by shifting some shipments from Kelowna to Kamloops.

**Influence Channel Decisions** Decisions regarding inventory management have a direct bearing on a producer's selection of channels and the location of intermediaries. Logistical considerations may become paramount, for example, when a company decides to decentralize its inventory. In this case management must determine (1) how many sites to establish and (2) whether to use wholesalers, the company's own warehouses, or public warehouses. One producer may select merchant wholesalers that perform storage and other warehousing services. Another may prefer to use a combination of (1) manufacturers' agents to provide aggressive selling and (2) public warehouses to distribute the products ordered.

**Minimize Shipping Costs** Managers with shipping responsibilities need to ensure that their companies enjoy the fastest routes *and* the lowest rates for whatever methods of transportation they use. The pricing of transportation services is one of the most complicated parts of North American business. The rate, or tariff, schedule is the carrier's price list. Typically it is complex; to cite one example, shipping rates vary for many different types of goods, depending on many factors including not only distance to the destination but also the bulk and weight of the products. Therefore, being able to interpret a tariff schedule properly is a money-saving skill for a manager with shipping responsibilities.

## MARKETING AT WORK

### FILE 16-4 LOGISTICS LESSONS FROM WAL-MART

Wal-Mart, Wal-Mart, Wal-Mart. . . The name seems to be on everybody's lips these days for it appears as if the giant U.S. discount retailer can do no wrong. While racking up the dollars and threatening to change the very nature of shopping as we know it, Wal-Mart has become a much venerated Marketing Muse, inspiring retailers all over Canada and leaving them begging to know the secrets of its success. George Stalk, Philip Evans, and Lawrence Shulman of the Boston Consulting Group uncovered some of these secrets in an article published in 1992 in *Harvard Business Review*.

When Wal-Mart was born, like any smart company, it was born with a vision that would motivate its every decision. In Wal-Mart's case, it was a complete dedication to fulfilling the needs of its customers that was to shape its goals: to provide customers with quality goods, to make these goods available where and when customers wanted them, to create a cost structure that would allow competitive pricing, and to develop a reputation for absolute trustworthiness. Of course, it is one thing to state such goals, and quite another to achieve them. Wal-Mart, however, hit on a valuable competitive strategy — "cross-docking." It was based on the way the company replenished its inventory, and it provided the nucleus for all its subsequent strategies.

A practically invisible logistics technique, "cross-docking" refers to a system whereby goods are constantly delivered to Wal-Mart's warehouses, where they are selected, repacked, and then transported to stores, often without having to sit in inventory. The expensive warehouse costs saved by simply moving rapidly moving products from one loading dock to another proved significant. This means that while bypassing the usual inventory and handling costs, Wal-Mart is able to reap the full savings that result from buying trucks carrying large volumes of goods. While competitor K mart is able to run only 50 percent of its goods through its warehouse system, Wal-Mart can boast that almost 90 percent of its products avoid these costs. Such savings reduce Wal-Mart's costs of sales by 2 to 3 percent, a significant difference that makes possible its strategy of everyday low prices.

These low prices in turn lead to further savings by eliminating the cost of frequent promotions, as well as stabilizing prices so that sales are more predictable, thus reducing stockouts and excess inventory. And, of course, low prices attract more customers, which means more sales per retail square foot.

If "cross-docking" is so successful, why don't all retailers use it? The reason is that it's very difficult to manage.

In order to make cross-docking work, Wal-Mart had to make strategic investments in a variety of interlocking support systems far beyond what could be justified by usual return-on-investment criteria. For example, cross-docking demands constant contact between Wal-Mart's distribution centres, suppliers, and every checkout in every store so that orders can flow in, be consolidated, and executed within a matter of mere hours. This could be done only by investing in a private satellite communication system that daily sends point-of-sale data directly to Wal-Mart's 4,000 vendors.

Another key investment was in the development of a rapid and responsive transportation system. Twenty distribution centres are serviced by a fleet of more than 2,000 company-owned trucks, allowing Wal-Mart to ship goods from warehouses to stores in less than 48 hours and to replenish store shelves twice a week, compared to the industry average of twice a month.

Finally, however, all the logistical facets of the cross-docking strategy could never have functioned if it weren't for the fundamental changes made on the management level. Traditionally in retail, decisions about merchandising, pricing, and promotions have remained in the highly centralized hands of a few corporate executives, but the very nature of cross-docking turned this command-and-control logic upside-down. For instead of the retailer pushing products into the system, cross-docking has customers "pulling" products when and where they need them. The upshot was a managerial style emphasizing frequent, informal co-operation between stores, distribution centres, and suppliers — with much less centralized control. Thus, instead of giving directives to individual store managers, senior managers at Wal-Mart are helping to create an environment where they can learn from the market — and from each other. In pursuing such goals, Wal-Mart has invested in information systems that provide store managers with detailed data about customer behaviour, while company airplanes regularly fly store managers to Wal-Mart's Bentonville, Arkansas, headquarters for conferences about market trends and merchandising.

In taking into account every aspect of the company's chain, Wal-Mart hasn't neglected the final link — its employees. Aware that its front-line employees play a pivotal role in satisfying customer needs, it has tried to improve motivation and a sense of teamwork by installing programs such as stock ownership and profit-sharing.

In Canada, Wal-Mart has contracted out its distribution services, marking a big change in approach. Toronto's Transcare supply chain management will run Wal-Mart's Canadian distribution. For Wal-Mart, while contracting out is new, and this puts extreme pressure on Transcare to be as good as Wal-Mart itself, it also means that if Transcare is successful, its British parent can be looking to work for Wal-Mart when it expands in Europe.

Source: Adapted from George Stalk, Philip Evans, and Lawrence Shulman, "Competing on Capabilities," *Harvard Business Review* 1992; and Paul Waldie, "Wal-Mart Revamps Distribution for Canada," *Financial Post*, March 30, 1994, p. 5.

## TASKS IN PHYSICAL DISTRIBUTION MANAGEMENT

*Physical distribution* refers to the actual physical flow of products. In contrast, **physical distribution management** is the development and operation of processes resulting in the effective and efficient physical flow of products. An effective physical distribution system is built around five interdependent subsystems: inventory location and warehousing, materials handling, inventory control, order processing, and transportation. Each must be carefully co-ordinated with the others.

### Inventory Location and Warehousing

The name of the game in physical distribution is inventory management. One important consideration is **warehousing**, which embraces a range of functions, such as assembling, dividing (bulk-breaking), and storing products and preparing them for reshipping. Management must also consider the size, location, and transporting of inventories. These four areas are interrelated. The number and locations of inventory sites, for example, influence inventory size and transportation methods. These interrelationships are often quite complex.

**Distribution Centres** An effective inventory-location strategy may involve the establishment of one or more **distribution centres**. Such facilities are planned around markets rather than transportation requirements. The idea is to develop under one roof an efficient, fully integrated system for the flow of products — taking orders, filling them, and preparing them for delivery to customers.

Distribution centres have been established by many well-known firms. They can cut distribution costs by reducing the number of warehouses, pruning excessive inventories, and eliminating out-of-stock conditions. Storage and delivery time have been cut to a minimum, recognizing the adage that companies are in business to *sell* goods, not to *store* them. IKEA, the Scandinavian furniture retailer, expanded very slowly in Canada and the United States because the company wanted to find locations and facilities that met the needs of its distribution centres.[7]

**Types of Warehouses** Any producer, wholesaler, or retailer has the option of operating its own private warehouse or using the services of a public warehouse. A **private warehouse** is more likely to be an advantage if (1) a company moves a large volume of products through a warehouse and (2) there is very little, if any, seasonal fluctuation in this flow.

**Distributors consider modern, efficient warehouses vital to their success.**

A **public warehouse** offers storage and handling facilities to individuals or companies. Public warehousing costs are a variable expense. Customers pay only for the space they use, and only when they use it. Public warehouses can also provide office and product display space, and accept and fill orders for sellers. Furthermore, warehouse receipts covering products stored in public warehouses may be used as collateral for bank loans.

### Materials Handling

Selecting the proper equipment to physically handle products, including the warehouse building itself, is the **materials handling** subsystem of physical distribution management. Equipment that is well matched to the task can minimize losses from breakage, spoilage, and theft. Efficient equipment can reduce handling costs as well as time required for handling.

Modern warehouses are often huge one-storey structures located in outlying areas where land is less expensive and loading platforms are easily accessed by trucks and trains. Conveyor belts, forklift trucks, and other mechanized equipment are used to move merchandise. In some warehouses the order fillers are even outfitted with roller skates!

**Containerization** is a cargo-handling system that has become standard practice in physical distribution. Shipments of products are enclosed in large metal or wood containers. The containers are then transported unopened from the time they leave the customer's facilities (such as a manufacturer's plant) until they reach their destination (such as a wholesaler's warehouse). Containerization minimizes physical handling, thereby reducing damage, lessening the risk of theft, and allowing for more efficient transportation.

### Inventory Control

Maintaining control over the size and composition of inventories, which represent a sizable investment for most companies, is essential to any physical distribution system. The goal of **inventory control** is to fill customers' orders promptly, completely, and accurately while minimizing both the investment and fluctuations in inventories.

#### Customer-Service Requirements

Inventory size is determined by balancing costs and desired levels of customer service. That is, what percentage of orders does the company expect to fill promptly from inventory on hand? Out-of-stock conditions result in lost sales, loss of goodwill, even loss of customers. Yet to be able to fill 100 percent of orders promptly may require an excessively large and costly inventory. Generally speaking, about 80 percent *more* inventory is required to fill 95 percent of the orders than to fill only 80 percent. For example, if a firm presently satisfies 80 percent of its requests by stocking 20,000 units, it would have to increase its inventory to 36,000 units to improve its rate of order fulfilment to 95 percent.

Perhaps the greatest boon to inventory control in recent years has been improvements in computer technology. These advancements have enabled management to shorten the order delivery time *and* substantially reduce the size of inventories. Canadian Tire is one of countless firms that has benefited from computer-based inventory control. Through its inventory-control system, goods reach the selling floor much more quickly when they are reordered electronically than they would under conventional inventory ordering systems.

#### Economic Order Quantity

Management must establish the optimal quantity for reorder when it is time to replenish inventory stocks. The **economic order quantity** (EOQ) is the volume at which the sum of inventory-carrying costs and order-processing costs are at a minimum. Typically, as order size increases, (1) inventory-carrying cost goes up (because the average inventory is larger) and (2) order-processing cost declines (because there are fewer orders).

In Figure 16-4, point EOQ represents the order quantity having the lowest total cost. Actually, the order quantity that a firm considers best (or optimal) often is larger than the EOQ. That's because management must try to balance the sometimes conflicting goals of low inventory costs and responsive customer service. For various reasons, such as gaining a differential advantage, a firm may place a higher priority on customer service than inventory costs. To completely fill orders in a timely manner may well call for a larger order quantity than the EOQ — for example, quantity X in Figure 16-4.

**FIGURE 16-4 Economic order quantity.**

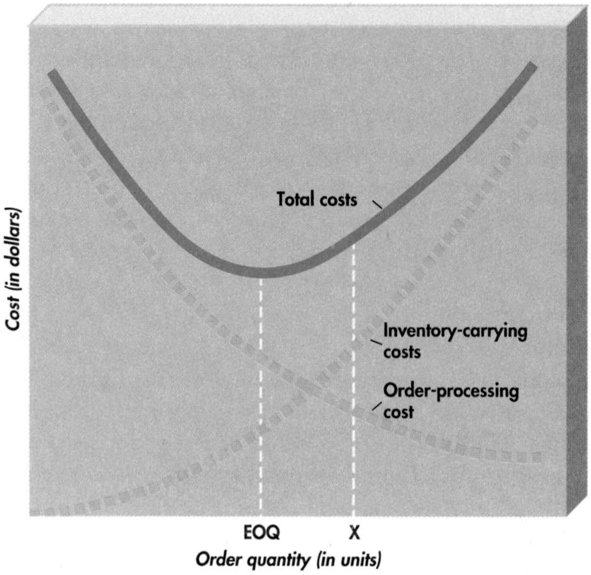


Just-in-Time A popular form of inventory control, purchasing, and production scheduling is the **just-in-time** (JIT) concept. The idea of JIT is that you buy in small quantities that arrive *just in time* for production and then produce in quantities *just in time* for sale. JIT has commanded the attention of *top* management — not just marketing or physical distribution management — in many North American companies.

When effectively implemented, the just-in-time concept has many benefits. By purchasing in small quantities and maintaining low inventory levels of parts and finished goods, a company can achieve dramatic cost savings because fewer items are damaged, stolen, or otherwise become unusable. Production and delivery schedules can be shortened and made more flexible and reliable. The Japanese have found that quality improves with JIT purchasing. When order quantities are small and deliveries frequent, a company can more quickly spot and then correct a quality problem in the products received.[8]

The JIT concept was adopted rather slowly in North America. The reasons are attributable largely to cultural differences between North America and Japan. Unlike Japan, channel relationships in the United States historically were adversarial, with each party negotiating forcefully to gain an advantage. Also, many North American producers felt more secure with a large inventory of parts and supplies. Suppliers, on the other hand, feared being cut off if producers relied on only one or a few sources of supply.

In Canada and the United States, the JIT philosophy was first adopted in the auto industry. But the concept has been picked up by leading firms in other industries, such as IBM, Xerox, Apple, Black & Decker, and General Electric. For some firms the results have been quite positive. Xerox eliminated 4,700 suppliers in one year, and Black & Decker cut more than 50 percent of its suppliers in two years.[9] A producer that relies on JIT tends to use fewer suppliers because they must be close to the producer's facilities and also because there must be strong partnerships with suppliers, which is not feasible with large numbers of suppliers. Channel members — even entire channels — that employ JIT effectively can gain a differential advantage. As JIT becomes widespread, firms or channels that ignore it risk a differential disadvantage.[10] Ford of Canada's JIT strategy allows it to bring to St. Thomas, Ontario, 2,600 different types of auto parts from every continent except Africa to allow it to assemble the Crown Victoria and the Mercury Grand Marquis.

### Order Processing

Still another part of the physical distribution system is a set of procedures for receiving, handling, and filling orders. This **order processing** subsystem should include provisions for billing, granting credit, preparing invoices, and collecting past-due accounts. Consumer ill will results if a company makes mistakes or is slow in filling orders. That's why more and more firms have turned to computers to execute most of their order-processing activities.

At the same time, some suppliers are providing retail stores with computer technology to use in placing orders. For example, a large distributor of drugs and health and beauty aids has equipped drugstores with handheld electronic devices. Orders assembed using such devices are transmitted to the wholesaler by telephone and can usually be assembled and shipped within 24 hours.

By providing customers with technology that assists them in placing orders, a supplier can gain in several ways. The orders are likely to be free of errors, increasing both the accuracy and efficiency of order processing. If better computer technology reduces the number of out-of-stock items at the next level of the distribution channel, then the supplier's sales should increase. For example, if a wholesaler's computer system aids rapid replenishment of a retailer's shelves and that contributes to greater sales at the retail level, manufacturers stand to gain through added sales from the wholesaler. Moreover, to the extent that improved technology produces time savings or other benefits for employees of the ordering firm, the customer is likely to exhibit loyalty to the supplier.

### Transportation

A major function of the physical distribution system in many companies is **transportation** — shipping products to customers. Management must decide on both the **mode of transportation** and the particular carriers. In this discussion we will focus on *intercity* shipments.

#### Major Modes

Railroads, trucks, ships, and airplanes are the leading modes of transportation. In Table 16-4 these four methods are compared on the basis of criteria likely to be used by physical distribution managers in selecting a mode of transportation. Of course, the comparisons in the table are generalizations, and the ratings of alternative modes of transportation can vary from one manager to the next, even within the same buying centre in an organization.[11]

The relative use of each of the four major modes is shown in Figure 16-5. Virtually all intracity freight movements are made by truck. The use of trucks has expanded greatly over the past 40 years while railway transport has declined.

#### Intermodal Transportation

When two or more modes of transportation are used to move freight, this is termed **intermodal transportation**. The intent of intermodal transportation is to seize the advantages of multiple forms of transportation.

One type of intermodal transportation involves trucks and railroads. So-called **piggyback service** involves carrying truck trailers on railroad flatcars. This type of intermodal transportation provides (1) more flexibility than railroads alone can offer, (2) lower freight costs than trucks alone, and (3) less handling of goods.

A similar type of intermodal transportation combines ships or barges with either railroads or trucks, or both. One version of **fishyback service** transports loaded trailers on barges or ships. The trailers may be carried piggyback fashion by railroad to the dock, where they are transferred to the ship. Then, at the other end of the water trip, the trailers are loaded back onto trains for completion of the haul. In an alternative use of the fishyback service, merchandise is trucked directly to ports, where the trailer vans are loaded on barges. At the end of the water journey, the vans are trucked to the receiving station.

TABLE 16-4 Comparison of transportation methods

| | Transportation method | | | |
|---|---|---|---|---|
| Selection criteria | Rail | Water | Highway | Air |
| Speed (door-to-door time) | Medium | Slowest | Fast | Fastest |
| Cost of transportation | Medium | Lowest | High | Highest |
| Reliability in meeting delivery schedules | Medium | Poor | Good | Good |
| Variety of products carried | Widest | Widest | Medium | Somewhat limited |
| Number of geographic locations served | Very many | Limited | Unlimited | Many |
| Most suitable products | Long hauls of carload quantities of bulky products, when freight costs are high in relation to product's value | Bulky, low value non-perishables | Short hauls of high-value goods | High-value perishables, where speed of delivery is all-important |

**FIGURE 16-5 Expenditure on transportation services as of third quarter, 1993 at annualized rate.**

AS A % OF DOMESTIC TRANSPORTATION INDUSTRY

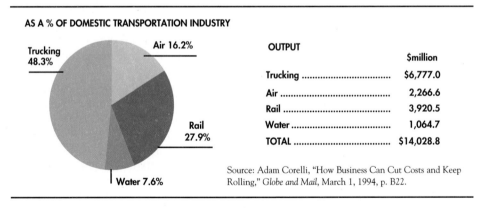

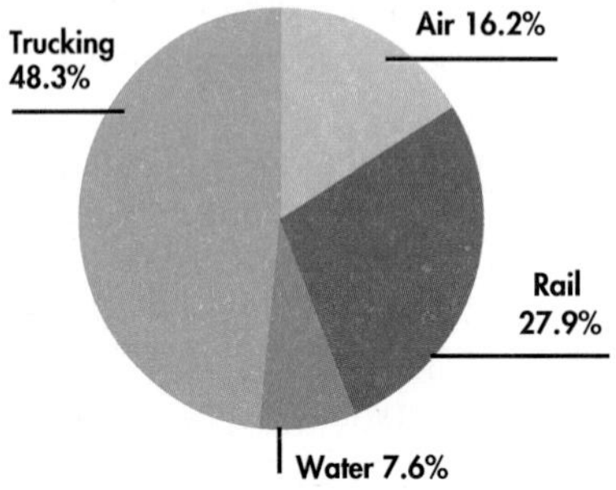


OUTPUT

| | $million |
|---|---|
| Trucking | $6,777.0 |
| Air | 2,266.6 |
| Rail | 3,920.5 |
| Water | 1,064.7 |
| TOTAL | $14,028.8 |

Source: Adam Corelli, "How Business Can Cut Costs and Keep Rolling," *Globe and Mail*, March 1, 1994, p. B22.

Freight Forwarders A specialized marketing institution serving firms that ship in less-than-carload quantities is called a **freight forwarder**. Its main function is to consolidate less-than-carload or less-than-truckload shipments from several shippers into carload and truckload quantities. The freight forwarder picks up the merchandise at the shipper's place of business and arranges for delivery at the buyer's door. A small shipper benefits from the speed and minimum handling associated with large shipments. A freight forwarder also provides the small shipper with traffic management services, such as selecting the best transportation methods and routes.

Package-Delivery Firms A major development of the past 25 years has been the formation of companies that deliver small shipments of packages and high-priority mail. You certainly are familiar with United Parcel Service (UPS), Federal Express (Fed Ex), and Loomis. All these firms compete directly with Canada Post.

## MARKETING AT WORK

### FILE 16-5 HOW MUCH PACKAGING IS ENOUGH?

One factor that determines in large part whether a shipment arrives unharmed is the type and amount of protective materials and wrapping used in preparing the package for shipment. Of course, if too much protection is used (thereby adding weight or bulk), the shipping cost goes up. Likewise, too much protection needlessly consumes natural resources (particularly trees) used in making protective materials and wrapping.

To assist customers in determining the optimal type and amount of protective packaging, United Parcel Service evaluates the packages of over 10,000 of its customers yearly. More than 100 UPS employees conduct the tests, aided by a variety of testing equipment. For instance, to determine whether a package will stand up to vibration, one device simulates the actual movement of a package in a tractor trailer during a long haul. Another piece of equipment is a drop-tester — the name suggests its function.

The results are used to develop guidelines regarding the amount and type of protective packaging that will ensure safe transit of a package. According to a UPS executive, the main goal of the testing program is "to minimize waste and maximize protection." To the extent that the program is successful, the company, its customers, *and the environment* all benefit.

Besides conservation of natural resources, what other benefits could UPS and its customers derive from this program of testing protective packaging?

Source: Tim Miniban, "UPS Gets Wrapped Up Building a Better Package," *Purchasing*, November 21, 1991, pp. 49, 51.

In many respects, these companies offer the same services as freight forwarders. However, whereas the typical freight forwarder does not have its own transportation equipment, package-delivery firms do. Companies such as UPS and Fed Ex essentially are integrated as cargo airlines and trucking companies. Furthermore, package-delivery firms, in effect, use intermodal transportation. Consider Fed Ex, for example. A package is picked up by truck, shipped intercity or overseas by plane, and delivered locally by truck.

## WHOLESALING AND PHYSICAL DISTRIBUTION IN THE FUTURE

To survive and prosper in the future, wholesaling intermediaries and physical distribution firms will have to identify and respond to certain trends in their operating environments.

### Trends in Wholesaling

Wholesaling intermediaries can expect serious challenges to their roles in the distribution process, including:

- Direct distribution where suppliers and customers bypass wholesaling intermediaries and deal directly with each other. In a weak economy, like the recent recession, manufacturers may seek to cut costs by eliminating intermediaries — often an agent.[12] (Of course, there's no guarantee that such a move will result in lower distribution costs.) In late 1991, Wal-Mart announced that it would stop dealing with intermediaries and do business directly with manufacturers in many cases. Intermediaries (especially manufacturers' reps and brokers) and their supporters claimed Wal-Mart took this step to obtain lower merchandise costs by eliminating intermediaries' markups or commissions. Wal-Mart contended the switch was made to ensure it has sufficient inventory.[13]
- Development of new wholesaling institutions that serve suppliers and customers in new and more satisfying ways. One fairly new institution is the **service merchandiser**, a merchant wholesaler that supplies retail stores (particularly supermarkets and other grocery stores) with nonfood items ranging from health and beauty products to automotive supplies.

- Continuing growth of vertical marketing systems. Producers and their customers, either intermediaries or end users, are forming various kinds of partnerships, which ordinarily are the administered type of system. For example, VWR Scientific Corp. sells glass beakers and lab equipment to Du Pont; however, the relationship goes a major step further in that the two firms' computer systems are linked for better inventory management.[14]
- The quest for improved quality and/or enhanced technology to maintain competitiveness and boost profits. This trend is most evident among merchant wholesalers that are providing added training to employees to improve customer service.

The total number of merchant wholesalers may decline due to mergers and acquisitions. Even large wholesalers are feeling the urge to merge. Some distributors believe they need to be larger to maintain their competitive edge. Smaller wholesalers will have to decide whether they intend to acquire, be acquired, or somehow isolate themselves from this trend — perhaps by serving small market niches.

For the foreseeable future, even if the number of merchant wholesalers does drop, they are likely to grab a larger share of total wholesale trade away from agent wholesaling intermediaries and manufacturers' sales facilities.

## Trends in Physical Distribution

Physical distribution management faces tremendous challenges and opportunities. Some will emanate from inside companies, while others will emerge from outside companies:

- The need for better co-ordination of physical distribution activities in most firms. Essentially, this is an organizational problem. If you ask, "Who's in charge of physical distribution?" too often the answer is "No one." To alleviate this problem, a number of firms are establishing separate departments responsible for all physical distribution activities. Even when this occurs in large firms, physical distribution usually is separated from the marketing department. This separation causes problems when a company is trying to formulate co-ordinated marketing strategies, including physical distribution.[15]
- The emergence or rejuvenation of firms providing specialized services related to physical distribution. One example is short-line railroads, each of which averages only 100 km of track. Since deregulation began, short-line railroads have sometimes picked up routes abandoned by CN or CP.

**What used to be a truck rental company now handles complex logistics for its customers.**

- The increasing — and necessary — applications of technology. Various forms of technology, particularly computers, are transforming the way various physical distribution activities are carried out. For instance, on-board computers (including rotating satellite antennas) allow trucking companies to monitor the progress of shipments.
- To gain strength in the field of physical distribution, some firms are forming logistics alliances. Under such an arrangement — called outsourcing — a manufacturer and one or more firms conducting specialized physical distribution activities join together to plan and implement the physical flows that will get the right goods to the right places in the right amounts at the right time. This type of alliance extends beyond normal business co-operation in several ways, including the ongoing nature of the relationship. Sears Business Systems has formed a logistics alliance with Itel Distribution Systems, and Procter & Gamble has done likewise.[16] Wal-Mart in Canada took an outsourcing approach for goods delivery unlike its method in the United States.

## SUMMARY

Wholesaling consists of the sale, and all activities directly related to the sale, of goods and services for resale, use in producing other goods or services, or for operating an organization. Firms engaged primarily in wholesaling, called wholesaling intermediaries, provide economies of skill, scale, and transactions to other firms involved in distribution.

Four categories of wholesaling intermediaries are: merchant wholesalers, agent wholesalers, primary products dealers, and manufacturers' sales facilities. The first two are independent firms; the last is owned by a manufacturer. Merchant wholesalers take title to products being distributed; agent wholesalers do not.

Merchant wholesalers, whose share of wholesale trade has increased in recent years, include both full-service and limited-service wholesalers. Of the major categories of wholesaling intermediaries, merchant wholesalers offer the widest range of services and consequently incur the highest operating expenses.

Agent wholesalers have lost ground to merchant wholesalers over the past several decades. The main types of agent wholesalers are manufacturers' agents and brokers. Because they perform more limited services, agent wholesalers' expenses tend to be lower than merchant wholesalers'.

Physical distribution is the flow of products from supply sources to the firm and then from the firm to its customers. The goal of physical distribution is to move the right amount of the right products to the right place at the right time. Physical distribution costs are a substantial part of total operating costs in many firms. Moreover, physical distribution is probably the only remaining source of possible cost reductions in many companies.

Although physical distribution activities are still fragmented operationally and organizationally in many firms, they should be treated as a system. The total cost concept should be applied to physical distribution — that is, the focus should be on the cost of physical distribution in its entirety, rather than on the costs of individual elements. However, management should strive *not* for the lowest total cost of physical distribution, but for the best balance between customer service and total cost. Effective management of physical distribution can help a company gain an advantage over competitors through better customer service and/or lower operating costs.

The operation of a physical distribution system requires management's attention and decision making in five areas: (1) inventory location and warehousing, (2) materials handling, (3) inventory control, (4) order processing, and (5) transportation. They should not be treated as individual activities but as interrelated components within a physical distribution system. Effective management of these five activities requires an understanding of distribution centres, economic order quantity, just-in-time processes, and intermodal transportation.

In the future, wholesaling intermediaries and physical distribution firms will face challenges to their roles in the distribution process. However, enterprising companies in the wholesaling and physical distribution fields will be able to seize profitable business opportunities. The challenges and opportunities include the continuing growth of vertical marketing systems, ongoing deregulation of transportation industries, mergers and acquisitions, and enhanced quality and technology. To succeed, wholesaling and physical distribution firms will have to monitor trends in distribution as well as their broader operating environments and then develop effective marketing strategies.

## KEY TERMS AND CONCEPTS

**Wholesaling (468)**
**Wholesaling intermediary (469)**
**Merchant wholesaler (470)**
**Manufacturer's sales branch and office (470)**
**Agents and brokers (471)**
**Full-service wholesaler (473)**
**Truck jobber (474)**
**Drop shipper (475)**
**Manufacturers' agent (manufacturers' representative) (475)**
**Broker (476)**
**Commission merchant (477)**
**Auction company (477)**
**Selling agent (478)**
**Import-export agents (478)**
**Physical distribution (logistics) (479)**
**Systems approach to physical distribution (480)**
**Total cost concept (481)**
**Physical distribution management (483)**
**Warehousing (484)**
**Distribution centre (484)**
**Private warehouse (484)**
**Public warehouse (484)**
**Materials handling (485)**
**Containerization (485)**
**Inventory control (485)**
**Economic order quantity (EOQ) (485)**
**"Just-in-time" (JIT) concept (486)**
**Order processing (487)**
**Transportation (487)**
**Mode of transportation (487)**
**Intermodal transportation (487)**
**Piggyback service (487)**
**Fishyback service (487)**
**Freight forwarder (488)**
**Service merchandiser (489)**

## QUESTIONS AND PROBLEMS

1. Which of the following are wholesaling transactions?
   a. Colour Tile sells wallpaper to an apartment building contractor and also to the contractor's wife for her home.
   b. General Electric sells motors to Whirlpool for its washing machines.
   c. A fish "farmer" sells fish to a local restaurant.
   d. A family orders carpet from a friend, who is a home decorating consultant, at 50 percent off the suggested retail price. The carpet is delivered directly to the home.
2. Why is it that manufacturers' agents often can penetrate a market faster and at a lower cost than a manufacturer's sales force?
3. Which type of wholesaling intermediary, if any, is most likely to be used by each of the following firms? Explain your choice in each instance.
   a. A small manufacturer of a liquid glass cleaner to be sold through supermarkets.
   b. A small canner in Nova Scotia packing a high-quality, unbranded fruit product.
   c. A small-tools manufacturing firm that has its own sales force selling to the business market and now wants to add backyard barbecue equipment to its product mix.
   d. A Quebec textile mill producing unbranded towels, sheets, pillowcases, and blankets.
4. Looking to the future, which types of wholesaling intermediaries do you think will increase in importance and which ones will decline? Explain.
5. "The goal of a modern physical distribution system in a firm should be to operate at the lowest possible *total* costs." Do you agree?
6. Name some products for which you think the cost of physical distribution constitutes at least one-half the total price of the goods at the wholesale level. Can you suggest ways of decreasing the physical distribution cost of these products?
7. "A manufacturer follows an inventory-location strategy of concentration rather than dispersion. This company's inventory size will be smaller, but its transportation and warehousing expenses will be larger than if its inventory were dispersed." Do you agree? Explain.
8. "The use of public warehouse facilities makes it possible for manufacturers to bypass wholesalers in their channels of distribution." Explain.
9. For each of the following products, determine the best transportation method for shipping them to a distribution centre in the community where your school is located. In each case the buyer (not the seller) will pay all freight charges, and, unless specifically noted, time is not important. The distribution centre has a rail siding and a loading/unloading dock for trucks.
   a. Disposable diapers from Ontario. Total shipment weight is 60 000 kg.
   b. A replacement memory card for your computer, which is now inoperative. Weight of shipment is 1 kg and you need this card in a hurry.
   c. Blank payroll cheques for your company. (There is a sufficient number of cheques on hand for the next two weekly paydays.) Shipment weight is 50 kg.
   d. Ice cream from London, Ontario. Total shipment weight is 21 000 kg.

## HANDS-ON MARKETING

1. Interview the owner or a manager at a firm that is a type of merchant wholesaler (such as a full-service wholesaler). Ask the owner or manager to describe the firm's activities, its differential advantage or disadvantage at the present time, and the company's prospects for the future. Conduct a similar interview with the owner or a manager at a firm that is a type of agent wholesaler (such as a broker). How do you explain any discrepancies between the interview results and the content of this chapter (other than saying that the chapter must be wrong)?
2. A manufacturer of precision lenses used in medical and hospital equipment wants to ship a 5-kg box of these lenses from your town to a laboratory in Stockholm, Sweden. The lab wants delivery in five days or less. The manufacturer wants to use a package-delivery service but is undecided as to which shipper to choose. Compile and compare the types of services provided and prices charged by Federal Express, United Parcel Service, and one other package-delivery firm.

## NOTES AND REFERENCES


1. Adapted, in part, from Andrew Trimble, "Quick Service Put Firm in Top Computer Group," *Toronto Star*, May 23, 1994, p. B1; and Computer Brokers of Canada Inc., 1993 Annual Report, pp. 1-6.
2. The term *merchant wholesaler*, or *wholesaler*, is sometimes used synonymously with *wholesaling intermediary*. This is not accurate, however. *Wholesaling intermediary* is the all-inclusive term, covering the major categories of firms engaged in wholesale trade, whereas *wholesaler* is more restrictive, applying to only one category, namely, merchant wholesaling intermediaries.
3. Jeffrey A. Tannenbaum, "Cold War: Amana Refrigeration Fights Tiny Distributor," *The Wall Street Journal*, February 26, 1992, p. B2.
4. Anil Kumar and Graham Sharman, "We Love Your Product, But Where Is It?" *Business Edge*, October 1992, p. 21.
5. See Lewis M. Schneider, "New Era in Transportation Strategy," *Harvard Business Review*, March-April 1985, pp. 118-126.
6. For a report on how a well-designed physical distribution system can implement a company's strategic marketing plan, see Roy D. Shapiro, "Get Leverage from Logistics," *Harvard Business Review*, May-June 1984, pp. 119-126.
7. Janet Bamford, "Why Competitors Shop for Ideas at IKEA," *Business Week*, October 9, 1989, p. 88.
8. For further discussion of the JIT concept, see Claudia H. Deutsch, "Just in Time: The New Partnerships," *The New York Times*, October 28, 1990, Section 3, p. 25; Gary L. Frazier, Robert E. Spekman, and Charles R. O'Neal, "Just-in-Time Exchange Relationships in Industrial Markets," *Journal of Marketing*, October 1988, pp. 52-67; William D. Presutti, Jr., "Just-in-Time Manufacturing and Marketing — Strategic Relationship for Competitive Advantage," *Journal of Business and Industrial Marketing*, Summer 1988, pp. 27-35.
9. Earnest C. Raia, "Journey to World Class (JIT in USA)," *Purchasing*, September 24, 1987, p. 48.
10. Steve McDaniel, Joseph G. Ormsby, and Alicia B. Gresham, "The Effect of JIT on Distributors," *Industrial Marketing Management*, May 1992, pp. 145-149.
11. For research results indicating that perceptions of different modes vary across members of the buying centre, see James H. Martin, James M. Daley, and Henry B. Burdg, "Buying Influences and Perceptions of Transportation Services," *Industrial Marketing Management*, November 1988, pp. 305-314.
12. Michael Selz, "Independent Sales Reps Are Squeezed by the Recession," *The Wall Street Journal*, December 27, 1991, p. B2.
13. Karen Blumenthal, "Wal-Mart Set to Eliminate Reps, Brokers," *The Wall Street Journal*, December 2, 1991, p. A3; Selz, loc. cit.
14. Joseph Weber, "Getting Cozy with Their Customers," *Business Week*, January 8, 1990, p. 86.
15. For a report that examines why marketing and physical distribution have been separated and reasons they should be put back together to form a stronger basis for business strategies in the 1990s, see Roy Dale Vorhees and John I. Coppett, "Marketing-Logistics Opportunities for the 1990s," *Journal of Business Strategy*, Fall 1986, pp. 33-38.
16. For more details on this type of business arrangement, see Donald J. Bowersox, "The Strategic Benefits of Logistics Alliances," *Harvard Business Review*, July-August 1990, pp. 36-45.

## CHAPTER 17 GOALS

You have abundant experience with retailing — as a consumer. And perhaps you also have worked in retailing. This chapter builds on that experience and provides insights about retail markets, different types of retailers, and key strategies and trends in retailing. After studying this chapter, you should have an understanding of:

- The nature of retailing.
- What a retailer is.
- Types of retailers classified by form of ownership.
- Types of retailers classified by marketing strategies.
- Forms of nonstore retailing.
- Trends in retailing.

CHAPTER

17

# RETAILING: MARKETS AND INSTITUTIONS

## Occupying an Endurable Niche

Tilley hats are famous. They are not only the favourite headgear of some pretty well-known people, including Sir Edmund Hillary, Prince Charles, Pierre Trudeau, and Paul Newman, but they were prescribed as standard equipment for Canadian soldiers serving in the Gulf War and on peacekeeping missions in the world's trouble spots. What makes the Tilley hat so special and where can you buy one?

Alex Tilley is no ordinary retailer. He is a niche player in a multimillion-dollar retail clothing business. But he knows precisely what his position is: Quite simply, he makes and sells the best adventure clothing in the world. His hats are indestructible. And he is so confident of the quality of what he sells that all his products are guaranteed to the customer's satisfaction. No wonder he calls them Tilley Endurables.

But Tilley wasn't always a retail success, and even today his distribution system is a little unorthodox. Alex Tilley makes no secret of the fact that he more or less lucked into his success. He took six years to get a three-year degree and later flunked the MBA program at York University, even though he was president of his class. He worked briefly for a number of companies and "was fired by some of the best." He ran a business that rented hothouse flowers to offices — it failed. He operated a chain of six tutoring schools in Nassau and Montreal — it too failed. Then he spent 14 years operating an art rental business and simultaneously indulging his love for sailing. It was while sailing that he decided the world needed a better sailing hat, one that would not blow off, shrink, or discolour and would not sink when it fell overboard.

He worked for months with a sailmaker to design the world's best sailing hat. After a few months of selling the hat at boat shows, and some positive recognition from *Yachting Magazine*, Tilley was in business, and Alex Tilley, "art consultant," became Alex Tilley, "manufacturer of the best adventure clothing in the world." The hat was just the beginning of a complete line of adventure clothing that now includes double-seated Classic shorts, pickpocket-proof pants, and the famous "Vest of Many Pockets."

Tilley began distributing his line of clothing through mail order, and today this still represents a fair portion of his business. Orders are stimulated through a catalogue that is sent to customers around the world and through offbeat advertisements in the *Globe and Mail*, *New York Times*, *New Yorker*, *Smithsonian*, *Los Angeles Times*, and *Wall Street Journal*. His promotional approach is unusual because it relies almost exclusively on testimonials from his many satisfied customers. His catalogues and the walls of his stores are full of postcards and letters testifying to the durability of Tilley products and to their performance in dangerous and rugged circumstances.

Today, Tilley products are distributed through only five company-owned stores in Canada — Montreal, Toronto, two in Vancouver, and the "flagship" store in Don Mills, Ontario. The company has one outlet in upstate New York and distributes its clothing through associated retailers in Canada and the United States. But it is mail order that sends Tilley's Canadian-made clothing to discriminating customers all over the world.[1]

Distributing consumer products begins with the producer and ends with the ultimate consumer. Between the two there is usually at least one intermediary — a retailer. The many types of retailing institutions and their marketing activities are the subjects of this chapter.

## NATURE AND IMPORTANCE OF RETAILING

For every retail superstar like Eaton's, Tilley, or Loblaws, thousands of tiny retailers serve consumers only in very limited areas. Despite their differences, all these firms do have two common features: They link producers and ultimate consumers, and they perform valuable services for both parties. In all likelihood these firms are retailers, but all their activities may not qualify as retailing. How can that be? Explanations follow.

### Retailing and Retailers

If Safeway or Sobeys sells some floor wax to a gift-shop operator to polish the shop floor, is this a retail sale? When a Shell or Petro-Canada service station advertises that tires are being sold at the wholesale price, is this retailing? Can a wholesaler or manufacturer engage in retailing? When a service such as hair styling or auto repair is sold to an ultimate consumer, is this retailing? Obviously we need to define some terms, particularly *retailing* and *retailer*, to avoid misunderstandings later.

**Retailing** (or **retail trade**) consists of the sale, and all activities directly related to the sale, of goods and services to ultimate consumers for personal, nonbusiness use. While most retailing occurs through retail stores, it may be done by any institution. A manufacturer selling brushes or cosmetics door to door is engaged in retailing, as is a farmer selling vegetables at a roadside stand.

Any firm — manufacturer, wholesaler, or retailer — that sells something to ultimate consumers for their own nonbusiness use is making a retail sale. This is true regardless of *how* the product is sold (in person or by telephone, mail, or vending machine) or *where* it is sold (in a store or at the consumer's home). However, a firm engaged *primarily* in retailing is called a **retailer**. In this chapter, we will concentrate on retailers rather than on other types of businesses that make only occasional retail sales.

While this chapter focuses primarily on retailers of goods, much of what is said — particularly regarding marketing strategies — applies equally well to retailers of services. As we discussed in Chapter 12, one of the characteristics of services relates to the inseparability of the service from the individual or company that provides it. Although this is certainly the case, the marketing of services is often delegated to retailers. For example, travel agents are really retailers who sell to end consumers the services offered by airlines, hotels, railways, and car rental companies. Banks and other financial services companies retail Canada Savings Bonds on behalf of the Government of Canada.

### Economic Justification for Retailing

All intermediaries basically serve as purchasing agents for their customers and as sales specialists for their suppliers. To carry out these roles, retailers perform many activities, including anticipating customers' wants, developing assortments of products, acquiring market information, and financing.

It is relatively easy to become a retailer. No large investment in production equipment is required, merchandise can often be purchased on credit, and store space can be leased with no "down payment." This ease of entry results in fierce competition and better value for consumers.

To get into retailing is easy but to be forced out is just as easy. To survive in retailing, a company must do a satisfactory job in its primary role — catering to consumers — as well as in its secondary role — serving producers and wholesalers. This dual responsibility is both the justification for retailing and the key to success in retailing.

**Size of the Retail Market** There were about 206,000 retail stores in Canada in 1992, and their total sales volume was more than $185 *billion* (see Figure 17-1). In spite of growth in total population and consumer incomes over the past 30 years, the total number of retail stores has not increased dramatically. In fact, the volatility of the retail business is reflected in the fact that the total number of retail stores in Canada actually *dropped* from 227,200 in 1988 to 206,300 in 1991, when Canada was struggling through the throes of a recession and consumer spending was down. Total sales actually dropped from $185.19 billion in 1991 to $184.90 billion in 1992, a level virtually unchanged from total retail sales in 1988. The turbulent retail industry of the early 1990s was a dramatic change from the rapid growth experienced during the 1980s. Nevertheless, despite the retail downturn of that period and the resulting departure of some retailers from the market, the Canadian retail market will return to a state of steady growth as the Canadian economy improves, and the increases in volume and value of goods that have characterized the last 30 years or so will continue.

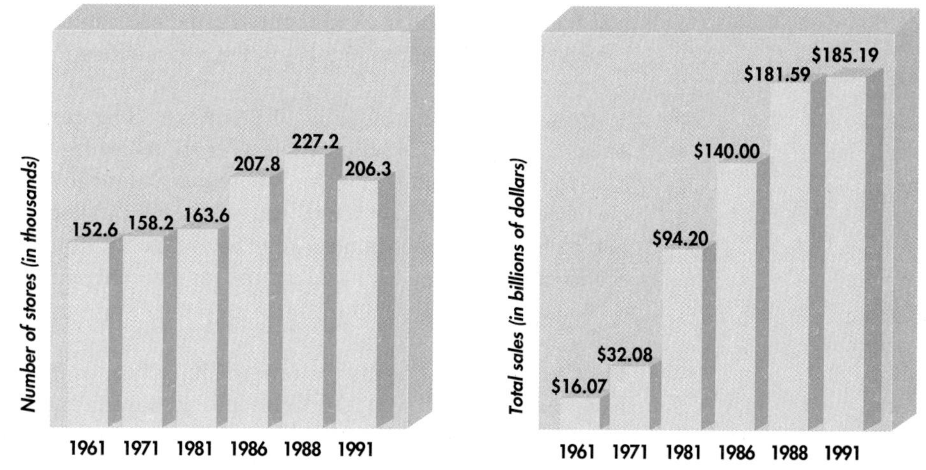


**FIGURE 17-1**
**Total retail trade in Canada, selected years.**

**Sales volume has increased tremendously. However, note the stabilizing of sales and reduction in number of stores in 1991.**
**(Source: Statistics Canada)**

TABLE 17-1 Total retail trade in Canada, 1961-1991

| | 1961 | 1971 | 1981 | 1986 | 1988 | 1991 |
|---|---|---|---|---|---|---|
| Number of stores (thousands) | 152.6 | 158.2 | 163.6 | 207.8 | 227.2 | 206.3 |
| Total sales ($ billions) | $16.07 | $32.08 | $94.20 | $140.00 | $181.59 | $185.19 |
| Average sales per store | $105,504 | $202,781 | $576,363 | $673,706 | $799,252 | $897,683 |

Source: Statistics Canada. *Annual Retail Trade*, Catalogue Number 63-223, Annual. Reproduced with permission of Supply and Services Canada.

## Costs and Profits of Retailers

Information regarding the costs of retailing is very meagre. By gleaning data from several sources, however, we can make some rough generalizations.

**Total Costs and Profits** As nearly as can be estimated, the total average operating expense for all retailers combined is about 25 to 27 percent of retail sales. Wholesaling expenses are estimated at about 8 percent of the *retail* dollar or about 10 to 11 percent of wholesaling sales. Thus, retailing costs are about $2^1/_2$ times the costs of wholesaling, when both are stated as a percentage of sales of the intermediaries in question. (See Figure 17-2.)

**FIGURE 17-2**
**Average costs of retailing and wholesaling.**

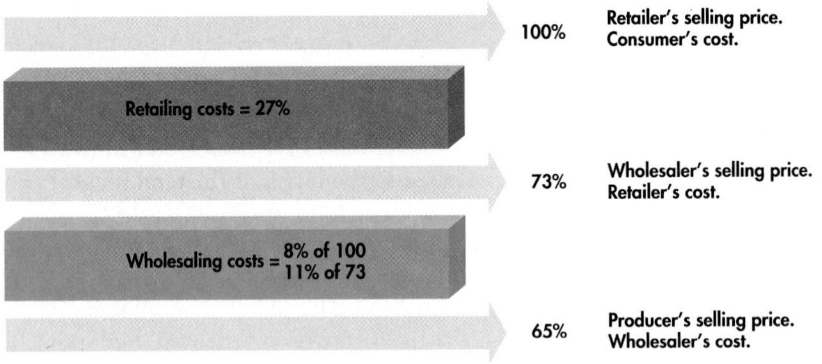


The proportionately higher retailing costs are generally related to the expense of dealing directly with the consumer. In comparison with wholesalers' customers, end consumers demand more services. The average retail sale is smaller, the rate of merchandise turnover is lower, merchandise is bought in smaller lots, rent is higher, and expenses for furniture and fixtures are greater. And retail sales people cannot be used efficiently because customers do not come into retail stores at a steady rate.

**Costs and Profits by Kind of Business** The expense ratios of retailers vary from one type of store to another. Table 17-2 shows average gross margins as a percentage of sales for different kinds of stores. These margins range from 15.4 percent for motor vehicle dealers to 51 percent for motor vehicle repair shops. Table 17-2 also shows average net profit (after income taxes) for each type of store. These data were produced by Statistics Canada for 1987 and are the most recent available.

## Store Size

Most retail establishments are very small. In fact, as many as 20 percent of all retailers have annual sales of $100,000 or less. However, despite their numbers, such stores account for a very small percentage of total retail sales.

TABLE 17-2 Gross margin and net profit as percentage of net sales of selected types of retailers

**Gross margin (net sales minus cost of goods sold) is the amount needed to cover a company's operating expenses and still leave a profit. How do you account for the differences in operating expenses among the various types of retailers?**

| Line of business | Gross margin % | Net profit % after income taxes |
|---|---|---|
| Food stores | 22.3 | 1.0 |
| Department stores | 31.0 | 1.4 |
| Variety stores | 27.4 | 1.7 |
| General merchandise | 20.7 | 1.7 |
| Automobile accessories and parts | 27.0 | 2.2 |
| Gasoline service stations | 14.8 | 1.4 |
| Motor vehicle dealers | 9.1 | –0.7 |
| Motor vehicle repair shops | 32.5 | 2.9 |
| Shoe stores | 42.7 | 1.8 |
| Men's clothing stores | 40.8 | 3.5 |
| Women's clothing stores | 42.7 | 1.9 |
| Dry goods stores | 39.4 | 1.3 |
| Hardware stores | 31.3 | 2.5 |
| Book and stationery stores | 35.6 | 2.2 |
| Florist shops | 49.1 | 2.3 |
| Fuel dealers | 17.9 | 3.0 |
| Furniture and appliance stores | 29.9 | 1.9 |
| Jewellery stores | 41.3 | 3.2 |
| Tobacconists | 40.0 | 4.3 |
| Drugstores | 27.2 | 2.2 |
| TOTAL RETAIL TRADE | 24.8 | 3.6 |

Source: Statistics Canada, *Corporation Financial Statistics*, 1987, cat. no. 61-207. Reproduced with permission of Supply and Services Canada.

At the same time, there is a high degree of concentration in retailing. A small number of companies account for a substantial share of total retail trade. These companies, such as Loblaws (part of the George Weston group of companies) and the Hudson's Bay Company (The Bay and Zellers), own many individual stores and account for the considerable degree of concentration in the industry. For example, the companies listed in Table 17-3, while numbering fewer than 40, probably account for close to half of all retail sales in Canada, particularly when one adds to the list some privately owned retail giants such as Eaton's and Sobeys.

Stores of different sizes present different management challenges and opportunities. Buying, promotion, personnel relations, and expense control are influenced significantly by whether a store's sales volume is large or small.

Size, or the lack thereof, brings with it certain advantages, several of which are evaluated in Table 17-4. This assessment suggests that relatively large stores have a competitive advantage over small stores. Small retailers do face many difficulties. The ones that cannot meet the challenges fail. If that's the case, how do so many small retailers succeed? The answer is twofold:

TABLE 17-3 Canada's largest retailers (1993-94 sales and profits)

| Company | Revenue $000 | Profit $000 |
|---|---|---|
| DEPARTMENT STORES | | |
| Hudson's Bay Co. | 5,441,498 | 147,701 |
| Sears Canada | 4,009,100 | 4,400 |
| Zellers Inc. | 3,159,500 | na |
| F.W. Woolworth Co. | 2,143,355 | 4,151 |
| Price Costco Canada | 1,675,648 | na |
| K mart Canada | 1,235,072 | –8,831 |
| CLOTHING STORES | | |
| Dylex Ltd. | 1,940,627 | –21,945 |
| Reitmans (Canada) | 346,442 | 14,510 |
| Suzy Shier | 209,562 | 9,028 |
| Château Stores of Canada | 156,900 | 4,509 |
| Mark's Work Wearhouse | 137,026 | –2,746 |
| Pantorama Industries | 119,960 | 5,017 |
| SPECIALTY STORES | | |
| Canadian Tire Corp. | 3,486,961 | 81,405 |
| Kinney Canada | 660,216 | –8,020 |
| Big V Pharmacies | 480,556 | 10,854 |
| Groupe Ro-na Dismat | 477,696 | 5,553 |
| Speedy Muffler King | 477,311 | 6,738 |
| Pharma Plus Drugmarts | 417,700 | na |
| Future Shop | 334,866 | 6,712 |
| Leon's Furniture | 277,975 | 16,188 |
| FOOD DISTRIBUTION | | |
| George Weston Ltd. | 11,931,000 | 57,000 |
| Loblaw Cos. | 9,359,700 | 93,400 |
| Univa Inc. | 6,213,700 | –108,200 |
| Oshawa Group | 5,730,600 | 50,200 |
| Canada Safeway | 4,456, 600 | na |
| Métro-Richelieu Inc. | 2,772,700 | 26,200 |
| Great A&P Tea Co. | 2,710,200 | –36,894 |
| HOSPITALITY SERVICES | | |
| McDonald's Restaurants of Can. | 1,520,363 | na |
| Cara Operations | 783,229 | 30,492 |
| C.P. Hotels & Resorts | 488,645 | 10,195 |
| Versa Services | 395,750 | 5,494 |
| Groupe St-Hubert | 190,044 | na |
| A&W Food Services of Can. | 108,610 | 1,107 |
| Four Seasons Hotels | 105,886 | –119,233 |
| Commonwealth Hospitality | 98,792 | na |
| Hilton Canada | 70,758 | –2,929 |

Note: This list of Canadian retail chains is incomplete in that certain large privately owned companies are not included. Also, the reader may be unfamiliar with certain of the corporate names listed here: for example, Cara Operations operates Harvey's and Swiss Chalet restaurants; Dylex Limited operates a large number of clothing retailers including Tip Top Tailors, Harry Rosen, Fairweather, and Braemar. The F.W. Woolworth Company sold 122 of its Woolco stores to Wal-Mart in 1994.

Source: "The Top 1000," *Report on Business Magazine*, July 1994.

## MARKETING AT WORK

### FILE 17-1 CATEGORY KILLERS PLAY HARDBALL

It didn't take HMV Canada long to move into the top spot in a sluggish Canadian retail music business. Only five years after opening its first Canadian store, HMV has taken 20 percent of the industry, whose unit sales (CDs, tapes, and LPs) totalled 52 million in 1992, down from an estimated 95 million units in 1979. In an industry now worth $750 million annually, HMV took the market leader position from Sam the Record Man, even though Sam operates 91 stores to HMV's 65. The cutthroat marketing that characterizes the retail record business is also said to have contributed to the bankruptcy of A&A Records in early 1994.

HMV's rapid rise is a result of some clever marketing, super-modern store design, youthful managers, and a great deal of hype, all designed to appeal to HMV's target customer, "the committed music addict." One-third of all the company's sales come from customers aged 19 to 24. HMV's Toronto flagship store is huge; at more than 25,000 square feet, it is big enough to host in-store concerts by stars like jazz great Oscar Peterson, cellist Yo Yo Ma, and concert violinist Nigel Kennedy. A few years ago, a roof-top concert by rocker Alice Cooper at the store blocked traffic on Yonge Street.

HMV's position as the largest record retailer in Canada also allows it to wield considerable power when dealing with suppliers, including the large recording companies. When Sony Canada, the label that records big-name artists like Michael Jackson and Pearl Jam, refused a request from HMV president Paul Alofs for volume discounts, Alofs sent instructions to store managers to cut purchases from Sony by 20 to 25 percent. Some Sony products were barred from in-store listening posts and window displays, and the new Sony mini-discs were immediately removed from all HMV stores. While some industry people feel Alofs may be playing hardball a little too hard, his company has the sales that allow him to exercise a little muscle. Along with other Canadian retailers who have come to dominate their product category in recent years, HMV enjoys being a "category killer" and having the power that goes along with it.

Source: John Heinzl, "HMV Plays Musical Hardball," *Globe and Mail*, November 22, 1993, pp. B1, B8.

- Some small retailers have formed or joined contractual vertical marketing systems. These entities — called retailer co-operatives, voluntary chains, or franchise systems — give individual members certain advantages of large stores, such as specialized management, buying power, and a well-known store name.
- Many consumers seek benefits that small stores can often provide better than large stores can. For instance, some people seek high levels of shopping convenience. Small outlets located near residential areas offer such convenience. Other consumers desire high levels of personal service. A small store's highly motivated owner-manager and well-supervised sales staff may surpass a large store on this important shopping dimension.

Many small stores take advantage of their comparative strengths and compete successfully against other retailers of varying sizes and types.

### Physical Facilities

Later in this chapter we will classify retailers according to their product assortments, price strategies, and promotional methods. Here, we'll look at **physical facilities**, which represents the distribution element of a retailer's marketing mix.

Some firms engage in *nonstore* retailing — by selling through catalogues or door to door, for example — but many more firms rely on retail *stores*. Firms that operate retail stores must consider three aspects of physical facilities:

TABLE 17-4 Competitive positions of large and small retail stores

| Selected bases for evaluation | Who has the advantage? |
|---|---|
| Division of labour and specialization of management | Large-scale retailers — their biggest advantage |
| Flexibility of operations — merchandise selection, services offered, store design, reflection of owner's personality | Small retailers — their biggest advantage |
| Buying power | Large retailers buy in bigger quantities and thus get lower costs |
| Access to desirable merchandise | Large retailers promise suppliers access to large numbers of customers whereas a single small retailer may be viewed as insignificant |
| Development and promotion of retailer's own brand | Large retailers |
| Efficient use of advertising, especially in citywide media | Large retailers' markets match better with media circulation |
| Ability to provide top-quality personal service | Small retailers if owners pay personal attention to customers and also to selecting and supervising sales staff |
| Opportunity to experiment with new products and selling methods | Large retailers can better afford the risks |
| Financial strength | Large retailers have resources to gain some of the advantages noted above (such as private brands and experimentation) |
| Public image | Small retailers enjoy public support and sympathy. However, this same public often votes with its wallet by shopping at big stores. |

- **Location.** It is frequently stated that there are three keys to success in retailing: location, location, and location! Although overstated, this axiom does suggest the importance that retailers attach to location. Thus a store's site should be the first decision made about facilities. Considerations such as surrounding population, traffic, and cost determine where a store should be located.
- **Design.** This factor refers to a store's appearance, both exterior and interior.
- **Layout.** The amount of space allocated to various product lines, specific locations of products, and a floor plan of display tables and racks make up the store's layout.

As might be expected, retail locations tend to follow the population. Consequently, the bulk of retail sales occur in urban, rather than rural, areas. And suburban shopping areas have become more and more popular, while many downtown areas have declined.

Shopping centres have become the predominant type of retail location in most suburban areas. A **shopping centre** consists of a planned grouping of retail stores that lease space in a structure that is typically owned by a single organization and that can accommodate multiple tenants. Shopping centres can be classified by size and market served:

Hazelton Lanes in Toronto designs to attract.

- **Convenience centre.** Usually consists of 5 to 10 outlets, such as a dry cleaner, branch bank, convenience grocery store, and video rental store.
- **Neighbourhood centre.** Has 10 to 25 tenants, including a large supermarket and perhaps a drugstore.
- **Community centre.** Includes 25 to 50 stores and features a discount house or junior department store. It may also include a supermarket. Given its composition of stores, a community centre draws shoppers from a larger area than does a neighbourhood centre.
- **Regional centre.** Anchored by one or more department stores and supermarkets and complemented by as many as 200 smaller retail outlets; typically an enclosed climate-controlled mall.

Many regional shopping centres are very large. They have become the hub of shopping and social activities in many communities; in fact they are "the meeting place" for many seniors and high school students. During the 1980s, construction of new regional centres slowed considerably as the market became saturated. It is expected that relatively few shopping malls will be built in the 1990s, but many existing ones will be renovated and modernized.

The growth of suburban shopping, especially in regional malls, led to decreased retail sales in many urban downtown areas. In recent years, therefore, some cities have worked to revitalize their downtown shopping districts. Often historical buildings or neighbourhoods are converted to shopping areas (for example, St. Lawrence Market in Toronto and the Cours de Mont Royal in Montreal). Enclosed shopping malls featuring distinctive designs have also been built in all major cities. Possibly the best known of these shopping centres is the West Edmonton Mall, which has become something of a tourist attraction in Western Canada.

## Classification of Retailers

To understand how retailers serve both suppliers and customers, we will classify retailers on two bases:

1. Form of ownership
2. Marketing strategies

Any retail store can be classified according to both bases, as illustrated by the following comparison of Eaton's and a neighbourhood paint store:

| | Classification bases | |
|---|---|---|
| Sample stores | Form of ownership | Marketing strategies |
| **Eaton's** | **Corporate chain** | **Department store with broad, relatively deep assortments, moderate prices, and levels of personal service that vary across departments.** |
| **Neighbourhood paint store** | **Independent** | **Limited-line store that has narrow, relatively deep assortments, avoids price competition, and provides extensive personal service.** |

**Although both are retailers, Eaton's and North's differ in important ways.**

## RETAILERS CLASSIFIED BY FORM OF OWNERSHIP

The major forms of ownership in retailing are corporate chain, independent, and vertical marketing system (VMS). Within the VMS category are several types of organizations: wholesaler-sponsored voluntary chains, retailer-owned co-operatives, and franchise systems.

### Corporate Chains

A **corporate chain**, sometimes called a *chain-store system*, is an organization of two or more centrally owned and managed stores that generally handle the same lines of products. Three factors differentiate a chain from an independent store and contractual vertical marketing system:

- Technically, two or more units constitute a chain. Today, however, many small-scale merchants have opened two or three units in shopping centres and in newly populated areas. These retailers ordinarily do not think of themselves as chains. Having four or more units is a good definitional basis for discussing chain stores.
- Central ownership distinguishes corporate chains from contractual vertical marketing systems.
- Due to centralized management, individual units in a chain typically have little autonomy. Strategic decisions are made at headquarters, and there is considerable standardization of operating policies for all the units in a chain.

Corporate chains continue to increase their share of total retail trade, as shown in Table 17-5. The predominance of chains varies considerably, however, depending on the kind of business. Organizations with four or more stores did almost 40 percent of all retail business in Canada in 1989 (latest data available). The importance of chains varies considerably from one type of business to another. Chains account for 70 percent or more of total sales in the general merchandise and variety stores categories and in family clothing and shoes. Among grocery stores, hardware stores, and pharmacies, however, chains account for 30 percent of sales or less. In the retail food business, there are several giant food chains (Loblaws, Steinberg, A&P, Provigo, Sobeys, Safeway, etc.), yet chains still account for only about 63 percent of all food sales. This is explained in part by the large number of independent food retailers in small towns and neighbourhoods throughout Canada.

**Competitive Strengths and Weaknesses** Chain-store organizations are large-scale retailing institutions. As such, they are subject to the general advantages and limitations

TABLE 17-5 Chains' share of total retail sales volume by kind of business, 1966 to 1989

| | Percent of Sales | | | | |
|---|---|---|---|---|---|
| Kind of Business | 1966 | 1974 | 1979 | 1986 | 1989 |
| Total retail sales | 33.4 | 41.1 | 41.5 | 41.5 | 39.3 |
| Grocery and combination stores | 44.9 | 57.5 | 60.4 | | |
| Combination stores (groceries and meat) | | | | 64.8 | 63.5 |
| Grocery, confectionery and sundries | | | | 29.8 | 25.5 |
| Other food stores | 8.7 | 8.1 | 8.5 | 9.4 | 11.2 |
| Department stores* | 100.00 | 100.00 | 100.00 | 100.00 | 100.00 |
| General merchandise | 74.7 | 80.4 | 79.8 | 75.6 | 73.3 |
| Variety stores | 86.7 | 83.2 | 76.3 | 87.2 | 85.4 |
| Men's clothing | 13.2 | 18.6 | 34.3 | 54.9 | 58.8 |
| Women's clothing | 26.5 | 40.9 | 53.3 | 65.6 | 67.4 |
| Family clothing | 21.9 | 28.5 | 49.9 | 68.3 | 70.3 |
| Shoe stores | 45.0 | 51.8 | 66.0 | 71.7 | 73.5 |
| Hardware stores | 15.5 | 19.0 | n/a | 21.2 | 14.8 |
| Furniture stores | 19.2 | 19.2 | 19.5 | 50.9 | 58.3 |
| Pharmacy stores | 13.4 | 18.5 | 22.4 | 29.6 | 31.0 |
| Jewellery stores | 33.7 | 39.4 | 45.4 | 49.3 | 48.0 |

***All department stores are considered chains by Statistics Canada.**

Source: Statistics Canada, *Market Research Handbook*, cat. no. 63-224, various years. Reproduced with permission of Supply and Services Canada.

of all large retailers that we discussed earlier in this chapter. Let's look at a few of these points, especially as they relate to chain stores.

**Lower selling prices** Chain stores have traditionally been credited with selling at lower prices than independents. But the claim of lower prices needs careful scrutiny because it can be misleading. It was probably more justified in the past than it is today. Many independents have pooled their buying power so that, in many instances, they can buy products at the same price as the chains. However, it is almost certainly true that chains will have a cost advantage over independents.

It is very difficult to compare the prices of chains with those of independents. The merchandise is often not exactly comparable, because many chains sell items under their own brands. It is difficult to compare the prices of Del Monte peaches with Loblaws', Steinberg's, or Safeway's brand of peaches. Also, it is not accurate to compare the price of the product sold in a cash-and-carry, no-customer-service store with the price of an identically branded product in a full-service store. The value of services should be included in the comparison.

**Multistore feature of chains** Chain stores do not have all their eggs in one basket (or in one store). Even large-scale independent department stores or supermarkets cannot match this advantage of the chains. A multiunit operation has automatically *spread its risks* among many units. Losses in one store can be offset by profits in other units.

Multistore organizations can *experiment* quite easily. They can try a new store layout or a new type of merchandise in one store without committing the entire firm.

A chain can make more *effective use of advertising* than even a giant single-unit independent store. To illustrate, a grocery chain may have 15 medium-sized stores blanketing a city. An independent competitor may have one huge supermarket doing three to four times the business of any single unit of the chain. Yet the chain can use the metropolitan daily newspaper as an advertising medium with much less waste in circulation than the independent can. Many chains can also make effective use of national advertising media.

**On the negative side** Standardization, the hallmark of a chain-store system and a major factor in its success, is a mixed blessing. Standardization also means inflexibility. Often a chain cannot adjust rapidly to a local market situation. Chains are well aware of this weakness, however, and have consequently given local store managers somewhat greater freedom to act in various situations. Also, with improved information systems, chains can better tailor their merchandising efforts to local markets.

### Independent Stores

An **independent retailer** is a company with a single retail store that is not affiliated with any type of contractual vertical marketing system. Most retailers are independents, and most independents are quite small. Of course, an independent department store or supermarket can have $10 million or more in annual sales, so it may have more economic power than small chains consisting of only a few stores. Still, independents usually have the characteristics of small retailers that were presented in Table 17-4.

Independents typically are viewed as having higher prices than chain stores. However, due to differences in merchandise and services, it is difficult to compare directly the prices of chains and independents. For instance, chains often have their own private brands that are not sold by independents. Also the two types of retailers frequently provide customers with different levels — and perhaps quality — of services. Many customers are willing to pay extra for services that are valuable to them, such as credit, delivery, alterations, installation, a liberal return policy, and friendly, knowledgeable personal service.[2]

### Contractual Vertical Marketing Systems

In a **contractual vertical marketing system**, independently owned firms join together under a contract specifying how they will operate. The three types of contractual VMS are discussed below.

#### Retailer Co-operatives and Voluntary Chains

Co-operatives and voluntary chains have the same basic purposes:

- To enable independent retailers to compete effectively with corporate chains through increased buying power.
- To provide members with management assistance in store layout, employee and management training programs, promotion, accounting, and inventory control systems.

The main difference between these two types of systems is who organizes them. A voluntary chain is sponsored by a wholesaler that enters into a contract with interested retailers. In contrast, a retailer co-operative is formed by a group of small retailers that agree to establish and operate a wholesale warehouse.

Historically these two forms of contractual VMS have been organized for defensive reasons — to maintain a competitive position against large, strong chains. Some differences between the two groups are as follows:

## MARKETING AT WORK

### FILE 17-2 SUPER-AUTOMATED SUPERMARKET

Possibly the most automated supermarket in Canada has opened in an east-side Vancouver neighbourhood. The Smart! Market is the latest market entry of the Jim Pattison Group and offers a combination of technology and logistics to cut costs and offer low prices to customers.

Smart! Market computers count customers as they enter and leave the store and schedule checkout openings accordingly. Shelves have electronic price displays that can be changed from a central computer. But it is at the checkout that the customer will notice the greatest difference between this store and conventional supermarkets. At Smart! Market the customer has no choice but to check out his or her own groceries. The customer slides the items through the scanner and the bill is tallied on a computer screen. The customer then pays at a single pay station. Security sensors measure and weigh each order to ensure that the items being carted away have actually been scanned.

The electronic checkouts not only reduce costs at the checkout, but also print a checkout tape that contains a column of prices that the customer would have paid for the same items at a competing supermarket nearby. Finally, the computer then orders replacement stock from a central warehouse for overnight delivery and restocking.

To keep costs down, Smart! Market will offer only 4,000 items, compare with the 25,000 carried by a typical supermarket. This may represent an issue that will determine the acceptance of the new retail concept. Will customers be prepared to accept the new technology in the interest of saving money on their food bills, or will they continue to pay possibly a little more for the variety offered by their regular supermarket?

Source: Robert Williamson, "A Brave New Grocery Store," *Globe and Mail*, July 11, 1994, pp. B1, B10.

| Voluntary chain | Retailer co-operative chain |
|---|---|
| 1. Sponsored by wholesalers, with a contract between wholesalers and independent retailer members. | 1. Sponsored by retailers. They combine to form and operate a wholesale warehouse corporation. |
| 2. Wholesaler provides a wide variety of management services — buying, advertising, store layout, accounting, and inventory control. Retailers agree to buy all (or almost all) their merchandise from wholesaler. Members agree to use common store name and design and to follow common managerial procedures. | 2. Services to retailer members are primarily large-scale buying and warehousing operations. Members maintain their separate identities. |
| 3. Most prevalent in grocery field (IGA). These chains also exist in hardware and building supplies (Castle), auto supplies (Western Auto), and variety stores. | 3. Quite significant in grocery field in local areas, but not in other lines. |

Franchise Systems **Franchising** involves a continuing relationship in which a franchiser (the parent company) provides the right to use a trademark and management assistance in return for financial considerations from a franchisee (the owner of the individual business unit). The combination of franchiser and franchisees is called a **franchise system**. This type of contractual VMS is growing rapidly.

There are two kinds of franchising:

- **Product and trade name franchising.** Historically the dominant kind, product and trade name franchising is most prevalent in the automobile (Ford, Honda) and petroleum (Esso, Ultramar, Petro-Canada) industries. It is a distribution agreement wherein a franchiser authorizes a franchisee-dealer to sell a product line, using the parent company's trade name for promotional purposes. The franchisee agrees to buy from the franchiser-supplier and also to abide by specified policies. The focus in product and trade name franchising is on *what is sold.*

- **Business format franchising.** Much of franchising's growth and publicity over the past two decades has been associated with business-format franchising (including names such as Kentucky Fried Chicken, Harvey's, Midas, and H & R Block). This kind of franchising covers an entire format for operating a business. A firm with a successful retail business sells the right to operate the same business in different geographic areas. Quite simply, the franchisee expects to receive from the parent company a proven business format; in return, the franchiser receives from the individual business owner payments and also conformance to policies and standards. The focus here is on *how the business is run.*

  In business-format franchising, the franchiser may be a manufacturer that provides franchisees with merchandise. More often, though, this is not the case. For example, some such franchisers do not sell products to their franchised stores; rather the stores buy their inventory from wholesalers. What the franchiser provides to franchisees in this case is management assistance, especially marketing expertise.

For a successful retail business that wants to expand, franchising provides critical advantages:

- Rapid expansion is facilitated because franchisees provide capital when they purchase franchises.
- Because they have an investment at risk, franchisees typically are highly motivated to work hard and adhere to the parent company's proven format.

**The legendary White Spot looks for franchisees as it expands operations.**

TABLE 17-6 Numerous products reach consumer markets through business-format franchises

| Product/Service Category | Sample franchises |
|---|---|
| Fast Food | McDonald's, Tim Horton's, A. L. Van Houtte, Harvey's, Druxy's, Pizza Hut, Second Cup, Grandma Lee's, Pizza Pizza, Treats |
| Auto Rental | Avis, Hertz, Tilden, Thrifty, Budget |
| Auto Repair | Midas, Speedy, Apple Auto Glass, Jiffy Lube, Thruway Muffler, Mister Transmission, Ziebart |
| Personal Care/Services | Magicuts, Body Shop, H & R Block, Faces, Money Concepts, Uniglobe Travel, Nautilus Fitness |
| Home Decor/Services | Color Your World, St. Clair, The Bathtub Doctor, College Pro Painters, Molly Maid, Weed Man, The Lawn Rangers |
| Printing/Photography | Kwik-Kopy Printing, Japan Camera, U Frame It, The Frame UP, Direct Film |
| Clothing | Athlete's Foot, Benetton, Cotton Ginny, Kettle Creek Canvas, Mark's Work Wearhouse, Rodier |
| Computers and Video | Compucentres, Computerland, Jumbo Video, Captain Video, Radio Shack |
| Health and Personal Care | Nutri/system, Shoppers Drug Mart, Optical Factory, Tridont Health Care, People's Drug Mart |
| Convenience Stores | 7-Eleven, Mac's, Beckers, Red & White |

For an independent store facing stiff competition from chains and for a prospective new retail store, franchising offers advantages:

- Franchisees can use the parent company's well-known name, which should help attract customers.
- Various forms of management assistance are provided to franchisees prior to, as well as after, opening the store, including site selection and store-layout guidance, technical and management training, promotional programs, and inventory control systems.

Franchising is not without problems. Some franchises are based on poor products or unsound business practices and consequently fail. Further, a number of franchisees criticize franchisers for practices such as the following: enticing prospective franchisees by projecting unrealistically high revenues or unrealistically low operating costs; not providing franchisees with the promised and necessary levels of business support; locating too many of the company's outlets in the same market; or unjustifiably terminating or not renewing the franchise agreement. Conversely, franchisers have their own complaints, notably that some franchisees deviate from the system's policies and practices. As in most business fields, if self-regulation is ineffective, added regulation at the federal and provincial levels is likely.

Despite some challenges, continued growth in franchising is expected. Ambitious, successful retailers will exploit it as an offensive tool — for rapid expansion. Many small retailers will use it defensively — to achieve a viable competitive position against corporate chains. And prospective business owners will continue to buy franchises because of the two key attributes — a degree of independence and a variety of management assistance. In fact, many people with little or no business experience have purchased franchises for this reason.

A growing share of franchise buyers are people who were employed previously by large corporations. New franchisees include laid-off production and office employees as well as numerous managers and executives who were victims of corporate restructuring or who accepted early retirement. Such new entrants view franchising as a way of determining their own financial destiny.

## RETAILERS CLASSIFIED BY MARKETING STRATEGIES

Whatever its form of ownership, a retailer must develop marketing-mix strategies to succeed in its chosen target markets. In retailing, the marketing mix emphasizes product assortment, price, location, promotion, and customer services. This last element consists of services designed to aid in the sale of a product. They include credit, delivery, gift wrapping, product installation, merchandise returns, store hours, parking, and — very importantly — personal service. (When personal service is intended to create a sale, then it is personal selling — a type of promotion.)

We will now describe the major types of retail stores, paying particular attention to three elements of their marketing mixes:

- Breadth and depth of product assortment.
- Price level.
- Number of customer services.

Table 17-7 classifies retail stores on the basis of these three elements.

Some types of retail stores, such as category-killer stores, are new and growing rapidly. Others, notably variety stores, are diminishing in importance. And still others, particularly department stores, are under competitive pressure to modify some strategies. We will see that certain retailers are similar to others because new or modified institutions have filled the "strategic gaps" that once separated different types of retail institutions.

### Department Stores

A mainstay of retailing in Canada is the **department store**, a large-scale retailing institution that has a very broad and deep product assortment, tries not to compete on the basis of price and provides a wide array of customer services. Familiar department store names include Eaton's, Sears, and The Bay.

Traditional department stores offer a greater variety of merchandise and services than any other type of retail stores. They feature both "soft goods" — such as apparel, sheets, towels, and bedding — and "hard goods" — including furniture, appliances, and consumer electronics. Department stores also attract — and satisfy — consumers by offering many customer services. The combination of distinctive, appealing merchandise and numerous customer services is designed to allow the stores to maintain the manufacturers' suggested retail prices. That is, department stores strive to charge "full" or "nondiscounted" prices.

Department stores face mounting problems, however. Largely due to their prime locations and customer services, their operating expenses are considerably higher than those of most other kinds of retail business. Many manufacturers' brands that used to be available exclusively through department stores are now widely distributed and often carry discounted prices in other outlets. And the quality of personal service, especially knowledgeable sales help, has deteriorated in some department stores.

TABLE 17-7 Retail stores classified by key marketing strategies

| Type of store | Breadth and depth of assortment | Price level | Number of customer services |
|---|---|---|---|
| Department store | Very broad, deep | Avoids price competition | Wide array |
| Discount house | Broad, shallow | Emphasizes low prices | Relatively few |
| Catalogue showroom | Broad, shallow | Emphasizes low prices | Few |
| Limited-line store | Narrow, deep | Traditional types avoid price competition; newer kinds emphasize low prices | Vary by type |
| Specialty store | Very narrow, deep | Avoids price competition | At least standard and extensive in some |
| Off-price retailer | Narrow, deep | Emphasizes low prices | Few |
| Category killer store | Narrow, very deep | Emphasizes low prices | Few to moderate |
| Supermarket | Broad, deep | Some emphasize low prices; others avoid price disadvantages | Few |
| Convenience store | Narrow, shallow | High prices | Few |
| Warehouse club | Very broad, very shallow | Emphasizes very low prices | Few (open only to members) |
| Hypermarket | Very broad, deep | Emphasizes low prices | Some |

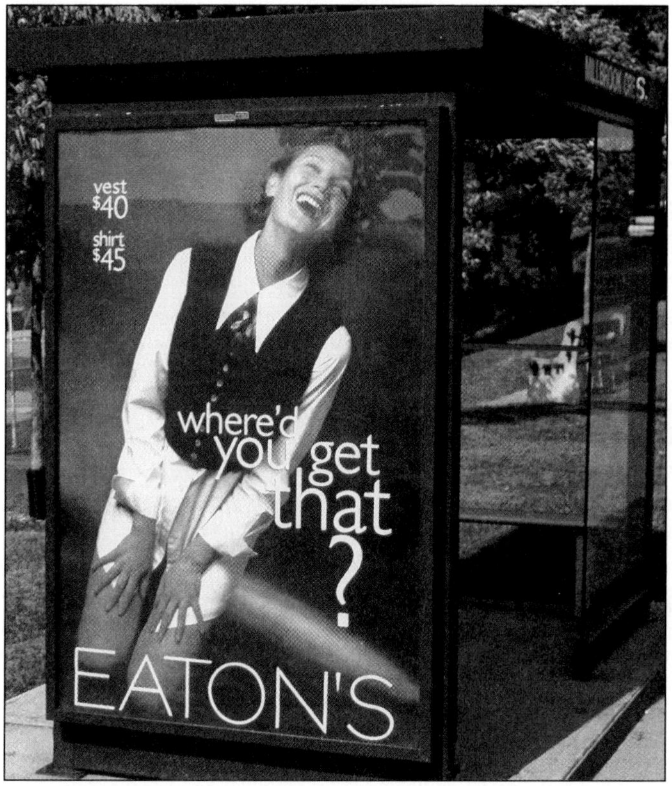


Department stores such as Eaton's attempt to differentiate themselves from major new competitors.

Intense horizontal competition is also hurting department stores. Other types of retailers are aiming at consumers who have long supported department stores. Specialty stores, off-price retailers, and even some discount houses have been particularly aggressive in trying to lure shoppers away from department stores. To varying degrees, retail chains such as K mart, Wal-Mart, and Zellers compete directly against the department stores.

As a result of competitive pressures, primarily from large discount chains, some department stores have disappeared from the Canadian market in recent years. Simpsons, one of Canada's oldest retailing institutions, was closed by its parent company, Hudson's Bay Company, and some of its stores were converted to The Bay. Woodwards, a fixture in retailing in western Canada for generations, ran into difficulties in the early 1990s and closed many stores. The remainder were acquired by The Bay in early 1993.

## MARKETING AT WORK

### FILE 17-3 SHAKING UP CANADIAN RETAILING

Without doubt the biggest news in Canadian retailing in recent years was the announcement in early 1994 that Wal-Mart, the world's largest and most successful retailer, had bought the 122 Woolco stores in Canada and would convert them to Wal-Marts. This was the latest and largest in a series of forays by big American retailers into the Canadian market, and Canadian retailers are paying attention. Spurred on in part by the devalued Canadian dollar, large U.S. chains see Canada as a cheap market into which to expand.

Wal-Mart's lead is being followed by other giant retail chains from south of the border, including Price Costco (general merchandise warehouse club), Sportmart (sporting goods), Computer City (computer equipment), and Michaels Stores (arts and crafts supplies). If they aren't opening their own massive stores, they are buying up Canadian retailers, as Home Depot did with the Aikenheads Home Improvement Warehouse chain. The American formula is simple; offer low prices, a wide product selection, and sales clerks who smile and make the customer feel welcome.

The new entrants to the marketplace are typically large square-shaped "big box" stores that operate like warehouse clubs, offering customers low prices, but few frills, or they are "category killers," who carry such a vast array of products in a particular category that they dominate the field. They gain advantage over their smaller and usually local competitors through their enormous buying power — Wal-Mart's sales in 1993 were $68 billion (U.S.), compared with $3.2 billion (Canadian) for Zellers — and because they can place demands on suppliers to keep prices low and to deliver on time and to their specifications.

Most also operate highly efficient distribution systems that permit just-in-time delivery of stock, thereby making the supplier carry the cost of inventory. Wal-Mart's famous "cross-docking" warehouse system (described in Marketing at Work File 16-4) moves products through central distribution centres so fast that much of the stock never ends up in inventory. Products arrive in suppliers' trucks and move quickly to another loading dock where they are shipped to a Wal-Mart store. Such a system requires sophisticated inventory and logistics systems and superior communications with suppliers.

Wal-Mart adds a number of other dimensions to its already formidable array of competitive advantages. Probably the most notable of these from a customer's perspective is the level of service provided in Wal-Mart stores and the effort made to pay attention to the customer. Wal-Mart employs "greeters," often retired local people, who meet customers at the door, welcome them, and offer a shopping cart. Staff are referred to as "associates" and are trained to provide a high level of customer service. Some customers and even some staff feel a little uncomfortable about the almost-religious zeal of Wal-Mart, which is characterized by slogans and morning staff meetings where the national anthem is sung and staff yell the company cheer. Staff are encouraged to approach customers and to call them by their first names. All this is reinforced by a human resources system that offers employees stock ownership and profit sharing.

The invasion of Wal-Mart and the other major American retailers has prompted a response from Canadian retailers such as The Bay, Zellers, Consumers Distributing, and K mart, itself American-owned. Many have announced that they too will be opening larger stores; existing outlets are being renovated, and there is a move towards generating better information on sales and inventory, establishing everyday low prices, and spending more time and money on listening to the customer through research. The net effect will be a more efficient Canadian retail industry, which will undoubtedly mean better deals for consumers, and one where the most efficient and strongest will survive.

Source: Mark Stevenson, "The Store to End All Stores," *Canadian Business*, May 1994, pp. 20-29; "The Wal-Mart Advantage? It's All about Inventory," *Globe and Mail*, January 18, 1994, p. B26; John Heinzl, "Hudson's Bay Dismisses 'Overreaction' to Wal-Mart," *Globe and Mail*, May 26, 1994, pp. B1, B5; and John Heinzl, "The Battle of the Buck," *Globe and Mail*, July 30, 1994, pp. A1, A5.

Seeking to gain a competitive advantage in a market increasingly dominated by the large discounters and category killers, the more conventional department stores have had to adopt new ways of doing business. Eaton's, for example, in 1993 announced a reorganization by removing a layer of management and appointed business managers to oversee operations on the floor of its stores. These managers were to ensure that staff is more attentive to the customer to ensure higher levels of customer service. At the same time, Eaton's established a computerized buying system that would link the company directly with more than 500 suppliers, eliminating purchase orders and reducing merchandise storage and handling.[3]

Sears, Canada's leading department store chain, modified its approach to defining its target markets by moving to a psychographic segmentation, rather than concentrating on the demographic characteristics of customers. Sears, working with Goldfarb Consultants, defined two principal target segments, the "day-to-day watchers" (fairly conservative people who tend to conform to modern trends), and the "joiner-activists" (less conservative, more prepared to embrace new ideas). Sears now creates advertising and places it in media that will appeal to consumers in those target segments. Also, Sears has increased its commitment to direct marketing, to take advantage of its data base of 7 million credit card holders. The company is also renovating many of its stores, particularly those that share shopping centre locations with Wal-Mart. Among other merchandising changes, Sears is placing more emphasis on its catalogue operations, by developing distinct catalogues for urban and rural markets, and by testing direct-response television, whereby customers call a 1-800 number to order merchandise that Sears advertises on TV.[4]

### Discount Houses

**Discount retailing** uses price as a major selling point by combining comparatively low prices and reduced costs of doing business. Several institutions, including off-price retailers and warehouse clubs, rely on discount retailing as their main marketing strategy.

Not surprisingly, the prime example of discount retailing is the **discount house**, a large-scale retailing institution that has a broad, shallow product assortment, emphasizes low prices, and offers relatively few customer services. A discount house normally carries a broad assortment of soft goods (particularly apparel) and well-known brands of hard goods (including appliances and home furnishings). It also advertises extensively. K mart, Zellers, and Wal-Mart are leading discount-house chains.

The success of discount houses can be attributed to two factors: First, other types of retailers normally had large markups on appliances and other merchandise, thereby providing discount houses with the opportunity to set smaller margins and charge lower prices. Second, consumers were receptive to a low-price, limited-service format. Discount houses have had a major impact on retailing, prompting many retailers to lower their prices.

Certainly, the most important development in the discount store scene in Canada was the 1994 acquisition of 122 Woolco stores by Wal-Mart, the world's biggest retail chain, with annual sales approaching $68 billion (U.S.). With its dramatic entry into the Canadian market, Wal-Mart brought its own brand of retailing, one characterized by wide selection, low prices, and friendly service. The response from competing retailers was immediate and dramatic. Literally within days of Wal-Mart's purchase of Woolco, competing stores in some markets had begun opening at 8:00 A.M. and were employing "greeters" at the front of their stores — a Wal-Mart trademark. With its behind-the-scenes ordering and inventory management systems and its up-front emphasis on customer service, Wal-Mart promises to have a considerable effect on how discounters and other retailers do business in the future.[5]

### Catalogue Showrooms

By placing a complete catalogue and a number of sample items in a showroom and the remaining inventory in an attached warehouse, a **catalogue showroom** sets itself apart from other types of stores. If offers a broad but shallow assortment of merchandise, low prices, and few customer services. Catalogue showrooms stress selected product lines, such as photographic equipment, consumer electronics, jewellery, small appliances, luggage, and gift items.

Shoppers examine the samples and catalogue available in the showroom. Or they may have already received an abridged catalogue in the mail or inserted in their newspapers. To purchase an item, the consumer fills out an order form and gives it to a clerk at the central counter. An employee takes the form and goes to the warehouse to obtain the desired merchandise.

The unopposed leader in the Canadian catalogue showroom business is Consumers Distributing Limited, which operates outlets across the country. Although Consumers pioneered the market in this country and successfully defended itself against a number of competitors in its early days, in the 1980s the company faced tough competition. Their price advantage disappeared as large discounters and new "category killer" stores (discussed shortly) also stressed low prices. Consequently, in the 1990s, catalogue showrooms in Canada and other countries were trying to maintain their price advantage or to trade up and encourage shoppers to spend more time in their stores (see Marketing at Work File 17-4).

### Limited-Line Stores

Much of the "action" in retailing in recent years has been in **limited-line stores**. This type of institution has a narrow but deep product assortment and customer services that vary from store to store. Traditionally, limited-line stores strived for full or nondiscounted prices. Currently, however, new types of limited-line retailers have gained a foothold by emphasizing low prices.

Breadth of assortment varies somewhat across limited-line stores. A store may choose to concentrate on:

- Several related product lines (shoes, sportswear, and accessories),
- A single product line (shoes), or
- Part of one product line (athletic footwear).

We identify limited-line stores by the name of the primary product line — furniture store, hardware store, clothing store, for example. Some retailers such as grocery stores and drugstores that used to be limited-line stores now carry much broader assortments because of scrambled merchandising.

Specialty Stores A very narrow and deep product assortment, often concentrating on a specialized product line (baked goods) or even part of a specialized product line (cookies), is offered to consumers by a **specialty store**. Examples of specialty stores are bake shops, furriers, athletic footwear stores, meat markets, and dress shops. (Specialty *stores* should not be confused with specialty *goods*. In a sense, specialty stores are misnamed because they may carry any category of consumer goods, not just specialty goods.)

Most specialty stores strive to maintain manufacturers' suggested prices and provide at least standard customer services. Some specialty stores, however, emphasize extensive customer services and particularly knowledgeable and friendly sales help. The success of specialty stores depends on their ability to attract and then serve well customers whose two primary concerns are deep assortments and extensive, top-quality services.

Off-Price Retailers While many discount houses attempted to trade up during the 1980s, **off-price retailers** positioned themselves below discount houses with lower prices on selected product lines. These new discount retailers are most in evidence in the areas of clothing and consumer electronics; they offer a narrow, deep product assortment, emphasize low prices, and offer few customer services. Store names such as BiWay, Future Shop, and Majestic Electronic Superstore are now well known to consumers in many cities in Canada. A number of chains of off-price retailers now operate in various regions of the country.

Off-price retailers often buy manufacturers' excess output, inventory remaining at the end of a fashion season, or irregular merchandise at lower-than-normal wholesale costs. In turn, their retail prices are much lower than those for regular, in-season merchandise sold in other stores. Customers are attracted by the low prices and fairly current fashions.

**Factory outlets** are a special type of off-price retailer. They are owned by manufacturers and usually sell a single manufacturer's clearance items, regular merchandise, and perhaps even otherwise unavailable items. Many well-known and popular brands such as L. L. Bean, Esprit, Calvin Klein, Royal Doulton, and Wabasso can be found in factory outlets in the United States and occasionally in Canada. This is a retailing form that is well established south of the border, but that has not yet made its presence felt in this country. As Canadian consumers become more familiar with shopping at factory outlets in the United States and as cross-border shopping continues to be part of the retailing scene in this country, we can expect the factory outlet to emerge here as well.

Category-Killer Stores Another phenomenon of the 1980s, a **category-killer store** has a narrow but very deep assortment, emphasizes low prices, and has few to moderate customer services. It is so named because it is designed to destroy all competition in a specific product category. Highly successful category killers include IKEA in assemble-it-yourself furniture, Majestic, and Future Shop in consumer electronics, and Toys " Я " Us. Other product areas where category killers tend to operate include office supplies, sporting goods, housewares, and records, tapes and discs.

This relatively new form of retail institution concentrates on a single product line or several closely related lines. The distinguishing feature of a category killer is a combination of many different sizes, models, styles, and colours of the product, *coupled with* low prices. For example, IKEA stocks literally thousands of furniture and home furnishing items. Record retailers such as the major stores of Sam's and HMV carry such an assortment that the consumer needs to make only one stop to ensure that he or she can find a particular tape or compact disc.

## MARKETING AT WORK

### FILE 17-4 CATALOGUE SHOWROOMS GET BIGGER

Increasing competition from U.S. retailers, a trend towards larger stores, and demands from consumers for more convenience and for a value-added shopping experience has led Consumers Distributing to respond with larger stores. The company, Canada's largest catalogue showroom retailer, expected to have 250 stores operating in Canada by the end of 1994 and planned to spend $100 million on opening a number of "superstores" in 1994 and 1995 that would change its approach to retailing.

In an attempt to draw customers from wider trading areas, Consumers will open 20 to 25 large stores, first in urban centres in Ontario, and then across the country. The new stores will have showrooms averaging 13,000 to 15,000 square feet, more than six times the size of typical existing Consumers' stores. The total size of the new premises will be 25,000 to 30,000 square feet, compared with the 10,000 square feet in existing stores.

The new format will allow the company to display virtually every item in its catalogue. Interactive kiosks will allow customers to view the catalogue on screens and to order and pay for their merchandise with a credit card. Those customers who prefer to will still be able to place their orders in the conventional way, by completing an order form and handing it to a store employee. Customers will find the new Consumers' stores arranged by department where they can examine merchandise before they buy it.

In a further move to encourage sales from its catalogues, Consumers will participate in Groupe Videotron's UBI interactive television project in Chicoutimi, Quebec. Consumers' catalogues will go on-line on the UBI channel in 1995, and customers will be able to order merchandise and pay for it from their own homes. These moves by Consumers' Distributing represent further evidence of the dramatic changes taking place in retailing, with the move towards larger stores and direct shopping from home.

Source: David Chilton, "Retailers Try New Tactics to Keep Their Edge," *Strategy*, March 21, 1994, pp. 4, 10.

That is the objective of the category killer in retailing, to dominate a category in such a way that the consumer believes this is the first store to visit and the value will be better there. Although the major category killers tend to be found in large metropolitan markets such as Toronto, Montreal, and Vancouver, it is in fact easier for a major retailer to dominate a category in a smaller market, where the competition is not likely to be as fierce and where competitors tend to be smaller, local independents.

Sustained growth is forecast for category killers. However, most kinds of merchandise as well as many geographic areas will not generate the large sales levels that permit low prices through high-volume buying power. Furthermore, existing category killers are not without problems. In particular, they face a major challenge in maintaining inventories that are large enough to satisfy customer demand but not so large as to result in excess inventories requiring significant markdowns.

### Supermarkets

As was the case with *discount*, the word *supermarket* can be used to describe a method of retailing *and* a type of institution. As a method, **supermarket retailing** features several related product lines, a high degree of self-service, largely centralized checkouts, and competitive prices. The supermarket approach to retailing is used to sell various kinds of merchandise, including building materials, office products, and — of course — groceries.

The term *supermarket* usually refers to an institution in the grocery retailing field. In this context a **supermarket** is a retailing institution that has a moderately broad, moderately deep product assortment spanning groceries and some nonfood lines and offers relatively few customer services. Most supermarkets emphasize price. Some use price *offensively* by featuring low prices in order to attract customers. Other supermarkets use price more *defensively* by relying on leader pricing to avoid a price disadvantage. Since supermarkets typically have very thin gross margins, they need high levels of inventory turnover to achieve satisfactory returns on invested capital.

Supermarkets originated in the early 1930s. They were established by *independents* to compete with grocery chains. Supermarkets were an immediate success, and the innovation was soon adopted by chain stores. In recent decades supermarkets have added various nonfood lines to provide customers with one-stop shopping convenience and to improve overall gross margins.

Today, stores using the supermarket *method* of retailing are dominant in grocery retailing. However, different names are used to distinguish these institutions by size and assortment:

- A *superstore* is a larger version of the supermarket. It offers more grocery and nonfood items than a conventional supermarket does. Many supermarket chains are emphasizing superstores in their new construction.
- *Combination stores* are usually even larger than superstores. They, too, offer more groceries and nonfoods than a supermarket but also most product lines found in a large drugstore.

For many years the supermarket has been under attack from numerous competitors. For example, a grocery shopper can choose among not only many brands of supermarkets (Loblaws, Safeway, A&P, Sobey's and Steinbergs) but also various types of institutions (warehouse clubs, gourmet shops, meat and fish markets, and convenience stores). Supermarkets have reacted to competitive pressures primarily in either of two ways: Some cut costs and stressed low prices by offering more private brands and generic products and few customer services. Others expanded their store size and assortments by adding more nonfood lines (especially products found in drugstores), groceries attuned to a particular market area (foods that appeal to a specific ethnic group, for example), and various service departments (including video rentals, restaurants, delicatessens, financial institutions, and pharmacies).

### Convenience Stores

To satisfy increasing consumer demand for convenience, particularly in suburban areas, the **convenience store** emerged several decades ago. This retailing institution concentrates on convenience groceries and nonfoods, has higher prices than most other grocery stores, and offers few customer services. Gasoline, fast foods, and selected services (such as car washes and automated teller machines) can also be found in many convenience stores.

The name *convenience store* reflects its main appeal and explains how the somewhat higher prices are justified. Convenience stores are typically located near residential areas and are open extended hours; in fact, some never close. Examples of convenience-store chains are 7-Eleven (originally open from 7 A.M. to 11 P.M. but now open 24 hours in most locations), Mac's, and Beckers.

Convenience stores compete to some extent with both supermarkets and fast-food restaurants. Furthermore, since the 1980s, gasoline companies have modified many service stations by phasing out auto repairs and adding a convenience groceries section.

### Warehouse Clubs

Another institution that mushroomed during the 1980s is the **warehouse club**, sometimes called a **wholesale club**. A combined retailing and wholesaling institution, it has very broad but very shallow product assortments, extremely low prices, and few customer services, and is open only to members. This format originated in Europe many years ago and was first applied successfully in the United States in the mid-1970s by the Price Club. In this country, Price/Costco is the major warehouse club chain, although others also operate, primarily in Quebec, Alberta and British Columbia.[6]

Warehouse clubs' target markets are small businesses (some purchasing merchandise for resale) and select groups of employees (government workers and school personnel, for example) as well as members of credit unions. Prices paid by ultimate consumers are usually about 5 percent higher than those paid by business members.

A warehouse club carries about the same breadth of assortment as a large discount house but in much less depth. For each item, the club stocks only one or two brands and a limited number of sizes and models. It is housed in a warehouse-type building with tall metal racks that display merchandise at ground level and store it at higher levels. Customers pay cash (credit cards are not accepted) and handle their own merchandise — even bulky, heavy items.

Further growth of warehouse clubs is expected during the remainder of the 1990s. As with other retailing institutions, modifications and refinements can be anticipated as competition intensifies. Some warehouse clubs, for instance, are already experimenting with more service departments.

## NONSTORE RETAILING

A large majority — perhaps 85 percent — of retail transactions are made in stores. However, a growing volume of sales is taking place away from stores. Retailing activities resulting in transactions that occur away from a retail store are termed **nonstore retailing.**

We will consider four types of nonstore retailing: direct selling, telemarketing, automatic vending, and direct marketing. (These names may be confusing so don't worry about the names. Focus instead on the distinctive features and competitive standings of the four types.) Each type may be used by producers and/or retailers.

### Direct Selling

Statistics Canada defines **direct selling** as the retail marketing of consumer goods to household consumers by other than the regular retail store outlet. This represents a major growth area in Canadian retailing, as consumers increasingly turn to nonstore retailers for the purchase of many products. In Canada, sales by direct selling exceeded almost $3 billion in 1989, a figure that does not include sales by foreign mail-order retailers, direct sales made to Canadians by the mail-order divisions of department stores (such as the Sears catalogue), or direct sales through vending machines or by wholesalers. We can expect the impact of nonstore retailers to increase through the 1990s as consumers demand the convenience of shopping from locations that are convenient *to them* and at times at which *they* are available.

The annual volume of direct selling in Canada has increased from approximately $772 million in 1969 to more than $3 billion in 1989.[7] An increasing number of companies are turning to the direct-selling route to reach consumers in their own homes. There are many well-known direct-selling companies, including Avon, Tupperware, Mary Kay, Amway, Electrolux, and Encyclopedia Britannica. Many diverse products are sold through the direct-selling route, most of which require some form of testing or demonstration (cosmetics, water purifiers, vacuum cleaners). Essentially, the direct-selling approach involves a sales person contacting potential customers outside of a conventional retail store environment.

The two major kinds of direct selling are **door to door** and **party plan**. Sometimes door-to-door selling simply involves "cold canvassing" without any advance selection of prospects. More often there is an initial contact in a store, by telephone, or by a mailed-in coupon. A relatively new form of direct selling has emerged in recent years, known as network marketing. This approach to nonstore retailing involves a series of levels of sales personnel, each of whom reports to an area or territory manager or captain. Sales are generated by sales people contacting prospects directly, usually in their homes. Commissions on sales are paid to each level in the sales hierarchy. Products currently sold by this method include cosmetics (Nu-Skin) and water purification systems (NSA).

With the party-plan approach, a host or hostess invites some friends to a party. These guests understand that a sales person — say, for a cosmetics or a housewares company — will make a sales presentation. The sales rep has a larger prospective market and more favourable selling conditions than if these people were approached individually door to door. And the guests get to shop in a friendly, social atmosphere.

With so many women now working outside the home, direct-selling firms have had to find new ways of making contact with prospective customers. For instance, Avon has moved in recent years to reach its target customers at their place of work by distributing catalogues at offices. Tupperware, possibly the best known of the party-plan retailers, continues to market its extensive range of plastic houseware products primarily through in-home parties, involving its 374,000 dealers in more than 40 countries. However, because of the changing nature of the North American market, Tupperware is now also marketed through catalogues and Tupperware parties held at the office.[8]

There are other drawbacks to direct selling. It is the most expensive form of retailing, with sales commissions as high as 40 to 50 percent of the retail price. Also, good sales people are extremely hard to recruit and retain. Some sales people have been too persistent or even fraudulent. As a result, a number of provinces have "cooling off" laws that permit consumers to nullify a door-to-door or party-plan sale during a period up to several days after the transaction.

Direct selling does give consumers the opportunity to buy at home or another convenient nonstore location. For the seller, direct selling provides the most aggressive form of retail promotion as well as the chance to demonstrate a product in the shopper's (rather than the seller's) environment.

### Telemarketing

Sometimes called *telephone selling*, **telemarketing** refers to a sales person initiating contact with a shopper and also closing a sale over the telephone. As with door-to-door selling, telemarketing may mean cold canvassing from the phone directory. Or it may rely on prospects who have requested information from the company or whose demographics match those of the firm's target market.

The telemarketing business has really developed only within the past ten years, as marketers found it increasingly difficult to reach consumers through conventional means. Also, the development of computerized mailing or calling lists and auto-dialling technology have meant that literally hundreds of calls can be made during a day by a single telemarketer. Many products that can be bought without being seen are sold over the telephone. Examples include home cleaning and pest-control services, magazine subscriptions, credit card and other financial services, and athletic club memberships.

Telemarketing's reputation has been damaged by the unethical sales practices of some firms. These firms tell consumers that they are conducting marketing research and "are not selling anything." Such unethical procedures hurt other telemarketing companies as well as legitimate research firms that conduct telephone surveys. Such practices are known as "sugging" — selling under the guise of research. The approaches used by some telemarketing companies, coupled with a desire on the part of many consumers not to be bothered at home, has led to a consumer backlash against telemarketing in some areas.[9]

Despite this problem, telemarketing sales have been increasing for several reasons. Certain consumers appreciate the convenience of making a purchase by phone. Also, the introduction of outgoing WATS lines about 25 years ago made telemarketing to consumers in distant locations more cost effective. Finally, computer systems today can automatically dial a telephone number or, going a step further, play a taped message and then record information that the consumer gives to complete the sale. Such systems reduce the normally high labour costs associated with telemarketing. These advances in technology, despite their obvious contribution to the efficiency of the process, contribute further to the negative feeling that many consumers have towards being sold products and services in such an intrusive manner. The truly effective telemarketing programs are being run by companies that have adopted an approach to telemarketing that involves doing a better job of targeting those customers who are likely to be interested in the products or service being offered (rather than the blanket calling of all households in a region) and conveying the message to the consumer in a polite and caring manner.

### Direct Marketing

There is no consensus on the exact nature of direct marketing; in a sense, it comprises all types of nonstore retailing other than the three already discussed. We define **direct marketing** as the use of nonpersonal media to contact consumers who, in turn, purchase products without visiting a retail store. (Be sure to distinguish among the terms direct *marketing*, direct *selling*, and direct *distribution*.)

To contact consumers, direct marketers use one or more of the following media: radio, TV, newspapers, magazines, catalogues, and mailings (direct mail). Consumers typically place orders by telephone or mail. Direct marketing is big business. Everywhere we go today, we are exposed to direct-marketing efforts. We see advertisements on television from direct-marketing retailers of records and exercise aids, and we are encouraged to telephone a 1-800 number with our VISA or MasterCard number. We receive "bill stuffers" with our monthly gasoline bills, retail store, and credit card statements. We order clothing and other items from mail-order catalogues, by either mailing back an order form, or more likely calling a toll-free long-distance telephone number. A large volume of direct-marketing effort is rarely seen by end consumers as it is directed at the business-to-business market, where direct marketers have relied on catalogues and mailing pieces for many years.

Given its broad definition, there are many forms of direct marketing. The major types are as follows:

- **Direct mail.** Companies mail consumers letters, brochures, and even product samples, and ask that orders be placed by mail or telephone.
- **Catalogue retailing.** Companies mail catalogues to consumers and to businesses or make them available at retail stores. Examples of the latter include Tilley Endurables, Canadian Tire, and Consumers Distributing.
- **Television shopping.** There are basically two approaches to retailing through television. One we have mentioned above, in which individual products are advertised and the consumer places an order by telephoning a toll-free number and giving his or her credit card number. The second involves the use of a dedicated television channel such as the Canadian Home Shopping Network, which represents a continuous advertisement for a variety of products such as housewares, jewellery, and other items that can be sold without the need for demonstration or trial.

Some companies operate mail-order divisions as components of their department store operations — Sears being the best example. Others have launched catalogues as an additional vehicle for the distribution of their products. Others, such as The Added Touch, distribute only through their catalogues. Direct marketers can be classified as either general-merchandise firms, which offer a wide variety of product lines, or specialty firms, which carry merchandise in only one or two product categories.

Direct marketing represents a major growth area in retailing. Its advantages relate particularly to its ability to direct the marketing effort to those consumers who are most likely to respond positively. Also, it offers products and services in a way that is most convenient for the consumer. Companies that are using catalogues and direct mail to reach their target customers maximize the effectiveness of their marketing programs by having the most accurate and complete mailing list possible. In fact, the success of most direct-marketing programs lies to a very great extent in the preparation and maintenance of an accurate mailing list.

Technology has kept pace with (or even led) developments in the direct-marketing field as companies are now developing sophisticated computer data bases of customers and prospective customers.[10] These data bases contain not only mailing addresses, but other data on the characteristics of the consumer and his or her household, and a history of purchases that the consumer has made. Companies such as American Express make very effective use of such data bases to direct mailings to cardholders in their monthly statements. The types of advertisements that are sent to certain customers are determined to an extent by an analysis of their purchasing history using the American Express card.[11]

Like other types of nonstore retailing, direct marketing provides consumers with shopping convenience. Direct marketers often benefit from relatively low operating expenses because they do not have the overhead of retail stores. There are drawbacks to direct marketing, however. Consumers must place orders without seeing or trying on the actual merchandise (although they may see a picture of it). To offset this limitation, direct marketers must offer liberal return policies. Furthermore, catalogues and, to some extent, direct-mail pieces are costly and must be prepared long before they are issued. Price changes and new products can be announced only through supplementary catalogues or brochures.

In addition, some consumers have reacted negatively to receiving unsolicited mailing pieces at their homes, in much the same way that they are not exactly delighted to receive telemarketing solicitations. This negative reaction to direct-mail advertising in particular is exacerbated by the opinion shared by many that direct mail is "junk mail" in that much of it is wasted and represents a waste of paper at a time when more and more people are interested in conserving forest products. Some equate the receiving of "junk mail" to killing a tree and request that their names are taken off mailing lists to reduce the amount of unsolicited printed materials sent through the mail. The Canadian Direct Marketing Association has encouraged its 450 members to comply with these requests.

### Automatic Vending

The sale of products through a machine with no personal contact between buyer and seller is called **automatic vending** (or *automated merchandising*). Most products sold by automatic vending are convenience-oriented or are purchased on impulse. They are usually well-known, presold brands with a high rate of turnover. For many years, the bulk of automatic vending sales has come from four main product categories: coffee, soft drinks, confectionery items, and cigarettes. In Canada, sales made through 196,000 vending machines in 1992 totalled $393 million, with sales coming increasingly from hot and cold drinks and confectionery items, and less from cigarettes. As with retail sales in general, sales through vending machines fell in the early 1990s, in part because of the recession, but also related to the fact that sales of cigarettes, a major vending machine category, continued to fall. Total vending machine sales stood at $363 million in 1982 and peaked at $479 million in 1990.

In 1992, total vending machine sales of $393 million comprised 31.2 percent coffee and 25.6 percent soft drinks. Confectionery items, including ice cream, accounted for 19.5 percent of vending machine sales, while sales of cigarettes accounted for only 14.6 percent, down from 20.5 percent in 1989.

Vending machines can expand a firm's market by reaching customers where and when it is not feasible for stores to do so. Thus they are found virtually everywhere, particularly in schools, workplaces, and public facilities. Automatic vending has to overcome major challenges, however. Operating costs are high because of the need to continually replenish inventories. The machines also require occasional maintenance and repairs.

While sales through vending machines have been somewhat volatile in recent years, there is reason to believe that we can expect to see more products sold through this form of nonstore retailing in the future. The reason for this optimism relates to changes in vending machine technology. One example of the new wave of vending machines is the machines introduced by DataWave Vending of Vancouver. This company recently launched a vending machine that dispenses single-use Kodak cameras and film for regular cameras. These machines will be located at popular tourist spots and will accept credit cards as payment. The DataWave machines are unique in that they not only accept credit cards but obtain authorization at the same time, providing protection against fraud.[12] Developments such as these, which result from improved technology, make it possible to retail much more expensive items through vending machines, thereby expanding the base of this form of retailing beyond the small beverage and confectionery items that have been its mainstay for years.

## RETAILING MANAGEMENT

Fundamental to managing a retailing firm is the planning of sound strategies. Central to strategic planning are the selection of target markets and development of customer relationships. Also, during the turbulent 1990s, a factor called retail positioning will probably be critical. Let's briefly discuss these topics.

### Positioning

Retailers are increasingly thinking about positioning as they develop marketing plans. **Positioning** refers to a retailer's strategies and actions designed to favourably distinguish itself from competitors in the minds (and hearts) of targeted groups of consumers. Positioning centres on the three variables we have stressed in this chapter: product assortment, price, and customer services.

Let's briefly examine several positioning strategies.[13] When only price and service levels are considered, two strategies that have potential value are *high price-high service* and *low price-low service*. The former is difficult to implement because it requires skilled, motivated employees (especially sales people); the latter necessitates careful management of operating expenses because gross margins are small.

When all three variables — product assortment, price, and customer services — are considered, two new options emerge. One is *product differentiation*, in which a retailer offers different brands or styles than those sold in competing stores. A second is *service and personality augmentation*, where a retailer offers similar products but sets itself apart by providing special services and also creating a distinctive personality or atmosphere for its stores.

A retailer's positioning strategy may include one or a combination of these options. Retail executives need to exhibit creativity and skill in selecting positioning strategies and then in implementing them.

### Customer Retention

In recent years, marketers in many businesses, and especially in retailing, have begun to subscribe in increasing numbers to the philosophy that it makes considerably greater sense to retain the customers they have rather than having to compete vigorously to attract new ones. This viewpoint acknowledges what should have been obvious to all marketers, namely that a company's most valuable assets are loyal customers. While not denying the importance of going out to attract new customers, this approach to doing business places at least equal emphasis on keeping existing customers happy.

Two elements of a customer-retention strategy involve getting to know customers in as much detail as possible and rewarding those who are loyal and continue to give us their business. The former implies the development and maintenance of a customer data base and the latter often involves the establishment of a bonus program for frequent shoppers. Some of the most effective customer-retention programs combine these elements.

The best example of a customer-retention program, often called *loyalty programs*, in Canadian retailing is Club Z, operated by Zellers, the successful discount arm of the Hudson's Bay Company. Established in 1986 as a frequent-buyer program, modelled along the lines of the airlines' frequent-flyer programs, Club Z awards "points" to Zellers' shoppers based on the amount of their purchases. These points may be redeemed for premiums from a Club Z gift catalogue. The program has been wildly successful in differentiating Zellers from the competition and in creating a very loyal customer base, as now close to half of all Canadian households are Club Z members.[14]

Other retailers have had or have recently established similar programs to encourage shopper loyalty. Canadian Tire has issued its well-known "Canadian Tire money" for many years, essentially giving customers discounts of up to 5 percent on purchases made in the store. Sears Canada relaunched its Sears Club, a frequent-shopper program that rewards users of the Sears credit card with savings of up to 4 percent on purchases. These reward programs are really modern-day, electronic versions of trading stamps, which were distributed by many retailers primarily in the 1940s and 1950s.

## RETAILING IN THE FUTURE

Retailers are facing challenges perhaps unequaled since the Depression of the 1930s. Many trends represent threats to retailers. But as we know, a threat perceived and handled properly is really an opportunity. We will illustrate the dynamics of retailing by focusing on seven diverse, significant trends.

- **Changing demographics and industry structure.** The Canadian population is growing older, with proportional decreases in the 16-to-34 age group and increases in the 45-and-over age group. Real growth in retail sales is expected to be substantially less than in the 1970s and 1980s. Thus there may be too many shopping centres and retail stores, particularly as we see so many major chains enter the market in the mid-1990s.
- **Expanding computer technology.** Advancing technology dramatically affects both consumer behaviour and retail management. In particular, sophisticated computer systems that capture sales and inventory data influence the items retailers stock as well as what and when they reorder. Newer systems permit retailers to automatically place orders and reorders with suppliers that are linked to them via computer.[15]
- **Emphasis on lower prices and lower costs.** An expanding number of retailers are expected to stress value. For most of them, that strategy will dictate reducing prices and — if they intend to remain profitable — cutting costs. To pare their expenses over a period of years, more and more chains will need to take steps such as eliminating one or more layers of management, cutting advertising, and investing in labour-saving equipment such as computers that monitor inventory levels and automatically reorder merchandise as needed.
- **Accent on convenience and service.** Compared to past decades, consumers are busier, are older, and have more money to spend. They want products and ways to buy them that provide maximum convenience and service. Convenience means nearby loca-

tions, extended hours, short waiting times, and other factors that make shopping easier. Service also includes friendly, knowledgeable sales staff, easy credit, liberal return policies, and ample postsale service.

- **Experimentation.** Largely because of competitive pressures, many retailers are experimenting with new or modified formats and also with nontraditional locations. For example, department stores are scaling back product assortments by eliminating "commodity" lines (such as fabrics and mattresses) and stressing fashion and quality. Discount houses are either trading up to become so-called promotional department stores or are digging in for price battles. Some retailers are expanding their markets through new types of locations, or by moving towards more nonstore retailing. Others are welcoming smaller, specialized retailers into their stores to operate specific departments as tenants or partners. For example, Bestsellers, a Toronto-based chain of 26 stores that sell fast-selling books, CDs, and videos, is planning to open outlets in selected Loblaws, Zehrs, and Real Canadian Superstores locations across Canada.[16]
- **Emphasis on productivity.** Extremely small profits are forcing retailers to squeeze more revenues out of their resources (floor space, people, and inventories). Hence, virtually all products are being sold, at least to some extent, on a self-service basis. To boost motivation, some retailers have put sales people completely on commissions rather than salaries plus commissions. Computer systems, as discussed above can also help achieve greater productivity.
- **Continuing growth of nonstore retailing.** Retail stores will continue to be dominant. But more and more retailers are complementing their stores with one or more types of nonstore retailing. Many consumers prefer the novelty or convenience of nonstore retailing.

As consumers change, so do forms of retailing. Retail executives would like to anticipate changes in retailing before they occur. To some extent this is possible, as many of the evolutionary changes in retailing have followed a cyclical pattern called the **wheel of retailing.**[17] This theory states that a new type of retailer often enters the market as a low-cost, low-price store. Other retailers as well as financial firms do not take the new type seriously. However, consumers respond favourably to the low prices and shop at the new institution. Over time this store takes business away from other retailers that initially ignored it and retained their old strategies.

Eventually, according to the wheel of retailing, the successful new institution trades up in order to attract a broader market, achieve higher margins, and/or gain more status. Trading up entails improving the quality of products sold and adding customer services. Sooner or later, high costs and, ultimately, high prices (at least as perceived by its target markets) make the institution vulnerable to new retail types as the wheel revolves. The next innovator enters as a low-cost, low-price form of retailing, and the evolutionary process continues.

There are many examples of the wheel of retailing. To mention a few, chain stores grew at the expense of independents during the 1920s, particularly in the grocery field. In the 1950s, discount houses placed tremendous pressure on department stores, which had become staid, stagnant institutions. The 1980s saw the expansion of warehouse clubs and off-price retailers, which have forced many institutions — supermarkets, specialty stores, and department stores — to modify their marketing strategies.

What will be the retailing innovations of the 1990s? Perhaps electronic retailing, some other form of nonstore retailing, or a new type of low-cost, low-price store. The wheel of retailing can help retailers identify changes in retail institutions. Retail firms must identify and respond to significant trends that affect retailing, including institutional changes, by developing customer want-satisfying marketing strategies.

## SUMMARY

Retailing is the sale of goods and services to ultimate consumers for personal, nonbusiness use. Any institution (such as a manufacturer) may engage in retailing, but a firm engaged primarily in retailing is called a retailer.

Retailers serve as purchasing agents for consumers and as sales specialists for wholesaling intermediaries and producers. They perform many specific activities such as anticipating customers' wants, developing product assortments, and financing.

More than 200,000 retail stores in Canada collectively generate almost $200 billion in annual sales. Retailers' operating expenses run about 27 percent of the retail selling price; profits are usually a very small percentage of sales.

Most retail firms are very small. However, small retailers can survive — and even prosper — if they remain flexible and pay careful attention to personally serving customers' needs.

Retailers can be classified in two ways: (1) by form of ownership, including corporate chain, independent store, and various kinds of contractual vertical marketing systems such as franchising; and (2) by key marketing strategies. Retailer types are distinguished according to product assortment, price levels, and customer service levels: department store, discount house, catalogue showroom, limited-line store (including specialty store, off-price retailer, and category-killer store), supermarket, convenience store, and warehouse club. Mature institutions such as department stores, discount houses, and supermarkets face strong challenges from new competitors, particularly different kinds of limited-line stores.

Although the large majority of retail sales are made in stores, an increasing percentage now occur away from stores. And this proportion is growing steadily. Four major forms of nonstore retailing are direct selling, telemarketing, automatic vending, and direct marketing. Each type has advantages as well as drawbacks.

Retailers need to carefully select markets and plan marketing mixes. Besides product, price, promotion, and customer services, executives also must make strategic decisions regarding physical facilities. Specific decisions concern location, design, and layout of the store. Downtown shopping areas have suffered while suburban shopping centres have grown in number and importance. Retailers also should consider positioning — how to favourably distinguish their stores from competitors' stores in the minds of consumers.

Various trends present opportunities or pose threats for retailers. Institutional changes in retailing can frequently be explained by a theory called the wheel of retailing. To succeed, retailers need to identify significant trends and ensure that they develop marketing strategies to satisfy consumers.

## KEY TERMS AND CONCEPTS

**Retailing (retail trade) (496)**
**Retailer (496)**
**Physical facilities (501)**
**Shopping centre (502)**
**Convenience centre (503)**
**Neighbourhood centre (503)**
**Community centre (503)**
**Regional centre (503)**
**Corporate chain (504)**
**Independent retailer (506)**
**Contractual vertical marketing system (506)**
**Retailer co-operative (506)**
**Voluntary chain (506)**
**Franchising (507)**
- **Product and trade name franchising (508)**
- **Business format franchising (508)**

**Franchise system (507)**
**Department store (510)**
**Discount retailing (513)**
**Discount house (513)**
**Catalogue showroom (514)**
**Limited-line store (514)**
**Specialty store (515)**
**Off-price retailer (515)**
**Factory outlet (515)**
**Category-killer store (515)**
**Supermarket retailing (516)**
**Supermarket (516)**
**Convenience store (517)**
**Warehouse club (wholesale club) (517)**
**Nonstore retailing (518)**
**Direct selling (518)**
- **Door-to-door selling (518)**
- **Party-plan selling (518)**

**Telemarketing (519)**
**Direct marketing (520)**
- **Direct mail (520)**
- **Catalogue retailing (520)**
- **Television shopping (520)**

**Automatic vending (521)**
**Positioning (522)**
**Wheel of retailing (524)**

## QUESTIONS AND PROBLEMS

1. Explain the terms *retailing*, *retail sale*, and *retailer* in light of the following situations:
   a. Avon cosmetics sales person selling door to door.
   b. Farmer selling produce door to door.
   c. Farmer selling produce at a roadside stand.
   d. Sporting goods store selling uniforms to a semi-professional baseball team.
2. How do you explain the wide differences in operating expenses among the various types of retailers shown in Table 17-2?
3. What recommendations do you have for reducing retailing costs?
4. Reconcile the following statements, using facts and statistics where appropriate:
   a. "Retailing is typically small-scale business."
   b. "There is a high degree of concentration in retailing today; the giants control the field."
5. Of the criteria given in this chapter for evaluating the competitive positions of large-scale and small-scale retailers, which ones show small stores to be in a stronger position than large-scale retailers? Do your findings conflict with the fact that most retail firms are quite small?
6. The ease of entry into retailing undoubtedly contributes to the high failure rate among retailers, which — in the view of some — creates economic waste. Should entry into retailing be restricted? If so, how could this be done?
7. What course of action might small retailers take to improve their competitive position?
8. In what ways does a corporate chain (Loblaws, Zellers, or Sears) differ from a voluntary chain such as IGA?
9. What can department stores do to strengthen their competitive positions?
10. "The supermarket, with its operating expense ratio of 20 percent, is the most efficient institution in retailing today." Do you agree with this statement? In what ways might supermarkets further reduce their expenses?
11. "Door-to-door selling is the most efficient form of retailing because it eliminates wholesalers and retail stores." Discuss.
12. What is the relationship between the growth and successful development of regional shopping centres in suburban areas and the material you studied in Chapters 4, 5, and 6 regarding consumers?
13. Which of the retailing trends discussed in the last section of the chapter do you think represents the greatest opportunity for retailers? The greatest threat?
14. Do you agree with the axiom that there are three keys to success in retailing — location, location, and location? How do you reconcile this axiom with the fact that there is so much price competition in retailing at the present time?
15. Of the types of retail stores discussed in the chapter, which one(s) do you think have been or would be most successful in foreign countries? Which one(s) have been or would be unsuccessful in other countries? Explain your answers.

## HANDS-ON MARKETING

1. Arrange an interview with a small retailer. Discuss with this merchant the general positions of small and large retailers, as covered in this chapter. Which if any of these points does the small retailer disagree with, and why? Also ask what courses of action this merchant takes to achieve or maintain a viable competitive position. Interview a second small retailer, ask the same questions, and compare your answers.
2. Write to the headquarters of two retail franchise systems with which you are familiar and request information provided to prospective purchasers of a franchise. (Local units of the franchise systems should be able to supply you with the headquarters' mailing addresses.) Once you have received the information, evaluate whether you would like to own either of these franchises. What criteria did you use in making this evaluation?

## NOTES AND REFERENCES


1. From information supplied by Diane Hargrave of Tilley Endurables, and from Andrew Vowles, "Hats Off to Tilley," *Retail Directions*, July/August 1991, pp. 23-37; Thelma Dickman, "Canada's Glad Hatter," *Leisureways*, April 1992, pp. 34-35; and Bernadette Morra, "Alex Tilley Just Can't Keep a Lid on His Success," *Toronto Star*, April 29, 1993, p. FA9.
2. For an interesting insight into how a small family-owned kitchenware retailer in Calgary operates with an emphasis on personalized service, see Cathryn Motherwell, "Where the Business Is Cooking," *Globe and Mail*, August 24, 1993, p. B28.
3. Robert Williamson, "Eaton's Has Changes in Store," *Globe and Mail*, July 29, 1993, pp. B1, B4.
4. James Pollock, "Sears' New Tack," *Marketing*, March 14, 1994, pp. 9-10.
5. James Pollock, "Delivering the Goods," *Marketing*, August 1/8, 1994, pp. 17-18.
6. See Marina Strauss, "Discounters Bite into Groceries," *Globe and Mail*, September 16, 1993, p. B4; and Marina Strauss, "Supermarket Price War Flares Again," *Globe and Mail*, May 5, 1994, p. B4.
7. Statistics Canada, *Direct Selling in Canada*, cat. no. 63-218, annual.
8. Kathy Hogan Trocheck, "The Party's Not Over," *Globe and Mail*, March 21, 1991, p. B8.
9. Michael W. Miller, "You're Selling What? Hold on, I'll Let You Speak to My Dog," *Globe and Mail*, June 29, 1991, p. B18,
10. Mary Gooderham, "Your Supermarket Knows Who You Are," *Globe and Mail*, August 17, 1993, pp. A1, A4.
11. Statistics Canada, *Vending Machine Operators*, cat. no. 63-213, annual.
12. Marina Strauss, "Vending Machines Get the Picture," *Globe and Mail*, August 18, 1994, p. B6.
13. Positioning based on price and service is discussed in George H. Lucas, Jr., and Larry G. Gresham, "How to Position for Retail Success," *Business*, April-June 1988, pp. 3-13. Positioning that combines all three variables is presented in Lawrence H. Wortzel, "Retailing Strategies for Today's Mature Marketplace," *The Journal of Business Strategy*, Spring 1987, pp. 45-56.
14. For more on the use of frequent-shopper programs and other techniques designed to encourage customer retention, see Kenneth R. Wightman, "The Marriage of Retail Marketing and Information Systems Technology: The Zellers Club Z Experience," *MIS Quarterly*, December 1990, pp. 359-366; and Mark Evans, "Retailers in Battle for Frequent Buyer," *The Financial Post*, May 13, 1991, p. 8.
15. For an interesting insight into how Canadian retailers and their suppliers are using technology to make their operations more efficient, see James Pollock, "Faster, Cheaper, Better," *Marketing*, February 7, 1994, p. 11; and Gerald Levitch, "Mapping the Market," *Marketing*, February 7, 1994, p. 12.
16. James Pollock, "Stores within Stores: A Growing Trend," *Marketing*, February 14, 1994, p. 4.
17. The wheel of retailing was first described in M. P. McNair, "Significant Trends and Developments in the Postwar Period," in A. B. Smith (ed.), *Competitive Distribution in a Free, High-Level Economy and Its Implications for the University*, Pittsburgh: The University of Pittsburgh Press, 1958, pp. 17-18.

## CASES FOR PART 5

# CASE 5–1

# TORONTO DOMINION BANK

It was 7:30 on a very warm morning in early July 1991. Although the thermometer on the clock at the service station across the street read 26 degrees, Marilyn Krauss had not minded walking the three blocks from the hotel to the branch. There were already a number of people on the streets of Melfort. She couldn't help thinking how much earlier people started the day here, as compared with Saskatoon. She was eager to get to the branch as she had scheduled a meeting at 8 o'clock with her senior staff to learn more about the Melfort area and to begin the process of preparing a marketing plan for the branch. It was her third week in her new job, and she had not had an opportunity to meet with her staff as she had spent the first two weeks familiarizing herself with the town and the branch.

Marilyn had been transferred from main office in Saskatoon to the position of manager of the Toronto Dominion Bank's branch in Melfort. She was looking forward to the new assignment, as she was happy to be in rural Saskatchewan. Marilyn had grown up near Regina, but moved to Saskatoon to attend the University of Saskatchewan. After graduation, she had joined the TD Bank as a management trainee. That was nine years ago, and she had moved steadily up the management ladder in two branches in Saskatoon, serving first as a loans officer and later as an account manager. Two years ago, she had moved to main office as a senior account manager. She expected the Melfort assignment to be a challenging one, as she knew that rural bank customers were likely to be different in many ways from those with whom she had been dealing in Saskatoon for the past nine years.

Marilyn was taking over the manager's job in Melfort from Fred Simpson, who had retired at the end of June. Fred had worked for the TD for more than 40 years, the last 15 as manager in Melfort. Marilyn wished that she had been able to spend more time with Fred before he and his wife had left for Regina, but the Simpsons had wanted to move as soon as possible after Fred retired, to be closer to their children and grandchildren, all of whom lived in Regina. In May, when Marilyn had visited Melfort to meet the staff of the branch, she and Fred had spent one afternoon meeting in Fred's office. Marilyn remembered that at the time she wondered whether she would ever be able to know the community as well as Fred did.

### MELFORT, SASKATCHEWAN

Melfort is a small Saskatchewan city located in the northeast part of the province, in the heart of the Carrot River Valley. Although there has not been much population growth in the city itself in the past ten years, Melfort is an economically stable community, located as it is in one of the richest and most productive farming areas of Canada. The city is an agriculture service centre, and most of the businesses in Melfort are related to the agriculture industry. The farmers in the area grow primarily grains, including wheat, oats, barley, rye, flax, and rapeseed. There are four grain elevators in Melfort.

The Melfort Union Hospital was replaced with a completely new facility in 1985-86 at a cost of $8 million. The 85-bed hospital is staffed by 14 physicians. In addition, three long-stay nursing homes accommodate 226 residents. Although only 38 permits for residential construction were issued in Melfort in 1990, construction in the city was booming as more than $8 million had been spent on the first phase of the new North East Leisure Centre, including a gymnasium, meeting rooms, crafts areas, exercise rooms, and catering facilities. The second phase, containing a 25-metre swimming pool, whirlpool, saunas, waterslide, snack bar, and spectator area, was scheduled for completion in late 1991.

Although she had not yet found a place to live, Marilyn had noted in the *Melfort Journal* that there were a small

---

 This case has been prepared by James G. Barnes of Memorial University of Newfoundland. It has been written to illustrate and stimulate discussion of a hypothetical marketing situation, and not to indicate either effective or ineffective handling of that situation. The author wishes to thank Al Cotton, David Thomson, and David Ross of the Toronto Dominion Bank for providing advice and data on the rural market for financial services; Gérard Cussom of Statistics Canada in Ottawa, and Dr. John Leyes, Director of the Small Area and Administrative Data Division of Statistics Canada. The preparation of this case was made possible through a grant from Statistics Canada.

number of homes available for sale. As she had driven around the town over the Canada Day weekend, she had made a number of enquiries. At the local Realty World real estate office, she had been advised that homes in Melfort generally sold in the range of $50,000 to $75,000 and that there was a small number currently on the market. Alternatively, she could rent a two-bedroom home quite near the business district for $400 per month. She had to make a decision on housing soon as she did not want to stay at the hotel more than another few days.

Marilyn was already aware that the TD Bank's competition in Melfort came from branches of the CIBC, Bank of Nova Scotia, and Royal Bank of Canada, and from the Melfort Credit Union. There were four small investment company offices in town, including The Co-operators, and four real estate companies. In addition to the downtown business and retail district, there were three small shopping plazas in Melfort and a 30-store enclosed shopping mall.

Several weeks ago, when she had been informed that the manager's position in Melfort was to be offered to her, she asked the bank's regional office to send her information about the city. Data on Melfort's population (Exhibit 1) and the mix of businesses in the city (Exhibit 2) were of particular interest to her. She had also called the office of Statistics Canada in Regina to send her information about the population of the Melfort area.

## THE STAFF MEETING

Precisely at 8 o'clock, Marilyn was joined in her office by Wendy Parmiter and Tony Wroblewski, the most senior members of the staff of 12. Wendy is the assistant manager of the Melfort branch and Tony had come to the branch as accountant just six months ago. Marilyn explained that she would like to spend the next two hours or so discussing the Melfort area and reviewing some of the data she had been able to compile on the area. She knew that they would soon have to begin preparing plans for 1992 and she wanted to make sure that they were ready and as well informed as possible.

Since Wendy had worked in the branch for more than ten years, Marilyn asked her to begin the discussion by providing an overview of the bank's customers and the way business is done in the area. Wendy explained that Melfort, with a population within the city itself of only approximately 6,000, was really quite a small market where business often was done on a more informal basis than would be the case in a larger city. As Wendy explained, "Everyone here knows each other, and it's hard to keep a secret in this town." As a result, she explained, many people are quite concerned about the confidentiality of their banking arrangements. They want to make sure that they can trust their banker to keep their financial affairs totally confidential.

Tony added that most of the TD customers are in the branch at least once a week, generally combining a visit to the bank with a shopping trip. Marilyn observed that this was quite different from her experience in Saskatoon, where the increased use of automated banking machines has meant that many customers rarely come into the branch. Tony also added that many of the customers also want to see the manager when they visit, even for relatively minor matters. He suggested that Marilyn should expect to be quite busy meeting customers, as maintaining the relationship with customers is an important element in keeping their business.

Marilyn asked Wendy and Tony to give her an overview of the competition in Melfort and the position that the TD is perceived to occupy. They explained that the four banks in town were quite competitive, each with its own solid core of loyal customers. Wendy observed that there had been some indication in recent years that some of the small investment companies in Melfort had been building business in the financial planning area, in some cases taking away business by providing services that she felt could have been provided by the banks. Tony felt that this may reflect something he had noted since coming to Melfort, namely that some of the business customers in the city seemed to want to keep their business and personal banking separate.

**EXHIBIT 1 Population, City of Melfort, 1980-1990**

| Population | | | | Age Groups | | | |
|---|---|---|---|---|---|---|---|
| | Total | Male | Female | 0-19 | 20-44 | 45-64 | 65 and over |
| 1980 | 6136 | 2960 | 3176 | 2006 | 1977 | 1146 | 1007 |
| 1985 | 6542 | 3154 | 3388 | 1922 | 2361 | 1108 | 1151 |
| 1988 | 6296 | 3022 | 3274 | 1812 | 2175 | 1084 | 1225 |
| 1990 | 6211 | 2954 | 3257 | 1785 | 2079 | 1095 | 1252 |

Source: Saskatchewan Department of Rural Development, *Community Profile*, *Melfort*, 1990

**EXHIBIT 2 Profile of Businesses, City of Melfort 1990**

| Type of Business | No. of Firms | Employment | Employment of Largest |
|---|---|---|---|
| Agriculture | | | |
| Nurseries | 1 | 3 | 3 |
| Feedlots | 1 | 4 | 4 |
| Dairy Farms | 3 | 7 | 3 |
| Hatcheries | 1 | 6 | 6 |
| Others | 13 | 67 | 20 |
| Construction | | | |
| General Building Contractors | 3 | 20 | 6 |
| Plumbing and Heating | 5 | 20 | 6 |
| Painting and Decorating | 5 | 15 | — |
| Electrical | 3 | 15 | 5 |
| Masonry | 1 | 2 | 2 |
| Plastering and Drywall | 2 | 5 | 3 |
| Carpenters | 1 | 2 | 2 |
| Others | 9 | 46 | 15 |
| Manufacturing | | | |
| Food Products | 5 | 61 | 21 |
| Printing, Publishing | 1 | 27 | 27 |
| Chemical Products | 4 | 5 | 5 |
| Metal Products | 2 | 3 | 3 |
| Others | 2 | 17 | 12 |
| Retail Trade | | | |
| Bulk Oil | 3 | 12 | 4 |
| Lumber Yards | 2 | 18 | 8 |
| Hardware Stores | 2 | 11 | 7 |
| Farm Equipment | 7 | 84 | 25 |
| General Merchandise | 6 | 56 | 26 |
| Grocery Stores | 9 | 40 | — |
| Meat and Fish Markets | 2 | 18 | 14 |
| Confectioneries | 4 | 15 | 3 |
| Bakeries | 3 | 11 | 6 |
| Motor Vehicle Dealers | 5 | 70 | 26 |
| Auto Supply Stores | 4 | 20 | 7 |
| Service Stations | 5 | 30 | 15 |
| Men's and Boys' Clothing | 4 | 6 | 3 |
| Women's Clothing | 4 | 10 | 3 |
| Children's Clothing | 1 | 2 | — |
| Family Clothing | 3 | 20 | 6 |
| Furniture Stores | 1 | 8 | — |
| Eating Places | 23 | 168 | 50 |
| Drugstores | 3 | 25 | 7 |
| Sporting Goods | 1 | 4 | 4 |
| Jewellery Stores | 2 | 5 | — |
| Gift Shops | 1 | 4 | 4 |
| Book and Stationery | 4 | 12 | 3 |
| Others | 8 | 17 | 4 |

| Type of Business | No. of Firms | Employment | Employment of Largest |
|---|---|---|---|
| Transportation | | | |
| Local and Suburban Transit | 1 | 6 | 6 |
| Taxicabs | 1 | 3 | 3 |
| Motor Freight Transport | | | |
| Local Trucking Firms | 7 | 12 | 5 |
| Nonlocal Trucking | 2 | 13 | 7 |
| Aircraft Servicing | 1 | 1 | 1 |
| Personal Services | | | |
| Coin Laundries | 1 | 3 | 3 |
| Dry Cleaners | 2 | 8 | 4 |
| Photo Studios | 3 | 6 | 3 |
| Beauty Shops | 6 | 16 | 5 |
| Barber Shops | 3 | 4 | 2 |
| Funeral Parlours | 1 | 6 | 6 |
| Other Personal Services | 1 | 4 | 4 |
| Business Services | | | |
| Cleaning and Maintenance | 3 | 7 | 4 |
| Real Estate | 3 | 27 | 8 |
| Insurance Agencies | 5 | 27 | 8 |
| Accounting Firms | 6 | 17 | 8 |
| Other Business Services | 4 | 20 | 10 |
| Auto Services | | | |
| Auto Body Repair Shops | 3 | 18 | 6 |
| Auto Repair | 8 | 25 | 6 |
| Car Washes | 2 | 4 | 4 |
| Other Auto Services | 5 | 16 | 4 |
| Repair Shops | | | |
| Radio and Television | 3 | 3 | 2 |
| Furniture and Repair | 2 | 1 | 1 |
| Other Repair Shops | 1 | 1 | 1 |
| Entertainment and Recreation | | | |
| Movie Theatres | 1 | 6 | 6 |
| Pool Halls | 2 | 2 | 1 |
| Bowling Alleys | 1 | 3 | 3 |
| Public Golf Courses | 2 | 25 | 25 |
| Others | 10 | 130 | 45 |

Source: Saskatchewan Department of Rural Development, *Community Profile*, *Melfort*, 1990

Marilyn wanted to know whether Wendy and Tony felt that there were any particular opportunities she could address in the short term that might bring additional business to the branch. Both felt that the market for financial services in the area was quite stable and slow to change, although there had been a rumour recently that one of the other banks was planning to move its commercial lending department out of its Melfort branch to centralize it in a regional office in Prince Albert, 97 km away. Tony felt that this might open up some commercial credit business.

## THE PLANNING PROCESS

As 10 o'clock approached, Marilyn could not help feeling that she had a challenge ahead of her. She was new to Melfort and the first woman to be manager of a bank in the city. In addition to wondering whether she would be accepted in her new role, she was concerned about how she would be able to build business for the bank in a market that seemed to be quite stable.

To demonstrate her commitment to planning and to the development of the Melfort branch, she had decided to send a report by the end of August to the TD Bank's divisional marketing manager in Regina, outlining her views on the prospects and opportunities facing the Melfort branch. To begin the process of preparing this report, she took out of her briefcase the information she had obtained from the office of Statistics Canada in Regina.

The data presented in Tables 3 to 10 represent information obtained from Statistics Canada's FSA and Postal Code Data Bank System on the Forward Sortation Area (FSA) around Melfort, the province of Saskatchewan, and all of Canada. Marilyn had asked for these data so that she could compare the postal area around Melfort (the S0E 1A0 postal area) with the province and the rest of the country. She was particularly interested in being able to identify any obvious areas where the Melfort area was different from Saskatchewan as a whole on various data obtained from tax returns.

The data from Statistics Canada were for the 1989 taxation year; that is, tax returns filed before April 30, 1990. The information indicated that there were 5,600 people who had filed tax returns from the Melfort area (Exhibit 3), and that the median income for all Melfort tax filers was $14,500, compared with $15,600 for Saskatchewan and $18,100 for all of Canada (Exhibit 4). She also noted that only 4 percent of Melfort taxfilers reported income of more than $50,000 in 1989, compared with 5 percent in Saskatchewan and 8 percent in the country as a whole (Exhibit 10a). She was also interested in the fact that, of the 5,600 taxfilers in Melfort, 2,950 had declared income from dividends (Exhibit 10c), and 1,200 had made a contribution to a Registered Retirement Savings Plan (Exhibit 10d).

Marilyn concluded that there was a great deal of information contained in the data that she had obtained from Statistics Canada. She was looking forward to having an opportunity to interpret the tables in greater detail and to incorporate the results of her analysis into her report to the divisional marketing manager.

## QUESTIONS

1. Identify as many factors as you can that would contribute to Marilyn Krauss's analysis of the differences between the marketing of financial services in rural as compared with urban markets.
2. Prepare a detailed analysis of the characteristics of the Melfort area as compared with the rest of Saskatchewan and Canada as a whole that would assist Marilyn Krauss in developing a profile of her market area.
3. Suggest a number of marketing strategies she should employ in developing business for the Toronto Dominion Bank in the Melfort area.

**EXHIBIT 3 Number of Taxfilers by Total Income by Sex, 1989**

| | Melfort | | | Saskatchewan | | | Canada | | |
|---|---|---|---|---|---|---|---|---|---|
| (Thousands of Dollars) | Males | Females | Total | Males | Females | Total | Males | Females | Total |
| $ Under 5.0 | 275 | 625 | 900 | 32,775 | 72,800 | 105,575 | 841,250 | 1,947,025 | 2,788,275 |
| 5.0 – 9.9 | 475 | 625 | 1,100 | 43,675 | 62,075 | 105,750 | 979,250 | 1,610,325 | 2,589,575 |
| 10.0 – 14.9 | 450 | 450 | 900 | 41,500 | 49,650 | 91,150 | 955,850 | 1,323,175 | 2,279,025 |
| 15.0 – 19.9 | 350 | 325 | 700 | 35,150 | 36,625 | 71,775 | 931,625 | 1,083,800 | 2,015,400 |
| 20.0 – 24.9 | 325 | 300 | 625 | 31,925 | 29,950 | 61,900 | 889,575 | 900,750 | 1,790,325 |
| 25.0 – 34.9 | 450 | 250 | 700 | 55,725 | 31,900 | 87,600 | 1,638,125 | 1,082,150 | 2,720,275 |
| 35.0 – 49.9 | 375 | 125 | 500 | 48,975 | 16,400 | 65,375 | 1,658,000 | 582,675 | 2,240,675 |
| 50.0 – 74.9 | 125 | — | 150 | 21,700 | 3,450 | 25,150 | 857,050 | 181,825 | 1,038,875 |
| 75.0 – 99.9 | 25 | — | 25 | 4,150 | 525 | 4,675 | 167,800 | 31,000 | 198,800 |
| 100.0 + | — | — | — | 3,075 | 350 | 3,425 | 161,325 | 25,950 | 187,275 |
| Total | 2,875 | 2,725 | 5,600 | 318,650 | 303,725 | 622,375 | 9,079,850 | 8,768,650 | 17,848,500 |
| Median, 1984 | 16,700 | 10,000 | 13,100 | 18,800 | 9,200 | 13,600 | 20,400 | 9,800 | 14,500 |
| Median, 1989 | 18,500 | 11,400 | 14,500 | 21,000 | 11,600 | 15,600 | 24,700 | 13,000 | 18,100 |
| % Change, 1984-1989 | 11 | 14 | 11 | 12 | 26 | 15 | 21 | 33 | 25 |

Table includes only the taxfilers who reported some income.

Source: Statistics Canada

**EXHIBIT 4** Number of Taxfilers in the Labour Force, 1984 and 1989

| | Melfort | | | Saskatchewan | | | Canada | | |
|---|---|---|---|---|---|---|---|---|---|
| | 1984 | 1989 | % Change 1984-89 | 1984 | 1989 | % Change 1984-89 | 1984 | 1989 | % Change 1984-89 |
| MALES | | | | | | | | | |
| With Employment Income | 2,375 | 2,425 | 2 | 279,225 | 270,650 | −3 | 7,027,800 | 7,650,425 | 9 |
| With Unemployment Insurance Income | 425 | 425 | 0 | 48,675 | 46,800 | −4 | 1,699,225 | 1,451,025 | −15 |
| Total | 2,375 | 2,450 | 3 | 282,025 | 273,425 | −3 | 7,144,825 | 7,731,500 | 8 |
| Median Employment Income | 14,000 | 15,300 | 9 | 16,300 | 18,100 | 11 | 19,500 | 24,600 | 26 |
| FEMALES | | | | | | | | | |
| With Employment Income | 1,675 | 1,875 | 12 | 195,625 | 211,125 | 8 | 5,216,025 | 6,255,450 | 20 |
| With Unemployment Insurance Income | 250 | 300 | 20 | 33,550 | 36,175 | 8 | 1,298,900 | 1,365,175 | 5 |
| Total | 1,675 | 1,925 | 15 | 199,250 | 214,900 | 8 | 5,352,075 | 6,375,600 | 19 |
| Median Employment Income | 9,800 | 11,300 | 15 | 9,500 | 11,400 | 20 | 10,500 | 13,700 | 30 |
| BOTH | | | | | | | | | |
| With Employment Income | 4,025 | 4,300 | 7 | 474,875 | 481,775 | 1 | 12,243,825 | 13,905,875 | 14 |
| With Unemployment Insurance Income | 675 | 725 | 7 | 82,200 | 83,000 | 1 | 2,998,125 | 2,816,225 | −6 |
| Total | 4,075 | 4,350 | 7 | 481,250 | 488,300 | 1 | 12,496,900 | 14,107,100 | 13 |
| Median Employment Income | 12,000 | 12,800 | 7 | 12,700 | 14,400 | 13 | 14,700 | 18,700 | 27 |

All counts are rounded to the nearest multiple of 25.

"Total" includes those with employment income and/or U.I. income. Because a number of taxfilers report both sources of income, the "Total" may be less than the sum of the counts for the two sources.

Source: Statistics Canada

**EXHIBIT 5 Number of Taxfilers Reporting Each Source of Income, 1989**

| Source of Income | Melfort Males | Melfort Females | Melfort Total | Saskatchewan Males | Saskatchewan Females | Saskatchewan Total | Canada Males | Canada Females | Canada Total |
|---|---|---|---|---|---|---|---|---|---|
| Wages/Salaries/Commissions | 1,750 | 1,700 | 3,450 | 210,575 | 193,425 | 404,000 | 6,990,350 | 5,969,400 | 12,959,750 |
| Self-Employment | 1,200 | 375 | 1,575 | 103,250 | 33,575 | 136,825 | 1,264,325 | 559,000 | 1,823,325 |
| Dividends | 325 | 125 | 475 | 27,200 | 16,575 | 43,750 | 867,975 | 633,325 | 1,501,300 |
| Interest | 1,775 | 1,575 | 3,350 | 179,450 | 162,450 | 341,925 | 4,473,100 | 4,326,325 | 8,799,425 |
| Family Allowances | 800 | 400 | 1,225 | 91,375 | 51,200 | 142,575 | 2,440,775 | 1,291,075 | 3,731,850 |
| Unemployment Insurance | 425 | 300 | 725 | 46,800 | 36,175 | 83,000 | 1,451,025 | 1,365,175 | 2,816,225 |
| Pensions | 750 | 725 | 1,475 | 70,475 | 68,100 | 138,575 | 1,670,650 | 1,751,700 | 3,422,375 |
| Other Income | 600 | 450 | 1,050 | 70,925 | 53,875 | 124,825 | 1,980,575 | 1,601,775 | 3,582,350 |
| Child Tax Credit | 25 | 925 | 975 | 2,975 | 101,625 | 104,600 | 69,250 | 2,193,800 | 2,263,025 |
| Federal Sales Tax Credit | 800 | 900 | 1,725 | 89,200 | 97,775 | 186,950 | 2,170,425 | 2,662,500 | 4,832,950 |

All counts are rounded to the nearest multiple of 25.
Taxfilers can report more than one source of income.

**EXHIBIT 6 Income Reported by Source of Income, 1989**

| (Millions of Dollars) | Melfort Males | Melfort Females | Melfort Total | Saskatchewan Males | Saskatchewan Females | Saskatchewan Total | Canada Males | Canada Females | Canada Total |
|---|---|---|---|---|---|---|---|---|---|
| Wages/Salaries/Commissions | 35.7 | 23.4 | 59.1 | 5,046.1 | 2,821.5 | 7,867.6 | 203,002.8 | 99,590.2 | 302,592.7 |
| Self-Employment | 10.6 | 1.5 | 12.0 | 997.6 | 162.3 | 1,159.9 | 17,086.1 | 3,726.3 | 20,812.4 |
| Dividends | 1.1 | 0.2 | 1.3 | 89.0 | 44.1 | 133.1 | 4,403.8 | 2,287.8 | 6,691.6 |
| Interest | 6.2 | 4.8 | 11.0 | 647.7 | 526.4 | 1,174.1 | 13,328.4 | 14,373.5 | 27,701.9 |
| Family Allowances | 0.6 | 0.3 | 0.9 | 70.9 | 36.7 | 107.6 | 1,725.0 | 795.9 | 2,520.9 |
| Unemployment Insurance | 1.7 | 0.8 | 2.5 | 192.4 | 102.5 | 295.0 | 6,293.1 | 4,359.3 | 10,652.4 |
| Pensions | 7.0 | 4.5 | 11.5 | 784.1 | 482.4 | 1,266.5 | 20,893.4 | 12,751.2 | 33,644.5 |
| Other Income | 1.7 | 1.0 | 2.8 | 210.6 | 152.7 | 363.3 | 5,655.2 | 4,845.1 | 10,500.2 |
| Child Tax Credit | 0.0 | 1.0 | 1.0 | 2.7 | 113.2 | 115.8 | 52.1 | 2,041.3 | 2,093.4 |
| Federal Sales Tax Credit | 0.1 | 0.1 | 0.2 | 11.2 | 13.9 | 25.1 | 250.5 | 329.3 | 579.8 |

Totals are independently rounded and do not necessarily equal the sum of individual rounded figures in the distribution.

Source: Statistics Canada

**EXHIBIT 7** Number of Taxfilers by Marital Status, 1989

| | Melfort | | | Saskatchewan | | | Canada | | |
|---|---|---|---|---|---|---|---|---|---|
| Marital Status | Males | Females | Total | Males | Females | Total | Males | Females | Total |
| Single | 700 | 450 | 1,150 | 91,600 | 67,350 | 158,950 | 2,899,275 | 2,405,650 | 5,304,950 |
| Married | 1,950 | 1,675 | 3,625 | 202,100 | 177,025 | 379,125 | 5,315,275 | 4,545,475 | 9,860,750 |
| Separated/Divorced | 150 | 175 | 325 | 17,950 | 23,825 | 41,775 | 680,100 | 919,875 | 1,599,975 |
| Widow/Widower | 75 | 425 | 500 | 7,525 | 36,200 | 43,750 | 206,875 | 929,325 | 1,136,200 |
| Total Taxfilers, 1989 | 2,875 | 2,725 | 5,600 | 319,200 | 304,400 | 623,600 | 9,101,525 | 8,800,325 | 17,901,850 |
| % Change 1984-89 | 7 | 21 | 14 | 3 | 11 | 7 | 14 | 19 | 16 |

All counts are rounded to the nearest multiple of 25.
Marital status is reported as of December 31, 1989.

Source: Statistics Canada

**EXHIBIT 8**  Demographic and Income Data for Postal Code Areas, 1989

| Melfort | | Saskatchewan | | Canada | |
|---|---|---|---|---|---|
| **All taxfilers** | | **All taxfilers** | | **All taxfilers** | |
| Number | 5,600 | Number | 623,600 | Number | 17,901,850 |
| % Change, 1984-89 | 14 | % Change, 1984-89 | 7 | % Change, 1984-89 | 16 |
| % Female | 49 | % Female | 49 | % Female | 49 |
| % Married | 65 | % Married | 61 | % Married | 55 |
| | | | | | |
| % By age | | % By age | | % By age | |
| < 25 | 13 | <25 | 15 | < 25 | 15 |
| 25-44 | 40 | 25-44 | 45 | 25-44 | 47 |
| 45-64 | 26 | 45-64 | 24 | 45-64 | 25 |
| > 64 | 20 | > 64 | 16 | > 64 | 13 |
| | | | | | |
| % Apartment | — | % Apartment | — | % Apartment | — |
| **Taxfilers reporting income** | | **Taxfilers reporting income** | | **Taxfilers reporting income** | |
| Number | 5,600 | Number | 622,375 | Number | 17,848,500 |
| | | | | | |
| % With income | | % With income | | % With income | |
| > $ 15,000 | 48 | > $ 15,000 | 51 | > $ 15,000 | 57 |
| > $ 25,000 | 25 | > $ 25,000 | 30 | > $ 25,000 | 36 |
| > $ 35,000 | 13 | > $ 35,000 | 16 | > $ 35,000 | 20 |
| > $ 50,000 | 4 | > $ 50,000 | 5 | > $ 50,000 | 8 |
| > $ 75,000 | 1 | > $ 75,000 | 1 | > $ 75,000 | 2 |
| > $100,000 | — | > $100,000 | 1 | > $100,000 | 1 |
| **Median total income** | | **Median total income** | | **Median total income** | |
| Male | 18,500 | Male | 21,000 | Male | 24,700 |
| Female | 11,400 | Female | 11,600 | Female | 13,000 |
| Both Sexes | 14,500 | Both Sexes | 15,600 | Both Sexes | 18,100 |
| Canadian Index | 80 | Canadian Index | 86 | Canadian Index | 100 |
| Provincial Index | 93 | Provincial Index | 100 | Provincial Index | — |
| % Change, 1984-89 | 11 | % Change, 1984-89 | 15 | % Change, 1984-89 | 25 |
| **Taxfilers reporting employment income and/or U.I.** | | **Taxfilers reporting employment income and/or U.I.** | | **Taxfilers reporting employment income and/or U.I.** | |
| Number | 4,350 | Number | 488,300 | Number | 14,107,100 |
| % Female | 44 | % Female | 44 | % Female | 45 |
| % U.I. | 17 | % U.I. | 17 | % U.I. | 20 |
| | | | | | |
| Median employment income | | Median employment income | | Median employment income | |
| Male | 15,300 | Male | 18,100 | Male | 24,600 |
| Female | 11,300 | Female | 11,400 | Female | 13,700 |
| Both Sexes | 12,800 | Both Sexes | 14,400 | Both Sexes | 18,700 |
| **Taxfilers reporting Family Allowance income** | | **Taxfilers reporting Family Allowance income** | | **Taxfilers reporting Family Allowance income** | |
| Number | 1,225 | Number | 142,575 | Number | 3,731,850 |
| Dollars ($'000) | 922 | Dollars ($'000) | 107,575 | Dollars ($'000) | 2,520,860 |

Source: Statistics Canada

EXHIBIT 9 Age Distribution of Taxfilers, 1989

| | Melfort | | | | | | Saskatchewan | | | | | | Canada | | | | | |
|---|---|---|---|---|---|---|---|---|---|---|---|---|---|---|---|---|---|---|
| Age group | Males | % | Females | % | Total | % | Males | % | Females | % | Total | % | Males | % | Females | % | Total | % |
| Under 20 | 125 | 4 | 125 | 5 | 225 | 4 | 14,450 | 5 | 13,150 | 4 | 27,600 | 4 | 479,375 | 5 | 417,875 | 5 | 897,225 | 5 |
| 20-24 | 250 | 9 | 225 | 8 | 475 | 8 | 31,825 | 10 | 32,350 | 11 | 64,175 | 10 | 931,375 | 10 | 936,800 | 11 | 1,868,175 | 10 |
| 25-29 | 275 | 9 | 300 | 11 | 550 | 10 | 38,075 | 12 | 39,800 | 13 | 77,875 | 12 | 1,137,125 | 12 | 1,157,000 | 13 | 2,294,125 | 13 |
| 30-34 | 300 | 10 | 300 | 11 | 600 | 11 | 38,950 | 12 | 39,250 | 13 | 78,225 | 13 | 1,122,250 | 12 | 1,136,000 | 13 | 2,258,250 | 13 |
| 35-39 | 300 | 10 | 325 | 12 | 625 | 11 | 34,225 | 11 | 33,750 | 11 | 67,975 | 11 | 1,010,975 | 11 | 1,015,325 | 12 | 2,026,300 | 11 |
| 40-44 | 275 | 9 | 225 | 8 | 500 | 9 | 28,325 | 9 | 27,450 | 9 | 55,775 | 9 | 914,100 | 10 | 888,425 | 10 | 1,802,525 | 10 |
| 45-49 | 250 | 9 | 225 | 8 | 475 | 8 | 21,875 | 7 | 20,525 | 7 | 42,400 | 7 | 714,550 | 8 | 655,725 | 7 | 1,370,275 | 8 |
| 50-54 | 150 | 5 | 150 | 5 | 325 | 6 | 19,575 | 6 | 17,450 | 6 | 37,025 | 6 | 591,875 | 7 | 509,000 | 6 | 1,100,875 | 6 |
| 55-59 | 175 | 6 | 175 | 6 | 350 | 6 | 19,875 | 6 | 16,250 | 5 | 36,125 | 6 | 566,550 | 6 | 450,450 | 5 | 1,017,025 | 6 |
| 60-64 | 200 | 7 | 150 | 5 | 350 | 6 | 19,450 | 6 | 14,950 | 5 | 34,375 | 6 | 516,025 | 6 | 407,525 | 5 | 923,575 | 5 |
| 65+ | 600 | 21 | 550 | 20 | 1,150 | 20 | 52,525 | 16 | 49,525 | 16 | 102,050 | 16 | 1,117,300 | 12 | 1,226,225 | 14 | 2,343,525 | 13 |
| Total | 2,875 | 100 | 2,725 | 100 | 5,600 | 100 | 319,200 | 100 | 304,400 | 100 | 623,600 | 100 | 9,101,525 | 100 | 8,800,325 | 100 | 17,901,850 | 100 |

All counts are rounded to the nearest multiple of 25.
Age is calculated as of December 31, 1989.

Source: Statistics Canada

**Exhibit 10 Interest and Investment Income**

**(a) Demographic and Income Report**

| Postal Areas | Number Taxfilers | % Age <25 | % 25-44 | % 45-59 | % >60 | Median Tot Inc | % >35K | % >50K |
|---|---|---|---|---|---|---|---|---|
| Melfort | 5600 | 13 | 41 | 20 | 26 | 14,600 | 13 | 4 |
| Saskatchewan | 619,125 | 15 | 45 | 19 | 21 | 15,700 | 16 | 5 |
| Canada | 17,716,325 | 15 | 47 | 20 | 18 | 18,200 | 21 | 8 |

**(b) Report on Savers**

| Postal Areas | Number Taxfilers | Number of Interest Filers | Amount Interest (000$) | Median Interest ($) | Median Age of Interest Filers |
|---|---|---|---|---|---|
| Melfort | 5600 | 2950 | 8667 | 900 | 50 |
| Saskatchewan | 619,125 | 301,025 | 906,280 | 800 | 48 |
| Canada | 17,716,325 | 7,436,500 | 18,448,377 | 700 | 45 |

**(c) Report on Investors**

| Postal Areas | Number Taxfilers | Number of Dividend Filers | Amount Invested (000$) | Median Invested ($) | Median Age of Dividend Filers |
|---|---|---|---|---|---|
| Melfort | 5600 | 475 | 3478 | 3300 | 50 |
| Saskatchewan | 619,125 | 43,700 | 396,280 | 3500 | 51 |
| Canada | 17,716,325 | 1,490,000 | 15,587,673 | 3000 | 49 |

**(d) RRSP Report**

| Postal Areas | Number Taxfilers | Number RRSP Filers | Amount RRSP (000$) | Median Age RRSP Filers |
|---|---|---|---|---|
| Melfort | 5600 | 1200 | 3415 | 42 |
| Saskatchewan | 619,125 | 145,050 | 435,405 | 42 |
| Canada | 17,716,325 | 4,136,650 | 13,337,526 | 42 |

Source: Statistics Canada

# CASE 5-2

# CATALOGUE RETAILING

Catalogue retailing accounts for more than $85 billion a year in North American consumer purchases. In Canada, sales are about $3 billion annually, employment in catalogue retailing is more than 35,000 and growth has been about 3.8% annually since 1986. In the United States sales are more than $82 billion, more than 250,000 people are employed, and growth since 1987 has been more than 8% annually. The industry has had a long and, until recently, relatively uneventful history. However, some recent developments have catalogue retailers rethinking the way they do business.

Many mark the 1890s as the time that catalogue retailing began in earnest. It was at that time that Sears, Roebuck & Co. distributed its general merchandise catalogue in the United States, and Eaton's followed with its catalogue for Canadians. Early catalogue retailers targeted rural consumers who found it impossible to visit large cities to shop in the stores. Catalogues not only brought these consumers access to a wide array of otherwise unavailable merchandise, they also provided a form of entertainment for the whole family. Thumbing through a catalogue and developing "wish lists" was a common leisure-time activity. Many urban consumers were also attracted to catalogues. However, their motivation was the shopping convenience that catalogues provided.

As the industry grew, a few large firms achieved dominant positions. Some, notably Eaton's in Canada and, in the United States, Sears, Montgomery Ward, and J. C. Penney, also operated retail stores, and others, such as Spiegel and Fingerhut, did all their business through catalogues. For more than 50 years, catalogue retailing experienced a steady if not spectacular growth that paralleled the increase in the population.

The Sears catalogue generated the most sales volume and was generally viewed as the industry leader in the United States while the Eaton's catalogue latterly had to compete with the newly developed Sears Canada catalogue. But in recent years the market changed, and Sears in the United States and Eaton's in Canada were unable to adapt their catalogue operations. Sears Canada maintained its "book" but it too had competitive problems.

By the 1970s, the majority of consumers, including those in rural areas, had relatively easy access to stores where they could actually see and touch merchandise. In addition, discounters such as K mart and Wal-Mart in the United States and Woolco, Zellers, and K mart in Canada were offering prices that were often lower than those found in catalogues. As a result, the differential advantages of the traditional general-merchandise catalogue, access to merchandise and reasonable prices, declined in importance.

In the 1980s, catalogue retailing took a new turn in response to changing demographics and life-styles. The increase in two-income households meant less time available for shopping but more discretionary income. Catalogue retailers that offered 24-hour, toll-free telephone ordering, quick delivery, and no-hassle return policies made shopping from home very convenient for time-starved consumers. These catalogue retailers grew more rapidly in the United States than in Canada at this stage due to sheer scale of market and the ability to introduce expensive new rapid-response and inventory technology.

Another change was the focus of catalogues. When it served as a substitute for a store, the ideal catalogue offered a complete assortment of staple items. These general-merchandise catalogues were often referred to as "browsing books" because of the way consumers used them. A different type of catalogue, offering highly targeted, specialized merchandise and lively, colourful presentations, flourished in the 1980s. Clothing is a category of merchandise in which catalogue retailing has been particularly successful, with American firms such as Lands' End, J. Crew, Tweeds, Talbot's, and L. L. Bean becoming familiar to many consumers.

There are, in fact, very few North American product categories that are not represented in the catalogue industry.

---

Sources: Cyndee Miller, "Sears Closes Book on Era: Competitors Hope to Improve Own Success Stories," *Marketing News*, March 15, 1993, p. 1; Lisa Coleman, "I Went Out and Did It," *Forbes*, August 17, 1992, pp. 102-104; Cathy Dydahl, "Catalog Retailing Cools Down after Growth of 1980s," *Chain Store Age Executive*, August 1992, pp. 38A-39A; "Cost Squeeze for Catalogs," *St. Louis Post-Dispatch*, April 14, 1991, p. 8E; John B. Hinge, "Catalog Houses That Once Boomed Find the Checks Are No Longer in the Mail," *The Wall Street Journal*, April 4, 1991, p. B1; Brian Bremner and Keith H. Hammond, "Lands' End Looks a Bit Frayed at the Edges," *Business Week*, March 19, 1990, p. 42; Mariann Caprino, "$1 Billion Is Spent on Edible Mail," *St. Louis Post-Dispatch*, November 25, 1990, p. E1.

For example, consumers can buy electronic goods, pets, furniture, toys, cosmetics, plants, antiques, and coins through catalogues. Some may question whether there is any limit to what can be sold through a catalogue. The change in focus of catalogues was a boon to IKEA Canada, but it was finally responsible for the demise of the Eaton's "book," leaving Sears Canada as the only "big book" retailer in Canada.

From 1985 to 1990, U.S. catalogue sales grew at a 12.5 percent annual rate while those in Canada grew at a much slower rate. But the increase in the number of catalogues began to slow in 1989, and actually declined in 1991. In both 1990 and 1991, the growth in sales slowed to a rate not much higher than inflation. The number of U.S. adults who shopped by phone or mail declined from an all-time high of 54.4 percent in 1990 to 52.6 percent in 1991.

In 1993, after eight consecutive years of losses ($130 million U.S. in 1992 alone), Sears in the United States announced the closing of its catalogue division. Despite annual sales of over $3.3 billion (U.S.), the company was unable to make the operation profitable. Rather than continue its efforts to revitalize the catalogue, Sears decided to eliminate it. Though its demise was not a complete surprise, the failure of the Sears U.S. catalogue sent shock waves through the industry.

The slowdown has affected most U.S. and Canadian catalogue retailers. Some firms with retail stores have got out of catalogues or cut back their operations. One result of the slowdown of the U.S. catalogue sales market has been increased attention paid to the development of the Canadian one. While U.S. catalogues do not have a great presence in Canada, they are expected to build. According to a 1991 survey by the Retail Council of Canada, only about 5 percent of Canadian consumers bought from U.S. books. Regardless of exchange rates, the GST, and various PSTs, U.S. cataloguers have discovered the Canadian market, and because they already have the vehicles and have paid for the development costs, they will keep pursuing it as their own sales continue to be harder to increase.

Several factors contributed to the problems in catalogue retailing:

- Lack of flexibility. Imagine a retail store where the merchandise assortment and displays can be altered only two or three times a year. That's what catalogue retailers are faced with. Once a catalogue is printed, the seller is limited to the items displayed until the next catalogue is produced. In contrast, retail stores are constantly offering consumers new and different merchandise.
- Nature of the goods. Most goods offered through catalogues are nonessential items. Catalogue retailers have learned from the experience of Eaton's that they cannot rely for their success on comparably priced goods that are readily available in stores. As a result, because nonessential purchases are postponable, they are the first to be deleted when consumers feel the need to cut back, as they did during the recent recession.
- Increases in mail and shipping rates. Third-class postal rates (used for most catalogues) increased and United Parcel Service, the carrier that delivers 90 percent of merchandise ordered through catalogues, raised its rates for home delivery. It is likely that these rates will continue to escalate.

There are also a number of issues that have catalogue retailers nervous about the future:

- Increasing competition. The number of U.S. catalogues increased by 16.5 percent a year in the 1980s. As the market became saturated, established firms attempted to reach more highly targeted audiences with additional specialized catalogues. For example, along with its adult clothing catalogue, Lands' End developed a catalogue with merchandise for children and another for bath and bedroom items. Also, because there are few barriers to entry, many new firms entered the industry. As a result, consumers are inundated with catalogues, many offering very similar products.
- Privacy concerns. The increasing sophistication of methods for gathering, storing, and using information about consumers has created concerns over catalogue firms (and other direct marketers) becoming too intrusive in consumers' lives. Some jursidictions have considered legislation that would make it illegal for a catalogue retailer to contact consumers without their prior consent. Industry experts fear that such legislation would destroy catalogue retailing.
- Environmental impact. With over 13 billion catalogues printed and distributed in North America yearly, the catalogue industry has upset many environmentalists. In response, catalogue companies are printing their books on recycled paper, using packaging material that is less damaging to the environment, and offering more environmentally sensitive products.

Catalogue retailing is based on reaching the consumer with the right merchandise and providing excellent service — ease of ordering, rapid delivery of the correct merchandise, and guaranteed satisfaction. But for many catalogue firms, that is not enough. Therefore, they are trying other strategies:

- Refined target marketing. The key to successful catalogue retailing is a good mailing list. By spending more time developing customer data bases and analyzing the information on target customers, catalogue retailers are able to develop more sharply focused and appropriately priced goods. As a result, they are able to target more narrowly defined market segments with more specialized catalogues.

- Operating adjustments. It is not difficult to cut back the scale of operation in the catalogue business. By reducing the size of the catalogue and the weight of the paper, using simpler layouts, and shortening the mailing list, costs can be reduced.
- Joint mailings. Another cost-cutting technique is to shrink-wrap catalogues with magazines that are being sent to subscribers. Another option is to mail noncompeting catalogues together and share the costs.
- Private delivery services. Some catalogue retailers are considering alternatives to the postal service for distributing catalogues. As yet, these services are available only on a regional basis.
- Shifting costs to consumers. Some catalogue retailers have shifted from a policy of absorbing the shipping costs to adding a flat fee to all orders. For the first time in its 80-year history, L. L. Bean has added a shipping charge. Others have begun charging for their catalogues and requiring that customers pay the shipping costs on returned goods.
- Exploring offshore international markets. Some catalogue retailers have begun to explore offshore international sales. L. L. Bean, in a joint venture with Seiyu and Matsushita, had sales of $14 million (U.S.) in Japan in 1991. Lands' End has entered Great Britain and France.

The biggest change today from the early days of catalogues is focus. Just like the trend in retail stores is away from general merchandisers to specialty outlets, catalogues have also become more specialized. Even with years of experience selling traditional, classic apparel, Lands' End has recently had difficulty satisfying its customers. The firm walks a tightrope between maintaining the styles that made it successful and offering fresher, more fashionable merchandise.

## QUESTIONS

1. How does catalogue retailing differ from in-store retailing? What are the requirements for success in catalogue retailing?
2. What characteristics make merchandise appropriate for catalogue retailing? What role do the breadth and depth of assortment play in the success of a catalogue retailer?
3. What factors will influence the future of catalogue retailing?

# CASE 5-3

# MURRAY INDUSTRIAL LIMITED

Murray Industrial Limited (MIL) was advertised as Newfoundland's most complete industrial supplier and sold to industrial accounts throughout Newfoundland and Labrador from three locations across the province. Products sold included hydraulic hose and fittings, bearings, conveyor products, hand power tools, fasteners (nuts, bolts, etc.), chain, packing, and general mill supply items.

According to Dave Rowe, general manager of MIL, "Our success has been largely due to our customer service strategy. We aim to provide superior service with a well-trained, motivated staff and a broad inventory of quality products. We have an on-going commitment to in-house training and product seminars, and we have a 24-hour emergency service for all of our accounts."

Prior to 1991, MIL was subdistributor for Snowden Rubber, a Gates Rubber distributor located in Dartmouth, Nova Scotia. In 1991, an opportunity arose to become a distributor for one of North America's largest and best known manufacturers of hydraulic hose and fittings when its Newfoundland distributor, Newfoundland Armature Works, became bankrupt.

Industrial distributors that sold hydraulic hose and fittings usually bought the more popular sizes and types of hose in full reel lengths and then cut it to fit particular customer applications. Frequently, distributors would attach hydraulic fittings or other special attachments to the shorter hose lengths as required by customers. When distributors bought full-length reels of hose (which varied in length depending on the size of the hose) or full-box quantities of fittings (which also varied depending on the size and style of fitting), they paid a standard distributor price for their inventory. If they desired to buy a cut-to-length piece of hose or a small quantity of fittings for special applications that might arise infrequently, they paid a 10 percent surcharge on the distributor price. For shipments that were needed urgently, manufacturers would often guarantee shipment within 24 hours but charged a $10 special-order handling charge.

At the time negotiations between MIL and the manufacturer began, the manufacturer had a distribution centre in Dartmouth, Nova Scotia, and prepaid shipments from there to distributors throughout Atlantic Canada. It offered a discount of 2 percent for payment by the twenty-fifth of the following month and co-op allowances to share promotion costs with distributors. Within a month (and before an agreement was signed), the Dartmouth warehouse was closed and the sales person was let go. Shipments were still prepaid but came from Toronto, and the sales person who serviced the Atlantic Provinces operated from Quebec. After about three months, the manufacturer's policy changed, and shipments became f.o.b. Toronto, and the prompt-payment discount was eliminated.

MIL increased sales by establishing subdistributors in remote regions; hydraulic hose eventually accounted for about 8 percent of the company's total sales and helped increase sales for complementary products. The largest customer MIL had was Royal Oak Mines, a gold mine located about one and a half hours from Port aux Basques and accessible only by air or water. It accounted for 35 percent of MIL's hydraulic hose sales.

Within a year, MIL began to have problems getting inventory. Back-order rates increased. The manufacturer closed its Toronto and Edmonton distribution centres in 1993 and decided to supply the Canadian market from the United States. The manufacturer sales force was reduced from six to two representatives in Canada. Distributors were reduced from 140 to 40 (MIL was the twenty-second largest at the time). All co-op policies were eliminated, and the Canadian price sheets were removed so that Canadian distributors had to purchase from U.S. price sheets and add exchange, duty, brokerage, transportation, and whatever markup they needed.

"Our biggest problem," said Dave Rowe, "was that they didn't plan for the change to the distribution system. Service continued to worsen from Toronto as inventory that was sold from there was not replaced, and we were told we couldn't order from the United States until July 1, 1993, when it would be organized to serve us. We haven't seen a sales person since early 1993, and any contact we have had with them since then has been initiated by us. Service started to affect our relationships with our customers. We eventually lost the Royal Oak Mines account, and they started buying Gates Rubber products. We were stuck with about $50,000 in inventory that we stocked specifically for them. When we approached the manufacturer, they refused to help us beyond their normal return goods policy. They were willing to take back up to 2 percent of our annual purchases as long as the material was still in new condition and was still a standard item listed in their catalogue. We had to pay return freight and a 15 percent restocking charge. It was also their policy not to accept return of any hose products after one year as hose quality deteriorated with time. While their pricing and inventory management practices were standard for the industry, we felt they had no obligation to help us as they were largely to blame for our lost customer."

## QUESTIONS

1. What responsibility should the manufacturer have for the lost account (Royal Oak Mines)?
2. What can Dave Rowe do? What must he consider before taking any action?

PART

6

# PROMOTION

**Designing and managing the marketing-mix element to inform, persuade, and remind current and potential customers**

We have examined product, price, and distribution — three of the four marketing-mix elements to reach an organization's target markets and achieve its marketing goals. To complete the marketing mix, we now turn our attention to promotion.

In Chapter 18 we present an overview of promotion, including the types of promotion, promotion as a form of communication, the management of promotion including the promotion mix, the promotion budget, the campaign concept, and the regulation of promotion. Chapter 19 looks at the personal selling process and sales-force management. Advertising, sales promotion, public relations, and publicity are the subjects of Chapter 20.

# CHAPTER 18 GOALS

This chapter will help you understand how promotion decisions are made by describing what promotion is and how it fits into a firm's total marketing program. After studying this chapter, you should have an understanding of:

- The components of promotion and how they differ.
- The role promotion plays in an organization and in the economy.
- How the process of communicating relates to effective promotion.
- The concept and design of the promotional mix.
- The promotional campaign.
- Alternative promotional budgeting methods.
- Regulation of promotion.

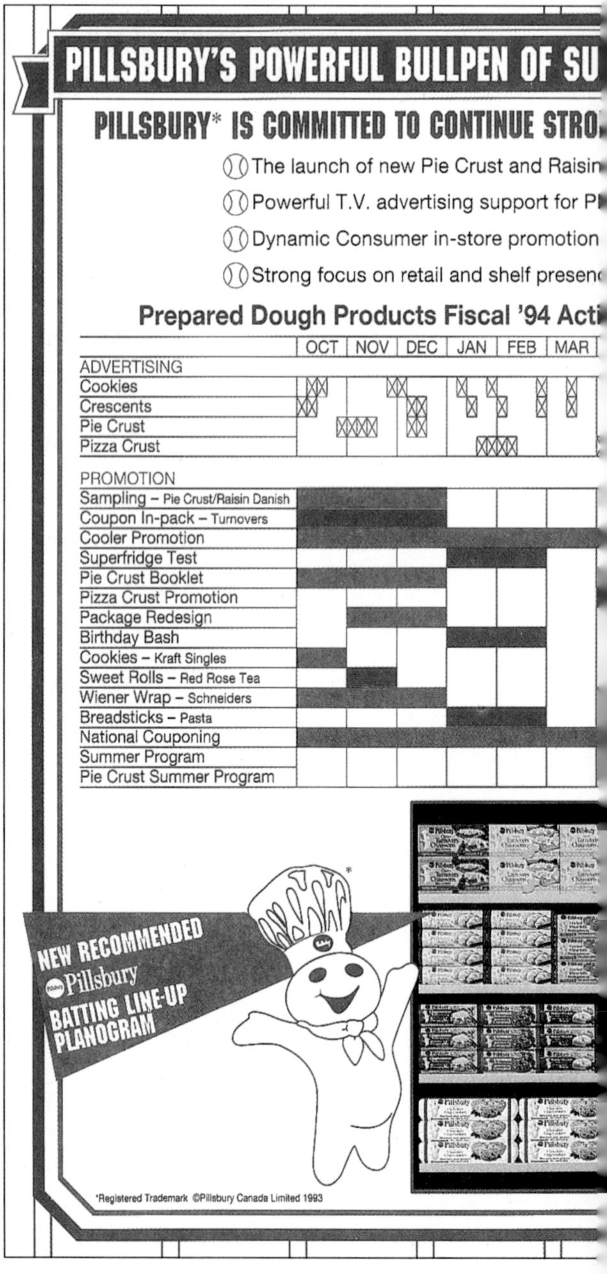

CHAPTER 18

# THE PROMOTIONAL PROGRAM

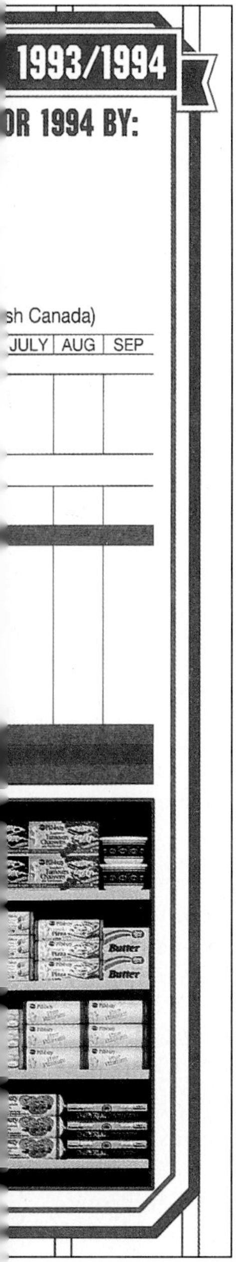


## Complex Promotional Program Supports New Product Launch

The back cover of the Pillsbury Canada Limited trade brochure, used to communicate with retailers, carries an outline of the promotional program prepared for 1993-94 to support the Pillsbury line of prepared dough products.

The 1993-94 promotional program was designed to support existing products in the category and launch two new ones — Pie Crust and Danish Rolls. For the pie crust, the product launch objectives were:

- To successfully introduce Pillsbury Pie Crust into the Canadian market nationally;
- To achieve agreement from all retailers to carry the product (listing authorization) by August 15, 1993;
- To obtain initial orders from all retailers by August 15, 1993, prior to TV advertising;
- To achieve retail distribution in 70 percent of retail stores by December 15, 1993.

Achieving these objectives meant designing a promotional program that had to be well planned, well detailed, well co-ordinated, and, of course, well supported by budgets, the efforts of the sales force in the field, and the co-operation and creativity of retailers. A consumer support program consisting of advertising and promotion was developed. In total, 8 million coupons were to be distributed. The budget to introduce Pillsbury Pie Crust was $1.5 million.

The advertising component of the program was made up of 10 weeks of television advertising for the pie crust in October, November, and December, scheduled in weekly blocks during the key baking season. The advertising was tested in focus groups and was considered to be successful in conveying the Pillsbury Pie Crust key attributes in an entertaining fashion.

An important element in the promotional program was a national recipe booklet distributed via:

- In-store demonstrations
- Refrigerated cooler units
- Information booklets — with coupons — to be placed on product shelves
- Eye-catching posters with the booklets and coupons in high traffic locations
- Mail-in offer on package

The booklet was designed to attract consumers looking for new pie ideas and included cents-off coupons. The 200 national demonstrations illustrated and reinforced the key attributes of Pillsbury Pie Crust. Regional cross-promotions were designed with the co-operation of producers of complementary products; the promotions were extended to the dairy case (cream cheese, whipping cream, yogurt), produce section (berries, peaches, apples), and the meat case (bacon, chicken, ground beef). A summer-long coupon program was scheduled for 1994.

The 1994 advertising and promotion activity grid for other Pillsbury dough products, reproduced on the preceding pages, shows what integration and co-ordination really mean.[1]

## NATURE OF PROMOTION

The marketing-mix activities of product planning, pricing, and distribution are performed mainly within a business or between a business and the members of its distribution channels. However, through its promotional activities, a firm communicates directly with potential customers. And, as we will see, it is not a simple process.

Basically, promotion is an attempt to influence. More specifically, **promotion** is the element in an organization's marketing mix that serves to inform, persuade, and remind the market of a product and/or the organization selling it, in hopes of influencing the recipients' feelings, beliefs, or behaviour.

### Promotional Methods

There are five forms of promotion: personal selling, advertising, sales promotion, public relations, and publicity. Each has distinct features that determine in what situations it will be most effective.

- **Personal selling** is the direct presentation of a product to a prospective customer by a representative of the organization selling it. Personal selling takes place face to face or over the phone, and it may be directed to an intermediary or a final consumer. We list it first because, across all businesses, more money is spent on personal selling than on any other form of promotion.
- **Advertising** is impersonal mass communication that the sponsor has paid for and in which the sponsor is clearly identified. The most familiar forms of ads are found in the broadcast (TV and radio) and print (newspapers and magazines) media. However, there are many other advertising alternatives, from direct mail to billboards and the telephone directory Yellow Pages.
- **Sales promotion** is demand-stimulating activity designed to supplement advertising and facilitate personal selling. It is paid for by the sponsor and frequently involves a

temporary incentive to encourage a purchase. Many sales promotions are directed at consumers. The majority, however, are designed to encourage the company's sales force or other members of its distribution channel to sell its products more aggressively. This latter category is called trade promotion. Included in sales promotion are a wide spectrum of activities, such as contests, trade shows, in-store displays, rebates, samples, premiums, discounts, and coupons.

- **Public relations** encompasses a wide variety of communication efforts to contribute to generally favourable attitudes and opinions towards an organization and its products. Unlike most advertising and personal selling, it does not include a specific sales message. The targets may be customers, stockholders, a government agency, or a special-interest group. Public relations can take many forms, including newsletters, annual reports, lobbying, and sponsorship of charitable or civic events. The Goodyear blimp is a familiar example of a public relations device.
- **Publicity** is a special form of public relations that involves news stories about an organization or its products. Like advertising, it involves an impersonal message that reaches a mass audience through the media. But several things distinguish publicity from advertising: It is *not* paid for, the organization that is the subject of the publicity has no control over it, and it appears as news and therefore has greater credibility than advertising. Organizations seek good publicity and frequently provide the material for it in the form of news releases, press conferences, and photographs. There is, of course, also bad publicity, which organizations try to avoid or deflect.

## The Communication Process and Promotion

**Communication** is the verbal or nonverbal transmission of information between someone wanting to express an idea and someone else expected or expecting to get that idea. Because promotion is a form of communication, much can be learned about structuring effective promotion by examining the communication process.

Fundamentally, communication requires only four elements: a *message*, a *source* of the message, a *communication channel*, and a *receiver*. In practice, however, important additional components come into play:

- The information that the sending source wants to share must first be **encoded** into a transmittable form. In marketing this means changing an idea ("An airline like Canadian Airlines International must find a way to personalize its image") into words ("We bring Canada to the rest of the world"), pictures, or some other form such as a sample.
- Once the message has been transmitted through some communication channel, the symbols must be **decoded**, or given meaning, by the receiver. The received message may be what the sender intended ("More foreign routes than you would expect") or something else ("I wonder if CAI is substituting interchanges for direct flights"), depending on the recipient's knowledge and experience.
- If the message has been transmitted successfully, there is some change in the receiver's knowledge, beliefs, or feelings. As a result of this change the receiver formulates a **response**. The response could be nonverbal (a smile while watching the Canadian Airlines International ad), verbal (suggesting to a friend to try Canadian Airlines International), or behavioural (purchasing a ticket on Canadian Airlines International).
- The response serves as **feedback**, telling the sender whether the message was received and how it was perceived by the recipient. Through feedback the sender can learn why a communication failed and how to improve future communication.
- All stages of the process can be affected by **noise** — that is, any external factor that interferes with successful communication. (For CAI, ads by Air Canada and other airlines are noise.)

Canadian Airlines
International uses many
different channels and
messages to communi-
cate with prospective
travellers.

WE BRING CANADA TO *the* REST OF THE WORLD.

Canadian provides direct service to Rome and Milan. They're just two of the 22 international destinations
Canadian Airlines serves. In Europe, we also fly to London, Manchester, Frankfurt, Munich and Paris.

Canadian
Canadian Airlines International

Canadian is a registered trademark of Canadian Airlines International Ltd.

Figure 18-1 illustrates these components of a communication process and relates them
to promotion activities.

What does the communication process tell us about promotion? First, the act of encoding
reminds us that messages can take many forms. Messages can be physical (a sample, a premium) or symbolic (verbal, visual), and there are a myriad of options within each of these
categories. For example, a verbal message can be factual, humorous, or even threatening.

Second, the number of channels or methods of transmitting a message are limited only
by the imagination and creativity of the sender. Most promotional messages are transmitted by familiar channels such as the voice of a sales person, the airwaves of radio, the
mail, the side of a bus, or the lead-in to a feature in a movie theatre. Each channel has
its own characteristics in terms of audience reach, flexibility, permanence, credibility, and
cost. In selecting a channel, a marketer must have clearly defined objectives and a familiarity with the features of the many alternatives. McDonald's shifted money from network
TV and made a large purchase of outdoor advertising when it purchased 20,000 billboards

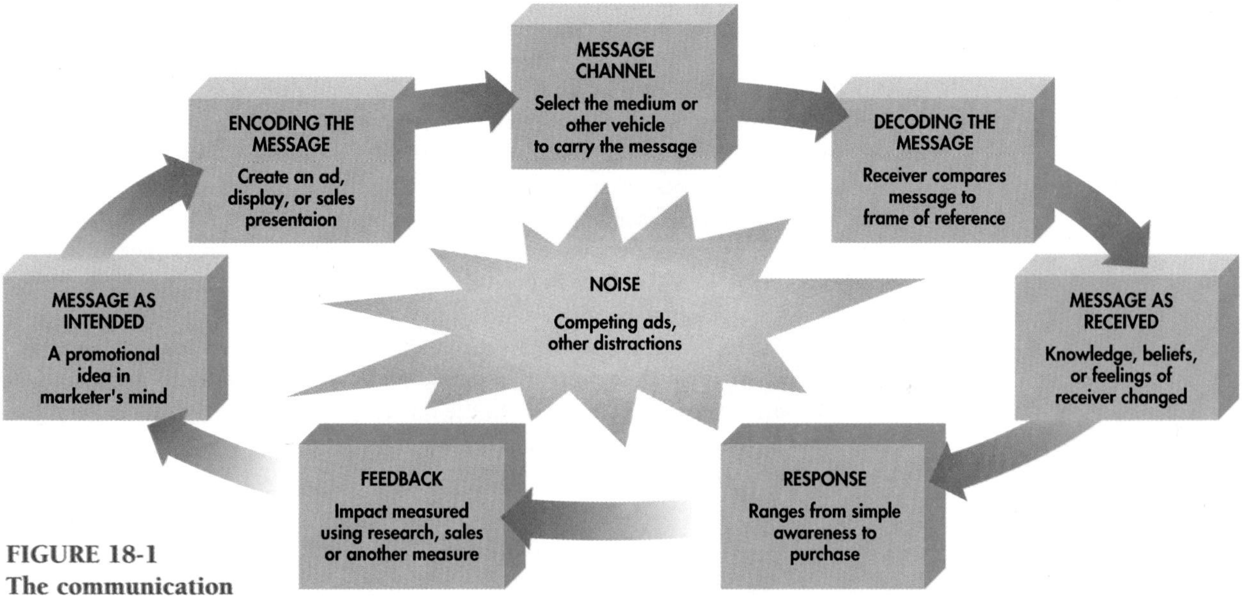


**FIGURE 18-1 The communication process in promotion.**

throughout North America to reach consumers on the road and within minutes of a purchase decision.[2]

Third, how the message is decoded or interpreted depends on its form (encoding and transmission) and the capability and interest of the recipient. In designing and sending messages, marketers must be sensitive to the audience. What is their vocabulary and level of verbal sophistication? What other messages have they received? What experiences have they had? What will get and hold their attention?

Finally, every promotion should have a measurable objective that can be determined from the response and feedback provided by the recipients. Feedback may be collected in many forms — changes in sales, recall of advertising messages, more favourable attitudes, increased awareness of a product or an organization — depending on the objective of the promotion. For some promotional activities the objective may be modest, for example, an increase in the audience's awareness of a brand. For others, such as a direct mail solicitation, the objective would be a particular level of sales. Without objectives, there is no way of evaluating the effectiveness of a message.

## THE PURPOSES OF PROMOTION

One of the attributes of a free market system is the right to use communication as a tool of influence. In our socioeconomic system, that freedom is reflected in the promotional efforts by businesses to influence the feelings, beliefs, and behaviour of prospective customers. Let's examine how promotion works from an economic perspective and from a marketing perspective.

### Promotion and Imperfect Competition

The North American marketplace operates under conditions of imperfect competition, characterized by product differentiation, emotional buying behaviour, and incomplete market information. A company uses promotion to provide more information for the decision maker's buying-decision process, to assist in differentiating its product, and to persuade potential buyers.

In economic terms, the purpose of promotion is to change the location and shape of the **demand** (revenue) **curve** for a company's product. (See Figure 18-2 and recall the discussion of nonprice competition in Chapter 14.) Through promotion a company strives to increase its product's sales volume at any given price (Figure 18-2a), or shift its demand curve to the right. Simply stated, promotion is intended to make a product more attractive to prospective buyers. Alcan has done this by having its sales people identify opportunities where aluminum is able to replace steel or other raw materials and then finding ways to make its use cost effective. One example is the beverage can market, which was once exclusively steel and is now 96 percent aluminum.[3]

A firm also hopes that promotion will affect the demand elasticity for its product (Figure 18-2b). The intent is to make the demand more *inelastic* when price increases, and more *elastic* when price decreases. In other words, management wants promotion to increase the attractiveness of a product so the quantity demanded will decline very little if price goes up (inelastic demand), and sales will increase considerably if price goes down (elastic demand).

**FIGURE 18-2**
**The goal of promotion is to change the pattern of demand for a product.**

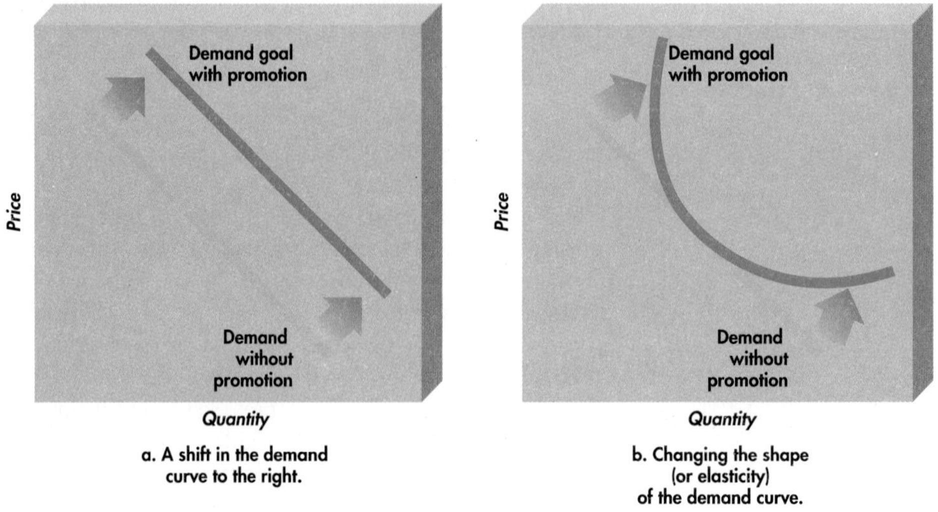


## Promotion and Marketing

Promotion serves three essential roles — it informs, persuades, and reminds prospective customers about a company and its products. The relative importance of these roles varies according to the circumstances faced by a firm.

The most useful product or brand will be a failure if no one knows it is available! Because distribution channels are often long, a product may pass through many hands between a producer and consumers. Therefore, a producer must *inform* intermediaries as well as the ultimate consumers or business users about the product. Wholesalers, in turn, must inform retailers, and retailers must inform consumers. As the number of potential customers grows and the geographic dimensions of a market expand, the problems and cost of informing the market increase.

Another purpose of promotion is *persuasion*. The intense competition among different industries, as well as among different firms in the same industry, puts tremendous pressure on the promotional programs of sellers. In our economy, even a product designed to satisfy a basic physiological need requires strong persuasive promotion, since consumers have many alternatives to choose from. Campbell Soup Company has been selling soup for over 120 years and has annual soup sales of over $1.6 billion. Studies show that virtually every

North American household has some Campbell's soup in the pantry. Yet the firm spends over $50 million a year advertising soup because of strong competition from existing brands and newer products such as single-portion packaged soups.[4] In the case of a luxury product, for which demand depends on a seller's ability to convince consumers that the product's benefits exceed those of other luxuries, persuasion is even more important.

Consumers also must be *reminded* about a product's availability and its potential to satisfy. Sellers bombard the marketplace with thousands of messages every day in the hope of attracting new consumers and establishing markets for new products. Given the intense competition for consumers' attention, even an established firm must constantly remind people about its brand to retain a place in their minds. It is unlikely that a day goes by, for example, in which you don't see some form of promotion (an ad, in-store display, counter sign, billboard, or imprinted T-shirt) for Coca-Cola. Thus, much of a firm's promotion may be intended simply to offset competitors' marketing activity by keeping its brand in front of the market.

### Promotion and Strategic Marketing Planning

A company's personal selling, advertising, and other promotional activities should form a co-ordinated promotional program within its total marketing plan. These activities are fragmented in many firms, with potentially damaging consequences. For example, advertising managers and sales-force managers may come into conflict over resources. But this wouldn't happen if the elements making up promotion were a co-ordinated part of a firm's overall strategic marketing plan.

To be effective, promotional activities must also be co-ordinated with product planning, pricing, and distribution, the other marketing-mix elements. Promotion is influenced, for instance, by how distinctive a product is and whether its price is above or below the competition. A manufacturer or intermediary must also consider its promotional interdependence with other firms in the distribution channel. For example, Chrysler recognizes that its success is closely tied to the performance of its dealers. Therefore, in addition to advertising its automobiles directly to consumers, Chrysler offers cash incentives to dealers with high customer satisfaction scores and trains the dealers' sales people in how to show a car and conduct a test drive.[5]

Promotion should also contribute to a firm's overall strategic plan. Bausch & Lomb has achieved success with contact lenses by concentrating much of its promotional efforts on educating physicians. However, with the growing popularity of disposable lenses, the distribution of contacts has shifted from doctors' offices to optical retailers. To maintain its market position, Bausch & Lomb found it necessary to shift its promotional efforts from physicians to lens wearers and to focus its efforts on teenagers. To reach this market, the firm offered certificates for free-trial pairs of disposable lenses via a 1-800 number on MTV, advertised free-trial offers in teen magazines, and distributed book covers and gym bags in high schools. In Canada, major competitor Johnson & Johnson made the same "Free Trial Pair" offer using a coupon in its advertising.

## DETERMINING THE PROMOTIONAL MIX

An organization's combination of personal selling, advertising, sales promotion, public relations, and publicity to help in achieving its marketing objectives is its **promotional mix**. An effective promotional mix is a critical part of virtually all marketing strategies. Product differentiation, market segmentation, trading up and trading down, and branding all require effective promotion. Designing an effective promotional mix involves a number of strategic decisions, as we shall now see.

**Johnson & Johnson stimulates no-risk trial of their lenses.**

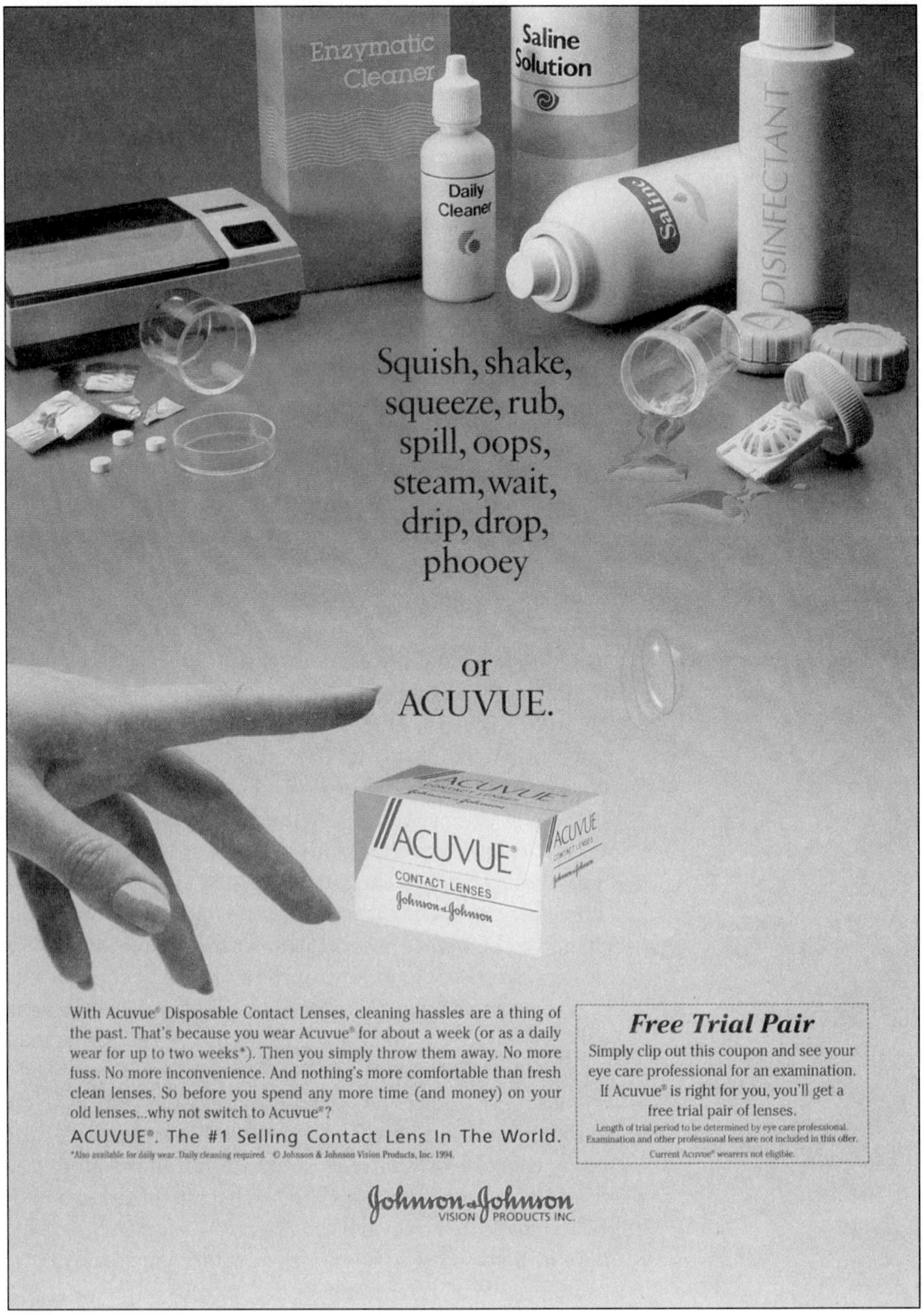


### Factors Influencing the Promotional Mix

These four factors should be taken into account when determining the promotional mix: (1) the target market, (2) the nature of the product, (3) the stage of the product's life cycle, and (4) the amount of money available for promotion.

**Target Market** As in most areas of marketing, decisions on the promotional mix will be greatly influenced by the audience or target market. At least four variables affect the choice of a promotional method for a particular market:

## MARKETING AT WORK

### FILE 18-1 AN INTERNATIONAL PERSPECTIVE ON SALES PROMOTION

As more firms become multinational in their operations, it becomes less clear that there is one most effective way to promote their products. Coca-Cola, for example, has successfully used the advertising slogan "Can't Beat the Feeling" in many parts of the world. But could it also standardize its sales promotion? There are several reasons why this may not be possible:

- **Level of economic development.** Limited purchasing power combined with low literacy levels restricts the number of sales promotion options in developing countries. In the Philippines most consumers buy in such small quantities (individual cigarettes and single portions of shampoo, for example) that in-package premiums are not possible. In developing countries, samples and demonstrations are the most common sales promotion tools, while coupons, common in developed countries, are seldom used.
- **Stage of market development.** The same product is frequently sold in mature markets where there are numerous competitors and consumers are familiar with alternative brands, and in new markets where not only is the brand unknown, but the product class is also new to consumers. In mature markets, greater emphasis is placed on increasing the number of stores that stock the product by using promotional tools such as trade allowances to intermediaries, while in new markets getting consumers to try the product through sampling and couponing is most appropriate.
- **Consumer values.** Sales promotion techniques are evaluated differently from culture to culture. In Japan, where coupons were first issued in 1976, some consumers are embarrassed to be seen using them. Thus what might be seen as a valuable premium in one country may be viewed as an indication of poverty in another.
- **Government regulations.** Laws governing what is permissible and the manner in which promotions can be carried out differ across countries. In Japan, the value of a premium cannot exceed 10 percent of a product's price and cannot be more than 100 yen (about 80 cents). In Malaysia, promotional contests can be games of skill but not chance. The only sales promotions permitted by all member countries in the European Union are free samples, in-store demonstrations, and reusable packages.
- **Structure of retail trade.** The dominance of large and powerful chain stores versus small independent retailers in a market will influence the success of promotions. Chains prefer trade promotions that provide price discounts and in-store customer promotions. However, smaller stores do not buy in large enough quantities to benefit significantly from trade discounts. In Japan, where stores are very small, in-store displays take up too much space and create congestion.

Because the goal of advertising is to build awareness and familiarity with a brand, the use of common themes around the world can be effective. But the objective of sales promotion is action — trial, purchase, repurchase, purchase of a larger quantity, and so forth. Thus it must be adapted to the particular conditions of a market.

Source: Kamran Kashani and John A. Quelch, "Can Sales Promotion Go Global?" *Business Horizons*, May-June 1990, pp. 37-44.

- **Readiness to buy.** A target market can be in any one of six stages of buying readiness. These stages — awareness, knowledge, liking, preference, conviction, and purchase — are called the **hierarchy of effects** because they represent stages a buyer goes through in moving towards a purchase and each defines a possible goal or effect of promotion.

  At the *awareness* stage the seller's task is to let the buyers know the product or brand exists. Here the objective is to build familiarity with the product and the brand name. Recall the unconventional ads that preceded the introduction of the Infiniti automobile. In a market already cluttered with many brands, the off-beat ads of nature scenes created a high level of brand-name awareness before anyone had even seen the car.

  *Knowledge* goes beyond awareness to learning about a product's features. Goodyear and BF Goodrich are tire companies that are often confused simply because the founders had similar names. And the effectiveness of the Goodyear blimp as a corporate symbol led many consumers to confuse the two companies. For example, Goodrich introduced steel-belted radial tires to the North American market, but most consumers attribute the innovation to Goodyear. To establish itself as an industry leader in consumers' minds, Goodrich developed an information campaign to increase the knowledge of consumers about the company's innovations.

*Liking* refers to how the market feels about the product or brand. Promotion can be used to move a knowledgeable audience from being indifferent to liking a brand. A common technique is to associate the item with an attractive symbol or person, which explains why Nokia, cell phone manufacturers, chose Elvis Stojko as their spokesman. "In the arena of skating, Elvis is the one to watch. In the arena of telecommunications, Nokia holds the same distinction."

Creating *preference* involves distinguishing among brands such that the market prefers yours. It is not uncommon to like several brands of the same product, but the customer can't make a decision until one brand is preferred over the alternatives. Ads that make direct comparisons with the competition are intended to create a preference. In the competition for long-distance customers, Unitel compares its price to Bell Canada's.

*Conviction* entails the actual decision or commitment to purchase. A student may prefer an IBM PC over a clone, but not yet be convinced to buy a computer. The promotion objective here is to increase the strength of the buyer's need. Trying a product and experiencing the benefits that come from using it are very effective in strengthening the conviction to own it. Being allowed to play with a Nintendo in a store display is an example.

*Purchase* can be delayed or postponed indefinitely, even for customers who are convinced they should buy a product. The inhibitor might be a situational factor such as not having enough money at the moment, or a natural resistance to change. Action may be triggered through a promotional price discount or offering additional incentives.

- **Geographic scope of the market.** Personal selling may be adequate in a small local market, but as the market broadens geographically, greater emphasis must be placed on advertising. The exception would be a firm that sells to concentrated pockets of customers scattered around the country. For example, the market for certain plastics is heaviest in Ontario and Quebec, because these plastics are used by component suppliers to the auto industry. In this case, emphasis on personal selling may be feasible.
- **Type of customer.** Promotional strategy depends in part on what level of the distribution channel the organization hopes to influence. Final consumers and intermediaries sometimes buy the same product, but they require different promotion. To illustrate, 3M Company sells its computer diskettes to final consumers through computer and office supply stores. Promotion to dealers includes sharing the cost of Yellow Pages ads and advertising in specialized business magazines such as *Office Products Dealer*. Different ads aimed at final consumers are run in magazines such as *Personal Computing*. In many situations intermediaries may strongly affect a manufacturer's promotional strategy. Large retail chains may refuse to stock a product unless the manufacturer agrees to provide a certain amount of promotional support.

Another consideration is the variety among the target markets for a product. A market with only one type of customer will call for a different promotional mix than a market with many target markets. A firm selling large power saws used exclusively by lumber manufacturers may rely only on personal selling. In contrast, a company selling portable hand saws to consumers and to construction firms will probably include an ample portion of advertising in its mix. Personal selling would be prohibitively expensive in reaching the firm's many customers.

Congratulations Elvis.
Being an innovator is never easy. Acceptance is never guaranteed. It takes courage and perseverance, as well as talent, to conquer new frontiers, to push the envelope – to leave an indelible mark in any field of endeavour.
At the 1994 Winter Olympics in Lillehammer, Canada's Elvis Stojko did just that. Winning the silver medal with a unique freestyle performance that combined ancient martial arts with modern skating, he created a truly innovative program of power and grace.
One month later at the World Figure Skating Championships, Elvis went on to win the gold medal and became the World Champion.
In the arena of skating, Elvis is indisputably the one to watch. In the arena of telecommunications, Nokia holds the same distinction. We're the second largest manufacturer of cellular phones in the world. And in our quest to become number one, we too have been leading the way with innovations like helping to build the world's first cellular system and making the world's first digital cellular call.
So when the time came to choose a spokesman for our cutting-edge technology, there was really only one choice.
Elvis, we look forward to a long association with you, as we both continue the drive toward new levels of excellence. And once again on behalf of all Canadians, congratulations. You did us proud.
NOKIA
CONNECTING PEOPLE
For more information about our complete line of Digital and Analogue Cellular Phones, call us at (905) 427-6654

**Nokia takes advantage of Elvis's success to make a connection.**

- **Concentration of the market.** The total number of prospective buyers is another consideration. The fewer potential buyers there are, the more effective personal selling is, compared with advertising. For example, in Canada there are only a handful of manufacturers of household vacuum cleaners. Clearly, for a firm selling a component part for vacuum cleaners, personal selling would be the best way to reach this market.

Nature of the Product Several product attributes influence promotional strategy. The most important are:

- **Unit value.** A product with low unit value is usually relatively uncomplicated, involves little risk for the buyer, and must appeal to a mass market to survive. As a result, advertising would be the primary promotional tool. In contrast, high-unit-value products often are complex and expensive. These features suggest the need for personal selling. BMW dealers are being encouraged to have sales people get out of the showroom and call on prospects. By increasing the personal selling effort through techniques such as delivering cars to potential customers for test drives, BMW hopes to stimulate declining North American sales.[6]
- **Degree of customization.** If a product must be adapted to the individual customer's needs, personal selling is necessary. Thus, you would expect to find an emphasis on personal selling for something like home remodelling or an expensive suit of clothing. However, the benefits of most standardized products can be effectively communicated in advertising.
- **Presale and postsale service.** Products that must be demonstrated, for which there are trade-ins, or that require frequent servicing to keep them in good working order lend themselves to personal selling. Typical examples are riding lawn mowers, power boats, and personal computers.

Stage of the Product Life Cycle Promotion strategies are influenced by a product's life-cycle stage. When a new product is introduced, prospective buyers must be informed about its existence and its benefits, and intermediaries must be convinced to carry it. Thus both advertising (to consumers) and personal selling (to intermediaries) are critical in a product's introductory stage. At introduction a new product also may be something of a novelty, offering excellent opportunities for publicity. Later, if a product becomes successful, competition intensifies and more emphasis is placed on persuasive advertising. Table 18-1 shows how promotional strategies change as a product moves through its life cycle.

Funds Available Regardless of what may be the most desirable promotional mix, the amount of money available for promotion is the ultimate determinant of the mix. A business with ample funds can make more effective use of advertising than a firm with limited financial resources. Small or financially weak companies are likely to rely on personal

TABLE 18-1 Promotional strategies for different product life-cycle stages

| Market situation | Promotional strategy |
|---|---|
| | Introduction Stage |
| **Customers are not aware of the product's features, nor do they understand how it will benefit them.** | **Inform and educate potential customers that the product exists, how it might be used, and what want-satisfying benefits it provides.<br>In this stage, a seller must stimulate *primary demand* — the demand for a type of product — as contrasted with *selective demand* — the demand for a particular brand. For example, producers had to sell consumers on the value of compact discs in general before it was feasible to promote a particular brand.<br>Normally, heavy emphasis must be placed on personal selling. Exhibits at trade shows are also used extensively in the promotional mix. A trade show gives a new product broad exposure to many intermediaries. Manufacturers also rely heavily on personal selling to attract intermediaries to handle a new product.** |
| | Growth Stage |
| **Customers are aware of product's benefits.<br>The product is selling well, and intermediaries want to handle it.** | **Stimulate selective (brand) demand as competition grows. Increase emphasis on advertising. Intermediaries share more of the total promotional effort.** |
| | Maturity Stage |
| **Competition intensifies and sales level off.** | **Advertising is used more to persuade rather than only to provide information. Intense competition forces sellers to devote larger sums to advertising and thus contributes to the declining profits experienced in this stage.** |
| | Decline Stage |
| **Sales and profits are declining. New and better products are coming into the market.** | **All promotional efforts are cut back substantially. The focus becomes reminding remaining customers.** |

selling, dealer displays, or joint manufacturer–retailer promotions. For example, at a cost of $300,000 a year, K-Swiss, an athletic shoe manufacturer, and Foot Locker, a retailer, jointly sponsor video production contests for middle-school students in several major cities. For less than the cost of one national TV ad, the contests achieve a high level of brand awareness among the firms' prime prospects.[7]

Lack of money may limit the options a firm has for its promotional effort. For example, television advertising can carry a particular promotional message to far more people and at a lower cost *per person* than can most other media. Yet a firm may have to rely on less expensive media, such as Yellow Pages advertising, because it lacks the funds to take advantage of television's efficiency.

### Choosing a Push or a Pull Strategy

As we have seen, producers aim their promotional mix at both intermediaries and end users. A promotion program aimed primarily at intermediaries is called a **push strategy**, and a promotion program directed primarily at end users is called a **pull strategy**. Figure 18-3 contrasts these two strategies.

Using a *push* strategy means a channel member directs its promotion primarily at the intermediaries that are the next link forward in the distribution channel. The product is "pushed" through the channel. Take the case of a hardware producer that sells its tools and replacement parts to household consumers through wholesalers and retailers such as True Value. The producer will promote heavily to wholesalers, which then also use a push strategy to retailers. In turn, the retailers promote to consumers. A push strategy usually involves a lot of personal selling and sales promotion, including contests for sales people and displays at trade shows. This promotional strategy is appropriate for many manufacturers of business products, as well as for various consumer goods.

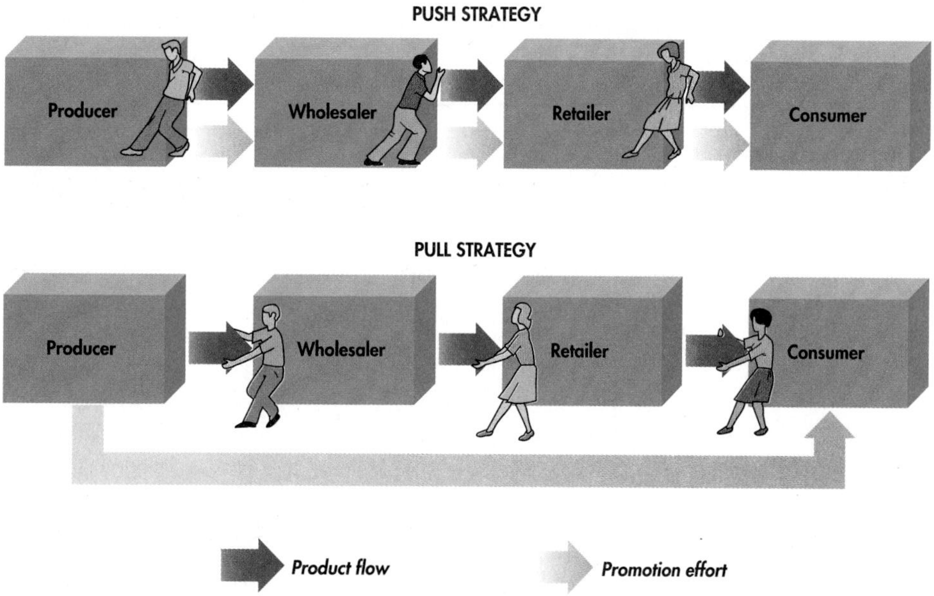


**FIGURE 18-3 Push and pull promotional strategies.**

With a *pull* strategy, promotion is directed at end users — usually ultimate consumers. The intention is to motivate them to ask retailers for the product. The retailers, in turn, will request the product from wholesalers, and wholesalers will order it from the producer. In effect, promotion to consumers is designed to "pull" the product through the channel. This strategy relies on heavy advertising and various forms of sales promotion such as premiums, samples, or in-store demonstrations.

There is little incentive for retailers to provide shelf space for minor variations of existing brands unless they are confident that they will sell. So manufacturers of consumer packaged goods often use a pull strategy to get new products stocked on supermarket shelves. For example, Johnson & Johnson spent over $40 million on North American advertising and sales promotion to introduce Tylenol Extra Strength Headache Plus, a line extension. At this spending level, retailers had some assurance that the brand would sell.

## WHAT MAKES A PRODUCT ADVERTISABLE?

Beyond the conditions mentioned in this section, advertising authority Neil Borden identified five product criteria that simply make certain products more "advertisable" than others. The criteria are:

- **Positive demand for the product.** Contrary to the opinion of many, advertising cannot successfully sell a product that people do not want. For example, despite the continuing efforts by an industry trade association, it is unlikely that advertising is going to produce a significant increase in the demand for Belgian endive, because consumers dislike its bitter taste.
- **The presence of physical features that provide opportunities to differentiate the product.** A differentiated product gives the advertiser more things to say. For this reason President's Choice cookies are easier to advertise than Sifto salt. Products that are not easy to differentiate by *brand* may still be advertised by a trade association.
- **Hidden qualities in the product.** This condition affords the seller opportunities for educating the market through advertising. Based on this criterion, a Kodak camera is simpler to advertise than Hallmark greeting cards.
- **The existence of emotional buying motives.** Society has attached powerful emotional buying motives to some products. Buying action can be stimulated by appealing to these motives. It is easier to build an effective advertising campaign for Obsession perfume than for Craftsman socket wrenches.
- **Sufficient funds to support an advertising program adequately.** Gillette spent $100 million to launch the Sensor razor and $50 million to introduce a line of men's toiletries just in the North American market.

If all these criteria are met, there is an excellent opportunity to advertise. When a product meets some, but not all, of these conditions, advertising may be less effective.

**This advertisement is placed by a trade association.**

## THE CAMPAIGN CONCEPT

Having examined the factors that influence the promotional mix, we turn our attention to a promotional campaign. In planning the promotional program for an organization, management should think in terms of the campaign concept. A **campaign** is a co-ordinated series of promotional efforts built around a single theme and designed to reach a specific goal in a defined period of time. In effect, a campaign is an exercise in strategic planning.

Although the term *campaign* is probably thought of most often in connection with the advertising component of promotion, it should embrace the entire promotional program. In developing a campaign, a company co-ordinates its advertising, personal selling, sales promotion, public relations, and publicity to accomplish an objective. For example, H. J. Heinz set rapid sales growth as one of its objectives for 1993. To achieve the goal, Heinz cut its ad budget by 43 percent and increased its sales promotion budget for activities such as coupons, contests, and in-store promotions by 100 percent, because sales promotion activity can provide a quicker increase in sales than advertising.[8]

A company may conduct many types of promotional campaigns, and even run some concurrently. Depending on objectives and available funds, a firm may have local, regional, national, and international campaigns all running at the same time. Moreover, a firm may have one campaign aimed at consumers, and another at wholesalers and retailers.

A promotional campaign begins with an objective. Pepsi set obtaining a 2 percent share of the soft drink market in both Canada and the United States as its goal for Crystal Pepsi. Next, the buying motives of the target market are examined to determine the best selling appeal. To be successful, the promotion campaign must offer ways that customers can solve their problems, satisfy their desires, or reach their goals. Pepsi believes that many adults who were raised on colas are now looking for alternative drinks that are lighter and free of caffeine and preservatives. Thus, they see the natural flavouring and clean, clear appearance of Crystal Pepsi as its selling appeal.

A campaign revolves around a theme or central idea. A **campaign theme** is simply the promotional appeals dressed up in a distinctive, attention-getting form. The theme for Crystal Pepsi is "You've never seen a taste like this." It expresses the product's benefits — clear, pure, and good tasting. Frequently, as with Crystal Pepsi, the theme takes the form of a slogan.

The theme permeates all promotional efforts and helps to unify the campaign. Some companies use the same theme for several campaigns; others develop a different theme for each new campaign. After using "Can't Beat the Real Thing" for five years in the United States, and "Can't Beat the Feeling" abroad, Coca-Cola looked for a new theme that can be used worldwide.[9]

With the theme established, each of the promotion-mix components must be carefully co-ordinated to communicate the desired message. This means that:

- The *advertising program* consists of a series of related, well-timed, carefully placed ads that reinforce personal selling and sales promotional efforts.
- The *personal selling effort* is co-ordinated with the advertising program. The sales people must be fully informed about the advertising part of the campaign — the theme, the media used, and the schedule for the appearance of ads. The sales force should be prepared to explain and demonstrate the product benefits stressed in the ads. The sales people also should transmit the promotional message to intermediaries so that they can take part in the campaign.
- The *sales promotional devices*, such as point-of-purchase display materials, are co-ordinated with other aspects of the campaign. New display materials must be prepared for each campaign. They should reflect the ads and appeals used in the current campaign to maximize the campaign's impact at the point of sale.
- *Publicity and public relations* efforts are scheduled to coincide with the other mix components and to emphasize the same theme.

The last step in a campaign is to evaluate the results. The outcome is compared with the objective to determine if the promotional effort was successful. Unfortunately, in evaluating promotion it is impossible to separate precisely the effects caused by a campaign from what would have occurred without it. As a result, it is impossible to determine exactly the value of a campaign. However, by comparing the cost of a campaign with the results, a firm can decide if the campaign was generally a success or a failure and identify ways of improving future efforts.

## MARKETING AT WORK

### FILE 18-2 THE TELEPHONE PROMOTIONAL WARS

It's a furious battle, the old boys' network against the upstarts. With deregulation and other changes in telecommunications, the telephone companies no longer have a monopoly on calling nor on the use of their long-distance lines. Now they must sell access at wholesale prices to firms that wish to buy in bulk. As a result, we have the Stentor Alliance, made up of Bell Canada in Ontario and Quebec, BC Tel, and the seven other regional telephone monopolies — the old boys, fighting for shares in the $3-billion residential market. Who is the new competition? Unitel has its own communications network and $427 million in revenues — mostly from its business market. Sprint Canada expects up to $200 million in sales in 1994, again mostly from the business market but with a growing share from the residential market. STN is the fastest growing company in the residential market with 474,000 customers. And then there is Call-net, based in Vancouver, also currently strong in the residential market with 100,000 residential customers. All the upstarts but Unitel buy in bulk from Stentor members or Unitel.

Each of these firms has different goals and objectives for the residential market with a different marketing strategy and different promotional program. In total, these competitors are using door-to-door appeals, television, radio, newspaper, direct mail, telemarketing, and just about every other vehicle imaginable including windshield flyers.

- Bell Canada is using a promotional program that includes heavy television usage, newspapers, magazines, and billing inserts to communicate its basic service and value message and is backing this up with special efforts to make its employees (25,000 in Ontario alone) into direct and indirect marketing representatives.
- Unitel relies mainly on television, but also uses newspapers, magazines, inserts, and brochures. It also has an agreement with Amway so that Amway's 100,000 Canadian reps can sell long-distance services in addition to its private-label consumer products.
- STN, on the other hand, uses a campaign that concentrates heavily on door-to-door efforts but it also has a 200-person telemarketing sales force, an exclusive direct mail campaign with Eaton's to reach its 1.5 million credit card customers and a two-minute television spot that ran for two months.
- Sprint Canada uses a television-spokesperson strategy featuring Candice Bergen, who has been extremely successful in the U.S. telephone wars for Sprint U.S. Sprint has also signed an agreement with Zellers to sell its services package in Zellers stores, through weekly flyers and offering 4 million Zellers credit card holders the opportunity of charging Sprint calls on their cards.
- Call-net's campaign includes national and local television, newspaper ads, several hundred direct sales people, and a massive direct-mail program that distributes 30,000 application forms per month.

The telephone wars will continue until the point when firms cannot generate the revenue to cover their promotional costs. Experts don't expect Stentor members to be casualties, but they are certainly looking for others. Based on your view of consumer behaviour and the promotional programs described above, who do you think will be in business three years from now?

Source: Adapted, in part, from Beppi Crosariol, "War of the Wires," *Globe and Mail Report on Business Magazine*, May, 1994, pp. 32-46, and Lawrence Surtees, "Call-net Predicts Profit in Two Years," *Globe and Mail*, June 9, 1994, p. B14.

## THE PROMOTIONAL BUDGET

Establishing promotional budgets is extremely challenging because management lacks reliable standards for determining how much to spend altogether on advertising or personal selling, and how much of the total budget to allocate to each promotional-mix element. A firm may have the alternative of adding seven sales people or increasing its trade show budget by $200,000 a year, but it cannot determine precisely what increase in sales or profits to expect from either expenditure. As a result, rather than one generally accepted approach to setting promotional budgets, there are four common **promotional budgeting methods**: percentage of sales, all available funds, following the competition, and budgeting by task or objective. These methods are frequently discussed in connection with the advertising budget, but they may be applied to any promotional activity as well as to determine the total promotional budget.

### Percentage of Sales

The promotional budget may be related in some way to company income, as a percentage of either past or anticipated sales. A common approach for determining the sales base is to compute an average between the previous year's actual sales and expected sales for the coming year. Some businesses prefer to budget a fixed amount of money per *unit* of past or expected future sales. Manufacturers of products with a high unit value and a low rate of turnover (automobiles or appliances, for example) frequently use the unit method.

Because the *percentage-of-sales method* is simple to calculate, it is probably the most widely used budgeting method. Moreover, it sets the cost of promotion in relation to sales income, making it a variable rather than a fixed expense.

There are two things you need to realize about basing promotional expenditures on past sales. First, management is effectively making promotion a *result* of sales when, in fact, it is a *cause* of sales. Second, a percentage of past sales method reduces promotional expenditures when sales are declining — just when promotion usually is most needed.

### All Available Funds

A new company or a firm introducing a new product frequently ploughs all available funds into its promotional program. The objective is to build sales and market share as rapidly as possible during those early, critical years. After a time, management generally finds it necessary to invest in other things, such as new equipment or expanded production capacity, so the method of setting the promotional budget is changed.

### Follow Competition

A weak method of determining the promotional budget, but one that is used occasionally, is to match the promotional expenditures of competitors or to spend in proportion to market share. Sometimes only one competitor is followed. In other cases, if management has access to industry average expenditures on promotion through a trade association, these become company benchmarks.

## MARKETING AT WORK

### FILE 18-3 YOU MAKE THE DECISION: IS PROMOTION AN EXPENSE OR AN INVESTMENT?

Promotional activities generally are budgeted as current operating expenses, implying that their benefits are used up immediately. Through the years, however, several economists and executives have proposed that advertising (and presumably other promotional efforts) be treated as a capital investment. Their reason is that the benefits and returns on these expenditures are like investments, often not immediately evident, instead accruing over several years. For example, a company like Hertz may build awareness and familiarity with a consumer for years through its advertising before it actually realizes a sale.

How would it affect management's thinking to treat promotion as an expense for accounting purposes, but as an investment for marketing purposes?

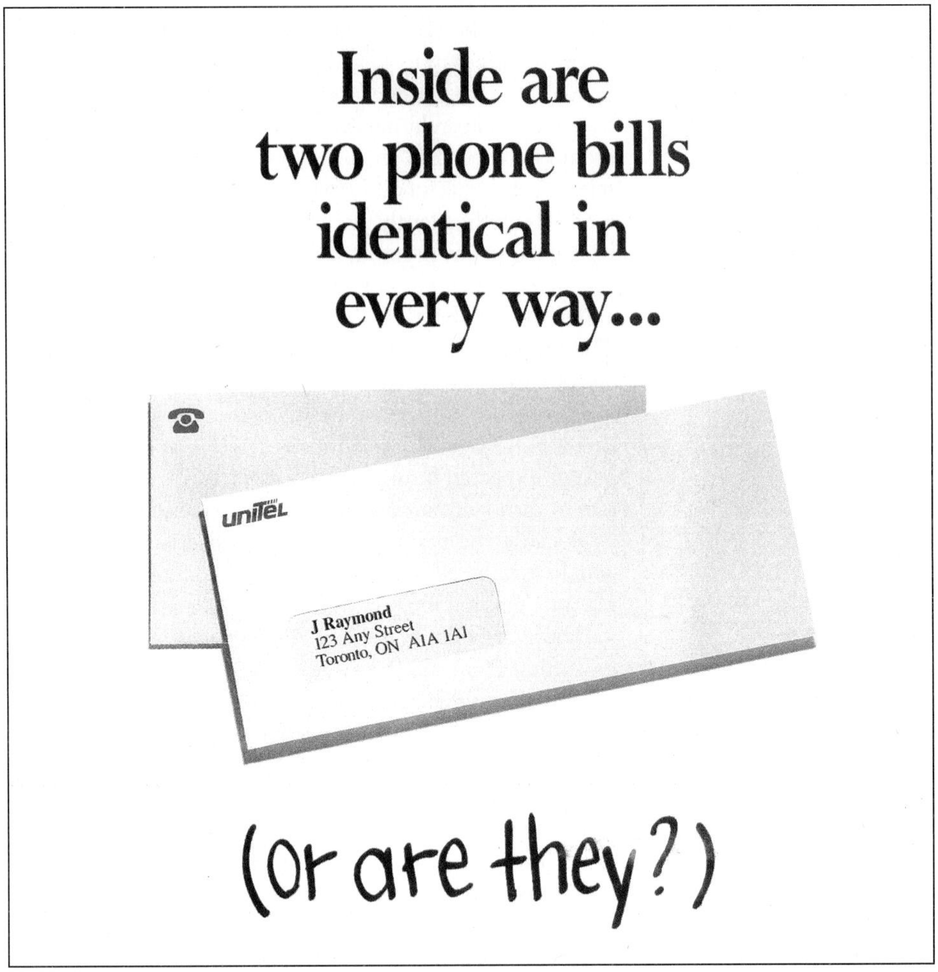


There are at least two problems with this approach. First, a firm's competitors may be just as much in the dark regarding how to set a promotional budget. Second, a company's promotional goals may be quite different from its competitors' because of differences in strategic marketing planning.

### Task or Objective

The best approach for establishing the promotional budget is to determine the tasks or objectives the promotional program must accomplish and then decide what they will cost. The task method forces management to define realistically the goals of its promotional program.

Sometimes this is called the *buildup method* because of the way it is constructed. For example, a company may elect to enter a new geographic market. Management determines this venture will require 10 additional sales people. Compensation and expenses of these people will cost a total of $520,000 per year. Salary for an additional sales supervisor and expenses for an extra office and administrative needs will cost $70,000. Thus in the personal selling part of the promotional mix, an extra $590,000 must be budgeted. Similar estimates can be made for the anticipated costs of advertising, sales promotion, and other promotional tools. The promotional budget is *built up* by adding up the costs of the individual promotional tasks needed to reach the goal of entering a new territory.

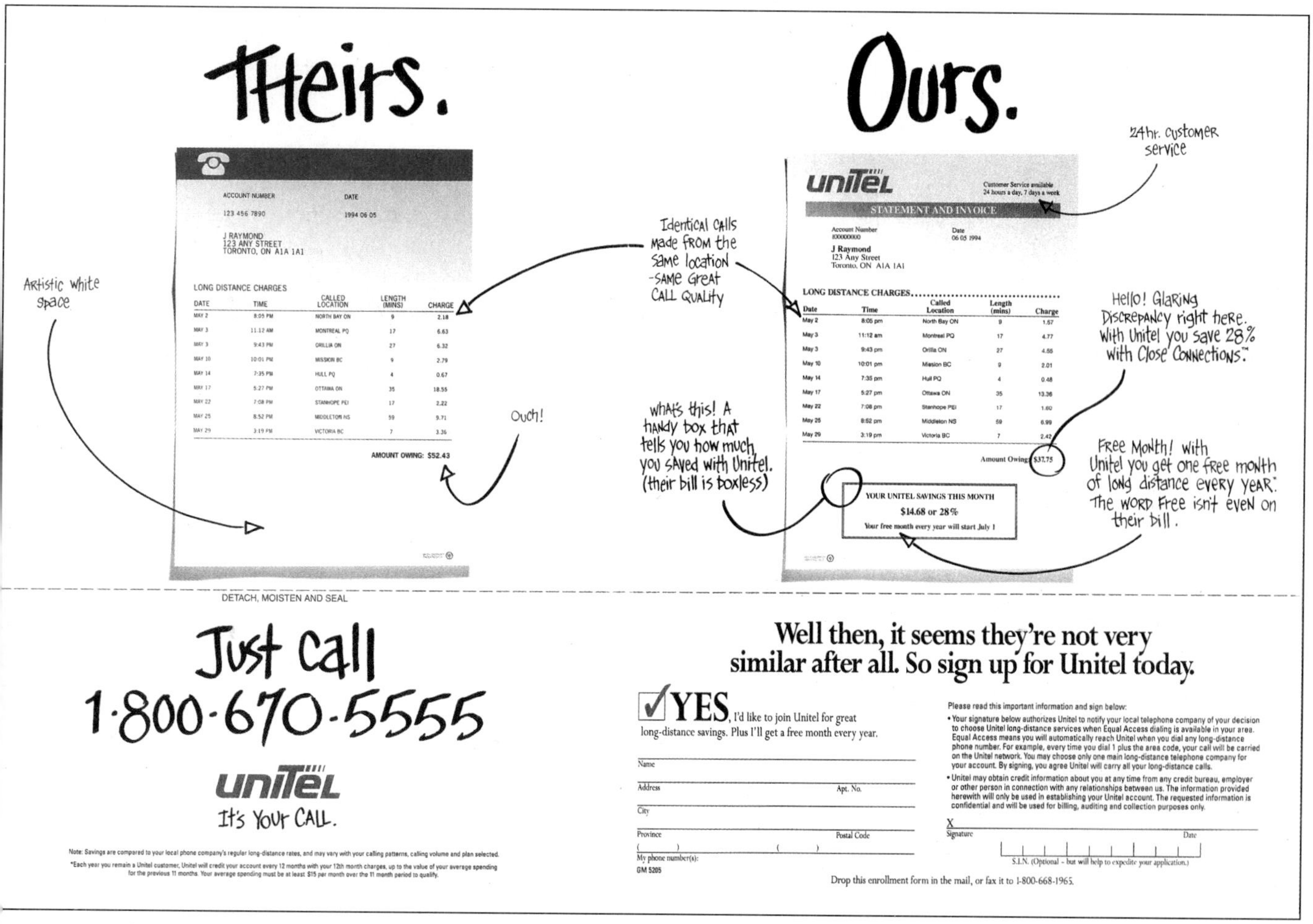


**Unitel's comparative approach is repeated on television, in newspapers, as inserts, and as brochures asking to call or clip.**

## REGULATION OF PROMOTIONAL ACTIVITIES

Because the primary objective of promotion is to sell something by communicating with a market, promotional activities attract attention. Consequently, abuses by individual firms are easily and quickly noted by the public. This situation in turn soon leads to (1) public demand for correction of the abuses, (2) assurances that they will not be repeated, and (3) general restraints on promotional activities. To answer public demand, laws and regulations have been enacted by the federal government and by most provincial governments. In addition, many private business organizations have established voluntary codes of advertising and promotional standards to guide their own promotional activities. In addition, the advertising industry itself, through the Advertising Advisory Board and its Advertising Standards Councils, does a considerable amount of self-regulation.

### The Federal Role

A number of departments of the federal government administer Acts aimed at controlling various aspects of promotion, particularly advertising. The **Broadcasting Act** established the Canadian Radio-television and Telecommunications Commission (CRTC) in 1968 and provided for sweeping powers of advertising regulation. Under section 16 of the Act, the Commission may make regulations concerning the character of broadcast advertising and the amount of time that may be devoted to it. While the potential for substantial control exists, the Commission does not in reality pass on each commercial message. What it has done is to delegate authority in certain fields to other agencies such as the Health Protection Branch of Health Canada and the Combines Investigation Branch of Industry Canada.

The Health Protection Branch deals with advertising in the fields of drugs, cosmetics, and devices (officialese for birth-control products), and it has sweeping powers to limit, control, rewrite, or ban promotion for the products under its authority. The authority itself is embodied in such Acts, and regulations associated with them, as the Health and Welfare Department Act, the Proprietary or Patent Medicine Act, the Food and Drug Act, the Criminal Code of Canada, and the Broadcasting Act. The various Acts and regulations result in general types of prohibition aimed at preventing the treatment, processing, packaging, labelling, advertising, and selling of foods, drugs, and devices in such a manner as to mislead or deceive, or even to be likely to create an erroneous impression concerning the nature of the products.

The Branch also prohibits the advertising of whole classes of drugs. It has developed a list of diseases or conditions for which a cure may not be advertised under any circumstances. This prohibition stands even if a professionally accepted cure exists. The logic for the prohibition of advertising, in spite of the existence of a cure, is that the Branch does not wish members of the general public to engage in self-diagnosis of the condition that can be treated.

By virtue of the powers delegated to it by the Commission, the Branch has absolute control over radio and television advertisements for the products under its jurisdiction. All such advertisements must be submitted to it at least 15 days prior to airing, and no radio or television station can air an ad without its having been approved by the Branch and, thereby, the Commission. In practical terms, the Health Protection Branch, even though an appeal route to the CRTC is available, has complete authority and advertisers have no resource of any consequence.

In contrast to the delegated review powers the Health Protection Branch has over advertisements using the broadcast media, its position with reference to the print media is weak. Its formal control is over alleged Food and Drug violations, which must be prosecuted in court. Given the lack of jurisprudence in this area, the Branch is loath to go to court in case it loses and thus sets a precedent or in case its regulations (many of which have not been tested in court) are found to be illegal. What the Branch does is advise advertisers of its opinion of advertisements that are prepared for the print media. This opinion is not a ruling, and ads submitted, as well as those that are not, are still subject to the regulations for which the Branch has responsibility. This does not mean that the Branch does not monitor the print media. Newspapers and magazines are sampled and advertisements examined.

Industry Canada has substantial and major responsibility in the area of regulating promotion. The Bureau of Competition Policy of the Department carries the major burden of promotional regulation. The Acts administered include: (1) the Hazardous Products Act (concerning poisonous compounds for household use), (2) the Precious Metals Marketing Act (i.e., definitions of sterling and carat weight), (3) the Trade Marks Act, (4) the Consumer Packaging and Labelling Act, and of greatest significance, (5) the Competition Act. Within the **Competition Act**, a number of sections pertain directly to the regulation of advertising and promotional activities. Section 35, for example, requires that manufacturers or wholesalers who offer promotional allowances to retailers must offer such allowances on proportionate terms to all competing purchasers. Section 36 of the Act regulates misleading advertising in general, while section 37 pertains specifically to "bait and switch" advertising.[10]

Section 36 of the Competition Act makes it illegal for an advertiser to make any false or misleading statement to the public in advertising or promotional materials or with respect to warranties. This section also regulates the use of false statements regarding the expected performance or length of life of a product and the use of testimonials in advertising. Section 36.2 of the Act regulates the use of "double ticketing" in retail selling and requires that, where a retailer promotes a product at two different prices or where two prices appear on a product or at the point of sale, the retailer must sell the product at the lower of the prices. Businesses or individuals who are convicted of violating section 36 are subject to fines as large as $25,000 or to imprisonment for up to one year.

Paragraph 36(1)(*d*) of the Competition Act regulates "sale" advertising and would apply particularly to retail advertisers. Section 37 requires that an advertiser who promotes a product at a "sale" price have sufficient quantities of the product on hand to satisfy reasonable market demand. Section 37.1 prohibits an advertiser from selling a "sale" item at a price higher than the advertised "sale" price. Finally, section 37.2 regulates the conduct of contests, lotteries, and games of chance. This section requires that advertisers who promote such contests disclose the number and value of prizes and the areas in which prizes are to be distributed, and further requires that prizes be distributed on a basis of skill or on a basis of random selection.

The provisions of the Competition Act relating to misleading advertising do not apply to publishers and broadcasters who actually distribute the advertising in question to the general public, provided that these publishers have accepted the contents of the advertising in good faith. In essence, this means that a newspaper cannot be prosecuted for misleading advertising if it accepted the advertising on the assumption that its contents were not misleading. Although no newspaper can be prosecuted for misleading advertising if it accepted the advertising in good faith, there is still some question concerning whether media production departments and advertising agencies, which actually participate with the advertiser in the production of misleading advertising, might not in the future be considered jointly responsible with the advertiser for the contents of the offending advertisement. This is a question with which the Canadian courts may deal in the future.

### The Provincial Role

In each of the provinces, a considerable variety of legislation exists that is aimed at controlling various promotional practices. For instance, in Ontario, various degrees of control are exercised by the Liquor Control Board of Ontario, the Ontario Board of Film Censors, the Ontario Superintendent of Insurance, the Ontario Human Rights Commission, the Ontario Securities Commission, the Ontario Police Commission, the Ontario Racing Commission, various ministries of the Ontario government responsible for financial, commercial, consumer, and transportation functions and services, and yet more. Most of the provinces have similar sets of legislation, regulatory bodies, and provincial departments. While much of the federal regulation must in the end result in argument and prosecution in a courtroom, the provincial machinery would appear to be much more flexible and potentially regulatory in nature, and if pursued, may have a more substantial effect on undesirable practices.

The powers of provincial governments in relation to the regulation of misleading advertising have been increased considerably in recent years. Since the mid-1970s, a number of provinces have passed legislation dealing with unfair and unconscionable trade practices. The "trade practices" Acts passed by British Columbia, Alberta, and Ontario contain "shopping lists" of practices that are made illegal by these Acts. In reality, these pieces of legislation write into law practices that have been considered illegal by federal prosecutors for a number of years. Relating to advertising, these Acts prohibit

## MARKETING AT WORK

### FILE 18-4 RUNNING AFOUL OF THE MISLEADING ADVERTISING PROVISIONS OF THE COMPETITION ACT: A WORD FROM THE DIRECTOR

**SECTION 52(1)(a):** all representations, in any form whatever, that are false or misleading in a material respect are prohibited.

In promoting the sale of radios, K mart Canada Ltd. represented on in-store signs:

"Our Price 19.99 Sale Price 9.99"

Investigation revealed that "19.99" represented neither the regular selling price in the relevant market nor K mart's regular selling price. The accused pleaded guilty and was fined $10,000.

**SECTION 52(1)(b):** Any representation in the form of statement, warranty or guarantee of the performance, efficacy or length of life of a product, not based on an adequate or proper test, is prohibited. The onus is on the one making the claim to prove that it is so based.

Remington Products (Canada) Inc., in promoting the sale of electric shavers, represented in television commercials:

"Shaves as close as a blade and closer than any other electric shaver . . . Gets whiskers other shavers leave behind . . . Remington Ultimate *tests prove it.* In independent tests approximately 70 percent said it shaves closer than any other electric shaver."

Investigation revealed that these claims were not based on adequate and proper tests. The accused pleaded guilty and was fined $75,000.

**SECTION 59:** Any contest that does not disclose the number and approximate value of prizes or important information relating to the chances of winning in the contest, that does not select participants or distribute prizes on the basis of skill or on a random basis, or in which the distribution of prizes is unduly delayed, is prohibited.

In promoting the sale of health club memberships, Hatcher and Day represented on a ballot:

"Sunshine Sweepstakes — No Purchase Necessary.
Limit One per person. . ."

Investigation revealed that the accused unduly delayed the distribution of prizes. Hatcher and Day pleaded guilty and were each fined $2,500 for a total of $5,000.

Source: Adapted from Director of Investigation and Research, *Misleading Advertising Bulletin*, Consumer and Corporate Affairs Canada, January, 1991, pp. 11, 16, 18, 19.

such practices as advertising a product as new when it is in fact used; advertising that fails to state a material fact, thereby deceiving the consumer; and advertising that gives greater prominence to low down payments or monthly payments rather than to the actual price of the product. The Alberta Unfair Trade Practices Act also contains a provision for corrective advertising. This provision means that a court, upon convicting an advertiser for misleading advertising, can order that advertiser to devote some or all of its advertising for a certain period to informing customers that the advertiser had been advertising falsely in the past and to correcting the misleading information that had been communicated in the offending advertisements.

The Province of Quebec has within its Consumer Protection Act a section that regulates advertising directed at children. This section forbids the use of exaggeration, endorsements, cartoon characters, and statements that urge children to buy. Quebec's Official Language Act also contains a number of sections that govern the use of French and English in advertising in that province.

### Regulation by Private Organizations

Several kinds of private organizations also exert considerable control over promotional practices of businesses. Magazines, newspapers, and radio and television stations regularly refuse to accept advertisements that they feel are false, misleading, or generally in bad taste, and in so doing they are being "reasonable" in the ordinary course of doing business. Some trade associations have established a "code of ethics" that includes points pertaining to sales-force and advertising activities. Some trade associations regularly censor advertising appearing in their trade or professional journals. Better Business Bureaus located in major cities all over the country are working to control some very difficult situations. The Advertising Advisory Board administers the Canadian Code of Advertising Standards, a number of other advertising codes, including the Broadcast Code for Advertising to Children (on behalf of the Canadian Association of Broadcasters), and a code regulating the advertising of over-the-counter drugs, which was developed in co-operation with the Proprietary Association and Health and Welfare Canada.

## SUMMARY

Promotion, the fourth component of a company's total marketing mix, is essential in modern marketing. The three primary methods of promotion are personal selling, advertising, and sales promotion. Other forms include public relations and publicity.

Promotion is communication. Fundamentally, the communication process consists of a source sending a message through a channel to a receiver. The success of communication depends on how well the message is encoded, how easily and clearly it can be decoded, and whether any noise interferes with its transmission. Feedback, the response created by a message, is a measure of how effective a communication has been.

The purposes of promotion are to inform, persuade, and remind customers. In economic terms, that means changing a firm's demand curve — shifting it to the right and changing its shape to make demand inelastic when prices increase and elastic when prices decrease.

Promotion must be integrated into a firm's strategic planning because effective execution requires that all elements of the marketing mix — product, price, distribution, and promotion — be co-ordinated. When deciding on the promotional mix (the combination of advertising, personal selling, and other promotional tools), management should consider: (1) the nature of the market, including the type of customer, the prospect's readiness to buy, and the geographic scope of the market; (2) the nature of the product, including unit value, the degree of customization required, and the amount of presale and postsale service; (3) the stage of the product's life cycle; and (4) the funds available for promotion.

A basic decision is how much promotional effort should be focused on intermediaries and how much should be directed to end users. The options are a push strategy, which involves concentrating promotional effort on the next link forward in the distribution channel, and a pull strategy, in which promotion is focused primarily on the final buyer.

A promotion campaign is a co-ordinated series of efforts built around a single theme and designed to reach a predetermined goal. The key to a successful promotional campaign is to carefully plan and co-ordinate advertising, sales promotion, personal selling, public relations, and publicity.

Because the effects of promotion are unpredictable, it is difficult to set a dollar figure for the total promotional budget. The most common method is to set the budget as a percentage of past or anticipated sales. A better approach is to establish the promotional objectives and then estimate how much it will cost to achieve them.

As a result of criticism and concern regarding the use of advertising and promotional techniques, the federal government has enacted legislation that regulates promotion. The main federal laws are the Competition Act and the Broadcasting Act. The Department of Consumer and Corporate Affairs and the Canadian Radio-Television and Telecommunications Commission are charged with administering the legislation in this area. Promotional practices are also regulated at the provincial level through trade practices legislation, through voluntary codes of businesses and trade associations, and by the advertising industry itself.

## KEY TERMS AND CONCEPTS

**Promotion (548)**
**Personal selling (548)**
**Advertising (548)**
**Sales promotion (548)**
**Public relations (549)**
**Publicity (549)**
**Communication (549)**
**Encoding (549)**
**Decoding (549)**
**Response (549)**
**Feedback (549)**
**Noise (549)**
**Promotion and the demand curve (552)**
**Promotional mix (553)**
**Hierarchy of effects (555)**
**Push strategy (559)**
**Pull strategy (559)**
**Campaign (560)**
**Campaign theme (561)**
**Promotional budgeting methods (563)**
**Broadcasting Act (565)**
**Competition Act (566)**
**Provincial role in regulating promotion (567)**
**Regulation by industry itself (568)**

## QUESTIONS AND PROBLEMS

1. Describe and explain the components of the communication process in the following situations:
   a. A college student trying to convince her father to buy her a used car.
   b. A sales person trying to sell a car to a college student.
2. Explain how the nature of the market affects the promotional mix for the following products:
   a. Contact lenses.
   b. Golf balls.
   c. Plywood.
   d. Take-out fried chicken.
   e. Compact discs.
   f. Mainframe computers.
3. Describe how classifying consumer goods as convenience, shopping, or specialty goods helps determine the best promotional mix.
4. Evaluate each of the following products with respect to the criteria for advertisability. Assume that sufficient funds are available.
   a. Automobile tires.
   b. Revlon cosmetics.
   c. Light bulbs.
   d. 10-minute automobile oil changes.
   e. College or university education.
   f. Luggage.
5. Explain whether personal selling is likely to be the main ingredient in the promotional mix for each of the following products:
   a. Chequing accounts.
   b. Home swimming pools.
   c. Liquid laundry detergent.
   d. Large order of McDonald's french fries.
6. Explain whether retailer promotional efforts should be stressed in the promotional mix for the following:
   a. Levi's jeans.
   b. Sunkist oranges.
   c. Women's cosmetics.
   d. Bank credit card.
7. Identify the central idea — the theme — in three current promotional campaigns.
8. Assume you are marketing a liquid that removes creosote (and the danger of fire) from chimneys used for wood-burning stoves. Briefly describe the roles you would assign to advertising, personal selling, sales promotion, and publicity in your promotional campaign.
9. Do you think we need additional legislation to regulate advertising? To regulate personal selling? If so, explain what you would recommend.

## HANDS-ON MARKETING

1. An ad should have a particular objective that should be apparent to a careful observer. For each of the following promotional objectives, find an example of a print ad:
   a. Primarily designed to inform.
   b. Primarily designed to persuade.
   c. Primarily designed to remind.
2. A promotional campaign is a co-ordinated series of promotional efforts built around a single theme and designed to reach a predetermined goal. A campaign often includes advertising, sales promotion, personal selling, public relations, and publicity. For an important event at your school (such as homecoming, recruiting new students, fund raising), describe the promotional tools used in the campaign and evaluate their appropriateness based on the criteria in the chapter for designing a promotional mix.

## NOTES AND REFERENCES

1. Adapted, in part, from promotional material kindly provided by Pillsbury Canada Ltd.
2. Richard Gibson, "McDonald's Ads Will Combine Food and Board," *The Wall Street Journal*, March 26, 1992, p. B1.
3. Dana Millbank, "Aluminum Producers, Aggressive and Agile, Outfight Steelmakers," *The Wall Street Journal*, July 1, 1992, p. A1.
4. Joseph Weber, "From Soup to Nuts and Back Again," *Business Week*, November 5, 1990, p. 114.
5. Bradley A. Stertz, "For LH Models, Chrysler Maps New Way to Sell," *The Wall Street Journal*, June 30, 1992, p. B1.
6. Bruce Hager and John Templeman, "Now, They're Selling BMWs Door-to-Door — Almost," *Business Week*, May 14, 1990, p. 65.
7. Ann de Rouffignac, "School Contests Help Concerns Promote Brands," *The Wall Street Journal*, July 3, 1992, p. B1.
8. Joanne Lipman, "Food Companies Cut Ad Budgets While Beefing Up Promotions," *The Wall Street Journal*, April 2, 1992, p. B6.
9. Michael J. McCarthy, "Coca-Cola Plans a New Slogan for Coke Classic," *The Wall Street Journal*, May 12, 1992, p. B1.
10. For a review of court decisions in misleading advertising cases in Canada, refer to James G. Barnes, "Advertising and the Courts," *The Canadian Business Review*, Autumn 1975, pp. 51-54. The Misleading Advertising Division of Industry Canada also publishes a quarterly review of misleading advertising cases entitled the *Misleading Advertising Bulletin*. Individuals interested in receiving this bulletin can have their names placed on the mailing list simply by writing to Industry Canada.

## CHAPTER 19 GOALS

This chapter examines personal selling, directing a sales force, and evaluating a sales person's performance. After studying this chapter, you should have an understanding of:

- The part that personal selling plays in our economy and in an organization's marketing program.
- The variety of personal selling jobs.
- The changing patterns in personal selling.
- The major tasks in staffing and operating a sales force.
- Key issues in evaluating a sales person's performance.

CHAPTER 19

# MANAGEMENT OF PERSONAL SELLING

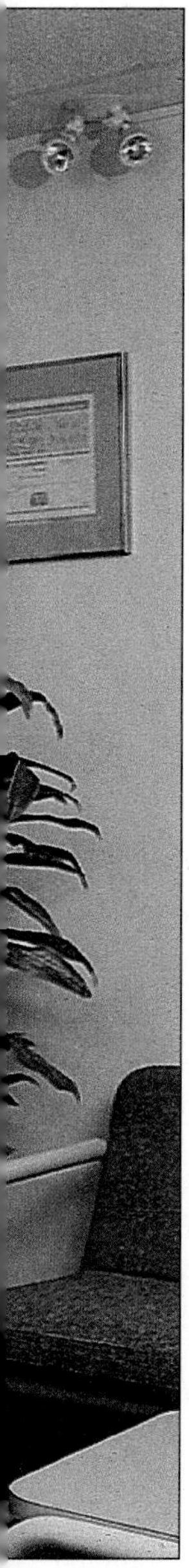

## Love Committed to Building Relationships

Love Printing is a highly successful firm in the Ottawa region. For a number of years, it has been the only printing house in the area to have its own state-of-the-art high-resolution colour scanner. With the progression of electronic imaging and computer graphics, Love has become a leader in using computer wizardry to produce the ultimate in colour reproduction and graphics manipulation.

In a service business, the scope of the service and the quality of work is difficult to communicate, in spite of being able to show examples of previous jobs, so Love has chosen to provide a simulated plant tour in its trade advertising and to invite people in for a real tour in order to drive home the message in the most credible fashion. The advertising does the prospecting — and identifies potential clients when they respond to the ad. The copy and photos present a plant tour starting with an invitation, the outstretched welcoming hand you see opposite, scenes of employees at work supported with copy about processes, equipment, and performance. The ad ends with the line "Discover the difference by yourself by coming to Stittsville for a tour. We're convinced that once you see our plant operations and our print professionals in action, our services will sell themselves."

That last line tells the story at Love. Being face to face, explaining, asking questions, answering questions, getting to know a person, even if the plant tour is a brief one, involving your professionals — these exchanges and small encounters come together to do two things. The first is to lend credibility to the service being marketed by showing what it's about and by introducing the people who take part in providing the business service. The second is to begin to build a relationship — it may not result in a sale now, it may result in a one-time piece of business, or it may result in a lasting business relationship.

All the personnel at Love Printing who are part of the plant tour play a role in a relationship selling approach to their business. For Love sales and marketing management, this means explaining, training, motivating, and providing feedback to its staff so they can do the job that needs to be done and be pleased to do it. In order to be successful at this, the "plant tour team" has to demonstrate candour, dependability, competence, a customer orientation, and likability. And when the team has these things right, "the services will sell themselves."

If the personal selling effort in an organization falters, then the economic fortunes of that organization will likely decline. The extent of Love Printing's success in strengthening its personal selling and sales-force management will largely determine the company's financial future.[1]

## NATURE OF PERSONAL SELLING

"Everybody lives by selling something." This statement is just as true today as when Robert Louis Stevenson wrote it over 100 years ago. In fact, we can define **personal selling** as the personal communication of information to persuade somebody to buy something.

Most of us recognize that some personal selling is involved when a student buys a Honda motorcycle or a Laura Ashley store sells a dress to a woman who works in an advertising agency. But let's recognize that some personal selling is involved (1) when the Bank of Montreal recruits a graduating senior who majored in finance or, conversely, when a student tries to convince the Bank of Montreal to hire her; (2) when a minister talks to a group of students to encourage them to attend church services; (3) when a lawyer tries to persuade a jury that her client is innocent; or even (4) when a child persuades his mother to give him some chocolate chip cookies. Yes, personal selling occurs in nearly every human interaction.

The goal of all marketing efforts is to increase profitable sales by offering want-satisfaction to consumers over the long run. Personal selling is by far the major promotional method used to reach this goal. The number of people employed in advertising is a small fraction of the number employed in personal selling. In many companies, personal selling is the largest single operating expense, often equalling 8 to 15 percent of sales. In contrast, advertising costs average 1 to 3 percent of sales.

In Chapter 18 we discussed four factors that influence an organization's promotional mix — the market, the product, the product's life-cycle stage, and the money available for promotion. Referring to those four factors, personal selling is likely to carry the bulk of the promotional load when:

- The market is concentrated either geographically, or in a few industries, or in a few large customers.
- The product has a high unit value, is quite technical in nature, or requires a demonstration.
- The product must be fitted to an individual customer's need, as in the case of securities or insurance.
- The sale involves a trade-in.
- The product is in the introductory stage of its life cycle.
- The organization does not have enough money for an adequate advertising campaign.

### Merits of Personal Selling

Personal selling is the *individual, personal* communication of information, in contrast to the *mass, impersonal* communication of advertising, sales promotion, and other promo-

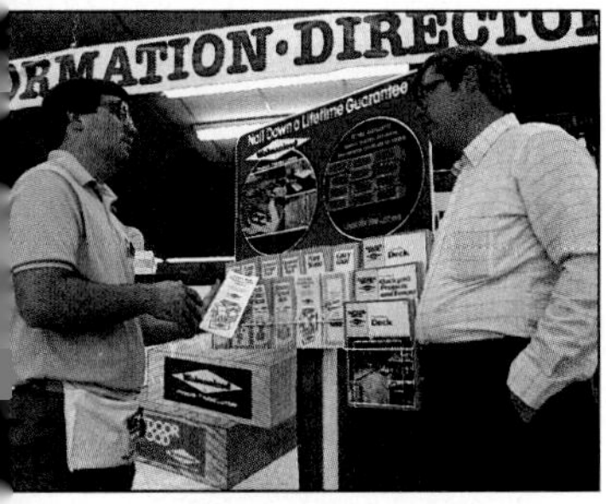

**In a personal-selling situation, a well-informed sales person is extremely valuable.**

tional tools. This means that personal selling is more *flexible* than these other tools. Sales people can tailor their presentations to fit the needs and behaviour of individual customers. Sales people can see their customers' reaction to a particular sales approach and make adjustments on the spot.

Also, personal selling usually can be *focused* or *pinpointed* on prospective customers, thus minimizing wasted effort. In contrast, much of the cost of advertising is spent on sending messages to people who in no way are real prospects.

Another advantage of personal selling is that its goal is to *actually make a sale*. Other forms of promotion are designed to move a prospect closer to a sale. Advertising can attract attention, provide information, and arouse desire, but seldom does it stimulate buying action or complete the transfer of title from seller to buyer.

A major limitation of personal selling is its *high cost*. Even though personal selling can minimize wasted effort, the cost of developing and operating a sales force is high. Another disadvantage is that a company often is *unable to attract the quality of people needed* to do the job. At the retail level, many firms have abandoned their sales forces and shifted to self-service selling for this very reason.

## Scope of Personal Selling

There are two kinds of personal selling, as shown in Figure 19-1. One is where the *customers come to the sales people*. Sometimes called **across-the-counter selling**, it primarily involves *retail-store selling*. In this kind of selling, we also include the sales people at catalogue retailers such as Sears Canada and Consumers' Distributing, who may take telephone orders as well. By far, most sales people in Canada fall into this first category.

The other kind of personal selling is where the *sales people go to the customers*. In this group are what we call **outside sales forces** — that is, sales reps engaged in field selling. These people sell in person at a customer's place of business or home.

Outside sales forces usually represent producers or wholesaling intermediaries, selling to business users and not to household consumers. However, in our definition of an outside sales force we also include: (1) producers who sell directly to household consumers — for example, insurance companies such as Mutual Life, and in-home sellers such as Avon Products; (2) retail sales people such as those from home heating and insulation

**FIGURE 19-1**
**Scope of personal selling.**

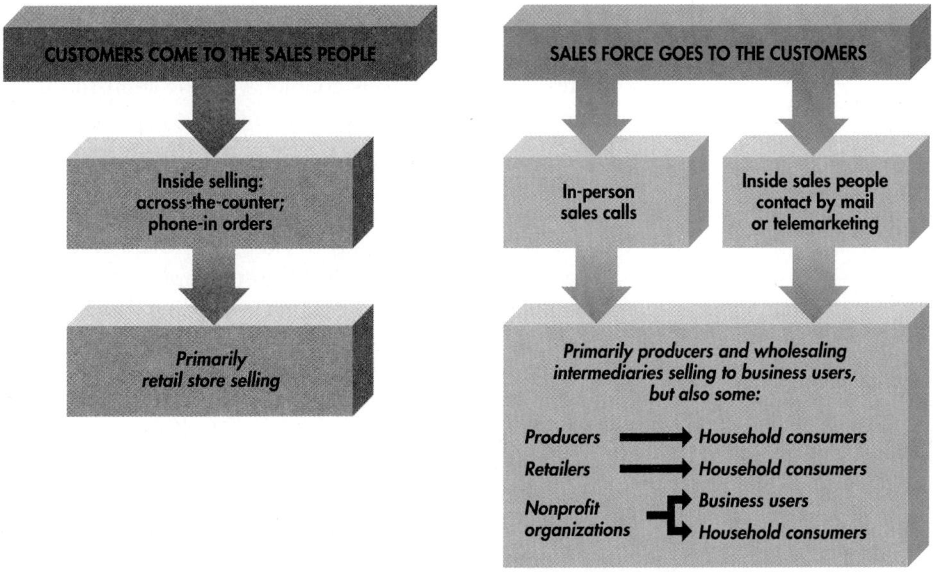

retailers; and (3) outside sales forces for not-for-profit organizations — for example, charity fund raisers, religious missionaries, and workers for political candidates.

Today some companies have a sales force that goes to the customers, but not in person. Instead, these reps are "going to the customers" by means of telephone, computer, and facsimile (fax) machines. In effect, some outside selling is becoming electronic, and the term **telemarketing** describes such communications systems. Many firms have used telephone selling for decades, and some sales reps regularly contact customers by mail or phone. What is different about telemarketing is the new telecommunications equipment used in "going to the customer."

### Nature of Sales Jobs

The sales job of today is quite different from that of years gone by. No longer appropriate is the stereotype of the cigar-smoking, back-slapping, joke-telling salesmen (and nearly all outside sales reps were men not so long ago). True, high-pressure selling may always exist in some fields. But it is no longer typical.

**The Professional Sales Person** A new type of sales rep is emerging — the **professional sales person**. Today these reps are managers of a market area — their territories. They engage in a *total* selling job — servicing their customers, building goodwill, selling their products, and training their customers' sales people. Today's reps act as a mirror of the market by relaying market information back to the firm. They organize much of their own time and effort. They often take part in recruiting new sales people, sales planning in their territories, and other managerial activities.

**Role Ambiguity and Role Conflict** Professional sales people typically occupy many roles with many different partners. For example, sales reps persuade prospective customers, expedite orders, co-ordinate deliveries, set up displays, service their accounts, gather market information, and help solve customers' problems. In performing these activities, sales people experience two related problems — role ambiguity and role conflict.

**Role ambiguity** occurs when a sales rep is uncertain about what to do when there is no company policy covering a given situation. When a large account asks for an additional promotional allowance or a good customer demands expensive entertainment, how should a rep respond?

**Role conflict** occurs when several groups present conflicting demands on the sales person. The marketing concept emphasizes satisfying the customer. But sometimes the best interests of the customers conflict with the short-run interests of the sales person or the company. For example, the auto centre in a department store pays its sales force a commission on sales. The sales people then may recommend unnecessary work on customers' cars in order to increase the reps' pay or to meet a high sales quota set by management. When customers' wants conflict with a seller's policies, sales reps can be caught in the middle. A case in point: A rep is ready to close a big sale, but the finance department won't approve the customer's credit. Sales reps must identify with their company and also with their customers, and often there is a conflict regarding whose position a rep should support.

**Wide Variety of Sales Jobs** The types of selling jobs and the activities involved in them cover a wide range. Consider the job of a Coca-Cola driver-sales person who calls routinely on a group of retail stores. That job is in another world from the IBM rep who sells a system for managing reservations to a hotel. Similarly, a sales rep for Avon Products selling door to door in Japan or China has a job only remotely related to that of a Canadair airplane rep who sells executive-type aircraft to Dow Chemical and other large firms around the world.

One way to classify sales jobs is on the basis of the creative selling skills required, from the simple to the complex. Our classification that follows is adapted from one developed years ago by Robert McMurry, a noted industrial psychologist.

1. **Driver-sales person.** In this job the sales person primarily delivers the product — for example, soft drinks or fuel oil. The selling responsibilities are secondary; few of these people originate sales.
2. **Inside order taker.** This is a position in which the sales person takes orders at the seller's place of business — for example, a retail clerk standing behind the counter at an Eaton's store or a telephone representative at a catalogue retailer. Most customers have already decided to buy, and the sales person's job is to serve them efficiently.
3. **Outside order taker.** In this position the sales person goes to the customer in the field and accepts an order. An example is a Home Hardware sales person calling on a retail affiliate store, or a sales rep for a radio station who sells advertising time to local businesses. The majority of these sales are repeat orders to established customers, although these sales people occasionally do introduce new products to customers.
4. **Missionary sales person.** This types of sales job is intended to build goodwill, perform promotional activities, and provide information and other services for the customers. This sales person is not expected to solicit an order. An example of this job is a missionary sales rep for Seagram's distillery or Procter & Gamble foods division, or a detail sales person for a pharmaceutical firm such as Merck or Lilly.
5. **Sales engineer.** In this position the major emphasis is on the sales person's ability to explain the product to a prospective customer, and also to adapt the product to the customer's particular needs. The products involved here typically are complex, technically sophisticated items. A sales engineer usually provides technical support and works with another sales rep who calls regularly on a given account.
6. **Creative sales person — an order getter.** This involves the creative selling of goods and intangibles — primarily services, but also social causes and ideas (don't do drugs, stop smoking, obey speed limit, as examples). This category contains the most complex, difficult selling jobs — especially the creative selling of intangibles, because you can't see, touch, taste, or smell them. Customers often are not aware of their need for a seller's product. Or they may not realize how that product can satisfy their wants better than the product they are now using. Creative selling often involves designing a system to fit the needs of a particular customer. For example, to make a sale, Northern Telecom may design a communications system for a hospital, or Otis elevator may develop a vertical lift system especially for a new office building.

**An effective inside order taker can adjust to a customer's reactions and can build good customer relations.**

In summary, the above six types of sales jobs fall into three groups: **order taker** (categories 1, 2, and 3), **sales-support personnel** (categories 4 and 5), and **order getter** (category 6). One organization may have several different types of sales jobs. IBM, for instance, has sales people in all of the above categories except driver-sales person.

**Sales Jobs Differ from Other Jobs** The features that differentiate sales jobs from other jobs are:

- **The sales force is largely responsible for implementing a firm's marketing strategies.** Moreover, it's the sales reps who generate the revenues that are managed by the financial people and used by the production people.
- **Sales people represent their company to customers and to society in general.** Many sales jobs require the rep to socialize with customers who frequently are upper-level people in their companies. Opinions of the firm and its products are formed on the

basis of impressions made by sales people in their work and outside activities. The public ordinarily does not judge a company by its factory or office workers.

- **Sales reps operate with little or no direct supervision.** For success in selling, a sales rep must work hard physically and mentally, be creative and persistent, and show considerable initiative. This all requires a high degree of motivation.
- **Sales jobs frequently involve considerable travelling and time away from home.** Many companies have reduced sales travel time by redesigning sales territories, routing sales trips better, and relying more on telemarketing. Nevertheless, being in the field, sales people must deal with an endless stream of customers who may seem determined not to buy their products. These stresses, coupled with long hours and travelling, require a mental toughness and physical stamina rarely demanded in other jobs. Personal selling is hard work!

**Today, personal selling requires a professional approach.**

## CHANGING PATTERNS IN PERSONAL SELLING

Traditionally, personal selling was a face-to-face, one-on-one situation between a sales person and a buyer. This situation existed both in retail sales involving ultimate consumers and also in business-to-business transactions. In recent years, however, some very different selling patterns have emerged. These new patterns reflect a growing purchasing expertise among consumers and business buyers, which, in turn, has fostered a growing professionalism in personal selling. Let's discuss four of these emerging patterns.

### Selling Centres — Team Selling

To match the expertise on the buying side, especially in business markets, a growing number of firms on the selling side have adopted the organizational concept of a **selling centre**. This is sometimes called a *sales team* or *team selling*. A selling centre is a group of people representing a sales department as well as other functional areas in a firm such as finance, production, and research and development (R&D). Team selling is expensive and is used only when there is a potential for high sales volume and profit.

Procter & Gamble, for example, has selling teams comprising sales people and representatives from finance, distribution, and manufacturing. Each team is assigned to cover a large retailer. When Bell Canada sells to a large multinational firm such as Nestlé, then it will send a separate selling team to deal with each of Nestlé's major divisions located in Ontario and Quebec.

**A sales rep practises relationship selling as she travels to customers' factories to learn first-hand about their needs.**

### Systems Selling

The concept of **systems selling** means selling a total package of related goods and services — a system — to solve a customer's problem. The idea is that the system — the total package of goods and services — will satisfy the buyer's needs more effectively than selling individual products separately. Xerox, for example, originally sold individual products, using a separate sales force for each major product line. Today, using a systems-selling approach, Xerox studies a customer's office information and operating problems. Then Xerox provides a total automated system of machines and accompanying services to solve that customer's office problems.

### Relationship Selling

Developing a mutually beneficial relationship with selected customers over time is **relationship selling**. It may be an extension of team selling, or it may be developed by individual sales reps in their dealings with customers. In relationship selling, a seller discontinues the usual territorial practice of covering many accounts. Instead, the seller attempts to develop a deeper, longer-lasting relationship built on trust with key customers — usually larger accounts.

Unfortunately, often there is not much trust found in buyer-seller relationships, neither in retailer-consumer selling nor in business-to-business selling. How do you build this trust? The following behavioural traits in selling can be effective trust builders:[2]

- **Candour** — be truthful in what you say.
- **Dependability** — behave in a reliable manner.
- **Competence** — display your ability, knowledge, and resources.
- **Customer orientation** — place your customers' needs and interests on a par with your own.
- **Likability** — seek a similarity of personality between you and the customers, and a commonality of interests and goals.

Many large companies, operating both in Canada and the United States — Procter & Gamble, Hyatt Hotels, RJR Nabisco, Kraft General Foods, and ABB (Asea Brown Boveri, a Swiss-based manufacturer of industrial equipment), to name just a few — are realigning their sales forces to engage in relationship selling. What they hope to achieve, and what appears to be developing for them, is long-run sales growth at a lower cost of selling.

### Telemarketing

Earlier we described *telemarketing* as the innovative use of telecommunications equipment and systems as part of the "going to the customer" category of personal selling. Telemarketing is growing because: (1) many buyers prefer it over personal sales calls in *certain selling situations*, and (2) many marketers find that it increases selling efficiency. Buyers placing routine reorders or new orders for standardized products by telephone or computer use less of their time than in-person sales calls. Sellers face increasingly high costs keeping sales people on the road; selling by telemarketing reduces that expense. Also, routine selling by telemarketing allows the field sales force to devote more time to creative selling, major account selling, and other more profitable selling activities.

## MARKETING AT WORK

### FILE 19-1 A COMMITMENT TO CUSTOMER SATISFACTION THROUGH SMART SELLING

Companies attract today's tougher customers through "smart selling" — which means focusing the entire company on selling and customer service. In the 1980s the business battles were to improve quality and reduce costs. Many companies have gone a long way towards winning those battles. In fact, "these days the product has to be great just to stay in the game," said an executive at Learning International, a sales training firm. Now, in the 1990s, the competitive battleground has shifted to selling and customer service.

Forward-looking companies have identified six guidelines for reaching the goal of smart selling:

- ***Focus the entire organization on sales and customer service.*** Du Pont's flexible sales teams, drawn from sales reps, technicians, chemists, factory managers, and financial people, work together developing and selling new products. One such product—a herbicide that growers can apply less often — topped $57 million in North American sales during its first year.
- ***Involve top management in smart selling.*** The founders and top executives of Home Depot stores regularly help prepare and participate in their sales training programs.
- ***Build deep, long-lasting relationships with customers.*** Make frequent phone calls to customers, or write a note to frequent shoppers at a store. Use computerized technology to keep track of relations with customers, ensuring that the right products get to the right place at the right time. General Electric has engineers stationed full time at a customer's plant — Praxair, maker of industrial gases — to help improve that customer's productivity.
- ***Rethink the sales training program.*** Forget the high-pressure selling and teach new skills to sales reps. New sales training firms emphasize new approaches such as teaching team selling, how to spot service problems, and ways to develop long-term relationships with customers.
- ***Change the motivation program — especially compensation.*** Avoid traditional commission-based pay plans that encourage short-term, high-pressure selling. Reward sales people for working to retain customers and improving long-term customer satisfaction.
- ***Use sales people to solve customers' problems, not just take their orders.*** Kraft General Foods sales people now offer research and tips for improving a store's profit. The reps no longer limit their efforts to designing in-store promotions.

Are these guidelines realistic, or are they just a bunch of nice, but meaningless, words?

Source: Christopher Power, "Smart Selling," *Business Week*, August 3, 1992, p. 46.

Here are examples of selling activities that lend themselves nicely to a telemarketing program:

- Seeking leads to new accounts and identifying potentially good customers that sales reps can follow up with in-person calls.
- Processing orders for standardized products. In Baxter Hospital Supply Co. Ltd., and some of its customers, for example, the buyer's computer talks with Baxter's computer to determine shipping dates and to place orders.
- Dealing with small-order customers, especially where the seller would lose money if field sales calls were used.
- Improving relations with intermediaries. Deere & Co. (farm equipment) "talks" via computers with its dealers about inventories, service, and financial management.
- Improving communications with intermediaries in foreign countries and competing better against manufacturers in those countries. In Europe, for example, the auto, chemical, steel, and shipbuilding industries have developed electronic communication systems involving manufacturers, suppliers, and even customs and shipping agents.

## THE PERSONAL SELLING PROCESS

The personal selling process is a logical sequence of four steps that a sales person takes in dealing with a prospective buyer. See Figure 19-2. This process leads, hopefully, to some desired customer action and ends with a follow-up to ensure customer satisfaction. The desired action usually is to get the customer to buy a product or a service. However, the same four-step process may be used equally well in other selling situations. For example, RJR Nabisco persuades Safeway and Sobey's to give Oreo cookies a good shelf location in a special promotion program; or Carleton University persuades alumni to contribute to a special fund-raising effort; or BMW wants its dealers to do some local advertising of their automobiles.

**FIGURE 19-2**
**The personal selling process.**

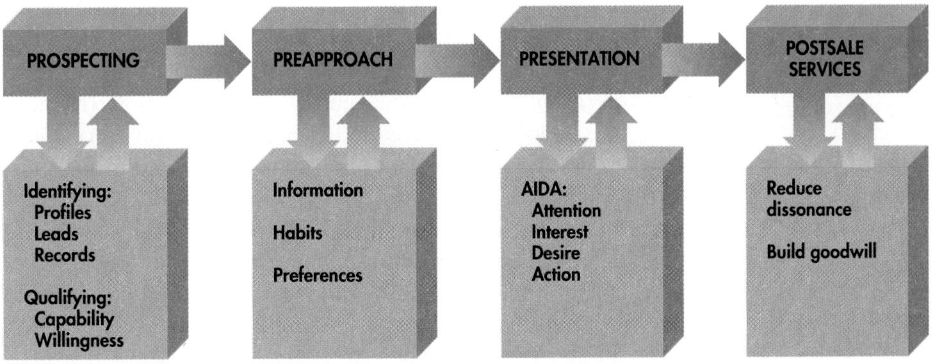


### Prospecting

The first step in the personal selling process is called **prospecting**. It consists of first identifying potential customers and then qualifying them — that is, determining whether they have the necessary purchasing power, authority, and willingness to buy.

**Identifying Prospective Customers** A rep may start the identification process by drawing up a profile of the ideal prospect. Records of past and current customers can help determine characteristics of an ideal prospect. From this profile a seller can start a list of potential customers.

Many other sources can be used to build the list of prospects. The rep's sales manager may prepare a list; current customers may suggest new leads; trade association and industry directories can be a good source; and leads can come from people mailing in a coupon or phoning a 1-800 number stated in an ad.

And a little thought often will suggest logical prospects. For example, the Brick (furniture store) can find prospects in lists of building permits issued. Toyota and Nissan auto dealers in Japan go door to door to seek prospects for new-car sales. Insurance companies, real estate firms, and even local diaper services use such sources as marriage and birth announcements in newspapers.

#### Qualifying the Prospects

After identifying prospective customers, a seller should **qualify** them — that is, determine whether they have the necessary willingness, purchasing power, and authority to buy. To determine *willingness to buy*, a seller can seek information about a prospect's relationship with its present suppliers. For example, a business firm or a household consumer may have had a long, satisfying relationship with The Cooperators for auto insurance. In this case there would seem to be little chance that an Allstate sales person could get that prospect's business. So they should spend their time elsewhere.

To determine a prospect's *financial ability to pay*, a seller can refer to credit-rating services such as Dun & Bradstreet. For household consumers or small businesses in an area, a seller can get credit information from a local credit bureau. Identifying who has the *authority to buy* in a business or a household can be difficult, as we saw back in Chapters 6 and 7. In a business, the buying authority may rest with a committee or an executive in a distant location. Besides determining the buying authority, a seller also should identify the one or more persons who *influence* the buying decision. A purchasing agent may have buying authority, but what he or she buys may depend on the recommendation of an office secretary or a factory engineer.

### Preapproach to Individual Prospects

Before calling on prospects, sales people should learn all they can about the persons or companies to whom they hope to sell. This **preapproach in selling** might include finding out what products the prospects are now using and their reactions to these products. In business-to-business selling, a sales person or selling team should find out how buying decisions are made in the customer's organization. (Remember, in Chapter 7 we discussed the various roles played in the buying-decision process in business firms.) A sales rep can target the right people if he or she knows who is the information gatekeeper, who influences and/or makes the buying decision, and who actually makes the purchase.

Sales people also should try to find out the personal habits and preferences of a prospect. Sales people should try to get all the information they can, so that they will be able to tailor their presentations to individual buyers.

### Presenting the Sales Message

With the appropriate preapproach information, a sales person can design a **sales presentation** that will attract the prospect's *attention*. The sales person will then try to hold the prospect's *interest* while building a *desire* for the product, and when the time is right, attempt to stimulate *action* by closing the sale. This approach, called **AIDA** (an acronym formed by the first letters of Attention, Interest, Desire, and Action) is used by many organizations.

#### Attract Attention — the Approach

The first task in a sales presentation is to attract the prospect's attention and to generate curiosity. In cases where the prospect is aware of a need and is seeking a solution, simply stating the seller's company and product will be enough. However, more creativity often is required.

For instance, if the sales person was referred to the prospect by a customer, the right approach might be to start out by mentioning this common acquaintance. Sometimes

**In-home personal sales presentations can be very effective for some products such as Encyclopedia Britannica.**

this is called the "Joe sent me" approach. Or a sales person might suggest the product benefits by making some startling statement. One sales training consultant often greets a prospect with the question, "If I can cut your selling costs in half, and at the same time double your sales volume, are you interested?"

**Hold Interest and Arouse Desire** After attracting the prospect's attention, the sales rep can hold it and stimulate a desire for the product with a sales talk. There is no common pattern here. Usually, however, a product demonstration is invaluable. Whatever pattern is followed in the talk, the sales person must always show how the product will benefit the prospect.

Some companies train their sales people to use a **canned sales talk** — a memorized sales presentation designed to cover all points set by management. All reps give the same presentation, verbatim or with minor changes. Companies engaging in telephone selling or door-to-door selling (Encyclopedia Britannica, for example) use canned sales talks. Although many people feel that this is a poor practice, canned talks have time and again proved to be effective. Nevertheless, they are used less and less today, because companies believe that flexible presentations can be more personal and tailored for individual customers' needs.

**Meet Objections and Close the Sale** After explaining the product and its benefits, a sales person should try to **close the sale** — that is, obtain the customer's agreement to buy. (This is the final A in AIDA — achieving the desired *action*.)

As part of the presentation, the sales person may periodically venture a **trial close** to test the prospect's willingness to buy. By posing some "either-or" questions, a sales person can bring the presentation to a head. For example, "Would you prefer the grey or the green model?" or "Do you plan to charge this or pay cash?"

The trial close is important because it gives the sales person an indication of how near the prospect is to a decision. Sometimes sales are lost simply because the rep fails to ask for the order.

The trial close also tends to bring out the buyer's objections. A sales person should encourage buyers to state their objections. Then the sales person has an opportunity to **meet the objections** and to bring out additional product benefits or re-emphasize previously stated points. The toughest objections to answer are those that are unspoken. A sales person must uncover the real objections before being able to close a sale.

### Postsale Services

An effective selling job does not end when the order is written up. The final stage of a selling process is a series of **postsale activities** that can build customer goodwill and lay the groundwork for future business. An alert sales person will follow up sales to ensure that no problems occur in delivery, financing, installation, employee training, and other areas that are important to customer satisfaction.

These activities reduce the customer's postpurchase anxiety (*cognitive dissonance*, as discussed in Chapter 6) — the anxiety that usually occurs after a person makes a buying decision. In this final stage of the selling process, a sales person can minimize the customer's dissonance by (1) summarizing the product's benefits after the purchase, (2) repeating why the product is better than alternatives not chosen, and (3) emphasizing how satisfied the customer will be with the product.[3]

## STRATEGIC SALES-FORCE MANAGEMENT

Managing the personal selling function is a matter of applying the three-stage management process (planning, implementation, and evaluation) to a sales force and its activities. Sales executives begin by setting sales goals and planning sales-force activities. This involves forecasting sales, preparing sales budgets, establishing sales territories, and setting sales quotas.

Then a sales force must be organized, staffed, and operated to implement the strategic plans and reach the goals that were set. The final stage involves evaluating the performance of individual sales people as well as appraising the total sales performance.

Effective sales-force management starts with a qualified sales manager. Finding the right person for this job is not easy. In many organizations the common practice when a sales management position becomes available is to reward the most productive sales person with a promotion. The assumption is that as a manager, an effective sales person will be able to impart the necessary wisdom to make others equally successful. However, as the following statements suggest, the qualities that lead to effective sales management are often diametrically opposed to the attributes of a successful sales person.[4]

- A sales person must be self-driven in order to achieve results. A sales manager must be careful not to drive people to achieve results.
- A sales person must be impatient. A sales manager must let situations develop and ripen.
- A sales person requires constant recognition for results. A sales manager must learn to give recognition and accept a secondary role.
- A sales person must "make the numbers" in the short run. A sales manager must take a longer-term view of business growth and personnel development.
- A sales person must be self-reliant. A sales manager must rely almost completely on others.
- A sales person is a doer. A sales manager is an organizer.
- A sales person builds account loyalty. A sales manager builds company loyalty.
- A sales person must be tenacious, confident that with enough time and effort any prospect can be sold. A sales manager must learn to cut losses quickly and move resources to more productive opportunities.
- A sales person has considerable freedom as long as results are forthcoming. A sales manager must conform to policies and procedures and play by the rules.

## STAFFING AND OPERATING A SALES FORCE

Most sales executives spend the bulk of their time in staffing and operating their sales forces. Hence, we now discuss what they do in these activities, as shown in Figure 19-3.

**FIGURE 19-3 Staffing and operating a sales force.**

## Recruiting and Selecting a Sales Force

Staffing (personnel selection) is the most important management activity in any organization. This is true whether the organization is a business, an athletic team, or a university or college faculty. Consequently, the key to success in managing a sales force is selecting the right people. No matter what the calibre of sales management, if a sales force is distinctly inferior to that of a competitor, the competitor will win.

**Sales-force selection** includes three tasks:

1. Determine the type of people wanted by preparing a written job description.
2. Recruit an adequate number of applicants.
3. Select the most qualified persons from among the applicants.

**Determining Hiring Specifications** The first step is to establish the proper hiring specifications, just as if the company were purchasing equipment or supplies rather than labour. To establish these specifications, management must first know what the particular sales job entails. This calls for a detailed job analysis and a written description. This written description will later be invaluable in training, compensation, and supervision.

Determining the qualifications needed to fill the job is the most difficult part of the selection function. We still really do not know all the characteristics that make a good sales person. We cannot measure to what degree each quality should be present. Nor do we know to what extent an abundance of one can offset the lack of another.

The search for the qualities that make a good sales person continues. As one approach, some companies have analyzed the personal histories of their past sales representatives in an effort to determine the traits common to successful (and unsuccessful) performers.

**Recruiting Applicants** A planned system for recruiting a sufficient number of applicants is the next step in selection. A good recruiting system:

- Operates continuously, not only when sales-force vacancies occur.
- Is systematic in reaching all appropriate sources of applicants.
- Provides a flow of more qualified applicants than is needed.

### MARKETING AT WORK

### FILE 19-2 DOES "PIRATING" CREATE AN ETHICAL DILEMMA?

Qualified sales people are hard to find, especially experienced sales people who are familiar with a recruiter's industry. One way to get such people is to recruit them aggressively from a competitor's sales force. Not only do these reps know the business, they might also bring along some of their customers. Competitors object strongly to this "pirating," as they call it. They have spent much money training these reps, and they now benefit from the reps' sales productivity. The recruiting companies believe that taking sales people from competitors is no different from taking customers — that's called competition.

Is it ethical for a sales manager to approach a competitor's sales rep directly with a job offer? Would you answer any differently if you were the sales rep?

To identify recruits, large organizations often use placement services on university and college campuses or professional employment agencies. Smaller firms that need fewer new sales people may place classified ads in trade publications and daily newspapers. Many firms solicit recommendations from company employees, customers, or suppliers.

**Matching Applicants with Hiring Specifications** Sales managers use a variety of techniques to determine which applicants possess the desired qualifications, including application forms, interviews, references, credit reports, psychological tests, aptitude tests, and physical examinations. Virtually all companies ask candidates to fill out application forms. In addition to providing basic screening information, the application indicates areas that should be explored in an interview.

No sales person should be hired without at least one personal interview. And it is usually desirable to have several interviews conducted by different people in different physical settings. Pooling the opinions of a number of people increases the likelihood of discovering any undesirable characteristics and reduces the effects of one interviewer's possible bias. An interview helps an employer to determine (1) the applicant's degree of interest in the job, (2) the match between the requirements of the job and the applicant's skills, and (3) the applicant's motivation to work hard.

Testing for intelligence, attributes, or personality is somewhat controversial. Some companies avoid testing for fear that they will be accused of discrimination. However, employment tests are legitimate selection tools as long as they can be shown to predict job performance accurately.

### Assimilating New Sales People

After sales people are hired, management should integrate them into the company family. Often this step is overlooked entirely. Potential sales people are carefully selected and are wined and dined to recruit them into the firm. Then, as soon as they are hired, the honeymoon is over, and they are left to fend for themselves. In such cases, the new people often become discouraged and may even quit. A wise sales manager will recognize that the new people know very little about the details of the job, their fellow workers, or their status in the firm.

### Training a Sales Force

Both new and experienced sales people need an effective training program to improve their selling skills, learn about new products, and improve their time and territory management practices. Management should answer the following questions in the course of designing a **sales training program**:

- **What are the goals of the program?** In very general terms, the aim of the program should be to increase productivity and stimulate the sales force. In addition, executives must determine what specific goals they want to reach. For instance, the goal may be to increase sales of high-profit items or to improve prospecting methods for generating new accounts.
- **Who should do the training?** The training program may be conducted by line sales executives, by a company training department, by outside training specialists, or by some combination of the three.
- **What should be the content of the program?** A well-rounded sales training program should cover three general topics: product knowledge, company policies, and selling techniques.
- **When and where should training be done?** Some companies believe in training new people before they go into the field. Others let new people first prove that they have the desire and ability to sell, and then bring them back into the office for intensive

training. Firms may employ either centralized or decentralized training programs. A centralized program, usually at the home office, may take the form of a periodic meeting attended by all sales people. A decentralized program may be held in branch offices or during on-the-job training.

- **What instructional methods should be used?** The lecture method may be employed to inform trainees about company history and practices. Demonstrations may be used to impart product knowledge or selling techniques. Role playing is an excellent device for training a person in proper selling techniques. On-the-job training may be used in almost any phase of the program.

## Motivating a Sales Force

Sales people, especially outside sales forces, require a high degree of motivation. Think back to our earlier discussion about the nature of a sales job — the pressures of role ambiguity and role conflict, for example. Also consider how a sales job is different from most other jobs. Sales people often work independently, without supervision and guidance from management. Outside sales people work most of the time away from the support and comfort of home-office surroundings.

Consequently, management faces a challenge in **motivating sales people**. One key is to determine what motivates the sales reps — is it a need for status, control, accomplishment, or something else? Another key is to design a motivational program that as much as possible will reach the reps individually.

Sales executives can draw from a wide assortment of specific motivational tools. Financial incentives — compensation plans, expense accounts, fringe benefits — usually are sure-fire motivators. But not always. Nonfinancial awards — job enrichment, praise from management, recognition and honour awards (pin, trophy, certificate) — may be the ticket to stimulate some reps. Sales meetings and sales contests are often-used alternatives. Today many firms provide cruises, resort trips, and other travel incentives as rewards to top-performing sales reps.[5]

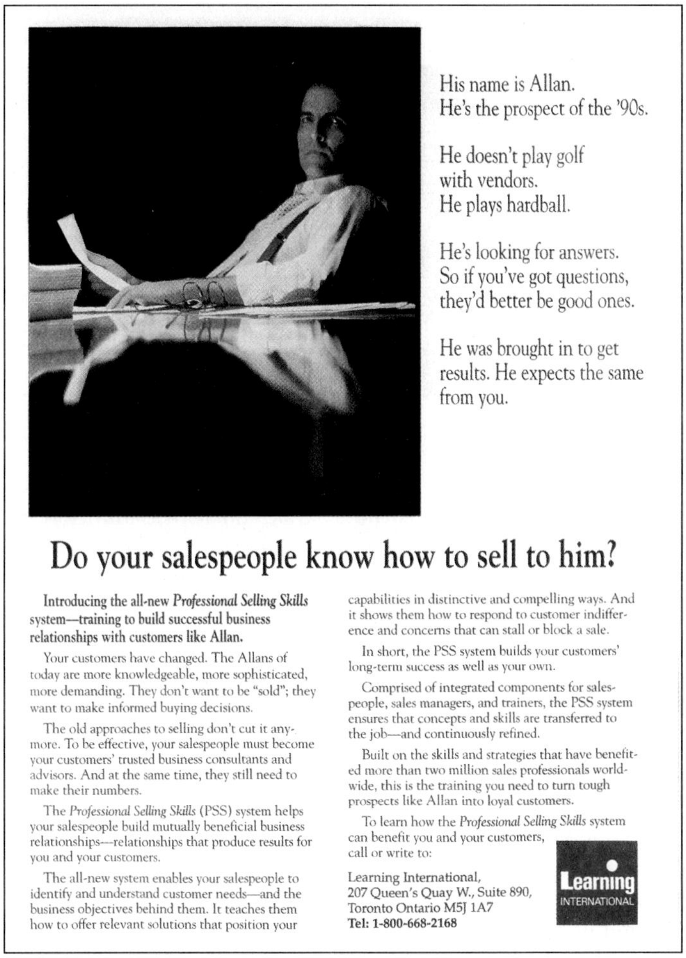


**This company provides sales training to prepare sales people to deal with tough customers.**

## Compensating a Sales Force

Financial rewards are still by far the most widely used tool for motivating sales people. Consequently, designing and administering an effective **sales compensation plan** is a big part of a sales manager's job. Financial rewards may be *direct* monetary payments (salary, commission) or *indirect* monetary compensation (paid vacations, pensions, insurance plans).

Establishing a compensation system calls for decisions concerning the level of compensation as well as the method of compensation. The *level* refers to the total dollar income that a sales person earns over a period of time. Level is influenced by the type of person required and the competitive rate of pay for similar positions. The *method* is the system or plan by which the sales person will reach the intended level.

## MARKETING AT WORK

### FILE 19-3 CASH INCENTIVES SOMETIMES WORK BEST

Some experts say, "Never use cash." Other say, "Cash never fails." A lot of Canadian companies are finding out that providing a cash bonus for a job well done works best in order to establish a connection between effort and desired behaviour. Congoleum, the Winnipeg-based floor covering manufacturer, devises its incentive programs so that as many people as possible can win, and so that there is variety in incentives to match the variety of personal interests. Cash incentive programs are designed to reward sales people who are promoting the Congoleum brand at home furnishing centres across the country at the rate of between $1 and $3 for each square foot of product sold. Such incentive programs usually last between four and eight weeks and are now common throughout the home furnishings industry.

Bill Reid, Congoleum's general manager, says that the company's incentive programs have two main objectives, increasing sales and increasing profits, followed closely by a third — improving service to buyers. "We don't just offer $2 a square foot and that's it," he says. "We also offer information to sales people about our products' features, functions, and benefits." Besides cash incentives, staff selling Congoleum can also accumulate points on products sold over a longer period of time. Eventually, points can be redeemed for quality merchandise from a specially developed catalogue. Congoleum also has the flexibility to target provincial and urban markets or even specific outlets with in-store contents.

Congoleum's cash incentive programs are implemented through its distributors' sales force. Each distributor has about 25 retail accounts. As an incentive for the distributor's implementation efforts, the company provides an override. For example, the distributor could receive an additional five cents, over and above normal margins, for every $1 of product sold during a particular incentive program. The merchandise incentive programs are contracted out to a merchandise fulfilment house, which operates within the merchandise incentive budget.

Cash incentive programs have a way of working again and again for the simple reason that when an individual receives cash, he or she can decide what to do with it; cash provides added value as an incentive. Merchandise incentive programs have to be kept creative and fresh since the incentive has been chosen by the company or the merchandise house and could end up being less than appealing. While incentive programs can be difficult to implement, and can sometimes result in providing rewards for effort that would have been expended without the incentive, the programs do attract attention and help make new product launches and promotions more interesting than would otherwise be the case.

Source: Adapted, in part, from "Incentives for the Sales Force: Special Report," *Strategy*, February 8, 1993, pp. 20, 22-25.

The three widely used methods of compensating a sales force are straight salary, straight commission, and a combination plan. A **salary** is a fixed payment for a period of time during which the sales person is working. A salary-only plan (called a *straight salary*) provides security and stability of earnings for a sales rep. This plan gives management control over a rep's efforts, and the reps are likely to cater to the customer's best interests. The main drawback of a straight salary is that it does not offer adequate incentive for sales people to increase their sales volume. Also, a straight salary is a fixed cost, unrelated to sales volume or gross margin.

Straight-salary plans typically are used when:

- Compensating new sales people or missionary sales people.
- Opening new territories.
- Selling a technical product with a lengthy period of negotiation.

A **commission** is a payment tied to a specific unit of accomplishment. Thus a rep may be paid 5 percent of every dollar of sales or 8 percent on each dollar of gross margin. A *straight-commission* plan (commission only) tends to have just the opposite merits and limitations of a straight salary. A straight commission provides considerable incentive for sales people, and it is a variable cost related directly to a rep's sales volume or gross margin. On the other hand, it is difficult to control straight-commission people. And it is especially difficult to get them to perform tasks for which no commission is paid.

Straight-commission plans may work well when:

- Great incentive is needed to get the sales.
- Very little nonselling work is required, such as setting up displays in retail stores.
- The company is financially weak and must relate its compensation expenses directly to sales or gross margins.
- The company is unable to supervise the sales force when they are outside the company's offices.

The ideal **combination compensation plan** has the best features of both the straight-salary and the straight-commission plans, with as few of their drawbacks as possible. To reach this ideal, a combination plan must be tailored to a particular firm, product, market, and type of selling.

Today about three-quarters of the firms in North America use some kind of a combination plan. In the early 1990s, however, several major department stores switched from a combination plan to straight commission. But a couple of years later some of these companies began to scale back their aggressive commission-pay plans — for two reasons. One was that the sales people themselves objected strenuously to losing the salary feature of a combination plan. The other reason was that the commission plans triggered a decline in the quality of customer service. Sears, for example, abandoned the commission plan in its Auto Centres after it was alleged that the sales reps were recommending unnecessary auto repairs. The reps were doing this to meet quotas and boost their commissions. As one Sears official said, "You have to strike the proper balance between motivating employees [via the pay plan] and good customer service."[6]

### Supervising a Sales Force

Supervising a sales force is difficult because sales people often work independently and where they cannot be continually observed. And yet supervision serves both as a means of continuing training and as a device to ensure that company policies are being carried out.

An issue that management must resolve is how closely to supervise. If too close, it can create a role conflict for the sales person. One of the attractions of selling is the freedom it affords sales people to develop creative solutions to customers' problems. Close supervision can stifle that sense of independence. Conversely, too little supervision can contribute to role ambiguity. Sales people who are not closely supervised may lack an understanding of the expectations of their supervisors and companies. They may not know, for example, how much time should be spent servicing existing accounts and how much developing new business.

The most effective supervisory method is personal observation in the field. Typically, at least half of a sales manager's time is spent travelling with sales people. Other supervisory tools are reports, correspondence, and sales meetings.

## EVALUATING A SALES PERSON'S PERFORMANCE

Managing a sales force includes **evaluating the performance** of sales people. Sales executives must know what the sales force is doing in order to reward them or to make constructive proposals for improvement. By establishing performance standards and studying sales people's activities, management can develop new training programs for upgrading the sales force's efforts. And, of course, performance evaluation should be the basis for compensation decisions and other rewards.

## MARKETING AT WORK

### FILE 19-4 MASTERING MOTIVATION

In November, after 24 years with Avon's Canadian division, Christina Gold was called to New York to become the first woman to head the U.S., Canadian, and Puerto Rican operations of the direct-sales beauty company. Ms. Gold's division represents 40 percent of Avon's $4 billion worldwide sales. In 1993, before Ms. Gold took over in New York, U.S. sales fell 1 percent but profits tumbled 22 percent, partly due to a general slackening in the motivation among the Avon ladies — not politically correct but commonly so referred to. Ms. Gold reviewed the scene and concluded, "The sales reps were worried [by her predecessor's approach] and they were alienated and were simply not selling as aggressively as we would like." During Ms. Gold's predecessor's reign at Avon, the value of trips, prizes, and commission guarantees was reduced. Birthday presents stopped arriving for high performers. Porcelain statuettes of the first Avon lady ceased to be distributed to productive reps. This latter move caused district managers to rise up like a tidal wave.

What Ms. Gold is now in the process of doing is adding new products, streamlining the flow of information from order processors to distribution so as to ensure that sales reps can get products to customers rapidly, and most importantly, cutting spending on flyers and brochures and putting the money into sales incentives. Her predecessor did the former as well, but he did not do the latter. Ms. Gold has also resumed the sending of birthday gifts to high performers and she asked every salaried employee to hand-write 100 brief thank-you notes to sales reps to commemorate Avon Representative Day, held annually on March 19. Outstanding work is recognized personally by Ms. Gold with a note or a call to sales reps. And they like it.

Ms. Gold achieves results not because she doesn't worry about the bottom line, but because she gets her results through people. In her Point Claire, Quebec, headquarters, she would gather her Canadian district managers together for three days twice a year and sound them out on such issues as proposed pricing and ways to change and improve commission rates. She offered training in time management and sales techniques to reps and often joined them on sales calls. "I'd go out with the sales reps who were doing well and with the ones who were doing badly and I'd pass what the successful ones were doing on to the others," Ms. Gold said. But her success in Canada and, presumably the United States, is based on her idea that "motivation isn't all prizes and things, it's listening."

Source: Adapted from Claudia Deutsch, "Avon's Montreal Recruit Has Gold Touch with Reps," *Globe and Mail*, April 5, 1994, p. B10.

Performance evaluation can also help sales people identify opportunities for improving their efforts. Employees with poor sales records know they are doing something wrong. However, they may not know what the problem is if they lack objective standards by which to measure their performance.

Both quantitative and qualitative factors should be used as bases for performance evaluation. **Quantitative bases** generally have the advantage of being specific and objective. **Qualitative factors**, although often reflecting broader dimensions of behaviour, are limited by the subjective judgement of the evaluators. For either type of appraisal, however, management faces the difficult task of setting standards against which a rep's performance can be measured.

### Quantitative Bases

Sales performance should be evaluated in terms of *inputs* (efforts) and *outputs* (results). Together, inputs such as number of sales calls per day or customer service activity, and outputs such as sales volume or gross margin, provide a measure of selling effectiveness.

Some *quantitative output* measures useful as evaluation criteria are:

- Sales volume by product, customer group, and territory.
- Sales volume as a percentage of quota or territory potential.

- Gross margin by product line, customer group, and territory.
- Orders — number and average dollar amount.
- Closing rate — number of orders divided by number of calls.
- Accounts — percentage of existing accounts sold and number of new accounts opened.

Useful *quantitative input* measures include:

- Call rate — number of calls per day or week.
- Direct selling expenses — total dollars or as a percentage of sales.
- Nonselling activities — promotion displays set up, training sessions held with distributors or dealers.

### Qualitative Factors

Performance evaluation would be much easier if it could be based only on quantitative criteria. It would minimize the subjectivity and personal bias of the evaluators. However, many *qualitative* factors must be considered because they influence a sales person's performance. Some of these factors are:

- Knowledge of products, company policies, and competitors.
- Time management and preparation for sales calls.
- Customer relations.
- Personal appearance.
- Personality and attitude — co-operation, creativity, resourcefulness.

A successful evaluation program will appraise a sales person's performance on as many different bases as possible. Otherwise management may be misled. A high daily call rate may look good, but it tells us nothing about how many orders are being written up. A high closing rate (orders divided by calls) may be camouflaging a low average order size or a high sales volume on low-profit items.

## SUMMARY

Personal selling is the main promotional method used in North American business — whether measured by number of people employed, by total expenditures, or by expenses as a percentage of sales. The total field of personal selling comprises two broad categories. One covers selling activities where the customers come to the sales people — primarily retail-store or retail-catalogue selling. The other includes all selling situations where the sales people go to the customer — primarily outside sales forces.

The sales job today is not what it used to be. A new type of sales rep — a professional sales person — has been developing over the past few decades. But this new breed of sales rep still faces problems of role ambiguity and role conflict. Sales jobs today range from order takers through support sales people (missionary sellers, sales engineers) to order getters (creative sellers). Sales jobs differ from other jobs in several respects. Some changing patterns in personal selling have emerged in recent years — patterns such as selling centres (team selling), systems selling, relationship selling, and telemarketing.

The personal selling process consists of four steps, starting with prospecting for potential buyers and then preapproaching each prospect. The third step is the sales presentation, which includes attracting attention, arousing buyer interest and desire, meeting objections, and then hopefully closing the sale. Finally, postsale activities involve follow-up services to ensure customer satisfaction and reduce dissonance regarding the purchase.

The sales management process involves planning, implementing, and evaluating sales-force activities within the guidelines set by the company's strategic marketing planning. The tasks of staffing and operating a sales force present managerial challenges in several areas. The key to successful sales-force management is to do a good job in selecting sales people. Then plans must be made to assimilate these new people into the company and to train them. Management must set up programs to motivate, compensate, and supervise a sales force. The final stage in sales-force management is to evaluate the performance of the individual sales people.

## KEY TERMS AND CONCEPTS

**Personal selling (574)**
**Across-the-counter selling (575)**
**Outside sales forces (575)**
**Telemarketing (576)**
**Professional sales person (576)**
**Role ambiguity (576)**
**Role conflict (576)**
**Driver-sales person (577)**
**Inside order taker (577)**
**Outside order taker (577)**
**Missionary sales person (577)**
**Sales engineer (577)**
**Creative sales person (577)**
**Order taker (577)**
**Sales-support personnel (577)**
**Order getter (577)**
**Selling centre (579)**
**Systems selling (579)**
**Relationship selling (579)**
**Prospecting (581)**
**Qualifying (582)**
**Preapproach in selling (582)**
**Sales presentation (582)**
**AIDA (582)**
**Canned sales talk (583)**
**Closing a sale (583)**
**Trial close (583)**
**Meeting objections (583)**
**Postsale activities (584)**
**Sales-force selection (585)**
**Sales training program (586)**
**Motivating sales people (587)**
**Sales compensation plan (587)**
**Salary (588)**
**Commission (588)**
**Combination compensation plan (589)**
**Evaluating rep's performance (589)**
**Quantitative evaluation bases (590)**
**Qualitative evaluation factors (590)**

## QUESTIONS AND PROBLEMS

1. The cost of a full-page, four-colour advertisement in one issue of *Sports Illustrated* magazine is much more than the cost of employing two sales people for a full year. A sales-force executive is urging her company to eliminate a few of these ads and, instead, to hire a few more sales people. This executive believes that one good sales person working for an entire year can sell more than one ad in one issue of *Sports Illustrated.* How would you respond?
2. Refer to the classification of sales jobs from driver-sales person to creative seller and answer the following questions:
   a. In which types of jobs are sales people most likely to be free from close supervision?
   b. Which types are likely to be the highest paid?
   c. For which types of jobs is the highest degree of motivation necessary?
3. What are some sources you might use to acquire a list of prospects for the following products?
   a. Bank accounts for new area residents.
   b. Dental X-ray equipment.
   c. Laptop computers.
   d. Contributors to the United Way.
   e. Baby furniture and clothes.
4. If you were preparing a sales presentation for the following products, what information about a prospect would you seek as part of your preparation?
   a. Two-bedroom condominium.
   b. New automobile.
   c. Carpeting for a home redecorating project.
5. What sources should be used for recruiting sales applicants in each of the following firms? Explain your choice in each case.
   a. A Delta hotel that wants companies to use the hotel for conventions.
   b. IBM, for sales of mainframe (large) computers.
6. For a multinational corporation hiring a sales force in a developing country, what applicant characteristics should be added to its selection criteria?
7. Compare the merits of straight-salary and straight-commission plans of sales compensation. What are two types of sales jobs in which each plan might be desirable?
8. How might a firm determine whether a sales person is using high-pressure selling tactics that might injure customer relations?
9. How can a sales manager evaluate the performance of sales people in getting new business?

## HANDS-ON MARKETING

1. Review your activities of the past few days and identify those in which:
   a. You did some personal selling.
   b. People tried to sell something to you.
   Select one situation in each category where you thought the selling was particularly effective, and tell why it was so.
2. Interview three students from your school who recently have gone through the job-interviewing process conducted by companies using your school's placement office. Ask the students to compare, contrast, and generally evaluate the recruiting practices of the companies they interviewed. Prepare a report covering your findings.

## NOTES AND REFERENCES


1. Adapted from promotional material supplied by Love Printing.
2. Stephen X. Doyle and George T. Roth, "The Use of Insight Coaching to Improve Relationship Selling," *Journal of Personal Selling & Sales Management*, Winter 1992, pp. 61-63. For further insights on relationship selling, see David Shani and Sujana Chalasani, "Exploiting Niches Using Relationship Marketing," *Journal of Consumer Marketing*, Summer 1992, pp. 33-42; Naoko Oikawa and John F. Tanner, Jr., "The Influence of Japanese Culture on Business Relationships and Negotiations," *Journal of Consumer Marketing*, Summer 1992, pp. 67-74; and Barry J. Farber and Joyce Wycott, "Relationships: Six Steps to Success," *Sales & Marketing Management*, April 1992, p. 50.
3. For more on postsale activities, especially in international competition, see A. Coskun Samli, Laurence W. Jacobs, and James Wills, "What Presale and Postsale Services Do You Need to Be Competitive?" *Industrial Marketing Management*, February 1992, pp. 33-41.
4. Adapted from Jack Falvey, "The Making of a Manager," *Sales & Marketing Management*, March 1989, p. 42.
5. "Travel Incentives: Case Studies," *Marketing Insights*, Summer 1991, p. 98. Also see James Feldman, "Targeted Motivation," *Marketing Insights*, Summer 1991, p. 91.
6. Gregory A. Patterson, "Distressed Shoppers, Disaffected Workers Prompt Stores to Alter Sales Commissions," *The Wall Street Journal*, July 1, 1992, p. B1.

## CHAPTER 20 GOALS

This chapter examines nonpersonal, mass communication promotional tools — advertising, sales promotion, and public relations. After studying this chapter, you should have an understanding of:

- The nature of advertising, what it means to the individual firm, and its importance in our economy.
- Characteristics of the major types of advertising.
- How advertising campaigns are developed and advertising media are selected.
- What sales promotion is and how to manage it.
- The role of public relations and publicity in the promotional mix.

CHAPTER 20

# MANAGEMENT OF ADVERTISING, SALES PROMOTION, AND PUBLIC RELATIONS

## The Media Aren't What They Used To Be

Most major advertisers have for many years relied on the traditional mass media to get their advertising messages to the widest possible audiences. Their objective, of course, is to reach a wide audience in a cost-effective manner, with a message that gets noticed.

The mass media that have received the greatest use over the years have been the "Big 4" of newspapers and magazines (generally referred to as "print"), and radio and television (known as "broadcast"). While these media have been effective in getting the message out to the public, a number of changes in recent years have turned the attention of advertisers towards other means of reaching their target audiences. The three developments that have brought about this change are the changing life-styles of Canadians, the technological advances that have made new media available, and what is generally referred to as the "fragmentation" of the traditional mass media.

One medium that holds considerable promise for the future is interactive television. Picture the following. A car buyer, sitting in the comfort of her living room, calls up a selection of cars on her television screen, experiments with different colours, two-door or four-door, convertible, sports options, and eventually decides on her preferred model. Then, with a click of the mouse, she requests a test drive from the nearest dealer. The dealer's representative shows up at her home with the car ready for her to drive it. When she is ready to talk details, the sales person takes out a laptop computer on which they check availability of inventory, examine various leasing and purchase options, and complete all the necessary "paperwork."

Sound farfetched? Not really. Ford Canada is already moving into the exciting new frontier of interactive advertising. In launching its new cars in 1994, Ford ran ads that were hooked into the Videoway interactive television network in Quebec during the coverage of the Winter Olympics. Videoway, with 220,000 subscribers, is the only interactive television system in Canada and a North American leader. The interactive campaign for Ford allowed viewers to click into ads for the vehicles they were interested in, using their television remote controls.

Ford was delighted with the results. Advertising manager Ron Dodds commented, "We end up targeting those folks who really want information on a specific vehicle, and not on other vehicles. You're ultimately hitting the folks with exactly what they want to see . . . . It's a home run."[1]

Advertising, sales promotion, and public relations are the mass communication tools available to marketers. As its name suggests, mass communication uses the same message for everyone in an audience. The mass communicator trades off the advantage of personal selling, the opportunity to tailor a message to each prospective customer, for the advantage of reaching many people at a lower cost per person. However, as the opening example of interactive television advertising illustrates, mass communication is not indiscriminate. Advertisers are constantly seeking ways to present their messages to well-defined target audiences.

## NATURE AND SCOPE OF ADVERTISING

All advertisements have four features:

- A verbal and/or visual message.
- A sponsor who is identified.
- Delivery through one or more media.
- Payment by the sponsor to the media carrying the message.

**Advertising**, then, consists of all the activities involved in presenting to an audience a nonpersonal, sponsor-identified, paid-for message about a product or organization. Advertising in one form or another is used by most organizations.

### Types of Advertising

Advertising can be classified according to (1) the target audience, either consumers or businesses; (2) what is being advertised, a product versus an institution; and (3) the objective sought, the stimulation of primary or selective demand. To fully appreciate the scope of advertising, it is essential to understand these three classifications.

**Consumer and Business-to-Business Advertising** An ad is directed at either consumers or businesses, thus it is either **consumer advertising** or **business-to-business advertising**. Retailers by definition sell only to consumers, thus they are the only organizations that are not faced with this choice. The publishers of *Money* magazine, for example, must decide what portion of its advertising budget will be used to attract businesses to advertise in the magazine (called trade advertising), and what portion will go towards gaining subscribers and selling magazines.

**Product and Institutional Advertising** All advertising may be classified as product or institutional. **Product advertising** focuses on a particular product or brand.

Product advertising is subdivided into direct-action and indirect-action advertising:

- **Direct-action advertising** seeks a quick response — for instance, a magazine ad containing a coupon or a 1-800 number may urge the reader to send or call immediately for a free sample, or a supermarket ad in a local newspaper stresses this week's specials.
- **Indirect-action advertising** is designed to stimulate demand over a longer period of time. It is intended to inform or remind consumers that the product exists and to point out its benefits. Most television advertising is of this type.

**Institutional advertising** presents information about the advertiser's business or tries to create a good attitude — build goodwill — towards the organization. This type of advertising is not intended to sell a specific product. Two forms of institutional advertising are:

- **Customer service advertising**, which presents information about the advertiser's operations. Advertisements describing the variety of automobile repairs and services available at Petro-Canada stations are an example.
- **Public service advertising**, which is designed to improve the quality of life and show that the advertiser is a responsible member of the community. Such ads may urge the public to avoid drugs or to support a local antipollution campaign.

Primary- and Selective-Demand Advertising **Primary-demand advertising** is designed to stimulate demand for a generic category of a product such as Colombian coffee, B.C. apples, or garments made from cotton. This is in contrast to **selective-demand advertising**, intended to stimulate demand for individual brands such as Nabob Coffee, Sunkist oranges, and clothing from The Gap.

Primary demand advertising is used in either of two situations. The first is when the product is in the introductory stage of its life cycle. This is called **pioneering advertising**. A firm may run an ad about its new product, explaining the product's benefits, but not emphasizing the brand name. The objective of pioneering primary demand advertising is to inform, not to persuade, the target market. The buying decision process model explains why such ads are limited to information. Recall from our discussion in Chapter 6 that a consumer must first be made *aware* of a product before becoming *interested* in or *desiring* it. Combine this with the fact that only so much information can be communicated in a single ad, and it becomes clear that only one objective can be accomplished at a time. In recent years, pioneering demand ads have been run for cellular telephones and video camcorders.

The second use of primary-demand advertising occurs throughout the product life cycle. It is usually done by trade associations trying to stimulate demand for their industry's product. Thus the Dairy Bureau of Canada's ads urge us to drink more milk. The bureau doesn't care what brand of milk and dairy products we buy, just that we use more of them. Similarly, the Pork Council encourages us to eat more pork.

Selective-demand advertising essentially is competitive advertising — it pits one brand against another. This type of advertising typically is employed when a product has gone beyond the introductory life-cycle stage. The product is reasonably well known and in competition for market share with several brands. The objective of selective-demand advertising is to increase the demand for a brand. To accomplish this goal, it emphasizes the particular benefits — the **differential advantages** — of the brand being advertised.

**Comparative advertising** is an important kind of selective-demand advertising that is used for a wide variety of products. In comparative advertising, the advertiser either directly — by naming a rival brand — or indirectly — through inference — points out differences between the brands. We have all seen the comparative advertising for Coke and Pepsi, both of which show the competitor's brand. In some comparative advertising, the competitor's name is not mentioned, but is obvious to the reader or viewer. In other cases, the competitor's product is named or even shown. In the increasingly competitive market for advertising long-distance telephone services, Bell Canada and the other major telephone companies across Canada have been exposed to explicit comparative ads from Unitel that point out the savings Unitel alleges a telephone customer can realize by purchasing long-distance telephone service from them rather than from his or her telephone company. Bell Canada responded with a subtle comparative advertisement of its own that observed, "The telephone wasn't invented by Alexander Graham Unitel."

The Bureau of Competition Policy of the federal Department of Consumer and Corporate Affairs has taken the position that truthful comparative advertising can be a pro-competitive force in the marketplace. In fact, the Bureau has periodically published guidelines for the consideration of advertisers. The main point to be learned from the discussion of comparative advertising and its regulation is that a company planning to use the technique had better be very sure that what is being said in its advertising about the competition is completely accurate.

Co-operative Advertising **Co-operative advertising** promotes products of two or more firms that share the cost of the advertising. There are two types — vertical and horizontal. **Vertical co-operative advertising** involves firms on different levels of distribution. For example, a manufacturer and a retailer share the cost of the retailer's advertising of that manufacturer's product. Frequently the manufacturer prepares the actual ad, leaving space for the retailer's name and location. Then the manufacturer and retailer share the media cost of placing the ad. Many retail ads in newspapers are co-operative ads. Co-operative ads are also common on radio but appear less frequently on TV.

Another type of vertical co-operative advertising uses an **advertising allowance**, or cash discount offered by a manufacturer to a retailer, to encourage the retailer to advertise or prominently display a product. The difference between co-operative advertising and allowances is the amount of control exerted by the manufacturer over how the money is actually spent.

These arrangements benefit retailers by providing them with extra funds for promotion. Manufacturers benefit from advertising at the local level. In addition, ad dollars go farther because rates for local media are typically lower for ads placed by local firms than for ads placed by national advertisers.

**Horizontal co-operative advertising** is undertaken by firms on the same level of distribution — such as a group of retailers — that share the costs of advertising. For example, all stores in a suburban shopping centre may run a joint newspaper ad. The principal benefit is that by pooling their funds, the firms can achieve much greater exposure than if they advertised individually.

Companies that normally would not have a close association often co-operate in joint promotions. More and more companies are realizing that they can stretch their promotion dollars, benefit from the reputation of noncompeting successful brands, and open new markets with joint promotional programs. Evian, the French spring water company, launched a special promotion with Kellogg's Special K breakfast cereal, the main focus of which was a sweepstakes with trips to the French Alps as grand prizes. By entering into the joint arrangement, Evian had two objectives in mind. The company wanted to increase sales in the short term but, more importantly, was interested in increasing brand awareness and spreading the message of proper hydration. By associating with Kellogg, Evian moved from being a "niche" brand to a major player in the competitive bottled water market. In another joint promotion, Campbell's Soup and Shell gasoline collaborated on a self-liquidating cross-promotion which offered consumers free Campbell's soups mugs when they visited Shell stations in Ontario.

## Cost of Advertising

Advertising in one form or another is used by most marketers. The significance of advertising is indicated by the amount of money spent on it. In 1990, the gross expenditures on advertising in Canada totalled $10.86 billion, up from $7.3 billion just three years earlier. Table 20-1 shows the total expenditure by medium and the percentage of the total accounted for by each of the major advertising media. For many years, daily newspapers have been the most widely used medium, but the percentage of total expenditures accounted for by newspapers has been declining steadily from approximately 30 percent in the mid-1970s to 22.9 percent in 1990. In fact, the percentage of total advertising expenditures going to the traditional mass media — radio, television, newspapers, and magazines — has been declining steadily, as many advertisers have been switching at least part of their advertising budgets to media such as direct mail, directories, and weekly papers, which can often do a better job of reaching targeted segments.

TABLE 20-1 Advertising revenues in Canada, by medium
Net Canadian Advertising Revenues: 1992-93

| Medium | Revenues ($M) in current $* 1993 | 1992 | % Change 1992-93 Current $* | Real $* |
|---|---|---|---|---|
| Catalogues, Direct Mail | 1,968.0 | 1,901.0 | 3.5 | 2.0 |
| Daily Newspapers | 1,862.6 | 1,736.1 | 7.3 | 5.7 |
| Television[1] | 1,708.8 | 1,735.0 | –1.5 | –3.0 |
| Yellow Pages[2] | 855.5 | 861.8 | –0.7 | –2.2 |
| Outdoor | 771.0 | 756.0 | 2.0 | 0.5 |
| Radio | 721.6 | 745.3 | –3.2 | –4.6 |
| Weeklies, Semi-weeklies, Tri-weeklies | 552.0 | 570.3 | –3.2 | –4.6 |
| General Magazines | 305.6 | 315.0 | –3.0 | –4.4 |
| Business Papers | 152.9 | 157.6 | –3.0 | –4.4 |
| Other[3] | 119.4 | 119.3 | 0.1 | –1.4 |
| Total | 9,017.5 | 8,897.4 | 1.3 | –0.1 |

* Current dollars includes inflation of 1.5% during 1993; real dollars excludes inflation
[1] Includes specialty services
[2] Excludes city directories
[3] Religious and school publications, farm papers and weekend supplements
Source: "*A Report of Advertising Revenues in Canada*" *The CARD Group*, Maclean Hunter, Toronto

Source: Jim McElgunn, "Canadian Ad Revenues Stayed Flat in 1993," *Marketing*, September 5, 1994, p. 2

**Advertising as a Percentage of Sales** When gauging the importance of advertising, we should measure expenditures against a benchmark rather than simply look at the total. Frequently, advertising expenses are expressed as a percentage of a company's sales. Table 20-2 shows the 10 largest advertisers in Canada for 1993. Note how these large advertisers differ in the way they allocate their advertising expenditures across the major advertising media. It is important also to note that some of the advertisers who spend a large amount of

TABLE 20-2 Top 10 national advertisers in Canada, with expenditures by medium, 1993

| | Total ($000s)* | Television | Daily Newspapers | Magazines | Out-of-Home | Radio |
|---|---|---|---|---|---|---|
| 1 General Motors of Canada | 113,048.4 | 63,708.3 | 36,623.4 | 6,894.1 | 2,282.3 | 3,540.3 |
| 2 Procter & Gamble | 84,499.5 | 76,377.3 | 5.5 | 7,763.8 | 72.4 | 280.5 |
| 3 The Thomson Group | 70,159.3 | 25,934.9 | 41,155.8 | 1,600.4 | 406.0 | 1,062.2 |
| 4 BCE | 53,972.9 | 22,513.0 | 20,654.0 | 3,164.5 | 3,102.4 | 4,539.0 |
| 5 John Labatt Ltd. | 50,036.0 | 33,697.4 | 4,550.4 | 580.9 | 4,523.6 | 6,683.7 |
| 6 Eaton's of Canada | 47,135.9 | 9,198.8 | 31,634.4 | 2,069.5 | 213.0 | 4,020.2 |
| 7 Sears Canada | 46,582.1 | 13,144.5 | 26,184.9 | 4,735.1 | 2.9 | 2,514.7 |
| 8 Government of Canada | 43,928.7 | 21,706.8 | 11,581.3 | 3,482.4 | 2,126.5 | 5,031.7 |
| 9 The Molson Companies | 42,873.6 | 26,448.0 | 8,251.2 | 830.9 | 2,076.1 | 5,267.4 |
| 10 Chrysler Canada | 41,171.5 | 23,135.2 | 12,830.0 | 3,061.5 | 1,891.5 | 253.3 |

Source: Jim McElgunn, "Canada's Top 100 Advertisers," *Marketing*, May 2, 1994, pp. 1, 4, 21, 22.

money on advertising each year actually devote a very small percentage of their total sales to advertising. Data collected by Statistics Canada indicate that the largest percentage of sales spent on advertising is by companies that manufacture health and beauty aids and soaps and cleaning products. In general, companies in the consumer products field spend a higher percentage of sales on advertising than do manufacturers of industrial products. In general, major companies spend an average of about 2 percent of total sales on advertising, with companies that manufacture consumer products spending approximately 3 percent on average.

**Advertising Cost Versus Personal Selling Cost** While we do not have accurate totals for the costs of personal selling, we do know they far surpass advertising expenditures. In manufacturing, only a few industries, such as drugs, toiletries, cleaning products, tobacco, and beverages, spend more on advertising than on personal selling. Advertising runs 1 to 3 percent of net sales in many firms, whereas the expenses of recruiting and operating a sales force are typically 8 to 15 percent of sales.

At the wholesale level, advertising costs are very low. Personal selling expenses, however, may run 10 to 15 times as high. Even among retailers in total — and this includes those with self-service operations — the cost of personal selling is substantially higher than that of advertising.

## DEVELOPING AN ADVERTISING CAMPAIGN

An **advertising campaign** consists of all the tasks involved in transforming a theme into a co-ordinated advertising program to accomplish a specific goal for a product or brand. For example, you have probably noticed the transit advertising campaign for Neilson's Mr. Big chocolate bar, which uses the line, "When you're this big they call you mister," and relies on a blend of humour and exaggeration. An advertising campaign is planned within the framework of the overall strategic marketing program and the promotional campaign. Before designing an advertising campaign, management must:

- Know who the target audience is.
- Establish the overall promotional goals.
- Set the total promotional budget.
- Determine the overall promotional theme.

With these tasks completed, the firm can begin formulating an advertising campaign. The steps in developing a campaign are: defining objectives, establishing a budget, creating a message, selecting media, and evaluating effectiveness.

### Defining Objectives

The purpose of advertising is to sell something — product, service, idea, person, or place — either now or later. This goal is reached by setting specific objectives that can be expressed in individual ads that are incorporated into an advertising campaign. Recall again from the buying-decision process that buyers go through a series of stages from unawareness to purchase. Thus the immediate objective of an ad may be to move target customers to the next stage in the hierarchy — say, from awareness to interest. Note also that advertising seldom is the only promotional tool used by a firm. Rather, it is typically one part of a strategy that may also include personal selling, sales promotion, and other tools. Therefore, the objective of advertising may be to "open doors" for the sales force.

Specific advertising objectives will be dictated by the firm's overall marketing strategy. Typical objectives are:

- **Support personal selling.** Advertising may be used to acquaint prospects with the seller's company and products, easing the way for the sales force.
- **Improve dealer relations.** Wholesalers and retailers like to see a manufacturer support its products.

**This ad is one in a series that constituted an effective campaign for Mr. Big.**

**Pick one up on your way home.**

**When you're this big they call you mister.™**

## MARKETING AT WORK

### FILE 20-1 HO! HO! HO! GREEN GIANT GROWS EVEN BIGGER

Green Giant is a brand that has long been synonymous with vegetables, and the Green Giant figure has been familiar to generations of Canadians. But the Green Giant division of Pillsbury Canada has recently seized an opportunity to expand the business in canned and frozen vegetables for which the brand is famous. For 1993-94, the company set out to increase volume and market share significantly.

In an integrated advertising and promotion campaign, Green Giant wished to take advantage of the fact that the canned and frozen vegetable market had been showing growth in sales volume of 2 to 3 percent over the previous year. The company knew that it owned a 50 percent market share in the use of canned or frozen vegetables as a side dish. They wanted to increase that share further and to build sales in the entire category by encouraging use of Green Giant vegetables as a main dish. To accomplish the latter objective, the company developed an extended-use campaign, relying primarily on the dissemination of main-dish recipes to users of Green Giant products.

The result was an integrated advertising and promotions campaign that involved the following elements:

- 30-second television commercials for Green Giant products, including such line extensions as International Mixtures;
- New labelling printed with main-dish recipes;
- Magazine advertising featuring main-dish uses for Green Giant vegetables;
- On-shelf cents-off coupons to stimulate trial;
- Trade brochures and promotions to support the launch of new products, such as the Green Giant Pasta Garden, a frozen side-dish combination of pasta and Green Giant vegetables.

The use of a number of advertising and promotional vehicles by Green Giant reflects the fact that marketers can rarely rely on a single promotional tool to accomplish their objectives. Also, the application of advertising and promotional strategies must be undertaken in a way that is consistent with the company's objectives — in this case, to expand market share and to encourage new uses for the product and brand.

- **Introduce a new product.** Consumers need to be informed even about line extensions that make use of familiar brand names.
- **Expand the use of a product.** Advertising may be used to lengthen the season for a product (as Lipton did for iced tea); increase the frequency of replacement (as Fram and Purolator did for oil filters); or increase the variety of product uses (as Arm & Hammer did for baking soda).
- **Counteract substitution.** Advertising reinforces the decisions of existing customers and reduces the likelihood that they will switch to alternative brands.

### Establishing a Budget

Once a promotional budget has been established (discussed in Chapter 18), it must be allocated among the various activities making up the overall promotional program. In the case of a particular brand, a firm may wish to have several ads, as well as sales promotion and public relations activities, directed at different target audiences all under way at the same time. When Pepsi launched the "Taste it all" campaign for Diet Pepsi, it was the first totally new campaign for the soft drink since 1982. The theme of the $60-million-a-year campaign is that Diet Pepsi fits into the life-styles of people who get the most out of life. It involves advertising, label changes, point-of-sale displays, and consumer sweepstakes with prizes of white-water rafting and dude ranch vacations. Since all these efforts must be paid for from the promotional budget, the potential value of each must be weighed and allocations made accordingly.

Now they can be yours.
FUSS-FREE FIESTA FAJITAS
SENSATIONAL SINGLE SKILLET CHICKEN DINNER
Here's ours.
CLIENT: PILLSBURY CANADA
PRODUCT: Green Giant International Mixtures
TITLE: "World Traveller"
LENGTH: :30 sec. TV
VENDOR: (FRENCH ACCENT) Ah, monsieur, try this beautiful combination of crisp cauliflower, tender carrots and tasty asparagus?
ANNCR VO: ...to find new ideas for his vegetable combinations.
ANNCR VO: Green Giants International Mixtures.
Six original frozen vegetable combinations inspired by the Giant's travels.
SINGER: Ho, ho,
Green Giant.
CREAM STYLE CORN MADE WITH NIBLETS*
RECIPE
MIRACLE MEATLOAF
SEE REVERSE OF LABEL
GéantVert.
Buy Some Yellow
SAVE 20¢ NOW
On a 12 oz. can of Green Giant* Peaches & Cream Whole Kernel Corn When You Buy Butter
Green Giant.
PEACHES & CREAM
Yellow and white and sweet all over.
SAVE 20¢
Peaches & Cream corn is a special variety of two-coloured corn with a supersweet taste. Try some today!
Save 20¢ NOW! on Green Giant*
WHOLE BABY BEETS
SLICED BEETS
DICED BEETS WITH HARVARD SAUCE
SAVE 20¢ NOW!
100% FLAVOUR
33% Less Salt
NIBLETS* WHOLE KERNEL CORN
1/3 Less Salt
NEW
See reverse for details.

One method that firms use to extend their advertising budgets is co-operative advertising, discussed earlier in this chapter. But not all firms are in a position to participate in co-operative advertising programs. Generally, such programs are available only to retailers and wholesalers who distribute the products of large manufacturers, and who can take advantage of the co-operative budgets made available by those companies. This leaves many companies and other organizations who must plan and execute their own advertising programs and must pay the entire cost. There is little question that many firms, particularly smaller ones, find the establishment of an advertising budget to be a very difficult exercise indeed. This is related to the fact that most business people find it equally difficult to measure the payback from advertising and, therefore, do not feel that they are in a position to decide where to place their advertising dollars to get the greatest return. The result is that a lot of advertising money is wasted, and many companies probably pay much more than they should for effective advertising.

### Creating a Message

Whatever the objective of an advertising campaign, the individual ads must accomplish two things: get and hold the **attention** of the intended audience, and **influence** that audience in the desired way. Remember that the ultimate purpose of advertising is to sell something, and that the ad itself is a sales message. The ad may be a fast-paced sales talk, as in a direct-action TV ad by a car dealership. Or it may be a very long-range, low-key message, as are many institutional ads. Whatever the method, the goal is to sell something sooner or later.

Attention can be achieved in many ways. (Recall our discussion of perception in Chapter 6). The most common approach is to present the material in an unexpected manner or use an unconventional technique to capture the attention of the audience. Thus a print ad may be mostly white space or a television commercial might show the product in an unusual setting or address a topic from a new perspective. Thus American Express gets attention when it features well-known personalities in the advertising for its credit cards. Nike uses dramatic special effects in its television commercials. Some advertising for social programs, such as anti-smoking campaigns and appeals against drinking and driving, will use dramatic emotional content to shock viewers and to get their attention.

If the ad succeeds in getting the audience's attention, the advertiser has a few seconds to communicate a message intended to influence beliefs and/or behaviour. The message has two elements, the appeal and the execution. The **appeal** in an ad is the reason or justification for believing or behaving. It is the benefit that the individual will receive as a result of accepting the message.

Some advertisers mistakenly focus their appeal on product features or attributes. They either confuse attributes with benefits, or assume that if they present the product's attributes, the audience will infer the correct benefits. Telling customers that a cereal contains fibre (an attribute) is much less meaningful than telling them that because it contains fibre, consuming it reduces the likelihood of colon cancer (the benefit). Common appeals or benefits and examples of product categories in which they are frequently used include:

- Health (food, nonprescription drugs).
- Social acceptance (cosmetics, health and beauty aids).
- Material success (automobiles, investments).
- Recognition (clothing, jewellery).
- Sensory pleasure (movies, candy).
- Time savings (prepared foods, convenience stores).
- Peace of mind (insurance, tires).

John Cleese Cardmember since 1971.
Membership Has Its Privileges.*
Don't leave home without it.*
Call 1-800-THE CARD to apply

**When American Express dresses John Cleese like this, it really gets attention.**

**Execution** is combining in a convincing, compatible way the feature or device that gets attention with the appeal. An appeal can be executed in different ways. Consider the ways you could communicate the benefit of reliable performance in a home appliance — presenting operating statistics, obtaining the endorsement of a respected person or organization, collecting testimonials from satisfied owners, or describing the meticulous manufacturing process. Rather than any of these, Maytag opted for "the lonely repairman," an amusing and memorable execution that gets attention and conveys the benefit of reliability. Other common executions and examples are shown in Table 20-3.

Creating an advertisement involves writing the copy, selecting the illustration (for visual media), preparing the visual or verbal layout, and reproducing the ad for the selected media. The **copy** in an ad is all the written or spoken material in it. Copy in a print ad includes the headline, coupons, advertiser's identification, and the main body of the message. In a broadcast ad the copy is the script.

For visual ads, the **illustration** is a powerful feature. The main points to consider about illustrations are (1) whether they are totally appropriate to the product advertised and (2) despite the adage "a picture is worth a thousand words," whether they are the best use of the space. The **layout** is the physical arrangement of all the elements in an advertisement. In print ads, it is the appearance of the page. For television, layout is the set as well as the positioning of actors and props. The layout of a radio ad is the sequence in which information is presented. A good layout can hold interest as well as attract attention. It should lead the audience through the entire ad in an orderly fashion.

TABLE 20-3 Frequently used advertising executions

**_Endorsement._ An authority figure or celebrity presents the product. The advertiser hopes the credibility or attractiveness of the spokesperson will spill over to the product. Examples: American Express, with its "Cardholder since . . ." campaign; Doug Gilmour for Head and Shoulders, Candice Bergen for Sprint, and many famous athletes for Nike.**

**_Slice of life._ Typical format is to depict "real people" experiencing a dilemma or crisis, interrupt this story with some information about the brand, then return to the story and show how the brand resolves the problem. The advertiser hopes the audience will relate to the story and associate the brand with the happy ending. Examples: The ongoing saga of a man and woman who both love Taster's Choice coffee; CIBC's "personal vision" ads; Ford's use of actual owners of their cars.**

**_Demonstration._ Show the product in action. May be particularly useful for a new product or one that is complicated to use. The purpose is to show how to use the product correctly and what benefits can be obtained. Examples: Luvs diapers absorbing the contents of a leaking water balloon; many detergents, razors, and dishwashing liquids regularly show their brand in action.**

**_Comparison._ Demonstrate how the product differs from the competition. Often used by the number 2, 3, or lower brand to associate itself with the sales leader in the minds of consumers. Examples: Pepsi versus Coca-Cola; many automobile companies use this approach.**

**_Symbolism._ A symbol is used to depict the benefits of the product in a concrete fashion. Common for services where visualization of a good is not possible. Examples: Prudential's Rock of Gibraltar; Michelin Tire's use of babies in their ads.**

**_Humour._ Using exaggeration, slapstick comedy, or humorous stories, advertisers attempt to draw the audience into the message. Examples: Nike's use of impossible basketball shots, the Energizer pink bunny.**

**This is not a complete list of possible executions. Others include fantasy, nostalgia, sex, and human interest. Can you think of examples of campaigns using these other executions?**

The cost of creating an ad can vary from almost nothing for a local radio spot written by the staff at a radio station to as much as $400,000 for a television commercial. In recent years, production costs for network TV ads have escalated dramatically. As a result, fewer ads are being made and they are kept on the air longer.

### Selecting Media

In describing the steps in developing an advertising campaign, we have discussed creating an advertising message before describing the selection of **advertising media** in which to place the ad. In reality these decisions are made simultaneously. Both the message and the choice of media are determined by the appeal and the target audience.

Advertisers need to make decisions at each of three successive levels to determine which specific advertising medium to use:

1. Which *type* of medium will be used — newspaper, television, radio, magazine, or direct mail? What about the less prominent media of billboards, specialty items, and Yellow Pages?

## MARKETING AT WORK

### FILE 20-2 JOE GOES TO THE WALL FOR NIKE

Nike has demonstrated over and over that it can produce some of the most creative and noticeable advertising anywhere. Few examples of Nike's flair for attention-grabbing advertising can be more dramatic than the five-storey wall ad in downtown Toronto that features Joe Carter hitting his World Series-winning home run in October 1993. The mural, on the wall of a building near SkyDome, is seen by 50,000 people an evening during baseball season — practically all of whom would undoubtedly be in Nike's target audience.

There is little to identify Nike on the ad, other than the company's logo in the upper left corner and the Nike "swoosh" on Carter's shoes. With five Nike-sponsored players on the Blue Jays, Nike found that it wasn't easy choosing which one to feature on its wall. John Olerud had won the batting championship in 1993, and Carter had made it seven consecutive 100-RBI seasons. But, as Stan Wong, Nike Canada's advertising and sports-marketing supervisor, observed, "The homer made the decision easy."

The Toronto wall is only one of a series of "local hero" wall ads that Nike features in other cities — Michael Jordan in Chicago, Barry Bonds in San Francisco, Ken Griffey Jr. in Seattle, Kirby Puckett in Minneapolis, and Deion Sanders in Atlanta. Nike plans to continue with a baseball theme for its wall ads in Toronto until October 1995, when it will switch to advertising that will feature the Raptors, Toronto's new NBA franchise. The company also plans local hero wall ads in Montreal and Vancouver.

Source: James Christie, "Shoe Firm Foots Bill for Carter Mural," *Globe and Mail*, May 7, 1994, p. A22.

2. Which *category* of the selected medium will be used? Television has network and cable; magazines include general-interest (*Maclean's*, *Time*) and special-interest (*Chatelaine*, *Canadian Business*) categories; and there are national as well as local newspapers.
3. Which *specific media vehicles* will be used? An advertiser who decides first on radio and then on local stations must determine which stations to use in each city.

Here are some general factors that will influence media choice:

- **Objectives of the ad.** The purpose of a particular ad and the goals of the entire campaign influence which media to use. For example, if the campaign goal is to generate appointments for sales people, the company may rely on direct mail. If an advertiser wants to induce quick action, newspaper or radio may be the medium to use.
- **Audience coverage.** The audience reached by the medium should match the *geographic* area in which the product is distributed. Furthermore, the selected medium should reach the desired *types of prospects* with a minimum of wasted coverage. Wasted coverage occurs when an ad reaches people who are not prospects for the product. Many media — even national and other large-market media — can be targeted at small, specialized market segments. For example, *Maclean's* magazine publishes regional editions with different ads in the Atlantic, Ontario, and Western editions, and a French-language edition for Quebec.
- **Requirements of the message.** The medium should fit the message. For example, food products, floor coverings, and apparel are best presented visually. If the advertiser can use a very brief message (the rule of thumb is six words or less), as is common with reminder advertising, billboards may be a suitable medium.
- **Time and location of the buying decision.** The medium should reach prospective customers when and where they are about to make their buying decisions. Research shows that radio scores the highest in immediacy of exposure. Over 50 percent of adults were last exposed to radio within one hour of making their largest purchase of the day. This

SCHOOL OF ECONOMICS
It figures.
Since the Beetle first made its way to these shores, Volkswagens have appealed to those who appreciate the value of a dollar.
So in this particular parking lot, the trusty Jetta is a natural. It's not hard to figure out why.
Buying one isn't a proposition that breaks the bank. Running one isn't, either. (The junior professor's diesel is especially frugal.)
And while Jetta is thrifty in this respect, the quality of its German engineering is unstinting.
The car handles with the precision you expect in a German sedan. The doors close with a 'thunk'. Repeatedly.
Inside, Jetta's space and comfort are a pleasant surprise. The trunk is huge. (The professors appreciate this. Economics texts are notoriously bulky.)
And like all Volkswagens, a Jetta tends to stick around (a 3 year/60,000 km warranty and a 6 year corrosion warranty help see to that).
Needless to say, you don't have to be an economist to own one.
Just someone who appreciates good value. But we suspect you already had that figured.
Jetta $13,715*


**Volkswagen has used the same format in executing its print advertisements for many years, incorporating subtle humour.**

factor highlights one of the strengths of place-based advertising. Likewise, in-store ads — for example, on shopping carts and in the aisles of supermarkets — reach consumers at the actual time of purchase.

- **Media cost.** The cost of each medium should be considered in relation to the amount of funds available to pay for it and its reach or circulation. For example, the cost of network television exceeds the available funds of many advertisers.

**Cost per thousand (CPM)** persons reached (M is the Roman numeral for a thousand) is a standard measure routinely provided to prospective advertisers by all media. It allows an advertiser to compare costs across media. CPM is computed as follows:

$$\text{CPM} = \frac{\text{ad cost} \times 1{,}000}{\text{circulation}}$$

For example, the advertising rate for a four-colour, one-page ad in *Travel & Leisure*, a magazine with an international circulation, is $42,000 and the circulation is 1,200,000. Therefore, CPM for the magazine is:

$$\text{CPM} = \frac{(\$42{,}000 \times 1{,}000)}{1{,}200{,}000} = \$35$$

Of course, it is essential to estimate what proportion of all persons reached are truly prospects for the advertiser's product. If an advertiser is interested only in females over 50 years of age, we might find that there are 650,000 *Travel & Leisure* readers in this category. Therefore, we would have to calculate a *weighted* CPM:

$$\text{Weighted CPM} = \frac{(\$42{,}000 \times 1{,}000)}{650{,}000} = \$64.62$$

Beyond these general factors, management must evaluate the advertising characteristics of each medium it is considering. We have carefully chosen the term *characteristics* instead of advantages and disadvantages because a medium that works well for one product is not necessarily the best choice for another product. To illustrate, a characteristic of radio is that it makes its impressions through sound and imagination. The roar of a crowd, running water, the rumbling of thunder, or screeching tires can be used to create mental images quickly and easily. But radio will not do the job for products that benefit from colour photography. Let's examine the characteristics of the major media.

## MARKETING AT WORK

### FILE 20-3 MORE THAN ONE WAY TO REACH THEM

How do you get through to 1.1 million kids in Quebec when provincial laws prohibit commercial advertising to children under 13? Sound sticky? Initially, perhaps. But creative marketers can find loopholes such as producing "adult" commercials that appeal visually to children and broadcasting them during "adult" television programs, probably watched by more kids than the prohibited "children's" shows. They can also resort to store windows, displays, and packaging. Or to ads that announce an event geared towards children.

Nestlé chose this latter route when, aiming to build popularity with its Smarties brand amidst the junior set, the company decided to sponsor a tour and a lip-sync show contest that was linked to 40 local festivals throughout the province. The tour was associated with Radio-Québec's "Le Club des 100 Watts," the most popular kids' show in the province, which both kicked off the tour and broadcast the finals. The tour revolved around the new purple "Cool Dude" Smarties, whose spokesperson was a Cool Dude mascot and master of ceremonies. Under Quebec's "exceptions to the law," TV and radio commercials as well as local and regional ads promoted both the tour and Smarties. Local organizers received press kits and posters, while contestants and spectators at every show were plied with free Smarties and promotional T-shirts. Although at every step of the way Smarties was highly visible, technically the brand was never advertised.

With each show attracting more than 25,000 people, it was hardly surprising when Smarties sales increased by a total of 46 percent through all channels during the four months of the promotion. And, boosted by special displays, single-pack sales at convenience stores skyrocketed by over 80 percent, considerably expanding the brand's former 4 percent share of Canada's $804-million chocolate bar market. With such sweet success, it seems as if the Smarties brand is bent on living up to its name.

Source: Gail Chaisson, "A Sweet Solution," *Marketing*, February 28, 1994, p. 18.

**Newspapers** As an advertising medium, newspapers are flexible and timely. They account for the largest portion of total advertising dollars spent in Canada. They can be used to cover a single city or a number of urban centres. With the development of computer technology and regional printing in the publishing industry, once-local newspapers may now be printed in regional centres for distribution across the country. The daily *Financial Post* and the *Globe and Mail*, for example, are headquartered in Toronto, but are printed regionally and are now true national daily papers.

While newspapers are becoming more attractive to the national advertiser, they remain the principal advertising vehicle for the local advertiser. Ads can be cancelled on a few days' notice or inserted on one day's notice. Newspapers can give an advertiser an intense coverage of a local market because almost everybody reads newspapers. The local feature also helps in that the ads can be adapted to local social and economic conditions. Circulation costs per prospect are low. On the other hand, the life of a newspaper advertisement is very short.[2]

**Television** Television is probably the most versatile of all media. It makes its appeal through both the eye and the ear; products can be demonstrated as well as explained. It offers considerable flexibility in the geographic market covered and the time of message presentation. By making part of its impression through the ear, television can take advantage of the personal, dramatic impact of the spoken word.

On the other hand, television is an extremely expensive medium. The message is not permanently recorded for the message receiver. Thus the prospect who is not reached the first time is lost forever, as far as a particular message is concerned. Television does not lend itself to long advertising copy, nor does it present pictures as clearly as magazines do. As with direct mail and radio, television advertisers must create their own audiences.

Cable is also changing television as an advertising medium. Canada is among the most heavily "cabled" nations in the world, with well over 80 percent of homes in many urban areas wired for cable. In this country, having cable television has given Canadians access to as many as 30 channels, many of which originate in the United States or carry specialized programming, including sports, movies, youth programs, arts and entertainment, and popular music videos. This increased access to television channels has resulted in a dramatic change in the nature and effect of television as an advertising medium.

In households with cable, television is now a much more focused medium, offering specialized television channels to people with particular interests. The sheer variety of channels has led to a situation described as **fragmentation**, where viewers regularly "zap" their way through the range of channels available, often when a commercial appears. This proliferation of channels through cable, coupled with the use of VCRs, remote control devices, and video games, has meant that the audience likely to be exposed to a television commercial is reduced, thereby limiting the effectiveness of television in reaching a mass market. As a result, some advertisers have begun to use shorter, more attention-getting commercials, or have moved some of their advertising budgets away from television to other media.

In the cluttered world of television, advertisers are constantly looking for ways to reach targeted audiences and to make their advertising messages stand out. As we saw in the opening pages of this chapter, Ford and other large advertisers are experimenting with interactive television, which many feel will become a major element in media advertising in the near future. Others are developing infomercials, which are intended to stand out from other forms of advertising on television. We will discuss infomercials in a later section of this chapter. Finally, some companies have moved their advertising from the mainstream television networks to specialty channels in order to increase the likelihood of reaching their targeted audiences. Advertising on such specialty channels as CBC Newsworld, The Weather Network, MétéoMédia, TSN, RDS, MuchMusic, MusiquePlus, YTV, and Vision TV reached more than $97 million in 1993, having more than quintupled since 1987-88.[3]

**Direct Mail** Direct mail is probably the most personal and selective of all the media. Because it reaches only the market that the advertiser wishes to contact, there is a minimum of waste circulation. Direct mail is not accompanied by articles or other editorial matter, however, unless the advertiser provides it. That is, most direct mail is pure advertising. As a result, a direct-mail ad creates its own circulation and attracts its own readers. The cost of direct mail per prospect reached is quite high compared with other media. But other media reach many people who are not real prospects and thus have higher waste-circulation costs. A severe limitation of direct mail is the difficulty of getting and maintaining good mailing lists. Direct-mail advertising also suffers from the stigma of being classed as "junk mail."

The effectiveness of direct mail has been increased in recent years through the application of technology to the process of identifying prospects to whom advertising materials are to be mailed. Highly specialized mailing lists can be purchased from mailing-list brokers. These lists can be expensive, but do offer the advertisers the ability to target precisely the group in which they are interested. Many companies have developed their own mailing lists through effective design of their internal information systems. By capturing sales data in an appropriate way, for example, a travel agency can produce a list of all the clients who made a business trip to Europe in the past year, or took a vacation in the southern United States, or made more than 15 business trips. These individuals then represent target segments for special-interest mailings. Wastage is dramatically reduced because the advertising reaches precisely those people who are most likely interested.

While direct mail is widely regarded as one of the most cost-effective of advertising media, it is also one that must be managed very carefully. In the first place, the effectiveness of a direct mail advertising program is very heavily dependent on the accuracy of the mailing list being used. Some users of direct mail spend too little time on ensuring the accuracy of the mailing list, with the result that many people on the list may not be at all interested in the product or service, while some will receive two or three mailing pieces because their names appear on the list in a number of different forms. You have probably received advertising material in the mail that you are not the least bit interested in. This contributes to the fact that many people have a low opinion of direct mail. In a study conducted for National Public Relations, seven out of ten respondents considered direct mail to be the least credible way for them to learn about a company's new product or service.[4] However, many companies do use direct mail very effectively and in a manner that does not offend recipients. One good example is the large international catalogue companies such as Lands' End and L. L. Bean who rely totally on direct mail to distribute their catalogues.[5]

**Radio** Radio is enjoying a renaissance as an advertising and cultural medium and as a financial investment. When interest in television soared after World War II, radio audiences (especially for national network radio), declined so much that people were predicting radio's demise. But for the past 10 years or so, this medium has been making a real comeback. Local radio (as contrasted with national networks) is especially strong. Radio accounts for almost 10 percent of all advertising revenues in Canada, attracting more than $700 million in sales annually.

As an advertising medium, radio's big advantage is its relatively low cost. You can reach almost everybody with radio. At the same time, with special-interest, targeted programming, certain radio stations can do a very effective job of reaching specific target market segments. In recent years, for example, a number of Canadian radio stations began to pay more attention to the growing segment of the market in the 30-to-50 age group. As a result, the top three formats in Canadian radio stations are country and western, adult contemporary, and news/talk, all of which are likely to appeal to a more mature audience than are the rock music stations that were more popular in the 1970s and 1980s. Other specialty stations have emerged in many of the larger radio markets in Canada, ranging from The FAN, Toronto's all-sports station, to Vancouver's "The Bridge" (CKBD), which bills itself as Canada's first contemporary Christian music station.[6]

Although radio is one of the more targeted of the mass media and can deliver an audience at a fairly low CPM (cost per thousand), it does have its limitations. On the one hand, it makes only an audio impression, so it is of limited value where a visual impact is needed. On the other hand, some advertisers who believe in the value of radio consider this to be one of radio's strong points, that it is able to stimulate the imagination of the listener. Radio also does not have a captive audience, in that many people listen to the radio for "background" entertainment while they are working around the house, driving in their cars, or doing homework! The exposure life of a radio commercial is quite short, resulting in a need to deliver multiple exposures to gain impact.

**Magazines** Magazines are an excellent medium when high-quality printing and colour are desired in an ad. Magazines can reach a national market at a relatively low cost per reader. Through special-interest or regional editions of general-interest magazines, an advertiser can reach a selected audience with a minimum of waste circulation. Magazines are usually read in a leisurely fashion, in contrast to the haste in which other print media are read. This feature is especially valuable to the advertiser with a lengthy or complicated message. Magazines have a relatively long life, anywhere from a week to a month, and a high pass-along readership.

With less flexible production schedules than newspapers, magazines require ads to be submitted several weeks before publication. In addition, because they are published weekly or monthly, it is more difficult to use topical messages. Magazines are often read at times or in places — on planes or in doctors' offices, for instance — far removed from where a buying impulse can be acted on.

**Outdoor Advertising** Outdoor advertising has a low cost per exposure. Because of the mobile nature of our society, outdoor ads reach a large percentage of the population. But because it is typically seen by people "on the go," billboard advertising is appropriate only for brief messages. It is excellent for reminder advertising, and it carries the impact of large size and colour. Motion and three-dimensional figures can be incorporated in a billboard's design for increased attention-getting ability. Billboards provide flexibility in geographic coverage and intensity of market coverage within an area. However, unless the advertised product is a widely used good or service, considerable waste circulation will occur. Although the cost of reaching an individual person is low, the total cost of a national billboard campaign can be quite high. Finally, the landscape-defacing aspect of outdoor advertising has aroused considerable public criticism.

## MARKETING AT WORK

### FILE 20-4 GETTING THE McDONALD'S MESSAGE TO MOMMY

In Canada, McDonald's has always tried to groom its image as a family restaurant, in particular, by appealing to children's appetites. Yet, since its strings of television commercials have gone unwatched by busy mothers who tend to watch little or no television at all, McDonald's in Ontario is attempting to reach out to them in a new manner — through ads in women's magazines. Acknowledging the targeting power of *Chatelaine*, *Modern Woman*, and *Today's Parent*, McDonald's has run two-page, four-colour, pull-out ads in order to promote its Happy Meals to mothers with young children. Kids are invited to draw a picture of a happy moment with Mommy and the family on the pull-out and then drop it off at McDonald's for the chance to win a Club Med family vacation in the Dominican Republic. With this medium so far free of competitors, it seems likely that this marketing marriage of french fries and family values will prove successful.

Source: "McDonald's Tries Promotion in Women's Mags," *Marketing*, April 4, 1994, p. 1.

**Sometimes a complex message can be communicated in a few words on a billboard.**

**Specialty Advertising** An item of merchandise imprinted with the advertiser's name, message, or logo and given free is specialty advertising. According to the Specialty Advertising Association International, more than 15,000 different items, from pens to coffee cups and calendars, are used in specialty advertising, and annual expenditures are more than $5 billion in North America.

Specialty advertising is usually used in conjunction with other promotional activities, though it is sometimes used alone by firms with very small advertising budgets. Its greatest strength is its long life. Every time the specialty item is used, the advertising message is repeated.

**Emerging Media** Many advertisers consider several lesser-known media to be valuable, especially when used in conjunction with the better-known media:

- **Yellow Pages.** The Yellow Pages as we have come to know it is a directory of local businesses and their telephone numbers organized by type of product or service. While such advertising media have been around for many years, there are some new twists as "Yellow Pages" directories are being printed by companies in competition with the telephone companies, and directories of fax numbers are being issued.
- **Infomercials.** These are the lengthy television advertisements that generally run for up to 60 minutes and combine information with entertainment and product promotions. They have been popular in the United States for many years, and many have been beamed into Canada on American channels, featuring such well-known presenters as Victoria Principal and Tony Robbins, promoting everything from diet plans and personal-improvement programs to baldness remedies and auto paint protectors. The use of infomercials has been restricted on Canadian television by a ruling of the CRTC that channels cannot carry more than 12 minutes of advertising during an hour of programming. In early 1994, the CRTC relaxed the restrictions to allow infomercials during the hours from midnight to 6 A.M., with their use during daytime and evening hours restricted to still photographs, such as the format used on the Home Shopping Network. Despite these restrictions, some Canadian firms such as the Royal Bank of Canada and Ford Canada are experimenting with infomercials, using the still-photo format.[7]

- **Place-based media.** As we have discussed earlier in this chapter, certain attractive target segments such as young professionals, teenagers, and dual-career families have become increasingly difficult to reach through traditional advertising media. The solution is to place the advertising where the people are. Consequently, we have seen an increase in advertising in airports, shopping malls, waiting rooms, supermarkets, phone booths, and even public washrooms. A Calgary company, AdWall Advertising, has installed its AdWalls in airports across Canada. Each AdWall consists of a bank of video monitors stacked four by four, to form a 50-foot-square image. Commercials are beamed to the AdWall over telephone lines from the company's Calgary headquarters.[8]
- **Videos.** Bothered by the erosion of their network television audience by videos, some national advertisers have moved their advertising to reach the video watchers by placing ads on rental video movies or by co-sponsoring or co-producing them.
- **Exterior transit ads.** Transit ads now appear on the exterior as well as the interior of buses and subway cars, both on the rear and the front of the bus; in fact, one of the newest forms of transit advertising is to paint the entire bus as a mobile billboard.

## Evaluating the Advertising Effort

In managing its advertising program, a company should carefully evaluate the effectiveness of previous ads and use the results to improve the quality of future ads. Shrinking profit margins and increasing competition — both foreign and domestic — force management to appraise all expenditures. Top executives want proof that advertising is worthwhile. They want to know whether dollars spent on advertising are producing as many sales as could be reaped from the same dollars spent on other marketing activities.

**Difficulty of Evaluation** It is hard to measure the sales effectiveness of advertising. By the very nature of the marketing mix, all elements — including advertising — are so intertwined that it is nearly impossible to measure the effect of any one by itself. Factors that contribute to the difficulty of measuring the sales impact of advertising are:

- **Ads have different objectives.** Though all advertising is ultimately intended to increase sales, individual ads may not be aimed at producing immediate results. Some ads simply announce new store hours or service policies. Other ads build goodwill or contribute to a company's image.
- **Ads can have an effect over time.** Even an ad designed to have an immediate sales impact may produce results weeks or months after it appears. A consumer may be influenced by an ad but not be able to act on it immediately. Or an ad may plant in the consumer's mind a seed that doesn't blossom into a sale for several weeks. It is impossible to determine, with the exception of mail-order advertising, when a particular ad or campaign produced results.
- **Measurement problems.** Consumers cannot usually say when or if a specific ad influenced their behaviour, let alone if it caused them to buy. Human motivation is too complicated to be explained by a single factor.

In spite of these problems, advertisers try to measure advertising effectiveness because they must — and some knowledge is better than none. An ad's effectiveness may be tested before it is presented to the target audience, while it is being presented, or after it has completed its run.

**Methods Used to Measure Effectiveness** Ad effectiveness can be measured directly and indirectly. **Direct tests**, which measure or predict the sales volume attributable to an ad or a campaign, can be used only with a few types of ads. Tabulating the number of redemp-

**Since few dogs read magazines regularly, how would you measure the effectiveness of this ad?**

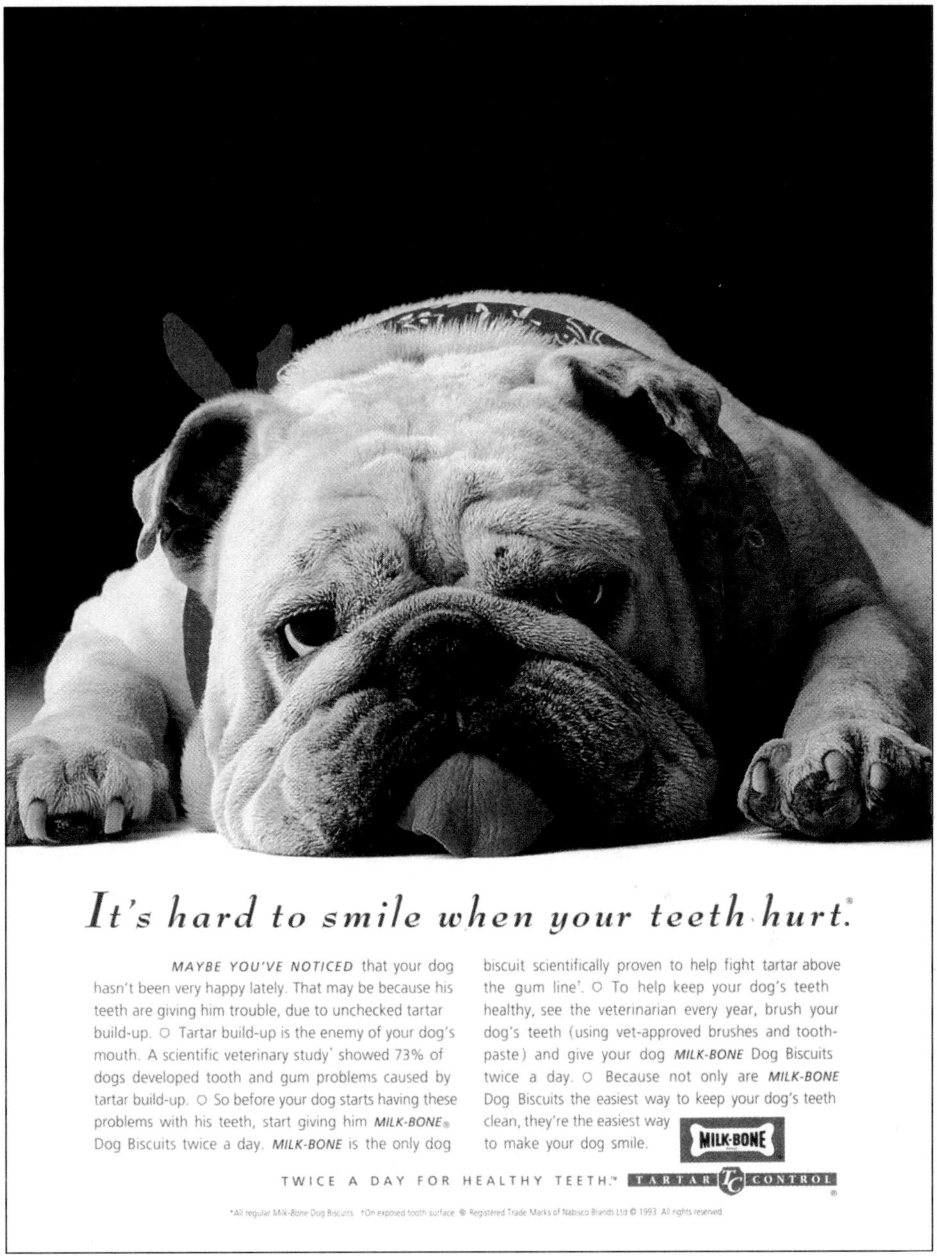

It's hard to smile when your teeth hurt.
MAYBE YOU'VE NOTICED that your dog hasn't been very happy lately. That may be because his teeth are giving him trouble, due to unchecked tartar build-up. ○ Tartar build-up is the enemy of your dog's mouth. A scientific veterinary study* showed 73% of dogs developed tooth and gum problems caused by tartar build-up. ○ So before your dog starts having these problems with his teeth, start giving him MILK-BONE® Dog Biscuits twice a day. MILK-BONE is the only dog biscuit scientifically proven to help fight tartar above the gum line†. ○ To help keep your dog's teeth healthy, see the veterinarian every year, brush your dog's teeth (using vet-approved brushes and toothpaste) and give your dog MILK-BONE Dog Biscuits twice a day. ○ Because not only are MILK-BONE Dog Biscuits the easiest way to keep your dog's teeth clean, they're the easiest way to make your dog smile.
MILK-BONE
TWICE A DAY FOR HEALTHY TEETH.™
TARTAR TC CONTROL
*All regular Milk-Bone Dog Biscuits †On exposed tooth surface ® Registered Trade Marks of Nabisco Brands Ltd © 1993 All rights reserved

tions of a reduced-price coupon incorporated in an ad will indicate its effectiveness. Coupons frequently are coded so they can also be traced to the publications from which they came. Another direct test that is used to predict sales measures the number of inquiries received from an ad that offers additional information to prospects who call or write in.

Most other types of measures are **indirect tests** of effectiveness, or measures of something other than actual behaviour. One of the most frequently used measures is **advertising recall.** Recall tests are based on the premise that an ad can have an effect only if it is perceived and remembered. Three common recall tests are:

- **Recognition** — showing people an ad and asking if they have seen it before.
- **Aided recall** — asking people if they can recall seeing any ads for a particular brand.

- **Unaided recall** — asking people if they can remember seeing any ads within an identified product category.

For broadcast media this kind of testing can be conducted using a telephone survey, calling people at home within a few hours after an ad is aired.

A well-known indirect measure of print ads is the Starch Readership Test. To measure readership, the Starch researcher pages through a magazine with a person who has previously read it, and records whether the person remembers noticing the ads in that particular magazine, how much of the copy was read, and whether the ad was associated with the sponsor. The responses from a representative sample of the target audience are presented as percentage scores for the ad. For example, a typical ad for a credit card in *Time* magazine might get scores of:

- 42 percent recall noticing the ad.
- 23 percent read most of the copy in the ad.
- 16 percent read the portion of the ad that includes the sponsor's name.

Advertisers use these results to compare scores for alternative executions of the same message or the same execution in different publications. They also use the scores to compare readership of their ads with readership of their competitors' ads. Critics of the method question the ability of consumers to accurately recall seeing a particular ad in a particular magazine and the artificiality of the data-gathering situation.

Television ads are often tested before they are presented to the general public in what are called **pretests**. Commercials in finished or nearly finished form (to save production costs) are presented to panels of consumers for their reactions. This is often done in theatre settings, with the test ad shown along with other ads in the context of a regular TV program. After viewing the program and the ads, the consumers are quizzed about the commercial being tested.

A criticism of pretests is that the situation is unrealistic. The ads often are not in the final forms that the actual target audience would see, the research respondents have been invited to a theatre to participate, and the respondents are usually given an incentive for their involvement. The testers argue that since these factors exist across all commercials tested, they in effect "wash out" and the scores provide useful comparative information.

Refinements are constantly being made in advertising testing. Developments in areas such as laboratory test markets and computer simulations hold promise for the future. However, the complexity of decision making, combined with the multitude of influences on the buyer, will continue to make measuring the effectiveness of advertising a difficult task.

## ORGANIZING FOR ADVERTISING

There are three ways a firm can manage its advertising:

- Develop an internal advertising department.
- Use an outside advertising agency.
- Use a combination of an internal department and an outside advertising agency.

Regardless of which alternative is selected, generally the same specialized skills are necessary to do the advertising job. Creative people are needed to prepare the copy, generate illustrative material, and design the layouts. Media experts are required to select the appropriate media, buy the time or space, and arrange for the scheduled appearance of the ads. And managerial skills are essential to plan and administer the entire advertising program.

### Internal Departments

All these advertising tasks, some of them, or just overall direction can be performed by an internal department. A company whose advertising is a substantial part of its marketing mix will usually have its own advertising department. Large retailers, for example, have their own advertising departments, and many do not use advertising agencies at all. If a company with an internal department has adopted the marketing concept, the advertising department head will report to the organization's top marketing executive.

### Advertising Agencies

Many companies, especially producers, use advertising agencies to carry out some or all of their advertising activities. An **advertising agency** is an independent company that provides specialized advertising services and may also offer more general marketing assistance.

Advertising agencies plan and execute entire advertising campaigns. They employ more advertising specialists than their clients do, because they spread the cost over many accounts. A client company can benefit from an agency's experience gained from other products and clients. Many large agencies have expanded the services they offer to include sales promotion and public relations, and they are frequently called upon to assist in new-product development, package design, and selecting product names. In fact, many of these firms have become *integrated* agencies, offering a full range of services from strategic planning to market research that heretofore were performed by other outside specialists or by the advertisers themselves.

### Inside Department and Outside Agency

Many firms have their own advertising department and also use an advertising agency. The internal advertising department acts as a liaison with the agency, giving the company greater control over this major expenditure. The advertising department approves the agency's plans and ads, is responsible for preparing and administering the advertising budget, and co-ordinates advertising with personal selling. It may also handle direct marketing, dealer displays, and other promotional activities if they are not handled by the agency.

## SALES PROMOTION

Sales promotion is one of the most loosely used terms in the marketing vocabulary. We define **sales promotion** as demand-stimulating devices designed to supplement advertising and facilitate personal selling. Examples of sales promotion devices are coupons, premiums, in-store displays, trade shows, samples, in-store demonstrations, and contests.

Sales promotions are conducted by producers and intermediaries. The target for producers' sales promotions may be intermediaries, end users — households or business users — or the producer's own sales force. Intermediaries direct sales promotion at their sales people or prospects further down the channel of distribution.

### Nature and Scope of Sales Promotion

Sales promotion is distinct from advertising or personal selling, but these three forms of promotion are often used together in a co-ordinated fashion. For example, an in-store display (sales promotion) furnished by Michelin to stores selling its tires may feature a slogan and illustrations (including, of course, the Michelin Man) from Michelin's current advertising campaign. This display, which helps retailers sell tires, also makes them more receptive to talking with Michelin sales people. Or, as another example, prospective customers may be generated from people who enter a contest at the Canon copy machines exhibit at an office equipment trade show. These prospects might be sent some direct-mail advertising and then be contacted by a sales person.

There are two categories of sales promotion: **trade promotions**, directed to the members of the distribution channel; and **consumer promotions**, aimed at consumers. Manufacturers as a group spend about twice as much on trade promotion as they do on advertising, and an amount about equal to their advertising on consumer promotions.

The numbers attached to some sales promotion activities are mind-boggling. Almost 22 billion cents-off coupons were distributed in Canada in 1993 by packaged-goods manufacturers, and of these, 327 million were redeemed. These numbers do not even include coupons issued by restaurants and other major users such as McDonald's, who in a recent promotion sent coupons to *every household in Canada*. Between 1988 and 1992, the face value of these coupons actually increased by 33 percent, while redemption rates went down. This is partly a result of increasing acceptance of technology in the distribution of coupons, as some retailers use a system to distribute coupons selectively — for example, targeting them only to customers who purchase a competitor's product. Some supermarket chains such as A&P no longer issue paper coupons at all, rather using electronic couponing that involves issuing discounts automatically to all A&P purchasers who have a special card that automatically scans for discounts as the customer's groceries are being checked in.[9]

Several factors in the marketing environment contribute to the surging popularity of sales promotion:

- **Short-term results.** Sales promotions such as couponing and trade allowances produce quicker, more measurable sales results. However, critics of this strategy argue that these immediate benefits come at the expense of building brand equity. They feel that an overemphasis on sales promotion may undermine a brand's future.
- **Competitive pressure.** If competitors are offering buyers price reductions, contests, or other incentives, a firm may feel forced to retaliate with its own sales promotions.
- **Buyers' expectations.** Once they are offered purchase incentives, consumers and channel members get used to them and soon begin expecting them. The resistance among retailers to Procter & Gamble's Every Day Low Prices program illustrates this point.
- **Low quality of retail selling.** Many retailers use inadequately trained sales clerks or have switched to self-service. For these outlets, sales promotion devices such as product displays and samples often are the only effective promotional tools available at the point of purchase.

## Management of Sales Promotion

Sales promotion should be included in a company's promotion plans, along with advertising and personal selling. This means setting sales promotion objectives and strategies, determining a sales promotion budget, selecting appropriate sales promotion techniques, and evaluating the performance of sales promotion activities.

One problem management faces is that many sales promotion techniques are short-run, tactical actions. Coupons, premiums, and contests, for example, are designed to produce immediate (but short-lived) responses. As a result, they tend to be used as stopgap measures to reverse unexpected sales declines rather than as integrated parts of a marketing program.

**Determining Objectives and Strategies** We identified three broad objectives of sales promotion when we defined the term:

- Stimulating business-user or household demand for a product.
- Improving the marketing performance of intermediaries and sales people.
- Supplementing advertising and facilitating personal selling.

One sales promotion technique may accomplish one or two — but probably not all — of these objectives.

More specific objectives of sales promotion are much like those for advertising and personal selling. Examples are:

- *To gain trial for a new or improved product.* Procter & Gamble or Lever Brothers might send a free sample through the mail.
- *To disrupt existing buying habits.* A coupon offering a large discount might cause a consumer to switch brands of a product that is viewed as generic, such as orange juice or motor oil.
- *To attract new customers.* Financial institutions have offered small appliances and other premiums to encourage consumers to open accounts.
- *To encourage greater use by existing customers.* Air Canada and most other airlines have "frequent flyer" programs to encourage travellers to use their airlines more often. Other businesses have established similar "loyalty" programs.
- *To combat a competitor's promotional activity.* One supermarket chain runs a lottery or game to attract shoppers and a competitor retaliates by offering triple-value coupons.
- *To increase impulse buying.* End-of-aisle and island displays in supermarkets can increase sales of a product by as much as 50 percent.
- *To get greater retailer co-operation.* A sporting-goods manufacturer gets additional shelf space by setting up excellent point-of-purchase displays, training retailers' sales people, and providing tote bags to be given away with purchases.

The choice of sales promotion tools derives directly from the objectives of the total marketing program. Consider the following situations and the different strategies available:

- A firm's objective is to increase sales, which calls for entering new geographic markets using a *pull strategy*. To encourage product trial and attract consumers away from familiar brands, possible sales promotion tactics are coupons, cash rebates, free samples, and premiums.
- A firm's objective is to protect market share in the face of intense competition. This goal suggests a *push strategy* to improve retailer performance and goodwill. Training retailers' sales forces, supplying effective point-of-purchase displays, and granting advertising allowances would be appropriate sales promotion options.

**Determining Budgets** The sales promotion budget should be established as a specific part of the budget for the total promotional mix. Including sales promotion in an advertising or public relations budget is not likely to foster the development of a separate sales promotion strategy. And as a result, sales promotion may be overlooked or poorly integrated with the other components of promotion. Setting a separate budget for sales promotion forces a company to recognize and manage it.

Within the concept of developing an integrated promotion strategy, the amount budgeted for sales promotion should be determined by the task method. This forces management to consider specific objectives and the sales promotion techniques that will be used to accomplish them.

**Selecting the Appropriate Techniques** Common sales promotion techniques are shown in Table 20-4, where they are divided into three categories based on the target audience:

- **Sales promotion directed at final consumers.** Many of the tools in Table 20-4 probably are quite familiar to you, but a brief discussion of some of them will give you a better sense of their significance. In just four years the number of coupons distributed by marketers has increased by almost 400 percent (from 6.8 billion in 1986 to 21.7 billion in 1993) with no end in sight.

TABLE 20-4 Major sales promotion tools, grouped by target audience

| End users (consumer or business) | Intermediaries and their sales forces | Producers' own sales force |
|---|---|---|
| Coupons | Trade shows and exhibitions | Sales contests |
| Cash rebates | Point-of-purchase displays | Sales training manuals |
| Premiums (gifts) | Free goods | Sales meetings |
| Free samples | Advertising allowances | Packets with promotional materials |
| Contests and sweepstakes | Contests for sales people | Demonstration model of product |
| Point-of-purchase displays | Training intermediaries' sales force | |
| Product demonstrations | Product demonstrations | |
| Trade shows and exhibitions | Advertising specialties | |
| Advertising specialties | | |

"Advertising specialties" is a miscellaneous category of small, usually inexpensive items imprinted with a company's name or logo that are given or sold by producers or intermediaries to customers and prospects. Examples are pens, calendars, key rings, paperweights, coffee cups, hats, and jackets.

- **Sales promotion directed at intermediaries.** Some of the tools just discussed may also be directed at intermediaries and their sales forces. In addition, trade associations in industries as diverse as shoes, travel, and furniture sponsor trade shows that are open

## MARKETING AT WORK

### FILE 20-5 OIL COMPANIES TURN TO LONGER-TERM PROMOTIONS

The industry that has probably relied more heavily than any other on sales promotions over the years is the retail gasoline business. The major companies such as Imperial Oil, Ultramar, Petro-Canada, and Irving have probably pumped out almost as many packages of garbage bags, cookbooks, toys, panty hose, and photo placemats as they have litres of gasoline. But there is a change taking place.

There are a couple of reasons that gasoline retailers have been so enamoured of promotions in the past. The first is that a fairly large percentage of drivers are "switchers"; that is, they don't always buy the same brand of gasoline, therefore they are attracted by promotional deals and giveaways. Second, the companies are selling a product that is essentially nondifferentiated. Finally, the use of promotions allows the companies to avoid price wars, from which they are unlikely to benefit.

But, in an industry where it is difficult to convince customers of product differences, companies have recently set out to differentiate themselves at the corporate level. Shell has linked up with Air Miles frequent flyer program, and Imperial Oil's advertising now features service and guaranteed product quality. Imperial has also moved to build customer loyalty by linking with Zellers and allowing Esso credit card holders to accumulate Club Z points every time they buy gasoline.

Ultramar has also teamed up with Zellers in a different way. While Ultramar has been running a rewards program for several years in which customers could accumulate points to be redeemed on merchandise, those Ultramar customers can now redeem the points for merchandise from Club Z catalogues, thereby eliminating the need for Ultramar to manage a points redemption service.

As with other frequent-buyer programs, those of the oil companies are designed to encourage customers to establish a loyalty to a single supplier, or at least to buy more of their gasoline from that company. What is also very interesting in the case of Esso and Ultramar is that both have linked with Zellers, a non-competing retailer, who happens to run the largest and most successful loyalty program in Canada.

Source: Ken Riddell, "Pumping up Promos," *Marketing*, April 18, 1994, p. 12.

only to wholesalers and retailers. Many producers also spend considerable time and money to train the sales forces of their wholesalers and retailers.

- **Sales promotion directed at a producer's own sales force.** Again, there is overlap between the tools directed at intermediaries and those designed for the producer's own sales force. Sales contests are probably the most significant of these tools, with many firms offering one kind or another. The most common incentive is cash, used in over half of all contests. Other incentives include merchandise, plaques, jewellery, and travel. Visual sales aids (flipcharts, slides) are prepared for sales people and brochures are developed to reinforce sales presentations.

A key step in sales promotion management is deciding which devices will help the organization reach its promotional goals. Factors that influence the choice of promotional devices include:

- **Nature of the target audience.** Is the target group loyal to a competing brand? If so, a high-value coupon may be necessary to disrupt customers' purchase patterns. Is the product bought on impulse? If so, an eye-catching point-of-purchase display may be enough to generate sales.
- **The organization's promotional objectives.** Does a pull or a push strategy best complement the rest of the promotion program?
- **Nature of the product.** Does the product lend itself to sampling, demonstration, or multiple-item purchases?
- **Cost of the device.** Sampling to a large market may be prohibitively expensive.
- **Current economic conditions.** Coupons, premiums, and rebates are good options during periods of recession or inflation, when consumers are particularly price conscious.

**Evaluating Sales Promotion** Evaluating the effectiveness of sales promotions is much easier and the results more accurate than evaluating the effectiveness of advertising. For example, responses to a premium offer or a coupon with a specified closing date can be counted and compared to a similar period when there were no premiums or coupons offered. It is easier to measure sales promotion because:

- **Most sales promotions have definite starting and ending points.** Coupons must be redeemed by a certain date. Contest entries must be submitted before a particular deadline. Contests for the sales force include only the sales made during a specified period. This is quite different from advertising, where there can be significant residual effects and the results of one campaign may overlap another.
- **Most sales promotions are designed to affect sales directly.** It is more difficult to measure a change in attitude or an increase in information about a product or brand than it is to count sales.

However, there are some pitfalls in measuring sales promotion effects. First, not all sales promotions meet the conditions just mentioned. For instance, training given to a distributor's sales force may be valuable, but may not produce immediate results. Second, current sales promotion results may be inflated by sales "stolen" from the future. That is, a sales promotion may get buyers to act now when they would have bought the product in the future anyway. An indication of this cannibalizing effect is a lower level of sales *after* the promotion ends compared to *before* the sales promotion began. Third, any attempt at measurement must take into consideration external conditions such as the behaviour of competitors and the state of the economy. A firm's market share may not increase following an expensive sales promotion, for example, but the promotion may have offset the potentially damaging impact of a competitor's promotional activity.

## PUBLIC RELATIONS[10]

**Public relations** is a management tool designed to favourably influence attitudes towards an organization, its products, and its policies. It is an often overlooked form of promotion. In most organizations this promotional tool is typically a stepchild, relegated far behind personal selling, advertising, and sales promotion. There are several reasons for management's lack of attention to public relations:

- **Organizational structure.** In most companies, public relations is not the responsibility of the marketing department. If there is an organized effort, it is usually handled by a small public relations department that reports directly to top management.
- **Inadequate definitions.** The term *public relations* is used loosely by both businesses and the public. There are no generally accepted definitions of the term. As a result, what actually constitutes an organized public relations effort often is not clearly defined.
- **Unrecognized benefits.** Only recently have many organizations come to appreciate the value of good public relations. As the cost of promotion has gone up, firms are realizing that positive exposure through the media or as a result of community involvement can produce a high return on the investment of time and effort.

### Nature and Scope of Public Relations

Public relations activities typically are designed to build or maintain a favourable image for an organization and a favourable relationship with its various publics — customers, prospects, stockholders, employees, labour unions, the local community, and the government. We're aware that this description is quite similar to our definition of institutional advertising. However, unlike advertising, public relations need not use the media to communicate its message.

Good public relations can be achieved by supporting charitable projects (by supplying volunteer labour or other resources), participating in community service events, sponsoring athletic teams, funding the arts, producing an employee or customer newsletter, and disseminating information through exhibits, displays, and tours. Major companies often sponsor public events or special programs on television as part of their public relations efforts. Cultural organizations such as ballet companies and symphony orchestras would not survive without the support they receive from major corporations. As a result, we see interesting sponsorships such as the support the Hongkong Bank of Canada gave to an exhibition of photographs of children that appeared in art galleries across Canada.

### Publicity as a Form of Public Relations

**Publicity** is any communication about an organization, its products, or policies through the media that is *not* paid for by the organization. Publicity usually takes the form of a news story appearing in a mass medium or an endorsement provided by an individual, either informally or in a speech or interview. This is good publicity.

There is also, of course, bad publicity — a negative story about a firm or its product appearing in the media. In a society that is increasingly sensitive about the environment and in which news media are quick to report mistakes, organizations tend to focus on this negative dimension of publicity. As a result, managers are so concerned with avoiding bad publicity that they overlook the potential of good publicity.

There are three means for gaining good publicity:

- Prepare a story (called a *news release*) and circulate it to the media . The intention is for the selected newspapers, television stations, or other media to report the information as news.

- Personal communication with a group. A press conference will draw media representatives if they feel the subject or speaker has news value. Company tours and speeches to civic or professional groups are other forms of individual-to-group communications.
- One-on-one personal communication, often called *lobbying*. Companies lobby legislators or other powerful people in an attempt to influence their opinions, and subsequently their decisions.

Publicity can help to accomplish any communication objective. It can be used to announce new products, publicize new policies, recognize employees, describe research breakthroughs, or report financial performance — if the message, person, group, or event is viewed by the media as newsworthy. This is what distinguishes publicity from advertising — publicity is not "forced" on the audience. This is also the source of its primary benefit. The credibility of publicity typically is much higher than advertising. If we tell you our product is great, you may well be sceptical. But if an independent, objective third party says on the evening news that our product is great, you are more likely to believe it.

Other benefits of publicity are:

- **Lower cost than advertising or personal selling.** Publicity usually costs less because there are no media space or time costs for conveying the message and no sales people to support.
- **Increased readership.** Many consumers are conditioned to ignore advertising or at least pay it scant attention. Publicity is presented as editorial material or news, so it gets greater readership.
- **More information.** Because it is presented as editorial material, publicity can contain greater detail than the usual ad. More information and persuasive content can be included in the message.
- **Timeliness.** A company can put out a news release very quickly when some unexpected event occurs.

Of course, publicity also has limitations:

- **Loss of control over the message.** An organization has no guarantee that a news release will appear in the media. In fact, only a small proportion of all the news releases a firm prepares are ever used. In addition, there is no way to control how much or what portion of a publicity release the media will print or broadcast.
- **Limited exposure.** The media will typically use publicity material to fill space when there is a lack of other news and only use it once. If the target audience misses the message when it is presented, there is no second or third chance. There is no opportunity for repetition as in advertising.
- **Publicity is not free.** Even though there are no media time and space costs, there are expenses in staffing a publicity department and in preparing and disseminating news releases.

Recognizing the value of publicity, some organizations have special units or programs to generate information. For example, Campbell Soup Company sponsors a major national survey of the attitudes of Canadians towards health and nutrition; Christie's, the cookie company, sponsors the Christie Children's Book Awards; and The Body Shop actively supports the World Wildlife Fund and other environmental groups. All these activities are designed to link the companies involved with causes and activities consumers believe to be important. Through their association, the companies intend to improve their corporate image. To fulfil its potential, however, publicity must be treated as part of the promotional strategy of the firm and be co-ordinated with the other promotional tools.

### Evaluating Public Relations

Although few executives would argue that having a good image and staying in touch with an organization's publics are unimportant, evaluating public relations and publicity is difficult. In the past, evaluation usually involved a report of activities rather than results. Public relations departments maintained "scrapbooks" to show management how many stories were written and published, the number of employees who volunteered for civic projects, and the like. These days, to justify expenditures, more organizations are requiring publicity departments to provide specific public relations objectives and show measurable results. Because it is impossible to relate public relations and publicity directly to sales, other measures must be used. One is behavioural research to show, for example, increased awareness of a product or brand name, or changes in attitudes and beliefs about a firm.

## SUMMARY

Advertising is the nonpersonal, mass-communications component in a company's promotional mix. Advertising can be directed to consumers or businesses, and focus on products or institutions. Direct-action product ads call for immediate action, while indirect-action product ads are intended to stimulate demand over a longer time period. Product ads are also classified as primary-demand and selective-demand stimulating. Primary-demand ads are designed to introduce a new product, to stimulate demand for a generic product, or to sustain demand for an industry's products. Selective-demand ads, which include competitive and comparative advertising, are intended to increase the demand for a particular brand.

In vertical co-operative advertising, manufacturers and their retail dealers share the cost of advertising the manufacturers' product at the local level. Horizontal co-operative advertising involves joint sponsorship of ads by firms at the same level of distribution.

Advertising expenditures are large, but the average cost of advertising in a firm is typically 1 to 3 percent of sales. This is considerably less than the average cost of personal selling. Other frequently used advertising media are radio, magazines, Yellow Pages, and outdoor displays.

An advertising campaign should be part of a total promotional program. The steps in designing a campaign include defining specific objectives, establishing a budget, creating a message, selecting media, and evaluating the advertising effort. Objectives can range from creating awareness of a brand to generating sales. Vertical and horizontal co-operative arrangements can have a significant impact on advertising budgets. The advertising message — consisting of the appeal and the execution of the ad — is influenced by the target audience and the media used to deliver the message.

A major task in developing a campaign is to select the advertising media — the general type, the particular category, and the specific vehicle. The choice should be based on the characteristics of the medium, which determine how effectively it conveys the message, and its ability to reach the target audience.

A difficult task in advertising management is evaluating the effectiveness of the advertising effort — both the entire campaign and individual ads. Except for sales results tests, commonly used techniques measure only recall of an ad. To operate an advertising program, a firm may rely on its own advertising department, an advertising agency, or a combination of the two.

Sales promotion consists of demand-stimulating devices designed to supplement advertising and facilitate personal selling. The amount of sales promotion has increased considerably in recent years, as management has sought measurable, short-term sales results.

Sales promotion should receive the same strategic attention that a company gives to advertising and personal selling, including setting objectives and establishing a budget. Sales promotion can be directed towards final consumers, intermediaries, or a company's own employees. To implement its strategic plans, management can choose from a variety of sales promotion devices. Sales promotion performance also should be evaluated.

Public relations is a management tool designed to favourably influence attitudes towards an organization, its products, and its policies. It is a frequently overlooked form of promotion. Publicity, a part of public relations, is any communication about an organization, its products, or policies through the media that is *not* paid for by the organization. Typically these two activities are handled in a department separate from the marketing department in a firm. Nevertheless, the management process of planning, implementing, and evaluating should be applied to their performance in the same way it is applied to advertising, sales promotion, and personal selling.

## KEY TERMS AND CONCEPTS

**Advertising (596)**
**Consumer advertising (596)**
**Business-to-business advertising (596)**
**Product advertising (596)**
**Direct-action advertising (597)**
**Indirect-action advertising (597)**
**Institutional advertising (597)**
**Primary-demand advertising (597)**
**Selective-demand advertising (597)**
**Pioneering advertising (597)**
**Differential advantage (597)**
**Comparative advertising (597)**
**Co-operative advertising (598)**
**Vertical co-operative advertising (598)**
**Advertising allowance (598)**
**Horizontal co-operative advertising (598)**
**Advertising campaign (601)**
**Attention (604)**
**Influence (604)**
**Appeal (604)**
**Execution (604)**
**Copy (604)**
**Illustration (604)**
**Layout (604)**
**Advertising media (606)**
**Cost per thousand (CPM) (608)**
**Fragmentation (610)**
**Direct tests (614)**
**Indirect tests (615)**
**Advertising recall (615)**
**Pretests (616)**
**Advertising agency (617)**
**Sales promotion (617)**
**Trade promotion (618)**
**Consumer promotion (618)**
**Public relations (622)**
**Publicity (622)**

## QUESTIONS AND PROBLEMS

1. Businesses in different industries demonstrate quite different patterns in their advertising expenditures. Some are heavy advertisers on television, while others use no television at all. Some advertise heavily in daily newspapers, while others rely on magazines. Some firms, such as those in the consumer products field, spend as much as 15 percent of sales on advertising, while others, including many industrial marketers, spend less than 1 percent. How do you account for such variations in advertising expenditures?
2. Find an example of a print, TV, or radio ad that represents each of the executions described in Table 20-3.
3. Which advertising medium would you recommend as best for each of these products?
   a. Wooden pallets.
   b. Pantyhose.
   c. Tax preparation service.
   d. Funeral services.
   e. Toys for young children.
   f. Plastic clothespins.
4. Many grocery product and candy manufacturers earmark a good portion of their advertising budgets for use in magazines. Is this a wise choice of media for these firms? Explain.
5. Why do department stores use newspapers more than local radio stations as an advertising medium?
6. Why is it worthwhile to pretest advertisements before they appear in the media? How could a test market be used to pretest an ad? (You may want to refresh your memory with a review of test marketing in Chapter 8.)
7. What procedures can a firm use to determine how many sales dollars resulted from a direct-mail ad? How would you determine whether any sales were cannibalized?
8. If a manufacturing firm finds a good ad agency, should it discontinue its own advertising department? Should it consider any changes?
9. Visit a supermarket, a hardware store, or a movie theatre and make a list of all the sales promotion tools that you observe. Which do you feel are particularly effective and why?
10. Is sales promotion effective for selling expensive consumer products such as houses, automobiles, or cruise trips? Is your answer the same for expensive business products?
11. Explain how sales promotion might be used to offset weak personal selling in retail stores.
12. Describe a recent public relations event in your community. How did it benefit the sponsor?
13. How does publicity differ from advertising?
14. Bring to class an article from a daily newspaper that appears to be the result of a firm's publicity efforts. Summarize the points made in the article that may benefit the firm. Could the same benefits be obtained through advertising?
15. Give a recent example of a company or other organization with which you are familiar that encountered unfavourable publicity. How well do you feel the organization handled the situation? What public relations or publicity tools did it use?

## HANDS-ON MARKETING

1. Bring to class four print ads or describe four radio or television ads that illustrate at least four of the specific advertising objectives outlined early in the chapter. As an alternative, find and describe two ads for the same brand that appear to be directed at different objectives.
2. Visit a supermarket, drugstore, or hardware store, and make a list of all the sales promotion tools that you observe. Describe how each one relates to the sales promotion objectives described in the chapter. Which do you feel are particularly effective, and why?

## NOTES AND REFERENCES

1. Marina Strauss, "Ford Interacts with New Frontier," *Globe and Mail*, April 28, 1994, p. B6; and Jonathan Berry, "What Is an Ad in the Interactive Future?" *International Business Week*, May 2, 1994, p. 43.
2. For additional insight into the characteristics of newspapers as an advertising medium and on developments in the newspaper business, see special sections of *Marketing*, published October 16, 1993, and May 20, 1994.
3. Jim McElgunn, "Boom Times for Specialty Services," *Marketing*, May 16, 1994, p. 16.
4. "TV, Print Still the Most Credible Ad Media," *Marketing*, November 8, 1993, p. 1.
5. David Chilton, "Lands' End Campaign Targets Canadians," *Strategy*, November 1, 1993, p. B4.
6. Bob Mackin Jr., "Take Risks, Find a Niche, and Dare to Be Different," *Marketing*, March 7, 1994, pp. 20-21.
7. See David Bosworth, "Infomercials May See Light of Daytime Television," *Direct Marketing News*, April 1994, pp. 1, 4; Marina Strauss, "Royal to Continue Using Infomercials," *Globe and Mail*, August 11, 1994, p. B5; and Jim McElgunn, "Ford Taps the Power of Infomercials," *Marketing*, March 21, 1994, p. 2; for a comment on the CRTC restrictions on infomercials, see "Who's Afraid of a Good Infomercial?" *Marketing*, March 21, 1994, p. 23.
8. "AdWall Maximizes Computer Technology," *Strategy*, November 1, 1993, p. 7; and Jim McElgunn, "Digital Graffiti It Isn't," *Marketing*, November 8, 1993, p. 2.
9. See Terry Brodie, "A Renaissance in Coupon-Clipping," *Financial Times of Canada*, December 11, 1993, p. 8; and Wayne Mouland, "Coupon Dynamics," *Marketing*, February 14, 1994, p. 17.
10. For additional insight into the nature and management of public relations in Canada, you might wish to refer to a feature report on public relations that appeared in *Marketing*, February 21, 1994, pp. 11-17, and to a report on public relations in the *Globe and Mail*, July 19, 1994, pp. 21-23.

## CASES FOR PART 6

# CASE 6-1

# W. K. BUCKLEY LIMITED (A)

It was April 1985, and Frank Buckley was faced with an important decision concerning the advertising program for Buckley's Mixture for the 1985-86 advertising season. At the suggestion of his advertising agency, Mr. Buckley had done no advertising during 1984-85 for the principal product in the Buckley product line, using that year to conduct consumer research and to prepare an advertising strategy for the future. The research was now complete and Mr. Buckley had received the recommendations of the agency. The approach they were proposing would involve a major departure from the approach that had been used to advertise Buckley's Mixture in the past.

### W. K. BUCKLEY LIMITED

The over-the-counter drug industry is constantly changing. With continuous advances in the treatment of illness, many pharmaceutical products become outdated in a very short time. Continual success of a formula over any extended period in this industry would seem almost impossible. Apparently, W. K. Buckley discovered a product that has maintained its success even after more than 70 years of treating Canadians who suffer from coughs and colds. The product is Buckley's Mixture.

W. K. Buckley Limited is a privately owned, Toronto-based company founded by William K. Buckley in 1920. The founder's son, Frank Buckley, joined the company in 1946 and is the current owner and president. It was 1919 when W. K. Buckley, the owner of a small Toronto drugstore, noticed the increasing popularity of one of his cough remedies. He decided to introduce the product to a wider market as Buckley's Mixture, a sugar-free, expectorant-type, non-prescription product, developed as an effective relief from coughs, colds, and bronchitis. The product was known for its distinctive taste and its effectiveness in combating coughs and colds. Among the ingredients that Mr. Buckley included and that are still found in Buckley's Mixture are ammonium carbonate, potassium bicarbonate, menthol, camphor, Canada Balsam, and pine needle oil. When other over-the-counter preparations were selling at 25 to 35 cents each, Mr. Buckley introduced Buckley's Mixture to the Toronto market at 75 cents. This higher price allowed him to advertise the product widely and gave him a better financial return. He continued this pricing policy when he expanded distribution to a network of retail drugstores in Toronto. Because it was so successful, he also priced Buckley's higher than competitive products when he began to distribute it throughout Ontario.

Although known primarily as the manufacturer of Buckley's Mixture, now available in 100 mL and 200 mL sizes, W. K. Buckley Limited today also produces and distributes a variety of other cough and cold remedies, as well as a veterinary line. Some of the company's other products include Jack and Jill cough syrup, Lemon Time, and Buckley's White Rub. A 1984 report indicated that 65 to 70 percent of Buckley's volume was sold through non-pharmacy outlets, including supermarkets and convenience stores. This was considerably different from sales patterns of cough medicines generally in Canada, as a recent Gallup study revealed that 84.5 percent of cough and cold remedies are sold through drugstores.

W. K. Buckley Limited distributes its products in Canada, the United States, and the Caribbean, and operates under licensing agreements in Australia, New Zealand, and Holland. The company has remained small, employing only 20 people, all at the company's Toronto plant. Brokers and agents are employed on a regional basis across Canada, eliminating the requirement for the company to employ a sales force.

Numerous changes have taken place in the proprietary medicine industry since the introduction of Buckley's Mixture. As the role of the independent drugstore began to

---

 This case was written by Leanne O'Leary and James G. Barnes of Memorial University of Newfoundland. The case was prepared with the co-operation and permission of W. K. Buckley Limited to illustrate the marketing initiatives of that company and not to indicate a correct or incorrect approach to the solution of marketing problems. The authors acknowledge the co-operation and support of Frank C. Buckley, President, John J. Meehan, Vice-President, and David Rieger, Manager of Sales and Marketing, of W. K. Buckley Limited, and Jackie Robertson of Ambrose Carr Linton Kelly, Inc., in the preparation of this case.

decline in the 1960s, large drug supermarkets emerged as the principal outlet for health and personal care products. Another significant change occurred in the 1970s when national and international pharmaceutical companies began to use some of the marketing and creative advertising strategies that had been employed successfully by W. K. Buckley. Fierce competition from large multinational companies and the introduction of many new products to the Canadian market caused a decline in popularity for Buckley's products during the 1970s and early 1980s.

## EARLY MARKETING STRATEGIES

Always one to take advantage of every opportunity, the founder of the company realized the potential that advertising offered for increased sales. During an era when advertising was a relatively new and poorly understood business tool, W. K. Buckley invested in newspaper space and used radio extensively to promote his product. Efficient use of national radio helped establish Buckley's Mixture as a household name in the 1930s and 1940s. Radio spots were purchased adjacent to the news each morning at 8 o'clock, and just before the CBC Noon Farm Broadcast to reach rural areas. Mr. Buckley maintained that this timing and continuity were more economical, equalling more media buys, built market loyalty, and reached his audience. People in rural Canada may be too busy to listen to the radio, but W. K. Buckley knew they stopped everything to listen to the CBC Farm Broadcast. Even today, the sales of Buckley's Mixture in rural Canada reflect the loyalty established over 50 years ago.

The 1920s was a period of rapid growth at W. K. Buckley Limited, with new products introduced and distribution expanded into Quebec, the Maritimes, and the Prairies. With the Depression of the 1930s, the company consolidated its operations in what it did best, the manufacture of cold and cough preparations. By the end of that decade, W. K. Buckley had also recruited commission sales representatives, hand-picked and trained, to establish a sales force for the company's product line. A business graduate from the University of Toronto, Frank Buckley joined the company in 1946, about the same time his father was expanding its operations into international markets, and the domestic market began to pose increasing challenges. The growth of the non-drugstore market was an early indicator of major changes to come later in the decade. Two major changes swept the industry in the 1960s and 1970s: the transition from the small, independent drugstore to the larger drug supermarket, and the impact of marketing and creative advertising strategies on the promotion of the industry and its products. Frank Buckley believed that the 1980s represented an opportunity for his company to return to a "back to the basics" strategy.

## THE MARKET

The Canadian market for cough and cold remedies is highly competitive. In 1984, the industry generated approximately $70 million in sales. Within this total market, the over-the-counter category had remained relatively stable during the preceding 10 years. However, this sector of the market was dominated by large multinational pharmaceutical companies who used their size to gain a lead in product development, media spending, and shelf positioning. The key competitive brands in this industry include Benylin (Parke Davis), Novahistine (Dow), Triaminic (Ancalab), Robitussin (A. H. Robins), Vicks (Proctor & Gamble), and Buckley's Mixture (W. K. Buckley Ltd.).

Exhibit 1 presents some of the results of a 1984 research study of the liquid cough remedy market, carried out with the objective of defining the national market. The research, conducted by Butler Research Associates, using the data collection services of the Gallup National Omnibus, surveyed 2,100 adults across the country in their own homes. The exhibit presents market share and level of awareness data for the top seven brands in the market. Benylin was the leading brand in all five regions of Canada where data were collected. While Vicks had very high levels of awareness, it had considerably lower incidence of usage. The leading brands of cough and cold remedies listed in this exhibit must also compete with antihistamine and cold products, such as Tylenol, Hismanal, Sudafed and Contac-C, for the same consumer dollar.

Buckley's, with an estimated share of market of 5.2 percent nationally, was strongest on the Prairies and in Ontario. The brand held an 8.6 percent share of market among users aged 60 and older, 5.5 percent with those in the 45-to-59 age bracket, but only 3.6 percent among those aged 18 to 29. When asked what they liked most about the product, users of Buckley's Mixture most often referred to its effectiveness, the fact that it relieves cold symptoms and soothes a cough, that it relieves congestion and is fast-acting. When asked to list what they disliked about the product, users mentioned its taste and its bitter, menthol flavour.

Advertising campaigns in the liquid cough remedy industry are conducted primarily in the winter season, when most colds and coughs are likely to occur. Advertising for Buckley's Mixture in the early 1980s was focused on a "tastes strong" message. To a large extent, the advertising budget consisted of national radio spots aimed at the working person (both male and female) in the 39 and over bracket. The advertising was also directed to rural areas where it was thought that most frequent users of Buckley's Mixture lived. Advertisements were also placed in *Reader's Digest* and *TV Guide*. Exhibit 2 presents radio scripts of three commercials for Buckley's Mixture that were used in the early 1980s.

EXHIBIT 1 Research Results
Canadian Cough Remedy Market, 1984

| | Top of Mind | Share of Mind | Total Awareness | Market Share* |
|---|---|---|---|---|
| BUCKLEY'S MIXTURE | 5.4% | 12.1% | 64.6% | 5.2% |
| Benylin | 22.9 | 33.8 | 73.0 | 29.2 |
| Vicks | 19.5 | 36.8 | 86.8 | 14.3 |
| Triaminic | 6.4 | 12.9 | 42.1 | 13.6 |
| Dimetapp | 2.0 | 4.8 | 33.3 | 6.1 |
| Robitussin | 4.1 | 9.1 | 46.8 | 5.8 |
| Novahistine | 1.2 | 3.6 | 45.4 | 4.0 |

* brand bought most recently

In April 1984, a new advertising agency was appointed to handle Buckley's advertising, replacing the previous agency, which had closed operations. The new agency, Ambrose, Carr, DeForest, and Linton, Ltd. of Toronto (later to become Ambrose Carr Linton Kelly, Inc.), determined that, although a specific target market had been defined for Buckley's products, there was no market research to confirm the accuracy of that definition. Considering the recent decline in the market share enjoyed by Buckley's Mixture, Ambrose Carr recommended that, before the $250,000 advertising budget was spent on promotion, it should be determined if the budget was being allocated effectively. Following the suggestion of his new advertising agency, Frank Buckley decided to do no advertising during the 1984-85 season; instead the company commissioned marketing research to learn more about its market.

## RESEARCH RESULTS

The research project was conducted by Butler Research Associates, a Toronto marketing research company, using the data-collection capabilities of the Gallup National Omnibus service. The data were collected during a two-week period in November 1984. The project was a national survey and involved interviews with 2,100 adults, 18 years of age and over, in their own homes, in population centres of at least 1,000. A random block sampling procedure was used in urban centres, and a quota sample based on sex and age in rural areas. The research objectives established for this project included: (1) determining the level of awareness and share of market of Buckley's Mixture and of competitive brands; (2) determining the strengths and weaknesses of Buckley's Mixture; (3) examining the usage and purchase patterns of the users of liquid cough remedies; and (4) developing a profile of Buckley's users. Some of the significant findings were:

- The liquid-cough-remedy market was strongest in Ontario and Quebec, which together represented 63.1 percent of users.
- The largest user segments were 18 to 44 years of age (67.2 percent) and families with children (55.4 percent).
- 52 percent of respondents had a cold during the 1983-84 winter.
- 75 percent of cough sufferers decided on and bought their own remedy.
- 66 percent of cough and cold remedies were bought by an individual for his/her own use.
- Almost all purchases were made after a cough and/or cold had started.
- The market was not homogeneous nationally and brand preferences differed across regions.
- Usage of and preference for Vicks was skewed towards the younger age segment (18 to 19).
- Benylin and Triaminic had the highest incidence of usage among families with children.
- Approximately 85 percent of liquid cough remedies are purchased in drugstores, and this statistic is even higher in urban centres.
- The most recent purchase was made by the female head of the household (73 percent).
- Consumers do not generally stock cough syrup, preferring to purchase it as required.

The research revealed some valuable information for the marketing of Buckley's Mixture. From the research, Frank Buckley and the creative staff of Ambrose Carr concluded that Buckley's Mixture was performing best in small communities (population fewer than 30,000), sales were skewed towards the less well educated, were strongest in the Prairies and Ontario, but were extremely weak in Quebec. Preference for Buckley's Mixture tended to be strongest among males and the oldest age segment. The research revealed that the total awareness of Buckley's was 64.6 percent, but the brand's market share was only 5.2 percent nationally. This invited the conclusion that Buckley's Mixture was either failing to elicit trial among consumers or failing to deliver after trial and was not being repurchased. Among current users, the strongest feature of Buckley's Mixture was its effectiveness in relieving coughs and congestion. This attribute was mentioned significantly more often by Buckley's users than by users of other liquid cough remedies. Buckley's sugar-free feature, however, was not particularly important to users in general or to Buckley's users.

In addition to the quantitative Gallup survey, W. K. Buckley Limited also commissioned a qualitative study of the market. A series of focus groups were conducted, two each in Montreal and Toronto. The principal objectives of the focus group discussions were to reveal usage and purchase patterns, identify key variables influencing brand selection, and determine the perceptions of and attitudes towards Buckley's Mixture in relation to competing brands. Consumers appeared to be loyal to a specific brand, with neither the price nor the ingredients of the product being particularly important in the selection of the brand. The discussions revealed that differences in usage patterns appeared not to be related to gender or culture. In most cases, consumers revealed that they used one brand for children and a different brand for adults. Heavy users of cough remedies were more likely than were light users to believe that the products were effective in dealing with a cold or cough. When the preferred brand could not be purchased, a pharmacist was consulted for recommendations. It was also noted that few consumers purchased liquid cough remedies on the basis of packaging.

The qualitative research revealed some key factors about Buckley's Mixture. Most of the participants recognized the brand, though few had tried the product recently. The focus group participants commented that the name had a connotation of old-fashioned reliability, trustworthiness, and security. Its major strengths, as indicated by focus group participants, included effective, old-fashioned strength, based on its sugar-free, natural ingredients. The participants commented that the product works well as a decongestant, coats the throat, and does not cause drowsiness. They also discussed the brand's weaknesses, which included its aroma, colour, taste, and consistency.

**EXHIBIT 2 Radio Commercial Scripts — Buckley's Mixture**

1:
SOUNDS OF TRAFFIC IN BACKGROUND
CAB DRIVER:

"I drive a cab, and when I get a cough from a cold, I don't want to cough all over the customers.

"I take Buckley's Mixture, 'cause it works. It checks my coughing, but it doesn't stop me driving. Buckley's loosens congestion, helps me breathe easy, and clears that stuffy feeling; you know what I mean?

"Personally, I take it straight, but some people mix it with honey. Either way, when you take Buckley's Mixture, you know you've taken cough medicine.

"It tastes strong (HORN BLOWS) but it beats coughing."

2:
SOUND OF VACUUM CLEANER IN BACKGROUND
HOMEMAKER:

"When I get a cough from a cold, I take Buckley's Mixture, because it works and you can't let a cough stop you when there are meals to cook and children to worry about.

"Buckley's Mixture loosens congestion and helps clear that stuffy, chesty feeling. It helps during the day, and it helps at night.

"No point pretending I like the taste; I don't. So, I mix it with honey. Even so, you know you've taken cough medicine when you take Buckley's.

"It tastes strong, but it beats coughing."

3.
SOUNDS OF FACTORY MACHINERY OPERATING IN BACKGROUND
EQUIPMENT OPERATOR:

"When I get a cough from a cold, I take Buckley's Mixture; because it works and because you can't operate machinery if you are coughing all the time.

"Buckley's loosens congestion, helps me breathe without wheezing and spluttering. It checks my coughing, but it doesn't stop me working, and it's sugar-free, which is important to me.

"The thing is that when you've taken Buckley's Mixture, you know you've taken cough medicine.

"It tastes strong (WHISTLE BLOWS) but it sure beats coughing."

## CONCLUSIONS

Once the research had been conducted and results analyzed, a strategy document presented to the Buckley management team by Ambrose Carr in March 1985 identified five key problems with Buckley's Mixture that were apparent from the consumer research:

1. Low top-of-mind awareness,
2. Low rate of trial,
3. Low awareness of its strength and effectiveness,
4. Perception of the product as being old-fashioned,
5. Negative perception of the taste, aroma, and texture.

After a comprehensive review of the results of both the national study and the qualitative focus groups, Peter Byrne, creative director of Ambrose Carr, presented several advertising campaign recommendations to Frank Buckley and his management team. One of the suggested campaigns involved Frank Buckley promoting his own product. This would continue the tradition of a face behind the name of W. K. Buckley Limited, a tradition that had been maintained over seven decades. The agency believed that Frank Buckley would portray the desired image of an honest businessman who believes in the effectiveness of his product and who promotes it on the basis of its true attributes. Another proposal was intended to turn the negative perceptions of the strong taste, aroma, and texture of Buckley's Mixture into positive aspects for the promotion efforts. The proposal from the agency involved the use of humorous phrases to illustrate the "awful" taste of Buckley's Mixture, simultaneously establishing it as an effective remedy.

## QUESTIONS

1. What objectives should Frank Buckley and his management team have in determining the marketing program to support Buckley's Mixture in 1985-86?
2. As a fairly small company, operating in an industry where the competition consists primarily of large companies with many products in their product lines, what strategy would be most appropriate for Mr. Buckley to adopt for Buckley's Mixture?
3. Considering the recent slippage in the market share of Buckley's Mixture and the limited advertising budget available to W. K. Buckley Limited, would you recommend to Frank Buckley that he accept the recommendations of his advertising agency?
4. What are the implications for Mr. Buckley of appearing in his own advertising and of promoting negative aspects of the product? What consumer or market characteristics or trends would such an approach address?

# CASE 6-2

# THE TEA COUNCIL OF CANADA (A)

The Tea Council of Canada is a not-for-profit organization with an international flavour. The concept of a tea council emerged in 1954 when the International Tea Agreement lapsed and was not renewed. Under that agreement, the International Tea Market Extension Board (ITMEB) had promoted tea globally. Major tea producers felt the need to continue the work started by the ITMEB, in co-operation with the tea trade in importing companies.

The Tea Council of Canada was among the first collaborative efforts to be established and, in 1954, it undertook the job of generic tea promotion. The council, funded by Sri Lanka and India as producer members, was chartered and supported by well-known tea importers and processors, including Salada, Brooke Bond, Lipton, and Mother Parker's. The council had since expanded its membership to include Kenya, Nestlé Enterprises, Northern Tea, North American Tea and Coffee, Inc., National Importers Canada Limited, and the Tetley Tea Company. Members of the council serve on its various committees and as financial supporters of its promotional programs.

In 1981, the Tea Council embarked on a planned promotional program with concentrated activities in four key areas: promotion and publicity, school education, special events, and the food services sector. These activities have come to be known as the "core program." Several committees within the council help ensure that the continuity and synergy of message are maintained under this program. These committees are the Marketing Committee, the Food Service Committee, and the Tea Grading Committee.

## THE TEA INDUSTRY

Just as the Tea Council has experienced changes over the years, so too has the tea industry as a whole. Although Europe (especially Britain) and tea often seem synonymous, tea originated in China. The first tea pots on record were discovered near Shanghai around 1500 A.D. Tea was then produced by India, Sri Lanka, and Java and these nations soon became major tea producers for the world's consumers. The first tea to arrive in Canada was brought by the Hudson's Bay Company to its trading posts as early as 1716. It soon became one of the company's most important trading commodities.

It was not until the end of the nineteenth century, however, that producers began to package tea in the now familiar tea bag. Today, many types, varieties, and blends of tea in tea bags are enjoyed daily in Canada. The industry has also become highly competitive, with an increased number of companies competing for segments of the market. A number of packaging innovations, including drinking boxes, envelope packs, and round tea bags, have been introduced by companies in an effort to carve out a larger share of the tea market.

## TRENDS IN TEA CONSUMPTION

Herbal and specialty teas have been enjoying a growth in popularity in the Canadian market in recent years. A study conducted in 1990 detailed a 5-to-7 percent annual increase in sales in this sector of the market. This positive movement has been a welcome development from the perspective of the tea industry as hot-drink consumption, and more specifically regular black tea consumption, has shown a clear downward trend since 1985. Black tea is also known as Orange Pekoe, and the term is used to describe domestic blends marketed by the various tea packers. Generally, hot beverages are losing sales to cold, light, unsweetened drinks. This is in part a result of dramatically increased promotion and publicity by marketers of certain drinks within the beverage industry, including milk, soft drinks, fruit juices, and mineral waters.

During the period from 1980 to 1988, tea sales in retail grocery stores declined from 26 percent to 21 percent of the beverage market, while coffee experienced a drop from 36 percent to 31 percent. During this same period, however, soft drink sales jumped from 17 percent to 23 percent, and juice and other non-alcoholic beverages climbed from 20 percent to 24 percent of this market.

---

© 1991. This case was written by Robert Power and Leanne O'Leary of Memorial University of Newfoundland, under the direction of Dr. James G. Barnes. The case was prepared with the co-operation and permission of the Tea Council of Canada to illustrate the marketing initiatives of that organization and not to indicate a correct or incorrect approach to the solution of marketing problems. The authors acknowledge the co-operation and support of Gordon F. Reynolds, Executive Director of the Tea Council of Canada, in preparation of this case.

In an industry that claims overall worldwide growth in tea volume per year of approximately 3 percent, Canada still manages to remain one of the world's leading tea-consuming nations with a per capita consumption of 1.6 pounds (0.72 kg) annually or the equivalent of one cup per day. In fact, Canada is the foremost tea-drinking country in the western hemisphere. While this may be true, Canadian consumption has seen better days. The mid-1970s saw annual tea consumption in Canada hit an all-time high of 1.3 kg per person. Canadian consumption is well behind that of residents of Qatar, a part of the United Arab Emirates. This nation consumes 12 pounds (5.4 kg) of tea annually or the equivalent of eight cups per person per day.

## THE MARKETING COMMITTEE'S PROPOSAL

In 1981, the Tea Council of Canada embarked on a planned promotional program with concentrated activities in three key areas. Members agreed that tea was likely to gain in image and consumption from improved awareness, through the provision of information about social, cultural, geographic, and historic implications of the tea industry. The promotional activities of the council were, therefore, geared to increasing general knowledge and attitudes, as well as improving the quality of tea and service in the out-of-home market.

For some time, however, there had existed a desire among some Tea Council members to test the effectiveness of a carefully planned, strategically defined, generic advertising campaign. In late 1989, the marketing committee of the Tea Council of Canada developed a proposal outlining their goals and methodology to undertake such a campaign. Following some revisions, the proposal was approved by the board of directors and each council member was assessed incremental funding of 0.25 cents per pound (0.45 kg), in addition to their regular contribution; this yielded approximately $250,000. While this funding certainly helped defray the costs associated with the project, the campaign would be primarily funded from core program budgets in 1990 and 1991.

Having received the approval of the board, the marketing committee began by undertaking a comprehensive usage and attitude study of the Canadian population. In conducting this research, the objective of the committee was to obtain information that would allow them to develop the marketing and communications strategy for their future promotional campaign. The research was conducted by the Custom Research Division of ISL — International Surveys Limited. The objectives of the research were to:

1. ascertain the prevalent images and attitudes that exist towards tea and tea drinking, and
2. test with consumers several strategic concepts in order to provide direction regarding an advertising and communications approach for tea in the near future.

In order to achieve this, a telephone survey was conducted in which randomly selected individuals were surveyed. The following quotas were followed in selecting the sample for the survey:

1. 60 percent of respondents were to be female and 40 percent male;
2. a total of 600 interviews were to be completed in five regional markets as follows: Halifax, Calgary, and Vancouver, 100 each; Montreal and Toronto, 150 each;
3. 54 percent of respondents were to drink tea daily; 18 percent at least weekly; and 28 percent at least occasionally.

## SUMMARY OF FINDINGS

Upon completion of the research, the conclusions presented by ISL reaffirmed some known facts and also provided key directional information for the council's marketing committee. The following conclusions were a result of the ISL research:

1. Hot drink consumption, and more specifically the consumption of tea, has been in decline since 1985.
2. Water, fruit juice, and milk appear to be the most obvious growth beverages.
3. While tea is not currently viewed as an overly healthy beverage, it clearly carries some health-related connotations.
4. Positioning tea on a health platform would require a considerable effort and a substantial budget since it would necessitate the changing of currently held beliefs, rather than the reinforcement of existing ones.
5. Promoting tea among those aged 60 and over had obvious limitations and promoting it among those aged under 30 means competing in a group of beverages that is already heavily targeted by competing products. The 30-to-49 age segment would therefore appear to be the most appropriate segment on which to concentrate.
6. With limited resources, the most appropriate strategy may be to focus on the soothing, refreshing, and natural taste elements against an executional background of health.
7. Recognizing the move by Canadians towards cold drinks, it may still be best to sell tea on the basis of what it is, a hot drink.

Other life-style research available to the Tea Council provided additional insights and input into the development of the committee's strategies. One survey, for example, found that consumers believe that life is too chaotic and turbulent and that people are looking for anchors and controls of life. Today, consumers want to "relax and take the edge off." People are searching for balance and moderation in their lives.

Another survey found people are working long hours, experiencing high levels of stress, and spending little time with their families. Women, in particular, are juggling the demands of a career and family. Unfortunately, consumers' real and perceived time pressures are likely to get worse during the next decade.

Having reached these conclusions, the council's marketing committee proceeded to prepare their case for approval of a formal promotional campaign for presentation to the board of directors.

## QUESTIONS

1. As chairman of the board of directors of the Tea Council of Canada, would you approve the council launching an advertising and promotional campaign designed to increase consumption of tea among Canadians?
2. What do you feel the objectives of such a campaign should be?
3. To whom should such a campaign be directed and what should be its principal messages and components?

# CASE 6-3

# THE SALVATION ARMY RED SHIELD APPEAL (B)

As meetings between the senior public relations staff of the Salvation Army and its advertising agency, BBDO Canada, continued through 1993, it became obvious that a new approach to advertising the Red Shield Appeal would be necessary for 1994. The prolonged economic downturn being experienced in Canada had meant that the demands being placed upon the Salvation Army for assistance were increasing to the point where more resources were needed.

Finally, in late 1993, a decision was reached to depart somewhat from the slogans that had been used during the past nine years (see the Salvation Army Red Shield Appeal (A) case for background information on the Red Shield Appeal and earlier advertising campaigns). The overt reference to God which had been used in recent advertising was deleted in favour of a more straightforward, aggressive appeal for funds in light of the increased needs being addressed by the Salvation Army on behalf of these people who were being affected by the prolonged economic downturn in Canada. The slogan adopted for the 1994 campaign, which The Army and its agency expected to be used for two or three years, was "Help us help others."

The "Help us help others" slogan was arrived at after many other slogans and themes had been developed and screened by agency and Salvation Army personnel at various levels in the organizations. Elwes observed that "Help us help others" was found to be the most simple and direct communication, expressing a call to action that was in keeping with the strategic decision to be less subtle in asking for donations. While the slogan was direct and easily understood, much of what The Salvation Army stands for was to be communicated through the execution of the various advertising materials.

As Julian Elwes prepared to involve his creative people at BBDO Canada in the preparation of the 1994 Red Shield Appeal advertising, he issued to his staff the communications brief presented in Exhibit 1. This brief was intended to clarify the objectives and desired effect of the 1994 advertising campaign.

## THE 1994 RED SHIELD APPEAL CAMPAIGN

Centred on the theme "Help us help others," the 1994 Red Shield Appeal campaign was launched in April 1994 to support the annual door-to-door canvass "Blitz Night" on May 2, 1994. The co-ordinated preparation of the various media materials included television and radio commercials, newspaper and magazine advertisements, and transit, outdoor and mall posters. While the campaign focused on the six-week period leading up to "Blitz Night," BBDO Canada expected the materials to be used throughout the year as advertising media across Canada provided the Salvation Army with public service announcements and donated advertising time and space. The total budget for the development of the commercials and other advertising materials and for paid media time was set at less than $700,000 for 1994, with less than half that amount being devoted to production, an amount that could be amortized by the Salvation Army over three or four years. BBDO Canada expected that the total value of advertising the Salvation Army would obtain would total close to $1.4 million when the contributions of free time and space by the various media are taken into consideration.

Examples of print advertisements developed by BBDO Canada for the 1994 Red Shield Appeal campaign are presented in Exhibit 2.

## QUESTIONS

1. Consider the decision to adopt "Help us help others" as the slogan for the 1994 Red Shield Appeal. Does this slogan accomplish the objectives of the Salvation Army and its advertising agency in light of the changing environment in which the Army is operating?
2. Evaluate the execution of the print and television advertising materials against the objectives of both the Salvation Army and its advertising agency. How would you propose to evaluate the success of these advertising materials in accomplishing these objectives?
3. What are the aspects of the Red Shield Appeal advertising campaign that makes it different from most client-agency relationships and from situations that would likely apply in the marketing of most products and services in the private sector?

---

Copyright © 1995 by James G. Barnes and Kerry Lynn Chaytor, Memorial University of Newfoundland. This case has been prepared as a basis for class discussion and is not intended to reflect either an effective or ineffective handling of a management problem. The authors wish to thank Lt. Col. Mel Bond of the Salvation Army and Julian Elwes of BBDO Canada for their support and assistance in the preparation of this case.

EXHIBIT 1

# THE SALVATION ARMY
# "HELP US HELP OTHERS" RED SHIELD CAMPAIGN
# COMMUNICATIONS BRIEF

**PURPOSE:**

(Specifically, what do we want consumers to do as a result of seeing the advertising?)

To heighten awareness of the Salvation Army and solicit donations via its annual Red Shield Appeal. To persuade the target group to make generous financial contributions to the Red Shield Appeal. This is two-pronged in that we want existing donors to maintain/increase their contributions *and* we want to motivate new donors.

**TARGET AUDIENCE:**

(Who are they — demographics? What are they like — psychographics, attitudes, values? What are their current beliefs about the category and the brand?)

All adults with additional skew towards 18-34. Broad income and education base. English and French.

**MEDIA:**

National — TV, radio, magazines, newspaper, transit, outdoor, mall posters. Campaign start date April 18. House to house canvass is "Blitz Night," Monday, May 2, 1994.

**BACKGROUND:**

The Salvation Army develops a new Red Shield Appeal campaign every four or five years. The 1994 campaign is designed to be harder hitting, i.e., with greater emotional appeal, because:

1. Downturn in economy has led to higher unemployment, greater need for welfare and therefore, overall, a significant increase in demands for Salvation Army services. Without dramatic increase in contributions there will be a significant shortfall in public demand/Army services supply.
2. Competitive charities are proliferating.

**PROMISE:**

(What is the single most important performance or emotional reward we are promising the target for buying/trying the product/service?)

Our target audience should feel that by making a financial donation they are signifcantly contributing to helping fulfil the needs of others less fortunate. Possibly, one day, it could be themselves or a relative/friend.

**SUPPORT:**

(Why they should believe what we say?)

The work of the Salvation Army is widely acknowledged and oftentimes the caring support the Army provides has personally touched the lives of our target group. There is great credibility in the ministry of the Army.

**DESIRED RESPONSE:**

(How do we want the consumer to respond or feel after seeing the advertising? How will it reinforce or alter his or her current beliefs?)

Existing donors should maintain/increase their annual contribution; new donors should be motivated to contribute. Make a difference — act now — make a donation and contribute to the caring of the less fortunate.

**RED SHIELD PERSONALITY/ PROFILE:**

(What characteristics does the Red Shield Appeal have that distinguish it from competitors? Is there anything we need to modify?)

Unlike other fund-raising drives, charity appeals, etc., NRSA has a religious motivation, its workers are genuinely caring people, and the services provided have high visibility and extreme credibility. Funds raised by the appeal are used to legitimately reduce suffering and provide encouragement and care for those less fortunate in life.

**COMMENTS:**

(What constraints, restrictions — legal or otherwise — do we need to consider?)

Funds for creative development and media placement are limited and traditionally have been bolstered by generous voluntary contributions of time by talent, production and recording studios, and the media (P.S.A.s, bonus outdoor postings, etc.).

*Creative materials requiring development include:*

2 English and 2 French TV spots (minimum)
2 English and 2 French Radio spots (minimum)

Newspaper/magazine ads — English and French
Outdoor paper — English and French
Transit — Interior and Bus Shelters — English and French
Direct Mail — English and French

EXHIBIT 2

OUR SOLDIERS
ARE EXPERTS IN
HAND TO HAND COMBAT.
THE SALVATION ARMY
S
S
HELP US HELP OTHERS.
THE SALVATION ARMY

# CASE 6-4

# ADVERTISING: A REFLECTION OR A SHAPER OF SOCIETY'S VALUES?

The typical North American consumer watches television for nearly 30 hours a week. In the course of a year, the average person also listens to 1,200 hours of radio, spends 180 hours reading newspapers, and 110 hours reading magazines. Of course, all these media include advertising that the viewer, listener, or reader sees or hears. Advertising messages are also presented to consumers on billboards, through the mail, on buses, taxis, and subway trains — some say, nearly everywhere you look. In fact, the average American consumer will see or hear more than 7 million ads in a lifetime. The average Canadian consumer will see or hear about 25% to 35% fewer.

The ultimate goal of advertising by for-profit organizations is to sell products. The goal is accomplished by informing, persuading, and reminding current and prospective customers. There are many who question what advertising attempts to do and the way it does it. In fact, for nearly as long as there has been advertising, there have been debates over its impact on society.

One category of criticisms is economic in nature. The main economic questions deal with the effects of advertising on competition and prices. In terms of competition, critics contend that the huge amounts of advertising done by large firms simply overwhelm smaller competitors. Through their advertising, large firms capture the attention of consumers and thereby may prevent smaller or new firms from being noticed. If this is true, advertising may serve as a barrier to new firms entering a market, restricting competition to the detriment of consumers. The counterargument is that consumers are not so gullible that they will accept heavily advertised brands that do not meet their needs. Advertising may get people to try a product once, but if they are dissatisfied, they will look elsewhere the next time the need arises.

The other major economic argument concerns the effect of advertising on prices. Obviously, advertising has to be paid for in the price consumers pay for a product. According to this argument, advertised products cost more than unadvertised products. The question is whether the additional cost is justified in terms of the benefits produced by the advertising. Few would argue with the informative role of advertising. Finding out when and where a product is available, its price, and its features through advertising saves consumers a considerable amount of time and effort.

However, critics contend that the purpose of much of advertising is not information, but persuasion; that all it does is shift demand back and forth among brands that are essentially the same while adding to the total cost of the products. The counterargument suggests that advertising can actually result in lower prices. If advertising can expand the market for a product by causing more people to purchase it, a firm will produce larger quantities and achieve economies of scale that result in lower unit costs. These cost savings can then be passed along to consumers in the form of lower prices.

All sides of these debates can cite specific instances to support their particular positions. Thus there is no clear, generalizable answer to the question of whether advertising always has a positive or a negative economic impact.

Another question that may be even murkier is the social role of advertising. Even if it contributes to the economic good, there are those who feel that advertising has socially undesirable effects. Several of the criticisms are described below.

- Advertising emphasizes materialism. As was mentioned, the ultimate objective of advertising is to create a sale. Thus, by its very nature, product advertising focuses on material pursuits. It does this by communicating the message that the consumption of goods and services solves problems and provides happiness. Critics contend, however, that advertising goes beyond just selling goods and services to moulding values as well. Because advertising

---

Sources: Richard W. Pollay, "The Distorted Mirror: Reflections on the Unintended Consequences of Advertising," *Journal of Marketing*, April 1986, pp. 18-36; Morris B. Holbrook, "Mirror, Mirror, on the Wall, What's Unfair in the Reflections on Advertising?" *Journal of Marketing*, July 1987, pp. 95-103; Richard W. Pollay, "On the Value of Reflections on the Values in 'The Distorted Mirror,'" *Journal of Marketing*, July 1987, pp. 104-110; William L. Wilkie, *Consumer Behavior*, 2nd ed., John Wiley, New York, 1991, pp. 545-552.

presents the same materialistic messages so frequently in such a professional, convincing fashion, consumers come to accept them as the norm or standard of correct behaviour. As a result, people judge their worth and the worth of others by what and how much they own.

- Advertising is intrusive. Before an ad can have any effect, it must get your attention. Thus, one feature of all advertising is that it intrudes on whatever else you may be doing. Some critics complain that it is virtually impossible to escape advertising. Not only is it in the media, it is printed on clothing, posted in public restrooms, broadcast to telephone users on hold, included on rented videotapes, plastered on sports scoreboards, and placed everywhere else advertisers feel consumers might see or hear it. Some feel there is so much advertising that consumers have become immune to its messages. Because advertising is always around in one form or another, consumers learn to ignore it. Others contend that there is so much advertising that consumers no longer question it. Instead, they just passively accept it and the messages it carries. How else, they ask, do jingles, slogans, and selling phrases get lodged in our heads without any conscious effort?
- Advertising is exploitive. The effectiveness of many ads depends on their ability to provoke an emotional response. The response can be a positive emotion such as generosity, affection, patriotism, security, or sociability. However, advertising also often plays on people's anxieties and fears as well as the darker side of a person's personality. Self-doubt, insecurity, envy, rejection, greed, and lust are common appeals. In a similar vein, advertising disguises self-indulgence as a virtue. A self-indulgent life-style is rationalized with slogans about having earned rewards through hard work ("You deserve a break today") or for just being alive ("You only go around once").
- Advertising creates unrealistic images. The portrayal of the ideal man or woman in advertising is based on physical appearance and social status. These messages create simplistic stereotypes of what it takes to be happy and successful. As a result, consumers develop superficial criteria for evaluating themselves and others.
- Advertising employs bad taste and contributes to a lower standard of decency. In advertising, nothing is sacred or private. Almost any bodily function, physical discomfort, or issue of hygiene is fair game to be graphically described and discussed. The use of sexual themes and innuendos, provocative poses, and scantily clad models to attract attention and make products seem desirable often exceeds the boundaries of good taste.
- Advertising exploits the naïveté of children. Advertisers recognize that children influence many of the purchases of their parents as well as spend a considerable amount of money themselves. As a result, firms try to take advantage of the lack of sophistication of children in encouraging the unrestrained consumption of junk food, overstating the pleasure that can be derived from toys and other products, and creating materialistic values.
- Advertising promotes distrust and cynicism. It is generally and even legally accepted that advertisers can engage in "puffery." That is a nice way of saying that advertisers are allowed to exaggerate the truth. The result is that, over time, puffery in advertising has instilled in consumers a tolerance for distortion and deception. The critics reason, if advertising can convey half-truths and misleading statements, then why shouldn't it be acceptable in all communications? And if that is the case, it behooves us all to be distrustful of communicators, regardless of their position or status.

The counterargument to these criticisms is that advertising is intended to sell products, not to shape the values of society. It can be effective only if it is accepted by the audience, and that will happen only if it reflects society's norms and beliefs. If advertising presents images that are contrary to values, it will be rejected along with the product it is selling. Thus, advertising — for better or worse — is a reflection of society.

## QUESTIONS

1. What should be the role of advertising in a free-enterprise economy?
2. How legitimate are the concerns that critics of advertising have expressed?
3. What, if anything, should be done about these concerns?

PART

7

# MANAGING THE MARKETING EFFORT

**Implementing a company's international marketing program, examining the issues involved in not-for-profit marketing, evaluating a company's total performance, appraising the role of marketing in our society today, and considering what it may be tomorrow**

Up to this point, we have dealt separately with how a firm selects its target markets and then develops and manages the four elements of its marketing mix for those markets. Now we bring those separate areas together as we present an overview of an organization's total marketing program.

We will apply the basic management process to a company's international marketing program in Chapter 21. In Chapter 22, we will examine not-for-profit marketing from a total marketing perspective. Following on the strategic planning stage introduced in Chapter 3, we will discuss the implementation and evaluation stages of the management process in Chapter 23. Then, in the final chapter, we will appraise the current position of marketing in our socioeconomic system and consider where marketing is headed.

# CHAPTER 21 GOALS

In selling abroad, a firm is often faced with cultural, economic, and legal systems that are quite different from those in its home country. Thus it must understand and adapt to a new and unfamiliar environment. Furthermore, for the firm interested in international marketing, its level of involvement can range from simply selling goods that will be exported to investing abroad. Thus we need to examine international marketing in some detail.

After studying this chapter, you should have an understanding of:

- The importance of international marketing to firms and countries.
- The impact of the macroenvironmental factors of culture, economics, and political/legal forces on international marketing.
- Alternative organizational structures for operating in foreign markets.
- Strategic considerations in formulating international marketing programs.
- The role of trade balances in international marketing.

Colin Korte

CHAPTER 21

# INTERNATIONAL MARKETING

## Success in Foreign Markets Requires Close Partnerships

Japan is frequently viewed as one of the toughest international markets to enter. But Canadian marketers are learning that despite the language barrier, despite the legal complexities involved in operating there, and despite the complexities and subtleties of distribution and retailing, bending over backwards to provide the best quality and service does bring success.

Develcon Electronics Ltd., based in Saskatoon, manufactures a computer hardware device called a local area network bridge-router. This device allows two different PC networks to communicate with each other. With the North American market slowing down in growth in the last few years, Develcon looked to markets outside Canada and the United States to maintain and increase its volume and profits. Develcon targeted the Japanese market for its export expansion strategy and began the search for distribution. Relationship marketing is an element of being successful in Japan and meeting, knowing, and getting along with the "right" people is a crucial part of gaining market access. "You have to choose your distributor carefully," says Don Friesen, Develcon's marketing director. "You can't afford to start a relationship with one distributor, dump him, and then try another one." Develcon was careful in choosing and is relentless in maintaining a good relationship with its three distributors located in Tokyo.

This means that Colin Korte, Develcon's Asia Pacific sales representative, visits with his distributors four times a year. He meets each distributor for a full day of conferences dealing with plans, program and product information, and sales call analysis discussions. Korte says that "when you keep the relationship close and open, the distributors feel like they are an important part of our sales team, and that arms them with the knowledge they require to succeed and equally important, motivates them." This is important since two-way communication gets difficult when one is using phones and faxes across 16 time zones. "They're interested in hearing what Canadians are doing, updates on promotions and new features. It's a good time to clear the air and hear them when we're getting beat up on," he says.

Korte's working day with his distributors ends with three-hour dinners where he frequently meets with resellers as well. This Japanese ritual allows business colleagues to develop a more personal relationship with each other and strong loyalties can develop. The evening, however, can be expensive, $600 to $1,200, and this can strain the budget of a small firm. But results are worth waiting for; more than 60 percent of Develcon's revenues now come from exports. Over the last three years, Japanese sales have exceeded $1 million and revenues are growing at over 8 percent per year. The real benefits lie in being able to expand production, sales, and profits at a time when the home market is growing very slowly.[1]

## THE ATTRACTION OF INTERNATIONAL MARKETING

What do we mean by international marketing? An organization whose products are marketed in two or more countries is engaged in **international marketing**. The fundamentals of marketing apply to international marketing in the same way they apply to domestic marketing.

Canadians have known for a long time that our economic welfare depended, to an important degree, on our success as international traders and marketers. For many years, our exports have ranged from 22 to 25 percent of our gross national product, compared with such current proportions as 6 percent for the United States, 17 percent for France, 26 percent for Germany, 44 percent for the Netherlands, 19 percent for the United Kingdom, and 10 percent for Japan. Clearly, how we do abroad is important to our welfare.

Our most important markets continue to be: (1) the United States — accounting for about 75 percent of our international trade; (2) Japan with 7 percent; (3) the European Union (EU) countries with 7 percent and, (4) all other countries of the world with about 11 percent. These proportions have not changed appreciably in the last few years. The overwhelming importance of the American market to each and every one of us is clearly obvious. A very high proportion of the sales made to the United States are of a business marketing nature involving raw materials, components, and parts rather than completely fabricated products. Direct consumer marketing activity plays a minor but growing role. Both forms of international marketing, business and consumer, are increasingly being pursued by more and more Canadian firms as our home market becomes more competitive and as the attractiveness of United States and other opportunities becomes more apparent.

International marketing is a two-way street, however. The same expanding foreign markets that offer growth opportunities for Canadian firms also have their own producers. Foreign firms are providing substantial competition in Canada, the United States, and abroad. Consumers in Canada and around the world have responded favourably, for example, to Japanese radio and TV products (Sony), motorcycles (Yamaha), cameras (Canon, Nikon), and autos (Nissan, Toyota). We continue to buy Italian shoes, German autos, Dutch electric razors, French wines, Austrian skis, Swiss watches, Chinese textiles, and so on. And we increasingly make our purchases in U.S.-owned retail outlets such as The Gap, Wal-Mart, and A & P.

## DOMESTIC MARKETING AND INTERNATIONAL MARKETING

Marketing fundamentals are universally applicable. Every preceding chapter can be applied in an international context. Whether ATCO, an Alberta firm that produces portable and mobile homes and buildings, sells in Toronto, Trois Rivières, Toledo, Taiwan, or Timbuktu, its marketing program should be built around a good product that is properly priced, promoted, and distributed to a market that has been carefully selected. However, strategies used to implement marketing programs in foreign countries often need to be quite different from domestic marketing strategies. And, of course, the international strategies have to be developed in the context of the domestic ones.

Canada's historic major foreign market has been the United States. Because of language, cultural, and social similarities between English-speaking Canadians and Americans, the American market has not been perceived as being very foreign — although it qualifies as such since it is another country. At the same time, the Quebec market — as described in Chapter 6 — is not usually perceived as being foreign. And yet, except for the legal and monetary status of Quebec, the province exhibits for companies outside that province many of the characteristics of a foreign market. As Canadians, we are able to have a unique perspective on international marketing and its opportunities and pitfalls. We engage in "near" international marketing domestically in Quebec with all the problems of translation, different meanings, different values, and different preferences — and we have seen examples of how well or badly we have recognized the differences. On the other hand, we also seem to engage in "near" domestic marketing internationally when dealing with the United States. Here again, we have seen examples of how we have failed to recognize differences.

Our domestic history provides us with a basic message: we have two major language and culture groups and numerous smaller ones; insofar as we recognize our multiculturalism in domestic marketing strategies and tactics, this provides us with the ability to do so in an international marketing context. For us, compared with many other countries that are much more homogeneous domestically, there is no reason not to be sensitive to the nuances of international marketing and less reason not to be successful at it. We have the domestic advantages and experience to deal with such issues as understanding foreign markets, determining the strategic question of degree of involvement in them, and being able to organize for operating in each.

Canadian firms move beyond the domestic market into international ones for several reasons. The first is simply the existence of foreign markets, with the biggest single one being right next to us. There is a strong demand for a wide variety of consumer products in the developed nations of the world. And within the developing as well as the developed nations of the world, there is a demand for business products such as machine tools, construction equipment, and business and consumer software.

Second, as domestic markets become saturated, producers — even those with no previous international experience — look to foreign markets. Labatt Breweries found U.S. and British markets highly attractive, in part due to strong competitors such as Molson and Fosters of Australia.

Third, some countries possess unique natural or human resources that give them a **comparative advantage** when it comes to producing particular products. This factor, for example, explains South Africa's dominance in diamonds, and the ability of developing countries in Asia with low wage rates to compete successfully in products assembled by hand. It also explains the high proportion of resources in our exports to the United States and elsewhere.

Another factor in international expansion is the possession of a **technological advantage**. In one country a particular industry, often encouraged by government and spurred by the efforts of a few firms, develops a technological advantage over the rest of the world.

**M&M/Mars may not have a technological or comparative advantage, but the worldwide love of chocolate creates an international marketing opportunity.**

For example, the Spar Aerospace-produced Canadarm appeals to niche markets around the world. We are world leaders in specialized aspects of marine and geo-physical measurement devices as well as pollution control devices. Who has the general technological advantage today? An index of technological strength, based on the number and quality of patents granted in a year, has been developed by *Business Week* magazine. In 1991, the four highest scores in the world went to Japanese firms (Toshiba, Hitachi, Canon, and Mitsubishi), and all the top 10 were either Japanese or U.S. firms. (Eastman Kodak, IBM, General Motors, and General Electric ranked fifth through eighth.)[2] Each operated globally with technology being applied in worldwide markets.

International markets create attractive opportunities, but the competition is intense. Success goes to the firms that understand and adapt to the environmental factors that influence international marketing.

## ORGANIZATION STRUCTURES FOR OPERATING IN INTERNATIONAL MARKETS

In deciding to market in a foreign country, management must select an appropriate organizational structure. There is a range of methods for operating in foreign markets (see Table 21-1), representing successively greater international involvement.

TABLE 21-1 The range of structures for operating in foreign markets

| Exporting directly or through import-export intermediaries | Company sales branches | Licensing foreign producers | Contract manufacturing by foreign producers | Joint ventures and strategic alliances | Wholly owned subsidiaries | Multinational corporation |
|---|---|---|---|---|---|---|
| Low involvement abroad | | | | | | **High involvement abroad** |

**International trade specialists like John V. Carr make getting into the U.S. market much easier for the inexperienced.**

## Exporting

The simplest way of operating in foreign markets is by **exporting**, either directly to foreign importers or through import-export intermediaries. In international markets, just as in domestic markets, there are both merchant and agent wholesalers.

An **export merchant** is an intermediary operating in the manufacturer's country that buys goods and exports them. Very little risk or investment is involved. Also, minimal time and effort are required on the part of the exporting producer. However, the exporter has little or no control over merchant wholesalers.

An **export agent** may be located in either the manufacturer's country or in the destination country. The agent negotiates the sale of the product and may provide additional services such as arranging for international financing, shipping, and insurance on behalf of the manufacturer. Greater risk is involved, because the manufacturer retains title to the goods. Because they typically deal with a number of manufacturers, both of these types of intermediaries generally are not aggressive marketers, nor do they generate a large sales volume.

To counteract some of these deficiencies, management can export through its own **company sales branches** located in foreign markets. Operating a sales branch enables a company to (1) promote its products more aggressively, (2) develop its foreign markets more effectively, and (3) control its sales effort more completely. Of course, with an international sales branch, management now has the task of managing a sales force. The difficulty is that these sales people are either employees sent from the home country who are unfamiliar with the local market, or foreign nationals who are unfamiliar with the product and the company's marketing practices. Because it is the easiest way to get into international markets, exporting is popular with small firms.

## Contracting

**Contracting** involves a legal relationship that allows a firm to enter a foreign market indirectly, quickly establish a market presence, and experience a limited amount of risk. One form of contracting is a licensing arrangement. **Licensing** means granting to another producer — for a fee or royalty payment — the right to use one's production process, patents, trademarks, or other assets. For example, in Japan, the Suntory brewery is licensed by Anheuser-Busch to produce Budweiser beer, while in England, Budweiser is brewed under licence by the Watney brewery.

**Franchising** has allowed Canadian service retailers, such as Pizza Pizza, Swiss Chalet, and Uniglobe Travel, to expand overseas. Franchising combines a proven operating formula with local knowledge and entrepreneurial initiative.

In **contract manufacturing**, a marketer, such as The Bay, contracts with a foreign producer to supply products that are then marketed in the producer's country. For example, rather than import certain tools and hardware for its planned stores in China, The Bay contracts with local manufacturers to supply certain items.

Contracting offers companies flexibility with minimal investment. It allows a producer to enter a market that might otherwise be closed to it because of exchange restrictions, import quotas, or prohibitive tariffs. At the same time, by licensing, producers may be building future competitors. A licensee may learn all it can from the producer and then proceed independently when the licensing agreement expires.

## MARKETING AT WORK

### FILE 21-1 EXPORTING TO A NICHE MARKET

Glegg Water Conditioning Inc. of Guelph, Ontario, produces equipment that makes water so pure it's not fit for human consumption — if you drank it, it would soon be drawing particles from the lining of your stomach. Water this pure is used in factories around the world to make everything from computer chips to insulin, from semiconductors to power generation.

Started in 1978, the company has grown to $53 million in sales in 1994. More than 96 percent of its sales are made outside Canada. Right from the beginning, Robert Glegg treated Canada and the United States as one market instead of focusing on the Canadian market alone. It has been estimated that in the U.S. market, for every $5 spent on equipment to purify water for heavy industrial use, $1 was spent with Glegg. Glegg's ambitions have not stopped at the United States. Currently, about 10 percent of sales are to Western Europe, 10 percent to Latin America, and 5 percent to Asia. The company is now targeting three sets of countries for expansion: Britain, France, and Ireland; Chile, Venezuela, and Mexico; and Thailand, China, and Taiwan. Its long-term goal is to make 70 percent of its sales in offshore markets with the remainder in North America.

The Glegg product is designed and engineered in Guelph, then contracted out for manufacturing with assembly and testing again in Guelph. This allows for tight cost and quality control. Once testing is complete, the system is taken apart again and shipped. A typical $1-million system is shipped in 10 tractor trailer loads, although some have taken 50 trailers. One of Glegg's innovations that helps it be extremely competitive is its reference design systems, which allows buyers to order a large system from a catalogue rather than have it custom designed; reference design products account for 50 percent of sales.

International export sales have come through a network of 42 independent manufacturer's representatives; each works on commission and represents Glegg in a specific geographic market. Glegg supports the reps with eight salaried sales executives who are spread across North America and Europe and who travel extensively in order to meet customers and help work out their needs with the reps.

Glegg has set a 10-year goal of becoming the leading world supplier of equipment in its specialized niche. Its sales staff will have to grow, it will have to target new markets, it will have to control costs and increase value, and it will have to have parts manufactured and assembled and tested in the United States, Europe, and Asia rather than in Guelph if it is to maintain its edge as competition increases. But Glegg says that head office and core engineering will stay in Guelph: "We're a Canadian company."

Source: Adapted from Casey Mahood, "Glegg Makes a Splash Abroad," *Globe and Mail*, April 12, 1994, pp. B1-2.

**Budapest consumers are willing to stand in the rain for a chance to purchase authentic Levi's.**

### Direct Investment

Another alternative is **direct investment** — a company can build or acquire its own production facilities in a foreign country. The organizational structure can be a joint venture or a wholly owned foreign subsidiary.

A **joint venture** is a partnership arrangement in which the foreign operation is owned in part by the domestic company and in part by a foreign company. A Canadian manufacturer of children's clothing with a well-accepted brand name operates a joint venture with a foreign producer of children's apparel. This arrangement provides a network of manufacturing, sales, and distribution operations in the market. Goldstar, a Korean electronics firm, has a joint venture with Iberna (Italy) and Gepi (Germany) to produce refrigerators. The appliances are designed in Goldstar's Ireland facility, made with components supplied by Gepi, and manufactured in Italy by Iberna.[3] When the controlling interest (more than 50 percent) is owned by foreign nationals, the domestic firm has no real control over the marketing or production activities. However, a joint venture may be the only structure, other than licensing, through which a firm is legally permitted to enter some foreign markets.

Joint ventures are frequently undertaken on a country-by-country basis. For example, a Canadian or U.S. firm may have joint ventures with different partners in Britain, Mexico, and Australia. Some major corporations have taken the notion of a joint venture to a higher level and formed strategic alliances. A **strategic alliance** is a formal, long-term agreement between firms to combine their capabilities and resources to accomplish global objectives. For example, British Air and USAir have formed a strategic alliance that may eventually become a single organization. For the time being, they are integrating their flight schedules, ticketing, prices, catering, and advertising. The arrangement gives British Airways access to U.S. cities and allows USAir to offer its customers convenient routes to over 70 countries.[4] Both Air Canada and CAI are developing similar strategic alliances.

## MARKETING AT WORK

### FILE 21-2 HUDSON'S BAY JOINT VENTURES TO ASIA

Competition in a mature market gets intense at the best of times, and retailing in Canada is quite mature, with little room for growth. The entry of Wal-Mart and other tough global competitors whose own markets have become mature has made competition in the Canadian retailing scene even more intense. So Canadian companies such as the Hudson's Bay Company are taking the next logical step — they're going abroad to growth markets.

Canada's oldest retailer has made public its plans for expanding into the Chinese and other Asian markets. "Asia, to us, is the world," president and chief executive officer George Kosich told the Hong Kong Chamber of Commerce. At present, Asia has strong economic conditions that look as if they can continue for a good period. Asian consumers are keen to expand their household goods as they begin to desire many products that North American consumers already have. North American retailers are very much under-represented in Asian markets. Hudson's Bay, with 25 years of experience in China and other Asian countries as a buyer, is well recognized by the trades and has valuable insights into doing business in Asia.

The Bay's plan is to enter Asian markets through establishing a new Asian company and/or being involved in joint ventures being proposed with a number of large Asian-based organizations. It plans to establish hybrids of Bay and Zellers stores in downtown areas and put its Zellers discount chain in suburban locations. While key positions would be staffed by Canadians, all other employees would be local. In the past two years, a number of Hong Kong, Japanese, and Australian retailers have entered the China market. The Bay will be scouting for similar opportunities in China, as well as joint ventures in Singapore, Malaysia, and Thailand.

Source: Adapted from Michael Bociurkiw, "Hudson's Bay Unveils Plans for Asian Expansion," *Globe and Mail*, February 25, 1994, p. B6.

**Wholly owned subsidiaries** in foreign markets are commonly used by Canadian companies operating in the United States and by firms that have evolved to an advanced stage of international business. With a wholly owned foreign subsidiary, a company has maximum control over its marketing program and production operations. Quebecor Printing Inc. of Montreal purchased Arcata Corp. in the United States to move from being North America's seventh largest book manufacturer to being the second largest. Much of the success of Levi Strauss's 501 jeans is attributed to its association with the American West. As a result, authenticity is important. To ensure that the product is made and presented in the same way around the world, the company makes use of subsidiaries rather than licensees.[5] A wholly owned subsidiary, however, requires a substantial investment of money, labour, and managerial attention. For example, Cadbury Schweppes, a British company, purchased Aguas Minerales, Mexico's largest producer of mineral water. Cadbury got a firm with an 80 percent share of the Mexican mineral water market plus a distribution system for its soft drinks, Canada Dry and Orange Crush. To further develop the market, Cadbury introduced new bottling techniques and spent $13 million on marketing research.[6] John Labatt Ltd. spent $210 million to acquire 168 U.K. pubs so that Labatt U.K. could expand beyond its current market share.

### Multinational Corporation

This leads us to the highest level of international involvement — one reached by very few companies as yet. It is the truly worldwide enterprise — the **multinational corporation**. Both the foreign and the domestic operations are integrated and are not separately identified. A regional sales office in Atlanta is basically the same as one in Toronto or Paris. Business opportunities abroad are viewed in the same way as those in the home country. That is, domestic opportunities are no longer automatically considered to be more attractive. From a strategic point of view, a true multinational firm does *not* view itself as a Canadian firm (Northern Telecom), or a Swiss firm (Nestlé), or a Dutch firm (Shell Oil) that happens to have plants and markets in other countries. In a truly worldwide enterprise, strategic marketing planning is done on a global basis.

## STRATEGIC PLANNING FOR INTERNATIONAL MARKETING

Firms that have been very successful in domestic marketing have no assurance whatsoever that their success will be duplicated in foreign markets. Satisfactory performance overseas lies in: (1) understanding the environment of a foreign market, and (2) gauging which domestic management practices and marketing-mix elements should be transferred directly to foreign markets, which ones modified, and which ones not used at all.

The term **global marketing** describes a strategy in which essentially the same marketing program is employed around the world.

The firm probably most easily associated with a globalized strategy is Coca-Cola. However, despite selling the same products and using common promotional themes all over the world, even Coca-Cola adapts its strategy to local markets. For example, the size and type of container (bottle and/or can) must conform to local regulations and customs. In this section we will examine the primary considerations in developing an international strategic marketing plan.

### Analysis of the Environment

Throughout the world, market demand is determined by the number of people, the ability to buy, and buying behaviour. Also, human wants and needs have a universal similarity. People need food, clothing, and shelter. They seek a better quality of life with lighter work loads, more leisure time, and social recognition and acceptance. But at about this point, the similarities in foreign and domestic markets seem to end, and the differences in culture, the economic environment, and political and legal forces must be considered.

#### Social and Cultural Forces

Culture is a set of shared values passed down from generation to generation in a society. These values determine what is socially acceptable behaviour. Some of the many cultural elements that can influence a company's marketing program are described below.

**Family.** In some countries the family is an extremely close-knit unit, whereas in others the family members act more independently. The family situations in each country may require a distinctive type of promotion, and perhaps even different types of products.

**Social Customs and Behaviour.** Customary behaviour is often hard to understand. In taking medicine, for example, British and Dutch consumers prefer white pills, the French like purple, and all three dislike red, which is the most popular colour in the

United States. In other instances, preferences are quite easily explained. Such is the case with prepared cookie dough, which is sold in tubes in the United States by Pillsbury. But because British consumers expect plastic tubes to contain sausage, Pillsbury repackaged the cookie dough in tubs for sale in Great Britain.[7]

**Education.** The educational level in a country affects the literacy rate, which in turn influences advertising, branding, and labelling. The brand mark may become the dominant marketing strategy feature if potential customers cannot read and must recognize the article by the picture on the label.

**Language Differences.** Language differences also pose problems. A literal translation of advertising copy or brand name may result in ridicule of a product, or even enmity towards it. Some words even have different meanings in countries that claim to speak the same language. Mars, the U.S. candy maker, introduced its Snickers candy bar in England under the name Marathon, because snickers sounds too much like knickers, the British term for women's underpants.[8] When Wal-Mart first began operating in Quebec, it discovered that communicating with employees in English only was illegal.

Economic Environment In international marketing a firm must closely examine the economic conditions in a particular country. A nation's infrastructure and stage of economic development are key economic factors that affect the attractiveness of a market and suggest what might be an appropriate marketing strategy.

**Infrastructure.** A country's ability to provide transportation, communications, and energy is its **infrastructure**. Depending on the product and the method of marketing, an international marketer will need certain levels of infrastructure development. For example, a consumer-goods manufacturer selling a low-priced product requires a transportation system that will permit widespread distribution. How about communications? Some firms would find it impossible to do business without the availability of newspapers in which to advertise or telephones with which to contact other businesses.

There is a danger in assuming that systems a marketer takes for granted domestically will be available elsewhere. The international marketer must recognize what infrastructure is needed and what is available. For example, in North America there are 50 phones for every 100 people, while in the former East Germany there are about 1.5 phones for every 100 people.[9]

**Level of Economic Development.** The **level of economic development** in a country is a general indication of the types of products that are likely to be in demand. Thus, a firm can use some indication of the level of development in identifying potential markets. The most common criterion for assessing development is gross national product (GNP), a measure of the value of all goods and services produced in a country during a year.

Among the world's approximately 150 nations, about 80 countries have a GNP of less than $1,700 U.S. per capita. These countries lack most or all of the resources for growth and often rely heavily on foreign aid. They frequently have unstable governments and overpopulation problems. Countries in this category include Ethiopia, Somalia, Sudan, Afghanistan, Burma, Vietnam, Haiti, and Bangladesh. Most of these **less developed countries** are not attractive markets for most consumer goods or for highly technical products. However, they should not be totally ignored. Less developed countries are very eager to acquire technology that will, for example, allow them to increase agricultural output. To attract technology and management know-how as well as to provide jobs for citizens, the governments in less developed countries often offer incentives to foreign businesses. For example, the government might guarantee payment for goods sold to local businesses on credit.

## MARKETING AT WORK

### FILE 21-3 SHOULD MANAGERS BE TRAINED IN CULTURAL DIFFERENCES?

Behaviour can be interpreted differently depending on where in the world it occurs. Consider these examples that could cause problems for an uninformed marketer.

**Body Language**

- Standing with your hands on your hips is a gesture of defiance in Indonesia.
- Carrying on a conversation with your hands in your pockets makes a poor impression in France, Belgium, Finland, and Sweden.
- When you shake your head from side to side, that means "yes" in Bulgaria and Sri Lanka.
- Crossing your legs to expose the sole of your shoe is unacceptable in Muslim countries.

**Physical Contact**

- Patting a child on the head is a grave offence in Thailand or Singapore, since the head is revered as the location of the soul.
- In an Oriental culture, touching another person is considered an invasion of privacy, while in Southern European and Arabic countries it is a sign of warmth and friendship.

**Promptness**

- Being on time is a sign of respect in Denmark and China.
- In Latin countries, your host or business associate would be surprised (and probably not prepared) if you arrived at the appointed hour.

**Eating**

- It is rude to leave anything on your plate when eating in Norway, Malaysia, or Singapore.
- In Egypt, it is rude *not* to leave something.

What are some cultural differences in Canada that foreign managers should be aware of?

The next level of countries have an average GNP between $1,700 U.S. and $5,500 U.S. This group of about 35 nations, including Singapore, South Korea, and Taiwan, are described as **newly industrialized countries**. They combine an eager work force, low wages, and stable governments to produce high rates of economic growth. They typically export manufactured goods and import technology and consumer goods. These are highly attractive markets for firms that have a technological advantage.

Finally, there are the **highly industrialized countries**, which have an average per capita GNP over $5,500 U.S. About 35 nations fall into this category, led by the United States, Canada, Japan, Germany, Italy, France, and Great Britain. They have well-developed infrastructures, high levels of education and literacy, stable governments, constantly advancing technology, and well-trained work forces. These countries are heavily involved in exporting a wide variety of goods. Although these are the wealthiest countries, they are also the ones in which an importer faces the stiffest competition.

Note that a classification like this can be useful, but it must be combined with other indicators in evaluating a market's potential. For example, averages can be misleading. Saudi Arabia, because of its oil revenues and small population, is in the same group as Switzerland, Japan, and Canada. However, Saudi Arabia's level of economic development is quite different. Thus, when analyzing *economic ability to buy* in a given foreign market, management must also examine such things as the (1) distribution of income, (2) rate of growth of buying power, and (3) extent of available financing.

**Political and Legal Forces** The principal political concerns of international marketers are the stability of governments and their attitudes towards free trade. Obviously, an unstable government adds to the risk of doing business in a country. For example, the frequent coups in Thailand make it a less attractive place to do business than some other Southeast Asian countries. The other political concern is the risk of **expropriation**, or having an investment in a country taken by the host government. Expropriation has become relatively uncommon — the most recent major occurrences were in the oil-producing countries in the Persian Gulf — because it has such a long-term negative effect on any future investments.

**Trade Barriers.** The major legal forces affecting international marketers are barriers created by governments to restrict trade and protect domestic industries. Examples include the following.

- **Tariff.** A tax imposed on a product entering a country. Tariffs are used to protect domestic producers and/or to raise revenue. Japan has a high tariff on imported rice, for example. The United States, from time to time, levies punitive tariffs on Canadian goods such as lumber.
- **Import quota.** A limit on the amount of a particular product that can be brought into a country. Like tariffs, quotas are intended to protect local industry.
- **Local-content law.** A regulation specifying the proportion of a finished product's components and labour that must be provided by the importing country. For example, to be sold in Taiwan, Japanese cars must be at least partially assembled there. To comply with a local-content law, a firm may import most of a product's parts, buy some locally, and have the final product assembled locally. These laws are used to provide jobs and protect domestic businesses.
- **Boycott.** A refusal to buy products from a particular company or country. Boycotts, also called embargos, are used by a government to punish another country for what are perceived to be unfair importation rules.

**Trade Agreements.** Trade agreements reduce trade barriers by giving preferential treatment to firms in the member countries. However, they may also result in member countries establishing barriers to trade with the rest of the world. Thus they have implications for all marketers. By examining three major trade agreements, we can form an impression of the role they play in international marketing:

- **The General Agreement on Tariffs and Trade (GATT).** This organization is the senior and guiding trade group with which most other groups conform. It was created in 1948 to develop fair-trade practices among its members. Today over 100 countries participate in periodic negotiations on issues such as tariff reductions, import restrictions, local-content rules, and subsidization of industry by government.

  A recent interesting issue brought before GATT is the protection of intellectual property through uniform copyright and patent laws. An example will illustrate the problem. A firm such as Pfizer Pharmaceuticals spends an average of $230 million and 10 years developing a new drug. However, once it is on the market, it can be duplicated by a well-trained chemist in a few weeks. Because patent law varies by country, the drug could be produced and sold in many parts of the world with no benefits going to Pfizer.

  Another GATT issue for many less developed countries are the developed country's regulations protecting textile and apparel industries. It is estimated that these regulations add 50 percent to wholesale clothing costs in North America. GATT provides a forum for negotiations, but it does not guarantee that solutions to disagreements will be found.
- **The North American Free Trade Agreement (NAFTA).** After three failed tries during this century, Canada and the United States negotiated and signed a free trade agreement that went into effect on January 1, 1989. A sectoral free trade arrangement had existed for the automobile industry for the last 24 years and this has proven to be

very effective. The 1989 agreement created a single comprehensive market that was 10 percent larger than that of the United States on its own and 15 percent larger than that of the European Union. In 1993, the agreement was extended by including Mexico in a North American Free Trade Agreement, thereby adding close to 90 million consumers to the trading zone, creating a combined market of approximately 370 million. As a result of the agreement, duties among the countries are to be eliminated in stages over the next 15 years.

Canada is already the United States' largest trading partner, and Mexico is third (behind Japan). As a result, NAFTA is unlikely to produce a dramatic increase in trade for Canada or the United States but will cause a substantial increase for Mexico. Most analysts expect to see some manufacturing and assembly jobs move from the United States, and possibly some from Canada, to Mexico as firms seek lower labour costs. This, in turn, will raise incomes in Mexico and create greater demand for U.S. and Canadian goods. Canadian firms have now begun to investigate Mexico's potential in earnest.

## MARKETING AT WORK

### FILE 21-4 FINDING FAVOUR IN MEXICO

One way to test the Mexican market is by attending or participating in trade fairs. One company, the Trimex Group of Kitchener, Ontario, used this approach and gained access to 425 companies, a potential of $100 million in sales, and 17,000 business people. It attended the largest trade fair ever arranged by the Canadian government; the fair made it possible for such firms to take advantage of what NAFTA has to offer.

What do these small firms have that larger ones — particularly larger American firms — do not? It seems that there is a perception in Mexico that large American firms sometimes come into Mexico looking for a quick sale, according to one business person, with an attitude of "sign on the dotted line or don't waste my time." "That puts off a lot of Mexican business people," he says. These smaller Canadian businesses seem to be more willing to take the time to listen to their potential customers, see if products can be adapted to the market, and work to build long-term relationships.

Dennis Kuchma, international director of Trimex, sees Mexico as a great market. A construction engineering firm that builds turnkey plants, Trimex has been in the Mexican market for 10 years and cautions Canadians about being alarmed by political events. Kuchma said his company generated $15 million in new business at the fair. He feels that the fact that Mexicans are happy with Canadian products makes it much easier to open the door to sales in other Latin American countries since if Mexicans like to deal with Canadians, that is seen as a strong endorsement in the rest of Latin America.

Robert Gregory, a rep from BJB Polymer Systems Ltd. in Brampton, Ontario, feels that Mexican businesses have learned they can get world-class products from Canada and that Canadian firms will take the time to work with them. Gregory picked up 14 new leads at the trade fair, a few of them so urgent that his company immediately flew in a team of executives to begin negotiations. One contact for his company resulted in BJB becoming the supplier of body mouldings for a Nissan plant in Mexico with a world mandate for one of its 1995 models. In becoming supplier to this plant, BJB replaced a Japanese source.

With a beginning like this for the Mexican side of NAFTA, Canadian business people will soon be looking for Chile, Argentina, Venezuela, Colombia, and Brazil to make their "applications" for entry.

Source: Adapted from Jeff Sallot, "Canadian Firms Find Favour in Mexico," *Globe and Mail*, May 28, 1994, pp. B1, B10.

- **The European Union (EU)**. This political and economic alliance evolved from the six-nation (France, Italy, Belgium, West Germany, Luxembourg, and the Netherlands) Treaty of Rome in 1957 and was originally called the European Common Market. Over the years the membership has grown (by 1993 Denmark, Great Britain, Greece, Spain, Ireland, and Portugal had been added, and several other countries have applied for admission); (see Figure 21-1). Its overriding objective is liberalizing trade among its members. More specifically, the goal of the EU is a single market for its members that would permit the free movement of goods, services, people, and capital. In addition, the members would be governed by the same set of rules for transporting goods, regulating business, and protecting the environment.

The timetable for accomplishing this dramatic plan was the end of 1992. While much progress had been made by then, some issues were unresolved. For example, automakers still had to produce a variety of engines to satisfy different national regulations, and an EU-based firm had to establish an Italian subsidiary to sell securities in Italy.[10] Despite delays and setbacks, it is clear that greater liberalization of trade in Europe is progressing well.

The prospect of a market of 325 million consumers with common regulations for advertising, packaging, and distribution is very attractive. To illustrate, because of

**FIGURE 21-1 The European Union countries in 1994 (with population figures in millions).**

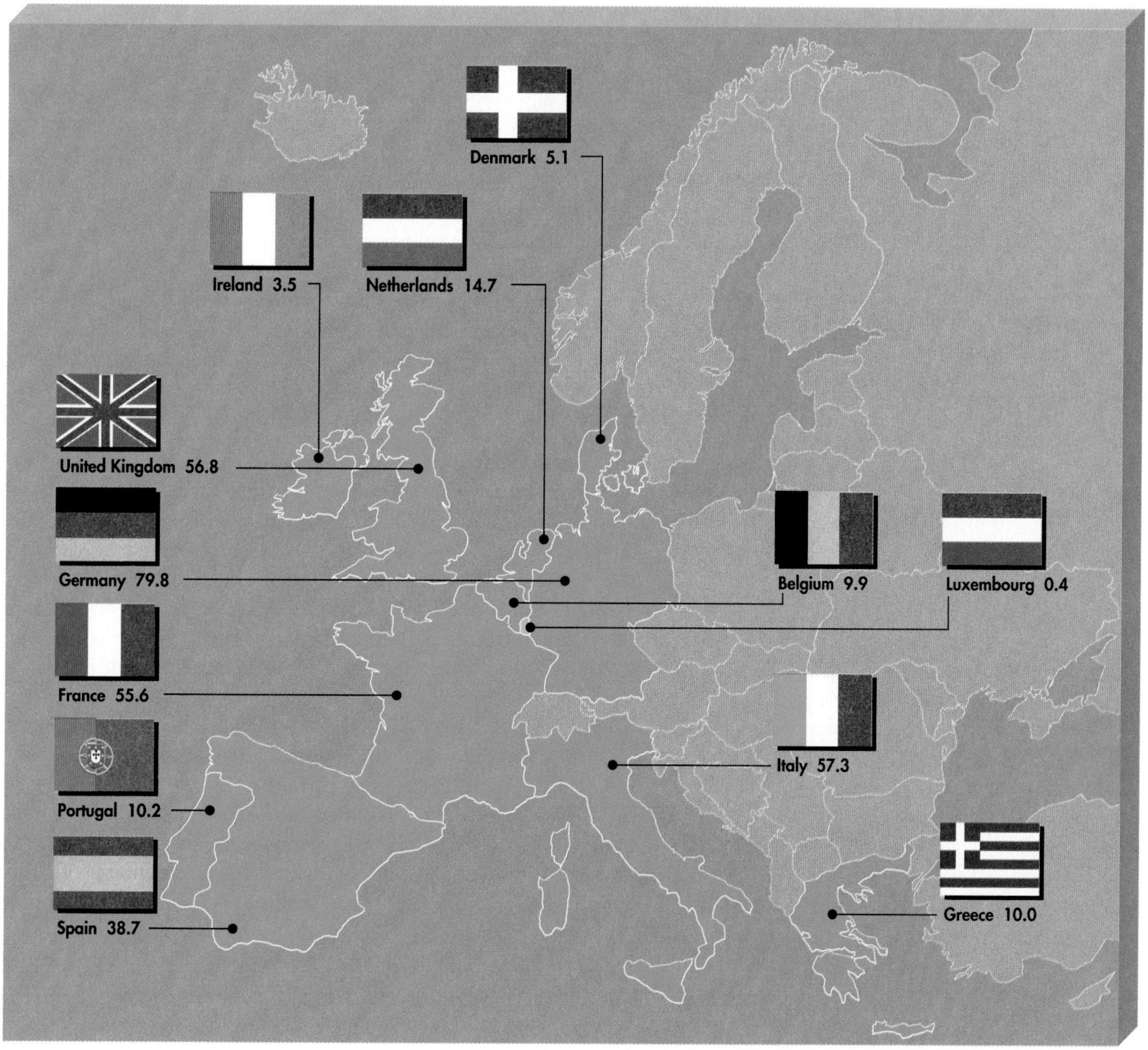

national border restrictions and administrative delays, a truck travelling from London to Milan under the old system could be expected to average only about 19 km per hour. Without the delays, the duration of the trip would be reduced by at least 50 percent.[11]

What does this mean for the rest of the world? While the EU economic unification is likely to eventually eliminate internal trade barriers, non-European firms fear that external trade barriers may restrict entry of products from outside the EU. These organizations anticipate a "Fortress Europe" that will limit outside competition in EU countries. At the same time, the EU will be a major competitive force as an exporter in world markets. Consequently, there was a flurry of foreign investments as many firms moved to establish production facilities, sales branches, and other forms of business in EU countries prior to the end of 1992. For example, International Paper bought paper companies in France, Switzerland, and Germany in 1989 and 1990;[12] Northern Telecom and Bombardier expanded into European locations.

The EU almost surely will continue to expand as several Central and Eastern European countries first become associate members (having the same trading privileges) and then become full members (with a say in policy making). These countries, which now consume very small amounts of Western goods, are seen as primary growth markets.[13]

- **The European Free Trade Association (EFTA).** This association, which was formed in 1960, has been successful in eliminating most of the trade barriers between its member countries. It is made up of Austria, Finland, Iceland, Liechtenstein, Norway, Sweden, and Switzerland (see Figure 21-2; Denmark, England, and Portugal were members, but left to join the EU). Despite the fact that the population of all the EFTA countries is less than that of Spain, they are an attractive market because their per capita income is twice the average per capita income in the EU.

  In 1992 an agreement was reached between the EFTA and the EC (as it was still called then) that brought the EFTA countries into compliance with the EC's single-market concept. In effect, this accord creates a 19-nation free-trade zone of 380 million people known as the **European Economic Area (EEA)**. Though the two organizations will remain distinct entities, many see the accord as a first step towards several EFTA members joining the EU.

The growth of regional economic trading blocs is a significant development that will create both opportunities and challenges for international marketers. However, these accords should not cause us to overlook other areas of the world.

The worldwide economic power of Japanese business is widely recognized. What might not be so obvious is the growth of four other Asian economies — South Korea, Taiwan, Hong Kong, and Singapore — sometimes referred to as Asia's "Four Tigers" or "Four Dragons." The primary economic countries of Asia are shown in Figure 21-3. An unknown at this time is the potential in Eastern Europe and the former Soviet Union. It is impossible to predict how successful these countries will be in moving towards capitalism, or how long it will take. However, the potential of the Commonwealth of Independent States (CIS), headed by Russia, and other countries such as Poland and Hungary, is enormous.

Looking ahead to the year 2000 and thereafter, perhaps the area with the greatest international marketing potential might be China, with its *1 billion* consumers. And, conversely, China has significant potential as an exporter of low-priced products. Already we have seen glimpses of these possibilities. By 1990, China was a major exporter of clothing. Foreign cosmetic sales in China, unheard of a few years ago, are soaring. Kentucky Fried Chicken opened the largest store in its chain on the square across from Chairman Mao's mausoleum in Beijing. And Coca-Cola and Pepsi-Cola are aggressively competing for larger Chinese market shares. Canadian General Electric is a major supplier of equipment for the massive Yangtze River power development project.

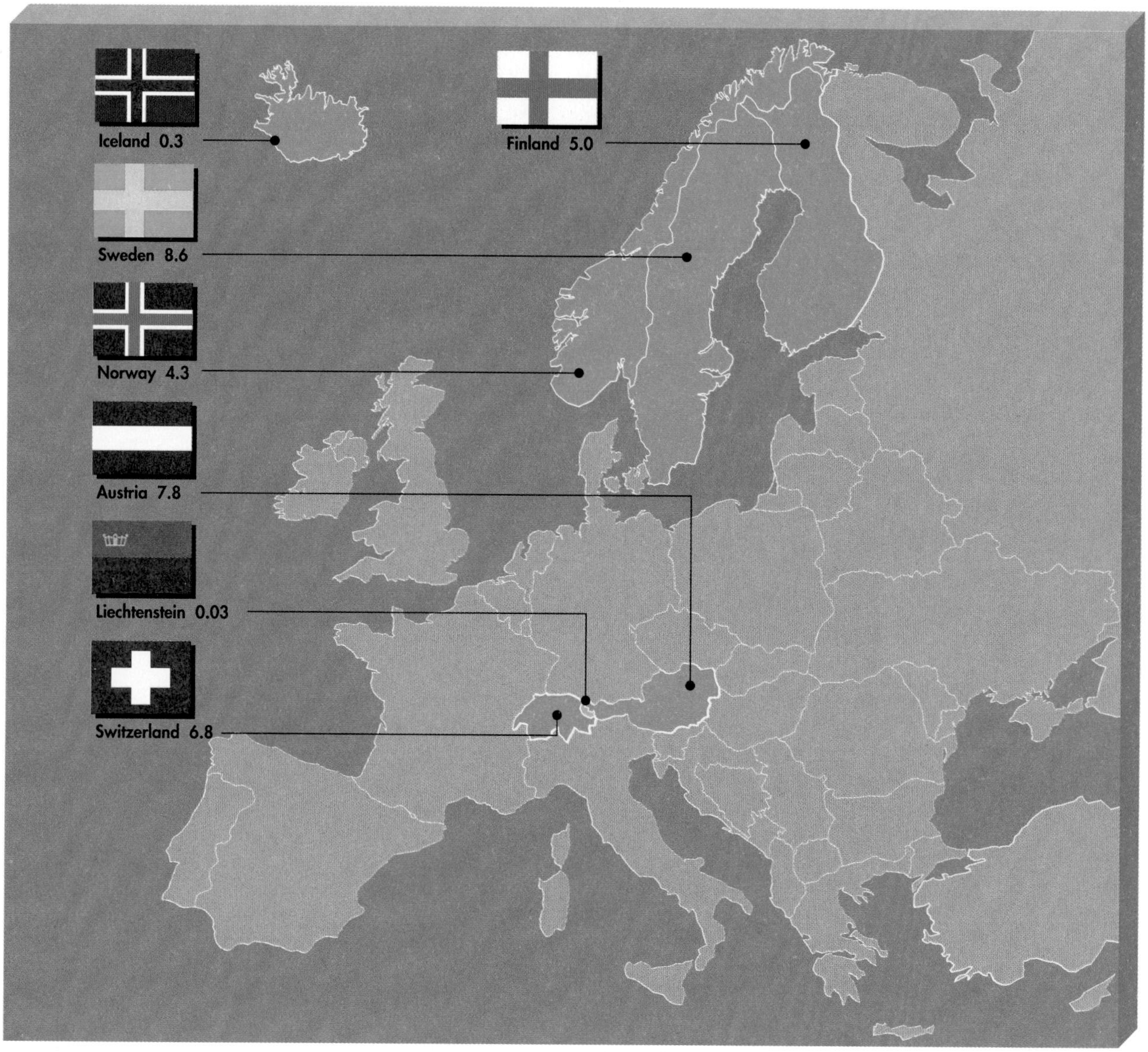


**FIGURE 21-2 The European Free Trade Association countries in 1994 (with population figures in millions).**

## Designing the Marketing Mix

Having examined the environment of a foreign market, the manager is prepared to design a marketing mix that will effectively meet the needs of customers and accomplish the organization's objectives. As the following discussion suggests, domestic practices have to be modified or entirely replaced in international marketing.

**Marketing Research** The scarcity of *reliable statistical data* may be the single biggest problem in certain foreign markets. Canadian firms have been spoiled by Statistics Canada, recognized globally as one of the most accurate and reliable suppliers of information. Typically, the quality of the data is related directly to a country's level of economic development. However, that is not always the case. For example, most nations (including England, Japan, France, Spain, and Italy) do not ask about income in their national censuses.[14] In some parts of the world, figures on population and production may be only crude estimates. In undeveloped countries, studies on such things as buying habits

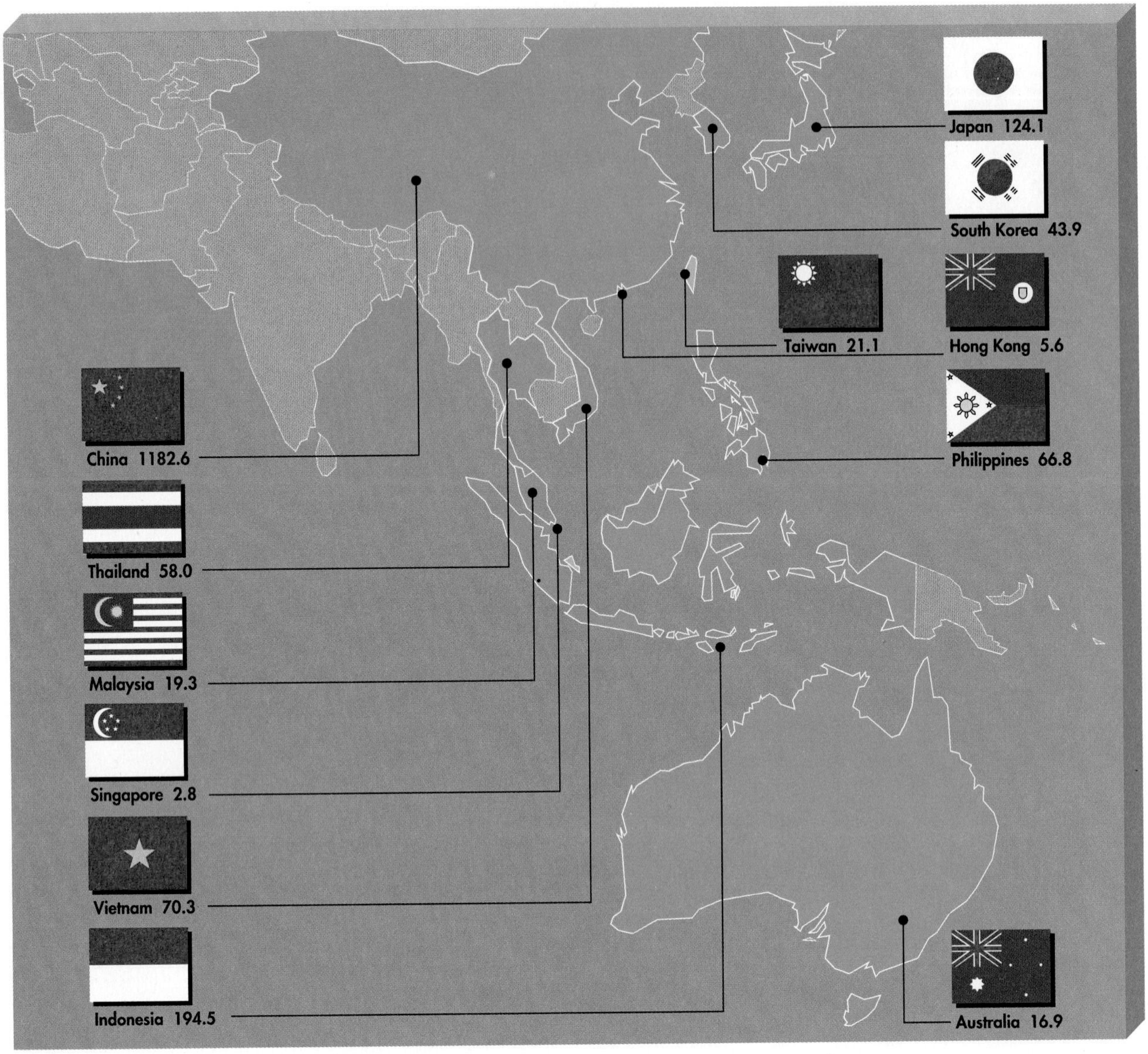


**FIGURE 21-3**
**The Asian side of the Pacific Rim (with population figures in millions).**

or media coverage are even less likely. In the design of a research project, the lack of reliable lists makes it very difficult even to select a representative sample. Another problem is a lack of uniformity among countries in how they define measures such as unemployment and the cost of living. As a result, comparisons across countries are often unreliable.

Another problem is associated with collecting data directly from customers and prospects. Telephone surveys, for example, are likely to be invalid if telephone service is not available to virtually the entire population of a country. The quality of data also depends on the willingness of people to respond accurately when researchers pose questions about attitudes or buying habits. Conducting surveys is very difficult in societies where opinion polls are relatively uncommon, strangers are viewed with suspicion, government is not trusted, or individuals feel that purchase choices and opinions are a private matter.

Product Planning A critical question in product planning concerns the extent to which a company can market the same product in several different countries. **Product**

**extension** describes the situation in which a standard product is sold in two or more countries. For example, cereal makers Kellogg and General Mills have extended the market for popular brands such as Cheerios and Rice Krispies to many parts of the world. Levi Strauss also has been successful in marketing its 501 brand of jeans in many countries.

We can make a few broad generalizations regarding product extensions. The best bet for standardization is in the area of durable business goods. In such industries as aircraft, computers, and tractors, the worldwide market (at least among industrialized nations) is quite uniform. Somewhere in the middle of our standardization spectrum, we can place consumer durable goods such as cameras, watches, pocket calculators, small appliances, and television sets. The most difficult goods to standardize globally are food and drink products and wearing apparel. (Here Coca-Cola and Levi Strauss are exceptions.) This difficulty can be traced to national tastes and habits. For example, in France the per capita consumption of dry cereal is only 0.5 kg per year, compared to 6 kg per year in the U.S.[15] Even with national markets, we often find strong regional differences in food and clothing preferences.

A second option is **product adaptation**, modifying a product that sells successfully in one market to suit the unique needs or requirements of other markets. When it entered the British market, Sara Lee Corp. changed the topping on its cheesecake from the North American favourite of strawberry to black currant.[16]

**Disney's Tokyo Disneyland has been a much more successful product extension than EuroDisney in France.**

The third alternative product strategy is **invention**, the development of an entirely new product for a foreign market. Concentrated laundry detergent in compact boxes was developed to accommodate the smaller storage areas in Japanese homes.

Marketers must study carefully the cultural and economic environment of any market — foreign or domestic — before planning products for that particular market. In Europe, for example, a 6-cubic-foot refrigerator is the most popular size, in contrast to the larger units preferred in Canada. It's true that the cost difference and the prevalence of smaller kitchens in Europe are decision factors. However, the basic reasons lie in cultural behaviour patterns of the consumers. Many Europeans shop for food daily and thus do not buy large quantities that must be stored for several days in a refrigerator. Many also do not have a car, so they walk to the store and do not want to carry large quantities. And Europeans eat only about one-half as much frozen foods as North Americans, so freezer storage space is not as important.

Branding and labelling are other considerations in foreign marketing. As suggested earlier, the brand mark may be the only part of the label that consumers in some countries can recognize. We also noted the problems with language that may make a brand name inappropriate in some markets. Most firms would prefer to use the same brand name in domestic and foreign markets, since it provides greater overall familiarity and recognition and can also produce some economies in promotion. However, it may be inappropriate. Heinz uses the Weight Watchers brand name on its frozen dinners in Great Britain, just as it has successfully done in the Canada and the United States. Unilever is more successful in the same market with a similar product it calls Healthy Options. Unlike their North American counterparts, apparently the British are more influenced by an appeal to their health than their weight.[17]

**Pricing** In earlier chapters, we recognized that determining the base price and formulating pricing strategies are complex tasks, frequently involving trial-and-error decision making. These tasks become even more complex in international marketing. An exporter faces variables such as currency conversion, differences in what is included in price quotations, and often a lack of control over intermediaries' pricing.

Cost-plus pricing is relatively common in export marketing. Because of additional physical distribution expenses, tariffs, and other export costs, foreign prices usually are considerably higher than domestic prices for the same product. For example, the Jeep Cherokee costs about $12,000 U.S. more in Japan than in the United States.[18] At the retail level, price bargaining is quite prevalent in many foreign markets — especially in Asia, Africa, and South America — and must be taken into consideration in setting the initial price.

Occasionally a firm's foreign price is lower than its domestic price. The price may be lowered to meet foreign competition or to dispose of outmoded products. Sometimes companies engage in **dumping** — selling products in foreign markets at prices below the prices charged for these goods in their home market. There have been frequent charges by Americans that Japanese auto and electronics firms have engaged in dumping in the United States to increase sales and build their market shares. Dumping, which frequently involves selling goods below cost, is viewed as an unfair business practice by most governments, and generally results in threats of tariffs or establishment of quotas.

Foreign intermediaries often are not aggressive in their pricing strategies. They prefer high unit margins from low sales volumes, so they do not lower prices to generate large sales volume. In fact, there is considerable price rigidity in many foreign markets. In some cases the inflexibility stems from agreements among firms that restrain independent pricing. The rigidity may also result from legislation. For example, British law prohibits wholesalers from selling to final consumers. This has created problems for Costco, a North American warehouse club trying to expand into England. Costco's operating formula is designed to generate two-thirds of its sales from small businesses who buy at wholesale prices, and one-third from consumers.[19]

Prices may be quoted in the seller's currency or in the currency of the foreign buyer. Here we encounter problems of foreign exchange and conversion of currencies. As a general rule, a firm engaged in foreign trade — whether it is exporting or importing — prefers to have the price quoted in its own national currency. Risks from fluctuations in foreign exchange then are shifted to the other party in the transaction.

An alternative to currency-based pricing is barter or **countertrade**. Rather than buy goods with cash, some countries arrange to trade domestically made products for imported goods. PepsiCo, for example, has traded soft drinks to Poland for wooden chairs that are used in its U.S. Pizza Hut stores.[20] Two reasons for countertrade are:[21]

- **Lack of hard currency.** Less developed countries may not have enough "hard" currency (the money of countries viewed in world markets as reasonably stable) to buy needed capital goods. So they trade their less sophisticated products for equipment and technology. A Canadian firm selling steel in Indonesia was compensated in palm oil, coffee, timber, and rattan furniture.
- **Inadequate marketing structure.** Some countries do not have a marketing structure that encourages or permits international trade. Without global distribution systems, adequate promotion, or the ability to provide service, they cannot sell their domestic goods overseas. To overcome this problem, these countries may require foreign firms that import products into the country to accept local goods in total or partial payment. Both China and Romania require importers to accept countertrade.

Combinations of manufacturers and intermediaries are tolerated to a far greater extent in many foreign countries than in Canada and the United States. They are allowed even when the avowed purpose of the combination is to restrain trade and reduce competition.

The best known of these international marketing combinations is the cartel. A **cartel** is a group of companies that produce similar products and act collectively to restrain competition in manufacturing and marketing. Cartels exist to varying degrees in steel, aluminum, fertilizers, electrical products, petroleum products, rayon, dyes, and sulphur. Probably the world's best-known cartel is OPEC, the Organization of Petroleum Exporting Countries, which has tried — with varying degrees of success — to control the price of crude oil.

**Distribution Systems** Studying the environment in a foreign market helps in understanding the distribution system, because marketing institutions such as various types of retailers result from their environment. For example, one-stop shopping is still unknown in most parts of the world. In many countries, people buy in small units, sometimes literally on a meal-to-meal basis. Also, they buy in small specialty stores. In contrast to North America, where shopping is often viewed as a chore, in many places it is a major part of social life.

In Western European countries, some of the traditional shopping patterns are changing, however. Astute retailers will capitalize on environmental change by introducing innovations that anticipate trends in the environment. Several European retailers have done a good job of innovating. Within a few years, they have moved from the stage of small, specialized stores to a variety of retailing concepts as advanced as any in the world.

These innovative retailers leapfrogged several stages of institutional development. In mass retailing, the *hypermarché* in France and the *Verbrauchermarkt* in Germany are huge self-service superstores operating very profitably and at much lower gross margins than similar Canadian and American stores. Conversely, distribution systems in Japan are another story. Producers, both foreign and Japanese, must contend with a culture-bound, high-cost channel structure composed of small retail stores and multiple layers of wholesalers.

**Intermediaries and Channels of Distribution.** Four groups of intermediaries operating in international trade are:

- Domestic foreign-trade intermediaries: Wholesalers located in the seller's home country that sell abroad.
- Foreign-trade intermediaries located abroad: Wholesalers located in countries other than the seller's country that buy goods from abroad.
- Wholesalers and retailers operating within foreign markets.
- Manufacturers' sales branches and sales offices located in foreign countries.

International intermediaries were introduced earlier in this chapter in connection with organizational structures for international marketing. Intermediaries operating *within* foreign countries are, in general, less aggressive and perform fewer marketing services than their domestic counterparts. The foreign marketing situation, however, usually argues against bypassing these intermediaries. Often the demand is too small to warrant establishing a sales office or branch in the foreign country. Also, in many countries, knowledge of the market may be more important than knowledge of the product, even for high-technology products. And sometimes government controls preclude the use of a firm's sales organization abroad. Thus, intermediaries in foreign countries ordinarily are a part of the channel structure.

**Physical Distribution.** Various aspects of physical distribution in foreign marketing are quite different from anything found on the domestic scene. Generally, physical distribution expenses account for a much larger share of the final selling price in foreign markets than in domestic markets. Problems caused by humidity, pilferage, handling, and inadequate marking must be considered in international shipments. Requirements regarding commercial shipping, insurance, and government documents complicate the paperwork in foreign shipping. As noted earlier, one of the primary benefits of economic alliances like the EEA is the efficiency they bring to physical distribution. With the free movement of goods across European borders, distribution time and expense will be drastically reduced.

**Bribery in International Distribution.** Bribes, kickbacks, and sometimes even extortion payments are facts of life in international distribution. Bribery is so rooted in many cultures that it is described with special slang words. It's called *mordida* (small bite) in Latin America, *dash* in West Africa, and *baksheesh* in the Middle East. The French call it *pot de vin* (jug of wine). In Italy there is *la bustarella* (the little envelope), left on a bureaucrat's desk to cut the red tape. In Chicago they use *a little grease* to get things done.

Bribery in marketing became an international scandal in the mid-1970s. Subsequent political sensitivity resulted in several companies' establishing written ethical guidelines.

What complicates this situation is the fact that bribery is not a sharply defined activity. Sometimes the lines are blurred between a bribe, a gift to show appreciation, a reasonable commission for services rendered, and a finder's fee to open a distribution channel. Realistically, in some foreign markets a seller must pay a fee or commission to an agent to get in touch with prospective buyers. Without paying such fees, there is simply no effective access to those markets.

**Advertising** Rather than discuss promotion in its entirety, we limit our discussion to advertising as being illustrative of the strategic problems in international promotion. Recognize, however, that there are issues related to personal selling and sales promotion that international marketers must deal with.

**Standardizing Advertising.** A controversial issue is the extent to which advertising can be standardized in international markets. In the past, little thought was given to standardization, and separate programs (copy, appeals, and media) were tailored for each country, or even for regions within a country. For example, in 1988, Parker Pens were advertised around the world using more than 30 different themes. While complete uniformity is not typical, today there is much support for the idea of commonality in international ad campaigns. Many companies use basically the same appeals, theme, copy, and layout in all or much of their international advertising — particularly in Western European countries. Unilever successfully uses the same appeal for Dove bar soap — contains "one-quarter cleansing cream" — in Australia, France, Germany, Italy, and the United States.[22] Similarly, Toys " Я " Us only slightly modifies television ads developed in the United States for use in Germany and Japan.

Standardization of advertising is spurred by the increase in international communications and entertainment. Many TV broadcasts reach audiences all over the world via satellite and cable networks. Annual sales of U.S. television programming to Europe are estimated to be about $500 million. Reruns of Alf and Cosby are seen around the world. Many European magazines and newspapers circulate across national borders. In addition, vacation and business travel from one country to another is quite common. In the last three years, 38 percent of Western Europeans have taken a foreign vacation.[23]

A second factor contributing to the standardization of advertising is production costs. Producing quality advertising is very expensive, so the opportunity to achieve savings by using the same ideas or executions around the world is attractive. IBM used a uniform television ad across Europe for its PS/1 personal computer, changing only the language of the spokesperson. The result was a $2 million savings in creative and production costs.[24] Levi Strauss has gone a step further, producing TV ads for global use that include 1960s American rock music and nonspeaking actors. By not having the actors speak, the problem of language differences is overcome and the same ads can be used in many parts of the world.[25]

Perhaps the issue comes down to this point: The goal of advertising is the same in any country, namely, to communicate information and persuasive appeals effectively. For some products, the appeals are sufficiently universal and the markets are sufficiently homogeneous to permit the use of very similar advertising in several countries. It is only the media strategy and the details of a message that must be fine-tuned to each country's cultural, economic, and political environment. However, care must be taken to recognize differences in national identity and characteristics that may require specialized advertising in a particular country.

## ADVERTISING REGULATION TAKES MANY FORMS

In some parts of the world, negative attitudes towards marketing in general and towards advertising in particular are a hardship for firms. Governments in some countries believe that consumers are at a severe disadvantage to the skills of advertising experts and therefore deserve special protection. People in many foreign countries object especially to hard-sell advertising. Like many countries, Brazil has a law to protect consumers against false or exaggerated advertising claims. However, the Brazilian law places the burden of proof on the advertiser rather than requiring the consumer to prove damages. And the penalties for violations can range up to $500,000, a five-year prison sentence, and closure of the business!

Advertising regulations differ from country to country, creating problems for firms that desire to globalize their advertising. Consider these regulatory examples:

- MTV Europe cannot show low-alcohol beer ads in Norway.
- In Poland the lyrics in musical commercials must be in Polish.
- Brazil requires that all ads shown in the country have some local content.
- Australia prohibits all foreign commercials.
- Until recently, Switzerland banned the use of children in commercials.
- Direct-comparison ads are not permitted in Austria.

Sources: Julia Michaels, "Strict Ad Code Puts Hex on Brazil Shops," *Advertising Age*, April 15, 1991, p. 44; Ken Wells, "Selling to the World: Global Ad Campaigns, after Many Missteps, Finally Pay Dividends," *The Wall Street Journal*, Aug. 27, 1992, p. A1.

For example, a Procter & Gamble ad for Camay that showed a husband walking in on his wife who was sitting in a bathtub was very successful in France and Britain. The same execution failed in Japan, where the viewers considered the husband's intrusion to be rude.[26]

## GOVERNMENT SUPPORT FOR INTERNATIONAL MARKETING

In most of the decision-making areas in international marketing, the federal government, as well as many provincial governments, provides contacts, information, guidance, and even financing for Canadian firms. For example, international marketing efforts are aided by the Department of Foreign Affairs and International Trade and the Export Development Corporation. The department attempts to assist firms from the research and development stage through to the international marketing of finished products. The Export Development Corporation provides insurance, guarantees, loans, and other financial facilities to help Canadian exporters.

Within the federal department, a number of units exist that work on specific problems associated with international marketing. The Office of General Relations is responsible for advance planning of Canada's external trade policies and general policy affecting primary and secondary industry. The Office of Area Relations protects and improves the access of Canadian goods to export markets. The Industry, Trade and Traffic Services Branch deals with shipping problems and trade control and provides information on Canadian products and companies. The Fairs and Missions Branch coordinates all departmental activities designed to promote the sale of Canadian products and services abroad. The International Defence Programs Branch promotes defence and export trade. The Trade Commissioners Service, with 76 offices in 55 countries, promotes export trade and protects commercial interests abroad. The Publicity Branch supports foreign trade promotion programs. The operational branches within the department (Aerospace; Marine and Rail; Agriculture; Fisheries and Food Products; Apparel and Textiles; Chemicals; Electrical and Electronics; Machinery; Materials; Mechanical Transport; and Wood Products) work to promote the sales of products and services in international markets.

## SUMMARY

Many companies in Canada and abroad derive a substantial share of their total sales and profits from their foreign marketing operations. Firms engage in international marketing because of demand abroad and the saturation of domestic markets, and because they have either a comparative or a technological advantage.

As in domestic marketing, international marketers must adapt to the macroenvironment. Differences in the social and cultural environment are reflected in family values, customs, education, and language. Critical economic conditions include the infrastructure in a market and a country's stage of economic development. Political and legal forces unique to international marketing are trade barriers and international trade agreements. Economic alliances in Europe (EU) and North America (NAFTA) have implications for marketers in both member and nonmember nations.

In terms of organizational structure, the simplest way to operate in a foreign market is to export through intermediaries specializing in foreign trade. Another method is to export through company sales branches located in foreign countries. More involved approaches include contracting, engaging in a joint venture, or forming a wholly owned subsidiary. The most fully developed organization structure for international marketing is the multinational corporation.

To develop an international marketing program, a basic issue is how global or standardized the marketing can be. In some cases each of the marketing-mix elements requires modification or adaptation. This is made more difficult by the fact that marketing research is quite primitive in many parts of the world.

International trade contributes to the growth of a nation's economy. The Canadian government is interested in boosting sales of Canadian products and services abroad in order to generate revenues to offset the purchase of foreign goods and services by Canadian companies and consumers. The globalization of the marketplace has meant that, in recent years, Canadians have been faced with attractive international options in their purchase of products and services. Canadian companies must not only ensure that they are able to compete in foreign markets, but that they can also compete with foreign competitors in the Canadian market.

## KEY TERMS AND CONCEPTS

**International marketing (644)**
**Comparative advantage (645)**
**Technological advantage (645)**
**Exporting (647)**
**Export merchant (647)**
**Export agent (647)**
**Company sales branch (647)**
**Contracting (647)**
**Licensing (647)**
**Franchising (647)**
**Contract manufacturing (647)**
**Direct investment (648)**
**Joint venture (648)**
**Strategic alliance (649)**
**Wholly owned subsidiary (649)**
**Multinational corporation (650)**
**Global marketing (650)**
**Infrastructure (651)**
**Level of economic development (651)**
**Less developed countries (651)**
**Newly industrialized countries (652)**
**Highly industrialized countries (652)**
**Expropriation (653)**
**Tariff (653)**
**Import quota (653)**
**Local-content law (653)**
**Boycott (653)**
**General Agreement on Tariffs and Trade (GATT) (653)**
**North American Free Trade Agreement (NAFTA) (653)**
**European Union (EU) (654)**
**European Free Trade Association (EFTA) (656)**
**European Economic Area (EEA) (656)**
**Product extension (658)**
**Product adaptation (659)**
**Invention (659)**
**Dumping (660)**
**Countertrade (660)**
**Cartel (660)**
**Government support for international programs (663)**

## QUESTIONS AND PROBLEMS

1. A luggage-manufacturing company with annual sales over $20 million has decided to market its products in Western Europe. Describe the alternative organizational structures this company should consider.
2. Interview some foreign students on your campus to determine how their native buying habits differ from yours. Consider such factors as when, where, and how people in their country buy. What roles do various family members play in buying decisions?
3. Many countries have a low literacy rate. In what ways might a company adjust its marketing program to overcome this problem?

4. If a company uses foreign intermediaries, it must usually stand ready to supply them with financial, technical, and promotional help. If this is the case, why is it not customary to bypass these intermediaries and deal directly with the ultimate foreign buyers?
5. Why do exporters normally prefer to have prices stated in U.S. dollars? Why should foreign importers prefer that quotations be in the currency of their country?
6. To become more competitive in world markets, Canadian manufacturers must continue improving product quality. Locate a recent article from a business publication that describes the efforts of a Canadian firm to improve quality and summarize it for the class.
7. Examine the ads in a foreign magazine in your college or city library. Particularly note the ads for North American products, and compare these with the ads for the same products in North American magazines. In what respect do the foreign ads differ from the domestic ads? Are there significant similarities?
8. "Prices of products are always higher in foreign countries than at home because of the additional risks, expenses of physical distribution, and extra intermediaries involved." Discuss.

## HANDS-ON MARKETING

1. Report on export marketing activities of companies in the province where your school is located. Consider such topics as the following. What products are exported? How many jobs are created by export marketing? What is the dollar value of exports? How does this figure compare with the value of foreign-made goods imported into the province?
2. Select one product — manufactured or nonmanufactured — for export, and choose the country to which you would like to export it. Examine the macroenvironmental factors described in the chapter and prepare an analysis of the market for this product in the selected country. Be sure to include the sources of information you used.

## NOTES AND REFERENCES


1. Adapted from Nattalia Lea, "Mission: Japan," *Profit*, Fall 1993, vol. 12, no. 3, pp. 29-35.
2. Robert Buderi, John Carey, Neil Gross, and Karen Lowey Miller, "Global Innovation: Who's in the Lead," *Business Week*, August 3, 1992, pp. 68-69.
3. Laxmi Nakarmi and Igor Reichlin, "Daewoo, Samsung, and Goldstar: Made in Europe?" *Business Week*, August 24, 1992, p. 43.
4. Paula Dwyer, Andrea Rothman, Seth Payne, and Stewart Toy, "Air Raid: British Air's Bold Global Push," *Business Week*, August 24, 1992, pp. 54-61.
5. Mario Shao, Robert Neff, and Jeffery Ryser, "For Levi's, a Flattering Fit Overseas," *Business Week*, November 5, 1990, pp. 76-77.
6. Elisabeth Malkin, "Schweppes Set with Expansion in Mexico," *Advertising Age*, April 27, 1992, p. I-14.
7. Phil Davies, "Europe Unbound," *Express Magazine*, Spring 1992, pp. 16-19.
8. Joann S. Lublin, "Slim Pickings: U.S. Food Firms Find Europe's Huge Market Hardly a Piece of Cake," *The Wall Street Journal*, May 15, 1990, p. A1.
9. Rick Arons, *EuroMarketing*, Probus, Chicago, 1991, p. 186.
10. Craig Forman, "Europe Crossroads: As EC Leaders Gather, the Program for 1992 Is Facing Big Problems," *The Wall Street Journal*, December 6, 1991, p. A1.
11. Arons, op. cit., p. 75.
12. Arons, op. cit., p. 160.
13. Shawn Tully, "Now the New New Europe," *Fortune*, December 2, 1991, pp. 136-145.
14. Donald B. Pittenger, "Gathering Foreign Demographics Is No Easy Task," *Marketing News*, January 8, 1990, p. 23.
15. Christopher Knowlton, "Europe Cooks Up a Cereal Brawl," *Fortune*, June 3, 1991, pp. 175-179.
16. Lublin, loc. cit.
17. Lublin, loc. cit.
18. Clay Chandler, "Why Cherokee Jeep Sales Slump in Japan," *The Wall Street Journal*, January 14, 1992, p. A10.
19. Eva Pomice, John Marks, Jonathan Kapstein, Kathy Burton, and Dana Hawkins, "Locking Up Tomorrow's Profits," *U.S. News & World Report*, June 29, 1992, pp. 57-60.
20. Arons, op. cit., p. 204.
21. Lee D. Dahringer and Hans Muhlbacher, *International Marketing*, Addison-Wesley, Reading, Mass., 1991.
22. Ken Wells, "Selling to the World: Global Ad Campaigns, after Many Missteps, Finally Pay Dividends," *The Wall Street Journal*, August 27, 1992, p. A1.
23. Nancy Giges, "Great Change in Europe Lifestyles: Study," *Advertising Age*, February 25, 1991, p. 17.
24. Richard L. Hudson, "IBM Strives for a Single Image in Europe," *The Wall Street Journal*, April 16, 1991, p. B6.
25. Wells, loc. cit.
26. Wells, loc. cit.

## CHAPTER 22 GOALS

In this chapter we apply many of the concepts and techniques of modern marketing to not-for-profit organizations. After studying this chapter, you should have an understanding of:

- The exchange concept as applied to not-for-profit organizations.
- The importance of marketing in not-for-profit organizations.
- The concept of contributor markets and client markets.
- The attitudes of not-for-profit organizations towards marketing.
- How market analysis and the marketing mix apply in not-for-profit marketing.
- The status of marketing programs in not-for-profit organizations.

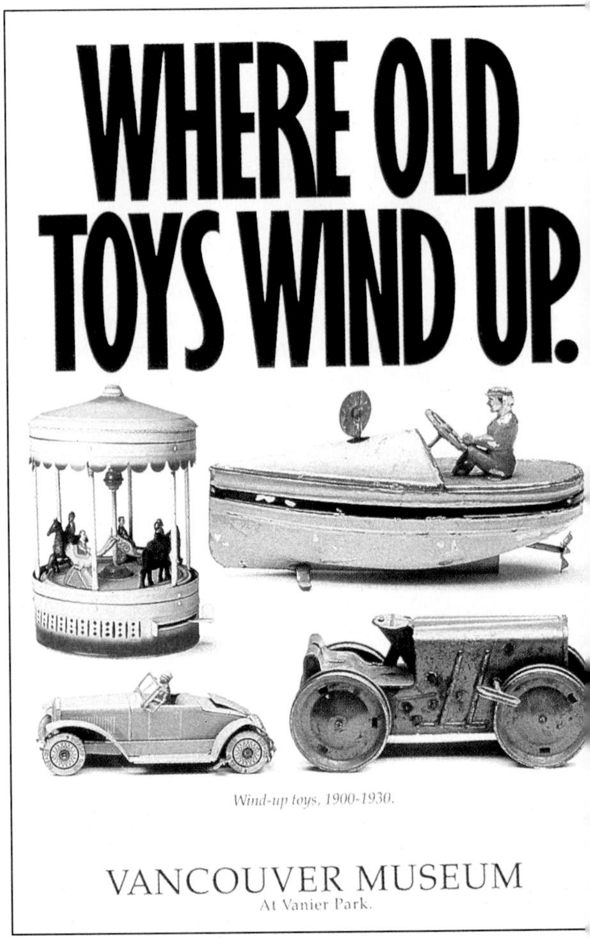

CHAPTER 22

# MARKETING IN NOT-FOR-PROFIT ORGANIZATIONS

## For the Greater Good of the Community

To attract members of the public to their concerts and performances, most Canadian performing arts groups engage in a series of activities that bear remarkable similarity to the marketing programs of companies such as Eaton's, Northern Telecom, and Bombardier. The difference is that the Canadian Opera Company, the Vancouver Symphony, and the Neptune Theatre are not marketing conventional products or services, but are trying to sell tickets and fill seats. They are examples of many different types of not-for-profit organizations that rely on the general public to provide the funding and support that will allow them to accomplish their goals.

Universities and colleges conduct advertising campaigns and other promotional activities to attract students. Many museums, art galleries, zoos, and social agencies, such as Scouts Canada, the YM-YWCA, and the Canadian Red Cross, use similar techniques to attract visitors, members, and donors (of money, time, and even blood!) who contribute to their success, and even to their very survival. Political candidates use advertising to attract voters and rely on "polling" and survey research to determine public opinion and voting preferences. Many religious organizations use television advertising, door-to-door visits, and other marketing techniques to put forth their message and to attract members and contributions. Symphony orchestras offer free lunch-time concerts to attract new patrons — a form of sampling. Universities offer evening programs and distance education courses to broaden the market for their "products." Many social agencies mount sophisticated advertising and public awareness campaigns to warn the public of the dangers of smoking, unprotected sex, and drug abuse, and to encourage responsible behaviour, such as the use of bicycle helmets.

A number of common threads run through these examples. In the first place, all of the organizations mentioned are *not-for-profit* organizations; that is, profit is not an organizational objective. Second, all are engaged in the business of encouraging socially responsible behaviour or the support of programs and activities that are generally regarded as being good for the community and its residents. In all cases, such groups and organizations regularly rely on concepts and activities that represent a different application of *marketing* as we have been studying it.

While there are many similarities between the activities of not-for-profit organizations and those of "for-profit" businesses, there are dramatic differences as well. In the first place, very few of the organizations mentioned are selling a tangible product; most are marketing cultural services, social causes and ideas, and "good works." Second, and this is a very important distinction, they are not marketing only to a single group of target customers. While most companies target their products and services at selected "consumers" who are in the market for breakfast cereal, a new car, or a trip to a holiday destination, many not-for-profit organizations are really targeting three groups: *customers or patrons* who will buy tickets to attend a performance of an orchestra or a theatre company or to visit a zoo or botanical garden, *donors* who will contribute to fund-raising activities, and *volunteers* who will perform the many activities that are necessary for the organization to succeed in its good work.

## NATURE AND SCOPE OF NOT-FOR-PROFIT MARKETING

The marketing fundamentals for not-for-profit, nonbusiness organizations are the same as for the business sector. A marketing program should be strategically planned around a product or service that is effectively priced, promoted, and distributed to satisfy wants in a predetermined market. However, there are important differences in the implementation of the marketing program and in not-for-profit management's understanding of and attitudes towards marketing. These differences tend to limit the marketing activities of not-for-profit, nonbusiness organizations, even though these organizations need effective marketing.

Most not-for-profit companies market services, rather than tangible products. Consequently, many of the concepts discussed in Chapter 12 are relevant in this chapter.

### Types of Not-for-profit Organizations

Not-for-profit organizations number in the thousands and engage in a very wide range of activities. The following groupings will give you some idea of this broad spectrum:

- *Educational:* Private schools, high schools, colleges, universities.
- *Cultural:* Museums, zoos, symphony orchestras, opera and theatre groups.
- *Religious:* Churches, synagogues, temples, mosques.
- *Charitable and philanthropic:* Social welfare groups (Salvation Army, United Way, Red Cross), research foundations, fund-raising groups.
- *Social cause:* Organizations dealing with family planning, literacy, stopping smoking, preventing heart disease, environmental concerns, those for or against abortion, or for or against nuclear energy.
- *Social:* Fraternal organizations, civic clubs (Lions, Rotary, Kinsmen).
- *Health care:* Hospitals, nursing homes, health research organizations (Canadian Cancer Society, Heart and Stroke Foundation).
- *Political:* Political parties, individual politicians.

## MARKETING AT WORK

### FILE 22-1 NOT LIKE FLOGGING SOAP

Eric Young is a Toronto-based marketing consultant. Nothing new in that, you say; Toronto must be full of marketing consultants. But Young is a different type of consultant who numbers among his clients the Canadian Civil Liberties Association, the Canadian Centre for Drug-Free Sport, and McMaster University. Eric Young is a specialist in "social marketing." He sees his job as one of advising not-for-profit organizations on how they can "harness the energy of societal shifts."

As a social marketer, Young is one of a small group of individuals and firms who see their role as one of bringing about change in how Canadians view social issues and in how they support social causes and ideas. They work with a variety of social agencies to accomplish objectives as diverse as increasing attendance at performances of arts organizations, to shunning drugs, to supporting literacy programs and concepts like employment equity.

One of the major challenges for Eric Young and other social marketing consultants who work with social organizations is to obtain the support of corporate sponsors who will provide much-needed funding and exposure for their marketing programs. One such example is Roots Canada, which works with Young's client, the Canadian Centre for Drug-Free Sport. The Roots logo appears modestly on the sleeves of T-shirts that the company pays for and that bear the campaign's emblem, Spirit of Sport. Such corporate involvement in social marketing is referred to by some as "decency positioning," enhancing the company's image in the eyes of the public by associating with good causes.

Source: Vivian Smith, "Society's Salesman," *Globe and Mail*, September 28, 1993, p. B26.

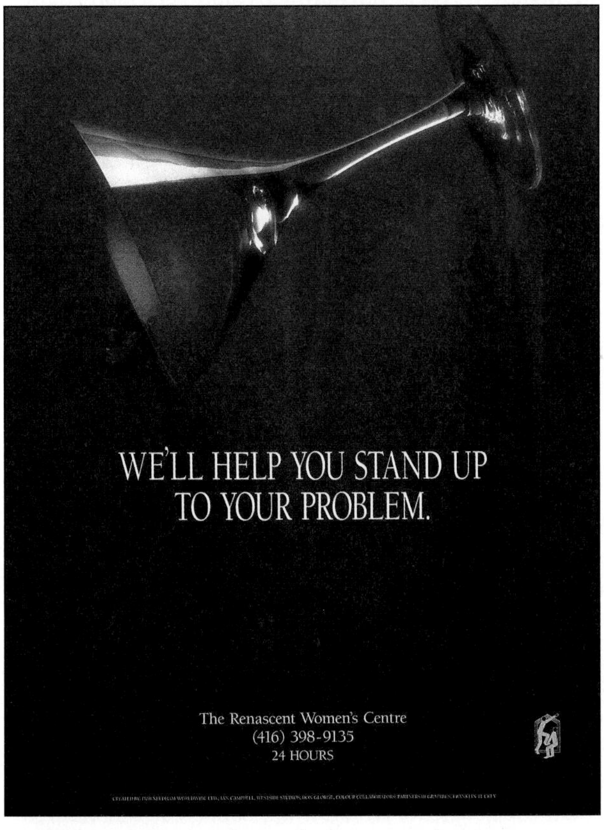
WE'LL HELP YOU STAND UP
TO YOUR PROBLEM.
The Renascent Women's Centre
(416) 398-9135
24 HOURS

**What is being exchanged when one donates to The Renascent Centres?**

While this list generally is a classification of not-for-profit organizations, note that there are some exceptions. A number of organizations within these groups — certain museums and performing-arts groups, for example — are *profit-seeking* organizations.

### The Exchange Concept and Not-For-Profit Marketing

In Chapter 1, marketing was broadly defined as an exchange intended to satisfy the wants of all parties involved in the exchange. And marketing consists of all activities designed to facilitate such exchanges. A discussion of marketing in not-for-profit organizations is certainly consistent with this broad, exchange-concept definition of marketing, for not-for-profit organizations are also involved in exchanges.

As an example, Roots, a business organization, sells you a sweatshirt or jacket in exchange for a sum of money. In a similar vein, a local theatre company, a not-for-profit organization, may provide you with an evening's entertainment in exchange for money. A charitable organization, such as the Salvation Army, provides you with a feeling of satisfaction and of having helped others, in exchange for a donation. The Canadian Red Cross may provide you with a similar, intangible feeling when you donate blood. Finally, your university or college, another not-for-profit organization, offers you access to education and other experiences, in return for your money, time, and commitment.

### Markets Involved in Not-for-Profit Marketing

A major difference between business and not-for-profit marketing is that not-for-profit organizations must reach more than one group with their marketing efforts. Business executives have traditionally defined their basic market as being made up of present and potential customers. They have thus directed their marketing efforts primarily towards this one group. In contrast, most not-for-profit organizations are involved with *three* major markets. One of these groups consists of the **contributors** (of money, labour, services, or materials) to the organization. Here the not-for-profit organization's task is that of "resource attraction."

The other major target market is the organization's **clients** — the recipient of its money or services. This recipient market is much like that of the customers of a business company. However, not-for-profit organization — such churches, charities, nursing homes, symphony orchestras, or universities — are unlikely to refer to their client-recipients as customers. Instead these organizations use such terms as *parishioners*, *members*, *patients*, *audience*, or *students*.

A third very important group for most not-for-profit organizations is **volunteers**. Some writers may group them under contributors, but they are a special group of contributors who deserve special attention. They may also be donors of money, but they are for the most part people who devote their time and energy to ensuring that the organization functions. They are the Scout leaders, the Big Brothers and Big Sisters, the soccer coaches, the "candy stripers" at the local hospital, the "friends" of the botanical garden, and the behind-the-scenes people at the production of the summer theatre. They are in many cases what makes not-for-profit organizations work. Without volunteers, many not-for-profits would not exist.

**Bishop Strachan starts early to recruit students.**

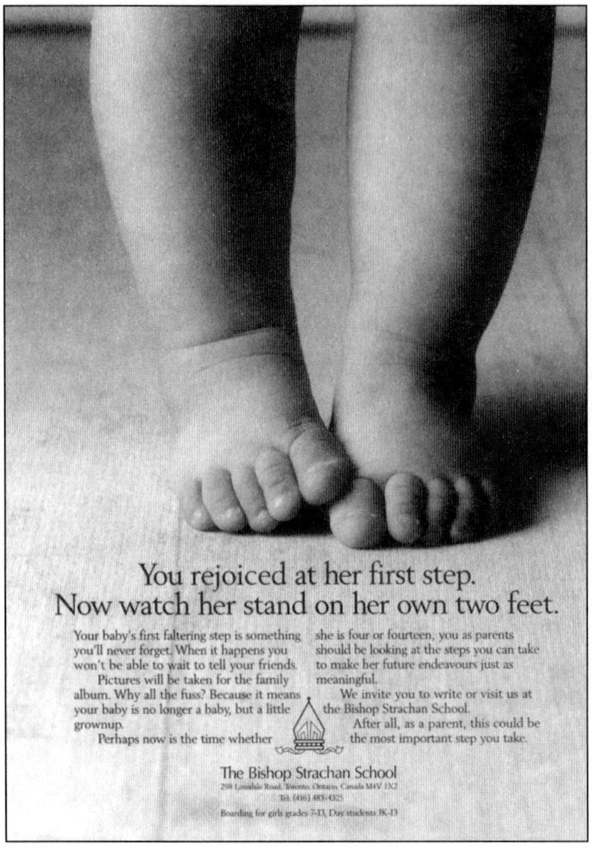

You rejoiced at her first step.
Now watch her stand on her own two feet.
Your baby's first faltering step is something you'll never forget. When it happens you won't be able to wait to tell your friends.
Pictures will be taken for the family album. Why all the fuss? Because it means your baby is no longer a baby, but a little grownup.
Perhaps now is the time whether she is four or fourteen, you as parents should be looking at the steps you can take to make her future endeavours just as meaningful.
We invite you to write or visit us at the Bishop Strachan School.
After all, as a parent, this could be the most important step you take.
The Bishop Strachan School
298 Lonsdale Road, Toronto, Ontario, Canada M4V 1X2
Boarding for girls grades 7-13, Day students JK-13

This distinction between business and not-for-profit marketing, based on the major markets involved, is significant for this reason: A not-for-profit organization must develop two separate marketing programs — one looking "back" to its contributors and volunteers, and the other looking "forward" to its clients. Moreover, like businesses, not-for-profit organizations also have relationships with several publics in addition to their main markets. A university, for example, must deal with government agencies, environmentalists, mass media, its faculty and staff, and the local community.

**Importance of Not-for-Profit Marketing** The attention that has been devoted to marketing by not-for-profit organizations in recent years is long overdue. Thousands of such organizations handle many millions of dollars each year and affect the lives of millions of people. Their work is extremely important in promoting behaviour and ideas that are in the broad public interest. Yet there are situations where the operation of not-for-profit organizations is not as efficient as it might be, in part because they do not have the resources to ensure efficiency. In some cases, we hear of a large portion of the money raised by some organizations going to cover administrative costs rather than being used to benefit the people for whom it was collected. When such events occur, there is a dual social and economic loss — donors' gifts are wasted and clients are not served efficiently.

Marketing's significance also becomes apparent when not-for-profit organizations fail to do an effective marketing job. The result may be additional social and economic costs and waste. If the death rate from smoking rises because the Canadian Cancer Society and other similar organizations cannot persuade people of the harm of smoking, we all lose. When anti-litter organizations fail to convince people to control their solid-waste disposal, we all lose. When good museums or good symphony orchestras must cease operating because of lack of contributions or lack of attendance, again there are social and economic losses.

By developing an effective marketing program, a not-for-profit organization can increase immeasurably its chance of (1) satisfactorily serving both its contributor and client markets and (2) improving the overall efficiency of its operations.

## NOT-FOR-PROFIT ATTITUDE TOWARDS MARKETING

People in not-for-profit organizations often do not realize that they are "running a business" and should therefore employ business management techniques. It is true that making a profit is not the goal of these organizations. Nevertheless, they do need to identify goals, plan strategies and tactics to reach these goals, effectively execute their plans, and evaluate their performance. Yet only very recently have many not-for-profit organizations started to employ accounting systems, financial controls, personnel management and labour relations, and other business management techniques.

Unfortunately, the acceptance of business management techniques often does not include planned marketing programs. Some not-for-profit organizations do not seem at all comfortable with marketing. To many of these groups, marketing means some form of promotion, such as advertising or personal selling. These organizations often do not understand the concept of a total marketing program.

Many not-for-profit groups speak about marketing and even believe they are practising it. But in many cases they still have a strong production orientation or, at best, a selling orientation. These organizations tend to select — on their own — the goods, services, or ideas that they *think* their customers want (or should want). Then they decide how to distribute or sell these products. Only at the end of the process do these groups analyze their markets. This really is not a marketing orientation.

People working in not-for-profit organizations sometimes have a negative attitude towards marketing. They are apt to think that having a marketing program — and using the term *marketing* — is demeaning and in bad taste. They may even feel that it is unethical to use marketing in their organizations.

Perhaps the choice of words is important. The governing body in a church, for instance, will not object to "informational notices" (don't call it "advertising") in newspapers or in church bulletins regarding church activities. When church members go to foreign lands to bring new members into the fold, the churches don't call this activity "personal selling." It is "missionary work."

Not-for-profit groups seem to face a dilemma. On the one hand, they often are unaware of what marketing is all about or may have a negative attitude towards it. Yet, on the other hand, these organizations typically are in great need of effective marketing programs. However, as we move through the late 1990s, the marketing climate in not-for-profit organizations is continually improving as the need for marketing is finally recognized.

While most not-for-profit organizations have been slower than their profit-oriented counterparts to employ modern marketing strategies and techniques, changing economic and social conditions have made many realize that they must do a better job of examining and understanding their "markets" and of marketing their operations. Not-for-profit organizations can no longer count on contributions from federal and provincial government sources as they have in the past — health care and education organizations have been par-

## MARKETING AT WORK

### FILE 22-2 THE PHANTOM COMES TO CALGARY

As soon as it was announced in February 1990 that the hit Andrew Lloyd Webber musical *Phantom of the Opera* would tour Canada, officials of the Calgary District Hospital Group (CDHG) got to work. Their plan was to organize a gala opening-night benefit performance that would raise funds for their hospitals. The CDHG had gained valuable experience organizing benefits in the past, including the successful 1991 gala opening of the Calgary Eaton Centre and an annual Fascinatin' Rhythm benefit dinner and dance, and soon got the support from the executive committee and board of trustees. The hard work then began to convince the Live Entertainment Corporation of Canada, producers of *Phantom*, to allow CDHG to stage an opening-night charity gala.

More than two years passed before *Phantom* finally opened in Calgary on June 2, 1992. The process that led to the successful opening-night gala began with an elaborate proposal to Live Entertainment consisting of numerous examples of CDHG's ability to host such an event: press clippings of previous events, sample programs, testimonials, and proposed ticket prices ranging from $150 to $250 per seat. The chairman of the project committee, Peter Burgener, presented the proposal in person to Live Entertainment in Toronto. Lynda Friendly, Live Entertainment's executive vice-president, later said the CDHG's was one of more than 100 suggestions for an opening-night program for Calgary, but was "by far the most comprehensive and persistent proposal we've ever received for a benefit gala."

Once the proposal had been accepted, the work really began to line up co-sponsors, arrange caterers and a band, secure door prizes, and generally attend to details that would make opening night a major success. In the end, corporate sponsorship was arranged with members of the Calgary business community, including Calgary Eaton Centre, TD Square, Western Gas Marketing, Canada Safeway, Pepsi-Cola, Royal Bank of Canada, AGT Limited, Seagrams, The Westin Hotel, and Canadian Airlines International. An opening-night lottery was organized with a grand prize of $100,000 and attractive door prizes, such as trips to San Francisco and custom-designed Phantom jewellery, were offered.

After two years of planning and attention to detail, with the support of many members of the Calgary business community and the untiring work of hundreds of volunteers, the CDHG's sponsorship of the opening night of *Phantom of the Opera* was a resounding success, netting the hospital almost $300,000 to be put to good use supporting hospital programs and services.

Source: Lyle Walton, "The Phantom Strikes Again," *Fund Raising Management*, April 1993, pp. 38-40.

ticularly hard hit as budgets are slashed. Changes to federal tax laws have made it less attractive to donate to charities as amounts that can be claimed as deductions have been reduced. With the slow economic times of the early 1990s, corporations and individuals have been less able and less willing to donate to charities. At the same time, competition for funds has been coming from a new generation of social causes, including AIDS education, Alzheimer's disease, child and sexual abuse, and drunk driving. Similarly, the demands being placed on many social agencies such as the Salvation Army, food banks, churches, and shelters, have never been greater. These changes have caused many not-for-profit organizations to realize that they must be professionally managed if they are to survive.

## DEVELOPING A STRATEGIC PROGRAM FOR NOT-FOR-PROFIT MARKETING

The basic procedure for planning and developing a marketing program is the same in any organization — profit or not-for-profit. That is, first we identify and analyze the target markets, and then we develop a strategic marketing mix that will provide want-satisfaction to those markets. Throughout the process we use marketing research to help in our decision making.

**The Metro Toronto Zoo uses humour to attract visitors.**

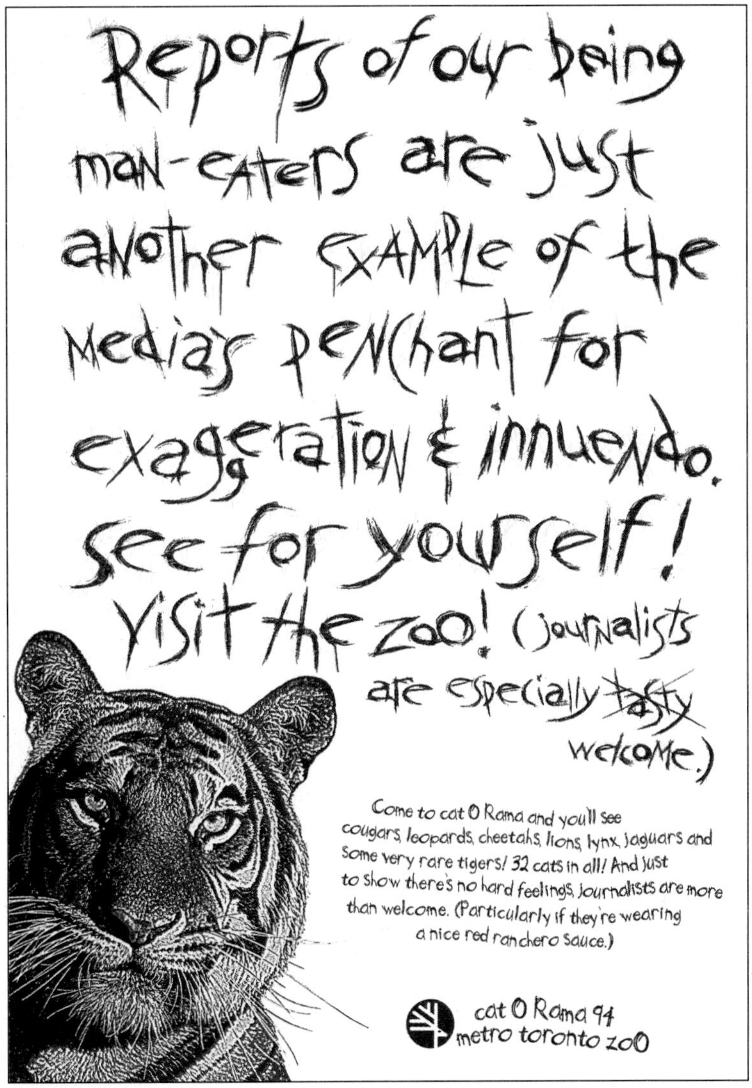

Reports of our being man-eaters are just another example of the media's penchant for exaggeration & innuendo.
see for yourself! Visit the zoo! (journalists are especially tasty welcome.)
Come to cat O Rama and you'll see cougars, leopards, cheetahs, lions, lynx, jaguars and some very rare tigers! 32 cats in all! And just to show there's no hard feelings, journalists are more than welcome. (Particularly if they're wearing a nice red ranchero sauce.)
cat O Rama 94
metro toronto zoo

### Target-Market Analysis

Not-for-profit organizations need two major marketing programs — one for the contributor market and one for the client market. It is important to pinpoint each market in some detail. Market pinpointing means using market segmentation. A broad (nonsegmented) appeal to the *donor* market is likely to result in a low return. Trying to be all things to all people in the *recipient* market is likely to result in being "nothing to nobody" and going broke in the process.

The possible bases for market segmentation for not-for-profit groups are generally the same as those discussed in Chapters 4 and 5. In trying to reach its *contributor* market, for example, an organization may segment its appeals by age group, geographic place of residence, record of past donations, or size of past donations. Recently, research has been devoted to segmenting donor markets on the basis of the benefits that donors derive from giving, their motivations, and the relationships that they establish with the not-for-profit organizations they support.[1] Segmentation analysis, involving examination of the demographic characteristics, needs, motivations and life-styles of donors, is critical to better understanding the segment of the market that supports charitable and social causes.

Many not-for-profit organizations segment their *client* markets, although they probably do not refer to this technique as market segmentation. For instance, political parties and major charities conduct fund-raising efforts that are directed at large corporate donors, smaller local businesses, professional groups such as lawyers and doctors, and former members or supporters. Country clubs develop different programs and membership categories for golfers, tennis players, swimmers, and curlers. Universities and colleges segment prospective students on the basis of age (current high school graduates and older people who are returning to university as "mature" students) and on their area of interest (engineering, science, business, etc.).

A decision to employ market segmentation means that a not-for-profit organization must tailor all or part of its marketing program to reach each segment — be it donor or client. Thus the product offering and the promotion may have to be adapted to each major segment.

Careful market analysis requires sophisticated marketing research to identify the various markets. This poses a problem because many not-for-profit organizations are not familiar with marketing research. But there are encouraging prospects in this area. Political parties and individual politicians, for example, are frequent users of opinion polls to determine voters' preferences on candidates and issues. Segmentation research also has been used to identify the characteristics of various market segments attending art museums and presentations of the performing arts (opera, concerts, theatres).

## Product Planning

Like a profit-seeking business firm, a not-for-profit organization must decide (1) what products it will offer, (2) what will be the nature of its product mix, and (3) what, if anything, it will do about product attributes such as branding and labelling. In not-for-profit marketing, again, an organization needs two sets of product strategies — one for its contributor market and one for its client market.

**Product Offering** In most not-for-profit organizations, the "product offering" to *clients* typically is a service, an idea, a person (in politics), or a cause. In the case of foundations and charitable organizations, the product offering often is a cash grant — a form of tangible product. Other organizations may offer such tangible products as food and clothing, printed materials, or birth control devices. However, in such cases the tangible products are incidental to the main services provided by the organization.

The key to selecting a product offering is for an organization to decide (1) what "business" it is in and (2) what client markets it wants to reach. If a church views its mission only as providing religious services, its product offering will be relatively limited. On the other hand, if this church views its mission more broadly — as providing fellowship, spirituality, and personal development — it will offer more services to more markets. The church may then offer family counselling services, day-care services, religious education courses, and social activities for seniors.

Planning the product offering to the *contributor* market is more difficult. An organization asks people to donate their money or time to a cause. The money or time is the price that contributors pay for the organization's "product." But what are they getting for this price? What is the product that contributors are buying with their donations? The product is an assortment of benefits for donors and volunteers that includes:

- Making donors and volunteers feel good.
- Supporting their favourite organizations.
- Providing them with a tax deduction for donations.
- Contributing to their status in reference groups.
- Supporting their religious beliefs.

**How would you describe the product offering of ABC Canada?**

A child's *mind* is an *open* book.
As a parent, it is your responsibility to fill the pages of a child's mind with wonder and joy. Reading together is a delightful way of accomplishing this and a means of ensuring that your child's future remains an open book.
Prepare a young mind for tomorrow. Open a book today.
ABC
CANADA
Literacy Foundation
Fondation pour l'alphabétisation
Distribution of this message was made possible by the Canadian Advertising Foundation
ABC-92-1025
"Open Book"
English
Trade Size Magazine
Revised/CAF


Management's task in product planning is to match a given benefit with the market segment that wants that benefit. Thus, the benefit of a tax deduction would be the product offering to one market segment, while another segment would be offered the benefit of furthering the organization's work. The difficulty lies in identifying the group of potential contributors (buyers) that want a particular benefit.

**Product-Mix Strategies** Several of the product-mix strategies discussed in Chapter 8 can be employed in not-for-profit marketing. Consider, for instance, the strategy of *expanding the product line*. Symphony orchestras have broadened their lines by offering concerts appealing to children and popular-music concerts for teenagers and college-age people. Universities expanded their mix when they added adult night courses, off-campus extension programs, and concentrated between-semester courses. Many larger hospitals have added hostels for the families of long-stay patients, diet counselling programs, and home-care programs.

The strategy of *product differentiation* is as important in not-for-profit organizations as it is in business. The principle is to set one's organization or program apart from the "competition" so as to encourage donations or support, or to attract clients. Many universities have differentiated their programs to attract students. Universities that serve populations scattered over wide geographic areas, such as Athabaska University and Memorial University of Newfoundland, deliver many courses and degree programs through distance education. Queen's University redesigned its MBA program so that it can be taken in cities across Canada through teleconferencing, or on the Kingston campus in a 12-month format. Many Canadian universities, including Memorial, Queen's, and the University of Guelph, offer degree programs that give students an option to study at the universities' campuses in Britain for a semester or more.

The *product life cycle* concept can be applied to not-for-profit marketing. Just as many business products and services become outdated and are replaced with new market entrants, so too do some not-for-profit organizations find that their entire reason for existence may no longer be relevant. This is especially the case in health-related organizations where (thankfully) progress is made in treating or even eradicating a particular disease. For example, organizations that were started many years ago to fight polio found that, particularly after the development of the Salk vaccine, they were headed into the decline stage of the life cycle. As a result, some health organizations alter their mandate to take in a broader range of health problems. Thus, the Canadian Heart Foundation became the Heart and Stroke Foundation, and the Canadian Tuberculosis Association became the Lung Association, as tuberculosis became much less prevalent in Canada. Unfortunately, such health issues as AIDS and Alzheimer's disease are in the growth stage of their life cycles.

**Product Attributes** Not-for-profit groups generally do not use product strategies such as branding and labelling. The little that has been done in this area, however, suggests that a not-for-profit organization can make its marketing more effective by emphasizing product attributes. For many years, colleges and universities have used nicknames (a form of brand name) primarily for their athletic teams, but also to identify their students and alumni. Most colleges and universities have school colours — another product attribute that helps increase the market's recognition and identification of the school.

Among health-research organizations, the Lung Association has registered as a trademark its double-barred Christmas-seal cross. The trademarks of the Girl Guides, the YM-YWCA, and Rotary International are recognized and remembered by many people.

### Price Determination

Pricing in many not-for-profit organizations is quite different from pricing in a business firm. Pricing becomes less important when profit making is not an organizational goal. Also, many not-for-profit groups believe there are no client-market pricing considerations in their marketing because there is no charge to the client. The organization's basic function is to help those who cannot afford to pay.

Actually, the goods or services received by clients rarely are free — that is, without a price of some kind. True, the price may not be a monetary charge. Often, however, the client pays a price — in the form of travel and waiting time and, perhaps, degrading treatment — that a money-paying client-customer would not have to pay for the same service. Poor children who have to wear donated, secondhand clothes certainly are paying a price if their classmates ridicule these clothes. Alcoholics Anonymous and some drug rehabilitation organizations that provide "free" services do exact a price. They require active participation by their clients as well as a very strongly expressed resolve by clients to help themselves.

Some not-for-profit groups do face the same pricing problems discussed in Chapters 13 and 14. Museums and opera companies must decide on admission prices; membership organizations must set a dues schedule; and colleges and universities must determine how much to charge for tuition. Not-for-profit organizations must (1) determine the base price for their product offering and (2) establish pricing strategies in several areas of their pricing structure.

**Setting the Base Price** Here again we are faced with two market situations — pricing in the contributor market and pricing in the client market.

When dealing with the contributor market, not-for-profit organizations really do not set the price of the donation. That price is set by contributors when they decide how much they are willing to pay for the benefits they expect to receive in return for their gifts. However, the organization may suggest a price. A charitable organization, for example, may suggest that you donate one day's pay or that you donate your time for one day a month.

Some of our discussion regarding the pricing of services (Chapter 12) is appropriate to the client market — for instance, in pricing admissions to museums, concerts, or theatre performances. But for most not-for-profit groups, the pricing methods used by business firms — cost-plus, balance of supply and demand, market alone — simply are not appropriate. Many organizations know they cannot cover their costs with prices charged to clients. The gap between anticipated revenues and costs must be made up by contributions.

As yet, there are no real guidelines — no methodology — for much not-for-profit pricing. A major problem here is that most not-for-profit organizations do not know the cost of the goods and services they offer in their client markets.

**Pricing Strategies** Some of the pricing strategies discussed in Chapter 14 are also applicable in not-for-profit marketing. Discount strategies have widespread use, for example. Some museums offer discount prices to students and senior citizens. A season ticket for many theatre companies or symphony orchestras costs less per performance than tickets purchased on an individual-performance basis. This is a form of quantity discount.

Considerations regarding one price versus variable price also are strategies applicable in not-for-profit marketing. Some charities provide services according to the client's ability to pay — a variable-price strategy. A one-price strategy typically is followed by universities. That is, all students pay the same tuition for a full load of coursework in a particular degree program.

### Distribution System

Setting up a distribution system in a not-for-profit organization involves two tasks. One is to establish channels of distribution back to contributors and forward to clients. The other task, usually the more important one, is to set up a physical distribution system to reach these two markets.

**Channels of Distribution** The channels of distribution used in not-for-profit marketing ordinarily are quite simple and short. The not-for-profit organization usually deals directly with its two major publics — no intermediaries are involved.

When an intermediary is used, it is an agent intermediary. For instance, to generate increased contributions, a political party or a university may employ an outside fund-raising organization. To reach potential customers, ballet companies, art galleries, and theatres may sell tickets through independent ticket agencies. In some cities programs like Neighbourhood Watch and Crime Stoppers effectively use local police personnel as intermediaries. They distribute crime-prevention literature and programs to schools and to the general public.

## MARKETING AT WORK

### FILE 22-3 HOW MUCH FOR SERGEANT MURPHY'S ROOKIE CARD?

The hottest trading cards in Calgary these days have little to do with the Flames or the Stampeders. You can't even buy them — not for any price. But, when you see one of Calgary's finest, just ask.

In an innovative public relations gesture, the constables and officers of Calgary's District Six have produced their own trading card collection, and they are handing them out free to anyone who asks. The project involved the printing of more than 60,000 cards: 1,000 each of 60 different cards, each of which has a photo of a police officer on the front and personal information on the back.

By providing the trading cards, Calgary police hope to build bridges between themselves and young people in the city of Calgary. The cards are aimed specifically at kids aged 8 to 15, but interest is being expressed from a much wider audience. Keith Davis, a civilian administrator with the Calgary Police Service, observed, "The cards show cops are human. We're trying to reach out to kids a bit and establish communication and also provide alternate role models. "

While Calgary is the first Canadian police force to issue its own trading cards, the idea began in California with the Campbelltown police force and spread to other American cities, including Houston, South Portland, and San Diego. The Calgary project is being funded entirely by the Calgary Real Estate Board. Davis indicates that the police force has been "bowled over by the response."

Source: Adapted from Terry Bullick, "Calgary Cop Cards Promote Community Relations," *Marketing*, April 25, 1994, p. 4.

Numerous not-for-profit organizations have established a separate marketing program whereby they serve as a retailer of goods that are related to the organization's primary service. Thus, we see art museums selling prints of paintings, colleges selling many items through the college bookstore, post offices selling stamps to collectors, and Planned Parenthood selling or giving away contraceptives. Over-the-counter and mail-order methods of retail selling may also be used in these situations.

**Physical Distribution** The primary goal in physical distribution is for a not-for-profit organization to locate where it can serve both contributors and clients most effectively. The organization should be as accessible as possible to its contributors so that giving is as easy and convenient as possible. Besides cash and cheques, charities use payroll deductions, installment plans, and credit cards. If the donor is contributing used goods, they may collect them at the donor's residence or at some other choice location instead of forcing the donor to haul the stuff across town to a central collection point.

Location is also critical in dealing with client markets. Thus, universities and colleges set up campuses in smaller cities and offer correspondence courses. Goodwill locates its stores in low-income neighbourhoods. Health-care organizations provide mobile units for lung X-rays, blood-pressure tests, and inoculations. City museums and art galleries arrange for portable exhibits to be taken to small towns.

### Promotion Program

Promotion is the part of the marketing mix that many not-for-profit organizations are most familiar with and most adept at. They have regularly used advertising, personal selling, sales promotion, and publicity — often very aggressively and effectively — to communicate with both their contributors and their clients. However, many of these organizations have not integrated their promotional mix into a total marketing program. In fact, many not-for-profit groups believe that promotion and marketing are one and the same thing.

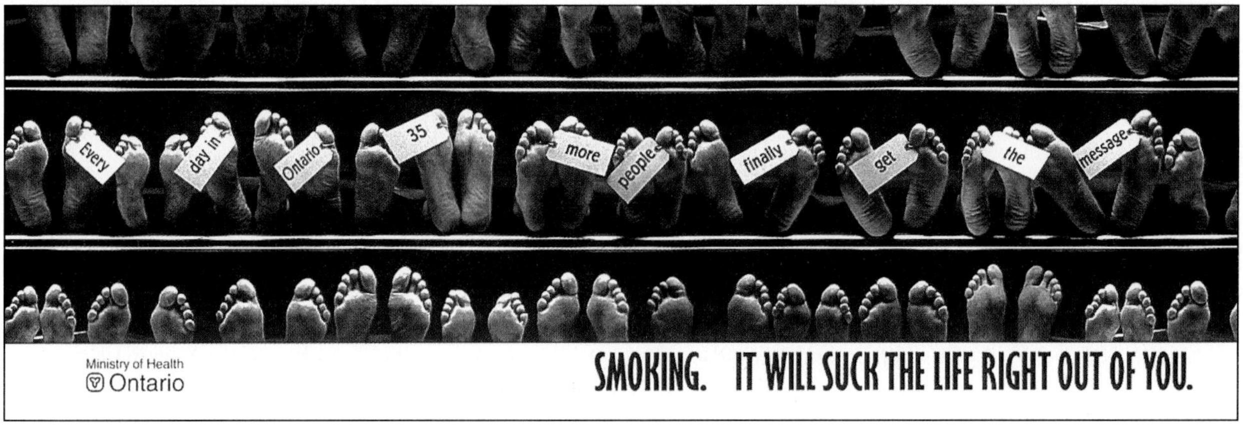

Every
day in
Ontario
35
more
people
finally
get
the
message
Ministry of Health
Ontario
SMOKING. IT WILL SUCK THE LIFE RIGHT OUT OF YOU.


**This is rather dramatic anti-smoking advertising.**

Advertising Advertising is used extensively to reach the donor market. Many not-for-profit organizations conduct annual fund-raising drives. Mass media (newspapers, magazines, television, radio) frequently are used in these efforts. Specific media also are used selectively to solicit funds. Direct mail can be especially effective in reaching segmented donor markets such as past contributors, religious or ethnic groups related to the organizations, or college alumni. Media such as alumni magazines and foreign-language newspapers can be used to pinpoint donor market segments.

Not-for-profit groups also can communicate with client markets through advertising. To offset declining enrolments, colleges and universities have run ads in a variety of media. A growing number of churches are advertising in print media and on radio and TV to increase their membership and attendance.

In some situations, a not-for-profit organization can reach both its contributor and its client markets with the same ad. The Heart and Stroke Association, the Canadian Cancer Society, or the Lung Association might advertise, asking you to contribute to its annual campaign. In the same ad, it might urge you to watch your diet, quit smoking, or get a medical checkup.

Personal Selling Personal selling is often employed in fund-raising efforts. A door-to-door campaign may be used. At Christmastime, Salvation Army volunteers, standing by their red kettles, collect donations in the downtown areas of many cities. And potential large donors may be approached by sales people.

Many not-for-profit organizations also use personal selling to reach their client public. These personal representatives may not be called sales people, but that is exactly what they are. For centuries, missionaries of countless religious groups have recruited new members by personal contact — personal selling. Personal selling also is employed to recruit new members for service organizations such as the YM-YWCA, Lions, Rotary, and Kiwanis. Colleges and universities send "sales people" — admission officers, alumni, current students — to talk to high school students, their parents, and their counsellors.

Using sales representatives to reach either contributors or clients poses some management problems for a not-for-profit organization. In effect, the organization has to manage a sales force, including recruiting, training, compensating, supervising, and evaluating performance. Not many not-for-profit organizations think in these terms, however, nor are they qualified to do this management job.

Sales Promotion Not-for-profit organizations have long recognized the value of sales promotion to reach their markets. Many organizations place exhibits (including donation boxes) in local stores and shopping centres and at sporting events. Usually there is no charge for this use of the space.

## IMPLEMENTATION OF MARKETING

In this final section we discuss briefly three topics that will affect the future development of marketing in not-for-profit organizations.

### Interest and Research in the Field

Marketing in not-for-profit organizations has a bright future. There is not only a growing interest in marketing among such organizations, but there is increasing evidence that volunteer leaders and full-time executives in the not-for-profit field really understand how the principles of marketing can be applied in a not-for-profit context and what marketing can contribute to their own organizations. Numerous books are being written on the subject, and journals with a specific interest in social and not-for profit marketing are being published.[2] Increasingly, marketing courses at universities and colleges are devoting time to the study of not-for-profit organizations and the application of marketing principles to their operations. There is considerable research being carried out on the subject in Canadian universities and special sessions on not-for-profit marketing are increasingly common at academic conferences.

Just a few years ago, research in not-for-profit marketing was initiated mainly by academicians and other people outside the not-for-profit field being studied. Now the marketing research is being generated by people working within various not-for-profit fields. This is a healthy sign for the future.

### Measuring Performance

A real managerial challenge is to establish some valid means of measuring the marketing performance of a not-for-profit organization. At present this is very difficult, if not impossible, for many of these organizations. A private business can evaluate its performance by using such quantitative measures as market share or return on investment, and then compare these figures with industry-wide averages and trends. For most not-for-profit organizations, however, there are no corresponding quantitative measures.

Not-for-profit organizations can quantify the contributions they receive, but the result reflects only their fund-raising abilities. It does not measure the services rendered to their clients. How do you quantitatively evaluate the performance of, say, the Red Cross? Perhaps by the number of people who donate blood or who receive donated blood, or by the number of people they train in first aid and lifesaving techniques?

Churches, museums, and YM-YWCAs can count their attendance, but how can they measure the services they provide for their clients? How does the Canadian Cancer Society or the Lung Association assess its performance? By the decline in death rates from cancer and respiratory diseases? Perhaps, but such a decline may be due in part to factors other than the work of these health-research organizations. These are not easy questions to answer.

Increasingly, however, not-for-profit organizations are employing the same tools as marketers in businesses to assess the performance of their programs and of the organizations themselves. The Coalition for Head Injury Prevention carried out research on a program designed to promote increased use of bicycle helmets among children in Barrie, Ontario. The research showed that helmet use among elementary school children increased from 5.4 percent to 15.4 percent in one year.[3] Similarly, many hospitals are using patient satisfaction and service quality questionnaires to assess how well they are meeting the needs of their patients.[4] Some universities and colleges are even asking students whether they are satisfied with the way they are being served.

Just a little pedal power....
...active living—moving a little more, a little more often—makes a healthy difference for you and the environment!
PARTICIPACTION
Moving Your Way · Every Day

## Managing the Marketing Effort

As stressed throughout this chapter, not-for-profit organizations are becoming increasingly familiar with the concepts of marketing. In fact, some have been practising marketing for some time, although they may not have been using marketing terminology. The marketing activities that are performed by not-for-profit organizations centre, in many cases, on advertising and promotion and are often not well co-ordinated. Typically, in many not-for-profit organizations, especially at the local and provincial levels, the organization of a marketing program depends on the availability of knowledgeable volunteers who are prepared to devote the time and effort needed to put a program together. In many situations, people who are given responsibility for what are actually marketing activities have no background in the field. Even in large organizations, like a university or a hospital, it is rare to find an individual with a marketing title, although this is becoming more common in not-for-profit organizations who actually market services directly to the general public, such as theatre groups, symphony orchestras, and public zoos.

**How does Participaction measure the success of its advertising?**

Ideally, to establish a more formal marketing structure, a not-for-profit organization may select a group of people — both volunteer leaders and full-time staff — first to decide what marketing objectives the organization wishes to accomplish. Such a group, in a series of marketing planning sessions, can define the organization's marketing goals and objectives and identify marketing strategies that will assist in reaching those goals. Decisions can even be made on the establishment of an internal marketing department. In smaller organizations, where there are few full-time staff, it generally falls to the executive director or senior full-time staff member to oversee marketing activities. In such a case, the organization may have to rely quite heavily on board members or other volunteers who have experience in marketing.

In larger not-for-profit organizations, as commitment to marketing activities increases and as a more formal structure develops, the organization may create a new middle-management position in marketing, with the title, for example, of director of marketing. In some cases, the marketing role is filled by individuals with titles such as patient relations manager or client services director. Eventually, as the function develops within the organization, a more senior marketing management position may be established at a level comparable with a vice-president of marketing in a business firm.

## SUMMARY

The marketing fundamentals apply to not-for-profit organizations as well as to firms in the business sector. But the development and implementation of a strategic marketing program are quite different in not-for-profit fields.

The not-for-profit field includes thousands of organizations spanning educational, cultural, religious, charitable, social, health-care, and political activities. Because of the large amounts of money and numbers of people involved in these organizations, marketing is quite important. Yet many people in not-for-profit organizations often seem opposed to marketing. Some do not understand what marketing is or what it can do for their organizations.

Most not-for-profit organizations must deal with two major groups (markets) — the contributors to the organization and the client-recipients of the organization's money or services. Consequently, a not-for-profit organization must develop two separate marketing programs — one to attract resources from contributors and one to serve its clients.

In developing its marketing programs, a not-for-profit organization first must identify and analyze its markets. Market segmentation is especially helpful at this stage. Then the organization is ready to develop its strategic marketing mix. The product offering will be determined largely by deciding what business the organization is in and what client markets it wants to reach. Product-mix strategies, such as expansion of mix or product differentiation, may well be used. Pricing in many not-for-profit organizations is quite different from the usual price determination in a business firm. Channels of distribution typically are quite simple in not-for-profit marketing. The main distribution challenge is to physically locate the organization where it can serve both contributors and clients. In promotion, many organizations have used advertising, personal selling, and other tools extensively, aggressively, and quite effectively.

Interest and research in not-for-profit marketing are growing. Both should be of help in implementing marketing programs in the future. Two important problems still to be solved are those of (1) measuring performance in a not-for-profit organization and (2) developing an internal structure to manage the marketing effort.

## KEY TERMS AND CONCEPTS

**Exchange concept in not-for-profit marketing (669)**
**Contributor (donor) markets (670)**
**Client (recipient) markets (670)**
**Volunteers (670)**
**Importance of not-for-profit marketing (670)**
**Market segmentation in not-for-profit organizations (673)**
**The marketing mix in not-for-profit organizations:**
- **Product offering (674)**
- **Pricing (676)**
- **Distribution (677)**
- **Promotion (678)**

**Measuring marketing performance in not-for-profit organizations (680)**
**Managing a marketing program in not-for-profit organizations (681)**

## QUESTIONS AND PROBLEMS

1. Are *nonbusiness organizations* and *not-for-profit organizations* synonymous terms? If not,
   a. Name some nonbusiness organizations in which profit making is a major goal.
   b. Name some business organizations that are intentionally not-for-profit.
2. In this chapter it is noted that some people in not-for-profit organizations have a negative attitude towards marketing. What suggestions do you have for changing this attitude so that these people will appreciate the value of marketing for their organizations?
3. Identify the various segments of the contributor market for your college or university.
4. Identify the client markets for:
   a. Your college or university.
   b. The United Way.
   c. Your church or other place of worship.
   d. Police department in your city.
5. What are some target markets (publics), other than contributors or clients, for each of the following organizations?
   a. YM-YWCA.
   b. Community hospital.
   c. Your school.
6. What benefits do contributors derive from gifts to each of the following?

a. The Royal Winnipeg Ballet.
b. The Boy Scouts.
c. A symphony orchestra.
d. A candidate for election to the House of Commons.

7. What is the product offering of each of the following?
   a. A political candidate.
   b. A family-planning organization.
   c. An organization opposed to nuclear energy.
8. A financial consultant for your university or college has suggested a change in the school's pricing methods. He recommended that the school discontinue its present one-price policy, under which all full-time students pay the same tuition. Instead he recommended that the tuition vary by department within the university. Thus students majoring in high-cost fields of study, such as engineering or a laboratory science, would pay higher tuition than students in lower-cost fields, such as English or history. Should the school adopt this recommendation?
9. Explain how the concept of the marketing mix (product, price, distribution, promotion) is applicable to the marketing of the following social causes:
   a. The use of returnable bottles, instead of the throwaway type.
   b. The prevention of heart ailments.
   c. A campaign against littering.
   d. Obeying the 100-km-per-hour speed limit.
10. How would you measure the marketing performance of each of the following?
    a. A church.
    b. Your school.
    c. The Liberal Party of Canada.
    d. A group in favour of animal rights.
11. The performance of a charitable organization may be measured by the percentage of contributions distributed among its clients. Explain why you think this is or isn't an effective measure of marketing performance.

## HANDS-ON MARKETING

1. Select a local arts organization or charity and arrange an interview with the executive director or senior person responsible for marketing. Identify the various elements of the marketing program of the organization that correspond to the elements of the marketing mix — product, price, promotion, and distribution. Also, try to identify the types of information that the organization relies on to make marketing decisions.
2. Assume that your college or university wants to hire a director of marketing. Prepare a job description for this position, indicating its scope, activities, location within the school's administration, and responsibilities.

## NOTES AND REFERENCES


1. Dianne S. P. Cermak, Karen Maru File, and Russ Alan Prince, "A Benefit Segmentation of the Major Donor Market," *Journal of Business Research*, vol. 29, no. 2, February 1994, pp. 121-130.
2. You might wish to refer to Siri Espy, *Marketing Strategies for Nonprofit Organizations*, published by Lyceum Books, Chicago; Alan R. Andreasen, *Marketing for Social Change*, published by Jossey-Bass, San Francisco; and the *Journal of Public Policy and Marketing*, published by the American Marketing Association.
3. Kevin Khayat and Brian Salter, "Patient Satisfaction Surveys as a Market Research Tool for General Practices," *British Journal of General Practice*, vol. 44, no. 382, 1994, pp. 215-219.
4. Brian A. P. Morris, Nancy E. Trimble, and Shawn J. Fendley, "Increasing Bicycle Helmet Use in the Community," *Canadian Family Physician*, vol. 40, June 1994, pp. 1126-1131.

## CHAPTER 23 GOALS

In Chapter 3 we defined the management process in marketing as planning, implementing, and evaluating marketing in an organization. This process is illustrated in Figure 23-1, which is identical to Figure 3-1. Most of this book has dealt with **planning** a marketing program. We discussed how to select target markets and how to design a strategic program to deliver want-satisfaction to those markets.

In this chapter we discuss the implementation and evaluation of a marketing program. **Implementation** is the operational stage — the stage during which an organization attempts to carry out its strategic plan. At the end of an operating period (or even during the period) management should conduct an **evaluation** of the organization's performance — that is, determine how well the organization is achieving the goals set in its strategic planning.

After studying this chapter, you should have an understanding of:

- The role of implementation in the management process.
- Organizational structures used to implement marketing.
- The tasks of staffing and operating in the implementation process.
- The role of a marketing audit in evaluating a marketing program.
- The meaning of misdirected marketing effort.
- Sales volume analysis.
- Marketing cost analysis.

CHAPTER 23

# MARKETING IMPLEMENTATION

## Marketing Internally for Great Customer Service

Four Seasons Hotels Inc. chairman Isadore Sharp believes that the company he founded "is now in the strongest position in its history." He believes that the hotel chain's brand image, its locations, and its staff enable it to dominate the high end of the hotel market. The first link in the Four Seasons chain was launched by Sharp in 1961 when he opened a motel on Jarvis Street in downtown Toronto. The modest motel has now grown to a company that manages 38 hotels scattered from Bangkok to Boston. The Four Seasons also owns pieces of many of the operations it manages. Success has come to Four Seasons because everyone involved in management and operations worries about the details, about how to make the chain's strategy a reality, and about implementation. By paying attention to the details of customer service, Four Seasons has become one of the finest names in luxury lodging.

The key to both the Four Seasons image and its reality is what is called "internal marketing." At Four Seasons, management works to ensure that the staff is committed to the goal of the best possible treatment for its customers. Management applies marketing principles to "sell the staff" on their role in providing customer satisfaction. After all, if the staff doesn't "buy" the strategy and the manner in which it is supposed to be implemented, then why should the customer? Management at Four Seasons has to be able to provide its core service, accommodation, at least as well as Hilton International or Hyatt. The Four Seasons' supplementary services are what distinguish it from Hilton, Hyatt, and others.

Whether a guest will return to the Four Seasons is influenced to a great extent by how he or she is treated. Good customer service — the positive interaction between customers and staff — is critical to a hotel's success. Various studies show that the staff at the Four Seasons is friendly, helpful, knowledgeable, polite, and personable — and not because they were born that way or "it just happened." It's because all personnel have been included in the process of examining what customer service means (the product to be internally marketed). They have been trained formally as well as having observed managers exemplifying good customer service (the distribution component of internal marketing). Employees have also seen the dollar investment that Four Seasons has made to achieve the goals of customer satisfaction (the price aspect of internal marketing). And, of course, Four Seasons personnel have been provided with information in various ways over their careers so that they can understand and internalize the important aspects of the Four Seasons' customer service program.

Successful internal marketing results in successful external marketing. It's not a surprise that Four Seasons has such a fine reputation. It's been earned within the organization so that it could be earned in the marketplace.[1]

## IMPLEMENTATION IN MARKETING MANAGEMENT

There should be a close relationship among planning, implementation, and evaluation. Without strategic planning, a company's operational activities — its implementation tactics — can go off in any direction, like an unguided missile. In the early 1980s, there was tremendous interest in strategic planning, sparked by management consulting firms. Then disenchantment set in, as many companies came to realize that strategic *planning* alone was not enough to ensure success. These plans had to be *effectively implemented.* Management began to realize that planners were great at telling them *what* to do — that is, designing a strategy. But planners often fell short when it came to telling *how* to do it — that is, how to implement the strategy.[2] As a marketing executive once said, "Too often those hot-shot planners could not sell a pair of shoes to a guy who is standing barefooted on a very hot sidewalk with a $50 bill in his hand."

No matter how good an organization's strategic planning may be, it is useless if those plans do not lead to effective action — that is, they are not implemented well. Good planning cannot overcome poor implementation. But effective implementation often can overcome poor planning. Fortunately, in the 1990s considerably more attention is being devoted to implementing a company's strategies. In the summer of 1992, for example, Chrysler spent $30 million to re-educate more than 100,000 employees in its dealerships. This training program supported (implemented) the introduction of the Chrysler

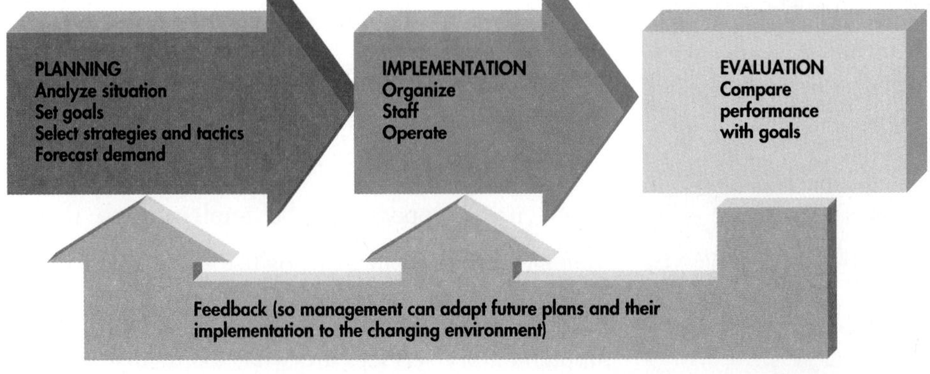


**FIGURE 23-1**
**The management process in marketing.**

Concorde, Dodge Intrepid, and Eagle Vision — the first completely new Chrysler cars since the early 1980s. Chrysler was concerned that dealers who had sold its earlier line of cars didn't know how to sell the sophisticated new cars to young, discerning customers.[3]

Implementation comprises three activities: (1) organizing the marketing effort, (2) staffing this organization, and (3) directing these people as they carry out the strategic plans.

## MARKETING AT WORK

### FILE 23-1 CAN A COMPANY SUCCESSFULLY PLAN GLOBALLY AND IMPLEMENT LOCALLY?

In the case of Bausch & Lomb (Ray-Ban sunglasses and contact lenses), the answer is "Yes, but it is not easy." The company found that the key lay in letting local managers make their own decisions. Prior to 1984, all production and marketing policies came from the company's headquarters in Rochester, New York. Since then, local managers have had considerably more control over implementation decisions. And in less than 10 years (1984-1992), international sales went from 25 percent to almost 50 percent of the company's total revenues.

Consider some examples. In Japan, Bausch & Lomb was going nowhere with its contact lenses, because they didn't meet the near-perfection requirements of Japanese ophthalmologists. In a new plant in Korea, the company developed a process to meet these requirements. By the early 1990s, Bausch & Lomb had boosted to 11 percent its share of the Japanese market.

Ray-Ban sunglasses provide another example of local implementation. They are recognized around the world, but until recently did not cater to foreign wants. In 1986 only one of the 25 new models was developed especially for foreign markets. In 1990 more than one-half of Ray-Ban's new products were developed for overseas markets. Europeans prefer a more flashy, costlier model than most North Americans do. In Asia, the company redesigned the glasses to better fit an Asian face, with its flatter nose bridge and higher cheekbones. Ray-Ban now holds about 40 percent of the world market for higher-priced ($40-$250) sunglasses.

**Ray-Ban sunglasses redesigned for the Asian market are hot sellers in stores like this one in Tokyo.**

In China, local Bausch & Lomb management decided to price contact lenses lower than anywhere else in the world. The company hoped to make up the revenue difference with an increase in the quantity of lenses sold. By 1992 China ranked number 3 in the world (behind the United States and Japan) in unit sales of contact lenses. The venture in China showed a profit after two years and repaid its initial investment in four years. Certainly there is something to be said for giving local managers some freedom in how they implement a company's strategic plans.

Source: Rahul Jacob, "Trust the Locals, Win Worldwide," *Fortune*, May 4, 1992, p. 76.

## ORGANIZING FOR IMPLEMENTATION

After setting a company's strategic marketing plan, an early activity is to organize the people who will be implementing it. This involves first defining the relationship between marketing and the other functional divisions of the firm. Then, *within* the marketing department, management must design an organization that will implement the plans.

**In addition to innovations in apprentice training and technology, Siemens today is applying its innovative spirit to its organizational structure.**

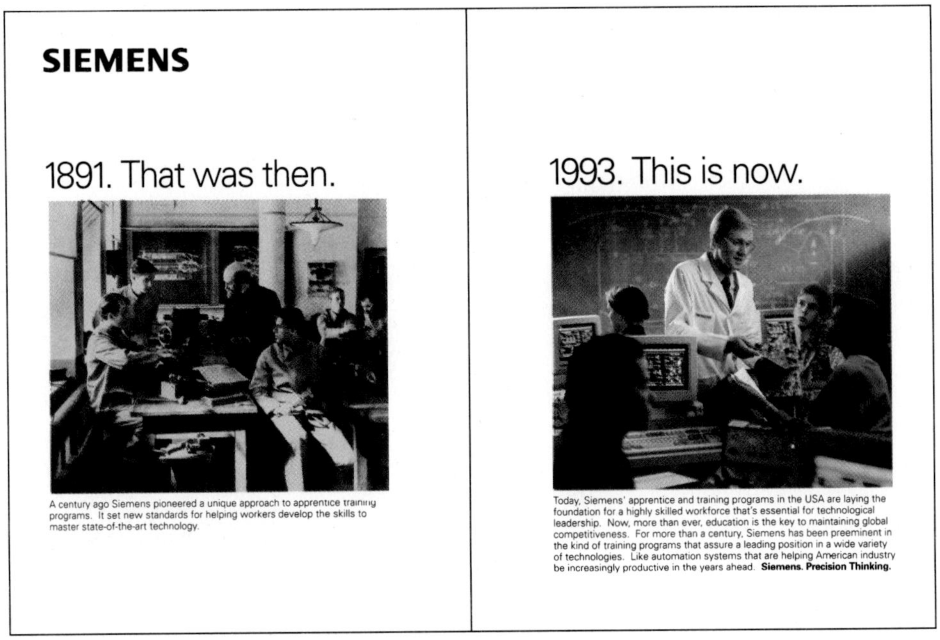

SIEMENS
1891. That was then.
A century ago Siemens pioneered a unique approach to apprentice training programs. It set new standards for helping workers develop the skills to master state-of-the-art technology.
1993. This is now.
Today, Siemens' apprentice and training programs in the USA are laying the foundation for a highly skilled workforce that's essential for technological leadership. Now, more than ever, education is the key to maintaining global competitiveness. For more than a century, Siemens has been preeminent in the kind of training programs that assure a leading position in a wide variety of technologies. Like automation systems that are helping American industry be increasingly productive in the years ahead. Siemens. Precision Thinking.

Organizational structures are receiving increasing attention in companies around the globe as management recognizes that yesterday's structures may hinder operations in today's dynamic environment. Hewlett-Packard, Xerox, Apple Computer, and the "Big 3" in North American autos are just a few of the companies that have made significant organizational changes in recent years.

Companies are streamlining their organizations by reducing the number of executive levels between the workers and the chief executive officer. To stimulate innovation, to reduce a smothering home-office bureaucracy, and to generate faster responses to market changes, firms are granting more authority to middle-level executives in decentralized locations. Siemens, the German electronics giant, for example, recently embarked on a major organizational overhaul designed to prepare the company for more intense competition, especially from the Japanese. Siemens wants to break from its traditional rigid executive hierarchy by developing 500 young middle managers with an entrepreneurial spirit. The company's new president, Heinrich Von Pierer, intends that these middle managers will couple Siemens' historical technical strength with innovative marketing to prepare the company for the next century.[4]

These changes show that firms today demand an organizational flexibility to respond quickly in a dynamic, information-driven marketing environment characterized by diversity and turbulence. Undoubtedly, new organization structures will continue to emerge in response to changing environments.[5]

### Company-Wide Organization

In Chapter 1 we stated that one of the three foundation stones of the marketing concept is to co-ordinate all marketing activities. In firms that are production-oriented or sales-oriented, typically we find that marketing activities are fragmented. The sales force is quite separate from advertising, and sales training may be under the personnel department.

In a marketing-oriented enterprise, all marketing activities are co-ordinated under one marketing executive, who usually is at the vice-presidential level. This executive reports directly to the president and is on an equal organizational footing with top executives in finance, production, and other major functions, as shown in Figure 23-2.

## MARKETING AT WORK

### FILE 23-2 EVALUATE, RE-ORGANIZE, AND IMPLEMENT AGAIN

J. D. Irving Ltd., a company primarily involved in forest products, was the owner of two New Brunswick newspapers: the *Telegraph-Journal*, which called itself a provincial paper, and the *Evening Times-Globe*, its sister paper. The fact was, however, that readers didn't see much difference between the two papers, which often carried identical stories. And advertisers didn't see any reason for choosing one over the other or, once the recession hit, for choosing either paper at all. For a while, it seemed as if the two were destined to go the way of many other Canadian papers — lost advertising revenue, diminished number of pages, staff layoffs, bankruptcy. . .

Valerie Millen, a corporate planning executive, was hired to evaluate the situation. She discovered a complete absence of management structure, financial controls, management information systems, reporting structures, and defined lines of responsibility. If advertising was in trouble, perhaps it had something to do with the fact that the advertising manager for both papers was very good at setting ambitious targets but had no way of measuring if they were met, because he had no access to financial results.

Once the evaluation was completed, it was time to implement some fast transformations, beginning with Millen being put in charge of change. "We changed everything in front of the press and everything behind the press — and all of the management," she said. One of the most significantly symbolic changes was her unconventional decision to call herself "general manager" of the papers, instead of the usual "publisher." The decision prompted tongues to wag at meetings of the Canadian Daily Newspaper Publishers Association, but Millen insisted on employees understanding that "this is a business like any other."

This vision of treating the papers as a business was to set the dominant tone for all subsequent changes Millen made. She introduced a new management structure with six department heads reporting to her and annual performance reviews. She replaced senior executives, created the new position of director of marketing, and brought a graphic designer in-house. She also daringly appointed as editor-in-chief, Neil Reynolds, the editor who had single-handedly converted the *Kingston Whig-Standard* from a sleepy, small-town paper into a nationally renowned, award-winning publication and whom she saw as "the best available person in Canada." "We needed somebody who could lead," she explained.

Once management was restructured and in place, Millen set her sights on the product at hand. Her objective was to reposition the two papers, making them into two distinct goods. Thus while the *Telegraph* became a provincial paper akin to a *Globe and Mail* of New Brunswick, the *Times-Globe* focused on becoming a local Saint John community paper. In order to modernize both papers and cut unnecessary costs, 50 jobs were eliminated so that manual paste-up could be replaced by computer pagination, and the mail room, telemarketing, and circulation systems could become fully automated. Several thousand subscribers in sparse rural areas of the province were dropped and mail subscriptions were curtailed. Finally, having dealt with production and distribution, Millen turned to packaging. Both papers were completely redesigned to present a bolder, more up-to-date look with a cleaner style, bigger print, and new banners and logos.

Of course it still remained to revamp the products themselves — in this case by changing the papers' editorial content, a responsibility that fell to Neil Reynolds. The first thing Reynolds did was to stop using the Canadian Press wire service at the *Times-Globe* and the many syndicated services employed by both papers. With the $500,000 he saved, more reporters were hired to improve local Saint John coverage in the *Times-Globe*; more correspondents were hired in *Telegraph-Journal* bureaus in Moncton and Fredericton. At a time when newspapers all over the country were busy laying off staff, 17 new editorial employees were being added to the papers, resulting in 55 workers in editorial out of a total work force of 194, compared with 46 out of 230 before the transformations. All of this seems like a minor miracle when one considers that no money had been added to the editorial budget. "It's all choices," explained Reynolds, noting that using Canadian Press for the two papers cost $350,000 a year.

Further cost cuts will be achieved by dropping the daily Toronto Stock Exchange listings in the *Telegraph-Journal*, publishing only the weekly TSE quotes on Saturday. "By habit, we were giving people things that weren't important to the majority of our readers," Reynolds said. Instead, he has introduced a supplementary magazine to the Saturday *Telegraph-Journal*.

From the outset, all these changes proved favourable with readers and advertisers alike and have subsequently given both papers a new lease on life. After its first few months, the reincarnated *Times-Globe* reported record circulation, up almost 10 percent from the previous year, and mostly in subscriptions as opposed to single-copy sales.

Source: Adapted from Harvey Enchin, "Irving Takes New Paper Route," *Globe and Mail*, November 27, 1993, pp. B1-2.

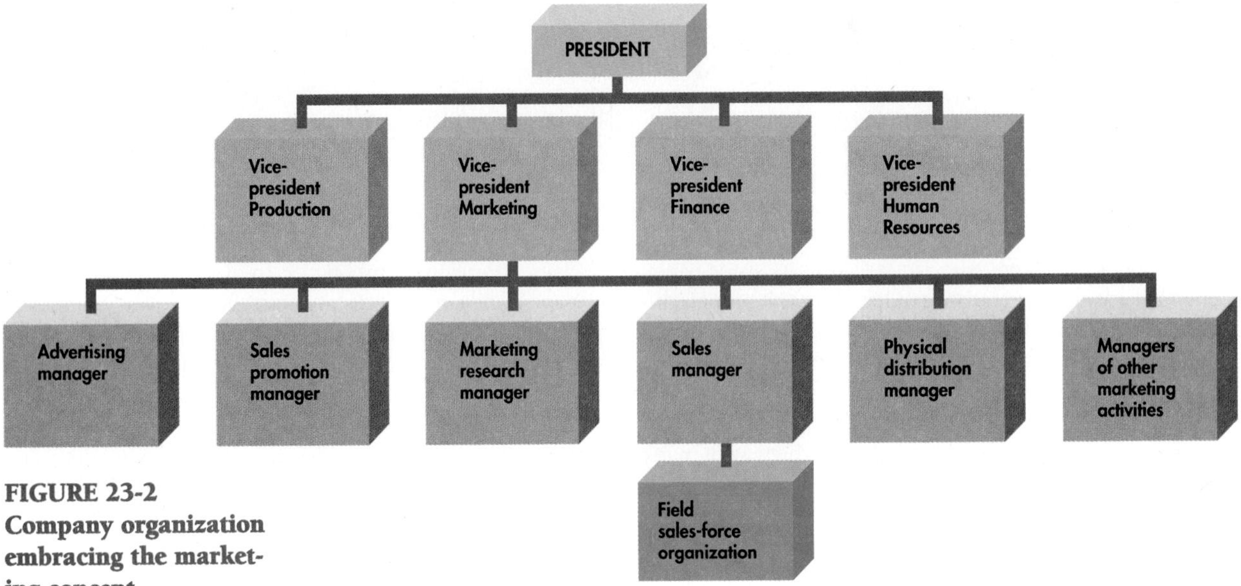


**FIGURE 23-2**
**Company organization embracing the marketing concept.**

Another aspect of organizational co-ordination is to establish effective working relationships between marketing and each of the other major functional areas. Marketing can help production, for example, by providing accurate sales forecasts. Production can return the favour with desired-quality products precisely when needed to fill customers' orders. Marketing and finance people can work together to establish pricing and credit policies.[6]

### Organization within the Marketing Department

Within the marketing department — especially in medium-sized or large firms — the sales force frequently is specialized in some organizational fashion. This is done to effectively implement the company's strategic marketing plan. The sales force may be organized in one of these three forms of specialization: geographic territory, product line, or customer type.

**Geographic Specialization** Probably the most widely used method of specializing selling activities is on the basis of **geographic specialization**. Each sales person is assigned a specific geographic area — called a *territory* — in which to sell. Several sales people representing contiguous territories are placed under a territorial sales executive, who reports directly to the general sales manager. These territorial executives usually are called *district* or *regional* sales managers, as shown in Figure 23-3A.

A geographic organization usually ensures better implementation of sales strategies in each local market and better control over the sales force. Customers can be serviced quickly and effectively, and local sales reps can respond better to competitors' actions in a given territory. As its major drawback, a geographic organization does not provide the product expertise or other specialized knowledge that some customers may want.

**Product Specialization** Another basis for organizing a sales force is **product specialization**, as illustrated in Figure 23-3B. A company such as a meat packer may divide all its products into two lines — meat products and fertilizers. One group of sales reps sells only the various meat products, while another group sells the fertilizer line. Each group reports to its own product sales manager, who in turn reports to the general sales manager.

**FIGURE 23-3**
**Major forms of sales organization.**

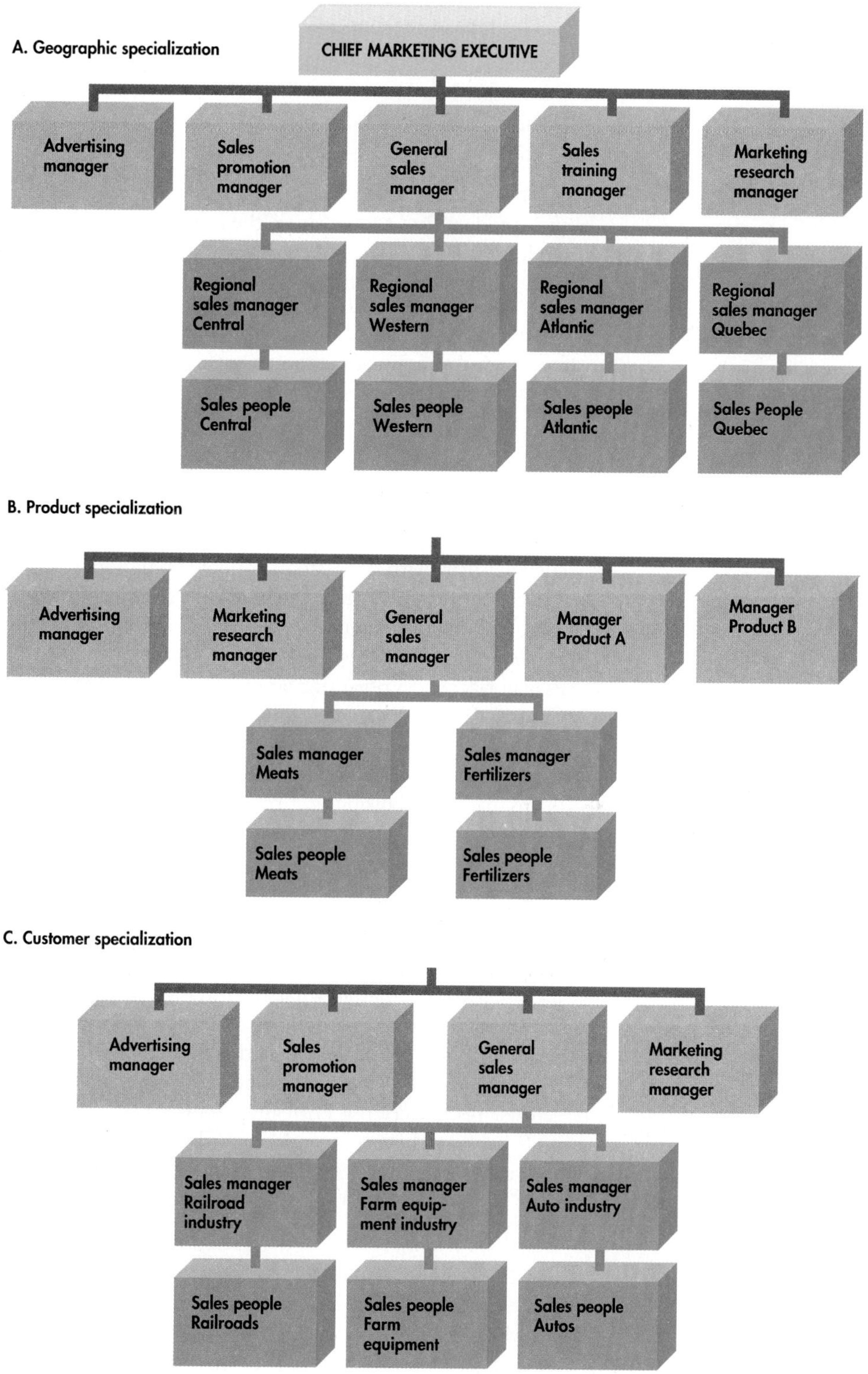

This type of organization is especially well suited for companies that are marketing:

- Complex technical products — a manufacturer of a variety of electronic products.
- Unrelated or dissimilar products — a company marketing luggage, folding tables and chairs, and toy building blocks.
- Thousands of items — a hardware wholesaler.

The main advantage of a product-specialized sales organization is the attention that each product line can get from the sales force. A drawback is that more than one sales rep from the same company may call on the same customer. This duplication is not only costly, but may also irritate customers.

Customer Specialization Many companies today have divided their sales departments on the basis of **customer specialization**. Customers may be grouped by type of industry or channel of distribution. An oil company may divide its markets by industries, such as railroads, auto manufacturers, and farm equipment producers, as shown in Figure 23-3C. A firm that specializes its sales operations by channel of distribution may have one sales force selling to wholesalers and another dealing directly with large retailers.

As more companies fully implement the marketing concept, the customer-specialization type of organization is likely to increase. Certainly the basis of customer specialization is commensurate with the customer-oriented philosophy that underlies the marketing concept. That is, the organizational emphasis is on customers and markets rather than on products.

A variation of customer specialization is the **major-accounts organization**. Many companies are adopting this structure as a better way to deal with large, important customers. A major-accounts organization usually involves team selling — a concept introduced in Chapter 19. A selling team, consisting perhaps of a sales rep, a sales engineer, a financial executive, and a manufacturing person, will negotiate with a buying team from the customer's organization. Procter & Gamble, for example, has established a series of selling teams, each specializing in a broad product category (cleaning products, food products) to better service key accounts such as Zellers and Wal-Mart.

## STAFFING THE ORGANIZATION

If your planning is going to work, you've got to select the right people to implement it. *Of all the stages in the management process, we believe that* **selection of people** *is the most important* — no matter what organization is being staffed. A football coach's success depends greatly on his ability to recruit the right players. A political party's success depends on its ability to select the candidate who will attract the most votes. A sales manager's success depends in great measure on the sales people whom the manager selects. Yes, selection is critically important in *any* organization.

In most marketing organizations, the sales force is primarily the unit that implements the strategic planning. In Chapter 19 we discussed a process for selecting sales people.

## DIRECTING THE MARKETING OPERATIONS

The third activity — directing and operating a marketing program — is the guts of the implementation process. This is where strategic plans are carried out, where the revenue is generated, and where management directs the work of the people who have been selected and organized.

The guidelines for operating the marketing-mix components (product, price, distribution, promotion) are probably pretty well set by virtue of the strategic marketing plan. It is up to the operating managers in the marketing department to follow these guidelines. Success in this stage depends on how well these executives can activate four concepts involved in managing people — delegation, co-ordination, motivation, and communication.

## MARKETING AT WORK

### FILE 23-3 TRAINING FOR CUSTOMER SERVICE ON A MAJOR SCALE

Canada Post may no longer be a monopoly, but many who work there still don't know it, according to chief executive George Clermont. Too many employees think of Canada Post as being a monopoly, but with the expanding telecommunications and cable fields, there are many communication alternatives. The post office is no longer a simple business. Letter mail accounts for only 40 percent of revenue. Post office services now include help for customers who want to develop targeted lists for ad mail and hybrid products such as Omnipost, which allows a message to be sent electronically to a certain point and then printed for delivery.

Since becoming a Crown corporation in 1981, Canada Post has been concentrating its efforts on streamlining its basic operations, breaking the cycle of repeated deficits, and increasing on-time delivery to 98 percent. Now that Canada Post has control of its basic operations, it is turning its attention from being very self-centred to looking at the outside world of the public being served — it is looking to develop customer satisfaction.

Making Canada Post more service- and customer-oriented is a massive undertaking. Half the 58,000 employees have been with the company for 10 to 20 years and half are in the age range of 40 to 50. Developing customer sensitivity and a different service concept usually means that extensive worker retraining is needed. To make the shift so that Canada Post can continue to implement its basic customer satisfaction strategy will require tripling spending on training to $56 million per year and setting up a new learning institute in conjunction with two business schools. The training funds will support education programs in areas such as customer service, product knowledge, and management training. Training will be offered in the workplace where possible, as well as through existing community colleges and universities. Pilot courses were started in the fall of 1994 in Calgary, Montreal, and Ottawa. Within three years, all the corporation's staff will have had customer training.

Clermont believes that if Canada Post can be more responsive to customers and implement all its programs to provide customers with what they need in a satisfying fashion, then the corporation can ensure its long-term survival.

Source: Adapted, in part, from Margot Gibb-Clark, "Post Office Triples Training Funding," *Globe and Mail*, June 8, 1994, p. B3.

### Delegate

An executive must be able to **delegate** authority and responsibility. Executives who try to do everything themselves — who are reluctant to delegate — fail to maximize the potential of their programs or their subordinates.

Delegation means giving a person a job to do (responsibility) and the tools to do it with (authority). This is what the new president at Siemens intended to do when he looked for 500 young, middle-level managers to provide new ideas, energy, and leadership for the company going into the twenty-first century.

In another example, the delegation system in the 3M Company (Scotch Tape, Post-it Notes, and a host of other goods) minimizes large-company bureaucratic rigidity. To stimulate new development, 3M sets up a small team (almost like a small company) with a new-product idea. Then the company delegates full authority to that team to develop the new product. This delegation system encourages the team to take initiatives and risks — all without fear of reprimand from higher-up executives. Sure, some projects will be winners and some will be losers. But if the company did a good job in selecting its people, there will be more winners than losers.

**Hallmark Cards expects to cut new-product development time in half by delegating authority to cross-functional teams like this one. Previously, artists, designers, printers, and financial people had been as far as a city block apart, while working on the same greeting card.**

### Co-ordinate

**Co-ordination** among divisions and among activities is essential in an organization, because people working together can accomplish a lot more than if they go off on their own. Effective co-ordination sometimes is difficult to achieve because of differences in interests, priorities, and personalities among the groups involved. At the *interdepartmental* level, for example, production people are interested in long production runs (and thus low unit costs) of standardized colours or sizes. Marketing people, on the other hand, want considerable variety in the output so as to cater to different market segments. Finance people want tight credit controls, while marketers know that easier credit means more sales. *Within* the marketing department, co-ordination and compromise also are essential because of limited funds and conflicting interests. The advertising people want increased advertising budgets, while the sales executives want to hire more sales reps.

To improve co-ordination across departments or even within the marketing department, some companies set up teams with representatives from each department to avoid potential problems. This, in effect, is what the 3M Company does regarding new-product development.

### Motivate

A successful leader of people in any field — be it athletics, education, politics, the military, or business — is able to **motivate** his or her people. Here we include *economic* motivation (monetary payments) as well as *psychological* motivation (honour awards, recognition by management, promotions, executive praise).

Motivational programs are more likely to succeed when workers' personal goals are compatible with the company's goals. Therefore, early on, the executives should make clear to the workers just what are the goals of that particular work group. Then the motivational reward (commission, bonus, honour award) should be tied directly to the workers' achieving these goals. Finally, a motivational program must be perceived by the workers as being fair and ethical.

### Communicate

To effectively implement a marketing plan — to organize, select people, delegate, co-ordinate, and motivate — you first have to **communicate** effectively. In early chapters, and again in Part 6 regarding promotion, we spoke about communicating with the market. Now we discuss the need for clear *internal* communication. There should always be communication both upward and downward in a company's hierarchy. Management should communicate with sales people, and these reps should have an open channel to communicate upward to management.

Often these things are easier said than done. Companies spend a lot of money to improve their executives' ability to communicate. But the workers still frequently misunderstand management's messages. And management often does not understand what the workers are saying. Let's face it — we have communication problems in most interpersonal relationships — for example, between professors and students, between boyfriends and girlfriends, between parents and their kids. Yet this is no reason to stop trying to improve communications.

Here are two guidelines to aid internal communication:

- Adopt a "walking-around" management style. That is, get out from behind the desk and visit with the workers. Convince the workers that management wants them to speak what's on their mind — with no recriminations against those who speak up.
- Bring a problem out in the open as soon as management is aware that one exists. Problems won't go away by ignoring them — like an ostrich with its head in the sand.

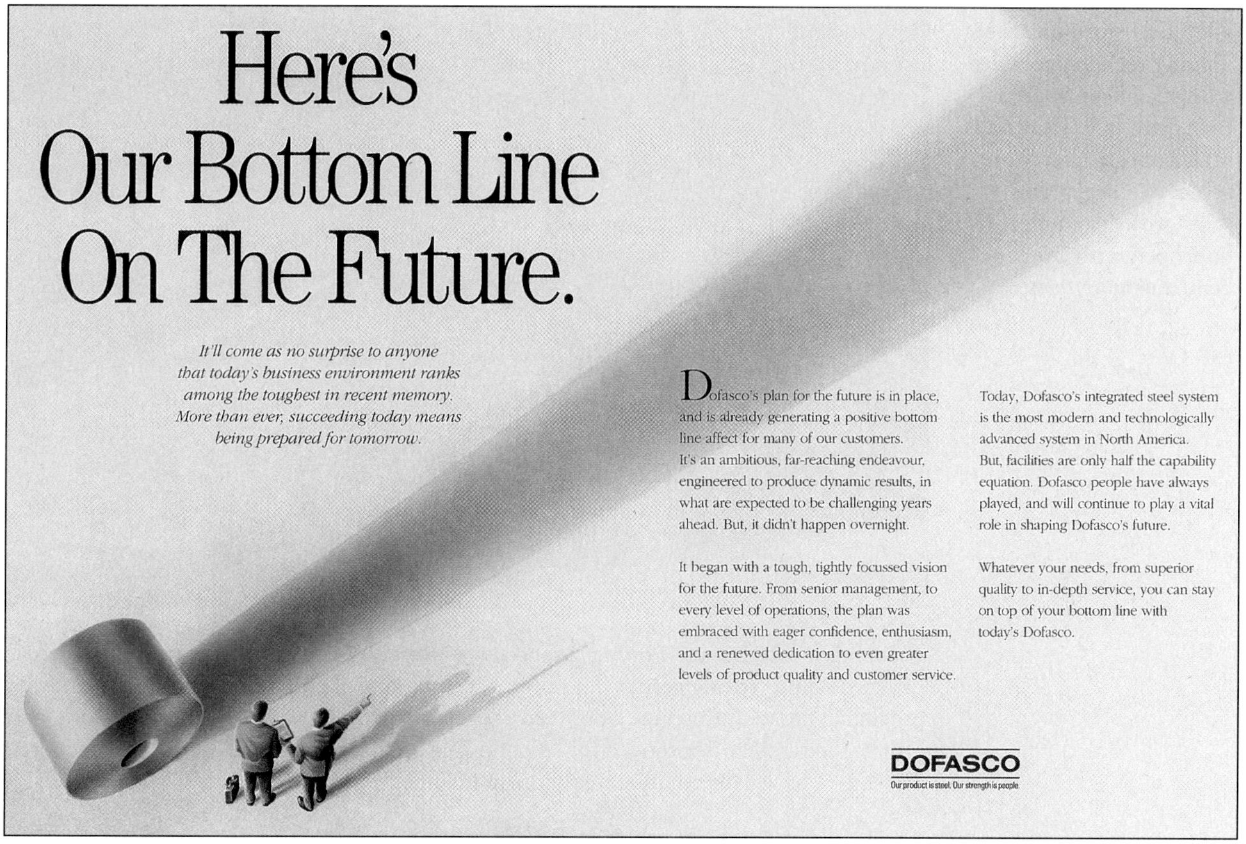


**Dofasco has been successfully implementing and promoting itself as a company that communicates to and works through its people.**

## EVALUATING MARKETING PERFORMANCE

Soon after a firm's plans have been set in operation, the process of evaluation should begin. Without evaluation, management cannot tell whether a plan is working and what factors are contributing to its success or failure. Evaluation logically follows planning and implementation. Planning sets forth what *should* be done. Evaluation shows what *really was* done. A circular relationship exists, as illustrated in Figure 23-4. Plans are made, they are put into action, the results of those actions are evaluated, and new plans are prepared on the basis of this evaluation.

Previously we discussed evaluation as it relates to individual parts of a marketing program — the product-planning process, the performance of the sales force, and the effectiveness of the advertising program, for instance. Now let's look at the evaluation of the *total marketing effort.*

**FIGURE 23-4**
**The circular relationship among management tasks.**

### The Marketing Audit: A Total Evaluation Program

A marketing audit is an essential element in a total evaluation program. An audit implies a review and evaluation of some activity. Thus, a **marketing audit** is a comprehensive review and evaluation of the marketing function in an organization — its philosophy, environment, goals, strategies, organizational structure, human and financial resources, and performance. A complete marketing audit is an extensive and difficult project. That's why it is conducted infrequently — perhaps every two or three years. However, a company should not delay a marketing audit until a major crisis arises.

The rewards of a marketing audit can be great. Management can identify problem areas in marketing. By reviewing its strategies, the firm is likely to keep abreast of its

**Taco Bell store manager, Tammy Ackers, receives a Pontiac Trans-Am as first prize in a Taco Bell sales contest. Her store achieved 45 percent sales growth in a neighbourhood with 30 percent unemployment.**

changing marketing environment. Successes can also be analyzed, so the company can capitalize on its strong points. The audit can spot lack of co-ordination in the marketing program, outdated strategies, or unrealistic goals. Furthermore, an audit should anticipate future situations. It is intended for "prognosis as well as diagnosis. . . . It is the practice of preventive as well as curative marketing medicine."[7]

### Misdirected Marketing Effort

One of the benefits of evaluation is that it helps correct **misdirected** (or misplaced) **marketing effort**.

The 80-20 Principle In most firms, a large proportion of the total orders, customers, territories, or products accounts for only a small share of total sales or profit. Conversely, a small proportion produces a large share of sales or profit. This relationship has been characterized as the **80-20 principle**. That is, 80 percent of the orders, customers, territories, or products contribute only 20 percent of sales or profit. On the other hand, 20 percent of these selling units account for 80 percent of the volume or profit. We use the 80-20 figure simply to highlight the misplacement of marketing effort. In reality, of course, the percentage split varies from one situation to another.

The basic reason for the 80-20 split is that almost every marketing program includes some misdirected effort. Marketing efforts and costs are proportional to the *number* of territories, customers, or products, rather than to their actual sales volume or profit. For example, in a Sears Canada department store, approximately the same order-filling, billing, and delivery expenses are involved whether a $500 suit or a $25 necktie is sold. Or a manufacturer such as Xerox may assign one sales person to each territory. Yet usually there are differences in the actual sales volume and profit among the territories. In each example the marketing effort (cost) is not in line with the actual return.

Reasons for Misdirected Marketing Effort Frequently, executives cannot uncover their misdirected effort because they lack sufficient information. The **iceberg principle** is an analogy that illustrates this situation. Only a small part of an iceberg is visible above the surface of the water, and the submerged 90 percent is the dangerous part. The figures representing total sales or total costs on an operating statement are like the visible part of an iceberg. The detailed figures representing sales, costs, and other performance measures for each territory or product correspond to the dangerous submerged segment.

*Total* sales or cost figures are too general to be useful in evaluation; in fact, they often are misleading. A company may show satisfactory overall sales and profit figures. But when these totals are subdivided by territory or products, serious weaknesses often are discovered. A manufacturer of audio equipment showed an overall annual increase of 12 percent in sales and 9 percent in net profit on one product line one year. But management wasn't satisfied with this "tip of the iceberg." When it analyzed the figures more closely, it found that the sales change within territories ranged from an increase of 19 percent to a decrease of 3 percent. In some territories profit increased as much as 14 percent, and in others it was down 20 percent.

A more basic cause of misplaced marketing effort is that executives must make decisions based on inadequate knowledge of the exact nature of marketing costs. In other words, management often lacks knowledge of: (1) the disproportionate spread of marketing effort; (2) reliable standards for determining what should be spent on marketing; and (3) what results should be expected from these expenditures.

As an illustration, a company may spend $250,000 more on advertising this year than last year. But management ordinarily cannot state what the resultant increase in sales volume or profit should be. Nor do the executives know what would have happened if they had spent the same amount on (1) new-product development, (2) management training seminars for intermediaries, or (3) some other aspect of the marketing program.

### The Evaluation Process

The evaluation process — whether a complete marketing audit or only an appraisal of individual components of the marketing program — is a three-step task:

1. Find out *what* happened. Get the facts, compare actual results with budgeted goals to determine where they differ.
2. Find out *why* it happened. Determine what specific factors in the marketing program accounted for the results.
3. Decide *what to do* about it. Plan the next period's program so as to improve on unsatisfactory performance and capitalize on the things that were done well.

To evaluate a total marketing program we need to analyze performance results. To do this, two tools are available — sales volume analysis and marketing cost analysis. We'll discuss both of these tools using the Great Western Company (GW) — a firm that markets office furniture. This company's market is divided into four sales districts, each with seven or eight sales people and a district sales manager. The company sells to office equipment wholesalers and directly to large business users. Great Western's product mix is divided into four groups — desks, chairs, filing equipment, and office accessories (wastebaskets and desk sets, for example). Some of these products are manufactured by GW and some are purchased from other firms.

## SALES VOLUME ANALYSIS

A **sales volume analysis** is a detailed study of the net sales section of a company's profit and loss statement (operating statement). Management should analyze its *total* sales volume, and its volume by *product lines* and *market segments* (territories and customer groups). These sales should be compared with company sales goals and industry sales.

We start with an analysis of Great Western's total sales volume, as shown in Table 23-1.

Annual sales doubled from $18 million to $36 million during the 10-year period ending with 1993. Furthermore, sales increased each year, with the exception of 1990. In most years, planned sales goals were met or surpassed. Thus far in our analysis the company's situation is encouraging.

However, a study of total sales volume alone is usually insufficient and may even be misleading. Remember the iceberg principle! To learn what is going on in the "submerged" parts of the market, we need to analyze sales volume by market segments — sales territories, for example.

TABLE 23-1 Annual sales volume of Great Western Company, industry volume, and company's share in market

| Year | Company volume (in millions) of dollars) | Industry volume in company's market (in millions of dollars | Company's percentage share of market |
|---|---|---|---|
| 1993 | 36.0 | 300 | 12.0 |
| 1992 | 34.7 | 275 | 12.6 |
| 1991 | 33.1 | 255 | 13.0 |
| 1990 | 30.4 | 220 | 13.8 |
| 1989 | 31.7 | 235 | 13.5 |
| 1988 | 28.0 | 200 | 14.0 |
| 1987 | 24.5 | 170 | 14.4 |
| 1986 | 22.5 | 155 | 14.5 |
| 1985 | 21.8 | 150 | 14.8 |
| 1984 | 18.0 | 120 | 15.0 |

Table 23-2 is a summary of the planned sales goals and actual sales results in Great Western's four sales districts. A key measurement is the *performance percentage* for each district — that is, actual sales divided by sales goal. A performance percentage of 100 means that the district did exactly what was expected. From the table we see that districts B and C did just a little better than was expected. District A passed its goal by a wide margin. But district D was quite a disappointment.

So far in our evaluation, we know a little about *what* happened in GW's districts. Now management has to figure out *why* it happened and *what should be done* about it. These are the difficult steps in evaluation. Great Western's executives need to determine why district D did so poorly. The fault may lie in some aspect of the marketing program, or competition may be especially strong in that district. They also should find out the reasons for district A's success, and whether this information can be used in the other regions.

This brief examination of two aspects of sales volume analysis shows how this evaluation tool may be used. However, for a more useful evaluation, GW's executives should go much further. They should analyze their sales volume by individual territories within districts and by product lines. Then they should carry their territorial analysis further by examining volume by product line and customer group *within* each territory. For instance, even though district A did well overall, the iceberg principle may be at work *within* the district. The fine *total* performance in district A may be covering up weaknesses in an individual product line or territory.

### Market-Share Analysis

Comparing a company's sales results with its goal is a useful evaluation, but it does not tell how the company is doing relative to its competitors. We need a **market-share analysis** to

TABLE 23-2 District sales volume in Great Western Company, 1993

| District | Sales goals (in millions of dollars) | Actual sales (in millions of dollars) | Performance percentage (actual ÷ goal) | Dollar variation (in millions) |
|---|---|---|---|---|
| A | $10.8 | $12.5 | 116 | +1.7 |
| B | 9.0 | 9.6 | 107 | +.6 |
| C | 7.6 | 7.7 | 101 | +.1 |
| D | 8.6 | 6.2 | 72 | –2.4 |
| Total | $36.0 | $36.0 | | |

compare the company's sales with the industry's sales. We should analyze the company's share of the market in total, as well as by product line and market segment.

Probably the major obstacle encountered in market-share analysis is in obtaining industry sales information in total and in sufficient detail. Trade associations and government agencies are sources for industry sales volume statistics in many fields.

Great Western Company is a good example of the value of market-share analysis. Recall from Table 23-1 that GW's total sales doubled over a 10-year period, with annual increases in nine of those years. *But,* during this decade the industry's annual sales increased from $120 million to $300 million (a 150 percent increase). Thus the company's share of this market actually *declined* from 15 to 12 percent. Although GW's annual sales increased 100 percent, its market share declined 20 percent.

The next step is to determine *why* Great Western's market position declined. The number of possible causes is quite large — and this is what makes management's task so difficult. A weakness in almost any aspect of GW's product line, distribution system, pricing structure, or promotional program may have contributed to the loss of market share. Or it may be that the culprit was competition. There may be new competitors in the market that were attracted by the rapid growth rates. Or competitors' marketing programs may be more effective than Great Western's.

## MARKETING COST ANALYSIS

An analysis of sales volume is helpful in evaluating and controlling a company's marketing effort. A volume analysis, however, does not tell us anything about the *profitability* of this effort. Management needs to conduct a marketing cost analysis to determine the relative profitability of its territories, product lines, or other marketing units. A **marketing cost analysis** is a detailed study of the operating expenses section of a company's profit and loss statement. As part of this analysis, management may establish budgetary goals, and then study the variations between budgeted costs and actual expenses.

### Types of Marketing Cost Analysis

A company's marketing costs may be analyzed:

- As they appear in its ledger accounts and profit and loss statement.
- After they are grouped into activity classifications.
- After these activity costs have been allocated to territories, products, or other marketing units.

**Analysis of Ledger Expenses** The simplest and least expensive marketing cost analysis is a study of the "object of expenditure" costs as they appear in the firm's profit and loss statement. These figures come from the company's accounting ledger records. The simplified operating statement for the Great Western Company on the left side of Table 23-3 is the model we shall use in this discussion.

The procedure is to analyze each cost item (salaries and media space, for example) in detail. We can compare this period's total with the totals for similar periods in the past, and observe the trends. We can compare actual costs with budgeted expense goals. We should also compute each expense as a percentage of net sales. Then, we should compare these expense ratios with industry figures, which are often available through trade associations.

**Analysis of Activity Expenses** Marketing costs should be allocated among the various marketing activities, such as advertising or warehousing, for more effective control. Management can then analyze the cost of each of these activities.

The procedure here is first to identify the major activities, and then to allocate each ledger expense among those activities. As indicated in the expense distribution sheet on the right-hand side of Table 23-3, we have decided on five activity cost groups in our Great Western example. Some items, such as the cost of media space, can be apportioned entirely to one activity (advertising). For other expenses, the cost must be spread among several activities. So management must decide on some reasonable basis for allocation among these activities. For example, property taxes may be allocated according to the proportion of total floor space occupied by each activity. Thus the warehouse accounts for 46 percent of the total area (square metres) of floor space in the firm, so the warehousing and shipping activity is charged with $60,000 (46 percent) of the property taxes.

An analysis of the costs of the marketing activities gives executives more information than they can get from an analysis of ledger accounts alone. Also, an analysis of activity expenses in total provides a starting point for management to analyze costs by territories, products, or other marketing units.

TABLE 23-3 Profit and loss statement and distribution of natural expenses to activity cost groups, Great Western Company, 1993

| Profit and loss statement (in $000) | | | | Expense distribution sheet (in $000) | | | | |
|---|---|---|---|---|---|---|---|---|
| | | | | Activity (functional) cost groups | | | | |
| | | | | Personal selling | Advertising | Warehousing and shipping | Order processing | Marketing administration |
| Net sales | | $36,000 | | | | | | |
| Cost of goods sold | | 23,400 | | | | | | |
| Gross margin | | 12,600 | | | | | | |
| Operating expenses: | | | | | | | | |
| Salaries and commissions | $2,710 | | → | $1,200 | $ 240 | $ 420 | $280 | $ 570 |
| Travel and entertainment | 1,440 | | → | 1,040 | | | | 400 |
| Media space | 1,480 | | → | | 1,480 | | | |
| Supplies | 440 | | → | 60 | 35 | 240 | 70 | 35 |
| Property taxes | 130 | | → | 16 | 5 | 60 | 30 | 19 |
| Freight out | 3,500 | | → | | | 3,500 | | |
| Total expenses | | 9,700 | | $2,316 | $1,760 | $4,220 | $380 | $1,024 |
| Net profit | | $ 2,900 | | | | | | |

**Analysis of Activity Costs by Market Segments** The third and most beneficial type of marketing cost analysis is a study of the costs and profitability of each segment of the market. This type of analysis divides the market by territories, products, customer groups, or order sizes. Cost analysis by market segment enables management to pinpoint trouble spots much more effectively than does an analysis of either ledger-account expenses or activity costs.

By combining a sales volume analysis with a marketing cost study, a researcher can prepare a complete operating statement for each of the product or market segments. These individual statements can then be analyzed to determine how they affect the total marketing program.

The procedure for a cost analysis by market segments is similar to that used to analyze activity expenses. The total of each activity cost (the right-hand part of Table 23-3) is allocated on some basis to each product or market segment being studied. Let's walk through an example of a cost analysis, by sales districts, for the Great Western Company, as shown in Tables 23-4 and 23-5.

TABLE 23-4 Allocation of activity costs to sales districts, Great Western Company, 1993

| Activity | | Personal selling | Advertising | Warehousing and shipping | Order processing | Marketing administration |
|---|---|---|---|---|---|---|
| | | | Allocation basis | | | |
| **Allocation basis** | | **Direct expense to each district** | **Number of pages of advertising** | **Number of orders shipped** | **Number of invoice lines** | **Equally among districts** |
| **Total activity cost** | | **$2,316,000** | **$1,760,000** | **$4,220,000** | **$380,000** | **$1,024,000** |
| **Number of allocation units** | | | **88 pages** | **10,550 orders** | **126,667 lines** | **4 districts** |
| **Cost per allocation unit** | | | **$20,000** | **$400** | **$3** | **$256,000** |
| | | | Allocation of costs | | | |
| **District A <** | **units** | — | 27 pages | 3,300 orders | 46,000 lines | — |
| | **cost** | $650,000 | $540,000 | $1,320,000 | $138,000 | $256,000 |
| **District B <** | **units** | — | 19 pages | 2,850 orders | 33,000 lines | — |
| | **cost** | $606,000 | $380,000 | $1,140,000 | $99,000 | $256,000 |
| **District C <** | **units** | — | 22 pages | 2,300 orders | 26,667 lines | — |
| | **cost** | $540,000 | $440,000 | $920,000 | $80,000 | $256,000 |
| **District D <** | **units** | — | 20 pages | 2,100 orders | 21,000 lines | — |
| | **cost** | $520,000 | $400,000 | $840,000 | $63,000 | $256,000 |

First, for each of the five GW activities, we select an allocation basis for distributing the cost of that activity among the four districts. These bases are shown in the top part of Table 23-4. Then we determine the number of allocation "units" that make up each activity cost, and we find the cost per unit. This completes the allocation scheme, which tells us how to allocate costs to the four districts:

- Personal selling activity expenses pose no problem because they are direct expenses, chargeable to the district in which they are incurred.
- Advertising expenses are allocated on the basis of the number of pages of advertising run in each district. GW purchased the equivalent of 88 pages of advertising during the year, at an average cost of $20,000 per page ($1,760,000 ÷ 88).

- Warehousing and shipping expenses are allocated on the basis of the number of orders shipped. Since 10,550 orders were shipped during the year at a total activity cost of $4,220,000, the cost per order is $400.
- Order-processing expenses are allocated according to the number of invoice lines typed during the year. Since there were 126,667 lines, then the cost per line is $3.
- Marketing administration — a totally indirect expense — is divided equally among the four districts, with each district being allocated $256,000.

The final step is to calculate the amount of each activity cost to be allocated to each district. The results are shown in the bottom part of Table 23-4. We see that $650,000 of personal selling expenses were charged directly to district A and $606,000 to district B, for example. Regarding advertising, the equivalent of 27 pages of advertising was run in district A, so that district is charged with $540,000 (27 pages × $20,000 per page). Similar calculations provide advertising activity cost allocations of $380,000 to district B; $440,000 to district C; and $400,000 to district D.

Regarding warehousing and shipping expenses, 3,300 orders were shipped to customers in district A, at a unit allocation cost of $400 per order, for a total allocated cost of $1,320,000. Warehousing and shipping charges are allocated to the other three districts as indicated in Table 23-4.

To allocate order-processing expenses, management determined that 46,000 invoice lines went to customers in district A. At $3 per line (the cost per allocation unit), district A is charged with $138,000. Each district is charged with $256,000 for marketing administration expenses.

After the activity costs have been allocated among the four districts, we can prepare a profit and loss statement for each district. These statements are shown in Table 23-5. Sales volume for each district is determined from the sales volume analysis (Table 23-2). Cost of goods sold and gross margin for each district are obtained by assuming that the company's gross margin of 35 percent ($12,600,000 ÷ $36,000,000) was maintained in each district.

Table 23-5 shows, for each district, what the firm's profit and loss statement shows for overall company operations. For example, we note that district A's net profit was 11.8 percent of sales ($1,471,000 ÷ $12,500,000). In sharp contrast, district D did rather poorly, earning a net profit of only 1.5 percent of net sales ($91,000 ÷ $6,200,000).

TABLE 23-5 Profit and loss statements for sales districts (in $000), Great Western Company, 1993

| | Total | District A | District B | District C | District D |
|---|---|---|---|---|---|
| Net sales | $36,000 | $12,500 | $9,600 | $7,700 | $6,200 |
| Cost of goods sold | 23,400 | 8,125 | 6,240 | 5,005 | 4,030 |
| Gross margin | 12,600 | 4,375 | 3,360 | 2,695 | 2,170 |
| Operating expenses: | | | | | |
| Personal selling | 2,316 | 650 | 606 | 540 | 520 |
| Advertising | 1,760 | 540 | 380 | 440 | 400 |
| Warehousing and shipping | 4,220 | 1,320 | 1,140 | 920 | 840 |
| Order processing, billing | 380 | 138 | 99 | 80 | 63 |
| Marketing administration | 1,024 | 256 | 256 | 256 | 256 |
| Total expenses | 9,700 | 2,904 | 2,481 | 2,236 | 2,079 |
| Net profit (in dollars) | $ 2,900 | $ 1,471 | $ 879 | $ 459 | $ 91 |
| Net profit (as percentage of sales) | 8.1% | 11.8% | 9.2% | 6.0% | 1.5% |

At this point in our performance evaluation, we have completed the *what happened* stage. The next stage is to determine *why* the results are as depicted in Table 23-5. As mentioned earlier, it is difficult to answer this question. In district D, for example, the sales force obtained only about two-thirds as many orders as in district A (2,100 versus 3,300). Was this because of poor selling, poor sales training, more severe competition in district D, or some other reason among a multitude of possibilities?

After a performance evaluation has determined why district results came out as they did, management can move to the third stage in its evaluation process. That final stage is, *what should management do about the situation?* This stage will be discussed briefly after we have reviewed major problem areas in marketing cost analysis.

### Problems in Cost Analysis

Marketing cost analysis can be expensive in time, money, and labour. In particular, the task of allocating costs is often quite difficult.

**Allocating Costs** The problem of allocating costs becomes evident when activity cost totals must be apportioned among individual territories, products, or other marketing units. Operating costs can be divided into direct and indirect expenses. **Direct costs,** also called *separable expenses*, are incurred totally in connection with one market segment or one unit of the sales organization. Thus salary and travel expenses of the sales representative in district A are direct expenses for that territory. The cost of newspaper space to advertise product C is a direct cost of marketing that product. Allocating direct expenses is easy. They can be charged entirely to the marketing unit that incurred them.

The allocation difficulty arises in connection with **indirect costs**, also called *common costs*. These expenses are incurred jointly for more than one marketing unit. Therefore, they cannot be charged totally to one market segment.

Within the category of indirect expenses, some costs are *partially* indirect and some are *totally* indirect. Order filling and shipping, for example, are partially indirect costs. They would *decrease* if some territories or products were eliminated. They would *increase* if new products or territories were added. On the other hand, marketing administrative expenses are totally indirect. The cost of the chief marketing executive's staff and office would remain about the same, whether or not the number of territories or product lines was changed.

Any method selected for allocating indirect expenses has obvious weaknesses that can distort the results and mislead management. Two commonly used allocation methods are to divide these costs (1) equally among the marketing units being studied (territories, for instance) or (2) in proportion to the sales volume in each marketing unit. But each method gives a different result for the total costs for each marketing unit.

**Full-Cost versus Contribution-Margin Approach** In a marketing cost analysis, two means of allocating indirect expenses are (1) the contribution-margin (also called contribution-to-overhead) method and (2) the full-cost method. A controversy exists regarding which of these two approaches is better for managerial control purposes.

In the **contribution-margin approach**, only direct expenses are allocated to each marketing unit being analyzed. These costs presumably would be eliminated if that marketing unit were eliminated. When direct expenses are deducted from the gross margin of the marketing unit, the remainder is the amount which that unit is contributing to cover total indirect expenses (or overhead).

All expenses — direct and indirect — are allocated among the marketing units under study in the **full-cost approach**. By allocating *all* costs, management can determine the net profit of each territory, product, or other marketing unit.

For any given marketing unit, these two methods can be summarized as follows:

| Contribution margin | Full cost |
|---|---|
| **Sales $** | **Sales $** |
| ***less*** | ***less*** |
| **Cost of goods sold** | **Cost of goods sold** |
| ***equals*** | ***equals*** |
| **Gross margin** | **Gross margin** |
| ***less*** | ***less*** |
| **Direct expenses** | **Direct expenses** |
| ***equals*** | ***less*** |
| **Contribution margin (the amount available to cover overhead expenses plus a profit)** | **Indirect expenses** ***equals*** |
| | **Net profit** |

Proponents of the *full-cost* approach contend that a marketing cost study is intended to determine the net profitability of the units being studied. They feel that the contribution-margin method does not fulfil this purpose and may be misleading. A given territory or product may be showing a contribution to overhead. Yet, after indirect costs are allocated, this product or territory may actually have a net loss. In effect, say the full-cost proponents, the contribution-margin approach is the iceberg principle in action. That is, the visible tip (the contribution margin) looks good, while the submerged part may be hiding a net loss.

*Contribution-margin* supporters contend that it is not possible to accurately allocate indirect costs among product or market segments. Furthermore, items such as administrative costs are not all related to any one territory or product. Therefore, the marketing units should not bear any of these costs. Advocates of the contribution-margin approach also say that a full-cost analysis may show that a product or territory has a net loss, but this unit may be contributing something to overhead. Some executives might recommend that the losing product or territory be eliminated. But they are overlooking the fact that the unit's contribution to overhead would then have to be borne by other units. With the contribution-margin approach, there would be no question about keeping this unit as long as there is no better alternative.

## USE OF FINDINGS FROM VOLUME AND COST ANALYSES

So far we have been dealing with the first two stages of marketing performance evaluation — finding out *what happened* and *why it happened*. Now we're ready to see some examples of how management might use the results from a combined sales volume analysis and marketing cost analysis.

### Territories

Knowing the net profit (or contribution to overhead) of territories in relation to their potential gives management several possibilities for action. It may decide to adjust (expand or contract) territories to bring them into line with current sales potential. Or territorial problems may stem from weaknesses in the distribution system, and changes in channels of distribution may be needed. Firms that use manufacturers' agents may find it advisable to establish their own sales forces in growing markets. Intense competition may be the cause of unprofitable volume in some districts, and changes in the promotional program may be necessary.

Of course, a losing territory might be abandoned completely. An abandoned region may have been contributing something to overhead, however, even though a net loss was shown. Management must recognize that this contribution must now be carried by the remaining territories.

### Products

When the profitability of each product or group of products is known, unprofitable models, sizes, or colours can be eliminated. Sales people's compensation plans may be altered to encourage the sale of high-margin items. Channels of distribution may be changed. Instead of selling all of its products directly to business users, for instance, a machine tools manufacturer shifted to industrial distributors for standard products of low unit value. The company thereby improved the profitability of these products.

Management may decide to discontinue carrying a losing product. But it should not do so without first considering the effect this decision will have on other items sold by the company. Often a low-volume or unprofitable product must be carried simply to round out the product assortment. Food supermarkets, for example, carry salt and sugar even though these are profitless for a store. Customers expect a supermarket to carry those items. If they are not available at one store, that seller will lose business, because shoppers will go to other stores that do carry a full complement of grocery products.

### Customer Classes and Order Sizes

By combining a sales volume analysis with a cost study, executives can determine the profitability of each group of customers. If one market segment generates an unsatisfactory net profit, then changes may be required in the pricing structure when selling to these customers. Or perhaps customers that have been sold directly by a producer's sales force should be turned over to wholesaling intermediaries. A manufacturer of air conditioners made just such a move when it found that direct sales to individual building contractors were not profitable.

A difficulty plaguing many firms today is the **small-order problem**. Many orders are below the break-even point. Revenue from each of these orders is actually less than allocated expenses. This problem occurs because several costs, such as billing or direct selling, are essentially the same whether the order amounts to \$10 or \$10,000. Management's immediate reaction may be that no order below the break-even point should be accepted. Or small-volume accounts should be dropped from the customer list. Such decisions may be harmful, however. Some of those small-order customers may, over time, grow into large, profitable accounts. Management should first determine *why* certain accounts are small-order problems and then figure out how to correct the situation. Proper handling can often turn a losing account into a satisfactory one. For example, a small-order handling charge, which customers would willingly pay, might change the profit picture entirely.

## MARKETING AT WORK

### FILE 23-4 AUDIT, DOWNSIZE, RESTRUCTURE — AND THAT INCLUDES SALES!

Until recently, restructuring a sales department was considered taboo. Companies would rather redesign their factories — and reap the usually large and measurable cost savings — than tamper with their sales force. After all, selling was considered an art and you couldn't analyze and then manipulate the efficiency of a sales person's art like you could that of machines. And besides, many firms argued, sellers were the ones who produce the revenue.

The problem with these views was that they fostered sales departments that were inefficient and technologically backward. Rick McCutcheon, a sales productivity consultant in Toronto, estimates that less than 10 percent of Canadian sales departments are sufficiently automated, because most sales managers have no computer experience and thus resist any efforts to computerize their operations. It is no wonder that most companies haven't a clue as to what exactly their sales force is up to all day. If they did, however, they'd be shocked to discover that only 23.7 percent of sales people's time was spent actually selling to customers. As well, every time an industrial sales person walks through a customer's door, whether he gets a sale or not, he costs the company $227. And that's just averaging the direct selling costs — salary, car allowance, travel and entertainment expenses. Then there are all the indirect expenses too, from secretaries and managers to laptop computers and office space, all of which often adds up to triple what most companies spend on advertising and promotion combined.

Faced with such statistics, some Canadian companies are finally and reluctantly beginning to restructure their sales departments. They are evaluating how sellers spend their time and they are ranking clients according to how much time they feel each needs, wants, or deserves. Then they cross-reference the two, trying to discover ways of offering the same service at reduced cost. Often, the answer is technology, which liberates sales people to spend more time actually selling. Another is to off-load tasks such as customer prospecting or after-sales service onto less expensive providers. This frequently results in a complete reorganization, applying a factory floor's productive discipline to the entire sales department. In this manner, according to Toronto-based consultant Dan Richards, "sales become much more a science and much less an art."

A major subscriber to this view is Kodak Canada Inc. Surveys revealed that the firm's 70-person sales force was spending only 50 percent of their time actually selling. The other 50 percent went to travel and administrative tasks. Call coverage — the number of personal calls per customer — was poor. And so was communication. For although sales reps had laptop computers, they had no business-forms software and no way to file electronic reports from the field, which resulted in thousands of pieces of paper being shifted from person to person, and from office to office. And how could sellers sell when they had to worry about rotating stock in retail outlets, verifying point-of-sale advertising, and replacing damaged or outdated products from sample kits in their cars?

So, in 1992, Kodak introduced its "strategic sales plan." Sales reps now had their laptops loaded with sophisticated software, allowing them to file reports electronically from the field to company-wide databank networks where managers could cross-reference and analyze them.

There was also a new emphasis on telemarketing. With businesses in general discovering that the average telephone telemarketing contact call cost one-tenth that of a field sales call, and that the average telemarketer could contact as many clients in a day as a field sales rep could in a week — usually at half the cost — it is slowly becoming *de rigueur* to hire telemarketers to handle time-consuming administrative tasks. Although at Kodak, telemarketing was formerly reserved exclusively for accounts that were either too small or remote for a sales rep to bother with, Kodak now encourages customers to take to their phones in order to acquire better ongoing services ranging from quicker inventory replenishment to more frequent updates on special offers. In order to keep the experience personal, Kodak sends clients pictures of its telesales reps accompanied by sales department flow charts. And in keeping with the changing nature of telemarketing itself, Kodak ceased hiring poorly educated part-timers who were simply punching out calls for minimum wage. Instead, the company recruited more experienced people whom they looked upon as *de facto* account managers, capable of screening calls, organizing information and quickly linking field reps with any orders, requests, and complaints made by clients in their absence.

Furthermore, an independent merchandiser was hired in order to free sales people from having to visit retail outlets, rotate stock, check point-of-sale advertising, and take care of other merchandising distractions. With all these implementations — coupled with some slimming and trimming of the sales force itself — Kodak's sales department could finally devote itself unconditionally to the art of selling.

Although the total cost savings of Kodak's plan have yet to be calculated, the company did witness a 7.5 percent drop in spending on travel, entertainment, and demonstration materials for field sales reps during 1993. Ken Shaddock, manager of sales administration, admitted that beyond this it's difficult to measure the results. He added, "But we are clearly reducing costs and saving people time. Call coverage has improved from terrible to excellent with negligible complaints from customers." And sales people no longer have to push thousands of sheets of paper around the company. "We're down to hundreds," he laughed.

Source: Mark Stevenson, "The Lean, Mean Sales Machine," *Canadian Business*, January 1994, pp. 32-36.

## SUMMARY

The management process in marketing is the planning, implementation, and evaluation of the marketing effort in an organization. Implementation is the stage in which an organization attempts to carry out its strategic planning. Strategic planning is virtually useless if it is not implemented effectively.

Implementation includes three activities — organizing, staffing, and operating. In organizing, the company first should co-ordinate all marketing activities into one department whose top executive reports directly to the president. Then, within the marketing department, the company may utilize some form of organizational specialization based on geographic territories, products, or customer types.

Selecting people is the most important step in the entire management process. To operate an organization effectively, management also needs to do a good job in delegation, co-ordination, motivation, and communication.

The evaluation stage in the management process involves measuring performance results against predetermined goals. Evaluation enables management to determine the effectiveness of its implementation and to plan corrective action where necessary.

A marketing audit is a key element in a total marketing evaluation program. Most companies are victims of at least some misdirected marketing effort. That is, the 80-20 and iceberg principles are at work in most firms because marketing costs are expended in relation to the number of marketing units (territories, products, customers), rather than to their profit potential. Fundamentally, companies do not know how much they should be spending for marketing activities, or what results they should get from these expenditures.

Two tools for identifying misdirected marketing efforts are a sales volume analysis and a marketing cost analysis. Given detailed analyses, management can study sales volume and marketing costs by product lines and market segments (sales territories, customer groups).

One problem in marketing cost analysis is allocating costs — especially indirect costs — to the marketing units. But the findings from these analyses are helpful in shaping decisions regarding a company's marketing program.

## KEY TERMS AND CONCEPTS

**Planning (684)**
**Implementation (684)**
**Evaluation (684)**
**Organizational structures for implementing strategic planning:**
- **Geographic specialization (689)**
- **Product specialization (689)**
- **Customer specialization (692)**
- **Major-accounts organization (692)**

**Importance of good selection (692)**
**Delegating authority and responsibility (693)**
**Co-ordinating marketing activities (694)**
**Motivating people (694)**
**Communicating inside a company (694)**
**Marketing audit (695)**
**Misdirected marketing effort (696)**
**80-20 principle (696)**
**Iceberg principle (696)**
**Sales volume analysis (697)**
**Market-share analysis (698)**
**Marketing cost analysis (699)**
**Direct costs (703)**
**Indirect costs (703)**
**Contribution-margin approach (703)**
**Full-cost approach (703)**
**Small-order problem (705)**

## QUESTIONS AND PROBLEMS

1. "Good implementation in an organization can overcome poor planning, but good planning cannot overcome poor implementation." Explain, using examples.
2. Give some examples of companies that are likely to organize their sales force by product groups.
3. A manufacturer of small aircraft (Cessna, for example) designed for executive transportation has decided to implement the concept of a selling centre. Who should be on this company's selling teams? What problems might this manufacturer encounter when it uses team selling?
4. Give examples of how advertising and personal selling activities might be co-ordinated in a company's marketing department.
5. As a sales manager, how would you motivate these two sales reps?
   a. An older salesman, who is satisfied with his present level of earnings. He intends to continue as a sales rep, with no promotion, until his retirement in five years.
   b. An excellent sales rep whose morale is shot because she did not receive an expected promotion. She has been with the company for three years.
6. A sales volume analysis by territories indicates that the sales of a manufacturer of roofing materials have increased 12 percent a year for the past three years in the territory comprising Manitoba, Saskatchewan and Alberta. Does this indicate conclusively that the company's sales volume performance is satisfactory in that territory?
7. A manufacturer found that one product accounted for 35 to 45 percent of the company's total sales in all but two of 10 territories across the country. In each of those two territories, this product accounted for only 14 percent of the company's volume. What factors might account for the relatively low sales of this article in the two districts?
8. What effects may a sales volume analysis by product have on training, supervising, and compensating the sales force?
9. "Firms should discontinue selling losing products." Discuss.
10. Should a company stop selling to an unprofitable customer? Why or why not? If not, then what steps might the company take to make the account a profitable one?

## HANDS-ON MARKETING

1. Interview a sales executive (a) in a manufacturing company and (b) in either a securities brokerage or a real estate brokerage firm to find out how they motivate their sales forces. As part of your report, give your evaluation of each motivational program.
2. Interview a marketing executive to find out how the total marketing performance is evaluated in his or her company. As part of your report, include your appraisal of this company's evaluation program.

## NOTES AND REFERENCES


1. Adapted from James Barnes, "The Role of Internal Marketing: If the Staff Won't Buy It, Why Should the Customer?" *Irish Marketing Review*, vol. 4, no. 2, 1989, pp. 11-17; and John Saunders and Carolyn Leitch, "Four Seasons Sees Storm Clouds Clearing," *Globe and Mail*, June 30, 1994, p. B7.
2. For some guidelines to aid in identifying implementation difficulties and suggestions for remedying them, see Thomas V. Bonoma, "Making Your Marketing Strategy Work," *Harvard Business Review*, March-April 1984, pp. 69-76; also see Thomas V. Bonoma, "Enough about Strategy! Let's See Some Clever Executions," *Marketing News*, February 13, 1989, p. 10.
3. Bradley A. Stertz, "For LH Models, Chrysler Maps New Way to Sell," *The Wall Street Journal*, June 30, 1992, p. B1.
4. Gail E. Schares, "The New Generation at Siemens," *Business Week*, March 9, 1992, p. 46.
5. For a discussion of two new organizational forms — a marketing exchange company and a marketing coalition company — needed to cope with complex and dynamic business environments, see Ravi S. Achrol, "Evolution of the Marketing Organization: New Forms for Turbulent Environments," *Journal of Marketing*, October 1991, pp. 77-93.
6. See Jeen-Su Lim and David A. Reid, "Vital Cross-Functional Linkages with Marketing," *Industrial Marketing Management*, Spring 1992, pp. 159-165.
7. Abe Schuchman, "The Marketing Audit: Its Nature, Purpose, and Problems," in *Analyzing and Improving Marketing Performance: "Marketing Audits" in Theory and Practice*, American Management Association, New York, Management Report No. 32, 1959, p. 14. This article is the classic introduction to the marketing audit concept.

## CHAPTER 24 GOALS

Our discussion touched on the societal dimensions of marketing when we briefly examined marketing's role in the total economy in Chapter 1 and described the environment in Chapter 2. For the most part, however, we have approached marketing from the viewpoint of the firm, as we addressed the challenges facing an individual producer or intermediary in managing its marketing activity. In this final chapter, we return to a broader perspective by identifying the major criticisms of marketing and responses to these criticisms. Then we will conclude our discussion of marketing by looking into the crystal ball and considering some prospects for the future that are certain to provide the inspiration for responses such as those illustrated on the opening page of this chapter.

After studying this chapter, you should have an understanding of:

- A societal perspective for evaluating marketing performance.
- The major criticisms of marketing.
- Consumer, government, and business responses to consumer discontent.
- Consumerism and its effect on marketing.
- The ethical responsibilities of marketers.
- Trends influencing future marketing activity.
- Some strategic adjustments necessary to cope with change.

CHAPTER 24

# MARKETING: ITS PERFORMANCE AND ITS FUTURE

## Changing With the Times

There can be little doubt that marketing is a most dynamic field in which to study and to work. Marketing must serve an ever-changing market in an environment that is itself characterized by constant change. Marketers simply can't stand still. They and their organizations must be constantly reacting to the change that is going on around them, so that they can keep current with what will be necessary to meet the needs of consumers and respond in a way that is accepted and perceived by consumers to be relevant to them. The following represent examples of how some Canadian companies have responded in recent years to the changing marketplace in which they operate.

- Avon Canada, a multinational direct marketer of cosmetics, announces a program that will involve a donation of $2 to the Breast Cancer International Centre for each of its Flame Pins that are sold.
- Petro-Canada announces its Environment Protection Policy and invites Canadians to write to the president and CEO with their comments.
- To encourage conservation of our energy resources, the major electrical utilities of Canada promote their "Power Smart" program that strives to educate consumers on how they can save on their use of electricity. The program also involves making available energy-saving devices such as low-flow shower heads and longer-lasting light bulbs at subsidized prices.

- Major brewers and distillers, including Molson, Labatt, and Seagrams, regularly advertise in magazines and newspapers and on billboards, advising Canadian not to drink and drive and not to consume alcohol during pregnancy.
- The Office Equipment Company of Canada announces that it will donate a portion of the price of every Canon Color Laser copier that it sells to the World Wildlife Fund.
- Molson Breweries announces that it is removing all preservatives from its beer in response to consumers' quest for healthier, more natural products. Some observers perceive the move to be a reaction to the growing success of Canada's microbrewers who have been brewing preservative-free beer for years.[1]
- The Government of Canada steps up its war against cigarette smoking by proposing that the tobacco industry be further regulated with the requirement that they use plain packaging only. The proposal is that the tobacco companies would not be permitted to use colour on cigarette packages, that as much as 30 to 40 percent of the surface area of the package be devoted to health warnings, and that one side panel would contain information on the "toxic constituents" of tobacco.[2]

What all these examples illustrate is that, even for the largest businesses and organizations, change and challenge are integral components of marketing. We have seen how companies are responding (or are being required to respond) to the change in the marketplace around them: to concern for the environment and for the prevention of illness, to consumer demands for safer, more healthy products, and to competitive actions that seem to appeal to consumers.

## EVALUATING MARKETING

Before we can begin to appraise marketing, we have to agree on a **basis for evaluating performance** — what the objective of marketing should be. In our discussion of the marketing concept, we said that an organization's objective is to determine consumers' wants and satisfy them. Thus, from the point of view of the *individual organization*, if the firm's target market is satisfied and the organization's objectives are being met, then the marketing effort can be judged successful.

However, this standard makes no distinction between organizations whose behaviour is detrimental to society and those whose activities are socially acceptable. Firms that pollute the environment or stimulate unwholesome demand would qualify as good marketers right along with firms that behave responsibly. Therefore, we must take a broader, societal view that incorporates the best interests of others as well as the desires of a particular target market and the objectives of the marketer to satisfy that market. Marketing must balance the wants of consumers, the objectives of the organization, *and* the welfare of society.

There is evidence all around us of the interrelationship of these three criteria. If a product does not *meet consumers' needs* or if a firm is unable to *provide the level of service* that customers want, the consumer will not buy that product or service. The business world is littered with companies that have gone out of business because they were unable to satisfy their customers. Likewise, if a firm behaves in a fashion that is viewed by consumers or the public to be *detrimental to society*, government will likely intervene, as it does in regulating the advertising of tobacco and other products judged to be potentially damaging to the health and safety of consumers. Finally, companies regularly change their advertising and promotional campaigns as their *organizational objectives* change.

## CRITICISMS OF MARKETING

Criticisms of marketing focus on actions (or inaction) that relate to the balance between organizational objectives and the wants of customers and/or the well-being of society. These issues can be categorized as follows:

- **Exploitation.** Marketers are sometimes accused of taking unfair advantage of a person or situation. Examples of exploitation are price gouging during a shortage and misleading prospects with false or incomplete information. These behaviours may meet the organization's goal of sales and profits, but they are detrimental to consumers, society, or both, and are clearly in conflict with marketing's goal of long-term customer satisfaction.
- **Inefficiency.** Some critics feel that marketing uses more resources than necessary. Accusations include ineffective promotional activity, unnecessary distribution functions, and excessive numbers of brands in many product categories. Inefficiency results in higher costs to organizations, higher prices to consumers, and a waste of society's resources.
- **Stimulating unwholesome demand.** A number of marketers have been accused of encouraging consumers or businesses to purchase products that are detrimental to the individual or the organization. For example, most people believe that the marketing of pornographic material is socially unacceptable. Though it may meet the needs of some consumers and satisfy the objectives of organizations that produce and sell it, the marketing of pornography is discouraged because society views it as detrimental.
- **Illegal behaviour.** Laws are passed to protect individuals, organizations, and society in general. Marketers are expected to abide by these laws, even when violating a law may benefit consumers or an organization. Price collusion, for instance, is likely to meet the needs of the organizations involved and might even result in lower prices for consumers than price competition. However, it is detrimental to competitors of the colluding firms. Therefore, since the behaviour is unfair to others in society, it is unacceptable.

Another way of looking at the criticisms of marketing is through the components of the marketing mix — product, price, distribution, and promotion. Some specific examples are described below, but keep in mind that these are *allegations*. Some are unsubstantiated by facts; others apply only to specific situations.

**Is this promotional sign misleading if all the shorts in the store aren't 30 percent off?**

**Product** Criticisms of products generally concentrate on how well they meet buyers' expectations. Critics charge that too many products are of poor quality or are unsafe. Examples cited include products that fail or break under normal use; prepared food that contains chemical preservatives, flavour enhancers, and colouring; commuter trains that run late; wash-and-wear clothing that needs ironing; products backed by confusing, inadequate warranties; and repair service that is unsatisfactory. Other examples include packages that appear to contain more of a product than they actually do; labels that provide insufficient or misleading information; and products advertised as "new" that appear to offer only trivial improvements. Critics also argue that style obsolescence, particularly in clothing, encourages consumers to discard products before they are worn out, and that there is an unnecessary proliferation of brands in many food and household product categories such as breakfast cereal, detergent, and pet food. As a result, buyers are confused and production capacity is wasted.

**Price** Everyone would like to pay less for products, but most buyers are satisfied with what they consider a fair exchange. Complaints about prices usually arise from the perception that the seller is making an excessive profit or that the buyer has been misled about prices or the terms of sale. We sometimes hear people say that prices are too high because they are controlled by the large firms in an industry. Sellers are accused of building in hidden charges or advertising false markdowns. Critics feel that price competition has been largely replaced by nonprice competition in the form of unnecessary product features that add more to the cost than to the value of a product.

**Distribution** Of the four marketing-mix variables, the least understood and appreciated by consumers is distribution. This is probably because distribution channels can take so many forms. In addition, a consumer comes in direct contact with only one level of the distribution channel — retailers — so it is difficult to appreciate the functions performed at other levels. Criticisms related to channels reflect this lack of familiarity. For example, channels are sometimes seen as having too many levels of intermediaries, and channel members are accused of performing needless functions. These criticisms overlook the pressure that competition exerts on channels to be efficient. On the other hand, some criticisms are valid. For example, when a manufacturer pressures channel members to carry its less attractive products in order to get its more attractive ones, the channel members have higher capital and inventory costs, which are passed along to customers.

**Promotion** The most frequent accusations against marketing focus on promotion — especially personal selling and advertising. Most of the complaints about personal selling are aimed at the retail level and the allegedly poor quality of retail selling and service.

Criticisms of advertising fall into two categories — social and economic. From a social viewpoint, advertising is charged with overemphasizing material standards of living and underemphasizing cultural and moral values. Advertising is accused of manipulating impressionable people, especially children; making statements that are false, deceptive, or in bad taste; making exaggerated claims for products; and overusing fear and sexual appeals. Critics also argue there is simply too much advertising and that ad placement is often offensive. For example, many people resent promotional messages and advertisements on rental videos.

The economic criticisms centre on the effect of advertising on prices and competition. The price argument goes like this. Advertising, particularly persuasive as opposed to informative ads, merely shifts demand from one brand to another. As a result, it only adds to the individual firms' marketing costs without increasing aggregate demand. Since the advertising must be paid for, the price of the product goes up. (There is a counterargument that advertising results in lower prices because it is an efficient method of reaching many people at a low cost per person. The mass market generated by the advertising results in economies of scale in purchasing, manufacturing, and distribution. These economies result in lower costs that more than offset the advertising expense, and the firm is able to charge lower prices than would be possible without the ads.)

The economic criticism of advertising is made from the perspective of competitive impact. It suggests that large firms can afford to differentiate their products through advertising. That is, through extensive advertising, they create the impression in consumers' minds that their brands are better than the brands of less well known rivals. In this way they create barriers to market entry for new or smaller firms. The result is an industry with a small number of firms, which leads to higher prices and higher profits. (The counterargument to this position is that advertising informs consumers about a product. If consumers find the information persuasive, they will try the product and return for more if they are satisfied. If they are not satisfied, no amount of advertising will bring them back. The fact that larger firms advertise more than smaller firms simply indicates that their products are valued by consumers.)

Right or wrong, marketers must take all allegations seriously because they reflect the perceptions of many people. We'll see next how marketers and society can deal with the allegations and the perceptions.

### Understanding the Criticisms

To evaluate the charges against marketing, we must understand what actually is being criticized. Is the object of the complaint ultimately the economic system? An entire industry? A particular firm? If the criticism applies to a firm, is the marketing department or some other department the culprit?

The free enterprise system encourages competition, and government regulatory bodies for many years have judged competition by the number of competitors in an industry. Thus when we complain about the number of toothpaste or cereal brands on the market, we are really criticizing the system. Within a particular firm, a faulty product may result from production, not marketing problems. Clearly, a failure in manufacturing does not make consumers' complaints less valid. The point is that marketing is not to blame for every business mistake.

We also need to consider the sources of criticism. Some critics are well intentioned and well informed. They point out real weaknesses or errors needing correction, such as deceptive packaging, misleading advertising, and irresponsible pricing. But some critics are simply ill informed. They do not understand the functions associated with distribution or are not aware of the costs of producing and selling a product. As a result, though their criticisms may have popular appeal, they cannot withstand careful scrutiny. There is still another type of critic whose views do not reflect the sentiments of society. Nevertheless, they vociferously criticize behaviour they find objectional to serve their own interests. Some of the protests against the use of advertising in political campaigns is an example. We must examine criticism carefully to separate the legitimate from the erroneous and self-serving.

Operating in a socially undesirable manner is unacceptable. Fortunately, this kind of behaviour is only a small part of all the marketing that occurs, although it is widely publicized. More common, and more disturbing, are the situations that are not clear-cut. These are debatable issues such as full disclosure in advertising (What is the meaning of "full"?); planned obsolescence (How long should a product last?); and the cost of marketing (How much should it cost to develop, distribute, and promote a product?).

## MARKETING AT WORK

### FILE 24-1 TAKING IT A LITTLE TOO FAR? UH-HUH

Pepsi-Cola recently succeeded in offending the Church of England when the Pepsi logo was laser-beamed on to an Anglican cathedral to promote a nightclub act. It seems Pepsi was sponsoring the Ministry of Sound, a London dance club that was taking its show on the road. To promote the tour, Pepsi decided to beam its logo on to well-known landmarks throughout Britain. But the world's second-largest maker of soft drinks met its match when it chose to decorate the tower of the cathedral in Liverpool.

"I'm astounded," said Very Rev. Derrick Walters, the church's Dean of Liverpool. "It is outrageous that the cathedral which is much loved would be used this way. I look forward to an apology from Pepsi."

A spokesman for Pepsi in London said that he had mailed apologies to the dean and to church lawyers. "It was never meant as any offence. It was a light-hearted stunt," he said.

The Pepsi logo had been beamed on to landmark buildings throughout Britain to promote the Ministry of Sound. "We chose the Anglican cathedral because it is one of the most prestigious buildings in the country," said Mark Rodol, a founder of the Ministry of Sound. "We just wanted people to know about the event."

The Pepsi spokesman said that the logo had been flashed on castles, the Houses of Parliament, and even a church in Portsmouth, with no complaints, but churches would be off-limits in the future.

Source: Adapted from "PepsiCo Apologizes for Religious Gaffe," *Globe and Mail*, June 11, 1994, p. B2.

## RESPONSES TO MARKETING ISSUES

Efforts to address the issues that arise from marketing activity have come from consumers, the government, and business organizations. In the following paragraphs we discuss some of these **responses to marketing issues**.

### Consumer Responses

One response to marketing misdeeds, both actual and alleged, has come from consumer activists. The term *consumerism* was popularized in the 1960s when, in response to increasing consumer protests against a variety of business practices, Canada became the first country in the world to establish a government department at the federal level to be responsible for the rights of consumers. There had been earlier "consumer movements" in this country — in the early 1900s and again during the Great Depression of the 1930s. In these, the emphasis had been on protecting consumers from harmful products and from false and misleading advertising.

The movement that began in the 1960s, however, is different in three ways from earlier consumer movements. First, the consumerism of the past 20 years has occurred in a setting of higher incomes and largely fills subsistence needs, in contrast to the harsher economic conditions that surrounded earlier movements. Second, the consumer-movement legislation since the 1960s has been intended first and foremost to protect the consumer's interests. Emphasis in earlier legislation was placed on the protection of competition and competitors.

Third, today's consumerism is much more likely to endure, because it has generated an institutional structure to support it. Government agencies have been established to administer the consumer-oriented laws and to protect consumer interests. The social sensitivity of many businesses has increased, and various consumer- and environment-oriented organizations have developed.

However, in the 1990s, as governments have been hard-pressed to meet the increasing demands being placed on public finances, consumer protection programs in some provinces and at the federal level have fallen victim to budget cuts.[3] In certain provinces, regional offices have been closed, staff levels have been reduced, and telephone counsellors have been replaced by automated phone information systems. At the federal level, the Department of Consumer and Corporate Affairs disappeared in 1993, as its function was assumed within the new Industry and Science Department. These developments are not only a result of government budget cuts, but may also reflect the fact that consumers are being protected in other ways, as many businesses and industry associations have adopted voluntary codes of behaviour to self-regulate their dealings with consumers, and as legislation that has been in place at the federal and provincial level affords a level of consumer protection that was not present before the 1970s.

At the same time as governments have been reducing their overt commitment to consumer issues, various consumer organizations have been struggling to maintain interest in their activities among the general public. For many of the same reasons that lie behind government's reduced involvement, consumers themselves seem to have placed consumer activism lower on their list of priorities in the 1990s. Many may feel that they have adequate protection as consumers, certainly better than they enjoyed in the era before consumer protection was institutionalized in legislation and self-regulatory programs of business. It may also be the case that consumers feel they have other, more pressing problems to address in the complex society and tough economic times that many now are facing. Regardless of the reasons, it is a fact that membership in the Consumers' Association of Canada has been declining in recent years, and subscriptions to its magazine, *Canadian Consumer*, have fallen from 153,000 at their peak in the 1980s, to only 65,000 in 1993, with the result that the CAC ceased publication of the magazine in June of that year.[4]

**Meaning and Scope of Consumerism** Consumerism includes three broad areas of dissatisfaction and remedial effort:

- Discontent with direct buyer-seller exchange relationships between consumers and businesses. This is the original and still main focus of consumerism. Efforts to ban MSG, a flavour enhancer and preservative that can cause a severe allergic reaction in some people, would be an example.
- Discontent with nonbusiness, not-for-profit organizations and governmental agencies. Consumerism extends to all exchange relationships. The performance of such diverse organizations as schools (quality of education, performance of students on standardized tests, number of class days per year), hospitals (medical care costs, smoking in rooms, malpractice), and public utilities (rate increases, eliminating service to people unable to pay their bills) has been scrutinized and subjected to organized and spirited consumer protests.
- Discontent of those indirectly affected by the behaviour of others. An exchange between two parties can sometimes have a negative impact on a third party. For example, farmers buy insecticides and pesticides from chemical companies. However, these products may pollute water supplies, rivers, and the air. Thus an exchange has created a problem for a third party or group. The effects of second-hand smoke is another example.

**Consumer Actions** Consumer reactions to marketing problems have ranged from complaints registered with offending organizations to boycotts (refusing to buy a particular product or shop at a certain store). Consumer groups have recognized their potential power and have become more active politically than ever. Some have organized mass letter-writing campaigns to editors, politicians, and business executives. They have supported consumer-oriented political candidates, conducted petition drives, and gained media attention through sit-ins and picketing.

More recently, many organized groups at both the local and national levels have become involved in a more broadly defined consumer movement. Some of these groups represent a variety of interests, dealing with the direct interaction of consumers with businesses as well as with broader issues such as environmentalism and animal rights. Others represent particular interest groups, including retired and elderly consumers, the urban poor, and victims of crime and fraud by businesses.

**Consumerism in the Future** Cultural conditions seem to have moved us away from brief periods of heightened consumerism to a more constant level of concern. Consumers today are generally more sensitive to social and environmental issues. Along with sources of dissatisfaction already described, the plight of the poor, air and water pollution, waste disposal, treatment of animals, and health and safety are other social and environmental causes receiving attention.

In addition, more people are willing and able to take an active role in consumerism. Compared to earlier generations, young people are better educated, more articulate, and more inclined to speak out. People of all ages are generally less intimidated by large organizations and less willing to accept the status quo. Responding to this increased public sensitivity, many politicians are also demonstrating greater concern for societal issues.

Since problems remain, consumerism in the remainder of the decade will focus on some of the same areas as in the past. For example, fair treatment for disadvantaged consumers and personal safety will be major concerns. In addition, waste management, efficient utilization of resources, and the preservation of natural beauty are environmental issues that will likely draw increased attention.

### Government Responses

Interest in consumer issues is not likely to disappear. The main reason for this forecast is that today it is politically popular to support various consumer, social, and environmental causes. Politicians may generally have been unresponsive to consumer needs in the years prior to the mid-1960s. Since then, however, consumer-oriented activity at both the federal and provincial levels has been carried on at an unprecedented rate. All the provinces have enacted legislation and put consumer protection programs in place.

A significant number of these laws are designed to protect the consumer's "right to safety" — especially in situations where consumers cannot judge for themselves the risk involved in the purchase and use of particular products. In Canada, we have such legislation as the Food and Drugs Act, which regulates and controls the manufacture, distribution, and sale of food, drugs, and cosmetic products. A very important piece of legislation, which also protects the consumer's right to safety, is the Hazardous Products Act. This law establishes standards for the manufacture of consumer products designed for household, garden, personal, recreational, or child use. Regulations under the Hazardous Products Act require that dangerous products be packaged as safely as possible and labelled with clear and adequate warnings. This law also makes provision for the removal of dangerous products from the marketplace.

One controversial area of product safety legislation is the paternalistic type of law that is intended to protect the consumer, whether he or she wants that protection. Thus, it is now mandatory to equip automobiles with seat belts, and in most provinces it is illegal to operate an automobile unless the seat belts are fastened. In some cities, it is required that bicycle riders wear helmets. In effect, somebody else is forcing a consumer to accept what the other person feels is in the consumer's best interests — truly a new and broadening approach to consumer legislation.

Another series of laws and government programs supports the consumer's "right to be informed." These measures help in such areas as reducing confusion and deception in packaging and labelling, identifying the ingredients and nutritional content in food products, advising consumers of the length of life of certain packaged food products, providing instructions and assistance in the care of various textile products, and determining the true rate of interest.

At the federal level, government has passed a number of pieces of legislation designed to provide consumers with more information. Possibly the most important of these is the Consumer Packaging and Labelling Act, which regulates the packaging, labelling, sale, and advertising of prepackaged products. The Textile Labelling Act requires manufacturers of textile products to place labels on most articles made from fabrics. These labels must name the fibres, show the amount of each fibre in the product by percentage, and identify the company for whom or by whom the article was made.

At the provincial level, a number of programs exist that provide information to consumers. For example, all provinces have passed consumer protection legislation, which requires that all consumer lending agencies and retail stores provide consumers with information concerning the true rate of interest that they are paying on borrowed money and on purchases made on credit.

Also at the provincial level, all provinces have passed a general Consumer Protection Act, which deals primarily with the granting of credit. All provinces also have legislation that provides for a "cooling off" period during which the purchaser of goods or services in a door-to-door sale may cancel the contract, return any merchandise, and obtain a full refund. In addition, most provinces have legislation that provides for the disposal of unsolicited goods and credit cards received through the mail. All provinces also administer legislation that regulates particular industries such as collection agencies, automobile dealerships, and insurance agents.

The consumer is also protected at both the federal and provincial levels in Canada in the area of misleading and dishonest advertising. The federal Competition Act contains a number of provisions dealing with misleading advertising; these have been discussed in Chapter 18.

One of the most significant responses to the consumer movement on the part of government has been a strengthened and expanded role of regulatory agencies involved in consumer affairs. At the provincial level, Public Utilities Boards hold public hearings and receive briefs from concerned citizens and consumer groups whenever a telephone or hydro company is seeking a rate increase or a change in its services. It has become quite common for organized consumer associations and ratepayer groups to intervene at such hearings as representatives of consumer interests.

Federally, two major regulatory agencies have emerged as powerful arms of government in recent years. The Canadian Transport Commission (CTC) regulates all aspects of interprovincial travel and companies that operate nationally, such as railways and the major airlines. Applications for route changes and fare increases must be filed with the CTC, and opportunities are presented at public hearings for consumer groups to make representations. Similarly, the Canadian Radio-television and Telecommunications Commission (CRTC) regulates the broadcasting and telephone industries in this country. This regulatory body has become very much involved in marketing-related areas in recent years. It is responsible for awarding broadcasting licences to AM and FM radio stations, television stations, and cable television operators. The CRTC also regulates these broadcasters in the content of the programming they use and also administers numerous codes of advertising standards in its role as the agency responsible for regulating broadcast advertising.

Also, at the federal level, many government departments play important regulatory roles that have a major impact on the way in which marketers do business. From the point of view of a marketer of consumer products, the two most important would likely be Industry Canada and Health Canada. Various branches of these departments administer federal regulations and legislation such as the Competition Act, the Hazardous Products Act, the Consumer Packaging and Labelling Act, and the Food and Drugs Act.

Finally, in all provinces and at the federal level in Canada there exist marketing boards that, to varying degrees, control the production, distribution, and pricing of products. These marketing boards, such as the Ontario Milk Marketing Board, the British Columbia Fruit Board, and the Canadian Egg Marketing Agency, wield considerable power over the marketing of the products that fall under their responsibility.[5] Most of these boards are involved in the distribution of agricultural products and were established to represent the interests of producers. However, through their efforts to promote marketing efficiency, marketing boards generally attempt to represent the best long-term interests of consumers.[6]

It is difficult to judge the effectiveness of government effort since it depends on one's perspective. From the point of view of many consumer advocates, the government is too slow and too many issues are ignored or overlooked. Alternatively, some free-market spokespersons would prefer less regulation and view government activity as interference. In evaluating consumer protection, it is important to recognize that there are trade-offs. For example, there are costs involved in providing consumers with more information, designing and manufacturing products to eliminate all hazards, and keeping the environment clean. These must be weighed against the expected benefits. Often these are difficult comparisons; some, for instance, involve costs that will be incurred now for benefits that may not be realized until some time in the future.

### Business Responses

An increasing number of businesses are making substantive responses to consumer problems. Here are a few examples:

- **Better communications with consumers.** Many firms have responded positively to the desire of consumers to be heard. Toll-free 1-800 phone numbers have become an integral part of customer service because they are easy to use and allow consumers to speak directly to a representative of the business.
- **More and better information for consumers.** Point-of-sale information is constantly improving. Manufacturers' instruction manuals on the use and care of their products are more detailed and easier to read. In many instances, package labels are more informative than in the past.
- **Product improvements.** More marketers are making a concerted effort to incorporate feedback from consumers in the designs of their products. As a result of consumer input or complaints, many companies have made improvements in their products. For example, detergent manufacturers have produced concentrated products that are more environmentally safe and scent-free products that contain no perfumes that may irritate people with allergies. Soft drink manufacturers have improved the design of the caps on their one- and two-litre bottles so that the product will retain its carbonation after opening.
- **Service quality measurement.** Many companies have realized that it is becoming increasingly difficult to gain a competitive advantage through product design, and that the key to success is to offer the customer the best possible service. Realizing also that they need feedback so they know how well they are doing, many have developed and introduced programs that allow them to measure consumers' perceptions of the level of service they are receiving.
- **More carefully prepared advertising**. Many advertisers are extremely cautious in approving agency-prepared ads, in sharp contrast to past practices. Advertisers are involving their legal departments in the approval process. They are sensitive to the fact that the CRTC may reject a commercial or the Advertising Standards Council may find that the advertisement violates some particular code of advertising standards. The advertising industry and the media are doing a much more effective self-regulation job than ever before, especially through the Advertising Advisory Board and its Advertising Standards Councils.
- **Customer service departments.** A growing number of companies have separate departments to handle consumer enquiries and complaints. Some even encourage customers to complain, or at least to provide feedback, by distributing short questionnaires in hotel rooms, airline seat pockets, and restaurants. In addition to dealing with complaints, customer service departments also gauge consumer tastes, act as sounding boards for new ideas, and often gain feedback on new products.

Some trade associations see themselves as defenders of their respective industry or profession. In that capacity, they try to moderate government antibusiness legislation through lobbying and head off criticism with arguments to justify almost any behaviour. More enlightened associations have recognized the necessity for responsible corporate behaviour. Though they still engage in lobbying, these groups actively respond to consumer problems by setting industry ethical standards, conducting consumer education, and promoting research among association members.

## ETHICS AND MARKETING

**Ethics** are standards of conduct. To act in an ethical fashion is to conform to an accepted standard of moral behaviour. Undoubtedly, virtually all people prefer to act ethically. It

**This magazine is taking steps to protect its readers with allergies.**

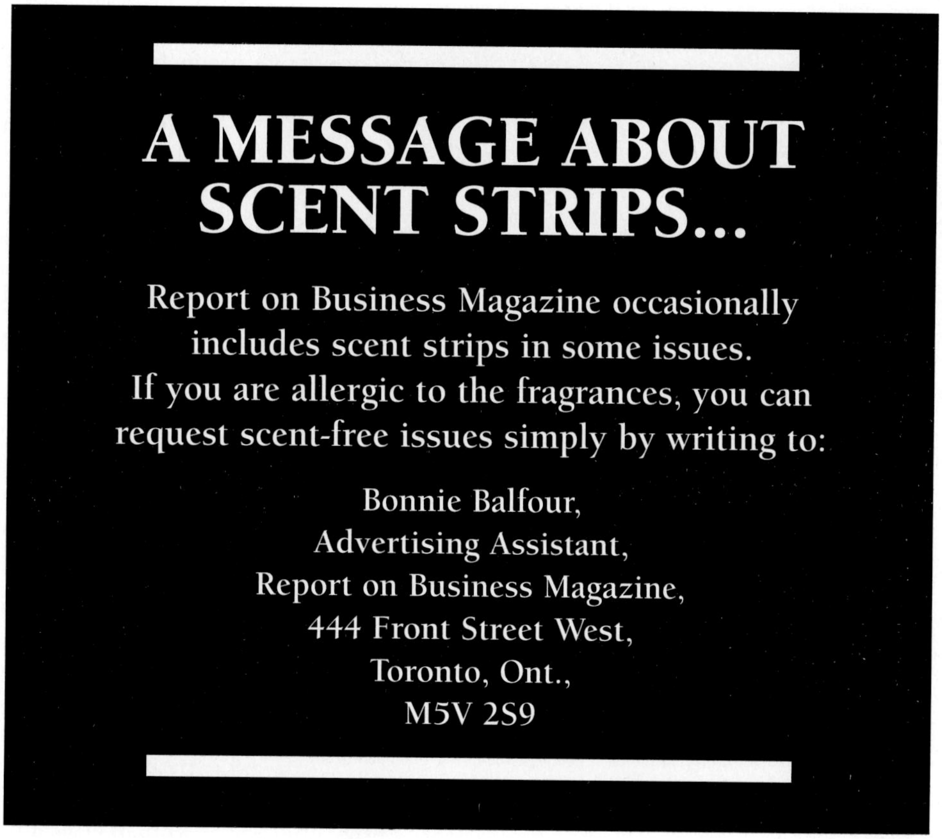


is easy to be ethical when no hardship is involved — when a person is winning and life is going well. The test comes when things are not going so well — when pressures build up. These pressures arise in all walks of life, and marketing is no exception.

Marketing executives face the challenge of balancing the best interests of consumers, the organization, and society into a workable guide for their daily activities. In any situation, they must be able to distinguish what is ethical from what is unethical and act accordingly, regardless of the possible consequences. However, there are many circumstances in which what constitutes ethical behaviour is far from straightforward.

### Setting Ethical Guidelines

Many organizations have formal codes of ethics that identify specific acts (bribery, accepting gifts) as unethical and describe the standards employees are expected to live up to. A large percentage of major corporations have ethics codes, as do many smaller businesses. These guidelines lessen the chance that an employee will knowingly or unknowingly violate a company's standards. In addition, ethics codes strengthen a company's hand in dealing with customers or prospects that encourage unethical behaviour. For young or inexperienced executives, these codes can be valuable guides, helping them to resist pressure to compromise personal ethics in order to move up in the firm.

However, every decision cannot be taken out of the hands of the manager. Furthermore, determining what is right and what is wrong can be extremely difficult. It is not realistic for an organization to construct a two-column list of all possible practices, one headed "ethical" and the other "unethical." Rather, a marketer must be able to evaluate a situation and formulate a response. Arthur Andersen and Co. has developed an ethical reasoning model that can be taught to current and future managers.[7] The model

DON'T FIND YOURSELF IN THE DARK ABOUT PRESCRIPTION MEDICINES.
There's really no reason anybody has to be in the dark about prescription medicines.
But if you take your medication without fully understanding the facts, then the very medicine designed to help you, could actually harm you.
The Pharmaceutical Manufacturers Association of Canada believes you owe it to yourself, not to mention your family, to be fully informed about prescription medicines.
That's why we're offering a free information kit. It outlines important facts about how to use medicines correctly, and questions you should ask your doctor or pharmacist.
So, if you take prescription medicines, we urge you to call 1-800-363-0203 for your information kit. And find out for yourself why knowledge is the best medicine.
Pharmaceutical Manufacturers Association of Canada

**This trade association is acting in a socially responsible way when it offers a free information kit.**

expands the traditional cost-benefit analysis to include all the individuals and groups affected, not just the decision maker's organization, to help clarify the ethical dimensions of a decision. The procedure consists of:

1. Identifying the decision options and the likely consequences of each.
2. Identifying all individuals and organizations that will be positively or negatively affected by the consequences of each option.
3. Estimating the negative impact (costs) and positive impact (benefits) of each option from the point of view of each affected party, taking into consideration their particular interests and needs.
4. Ranking the costs and the benefits of each option and making a decision.

This approach is an attempt to be systematic and logical in ethical decisions. It will work only if the decision maker can be objective and impartial. However, ethical situations are frequently charged with emotion. Thus, an alternative approach that attempts to personalize the situation may be more effective. When faced with an ethical problem, honest answers to the following questions should indicate which route to follow:

- Would I do this to a friend?
- Would I be willing to have this done to me?
- Would I be embarrassed if this action were publicized nationally?

### Pragmatic Reasons for Behaving Ethically

Marketing executives should practice ethical behaviour because it is morally correct. While this is simple and beautiful in concept, it is not sufficient motivation for everyone. So let's consider four pragmatic **reasons for ethical behaviour**:

- **To reverse declining public confidence in marketing.** Periodically we hear about misleading package labels, false claims in ads, phony list prices, and infringements of well-established trademarks. Though such practices are limited to only a small proportion of all marketing, the reputations of all marketers are damaged. To reverse this situation, business leaders must demonstrate convincingly that they are aware of their ethical responsibility and will fulfil it. Companies must set high ethical standards and enforce them. Moreover, it is in management's interest to be concerned with the well-being of consumers, since they are the lifeblood of a business.
- **To avoid increases in government regulation.** Our economic freedoms sometimes have a high price, just as our political freedoms do. Business apathy, resistance, or token responses to unethical behaviour simply increase the probability of more government regulation. Indeed, most of the governmental limitations on marketing are the result of management's failure to live up to its ethical responsibilities at one time

or other. Moreover, once some form of government control has been introduced, it is rarely removed.

- **To retain the power granted by society.** Marketing executives wield a great deal of social power as they influence markets and speak out on economic issues. However, there is responsibility tied to that power. If marketers do not use their power in a socially acceptable manner, that power will be lost in the long run.
- **To protect the image of the organization.** Buyers often form an impression of an entire organization based on their contact with one person. More often than not, that person represents the marketing function. You may base your opinion of a retail store on the behaviour of a single sales clerk. As Procter & Gamble put it in an annual report: "When a Procter & Gamble sales person walks into a customer's place of business . . . that sales person not only represents Procter & Gamble, but in a very real sense, that person is Procter & Gamble."

**Supporting environmental causes such as the World Wildlife Fund indicates a company's social responsibility.**

## Socially Responsible Behaviour

Ethical behaviour goes beyond avoiding wrongdoing. The ethical marketer recognizes that the position he or she holds in society carries with it certain obligations. This **social responsibility** involves improving the well-being of society. Besides obeying the law and meeting the normal and reasonable expectations of the public, socially responsible organizations and individuals lead the way in setting standards of business and community performance. Some companies encourage their employees to join volunteer groups and will pay the fees for staff to join service clubs that get involved in community projects. Many large corporations sponsor television specials on environmental and other social issues and generally support public broadcasting. Publishers, such as McGraw-Hill Ryerson, donate scholarships to universities and colleges and support literacy programs. Companies like Avon and The Office Equipment Company of Canada, which were mentioned in the chapter opener, donate money raised from the sale of certain items to charitable organizations.

## Protecting the Customer's Right to Privacy

One of the most troublesome issues facing marketers today relates to behaviour that threatens the customer's right to privacy. This is especially important today as more and more companies are collecting information on customers from a number of different sources and storing the data on data bases to be used for marketing purposes. Some consumers object to businesses having the information in the first place and to their use of it to sell them things. The point is that the technology is available today to permit the integration of data bases, making it possible to obtain information about the characteristics of consumers and their households and to match that information with data about purchases, credit card usage, and other consumption behaviour.[8]

Nowhere is the issue of privacy more pertinent than in the area of telemarketing. As the use of the telephone has increased to contact people in their homes for the purpose of marketing products and services, so too has the public outcry against such practices. Some less-scrupulous marketers have used automated-dialling devices that continually dial telephone numbers selected at random and play a recorded sales pitch when the telephone is answered. While the use of such tactics is not at all widespread, many members of the public object to being telephoned at home. Consequently, many have turned to installing answering machines or other technology that will allow them to screen calls, or they have paid for unlisted telephone numbers (although they will not be protected from random calling even with an unlisted number). As the case in the Marketing at Work File on page 725 illustrates, the CRTC has ruled that even the telephone companies themselves cannot call unlisted numbers for telemarketing purposes.

The direct marketing industry has taken steps to police itself with regard to offering protection to consumers against invasion of privacy. The industry association, the Canadian Direct Marketing Association, has adopted a code of standards that regulates its members, who account for about 80 percent of all direct marketers in Canada. The code, among other things, provides for the right of consumers to have their names deleted from mailing lists, provides for informing consumers of the source of their names appearing on any list, and ensures that data are protected against unauthorized use.[9]

One consumer in Sudbury, Ontario, was so angry, having received persistent mailings from Columbia House, the mail-order video and record company, even after he had asked in writing that his name be removed from their list, that he started sending the company $10 for each piece of unwanted mail that he received, later increasing it to $100. When the mailings continued, he took Columbia House to small claims court to try to collect the $480 that he claimed they owed him. He won his case, thereby setting a legal precedent.[10]

## Advertising and Social Responsibility

The issue of the social responsibility of marketing is also often related to the advertising that businesses present to their target consumers. For example, Benetton, the international Italian-owned clothing manufacturer and retailer, has in recent years employed rather controversial approaches in its advertising. Some consumers in many countries around the world have been shocked by the content of Benetton ads, which have featured black and white people embracing, multicoloured condoms, a car burning in an urban ghetto, a group of refugees clambering up the side of a rusty ship, a black Queen Elizabeth, a photo of a dying AIDS patient with his anguished family looking on, and the blood-stained clothing of a recently killed Bosnian soldier. Benetton maintains that its ads are intended to force people to think of important social issues; however, many are offended by them.[11]

Advertising is also criticized for the way in which certain groups in society are presented or for the effect that it may have upon them. There has been considerable objection, for example, to the portrayal of ultra-thin young models in fashion advertising for such brands as Club Monaco and The Gap. Critics suggest that such advertising promotes the view that thinness is glamorous and may contribute to eating disorders.[12]

## MARKETING AT WORK

### FILE 24-2 IT'S UNLISTED FOR A REASON

It's a good bet that Bell Canada wishes it had never telephoned Laura Sokoloski with a sales pitch for long-distance services. Sokoloski has an unlisted telephone number, and she proceeded to file complaints against Bell with the Canadian Radio-television and Telecommunications Commission (CRTC), the "regulator" of the telephone industry, and with the federal Privacy Commissioner. It seems she had arranged for an unlisted number so that she would not receive calls from people who wanted to sell her things.

As part of a telemarketing campaign, Bell Canada and other telephone companies across the country have been trying to sign up Canadian households for long-distance savings plans as competition heats up in the long-distance market. Sokoloski took exception to the fact that Bell included unlisted numbers in their telemarketing list, indicating that she pays $4.05 a month for her unlisted number. She first complained to Bell, but was told that the company did not consider it an invasion of privacy for the company to solicit its own unlisted customers by telephone.

The CRTC agreed with Sokoloski and ordered Canada's telephone companies not to solicit their own customers who have unlisted numbers. The commission ruled that, by paying to have their numbers unlisted, these customers have a right to be left alone — even by the telephone company.

Source: Lawrence Surtees, "Bell Telemarketers Phone Wrong Number," *Globe and Mail*, June 3, 1994, p. A1; and Lawrence Surtees, "Woman Wins Privacy Suit with Bell," *Globe and Mail*, June 30, 1994, p. A2.

Other advertising is criticized as being socially irresponsible primarily because of the product that is being advertised. For example, Labatt Breweries encountered a stream of protest when the company introduced its Maximum Ice brand, a beer with a 7.1 percent alcohol content. The advertising, with its heavy-metal look, was said to appeal most to young, male beer drinkers. The introduction of the brand and its provocative advertising have been soundly criticized by organizations such as MADD (Mothers Against Drunk Driving) and is seen to be a threat to the efforts of many groups to curb excessive drinking and drunk driving in particular.[13]

Much advertising that appears in the mass media is controversial for a number of reasons. What is often interesting to observe is that the most violent criticism and the most strident demands for the removal of the offending advertising often come from people who are clearly not in the advertiser's intended target consumer segment.

### Ethics and the Consumer

Acting ethically is not a one-way street. Consumers also have a responsibility to behave ethically in exchange situations. Business firms are increasingly experiencing unethical behaviour on the part of consumers. Shoplifting, fraudulent coupon redemption, vandalism, fraudulent cheque cashing, and other consumer abuses have become major expense items for organizations. Although determining exactly how much consumer fraud occurs is virtually impossible, reliable estimates place the annual cost to business in the billions of dollars.

Of course, the high incidence of unethical consumer behaviour does not excuse inappropriate business practices. These examples simply illustrate how widespread unethical behaviour has become. What the facts make abundantly clear is the need for a system-wide exploration of ways to reduce this problem in business, among consumers, and within all other social institutions.

## PROSPECTS FOR THE FUTURE

Let's move now from looking at how marketers can and should behave to a description of what lies ahead for marketing. More specifically, in order to be more effective and efficient, what do marketers need to know and what do they need to do?

### Market Trends and Reactions

Many trends bear watching. To illustrate their significance, we will look at three areas — demographic changes, shifts in values, and the growth of information.

**Consumer Demographics** Changes in demographics — the population's age distribution, income, education, ethnic composition, and household structure — all affect marketers' activities. For example, the population is getting older and senior citizens are the fastest-growing age group. This shift creates expanded marketing opportunities in such areas as travel and tourism and health and medical care. Another demographic change is the greater ethnic diversity resulting primarily from increases in the level of immigration from Asia and other areas. These groups are large enough to attract the attention of marketers, but they present interesting challenges.

Another important development is the decrease in household size. More people than ever live alone. Therefore, marketers of many consumer products must consider the impact of smaller households on meat preparation, the size of appliances, and package sizes, to cite several examples. Small households also mean fewer people to perform normal maintenance functions. Therefore, time has for many become the currency of the 1990s.

What do these demographic changes tell us? They indicate that some markets will disappear and new ones will emerge. Marketers must remain abreast of these developments and adjust strategies accordingly. For example, the aging population has created opportunities for products modified to accommodate the physical limitations of the elderly (labels and instructions in large print, easy-to-open containers), and time pressure has spawned firms that will do routine errands (getting the car serviced, picking up the dry cleaning, grocery shopping).

**Values** Values, the widely held beliefs in a society, change slowly. When they do, however, the impact on existing institutions and the opportunities for innovative marketers can be great. Value shifts often accompany demographic changes. As the Canadian population gets older, we can expect some adjustments in values. For example, we are seeing:[14]

- **Broadened perspectives.** Some forecasters see a shift away from a self-orientation to an "other-orientation." For example, volunteerism is on the upswing. Indications are that people may be disturbed by the materialism of the 1980s, a period where self-gratification governed many choices.
- **Increased scepticism.** Education is at its highest level ever. Consumers have more confidence in their ability to make judgements and are less willing to accept unsubstantiated claims. Authority is subject to challenge. Consumers demand information and are willing to question traditions. The difficulty North American automakers are having in winning back the confidence of consumers is an example of this development.
- **Balanced life-styles.** From a society that focused on work to produce a richer life-style, we are moving to a society that wants to balance work and leisure to enjoy a life-style. This will mean an increasing concern with wellness in the form of nutrition and exercise, the allocation of more time to home, family, and leisure, and a desire to become involved in activities viewed as worthwhile and fulfilling.

What do these changes mean for marketing? We are likely to see all increasing emphasis of quality over quantity in consumption and a more careful evaluation of the value of product features that seem to add more to style than substance. One area in which values are evident is a heightened interest in the future quality of life. International concern over the dissipation of the atmosphere's ozone layer, the disappearance of rainforests, increases in acid rain, and the "greenhouse effect" was reflected in the unprecedented Earth Summit Treaty signed by 143 nations in Rio de Janeiro in 1992. Other environmental issues of interest to consumers are waste disposal and landfills, air and water pollution, and biodegradability.

Any marketing activity of a firm that is intended to create a positive impact or lessen the negative impact of a product on the environment in order to capitalize on consumers' concerns about environmental issues is known as **green marketing**. Green marketing efforts range from simply altering advertising claims to the development of entirely new products.

Environmentally sensitive product packaging, alternatives to fossil fuel, and energy conservation are excellent marketing opportunities. Other prospects are not so obvious. One industry spawned by environmental interests and a desire to visit unspoiled, exotic locations is leisure travel to unusual destinations. But even this may have its downside. For example, there has been such an increase in the number of whale-watching tours in various parts of the world that some environmentalists are becoming concerned that the number of tourists may represent a threat to the animals they wish to protect.

The issues in the environmental debate are not at all clear. The complexity of the ecosystem means that it is possible for interest groups to argue that recyclable paper and cardboard containers are environmentally safer than polystyrene, while some scientists can make an equally rational case that the total use of energy is greater in the manufacture of the paper products. The net effect is that the consumer is probably confused. Inherently, however, the consumer is more likely to come down on the side of apparently "natural" products; therefore, cloth diapers are perceived to be less harmful to the environment than are disposables; cardboard fast-food containers are perceived to be less harmful than their "plastic" counterparts. Consequently, some companies have been accused of jumping on the bandwagon with respect to the environmental issue by labelling "green" some products that do not really offer an environmental advantage.[15]

The federal government has tried to make some sense of the environmental debate by establishing the Environmental Choice program. This is a program that sets certain standards for the testing of products and their impact on the environment. The logo of the program now appears on more than 500 products from 80 companies, including cloth diapers, re-refined motor oil, and environmentally safe paint. Canada's program is an example of similar initiatives that have been launched by many countries around the world. One challenge that comes out of such an initiative, which is all the more important as world trade increases, is the consistency of standards among countries. In other words, will a product that is considered environmentally friendly in Canada meet the environmental standards of the European Union or Japan? Some business people and economists are concerned that environmental restrictions may become trade barriers of the 1990s.

There are several indications that consumers will focus more on the home in the years ahead. Stressful jobs and time constraints have led people to seek a place where they can relax in comfort and security.[16] A home fulfils the desire for something stable in a dynamic world. As a result, consumers are spending more on their homes and on products that make their homes enjoyable. For instance, computerized television that will identify and record programs in preselected categories will probably be available in the 1990s. Home remodelling, lower-cost construction methods such as modular homes and prefab housing components, and fibre-optic systems to monitor lighting, security, and fire protection are predicted growth markets, as are traditional forms of leisure time activities.

**The service that Petro-Canada delivers at the pumps is backed by a corporate policy on environmental protection.**

The success of businesses such as Four Seasons Hotels and Bell Canada makes it clear that consumers reward good service. It is also apparent that many firms recognize this opportunity. The effective "lonely Maytag repairman" ad campaign that has run for many years and airline ads emphasizing on-time arrival records are just two examples. Recognizing the need to offer good service is often easier than finding and training employees to provide it. A major challenge for organizations in the 1990s will be to design and implement systems that provide consumers with high-calibre service.

**Market Information** Marketers have the ability to pinpoint customers as never before. Using scanner data that produces detailed purchase behaviour on a store-by-store basis, Statistics Canada data that provide demographic information down to the city block, and a variety of other sources such as warranty registration cards, contest entries, and rebate requests, firms can build detailed customer and prospect profiles. With this information, they are able to design products and assortments tailored specifically to a customer's needs. Consider the case of Black's Photo Corporation. Until recently, the company would make a decision on where to locate a new store primarily by the seat of its pants. Now it uses a software program from Toronto-based Compusearch Micromarketing to combine demographic and marketing data with mapping and topographical software to provide detailed information on the market potential of certain areas. The software, called Conquest/Canada, can provide the following: census data, consumer spending per household in more than 800 purchase categories, ownership data on household facilities and equipment, vehicle registrations, business activity in the area, and Compusearch's population and age group projections to the year 2004. The result is that much of the guesswork is taken out of marketing decisions such as store location.[17]

Knowing more about the market has led to **market fragmentation** — the identification of smaller and smaller market segments. There was a time when a packaged-goods manufacturer could develop a quality product, advertise it nationally using the national media, stock retailers' shelves, and have a reasonable chance of success. But the situation has changed. Marketers can no longer expect large numbers of consumers to compromise their needs and wants and buy standardized products. Rather, they must tailor goods and services to meet the needs of small market segments. Called **niche marketing**, this strategy significantly complicates the marketer's job. One version of a product is replaced by several. Different ads must be produced and new media found to reach different consumers. Retailers must choose among many product variations, not all of which can be stocked. The added variety complicates inventory management, distribution, and personal selling.

Evidence of this fragmentation is everywhere. McDonald's, the king of hamburgers, not only has expanded its variety of burgers, but has also test marketed fish-and-chips, lobster sandwiches, Mexican food, fried chicken, and pizza. From 1947 to 1984 Procter & Gamble had only one Tide. Today there are many versions, including Tide Ultra, Phosphate Free Tide, Liquid Tide, and Tide with bleach.

There are no indications that the trend to niche marketing will end. In fact, with more sophisticated electronic data collection methods being developed and the diversity of the population increasing, all indications point to even greater fragmentation in the future.

## Strategic Marketing Adjustments

We have highlighted just three of the many changes taking place in the market — demographic changes, shifts in values, and the growth in information — and some of the implications they have for marketers. One common response to change, as illustrated by the examples, is simply to react as it occurs. However, realizing that change is always occurring, marketers should initiate strategic proactive efforts to improve performance. Four are described in this section.

**Instilling a Market-Driven Orientation** Describing the marketing concept and implementing it in an organization are two different things. The concept — combining a customer orientation with co-ordinated marketing and the organization's goals — certainly has intuitive appeal, yet many organizations seem unable to practise it consistently. Despite having been taught in business schools for over 50 years, its effective implementation is the exception rather than the rule. What does practising the marketing concept require? At least the following:[18]

- The marketing concept involves a philosophy of business that focuses on the customer's needs. However, when faced with the choice of putting the customer first or meeting their own needs, employees often find it difficult to give the customer priority. Instilling this orientation requires top-management commitment. Lip service is not sufficient. Employees must see management putting the customer first.
- There must be a reward system encouraging a customer orientation. Employees must be empowered to make decisions that recognize the importance of customers and be publicly rewarded for those decisions. Take the case of the Federal Express driver who could not get a drop-box unlocked. Rather than give up and have the packages in the box fail to be delivered on time, he managed to load the 225 kg box in his truck and haul it back to the office where a mechanic could open it. For his decision (and his effort), he was given an award by the company.
- Organizations must stay in close contact with the market. This means having detailed, accurate market knowledge. Buyers are becoming less and less willing to compromise

to satisfy their desires. Marketers must develop more marketing programs for smaller markets. Good information and decision-support systems are needed in making these decisions. In consumer marketing this means conducting research on a continuous basis. In business-to-business marketing it may mean creating new structures. For example, Procter & Gamble has a marketing team located permanently at Wal-Mart headquarters to ensure that this key customer is served adequately.

- A sustainable differential advantage must be established by precisely matching the buyers' needs with the firm's capabilities. Following its enormous success in running shoes, Nike introduced a line of casual shoes that failed. Philip Knight, co-founder, chairman, and CEO of Nike, explained the failure in terms of focus.[19] Being skilled at producing and marketing athletic shoes did not automatically transfer to another product, even a closely related one. Nike's differential advantage is in sports and fitness products. That is what it does well and where its advantage exists.
- Offer consumers the best value possible. Many companies have realized that offering discounts and "specials" does little to build long-term customer loyalty and have instead turned to low, everyday prices. The concept of *adding value* is a very important one for marketers in the 1990s. The most effective way of adding value is often to provide exceptional service.[20]
- Listen to the customer. Successful companies no longer assume that they know what their customers want. Consequently, many are doing more marketing research than they have in the past. They have also learned that they can do nothing to improve the service to customers unless they know when customers are having problems or concerns. Consequently, many have implemented a program to *encourage* customers to complain and have then put in place a system that tracks every customer complaint and ensures that it is resolved to the customer's satisfaction.[21]
- All exchange partners, not just customers, must be satisfied. Exchange partners of an organization include its customers, suppliers, intermediaries, owners, regulators, and anyone else it interacts with. If suppliers, for example, feel their exchanges with an organization are unsatisfactory, they will not do everything in their power to ensure that the final customers' needs will be met. The same is true of employees. Essential to satisfying final customers are strong, positive relationships among all the parties who contribute to bringing a product or service to market.

**Adopting a Global Orientation** To be successful in the future, marketers must adopt a global orientation towards markets, products, and marketing activity. In the past most firms could be successful by focusing on the domestic market and outperforming local rivals. However, that has changed. Now firms, both large and small, are going where the markets are the most attractive.

The cliché that we live in a "small world" is a reality for marketers. Virtually instantaneous communications have greatly increased global awareness. Economic, social, and political developments on one side of the world have an impact everywhere else. On the evening television news we are as likely to hear about developments on the Japanese stock market as we are about activity on Bay Street.

As a result, foreign firms are now major investors in Canada and Canadian firms in search of new mass markets have a renewed interest in opportunities overseas. Growing buying power in Asia, the elimination of trade restrictions in the European Union in 1992, and political changes in Eastern Europe and the former Soviet Union have created interest among many Canadian businesses who are establishing their positions or launching initiatives to enter these markets. Canadian companies such as Northern Telecom and Bombardier now manufacture and export telecommunications and transportation equipment to many countries. McDonald's of Canada was responsible for that company's entry into Moscow. Canadian banks are major players in financing projects around the world and have long been among the leading domestic banks in regions such as the Caribbean. With the enormous potential established by the performance of the pioneering firms, many organizations are eagerly investigating global marketing. However, significant problems exist and the risks may well exceed the benefits in some cases.

Probably the biggest mistake global marketers make is a failure to recognize the diversity that exists in a target area. Some marketers, for example, envision the 320 million consumers in the European Union as a single market. They ignore the language, cultural, political, and historical differences that transcend any economic agreement. Even in a country as small as Finland, the population is a mixture of natives and immigrants from Russia, Germany, Sweden, and other Western European countries. There are two official languages and many dialects, as well as distinctive regional food preferences. These and other differences, within just one small country, suggest that global marketing faces many of the same challenges as domestic marketing.

A study of global marketing successes and failures identified five key reasons for poor performance.[22]

- Insufficient formal marketing research.
- Failure to adapt marketing to specific market differences.
- Lack of sustained marketing effort.
- Failure to decentralize decision making.
- Lack of local commitment and confidence.

Despite problems, the trend towards global marketing will accelerate. The lure of millions of consumers, combined with improved understanding of the markets and marketing practices necessary to be successful, will increase the attractiveness of such opportunities.

**Emphasizing Quality and Satisfaction** In the 1970s many businesses recognized that the quality of their products was significantly below the quality of competitors from other countries. To correct the problem, they adopted a variety of quality-instilling techniques. One of the most popular was developed by W. Edwards Deming and Joseph Juran and has been practised by the Japanese since the 1950s. It is called Total Quality Management (TQM). TQM is the application of quality principles to all endeavours of an organization, not just manufacturing. It is a business philosophy that stresses a teamwork approach that involves every employee of a company. Advocates of TQM believe that it is as important to satisfy "internal customers" as it is to satisfy final consumers. So, for example, marketing managers are viewed as customers of the marketing research staff. TQM also involves changes in the way things are done, from manufacturing processes to record keeping.[23]

The efforts that many organizations are now making to improve the quality of their output usually requires a complete change in the way in which managers see their business. It is also important to stress that an emphasis on quality is as important in organizations that deal in services as it is in companies that manufacture tangible products. This is a point that we have made in Chapter 12, but that bears reinforcing.

The emphasis on quality in products and services that is sweeping business today requires a rethinking of the role of marketing and even of what marketing means. If marketing, as we have observed very early in this book, means an emphasis on customer satisfaction, then the goals of the quality movement are not at all removed from that. In fact, there may be some justification in arguing that marketing and quality really refer to the same thing, namely efforts to produce satisfied customers. They both refer to intrinsic values in organizations that are customer-focused: an attitude, an orientation towards doing whatever is necessary to satisfy the customer. Some companies have gone so far as to dismantle their marketing departments, instead assigning responsibility for customer relationships and satisfaction to senior strategy-makers and to the plants and field staff who actually make and deliver the products and services.[24]

**Designing Environmentally Sound Strategies** Quality applies to more than making products that work better or longer. A broader issue is the general quality of everyday life and the way we treat the environment. In the past, commitments to single-issue efforts (for example, making a product biodegradable or eliminating chlorofluorocarbons) were enough to win consumer approval. However, in the future, environmental acceptance will be based on a product's entire life cycle, from design through disposal.

Firms will be forced to move away from looking for an exploitable or advertisable feature to making environmental concerns an integral part of the business system. This will require a new way of thinking about consumption. One example is to make products so that the materials, components, and packages can be used longer and reused either in part or whole, a process called **reconsumption.**[25] Forms of reconsumption include:

- **Refilling.** Rather than discarding a container when it is empty, if it is properly designed, it can be refilled. Over 30 million laser-printer cartridges are used and disposed of every year. Accutone has designed its cartridges so they can be refilled. Similarly, Xerox has introduced a copier with a recyclable printing cartridge.
- **Repairing.** With proper maintenance, products can be used longer. Thus, rather than waiting to act until after a product fails, SKF, a Swedish bearing manufacturer, has developed a series of preventive support services and diagnostic techniques that its customers can use to greatly lengthen the life of its bearings.
- **Restoring.** Some products can be returned to their original condition by replacing parts and reconditioning others. Restoration requires that parts be designed in such a way that they can be economically removed from a product, and made from materials that can be reconditioned. BMW and Mercedes are now restoring damaged auto parts that in the past were simply discarded.
- **Reusing.** Packaging material is often discarded long before it is unusable. Lego, the Danish toy manufacturer, delivers its products to retailers in large, durable boxes that are returned to Lego for reuse.

The key to making reconsumption work is developing methods of manufacturing and marketing that make it profitable. This isn't easy. McDonald's has recently invested nearly 60 percent of its R&D budget in attempting to develop a soluble plastic for packaging. It also requires new ways of thinking. For years manufacturers have focused on ways of assembling things efficiently. Now the focus must switch to developing technologies for separating materials. For example, finding a method to economically remove the ink from newspaper will be crucial to its recycling.

Marketing functions will also have to be rethought. Channels of distribution, for example, will have to flow both ways. For reconsumption, packages, products, and parts will have to be returned to the seller. Methods must be constructed to collect as well as distribute goods. To meet the needs of customers and gain their co-operation, these collection systems will have to be as easy to understand and operate as our existing one-way distribution methods.

Quality in many forms clearly is critical to customer satisfaction and therefore must have a high priority with management. The challenge for managers will be to identify or develop systems that can be successfully implemented and sustained within the existing business culture.

**Building Relationships** One of the most important aspects of the current new way of looking at marketing is the emphasis that many companies now have on the development of relationships with customers. There is a growing appreciation for the fact that it costs a company a great deal more to attract a new customer than it does to keep an existing customer happy. Therefore, we have seen a change in emphasis away from *getting* customers, towards *keeping* customers. In fact, some authors have suggested that in the future marketers must pay increasing attention to the "three R's" of marketing: relationships, retention, and recovery.[26] In this new way of thinking, marketers will stress building relationships with customers who will generate long-term profits for the company, developing strategies that will keep them satisfied so they will stay with the company, and creating strategies that will deal with recovering from problems and mistakes when they occur. As the following box reflects, there is a considerable difference between this new way of looking at marketing and what has been practised in the past.

| OLD MARKETING MODEL | NEW MARKETING MODEL |
|---|---|
| • Focus on the product. | • Focus on process for serving customers. |
| • Define the target group. | • Feed and nourish the relationship. |
| • Set brand objectives. | • Extend respect and value to customers. |
| • Opportunity comes from analysis. | • Opportunity comes from synergy. |
| • Focus on brand benefit. | • Develop and refresh relevance. |
| • Create strategic advertising. | • Open the doors for dialogue. |
| • Operate against a brand plan. | • Improvise to sustain the relationship. |
| • Driven by a marketing group. | • A pervasive inter-disciplinary attitude. |

Source: John Dalla Costa, "Towards a Model Relationship," *Marketing*, June 27, 1994, p. 12.

## MARKETING AT WORK

### FILE 24-3 IS THIS HOW TO ESTABLISH RELATIONSHIPS?

You are sitting at the keyboard of your new computer and suddenly a warning message appears on the screen advising you that the system has just crashed. But the helpful manufacturer has provided a toll-free telephone number that you can call for help in reactivating the system. You call the number and, sure enough, you find the person at the other end very knowledgeable and helpful. She asks you a few questions and then provides the information you need to get the computer up and running.

Your response? Great customer service! But what if the fault had been designed into the system by the manufacturer so that *all* computers crashed and *all* customers had to call the toll-free number to get back in operation?

This "innovation" in customer service was cited at a recent conference on "customer-centred" management as an example of an effective way to establish solid business-customer relationships. The speaker at the conference, a representative of *Fortune* magazine, refused to name the computer company and shrugged off the ethical implications of such a marketing tactic, saying that the inconvenience to the customer is worth the establishment of good communications with the manufacturer.

What do you think?

Source: Tamsen Tillson, "Customer Service with a Twist," *Globe and Mail*, June 22, 1994, p. B4.

A practice called trade loading reflects a short-term orientation in the relationship between manufacturers and intermediaries. **Trade loading**, which affects everything from cars to cigarettes, means using periodic discounts to induce wholesalers and retailers to buy more products than they can resell in a reasonable amount of time. Manufacturers use trade loading to achieve quarterly market share or profit goals. Intermediaries use it to get discounts. But the savings may be more imagined than real. Because of trade loading, the average grocery product takes much longer to travel from the factory to the retail store shelf, and the cost of maintaining this excess inventory adds millions to consumers' grocery bills. The presence of trade loading has influenced the buying behaviour of intermediaries and consumers. Wholesalers have grown to expect incentives when they buy products. Also, because some of these periodic discounts are passed along to consumers, they have become conditioned to buy products only when they are on sale.

Also pressured by the desire for short-term results, business-to-business marketers have emphasized immediate sales over the development of relationships. However, as in the examples above, the situation appears to be changing. Firms have discovered that it costs several times more to get a new customer than to retain an existing one. So in both consumer and business-to-business marketing, there has been an increased recognition of the value of relationship building and customer retention. The question is, will it spread throughout all businesses?

One final issue that should be addressed relates to the type of relationship that a company should establish with its customers. There are some who believe that having a customer's name in a data base and sending him or her regular mailings constitutes a relationship. But a genuine relationship that will last a long time requires the company to demonstrate a sincere interest in the customer and in his or her well-being — not really different from those factors that contribute to relationships between people.[27]

## SUMMARY

In addition to the financial analysis of marketing performance that was discussed in Chapter 23, a firm's marketing performance should also be appraised from a broad, societal perspective. Thus, evaluating an organization's marketing efforts must consider how well it satisfies the wants of its target customers, meets its own needs, and serves the best interests of society.

Marketing has been attacked for being exploitative, inefficient, illegal, and for stimulating unwholesome demand. There are specific allegations of wrongdoing in all four areas of the marketing mix. Many criticisms of marketing are valid. However, the offensive behaviour is confined to a small minority of all marketers, and some of the criticism is based on issues that are more complicated than they first appear.

Efforts to address marketing abuses have come from consumers, government, and business. Consumerism — protests against perceived institutional injustices and efforts to remedy them — has had a significant impact on business behaviour. Consumer responses to marketing problems have included protests, political activism, and support of special-interest groups. Conditions that provide an impetus for widespread consumerism — sensitivity to social and environmental concerns, and the willingness to become actively involved — are present today. Government at the federal, provincial, and local levels enforces consumer-protection legislation. Businesses have responded to criticism by improving communications, providing more and better information, upgrading products, and producing more sensitive advertising.

Ethical behaviour is the best remedy for the charges against marketing. Many organizations have established codes of conduct to help employees behave ethically. However, it is not possible to have a rule for every situation. Managers can use a form of cost-benefit analysis to evaluate the ethics of alternatives. Another method of judging the ethics of a particular act is to ask three questions: Would I do this to a friend? Would I be willing to have this done to me? Would I be embarrassed if this action were publicized nationally? Besides being morally correct, ethical behaviour by organizations can restore public confidence, avoid government regulation, retain the power granted by society, and protect the image of the organization.

Consumers also have a responsibility to act ethically. The volume of credit card misuse, fraud, coupon misredemption, and shoplifting suggests that a system-wide exploration of ways to reduce unethical behaviour is needed.

Prospects for the future of marketing are reflected in projected changes in consumer demographics, shifts in values, and the expansion of information. Marketers will react to these and other changes, but they will also have to make some basic strategic adjustments to compete in the twenty-first century. Among the needed adjustments are instilling a market-driven orientation, adopting a global orientation, emphasizing quality and satisfaction, and retaining customers by building relationships.

## KEY TERMS AND CONCEPTS

**Basis for evaluating performance (712)**
**Nature of marketing criticisms (712)**
**Responses to marketing issues (716)**
**Consumerism (716)**
**Ethics (720)**
**Reasons for ethical behaviour (722)**
**Social responsibility (723)**
**Green marketing (727)**
**Market fragmentation (729)**
**Niche marketing (729)**
**Reconsumption (732)**
**Trade loading (733)**

## QUESTIONS AND PROBLEMS

1. Can all the criticisms of marketing be dismissed on the basis of critics' being poorly informed or acting in their own interest?
2. Some people believe there are too many fast-food outlets in their communities. Suggest a method for reducing the number of these outlets.
3. React to the following criticisms of advertising:
   a. It costs too much.
   b. It is in bad taste.
   c. It is false and deceptive.
   d. It creates monopolies.
4. What proposals do you have for regulating advertising to reduce the occurrence of false or misleading claims?
5. What specific recommendations do you have for reducing the cost of advertising?
6. What information do you think should be included in ads for each of the following goods or services?
   a. Snack foods.
   b. Jogging shoes.
   c. Nursing homes.
   d. Credit cards.
7. What are the social and economic justifications for "paternalistic" laws such as seat-belt regulations and warnings on cigarette packages and alcoholic beverage containers?
8. How would you respond to the argument that companies can absorb the cost of coupon misredemption?
9. Describe a firm whose behaviour you feel reflects the adoption of a customer-focused strategy.
10. Within the overall college student segment, describe a smaller or fragmented market that you believe exists.
11. What does global marketing have in common with domestic marketing?
12. Describe how you interact with a business or other organization with which you feel you have a positive relationship.

## HANDS-ON MARKETING

1. Examine the following items:
   a. A snack-food package.
   b. An owner's manual for a power tool.
   c. An apartment lease.
   d. A credit card application.

   What information does each contain that would he helpful to a consumer in making a purchase decision? How clearly is the information presented? What additional information would be useful?
2. Ask the managers of three firms in the same industry:
   a. What foreseeable developments will have the greatest impact on marketing in their industry over the next five years.
   b. How they think the industry should respond to the developments.

## NOTES AND REFERENCES


1. Marina Strauss, "Brewer Goes Natural, Removes Preservatives," *Globe and Mail*, October 29, 1993, p. B4; and Terence Corcoran, "Tired of Beer Wars? Build a Bomb Shelter," *Globe and Mail*, October 29, 1993, p. B2.
2. David Chilton, "Smuggling Fuels Plain Pack Argument," *Strategy*, February 21, 1994, p. 1.
3. Wallace Immen, "Customers on Their Own as Protection Net Shrinks," *Globe and Mail*, December 13, 1993, p. A4.
4. Wallace Immen, "Consumer Watchdogs Lose Bite," *Globe and Mail*, July 12, 1993, pp. A1, A2.
5. For an interesting insight into the efforts of the Ontario Milk Marketing Board to reverse the trend in the sales of milk in Canada, see Jared Mitchell, "Moving the Moo," *Report on Business Magazine*, March 1994, pp. 65-69.
6. For an interesting discussion of the pros and cons of marketing boards, see Mary Janigan, "Why Chickens Don't Come Cheap," *Report on Business Magazine*, October 1990, pp. 87-99.
7. Mary L. Nicastro, "Infuse Business Ethics into Marketing Curriculum," *Marketing Educator*, Winter 1992, p. 1.
8. Mary Gooderham, "Nowhere to Hide in the Information Age," *Globe and Mail*, August 20, 1993, p. A4.
9. James Pollock, "New Privacy Guidelines May Save Direct Marketers from Government Legislation," *Marketing*, May 18, 1992, p. 1; and James Pollock, "Special Delivery Package," *Marketing*, June 20, 1994, p. 18.
10. Eric Swetsky, "Consumer Wins Case against Columbia House," *Direct Marketing News*, vol. 5, no. 8, May 1993, p. 11.
11. Norbert Ruebsaat and Richard Pinet, "When Advertisers Have Designs on Reality," *Globe and Mail*, May 29, 1992, p. A18; Randell Scotland, "Benetton's 'Black' Queen Sparks Ad Debate," *The Financial Post*, April 17, 1993, p. S14; and Stan Sutter, "A Controversial Ad and an Old Friend," *Marketing*, January 24, 1994, p. 8.
12. Angela Kryhul, "'Waif' Ads under Fire," *Marketing*, November 22, 1993, p. 2.
13. Laura Metcalf, "Labatt Strikes New Ice," *Marketing*, October 11, 1993, p. 2; and John Bates, "Point: Maximum Ice Undermines Responsible Use Efforts," *Marketing*, November 8, 1993, p. 8.
14. Examples are adapted from Ken Dychtwald and Greg Gable, "Portrait of a Changing Consumer," *Business Horizons*, January-February 1990, pp. 62-73.
15. For an interesting discussion of the confusion caused by the environmental debate, see Arthur Johnson, "Ecohype — Consumer Beware: 'Green' Products May Not Be What They Seem," *The Financial Post Magazine*, May 1991, pp. 17-23; and Jaclyn Fierman, "The Big Muddle in Green Marketing," *Fortune*, June 3, 1991, pp. 91-101.
16. Michael Posner, "The Death of Leisure," *Globe and Mail*, May 25, 1991, p. D1.
17. Gerald Levitch, "Mapping the Market," *Marketing*, February 7, 1994, p. 12.
18. Several of the following points are adapted from David W. Cravens, "Marketing Management's Future Challenges," *Journal of Marketing Management*, Fall 1991, pp. 1-10.
19. Geraldine E. Willigan, "High Performance Marketing: An Interview with Nike's Phil Knight," *Harvard Business Review*, July-August 1992, pp. 91-101.
20. "Stuck! How Companies Cope When They Can't Raise Prices," *Business Week*, November 15, 1993, pp. 146-155.
21. Jay Finegan, "The Rigorous Customer-Complaint Form," *Inc.*, March 1994, pp. 101-103.
22. These factors are adapted from Kamran Kashani, "Beware the Pitfalls of Global Marketing," *Harvard Business Review*, September-October 1989, pp. 91-98.
23. To learn more about the background of the quality movement, see Mary Walton, *The Deming Management Method*, Perigee Books, New York, 1986; Joseph M. Juran, ed., *Quality Control Handbook*, McGraw-Hill, New York, 1974; Philip Crosby, *Quality Is Free*, New American Library, New York, 1979; Robert Jacobson and David A. Aaker, "The Strategic Role of Product Quality," *Journal of Marketing*, October 1987, pp. 26-43.
24. John Dalla Costa, "A Commitment to Quality," *Marketing*, April 25, 1994, p. 8.
25. Sandra Vandermerwe and Michael Oliff, "Corporate Challenges for an Age of Reconsumption," *Columbia Journal of World Business*, Fall 1991, pp. 23-28.
26. Judith A. Cumby and James G. Barnes, "Strategic Investment in Service Quality: Protecting Profitable Customer Relationships," in Teresa A. Swartz, David E. Bowen, and Stephen W. Brown, eds. *Advances in Services Marketing and Management*, Volume 4, JAI Press, Inc., Greenwich, CT, 1995 (forthcoming).
27. James G. Barnes, "Close to the Customer: But Is It Really a Relationship?" *Proceedings of the 1994 Annual Conference of the Marketing Education Group*, vol. 1, University of Ulster, Coleraine, Northern Ireland, July 1994, pp. 71-80.

CASES FOR PART 7

# CASE 7–1

# W. K. BUCKLEY LIMITED (B)

It was the early summer of 1990, and a decision had to be made soon concerning the advertising approach to be used to promote Buckley's Mixture to the Canadian public during the 1990-91 "cough and cold" season. Frank Buckley and John Meehan realized that the advertising strategy adopted in 1985 had been very successful, contributing to dramatic increases in the sales of Buckley's Mixture. But the advertising that featured Frank Buckley and drew attention to the "awful" taste of the product had now been used for five seasons. While sales continued to increase, the management team at W. K. Buckley Limited wondered how much longer this advertising campaign would continue to work. Was 1990 the year when a new approach should be considered?

## BUCKLEY'S MIXTURE ADVERTISING

"It tastes awful. And it works." In 1984, Frank Buckley and his management team at W. K. Buckley Limited accepted the recommendation of its advertising agency and decided to use this simple yet honest advertising statement for their most important product, Buckley's Mixture. Since then, it has become a widely recognized and successful marketing slogan and has helped Buckley's Mixture increase its market share in the cough and cold remedy category. In the year ending February 1990, a time when the market for cold remedies had slipped by 2 percent, Buckley's Mixture had enjoyed a 16 percent increase in market share.

W. K. Buckley Limited is a privately owned Canadian company, founded in 1920 by William Buckley. The founder's son, Frank Buckley, joined the company in 1946 and is current owner and president. Primarily known for its flagship product, Buckley's Mixture, W. K. Buckley Limited also manufactures and distributes a variety of other cough and cold products, as well as a veterinary line. The Buckley product line includes Jack & Jill cough syrup, Buckley's White Rub, and Lemon Time. W. K. Buckley Limited operates in Canada, the United States, and the Caribbean and has products marketed under licensing agreements in Holland, Australia, and New Zealand.

First introduced by William Buckley from his Toronto corner drugstore in 1919, Buckley's Mixture became a household name in the 1930s and 1940s, especially in rural areas of Western Canada. Its sales were enhanced in the early years by the innovative use of advertising. Extensive promotion in the form of radio advertisements have been key to the success of Buckley's Mixture. Having realized the power of advertising in the consumer marketplace, major international pharmaceutical companies began using aggressive marketing and advertising strategies in the 1970s. This fierce competition contributed to a decline in the market share enjoyed by Buckley's flagship product.

## THE 1984-85 ADVERTISING DECISION

The peak season for the liquid cough remedy market is September to April. Before the beginning of the 1984-85 season, W. K. Buckley Limited appointed a new advertising agency, Ambrose, Carr, DeForest & Linton Limited (later to become Ambrose Carr Linton Kelly, Inc.) to co-ordinate the advertising programs for its products. Following its initial review of the W. K. Buckley account, the agency recommended marketing research to facilitate the definition of target market segments. For the 1984-85 season, on the advice of the new advertising agency, the company did not launch an advertising campaign, but undertook extensive research into the Canadian cough and cold remedy market.

From this research, five key problems became apparent. For Buckley's Mixture there was:

1. low top-of-mind awareness,
2. low rate of trial,

 The case was prepared with the co-operation and permission of W. K. Buckley Limited to illustrate the marketing initiatives of that company and not to indicate a correct or incorrect approach to the solution of marketing problems. The authors acknowledge the co-operation and support of Frank C. Buckley, President, John J. Meehan, Vice-President, and David Rieger, Manager of Sales and Marketing, of W. K. Buckley Limited, and Jackie Robertson of Ambrose Carr Linton Kelly, Inc., in the preparation of this case.

3. low awareness of its strength and effectiveness,
4. perception of it being old-fashioned,
5. negative perception of its taste, aroma, and texture.

Faced with a decreasing market share for Buckley's Mixture, the advertising agency decided that a different approach was required for the 1985-86 season. On the recommendation of Ambrose Carr, Frank Buckley took an unusual approach in promoting Buckley's Mixture. The agency recommended the use of radio and *Reader's Digest* as the chosen media for the season. The "It tastes awful. And it works" campaign actually drew attention to what some would consider a negative feature of Buckley's Mixture, its taste. The agency described this approach as an attempt to get away from the sameness of many ads that accentuate the positives and praise a product's good points. The objective was to draw attention to the advertisements and create a greater awareness of the product. Frank Buckley, the company's president, was to be featured in the advertisements to develop the concept of established effectiveness and trustworthiness. The agency proposed that Frank Buckley would represent an honest businessman who believed in his product and its attributes and was therefore willing to promote it straight, without gimmicks to hide its awful taste.

Traditionally, the market for Buckley's Mixture was in rural areas and in the lower income segment (less than $30,000 annual household income). While the maintenance and development of this current market segment was important, its definition left a large non-user market that could now be targeted. Based on market research conducted by the agency for W. K. Buckley Limited, the primary target group was redefined to be men aged 18 to 34 and, secondarily, women in the same age category, living in markets of more than 100,000 in Ontario only. The secondary target group remained adults aged 49 and older, living in markets with populations under 30,000. Although W. K. Buckley Limited was operating on a very limited advertising budget, both groups were targeted during the first year of the campaign. (See W. K. Buckley Limited [A] for a review of the 1984-85 marketing research and the recommended advertising strategy.)

## ADVERTISING CAMPAIGNS: 1985-86 TO 1989-90

For the 1985-86 advertising season, two radio commercials were produced, featuring lyrics promoting Buckley's Mixture with accompanying music and sung to the tune of a popular song. These were tested with 15 people from the target group (ages 18-34). Most liked the style of music (soft rock), found the lyrics interesting, and felt it was successful in encouraging listeners to try the product. The favourable reaction to these commercials was based on the appeal of using a song for advertising, rather than an announcer's voice. Respondents claimed that the terms "rot your socks," "strong taste," and "make you swoon" were creative in describing the taste of Buckley's Mixture and in catching the listener's attention. These commercials were subsequently launched in the Golden Horseshoe region of Toronto and southern Ontario.

Accompanying the product advertising campaign in the 1985-86 season was promotional support for new packaging for Buckley's Mixture. This represented the first package modification for the product in eight years. The new Buckley's Mixture package, although still available in 100 mL and 200 mL sizes, highlighted its sugar-free attribute. Advertisements ran in both English and French in *Reader's Digest* (see Exhibit 1).

During the 1986-87 season, transit advertisements were used extensively on a national basis. The transit campaign employed the same creative direction as the 1985-86 print campaign, with the reassurance that Buckley's Mixture is the same dependable product that Canadians had known since the 1920s. These advertisements featured Frank Buckley and used quotes such as, "I have recurring nightmares in which someone gives me a taste of my own medicine" and "I'm dedicated to ensuring that every new batch of Buckley's tastes as bad as the last" (see Exhibit 2). The main objectives for that season were to create consumer awareness of the Buckley's Mixture name, to increase awareness of the new package, and to retain trust in the brand as an effective, reliable product. National magazines *TV Guide* and *TV Hebdo* were used for the print component of the campaign (see Exhibit 3).

A television campaign was also initiated in Atlantic Canada in 1986-87, featuring a single commercial with a sea captain. It was felt that the association between the cold sea and coughs and colds would be appropriate to appeal to consumers in the Atlantic provinces.

This increased awareness also provided a foundation for the introduction of the "Buckley's DM" (Dextromethorphan) product. This addition to the Buckley's line was projected for a 1987-88 launch, but was postponed for a year because of product stability problems.

Transit advertising was continued for the 1987-88 season, as it provided good reach and high frequency with the target group and presented a strong, visual advertising message. Preparing for the upcoming announcement of the DM product, Buckley's redefined the target market to include higher income groups, as they were felt to represent the greatest sales opportunity for DM products.

**EXHIBIT 1** Buckley's Mixture Print Advertisement 1985-86

The only thing we've changed is our package, so it will be easier to spot on the shelf. And that's good. Because the sooner you spot it, the sooner you can start to get rid of that nasty cough that comes with a cold.

**EXHIBIT 3** Buckley's Mixture Print Advertisement 1986-87

"I came by my bad taste honestly. I inherited it from my father."
Fortunately, Buckley's Mixture works on coughs just the way it worked when my dad created it back in 1919.
Unfortunately, it also tastes just the way it tasted back in 1919. But dad always said, "I'll tell you two things about Buckley's. It tastes awful. And it works."
Buckley's
WE'VE HAD A FACELIFT. BUT OUR PERSONALITY IS JUST AS NASTY AS EVER.
IMPORTANT SUGAR FREE
Buckley's Mixture
coughs
colds


**EXHIBIT 2** Buckley's Mixture Transit Advertisement 1986-87

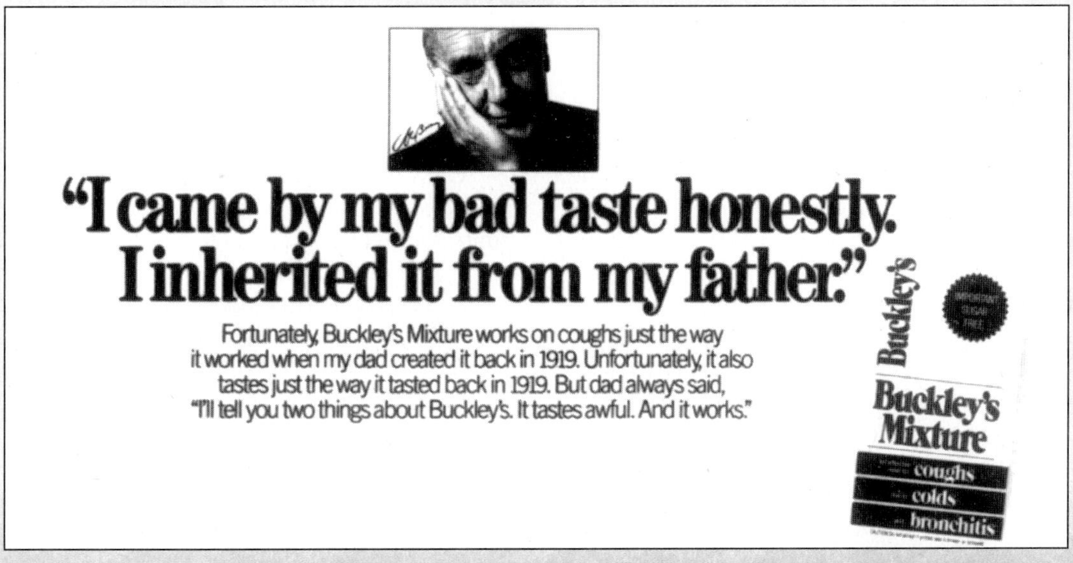

"I came by my bad taste honestly. I inherited it from my father."
Fortunately, Buckley's Mixture works on coughs just the way it worked when my dad created it back in 1919. Unfortunately, it also tastes just the way it tasted back in 1919. But dad always said, "I'll tell you two things about Buckley's. It tastes awful. And it works."
Buckley's
Buckley's Mixture
coughs
colds
bronchitis

**EXHIBIT 4 Buckley's Mixture Transit Advertisement 1987-88**

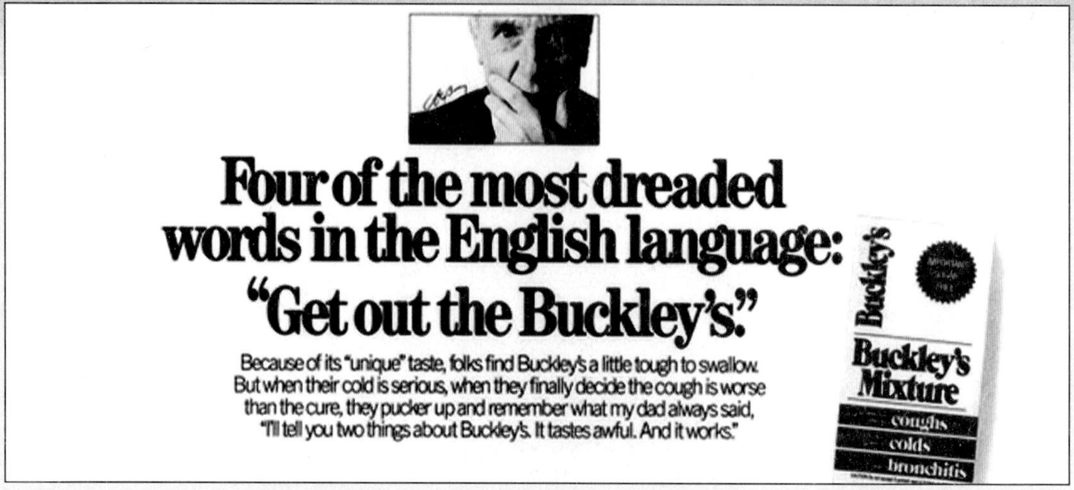


**EXHIBIT 5 Buckley's DM Mixture Transit Advertisement 1988-89**

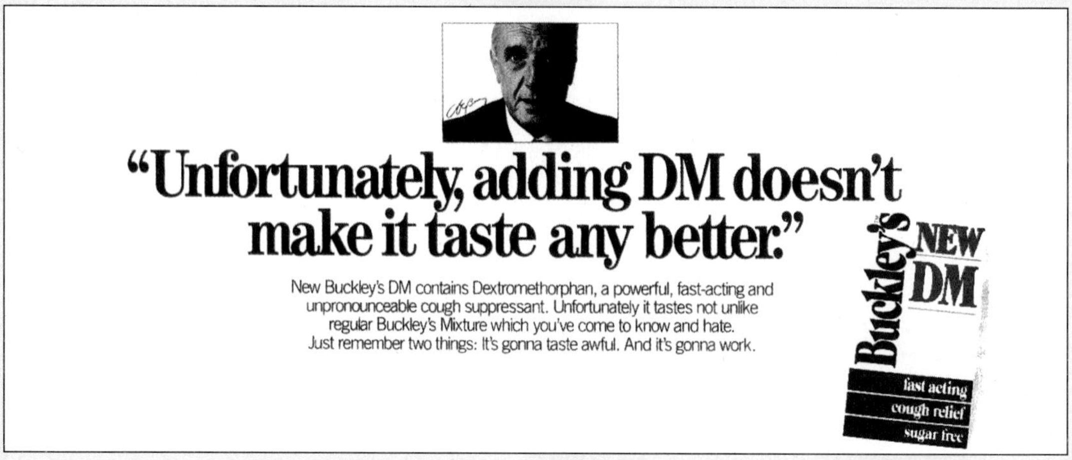

"Unfortunately, adding DM doesn't make it taste any better."
New Buckley's DM contains Dextromethorphan, a powerful, fast-acting and unpronounceable cough suppressant. Unfortunately it tastes not unlike regular Buckley's Mixture which you've come to know and hate. Just remember two things: It's gonna taste awful. And it's gonna work.
Buckley's NEW DM
fast acting
cough relief
sugar free


The 1987-88 transit ads were similar to those used during the previous year, with a picture of Frank Buckley and quotes such as "Four of the most dreaded words in the English language: Get out the Buckley's" and "Since 1919 we've been leaving Canadians with a bad taste in their mouths" (see Exhibit 4). The print advertising was continued in *TV Guide* and *TV Hebdo*, and the television campaign was used again in the Atlantic provinces.

In the 1988-89 season, Buckley's DM was introduced. This product was identical to the original Buckley's Mixture except it had added Dextromethorphan Hydrobromide (DM), an antitussive used for fast-acting suppression of a non-productive cough. DM products, although new to the Buckley product line, had been on the market for several years and were well known to consumers. Transit ads were used, which now promoted the DM product (see Exhibit 5).

W. K. Buckley's advertising agency, Ambrose Carr Linton Kelly, believed that interior transit was an efficient, strategically correct medium for reaching the target group. During this season, radio was used for the first time in three years and television was introduced as a new medium for Buckley's advertising. Commercials on radio featured Frank Buckley describing the taste of Buckley's Mixture and referring to its effectiveness (see Exhibit 6). These were run in major urban markets across the country. The campaign also involved regional efforts that were customized for regional market segments. For example, the television campaign in Atlantic Canada was continued in 1988-89.

**EXHIBIT 6 Buckley's Mixture Radio Commercial Scripts 1988-89 and 1989-90**

**DEDICATED**

Hi, I'm Frank Buckley, and I'm dedicated to ensuring that every batch of Buckley's Mixture tastes as bad as the last. You see, back in 1919 when my dad developed Buckley's Mixture, he used only ingredients that would make Buckley's Mixture provide fast, effective relief from coughs due to colds. He didn't particularly care how the stuff tasted. So just remember two things about Buckley's Mixture. It's going to taste awful and it's going to work.

**NIGHTMARES**

Hi, I'm Frank Buckley, and I have recurring nightmares in which someone gives me a taste of my own medicine. That medicine is Buckley's Mixture. Now, I'd be the first one to admit Buckley's Mixture has a taste that will rot your socks. But when you've got a nasty cough due to a cold, close your eyes, brace yourself, and remember just two things. It's going to taste awful and it's going to work.

**HONESTLY**

My name is Frank Buckley and I came by my bad taste honestly. I inherited it from my father. Back in 1919 he developed Buckley's Mixture. Buckley's Mixture became known for two things, how well it worked and how badly it tasted. But 69 years later, when folks have a cough due to a cold or bronchitis, they pucker up and remember what Dad always said about Buckley's Mixture. It's going to taste awful and it's going to work.

**1919**

Hi, I'm Frank Buckley for Buckley's Mixture. My father came up with Buckley's Mixture back in 1919. About the same time my folks came up with me. Back then, people expected medicine to taste like . . . well, medicine. So, to be real honest, it tastes real bad. But if you do have a nasty hacking cough, but don't have time to pamper it, try Buckley's Mixture. Just remember two things. It tastes awful and it works.

**SURPRISE**

Hi, I'm Frank Buckley for Buckley's Mixture. If you've never tried Buckley's Mixture before, you're going to be very surprised, twice. You'll be surprised at how quickly and effectively Buckley's relieves the nastiest coughs due to colds, bronchitis, and even smoker's cough. But, just before you're surprised by how effective Buckley's Mixture is, you'll be very surprised by how it tastes. Buckley's Mixture, it tastes awful and it works.

For the 1989-90 season, W. K. Buckley Limited expanded the advertising campaign by using television in the Toronto region for the first time. Commercials were aired nine times a week for four weeks on a Buffalo, N.Y., station that beamed its signal into the Toronto area. These commercials featured Frank Buckley, seated in a chair, holding a package of Buckley's Mixture. He explained in a lighthearted way how awful Buckley's tastes but how effectively it works. These TV commercials were also aired in the Atlantic provinces and featured a similar dialogue to the radio commercials, which were run in major markets across the country. The budget allocated to transit advertising was increased and aimed at a better-educated group. "It contains oil of pine needles. What did you expect it to taste like?" was one of the advertising slogans created for the campaign that demonstrates the continued focus on the actual attributes of Buckley's Mixture (see Exhibit 7).

Exhibit 8 contains a detailed overview of the advertising budget allocations at W. K. Buckley Limited for the years from 1983 to 1990. The chart details the season, media used, market and target group, and the allocated budget.

## MARKETING RESEARCH

Marketing research remained an essential component of the marketing program at W. K. Buckley Limited. In 1988, with the objective of acquiring further information about the consumer of Buckley's Mixture, the company distributed 10,680 survey cards to purchasers in packages of Buckley's Mixture. Although the cards were distributed only in Ontario, among the 357 replies were some cards returned by purchasers from other provinces and two from the United States.

Some of the more significant information from this research came in the form of demographics. Fifty-five percent of purchasers who returned survey cards were aged over 40 and 30 percent were over 60. In addition, 26 percent were retired and 19 percent were homemakers, with only 8 percent at the white-collar or executive level. The most common annual household income mentioned by those who returned cards was $20,000 or less (36 percent), while 53 percent made less than $30,000.

Nearly half the respondents had been using Buckley's Mixture for more than 10 years (49 percent) and only 22 percent had used it for two years or less. The "sugar-free" factor was important to 69 percent, while 14 percent were not aware of it. In addition, only 7 percent first became aware of Buckley's Mixture through advertisements (either bus, subway, or radio), while 61 percent learned of the product through friends or family. Ninety percent liked it most because of its effectiveness, 39 percent for its strength, and 7 percent actually liked the taste.

**EXHIBIT 7 Buckley's Mixture Transit Advertisement 1989-90**

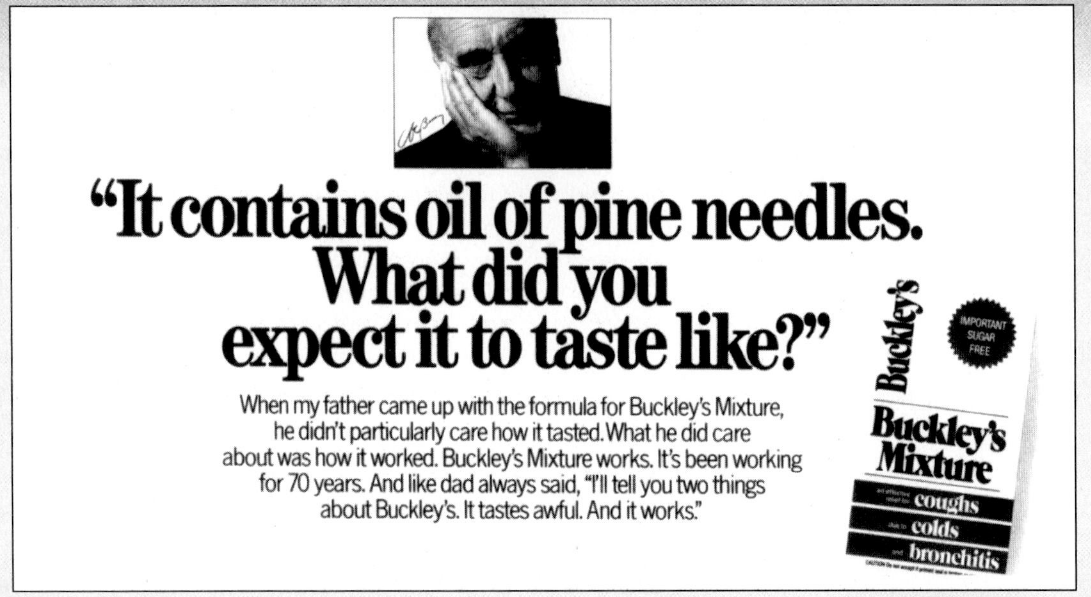

"It contains oil of pine needles. What did you expect it to taste like?"
When my father came up with the formula for Buckley's Mixture, he didn't particularly care how it tasted. What he did care about was how it worked. Buckley's Mixture works. It's been working for 70 years. And like dad always said, "I'll tell you two things about Buckley's. It tastes awful. And it works."
Buckley's
IMPORTANT SUGAR FREE
Buckley's Mixture
coughs
colds
bronchitis


A qualitative study was conducted in 1989 to determine the public's attitudes towards Buckley's Mixture and the advertising approach for the brand. Three focus group interviews were conducted by Ambrose Carr Linton Kelly. Two extended groups were conducted lasting two and one half hours. One of these groups contained current Buckley's users, the other non-triers of the brand. The third focus group consisted of one half triers and one half non-tries. This group discussion lasted three and one half hours.

Each group discussed exposure to other Buckley's products, the DM mixture, and price sensitivity in the market. The research concluded that a strong advertising foundation was being built on the message of honesty and efficacy, which is delivered in a humorous approach by Frank Buckley. In addition, it was found that Mr. Buckley successfully projects the strength of traditional values (honesty and sincerity) and also appears a contemporary businessman who understands today's needs. Participants concluded that, as a brand spokesperson, he is an honest champion of a product he believes in. The discussions concluded that the message was delivered most strongly in the transit medium, as the consumer could visually fit Frank Buckley's style to their expectations. Participants felt that the image tended to lose a little of its impact on radio, as the advertisement moves faster and is filled with more detail than most feel was necessary. However, participants did believe that radio was a "logical" extension to the transit ads and the message was clearly understood by listeners.

Research participants were open to the idea of advertising for Buckley's Mixture on television and radio, expecting the same relaxed but confident presentation. They felt that future advertising, particularly on radio, should portray a softer-spoken, slower-paced, less professional voice. The message communicated should concentrate on heightened efficacy (i.e., bronchitis, serious coughs) and reference to the taste should be softened somewhat. The study revealed that the participants were also receptive to the use of other settings and new generations of the Buckley family.

When questioned about Buckley's DM, few participants in the group interviews were aware of it. Many did not understand the difference between the original Buckley's Mixture and the DM product. Others were concerned that an addition of another ingredient would take away Buckley's "natural" image and would contradict some of the advertising. However, some felt it showed that W. K. Buckley Limited was "keeping up with the times."

The sales of Buckley's Mixture have improved markedly since the launch of the "Tastes Awful" advertising campaign. Some areas of the country are more responsible for the sales increase than are others. Ontario, Alberta, and the Atlantic provinces account for almost 70 percent of the sales of Buckley's Mixture. Alberta and the Atlantic provinces have accounted for the largest sales increases in recent years. Consistent with historic results, Quebec has had very low sales compared to the size of its market.

**EXHIBIT 8 Advertising Overview — Buckley's Mixture**

| Year | Media | Market | Target Group | Execution | Budget |
|---|---|---|---|---|---|
| 1983/84 | Radio | National excluding Atlantic | Adult 39+, Rural | N/A | $228,000 |
| | Television | Atlantic Canada | Adults 18-44 | N/A | $22,000 |
| 1984/85 | 1 Year Advertising Hiatus for Market Research | | | | |
| 1985/86 | Radio | Southern Ontario | Men 18-34 (Vicks users) (secondary: women 18-34) | All I Want [:60] | $172,000 |
| | | Ontario | Urban 100M+ population<br>Household income <$30M<br>Education: high school or less | Feelin' Low [:60] | |
| | Magazine *Reader's Digest* | National Markets | Adults 49+ (Buckley's users)<br>Under 30M population<br>Household income <$30M<br>High school and less | We've Had a Facelift (E&F) | $74,000 |
| | Trade Brochure Developed for sales force and Shelf Talker | | | | |
| 1986/87 | Interior Transit | National English only | Adults, 18-44 (Triaminic DM users)<br>Married, no children<br>Urban 100M+ population<br>Clerical or labourer | I have recurring nightmares. . .<br>I'm dedicated to ensuring. . .<br>I came by my bad taste. . . | $151,000 |
| | Magazine *TV Guide/ TV Hebdo* | National English/French | | We've Had a Facelift<br>I came by my bad taste. . . | $85,000 |
| | Television | Atlantic Canada | Adults, 18-44 | Sea Captain | $19,000 |
| 1987/88* | Interior Transit | National English/French | Adults, 18-44<br>Married, with/without children<br>Urban 100M+ population<br>Household income $30M+ | Since 1919. . .<br>Four of the Most. . . | $134,000 |
| | Magazine | National | | I came by my bad taste. . . | $77,000 |
| | Trade Magazine | National — English | Pharmacists/Drugstore owners | Here's Your Chance. . . | $10,000 |
| | Television | Atlantic Canada | | Sea Captain | $24,000 |
| 1988/89 | Transit | National English/French | Adults, 18-49<br>Household income $25M+<br>Average education<br>Urban 100M+ population | Sometimes Just the Right. . .<br>Unfortunately, adding DM. . . | $171,000 |
| | Radio | Major Markets | | Dedicated [:30]<br>Nightmares [:30]<br>Honesty [:30] | $186,000 |
| | Television | Atlantic Canada | | Sea Captain | $30,000 |
| 1989/90 | Transit | National English/French | Adults, 18+<br>Household income $25M+<br>High school education+<br>Professional | It contains oil of pine. . .<br>How bad does it taste. . . | $193,000 |
| | Radio | Major Markets | | 1919 [:30]<br>Surprise [:30] | $223,000 |
| | Television | Atlantic Canada<br>Toronto spill (WUTV Buffalo) | | 1919 [:30]<br>Surprise [:30] | $40,000<br>$5,000 |

*Buckley's Mint Flavour DM was scheduled for market introduction in 1987, but a decision was made not to launch because of problems with product instability.

**Percentage of Total Sales of Buckley's Mixture**

| | Year to date January 1989 | Year to date January 1988 | Regional Change |
|---|---|---|---|
| Atlantic | 14.3% | 13.7% | +22.6% |
| Quebec | 8.8 | 9.3 | +13.0 |
| Ontario | 36.6 | 38.4 | +13.0 |
| Man./Sask. | 11.9 | 12.5 | +13.1 |
| Alberta | 17.8 | 13.9 | +52.1 |
| British Columbia | 10.5 | 12.1 | + 2.8 |
| Total | 100 | 100 | +18.5 |

Qualitative research conducted for Ambrose Carr by CRT Information Services involved creative testing of Buckley's Mixture transit advertisements. The research involved personal, in-depth interviews with 13 English-speaking and 13 French-speaking respondents. Among the French-speaking respondents, the "bad taste" emphasis and its communication were not perceived to be particularly humorous and had a negative effect on the desire to purchase. This response interfered with the perception of Buckley's Mixture as an efficient product. Also the word "mixture" in French does not properly communicate the fact that the product is a cough syrup. These factors, as well as difficulty encountered in the consumers' ability to remember the name Buckley's, created very low stimulation to purchase in the Quebec market.

## THE 1990-91 CAMPAIGN

The time had come to decide on the advertising campaign for Buckley's Mixture for the 1990-91 season. Frank Buckley and vice-president John Meehan felt the company should give considerable thought to its future advertising efforts. The "Tastes Awful" campaign had been a great success, contributing to increased awareness of Buckley's Mixture and large increases in market share. Both Mr. Buckley and Mr. Meehan agreed that some of the key points that must be conveyed in advertising include:

- Buckley's Mixture is a natural product with no artificial flavours or sugar, and
- the product has enjoyed a good established name since 1919.

In addition to the development of an advertising campaign for the upcoming season, the Buckley's management team had established several business objectives for the coming year. The company is aiming to build awareness and interest in Buckley's Mixture, to increase the trial of their products, while increasing sales by 5 percent real growth during the year and market share by 10 percent by 1991-92. The achievement of these marketing goals would occur while maintaining profitability at current levels.

Since Buckley's Mixture is W. K. Buckley's best-known product, it is expected to lead the way in meeting these objectives. Recognizing that users of Buckley's Mixture are very brand loyal, Frank Buckley and John Meehan agreed that the best way to increase sales would be to attract new users.

## QUESTIONS

1. Evaluate the advertising strategy, use of budget, and media allocation used to promote Buckley's Mixture during the period from 1983 to 1990.
2. Recognizing the history of the Buckley's product line and the corporate goals established by W. K. Buckley Limited, what approach should be taken for promoting Buckley's Mixture in 1990-91?
3. Should Mr. Buckley and Mr. Meehan consider making a major change in the advertising strategy? Why?
4. What approach can W. K. Buckley Limited take to gain increased market share in Quebec?

# CASE 7-2

# THE TEA COUNCIL OF CANADA (B)

Canada is one of the world's leading tea-consuming countries. However, recent research on consumption habits indicates that, while tea is still a very popular drink in Canada, the historical "hard-core" tea drinkers are moving away from the beverage. Demographic changes in the Canadian market, complemented by trends towards cold, light unsweetened beverages and drinks, demonstrate that competition in the beverage industry is likely to intensify.

In the early 1980s, the Tea Council of Canada, a not-for-profit generic promotion organization, commenced a promotional program to improve awareness of tea and to facilitate an increase in the consumption of tea, to improve attitudes towards tea and the image of the product, and to contribute to increases in the quality of tea and in how it is served in the out-of-home market. In 1989, the marketing committee of the Tea Council of Canada established its objectives for testing the effectiveness of a strategically defined, generic advertising campaign. The committee proceeded to undertake a detailed usage and attitude study of the Canadian tea market. This research, conducted by ISL — International Surveys Limited, was designed to ascertain the images and attitudes held by the Canadian population towards tea and tea drinking. It was also intended to accumulate information that would provide direction to the advertising and communications approach for promoting regular black tea in the near future. The Tea Council's marketing committee received the results of the ISL usage and attitude study in October 1989. The findings, supplemented with other life-style research, reaffirmed some known facts about the market and provided key directional information for the council's marketing committee.

## DEVELOPING THE STRATEGY

After reviewing the conclusions reached through the usage and attitude study, the marketing committee's next step was to identify clearly the marketing and consumer communications strategies for the future campaign. The marketing strategy consisted of a clear definition of tea's current position in the beverage market. Hot tea would be positioned to tea drinkers as the only beverage that offers a calming, soothing respite from the rigours and routines of contemporary daily life. The marketing strategy would also incorporate the focus of the overall campaign to build awareness of hot tea in a contemporary manner. The communications strategy developed by Anderson Advertising of Toronto for the Tea Council of Canada consisted of three key factors: (1) communications focus; (2) target consumers; (3) basic consumer benefit. The council's marketing effort was targeted at adult consumers, aged 25 to 49, primarily female, in middle-income households whose life-styles have become considerably more demanding and compromising. Communication efforts were intended to persuade these consumers to reconsider tea over other beverages. Upon clarification of these points, the committee presented a second proposal to the board of directors of the Tea Council, outlining the potential opportunities for the promotional campaign. This proposal was accepted by the council and the committee was given permission to continue with the implementation process.

To launch the project, the council invited a number of advertising agencies to submit an integrated marketing communications plan with principal emphasis to be centred on an appropriate theme line or slogan to support the advertising position. Five agencies presented their positioning approach to the marketing committee and two were subsequently selected. The Tea Council decided to research these two approaches to determine the level of consumer understanding and acceptability. The two most appropriate theme lines chosen were:

"Tea. It also refreshes the mind."

"Tea. The break you savour."

Elliott Research Corporation was contacted to prepare a research proposal for a survey designed to investigate consumers' interpretations of the theme lines, their reactions towards them, and the images of tea conveyed through

Copyright © 1991. This case was written by Robert Power and Leanne O'Leary of Memorial University of Newfoundland, under the direction of Dr. James G. Barnes. The case was prepared with the co-operation and permission of the Tea Council of Canada to illustrate the marketing initiatives of that organization and not to indicate a correct or incorrect approach to the solution of marketing problems. The authors acknowledge the co-operation and support of Gordon F. Reynolds, Executive Director of the Tea Council of Canada, in the preparation of this case.

these advertising slogans. The results obtained through this consumer study would be used to decide the most effective theme line for promoting the desired black tea image.

## METHODOLOGY

The research study was completed by means of personal interviews with 100 adult females, 25 to 49 years of age, who drink tea at least once a month. Individual respondents were recruited among shoppers in the enclosed malls of shopping centres in Toronto and London, Ontario. Qualified respondents were interviewed at Elliott Research Corporation's permanent research facilities in those shopping centres.

Two versions of the questionnaire were prepared so that each of the theme lines to be tested was shown first to one-half of the respondents. Each of the theme lines was exposed at first with just the line, but later with appropriate additional copy related to the line. As each theme line was exposed, the respondent was asked to express in her own words the messages that she believed the advertiser is attempting to communicate. Additional questions were asked to investigate the suitability of the advertisement's body copy (text) with the theme line and the reasons for the participants' responses.

After each of the theme lines was evaluated, both with and without supporting copy, the respondent was asked to choose the theme line that she believed most effectively described her image of and attitude towards tea. The respondent was then asked to detail, using a list of selected attributes, her impressions of the beverage that would be promoted by that specific theme line.

## RESEARCH CONCLUSIONS

The study demonstrated that both of the proposed theme lines successfully conveyed the ideas expressed in the marketing strategy of the Tea Council of Canada: "Tea is the beverage which offers a calming, soothing respite from the rigours and routine of contemporary daily life."

Both of the advertising slogans conveyed a variety of relevant sales messages to the tea drinkers as they read them. While either theme line could be used, the research study showed the line, "Tea. The break you savour" to be superior in communicating a broader range of product attributes or consumer benefits, without eliciting a significant level of negative thoughts or ideas about the marketing messages. To a majority of respondents, this headline conveyed the desired idea that tea is refreshing. The theme line was also considered to be superior in the degree to which the words used were suited to the remainder of the advertisement, including the body copy. The message conveyed by the slogan and the additional body copy was related mainly to relaxation, enjoying a break, or a pleasurable moment.

As a result, the new theme line for the test advertising campaign and ultimately all other Council promotional activities became:

Tea — The Break You Savour

A break is a brief moment of the day set aside to relax — and that moment can be enhanced by the soothing, natural refreshment of tea.

And, unlike any other break, the time for tea is a simple, yet special, pleasure that is not just enjoyed but savoured.

Anderson Advertising of Toronto was also selected by the Tea Council of Canada to develop the promotional campaign.

## TEST ADVERTISING

Based on the conclusions of the Elliott research, the Anderson team developed an advertising campaign that was scheduled to undergo a market test from September 1990 through May 1991. A test period was required to measure the effectiveness of a carefully planned, strategically defined generic advertising campaign. The results of this test would assist in evaluating the viability of this campaign for use on a national level. Ontario was selected as the most suitable test market because of its importance to total hot tea consumption in Canada and because the region is representative of national tea drinking habits.

Considering the restricted budgets of the Tea Council for this program, television, radio, and newspapers were considered inappropriate and unaffordable vehicles to implement the plan. Other media that took into account vital, creative requirements were selected. Consumer magazines were recommended as the primary medium for the Tea Council's advertising campaign, with transit shelters, mall posters, and direct marketing as the support media. Consumer magazines would provide a cost-efficient means to establish a high level of frequency. Within Ontario, Toronto offered the means to duplicate most closely the national campaign since it offered both transit shelters and mall poster space and quality market-specific publications, such as *Toronto Magazine*, *Toronto Life*, and the Toronto edition of *Maclean's*. Exhibit 1 shows advertisements developed for the Tea Council's test campaign.

The test, supplemented by a comprehensive public relations campaign, as well as opportunistic marketing activities by the council's corporate members, is tremendously important to the future viability of the campaign at a national level. Pre- and post-campaign research will ultimately help determine the extent to which the new campaign affects the

**EXHIBIT 1**

opinions and attitudes of target segments, and more importantly, the consumption of "quality" black tea.

## QUESTIONS

1. Evaluate the process, as demonstrated in this case, for translating the objective into the advertising materials or campaigns.
2. Recognizing the research results and recommendations presented to the Tea Council of Canada, comment on the appropriateness of the advertising campaign with respect to target segment, slogan, and medium used.
3. What research would you advise the Tea Council of Canada to carry out before and after the test advertising campaign, so that they might be able to evaluate its success?

# CASE 7-3

# ETHICAL DILEMMAS IN BUSINESS-TO-BUSINESS SALES

The following were actual situations experienced by the case writer during more than 15 years in business-to-business sales and sales management. The names of firms and individuals have been disguised due to the nature of the material in this case.

## HALCO MANUFACTURING

Dave MacDonald was excited when he got the unexpected phone call from Nicki Steele, a senior buyer from Halco Manufacturing.

"I know it's a year since we bought that prototype reel from you, but we just got a contract from the government to build 10 more bear traps and we desperately need to hold our price on these units. Could you possibly sell us 10 new reels at the same price you charged last year?" Nicki inquired.

"I'll see what I can do and call you back today," Dave replied.

Dave immediately retrieved the file from the previous year and saw that they had supplied the reel for $6,990 f.o.b. the customer's warehouse. There was a breakdown of the pricing on the file:

| | |
|---|---|
| Manufacturer's list price | $4,000.00 |
| Special engineering charge (25%) | 1,000.00 |
| Total list price | 5,000.00 |
| Distributor discount (20%) | 1,000.00 |
| Distributor net cost | 4,000.00 |
| Estimated Currency Exchange (8%) | 320.00 |
| Estimated Duty (22-1/2%) | 972.00 |
| Estimated Freight | 245.00 |
| Estimated Brokerage | 55.00 |
| Estimated distributor cost, f.o.b. destination | 5,592.00 |
| Mark-up (25%) | 1,398.00 |
| Selling Price, f.o.b. destination | $6,990.00 |

There were some notes on the file that Dave reviewed. The reel was designed as part of a "bear trap" on Canadian navy ships. These bear traps would hook onto helicopters in rough weather and haul them safely onto landing pads on the ship decks. The reel was really a model SM heavy duty steel mill reel, except some of the exposed parts were to be made of stainless steel to provide longer life in the salt water atmosphere. There was a special engineering charge on the reel as it was a nonstandard item that had to be specially engineered. The manufacturer had suggested at the time they quoted that Dave could keep the full 20 percent discount as they thought there was only one other manufacturer capable of building this unit, and their price would likely be much higher.

When Dave got a price from the manufacturer on the 10 new units, he was surprised they quoted a price of only $3,200 each, less 40/10 percent instead of the 20 percent that was given on the original reel.

As Dave estimated his cost, things got better. The original reel was imported from the United States at 22-1/2 percent duty as "not otherwise provided for manufacturers of iron or steel, tariff item 44603-1." In the interim, the company Dave worked for got a duty remission on series SM steel mill reels as "machinery of a class or kind not manufactured in Canada, tariff item 42700-1" and the duty was remitted (and the savings supposedly passed on to the end customer). The currency exchange rate also improved in Dave's favour, and the estimated freight and brokerage charges per unit dropped considerably because of the increased shipment size. Dave estimated his new cost as follows:

| | |
|---|---|
| Manufacturer's list price | $3,200.00 |
| Distributor discount (40/10%) | 1,472.00 |
| Distributor net cost | 1,728.00 |
| Estimated Currency Exchange (2%) | 35.00 |
| Estimated Duty (remitted) | 0.00 |
| Estimated Freight | 85.00 |
| Estimated Brokerage | 14.50 |
| Estimated distributor cost, f.o.b. destination | $1,862.50 |

Now that he had all the figures, Dave had to decide what the selling price should be to his customer.

## CROWN PULP AND PAPER LTD.

Bill Siddall had been promoted to the position of salesperson, and he was pleased when he received an order for nearly $10,000 for stainless steel fittings from the new pulp mill being built in his territory. Unfortunately, he quoted a price that was 40 percent below his cost.

"We have to honour the price quoted," Bill insisted.

"I know if you let me talk to Rory, he'll let us raise the price," replied Dave MacDonald, the sales manager. "Rory used to be the purchasing agent at one of my best accounts before he came to the mill."

"No. You gave me responsibility for this account, and I want to build a good relationship with Rory myself. He gave us the order over two weeks ago. He can't change suppliers now because it would be unfair. Since this is our first order, I would like to supply it without any problems. We'll get back the money we lost on this order many times if we can get their future business. This material is needed for a small construction job, and they haven't even started to consider their stores inventory yet."

After much discussion, it was agreed that the order would stand, but Dave would call the fitting manufacturer's sales manager, Chuck Knowles, as the two men were good friends.

"We need some help on that last order we placed with you. Bill sold it at 40 percent below our cost," said Dave.

"How could that happen?" Chuck seemed amazed.

"Well," replied Dave, "you give us a 25 percent distributor discount and we gave 10 percent to the customer due to the size of the order. What we forgot was to double the list price because the customer wanted schedule 80 wall thickness on the fittings instead of standard schedule 40. This was Bill's first large inquiry and he made an honest mistake. He doesn't want me to get involved with the customer, and I don't want to force the issue with him, so I'm hoping you can help us on this one order. We expect to get a lot of business from this account over the next few years."

"I'll split the difference with you. What you're selling now for $0.90, you're paying $1.50 for, and if I give you an additional 20 percent discount, your cost will come down to $1.20. Can you live with that?" Chuck asked.

"It's a help. We appreciate it. We'll see you on your next trip to our territory, and I'll buy lunch."

"A deal. See you next month." The conversation ended.

When it was over, Dave went to the Brae Shore Golf Club. He was confident Rory would be there. Sure enough, at 8:00 A.M., Rory was scheduled to tee off. Dave sat on the bench at the first tee and waited for Rory to appear. Promptly, Rory arrived with Bob Arnold, one of his senior buyers. The three men greeted each other pleasantly and Rory asked who Dave was waiting for.

"Just one of my neighbours. He was supposed to be here an hour ago but I guess he won't show."

"Join us. We don't mind. Besides we might need a donation this fall when we have our company golf tournament. We'll invite you, of course, and we'll invite Bill if he plays golf."

"He doesn't play often, but he's pretty good. Beat me the last time we played. How is he doing at your mill? Is everything okay?" Dave asked.

"Checking up on him? Sure. He's fine. He made a mistake the other day when he went to see our millwright foreman without clearing it through my office first, but he'll learn. He'll do a lot of business with us because we want to buy locally where possible, and you have a lot of good product lines. I think he'll get along well with all of us as well. He seems a bit serious, but we'll break him in before long. We just gave him a big order for stainless fittings a few weeks ago, but we told him to visit at 10 o'clock next time and to bring the doughnuts."

"I know," replied Dave. "Unfortunately, we lost a lot of money on that order."

"Your price was very low. I couldn't understand it because I knew your material wasn't manufactured offshore. Did you quote the cheaper T304 grade of stainless instead of the T316 we use?"

"No. We quoted schedule 40 prices instead of schedule 80. The wall thickness for schedule 80 is twice as thick, and the price should have been double as well."

"Heck. Double the price. We'll pay it. I'll make a note on the file Monday. I know you're not trying to take us and I can appreciate an honest mistake. At double the price, you might be a bit high, but you know we want to place the order with you anyway because you're local. Eventually we'll want you to carry some inventory for us, so we might just as well make sure we're both happy with this business."

## STRAIT STRUCTURAL STEEL LTD.

Dave MacDonald was sitting in the outer office waiting to see Stan Hope, the purchasing agent for Strait Structural Steel, a new account that had just begun operations in a remote, coastal location about 65 km from the nearest city. Stan had telephoned Dave the previous week and had an urgent request for four large exhaust fans that were required to exhaust welding fumes from enclosed spaces where welders were at work. The union had threatened to stop the project unless working conditions were improved quickly, and although Dave didn't sell fans at the time, he found a line of fans and negotiated a discount from the manufacturer, along with an agreement to discuss the further possibility of representing the fan manufacturer on a national basis.

When Stan gave the order to Dave for the fans, the two men discussed other products that Dave sold. Dave sold products for a company that was both a general-line and specialty-line industrial distributor. Included in the general-line products were such items as hand and power tools, cutting tools (drills, taps, dies), safety equipment, wire rope and slings, fasteners (nuts, bolts), and fittings (stainless steel, bronze, and carbon steel flanges, elbows, tees). Included in the specialty-line products were such items as electric motors and generators, motor controls, hydraulic and pneumatic valves and cylinders, rubber dock fenders, and overhead cranes. When the men finally met, they were almost instantly friends, and it was obvious that the opportunities for them to do further business were great. "One item that really interests me," said Stan, "is PTFE tape. We need some and we will be using a lot of it."

"We have the largest stock of PTFE tape in the country," replied Dave. "We import it directly from Italy, but it's high quality and is the same standard size as all others on the market — 1/2 0wide, .003 0thick, and 4800long. How much are you interested in?"

"Let's start with 400 rolls," Stan suggested.

PTFE tape was a white, non-adhesive tape that was used as a pipe thread sealant. It was wrapped around the threads of pipe or fittings before they were screwed together to make a leak-proof seal. The tape first came on the market in the late 1960s at prices as high as $3.60 per roll, but since then prices had dropped considerably. North American manufacturers were still selling the tape for list prices near $1.80 and were offering dealer discounts between 25 and 50 percent depending on the quantities that dealers bought. Dave was importing the tape from Italy at a landed cost of $0.17 per roll.

"We have a standard price of $1 per roll as long as you buy 200 rolls," Dave offered.

"No question. You have an excellent price. How much would you charge M H Sales?"

"I don't know. Who is M H Sales?" asked Dave.

"A small industrial supply company located in my basement. The 'H' is for Hope. I share the company with Bruce Malcolm, the 'M,' and he's in purchasing at Central Power Corporation. M H Sales is a small company and we are looking for additional products to sell. Between Strait Structural and Central Power, we could sell several thousand rolls of PTFE tape each year."

## McCORMICK GLEASON LIMITED

Dave MacDonald telephoned Clarey Stanley, a senior buyer at McCormick Gleason Limited. "Clarey, I'm calling about that quote we made on Lufkin tapes. Can we have your order?"

"Sorry. Your price was high. I gave the order to Ken Stafford. You need a sharper pencil."

"How much sharper?" Dave asked.

"I can't tell you that. But you were close," Clarey replied. "By the way, Kenny called me from the stores department this morning and he has a large shipment of electric relays that was delivered yesterday. They weren't properly marked and he can't identify the ones with normally open contacts from the ones with normally closed contacts. Do you want them returned, or can someone see him and straighten it out here?"

"Tell him I'll see him immediately after lunch. I can tell them apart and I'll see they get properly identified."

When the conversation ended, Dave made a note to see Clarey about the tapes. There was a problem somewhere. Dave knew his cost on Lufkin tapes was the lowest available, and he quoted 12 percent on cost because he really wanted the order. The order was less than $1,500, but it meant that Dave could place a multiple-case order on the manufacturer and get the lowest possible cost for all replacement inventory. That would increase the margin on sales to other customers who bought smaller quantities. There was no possibility that Stafford Industrial, a local, one-person, "out-of-the-basement" operation that bought Lufkin tapes as a jobber, not as a distributor, could match his price.

That afternoon, while waiting to see Ken MacKay, the stores manager, Dave noticed a carton from Stafford Industrial Sales being unloaded from a local delivery van. Although he knew that Stafford supplied quite a few maintenance, repair and operating (MRO) supplies to this customer, Dave decided to play ignorant.

"What do you buy from Stafford Industrial?" he asked the young stores clerk who was handling the package.

Opening the carton, the clerk read the packing slip. "It says here we ordered 144 measuring tapes, 3/4 0wide by 25 feet long."

"Are those things expensive?" Dave asked.

"Don't know. There's no price on the packing slip. Clarey Stanley in purchasing ordered them. You could talk to him." The clerk continued to unpack the shipment. As he did, Dave noticed the tapes were manufactured offshore and were poor quality compared to the Lufkin tapes that he sold, and that he had quoted to Clarey Stanley the previous day.

"Aren't those supposed to be Lufkin tapes?" Dave asked.

"Not that I know. The packing slip just says tapes. Wait and I'll haul our copy of the purchase order." The clerk went to a filing cabinet next to his desk and returned with a carbon copy of the purchase order. "No, it just says tapes. It doesn't specify any brand."

There was something wrong, and Dave was determined to get an answer.

# CASE 7-4

# SNEAKERS: WHERE IS THE INDUSTRY GOING?

In North America sneakers are a nearly $6 billion market with $600 million in Canada. And after several years of annual growth exceeding 20 percent in both countries, sales have virtually flattened. As a result, the executives in all the sneaker companies — Nike, Reebok, L.A. Gear, and others — are wondering what marketing strategies their companies should employ to effectively meet the market conditions that are emerging in the mid-1990s.

What has happened to sneakers? Understanding the North American industry requires taking a look at the past 25 years. In the 1960s sneakers were purchased for function. Converse sold its Chuck Taylor All-Stars for basketball, Keds were popular for knocking around, and a few other manufacturers in both countries produced specialized shoes for track and court-related sports.

Then things changed in the 1970s. A strong adult health and physical-fitness movement seized Canadians and Americans and gained momentum during the decade. Jogging and running became very popular, especially with the large market of people in their 20s and 30s. Running marathons (a race of 26.2 miles), formerly the domain of a few élite athletes, became the goal of thousands. Weekend races and fun runs to raise money for charity became commonplace in towns and cities in both countries. Everyone seemed to be running — or at least wearing running shoes. Sneakers went from function to fashion, and the race among the makers was under way.

A Sporting Goods Manufacturers survey in the late 1980s indicated that more than 90 percent of the North American population has at least one pair of athletic shoes, and over 70 percent buy a new pair each year. According to their market research, there are four primary consumer segments:

- Pragmatists: concerned with economy, comfort, durability (30 percent).
- Performance conscious: focused on competition and athletic performance, mostly young adult males (30 percent).
- Appearance conscious: interested in style, colour, and wardrobe co-ordination (25 percent).
- Fashion leaders: want to set the trend, be the first to buy (15 percent).

Consider how the major competitors — Nike, Reebok, and L. A. Gear — approached the market.

In 1964 Phil Knight and his former track coach at the University of Oregon, Bill Bowerman, started Blue Ribbon Sports to distribute a brand of Japanese-made running shoes. A few years later, convinced they could design a superior shoe for the competitive runner, Knight and Bowerman formed Nike. The company name was taken from Greek mythology, in which Nike is the goddess of victory and the speedy messenger for "top management" — Zeus and Athena.

Nike initially focused on running shoes with a product-oriented philosophy. The feeling in the company was that well-designed, performance-enhancing shoes would create their own market. In fact, the company's initial marketing program consisted of Knight persuading several top U.S. distance runners to try out the new shoe. In effect, Nike employed the testimonial approach, relying on a type of reference group influence that is used on a much larger scale today by most athletic equipment marketers.

In the absence of significant competition, the strategy worked. Nike grew rapidly and was soon making shoes for other sports. By 1976 sales were $14 million; over the next five years, both sales and profits grew by more than 75 percent a year. The biggest factor contributing to Nike's growth was a change in fashion. For people under 25 years old, sneakers became a wardrobe staple. By the early 1980s, 80 percent of the athletic shoes purchased were being used primarily for non-athletic purposes.

But two events in the 1980s caused Nike to rethink its strategy:

---

Sources: Richard Sandomir, "Scrappy Reebok Aims at Aloof Nike," *The New York Times*, February 9, 1993, p. C1; "Pumping Up," *The Economist*, February 15, 1992, pp. 78-79; David J. Jefferson, "Reebok Primes the Pump While Rivals Stress Value," *The Wall Street Journal*, February 3, 1992, p. B1; Matthew Grimm, "Gearing Up for the Long Run," *Adweek's Marketing Week*, February 3, 1992, pp. 12-13; Geraldine E. Willigan, "High Performance Marketing: An Interview with Nike's Phil Knight," *Harvard Business Review*, July-August 1992, pp. 91-101; Joseph Pereira, "From Air to Pump to Puma's Disc System, Sneaker Gimmicks Bound to New Heights," *The Wall Street Journal*, October 31, 1991, p. B1; David Chilton, "Adidas Gets Back to Basics," *Playback Strategy*, March 11, 1991, pp. 1, 12; Patricia Davis, "Hot Shoes," *Report on Business Magazine*, May, 1990, pp. 91-94.

- An ill-advised extension of its product line. Anticipating that the running-shoe business would soon stop growing, management began looking for other alternatives. Because consumers often wore their running shoes at times when they weren't running, Nike reasoned there was a market for a casual shoe with the Nike name on it. Unfortunately, their approach to designing the shoe ignored fashion. As a result, the product Nike produced — a highly functional casual shoe that consumers thought was ugly — failed.
- Overlooking the aerobics boom. When the company finally did respond to the demand for a shoe designed for aerobics, it used the Nike approach of developing a sturdy but clunky shoe that was highly functional but unattractive.

These mistakes — combined with the success of competitors — caused Nike to slip from nearly 50 percent of the market in 1980 to 22 percent in 1986. To stem the slide, Nike management concluded a marketing orientation was necessary. Though function remained the most prominent component of Nike's strategy, it became more conscious of what consumers wanted in appearance, style, and image. According to Phil Knight, "We've come around to saying that Nike is a marketing-oriented company. . . . The design elements and functional characteristics of the product itself are just part of the overall marketing process."

Nowhere is this marketing orientation better reflected than in the evolution of "air technology." In 1979 Nike introduced a shoe with an air sac in the heel to act as a shock absorber. Over the next few years the technology was refined and incorporated in more shoes. By 1987 there were 50 Nike models with air sacs, generating sales of more than $40 million. However, Nike was able to match this sales figure with a single running shoe when it added a "window" to the side of the sole to make the air sac visible. What's the difference? Nike realized that consumers wanted to see the technology for which they were paying a premium price, and they wanted it to be visible to others as well.

With greater sensitivity to the market, Nike anticipated the importance of the basketball shoe category and secured the services of Michael Jordan as an endorser. It then introduced Air Jordans in 1988, a shoe that combined performance, style, and eye-catching advertising. As a result, it became the most successful line of all athletic shoes.

In its advertising, Nike has demonstrated an understanding of North American consumer motivation with flashy ads developed by film directors such as Spike Lee. The "Just Do It" advertising campaign appealed to every person's desire to improve, whatever their current level of performance. And the "Bo Knows" ad campaign featuring Bo Jackson effectively combined humour and the dream of exceptional performance in a highly memorable series of messages.

Finally, Nike has also become the industry leader in servicing retailers. It has improved delivery time, provided retailers with systems to keep better track of inventories, and installed a 24-hour hotline to respond to retailers' problems. As a result, Nike is the highest-rated firm in the sportswear industry for on-time delivery and responsiveness to customers.

Nike effectively shifted its focus from just products to the product and the customer. As a result, the firm has regained the top spot among sneaker makers with 30 percent of the market, and sales of more than $3.9 billion.

Before 1980 Reebok was a virtual unknown in the North American sneaker market. The firm was an offshoot of a British company, J. W. Foster & Sons, that had been making high-quality athletic shoes in England for more than 80 years. An enterprising outdoor equipment distributor, Paul Fireman, noticed the Reebok shoes at an international sportswear trade show and signed on as the firm's licensee. Though the first products Reebok introduced in North America were running shoes, it was clear in 1980 that Nike and other established firms like Adidas and Puma were pretty much in control of that market. So Fireman went looking for other opportunities. What he discovered was an overlooked segment and an emerging market.

Fireman observed that no one was making a shoe for women that could be colour-co-ordinated with athletic clothing. Quite the contrary, most shoes were decorated with garish, contrasting colours to draw attention to them. Second, a new athletic activity called aerobics was growing in popularity, and no manufacturer had developed a shoe especially for it. Responding to these two opportunities, Reebok produced a soft leather shoe trimmed in pastels that was less durable but more attractive than existing premium athletic lines.

The shoe was positioned as especially for aerobics and was promoted directly to aerobics instructors. It caught on, and sales by the end of 1983 amounted to $13 million. But that proved to be only the beginning. The comfort and good looks of Reebok's aerobic shoes led to their becoming a fashion item. The company expanded the line, and by 1986 sales of aerobic shoes alone reached nearly $300 million. With an established reputation, Reebok was able to move into specialized lines like tennis and children's sneakers (Weeboks), expand its efforts in running shoes, and go after the rapidly growing basketball shoe market. While Nike shoe sales declined from 1985 to 1987 ($625 million to $597 million), Reebok's soared from $300 million to $990 million.

In 1989 Reebok introduced its Pump — a shoe that incorporated an inflation device that allowed the wearer to create a snug fit. Nike was the first to introduce an inflatable shoe, but its version required a detachable pump. Reebok's shoe combined the functional advantage of greater convenience with the psychological value of a highly visible pump mechanism on the shoe's tongue.

To strengthen its position as a performance *and* fashion brand, Reebok secured the services of professional basketball star Shaquille O'Neal in 1993 with a $15 million, five-year contract. It is also refocusing its efforts on athletic shoes and sports apparel by selling two subsidiaries acquired in the 1980s, Boston Whaler (fishing boats) and Ellesse (an Italian sportswear manufacturer).

Having once outperformed Nike in sales only to see its major rival rebound and retake first place, Reebok's Fireman has set a goal of surpassing Nike again by 1995.

L.A. Gear is a smaller player in the sneaker market. The firm is less than 20 percent of the size of Nike, but it has had a significant effect on the industry. L.A. Gear is the creation of Robert Greenberg, who, after delving into a variety of businesses including hairdressing and rollerskate manufacturing, focused on marketing imported shoes. It wasn't until 1985 that his shoe line included sneakers. With total sales of his company just under $11 million, Greenberg decided to incorporate the "southern California life-style look" in sneakers for girls age 9 to 17. The shoes had leather tops that were decorated with sequins, fringe, and rhinestones, and included pictures of surfers, palm trees, and beaches. The line was an immediate hit and sales exploded to more than $220 million by 1988.

While Nike and Reebok used athletics as the basis for their marketing efforts, L.A. Gear adopted a different positioning. For example, its print ads were more likely to appear in *Cosmopolitan* and *Glamour* than in *Sports Illustrated*. And while the premier endorsers for Nike (Michael Jordan) and Reebok (Shaquille O'Neal) are athletes, L.A. Gear signed Michael Jackson.

There is also an important difference across the three firms with respect to distribution. The majority of Nike and Reebok retailers are athletic-shoe specialty stores, whereas L.A. Gear sells primarily through department stores and women's shoe stores.

To take advantage of its popularity, L.A. Gear moved quickly into styles for men and women and specialized shoes for a variety of sports. By 1990 the firm had sales of $900 million. But then the roof fell in. Growth in sneaker sales slowed, and L.A. Gear had made too large a commitment to performance-enhancing athletic shoes that were not doing well. Then its Catapult-model basketball shoe was hit with a design patent-infringement suit by Nike.

L.A. Gear had other problems as well. The product line had grown to 400 styles. And since the firm prided itself on shipping shoes to a retailer within a week of an order, it had to carry huge inventories. (The rest of the industry requires advance orders.) In addition, in 1989, L.A. Gear signed Michael Jackson to a $20-million contract to design and endorse a line of shoes, but the relationship soured. All L.A. Gear got was one commercial featuring Jackson.

In the first nine months of 1991, the firm lost $28 million. When L.A. Gear had trouble paying its bills, creditors forced the sale of controlling interest in the firm to a group of investors. Greenberg was replaced with a new management team.

The changes introduced by the new managers include reducing the product line to 150 styles, and reorganization of the firm into three divisions — casual, children's, and athletic. In the casual line, the styles are more conservative and less reliant on fashion or fad. The objective is to convince consumers and retailers that L.A. Gear is a stable company that produces quality products.

During the 1980s, growth in the sneaker market was spurred by free-spending consumers and a constant flow of new products positioned for many different athletic uses that included a wide variety of features and expensive advertising. To make all of this possible, prices reached as much as $170. But the market is fickle and unpredictable. Consider these developments:

- A brand called British Knights became high fashion until the "BK" insignia on the shoes became associated with gang violence. Sales dropped sharply.
- Air Jordans were the hottest-selling athletic shoe ever until Michael Jordan was injured and sat out most of a basketball season. While he was not playing, sales of the line dropped dramatically. When he got back on the court, sales picked up. In 1993, Jordan announced his retirement from basketball.
- Converse changed the name of a new basketball shoe from Run "N" Gun to Run "N" Slam when community groups complained that the original name, a common term to describe fast-paced play, might incite violence among young people.
- Saucony Jazz 3000 running shoe received *Consumer Reports'* best-buy rating for good value and sales immediately doubled. Since it is a small company, management is concerned it will not be able to capitalize on the publicity beyond a short-term sales spurt.

Now growth has slowed — to only 4 percent in 1991, and even less since then. What has been the response from the participants?

Nike, L.A. Gear, and others have gone back to the basics. They contend that the era of conspicuous consumption in sneakers is over. The consumers they see in the 1990s want performance, quality, and value. The trend is reflected in *Running World* magazine's "Shoe Buyer's Guide," which reports that many manufacturers improved the quality of their shoes while lowering the prices as much as 20 percent in 1994. Nike, for example, is producing adaptations of its Air Line priced in the $50 range. And L.A. Gear is adjusting its product mix so that 80 percent of its items will sell from $40 to $60.

Reebok has taken a different approach. It added two new designs to its Pump line — Insta-Pump and Pump Custom-Cushioning. The shoes contain bladders that are filled with carbon dioxide from hand-held gas canisters. The running shoe version, with two air chambers, even has tiny pressure gauges with digital readouts. The price is over $150.

## QUESTIONS

1. What implications do the demographic changes described in Chapter 24 have for segmenting the sneaker market?
2. The North American market for sneakers was stimulated by a change in the social/cultural environment in Canada and the United States. Is something similar happening or likely to happen elsewhere in the world? How should the sneaker manufacturers prepare for developments outside the North American market?
3. Which product-market strategies (discussed in Chapter 3) appear to be the most appropriate for sneaker marketers? How will the marketing-mix components be affected by the choice of a strategy?

# GLOSSARY

**accessory equipment** In the business market, capital goods used in the operation of an industrial firm.

**actual self** The way you really see yourself. To be distinguished from *ideal self*.

**ad** See *advertisement*.

**administered vertical marketing system** A distribution system in which channel control is maintained through the economic power of one firm in the channel.

**administration** See *management*.

**adoption process** The stages that an individual goes through in deciding whether to accept an innovation.

**advertisement** A sponsor-identified message regarding a product or organization that can be verbal and/or visual, and is disseminated through one or more media. Same as *ad*.

**advertising** All activities involved in presenting to a group a nonpersonal, sponsor-identified message regarding a product or organization.

**advertising agency** An independent company rendering specialized services in advertising in particular and in marketing in general.

**advertising allowance** A payment or cash discount offered by a manufacturer to a retailer to encourage the retailer to advertise or prominently display the manufacturer's product.

**advertising campaign** The total advertising program for a product or brand that involves co-ordination, central theme, and specific goals.

**advertising media** The communications vehicles (such as newspapers, radio, and television) that carry advertising.

**advertising recall** A measure of advertising effectiveness that is based on the premise that an ad can have an effect only if it is perceived and remembered.

**agent** A firm that never actually owns products that are being distributed but does actively assist in the transfer of title.

**agent wholesaler** An independent firm that primarily engages in wholesaling and does not take title to the products being distributed but does actively negotiate their sale or purchase on behalf of other firms.

**agents and brokers** A broad category of wholesaling intermediaries that do not take title to products. The category includes manufacturers' agents, selling agents, commission merchants, auctioneers, brokers, and others.

**agribusiness** The business side of farming. Usually involves large, highly mechanized farming operations.

**AIDA** A sequence of steps in various forms of promotion, notably personal selling and advertising, consisting of attracting Attention, holding Interest, arousing Desire, and generating buyer Action.

**annual marketing plan** A written document that details the planned marketing activities for the given business unit or product for the given year.

**assumptive close** In personal selling, the stage in the selling process when the sales person can often finalize the sale by asking questions that will settle the details of the purchase.

**attitude** A learned predisposition to respond to an object or class of objects in a consistently favourable or unfavourable way.

**auction company** An agent wholesaler that provides (1) auctioneers who do the selling and (2) physical facilities for displaying the sellers' products.

**automated merchandising** See *automatic vending*.

**automatic vending** A form of nonstore retailing where the products are sold through a machine with no personal contact between the buyer and seller. Same as *automated merchandising*.

**average fixed cost** The total fixed cost divided by the number of units produced.

**average fixed cost curve** A graph of average fixed cost levels, showing a decline as output increases, because the total of the fixed costs is spread over an increasing number of units.

**average revenue** The unit price at a given level of unit sales. It is calculated by dividing total revenue by the number of units sold.

**average total cost** The total cost divided by the number of units produced.
**average variable cost** The total variable cost divided by the number of units produced.
**average variable cost curve** A graph of average variable cost levels, which starts high, then declines to its lowest point, reflecting optimum output with respect to variable costs (not total costs), and then rises.
**balance of trade** In international business, the difference between the value of a nation's imports and the value of its exports.
**barter** The exchange of goods and/or services for other products.
**base price** The price of one unit of the product at its point of production or resale. Same as *list price*.
**battle of the brands** Market competition between producers' brands and intermediaries' brands. In recent years, generic products have entered this competitive struggle.
**behavioural segmentation** Market segmentation based on consumers' product-related behaviour, typically the benefits desired from a product and the rate at which the consumer uses the product.
**benefit segmentation** A basis for segmenting a market. A total market is divided into segments based on the customers' perceptions of the various benefits provided by a product.
**Boston Consulting Group (BCG) matrix** A strategic planning model that classifies strategic business units or major products according to market shares and growth rates.
**brand** A name, term, symbol, special design, or some combination of these elements that is intended to identify the products of one seller or a group of sellers.
**brand competition** Competition among marketers of branded products that are very similar and may be substituted for each other.
**brand licensing** See *trademark licensing*.
**brand manager** See *product manager*.
**brand mark** The part of a brand that appears in the form of a symbol, picture, design, or distinctive colour or type of lettering.
**brand name** The part of a brand that can be vocalized — words, letters, and/or numbers.
**breadth of product mix** The number of product lines offered for sale by a firm.
**break-even point** The level of output at which revenues equal costs, assuming a certain selling price.
**broker** An independent agent wholesaler that brings buyers and sellers together and provides market information to either party.
**build-up method** See *task method*.
**business cycle** The three recurring stages in an economy, typically prosperity, recession, and recovery.
**business marketing** The marketing of goods and services to business users.
**business product** A product that is intended for purchase and use in producing other products or in rendering services in a business.
**business user** An organization that buys goods or services to resell, use in its own business, or make other products.
**buy classes** Three typical buying situations in the business market — namely new-task buying, modified rebuy, and straight rebuy.
**buyers** The people in a buying centre who select the suppliers, arrange the terms of sale, and process the actual purchase orders.
**buying centre** All of the people in an organization who participate in the buying-decision process.
**buying-decision process** The series of logical stages a prospective purchaser goes through when faced with a buying problem. The stages differ for consumers and organizations.
**buying motive** The reason why a person buys a specific product or shops at a specific store.
**campaign** A co-ordinated series of promotional efforts built around a single theme and designed to reach a pre-determined goal.
**campaign theme** In promotion, the central idea or focal point in a promotional campaign.
**cartel** A group of companies that produce similar products and combine to restrain competition in manufacturing and marketing.
**cash cows** According to the Boston Consulting Group matrix, strategic business units that are characterized by high market shares and do business in mature industries (those with low growth rates).
**cash discount** A deduction from list price for paying a bill within a specified period of time.
**catalogue retailing** One form of direct marketing, in which companies mail catalogues to consumers or make them available at retail stores and consumers make their purchases from the catalogues.
**catalogue showroom** A type of retail institution that offers a complete catalogue and some sample items in the showroom and the remaining inventory in an attached warehouse. It offers a broad but shallow assortment of merchandise, emphasizes low prices, and offers few customer services.
**category killer store** A type of retail institution that has a narrow but very deep assortment, emphasizes

low prices, and few to moderate customer services. It is designed to "destroy" all competition in a specific product category.

**category-management system** A form of marketing organization in which an executive position called a category manager is established for each product category, and all the competing brand managers in each group report to this executive.

**Census Metropolitan Area** The major population centres of Canada as defined by Statistics Canada; generally containing population centres of 100,000 or more.

**chain store** One in a group of retail stores that carry the same type of merchandise. Corporate chain stores are centrally owned and managed. Voluntary chains are an association of independently owned stores.

**channel conflict** A situation in which one channel member perceives another channel member to be acting in a way that prevents the first member from achieving its distribution objectives.

**channel control** The ability to influence the behaviour of other channel members.

**client market** Individuals and/or organizations that are the recipients of a not-for-profit organization's money and/or services. Same as *recipient market.*

**closing** In personal selling, the stage in the selling process when the sales person gets the buyer to agree to buy.

**cognitive dissonance** The anxiety created by the fact that in most purchases the alternative selected has some negative features and the alternatives not selected have some positive features.

**combination salary plan** The method of sales force compensation that combines a base salary with a commission related to some task(s).

**commission** Compensation tied to a specific unit of accomplishment.

**commission merchant** An independent agent wholesaler, used primarily in the marketing of agricultural products, that may physically handle the seller's products in central markets and has authority regarding prices and terms of sale.

**communication process** A system of verbal and/or nonverbal transmission of information between a sender and a receiver. The four elements are message, source, communication channel, and receiver.

**community shopping centre** A shopping *centre* that is larger than a neighbourhood centre but smaller than a regional centre. Usually includes one or two department stores or discount stores, along with a number of shopping-goods stores and specialty stores.

**comparative advertising** Selective demand advertising in which the advertiser either directly (by naming a rival brand) or indirectly (through inference) points out how the advertised brand is better.

**Competition Act** The major piece of federal legislation in Canada that governs the marketing and advertising activities of companies and organizations operating in Canada.

**concept testing** The first three stages in the new-product development process — pretesting of the product idea, in contrast to later pretesting of the product itself and the market.

**consumer** An individual or organizational unit that uses or consumes a product.

**Consumer Packaging and Labelling Act** Federal legislation that regulates the packaging and labelling of consumer products in Canada.

**consumer product** A product that is intended for purchase and use by household consumers for nonbusiness purposes.

**consumerism** Protests by consumers against perceived injustices in marketing, and the efforts to remedy these injustices.

**containerization** A cargo-handling system in which shipments of products are enclosed in large metal or wood receptacles that are then transported unopened from the time they leave the customer's facilities until they reach their destination.

**contractual vertical market system** An arrangement under which independent firms — producers, wholesalers, and retailers — operate under a contract specifying how they will try to improve their distribution efficiency and effectiveness.

**contribution-margin allocation** In marketing cost analysis, an accounting approach in which only direct expenses are allocated to the marketing units being studied. A unit's gross margin minus its direct cost equals that unit's contribution to covering the company's indirect expenses (overhead).

**contributor market** Individuals and/or organizations that donate money, labour, services, and/or materials to a not-for-profit organization. Also called *donor market.*

**convenience goods** A class of consumer products that the consumer has prior knowledge of and purchases with minimum time and effort.

**convenience sample** A sample that is selected in a nonrandom way such that every member of the universe does not have an equal chance of being included.

**convenience store** A type of retailing institution that concentrates on convenience-oriented groceries and nonfoods, has higher prices than found at most other grocery stores, and offers few customer services.

**"cooling-off" laws** Provincial or municipal laws that permit a consumer to cancel an order for a product — usually within a period of three days after signing the order.

**co-operative advertising** Advertising in which two or more firms share the cost.

**copy** The written or spoken material in an ad that makes up the primary message.

**corporate chain** An organization of two or more centrally owned and managed stores that generally handle the same lines of products.

**corporate vertical marketing system** An arrangement under which a firm at one level of a distribution channel owns the firms at the next level or owns the entire channel.

**correlation analysis** A method of sales forecasting that is a statistical refinement of the direct-derivation method.

**cost per thousand (CPM)** The media cost of gaining exposure to 1,000 persons with an ad.

**cost-plus pricing** A major method of price determination in which the price of a unit of a product is set at a level equal to the unit's total cost plus a desired profit on the unit.

**creative selling** A selling job that often requires designing a system to fit the needs of the particular customer and may depend upon the expertise of several people who make up a sales team.

**cues** In learning theory, signals from the environment that determine the pattern of response.

**culture** A complex of symbols and artifacts created by a given society and handed down from generation to generation as determinants and regulators of human behaviour.

**cumulative discount** A quantity discount based on the total volume purchased over a period of time.

**customer** An individual or organization that makes a purchase decision.

**customer satisfaction** How closely experience with a product meets or exceeds a customer's expectations.

**customer service advertising** Advertising that presents information about the advertiser's operations.

**data base** A set of related data that is organized, stored, and updated in a computer.

**data base marketing** An approach to marketing that relies on the use of a data base of customers or prospective customers that is used to identify prospects for a direct marketing program.

**deciders** The people in a buying centre who make the actual buying decision regarding a product and/or supplier.

**decision support system (DSS)** A procedure that allows a manager to interact with data and methods of analysis to gather, analyze, and interpret information.

**decline stage** The fourth, and final, part of a product life cycle, during which the sales of a generic product category drop and most competitors abandon the market.

**decoding** The process of a receiver giving meaning to words, pictures, or both that have been transmitted by a sender.

**Delphi method** A forecasting technique, applicable to sales forecasting, in which a group of experts individually and anonymously assesses future sales and after which each member has the chance to offer a revised assessment as the group moves towards a consensus.

**demand forecasting** The process of estimating sales of a product during some future time period.

**demography** The statistical study of human population and its distribution.

**department store** A large-scale retailing institution that has a very broad and deep product assortment, prefers not to compete on the basis of price, and offers a wide array of customer services.

**depth of product line** The assortment within a product line.

**derived demand** A situation in which the demand for one product is dependent upon the demand for another product.

**descriptive label** A label that gives information regarding the use, care, performance, or other features of a product.

**differential advantage** Any feature of an organization or brand perceived by customers to be desirable and different from the competition.

**differentiation** According to Porter's generic-strategies model, a strategy of satisfying either a broad or narrow market by creating a distinctive product and then charging a higher-than-average price.

**diffusion of innovation** A process by which an innovation is spread through a social system over time.

**direct-action advertising** Product advertising that seeks a quick response.

**direct costs** Separate expenses that are incurred totally in connection with one market segment or one unit of the sales organization.

**direct-derivation method** A sales forecasting method used to translate market-factor behaviour into an estimate of future sales.

**direct distribution** A channel consisting only of producer and final customer with no intermediaries providing assistance.

**direct mail** An advertising medium whereby the advertiser contacts prospective customers by sending some form of advertisement through the mail.

**direct marketing** A form of nonstore retailing that uses nonpersonal media to contact consumers who, in turn, purchase products without visiting a retail store.

**direct purchase** A situation in which a customer makes a purchase directly from a producer.

**direct selling** A form of nonstore retailing in which personal contact between a sales person and a consumer occurs away from a retail store.

**direct tests (in advertising)** Measures of the sales volume produced by an ad or an entire advertising campaign.

**discount house** A large-scale retailing institution that has a broad and shallow product assortment, emphasizes low prices, and offers relatively few customer services.

**discount retailing** A retailing approach that uses price as a major selling point by combining comparatively low prices and reduced costs of doing business.

**discretionary purchasing power** The amount of disposable income remaining after fixed expenses and essential household needs are paid for.

**dispersion** In distribution, the intermediary's activities that distribute the correct amount of a product to its market.

**disposable personal income** Personal income remaining after all personal taxes are paid.

**distribution centre** A concept in warehousing that develops under one roof an efficient, fully integrated system for the flow of products — taking orders, filling them, and delivering them to customers.

**distribution channel** The set of people and firms involved in the flow of the title to a product as it moves from producer to ultimate consumer or business user.

**diversification** A product-market growth strategy in which a company develops new products to sell to new markets.

**dogs** According to the Boston Consulting Group matrix, strategic business units that are characterized by low market shares and operate in industries with low growth rates.

**door-to-door selling** One kind of direct selling, in which the personal contact between a sales person and an individual prospect occurs at the prospective customer's residence or business.

**donor market** See *contributor market.*

**drive** See *motive.*

**driver sales person** A selling job in which the job is primarily to deliver the product. Selling responsibilities, if any, are secondary to seeing that orders are filled correctly and on time.

**drop shipper** A limited-function merchant wholesaler that does not physically handle the product.

**dual distribution** The use by a producer of multiple and competing channels of distribution.

**dumping** The process of selling products in foreign markets at prices below the prices charged for these goods in their home market.

**early adopters** The second group (following the innovators) to adopt something new. This group includes the opinion leaders, is respected, and has much influence on its peers.

**early majority** A more deliberate group of innovation adopters that adopts just before the "average" adopter.

**economic order quantity (EOQ)** The optimal quantity for reorder when replenishing inventory stocks, as indicated by the volume at which the inventory-carrying cost plus the order-processing cost are at a minimum.

**ego** In Freudian psychology, the rational control centre in our minds that maintains a balance between (1) the uninhibited instincts of the id and (2) the socially oriented, constraining superego.

**80-20 principle** A situation in which a large proportion of a company's marketing units (products, territories, customers) accounts for a small share of the company's volume or profit, and vice versa.

**elastic demand** A price-volume relationship such that a change of one unit on the price scale results in a change of more than one unit on the volume scale.

**encoding** The process of translating an idea into a message in the form of words, pictures, or both in order that it can be transmitted from a sender to a receiver.

**environmental monitoring** The process of gathering information regarding a company's external environment, analyzing it, and forecasting the impact of whatever trends the analysis suggests. Same as *environmental scanning.*

**ethics** The rules and standards of moral behaviour that are generally accepted by a society.

**ethnographic research** The process of watching closely how consumers interact with a product and then deducing how it fits into their lives.

**European Union** A collection of countries in Western Europe and Scandinavia that have formed a political and economic alliance that has succeeded in liberalizing trade among its members. A number of Eastern European countries are expected to join in the future.

**evaluation** The process of determining what happened, why it happened, and what to do about it.

**exchange** The voluntary act of providing a person or organization something of value in order to acquire something else of value in return.

**execution** The step in creating an advertising message that tries to combine in a convincing, compatible way the feature or device that gets attention with the appeal.

**exclusive dealing** The practice by which a manufacturer prohibits its dealers from carrying products of competing manufacturers.

**exclusive distribution** A strategy in which a producer agrees to sell its product to only a single wholesaling intermediary and/or retailer in a given market.

**exclusive territory** The practice by which a manufacturer requires each intermediary to sell only to customers located within the intermediary's assigned territory.

**executive judgement** A method of sales forecasting that consists of obtaining opinions regarding future sales volume from one or more executives.

**expected price** The price at which customers consciously or unconsciously value a product — what they think the product is worth.

**experimental method** A method of gathering primary data in which the researcher is able to observe the results of changing one variable in a situation while holding all others constant.

**exporting** The activities by which a firm sells its product in another country, either directly to foreign importers or through import-export intermediaries.

**express warranty** A statement in written or spoken words regarding restitution from seller to customer if the seller's product does not perform up to reasonable expectations.

**fabricating materials** Business goods that have received some processing and will undergo further processing as they become part of another product.

**fabricating parts** Business goods that already have been processed to some extent and will be assembled in their present form (with no further change) as part of another product.

**factory outlet** A special type of off-price retail institution that is owned by a manufacturer and usually sells only that manufacturer's clearance items, regular merchandise, and perhaps even otherwise unavailable items.

**fad** A short-lived fashion that is usually based on some novelty feature.

**family** A group of two or more people related by blood, marriage, or adoption living together in a household.

**family brands** A branding strategy in which a group of products is given a single brand.

**family life cycle** The series of life stages that a family goes through, starting with young single people and progressing through married stages with young and then older children, and ending with older married and single people.

**family packaging** A strategy of using either highly similar packages for all products or packages with a common and clearly noticeable feature.

**fashion** A style that is popularly accepted by groups of people over a reasonably long period of time.

**fashion-adoption process** The process by which a style becomes popular in a market; similar to diffusion of an innovation.

**fashion cycle** Wavelike movements representing the introduction, rise, popular acceptance, and decline in popularity of a given style.

**fashion obsolescence** See *style obsolescence*.

**feedback** The component of communication that tells the sender whether the message was received and how it was perceived by the recipient.

**field experiment** An experiment in which the researcher has only limited control of the environment because the experiment is conducted in a real-world setting.

**fixed cost** A constant cost regardless of how many items are produced or sold.

**flexible-price strategy** A pricing strategy in which a company sells similar quantities of merchandise to similar buyers at different prices. Same as *variable-price strategy*.

**f.o.b. (free on board) factory price** A geographic pricing strategy whereby the buyer pays all freight charges from the f.o.b. location to the destination. Same as *f.o.b. mill price*.

**f.o.b. mill price** See *f.o.b. factory price*.

**focus** According to Porter's generic-strategies model, a strategy of satisfying part of a market with either a very low-priced or highly distinctive product.

**focus group** A preliminary data-gathering method involving an interactive interview of four to ten people.

**form utility** The utility that is created when a good is produced.

**forward dating** A combination of a seasonal discount and a cash discount under which a buyer places an order and receives shipment during the off-season but does not have to pay the bill until after the season has started and some sales revenue has been generated.

**fragmented markets** Small market segments that can be identified and isolated through increasingly sophisticated demographic, behavioural, and geographic data.

**franchise system** The combination of franchiser, franchisees, and franchiser-owned business units.

**franchising** A type of contractual vertical marketing system that involves a continuing relationship in which a franchiser (the parent company) provides the right to use a trademark plus various management assistance in opening and operating a business in return for financial considerations from a franchisee (the owner of the individual business unit).

**freight absorption** A geographic pricing strategy whereby the seller pays for (absorbs) some of the freight charges in order to penetrate more distant markets.

**freight forwarder** A specialized transportation agency that consolidates less-than-carload or less-than-truckload shipments into carload or truckload quantities and provides door-to-door shipping service.

**fulfilment** The process of filling orders as when a catalogue company selects the items from its inventory to be sent to a customer who has ordered them.

**full-cost allocation** In a marketing cost analysis, an accounting approach wherein all expenses — direct and indirect — are allocated to the marketing units being analyzed.

**full-service wholesaler** An independent merchant wholesaler that normally performs a full range of wholesaling functions.

**functional discount** See *trade discount*.

**gatekeepers** The people in a buying centre who control the flow of purchasing information within the organization and between the buying firm and potential vendors.

**General Agreement on Tariffs and Trade (GATT)** An organization, formed in 1948 and now comprising over 100 countries, that seeks to develop fair-trade practices among its members.

**generic product** A product that is packaged in a plain label and is sold with no advertising and without a brand name. The product goes by its generic name, such as "tomatoes" or "paper towels."

**generic use of brand names** General reference to a product by its brand name — cellophane, kerosene, zipper, for example — rather than its *generic name*. The owners of these brands no longer have exclusive use of the brand name.

**geodemographic clustering** The use of statistical population data along with information on where people live, usually obtained from postal code data, to identify clusters of consumers or households with similar characteristics.

**global marketing** A strategy in which essentially the same marketing program is employed around the world.

**goal** See *objective*.

**good** A set of tangible physical attributes assembled in an identifiable form to provide want-satisfaction to customers.

**government market** The segment of the business market that includes federal, provincial, and local units buying for government institutions such as schools, offices, hospitals, and research facilities.

**grade label** Identification of the quality (grade) of a product by means of a letter, number, or word.

**green marketing** Any marketing activity of a firm that is intended to create a positive impact or lessen the negative impact of a product on the environment in order to capitalize on consumers' concerns about environmental issues.

**growth stage** The second part of a product life cycle, during which the sales and profits of a generic product category rise and competitors enter the market, after which profits start to decline near the end of this part of the cycle.

**heterogeneity of a service** A characteristic of a service indicating that each unit is somewhat different from other "units" of the same service.

**hierarchy of effects** The stages a buyer goes through in moving towards a purchase — specifically, awareness, knowledge, liking, preference, conviction, and purchase.

**high involvement** A purchase decision that involves all six stages of the buying decision process.

**horizontal business market** A situation where a given product is usable in a wide variety of industries.

**horizontal conflict** A form of channel conflict occurring between firms on the same level of distribution — between intermediaries of the same type or between different types of intermediaries.

**horizontal co-operative advertising** Advertising that involves firms on the same level of distribution sharing the cost.

**household** A single person, a family, or any group of unrelated persons who occupy a housing unit.

**hypermarket** A type of exceedingly large-scale retailing institution that has a very broad and moderately deep product assortment, emphasizes low prices, and offers some customer services.

**hypothesis** A tentative supposition or a possible solution to a problem.

**iceberg principle** A concept related to performance evaluation stating that the summary data (tip of the iceberg) regarding an activity may hide significant variations among segments of this activity.

**id** In Freudian psychology, the part of the mind that houses the basic instinctive drives, many of which are antisocial.

**ideal self** The way you want to be seen or would like to see yourself. To be distinguished from *actual self*.

**illustration** The pictorial portion of an ad.

**image utility** The emotional or psychological value that a person attaches to a product or brand because of the reputation or social standing of that product or brand.

**implementation** The process of organizing for the marketing effort, staffing this organization, and directing the operational efforts of these people as they carry out the strategic plans.

**implied warranty** An intended but unstated assurance regarding restitution from seller to customer if the seller's product does not perform up to reasonable expectations.

**import-export agent** An agent wholesaler that arranges for distribution of goods in a foreign country.

**impulse buying** Low-involvement purchases made with little or no advance planning.

**independent retailer** A company with a single retail store that is not affiliated with any type of contractual vertical marketing system.

**indirect-action advertising** Product advertising that is intended to inform or remind consumers about a product and its benefits.

**indirect costs** Expenses that are incurred jointly for more than one marketing unit and therefore cannot be totally charged to one market segment.

**indirect distribution** A channel consisting of producer, final customer, and at least one level of intermediary.

**indirect tests (in advertising)** Measures of advertising effects that use something other than sales volume.

**inelastic demand** A price-volume relationship such that a change of one unit on the price scale results in a change of less than one unit on the volume scale.

**influencers** The people in a buying centre who set the specifications and aspects of buying decisions because of their technical expertise, financial position, or political power in the organization.

**infomercials** Television "programs" that may be 30 minutes or 60 minutes or longer in length and that are actually paid commercials for businesses or other advertisers.

**informal investigation** The stage in a marketing research study at which information is gathered from people outside the company — intermediaries, competitors, advertising agencies, and consumers.

**information utility** The want-satisfying capability that is created by informing prospective buyers that a product exists.

**in-home retailing** Retail selling in the customer's home. A personal sales representative may or may not be involved. In-home retailing includes door-to-door selling, party-plan selling, and selling by television and computer.

**innovators** The first group — a venturesome group — of people to adopt something new (good, service).

**inseparability** A characteristic of a service indicating that it cannot be separated from the creator-seller of the service.

**inside order taker** A selling job in which the primary function of the sales person is to take orders in person or by phone inside a store or other type of business.

**installations** In the business market, long-lived, expensive, major industrial capital goods that directly affect the scale of operation of an industrial firm.

**institutional advertising** Advertising designed either to present information about the advertiser's business or to create a good attitude — build goodwill — towards the organization.

**intangibility** A characteristic of a service indicating that it has no physical attributes and, as a result, is impossible for customers to taste, feel, see, hear, or smell before buying.

**intensity of distribution** The number of intermediaries used by a producer at the retailing and wholesaling levels of distribution.

**intensive distribution** A strategy in which a producer sells its product in every available outlet where a consumer might reasonably look for it. Same as *mass distribution*.

**interactive kiosks** Computer terminals which are usually located in retail stores, shopping malls, or other public locations that allow customers to order items or to obtain information.

**intermediary** A firm that renders services directly related to the purchase and/or sale of a product as it flows from producer to consumer.

**internal marketing** The process of directing programs to staff members with the intention of encouraging them to deliver superior service to customers and generally to adopt a customer focus in all that they do.

**introduction stage** The first part of a product life cycle, during which a generic product category is launched into the market in a full-scale marketing program. Same as *pioneering stage*.

**inventory control** The subsystem of physical distribution management that involves maintaining control over the size and composition of inventories in order to fill customers' orders promptly, completely, and accurately while minimizing both the investment and fluctuations in inventories.

**inverse demand** A price-volume relationship such that the higher the price, the greater the unit sales.

**involvement level** The amount of time and effort the consumer invests in a buying decision.

**joint venture** A partnership arrangement in which a foreign operation is owned in part by a Canadian company and in part by a foreign company.

**"just-in-time" concept** An inventory control system that involves buying parts and supplies in small quantities just in time for use in production and then producing in quantities just in time for sale.

**label** The part of a product that carries written information about the product or the seller.

**laboratory experiment** An experiment in which the researcher has complete control over the environment during the experiment.

**laggards** Tradition-bound people who are the last to adopt an innovation.

**late majority** The sceptical group of innovation adopters who adopt a new idea late in the game.

**layout** The physical arrangement of all of the elements of an ad.

**leader pricing** Temporary price cuts on well-known items. The price cut is made with the idea that these "specials" (loss leaders) will attract customers to the store.

**learning** Changes in behaviour resulting from previous experiences.

**leasing** A situation, found in both business and consumer markets, in which a good is rented rather than purchased outright.

**licensing** A business arrangement whereby one firm sells to another firm (for a fee or royalty) the right to use the first company's brand, patents, or manufacturing processes.

**life-style** A person's activities, interests, and opinions.

**limited-function wholesaler** A merchant wholesaler that performs only selected wholesaling functions.

**limited-line store** A type of retailing institution that has a narrow but deep product assortment, and its customer services tend to vary from store to store.

**line extension** One form of product-mix expansion in which a company adds a similar item to an existing product line with the same brand name.

**list price** See *base price*.

**logistics** See *physical distribution*.

**loss leaders** Products whose prices are cut with the idea that they will attract customers to the store.

**low involvement** A purchase decision in which the consumer moves directly from need recognition to purchase, skipping the stages in between.

**loyalty programs** Programs that reward loyal and frequent customers with points that can be redeemed for gifts, merchandise or services, such as the frequent-flyer programs operated by most airlines and the frequent-shopper programs of retailers such as Zellers and Sears.

**mail-order selling** A type of nonstore, nonpersonal retail or wholesale selling in which the customer mails in an order that is then delivered by mail or other parcel-delivery system.

**mall-intercept interview** Personal interview conducted in a shopping centre mall.

**mail survey** The method of gathering data by means of a questionnaire mailed to respondents and, when completed, returned by mail.

**management** The process of planning, implementing, and evaluating the efforts of a group of people working towards a common goal. Same as *administration*.

**manufacturers' agent** An independent agent wholesaler that sells part or all of a manufacturer's product mix in an assigned geographic territory.

**manufacturer's sales facility** An establishment that primarily engages in wholesaling and is owned and operated by a manufacturer but is physically separated from manufacturing plants.

**manufacturer's sales office** A manufacturer's sales facility that does not carry a stock of the product being sold.

**marginal analysis** A method of price setting that considers both demand and costs to determine the best price for profit maximization.

**marginal cost** The cost of producing and selling one more unit; that is, the cost of the last unit produced or sold.

**marginal revenue** The income derived from the sale of the last unit.

**markdown** A reduction from the original retailing selling price, usually made because the store was unable to sell the product at the original price.

**market** People or organizations with wants to satisfy, money to spend, and the willingness to spend it.

**market aggregation** A strategy whereby an organization treats its total market as a unit — that is, as one mass market whose parts are considered to be alike in all major respects.

**market development** A product-market growth strategy in which a company continues to sell its present products, but to a new market.

**market factor** An item or element that (1) exists in a market, (2) may be measured quantitatively, and (3) is related to the demand for a good or service.

**market-factor analysis** A sales forecasting method based on the assumption that future demand for a product is related to the behaviour of certain market factors.

**marketer** Any person or organization that desires to make exchanges.

**market fragmentation** The identification of smaller and smaller market segments.

**market index** A market factor expressed as a percentage, or in another quantitative form, relative to some base figure.

**market penetration** A product-market growth strategy in which a company tries to sell more of its present products to its present markets.

**market-penetration pricing** See *penetration pricing*.

**market potential** The total sales volume that all organizations selling a product during a stated time period in a specific market could expect to achieve under ideal conditions.

**market segmentation** The process of dividing the total market for a product into several parts, each of which tends to be homogeneous in all significant aspects.

**market share** The proportion of total sales of a product during a stated time period in a specific market that is captured by a single firm. Market share can refer to entire industries, narrow segments, or particular geographic areas and also can apply to past, present, or future time periods.

**market-share analysis** A detailed analysis of the company's share of the market in total as well as by product line and market segment.

**market-skimming pricing** See *skimming pricing*.

**marketing** A total system of business activities designed to plan, price, promote, and distribute want-satisfying products to target markets in order to achieve organizational objectives.

**marketing audit** A comprehensive review and evaluation of the marketing function in an organization — its philosophy, environment, goals, strategies, organizational structure, human and financial resources, and performance.

**marketing concept** A philosophy of doing business that emphasizes customer orientation and co-ordination of marketing activities in order to achieve the organization's performance objectives.

**marketing cost analysis** A detailed study of the "operating expenses" section of a company's profit and loss statement.

**marketing information system** An on-going organized set of procedures and methods designed to generate, analyze, disseminate, store, and retrieve information for use in making marketing decisions.

**marketing intermediary** An independent business organization that directly aids in the flow of products between a marketing organization and its markets.

**marketing mix** A combination of the four elements — product, pricing structure, distribution system, and promotional activities — that comprise a company's marketing program. Many marketers now consider service and the "people" side of marketing to be a fifth component of the marketing mix, especially in the marketing of services.

**marketing-orientation stage** The third stage in the evolution of marketing management, in which a company focuses on the needs of its customers and carries out a broad range of marketing activities.

**marketing research** The process of specifying, assembling, and analyzing information used to identify and define marketing opportunities and problems; generate, refine, and evaluate marketing actions; monitor marketing performance; and improve understanding of marketing as a process.

**markup** The dollar amount that is added to the acquisition cost of a product to determine the selling price.

**Maslow's needs hierarchy** A needs structure consisting of five levels and organized according to the order in which people seek need gratification.

**mass distribution** See *intensive distribution*.

**materials handling** The subsystem of physical distribution management that involves selecting and operating the equipment and warehouse building that is used in physically handling products.

**maturity stage** The third part of a product life cycle, during which the sales of a generic product category continue to increase (but at a decreasing rate), profits decline largely due to price competition, and some firms leave the market.

**membership programs** See *loyalty programs*.

**merchant wholesaler** An independently owned firm that primarily engages in wholesaling and ordinarily takes title to the products being distributed. Same as *wholesaler*.

**missionary seller** A selling job in which the sales people are not expected to solicit orders but are expected to influence decision makers by building goodwill, performing promotional activities, and providing service to customers. In pharmaceuticals marketing, called detail sales person.

**modified rebuy** In the business market, a purchasing situation between a new task and a straight rebuy in terms of time required, information needed, and alternatives considered.

**motive** A need sufficiently stimulated that an individual is moved to seek satisfaction. Same as *drive*.

**multiple-brand strategy** A strategy in which a firm has more than one brand of essentially the same product, aimed either at the same target market or at distinct target markets.

**multiple packaging** The practice of placing several units of the same product in one container.

**multiple buying influences** A situation in which a purchasing decision is influenced by more than one person in the buyer's organization.

**multiple-segment strategy** A strategy that involves two or more groups of potential customers selected as target markets.

**national brand** See *producer's brand*.

**need recognition** The stage in the buying decision process in which the consumer is moved to action by a need.

**neighbourhood shopping centre** A small group of stores situated around a supermarket and including other convenience-goods stores and specialty stores. Draws from a market located perhaps within 10 minutes by car.

**new product** A vague term that may refer to (1) really innovative, truly unique products; (2) replacements for existing products that are significantly different from existing ones; or (3) imitative products that are new to the given firm.

**new-product development process** Developmental stages that a new product goes through, starting with idea generation and continuing through idea screening, business analysis, limited production, test-marketing, and eventually commercialization (full-scale production and marketing.)

**new-product strategy** A plan as to what role new products are to play in helping the company achieve its corporate and marketing goals.

**new-task buying** In the business market, a purchasing situation in which a company for the first time considers buying a given item.

**niche marketing** A strategy in which goods and services are tailored to meet the needs of small market segments.

**noise** Any external factor that interferes with successful communication.

**nonadopters** Those consumers that never adopt an innovation.

**nonbusiness market** Such diverse institutions as churches, colleges and universities, museums, hospitals and other health institutions, political parties, labour unions, and charitable organizations.

**noncumulative discount** A quantity discount based on the size of an individual order of products.

**nonprice competition** A strategy in which a firm tries to compete based on some factor other than price — for example, promotion, product differentiation, or variety of services.

**nonstore retailing** Retailing activities resulting in transactions that occur away from a retail store.

**North American Free Trade Agreement (NAFTA)** An agreement among Canada, the United States, and Mexico to eliminate tariffs between the countries.

**not-for-profit organization** An organization in which profit is not an intended organizational goal.

**nutrition labelling** The part of a product that provides information about the amount of calories, fat, cholesterol, sodium, carbohydrates, and protein contained in the package's contents.

**objective** A desired outcome. Same as *goal*.

**observational method** Gathering data by observing personally or mechanically the actions of a person.

**odd pricing** A form of psychological pricing that consists of setting prices at odd amounts ($4.99 rather than $5.00, for example) in the belief that these seemingly low prices will result in larger sales volume.

**off-price retailer** A type of retail institution, often found in the areas of apparel and shoes, that has a narrow and deep product assortment, emphasizes low prices, and offers few customer services.

**off-price retailing** A strategy of selling well-known brands below the manufacturer's recommended retail price.

**one-price strategy** A strategy under which a seller charges the same price to all customers of the same type who buy the same quantity of goods.

**operating supplies** The "convenience goods" of the business market — short-lived, low-priced items purchased with a minimum of time and effort.

**opinion leader** The member of a reference group who is the information source and who influences the decision making of others in the group.

**order processing** The subsystem of physical distribution management that consists of the set of procedures for receiving, handling, and filling orders.

**order taker** One of three types of sales jobs, the others being sales-support personnel and order getter.

**organizational mission** The first step in strategic planning that defines the organization by asking the question, "What business are we in?"

**organizational portfolio analysis** A key step in strategic planning that identifies the present status of each strategic business unit and determines its future role in the company.

**organizational strategies** Broad, basic plans of action by which an organization intends to achieve its goals and fulfil its mission. These plans are for (1) the total organization in a small, single-product company or (2) each SBU in a large, multiproduct or multibusiness organization.

**outside order taker** A selling job in which sales people are primarily going to customers in the field.

**outside sales force** A group of sales reps engaged in field selling, that is, selling in person at a customer's place of business or home.

**overall cost leadership** According to Porter's generic-strategies model, a strategy of satisfying a broad market by producing a standard product at a low cost and then underpricing competitors.

**package** The actual container or wrapper for a product.

**packaging** The activities in product planning that involve designing and producing the container or wrapper for a product.

**party-plan selling** One kind of direct selling, in which a host or hostess invites some friends to a party at which a sales person makes a sales presentation.

**past-sales analysis** A method of sales forecasting that applies a flat percentage increase to the volume achieved last year, or to the average volume of the past few years, to predict future volume.

**patronage buying motives** The reasons why a consumer chooses to shop at a certain store.

**penetration pricing** A pricing strategy in which a low initial price is set to reach the mass market immediately. Same as *market-penetration pricing*.

**percentage-of-sales method** A method of determining the promotional budget in which the amount is set as a certain percentage of past or forecasted future sales.

**perception** Collecting and processing information from the environment in order to give meaning to the world around us.

**perishability** A characteristic of a service indicating that it is highly perishable and cannot be stored.

**personal interview** A face-to-face method of gathering data in a survey.

**personal selling** The personal communication of information to persuade a prospective customer to buy a good, service, idea, or other product.

**positive reinforcement** According to learning theory, receiving a desirable outcome as a result of behaviour.

**personality** An individual's pattern of traits that influences behavioural responses.

**physical distribution** Activities involved in the flow of products as they move physically from producer to consumer or industrial user. Same as *logistics*.

**physical distribution management** The development and operation of efficient flow systems for products.

**piggyback freight service** The service of transporting loaded truck trailers on railroad flatcars.

**pioneering advertising** Primary-demand advertising in the introductory stage of the product life cycle.

**place utility** The utility created when a product is made readily accessible to potential customers.

**planned obsolescence** A product strategy designed to make an existing product out of date and thus to increase the market for replacement products. There are two forms: technological and style.

**planning** The process of deciding now what we are going to do later, including when and how we are going to do it.

**positioning** A company's strategies and actions related to favourably distinguishing itself and its products from competitors in the minds (and hearts) of selected groups of consumers.

**possession utility** The utility created when a customer buys the product — that is, ownership is transferred to the buyer.

**postage-stamp pricing** See *uniform delivered price*.

**postpurchase behaviour** Efforts by the consumer to reduce the anxiety often accompanying purchase decisions.

**postpurchase service** The final stage of the selling process, including delivery, financing, installation, routine maintenance, employee training, billing, and other areas important to customer satisfaction.

**pretest** An activity in which commercials in finished or nearly finished form are presented to panels of consumers in order to gauge their reactions.

**price** The amount of money and/or products needed to acquire some combination of another product and its accompanying services.

**price competition** A strategy in which a firm regularly offers prices that are as low as possible, usually accompanied by a minimum of services.

**price discrimination** A situation in which different customers pay different prices for the same product.

**price lining** A retail pricing strategy whereby a store selects a limited number of prices and sells each item only at one of these selected prices.

**price war** A form of price competition that begins when one firm decreases its price in an effort to increase its sales volume and/or market share, the other firms retaliate by reducing prices on competing products, and additional price decreases by the original price cutter and/or its competitors usually follow.

**pricing objective** The goals that management tries to reach with its pricing structure and strategies.

**primary data** Original data gathered specifically for the project at hand.

**primary demand** The market demand for a general category of products (in contrast to the selective demand for a particular brand of the product).

**primary-demand advertising** Advertising designed to stimulate demand for a generic product.

**private label** A brand name that is owned by a retailer or wholesaler.

**private warehouse** A warehouse that is owned and operated by the firm whose products are being stored and handled at the facility.

**producer's brand** A brand that is owned by a manufacturer or other producer. Same as *national brand.*

**product** A set of tangible attributes, including packaging, colour, price, quality, and brand, plus the services and reputation of the seller. A product may be a good, service, place, person, or idea.

**product advertising** Advertising intended to inform or stimulate the market about an organization's products.

**product development** A product-market growth strategy that calls for a company to develop new products to sell to its existing markets.

**product differentiation** The strategy in which one firm promotes the features of its product over competitors' brands offered to the same market.

**product-liability claim** A legal action alleging that an illness, accident, or death resulted from the named product because it was harmful, faulty, or inadequately labelled.

**product life cycle** The stages a product goes through from its introduction, to its growth and maturity, to its eventual decline and death (withdrawal from the market or deletion from the company's offerings).

**product line** A broad group of products, intended for essentially similar uses and possessing reasonably similar physical characteristics.

**product manager** An executive responsible for planning the marketing program for a given product or group of products. Same as *brand manager*.

**product-market growth matrix** A planning model that consists of four alternative growth strategies based on whether an organization will be selling its present products or new products to its present markets or new markets.

**product mix** All products offered for sale by a company.

**product positioning** The decisions and activities involved in developing the intended image (in the customer's mind) for a product in relation to competitive products and to other products marketed by the same company.

**product-related segmentation** Market segmentation based on product usage rate or product benefits desired by consumers.

**production-orientation stage** The first stage in the evolution of marketing management, in which the basic assumption is that making a good product will ensure business success.

**promotion** The element in an organization's marketing mix that is used to inform, persuade, and remind the market regarding the organization and/or its products.

**promotional allowance** A price reduction granted by the seller as payment for promotional services rendered by the buyer.

**promotional mix** The combination of personal selling, advertising, sales promotion, publicity, and public relations that is intended to help an organization achieve its marketing objectives.

**prospecting** The stage in the personal selling process that involves developing a list of potential customers.

**psychographic segmentation** Market segmentation based on some aspect(s) of consumers' personality, life-style, or social class.

**psychographics** A concept in consumer behaviour that describes consumers in terms of a combination of psychological and sociological influences.

**public relations** A broad communications effort designed to build or maintain a favourable image for an organization with its various publics.

**public-service advertising** Advertising designed to improve the quality of life and indicate that the advertiser is a responsible member of the community.

**public warehouse** An independent firm that provides storage and handling facilities.

**publicity** A news presentation for a product or organization presented in any medium that is not paid for and has the credibility of editorial material.

**"pull" promotional strategy** Promotional effort directed primarily at intermediaries that are the next link forward in distribution channels.

**qualifying** The stage in the personal selling process in which the sales person determines if the prospect has both the willingness and capability to buy.

**qualitative performance bases** In sales force performance, judgmental indications of inputs and/or outputs.

**qualitative research** A form of marketing research that is usually employed for exploratory purposes that examines consumers' deeply held views, opinions, and feelings. Includes focus group interviews and one-on-one depth interviews.

**quality** How well a product or service meets the expectations of the customer.

**quantitative performance bases** In sales force performance, numerical measure of inputs and/or outputs.

**quantitative research** A form of marketing research that is intended to obtain statistical information about a sample of consumers or members of the public. Usually relies on surveys to collect the data.

**quantity discount** A reduction from list price when large quantities are purchased; offered to encourage buyers to purchase in large quantities.

**questionnaire** A data-gathering form used to collect the information in a personal, telephone, or mail survey.

**rack jobber** A merchant wholesaler that provides its customers with the display case or rack, stocks it, and price-marks the merchandise.

**random sample** A sample that is selected in such a way that every unit in the defined universe has an equal chance of being selected.

**raw materials** Business goods that have not been processed in any way and that will become part of another product.

**recipient market** See *client market.*

**reciprocity** The situation of "I'll buy from you if you'll buy from me."

**recovery** The process of correcting the situation when a customer is dissatisfied with service provided. A company may attempt to recover from a poor service experience by apologizing or by offering the customer a price reduction or other form of compensation.

**reference group** A group of people who influence a person's attitudes, values, and behaviour.

**refusal to deal** A situation in which a manufacturer desiring to select and perhaps control its channels may refuse to sell to some intermediaries.

**regional shopping centre** The largest type of planned suburban shopping centre (sometimes large enough to be a mini-downtown). Usually includes two or more department stores and many limited-line stores, along with service institutions such as banks, theatres, restaurants, hotels, and office buildings.

**reinforcement** In learning theory, the satisfaction or dissatisfaction experienced as a result of behaviour.

**relationship marketing** An attempt by a sales person or company to develop a deeper, longer-lasting relationship built on trust with key customers — usually larger accounts.

**repositioning** The process of moving a company or a store or a brand to a new position in the minds of target customers, usually by changing its image.

**resale price maintenance** A pricing policy whereby the manufacturer sets the retail price for a product.

**reseller market** Wholesaling and retailing intermediaries that buy products for resale to other business users or to consumers. A segment of the business market.

**resident buyer** Independent agent located in central market who buys for wholesalers and retailers located in outlying areas.

**responses** In learning theory, the behavioural reactions to the drive and cues.

**retail trade** See *retailing.*

**retailer** A firm engaged primarily in retailing.

**retailer co-operative** A type of contractual vertical marketing system that is formed by a group of small retailers who agree to establish and operate a wholesale warehouse.

**retailing** The sale, and all activities directly related to the sale, of goods and services to ultimate consumers for personal, nonbusiness use. Same as *retail trade.*

**retention** The objective of keeping existing customers; the understanding being that the longer a customer continues to do business with a company, the more profitable the customer becomes.

**role ambiguity** Confusion among sales people about how much responsibility to assume in dealing with customers.

**role conflict** The stress created for a sales person by the often contrary demands and expectations of his or her employer, customers, and family.

**sales engineer** A selling job, often involving technically trained individuals selling some kind of sophisticated equipment, in which the emphasis is on the sales person's ability to explain the product to the prospect and perhaps to adapt it to the customer's particular needs.

**sales-force composite** A method of forecasting sales that consists of collecting from all sales people and intermediaries an estimate of sales in their territories during the forecasting period.

**sales-force selection task** The three steps in assembling a sales force, consisting of (1) determining the number and type of people wanted by preparing a written job description, (2) recruiting an adequate number of applicants, and (3) selecting the most qualified persons from among the applicants.

**sales forecast** An estimate of likely sales for one company's brand of a product during a stated time period in a specific market and assuming the use of a predetermined marketing plan.

**sales-orientation stage** The second stage in the evolution of marketing management, in which the emphasis is on selling whatever the organization produces.

**sales potential** The portion of market potential, applying only to one company's brand of a product, that a specific company could expect to achieve under ideal conditions.

**sales promotion** Activities, including contests for sales people and consumers, trade shows, in-store displays, samples, premiums, and coupons, that are designed to supplement advertising and co-ordinate personal selling.

**sales-volume analysis** A detailed study of the "net sales" section of a company's profit and loss statement.

**satisfaction** The consumer condition when experience with a product or service equals or exceeds expectations.

**scrambled merchandising** A strategy under which an intermediary diversifies its assortment by adding product lines not traditionally carried by its type of business.

**seasonal discount** A discount for placing an order during the seller's slow season.

**secondary data** Information already gathered by somebody else for some other purpose.

**selective attention** The process that limits our perceptions such that, of all the marketing stimuli our senses are exposed to, only those able to capture and hold our attention have the potential of being perceived.

**selective demand** The market demand for an individual *brand* of a product, in contrast to the primary demand for the broad product category.

**selective-demand advertising** Advertising that is intended to stimulate demand for individual brands.

**selective distortion** The process of mentally altering information that is inconsistent with one's own beliefs or attitudes.

**selective distribution** A strategy in which a producer sells its product through multiple, but not all, wholesalers and/or retailers in a market where a consumer might reasonably look for it.

**selective retention** The process of retaining in memory some portion of what is perceived.

**self-concept** A person's self-image.

**self-image** The idea or image one has of oneself.

**selling agent** A type of independent intermediary that essentially takes the place of a manufacturer's marketing department, marketing the manufacturer's entire output and often influencing the design and/or pricing of the products.

**service** An activity that is separately identifiable, intangible, and the main object of a transaction designed to provide want-satisfaction for customers.

**service encounter** In services marketing, a customer's interaction with any service employee or with any tangible element, such as a service's physical surroundings.

**service quality** The value that consumers perceive they are receiving from their purchase of services; generally very difficult to measure.

**shopping centre** A planned grouping of retail stores in a multiunit structure, with the physical structure usually owned by a single organization.

**shopping goods** A class of consumer products that are purchased after the buyer has spent some time and effort comparing the price, quality, colour, and/or other attributes of alternative products.

**shopping-mall intercept** A method of gathering data by conducting personal interviews in central locations, typically regional shopping centres.

**simulated test market** A confidential variation of test marketing in which consumers are shown advertising for a product and then are allowed to "shop" in a test store in order to measure their reactions to the advertising, the product, or both.

**single-segment concentration strategy** The selection of one homogeneous segment from within a total market to be the target market.

**single-source data** A data-gathering method in which exposure to television advertising and product purchases can be traced to individual households.

**singles** Households that consist of just one person.

**situation analysis** The stage in a marketing research study that involves obtaining information about the company and its business environment by means of library research and extensive interviewing of company officials.

**situational influences** Temporary forces, associated with the immediate purchase environment, that affect behaviour.

**skimming pricing** A pricing strategy in which the initial price is set high in the range of expected prices. Same as *market-skimming pricing*.

**social and cultural forces** A set of factors, including life-styles, social values, and beliefs, that affect the marketing activities of an organization.

**social class** A division of society based on education, occupation, and type of residential neighbourhood.

**social environment** Family, friends, and acquaintances who directly or indirectly provide information about products.

**social responsibility** The commitment on the part of a company to improving the well-being of society.

**societal marketing concept** A revised version of the marketing concept under which a company recognizes that it should be concerned about not only the buyers of a firm's product but also other people directly affected by the firm's operations and not only with tomorrow but also with the long term.

**specialty goods** A class of consumer products with perceived unique characteristics such that consumers are willing to expend special effort to buy them.

**specialty store** A type of retail institution concentrating on a specialized product line, or even part of a specialized product line.

**stabilizing prices** A pricing goal designed to achieve steady, nonvolatile prices in an industry.

**Standard Industrial Classification (S.I.C.) system** A coding system developed by the federal government that groups firms into similar types of businesses and thus enables a company to identify and analyze small segments of its market.

**stars** According to the Boston Consulting Group matrix, strategic business units that are characterized by high market shares and high industry growth rates.

**stimulus-response theory** The theory that learning occurs as a person responds to some stimuli and is rewarded with need satisfaction for a correct response or penalized for an incorrect one.

**stockturn rate** The number of times the average inventory is turned over, or sold, during the period under study.

**storage** An activity in physical distribution that creates time utility by holding and preserving products from the time of production until their sale.

**straight commission compensation** The method of sales force compensation in which payment is directly related to the tasks performed, usually the volume of the product(s) sold.

**straight rebuy** In the business market, a routine purchase with minimal information needs.

**straight salary compensation** The method of sales force compensation in which the sales person is paid a fixed amount, regardless of tasks performed or level of performance.

**strategic business unit (SBU)** A separate division for a major product or market in a multiproduct or multibusiness organization.

**strategic company planning** The level of planning that consists of (1) defining the organization's mission, (2) setting organizational objectives, (3) evaluating the firm's strategic business units, and (4) selecting appropriate strategies so as to achieve the organization's objectives.

**strategic marketing planning** The level of planning that consists of (1) conducting a situation analysis, (2) determining marketing objectives, (3) selecting target markets and measuring the market, and (4) designing a strategic marketing mix.

**strategic planning** The managerial process of matching a firm's resources with its market opportunities over the long run.

**strategy** A broad plan of action by which an organization intends to reach its objective(s).

**style** A distinctive presentation or construction in any art, product, or activity.

**style obsolescence** A product strategy in which superficial characteristics of a product are altered so that the new model is easily differentiated from the old one in order to make people dissatisfied with the old model. Same as *fashion obsolescence*.

**subculture** Groups that exhibit characteristic behaviour patterns sufficient to distinguish them from other groups within the same culture.

**substitute products** Two or more products that satisfy essentially the same need(s).

**superego** In Freudian psychology, the part of the mind that houses the conscience and directs instinctive drives into socially acceptable channels.

**supermarket** A type of retailing institution that has a moderately broad and moderately deep product assortment spanning groceries and some nonfood lines, that offers relatively few customer services, and that ordinarily emphasizes price in either an offensive or defensive way.

**supermarket retailing** A retailing method that features several related product lines, a high degree of self-service, largely centralized checkout, and competitive prices.

**suppliers** The people or firms that supply the goods or services that an organization needs to produce what it sells.

**survey method** A method of gathering data by interviewing a limited number of people (a sample) in person or by telephone or mail.

**survey of buyer intentions** A form of sales forecasting in which a firm asks a sample of current or potential customers how much of a particular product they would buy at a given price during a specified future time period.

**SWOT analysis** Identifying and evaluating an organization's most significant strengths, weaknesses, opportunities, and threats.

**syndicated data** Research information that is purchased from a research supplier on a shared-cost basis by a number of clients.

**tactic** An operational means by which a strategy is to be implemented or activated.

**target market** A group of customers (people or organizations) at whom a seller aims its marketing effort.

**target return** A pricing goal that involves setting prices so as to achieve a certain percentage return on investment or on net sales.

**tariff** A tax imposed on a product entering a country.

**task method** A method of determining the promotional appropriation under which the organization first decides what is to be accomplished and then calculates how much it will cost to reach this goal. Same as buildup method.

**telemarketing** A form of nonstore retailing in which a sales person initiates contact with a shopper and also closes the sale over the telephone.

**telephone survey** A method of gathering data in a survey by interviewing people over the telephone.

**televised shopping** One form of direct marketing, in which TV channels and shows sell consumer electronics, jewellery, and other products at relatively low prices.

**test marketing** A marketing research technique in which a firm markets its product in a limited geographic area, measures the sales, and then — from this sample — projects (a) the company's sales over a larger area and/or (b) consumers' response to a strategy before committing to a major marketing effort.

**time utility** The utility created when a product is available to customers when they want it.

**total cost** The sum of total fixed costs and total variable costs, or the full cost of a specific quantity produced or sold.

**total cost concept** In physical distribution, the optimization of the cost-profit relationship for the entire physical distribution system, rather than for individual activities.

**total quality management (TQM)** A philosophy as well as specific procedures, policies, and practices that commit an organization to continuous quality improvement in all of its activities.

**trade discount** A reduction from the list price, offered by a seller to buyers in payment for marketing activities that they will perform. Same as *functional discount*.

**trade promotion** The type of sales promotion that is directed at members of a distribution channel.

**trademark** A brand that is legally protected.

**trademark licensing** A business arrangement in which the owner of a trademark grants permission to other firms to use the owner's brand name, logo-type, and/or character on the licensee's products in return for a royalty on sales of those products. Same as *brand licensing*.

**trading down** A product-line strategy wherein a company adds a lower-priced item to its line of prestige goods in order to reach a market that cannot afford the higher-priced items.

**trading up** A product-line strategy wherein a company adds a higher-priced, prestige product to its line in order to increase sales of the existing lower-priced products in that line and attract a higher-income market.

**trend analysis** A method of forecasting sales over the long term by using regression analysis, or over the short term by using a seasonal index of sales.

**trial close** The stage in the personal selling process when the sales person poses some "either-or" questions in such a way that the customer's answer is intended to close the sale.

**trickle-across cycle** In fashion adoption, a fashion cycle that moves horizontally within several social classes at the same time.

**trickle-down cycle** In fashion adoption, a fashion cycle that flows downward through several socioeconomic classes.

**trickle-up cycle** In fashion adoption, a fashion cycle by which a style becomes popular (fashionable) first with lower socioeconomic classes and then, later, with higher socioeconomic groups.

**truck jobber** A limited-function merchant wholesaler that carries a selected line of perishable products and delivers them by truck to retail stores.

**tying contract** A contract under which a manufacturer sells a product to an intermediary only under the condition that this intermediary also buys another (possibly unwanted) product from the manufacturer.

**ultimate consumers** People who buy products for their personal, nonbusiness use.

**uniform delivered price** A geographic pricing strategy whereby the same delivered price is quoted to all buyers regardless of their location. Same as *postage-stamp pricing*.

**unit pricing** A form of price reporting where the price is stated per kilogram, litre, or some other standard measure in order to aid consumers in comparison shopping.

**unsought goods** A type of consumer product that consists of new products the consumer is not yet aware of or products the consumer does not yet want.

**unstructured interview** In sales force selection, an interviewing procedure in which the interviewer is permitted the freedom to ask questions and explore issues as they develop in the flow of the interview.

**users** The people in a buying centre who actually use a particular product.

**utility** The attribute in an item that makes it capable of satisfying human wants.

**VALS** A psychographic segmentation tool, developed by a research firm, that divided adults into nine segments based on similarities in their values and life-styles.

**value** The quantitative measure of the worth of a product to attract other products in exchange.

**value added** The dollar value of a firm's output minus the value of the inputs it purchased from other firms.

**variable cost** A cost that varies of changes directly in relation to the number of units produced or sold.

**variable-price strategy** See *flexible-price strategy*.

**vertical business market** A situation where a given product is usable by virtually all the firms in only one or two industries.

**vertical conflict** A form of channel conflict occurring between firms at different levels of the same channel, typically producer versus wholesaler or producer versus retailer.

**vertical co-operative advertising** Advertising in which firms at different levels of the distribution channel share the cost.

**vertical marketing system (VMS)** A tightly co-ordinated distribution channel designed to achieve operating efficiencies and marketing effectiveness.

**voluntary chain** A type of contractual vertical marketing system that is sponsored by a wholesaler who enters into a contract with interested retailers.

**warehouse club** A combined retailing and wholesaling institution that has a very broad but very shallow product assortment with very low prices and few customer services and is open only to members. Same as *wholesale club*.

**warehousing** A broad range of physical distribution activities that include storage, assembling, bulk breaking, and preparing products for shipping.

**warning label** The part of a product that tells consumers not to misuse the product and informs them of almost every conceivable danger associated with using it.

**warranty** An assurance given to buyers that they will be compensated in case the product does not perform up to reasonable expectations.

**wheel of retailing** The cyclical pattern of changes in retailing, whereby a new type of store enters the market as a low-cost, low-price store and over time takes business away from unchanging competitors; eventually, the successful new retailer trades up, incurring higher costs and higher prices and making the institution vulnerable to a new type of retailer.

**wholesale club** See *warehouse club*.

**wholesaler** See *merchant wholesaler*.

**wholesaling** All activities directly related to the sale of goods and services to parties for resale, use in producing other goods and services, or operating an organization.

**wholesaling intermediary** A firm engaged primarily in wholesaling.

**wholly owned subsidiary** A business arrangement in foreign markets in which a company owns the foreign operation in order to gain maximum control over its marketing program and production operations.

**zone-delivered price** A geographic pricing strategy whereby the same delivered price is charged at any location within each geographic zone. Some as *parcel-post pricing*.

# TOPICAL INDEX

# COMPANY AND BRAND NAME INDEX

# CREDITS

CHAPTER 1

**Pages 2-3:** Reproduced with permission of Chuck Simpson, Challenger Motor Freight. Photography by Eden Robbins.
**Page 6:** Courtesy of Bell Ontario
**Page 12:** Courtesy of Frito-Lay, Inc.
**Page 19:** Courtesy of Domino's Pizza
**Page 20:** © (1992) The Rockport Company, Inc. All rights reserved. Reprinted by permission of The Rockport Company, Inc.
**Page 21:** Courtesy of Blue Cross of Atlantic Canada, Moncton, New Brunswick
**Page 22:** Canadian Cancer Society/Harrod Mirlin Inc. Photography by Edward Gajdel

CHAPTER 2

**Pages 38-39:** Courtesy of McDonald's Restaurants Canada Limited
**Page 45:** Reproduced with permission of Paige Sillcox, Cookie It Up! Photography by Kirk McGregor.
**Page 47:** Courtesy of Italpasta Ltd.
**Page 48:** Samsung Electronics Canada Inc.

CHAPTER 3

**Pages 58-59:** Reproduced with permission of Natasha Rajewski, SoapBerry Shops. Photography by Doug Forster.
**Page 61:** Nathan Holtz (both)
**Page 67:** Ontario Egg Producers' Marketing Board
**Page 69:** With the permission of *Canadian Grocer*.
**Page 76:** Courtesy of Sony Corporation of America

CHAPTER 4

**Pages 90-91:** H.J. Heinz Company of Canada Ltd.
**Page 103:** Daemmrich/The Image Works
**Page 104:** Courtesy of Levi Strauss & Co.
**Page 105:** Reproduced with permission of TD Trust. Advertisement prepared by Saatchi & Saatchi Advertising.
**Page 110:** Jeff Vinnick, Photographer
**Page 113:** Courtesy of Mercedes-Benz Canada Inc.

CHAPTER 5

**Pages 118-119:** Copyright © Montres Rolex S.A. Geneva. Reproduced with permission.
**Page 124:** Courtesy of General Motors
**Page 132:** Courtesy of Polaroid Canada Inc. Creative by BBDO Canada Inc.
**Page 136:** Used with permission of Ontario Hydro.

CHAPTER 6

**Page 146:** ™CIBC
**Page 151:** Gupton/Stock, Boston
**Page 155:** Natural Resources Canada
**Page 157:** Borden Catelli — Consumer Products
**Page 159:** Courtesy of Corporate Foods Limited
**Page 164:** Courtesy of Lever Canada
**Page 168:** Nathan Holtz

CHAPTER 7

**Pages 178-179:** Courtesy of TSN
**Page 182:** Heitner/Picture Cube
**Page 185:** Courtesy of Du Pont Company
**Page 190:** Ad developed and produced by Muller Hirayana Graves Advertising/Richard Muller, Creative Director
**Page 197:** Courtesy of Osler, Hoskin & Harcourt
**Page 201:** Courtesy of Fleet Bank. Ad agency: Arnold Fortuna Lawner & Cabot (Elizabeth Beebee)

CHAPTER 8

**Pages 204-205:** Courtesy of Volvo Canada Ltd.
**Page 218:** Courtesy of Bell Ontario
**Page 221:** Courtesy of the Creative Research Group Limited
**Page 225:** Courtesy of Paradise Bakery

CHAPTER 9

**Pages 258-259:** Courtesy of Logitech Canada
**Page 264:** Courtesy of Nikon Inc./Photography by Jay Brenner
**Page 266:** Courtesy of Talon Inc.
**Page 268:** Material courtesy of Sony of Canada Ltd. Sony is a registered ™ of Sony Corporation, Tokyo, Japan.
**Page 275:** Samsonite Canada Inc., Stratford, Ontario

CHAPTER 10

**Pages 286-287:** Courtesy of Coca-Cola Ltd./McCann-Erickson Advertising of Canada Limited
**Page 288:** LOWE SMS, 1993

**Page 290:** Courtesy of Intel Corporation
**Page 292:** Registered Trademark of Welch Foods Inc., A Cooperative Authorized User: Cadbury Beverages Canada
**Page 295:** Courtesy of Swatch, a division of SMH (US) Inc.

CHAPTER 11
**Pages 310-311:** Courtesy of Country Style Donuts CSD a member of Maple Leaf Foods Inc.
**Page 313:** Courtesy of Xerox Canada Inc.
**Page 315:** Oreo ® is a trade mark of Nabisco Brands Ltd., Toronto, Canada, © all rights reserved. Reproduced with permission of Nabisco Brands Ltd., Toronto, Ontario, Canada
**Page 328:** Control Data Systems

CHAPTER 12
**Pages 340-341:** Courtesy of the Toronto Dominion Bank. Used with permission
**Page 348:** Courtesy of Cathay Pacific
**Page 353:** Courtesy of United Parcel Service Canada Ltd. Used by permission
**Page 357:** Courtesy of Price Waterhouse

CHAPTER 13
**Pages 370-371:** Courtesy of IKEA Canada. Ad prepared by Geoffrey B. Roche & Partners Advertising Inc.
**Page 376:** Reproduced with the permission of General Motors of Canada Ltd. Advertising Agency; Cossette Communication-Marketing. Art Director: Brian Hickling. Copy Writer: Jim Garbutt
**Page 378:** Courtesy Petro-Canada
**Page 385:** Gruner/Light Images

CHAPTER 14
**Page 411:** Courtesy of National Ballet of Canada
**Page 413:** (top) Courtesy of Eastman Kodak
**Page 413:** (bottom) Courtesy of Compaq Computer Corporation
**Page 421:** Courtesy of Everything's $1.00
**Page 426:** Courtesy of Air Canada Cargo. Agency: FCB Direct Montreal

CHAPTER 15
**Pages 438-439:** Courtesy of International Hospitality Inc. Photography by Liam Sharp
**Page 442:** (top left) Barner/Stock, Boston
(bottom left) Winter/Stock, Boston
(right) Bachman/Stock, Boston
**Page 448:** Courtesy of Avon Products Inc.
**Page 451:** Photograph courtesy of the May Department Stores Company
**Page 456:** Peter Tym/Globe & Mail, March 1, 1994, p. B24

CHAPTER 16
**Pages 466-467:** Courtesy of Globelle
**Page 480:** Courtesy of RPS
**Page 484:** Courtesy of G.N. Johnston Equipment & Co. Ltd.
**Page 490:** Ryder Dedicated Logistics

CHAPTER 17
**Pages 494-495:** Courtesy of Tilley Endurables Inc.
**Page 503:** Photo courtesy of Viliam with special thanks, and *Marketing Magazine*
**Page 504:** (left) Courtesy of Eaton's
**Page 504:** (right) Courtesy of North's Decorating Services Ltd., Coboconk, Ontario
**Page 508:** (left) Courtesy of Whitespot Restaurants
**Page 508:** (right) Courtesy of Mr. Submarine Limited; Courtesy of First Choice® Haircutters; Courtesy of Ultramar Canada Inc.; Courtesy of Thrifty Car Rental; Courtesy of Kwik-Kopy Printing Canada Corporation; Courtesy of Midas Canada Inc.
**Page 511:** Courtesy of Eaton's
**Page 514:** Courtesy of Consumers Distributing Co. Ltd.

CHAPTER 18
**Pages 546-547:** Courtesy of Pillsbury Canada Limited
**Page 550:** Courtesy of Canadian Airlines International. Agency: Chiat/Day. Creative Director: Peter McHugh. Copywriter: Randy Diplock. Art Director: Jamie Way. Photographer: Richard Picton. Print Production Manager: Gina Shank. Separations: Batten Graphics
**Page 554:** Courtesy of Vistakon
**Page 557:** Picture courtesy of Nokia Products Ltd.
**Page 560:** Courtesy of Canada Pork Inc. and the provincial pork producer marketing organizations. Agency: Harrod & Mirlin. Photographer: Doug Bradshaw
**Pages 564-565:** Courtesy of Unitel Communications Inc. Used with permission.

CHAPTER 19
**Pages 572-573:** Courtesy of Love Printing Service Ltd., Stittsville, Ontario
**Page 575:** Daemmrich/The Image Works
**Page 577:** Courtesy of Radio Shack
**Page 578:** Courtesy of Canadian Professional Sales Association
**Page 579:** Bruce Zake
**Page 583:** Courtesy of World Book Educational Products
**Page 587:** Courtesy of Learning International

CHAPTER 20
**Pages 594-595:** Photo courtesy of the Vancouver Sun
**Pages 600-601:** Courtesy of Neilson Cadbury Limited. Agency: Leo Burnett Company Limited. Photography by Michael Assaly Photography
**Page 603:** Courtesy of Pillsbury Canada Limited
**Page 605:** Provided with the permission of American Express. Ad produced by Ogilvy & Mather Advertising
**Page 608:** Provided by Volkswagen Canada Inc.
**Page 613:** Courtesy of Rollerblade, Inc.

**Page 615:** Advertisement reproduced with the permission of Nabisco Brands Ltd., Toronto, Ontario Canada. Milk-Bone®™ is a trademark of Nabisco Brands Ltd., Toronto, Canada, © all rights reserved

CHAPTER 21

**Pages 642-643:** Used with permission of Colin Korte of Develcon. Photographer Ken Straiton/First Light

**Page 646:** Jeffrey Aaronson

**Page 647:** Ad created by W.B. Doner & Co. Used with permission of John V. Carr & Son, Inc.

**Page 648:** Peter Komiss

**Page 659:** Takeshi Yuzawa

CHAPTER 22

**Page 666:** Courtesy of Lanyon Phillips Brink Advertising Inc., and the Vancouver Museum

**Page 669:** Donated by DDB Needham Worldwide Ltd.; Ian Campbell, Westside Studios; Don George, Colour Collaborators; Partners III Graphics; Franklin Tuckey

**Page 670:** Judy Ankerman, Mark Walton, Prairie Flower Productions, Toronto, Courtesy of The Bishop Strachan School, Toronto, Ontario

**Page 673:** Client: The Metropolitan Toronto Zoo. Agency: Chiat Day Inc. Advertising. Art Director: Richard Mirabelli. Writer: Peter McHugh

**Page 675:** ABC Canada Literacy Foundation

**Page 679:** Ontario Ministry of Health

CHAPTER 23

**Pages 684-685:** Courtesy of Four Seasons Hotels and Resorts

**Page 687:** Seiji Ibuki

**Page 688:** Courtesy of Seimens Corporation

**Page 694:** James Schnepf

**Page 695:** Courtesy of Dofasco Inc.

**Page 696:** Courtesy of Taco Bell

CHAPTER 24

**Pages 710-711:** Courtesy of Avon

**Page 713:** Etra/Photo Edit

**Page 721:** Reprinted from *Report on Business Magazine*, with permission

**Page 722:** Courtesy of Pharmaceutical Manufacturers Association of Canada

**Page 723:** Courtesy of OE Inc. Office Equipment Company of Canada and the World Wildlife Fund. Red Throated Loon WWF/Kathleen Blanchard

**Page 728:** Petro-Canada photo by LaBounty & Johl

*cut here*

## STUDENT REPLY CARD

In order to improve future editions, we are seeking your comments on

*Fundamentals of Marketing*, Seventh Canadian Edition, by Sommers, Barnes, and Stanton

Please answer the following questions and return this form via Business Reply Mail.
Your opinions matter. Thank you in advance for sharing them with us!

Name of your college or university: ______________________________

Major program of study: ______________________________

Course title: ______________________________

Were you required to buy this book? __________ yes __________ no

Did you buy this book new or used? __________ new __________ used ($)

Do you plan to keep or sell this book? ________ keep __________ sell

Is the order of topic coverage consistent with what was taught in your course?

*cut here*

*fold here*

Are there chapters or sections of this text that were not assigned for your course?
Please specify:

Were there topics covered in your course that are not included in the text?
Please specify:

What did you like most about this text?

What did you like least?

If you would like to say more, we would appreciate hearing from you.
Please write to us at the address shown on the reverse of this page.

cut here

fold here

cut here

Postage will be paid by

MAIL POSTE
Canada Post Corporation/Société des postes
Postage Paid if mailed in Canada
Port payé si posté au Canada
Business Reply
Réponse d'affaires
0183560299 01

0183560299-L1N9B6-BR01

Attn.: Sponsoring Editor
College Division

**McGRAW-HILL RYERSON LIMITED**
**300 WATER ST.**
**WHITBY ON L1N 9Z9**